1,000,000 Books

are available to read at

Forgotten Books

www.ForgottenBooks.com

Read online
Download PDF
Purchase in print

ISBN 978-0-266-08112-8
PIBN 10948260

This book is a reproduction of an important historical work. Forgotten Books uses state-of-the-art technology to digitally reconstruct the work, preserving the original format whilst repairing imperfections present in the aged copy. In rare cases, an imperfection in the original, such as a blemish or missing page, may be replicated in our edition. We do, however, repair the vast majority of imperfections successfully; any imperfections that remain are intentionally left to preserve the state of such historical works.

Forgotten Books is a registered trademark of FB &c Ltd.
Copyright © 2018 FB &c Ltd.
FB &c Ltd, Dalton House, 60 Windsor Avenue, London, SW19 2RR.
Company number 08720141. Registered in England and Wales.

For support please visit www.forgottenbooks.com

1 MONTH OF FREE READING

at
www.ForgottenBooks.com

By purchasing this book you are eligible for one month membership to ForgottenBooks.com, giving you unlimited access to our entire collection of over 1,000,000 titles via our web site and mobile apps.

To claim your free month visit:
www.forgottenbooks.com/free948260

* Offer is valid for 45 days from date of purchase. Terms and conditions apply.

English
Français
Deutsche
Italiano
Español
Português

www.forgottenbooks.com

Mythology Photography **Fiction** Fishing Christianity **Art** Cooking Essays Buddhism Freemasonry Medicine **Biology** Music **Ancient Egypt** Evolution Carpentry Physics Dance Geology **Mathematics** Fitness Shakespeare **Folklore** Yoga Marketing **Confidence** Immortality Biographies Poetry **Psychology** Witchcraft Electronics Chemistry History **Law** Accounting **Philosophy** Anthropology Alchemy Drama Quantum Mechanics Atheism Sexual Health **Ancient History Entrepreneurship** Languages Sport Paleontology Needlework Islam **Metaphysics** Investment Archaeology Parenting Statistics Criminology **Motivational**

ANNUAL REPORT

OF THE

AMERICAN HISTORICAL ASSOCIATION

FOR

THE YEAR 1899.

IN TWO VOLUMES.

VOLUME I.

WASHINGTON:
GOVERNMENT PRINTING OFFICE.
1900.

LETTER OF SUBMITTAL.

SMITHSONIAN INSTITUTION,
Washington, D. C., June 6, 1900.

To the Congress of the United States:

In accordance with the act of incorporation of the American Historical Association, approved January 4, 1889, I have the honor to submit to Congress the annual report of that Association for the year 1899.

I have the honor to be, very respectfully, your obedient servant,

S. P. LANGLEY,
Secretary.

Hon. WILLIAM P. FRYE,
President pro tempore United States Senate.

ACT OF INCORPORATION.

Be it enacted by the Senate and House of Representatives of the United States of America in Congress assembled, That Andrew D. White, of Ithaca, in the State of New York; George Bancroft, of Washington, in the District of Columbia; Justin Winsor, of Cambridge, in the State of Massachusetts; William F. Poole, of Chicago, in the State of Illinois; Herbert B. Adams, of Baltimore, in the State of Maryland, Clarence W. Bowen, of Brooklyn, in the State of New York, their associates and successors, are hereby created, in the District of Columbia, a body corporate and politic, by the name of the American Historical Association, for the promotion of historical studies, the collection and preservation of historical manuscripts, and for kindred purposes in the interest of American history and of history in America. Said Association is authorized to hold real and personal estate in the District of Columbia so far only as may be necessary to its lawful ends to an amount not exceeding five hundred thousand dollars, to adopt a constitution, and to make by-laws not inconsistent with law. Said Association shall have its principal office at Washington, in the District of Columbia, and may hold its annual meetings in such places as the said incorporators shall determine. Said Association shall report annually to the Secretary of the Smithsonian Institution concerning its proceedings and the condition of historical study in America. Said Secretary shall communicate to Congress the whole of such reports, or such portions thereof as he shall see fit. The Regents of the Smithsonian Institution are authorized to permit said Association to deposit its collections, manuscripts, books, pamphlets, and other material for history in the Smithsonian Institution or in the National Museum at their discretion, upon such conditions and under such rules as they shall prescribe.

[Approved January 4, 1889.]

AMERICAN HISTORICAL ASSOCIATION,
OFFICE OF ASSISTANT SECRETARY.
SMITHSONIAN INSTITUTION,
Washington, D. C., May 9, 1900.

SIR: In accordance with the act of incorporation of the American Historical Association, I have the honor to transmit herewith a general report of the proceedings of the fifteenth annual meeting of the association held at Boston and Cambridge, December 27 to 29, 1899. Some of the papers read and discussed at that meeting have been printed elsewhere and some of them are recommended for publication in this report, as are also several papers read by title only. The most extensive and most important portion of the report consists of a large collection of letters from and to John C. Calhoun, gathered and prepared for publication at considerable expense to the association, under the direction of Prof. J. F. Jameson, chairman of the Historical Manuscripts Commission, and forming the fourth report of that commission. There is also included in the report a complete bibliography of Mississippi, compiled by Mr. J. M. Owen, on the same plan as the bibliography of Alabama, published in the 1897 report.

The association has enlarged its activities by the establishment of a Public Archives Commission for the special study of the character and the means taken for the preservation and publication of State and national archives. A bill has already been introduced in Congress calling upon the association for an investigation of this subject and making an appropriation for the purpose.

Very respectfully,

A. HOWARD CLARK,
Assistant Secretary.

Mr. S. P. LANGLEY,
Secretary of the Smithsonian Institution.

AMERICAN HISTORICAL ASSOCIATION.

Organized at Saratoga, N. Y., September, 10, 1884. Incorporated by Congress January 4, 1889.

OFFICERS FOR 1900.

PRESIDENT:
EDWARD EGGLESTON, L. H. D.,
Joshua's Rock, Lake George, N. Y.

VICE-PRESIDENTS:
MOSES COIT TYLER, L. H. D., LL. D.,
Professor Cornell University.
CHARLES FRANCIS ADAMS, LL. D.,
Boston, Mass.

SECRETARY:
HERBERT BAXTER ADAMS, Ph. D., LL. D.,
Professor Johns Hopkins University, Baltimore, Md.

ASSISTANT SECRETARY AND CURATOR:
A. HOWARD CLARK,
Curator Department American History, Smithsonian Institution, Washington, D. C.

SAMUEL MACAULEY JACKSON, D. D., LL. D.,
Secretary Church History Section, 692 West End avenue, New York.

TREASURER:
CLARENCE WINTHROP BOWEN, Ph. D.,
130 Fulton street, New York.

EXECUTIVE COUNCIL:
In addition to above-named officers.
(Ex-Presidents.)
Hon. ANDREW DICKSON WHITE, L. H. D., LL. D.,
Ithaca, N. Y.
CHARLES KENDALL ADAMS, LL. D.,
President Wisconsin University, Madison.
Hon. WILLIAM WIRT HENRY, LL. D.,
Richmond, Va.

AMERICAN HISTORICAL ASSOCIATION.

JAMES BURRILL ANGELL, LL. D.,
President University of Michigan.

HENRY ADAMS, LL. D.,
Washington, D. C.

Hon. GEORGE FRISBIE HOAR, LL. D.,
Worcester, Mass.

RICHARD SALTER STORRS, D. D., LL. D.,
Brooklyn, N. Y.

JAMES SCHOULER, LL. D.,
Boston, Mass.

GEORGE PARK FISHER, D. D., LL. D.,
Professor Yale University.

JAMES FORD RHODES, LL. D.,
Boston, Mass.

(Elected Councilors.)

GEORGE BURTON ADAMS, Ph. D.,
Professor Yale University.

Hon. MELVILLE WESTON FULLER, LL. D.,
Washington, D. C.

ALBERT BUSHNELL HART, Ph. D.,
Professor Harvard University.

A. C. McLAUGHLIN, A. M.,
Professor University of Michigan.

WILLIAM A. DUNNING, Ph. D.,
Professor Columbia University, New York.

Hon. PETER WHITE,
Marquette, Mich.

TERMS OF OFFICE.

EX-PRESIDENTS:

Hon. ANDREW DICKSON WHITE, L. H. D., LL. D., 1884-85.
†Hon. GEORGE BANCROFT, LL. D., 1885-86.
†JUSTIN WINSOR, LL. D., 1886-87.
†WILLIAM FREDERICK POOLE, LL. D., 1887-88.
CHARLES KENDALL ADAMS, LL. D., 1888-89.
†Hon. JOHN JAY, LL. D., 1889-90.
Hon. WILLIAM WIRT HENRY, LL., D., 1890-91.
JAMES BURRILL ANGELL, LL. D., 1891-93.
HENRY ADAMS, A. B., 1893-94.
Hon. GEORGE FRISBIE HOAR, LL. D., 1894-95.
†RICHARD SALTER STORRS, D. D., LL. D., 1895-96.
JAMES SCHOULER, LL. D., 1896-97.
GEORGE PARK FISHER, D. D., LL. D., 1897-98.
JAMES FORD RHODES, LL. D., 1898-99.

EX-VICE-PRESIDENTS:

†JUSTIN WINSOR, LL. D., 1884-86.
CHARLES KENDALL ADAMS, LL. D., 1884-88.
†WILLIAM FREDERICK POOLE, LL. D., 1886-87.
†Hon. JOHN JAY, LL. D., 1887-89.
Hon. WILLIAM WIRT HENRY, LL. D., 1888-90.
JAMES BURRILL ANGELL, LL. D., 1889-91.
HENRY ADAMS, A. B., 1890-93.
†EDWARD GAY MASON, A. M., 1891-93.
Hon. GEORGE FRISBIE HOAR, LL. D., 1893-94.
†RICHARD SALTER STORRS, D. D., LL. D., 1894-95.
JAMES SCHOULER, LL. D., 1895-96.
GEORGE PARK FISHER, D. D., LL. D., 1896-97.
JAMES FORD RHODES, LL. D., 1897-98.
EDWARD EGGLESTON, 1898-99.

SECRETARIES:

HERBERT BAXTER ADAMS, Ph. D., LL. D., 1884—
A. HOWARD CLARK, 1889—

TREASURER:

CLARENCE WINTHROP BOWEN, Ph. D., 1884—

EXECUTIVE COUNCIL:

(In addition to above-named officers.)

Hon. WILLIAM BABCOCK WEEDEN, A. M., 1884-86.
†CHARLES DEANE, LL. D., 1884-87.
MOSES COIT TYLER, L. H. D., LL. D., 1884-85.
EPHRAIM EMERTON, Ph. D., 1884-85.
FRANKLIN BOWDITCH DEXTER, A. M., 1885-87.
†WILLIAM FRANCIS ALLEN, A. M., 1885-87.

AMERICAN HISTORICAL ASSOCIATION.

Hon. WILLIAM WIRT HENRY, LL. D., 1886-88.
†Hon. RUTHERFORD BURCHARD HAYES, LL. D., 1887-88.
JOHN W. BURGESS, 1887-91.
ARTHUR MARTIN WHEELER, A. M., 1887-89.
GEORGE PARK FISHER, D. D., LL. D., 1888-91.
†GEORGE BROWN GOODE, LL. D., 1889-96.
JOHN GEORGE BOURINOT, D. C. L., LL. D., 1889-94.
JOHN BACH McMASTER, A. M., 1891-94.
GEORGE BURTON ADAMS, Ph. D., 1891-97; 1899—
HENRY MORSE STEPHENS, A. M., 1895-99.
FREDERICK JACKSON TURNER, Ph. D., 1895-99,
EDWARD MINER GALLAUDET, Ph. D., LL. D., 1896-97.
MELVILLE WESTON FULLER, LL. D., 1898—
ALBERT BUSHNELL HART, Ph. D., 1898—
A. C. McLAUGHLIN, A. M., 1898—
WILLIAM A. DUNNING, Ph. D., 1899—
Hon. PETER WHITE, 1899—

The term of office is indicated by the dates following the name.
Deceased officers are marked thus †.

CONTENTS.

VOLUME I.

		Page.
I.	Report of Proceedings of Fifteenth Annual Meeting in Boston and Cambridge, December 27-29, 1899, by A. Howard Clark, Assistant Secretary	2
II.	Inaugural Address by James Ford Rhodes, President	43
III.	Removal of Officials by the Presidents of the United States, by Carl Russell Fish	65
IV.	Legal Qualifications for Office in America (1619-1899), by Frank Hayden Miller	87
V.	The Proposed Absorption of Mexico in 1847-48, by Edward G. Bourne	155
VI.	The Problem of Chinese Immigration in Farther Asia, by F. W. Williams	171
VII.	The Droit de Banalité during the French Régime in Canada, by W. Bennett Munro	205
VIII.	The Restoration of the Proprietary of Maryland and the Legislation against the Roman Catholics during the Governorship of Capt. John Hart (1714-1720), by Bernard C. Steiner	229
IX.	The First Criminal Code of Virginia, by Walter F. Prince	309
X.	A Critical Examination of Gordon's History of the American Revolution, by Orin Grant Libby	365
XI.	A Recent Service of Church History to the Church, by W. G. Andrews	389
XII.	The Origin of the Local Interdict, by Arthur Charles Howland	429
XIII.	The Poor Priests; or, Study of the Rise of English Lollardy, by Henry Lewin Cannon	449
XIV.	The Roman City of Langres (France) in the Early Middle Ages, by Earle W. Dow	483
XV.	Robert Fruin, 1823-1899. A Memorial Sketch, by Ruth Putnam	513
XVI.	Sacred and Profane History, by J. H. Robinson	527
XVII.	Should recent European History Have a Place in the College Curriculum, by C. M. Andrews	537
XVIII.	The Colonial Problem, by Henry E. Bourne	549
XIX.	A Bibliography of the Study and Teaching of History, by James Ingersoll Wyer	559

		Page.
XX.	Titles of Books on English History published in 1897–1899, selected by W. Dawson Johnston	613
XXI.	A Bibliography of Mississippi, by Thomas McAdory Owen	633
XXII.	Bibliography of Publications of the American Historical Association, 1885 to 1900	829
	Index	845

VOLUME II.

Fourth Annual Report of the Manuscripts Commission. Correspondence of John C. Calhoun. Edited by J. F. Jameson.

I.—REPORT OF PROCEEDINGS OF FIFTEENTH ANNUAL MEETING OF THE AMERICAN HISTORICAL ASSOCIATION.

BOSTON AND CAMBRIDGE, MASS., DECEMBER 27-29, 1899.

REPORT OF PROCEEDINGS OF THE FIFTEENTH ANNUAL MEETING OF THE AMERICAN HISTORICAL ASSOCIATION.[1]

By A. HOWARD CLARK, Assistant Secretary and Curator.

The act of incorporation of the American Historical Association, approved January 4, 1889, provides that it shall have its principal office at Washington City, and that it may hold its annual meetings in such places as the incorporators shall determine. Under this authority meetings have been held in Washington, Chicago, Cleveland, New York, and New Haven. At the New Haven meeting in 1898 it was decided that future meetings be held alternately in the East, the West, and at Washington. Accordingly Boston was fixed upon for the 1899 meeting, Detroit for 1900, and Washington for 1901.

The fifteenth annual meeting convened in Boston on December 27, 1899, and for three days in that city and in Cambridge the association was busied with the reading and discussion of papers and topics pertaining to American history and to the study of history in America.

The condition of the association was shown by the reports of the officers and various commissions and committees to be very active and prosperous. The membership has more than doubled since 1894, the increase during the last two years being especially large, and the present number of members is nearly 1,500, residing in all parts of the country, and including the large majority of professional writers and teachers of American history, besides many representative men interested in the study of facts and problems connected with America's past and their relation to the future of the nation in all its phases of social and political life.

---

[1] An account of this meeting is printed in the April number of the American Historical Review, and has been used in part in preparing the present report.

Since its organization, in 1884, the association has published five volumes of papers and eleven volumes of reports, making a total of nearly 11,000 octavo printed pages, covering all branches of American history and of history study. As aids to investigators some extensive bibliographies have been published, and other important ones are in preparation. The Historical Manuscripts Commission has issued three reports containing very valuable material. One of the most important publications was the Report of the Committee of Seven on the Study of History in Schools. This work has also been published through the MacMillan Company, and is proving of great benefit in systematizing history study throughout the country, particularly in the secondary schools, and the entrance requirements in history in one at least of the larger universities have been modified in accordance with this committee's recommendations.

The association reports are printed as Congressional documents, and it has thus been possible to place them in the libraries of the principal historical societies of this country and in the libraries of the larger historical societies throughout the world.

The Boston meeting proved to be the largest and most enthusiastic in the association's history, the attendance of members being about two hundred, while several hundred persons showed by their presence their interest in the general work.

The sessions of the first day were devoted to the reading and discussion of papers on colonization, church history, and to the president's inaugural address. The second day's papers were on fields for historical study and on European history, while on the third day the topics pertained chiefly to foreign relations.

The opening session was called to order at 10.30 a. m., December 27, in the South Congregational Church, Boston. President James Ford Rhodes presided, and in the absence, through illness, of Secretary H. B. Adams, the assistant secretary, A. Howard Clark, of the Smithsonian Institution, discharged the duties of that office.

In his opening remarks President Rhodes said:

The members of the association will observe a new property. The history of it is graven neatly on this gavel and is: "This gavel is presented to the American Historical Association by Samuel Macauley Jackson, Boston,

December 28, 1899." It is made of the five following woods, four of which, forming the head, consist of the maple of Connecticut, the ash of Pennsylvania, the red birch of New Hampshire, and the oak of New York State. The gold band upon which this is engraved is from California. Upon the two silver bands are the words "From Nevada." The handle is made of the vermilion of Kentucky. In the name of the association I thank Mr. Jackson for this useful present.

Every member will notice with regret that our veteran secretary is not here with us, and everyone will know that it is an enforced absence. He has been secretary of the association from its formation, and until now has never missed a meeting. Overwork has unfortunately broken the health of Mr. Adams, and he is seeking recuperation by travel and rest. He has been a mighty worker for this association; he has done much to secure for it the place it occupies in the minds of historical students; he has been in diligence, discretion, and zeal an ideal permanent executive officer. Our sympathies and our good wishes go out to him. I recommend that at the business meeting Friday afternoon an appropriate resolution be adopted which shall express our regret at his inability to attend this meeting and our hope for the speedy recovery of his health.

I can not let this occasion pass without a word in the way of tribute to a member whom death has recently taken from us. I refer to Mr. John C. Ropes. The classmate, the professional associate, and the friend have at different times and on different occasions laid their chaplet on his bier. I have here to deplore the loss which history has sustained. Mr. Ropes did the work of two days in one; one was given to the duties of an exacting profession, the other to his chosen muse. His works on Napoleon, the two volumes of his military history of the civil war, testify to his diligence and impartiality in the common field of members of this association. As I turn over his volumes on the civil war I am struck with the modesty and reserve he showed in his footnotes, for he was not only a mine of knowledge, but his knowledge was at hand. Reading had made him a full man and conference a ready man. In every respect he was a true historian. It was a cruel fate which took him hence, and the muse of history may well drop a tear that he did not live to finish his Story of the Civil War. I now declare the fifteenth meeting of the American Historical Association open. Mayor Quincy, who was to have extended the welcome of the city, is unavoidably absent, and his place will be filled by Rev. Dr. Edward Everett Hale, pastor of this church, and well known to the most of you.

Dr. Hale said:

I am sure the city of Boston will cordially welcome you, and more cordially than any other city because we here feel the necessity of the proper working up of our own history. We welcome you to all criticisms of the past, to all the duty which we know you will do in the future in making more clear the history of New England, of the United States, and, as I see by the programme, of the whole world.

In December, 1898, the association appointed a committee on the history of colonies and dependencies, Prof. Henry E. Bourne, of Western Reserve University, being made its chairman. He reported that the committee had made some progress during the year, but very much remained to be done in its extensive field of operations. Professor Bourne read a paper on "Some difficulties of American colonization," and a paper was read by Prof. F. W. Williams on "Chinese emigrants in the Far East," both of which are printed in full in this volume.

Mr. A. Lawrence Lowell, of Boston, presented a valuable paper, of which an abstract is here given, on "The selection and training of colonial officials in England, Holland, and France," being a summary of a body of material to be later published as a book:

We can not copy the political form of any foreign country, but we can learn their principles [said Mr. Lowell in beginning]. In England, until the middle of this century the civil servants of India were appointed at the pleasure of the directors of the East India Company, and until about the beginning of the century they received no special training. In 1806 a college was established for their education at Haileybury, and it did very good work; but the students were admitted to it by the patronage of the directors of the company, and when the patronage system fell the college fell with it. A system of competitive examination was substituted, upon a plan drawn up by a commission, of which Macauley was chairman. This plan, which is carried out to-day, is based on two main principles: 1, that the candidates must have a very high general education; 2, that they must not be required to spend in preparing for the examination time which they will have wasted if unsuccessful. Hence the examination covers only subjects usually taught at universities and does not include subjects relating peculiarly to their duties in India. The examination is very much like an examination for graduation honors, and as the subjects are numerous and optional, a man from any university has a fair chance at it. Before going to India the successful competitors spend a year in England, usually at a university, studying Indian law and languages. The same competitive examination is used to select the Eastern cadets; that is, the appointees to the civil service of the other Asiatic colonies, including the Malay States.

Appointments to the civil service of the Dutch East Indies have been made in Holland by competitive examination since 1864. The only general education required is a diploma of a high school. The examination bears entirely upon the law, languages, history, religion, and customs of the Dutch Indies, and the candidates are in fact all prepared at the India Institute at Delft. The course there is three years, but only the men who rank highest at the examination get appointments, and they are a small part of those who go through the school. A commission recently appointed by the minister of the colonies has reported that the preparation for the examination is too much a mere effort to learn by heart a mass of unimportant details, and that the system is bad in not requiring a sufficiently high general education, and in having the competitive examination come at the end of a long course of technical study.

There are four methods of admission to the colonial service of France: (1) Promotion from a subordinate service; (2) appointment of military and other officers; (3) open competition; (4) the Colonial School at Paris. The proportion of these four is constantly changing and varies in different colonies. The open competition has not been very successful because there are only two or three places offered a year, and hence they do not attract many competitors; for graduates of the school are reserved only one-sixth of the places in Africa, but they get a larger proportion in Indo-China. The competitive examination comes at the entrance to the school, and only about as many are admitted as are likely to be employed. The course is two years and is devoted almost entirely to technical colonial studies and to law. The graduates in the service are well spoken of, but the school has only existed ten years and it is too soon to judge of its work by experience.

In the discussions which followed this group of papers Mr. Alleyne Ireland, author of the book on Tropical Colonization, spoke of the difficulties which attend the introduction of the system of contract labor, which was nevertheless, in his judgment, inevitable in the Philippines. Dr. Clive Day, of Yale University, speaking chiefly with respect to the 250,000 Chinamen in Java, showed wherein they were an economic necessity in such colonies, their function being that of middlemen on a small scale, and compared their position to that of the Jews in the Middle Ages. Mr. Arthur Lord, of Plymouth, spoke of the application of the principles of civil-service reform to the new possessions. Though we could not demand highly specialized training or provide pensions, it was possible to insist that appointees should have youth, health, some experience in administrative duties, and an acquaintance with Spanish and with the language of the district. Prof. H. Morse Stephens, of Cornell University, declared that if a system of patronage was followed in appointments a college to train the appointees was a necessity. English experience had shown, especially at the time of the mutiny, that it had also a high value in making the officials all brothers; yet with this went a tendency to become cliquey, and the government of India would have become an aristocratic tyranny had it not been for the constant practice of sending out as governors persons of commanding social position independent of the Indian service, and English barristers as judges.

In an editorial discussing the papers presented at this session the Boston Herald of December 29 said:

We are confronted with new and grave responsibilities, all the more grave for the reason that the experience of other nations has proved that it is the easiest of all possible mistakes to make to adopt a bad method of colonial control, one which will give constant offense to the people of the outlying possession and be at the same time demoralizing to the controlling country. From the time of ancient Greece and Rome up to the present day, we have had numerous instances afforded of the disastrous effects of improperly directed colonial administration, and, what is more, the list of colonial failures enormously exceeds the number of colonial successes. With this historical record before us, it is of the utmost importance that we should first endeavor to discover the methods adopted by those who have made successes in this class of work, and then try to frame our policy in close conformity with the broad general principles that have controlled these.

One of the most obvious means is to devise a plan by which those who are appointed to represent our Government in these distant parts of the world over which we are to exercise control shall be specially fitted for the work they are called upon to undertake. The English have had the largest experience in work of this kind, and after a number of experiments they have decided that a high grade of competitive examination produces the best results. The men who enter the Indian civil service have to pass an examination somewhat similar to that which a young man would be compelled to pass in order to obtain a university degree, and having in this way shown their intelligence, those who succeed, before they enter into active service, are compelled to study for a year or more subjects which have a peculiar bearing upon Indian service, such as the languages, laws, customs, and traditions of the people. The result has been that England has built up in her Indian civil service a force of men having remarkable ability and possessing an exceptional esprit de corps. The ease with which under Lord Cromer the administration of Egypt has been carried on is because the lines laid down for the administration of India have been reproduced in this new field.

It is, however, questionable whether public opinion could be obtained for, or Congressional sanction given to, a plan of appointments to our colonial service similar to that which controls the Indian civil service of Great Britain. We regret to say it, but our people have not yet brought themselves to believe that any large degree of intelligence or special knowledge is required in the civil administration of a country. If it was proposed to establish a colonial civil-service system which ruled out almost everyone who was not capable of passing an examination for university honors, a protest would go up, particularly from the demagogic politicians, that this was a species of class control, and that in a free democratic government every citizen should be given a chance to receive an official appointment. This is one of our weaknesses, and, if it is not in some way guarded against, it is likely to lead to colonial administration on the part of the United States which, in its results, will be no improvement on the administration by Spain of her American colonies, while administrative corruption in these outlying possessions will react, as in the past we know that it did, upon the home governments of Rome, Venice, Spain, and other imperial countries.

The suggestion was made in the discussion by the American Historical Association of this question that the best method of securing desired results, because the method most in line with our national practices in other directions, would be the establishment of a colonial academy under Government control, and managed in much the same manner that the academies at West Point and Annapolis are administered. The cadets to these army and navy schools are appointed as the result of official patronage, but after their years of tuition the young men who succeed in graduating have not only a thorough knowledge of their duties, but a high standard of honesty and honor, and a knowledge of and confidence in each other which make them most effective public servants.

It is not improbable that a Government colonial academy conducted on similar lines, guaranteeing to its graduates that same continuity and permanence of service, with promotion and retiring pension, such as are held out in the case of West Point and Annapolis, would, in a few years, produce a body of men which would be as admirable in its capacity, integrity, and service ability as the bodies made up of graduates of our Naval and Military academies. The method is one which is certainly worth trying, and as no time should be lost in providing the force with which our outlying possessions are to be governed, Congress, at its present session, could undertake no work of greater value than that of preparing the way for the foundation of an institution of this character.

The session of the church history section of the association was held in the rooms of the Massachusetts Historical Society on Wednesday afternoon. Prof. Moses Coit Tyler, second vice-president of the association, occupied the chair. The first paper presented was by Prof. Egbert C. Smyth, of Andover, Mass. Its subject was: "The prevalent view in the ancient church of the purpose of the death of Christ."

Professor Smyth stated that he had been led to investigate the subject anew by the frequency and positiveness of the assertion, in recent more or less influential publications, that "for one thousand years" the common view of the atonement was that the death of Christ was a ransom to Satan. The statements referred to indicate in various ways that they are made at second or third hand, and to some extent have a common source. Still they are widely current. The results of the writer's study were presented under the following heads:

1. The earliest view is not that of a ransom to the devil.

2. Some of the most important representatives of the ancient church either ignore or positively reject the theory in question.

3. The interpretation which supposes that there was held for centuries—"a thousand years," or "nearly" so—a theory of ransom to Satan, and that this was then followed and superseded by that of a Godward relation of Christ's death, is grossly incorrect.

4. The ransom to Satan theory never had the definiteness which is ascribed to it nowadays.

5. It is not sufficient in such a problem to confine the range of investigation to individval opinions, or merely to the testimony of church teachers. That of creeds, liturgies, hymns, the sacrament of the Lord's supper, is of weight. This lends no support to the representations referred to in the beginning of this paper. On the contrary, it affirms the constant presence to the church, however imperfectly discerned or inadequately appreciated, of Him who was "victor and victim," and the first because He was also the last.

The Rev. W. G. Andrews, of Guilford, Conn., read a paper on "A recent service of church history to the church," which is given in full in this report. The first third of the century in America was characterized by union and cooperation of denominations in Christian work. In the second third of the century this period of good feeling was over. The denominations became conscious of their distinctive mission, and division or hostility became the tendency. At the same time this self-consciousness of the denominations turned to the story of their past. Denominational histories wakened interest in a more general study of Christian history as a whole. The result of this has been a diminution of prejudice and an appreciation of what is common to all forms of Christianity. While uniformity in opinion and ritual is less valued, there is, as a result of this study of Christian history, a longing for essential unity.

The concluding paper of the afternoon was by Rev. H. S. Burrage, of Portland, Me., on the question, "Why was Roger Williams banished?"

Dr. Burrage referred at some length to the proceedings connected with the banishment of Roger Williams, and called attention to the attempt of the late Rev. Dr. Henry M. Dexter, in his As to Roger Williams, to show that banishment of Mr. Williams "took place for reasons purely political and having no relation to his views upon toleration, or upon any subject other than those which in their bearing upon the common rights of property, upon the sanctions of the oath, and upon due subordination to the powers that be in the state made him a subverter of the very foundations of the Government—with all his worthiness of character and general soundness of doctrine, a nuisance which it seemed to them they had no alternative but to abate in some way safe to them and kindest to him."

This position was strenuously combated. It was not denied that the members of the general court in their banishment of Roger Williams were influenced by other considerations than his unyielding attitude with reference to soul liberty.

Mr. Winthrop, in his account of the proceedings of the court, and Roger Williams himself, in his recital of the statement made by Governor Haynes in pronouncing the sentence of banishment, made it clear that other matters were before the court and doubtless did enter into its decision. But the very same testimony is equally valid proof that Mr. Williams's doctrine of soul liberty was also before the court. It was there in the form in which he held it all through his career. Nor is this all. It was expressly mentioned by Governor Haynes as one of the causes that led to the banishment.

The only new document bearing upon this matter is that which records the action of the council of the Bay Colony in 1676, offering Roger Williams an asylum in some one of the Massachusetts towns during the Indian troubles.

The remainder of the paper was an answer to the question, What light, if any, does this action throw upon the causes of Mr. Williams's banishment?

If, as Dr. Dexter says, the banishment was for reasons purely political and had no relation to Mr. Williams's notions upon toleration, it would seem that in the action of the council in 1676 we should find some indication of that fact. These are not to be found.

Mr. Williams was banished for having "broached and dyvulged dyvers newe and dangerous opinions," and for having maintained the same without retraction. It is noteworthy that in the action of the council in 1676 it is stated that Mr. Williams, hitherto restrained, might come into the colony for security to his person, "he behaving himself peaceably and inoffensively & not disseminating & venting any of his different opinions in matters of religion to the dissatisfaction of any." This may mean that Mr. Williams might have a refuge within the limits of the colony if he would so guard his utterances with reference to matters of religion as not to give offense to the Bay Colony people. Or it may mean that any expression whatever of his religious opinions would not be tolerated if they were displeasing to the people. In either view there is a recognition of the fact that Mr. Williams's doctrine of soul liberty was certainly one of the causes that led to his banishment.

The action of the Massachusetts council, however, is delightful evidence of the kindly feeling that was entertained for Roger Williams by the leaders of the Puritan colony, and while it must have awakened memories that were not altogether pleasing, it could hardly have failed to reach and touch his heart.

A brief discussion, opened by Dr. Ezra H. Byington and continued by Prof. George P. Fisher, brought the afternoon session to a close.

At the evening session in the Congregational Church two addresses were delivered. The first was a speech of welcome by the governor of the Commonwealth, Roger Wolcott, and the other the inaugural address by President Rhodes.

Governor Wolcott said:

In extending the greetings of the Commonwealth of Massachusetts to the American Historical Association, I feel that I am bidding them welcome to a soil and to an intellectual atmosphere which should be native and familiar to all students of American history, for here, within the limits of the old Commonwealth, has been enacted a fair share, and here has been written a preponderant share, of the history of the United States.

From the very earliest settlement at Plymouth and Massachusetts Bay, in the colony at Salem and at Boston, down through all the bloody period of the French and Indian wars, down through the period that introduced and made necessary the war of the Revolution, the earliest battles of that great period and of the century, and more that has passed since then, the Commonwealth of Massachusetts has never retired from a place in the forefront of her sister States.

And following this great series of events there has floated a constant stream of historical output, the fount of which is not yet dried up.

Beginning with the earliest times—the history of the Plymouth plantation by Governor Bradford, and the history of the colony of Massachusetts Bay by Governor Winthrop—began the very beginning of the life of our people in New England. Then somewhat later came the diary of Judge Sewall, carefully recording the events and giving an accurate picture of the life and habits of the time in which he lived. Then there were the stories of a more or less ecclesiastical character, such as Dr. Johnson's "Wonder-Working Providence," and the writings of Cotton Mather, especially the "Magnalia," or the ecclesiastical history of New England. Next came the careful chronological history of Thomas Prince, the pastor of the Old South Meeting House. Then Gov. Thomas Hutchinson's history—first a governor and afterwards an exile, a precedent which fortunately has not been followed in dealing with his successors in the office.

George Bancroft spent fifty years of his laborious life in collecting and editing the history of the period up to and including and following the war of the Revolution. Then we have had the careful and valuable history of Hildreth; the History of New England, by Palfrey;.the records in diary and the record of the page of written history of the Adamses, one of whom was your host to-day; the carefully collected historical papers which were edited by President Sparks, of Harvard College, and more recently the completed work of Schouler. That has expanded, as it necessarily must, as the continuous history written here in Massachusetts has expanded from the history of a mere colony or province or Commonwealth to the broader history of New England and the United States.

And then finally we have the charming histories of Prescott, Motley, and Parkman, describing the inroad of the Spaniards upon those peaceful islands and lands that had the curse of bearing gold put upon them, but which up to that time had slumbered peacefully beneath the Southern cross. And then we read the heroic struggle of the Netherlands against the cruel domination of Spain. Later we follow the courses of the Great Lakes and the lordly St. Lawrence, with the history written by Parkman, telling of the French domination and the final fall of the French power. These three latter historians whom I have mentioned have had the great good fortune of clothing historical events, picturesque and romantic as they were, in the charm of a perfect English style, and of therefore winning for themselves the name not only of historical students, but also, in a broader sense, of scholars and men of letters.

We have been very grasping, as men and States sometimes must be who win a forward place in the ranks of competition; and although, as I have said, the breed of our own historians has not been exhausted, we have stretched out and taken historical students from other cities.

One of those gentlemen, Mr. John Fiske, born, I believe, in the neighboring State of Connecticut has perhaps done more than any other writer to make American history readable and interesting to the children of our schools.

Another one, who is present to-night, and who is president of this association, we allured to ourselves from Ohio—not the only or the worst thing we have derived from Ohio during the recent quarter of a century.

I think that the coming of such students to Boston and to Massachusetts may be easily explained by the fact of the great collections of books in the Boston Public Library, in the library of Harvard College, and in the valuable collection in the rooms of the Massachusetts Historical Society. I think that more and more, as the value and the availability of those great collections become known, Massachusetts will continue to be in the future, as it has certainly been in the past, the State of the American Union where history—and the most valuable part of Americrn history—has heretofore been written.

But I must not detain you. I have spoken briefly, merely to show you why historical students should feel at home on the soil of the Commonwealth of Massachusetts, and having done that, I have robbed myself of the excuse or the opportunity of saying more. It needs no welcome from me to greet you on coming to a Commonwealth where the very spirit of the past and the opportunities of the present are your sufficient welcome. Yet I can not close without assuring you that the meeting of such a company of American historical students as constitute this American Historical Association can never be a matter of indifference to the Commonwealth of Massachusetts, and that such organizations of scholars as this are always heartily welcomed by the old Bay State.

In his address, printed in this volume, President Rhodes said that he thought no period so propitious for writing history as the present. It is the age of Darwin and Darwin's theory; the ideas of evolution, heredity, and environment have affected profoundly historical students and have given them great advantages in their tracing of the development of a people or the growth of an institution. He questioned, however, whether we wrote history better than the ancient writers. Scholars would generally agree that Thucydides and Tacitus were the greatest historians, and if they were to name a third choice they would undoubtedly specify Herodotus or Gibbon. Herodotus was characterized, and the secret of his hold upon men was thought to be expressed well by the London Times: "When Homer and Dante and Shakespeare are neglected, then will Herodotus cease to be read."

Diligence, accuracy, love of truth, and impartiality were the merits commonly ascribed to Thucydides, but Mr. Rhodes thought Samuel R. Gardiner the equal of the Athenian in these respects. In truth, Gardiner had to submit to a much harder test from the external evidence. Tacitus was characterized and deemed worthy of high praise, but in "diligence, accuracy, and love of truth" Gibbon was rated his equal; and with the remark, "Gibbon's work has richly deserved its life of more than one hundred years," the testimony to the merit of the Englishman by Niebuhr, Mommsen, and Frederic Harrison was cited.

Nevertheless, in the consensus of learned people Thucydides and Tacitus stand at the head of historians, and Mr. Rhodes ventured the suggestion that their special merit was their compressed narrative.

On Thursday, December 28, morning and evening sessions were held in the Congregational Church, and the afternoon was devoted to social matters. The first paper of the day was by Mr. Charles Francis Adams, president of the Massachusetts Historical Society, and was entitled "A plea for military history."

He began by quoting at some length from the address entitled "Historians and historical societies," delivered by him at the opening of the Fenway Building of the Massachusetts Historical Society last April. In these quotations the variety of special knowledge required by the modern historian was pointed out, and the consequent necessity that the history of the future should be the work of a literary artist and judicially minded philosopher, rather than a mere investigator, as it is manifestly impossible that any one man could have full special knowledge of so many subjects.

Referring to his own army experience during the civil war, Mr. Adams said:

> Since then I have read in books of history, and other works more avowedly of fiction, many accounts of campaigns and battles; and in so doing I have been most deeply impressed with the audacity, not of soldiers, but of authors.

He then referred to the late John C. Ropes as a brilliant exception to the foregoing criticism, quoting the opinion of General Schofield, when commander of the Army of the United States, that Mr. Ropes was the first of living military critics. He paid a high tribute to the value of Mr. Ropes's studies, and expressed the opinion that his loss, so far as the military history of the rebellion was concerned, was irreparable. There was no man living who could finish the work on the civil war which Mr. Ropes left incomplete.

Passing, then, to examples of the defective treatment of military operations by historians, Mr. Adams referred to five important military operations in American history—the capture of Quebec by Wolfe, the battle of Bunker Hill, the battle of Long Island, the battle of Bladensburg, and the battle of New Orleans.

As respects the capture of Quebec, and speaking from recent personal examination of the ground, he pointed out alleged deficiencies in the accounts of the several historians, especially of the late Francis Parkman. The ascent from the river to the Heights of Abraham he pronounced a by no means difficult operation under the circumstances, while the subsequent battle, in which both Wolfe and Montcalm were killed, he declared a most serious and fatal strategic blunder on the part of the latter; a blunder which probably saved Wolfe's army from destruction.

He then referred at length to the influence of the battles of Bunker Hill and Long Island, to the grave strategic and tactical errors which marked each of the struggles, and to the imminent danger in the latter case to which Washington exposed himself, his army, and the cause of American independence upon Long Island, all of which considerations had been ignored in the books of so-called history. The battle of New Orleans was the direct result, he asserted, of the battle of Bladensburg—its logical sequence. At Bladensburg the British had simply walked over the ill-defended American lines, and they had concluded that there was an excellent chance of their being able to repeat the operation at New Orleans. They got themselves slaughtered in consequence.

In the meanwhile, had they pursued a correct system of strategy and tactics, controlling, as they did, the Mississippi, they could have easily outflanked Jackson and compelled him to retreat, capturing the city of New Orleans without loss of life. All this, again, had escaped the civilian historical writer.

He closed by suggesting that in future the work of the historian of the highest class would be more of a judicial character than it had hitherto been; that is, he would inform himself as to the facts less by personal investigation than by passing upon the special knowledge and fairness of judgment of the writers of monographs, whether those monographs related to particular episodes or to those branches of human knowledge which entered into history, whether finance, diplomacy, military and naval operations, or social, economical, financial, and educational influences and developments. The historian of the future, submitting himself to the guidance of trained specialists, would exert himself mainly to make among those specialists a correct choice.

Prof. James H. Robinson, of Columbia, in a paper upon "Sacred and profane history," dwelt upon the extraordinary accumulation of historical knowledge during the past fifty years, which necessitated a division of our vast stock into two distinct parts. Everything of a technical or special nature should be viewed as purely professional. On the other hand, certain matters of general and permanent interest should be carefully presented for the benefit of the public and for the students in our schools and colleges. Hitherto we have confused these two classes of knowledge, and our histories for general use contain many details which have no business there, and, on the other hand, space enough is not given to describe clearly the great factors in mankind's past and to explain such mighty changes as the Renaissance, the Protestant revolution, and the French revolution. The paper is printed in full in subsequent pages of this volume.

The closing essay of the morning was by Prof. W. J. Ashley, of Harvard University, who made "A plea for economic history."

The paper was largely a definition of economic history and

a statement of its proper subject-matter. The speaker began by mentioning the extraordinary attention which was once given to theological controversies, and to the vast stores of erudition once heaped up by proposed historians of the church. Such an attitude had become foreign to us to-day, as was shown by the prevailing tendency to relegate church history to theological seminaries.

The speaker then dwelt on the fact that it was the era of constitution making ushered in by the French Revolution, which gave us our constitutional historians. Without 1830 and 1832 Guyot, Hallam, and Macauley were inexplicable.

The causes which had produced our modern economic histories were also discussed by the speaker. Socialist critics had been obliged to turn to history in support of their contentions. The existence of such questions as the labor question, the agricultural question, the tariff question, had all influenced the character of modern histories, as well as the facts selected for emphasis.

The preface to Green's Short History of the English People was a profession of faith, and not the least significant thing about it was its date, 1874. Much of the interest there displayed in the common people would doubtless expand itself; particulars of the material aspects of life, such as food, clothing, etc., were necessarily trivial until brought into relation to those economic conditions upon which reposed the structure of society at any particular epoch.

The speaker discussed the senses in which history might be called "economic." In one sense economic history was that complete portrayal of the whole evolution of society which all dreamt of as an ultimate ideal that should do justice to all its elements and aspects. Toward social history in this sense it was the task of economic history to furnish a very considerable contribution.

The discussion of the papers of this session was opened by Prof. Anson D. Morse, of Amherst College. He spoke on the utility of society, which he said was to permit the free and powerful action of personal influence. Society accomplishes the assumption of ideas and ideals by children and the less mature of its members. In order to do this work in the best way it should be so organized as to be a small, manageable community of from 2,000 to 12,000 persons. Within these groups personal influence is powerful, affecting only their members. The personal influence of a group of Catholics does not affect a group of Presbyterians or Baptists. This grouping has a decisive influence on American history and especially on politics. If the influence of the best people in each of these groups should be exerted the political "boss" would be unknown. Society was better established during the Colonial period than it is now.

Prof. John Winthrop Platner, of Harvard University, followed. Church history is becoming politely tolerated, he said. Scholars are recognizing that there is a unity in history, and that all branches of this history affect all mankind. Sacred history may be studied as that of a great institution and as including mythology the same as Christianity. There should be more attention paid to religious history in its largest sense, bearing upon all departments of human life.

Mrs. Robert Abbe, of New York, spoke on the necessity of inspiring children with a love for good citizenship. The child should be trained in this the same as he is taught respect for his parents and grandparents. She told what had been done in New York in organizing children into classes. There are 90 of these, with a membership of 2,000. One of these classes is composed of children who are detained in the Tombs awaiting trial for minor offenses. These children take the greatest interest in this study and show great aptitude. The methods pursued in reaching the poorer classes were described, and she said that she hoped to arouse a love for history in the children of the wealthier classes in time.

Prof. John M. Vincent, of Johns Hopkins University, spoke of the reign of Alfred the Great, which is to be celebrated in England in 1901. He thought it well to study this period of British history, not because there was hope of discovering anything new in the life of Alfred, but because it had such an important bearing on the history of the race.

The evening session was presided over by Dr. Moses Coit Tyler, second vice-president of the association.

The first paper read was an interesting account of "Robert Fruin, professor of Dutch history at Leyden, died 1899," contributed by Miss Ruth Putnam, of New York, and printed in full in this volume.

Prof. Charles M. Andrews, of Bryn Mawr College, next

answered the question, "Should recent European history have a place in the college curriculum?" Professor Andrews read a plea for the study of recent history in college classes, stating that the history of the last thirty years had not been considered available for scholarly historical treatment; he said that this view of the matter had been accepted rather too complacently by historical scholars.

Mr. James Breck Perkins, of Rochester, read a paper on French mistakes, meaning those mistakes in colonial policy which had prevented France from acquiring such an empire as that of England. Few would deny that at the present time the influence of the British Empire far exceeds that exercised by France. Two hundred and fifty years ago such a relative position would have seemed quite unlikely. At that time, though colonial development was in an embryonic state, France was, on the whole, in advance of her rival across the channel, and had every prospect of bringing into existence a great colonial empire. Among the causes of her failure a prominent place must be given to religious bigotry, but for which the French Huguenots might have done for France what the English Puritans did for Great Britain. Catholic Frenchmen, moreover, were not afforded in the colonies that free opportunity to better their economic condition, without which it was vain to expect men to emigrate. Even worse was the management of India, for while abundant attention, however misdirected, was applied to the attempt to build up an empire in the West, the French Government viewed with positive indifference the golden opportunity presented to it by Dupleix for acquiring an empire of boundless importance in the East. Dupleix essayed to create an empire by means closely resembling those which had been employed by the Romans. If the directors of the French East Indian Company or the authorities at Versailles had properly appreciated and seconded his efforts a French proconsul might now be ruling in Calcutta.

The discussion which followed related to the academic problem of the teaching of recent history. Prof. Ferdinand Schwill, of Chicago, agreed with Professor Andrews. If in some respects the materials for thorough work on this period seemed unsatisfactory, yet good opportunities for learning the elements of historical criticism were often presented by newspapers and such sources, in which good and bad were intermixed, but in which the bias or point of view was an obvious one, and certainly classes were always much interested in these most recent periods. Professor Haskins, of Wisconsin, while agreeing to the general proposition, especially if the study of these times was used as the culmination of a general course, thought that excessive attention to them was to be deprecated. The materials were too voluminous for the successful teaching of critical methods. The most successful seminaries were, as a rule, those occupied with mediæval history, which presented a small and compact body of material.

The closing sessions of the annual meeting were held on Friday, December 29, at Harvard University in Cambridge, the morning session for the reading of papers being in Sanders Theater and in the afternoon a business session in the Fogg Art Museum.

The discussions of the morning had "foreign relations" for their subject.

The first paper read was by Prof. John Bach McMaster, of the University of Pennsylvania. His topic was "The government of foreigners." He said that the government of Cuba, Porto Rico, and the Philippines had given us a new and hitherto untried problem. We were presented, in fact, with three pieces of foreign territory, presenting three types of civilization. In every sense of the word these people were foreign to us. It was not setting up a government in the wilderness that we were familiar with. The question raised was whether these people were under the Constitution or without it. Historically they were outside of the Constitution. When the war of independence was under way Congress proposed to take territory outside of the United States and sell it for the payment of the war debt. It was afterwards proposed to take that territory into the United States. This was objected to by the people of the thirteen States. When the territory acquired from France was taken into the United States many of the provisions of the Constitution were not observed, and laws in violation of those provisions were in force. Under the treaty with France when Louisiana was acquired regulations for the government of that territory were adopted in violation of the Constitution. The argument used was that the territory was outside of the provisions of the Constitution, and this contention had been upheld by the Supreme Court. It followed from this that our new possessions were outside the Constitution of the United States and Congress was at liberty to use its authority in governing the territories in question, the only obligation upon it being to do what was just and right.

Baron Speck von Sternburg, counselor of the German legation to the United States and a member of the recent international Samoan commission, read in admirable English a paper on the Samoan question. Beginning with the agreement obtained in 1872 by Commander Meade, U. S. N., by which the United States acquired the privilege of a Samoan naval station, the mission of Captain Steinburger in 1873, the American treaty of 1878 securing Pago-Pago, and the British and German treaties of 1878, he traced the history of Samoan affairs during the prime ministry of Steinburger and the subsequent petty war of consuls, down to the time of the great hurricane in Apia Harbor. He then gave a history of the Berlin conference of 1889, and of the results of the tripartite agreement then effected. Anarchy prevailing, the three powers sent out last May a joint high commission, which succeeded in disarming the two rival native armies, breaking up military rule, and establishing a strong temporary civil government. The proposals which they laid before the three powers, and which took effect in the treaty signed on December 2, 1899, were described, and the happiest auguries expressed as to the future quiet and prosperity of the islands under the new arrangements.

The next paper was by Prof. Edward G. Bourne, of Yale University, on "The United States and Mexico, 1847–1848." Professor Bourne compared the situation that existed after the capture of the City of Mexico with that in the Philippines after the battle of Manila, and raised the question how we then escaped the annexation of all Mexico, which was urged with all the arguments advanced for the retention of the Philippines.

He sketched the rise of this "all of Mexico" agitation, showing that it was the outcome of a genuine spirit of expansion and not identified with the pro-slavery interest, for it was violently opposed by some of the greatest champions of slavery and ardently advocated by the opponents of that institution. The paper is given in full in this volume.

A paper by Prof. S. M. Macvane, of Harvard University, on "Democracy and peace," consisted in a discussion of the effect which the rise and advance of modern democracy has had on the conduct of diplomatic negotiations, and of the question whether, on the whole, democratic government makes for peace, as its admirers of a hundred years ago unquestionably expected that it would. He contended that of the ten important wars which have occurred within the present century seven arose not from any inherent difficulty of effecting a peaceable solution, but from the exasperation of popular feeling. Under a democratic form of government national sentiment interferes with calm consideration. The telegraph and the cheap newspaper have within the last fifty years made diplomacy more difficult; excitement is sooner brought to bear, and the diplomat has not so free a hand. Secrecy is less possible; and while it is the abuses of publicity against which we object rather than the publicity itself, apparently the two are inseparable. Professor Macvane also argued against the doctrine that the citizen ought not to oppose an aggressive policy on the part of his government lest he encourage the enemy; and against the doctrine that the best mode by which to maintain peace is to be always prepared for war. This paper has already been published elsewhere.

Prof. J. B. Moore, of Columbia University, formerly Assistant Secretary of State, thought Professor Macvane's picture of the earlier diplomacy unhistoric. He maintained that there was no such contrast as had been indicated with respect to dependence of diplomacy upon the popular will. In monarchical times, also, wars had frequently arisen out of popular excitement. In reality, though popular excitement often appeared upon the surface to be the cause of war, a deeper consideration would often show that there had been conflicting national interests of sufficient magnitude to make war inevitable.

Prof. H. P. Judson, of the University of Chicago, spoke chiefly upon the problem discussed in Professor McMaster's paper. He contended that the term "United States" is used in the Constitution in two senses, one geographical and international, in which sense the Territories are a part of the United States, and the other constitutional, in which sense they are not. He believed that the limitations expressed in the Constitution with regard to taxes on imports applied to the States only, and that the maintenance of a revenue tariff in the islands while a protective tariff was maintained at home was not unconstitutional. As to citizenship, he believed that, since the United States and places subject to their jurisdiction were contrasted in the thirteenth amendment, in the fourteenth amendment also the phrase "United States" did not include the latter. Mr. Edwin V. Morgan, who had lately been secretary to the Samoan commission, set forth, upon the basis of their experiences in Samoa, the necessity that those who are to take part in governing our new possessions shall study upon the spot the languages, customs, and religions of the inhabitants.

At the close of the morning session the association was entertained in Memorial Hall by the President and Fellows of Harvard College. After the luncheon President Eliot made a short address of welcome to the guests, in which he said:

I think there is no place in all America more fitting for the meeting of a society such as you represent than Cambridge. A great deal of American history has been wrought in Cambridge; history military, civil, and ecclesiastic; and, as you are aware, a great deal of history has been written here. The names of Palfrey, Sparks, and Winsor immediately rise to memory.

Many graduates of this university spent their lives in this study, and its achievement in that line would have been highest had not so many devoted themselves to politics and literature. History is still written in Cambridge, and it is my belief that the present generation of writers will maintain the standard of excellence their predecessors set for them, though, in accordance with the age in which they live, their tone and spirit be different.

So Cambridge is a place peculiarly appropriate in which to welcome you. There is about the ancient buildings a charm which in this country we are seldom able to win. Massachusetts, once used as a dormitory, old Harvard Hall, and back of them the first college chapel, erected as a separate building, the gift of the widow of an alderman of London in the year 1740— all these you may yet see and feel the charm which lies about them.

Some time ago I met a man in the college yard who had all the appearance of one from the country. He was very curious about the buildings and was anxious to know their ages. I pointed out old Massachusetts to him and told him it was built in 1728. He looked at it for a moment and then ejaculated: "Great God!" A moment later he said: "I come from South Dakota."

Then, too, it gives an American a sensation to stand on the ground on which a company of American soldiers drilled one June evening before marching away to fight at Bunker Hill. On this same plot of ground there once stood a frame house which was once occupied by a predecessor of mine, a man who once came out to pray for the Continental cause as the troops marched away. The fact that a British garrison was quartered not 3 miles away makes me believe that the men of that day were not lacking in courage. The plot of ground is the triangle in front of the law school. I hope that all of you may visit and stand on these places.

I note with great pleasure the progress history is making both in and outside of the university recently. Much of its progress is, I am sure, due to this society.

Harvard college has lately made a revision of its entrance requirements, and one of the first studies changed was history. This will require a broader and more general knowledge of history in the work done in the secondary schools. In the education of young republicans I feel that the history of their own country should play an important part.

Short addresses were also made by Mr. Larned, of Buffalo; Professor Haskins, of Wisconsin; Rev. Samuel Crothers, Professor Morse, and Dr. Rhodes.

At the business meeting of the association in the Fogg Art Museum reports from the Executive Council and from the several commissions and committees were presented and acted upon, various questions of general interest were discussed, and officers were elected for the ensuing year. The election resulted in the choice of Mr. Edward Eggleston for president, Prof. Moses Coit Tyler and Mr. Charles Francis Adams, vice-presidents. Prof. W. A. Dunning and Hon. Peter White were elected in the council to fill vacancies caused by the resignation of Professors Turner and Stephens. Dr. Herbert B. Adams was reelected secretary, Mr. A. Howard Clark assistant secretary and curator, and Dr. C. W. Bowen treasurer. Prof. J. F. Jameson resigned the chairmanship of the Historical Manuscripts Commission, and Mr. R. G. Thwaites, secretary of the State Historical Society of Wisconsin, was chosen in his place. The association has, from the beginning of its history, had but one honorary member, the late Prof. Leopold von Ranke. It now elected as honorary members the Right Rev. Dr. William Stubbs, Bishop of Oxford, and Dr. Samuel Rawson Gardiner. Provision was made in the constitution for the addition of a class of corresponding members, limited, as is honorary membership, to persons not resident in the United States.

The association has projected several new lines of usefulness. It has established a Public Archives Commission, charged to investigate and report, from the point of view of historical study, upon the character, contents, and functions of our public repositories of manuscript records, and having power to appoint local agents in each State, through whom their inquiries may be in part conducted. A committee was also appointed to consider the possibility of preparing a general history of the United States, composed of monographs written by various scholars. Upon the invitation of several societies in England desiring cooperation in the expected approaching commemoration of the thousandth anniversary of the death of King Alfred, a committee was appointed to make arrangements for American participation in the expected celebration at Winchester.

The treasurer, Dr. C. W. Bowen, reported total assets of the association amounting to $12,581, a gain of more than a thousand dollars during the year. The assistant secretary reported the present number of members as 1,411, twice as many as were enrolled in December, 1896. For the Historical Manuscripts Commission Prof. J. F. Jameson reported the approaching completion of his edition of the Correspondence of John C. Calhoun, which will constitute the Fourth Report of the Commission; upon the termination of this work his chairmanship of the commission comes to an end. Professor Hart reported for the Board of Editors of the American Historical Review. For the committee on the Justin Winsor Prize Prof. C. M. Andrews reported that they had been unable to make any award this year, and asked for permission, which was granted, to draw up a definite code of rules to govern the competition for the prize. On behalf of the Committee on Bibliography Mr. A. Howard Clark made a report recommending that Mr. Iles's proposed select bibliography of American history be referred to the executive council, with power to act; that Mr. W. D. Johnston's annual Annotated Bibliography of English History be hereafter printed in the annual reports of the association; that the association print Mr. T. M. Owen's bibliography of Mississippi; that Mr. William Beer's projected bibliography of Louisiana and the Louisiana Territory be commended to the attention of the council, and that the project of an index to historical articles printed in serials not indexed in "Poole" be commended to the attention of the American Library Association.

After the passage of votes of thanks to the retiring president and others the American Historical Association adjourned. The next meeting is to be held in Detroit, on Thursday, Friday, and Saturday, December 27, 28, and 29, 1900.

The programme of the entire meeting was arranged by a committee under the chairmanship of Prof. Albert Bushnell Hart, of Harvard University, and the social features were arranged by a local committee under Mr. A. Lawrence Lowell, to whom votes of thanks were extended, as also to all who assisted in the entertainment of the association.

Mr. Lowell and his committee was aided by the hospitable kindness of the president of the association, Mr. James Ford Rhodes, and Mrs. Rhodes; of Mr. Charles Francis Adams, of the Technology Club; of the president and fellows of Harvard College, of the president and corporation of Radcliffe College, and of Miss Longfellow. On Wednesday afternoon, December 27, the first day of the meeting, Mr. Adams, president of the Massachusetts Historical Society, entertained the members of the association by a luncheon in the handsome new building of that society, and the society threw open its rooms for the session of the Church History Section and of the various committees of the association. After the president's address on Wednesday evening, the Boston Public Library and the Art Museum were thrown open to the members, and the Technology Club gave them a "smoker" at its clubhouse near the Institute of Technology. On Thursday afternoon the president and Mrs. Rhodes received the members at the Algonquin Club, where Mr. Rhodes again entertained them in the evening, after the session, at a second "smoker." On Friday noon the president and fellows of Harvard College gave a luncheon in the Memorial Hall. In the afternoon the ladies of the association were given tea at Fay House, where Miss Alice Longfellow read a paper on the Craigie House, once the headquarters of Washington, later the home of Longfellow; after which they were received by her in that historic mansion. Throughout the sessions a committee on places of historic interest, aided by members of the Old South Historical Society and the Harvard Memorial Society, furnished guidance and information to visitors. After the conclusion of the meeting there was opportunity, by invitation of the president and trustees of Wellesley College, the Pilgrim

Society, the Concord Antiquarian Society, the Lexington Historical Society, and the Essex Institute, to visit, on Saturday, Wellesley College, Plymouth, Concord, Lexington, and Salem.

In the evening about a hundred and fifty members of the association took part in a banquet at the Hotel Brunswick in Boston. Prof. H. Morse Stephens acted as toastmaster, and speeches were made by Col. Thomas Wentworth Higginson and by Professors Hart, J. B. Moore, and Judson.

VOTED BY THE EXECUTIVE COUNCIL AT MEETINGS DECEMBER 1 AND 28, 1899.

That the council recommend the amendment of Article III of the constitution by inserting the words "or corresponding" after the word "honorary."

That Right Rev. William Stubbs, D. D., Bishop of Oxford, and Samuel Rawson Gardiner, M. A., Fellow of Merton College, Oxford, be elected honorary members of the American Historical Association.

That the president appoint a committee of three, of which he shall be a member, to consider the unification of historical manuscripts and records now in the several Executive Departments at Washington not needed for current business of the Departments.

That Prof. H. Morse Stephens be reelected one of the board of editors of the American Historical Review from January 1, 1900.

That the treasurer be authorized to sell bank stock belonging to the association and to reinvest the funds as may be considered advisable by the committee on finance.

That appropriations be authorized for current expenses, for the Manuscripts Commission, and for the Historical Review, as in previous year.

That the resignations of Professors Jameson, Trent, and Turner, of the Manuscripts Commission, be accepted with regret.

That the committee on Justin Winsor prize be authorized to formulate and publish rules to govern the award of the prize.

That a committee on publications be appointed to serve for one year.

That the council recommend the organization of a Public Archives Commission of five members, with power to appoint adjunct members in the several States, to investigate and report on the character of the historical public archives of the several States and the United States and the means taken for their preservation and publication, and that $100 be appropriated for organization expenses of said commission.

That a committee be appointed to consider the advisability and feasibility of publishing a monographic history of the United States under the auspices of the association.

That a committee be appointed to cooperate with the Royal Societies of England in the celebration of the thousandth anniversary of the death of King Alfred the Great.

VOTED BY THE ASSOCIATION DECEMBER 29, 1899.

That Article III be amended by insertion of words "or corresponding" after the word "honorary," so that the sentence shall read: "Persons not residents in the United States may be elected as honorary or corresponding members, and be exempt from the payment of dues."

That the thanks of the association be extended to Professor Jameson for the very able manner in which he has carried on the work during his chairmanship of the Historical Manuscripts Commission.

That the recommendation of the Executive Council for the appointment of a Public Archives Commission be adopted and the appointment of members of the commission made by the council be confirmed.

That the report of the Treasurer be approved.

That the action of the Executive Council authorizing the Treasurer to sell certain bank stocks be approved.

That the recommendations of the Bibliographical Committee be adopted.

That the report and committee appointments of the Council be approved.

That a vote of thanks be extended to the retiring president.

That the assistant secretary be directed to present the thanks of the association to the chairmen and members of the several committees for their able management of the fifteenth annual meeting, and to the several colleges, organizations, and individuals who have extended hospitality to the association during the meeting.

That the association record its regret at the illness of Secretary Herbert B. Adams, and its hope for his early recovery to health.

PRESENT ACTIVITIES OF THE ASSOCIATION.

The following list enumerates the present leading activities of the American Historical Association:

(1) The annual meeting of the association held during the Christmas holidays in the East or the West or the District of Columbia in triennial succession.

(2) The annual report of the secretary of the association concerning the annual meeting and its proceedings, with the papers, bibliographies, and other historical materials submitted through the Secretary of the Smithsonian Institution for publication by Congress.

(3) The Historical Manuscripts Commission of five members, established in 1895, and now receiving from the association a subsidy of $500 a year for the collection and editing of important manuscripts. Mr. Reuben G. Thwaites, of Madison, Wisconsin, chairman.

(4) The preservation of historical exchanges, books, pamphlets, reports, and papers of the association in the National Museum at Washington, D. C., in the keeping of Mr. A. Howard Clark, assistant secretary of the association and curator of the historical collections.

(5) The Committee of Seven, established in 1896, for Promoting the Study of History in Secondary Schools, Prof. A. C. McLaughlin, chairman.

(6) The Public Archives Commission, established this year, for investigating the public archives of the several States and of the United States, under the chairmanship of Prof. William MacDonald, of Bowdoin College.

(7) Committee to consider the advisability and feasibility of publishing a monographic history of the United States under the auspices of the American Historical Association. The chairman of this committee is Prof. A. B. Hart, of Harvard University.

(8) Committee of Three, to consider the possibility of unifying the public repositories of historical manuscripts in Washington. Dr. James Ford Rhodes, chairman.

(9) Committee on bibliography, to advise the Executive Council and to cooperate with the American Library Association upon matters of bibliographical interest. Mr. A. Howard Clark, chairman.

(10) A general committee, representing the local and State historical interests of the association. This committee is being gradually appointed by authority of the Executive Council. A list of those who have accepted membership on this committee is given on another page.

(11) The "Justin Winsor Prize" of $100 for the best unpublished monographic work, based upon original investigation in American history. This prize has been awarded only once, and then in the year 1896 to Prof. Herman V. Ames, a graduate of Amherst College and a doctor of philosophy of Harvard University. Prof. C. M. Andrews, chairman of the committee.

(12) The Church History Section, which continues the work of the American Society of Church History, was originally an institutional off- shoot of the American Historical Association in 1888, but in 1896 it became an organic part of the association, with Dr. Samuel Macauley Jackson as secretary of the section.

(13) A Committee of Five for the Historical Study of Colonies and Dependencies. Prof. Henry E. Bourne, Western Reserve University, chairman.

(14) The American Historical Review, published quarterly, and now subsidized by the American Historical Association, whose Executive Council will henceforth fill vacancies in the board of editors.

The American Historical Association in account with Clarence W. Bowen, treasurer.

| 1899.
Dec. 23 | To paid treasurer's clerk hire, vouchers 2, 30-33, 49, 66... postage and stationery, treasurer, and assistant secretary, vouchers 6, 13, 14, 18, 25, 27, 33, 40, 44, 54, 61, 62, 63... secretary's clerk hire, ... hers 4, 18, 37, 53... assistant secretary's clerk hire, ... uhrs 3, 24, 46, 56... preparing index ... ual report 1898, voucher 35... American Historical Review, vouchers 1, 10, 11, 15, 17, 19, 21, 22, 23, 28, 29, 31, 33, 42, $347, 50, 51, 52, 57, 58... ...y of history in secondary schools, vouchers 5, 20, 60... ssion, vouchers historical manuscripts, 8, 34, 41, 55, 65... expenses last i ... ing, ... hers 7, 9, 12. bank collection of checks, vouchers 26, 39... Rific ... or, vouchers 45, 59... Tiffany & Co., certificates, voucher 32... stereotype-plate ... cks, voucher 36... Balance cash on ind... | $68.66
170.80
310.00
210.00
41.50
2,487.50
264.26
418.44
50.00
2.00
141.72
7.45
14.26
1,331.22
5,582.81 | 1898.
Dec. 27
1899.
Dec. 23 | By balance cash on hand......
1,275 annual dues, at $3...
21 life members, at $50...
dividends on bank stocks...
rebate of tax on bank stocks...
sales of publications...
interest on bond and mortgage...
1 annual dues...
dividend from executor, on annual dues... | $844.63
3,825.00
125.00
130.00
41.67
187.00
375.00
3.02
1.49
5,582.81 |
| | | | 1899.
Dec. 23 | By balance cash on hand......
The assets of the association are:
Bond and mortgage......
10 shares National Bank of Commerce, $250...
5 shares Bank of New York, N. B. A., $250...
Cash... | 1,331.22
7,500.00
2,500.00
1,250.00
1,331.22
12,581.22 |

An increase during the year of $1,041.59. Respectfully submitted.

CLARENCE W. BOWEN, *Treasurer.*

The undersigned auditing committee have examined the foregoing account of the treasurer, with accompanying voucher, and find the same to be correct. Satisfactory evidence of ownership of the assets of the association, as stated in this report, have also been submitted to our inspection.

A. MCF. DAVIS.
PETER WHITE.

BOSTON, *December 23, 1899.*

OFFICERS OF THE AMERICAN HISTORICAL ASSOCIATION ELECTED DECEMBER 29, 1899.

President: Edward Eggleston, L. H. D.
First Vice-President: Moses Coit Tyler, LL. D., L. H. D.
Second Vice-President: Charles Francis Adams, LL. D.
Secretary: Herbert B. Adams, Ph. D., LL. D.
Treasurer: Clarence W. Bowen, Ph. D.
Assistant Secretary and Curator: A. Howard Clark.
Secretary of the Church History Section: Samuel Macauley Jackson, D. D., LL. D.
Executive Council (in addition to the above-named officers): Ex-presidents of the association, Andrew D. White, LL. D., L. H. D.; Charles Kendall Adams, LL. D.; William Wirt Henry, LL. D.; James B. Angell, LL. D.; Henry Adams, LL. D.; George F. Hoar, LL. D.; Richard S. Storrs, LL. D.; James Schouler, LL. D.; George P. Fisher, D. D., LL. D.; James Ford Rhodes, LL. D. Elected, George Burton Adams, Ph. D.; Melville W. Fuller, LL. D.; Albert Bushnell Hart, Ph. D.; Andrew C. McLaughlin, A. M.; William A. Dunning, Ph. D.; Hon. Peter White.

LIST OF COMMITTEES.

Committee on programme for Detroit meeting: Prof. A. C. McLaughlin, University of Michigan, chairman; Prof. E. G. Bourne, Yale University; Mr. A. Howard Clark, Smithsonian Institution; Prof. H. P. Judson, Chicago University; Prof. J. H. Robinson, Columbia University; Prof. F. J. Turner, University of Wisconsin.

Local committee for Detroit meeting: Hon. Peter White, Marquette, Mich., chairman.

Historical Manuscripts Commission: Mr. Reuben G. Thwaites, Historical Society of Wisconsin, chairman; Mr. James Bain, jr., Toronto Public Library; Dr. Herbert Friedenwald, Library of Congress; Prof. F. W. Moore, Vanderbilt University; Mr. Robert N. Toppan, Prince Society, Boston.

Committee on bibliography: A. Howard Clark, Smithsonian Institution, chairman; William E. Foster, Providence Public Library; George Iles, New York City; J. N. Larned, Buffalo, N. Y.; W. C. Lane, librarian of Harvard University; Appleton Prentiss Clark Griffin, Library of Congress. (Herbert Putnam was appointed chairman but declined and Mr. Griffin was added by President Eggleston.)

Committee on historical study of colonies and dependencies: Prof. H. E. Bourne, Western Reserve University, chairman; A. Lawrence Lowell, Boston; Prof. H. L. Osgood, Columbia University; Prof. F. Wells Williams, Yale University; Prof. George M. Wrong, Toronto University.

Committee on Justin Winsor prize: Prof. C. M. Andrews, Bryn Mawr College, chairman; Prof. E. P. Cheyney, University of Pennsylvania; Prof. H. L. Osgood, Columbia University; Dr. Theo. Clarke Smith, Vassar College; Prof. Ferdinand Schwill, University of Chicago.

Committee on publications (for one year): Prof. E. G. Bourne, Yale University, chairman; A. Howard Clark, Smithsonian Institution; Prof. F. M. Fling, University of Nebraska; Prof. C. H. Haskins, University of Wisconsin; Samuel Macauley Jackson, New York City; Prof. A. D. Morse, Amherst College; Dr. James Schouler, Boston.

Public Archives Commission, with power to appoint adjunct members in the several States: Prof. William McDonald, Bowdoin College, chairman; (Dr. Frederic Bancroft, Washington, D. C., declined appointment.) L. G. Bugbee, University of Texas; H. W. Caldwell, University of Nebraska; Prof. J. H. Robinson, Columbia University.

Committee to consider the advisability and feasibility of publishing a monographic history of the United States under the auspices of the American Historical Association: Prof. A. B. Hart, Harvard University, chairman; Mr. Charles Francis Adams, president Massachusetts Historical Society; Dr. Herbert B. Adams, Johns Hopkins University; Prof. W. A. Dunning, Columbia University; Prof. John Bach McMaster, University of Pennsylvania; Prof. F. J. Turner, University of Wisconsin; Prof. Moses Coit Tyler, Cornell University.

Committee to cooperate with the Royal Societies of England in the international commemoration of the thousandth anniversary, in the year 1901, of the death of King Alfred the Great: Dr. J. M. Vincent, Johns Hopkins University; Prof. H. Morse Stephens, Cornell University; Dr. Melville M. Bigelow, Boston.

Finance committee: Mr. Ira Remsen Lane, New York; Mr. Robert N. Toppan, Cambridge.

Committee to consider the possibility of unifying the public repositories of historical manuscripts at Washington: Dr. James Ford Rhodes, Boston, chairman; Prof. Herbert B. Adams, Johns Hopkins University; Prof. William M. Sloane, Columbia University.

Committee on resolutions: Prof. H. E. Bourne, Western Reserve University; Prof. C. M. Andrews, Bryn Mawr College; Prof. W. P. Trent, University of the South.

General committee appointed under resolution of New Haven meeting to represent the local and historical interests of the Association:

The following members have thus far accepted:

I. NEW ENGLAND.

Maine: Prof. Wm. McDonald, Bowdoin College.
Connecticut: Prof. E. G. Bourne, Yale University; Prof. Max Farrand, Wesleyan University, Middletown.

II. MIDDLE STATES.

New Jersey: Prof. E. L. Stevenson, Rutgers College, New Brunswick; Dr. Ernest C. Richardson, Princeton.
Pennsylvania: Prof. Dana C. Munro, University of Pennsylvania, Philadelphia.

III. SOUTHERN STATES.

Virginia: President L. G. Tyler, William and Mary College, Williamsburg.
North Carolina: Prof. E. A. Alderman, University of North Carolina, Chapel Hill; Prof. J. S. Bassett, Trinity College, Durham.
Georgia: Prof. J. H. T. McPherson, University of Georgia, Athens.
Alabama: Prof. T. C. McCorvey, University of Alabama, Tuscaloosa.
Mississippi: Prof. F. L. Riley, University of Mississippi.
Louisiana: William Beer, Howard Memorial Library, New Orleans.
Kentucky: Prof. Arthur Yager, Georgetown College, Georgetown; Prof. Henry L. Trimble, Bethel College, Russellville; R. T. Durrett, LL. D., Louisville.
Tennessee: Prof. J. B. Henneman, University of Tennessee, Knoxville.
Missouri: Prof. Charles L. Smith, William Jewell College, Liberty: Prof. M. S. Snow, Washington University, St. Louis.

IV. NORTHWEST.

Ohio: Prof. J. W. Perrin, Adelbert College, Cleveland.
Indiana: Prof. U. G. Weatherly, Indiana University, Bloomington; Prof. J. A. Woodburn, Indiana University, Bloomington.
Illinois: Prof. H. P. Judson, University of Chicago; Prof. J. P. Cushing, Knox College, Galesburg.
Michigan: Hon. Peter White, Marquette.
Wisconsin: Reuben G. Thwaites, Madison.
Minnesota: Prof. F. M. Anderson, University of Minnesota, Minneapolis.

V FAR WEST.

Nebraska: Prof. F. M. Fling, University of Nebraska, Lincoln; Prof. H. W. Caldwell, University of Nebraska, Lincoln.
Iowa: Prof. B. F. Shambaugh, State University, Iowa City.
Oregon: Prof. F. G. Young, University of Oregon, Eugene.
Colorado: Prof. J. E. Le Rossignol, University of Denver, University Park.

VI. CANADA.

Montreal: Prof. C. W. Colby, McGill University.
Toronto: Prof. George M. Wrong, University of Toronto; James Bain, jr., Librarian of Public Library.

The committee on the Justin Winsor prize issued the following announcement, dated March 15, 1900:

The Justin Winsor prize of $100, offered by the American Historical Association for the encouragement of less well-known writers, will be awarded for the year 1900 to the best unpublished monographic work based upon original investigation in American history which shall be submitted to the committee of award on or before October 1, 1900. If not typewritten, the work must be written legibly upon only one side of the sheet, and must be in form ready for publication. In making the award the committee will take into consideration not only research and originality, but also clearness of expression, logical arrangement, and literary form. No prize will be awarded unless the work submitted shall be of a high degree of excellence. The successful essay will be published by the American Historical Association.

CHARLES M. ANDREWS, *Chairman.*

PROGRAMME OF FIFTEENTH ANNUAL MEETING, 1899.

WEDNESDAY MORNING, DECEMBER 27, 10.30 A. M.

PUBLIC SESSION ON COLONIZATION.

(South Congregational Church, corner of Newbury and Exeter streets.)

1. Address of welcome, by Hon. Josiah Quincy, mayor of Boston.
2. Some Difficulties of American Colonization, by Prof. H. E. Bourne, Western Reserve University.
3. Chinese Emigrants in the Far East, by Prof. F. W. Williams, Yale University.
4. The Selection and Training of Colonial Officials in England, Holland, and France, by Prof. A. Lawrence Lowell, Harvard University.
5. Discussion, by Mr. Alleyne Ireland, Boston; Dr. Clive Day, Yale University; Mr. Arthur Lord, Plymouth, Mass., and Prof. H. Morse Stephens.

WEDNESDAY AFTERNOON, DECEMBER 27.

1.30 p. m.

LUNCHEON GIVEN BY MR. CHARLES FRANCIS ADAMS, PRESIDENT OF THE MASSACHUSETTS HISTORICAL SOCIETY.

(The society's building, Boylston street, corner of the Fenway.)

3 p. m.

PUBLIC SESSION OF THE CHURCH HISTORY SECTION.

Under the chairmanship of Moses Coit Tyler, LL. D., second vice-president (building of the Massachusetts Historical Society.)

1. The Prevalent View in the Ancient Church of the Purpose of the Death of Christ, by Rev. Prof. E. C. Smyth, D. D., Andover, Mass.
2. A Recent Service of Church History to the Church, by Rev. W. G. Andrews, D. D., Guilford, Conn.
3. Why Was Roger Williams Banished? By Rev. H. S. Burrage, D. D., Portland, Me.
4. Discussion, by Dr. Ezra H. Byington, Newton, Mass., and Prof. George P. Fisher.

4.30 p. m.

MEETINGS OF THE COMMITTEES, COMMISSIONS, AND BOARDS.

(Building of the Massachusetts Historical Society.)

Historical Manuscripts Commission; Committee on the Justin Winsor Prize; Committee on the History of Colonies and Dependencies; Board of Editors of the American Historical Review; Bibliographical Committee.

WEDNESDAY EVENING, DECEMBER 27.

8 p. m.

PUBLIC SESSION, PRESIDENT'S INAUGURAL ADDRESS.

(South Congregational Church, corner of Newbury and Exeter streets.)

1. Address of welcome, by his excellency Roger Wolcott, LL. D., governor of the Commonwealth.
2. Inaugural address, by James Ford Rhodes, LL. D., president of the association.

9.30 p. m.

RECEPTION GIVEN BY THE MUSEUM OF FINE ARTS AND THE BOSTON PUBLIC LIBRARY.

10.30 p. m.

SMOKER GIVEN BY THE TECHNOLOGY CLUB (71 NEWBURY STREET).

THURSDAY MORNING, DECEMBER 28.

9 a. m.

MEETING OF THE COUNCIL.

(The study, South Congregational Church.)

10.30 a. m.

PUBLIC SESSION ON FIELDS OF HISTORICAL STUDY.

(South Congregational Church, corner of Newbury and Exeter streets.)

1. A Plea for Military History, by Charles Francis Adams, Boston.
2. Sacred and Profane History, by Prof. James H. Robinson, Columbia University.
3. A Plea for Economic History, by Prof. W. J. Ashley, Harvard University.
4. Discussion, by Prof. Anson D. Morse, Amherst College; Prof. John Winthrop Platner, Harvard University; Mrs. Robert Abbe, New York; Prof. John M. Vincent, Johns Hopkins University.
5. Appointment of committees.

THURSDAY AFTERNOON, DECEMBER 28.

4 p. m.

RECEPTION BY PRESIDENT AND MRS. RHODES (ALGONQUIN CLUB, 217 COMMONWEALTH AVENUE).

THURSDAY EVENING, DECEMBER 28.

8 p. m.

PUBLIC SESSION ON EUROPEAN HISTORY.

(South Congregational Church, corner of Newbury and Exeter streets.)

1. Robert Fruin, Professor of Dutch History at Leyden, died 1899, by Miss Ruth Putnam, New York.

2. Should Recent European History have a place in the College Curriculum, by Prof. Charles M. Andrews, Bryn Mawr College.
3. French Mistakes, by Mr. James Breck Perkins, Rochester.
4. Discussion, by Prof. Ferdinand Schwill, University of Chicago; Prof. Charles H. Haskins, University of Wisconsin; and Dr. E. F. Henderson, Chestnut Hill.

10.30 p. m.

SMOKER GIVEN BY THE PRESIDENT (ALGONQUIN CLUB, 217 COMMONWEALTH AVENUE).

FRIDAY MORNING, DECEMBER 29, 10.30 A. M.

PUBLIC SESSION ON FOREIGN RELATIONS.

(Sanders Theater, Memorial Hall, Cambridge.)

1. The Government of Foreigners, by Prof. John Bach McMaster, University of Pennsylvania.
2. The Samoan Question, by Baron Speck von Sternburg, German Commissioner to Samoa.
3. The Proposed Absorption of Mexico in 1847–48, by Prof. E. G. Bourne, Yale University.
4. Democracy and Peace, by Prof. S. M. Macvane, Harvard University.
5. Discussion, by Prof. John B. Moore, Columbia University; Prof. Harry Pratt Judson, University of Chicago; Mr. Edwin V. Morgan, Secretary of the Samoan Commission.

FRIDAY AFTERNOON, DECEMBER 29.

1 p. m.

LUNCH GIVEN BY HARVARD COLLEGE (MEMORIAL HALL). BRIEF ADDRESSES BY PRESIDENT CHARLES W. ELIOT AND OTHERS.

3.30 p. m.

LADIES' TEA GIVEN BY RADCLIFFE COLLEGE.

(Fay House, No. 10 Garden street.)

1. An Address of Welcome, by Mrs. Louis Agassiz, President of Radcliffe.
2. The History of the Craigie House, some time Headquarters of George Washington, by Miss Alice M. Longfellow, Cambridge. After the reading of the paper, Miss Longfellow will receive the ladies present at Craigie House.

4 p. m.

BUSINESS MEETING OF THE ASSOCIATION.

(Fogg Art Museum, Cambridge, opposite Memorial Hall.)

1. Report of the Council. (Honorary members; new activities; appointments; time and place of next meeting, etc.)
2. Reports of the Treasurer and Auditing Committee.

3. Report of the Historical Manuscripts Commission.
4. Report of the Committee on the Justin Winsor Prize.
5. Report of the Board of Editors of the American Historical Review.
6. Report of the Bibliographical Committee.
7. Vote upon the following amendment to the constitution, proposed by the Council: That in Article III, after the word "honorary," be inserted the words "or corresponding."
8. Election of officers.
9. Report of the Committee on Resolutions.

FRIDAY EVENING, DECEMBER 29, 7.30 P. M.

SUBSCRIPTION DINNER (HOTEL BRUNSWICK). PROF. H. MORSE STEPHENS, CORNELL UNIVERSITY, TOASTMASTER.

PAPERS READ BY TITLE.

American Power in the Pacific and the Far East, by James M. Callahan, Ph. D., Johns Hopkins University.

The Rise of the Lollards, by H. L. Cannon, Ph. D., Indianapolis High School.

Governmental Conditions at Langres in the Early Middle Ages, especially the Eleventh Century, by Earle W. Dow, Assistant Professor of History, University of Michigan.

Statistics of Removals by the President, derived from Official Sources, by Carl Russell Fish, A. M., Harvard University.

Origin of the Interdict, by A. C. Howland, Ph. D., Teachers' College, Columbia University.

Legal Qualifications for Office in the American Colonies and States, 1619-1899, by Frank Hayden Miller, Harvard University.

The Droit de Banalité during the French Régime in Canada, by William Bennett Munro, Harvard University.

The First Virginia Code of Laws; A Critical Study, by Walter F. Prince, Ph. D., New Haven.

The Administration of Captain John Hart and the Anti-Catholic Laws of Colonial Maryland, by Bernard C. Steiner, Ph. D., Johns Hopkins University.

HONORARY RECEPTION COMMITTEE OF THE AMERICAN HISTORICAL ASSOCIATION, BOSTON, 1899.

President of the committee: His Excellency Roger Wolcott, governor of the Commonwealth.

Vice-presidents.

Dr. Charles W. Eliot, president of Harvard University.
Dr. Franklin Carter, president of Williams College.
Dr. George Harris, president of Amherst College.
Mrs. Elizabeth S. Mead, president of Mount Holyoke College.
Dr. John F. Lehy, president of Holy Cross College, Worcester.
Dr. Elmer H. Capen, president of Tufts College.
Prof. James M. Crafts, president of Massachusetts Institute of Technology.
Rev. W. G. Read Mullan, S. J., president of Boston College.
Dr. Henry H. Goodell, president of Massachusetts Agricultural College.
Dr. T. C. Mendenhall, president of Worcester Polytechnic Institute.
Dr. William F. Warren, president of the Boston University.
Miss Caroline Hazard, president of Wellesley College.
Dr. L. Clark Seelye, president of Smith College.
Dr. G. Stanley Hall, president of Clark University.
Mrs. Louis Agassiz, president of Radcliffe College.
Mr. Alexander Agassiz, president of the American Academy of Arts and Sciences.
Mr. William Endicott, president of the Museum of Fine Arts.
Mr. Solomon Lincoln, president of the trustees of the Public Library of the City of Boston.
Mr. C. B. Tillinghast, librarian of State Library.

Members of the committee.

(The presidents of the historical societies of Massachusetts.)

Mr. Charles Francis Adams, president of the Massachusetts Historical Society and of the Quincy Historical Society.
Judge Ira A. Abbott, president of the Haverhill Historical Society.
Mr. Lewis Alden, president of the Holbrook Historical Society.
Mr. Joseph A. Allen, president of the Medfield Historical Society.
Dr. Justin Allen, president of the Topsfield Historical Society.
Mr. William H. Allen, president of the Manchester Historical Society.
Gen. Francis H. Appleton, president of the Society of the Sons of the American Revolution.
Mr. William F. Barnard, president of the Nantucket Historical Society.

Mr. Robert Batcheller, president of the Quaboag Historical Society, North Brookfield.
Dr. Franklin T. Beatty, president of the Society of the War of 1812.
Mrs. George B. Blake, president of the Society of the Colonial Dames of America.
Mr. George R. Blinn, president of the Bedford Historical Society.
Mr. C. K. Bolton, chairman of the Brookline Historical Publication Society.
Mr. Gamaliel Bradford, governor of the Society of the "Mayflower" Descendants.
Maj. Frank Harrison Briggs, president of the Society of the Sons of the Revolution.
Hon. William Claflin, president of the New England Methodist Historical Society.
Mr. Philip A. Chase, president of the Lynn Historical Society.
Mr. Charles G. Chick, president of the Hyde Park Historical Society.
Judge A. M. Copeland, president of the Connecticut Valley Historical Society.
Mr. Deloraine Pendre Corey, president of the Malden Historical Society.
Mr. Henry G. Denny, president of the Dorchester Antiquarian and Historical Society.
Gen. N. A. M. Dudley, president of the Roxbury Military Historical Society.
Rev. Richard Eddy, president of the Universalist Historical Society.
Mr. Charles D. Elliot, president of the Somerville Historical Society.
Rev. Samuel Hopkins Emery, president of the Old Colony Historical Society.
Hon. C. C. Esty, president of the Framingham Historical and Natural History Society.
Hon. Anson D. Fessenden, president of the Townsend Historical Society.
Mr. Edward S. Fessenden, president of the Arlington Historical Society.
Mr. Julius A. George, president of the Mendon Historical Society.
Dr. Samuel A. Green, president of the Groton Historical Society and of the Boston Numismatic Society.
Mr. Curtis Guild, president of the Bostonian Society.
Mr. Herbert J. Harwood, president of the Littleton Historical Society.
Hon. Benjamin W. Harris, president of the Old Bridgewater Historical Society.
Mr. Don Gleason Hill, president of the Dedham Historical Society.
Mrs. C. D. Hendrickson, president of the Orange Historical and Antiquarian Society.
Mr. W. Edgar Horton, president of the Foxborough Historical Society.
Hon. Joseph Sidney Howe, president of the Methuen Historical Society.
Mr. F. Lincoln Hutchins, president of the Worcester Society of Antiquity.
Hon. Edward T. Johnson, president of the Rumford Historical Society.
Hon. John S. Keyes, president of the Concord Antiquarian Society.
Mr. Warren D. King, president of the Peabody Historical Society.
Mr. William Little, president of the Historical Society of Old Newbury.
Col. Thomas L. Livermore, president of the Military Historical Society of Massachusetts.
Mr. Arthur Lord, president of the Pilgrim Society.

HONORARY RECEPTION COMMITTEE. 41

Mr. John J. Loud, president of the Weymouth Historical Society.
Mr. William F. Macy, president of the Society of Sons and Daughters of Nantucket.
Mr. Charles F. Mansfield, president of the Wakefield Historical Society.
Mr. John C. Marvel, president of the Rehoboth Antiquarian Society.
Mr. John J. May, president of the Dorchester Historical Society.
Rev. Alexander McKenzie, president of the Shepard Historical Society.
Mr. Edwin D. Mead, director of the Old South Work in American History.
Mr. Frederick A. Morey, president of the Billerica Historical Society.
Mr. Edward P. Nichols, president of the Lexington Historical Society.
Mr. A. D. Norcross, president of the Monson Historical Society.
Prof. Charles Eliot Norton, president of the Harvard Memorial Association.
Col. William H. Oakes, president of the Bunker Hill Historical Society.
Mr. W. Frank Parsons, president of the Cape Ann Historical Society.
Mr. J. Edward Plimpton, president of the Walpole Historical Society.
Rev. Edward Griffin Porter, president of the New England Historic Genealogical Society.
Rev. Alfred P. Putnam, president of the Danvers Historical Society.
Rev. Edward A. Rand, president of the Watertown Historical Society.
Hon. Robert S. Rantoul, president of the Essex Institute.
Mr. J. K. Richardson, president of the Backus Historical Society.
Hon. Stephen Salisbury, president of the American Antiquarian Society.
Mr. Edmund F. Slafter, president of the Prince Society.
Hon. George Sheldon, president of the Pocumtuck Valley Memorial Association.
Mr. Gustavus Smith, president of the Historical, Natural History, and Library Society of South Natick.
Mr. A. J. C. Sowdon, governor of the Society of Colonial Wars.
Mr. Solon W. Stevens, president of the Old Residents Historical Association of Lowell.
Judge C. C. Stone, president of the Clinton Historical Society.
Rev. John W. Suter, president of the Winchester Historical Genealogical Society.
Mr. George Frederick Sumner, president of the Canton Historical Society.
Mr. Charles F. Swift, president of the Cape Cod Historical Society.
Mr. William Cushing Wait, president of the Medford Historical Society.
Mr. M. H. Walker, president of the Westboro Historical Society.
Mr. Joseph P. Warren, president of the Old South Historical Society.
Mr. Charles E. Ward, president of the Oak Tree Association.
Hon. Winslow Warren, president of the Massachusetts Society of the Cincinnati.
Mr. T. Frank Waters, president of the Ipswich Historical Society.
Mr. Edward Wheelwright, president of the Colonial Society of Massachusetts.
Mr. A. B. Whipple, president of the Berkshire Historical and Scientific Society.
Prof. John Williams White, president of the Archæological Institute of America.
Mr. Henry A. Willis, president of the Fitchburg Historical Society.

Prof. George E. Woodberry, president of the Beverly Historical Society.
Mr. Carroll D. Wright, president of the American Statistical Association.

SPECIAL COMMITTEES.

LOCAL COMMITTEE OF ARRANGEMENTS.

A. Lawrence Lowell, *chairman;* Archibald Cary Coolidge, Andrew McFarland Davis, Albert Bushnell Hart, John O. Sumner.

PROGRAMME COMMITTEE.

Albert Bushnell Hart, *chairman;* Herbert B. Adams, Henry E. Bourne, William E. Dunning, Charles H. Haskins.

COMMITTEE ON GUESTS.

Archibald Cary Coolidge, *chairman;* Max Farrand, Elliot H. Goodwin, Gaillard T. Lapsley, Edwin V. Morgan.

LADIES' COMMITTEE.

Miss Elizabeth Kendall, *chairman;* Miss Mary Coes, Miss Louisa P. Haskell.

COMMITTEE ON PLACES OF HISTORIC INTEREST.

Joseph Parker Warren, *chairman;* Rev. Edward G. Porter, Carl Russell Fish, Horace H. Morse, Thomas H. Reed, George G. Wolkers.

II.—INAUGURAL ADDRESS OF JAMES FORD RHODES, PRESIDENT OF THE AMERICAN HISTORICAL ASSOCIATION, AT FIFTEENTH ANNUAL MEETING, DECEMBER 28, 1899.

HISTORY.

By JAMES FORD RHODES, President American Historical Association.

A miner from a far Western town describes Boston as "a city in whose streets respectability stalked about unchecked." Here was a high compliment. To be respectable is to be worthy of esteem, and I think if one were to set down seriously the qualities which entitle Boston to honor, not the least of them would be the high moral standard that prevails here among men. This is worthy of mention to members of an association which stands, above all, for honesty and truth. It is impossible to attend these meetings without gaining the impression that, however else we differ, we are at one in our endeavor to elicit the truth; that we are ready, by precept and example, to traverse the definition attributed to Napoleon, that history is lies agreed upon. I have thought, then, that no theme better suited to the company and the occasion could be chosen than simply "history."

It is an old subject, which has been discoursed about since Herodotus, and one would be vain indeed who flattered himself he could say aught new concerning the methods of writing it, when this subject has for so long a period engaged the minds of so many gifted men. Yet, to a sympathetic audience, to a people who love history, there is always the chance that a fresh treatment may present the commonplaces in some different combination, and augment for the moment an interest which is perennial.

Holding a brief for history as do I, your representative, let me at once concede that it is not the highest form of intellectual endeavor; let us at once agree that it were better that all the histories ever written were burned than for the world to lose Homer and Shakespeare. Yet, as it is generally true that an advocate rarely admits anything without qualification,

I should not be loyal to my client did I not urge that Shakespeare was historian as well as poet. We all prefer his Antony and Cleopatra and Julius Cæsar to the Lives in North's Plutarch which furnished him his materials. The history is in substance as true as Plutarch, the dramatic force greater, the language is better than that of Sir Thomas North, who himself did a remarkable piece of work when he gave his country a classic by Englishing a French version of the Stories of the Greek. It is true, as Macaulay wrote, the historical plays of Shakespeare have superseded history. When we think of Henry V it is of Prince Hal, the boon companion of Falstaff, who spent his youth in brawl and riot, and then became a sober and duty-loving king; and our idea of Richard III is a deceitful, dissembling, cruel wretch who knew no touch of pity, a bloody tyrant who knew no law of God or man.

The Achilles of Homer was a very living personage to Alexander. How happy he was, said the great general when he visited Troy, "in having while he lived so faithful a friend, and when he was dead so famous a poet to proclaim his actions." In our century, as more in consonance with society under the régime of contract, when force has largely given way to craft, we feel in greater sympathy with Ulysses. "The one person I would like to have met and talked with," Froude used to say, "was Ulysses. How interesting it would be to have his opinion on universal suffrage, and on a house of parliament where Thersites is listened to as patiently as the king of men."

We may also concede that in the realm of intellectual endeavor the mathematical and physical sciences should have the precedence of history. The present is more important than the past, and those sciences which contribute to our comfort place within the reach of the laborer and mechanic as common necessaries what would have been the highest luxury to the Roman emperor or to the king of the Middle Ages, contribute to health and the preservation of life, and by the development of railroads make possible such a gathering as this. These sciences, we cheerfully admit, outrank our modest enterprise, which, in the words of Herodotus, is "to preserve from decay the remembrance of what men have done." It may be true, as a geologist once said in extolling his study at the expense of the humanities, "Rocks do not lie, although men do," yet, on the other hand, the historic sense, which during our century has diffused itself widely, has invaded the domain of physical science. If you are unfortunate enough to be ill and consult a doctor he expatiates on the history of your disease. It was once my duty to attend the commencement exercises of a technical school, when one of the graduates had a thesis on bridges. He began by telling how they were built in Julius Cæsar's time, and tracing at some length the development of the art during the period of the material prosperity of the Roman Empire, he had little time and space left to consider their construction at the present day. One of the most brilliant surgeons I ever knew—the originator of a number of important surgical methods, who, being a physician as well, was remarkable in his expedients in saving life when called in counsel in grave and apparently hopeless cases— desired to write a book embodying his discoveries and devices, but said that the feeling was strong within him that he must begin his work with an account of medicine in Egypt and trace its development down to our own time; as he was a busy man in his profession, he lacked the leisure to make the preliminary historical study and his book was never written. Men of affairs who, taking "the present time by the top," are looked upon as devoted to the physical and mechanical sciences, continually pay tribute to our art. President Garfield, on his deathbed, asked one of his most trusted Cabinet advisers, in words that become pathetic as one thinks of the opportunities destroyed by the assassin's bullet, "Shall I live in history?" A clever politician, who knew more of ward meetings, caucuses, and the machinery of conventions than he did of history books, and who was earnest for the renomination of President Arthur in 1884, said to me, in the way of clinching his argument, "That Administration will live in history." So it was, according to Amyot, in the olden time. "Whensoever," he wrote, "the right sage and virtuous Emperor of Rome, Alexander Severus, was to consult of any matter of grave importance, whether it concerned war or government, he always called such to counsel as were reported to be well skilled in histories."

Proper concessions being made to poetry and the physical sciences, our place in the field remains secure. All of us here will accept fully these temperate conclusions of the committee of Seven of this association, namely, "Appreciation and sympathy for the present is best secured by a study of the past;" the study of history is a training in the handling of books; it is a training in citizenship, in judgment, in character. This committee have compassed their object and established their points. On their ground it is unnecessary to trench, and for me it would be presumptuous. My paper will take somewhat the form of a plea for general historians, and from their point of view will envisage the writing of history. On the first day of our meeting we should maintain a closed front against the advocates of other studies, and it shall be my purpose to steer clear of mooted questions. I shall not discuss the propositions whether history is the "handmaid of philosophy" or whether it is "philosophy teaching by examples," nor shall I enter upon the relations between history and political science, and I shall aim to avoid definitions. I shall not go into disputed matters unless by the nature of the case I touch upon them by indirection, believing what Huxley wrote in his prologue to Some Controverted Questions, that "controversy always tends to degenerate into quarreling, to swerve from the great issue of what is right and what is wrong to the very small question of who is right and who is wrong."

Was there ever so propitious a time for writing history as in the last forty years? There has been a general acquisition of the historic sense. The methods of teaching history have so improved that they may be called scientific. Even as the chemist and physicist, we talk of practice in the laboratory. Most biologists will accept Haeckel's designation of "the last forty years as the age of Darwin," for the theory of evolution is firmly established. The publication of the Origin of Species in 1859 converted it from a poet's dream and philosopher's speculation to a well-demonstrated scientific theory. Evolution, heredity, environment, have become household words, and their application to history has influenced everyone who has had to trace the development of a people, the growth of an institution, or the establishment of a cause. Other scientific theories and methods have affected physical science as potently, but no one has entered so vitally into the study of man. What hitherto the eye of genius alone could perceive may become the common property of everyone who cares to read a dozen books. But with all of our advantages, do we write better history than was written before the year 1859, which we may call the line of demarcation between the old and the new? If the English, German, and American historical scholars should vote as to who were the two best historians, I have little doubt that Thucydides and Tacitus would have a pretty large majority. If they were asked to name a third choice, it would undoubtedly lie between Herodotus and Gibbon. At the meeting of this association in Cleveland, when methods of historical teaching were under discussion, Herodotus and Thucydides, but no others, were mentioned as proper object lessons. What are the merits of Herodotus? Accuracy in details, as we understand it, was certainly not one of them. Neither does he sift critically his facts, but intimates that he will not make a positive decision in the case of conflicting testimony. "For myself," he wrote, "my duty is to report all that is said, but I am not obliged to believe it all alike—a remark which may be understood to apply to my whole history." He had none of the wholesome skepticism which we deem necessary in the weighing of historical evidence; on the contrary, he is frequently accused of credulity. Nevertheless, Percy Gardner calls his narrative nobler than that of Thucydides, and Mahaffy terms it an "incomparable history." "The truth is," wrote Macaulay in his diary, when he was 49 years old, "I admire no historians much except Herodotus, Thucydides, and Tacitus." Sir M. E. Grant Duff devoted his presidential address of 1895, before the Royal Historical Society, wholly to Herodotus, ending with the conclusion, "The fame of Herodotus, which has a little waned, will surely wax again." Whereupon the London Times devoted a leader to the subject. "We are concerned," it said, "to hear, on authority so eminent, that one of the most delightful writers of antiquity has a little waned of late in favor with the world. If this indeed be the case, so much the worse for the world. * * * When Homer and Dante and Shakespeare are neglected, then will Herodotus cease to be read."

There we have the secret of his hold upon the minds of men. "He knows how to tell a story," said Professor Hart, in the discussion previously referred to at Cleveland. He has "an epic unity of plan," writes Professor Jebb. Herodotus has furnished delight to all generations, while Polybius, more accurate and painstaking, a learned historian and a practical statesman, gathers dust on the shelf or is read as a penance. Nevertheless it may be demonstrated from the historical literature of England of our century that literary style and great power of narration alone will not give a man a niche in the temple of history. Herodotus showed diligence and honesty, without which his other qualities would have failed to secure him the place he holds in the estimation of historical scholars.

From Herodotus we naturally turn to Thucydides, who in the beginning charms historical students by his impression of the seriousness and dignity of his business. "History," he writes, "will be found profitable by those who desire an exact knowledge of the past as a key to the future, which in all human probability will repeat or resemble the past. My history is an everlasting possession, not a prize composition which is heard and forgotten." Diligence, accuracy, love of truth, and impartiality are merits commonly ascribed to Thucydides, and the internal evidence of the history bears out fully the general opinion. But there is, in my judgment, a tendency in the comparative estimates to rate the Athenian too high for the possession of these qualities, for certainly some modern writers have possessed all of these merits in an eminent degree. When Jowett wrote in the preface to his translation, "Thucydides stands absolutely alone among the historians not only of Hellas, but of the world, in his impartiality and love of truth," he was unaware that a son of his own university was writing the history of a momentous period of his own country in a manner to impugn the correctness of that statement. When the Jowett Thucydides appeared Samuel R. Gardiner had published eight of his volumes, but he had not reached the great civil war, and his reputation, which has since grown with a cumulative force, was not fully established, but I have now no hesitation in saying that the internal evidence demonstrates that in impartiality and love of truth Gardiner is the peer of Thucydides. From the point of view of external evidence the case is even stronger for Gardiner; he submits to a harder test. That he has been able to treat so stormy, so controverted, and so well-known a period as England of the seventeenth century with hardly a question of his impartiality is a wonderful tribute. In fact, in an excellent review of his work I have seen him criticised for being too impartial. On the other hand, Grote thinks that he has found Thucydides in error—in the long dialogue between the Athenian representatives and the Melians. "This dialogue," Grote writes, "can hardly represent what actually passed, except as to a few general points which the historian has followed out into deductions and illustrations, thus dramatizing the given situation in a powerful and characteristic manner." Those very words might characterize Shakespeare's account of the assassination of Julius Cæsar, his reproduction of the speeches of Brutus and Mark Antony. Compare the relation in Plutarch with the third act of the tragedy and see how, in his amplification of the story, Shakespeare has remained true to the essential facts of the time. Plutarch gives no account of the speeches of Brutus and Mark Antony, confining himself to an allusion to the one and a reference to the other, but Appian of Alexandria, in his history, has reported them. The speeches in Appian lack the force which they have in Shakespeare, nor do they seemingly fit into the situation as well.

I have adverted to this criticism of Grote, not that I love Thucydides less, but that I love Shakespeare more. For my part, the historian's candid acknowledgment in the beginning has convinced me of the essential, not the literal, truth of his accounts of speeches and dialogues. "As to the speeches," wrote the Athenian, "which were made either before or during the war, it was hard for me, and for others who reported them to me, to recollect the exact words. I have therefore put into the mouth of each speaker the sentiments proper to the occasion, expressed as I thought he would be likely to express them, while at the same time I endeavored, as nearly as I could, to give the general purport of what was actually said." That is the very essence of candor. But be the historian "as chaste as ice, as pure as snow, he shall not escape calumny." Mahaffy declares that, "although all modern historians quote Thucydides with more confidence than they would quote the gospels," the Athenian has exaggerated; he is one-sided, partial, misleading, dry, and surly. Other critics agree with Mahaffy that he has been unjust to Cleon and has screened Nicias from blame that was his due for defective generalship.

We approach Tacitus with respect. We rise from reading his Annals, his History, and Germany with reverence. We know that we have been in the society of a gentleman who had a high standard of morality and honor. We feel that our guide was a serious student, a solid thinker, and a man of the world; that he expressed his opinions and delivered his judgments with a remarkable freedom from prejudice. He draws us to him with sympathy. He sounds the same mournful note which we detect in Thucydides. Tacitus deplores the folly and dissoluteness of the rulers of his nation; he bewails the misfortunes of his country. The merits we ascribe to Thucydides—diligence, accuracy, love of truth, impartiality,—are his. The desire to quote from Tacitus is irresistible. "The more I meditate," he writes, "on the events of ancient and modern times the more I am struck with the capricious uncertainty which mocks the calculations of men in all their transactions." Again, "Possibly there is in all things a kind of cycle, and there may be moral revolutions just as there are changes of seasons." "Commonplaces," sneer the scientific historian. True enough, but they might not have been commonplaces if Tacitus had not uttered them and his works had not been read and reread until they have become a common possession of historical students. From a thinker who deemed the time "out of joint," as Tacitus obviously did, and who, had he not possessed great strength of mind and character, might have lapsed into a gloomy pessimism, what noble words are these:

This I regard as history's highest function: To let no worthy action be uncommemorated, and to hold out the reprobation of posterity as a terror to evil words and deeds.

The modesty of the Roman is fascinating. "Much of what I have related," he says, "and shall have to relate may perhaps, I am aware, seem petty trifles to record. * * * My labors are circumscribed and unproductive of renown to the author." How agreeable to place in contrast with this the prophecy of his friend, the younger Pliny, in a letter to the historian:

I augur, nor does my augury deceive me, that your histories will be immortal; hence all the more do I desire to find a place in them.

To my mind, one of the most charming things in historical literature is the praise which one great historian bestows upon another. Gibbon speaks of "the discerning eye" and "masterly pencil of Tacitus—the first of historians who applied the science of philosophy to the study of facts," "whose writings will instruct the last generations of mankind." He has produced an immortal work, "every sentence of which is pregnant with the deepest observations and most lively images." I mention Gibbon, for it is more than a strong probability that in diligence, accuracy, and love of truth he is the equal of Tacitus. A common edition of the History of the Decline and Fall of the Roman Empire is that with notes by Dean Milman, Guizot, and Dr. Smith. Niebuhr, Villemain, and Sir James Mackintosh are each drawn upon for criticism. Did ever such a fierce light beat upon a history? With what keen relish do the annotators pounce upon mistakes or inaccuracies, and in that portion of the work which ends with the fall of the Western Empire how few do they find. Would Tacitus stand the supreme test better? There is, so far as I know, only one case in which we may compare his Annals with an original record. On bronze tablets found at Lyons in the sixteenth century is engraved the same speech made by the Emperor Claudius to the senate that Tacitus reports. "Tacitus and the tablets," writes Professor Jebb, "disagree hopelessly in language and in nearly all the detail, but agree in the general line of argument." Gibbon's work has richly deserved its life of more than one hundred years, a period which I believe no other modern history has endured. Niebuhr, in a course of lectures at Bonn, in 1829, said that Gibbon's "work will never be excelled." At the Gibbon Centenary Commemoration in London, in 1894, many distinguished men, among whom the church had a distinct representation, gathered together to pay honor to him who, in the words of Frederic Harrison, had written "the most perfect book that English prose (outside its fiction) possesses." Mommsen, prevented by age and work from being present, sent his tribute. "No one," he said, "would in the future be able to read the history of the Roman Empire unless he read . . . Edward Gibbon." The Times, in a leader devoted to the subject, apparently expressed the general voice:

Back to Gibbon is already, both here and among the scholars of Germany and France, the watchword of the younger historians.

I have now set forth certain general propositions which, with time for adducing the evidence in detail, might, I think, be established: That in the consensus of learned people Thucydides and Tacitus stand at the head of historians, and that it is not alone their accuracy, love of truth, and impartiality which entitle them to this preeminence, since Gibbon and Gardiner among the moderns possess equally the same qualities. What is it, then, that makes these men supreme? In venturing a solution of this question, I confine myself necessarily to the English translations of the Greek and Latin authors. We have thus a common denominator of language, and need not take into account the unrivaled precision and terseness of the Greek and the force and clearness of the Latin. It seems to me that one special merit of Thucydides and Tacitus is their compressed narrative—that they have related so many events and put so much meaning in so few words. Our manner of writing history is really curious. The histories which cover long periods of time are brief; those which have to do with but a few years are long. The works of Thucydides and Tacitus are not like our compendiums of history, which merely touch on great affairs, since want of space precludes any elaboration. Tacitus treats of a comparatively short epoch, Thucydides of a much shorter one; both histories are brief. Thucydides and Macaulay are examples of extremes. The Athenian tells the story of twenty-four years in one volume; the Englishman takes nearly five volumes of equal size for his account of seventeen years. But it is safe to say that Thucydides tells us as much that is worth knowing as Macaulay. One is concise, the other is not. It is impossible to paraphrase the fine parts of Thucydides, but Macaulay lends himself readily to such an exercise. The thought of the Athenian is so close that he has got rid of all redundancies of expression; hence the effort to reproduce his ideas in other words fails. The account of the plague in Athens has been studied and imitated, and every imitation falls short of the original not only in vividness but in brevity. It is the triumph of art that in this and in other splendid portions we wish more had been told. As the French say, "the secret of wearying is to say all," and this the Athenian thoroughly understood. Between our compendiums, which tell too little, and our long general histories, which tell too much, are Thucydides and Tacitus.

Again, it is a common opinion that our condensed histories lack life and movement. This is due in part to their being written generally from a study of secondhand, not original, materials. Those of the Athenian and the Roman are mainly the original.

I do not think, however, that we may infer that we have a much greater mass of materials, and thereby excuse our modern prolixity. In written documents, of course, we exceed the ancients, for we have been flooded with these by the art of printing. Yet anyone who has investigated any period knows how the same facts are told over and over again in different ways by various writers; and if one can get beyond the mass of verbiage and down to the really significant original material, what a simplification of ideas there is, what a lightening of the load. I own that this process of reduction is painful, and thereby our work is made more difficult than that of the ancients. An historian will adapt himself naturally to the age in which he lives, and Thucydides made use of the matter that was at his hand. "Of the events of the war," he wrote, "I have not ventured to speak from any chance information, nor according to any notion of my own. I have described nothing but what I either saw myself or learned from others of whom I made the most careful and particular inquiry. The task was a laborious one, because eyewitnesses of the same occurrences gave different accounts of them, as they remembered or were interested in the actions of one side or the other." His materials, then, were what he saw and heard. His books and his manuscripts were living men. Our distinguished military historian, John C. Ropes, whose untimely death we deplore, might have written his history from the same sort of materials, for he was contemporary with our civil war and followed the daily events with intense interest. A brother of his was killed at Gettysburg, and he had many friends in the Army. He paid at least one memorable visit to Meade's headquarters in the field, and at the end of the war had a mass of memories and impressions of the great conflict. He never ceased his inquiries; he never lost a chance to get a particular account from those who took part in battles or campaigns, and before he began his Story of the Civil War he, too, could have said, "I made the most careful and particular inquiry" of generals and officers on both sides and of men in civil office privy to the great transactions. His knowledge drawn from living lips was marvelous, and his conversation, when he poured this knowledge forth, often took the form of a flowing narrative in an animated style. While there are not, so far as I remember, any direct references in his two volumes to these memories or to memoranda of conversations which he had with living actors after the close of the war drama, and while his main authority is the Official Records of the Union and Confederate Armies, which no one appreciated better than he were unique historical materials, nevertheless this personal knowledge trained his judgment and gave color to his narrative.

It is pretty clear that Thucydides spent a large part of a life of about three score years and ten in gathering materials and writing his history. The mass of facts which he set down or stored away in his memory must have been enormous. He was a man of business, and had a home in Thrace as well as in Athens, traveling, probably, at fairly frequent intervals between the two places; but the main portion of the first forty years of his life was undoubtedly spent in Athens, where, during those glorious years of peace and the process of beautifying the city, he received the best education a man could get. To walk about the city and view the buildings and statues was both directly and insensibly a refining influence. As Thucydides himself, in the funeral oration of Pericles, said of the works which the Athenian saw around him, "the daily delight of them banishes gloom." There was the opportunity to talk with as good conversers as the world has ever known, and he undoubtedly saw much of the men who were making history. There was the great theater and the sublime poetry. In a word, the life of Thucydides was adapted to the gathering of a mass of historical materials of the best sort, and his daily walk, his reading, his intense thought gave him an intellectual grasp of the facts he has so ably handled. Of course he was a genius, and he wrote in an effective literary style, but seemingly his natural parts and acquired talents are directed to this: A digestion of his materials and a compression of his narrative without taking the vigor out of his story in a manner I believe to be without parallel. He devoted a life to writing a volume. His years after the peace was broken, his career as a general, his banishment and enforced residence in Thrace, his visit to the countries of the Peloponnesian allies with whom Athens was at war, all these gave him a signal opportunity to gather materials and to assimilate them in the gathering. We may fancy him looking at an alleged fact on all sides and turning it over and over in his mind. We know that he must have meditated long on ideas, opinions, and events, and the result is a brief, pithy narrative. Tradition hath it that Demosthenes copied out this history eight times, or even learned it by heart. Chatham, urging the removal of the forces from Boston, had reason to refer to the history of Greece, and, that he might impress it upon the lords that he knew whereof he spoke, declared, "I have read Thucydides."

Of Tacitus likewise is conciseness a well-known merit. Living in an age of books and libraries, he drew more from the written word than did Thucydides; and his method of working, therefore, resembled more our own. These are common expressions of his: "It is related by most of the writers of those times;" I adopt the account "in which the authors are agreed;" this account "agrees with those of the other writers." Relating a case of recklessness of vice in Messalina, he acknowledges that it will appear fabulous, and asserts his truthfulness thus:

But I would not dress up my narrative with fictions to give it an air of marvel, rather than relate what has been stated to me or written by my seniors.

He also speaks of the authority of tradition, and tells what he remembers "to have heard from aged men." He will not paraphrase the eloquence of Seneca after he had his veins opened, because the very words of the philosopher had been published; but when, a little later, Flavius the tribune came to die, the historian gives this report of his defiance of Nero: "I hated you," the tribune said to the emperor; "nor had you a soldier more true to you while you deserved to be loved. I began to hate you from the time you showed yourself the impious murderer of your mother and your wife, a charioteer, a stage player, an incendiary." "I have given the very words," Tacitus adds, "because they were not, like those of Seneca, published, though the rough and vigorous sentiments of a soldier ought to be no less known." Everywhere we see in Tacitus, as in Thucydides, a dislike of superfluous detail, a closeness of thought, a compression of language. He was likewise a man of affairs, but his life work was his historical writings, which, had we all of them, would fill probably four moderate-sized octavo volumes.

To sum up, then, Thucydides and Tacitus are superior to the historians who have written in our century, because by long reflection and studious method they have better digested their materials and compressed their narrative. Unity in narration has been adhered to more rigidly. They stick closer to their subject. They are not allured into the fascinating bypaths of narration, which are so tempting to men who have accumulated a mass of facts, incidents, and opinions. One reason why Macaulay is so prolix is because he could not resist the temptation to treat events which had a picturesque side and which were suited to his literary style, so that, as John Morley says, "in many portions of his too elaborated history of William III he describes a large number of events about which, I think, no sensible man can in the least care either how they happened, or whether, indeed, they happened at all or not." If I am right in my supposition that Thucydides and Tacitus had a mass of materials, they showed reserve and discretion in throwing a large part of them away, as not being necessary or important to the posterity for which they were writing. This could only be the result of a careful comparison of their materials and of long meditation on their relative value. I suspect that they cared little whether a set daily task was accomplished or not; for if you propose to write only one large volume or four moderate-sized volumes in a lifetime, art is not long nor is life too short.

Another superiority of the classical historians, as I reckon, arose from the fact that they wrote what was practically contemporaneous history. Herodotus was born 484 B. C., and the most important and accurate part of his history is the account of the Persian invasion which took place four years later. The case of Thucydides is more remarkable. Born in 471 B. C., he relates the events which happened between 435 and 411, when he was between the ages of 36 and 60. Tacitus, born in 52 A. D., covered with his Annals and History the years between 14 and 97. "Herodotus and Thucydides belong to an age in which the historian draws from life and for life," writes Professor Jebb. It is manifestly easier to describe a life you know than one you must imagine, which is what you must do if you aim to relate events which took place before your own and your father's time. In many treatises which have been written demanding an extraordinary equipment for the historian, it is generally insisted that he shall have a fine constructive imagination; for how can he recreate his historic period unless he live in it? In the same treatises it is asserted that contemporary history can not be written correctly, for impartiality in the treatment of events near at hand is impossible. Therefore the canon requires the quality of a great poet, and denies that there may be had the merit of a judge in a country where there are no great poets, but where candid judges abound. Does not the common rating of Thucydides and Tacitus refute the dictum that history within the memory of men living can not be written truthfully and fairly? Given then the judicial mind, how much easier to write it. The rare quality of a poet's imagination is no longer necessary, for your boyhood recollections, your youthful experiences, your successes and failures of manhood, the grandfather's tales, the parent's recollections, the conversation in society—all these put you in vital touch with the life you seek to describe. These not only give color and freshness to the vivifying of the facts you must find in the record, but they are in a way materials themselves, not strictly authentic, but of the kind that direct you in search and verification. Not only is no extraordinary ability required to write contemporary history, but the labor of the historian is lightened, and Dryasdust is no longer his sole guide. The funeral oration of Pericles is pretty nearly what was actually spoken, or else it is the substance of the speech written out in the historian's own words. Its intensity of feeling and the fitting of it so well into the situation indicate it to be a living contemporaneous document, and at the same time it has that universal application which we note in so many speeches of Shakespeare. A few years after our civil war a lawyer in a city of the middle West, who had been selected to deliver the Decoration Day oration, came to a friend of his in despair because he could write nothing but the commonplaces about those who have died for the Union and for the freedom of a race which had been uttered many times before, and he asked for advice. "Take the funeral oration of Pericles for a model," was the reply. "Use his words where they will fit, and dress up the rest to suit our day." The orator was surp ised to find how much of the oration could be used bodily, and how much with adaptation was germane to his subject.

But slight alterations are necessary to make the opening sentence this:

> Most of those who have spoken here have commended the lawgiver who added this oration to our other customs; it seemed to them a worthy thing that such an honor should be given to the dead who have fallen on the field of battle.

In many places you may let the speech run on with hardly a change.

> In the face of death [these men] resolved to rely upon themselves alone. And when the moment came they were minded to resist and suffer rather than to fly and save their lives. They ran away from the word of dishonor, but on the battlefield their feet stood fast; and while for a moment they were in the hands of fortune, at the height, not of terror, but of glory, they passed away. Such was the end of these men; they were worthy of their country.

Consider for a moment, as the work of a contemporary, the book which continues the account of the Sicilian expedition and ends with the disaster at Syracuse. "In the describing and reporting whereof," Plutarch writes, "Thucydides hath gone beyond himself, both for variety and liveliness of narration as also in choice and excellent words." "There is no prose composition in the world," wrote Macaulay, "which I place so high as the seventh book of Thucydides. * * * I was delighted to find in Gray's letters, the other day, this query to Wharton: 'The retreat from Syracuse—is it or is it not the finest thing you ever read in your life?'" In the Annals of Tacitus we have an account of part of the reign of Emperor Nero which is intense in its interest as the picture of a state of society that would be incredible did we not know that our guide was a truthful man. One rises from a perusal of this with the trite expression, "Truth is stranger than fiction;" and one need only compare the account of Tacitus with the romance Quo Vadis to be convinced that true history is more interesting than a novel. One of the most vivid impressions I ever had came after reading the story of Nero and Agrippina in Tacitus, from a view immediately thereafterward of the statue of Agrippina in the National Museum at Naples.

It will be worth our while now to sum up what I think may be established with sufficient time and care. Natural ability being presupposed, the qualities necessary for an historian are diligence, accuracy, love of truth, impartiality, the thorough digestion of his materials by careful selection and long meditating, and the compression of his narrative into the smallest compass consistent with the life of his story. He must also have a power of expression suitable for his purpose. All these qualities, we have seen, were possessed by Thucydides and Tacitus, and we have seen, furthermore, that by bringing to bear these endowments and acquirements upon contemporary history their success has been greater than it would have been had they treated a more distant period. Applying these considerations to the writing of history in America, it would seem that all we have to gain in method, in order that when the genius appears he shall rival the great Greek and the great Roman, is thorough assimilation of materials and rigorous conciseness in relation. I admit that the two things we lack are difficult to get as our own. In the collection of materials, in criticism and detailed analysis, in the study of cause and effect, in applying the principle of growth, of evolution, we certainly surpass the ancients. But if we live in the age of Darwin we also live in an age of newspapers and magazines, when, as Lowell said, not only great events, but a vast "number of trivial incidents, are now recorded, and this dust of time gets in our eyes;" when distractions are manifold; when the desire to "see one's name in print" and make books takes possession of us all. When one has something like an original idea or a fresh combination of truisms, he obtains easily a hearing. The hearing once had, something of a success being made, the writer is urged by magazine editors and by publishers for more. The good side of this is apparent. It is certainly a wholesome indication that a demand exists for many serious books, but the evil is that one is pressed to publish his thoughts before he has them fully matured. The periods of fruitful meditation out of which emerged the works of Thucydides and Tacitus seem not to be a natural incident of our time. To change slightly the meaning of Lowell, "the bustle of our lives keeps breaking the thread of that attention which is the material of memory, till no one has patience to spin from it a continuous thread of thought." We have the defects of our qualities. Nevertheless, I am struck with the likeness between a common attribute of the Greeks and Matthew Arnold's characterization of the Americans. Greek thought, it is said, goes straight to the mark, and penetrates like an arrow. The Americans, Arnold wrote, "think straight and see clear." Greek life was adapted to meditation. American quickness and habit of taking the short cut to the goal make us averse to the patient and elaborate method of the ancients. We have improved, however, in manner of expression. The Fourth of July spread-eagle oration, not uncommon even in New England in former days, would now be listened to hardly anywhere without merriment. In a Lowell Institute lecture in 1855 Lowell said:

> In modern times the desire for startling expression is so strong that people hardly think a thought is good for anything unless it goes off with a *pop*, like a ginger-beer cork.

No one would thus characterize our present writing. Between reserve in expression and reserve in thought there must be interaction. We may hope, therefore, that the trend in the one will become the trend in the other and that we may look for as great historians in the future as in the past. The Thucydides or Tacitus of the future will write his history from the original materials, knowing that there only will he find the living spirit, but he will have the helps of the modern world. He will have at his hand monographs of students whom the professors of history in our colleges are teaching with diligence and wisdom, and he will accept these aids with thankfulness in his laborious search. He will have grasped the generalizations and methods of physical science, but he must know to the bottom his Thucydides and Tacitus. He will recognize in Homer and Shakespeare the great historians of human nature, and he will ever attempt, although feeling that failure is certain, to wrest from them their secret of narration, to acquire their art of portrayal of character. He must be a man of the world, but equally well a man of the Academy. If, like Thucydides and Tacitus, the American historian chooses the history of his own country as his field he may infuse his patriotism into his narrative. For he has a goodly heritage. He will speak of the broad acres and their products, the splendid industrial development due to the capacity and energy of the captains of industry; but he will like to dwell longer on the universities, and colleges, on the great numbers seeking a higher education, on the morality of the people, their purity of life, their domestic happiness.

He will never be weary of referring to Washington and Lincoln, feeling that a country with such exemplars is indeed one to awaken envy, and he will not forget the brave souls who followed where they led. I like to think of the Decoration Day orator, speaking thirty years ago, with his mind full of the civil war and our Revolution, giving utterance to these noble words of Pericles:

> I would have you day by day fix your eyes upon the greatness of your country until you become filled with love of her; and when you are impressed by the spectacle of her glory, reflect that this empire has been acquired by men who knew their duty and had the courage to do it, who in the hour of conflict had the fear of dishonor always present to them, and who, if ever they failed in an enterprise, would not allow their virtues to be lost to their country, but freely gave their lives to her as the fairest offering which they could present at her feast. They received each one for himself a praise which grows not old, and the noblest of all sepulchers. For the whole earth is the sepulcher of illustrious men; not only are they commemorated by columns and inscriptions in their own country, but in foreign lands there dwells also an unwritten memorial of them, graven not on stone but in the hearts of men.

III.—REMOVAL OF OFFICIALS BY THE PRESIDENTS OF THE UNITED STATES.

By CARL RUSSELL FISH,
CAMBRIDGE, MASS.

REMOVAL OF OFFICIALS BY THE PRESIDENTS OF THE UNITED STATES.

By CARL RUSSELL FISH, Harvard University.

The final authority on the subject of removals from Presidential offices is the Executive Journal of the Senate. This is not published from year to year, but at longer intervals, as the individuals mentioned in it disappear from public life. At present it has been made public through the Presidency of Andrew Johnson. This explains the limitation of the tables by that date.

While this Journal is the final source for such statistics, it is by no means an easy one to use, for the cases in which the removal is actually mentioned do not truly represent the total number in which the change is made by the direct authority of the President. Many cases are ambiguously worded; the usage of the several Presidents varies somewhat, and in some the fact of removal seems to be glossed over by such phrasing. This led to the device of separate columns, each representing a different form of expression, and differing also in the degree of certainty with which we can assume that the vacancy, which the appointment was to fill, was a forced one. With a brief explanation of each, the whole is left to the judgment and special purpose of the reader.

Column 1 represents the cases where the removal is distinctly mentioned in the Journal.

Column 2 gives the cases where the phrasing is exactly similar to that in column 1, except that the word "removed" is omitted. It is probable that these generally represent removals. Tench Coxe was, as we know from other sources, removed;[1] yet his case is thus entered.

Column 3 gives the cases of failure to reappoint at the end of an expired term; practically these are removals.

---

[1] American Historical Review, II, 259-261.

Column 4 gives the cases of appointments to fill the places of consuls whose exequaturs have been denied and officers who have been unable to qualify after appointment, as from inability to find bond, or have become disqualified.

Column 5 gives the cases of appointments to take the place of temporary appointees. These latter are, for the most part, men acting in the place of officers summarily dismissed for cause.

Column 6 gives the cases reported in the Journal thus: "A B, collector at C, commissioned during the recess." This phrase covers removals often enough to justify the inclusion of these cases in the tables; its special significance will be explained as far as possible for each separate table.

Column 7 occurs only twice, in the table for Jefferson and in the summary by Presidents. It contains the famous "midnight" appointments of Adams.

Jefferson refused to issue the commissions, although they had been fully made out, and his appointees retained their places, in spite of the adverse decision in Marbury *v.* Madison.

There are some cases of removal, or practical removal, besides these. When the entry states that the late occupant has resigned, the resignation may have been forced. This is more particularly true of the higher offices. Again, the simple announcement of an appointment may occasionally conceal a removal. These cases are, however, obviously too vague to warrant their inclusion here. They are mentioned merely to guard against a too complete acceptance of the following figures.

The sources from which the total number of offices (and these include only the Presidential offices in the civil service) are derived, are two. For 1801 a list of "persons having office or employment under the United States," submitted to Congress in 1802 by Jefferson, has been used; for the other data, the appropriate numbers of the Blue Book or Official Register, published in 1816, 1817, and thereafter biennially. These figures are not offered as accurate. The Register, especially in the earlier numbers, is not complete, is ill arranged, and the Presidential offices are not differentiated. It is impossible, therefore, to obtain a result more than approximately correct. The rough estimates find their excuse in the added significance they give to the more carefully prepared matter in the tables.

It is perhaps safer to call special attention to the fact that has several times been incidentally mentioned, that the only offices dealt with are the Presidential; that is, those filled by the President with the "advice and consent" of the Senate. It would be impossible to find material on the whole body of offices, nor would the value of such statistics be very great, unless they were arranged with special reference to locality, instead of to the country as a whole.

To the separate tables such appropriate notes as will serve to make the figures more intelligible are added. These general statements have to be given without any special authority for each. They are conclusions I have drawn from an immense mass of material, collected toward a thesis for the doctorate. I have, of course, omitted all about which there could be a dispute, and offer only those which, besides being necessary for an understanding of the tables, are most amply supported by my notes.

REMOVALS UNDER WASHINGTON, 1789-1797.

	(1) Removal mentioned.	(2) Name of last occupant, but not cause of the vacancy.	(3) Failure to reappoint.	(4) Appointment vice nonacting appointee.	(5) Appointment vice temporary appointee.	(6) Commissioned during the recess.	Total.
Ministers	2	1					3
Consul	1	1					2
Collectors	8						8
Surveyors	2	2					4
Total	13	4					17
Military	5	1					6
Grand total	18	5					23
Average per year							3—

REMOVALS UNDER JOHN ADAMS, 1797-1801.

	(1) Removal mentioned.	(2) Name of last occupant, but not cause of the vacancy.	(3) Failure to reappoint.	(4) Appointment vice nonacting appointee.	(5) Appointment vice temporary appointee.	(6) Commissioned during the recess.	Total.
Secretary of State	1						1
Minister		1					1
Consuls, etc	3	1					4
Marshal	1						1
Collectors	5	2					7
Surveyors	3		2				5
Supervisor	1						1
Commissioner of court		1					1
Total	14	5	2				21
Military	4	2					6
Grand total	18	7	2				27
Average per year							7—

REMOVALS UNDER JEFFERSON, 1801-1809.

It should be observed that practically all the removals which raise this number above the customary were made during 1801, 1802, and 1803; that is, the removals for political purposes were made gradually, but when they were completed the old method of conducting the service was resumed.

	(1) Removal mentioned.	(2) Name of last occupant, but not cause of the vacancy.	(3) Failure to reappoint.	(4) Appointment vice nonacting appointee.	(5) Appointment vice temporary appointee.	(6) Commissioned during the recess.	(7) Midnight appointments.	Total.
Minister	1							1
Consuls, etc	2	3		1			10	16
Attorneys	3	1					7	11
Marshals	9	1	5				3	18
Collectors	24	1					1	26
Surveyors	1	4		1				6
Naval officers	2	1						3
Supervisors	4							4
Commissioner of loans	1							1
Surveyor-general	1							1
Governor of Territory			1					1
Secretaries of Territories			2					2
Judge of orphans' court							1	1
Register of wills							1	1
Justices of the peace							17	17
Total	48	11	8	2			40	109
Military	10	4		1				15
Grand total	58	15	8	3			40	124
Average per year								15½
Probable number of offices, 1802								433

REMOVALS UNDER MADISON, 1809-1817.

The large number of military removals are, of course, due to the war of 1812. The exceptionally large number of civil officers, larger than the number we have thirteen years later, is also due to the war, and represents chiefly the officers of the direct tax.

	(1) Removal mentioned.	(2) Name of last occupant, but not cause of the vacancy.	(3) Failure to reappoint.	(4) Appointment vice nonacting appointee.	(5) Appointment vice temporary appointee.	(6) Commissioned during the recess.	Total.
Attorney		1					1
Marshal		1	1				2
Collectors	2	2					4
Surveyors	1	3					4
Naval officers					1		1
Assessors of direct tax		9	1				10
Collectors of direct tax		4					4
Register of land office	1						1
Total	4	20	2	1			27
Military	83	6					89
Grand total	87	26	2	1			116
Average per year							14½
Probable number of officers, 1816							824

REMOVALS UNDER MONROE, 1817-1825

It is interesting to note that Monroe made no use of the act of 1820, which, by setting a limit of four years to very many offices that had previously been held at the pleasure of the President, offered an unostentatious method of making removals. This bill was fathered by Crawford, was passed with little comment, but was afterwards strongly animadverted on by Monroe, Jefferson, Madison, and J. Q. Adams.

	(1) Removal mentioned.	(2) Name of last occupant, but not cause of the vacancy.	(3) Failure to reappoint.	(4) Appointment vice nonacting appointee.	(5) Appointment vice temporary appointee.	(6) Commissioned during the recess.	Total.
Minister		1					1
Consuls, etc.	6	2					8
Attorney	1						1
Marshal	1						1
Collectors		3					3
Surveyor	1						1
Naval officer	1						1
Collectors of direct tax	1	1					2
Surveyor-general	1						1
Surveyor of public lands	1						1
Register of land office		1					1
Receivers of public money	2						2
Indian agents	2	1					3
Bank director		1					1
Total	17	10					27
Military	35	6					41
Grand total	52	16					68
Average per year							8½

REMOVALS UNDER J. Q. ADAMS, 1825-1829.

	(1) Removal mentioned.	(2) Name of last occupant, but not cause of the vacancy.	(3) Failure to reappoint.	(4) Appointment vice nonacting appointee.	(5) Appointment vice temporary appointee.	(6) Commissioned during the recess.	Total.
Consuls	1	1		1			3
Attorneys	1	1					2
Collectors	2						2
Surveyor		1					1
Surveyor of public lands			1				1
Registers of land offices	1		2				3
Total	5	2	4	1			12
Military	11						11
Grand total	16	2	4	1			23
Average per year							6—

REMOVALS UNDER JACKSON, 1829-1837.

The comment made on the table for Jefferson should be renewed here and applied to all tables following. That is, that the larger number of removals were made early in the term, indicating that they were made with a political purpose, and not solely for the efficiency of the service.

It will be observed that the figures ordinarily given for removals under Jackson, where they are confined to Presidential offices, are more correct than those for most of the Presidents, the interest in the subject and the discussions to which the alleged practice of the "spoils system" led, having caused more careful investigation.

The table will doubtless cause some surprise at the moderate dimensions of the most famous "sweep" of the service in our history. Several things should here be taken into consideration: First, that many officers in the service were in favor of Jackson's election; second, that among those removed were many from the most important offices, men having many subordinates; finally, there is a consideration that holds good until Johnson's Administration—the "spoils system" did not prevail in and was not forced upon the South. This is a general truth, and as all such admits of many exceptions, but they are fewer than would be supposed. Lincoln might occur as a more probable President to have introduced the change.

It will be remembered, however, that he had no opportunity. The civil war delivered him from the most troublesome of the minor problems before him.

	(1) Removal mentioned.	(2) Name of last occupant, but not cause of the vacancy.	(3) Failure to reappoint.	(4) Appointment vice nonacting appointee.	(5) Appointment vice temporary appointee.	(6) Commissioned during the recess.	Total.
Ministers	5	2					7
Secretaries of legation	1	2					3
Consuls, etc.	21	13		4	1		39
Attorneys	11	3		5	3		22
Marshals	16	2	6		1		25
Collectors	31		16				47
Surveyors	5	1	6				12
Naval officers	6		1				7
Appraisers	9						9
Recorder of land titles	1						1
Surveyors of lands	2		2				4
Registers of land offices	15	1	3				19
Receivers of public money	25		6				31
Governors of Territories			2				2
Judges of Territories	1		6				7
Secretaries of Territories	2	1					3
Indian agents	5						5
Treasury officials	5						5
Mint official	1						1
Bank director		1					1
Special commissioners	2						2
Total	164	26	58	9	5		252
Military	25		2				27
Grand total	189	26	60	9	5		279
Average per year							35—
Probable number of officers, 1829							610

REMOVAL OF OFFICIALS BY PRESIDENTS.

REMOVALS UNDER VAN BUREN, 1837-1841.

This table illustrates how completely Van Buren was a successor to Jackson. The number of removals is small, and an unusually large number were made for cause, the service having become exceedingly disordered under Jackson.

	(1) Removal mentioned.	(2) Name of last occupant, but not cause of the vacancy.	(3) Failure to reappoint.	(4) Appointment vice nonacting appointee.	(5) Appointment vice temporary appointee.	(6) Commissioned during the recess.	Total.
Consuls	2	5	....	1	....	....	8
Collectors	4	8	....	1	....	....	13
Surveyors	2	....	7	1	1	....	11
Naval officer	1	....	....	....	....	....	1
Appraisers	2	....	....	....	....	....	2
Secretary of land office	....	....	1	....	....	....	1
Registers of land offices	2	....	6	1	....	....	9
Receivers of public money	7	....	10	2	....	....	19
Governor of Territory	....	1	....	....	....	....	1
Judge of Territory	....	....	1	....	....	....	1
Secretary of Territory	....	....	1	....	....	....	1
Indian agent	....	....	1	....	....	....	1
Treasury officials	1	1	....	....	....	....	2
Postmasters	5	2	3	....	....	....	10
Total	26	17	30	6	1	....	80
Military and naval	17	2	....	....	....	....	19
Grand total	43	19	30	6	1	....	99
Average per year							25 −
Probable number of offices, 1839							924

REMOVALS UNDER HARRISON AND TYLER, 1841-1845.

Harrison is combined with Tyler because, although he died before he had made any great actual change in the service, he prepared lists of removals and appointments, many of which were acted upon by Tyler. It is impossible, therefore, to disentangle the skein of their interaction.

The total number is somewhat increased by the fact that some offices were twice vacated. Tyler carried on a second proscription in the summer of 1845, not very extensive, but including some important offices.

	(1) Removal mentioned.	(2) Name of last occupant, but not cause of the vacancy.	(3) Failure to reappoint.	(4) Appointment vice nonacting appointee.	(5) Appointment vice temporary appointee.	(6) Commissioned during the recess.	Total.
Ministers	10						10
Secretaries of legation	1		1				2
Consuls	30			2			32
Attorneys	19	1	2				22
Marshals	36		3		1		40
Collectors	66		18				84
Surveyors	35	1	10	1			47
Naval officers	9		3				12
Appraisers	13	1					14
General Land Office	5						5
Surveyors of land	8		1				9
Registers of land offices	25		5	1			31
Receivers of public money	20	2	5				27
Governors of Territories	3		1				4
Secretaries of Territories	5						5
Indian agents, etc	5	1	2		1		9
Treasury officials	3						3
Mint officials	5				1		6
Postmasters	73	9	9	1			92
Special commissioners	3						3
Warden of penitentiary	1						1
Total	375	15	60	5	3		458
Military and naval	18		1				19
Grand total	393	15	61	5	3		477
Average per year							119+

REMOVALS UNDER POLK, 1845-1849.

	(1) Removal mentioned.	(2) Name of last occupant, but not cause of the vacancy.	(3) Failure to reappoint.	(4) Appointment vice nonacting appointee.	(5) Appointment vice temporary appointee.	(6) Commissioned during the recess.	Total.
Ministers, etc	8		2				10
Secretaries of legation	2						2
Consuls	35		3				38
Attorneys	13		7				20
Marshals	9		6				15
Collectors	39	1	22				62
Surveyors	14	1	13	2			30
Naval officers	7		5				12
Appraisers	2						2
General Land Office	2		1				3
Surveyors-general	4						4
Registers of land offices	21		11				32
Receivers of public money	14		11				25
Governors of Territories	2						2
Secretaries of Territories	2						2
Indian agents	4		1				5
Treasury officials	4			1			5
Mint officials	2						2
Postmasters	41	1	25				67
Justices of the peace			1	3			4
Total	225	3	108	6			342
Military and naval	20		2			2	24
Grand total	245	3	110	6		2	366
Average per year							92¼

REMOVALS UNDER TAYLOR, 1849–JULY 9, 1850.

The internal evidence of the journal combines with the external evidence to show that most of the officers commissioned during the recess were appointed to fill vacancies caused by removal.

	(1) Removal mentioned.	(2) Name of last occupant, but not cause of the vacancy.	(3) Failure to reappoint.	(4) Appointment vice nonacting appointee.	(5) Appointment vice temporary appointee.	(6) Commissioned during the recess.	Total.
Ministers, etc.	6	1					7
Secretaries of legation		3		1			4
Consuls	28			6		28	34
Attorneys			4			28	32
Marshals	2		3			30	35
Collectors	1	5				89	95
Surveyors		1	9			39	49
Naval officers			1			11	12
Appraisers		1				7	8
General Land Office						1	1
Surveyors-general			1			4	5
Registers of land offices	1		6			46	53
Receivers of public money			9			47	56
Indian agents, etc.			1			5	6
Governors of Territories						2	2
Judges of Territories						2	2
Secretary of Territory						1	1
Treasury officials						5	5
Mint officials	4						4
Postmasters	2	6	8	1		102	119
Justices of the peace		1				9	10
Total	44	17	43	8		428	540
Military and naval	8		3				11
Grand total	52	17	46	8		428	551
Average per year							414+
Probable number of offices,1849							929

REMOVAL OF OFFICIALS BY PRESIDENTS.

REMOVALS UNDER FILLMORE, JULY 9, 1850-1853.

	(1) Removal mentioned.	(2) Name of last occupant, but not cause of the vacancy.	(3) Failure to reappoint.	(4) Appointment vice nonacting appointee.	(5) Appointment vice temporary appointee.	(6) Commissioned during the recess.	Total.
Chargés	1						1
Secretary of legation	1						1
Consuls	13					1	14
Attorneys						2	2
Marshals	6		1				7
Collectors	7		1	1			9
Surveyors	3	1	4	1			9
Appraisers	2						2
Supervisor of steamboats	1						1
General Land Office						1	1
Surveyor-general						1	1
Registers of land offices	2		1			6	9
Receivers of public moneys	2	1	1			5	9
Judges of Territories	2		2				4
Secretary of Territory	1						1
Indian agents	4						4
Treasury officials						2	2
Mint officials						4	4
Commissioner of Pensions						1	1
Postmasters		3	3				6
Total	45	5	13	2		23	88
Military and naval	13	1					14
Grand total	58	6	13	2		23	102
Average per year							38+

REMOVALS UNDER PIERCE, 1853–1857.

	(1) Removal mentioned.	(2) Name of last occupant, but not cause of the vacancy.	(3) Failure to reappoint.	(4) Appointment vice nonacting appointee.	(5) Appointment vice temporary appointee.	(6) Commissioned during the recess.	Total.
Ministers, etc	9						9
Secretaries of legation	3						3
Consuls	66	2		4			72
Attorneys	35		1				36
Marshals	28	1	3	1			33
Collectors	83		7	1			91
Surveyors	73		5				78
Naval officers	12		2				14
Appraisers	20						20
Supervisors of steamboats	7						7
General Land Office	2			1			3
Surveyors-general	9						9
Registers of land offices	56	1	5			10	72
Receivers of public moneys	53		7	1		10	71
Governors of Territories	4	1	1				6
Judges of Territories	12	2		1			15
Secretaries of Territories	3						3
Indian agents, etc	30	3				1	34
Treasury officials	5		1				6
Mint officials	11						11
Commissioner of Pensions	1						1
Commissioner of Indian Affairs	1						1
Superintendent of Public Printing			1				1
First Assistant Postmaster-General	1						1
Postmasters	147	65	5	2			219
Special commissioners	3			1			4
Chief of bureau	1						1
Warden of penitentiary	1					1	2
Total	676	75	38	12		22	823
Military and naval	31	2	4				37
Grand total	707	77	42	12		22	860
Average per year							215

REMOVAL OF OFFICIALS BY PRESIDENTS.

REMOVALS UNDER BUCHANAN, 1857-1861.

It will be observed that this is the first true case in which the principle of rotation in office was carried out; that is, when the President acted on the theory that men should remain in office only four years, regardless of party. The size of the "sweep" will only be evident when it is remembered that resignation played a more important part than usual. Many officeholders resigned to preserve their good standing in the Democratic party.

	(1) Removal mentioned.	(2) Name of last occupant, but not cause of the vacancy.	(3) Failure to reappoint.	(4) Appointment vice nonacting appointee.	(5) Appointment vice temporary appointee.	(6) Commissioned during the recess.	Total.
Ministers, etc	2					1	3
Secretary of legation	1						1
Consuls	15	2					17
Attorneys	7	2	8				17
Marshals	11	1	14				26
Collectors	14	3	43				60
Surveyors	3	1	19	1	1		25
Naval officers			6				6
Appraisers	8						8
Inspector of steamboats	1						1
Surveyors-general	1		2				3
Registers of land offices	6	2	17			3	28
Receivers of public moneys	10	1	18			6	35
Governor of Territory			1				1
Judges of Territories	4		3				7
Secretaries of Territories	2						2
Indian agents, etc	13		7			1	21
Treasury officials	2		1				3
Mint officials	3						3
Solicitor of Court of Claims	1						1
Postmasters	93	1	64			1	159
Warden of penitentiary		1					1
Justices of the peace						30	30
Total	197	14	203	1	1	42	458
Military and naval	16	7	5				28
Grand total	213	21	208	1	1	42	486
Average per year							121¼
Probable number of officers, 1859							1,520

REMOVALS UNDER LINCOLN, 1861–APRIL 15, 1865.

Here, at least in the case of the 362 officers of the internal revenue, the officers commissioned during the recess represent appointments to vacancies created otherwise than by removal.

	(1) Removal mentioned.	(2) Name of last occupant, but not cause of the vacancy.	(3) Failure to reappoint.	(4) Appointment vice nonacting appointee.	(5) Appointment vice temporary appointee.	(6) Commissioned during the recess.	Total.
Ministers, etc.	22	1					23
Secretaries of legations	5	1					6
Consuls	134	3	1	1		7	146
Attorneys	33		5	1			39
Marshals	32	3	7	1			43
Collectors	81		6	1		2	90
Surveyors	43	1	9	1			54
Naval officers	12						12
Appraisers	10						10
Inspectors of steamboats	8	1					9
Commissioners of direct tax	1						1
Assessors of internal revenue	7					181	188
Collectors of internal revenue	5	2				181	188
Recorder of land titles	1						1
Surveyors-general	5					6	11
Registers of land offices	15	1	1			36	53
Receivers of public moneys	12		4			38	54
Governors of Territories	5						5
Judges of Territories	12			1			13
Secretaries of Territories	6						6
Commissioner of Pensions						1	1
Indian agents	25	2	4	1		43	75
Treasury officials	2		1				3
Mint officials	8						8
Solicitors for Court of Claims	2						2
Postmaster-General	1						1
Postmasters	373	10	8	4			395
Commissioner of buildings						1	1
Special commissioners	2						2
Secretaries to the President						2	2
Warden of penitentiary						1	1
Justices of the peace						14	14
Total	862	25	46	11		513	1,457
Military and naval	177	5					182
Grand total	1,039	30	46	11		513	1,639
Average per year							403

REMOVALS UNDER JOHNSON, APRIL 15, 1865-1869.

The removals by Johnson are not an instance of rotation in office. This idea had so impregnated the minds of the politicians that it had been generally expected that Lincoln would make a thorough change after his second inauguration. He decided against it, and Johnson attempted nothing of the kind until after his disagreement with Congress.

	(1) Removal mentioned.	(2) Name of last occupant, but not cause of the vacancy.	(3) Failure to reappoint.	(4) Appointment vice nonacting appointee.	(5) Appointment vice temporary appointee.	(6) Commissioned during the recess.	Total
Ministers, etc	7	2		1			10
Secretaries of legation	2						2
Consuls	36	3		1			40
Attorneys	11	1	5				17
Marshals	15	7					22
Collectors	24	6	6	3	2		41
Surveyors	12	6	4	2		2	26
Naval officers	4	3					7
Appraisers	4						4
Inspectors of steamboats	4	1				1	6
Commissioners of internal revenue	1	1					2
Assessors of internal revenue	80	7	32	1		4	124
Collectors of internal revenue	80	1	25	1		21	128
General Land Office			1			2	3
Surveyors-general		1	3			4	8
Registers of land offices	2					4	6
Receivers of public moneys	2	1	6			4	13
Governors of Territories	3		1				4
Judges of Territories	5		3				8
Secretaries of Territories	3	1					4
Commissioner of Indian Affairs						1	1
Indian agents, etc	1	4	5			27	37
Commissioner of Education		1					1
Commissioner of Agriculture	1						1
Secretary of War	1						1
Treasury officials	3	1				1	5
Mint officials	3			2			5
Pension agents	1	3	1				5
Postmasters	149	150	46	14	8		367
Commissioners of police			2				2
Wardens of penitentiary	1	1					2
Member of levy court			1				1
Total	455	200	142	25	10	71	903
Military and naval	127	3	1				131
Grand total	582	203	143	25	10	71	1,034
Average per year							264
Probable number of officers, 1869							2,669

SUMMARY BY PRESIDENTS.

These figures are for civil officers only, the military and naval removals having been left out of account.

	(1) Removal mentioned.	(2) Name of last occupant, but not cause of the vacancy.	(3) Failure to reappoint.	(4) Appointment vice nonacting appointee.	(5) Appointment vice temporary appointee.	(6) Commissioned during the recess.	(7) "Midnight" appointments.	(8) Total.	(9) Probable number of officers.
Washington	13	4						17	
John Adams	14	5	2					21	
Jefferson	48	11	8	2			40	109	433
Madison	4	20	2	1				27	824
Monroe	17	10						27	
J. Q. Adams	5	2	4	1				12	
Jackson	164	26	58	9	5			252	610
Van Buren	26	17	30	6	1			80	924
Harrison and Tyler	375	15	60	5	3			458	
Polk	225	3	108	6				342	
Taylor	44	17	43	8		428		540	929
Fillmore	45	5	13	2		23		88	
Pierce	676	75	38	12		22		823	
Buchanan	197	14	203	1	1	42		458	1,520
Lincoln	862	25	46	11		513		1,457	
Johnson	455	200	142	25	10	71		903	2,669
Total	3,169	445	762	89	20	1,089	40	5,614	

SUMMARY BY OFFICES.

	Washington.	J. Adams.	Jefferson.	Madison.	Monroe.	J. Q. Adams.	Jackson.	Van Buren.	Harrison and Tyler.	Polk.	Taylor.	Fillmore.	Pierce.	Buchanan.	Lincoln.	Johnson.	Total.
Secretary of State	1																1
Ministers, etc	3	1	1		1		7		10	10	7	1	9	3	23	10	86
Secretaries of legations							3		2	2	4	1	3	1	6	2	24
Consuls, etc	2	4	16		8	3	39	8	32	38	34	14	72	17	146	40	473
Attorneys			11	1	1	2	22		22	20	32	2	36	17	39	17	222
Marshals		1	18	2	1		25		40	15	35	7	33	26	43	22	268
Solicitors for Court of Claims													1		2		3
Collectors	8	7	26	4	3	2	47	13	84	62	95	9	91	60	90	41	642
Surveyors	4	5	6	4	1	1	12	11	47	30	49	9	78	25	54	26	362
Naval officers			3	1	1		7	1	12	12	12		14	6	12	7	88
Appraisers							9	2	14	2	8	2	20	8	10	4	79
Inspectors of steamboats												1	7	1	9	6	24
Supervisors		1	4														5
Commissioners of court		1	1														2
Commissioner of direct tax															1		1
Assessors of direct tax			10														10
Collectors of direct tax			4	2													6
Commissioners of internal revenue																2	2
Assessors of internal revenue															188	124	312
Collectors of internal revenue															188	128	316
General Land Office							1	1	5	3	1	1	3		1	3	19

SUMMARY OF OFFICES—Continued.

	Washington.	J. Adams.	Jefferson.	Madison.	Monroe	J. Q. Adams.	Jackson.	Van Buren.	Harrison and Tyler.	Polk.	Taylor.	Fillmore.	Pierce.	Buchanan.	Lincoln.	Johnson.	Total.
Surveyors-general, etc		1		2	1	4		9	4	5	1	9	3		11	8	58
Registers of land offices			1	1	3	19	9	31	32	53	9	72	28		53	6	317
Receivers of public moneys					2		31	19	27	25	56	9	71	35		54	13	342
Governors of Territories		1					2	1	4	2	2		6	1		5	4	28
Judges of Territories							7	1			2	4	15	7		13	8	57
Secretaries of Territories			2				3	1	5	2	1	1	3	2		6	4	30
Commissioners of Indian Affairs													1				1	2
Indian agents, etc					3		5	1	9	5	6	4	34	21		75	37	200
Commissioner of Education																	1	1
Commissioner of Agriculture																	1	1
Secretary of War																	1	1
Commissioners of Pensions												1	1			1		3
Pension agents																5		5
Treasury officials								5	2	3	5	5	2	6	3	3	5	39
Mint officials								1		6	2	4	4	11	3	8	5	44
Bank directors				1			1											2
Postmaster-General																1		1
First Assistant Postmaster-General													1					1
Postmasters								10	92	67	119	6	219	159		395	367	1,434
Superintendent of Printing													1					1
Special commissioners							2		3				4			2		11
Chief of bureau													1					1
Secretaries of the President																2		2
Commissioner of buildings																1		1
Commissioners of police																2		2
Wardens of penitentiary									1					2		1	2	7
Judge of orphans' court				1														1
Register of wills				1														1
Justices of the peace				17				4	10				30			14		75
Member of levy court																1		1
Total		17	21	109	27	27	12	252	80	458	342	540	88	823	458	1,457	903	5,614
Military and naval		6	6	15	89	41	11	27	19	19	24	11	14	37	28	182	131	660
Grand total		23	27	124	116	68	23	279	99	477	366	556	102	860	486	1,639	1,034	6,274

It will be observed that the significant elevation is that at the line marking the termination of each Administration.

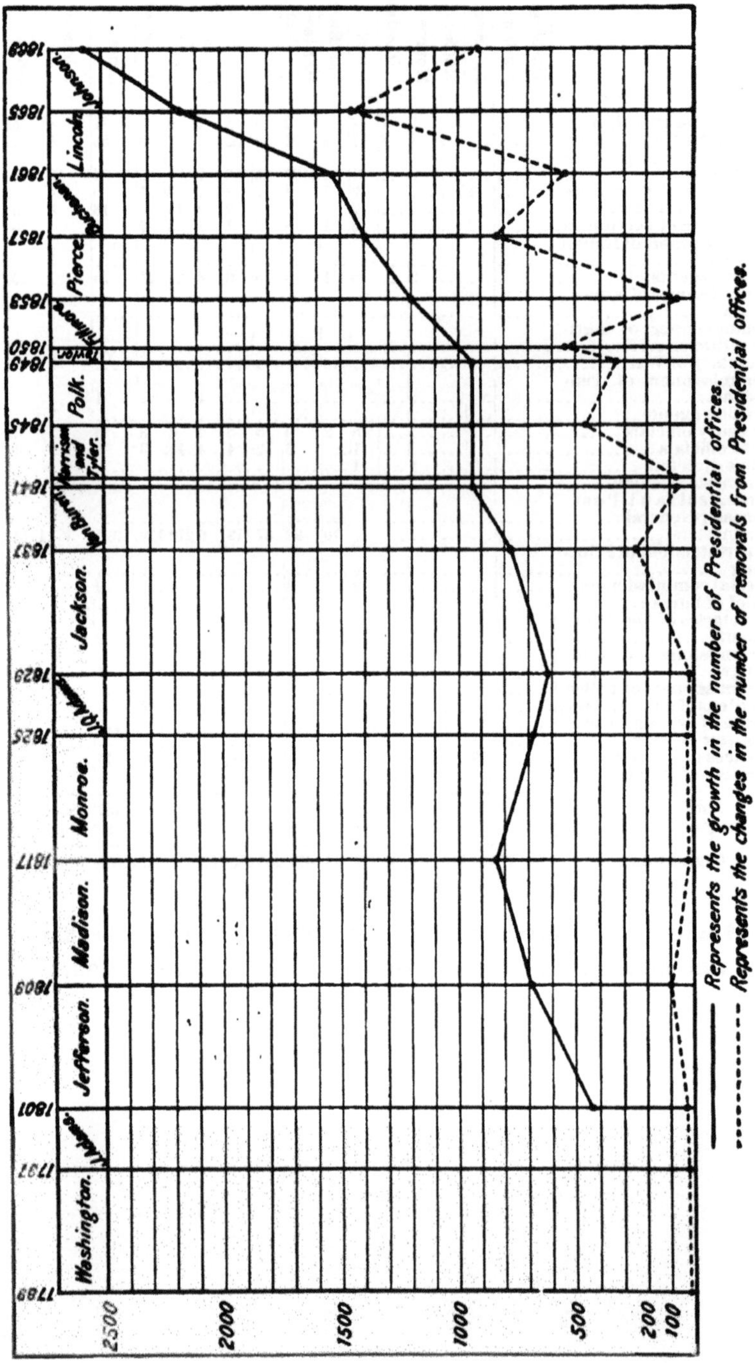

Washington.
Jefferson.
Madison.
Monroe.
Jackson.
Polk.
Pierce
Lincoln
1789
1797
1801
1809
1817
1825
1829
1837
1841
1845
1849
1850
1853
1857
1861
1865
1869
2500
2000
1500
1000
500
200
100
—— Represents the growth in the number of Presidential offices.
- - - - Represents the changes in the number of removals from Presidential offices.

IV.—LEGAL QUALIFICATIONS FOR OFFICE IN AMERICA, 1619-1899.

By FRANK HAYDEN MILLER,
CAMBRIDGE, MASS.

LEGAL QUALIFICATIONS FOR OFFICE IN AMERICA.

By Frank Hayden Miller.

INTRODUCTION.

This paper aims to give a brief history of the legal qualifications for office in the American colonies and States, to show what the general development has been, and to offer some explanations of this development. No attempt is made to treat of the civil-service regulations or of requirements for local officers, except in so far as they affect State or Federal officers. The sources used are the colonial records, statutes, and revisions, the State constitutions, statutes, journals, and debates of the constitutional conventions, pamphlets, and letters.

The suffrage question has only been treated where the connection with office holding was so close as to demand it.

Three general periods have been selected—the colonial, the Revolutionary, and the Federal. Within these periods the subject has been treated topically.

Two tables have been inserted in the text, one giving qualifications of all kinds in the colonies, the other stating the religious and property qualifications in the constitutions, with the dates when they have been omitted in revisions or abolished by amendments.

The colonial table is not exhaustive. It is simply an attempt to present graphically the chief data upon which the colonial chapter of the paper has been based. I have only used the Harvard and Boston libraries on the colonial period and have inserted no provision in the table which I was unable to verify in the documents.

In the second table I have included all States which had a property qualification beyond the payment of a tax, and all those which have provided any religious test. In Connecticut and Rhode Island, statutes on the subject are given for the period previous to the formation of their constitutions.

CHAPTER I.

The Colonial Period.

1. INTRODUCTION.

Two forces were actively at work in the legal development of the American colonies; the English precedents on the one hand, the local conditions on the other. Nearly all of the legislation can be traced, either to English influence—operating directly or indirectly through the conservative tendency of Englishmen to reproduce English institutions—or to the necessity of meeting new conditions. The colonists were practical and conservative; they preferred to meet particular cases resulting from varying conditions, rather than to provide by a detailed code, for all probable contingencies. The condition of the country, as well as the previous training of the settlers, favored this method. A primitive community needs few laws, and this would be especially true in regard to voting and officeholding. Where the political unit formed one social and economic unit, as was the case in the New England colonies at the time of their settlement, where each man was likely to know every other man in the colony, legal regulations in regard to suffrage and officeholding were not as necessary as they are in modern states. Furthermore, voting and officeholding were rather burdens thrust upon the citizen than privileges granted him. In most of the colonies service was compulsory, the pay of magistrates was small and the responsibility large. Hence laws were needed, rather to compel men to serve than to prevent improper persons from being chosen. The reason given, where a law was passed in New Jersey to allow Quakers to hold office, was that the burden of officeholding was too great for the remaining inhabitants.[1] The House of Burgesses in Virginia fined members for resigning;[2] and in Maryland, where one Weston pleaded that he was not a freeman, the assembly, disregarding his plea, compelled him to serve.[3]

Inasmuch, then, as the English precedents, British conservatism, and the colonial conditions all worked against elabo-

---

[1] Trott's Laws, 249.   [2] Hening, I, 540.   [3] Maryland Archives, I, 169.

rate provisions in regard to officeholding, we will not be surprised to find few regulations on the matter in early colonial times. In the colonial assemblies, too, a much greater power than at present was exercised in deciding upon the fitness of their members. In Plymouth it was expressly provided that if a deputy was found "unfit or troublesome," he could be sent back and a new election ordered. The Virginia Burgesses refused to receive a member elect because he was "notoriously of a scandalous character;" and rejected another on the ground that it was contrary to precedent that a clerk should act as a Burgess. Thus the tendency was to decide upon the fitness of a member after election, rather than to specify legal qualifications for candidates.

This chapter will treat of: Citizenship, property, religious and residence qualifications, prohibitions against plurality of office and reeligibility. It is not designed to treat the suffrage exhaustively; but the similarity, frequently amounting to identity of the requirements for electors and those for officeholders, necessitates a discussion of the one in a treatment of the other. While, in the latter part of the period, the qualifications for the suffrage and office diverge, it is interesting to compare the provisions. Where no enactments are found in regard to the qualifications for office, those for the suffrage have been given on the supposition that one who had not been admitted to the franchise would probably not have been considered qualified for office. Indeed there is a judicial decision to the effect that, in want of any statutory regulation, only voters could hold office.[1] While this decision was made in this century, it was based on the common law, and the reasoning would apply equally well to the colonial period.

II. CITIZENSHIP.

There were three stages of political rights in the colonies: First, the local franchise, or the right to vote in town meeting and to hold local offices; second, the full right of suffrage; third, full political rights, including officeholding. The distinction between the first and second stages occurs only in New England where there was a high degree of local self-government. Connecticut was the first colony to make this

---

[1] State v. Smith, in 14 Wis. 497.

distinction, which is closely connected with the New England method of the admission of freemen. There were two stages in this process of obtaining a "freedom;" first the candidate was to be admitted by the town, regularly assembled in town meeting;[1] then he was "propounded" at a meeting of the general court, or legislative body of the colony. After his admission by the town he became an *inhabitant* of the town; but only when the general court had accepted him did he obtain the full rights of citizenship indicated under the title "freeman of the colony" or "corporation."[2] An inhabitant of the town was permitted to vote in town matters, but only a freemen of the colony could vote for colonial officers, or hold office.

The provisions in regard to voting for deputies are interesting as indicating the point of view of the colonist in regard to the dividing line between local and colonial officers. At first inhabitants were allowed to vote for deputies, while only freemen were permitted to choose magistrates.[3] In 1663, however, the voters for deputies were required to be freemen.[3] The New Haven act permitting the Milford burgesses who were not church members to vote for town officers and for deputies, while they were forbidden to vote for magistrates, indicates the same opinion that the deputy was a local rather than a colonial officer.[4]

Plymouth made a distinction between inhabitants and freemen similar to that in Connecticut. The process of admission to the freedom was practically the same: First, a vote in the town meeting, then approval by the general court. There was one point of rather important variation, however. While in Connecticut all who had been admitted as *inhabitants* could vote in town meeting on the admission of inhabitants, on the other hand, in Plymouth, only *freemen* could vote on the question of admission.[5] That this was not an unimportant difference is shown by the fact that the general court stated, in the preamble to one of their acts on the subject, that there were many more voting *inhabitants* than freemen in each town.[6] Here, as in Connecticut, only freemen were allowed to vote for magistrates and assistants, while inhabitants were

---

[1] Conn. Col. Rec., I, 96.
[2] Col. Rec., I, 290.
[3] Ibid., I, 117.
[4] New Haven Col. Rec., I, 110.
[5] Plymouth Col. Rec., IX, 65.
[6] Col. Rec., IX, 92.

allowed to vote for deputies. After admission by the town the inhabitant was required to take the oath of fidelity before he was allowed to vote.[1]

In Massachusetts, also, admission by both the town and colony was required for obtaining the privileges of a freeman. Here, too, some local political privileges were granted to nonfreemen—voting on local matters and holding town office. Even this limited suffrage was carefully guarded, and only those who had been admitted by the freemen of the town, were 24 years of age, and had taken an oath were allowed the privileges. It was provided, furthermore, that a majority of the selectmen should be freemen.[2] It is clear that even in local matters the freemen would still retain control.

Freemen were probably admitted in Rhode Island in the same manner as in the other colonies of New England, but the matter is very obscure. Apparently, there was a higher degree of local control than in the colonies already considered. An act in 1652 requiring the consent of the whole colony for the naturalization of foreigners seems to indicate that the towns had the right to admit those who were not foreigners without any further action by the colony.[3] After the freehold qualification was adopted, lists of freemen had to be certified by the towns to the general court, but nothing is said in regard to any further action in regard to their admission. The provision was evidently for the purpose of deciding on the qualifications of their own members and enforcing the law in regard to the possession of a freehold. There was apparently an attempt to adopt the double system of admission in the eighteenth century, as is shown by the following act:

Whereas there was an act passed at the last session of this assembly prohibiting freemen of any town to choose or vote for deputies unless they were free of the colony, which being found inconvenient, it is repealed.[4]

This is the only indication I find of a distinction in Rhode Island between a freeman of the colony and a freeman of a town, and I am inclined to think that such a distinction existed only during the brief period between the enactment of the law cited in the preamble of the act quoted and its repeal.

---

[1] Col. Rec., IX, 31.
[2] Massachusetts Col. Rec., II, 197 (1647).
[3] Rhode Island Col. Rec., I, 246 (1652).
[4] Col. Rec., IV, 338.

There was evidently nothing in the colonies outside of New England corresponding to the admission of freemen by the towns. The suffrage was controlled by general laws, either incorporated into the charter, as in Pennsylvania, or passed by a colonial assembly. Hence, it follows naturally that no distinction is made between suffrage on local matters and the right to vote for colonial officers.

One phase of citizenship remains to be considered, namely, the naturalization of foreigners. In the acts regulating the admission of freemen in New England, aliens are seldom mentioned. The provision already mentioned in Rhode Island is the only one I find in any New England enactment indicating that aliens could be naturalized. An act of New Hampshire required that freemen should be Englishmen[1] and a Massachusetts act has the same provision.[2] Probably there were not foreigners enough in New England to call for legislation on the subject of naturalization. In the Middle and Southern colonies there was more immigration from non-British countries, and the subject of naturalization received the attention of the colonial legislatures. The process of naturalization adopted varied in the different colonies. Pennsylvania naturalized each person by a vote of the legislature.[3] Usually a large number were admitted by one act of the assembly, but each person was named. In New York there was an act in 1715 naturalizing all who had been in the province a certain length of time, and providing further for the naturalization of all Protestants.[4] There is nothing in the language of the act to indicate that it should not operate prospectively for the benefit of those coming into the colony after its enactment. It was evidently not so construed, however, as the governor in 1775 vetoed a naturalization bill and mentioned the fact with regret in his report to the lords of trade, alleging his instructions.[5] He said that the refusal of His Majesty to consent to a naturalization law worked to the disadvantage of the royal colonies, as foreigners were thus driven to the charter colonies, where they were encouraged.

In Delaware the assembly enacted that the governor might

---

[1] New Hampshire Prov. Pap. I, 396 (1680).
[2] Massachusetts Col. Rec., IV, Part II, 118 (1665).
[3] Laws, Code of 1742, 470. There are many such examples in this revision.
[4] Trotts Laws, 275.
[5] New York Col. Rec., VIII, 564. I am unable to find the instructions.

grant instruments of naturalization,[1] and in a later act[2] referred to aliens naturalized in England, Pennsylvania, or Delaware, apparently not recognizing the naturalization in the other colonies. I find no other act recognizing naturalization in another colony. South Carolina passed an act in 1697 naturalizing all foreigners who should take the oath of allegiance. They were "to have, use, and enjoy all the rights, privileges, powers, and immunities," the same as those of English parents.[3] An act in 1704, however, provided that this act of 1697 should not be so construed as to allow naturalized aliens to hold office, although they were permitted to vote.[4] This act of 1697 would seem to naturalize only those who were in the colony at the time, as it read, "All aliens * * * now inhabitants of South Carolina." Yet there seems to be no later act upon the subject.

It is apparent that the question of the political privileges of aliens was very inadequately dealt with by the colonial assemblies. It is not probable, however, that they were disfranchised in colonies where no acts on the subject are to be found. The assemblies legislated as little as possible, and were inclined rather to meet abuses when they occurred than to provide for all probable emergencies. Hence it is very likely that unobjectionable foreigners may have been allowed to vote where there was no legislation on the matter.

PROPERTY QUALIFICATIONS.

No property qualifications appear to have been required until the second half of the seventeenth century. In 1659 Connecticut required that a freeman should possess £30 "proper personal estate" or should have borne an office in the commonwealth.[5] This was reduced to £20 in 1862.[6] Virginia adopted a property qualification for the suffrage in 1655, but repealed the act the following year, because it was "hard and unagreeable that any persons should pay taxes and have no votes."[7] A freehold qualification for suffrage was adopted in 1670,[8] and for the Burgesses in 1705.[9] In a preamble to the act of 1670 it is stated that the elections

---

[1] Delaware Laws, 52. (1700.)
[2] Ibid, 148. (1734.)
[3] Cooper's Statutes, II, 131.
[4] Ibid., II, 232.
[5] Connecticut Col. Rec., I, 331.
[6] Ibid., I, 389.
[8] Hening's Statutes, I, 412.
[7] Ibid., II, 286.
[9] Ibid., III, 244.

had become tumultuous, owing to the voting of unworthy persons. The colonies settled after the middle of the seventeenth century had property qualifications from the start, and from 1691 on every colony provided some property requirement for suffrage and usually, also, for office. These provisions continued to exist in all of the colonies until the Revolution.

In most cases the amount required for suffrage and office was the same, the most common provision being the forty-shilling freehold. Rhode Island, starting with the forty-shilling freehold, increased it by successive enactments to £400 in 1746.[1] The reason given in one of the acts was that the "admission of necessitous persons" had given rise to bribery in the elections. The variations may have been due, however, to the fluctuations in the value of paper money.

Only three of the colonies made a marked difference in the amounts required for suffrage and office. South Carolina and New Jersey required £1,000 for members of the assembly; New Hampshire required £300.

A freehold was usually required. Pennsylvania, Delaware, and Virginia specified the number of acres of land: in other cases the value in money of the freehold was determined. In South Carolina land and slaves or an equivalent in personal property was demanded.

The location of the property was usually specified, the earlier statutes providing merely that the property should be in the colony. Later on, however, there was a tendency to require that deputies to the assembly should possess a freehold in the district represented. In New Jersey the deputy was to own property in the division—East or West Jersey—from which he was elected.

South Carolina had the most complicated provision. If a resident of the parish, the deputy might have real estate in the parish or property anywhere in the colony, but if a nonresident of the parish he must have the freehold in the parish and ten slaves in addition to the requirement for a resident: in short, he must either reside or have property in the parish which he represented. Where the property qualification was the same for voters and deputies, the latter must

---

[1] Revision of 1752, p. 13.

necessarily have had property in the district in order to be qualified as a voter.

Thus in Connecticut the deputy was to be a freeman; the freemen were to elect deputies from their own number and the freemen were required to own a certain amount of property in the town. Hence, although it was not directly so provided by statute, ownership of property in the town represented was required. Most of the colonies required it by statute. New Hampshire, on the other hand, provided that the property might be anywhere in the colony.[1]

In general, then, the colonies had at first a simple freehold qualification for office and suffrage; later, the amount of the freehold was specified and the location of it within a district was fixed. The freehold of to the value of £40 or yielding an income of 40 shillings per. annum, became quite common for both suffrage and office late in the seventeenth century, although it appeared much earlier in Rhode Island.

What has been said so far applies chiefly to deputies in the assemblies, and these were frequently the only officers whose qualifications were fixed by statute. There were, however, a number of provisions requiring property of other officers. In Massachusetts a freehold was required of assessors varying in amount according to the size of the town for which they were chosen.[2] The amount required varied from £50 to £500. Pennsylvania provided that coroners, sheriffs, and assessors should have the same qualifications as assemblymen. The instructions to the governor of New Jersey stated that judges, sheriffs, and councilors should be men of good estates.[3] Some of the colonies required that the property should have been held a certain length of time before the election.

There is abundant evidence that the freehold qualification caused a good deal of trouble to election inspectors: there were numerous regulations in regard to the transmission of certificates to the assemblies: there were acts fining inspectors for allowing those to vote who were improperly admitted or not qualified. Many of the colonies provided oaths which must be taken by the elector or candidate saying that their

---

[1] Revision of 1771, p. 166.
[2] Province Laws, I, 167.
[3] Instructions to Governor Bernard in New Jersey Archives, IX, 43.

property had not been fraudulently conveyed to them for the purpose of enfranchising them. There were laws respecting mortgagors in and out of possession. Some statutes provided that the estate must be clear of debt, and oaths were provided to this purpose. Acts were frequently passed explaining previous acts and determining how the qualification should be computed: in short, the provisions gave endless annoyance to the town and colonial authorities. Up to the time of the Revolution, however, no property qualification had been abolished, and the tendency was rather to increase than to diminish the amount required.

RESIDENCE.

Most of the colonies required a deputy to be a resident of the district which he represented. Massachusetts, in 1644, allowed them to reside in any part of the province,[1] but by the charter of 1691 residence in the town represented was necessary. The provision mentioned above, requiring a freehold in the district represented, would tend to fix their residence there. South Carolina required residence in the parish, or residence in the county with a freehold in the parish.

A number of colonies required a year's residence in the province before one could be elected to office. In Pennsylvania and Delaware a period of two years was necessary. In Massachusetts and Connecticut a person acquired a domicile in a year, but might be admitted to political privileges sooner. The length of the residence within the district was not usually fixed by statute. New Jersey, however, provided a year's residence in the county, city, or town as a prerequisite for voting.[2] The tendency to allow localities to be governed by officers chosen among themselves was carried to an extreme in New York. Here the sheriffs, who were chosen by the governor, were to be appointed from each riding of a county in turn.

On the whole, not much stress seems to have been laid on residence qualifications: the property qualification served the same purpose; that is, to require that the freemen should be identified with the interests of the province. In a number of colonies nonresidents could vote. Both Virginia and New

---

[1] Massachusetts Col. Rec., II, 88.
[2] Allinson's Laws of New Jersey, ch. 116 (1725).

Hampshire had provisions that a person could vote in a county where he had property, although not a resident. The elector's oath, however, prevented anyone from voting twice in the same election.

RELIGIOUS TESTS.

There were four stages of religious toleration in the colonies: (1) The absolute prohibition of nonconforming religions; (2) permission to remain in the colony and enjoy property rights; (3) an admission to the suffrage and to some minor offices; (4) equal political rights, including colonial offices. As long as a colony was in the first stage there would be no legislation in regard to voting and officeholding by those of the proscribed religion. Hence we seldom find a law in the seventeenth century excluding Quakers from the suffrage or office, as they were not supposed to be allowed to settle in the colony at all. Their refusal also to take the oaths disqualified them.

Toleration was only a question of degree in the colonies: no colony ever allowed all persons to hold office without regard to religious belief; some excluded all who did not belong to a particular church; others made Christianity the basis of the religious qualification; a third class—and this became quite general after the accession of William and Mary—allowed full rights to all Protestants.

Massachusetts Bay and New Haven expressly prohibited the admission of freemen who were not church members. The former required membership in a church of the colony,[1] the latter, membership in some of the approved churches of New England.[2] When Milford applied for admission to the New Haven colony, the petition states that the town, hitherto independent, has admitted six persons as free burgesses who are not church members; they request that these persons may be allowed to vote in town matters and for deputies to the general court; they pledge themselves not to elect these persons as deputies or allow them to vote for magistrates; they also promise not to admit any more burgesses who are not church members. The general court acceded to this request.[3] With this exception, only church members were allowed to

---

[1] Massachusetts Col. Rec., I, 87.
[2] New Haven Col. Rec., I, 15, 112.
[3] Ibid., 1, 110.

vote, even in town matters, in New Haven as long as the colony had a separate organization.

In the Massachusetts Bay colony the law was passed in 1631 and continued in existence until 1665, when it was modified at the request of the King. In his letter to the colony he demanded that the law be so modified that all freeholders of competent estates be allowed to become freemen. He used the expression "orthodox in religion (though differing in their judgment in regard to church government)." The commissioners who brought this letter demanded that the law be so changed as to include members of the Church of England. The general court thereupon passed a law providing that those not church members might be proposed for admission as freemen, upon presentation of a certificate of their orthodoxy from the minister of the place of which they were inhabitants, and a certificate from the selectmen that they paid 10 shillings to a single rate.[1] Church members were required merely to be householders.

It would probably have been somewhat difficult for one who was not a member of a church to satisfy the clergyman of his orthodoxy, and we can well understand why the commissioner should say that the King would feel himself deluded rather than satisfied by such a law. His objections were based, however, on the discrimination in the property qualification. He said that not three church members in a hundred paid 10 shillings to a single rate; hence the apparent concession was worthless.[2] In spite of this remonstrance, this law seems to have been retained until 1691.

Neither Plymouth nor Connecticut required church membership for freemen, but it is doubtful whether persons who were not church members would have been admitted by the towns. That discrimination was made on account of religion in Connecticut, is evident from the fact that Charles II made the same request to Connecticut as to Massachusetts, namely, that persons of competent estates, though differing in religion, should be admitted as freemen. The general court replied that this was in accord with their orders.[3] The only statute on the subject in Connecticut was that the governor should belong to an approved congregation.

---

[1] Massachusetts Col. Rec., IV.² 118.
[2] Ibid., 205.
[3] Connecticut Col. Rec., I, 439.

Pennsylvania required of all officeholders merely belief in Jesus Christ. Virginia disqualified Popish recusants from office. A later revision states that Rhode Island disqualified Catholics in 1663. The correctness of this statement has been disputed, and it seems doubtful whether any such law was actually made.[1]

During the seventeenth century, or at least until 1690, the regulations against the Catholics were rare; in only two cases do I find them specifically disqualified, and in one of these the authority is doubtful. The chief object of persecution in this period was the Quaker: where he was allowed to remain in the colony at all he was given no political rights, except in Pennsylvania and Rhode Island.

The next period, from 1691 to the Revolution, was characterized by the admission of all Protestants except Quakers to complete political rights and the amelioration of the laws against the Quakers. In all of the colonies they were allowed to settle and hold property, and in a number of them they acquired some political rights. In most of the colonies they were not specifically excluded from officeholding, but the oaths required prevented their acting. These oaths were not framed, however, in order to exclude them: their refusal to take any oath was the cause of their disqualification.

In New Jersey they were allowed to affirm, the reason given being that their number was so large that the burden of office-holding and service on juries had become too heavy for the inhabitants.[2] In New Hampshire the same regulation was made, owing to the need of Quakers as witnesses.[3] In Massachusetts[4] and in North Carolina[5] they were allowed to vote, but were not permitted to hold office. Virginia allowed electors to affirm, if Quakers, but made no such provision in regard to officeholders.[6] Maryland went a step further and permitted officeholders also to affirm if they had scruples against taking an oath.[7] Hence at the outbreak of the Revolution Quakers were allowed to vote in most of the colonies and to hold office in several of them.

The exclusion of Catholics from office in England by an act

---
[1] This provision was adopted, however, in the revision of 1745, p. 4. In regard to this law see Rider in R. I. Historical Tracts, 2d Series, I. (Providence, 1889.)
[2] Trott's Laws, p. 249.   [3] Ibid., p. 348.   [4] Massachusetts Bay Res., IV, 180.
[5] Trott's Laws, p. 102–103.   [6] Hening's Statutes.   [7] Trott's Laws, p. 187.

of 1689 had considerable influence in the colonies.[1] The commissioners of trade and plantations instructed the governors in the royal colonies to administer the oaths prescribed by that act to councilors and other officers appointed by them. Early in the eighteenth century most of the colonial legislatures required the same oaths of their members.

In New York and New Hampshire the oaths which would have excluded Catholics were administered to all males over 16 years of age. The governor's commission had given him power to administer the oaths to "such persons as he saw fit." There are other indications that the home government brought some pressure to bear on the colonies for the administering of these oaths. The test had been enacted in 1673, but was never applied in the colonies until after the Revolution of 1688. In some of the colonies, even after the oaths were taken by members of the assembly, they are spoken of simply as the oaths required by Parliament and no act of the assembly is mentioned. In New Hampshire upon the meeting of an assembly the oaths were administered to members by order of the governor.[2]

The only colony in which I find no oath required which would have disqualified Catholics, is Rhode Island. The oaths required of officers and freemen, many of which are to be found in the Colonial Records and revisions of the laws, simply required allegiance. A law was passed in 1756 giving assistants and judges power to swear all suspected persons: an oath of allegiance to the King was required and one abjuring the Pretender. Those refusing to take these oaths were to be known as "Popish recusant convicts;"[3] but the test and transubstantiation oaths were not mentioned, although the enactment was clearly directed against disloyal Catholics. As early as 1679 an oath was administered to the inhabitants of a town, denying the power of the Pope to depose the King, but the clause which in the other colonies usually accompanied this oath, denying the ecclesiastical power of the Pope over British subjects, was omitted.[4]

South Carolina, during a short period, required member-

---
[1] There were several later statutes on the subject: 3 W. & M., c. 2; 7 W. III, c. 34; 1 Geo. 1, Stat. 2, c. 13; 12 Geo. II, c. 13; 22 Geo. II, c. 46.
[2] New Hampshire Prov. Papers, VI, 128.
[3] Revision of 1767, p. 6.
[4] Col. Rec., III, 69.

ship in the Church of England for members of the assembly. As a reason for this enactment the law states that the admission of persons differing in religion "hath often caused great contentions and animosities . . . and all members of Parliament are obliged to conform to the Church of England."[1] There were laws in South Carolina and Virginia disqualifying those who publicly denied the Trinity. New York held that Jews were not qualified to vote or hold office: this was the decision of a contested election.[2] I find no statute, however, in which Jews are mentioned by name as disqualified; but the oaths for freemen and officers would, in many cases, have excluded them.

MORAL QUALIFICATIONS.

There were provisions in nearly all the colonies in regard to the moral character of freemen and officeholders. In Connecticut a person was required to have a certificate from the selectmen of his town that he was of an "honest, peaceable, and civil conversation" before he would be considered for admission as a freeman.[3] The selectmen were liable to a fine for certifying persons not properly qualified. There were similar provisions in the other New England colonies.

The right possessed by all of the assemblies to decide upon the qualifications of their own members was used very freely to exclude those whom they thought unfit. The Plymouth assembly provided by law that the House might refuse to admit any deputies who should prove "insufficient or troublesome."[4] There were laws disqualifying those convicted of scandalous offenses, bribery, and blasphemy. The person so disqualified could, in some cases, be restored by the civil courts. Sometimes, especially in the case of bribery, the disqualification was for a limited period only.

PLURALITY OF OFFICES AND REELIGIBILITY.

Provisions fixing the incompatibility of certain offices occur in most of the colonies. The Pennsylvania charter of 1682 provided that a person should hold only one public office at a time. No other colony established so complete an incom-

---
[1] Cooper's Statutes, II, 232.
[2] New York, Col. Doc., VI, 56, note.
[3] Connecticut Col. Rec., I, 389. Many such regulations were made.
[4] Plymouth Col. Rec., IX, 31.

patibility between different offices. Most of them simply specified certain offices which were not to be held simultaneously. Sheriffs were usually excluded from the assembly, sometimes for a period after they had ceased to hold office. Attorneys and clerks of courts were also frequently barred. Virginia and New Jersey had the parliamentary provision that persons accepting salaried places must stand for reelection in order to hold their seats in the assembly. In Virginia and Maryland, inspectors of tobacco were disqualified,[1] and in Massachusetts, purchasers and collectors of the excise.[2] The laws in regard to the former are numerous: one forbids them to be present at elections. It was their duty to issue certificates to individuals based on the valuation of their tobacco stored in public warehouses; these certificates circulated as money. It was evidently felt that their power of fixing the value of every man's personal property would give them undue influence in the election. The purchasers of excise in Massachusetts had the right to compound with a tavern keeper for a year's excise. In the case of sheriffs, inspectors, and purchasers of excise, the disqualification was probably due to a fear of the influence of these officers on the elections. This is evident from the provision in the case of sheriffs and inspectors that they should not be eligible for two years after the close of their term. There were other provisions which were due simply to the incompatibility of the two offices. Sheriffs, for example, could not also act as clerks, or attorneys. There seems to have been no incompatibility between town and colonial office. Maryland excluded ordinary keepers, probably on the ground that their business made them unfit for the assembly.[3]

Provisions limiting reeligibility were rare. There are some such regulations in regard to sheriffs, and in Connecticut the governor was ineligible to reelection for the succeeding year.

COLOR AND SEX.

Negroes, Indians, and mulattoes were disqualified for voting and office holding in three colonies.[4]

---

[1] Bacon's Laws of Maryland and Hening's Statutes contain numerous provisions on the subject.
[2] Massachusetts Bay Res., II, 921.
[3] Bacon's Laws, 1716, ch. 11, ¶. 5.
[4] South Carolina, Virginia, and Georgia.

In Maryland a woman claimed the right to vote in one of the early assemblies, but her demand was refused by that body; she then protested against any action taken by the assembly.

SUMMARY.

The colonial period falls roughly into two divisions: The first, from the beginning until 1691; the second from 1691 to the Revolution. The first period was characterized by the scarcity of general laws upon the subject and by the identity of the qualifications for suffrage and office. Objectionable persons were rejected by the assemblies or in New England by the towns. Quakers were usually disqualified by the oaths required of electors and officers. The second period was characterized by the control of the home government. This is seen especially in the 40-shilling freehold for the suffrage, the exclusion of Catholics from office by the oaths, and the gradual admission of Quakers to the privileges of the suffrage and office. There was also a tendency to differentiate the qualifications for suffrage and office, a number of the colonies requiring more property for members of the assembly than for voters.

CHAPTER II.

The Revolutionary Period.

I. THE EARLY CONSTITUTIONS.

In the first constitutions, adopted between 1776 and 1790, qualifications for State officers were usually specified in considerable detail. Some of the provisions were the same as had existed in the colonies, a strong tendency being evident to follow closely the colonial precedents. A new class of officers, however, had to be provided for—Senators and Delegates to the Continental Congress. The governors and executive councils, also, whose qualifications in most of the colonies had not been subject to regulation by the assemblies, were now under the control of the States.

The provisions for these officers are found partly in imitation of the provisions in the colonial statutes, partly in accordance with the political theory prevalent at the time. The property, religious, and residence qualifications follow the colonial precedents. The restrictions on reeligibility and the holding of two offices at one time are chiefly the result of doctrinaire considerations. In Virginia and Pennsylvania, where the influence of the principles of the Declaration of Independence was particularly strong, the religious tests were greatly modified, and in the latter the property qualification was abolished.

A comparison of the constitutional provisions with those existing at the outbreak of the Revolution in the colonies will illustrate the working of the two tendencies, that is, the conservative and the doctrinaire.

First. The religious qualifications were much the same, but the tendency is toward greater freedom. Seven of the States disqualified Catholics, and all except New York required some religious test.

Secondly. Property qualifications were retained except in Pennsylvania, and were extended to officers who had not been under the control of the colonial legislatures. The tendency was to increase rather than to diminish the amount required. An inspection of the tables will illustrate these points.

Thirdly. Residence qualifications were retained and increased.

Fourthly. Provisions limiting reeligibility, especially for executive officers, became quite general. In Pennsylvania this restriction was even extended to members of the legislature.

Fifthly. Clergymen were excluded from office in many States, an entirely new provision.

Sixthly. There was a tendency to differentiate qualifications for suffrage and office. The provisions in regard to suffrage usually remained the same, often not being specified in the constitutions.

II. DEBATES AND DISCUSSIONS.

The debates of the State constitutional conventions have not been preserved, but the discussions in the Federal conventions and the debates in the State conventions, called to ratify the Federal Constitution, give an excellent idea of the reasons for the provisions in the State constitutions. The Bills of Rights, Declaration of Rights, and addresses to the people also throw some light on the matter. Letters written by members of the conventions are also valuable as an index to the motives of the framers of the constitutions.

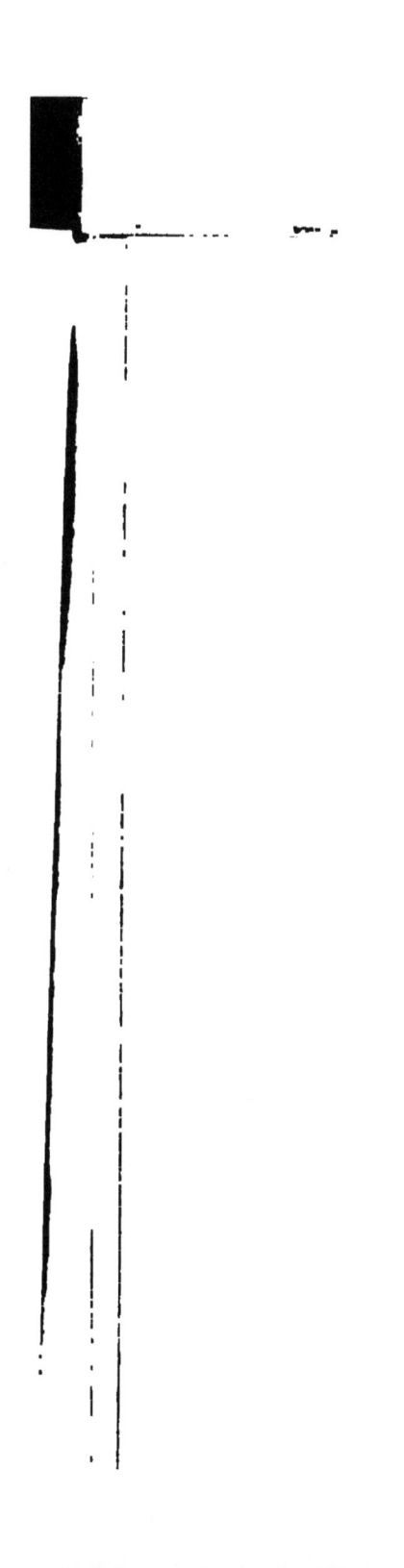

There was no attempt to insert religious qualifications in the Federal Constitution. In the convention Pinckney proposed to add to the oath a clause abolishing religious tests. Sherman thought it unnecessary, the prevailing liberality being a sufficient security against such tests. No one advocated religious tests as a matter of principle. The lack of such a provision, however, was criticised in some of the ratifying conventions.

In North Carolina a speaker objected that Papists and Mohammedans might become president:

> There is a disqualification, I believe, in every State in the Union. It ought to be so in this system.

Mr. Wilson wished that the constitution had excluded Popish priests from offices. As there was no test required and nothing to govern them but honor, he said that "when their interests clashed with their honor the latter would fly before the former."[1]

Abbot said that "some suppose that if no religious test is required, pagans, deists, and Mohammedans might obtain office among us and all our Senators and Representatives might be pagans."

Iredell replied with general arguments on religious toleration and added that the people would never choose men having no religion or a religion materially differing from their own.

> I met by accident with a pamphlet this morning, in which the author states, as a very serious danger, that the Pope of Rome might be elected President.

He then proceeded in all seriousness to demonstrate how exceedingly difficult it would be for the Pope to become President, admitting that it was possible.[2]

Mr. Caldwell objected that there was an invitation to Jews and pagans to come among us.

> All those who have any religion are against the emigration of those people from the Eastern Hemisphere.

Spencer was in favor of "securing every inalienable right," and that of worshiping God according to the dictates of conscience in particular.

---

[1] Elliot's Debates, IV, 215. [2] Ibid., IV, 198.

Religious tests are the foundation of persecutions in all countries.

Governor Johnston admitted that Jews and pagans might emigrate, but that more Christians would come and also the children of Jews would probably be Christians.[1]

In the Connecticut convention Oliver Wolcott argued that there was no necessity of such a test as some wish. The constitution enjoined an oath which was an appeal to God.[2] An objection was often urged that a person destitute of religion could not be bound by an oath.

In the Massachusetts convention the Rev. Mr. Shute objected to a test on the ground that unprincipled men would be perfectly willing to subscribe to anything, and only honest men would be barred out by the oath.

As all have an equal claim to the blessings of the government under which they live and which they support, so none should be excluded from them for being of any particular denomination in religion.

Rev. Mr. Payson objected to a test as "an impious encroachment on the prerogatives of God." These discussions, like the early constitutions, demonstrate that the sentiment in favor of religious tests was still strong in this period.

Several propositions were made in the Federal Convention in regard to property qualifications. A motion was carried, instructing the committee to fix upon such qualification for members of Congress.[3] The committee could not agree upon the amount and reported in favor of leaving the matter to the legislature.[4] Charles Pinckney objected to this plan as giving too much power to the first legislature:

He thought it essential that the members of the legislature, the executive, and the judges should be possessed of competent property to make them independent and respectable.

He suggested $100,000 for the President and $50,000 for the others.

Ellsworth objected to a property qualification on account of the difficulty of fixing the amount. If it was made high enough for the South, it would not be applicable to the Eastern States.[5] Franklin was the only speaker who opposed the proposition to require property on principle, saying that "some of the greatest rogues he was ever acquainted with were the

---

[1] Elliot's Debates, IV, 199. [2] Ibid., II. 202.
[3] Ibid., V, 370. [4] Ibid., V, 224. [5] Ibid., V. 402.

richest rogues." A resolution was also carried to require a property qualification for the Presidency.[1] Hence it was evident that the lack of all property requirements for office in the United States Constitution was not owing to any opposition of the convention to such qualifications per se.

The omission of the property qualifications was objected to in the Massachusetts convention. Rufus King replied that men destitute of property were often superior in knowledge and rectitude. No such qualification had been required by the Confederation, and it was difficult to fix upon the proper amount.[2]

Tench Coxe, in a pamphlet advocating the adoption of the Constitution, approved the omission of religious and property tests:

No qualification in moneyed or landed property is required by the proposed plan; nor does it admit of any preference from the preposterous distinctions of birth and rank. * * * Any wise, informed, and upright man, be his property what it may, can exercise the trusts and powers of the state, provided he possesses the moral, religious, and political virtues which are necessary to secure the confidence of his fellow-citizens.[3]

In January, 1776, John Adams, in a letter to Penn, a member of the North Carolina convention, sketched a plan of government in which he suggested the advisability of rotation in the executive and legislative departments. He proposed that officers should be eligible for three years, and then ineligible for the same length of time.[4]

Copies of this letter were sent to other conventions, and probably had considerable influence on the regulations pertaining to reeligibility. The Pennsylvania constitution gave as a reason for forced retirement that more men would be trained to public office, and an inconvenient aristocracy would thus be avoided.

In the Federal Convention a resolution making the President ineligible to reelection was at first adopted. By this plan the term was to be seven years.[5] The question was not debated in the Federal Convention, but in the States many objections were made to the Constitution on account of the reeligibility of the President.

Charles Pinckney replied to the objections in the South Car-

---

[1] Elliot's Debates, I, 219. [2] Ibid., II, 85.
[3] Ford Pamphlets, p. 146. [4] John Adams Works, IV, 20d. [5] Elliot's Debates, I, 219.

olina convention, saying that a man might be made dangerous if all hope of reelection were cut off. The term might close in the midst of war and the President be the most capable man for conducting affairs. The mode of electing the President made undue influence almost impossible.[1] Hamilton used similar arguments in the Federalist, contending that the limit to a single term would lessen the inducement to good behavior, impair the stability of the Government, and deprive the country in emergencies of the services of the best men. The people should not be deprived of the privilege of choosing men of experience.[2]

In the Virginia plan, Senators and Representatives were to be incapable of holding either a Federal or State office during the term for which they were elected.[3] In favor of this proposition it was urged that eligibility of members of the legislature to executive office would give too much power to the President to control Congress by using offices as rewards. Gerry said that "eligibility of members would have the effect of opening the batteries against good officers, in order to drive them out and make way for members of the legislature."

On the other hand, it was contended that the first legislature would be composed of the ablest men to be found. If they were ineligible, the great offices, even those of the judiciary department, which were to continue for life, must be filled, while those most capable of filling them would be under a disqualification.[3] The clause was amended to read as it appears in the Constitution.

In the Pennsylvania ratifying convention, Wilson, who had been a member of the Federal convention gave the reasons for the incompatibility of legislative and executive office.

The provision, I apprehend, would be found to be very extensive and very salutary. * * * to prevent those intrigues, those factions, that corruption, that would otherwise rise here and have risen so plentifully in every other country. The reason why it is necessary in England to continue such influence is that the Crown, in order to secure its own influence against two other branches of the legislature, must continue to bestow places; but these places produce the opposition which frequently runs so strong in the British Parliament. Members who do not enjoy offices combine against those who do enjoy them. It is not from principle that they thwart the ministry in all its operations. No, their cry is, "Let us turn

---

[1] Elliot's Debates, II, 315.
[2] Federalist, No. 7, p. 2481.
[3] Elliot's Debates, V, 127.
[4] Ibid., V, 505.

them out and succeed to their places." The great source of corruption in that country is that persons may hold offices under the Crown and seats in the legislature at the same time.[1]

Residence and citizenship qualifications were the subject of a good deal of debate in the Federal convention. Some members were in favor of admitting only natives to the legislature. It was feared that foreign powers would interfere in our affairs. But Madison replied that America was indebted to emigration for her settlement and prosperity; that part of America which had most encouraged emigration had advanced most rapidly in population, agriculture, and the arts; and that foreigners would seldom be elected, even if eligible. Wilson also opposed the proposition, quoting the example of Pennsylvania, which had become populous and prosperous by encouraging immigration.[2]

Governeur Morris wanted a long-citizenship qualification for Senators. He said that "men who can shake off their attachments to their own country can never love another." He did not wish to see any of these philosophical gentlemen who called themselves citizens of the world in our councils; he would not trust them.

Another speaker also urged the necessity of greater qualifications for Senators, as bribery and cabal could easily be practiced in the choice of Senators by the State legislatures. Franklin, Madison, Randolph, and Wilson opposed the proposition with arguments similar to those quoted above.[3]

Hamilton justified the longer-citizenship qualification for the Senate on the ground of the treaty-making power:

They ought to be thoroughly weaned from the prepossessions and habits incident to foreign birth and education. * * * A hasty admission of them might create a channel for foreign influence on the national councils.[4]

The provisions in regard to citizenship apparently aroused very little opposition, as they were not discussed in any of the ratifying conventions.

We see, then, by the debates, as by the constitutions, that the Revolutionary period was one of transition.

Many of the State constitutions retained the religious tests, but such provisions found no advocates in the Federal convention. In the matter of property qualifications, while the sen-

---

[1] Elliot's Debates, V, 398.
[2] Ibid, V, 411.
[3] Ibid., II, 483.
[4] Federalist No. 62, Ford's ed., p. 408.

timent in the convention favored them, the members did not consider it a vital point. This lack of all restrictions in regard to religion and property in the Federal Constitution was of great importance in the following period, when new States were founded, modeling their institutions upon those of the National Government.

CHAPTER III.

FEDERAL PERIOD.

I. PROPERTY QUALIFICATIONS.

We have seen that most of the colonial governments and their successors in the Revolutionary period required property for office-holding, varying from a simple freehold to £10,000.

In the later constitutions of these States there was no general tendency to reduce the property qualification during the eighteenth century. South Carolina is the only exception. In the constitution of 1790 the property qualification for governor was changed from £10,000 to £1,500, and those for members of the legislature in proportion.

On the other hand, Georgia, which by the constitution of 1777 had required a property qualification for members of the legislature only, in the constitution of 1789 required 500 acres of land or £1,000 for governor. Delaware, also, in 1792 increased the property qualification for senators from a simple freehold to 200 acres or £1,000.

Only three of the new constitutions of later States provided for a property qualification beyond the payment of a tax. Tennessee, in 1796, required 200 acres of land for members of the legislature and 500 acres for governor. Louisiana, in 1812, provided for a freehold valued at $500 for representatives, one of $1,000 for senators, and of $5,000 for governor. Mississippi, in 1817, required freeholds of $500, $1,000, and $2,000 for representatives, senators, and governor, respectively. Four States—Ohio, Indiana, Illinois, and Missouri—required that members of the legislature should be taxpayers. It is to be noted that the three States requiring a freehold qualification were all Southern States.

Mississippi, then, in 1817, was the last State to adopt any property qualification beyond that of the payment of a tax. At this date no State had abolished previous property qualifications except Maryland.

The era for abolishing property qualifications really began

in the fourth decade of this century.[1] A large part of the the States omitted or abolished the property qualification in the thirties and forties. As this movement begins in 1832, when Jacksonian democracy was at its height, it is fair to suppose that property qualifications for office were swept away on the wave of this great democratic movement. It is connected with the movement for a more extended franchise, but comes a little later and does not excite anything like the interest which is aroused by the suffrage question. In the New York convention of 1820, the Massachusetts convention of the same year, and the Virginia convention of 1830 the extension of the franchise was the great bone of contention and was hotly debated. The property qualifications for office, on the other hand, were hardly considered, and were only touched on in debate incidentally to the suffrage question.

In the Delaware convention of 1831 property qualifications underwent considerable discussion. A committee was appointed to consider the expediency of abolishing them entirely.[2] They reported in favor of dropping all those except for Senator.[3] This was a freehold of 200 acres or £1,000. Judge Hall spoke in favor of the property restriction. There was danger, he said, of the people regarding property as an actual disqualification. The legislature had power to tax, hence ought to be composed of taxpayers.[4]

Another speaker said that as the residence for suffrage had been reduced, the Senators might be elected by men from Maine and Massachusetts. This would be dangerous, and should be guarded against by a property qualification.[5] The provision, it was urged, was a good inducement to industry. Land could be bought for $2 an acre, hence the amount was not excessive.

It is necessary to protect us from the "workies." Abolish the property qualification and they will make us clothe and educate their children.

The free-school law was quoted as an example of what might be expected if men without property got control. No

---

[1] Property qualifications were omitted in new constitutions or abolished as follows: Maryland, 1810, abolished; Mississippi, 1832, omitted; Tennessee, 1834, omitted; Georgia (for legislature), 1835, abolished; Massachusetts (for legislature), 1840, abolished; New Jersey, 1844, omitted; Connecticut, 1845, abolished; Louisiana, 1845, omitted; New York, 1845, abolished; Georgia (for governor), 1847, abolished; South Carolina, 1865, omitted; North Carolina, 1868, omitted; Rhode Island, 1888, abolished; Massachusetts (for governor), 1892, abolished; Delaware, 1897, abolished.

[2] Delaware Debates, 1831, p. 7.   [3] Ibid., p. 16.   [4] Ibid., p. 126.   [5] Ibid., p. 128.

arguments were made on the other side, but the vote for the retention of the amendment stood 16 to 10, showing that there must have been considerable opposition.[1]

The property qualification for members of the lower house was abolished on grounds of expediency, it being merely nominal and giving rise to frauds. Only one other convention between 1830 and 1850 retained a property qualification of any considerable amount. This was the convention of North Carolina in 1835. This convention, however, was limited by the terms of the law calling it to the consideration of certain provisions, and qualifications for office were not among the number.

It is noteworthy that the only Southern States retaining property qualifications after this period are the Carolinas, where they remained until after the war. These States were always conservative and much less affected by Jacksonian Democracy than the other Southern States, and especially less than Mississippi, Tennessee, and Georgia, which abolished such requirements early in the period.

The retention of the property qualification for governor in Massachusetts until 1892, and for Senator in Delaware until 1897, may be regarded as accidental survivals, owing to the difficulty of amending the constitutions. That of Massachusetts was, in fact, abolished by the convention of 1853, but the constitution submitted to the people at that time was not ratified. In this convention there was general agreement that the property qualification ought to be abolished.[2] It might still be a part of the fundamental law but for a circumstance which aroused sufficient interest to procure its abolition.

In 1892 William E. Russell was elected governor. After his election it was found that he lacked the necessary property to qualify. Sufficient property was deeded over to him to fulfill the constitutional requirement before his inauguration. The danger of losing the services of so popular a candidate procured the amendment of 1892. In Delaware the constitution of 1897, abolishing the property qualification, is the first one adopted since 1832.

One more phase of this topic remains to be considered. Three Southern States have a property qualification for suffrage and office intended to bar negroes. The Mississippi

---

[1] Delaware Debates, 1831, pp. 204–207.   [2] Massachusetts Debates, 1853, I, 166.

constitution of 1890 provides that the legislature may require the payment of a poll tax for two preceding years. This tax is not to exceed $2 for the State and $1 for the county. The Louisiana constitution of 1898 gives an option between an educational qualification and property assessed at $300. In either case the payment of a poll tax is requisite. That this provision is intended for negroes only is shown by the exemptions. Foreigners naturalized before 1898 and those having the right of suffrage before 1867, their sons and grandsons, are not subject to the property or educational qualifications. Neither of these constitutions was submitted to the people for ratification, but were enacted by the conventions themselves.

The South Carolina constitution of 1896 had a provision modeled on that of Mississippi. Senator Tillman was chairman of the committee on suffrage. In an address to the convention at the end of the session he said:

> If we were free, instead of having negro suffrage, we would have negro slavery. Instead of having the United States Government, we would have the Confederate States Government. Instead of paying $3,000,000 pension tribute, we would be receiving it.

Considering the unfortunate necessity of remaining a subject State, he finds the constitution the best that can be expected. He then concludes:

> I hope, as South Carolinians, as white men and Democrats, we will go on as prosperously in the future as we have in the past.[1]

One of the members registered a protest against the educational clause which gave the election inspector power to decide upon the fitness of the challenged voter. He said that other provisions, evidently referring to the tax and property qualifications, which were above suspicion of unfairness, would accomplish the desired end; that is, securing white supremacy.[2] Thus we see that the purpose of disfranchising the negroes was openly avowed by the members of the convention.

These provisions, intended to disqualify negroes, are the only property qualifications remaining in State constitutions.

II. RELIGIOUS QUALIFICATIONS.

We have seen that in the Revolutionary constitutions two kinds of tests were required: (1) Belief in the Protestant re-

---

[1] South Carolina convention, 1896, Journal, pp. 731-734. [2] Ibid., p. 727.

ligion; (2) belief in the Christian religion. In constitutions adopted after 1792, whether of the original States or of newly admitted States, these tests are never required. In their place we find two others not as stringent as the former: (1) Belief in God and a future state of rewards and punishments; (2) belief in a Supreme Being. These tests still exist in several of the constitutions.

Let us consider these various tests in the order named. In the Revolutionary constitutions seven States excluded Catholics from office. In three of these—Georgia, Vermont, and South Carolina—these tests were dropped in the new constitutions adopted before the close of the eighteenth century. No religious test of any kind was adopted in their stead. In the four remaining States the provisions were retained for a considerable length of time. This is not significant, however, as they were dropped in every case upon the first general revision of the constitution. There is no case in which a test excluding Catholics from office was retained by a convention after 1792. There is one case in which a convention abolished the religious test which disqualified Catholics and the amendment was rejected by the people; this was in New Hampshire in 1852. There is no doubt that the amendment was rejected on its merits, as there were only three submitted. Those abolishing property qualifications were adopted, but the one removing the disabilities of Catholics was rejected. It is to be noted that a two-thirds vote was required for the adoption of the amendment, so that it may have been lost although favored by a majority of the voters. In Massachusetts all tests were abolished by amendment in 1822. Webster reported the article from the committee. There was considerable debate and strong opposition to the abolition of the test, but none of it seems to have been directed against the Catholics. Probably the convention did not consider that the oath disqualified them: it required the disavowal of the supremacy of any foreign prelate in matters ecclesiastical and civil. As the debate is on the question of requiring belief in Christianity, it will be treated under that head.

In North Carolina, in 1835, there was a bitter contest over the abolition of that part of the thirty-second article which disqualified "persons denying the truths of the Protestant religion" from holding civil office. In 1832 the senate had issued an address to the people advocating the expunging of the provision. The consideration of this article was recommended to the convention of 1835 by the legislature.

The arguments in favor of its retention were weak, and usually avoided the principle at issue. The main points urged in its favor were that it was a dead letter, did no harm, and as it had been in the constitution sixty years it was best not to disturb it. Some speakers, however, maintained that it might be necessary to exclude Catholics, and the delegates from Orange claimed instructions of their constituents in its favor. One speaker, admitting that it had been a dead letter, said it ought to be retained as "sleeping thunder." Cooper carried out the same line of argument:

> Our fathers saw the necessity of the article and placed it where it was. They knew what a Roman Catholic was, and were afraid, if they didn't put something of this kind in, they might hereafter have a harder struggle than they had just got out of.

He did not care how wise men were, if they did not agree with the general opinion in religion they ought to be looked after. Most of the speakers did not come out so squarely against the Catholics. The most characteristic argument is that of Shober. "The section under consideration," he said, "has done no harm. It has been a part of our constitution for fifty years; it has stood as a beacon to aspirants for office, as an axiom that we prize religion, and tells the world we are a Christian people."

The remarks against the test were of a very desultory character. Most speakers began by making a full exposition of their religious views and avowing their belief in the doctrines of some Protestant sect; nevertheless they believed in full toleration of other sects. The debaters seemed to fear that if they opposed the test they would be regarded as irreligious. Far the best exposition of the opposition to the test was made by Gaston, a Catholic and judge of the supreme court. He first gives his reasons for having accepted office, holding that Catholics were not disqualified by the test. (1) The article only disqualifies those who "deny;" that implies spoken or written denial, not simply profession of another faith; (2) there is no tribunal to define the Protestant religion; (3) Catholics do not deny the truths of the Protestant religion—they accept its truths and believe more; (4) the colonies had excluded Catholics by their tests which had been abolished. In proof of the ambiguity of the clause he speaks of the different interpretations which had been applied to it in the course of the debate:

> One informs us that it excludes nobody, * * * that the whole provision is a dead letter. Another thinks that it clearly excludes atheists, and such deists as make a parade of their infidelity by proclaiming the holy scriptures to be false. A third believes that it disqualifies atheists, deists, and Jews. A fourth believes that these are excluded, and that it was intended also to exclude Catholics, but that the language is not sufficiently explicit to warrant a judicial exposition to that effect. A fifth holds that it not only intended to exclude, but, by legal construction, does exclude them. A sixth is satisfied that Quakers, Memnonists, and Dunkards are disqualified because of their opposition to bearing arms.

Hence he urges upon the convention the necessity of amending the article so as to make it explicit. He also explained fully the relation between Catholics and the Pope to show that the latter has no civil jurisdiction in America, and that there is nothing incompatible between allegiance to the Pope and loyalty to the State. This had particular reference to the latter part of the test, which disqualified "those holding opinions incompatible with the safety and freedom of the State."

The most radical opponent of the provision was Wilson, who objected to a religious test of any kind whatever. He quoted Jefferson as saying:

> What is it to me, as a citizen of North Carolina, whether my neighbor believes in one God or in twenty? It neither picks my pocket nor breaks my shin.

"For shame," he said, at the close of a long speech, "that men should attempt to hide a wicked, persecuting spirit, a miserable scramble for power, behind such thin-woven subterfuges." His amendment abolishing all tests was lost by a vote of 76 to 32.

The convention finally adopted an amendment substituting "Christian" for "Protestant," by a vote of 74 to 51[1].

New Hampshire retained provisions disqualifying Catholics until 1877. These were clauses in the constitution of 1784, retained in that of 1792, requiring that the governor, representatives, and senators should be Protestants. All religious tests were abolished by an amendment ratified in 1877.

Inasmuch as no new constitution adopted after 1790 and no

---

[1] Debates in North Carolina Convention, pp. 242-312.

revised constitution after 1800 disqualified Catholics, the attitude of hostility to them may be said to end with the first constitutions. Probably their loyalty during the war had an influence in securing them full political rights. This was an argument made in the North Carolina convention. Thomas Carroll is mentioned as a distinguished example of a patriotic Catholic. In spite of the test, Thomas Burke, a Catholic, had been governor of North Carolina until he had resigned the position to accept an appointment in the continental army. Gaston, the Catholic judge who opposed the test so ably, was one of North Carolina's most honored citizens.

In five of the States the constitutions required officers to be Christians. The qualification in all of them was to be tested by an oath. Three of these oaths disappeared in the revisions of the eighteenth century. In Maryland in 1826 Jews were granted the right to substitute an oath of belief in God and a future state of rewards and punishments. In Massachusetts the oath was abolished by an amendment that was enacted in 1822. The amendment caused considerable debate in the convention. Webster reported for the committee in favor of dropping the test, basing his reasons on grounds of expediency. He said he would himself have been willing to retain it. It was opposed as useless, as interfering with inalienable rights, as a union of church and state, as conflicting with the United States Constitution, which insures a republican form of government. If this test were retained, the Declaration of Independence should read:

All *Christians* are born free and equal. It is antirepublican and repugnant to the liberties of the people.

It was favored on strong religious grounds:

Striking it out would be a disrespect to our fathers and a national sin. If it had excluded a man even as learned as Gibbon from the legislature, it would not have been unfortunate if he was capable of making such an insidious, unmanly attack on our holy religion. As to Jews, Mohametans, deists, and atheists, they are all opposed to the common religion of the Commonwealth and believe it an imposition, a mere fable, and that its professors are all under a wretched delusion. Are such persons suitable rulers of a Christian State?

One speaker expressed his surprise that so many ministers of the gospel were opposed to the test. "Are we not descendants of the Pilgrims?"[1]

---
[1] Journal of the Convention, p. 180 et seq.

In the address to the people submitted with the proposed amendments the test was adverted to in the following guarded manner:

We have agreed that the declaration of belief in the Christian religion ought not to be required in the future; because we do not think the assuming of civil office a suitable occasion for so declaring; and because it is implied that every man that is selected for office in this community must have such sentiments of religious duty as relate to his fitness for the place to which he is called.[1]

The latter reason indicates how careful the convention was to avoid the suspicion of irreligion which might attach to them for abolishing the test. It is also an indication of a sentiment very common in the later conventions that legal qualifications ought to be abolished in order to let the people judge themselves of the fitness of a candidate. The amendment was ratified by a vote of 17,552 to 9,244, the majority being smaller than that for any other amendment.[2] The debate in the convention and the vote indicate sufficiently that there was a strong sentiment in Massachusetts in 1822 in favor of limiting office holding to Christians.

In Pennsylvania the constitution of 1790 omitted the oath requiring belief in God and the inspiration of the Old and New Testaments and inserted in the Bill of Rights that no other oath except that of belief in God and a future state of rewards and punishments could ever be required for admission to office. This provision has been repeated in the later constitution. It must be noted that this is not a test, but a prohibition of tests beyond a certain limit. As a matter of fact, no religious test has been required in Pennsylvania since 1790. This clause was the subject of some debate in the convention of 1838. Many memorials were presented for its abolition. It was said to exclude Universalists and Quakers; the former because they did not believe in future punishment, the latter because they did not believe in a future state of rewards and punishments. The real grievance seemed to be that Quakers and Universalists had been disqualified from testifying in the courts.[3] The demand was for the abolition of all religious tests, both for

---
[1] Journal of the Convention, p. 630.
[2] Ibid., p. 633.
[3] Debates, IX, 227-236. Many memorials for the abolition of the test are mentioned in Vols. IX, X, and XI.

office and for giving testimony. But, as has been said, the article was retained as in the constitution of 1790.[1]

Tennessee, in her first constitution, adopted in 1796, provided that no person should hold office who did not believe in God and a future state of rewards and punishments. This provision was repeated in the later constitutions, and is still retained. As no oath was specified the enforcement of the provision was left to the legislature. The result is that no oath of such belief has ever been required and the provision is a dead letter. It is interesting to note that the same constitution which required this test said that, "no religious test as a qualification for office shall ever be required."[2] It is difficult to see how the two provisions could be reconciled. Probably the test was, in the language of the orator in the North Carolina convention—

A beacon to aspirants for office as an axiom that we prize religion, and tells the world that we are a Christian people.

A number of States have required belief in God as a qualification for office. Only three such provisions remain, those of Arkansas and North Carolina and South Carolina. Texas has a provision that no test further than that of belief in God shall be required.

In general these tests have remained longest in the constitutions of Southern States. None of these recent constitutions incorporate the test in the oath of office and there is no evidence that they have ever been enforced.

At present some thirty States prohibit religious tests in their constitutions and none is required by legislation in any State. Hence religious tests, although there are survivals in some half a dozen of the State constitutions, have entirely disappeared as an actual legal qualification for office.

III. RESIDENCE QUALIFICATIONS, 1789–1899.

In the constitutions adopted before 1789 only residence in the State or district was required.

After the Federal Constitution went into effect the States usually required citizenship of the United States for a given time for the chief officers. Before 1789 there was no uniform

---

[1] Stimson, Am. Statute Law, p. 9, classifies Pennsylvania as requiring a religious test for office. This is manifestly an error, as shown above.
[2] Constitution of 1796, Art. XI, sec. 4.

naturalization and the citizenship was always State citizenship. The word foreigner occurs in some of the early constitutions and always denotes a person not a citizen of the State. In these constitutions the residence qualification was not large, probably owing to the fact that the exclusion would operate chiefly against citizens of one State moving into another. The uniform naturalization provided for by the Federal Constitution and carried out by Congress gave an opportunity to discriminate between citizens of other States in the Union and citizens of foreign states. This was done in nearly every constitution by requiring, in addition to a certain period of residence in the State, citizenship of the United States for periods varying in the different States, and for different offices from one to thirty years, and, in the case of governor, for life.

The general tendency during the first half century under the Federal Constitution was to require long terms of citizenship, especially for the office of governor.

During the next half century the tendency was to decrease the residence term within the United States. There is a partial exception to this tendency in the Southern States since the war. The carpet-bag constitutions reduced the term of residence in the State and also, in many cases, the term of citizenship of the United States. The States which have adopted constitutions since the northern influence was withdrawn, have increased the residence qualification and, in some cases, also that of citizenship. The reason in both cases is the same—the dislike of outside influence, whether on the part of foreigners or of immigrants from the northern States.

In nearly all the constitutions longer residence and citizenship qualifications are required for governor than for senator and for senators than for members of the lower house.

An examination of the residence qualifications for governor will give an idea of the movement in general, as there is a tendency to maintain about the same ratio in the terms of residence required for the various officers.

First, let us remember that no State before 1789 required that the governor should be a native American. The residence demanded was not long, only one State requiring ten years. There is a marked change in this respect in the later constitutions of the original States and in those of new States. The constitutions of Kentucky and Tennessee were formed on the model of the earlier State constitutions, and citizenship of the United States was not required; but the constitutions drafted in the early part of this century required a long period of citizenship of the United States for the office of governor. Ohio in 1802 required twelve years; Indiana in 1816, ten years; Mississippi in 1817, twenty years; Illinois in 1818, thirty years.

The first State to require a native of the United States was Alabama in 1819. Five other States have had a similar provision in their constitutions; and in Maine the provision still remains. The list is as follows, with the dates at which the provision was adopted and at which it was dropped:

Alabama, 1819-1875; Maine, 1820; Missouri, 1820-1865; New York, 1821-1846; Virginia, 1830-1870; Arkansas, 1836-1868.

These provisions seem to have been inserted in the constitutions without opposition. In the three States in which I have had access to the debates in the convention there was no discussion of the residence qualifications. A member of the convention of 1846 in New York said the provision was adopted unanimously in 1821 in committee of the whole. My impression is that they were adopted in imitation of the constitution of the United States, and do not indicate any particular jealousy of foreign influence.

Four of the States were adopting new constitutions which followed closely that of the Federal Government. In New York and Virginia there had been no residence or citizenship qualification whatever in the previous constitutions. This was naturally regarded as a defect, and in remedying it the Federal Constitution was imitated. All of the other original States had provided a residence qualification, and when they came to revise their constitutions simply changed the residence within the State to citizenship of the United States, usually requiring a shorter term of residence within the State than before.

The retention of the provision in the constitution of Maine is probably owing to the fact that the constitution has never been revised, and there isn't sufficient opposition to the clause to secure its abolition by amendment. The lack of interest is probably due to the fact that the foreign element is not strong enough to make it worth while for a party to make an issue of this provision, and bid for the foreign vote by advocating its abolition.

The tendency to decrease the residence requirement is shown by the fact that, of sixteen States which required more than ten years' citizenship of the United States or the State, only nine have retained so large a qualification.[1] Only three of these States are north of Mason's and Dixon's line. Of these three, two adopted their present constitutions before the war, and Delaware, in the constitution of 1897, simply retained the residence qualifications of the old constitution. The contrast is brought out between the North and the South in this respect by observing that no northern State has increased its residence or citizenship qualification since 1850, while many of the southern States have done so since the war. In most cases the increase is in the residence required within the State, but some constitutions have also required a longer citizenship of the United States than heretofore.[2]

In five of the States the constitutions adopted under northern influence immediately after the war had decreased the residence qualification. The later revisions tended to do away with these changes and restore the antebellum provisions.

By one of the reconstruction articles of 1867, all persons excluded from holding office on account of rebellion were excluded from holding a seat in a constitutional convention and from voting for members of the convention. The sentiment of the South toward these constitutions is seen in the debates of the later conventions, and is summed up in an address submitting the Alabama Constitution of 1875 to the people for ratification. "The constitution of 1868," so runs the address, "was not the work of the people of Alabama. It is the off-

---

[1] The States still retaining long-residence qualifications are as follows, with the dates at which the present constitutions were adopted: Delaware, 1897, 12 years citizen of United States; Georgia, 1877, 15 years citizen of United States; Kansas, 1861, 20 years citizen of United States; Louisiana, 1898, 10 years citizen of United States and Louisiana; Maryland, 1867, 10 years citizen of Maryland; Mississippi, 1890, 20 years citizen of United States, Missouri, 1875, 10 years citizen of United States; New Jersey, 1844, 20 years citizen of United States; Maine, 1820, native of United States.

[2] The following table indicates these changes: Alabama, 1867, 4 years in State; 1875, 7 years in the State. Arkansas, 1868, 1 year in State; 1874, 7 years in the State. Georgia, 1868, 15 years in United States. 1877, 15 years citizen of United States. Kentucky, 1850, 6 years in Kentucky; 1891, 6 years citizen of Kentucky. Louisiana, 1868, 2 years citizen of United States and Louisiana; 1898, 10 years citizen of United States and Louisiana. Maryland, 1864, 5 years citizen of United States and in Maryland; 1867, 10 years citizen of Maryland. Mississippi, 1868, 2 years in Mississippi; 1890, 5 years in Mississippi. Missouri, 1820, 4 years in Missouri; 1865, 7 years in Missouri.

spring of usurpation and the contrivance of unscrupulous adventurers inflicted upon our people after they had solemnly rejected it. * * * It was manufactured for the benefit of alien and corrupt usurpers, and has been administered in an office-holding and governmental extravagance which in a few years has bankrupted the State and well-nigh ruined our people."[1] With such a prevailing sentiment one can well understand why the recent constitutions in the South have provided a long residence in the State as a prerequisite for holding the chief executive office. In no State can an alien be elected governor; but some twenty require merely citizenship of the United States. Most of the Western States have this provision, the tendency being strong to do away with all distinctions between native and naturalized citizens.

Most of the States require a period of State residence greater than that necessary for an elector. With the exception of the Southern States already considered, this period is not long, varying from two to five years. Massachusetts, New Hampshire, and Pennsylvania still retain the seven-year requirement of their early constitutions. There has not been the same tendency to decrease the residence qualification, as is seen in the provisions for citizenship. This is probably due to the fact that the residence required has never, in most States, been very long; and also to the fact that the immigrants from other States do not form a compact element, to which a political party can appeal and make an issue of removing their political disabilities. That this has been done in the case of aliens and foreign-born citizens can be abundantly proven.

The qualifications for members of the legislature are more uniform in the various States than are those for governor, and do not vary so much in the later constitutions from those of earlier ones. As a rule, also, the residence and citizenship qualification is alike for the two houses. The age qualification is the only one that differs.

All but six States require that members of both houses shall be citizens. In six States[2] the same qualification is required as for suffrage, and aliens having taken out their first papers are given the franchise. Residence in the State vary-

---
[1] Alabama convention, 1875. Journal, p 169.
[2] Florida convention of 1868; Kansas convention of 1861; Minnesota convention of 1857, Nebraska convention of 1875; North Dakota convention of 1889; Wisconsin convention of 1848.

ing from one to seven years is required. Residence in the district represented, for a period varying from six months to two years, is necessary in every State. Many States demand a year in the district, and then make no further residence qualification.

The age qualifications for both governor and members of the legislature are quite uniform in the various States. The prevailing provision in regard to the governor is that he should be 30 years of age. Senators must usually have attained the age of 25, and members of the lower house 21. Of course there are a good many slight variations, the tendency in the western States being to make the right of suffrage and eligibility to the legislature identical.

As judges have become elective, there has been a tendency to affix residence and age qualifications for judicial places also. As a rule these requirements correspond with those for governor in age and of senators in residence and citizenship qualifications. A number of States had an old-age limit when the judges were appointed during good behavior.[1] This provision naturally disappeared when they were elected for a term of years.

In the early conventions there was not much discussion on age and residence qualifications; but in the fifth decade of the century these questions were hotly debated. A theory seems to have been very widespread that the convention had no right to limit the people in their choice of officers by making any requirements whatever. It was an unwarranted interference with the sovereign rights of the people. This argument was used in nearly all of the conventions between 1840 and 1860.

In Louisiana in 1845 there was a long debate on the question of increasing the residence qualifications from two to five years. The chief opposition to outside influence seemed to be directed toward those coming from other States, although the dangers of foreign immigration were also referred to. The Native American movement was mentioned but condemned. The chief argument relied upon was that of the peculiar institutions of the State. Other States, it was said,

---

[1] In Alabama, 1819, Connecticut convention of 1818, and Maine convention of 1820, the age limit was 70 years; Mississippi convention of 1817, 65; New York convention of 1821, 60; Missouri convention of 1820, 65. The provision is still retained in New York.

had the common law, Louisiana the civil law, hence a longer residence was necessary in order to properly understand her institutions. Slavery was also referred to as requiring protection from the influence of intruders. "Can an inhabitant of Massachusetts," said one debater, "who removes among us, regard slavery in its true light? Will he submit to the perfect tolerance of religions, so remarkable in our community, not the result of law but of public opinion? It must be presumed that the attachments he has formed in his former home will preclude him from at once imbibing a relish for our institutions." In reply to these arguments, the theory of the right of the people to choose whom they please to office was advanced. This was answered as a cry of demagogues.

From the Peloponesiacuum Bellum to the present time it has always been the practice of demagogues to delude the dear people by flattering them.

The amendment was lost by a tie vote.[1]

Residence qualifications were most fully debated in the convention of 1846 in New York. The constitution of 1821 had provided that the governor should be a native of the United States. There was no attempt to retain this provision in 1846, but a five years' residence and a five years' citizenship were suggested. O'Connor opposed the five years' residence as illiberal. It was writing in the fundamental law a reproach upon the wisdom and good sense of the people of the State. It was "restricting the people in the exercise of supreme and legitimate sovereignty." Hunt followed along the same line of argument, saying that the convention was only acting as attorney for the people and could not limit their power or interfere with their freedom of elections. "Who, in framing a power of attorney for an agent, would even think of inserting any clause limiting his own powers, of tying his own hands in order to keep himself from picking his own pockets?" These arguments were well answered by Jordan and Angel. They ridiculed the idea of not restricting the sovereign people. If this were carried to its logical conclusion the convention could not prevent them from electing ten governors at once, or from electing judges to other office, or United States officers to State office. Angel maintained that it was

---

[1] Louisiana convention of 1844-45. Debates, pp. 53-94.

the very purpose of a constitution to bind the sovereign people and prevent the tyranny of the majority.[1]

The proposition to require five years' citizenship was also hotly debated. It was opposed on the ground of discriminating against naturalized citizens. In reply, Mr. Angel asked if they had no American feeling in that body. He had no desire to encourage the ambitious views of a foreigner who should come to our shores with aspirations for the chair of the chief magistrate of the State. Many formidable evils might arise from this indulgence to foreigners.

> Had the people of the State forgotten that we had a large Protestant body within our bosom, who were looking with great interest on this question? And could the feelings and opinions of that large and respectable class be disregarded?

This is the only mention I find of the American movement with anything like approval in any of the conventions of the period. The amendment for five years' citizenship was rejected—73 to 36.[2]

In the debates in the California convention in 1849 the ten-year-citizenship qualification for governor was opposed on the ground that foreigners knew our institutions on coming to this country. De Tocqueville was quoted as an example. The very fact of their coming proved that they understood and appreciated our form of government.[3]

In the Maryland convention of 1864 an amendment was proposed requiring a native of the United States for governor, but it was opposed on the ground of the services of foreigners in the war and was rejected by a vote of 51 to 3.[4]

In most of the conventions since 1845 propositions have been made that no qualification be required for officeholding beyond that for suffrage. In a number of States such a provision has been adopted, excepting qualifications specified in the Constitution. But in Rhode Island and Connecticut alone are qualifications for office and suffrage identical, and they have always been so since colonial times.

In specifying qualifications the language of the constitutions varies, and it is not always clear whether the candidate is to be qualified on the day of election, or whether it is suffi-

---

[1] New York convention of 1846. Debates, pp. 144-158.
[2] Ibid., pp. 268-270
[3] California convention of 1849, pp. 157-159.
[4] Maryland convention of 1864. Debates, p 1316.

cient if he can qualify at the time he takes his oath of office. In the cases of Commonwealth *v.* Pyle (18 Pa., 519) and Commonwealth *v.* Schoener (1 Leg. Chron., 177) it was held that where a person was declared ineligible without a certain qualification he must have been qualified at the time of the election; but where the prohibition is as to the enjoyment of the office it suffices that he is legally qualified before he is sworn. The Pyle case was argued in 1854 and quoted the decision of Congress in regard to contests in that body. According to this interpretation, where the constitutions do not expressly require that a candidate should be qualified at the time of election, it would generally be sufficient to qualify upon assuming the duties of the office.[1]

The decisions upon the qualifications of their own members is left to the respective houses;[2] and if they choose to admit those disqualified by law, there is no remedy in the courts.

The qualifications of other officers are subject to adjudication and decision in the courts. This was the decision in the case of Barker *v.* The People (3 Cowen, 77), tried in New York in 1824. The same opinion is expressed in the opinions submitted to the legislature by the supreme judicial court of Massachusetts.[3]

The Massachusetts constitution of 1780 provided that "every person shall be considered an inhabitant, for the purpose of electing and being elected in that town, district, or plantation where he dwelleth or hath his home." In specifying the qualification for office and suffrage this word inhabitant is always used. In 1811 the legislature called upon the supreme judicial court for an opinion as to the proper meaning of the term. The opinion submitted was as follows:

The words "inhabitants" or "residents" may comprehend aliens, or they may be restrained to such inhabitants who are citizens, according to the subject-matter to which they are applied. The latter construction comports with the general design of the constitution. There the words "people" and "citizens" are synonymous. The people are declared to make the constitution for themselves and their posterity, and the representation in the general court is a representation of the citizens. If, therefore, aliens could vote in the election of Representatives, the representation

---

[1] The most common form is that "no person shall be governor, senator, etc., who has not resided so long in the State, etc."

[2] There was an attempt in Pennsylvania in 1873 to give this power to the courts Debates of the convention, II, 561.

[3] 122 Massachusetts, 600.

would be not of citizens only, but of others, unless we should preposterously conclude that a legally authorized elector of a Representative is not represented. It may therefore seem superfluous to declare our opinion, that the authority given to *inhabitants* and *residents* to vote is restrained to such *inhabitants* and *residents* as are *citizens*.[1]

This ingenious interpretation of a constitutional provision, making it mean what it did not say for reasons of public policy, was carried a step further in 1877 in a similar opinion.[2]

The court quoted the opinion of 1811 and reaffirmed it. There were two questions, both pertaining to qualifications of members of the legislature. The questions were: First. Must an alien be naturalized before he can become a member of the legislature? Second. Can a naturalized citizen become a member under the same conditions as native citizens? This question hinged on the interpretation of the word "inhabitant" in an amendment fixing the qualifications of members. The court answered both questions in the affirmative, holding that the word inhabitant in the original constitution meant citizen and in the amendment "having a domicile in the district." After the word "citizen" began to be used in the constitution in a more precise sense, the word inhabitant had become more restricted. It is to be noted that these opinions were not decisions of contested cases and had no binding force, but they were doubtless followed by the legislature in deciding contests. Hence the constitution of Massachusetts, as interpreted, confined the rights of suffrage and officeholding to citizens.

IV. AGE QUALIFICATIONS.

Age qualifications were not much debated in the conventions. In Delaware, in 1831, a proposition was made to retire judges at 70. It was alleged in the debate that the provision in the New York constitution was adopted for party purposes and out of personal spite. Kent had thus been forced out at 60; Spencer also was "conventionized" off the bench. It was said that a similar proposition had been negatived in Virginia by a large majority. These arguments prevailed and the amendment was lost without a division.[3]

When the provision retiring judges at 60 was adopted in

---

[1] 7 Massachusetts, 525.
[2] 122 Massachusetts, 594.
[3] Delaware convention of 1831. Debates, pp. 197–199.

New York in 1821, John Adams wrote to a member of the convention:

I consider that provision a personal insult to me as an old man.

In the Virginia convention of 1829-30 there was considerable debate in regard to increasing the age qualification for Senators. The chief argument against the proposition was found in the many examples of brilliant ability under the specified age. There was also a hint at the theory so prevalent later, that it was not right to limit the people in their choice. John Randolph, it was said, became a member of the House of Representatives under the age of 25. When the Speaker asked him: "Are you 25, sir?" he replied, "Go and ask my constituents." Among other arguments in favor of the increased age was that a dissolution of the Union was possible, and then still more important duties would fall to the Senate.[1]

In the debates of 1845 the argument against age qualifications chiefly relied upon, is the unwarrantable restriction upon the rights of the sovereign people. In Ohio, in 1850, the thirty-year requirement for governor was advocated on the ground of keeping young men out of the temptations of politics. A speaker retorted that "it would be better to make them retire at 45, that they might have time to prepare their accounts for another world."[2] The age restrictions were also opposed on the ground that they would drive young men to other States where there were no such restrictions.[3] This was an argument which probably had great weight with all the Western States, which desired to attract immigrants, and goes far to explain the tendency to do away with all restrictions on suffrage and officeholding except a short period of residence in the State. This was carried so far that, as has been seen, in some States aliens could hold seats in the legislature and in nearly twenty States aliens have been allowed to vote. The Indiana convention, in their address to the people, said that the provision allowing aliens the suffrage would probably attract immigrants.[4]

In case no statute fixes the qualifications for an office it has

---

[1] Virginia convention of 1829-30. Debates, pp. 462, 463.
[2] Ohio convention of 1850. Debates, I, 299-306.
[3] Ibid., I, 227.
[4] Indiana convention of 1850. Address to the people, p. 26.

been held that a person not an elector can not hold the office.[1] Such person, however, can be elected and qualify before his term begins.[2]

V. EDUCATIONAL QUALIFICATIONS.

Educational qualifications are of two kinds—general and professional. General qualifications required for suffrage and officeholding are limited to the ability to read and write either in English or in one's native language. Such a requirement is found in but a few States. The first to adopt it was Connecticut in 1855. By an amendment to the constitution an elector must be able to read any article of the constitution or any section of the statutes before being admitted to vote. Massachusetts adopted a similar amendment in 1857. Maine also has such a provision, and the Delaware constitution of 1897 provides that after 1900 electors must be able to read and write. The Florida constitution of 1868 provided that the legislature might pass an act requiring an educational qualification for suffrage after 1880, but no such law has been enacted.

The recent constitutions of South Carolina, Mississippi, and Louisiana, offering an option between an educational and a property qualification, have already been considered. Their purpose was evidently to disfranchise the negro. In his address as president of the convention of 1895, in South Carolina, Governor Evans said:

> There should be an educational qualification for the right of suffrage if the supremacy of the intelligence is to be preserved. It is no injustice to any man, black or white, to have such a qualification, for only the intelligent are capable of governing. . . . We have experienced the cost and hardship of the rule of the ignorant and know what it means.[3]

The provisions on suffrage were adopted with little opposition in these Southern States. In fact, their enactment was the chief purpose in revising the constitutions. These constitutions were not submitted to the people for ratification, but were put into operation by the conventions. The suffrage provision of the Mississippi constitution has been contested in the courts, but has been held valid both by the supreme court of Mississippi[4] and by the Supreme Court of the United

---

[1] 14 Wisconsin, 497.
[2] 28 Wisconsin, 96.
[3] South Carolina convention of 1895, Journal, p. 39.
[4] Sproule v. Fredericks, 69 Miss., 898.

States.[1] While the purpose of these provisions is clearly to disfranchise negroes, yet they purport to treat all alike and do not discriminate against anyone on account of race, color, or previous condition of servitude, and hence are not in conflict with the fourteenth amendment of the Constitution of the United States.

Professional qualifications are confined chiefly to judges and attorneys. In the earlier constitutions the judges were usually appointed and no qualifications were specified. As the judges became elective qualifications of age and residence appeared, and later the requirement of a legal education.

The first trace I find of any educational requirement is in the constitution of Kentucky in 1799. This provided that clerks of the courts should have a certificate of fitness from the court of appeals.

Kentucky was also first in providing that judges must have a legal training. The constitution of 1850 required that judges of the higher courts should have had eight years' practice in the law. About twenty States have adopted provisions requiring some legal qualification for judges.[2]

The close connection between making the judgeship elective, and affixing an educational qualification is well exemplified by the Louisiana constitution. In 1868 district judges and attorneys were made elective, and the provision was added that the incumbents must be learned in the law. For the supreme judges, on the other hand, who were still appointed, no such requirement was made. In 1898 the supreme judges became elective, and a professional qualification was affixed to the office.

When the provision was adopted in Kentucky there was considerable opposition in the convention. It was opposed on the same ground as all other qualifications, viz, that it

---

[1] Williams v. Mississippi, 170 U. S., 213.
[2] Alabama, 1875, learned in the law; California, 1879, admitted to practice before Supreme Court; Colorado, 1876, learned in the law; Georgia, 1877, seven years' practice; Idaho, 1890 (district judge and attorney), learned in the law; Kentucky, 1850, learned in the law; Louisiana, 1868 (district judge), learned in the law, (supreme judges were appointed); Louisiana, 1898, ten years' practice in Louisiana; Maryland, 1867, practicing lawyers; Minnesota, 1857, learned in the law; Missouri, 1875, learned in the law; Montana, 1889, admitted to practice in Supreme Court; North Dakota, 1889, learned in the law; South Dakota, 1889, learned in the law; Virginia, 1870, five years' practice; Washington, 1889, admitted to practice in court of record; Wyoming, 1890, nine years' practice.

interfered with the free choice of the people. One speaker said:

> Gentlemen have so long been accustomed to the loaves and fishes, they have so long had a monopoly of every lucrative office in Kentucky, that they will now fight to the last. This is the last dying kick of aristocracy.

It was also characterized as legislation favoring the lawyers and opposed to the interests of the farmers.[1] This argument was also adverted to in the debate on the exclusion of clergymen from civil office, a clergyman being particularly bitter in regard to the favor shown to lawyers. A resolution requiring eight years' practice for circuit judges was rejected by a vote of 38 to 31.

The proposition most hotly debated, however, was the one requiring clerks of county courts to procure a certificate of fitness from the court of appeals. The following resolution was offered:

> That the good people of this Commonwealth are fully competent to judge of and decide upon the qualifications of all candidates for any office, whether the same be legislative, executive, or judicial, or ministerial; wherefore a certificate of election according to law is the only certificate of qualifications that shall ever be required to enable any citizen to enter upon the discharge of the duties of the office to which he may be elected.

It was argued in support of the resolution:

> If the principle be true, that all political power is inherent in the people; that the people are competent for self-government, and that they are the safest depositories of political power, why not leave with the people, who are directly interested in the subject, the power to judge of the qualifications of a clerk? You strike at the great principle that the people are competent for self-government, and you strike also at the principle that the people are the safest depositories of political power, when you attempt to withhold from them the exercise of that power.

He maintained, further, that the people are as well qualified to judge of the qualifications of minor as of more important officers.[2]

Qualifications were advocated as a restriction upon the power of stump orators and a bar against mobocracy. The real point of the necessity of technical or professional qualifications of which the people in general were unable to judge was not touched upon.

In most of the States, however, the professional requirement

---

[1] Kentucky convention of 1849. Debates, pp. 293 et seq.
[2] Kentucky convention of 1849. Debates, pp. 144 et seq.

for judges was adopted without opposition. But it is not found in the constitutions of half of the States and the prejudice against lawyers will probably prevent its ever being adopted by some of them. That it is not án entirely unnecessary provision, was proven in Kansas when the Farmers' Alliance got control of the State government. One of their principles was to elect no lawyer to office. The result was that judges were chosen with no legal training, judgments were entered contrary to law, and judges even refused to carry out the decisions of higher courts when they conflicted with their own.

VI. EXCLUSION OF CLERGYMEN.

Fourteen States in all have had provisions in their constitutions excluding clergymen from office. All of these provisions have excluded them from the legislature, and some of them from civil office generally. These restrictions have disappeared in all of the States except Maryland and Tennessee, whose constitutions still exclude ministers from the legislature.

These provisions have been the subject of a good deal of discussion in the conventions. In Florida the clause excluding clergymen was adopted in committee of the whole by a majority of one.[1] The question was most fully debated in the Kentucky convention of 1849. A memorial was presented from the ministers of Frankfort protesting against the exclusion of their profession from the legislature.[2] A curious argument was used against the exclusion to prove that it was sectarian and decided a great theological controversy between the Catholics and the Protestants. The substance of the argument was that the Catholics regarded the priesthood as forming a caste, possessed of a peculiarly sacred character and withdrawn from the affairs of secular life. The Protestants, on the other hand, deny this sacred character of the minister, and make him simply a teacher, a propounder of the Scriptures, and not an intermediary between God and man. The exclusion of clergymen from the legislature because, in the language of the constitution, "the duties of their high calling were incompatible with political life," was deciding the great theological controversy against the Protestants. The memorial objected to the exclusion also on other grounds. It

---

[1] Florida convention of 1838, Journal, p. 58.
[2] Kentucky convention of 1849, Debates, p. 747.

infringed upon the equal rights of citizenship by discrimination against a class. It was an unwarranted interference with the church by the state. A long debate on the memorial follows. Wallis, a clergyman, said, in the course of a long harangue:

> The bogtrotter of Ireland, the boor of Germany, the serf of Russia . . . who may become a citizen of the State, is eligible to all its offices; while you deny eligibility to a virtuous and intelligent class of native-born citizens simply because they serve God according to the dictates of their conscience.

He said the provision was inserted in the Virginia constitution in 1776 owing to the influence of Jefferson, who was imbued with the French philosophy, and on account of jealousy of the Episcopal clergy.

The arguments in opposition to the exclusion of clergymen were those stated in the memorial and the experience of other States where the exclusion did not exist. The reasons given for the provision were: The danger to the clergy of corruption by mixing in politics; the danger to the state from the interference of the church. There was a good deal of loose talk about the dangers of a union of church and state, the argument being used on both sides. The main point, however, was the sacredness of the mission of the clergy and the necessity of keeping them out of temptation.

There is something ludicrous in the juxtaposition of the two arguments: First, that clergymen were peculiarly sacred and pure, hence their exclusion from the mire of politics; second, that the clergy was a dangerous body, hence must be excluded. Nevertheless, the two arguments were often used by the same speaker. Whether the convention considered clergymen too pure or too dangerous to be allowed in the legislature, the provision excluding them was adopted by a vote of 74 to 17. In the Maryland convention of 1851 the provision of the constitution excluding clergymen was strongly opposed. Chandler, himself a clergyman, argued against it as class legislation, as an interference with the sovereign rights of the people. That it was unnecessary was shown by its non-existence in the Constitution of the United States and of 21 States. A member replied to him as follows:

> The moment you permit the ministers of religion to assume political power their whole character is changed. Whilst in the exercise of their religious duties exclusively they command the respect and veneration of

LEGAL QUALIFICATIONS FOR OFFICE. 137

all good men, no matter of what denomination. . . . The legislature is no place for ministers of the gospel. The pulpit is the sphere for their teachings.

Chandler's amendment striking out the clause excluding clergymen was lost by a vote of 22 to 44.[1]

In the convention of 1864, held in Maryland under Northern influence, to revise the constitution, there was a long debate on this clause. In addition to the arguments usually alleged against such a provision, it was said that it must be in some way connected with slavery, as it existed only in the constitutions of slave States. A reason was suggested for its prevalence in slave States: only in these States did the code of honor exist, from which ministers and women were excluded. Only gentlemen, subject to the code, could enter the political arena, as they could answer with a challenge anything which touched their honor. The restriction was abolished by a vote of 40 to 10,[2] but in the convention of 1867, where the Southern influence became again predominant, the provision was reinserted. Tennessee, the only other State which retains this disqualification of clergymen, readopted it in 1870 by a vote of 38 to 24.[3]

In the earlier constitutions probably the prevailing motive for excluding the clergy was the jealousy of their influence, as the provision appears chiefly in those States where an established church had existed. I am inclined to think that the prevailing motive in its retention in the revised constitutions in the second half century was the one so often urged in the conventions; that is, the feeling that clergymen were out of place in politics and would lose some of the sacredness of their character.

The conventions were composed of practical politicians, who might not have much knowledge of political philosophy, but who had too good practical sense to have much fear of the influence of the church which would result from the occasional admission of a clergyman to a seat in the legislature. In the debate on a proposition to exclude clergymen from the office of governor the case is well put:

Suppose you elect one of the best preachers in the land as governor. He has purity and political honesty beyond cavil, but how would you like to see him presiding at the punch bowl?[4]

---

[1] Maryland convention of 1851, Debates, I 389–395.
[2] Maryland convention of 1864, Debates, II 786–796.
[3] Tennessee convention of 1870, Journal, p. 390.
[4] Kentucky, 1890, Debates, Vol. I, 1070.

The fact that the restriction is found largely in the constitutions of Southern States is suggestive, but I hardly think it has anything to do with slavery. A better reason for its appearance in these States is that their constitutions were usually modeled after that of Virginia, especially in such general provisions. When the provision once got into a Southern constitution it was more liable to be retained on account of the greater conservatism there than in the North. In none of the debates are the clergymen charged with being abolitionists, although a clergyman in the Kentucky convention of 1849 denied that they had any leanings in that direction, evidently expecting such a charge.

Even in those States where they were excluded from the legislature clergymen were elected to and served in the conventions. This would indicate that there was no strong feeling against them as a class, as they might have been excluded.

VII. DISQUALIFICATIONS FOR DUELING.

About half of the States have provisions in their constitutions disqualifying anyone for office who should engage in a duel. These provisions are of the same general tenor, but vary somewhat in detail. Nearly all of them include accessories as well as principals in the disqualification. Most of them limit the time at which the act of dueling shall so disqualify from the adoption of the constitution.

The most important difference in these provisions is in regard to the proof of the act. Many of the constitutions provide that conviction in court is necessary in order to disqualify a duelist. Some States, however, require every officer to take an oath that he has not been engaged in a duel since the adoption of the constitution. One State requires the candidate to swear that he has not been engaged in a duel and will not be concerned in one during his term of office.[1] It was also a question much debated whether a duel fought outside of the State ought to disqualify. Most of the provisions are general in this respect and would seem to cover the case of a duel fought anywhere. Louisiana, in the constitution of 1812, made a distinction as to the party with whom the duel was fought. Only those were disqualified who fought a duel with a citizen of the State.

---

[1] Nevada constitution, Art. IV., sec. 2.

The dueling clauses were not usually the subject of much discussion in the conventions. In Ohio in 1850 there was considerable debate on the question of inserting a dueling disqualification, and it was finally defeated. It was opposed on the ground that it was unnecessary, public spirit against dueling being sufficient. It was also said that such provisions had been ineffectual in Southern States. Some further arguments used against the restriction were rather inconsistent with those already stated. One member said it would exclude two high-minded men whom he knew. Another remarked that if the measure had been in force some time ago certain members of the convention would have been excluded. Mr. Sawyer wished to know to whom the gentleman referred—whether he meant himself, Judge Hitchkock, or his friend over the way. Mr. London replied that "if the gentleman is acquainted with the chairman of the committee on military affairs he can pick him out."[1] It is evident from this discussion that the public sentiment in Ohio in 1850 was neither sufficiently strong against dueling to prevent its practice nor to keep men out of office who had engaged in it.

The dueling provisions were most fully debated, however, in the Kentucky conventions. There had been a law in Kentucky against dueling and disqualifying those convicted of the same for office, but the legislature had been in the habit of passing special laws to relieve persons from the disabilities thus incurred. It was proposed in the convention of 1849 to deal with the matter in the constitution, and thus take it out of the hands of the legislature. All agreed that the law had been a dead letter. A very stringent law was proposed, disqualifying all who should fight a duel or act as accessory in a duel. This was to be enforced by an oath requiring all officers to swear that they had not fought a duel since the adoption of the constitution and would not during their term of office. The proposition was objected to on the ground that it shut a duelist off from all chance of pardon and forever disqualified him, whereas an ordinary criminal was restored to political privileges by a pardon from the governor. This objection was met by a provision that the governor should be empowered to pardon a duelist and restore him to all his rights after five years.

---

[1] Ohio convention of 1850, Debates, I, 260.

Dueling was also defended on general grounds.

> That feeling of honor or chivalry, or by whatever name it may be called, which impels to self-defense is innate with the Kentuckian, and neither law nor constitution can destroy it.

One member defended the duel as a means of saving life by preventing street frays, which result more disastrously than duels. He said twelve or fourteen of his friends had perished in street frays, and only one in a fair and honorable duel. One speaker was especially opposed to penalizing a duel fought outside the State.

> We send a man to Congress, where he meets with men from every State. Many of them are aware that such a provision exists in the constitution of Kentucky. Will they not, seeing how his hands are tied, seek every opportunity to insult him?

In spite of the vigorous opposition the dueling section was adopted by a vote of 62 to 28.[1]

In the convention of 1890 similar arguments were used in favor of the duel as in 1849. Some claimed that the provision in the constitution of 1850 had put a stop to the practice. All were agreed that dueling had practically ceased in the State. One speaker regretted this, saying that the bowie knife and navy six had taken the place of the more refined duel. Street frays, it was alleged, had increased in frequency as the duel had declined. The code duello gave a man a chance to cool off before entering the encounter. Friends often intervened, and there was no fight at all. For a high-strung and spirited people like the Kentuckians it was a necessary and comparatively harmless safety valve. The oath was objected to on the ground that it compelled a man to testify against himself and as antagonistic to free government.

> You encourage a disregard for the sacredness of an oath by a frequent recurrence to them.

The speaker was asked if he had not himself been restrained by the dueling oath. "I have never been influenced by that oath one single particle," was the reply.

> If a man had given sufficient offense to cause me to challenge, I would have moved to some other State and then sent him the challenge. * * * I know of gentlemen who have done that in the State of Kentucky.

---

[1] Kentucky convention of 1849, Debates, pp. 815–827.

The section was carried by a vote of 29 to 27.[1] A provision was made, as in the constitution of 1850, for a pardon by the governor after five years.

The provision in the oath by which the candidate swore that he would not fight a duel during his term was omitted. The disqualifications and the oath enforcing the same are inconsistent. In the provision against dueling the disqualification is limited to those who fight "with a citizen of the State." On the other hand, the oath prescribed for all officers and members of the legislature requires them to swear that they have not fought a duel or acted as second "in or out of the State" since the adoption of the constitution.[2] This would evidently include duels fought with others than citizens of Kentucky.

The disappearance of dueling as a means of settling disputes has made a dead letter of these provisions, although they are still retained in most of the States where they have been adopted. It is difficult to say whether they ever had any effect. In States where an oath was required it seems probable that they did have some influence. It might be impossible to convict a duelist, but it seems at least doubtful whether an officer would readily perjure himself by taking the dueling oath, especially if it was well known that he had been engaged in a duel. The spirited opposition to the incorporating of these provisions in the constitution of Kentucky would indicate that they had some effect.[3] On the other hand, the provisions appear in constitutions of Northern States where dueling was never practiced. Here they had no practical bearing whatever and simply amounted to a disapproval of the practice.

VIII. BRIBERY.

There is a great variety of regulations in the constitutions on the subject of bribery and the disabilities resulting therefrom. Over thirty States have some provision in the constitution disqualifying for bribery. Some of these provisions merely state that anyone convicted of bribery shall be disqualified from holding office. In such cases the clause

---

[1] Kentucky convention of 1890, Debates, pp. 4690-4708.
[2] Kentucky constitution of 1891, secs. 228 and 239.
[3] In Cochran v. Jones (Am. Law Reg., 373) it was held that an election board might take cognizance of the fact that a candidate had fought a duel, although he had not been convicted in court. This case came up in Kentucky under the constitution of 1891.

appears as a part of the section dealing with disqualification for crimes in general.

Many of the constitutions disqualify for bribery in the election. The duration of this disqualification varies. In some States anyone disqualified for bribery in an election can never hold office again. In one State only the legislature can restore such a person to his political privileges.[1]

In other States the disqualification extends only to the particular office for which the bribe was given. Another class is that in which the disability extends to all offices, but only for the ensuing term. In yet another class the disability is fixed for a term of years. Such provisions are found in a number of the earlier constitutions, but have disappeared in the later revisions, except in Vermont and Tennessee. The disability is for one year in the former State and for six years in the latter.

In most cases both the giver and taker of a bribe are disqualified, but in four States only the giver of the bribe. This refers only to bribery at elections, and that was apparently the only kind which the earlier constitutions aimed to prevent.

Since the civil war another form of bribery has assumed importance and is referred to in a number of constitutions. This is the bribery of members of the legislature or other officers for their votes, or for the performance or nonperformance of an official duty. The first provision relating to bribery of this kind is in the constitution of Maryland, adopted in 1867. This provided for the punishment and disqualification to hold any office of profit or trust, both of any person bribing an officer and of an officer accepting such a bribe. West Virginia, in 1872, adopted a provision almost identical with that of Maryland. Pennsylvania followed suit with a similar provision in 1873, and required every officer to take an oath that he would not accept a bribe during his term of office. The Dakotas went a step farther in 1889 and defined logrolling as bribery and subject to the same penalties and disabilities. Wyoming made a similar provision in 1890. California has a provision disqualifying a member of the legislature who has accepted a bribe. The other States also disqualified those giving the bribe.

In some States the constitutions provided that the legislature may make laws in regard to bribery, disqualifying for

---

[1] Rhode Island constitution, IX, 2.

suffrage and office those convicted. In the constitutions of Maryland and West Virginia the provision is mandatory, the language being that "it shall be the duty of the general assembly at its first session" to make such laws.

It is interesting to note that, as in the case of dueling, only a conviction disqualifies in some States, while in others the officer is compelled to swear in his oath of office that he has not given a bribe during the election. Such oaths are found in some of the earliest constitutions: That of Georgia, framed in 1777, provided for such an oath for all members of the legislature; Kentucky, in the constitution of 1792, required it for all officers.

Some of the recent constitutions require such an oath and make it more stringent. The officer is compelled to swear not only that he has not given a bribe to procure his election, but also that he will not take a bribe during his term of office.[1] In Wyoming and South Dakota the member of the legislature must also swear that he will not give his vote on one measure in return for the vote of another member on some other measure. There are four States which thus attempt to bind an officer by a promise not to be dishonest, two of them including logrolling under bribery. There is something ludicrous about making a man swear that he has been, and will be, honest. The only effect which I can see that this provision could possibly have, would be to add the penalties of perjury to those of bribery in case of conviction.

The provisions in regard to bribery were not much discussed in the conventions. Probably members did not care to put themselves on record as favoring the practice, or opposed to any of the penalties which might be attached to it. The most extreme proposition on the subject appears in the convention in Pennsylvania in 1873. A resolution was submitted to subject members of the general assembly to an oath at the end of the term. The substance of the oath was as follows:

I have listened to no private solicitations by interested parties or their agents. * * * I have not voted or spoken on any matter in which I had or expected to have a private interest. I have not acted corruptly.[2]

---

[1] Nebraska, Pennsylvania, South Dakota, and Wyoming.
[2] Pennsylvania convention of 1873, Debates, II, 561.

Refusal to take the oath was to disqualify for all office; but the proposition was rejected.

In Nevada, in 1864, however, bribery was actually defended in the convention. Said a member:

> This clause seems to strike at the glorious privilege of electioneering for a man's friends. If I have a friend whom I believe to be particularly fitted for a particular office, and I have a desire for the sake of the public good to get him into that office, I have a right to use all honorable means to that end, and, if it is necessary, to buy a little whisky, too.[1].

The convention seemed to agree with the speaker, as the bribery clause was rejected.

In the Wyoming convention of 1889 there was considerable debate on the bribery clause. It was opposed as useless. The chief argument in its favor seemed to be that it would give the State a good reputation. A member regretted the striking out of one of the sections:

> I believe that it would have given us very good standing before the authorities at Washington. It would have indicated a disposition toward reform in Wyoming.[2]

An oath was proposed in the Kentucky convention of 1890 denying the use of money in the past election, to be taken by all officers, but it was rejected without debate by a vote of 40 to 33.[3]

IX. EXCLUSION OF OFFICERS OF CORPORATIONS.

The constitution of Indiana has a clause disqualifying the officers of banks from election to the general assembly, the disability to continue three months after they resign their position in the bank. The constitution was drafted in 1850, at the time of the war on the State banks. The provision was the subject of a spirited debate. It was advocated on the ground that the officer of the bank would represent the corporation and not the people. It was opposed as a demagogic trick and as unfair discrimination against a class. One proposition would have excluded railroad officers also. The State bank is called a monopoly, corrupt, and insolvent. Nicholas Biddle is referred to as an example of the dangerous power which may be obtained by banking officers. The provision was finally adopted by a vote of 67 to 62.[4]

---

[1] Nevada convention of 1864, Debates, p. 141.
[2] Wyoming convention of 1889, Debates, pp. 769-773.
[3] Kentucky convention of 1890, Debates, p. 4697.
[4] Indiana convention of 1850, Debates, II, 1203-1221.

Florida had a similar provision in her constitution from 1838 to 1865. It excluded banking officers from eligibility to the assembly and to the office of governor, extending the disability to one year after they had resigned their positions in the corporation. This provision was adopted by a vote of 30 to 26.[1]

In the Ohio convention of 1850 a proposition was made to exclude officers of banking and railroad corporations. This was amended so as to include the presidents of other incorporated companies in the State. It was proposed to amend by adding the borrowers or holders of any bank bills to the list of the exclusions. One member wished to include "money brokers, ministers of the gospel, and teachers of any religious sects."

There was no debate on the propositions, and they were finally voted down by a small majority.[2]

A proposition to exclude banking officers was made in Virginia in 1867, but was tabled by a vote of 46 to 39.[3] The only States which actually adopted such provisions were Florida and Indiana. In the former State the constitution was adopted soon after the panic of 1837, and naturally banking officers were in bad odor at that time. In Indiana in 1850 there was war on the State bank, and this provision grew out of the feeling engendered by that struggle.

X. PLURALITY OF OFFICES.

The provisions against the simultaneous holding of two offices are quite general, but vary greatly in detail. Nearly all of the constitutions have a section stating that the three departments of government should be kept distinct, and no officer of one department is to exercise the duties of another department except as directed in the constitution. While this clause is probably aimed more at the encroachment of one department upon another, it has been interpreted to prevent the simultaneous holding of offices in the different departments.[4]

---

[1] Florida convention of 1838, Journal, p. 55.
[2] Ohio convention of 1850, Debates, II, 182, 185.
[3] Virginia convention of 1867–68, Journal, p. 176. The resolution would also have excluded clergymen and attorneys of the Commonwealth.
[4] 3 Maine, 484. In an opinion rendered in 1830 by the supreme judicial court to the Senate, the office of justice of peace was held incompatible with that of sheriff. Const., III, cf. Bamford v. Melvin, 7 Maine, 14.

Many of the States also have a general provision to prevent anyone from holding two lucrative offices at the same time. An exception is usually made of officers in the militia and justices of the peace. In some cases, also, postmasters having an annual salary of less than five hundred dollars are excepted. Under this clause many contests have arisen in the courts as to what a lucrative office was. In the case of Doyle *v.* Raleigh (89 N. C., 133) it was held that an "office of trust or profit" must involve the exercise of functions affecting the public, in order to render the incumbent ineligible to hold a similar office or place. Acting as night watchman in the post-office at a salary of $60 per month was held not to disqualify the incumbent for office. In North Carolina the question came up whether railroad officials of those roads under State control were public officers. It was held that the directors appointed by the State were public officers.[1] In the case of Eliason *v.* Coleman (86 N. C., 235), however, it was held that the chief engineer of the Western North Carolina Railroad was not a public officer, although eight of the directors of this road were appointed by the government. The opinion stated:

The true test of a public office seems to be that it is parcel of the administration of government, civil or military, or is itself created directly by the lawmaking power.

All of the State constitutions forbid the simultaneous holding of a United States and State office, some of them making the exception of postmasters already mentioned. In addition to the incompatibility fixed by the constitutions there is a common-law incompatibility. This is seen in the case of Ryan *v.* Green (13 N. Y., 295). It was held in this case that the incompatibility between two offices is an inconsistency in the functions of the two; as, judge and clerk of the same court:

Physical impossibility is not the incompatibility of the common law, which existing, one office is ipso facto vacated by accepting another. * * * The offices must subordinate, one the other, and they must per se have the right to interfere, one with the other, before they are incompatible at common law.

Hence it was held that the defendant was not disqualified from holding two offices at the same time, although it would be physically impossible for him to discharge the functions of both.

---

[1] Clark *v.* Stanley, 66 North Carolina, 59.

DISQUALIFICATIONS TO HOLD OTHER OFFICE DURING THE TERM.

The disabilities to hold other office during the term for which the incumbent has been elected appear in many of the constitutions. They may be most conveniently treated under the heads of the three departments of government. The most common provision of this kind is that copied from the United States Constitution forbidding members of the legislature to hold any office which has been created, or the emoluments whereof have been increased, during the term for which they were elected. In some cases this provision is applied to all offices, but usually, as in the United States Constitution, it is limited to appointive offices. Many of the constitutions go further, however, and forbid the holding of any office in the gift of the legislature by a member during the term for which he was elected. A few States include appointment by the governor in the prohibition, and some go still further and make a member ineligible for all office during the term for which he was elected. At present some dozen States have provisions in their constitutions to prevent a member being elected to a position in the gift of the legislature.

The provision in regard to judges is the same in nearly all of the constitutions where any disability is specified. Judges are ineligible to other than a judicial office during the term for which they shall have been elected or appointed. Such a provision occurs in the constitutions of nine States. Virginia and West Virginia have had similar provisions in their constitutions, but they have been dropped in the later revisions. Michigan extends the disability to one year after the expiration of the term. In Virginia and West Virginia the prohibition was against holding "political office." Minnesota simply makes them ineligible while in office. This would require their resignation before the election, differing both from incompatibility and ineligibility for the term.

Only a few States have a provision in their constitutions disqualifying the governor from holding other office during his term. A number of States, however, attempt to prevent his election as United States Senator. As a similar attempt is made in regard to members of the legislature and judges, it will be best to consider them together.

Twelve States have had provisions in their constitutions evidently intended to disqualify State officers from being elected to the United States Senate. In six of them it was definitely stated that officers should not be elected to the United States Senate. These provisions do not appear at any particular period. The first State to adopt such a restriction was Georgia, in 1798. Florida, in 1838, made the governor and judges ineligible to election to the Senate of the United States or the House of Representatives during the term for which they were elected and one year thereafter. Provisions making either the governor or members of the legislature or both ineligible for their term to the United States Senate still remain in the constitutions of five States.[1] In three of these, New York, Michigan, and California, the Senate is specifically named. In the others the prohibition is against being elected by the general assembly. That these regulations are unconstitutional or, at least, unenforceable, is evident. The United States Senate is sole judge of the qualifications of its own members and would not consider State regulations in regard to eligibility. On the other hand, the State legislature might hesitate to elect a person Senator who was declared ineligible by the State constitution. That this check has not always been effective will appear in the consideration of the debates on the question.

The provisions disqualifying officers for other places during the term for which they were elected have been the subject of considerable debate in the conventions. The best general statement of the objects of these provisions is given in the address of the Vermont Council of Censors upon submitting amendments to the people in 1820. The part of the address in point is as follows:

> The third of the proposed amendments excludes the members of both branches of the legislature during the period for which they were elected from being appointed to certain civil offices within their gift. This provision, particularly so far as relates to judicial officers, is believed to be necessary to give full effect to the sixth section of the second chapter of the constitution, which provides that the legislative, judicial, and executive departments be distinct. And it may with confidence be asked whether it is not in accordance with the soundest maxims of republicanism that the legislator should be divested of other offices and of all tempting facilities for obtaining them, and that the framer of the laws should not be appointed to enforce their execution.[2]

---

[1] California convention of 1779; Illinois convention of 1870; Michigan convention of 1850; New York convention of 1895; South Dakota convention of 1889.
[2] Journal of Vermont Council of Censors, p. 40.

It is to be noted that while the purpose of the amendment is to keep the departments distinct, especially the legislative from the others, the emphasis is laid on the necessity of keeping the legislative and judicial departments distinct. In some States we will find that the emphasis is on the necessity of keeping the legislative and executive departments distinct. In the convention of 1847 in Illinois a resolution was introduced making all officers ineligible for the term for which they were elected or appointed, and two years thereafter. The resolution was referred to the committee on the judiciary, and the two-years clause was dropped in the draft of the constitution finally adopted.[1] In the debate in the Maryland convention of 1864 on the section disqualifying delegates from holding appointive offices during the term for which they were elected, it was said, "It is not expedient to encourage any species of illicit intercourse between the executive and legislative departments."[2]

In the Ohio convention of 1871 a member gives as a reason for making members of the legislature ineligible for their term, and not executive officers, that the legislature fixes salaries, and the object of the restriction is to prevent the misuse of patronage.[3]

The provisions disqualifying members of the legislature and governor from election to the United States Senate were usually adopted without debate. Such appears to have been the case in the Michigan convention of 1850; but in the convention of 1867 the provision was discussed.

The reasons given for disqualifying the governor were that he might not use his political influence for promotion, and that he ought to serve out the term in the position in which he had been placed by the people. One governor, it was said, had devoted all his energies to secure his election to the United States Senate; hence the restriction in the constitution. Against this disqualification it was alleged that the governor might be the best man for the Senatorship, and that at any rate the provision was unconstitutional and ineffectual. Indiana was quoted as having a similar restriction in its constitution, yet Governor Morton was elected in 1867 to the

---

[1] Illinois convention of 1847, Journal, p. 100.
[2] Maryland convention of 1864, Debates, II. 806–808.
[3] Ohio convention of 1871, Debates, I, 384, 391.

United States Senate. In Michigan, Governor Bingham had received 20 votes for United States Senator in spite of the restriction. The motion to strike out the provision was lost by a vote of 24 to 33.[1] It should be noted in this connection that the election of the governor to the United States Senate is a very common occurrence; hence this restriction was made to meet a real evil—or at any rate what was regarded as an evil—and not based on theoretical grounds, like most of the provisions on eligibility.[2]

An attempt has been made by a number of conventions to pass a self-denying ordinance, disqualifying members of the convention for office. In the Maryland convention of 1851 a resolution was submitted disqualifying anyone who should act as a member of a constitutional convention from ever thereafter acting as a judge. It was argued that judges should be kept out of politics.[3] A proposition was also made that "no member of any such convention shall hold any office, created or made vacant or regulated by such new constitution, within five years after the new constitution shall go into operation." This resolution was rejected, 24 to 36.[4]

A similar resolution was introduced in the Kentucky convention of 1849, extending the disqualification to ten years, but it does not appear to have come to a vote.

The reasons for such resolutions were given in the proposition submitted in the Louisiana convention of 1898.

> Whereas it has been publicly charged that many members of this convention were actuated by selfish motives, and that the main cause of the dissensions existing in the body was due to the fact that some of its members were shaping their course so as to obtain some political records or personal benefits in the near future * * * therefore *resolved* that members of this convention be disqualified for State and United States office until 1901.[5]

This, like all the similar resolutions in other States, was rejected.[6] One of the constitutions even provides expressly that members of the convention shall not be disqualified.[7]

---

[1] Michigan convention of 1867, Debates, I, 366–373.
[2] The Wisconsin constitution of 1846, rejected by the people, provided an oath for all State officers by which they promised not to accept a place in Congress during the term for which they were elected. Journal, p. 398.
[3] Maryland convention of 1851, Debates, I, 201.
[4] Ibid., II, 381.
[5] Louisiana convention of 1898, Journal, p. 130.
[6] Virginia convention of 1867–68. *Resolved*, that no member of this convention shall be eligible to any office in Virginia for the next five years. Journal, p. 156.
[7] Arkansas convention of 1868, XV, 19.

XI. REELIGIBILITY.

Many of the States have had provisions in their constitutions making the governor ineligible for reelection after a certain number of years.

These regulations appear in six of the eighteenth century constitutions and some eighteen States have had such restrictions. There seems to be a tendency to drop them, as they occur now in the constitutions of but nine States. As usual the Southern States are the more conservative in making the change, six retaining the restrictions, among them three States which have revised their constitutions in this decade.[1]

A number of States have a limited reeligibility for treasurer. The reason for this restriction is quaintly stated in the Massachusetts constitution of 1780:

That the citizens of this Commonwealth may be assured from time to time that the moneys remaining in the public treasury, upon the settlement and liquidation of the public accounts, are their property, no man shall be eligible as treasurer and receiver-general more than five years successively.

A similar purpose is served by the provision found in many of the constitutions, that no collector of public revenues shall be eligible to the legislature or to office until he has accounted for all the public moneys which he has handled. Some States also make administrative officers ineligible for reelection. The restriction upon the reeligibility of sheriffs is very general, usually providing that the office can be held by the same person only in alternate terms.

The provisions in regard to reeligibility were not the subject of much debate in the conventions. In Wisconsin, in 1847, a proposition to make the governor ineligible as his own successor was opposed as interfering with the free choice of the people. "It was aristocratic, unreasonable, and unfounded

---

[1] Mississippi convention of 1890, Kentucky convention of 1891, Louisiana convention of 1898. The following table will show the time when such restrictions have been adopted and abolished: Alabama, 1819, 4 years in 7; Florida, 1838-1865, 4 years in 8; Georgia, 1777-1789, 1 year in 3; Georgia, 1789-1877, no provision; Georgia, 1877, 4 years in 8; Illinois, 1818-1870, 4 years in 8; Indiana, 1851, 4 years in 8; Kentucky, 1799-1850, 4 years in 11; Kentucky, 1850, 4 years in 8; Louisiana, 1812, 4 years in 8; Maryland, 1837-1864, one term; Mississippi, 1832-1890, 4 years in 6; Mississippi, 1890, 4 years in 8; Ohio, 1802-1851, 6 years in 8; Oregon, 1857, 8 years in 12; Pennsylvania, 1873, 4 years in 8; South Carolina, 1778-1865, 4 years in 8; Tennessee, 1796, 6 years in 8; Texas, 1845-1866, 4 years in 6; Texas 1866-1868, 8 years in 12; Virginia, 1776-1830, 3 years in 7; Virginia, 1830-1870, 3 years in 6; Virginia, 1870, 4 years in 8.

in any principle of justice or sound policy."[1] Similar arguments were used in the California convention of 1849. The proposition was favored on the ground of rotation in office.[2] In Kentucky, in 1849, a proposition was made to limit sheriffs and judges to one term. In opposing it a member said:

> I believe it detracts from the competency and ability of the people to judge for themselves, and every page that bears the impress of such a sentiment, fixes upon the Commonwealth a blighting, withering stain, so dark, deep, and damning that neither time nor circumstances can obliterate it.[3]

In the Utah convention of 1895 an amendment was offered making State officers ineligible for reelection in order "to prevent the governor and executive officers from laying their wires for reelection."[4]

GENERAL SUMMARY.

In a word, this has been the general development. The colonies began with few or no restrictions upon office holding. Gradually qualifications were adopted to meet existing conditions. This period of tentative legislation continued until 1691, when the influence of the home government became strong and the laws in the colonies corresponded closely to those in England. In the early period the preamble of a statute usually stated that a qualification should be required in the future, because the lack of such a provision had given trouble. In the later period, on the other hand, an act of Parliament was frequently quoted as a reason for the colonial law. Hence the disqualification of Catholics and the restriction of voting and office holding to freeholders became quite general.

The foundation of the State constitutions is accompanied by a new element, the influence of political theory. The lawmaking in the colonies had been the result of experience either their own or that of the mother country. The political philosophy of the Revolution was liberal and tolerant; the practice of the colonies had been conservative and intolerant: the constitutions of the time were the result of these conflicting forces. In the Federal Constitution the liberal tendencies prevailed—at least as far as related to qualifications

---
[1] Wisconsin convention of 1847, debates, p. 59.
[2] California convention of 1849, debates, p. 156.
[3] Kentucky convention of 1849, debates, p. 413.
[4] Utah convention of 1895, debates, 1, 660.

for office. In the formation of the State constitutions the conservative influence was predominant, and the religious and property qualifications were retained.

The sentiment against these restrictions, however, was gaining, and they disappeared in most cases upon the first revision of the constitutions. The new States admitted after 1800 never required religious qualifications, and in only two cases was property beyond the payment of a tax demanded.

The first half of the nineteenth century was characterized by long residence and citizenship qualifications. The tendency of the latter half of the century has been to reduce these requirements. The argument chiefly used in the conventions was the injustice of limiting the people in their choice. Probably two other reasons had much more influence: the first was the desire of the new States to attract immigrants; the second was the determination of politicians to win the votes of the foreign-born population.

This has been carried so far that in many States aliens who have declared their intention to become citizens are allowed the suffrage, and in several they can hold seats in the legislatures. On the other hand, many Southern States have recently increased the residence and citizenship qualifications, being jealous of both Northern and foreign influence.

The exclusion of clergymen, appearing in a number of the Revolutionary constitutions and in some of the later ones, has disappeared in most of the States.

Provisions limiting the reeligibility of the governor, also dating back to the first constitutions, have been dropped in many States.

The disqualification for bribery, on the other hand, has become quite general, in many cases being enforced by an oath.

In no State can an officer hold either two State offices or a State and Federal office simultaneously.

The general tendency during the nineteenth century has been to do away with restrictions and to make the qualifications for office holding coincident with those for citizenship.

V.—THE PROPOSED ABSORPTION OF MEXICO IN 1847-48.

By EDWARD G. BOURNE, Ph. D.,
PROFESSOR, YALE UNIVERSITY.

THE PROPOSED ABSORPTION OF MEXICO IN 1847-48.[1]

By Prof. EDWARD G. BOURNE.

During the last eighteen months few students of our history can have failed to be struck with the points of similarity between some of the aspects and incidents of our recent public policy and some of the phases of the Mexican war. Not only in broad outlines is there a resemblance between the two situations, but it exists even in details. What a curious coincidence that in the one case we should have assisted the exiled Santa Anna to return to Mexico, counting on his friendly aid in attaining our demands, and that in the other the exiled Aguinaldo should have been brought home and his followers equipped as our allies! Indeed, let anyone who thinks this comparison forced read over his Biglow Papers. The famous epistle of Bird of freedom Sawin from Mexico echoes with contemporaneous discussion, and one long passage, with two or three changes in the names, might well serve the Anti-Imperialists as a tract for the times.

But it is not my purpose on this occasion to follow out in detail the comparison between the two wars and the issues arising from them, but rather, in view of the present persistent asseveration that the victory in Manila Bay imposed upon the United States at once the duty and the necessity of securing and retaining the Philippines, to inquire how we escaped annexing all of Mexico in 1848. This relic of New Spain, less populous than our antipodal islands, contiguous to our territory, a political wreck from the incessant turmoil of a generation, in the complete possession of our armies for months, with the flag flying from the Halls of the Montezumas, was finally relinquished, although the situation presented every argument urged for the retention of the Philippines more

---
[1] Read at the meeting of the American Historical Association at Cambridge, Mass., December 29, 1899.

cogently, and annexation would have involved fewer social, political, and constitutional difficulties. In the light of present events and of current opinion it is hardly credible that, if confronted to-day by that situation, our people would avoid their duty and leave the conquered to work out their own salvation, merely disburdened of some undeveloped territory.

That a policy so alien to our present ideas should have prevailed only a half century ago invites some explanation in addition to the obvious one that expansion and the extension of human slavery were, in the minds of an increasing number, inextricably bound together, and that therefore the deepening moral abhorrence of slavery, which was taking fast hold of the idealists, re-enforced the opposition of conservatism. As a consequence, just that idealist element which, to-day, leads the movement for expansion, under the banner of political altruism, shrank back fifty years ago from having anything to do with it.

It is to offer some further explanation beyond this obvious one that I undertake a brief inquiry into the rise, diffusion, and probable strength of a desire to acquire all of Mexico. For such an inquiry will show that the movement for expansion, although associated in the minds of many people with the extension of slavery, was by no means identical with it, being on the one hand strongly opposed by some of the ablest champions of the institution and on the other hand ardently advocated by its enemies, while the body of its support was in no inconsiderable degree made up of men on the whole indifferent to the slavery question. The emergence of this expansionist movement at this time, in spite of the obstacles to its success, prepares us for its triumphant career at the present day, when it has no substantial hindrance save the conservative spirit, to whose objections our sanguine people are wont to pay little attention.

It is well known that President Polk, on assuming office, announced to George Bancroft that he proposed during his term to settle the Oregon question and to acquire California.[1] He is, I think, with the possible exception of Grant, the only President who has entered office with a positive and definite policy of expansion. Polk was, in fact, an expansionist, not at the behest of slavery, as has been charged, but for the

---
[1] Schouler's History of the United States, IV, 498.

cause itself; yet a prudent expansionist, for he hesitated at the incorporation of large masses of alien people, refusing to countenance, as we shall see, the all-of-Mexico movement, and yielding only in the case of the proposed purchase of Cuba. To accomplish his purpose in regard to California, when negotiations failed, President Polk was ready to try conquest, and he welcomed, if he did not provoke, the war with Mexico.[1] The conquest of sparsely settled California and New Mexico was easily accomplished. The resistance of Mexico, although more desperate than was expected, was not effectual, and in April, 1847, Mr. Trist was dispatched with the project of a treaty. Our commissioner was authorized to offer peace on the cession of all territory east of the Rio Grande from its mouth to the southern boundary of New Mexico, New Mexico, Upper and Lower California, and a right of way across the Isthmus of Tehuantepec. "The boundary of the Rio Grande, and the cession to the United States of New Mexico and Upper California constituted an ultimatum," and less than that was under no circumstances to be accepted. The refusal of these terms was followed in September by the capture of the City of Mexico. The news of this triumph of the American arms, which reached Washington late in October, soon gave rise to an active agitation to incorporate all of Mexico into the Union.[2] The opponents of the administration averred this to be the design of the President, although it was not; and the suspicion was increased by the known fact that the Secretary of the Treasury, Robert J. Walker, was an advocate of this policy.[3]

Inasmuch as President Polk initiated his own policy and resolutely and independently pursued his own plans, no account of his presidency can be satisfactory to-day which is not based on a careful examination of the voluminous diary,[4] in whose

---

[1] Compare the narrative in Schouler's Historical Briefs, 149-151, which is a faithful presentation, in brief, of the material contained in Polk's diary.

[2] Cf. Von Holst, III, 341-344. It will be noticed that Von Holst, not having access to Polk's diary, worked in the dark in regard to the President's Mexican policy, and attributes designs to him which he did not entertain. The New York Sun asserted in October that it had advocated the occupation of Mexico in May. Niles, LXXIII, 113.

[3] Baltimore American, in Niles, LXXIII, 113.

[4] George Bancroft's typewritten copy of the manuscript of the diary is among the Bancroft papers in the Lenox Library. For an account of the diary see Schouler's Historical Briefs, 121-124. I may take the occasion here to express my appreciation of the courtesy of Mr. Eames and Mr. Paltsits in giving me every facility in the examination of the diary and correspondence of Polk.

pages are recorded not only his own views and intentions, but also brief reports of Cabinet meetings and of conferences with party leaders. Turning to this record we find that Polk told his Cabinet September 4, 1847, that if the war was still further prolonged he would "be unwilling to pay the sum which Mr. Trist had been authorized to pay in the settlement of a boundary by which it was contemplated that the United States would acquire New Mexico and the Californias, and that "if Mexico continued obstinately to refuse to treat, I was decidedly in favor of insisting on more territory than the provinces named." The question was discussed by the Cabinet on September 7, and Secretary Walker and Attorney-General Clifford are recorded as "in favor of acquiring in addition the department or State of Tamaulipas, which includes the port of Tampico." Secretary Buchanan, the Postmaster-General, and Secretary John Y. Mason opposed this proposition. The President declared himself "as being in favor of acquiring the cession of the Department of Tamaulipas, if it should be found practicable." Clifford proposed the recall of Trist and the prosecution of the war with the greatest vigor until Mexico should sue for peace. This was approved by Walker and by the President, except as regards the recall of Trist. A month later he changed his mind and Trist was recalled, as he notes, October 5, "because his remaining longer with the Army could not probably accomplish the objects of his mission, and because his remaining longer might and probably would impress the Mexican Government with the belief that the United States were so anxious for peace that they would ultimate (*sic*) conclude one on the Mexican terms. Mexico must now sue for peace, and when she does we will hear her propositions."

Another month passes and Secretary Buchanan has shifted his position, presumably in response to some indications of a changing public sentiment, such as the recent Democratic victory in Pennsylvania, and we are not surprised to learn that he "spoke in an unsettled tone" and "would express no opinion between these two plans," i. e., for the President in his message "to designate the part of Mexican territory which we intended to hold as an indemnity, or to occupy all Mexico by a largely increased force and subdue the country and promise protection to the inhabitants." Buchanan would, so Polk gathered from his utterances, favor the acquisition of Tamaulipas and the country east of the Sierra Madre Mountains and withdraw the troops to that line. This in fact Buchanan announced to the President nearly two months later, January 2:

> My views [records the President, November 9], were in substance that we would continue the prosecution of the war with an increased force, hold all the country we had conquered, or might conquer, and levy contributions upon the enemy to support the war until a just peace was obtained; that we must have indemnity in territory, and that as a part indemnity the Californias and New Mexico should under no circumstances be restored to Mexico, but that they should henceforward be considered a part of the United States and permanent territorial governments be established over them; and that if Mexico protracted the war additional territory must be acquired as further indemnity.

He adds in regard to Buchanan:

> His change of opinion will not alter my views; I am fixed in my course, and I think all the Cabinet except Mr. Buchanan still concur with me, and he may yet do so.

On November 18 Polk requested Buchanan to prepare a paragraph for the message to the effect—

> That failing to obtain a peace, we should continue to occupy Mexico with our troops, and encourage and protect the friends of peace in Mexico to establish and maintain a republican government, able and willing to make peace.

By this time Buchanan had come into an agreement with the President, and on the 20th the Cabinet all agreed that such a declaration should be inserted in the message. But if peace could not be obtained by this means the question was as to the next step.

In Mr. Buchanan's draft, he stated in that event "we must fulfill that destiny which Providence may have in store for both countries."

Experience warns us when a statesman proposes humble submission to the leadings of Providence that he is listening anxiously and intently to the voice of the people. President Polk was too independent a man to get his divine guidance by those channels and announced to his Cabinet:

> I thought this would be too indefinite and that it would be avoiding my constitutional responsibility. I preferred to state in substance that we should, in that event, take the measure of our indemnity into our own hands and dictate our own terms to Mexico.

Yet all the Cabinet except Clifford preferred with Buchanan to follow whither destiny should lead.[1] The paragraph was still troublesome, and Polk presented a third draft to the Cabinet November 23.

> Mr. Buchanan [records the diary] still preferred his own draft, and so did Mr. Walker, the latter avowing as a reason that he was for taking the whole of Mexico, if necessary, and he thought the construction placed upon Mr. Buchanan's draft by a large majority of the people would be that it looked to that object.

Polk's answer does him honor:

> I replied that I was not prepared to go to that extent, and furthermore, that I did not desire that anything I said in the message should be so obscure as to give rise to doubt or discussion as to what my true meaning was; that I had in my last message declared that I did not contemplate the conquest of Mexico, and that in another part of this paper I had said the same thing.

It will be noticed that on this occasion Robert J. Walker comes out squarely for all of Mexico. He seems to have improved the occasion again in his Treasury report to express his views, but the President required that to be in harmony with the message. Perhaps it will not be superfluous to remark that the most advanced expansionist in Polk's Cabinet always had been an expansionist; was opposed to slavery, although a Southerner by adoption, and was, during the civil war, a strong Union man.

Twice later this crucial paragraph was revised. In its final form it read:

> If we shall ultimately fail [i. e., to secure peace], then we shall have exhausted all honorable means in pursuit of peace, and must continue to occupy her country with our troops, taking the full measure of indemnity into our own hands, and must enforce the terms which our honor demands.[2]

An earlier passage, however, in explicit terms renounced the "all-of-Mexico" policy in these words:

> It has never been contemplated by me, as an object of the war, to make a permanent conquest of the Republic of Mexico, or to annihilate her separate existence as an independent nation.[3]

The opening of Congress gave an opportunity for the rising feeling for all of Mexico to show its strength. Yet it must

---
[1] It is interesting to note that Buchanan used this rejected paragraph in a letter to a Democratic meeting in Philadelphia. Von Holst, III, 341 n.
[2] Niles' Register LXXIII, 230.
[3] Ibid.

not be forgotten that the new House had been elected over a year earlier, when the opposition to the war was perhaps at its height and not yet counterbalanced by the excitement of the victories of 1847. During the first weeks of the session many series of resolutions in favor of and against the policy of all of Mexico were presented. Several of the latter were offered by Southern Whigs like Botts of Virginia and Toombs of Georgia, and illustrate the point that the slavery and expansion interests were not identical. Similarly, as Calhoun made the ablest speech against the absorption of Mexico, so the most outspoken advocates of it were Senator Dickinson of New York, a Hunker Democrat, and Senator Hannegan, of Indiana. Hannegan offered the following resolution January 10:

That it may become necessary and proper, as it is within the constitutional capacity of this Government, for the United States to hold Mexico as a territorial appendage.[1]

Senator Dickinson, who at the Jackson dinner on the 8th had offered the toast "A more perfect union, embracing the entire North American continent,"[2] on the 12th made a speech in the Senate advocating expansion, in which he declared for all of Mexico and asserted that it was our destiny to embrace all of North America. Said he:

Neither national justice nor national morality requires us tamely to surrender our Mexican conquests, nor should such be the policy of the Government if it would advance the cause of national freedom or secure its enjoyment to the people of Mexico.

Calhoun at the earliest opportunity, December 15, had offered these trenchant resolutions:

That to conquer Mexico or to hold it either as a province or to incorporate it in the Union would be inconsistent with the avowed object for which the war has been prosecuted; a departure from the settled policy of the Government; in conflict with its character and genius, and in the end subversive of our free and popular institutions.[3]

These resolutions drew from Cass a few days later the wonderful assertion that "there is no man in this nation in favor of the extinction of the nationality of Mexico." Whereupon Calhoun rejoined:

Why, you can hardly read a newspaper without finding it filled with speculation upon this subject. The proceedings that took place in Ohio

---
[1] Cong. Globe, Thirtieth Congress, first session, p. 136.
[2] Niles's Register, LXXIII, 336.
[3] Cong. Globe, Thirtieth Congress, first session, p. 26.

at a dinner given to one of the volunteer officers of the army returned from Mexico show conclusively that the impression entertained by the persons present was that our troops would never leave Mexico until they had conquered the whole country. This was the sentiment advanced by the officer, and it was applauded by the assembly and indorsed by the official paper of that State.[1]

Calhoun put the case even more strongly in his speech in the Senate January 4:

There was at that time [i. e., at the beginning of the session] a party scattered all over every portion of the country in favor of conquering the whole of Mexico. To prove that such was the case it is only necessary to refer to the proceedings of numerous large public meetings, to declarations repeatedly made in the public journals, and to the opinions expressed by the officers of the Army and individuals of standing and influence, to say nothing of declarations made here and in the other House of Congress.[2]

Some of these expressions may be briefly noticed. Gen. John A. Quitman, one of the most energetic of the army officers, subsequently a persistent advocate of the acquisition of Cuba, arrived in Washington in December and presented a plan to the President for a permanent occupation of Mexico.[3] Commodore Stockton, the Dewey of the conquest of California, at a great dinner given in his honor the 30th of December advocated not the annexation but the occupation of Mexico until that people should be completely regenerated and would accept civil and religious liberty and maintain a genuine republic.[4] Among the newspapers advocating the retention of all of Mexico we find, strange as it seems, the New York Evening Post, with such language as this:

Now, we ask whether any man can coolly contemplate the idea of recalling our troops from the territory we at present occupy—from Mexico, from San Juan de Ulloa, from Monterey, from Puebla—and thus by one stroke of a secretary's pen resign this beautiful country to the custody of the ignorant cowards and profligate ruffians who have ruled it the last twenty-five years. Why, humanity cries out against it. Civilization and Christianity protest against this reflux of the tide of barbarism and anarchy.[5]

The National Era, the organ of antislavery, advocated the absorption of Mexico by the admission to the Union of indi-

---

[1] Cong. Globe, Thirtieth Congress, first session, p. 54.
[2] Quoted by Von Holst, III, 343. Cf. Niles's Register, LXXIII, 334. A writer in the Charleston Courier affirmed, "Most of the leading Democratic papers openly advocate that policy." Niles, LXXIII, 354.
[3] Claiborne's Quitman, II, 7-9.
[4] Niles's Register, LXXIII, 335.
[5] Quoted in Niles's Register, LXXIII, 334, in article on "Manifest destiny."

vidual Mexican States as fast as they should apply. The disrupted condition of Mexico favored this solution.[1]

In New York the Hunker Democrats came out strongly. The "Address to the Democracy of New York" unanimously adopted by the Syracuse convention explains that as the purpose of the occupation of Mexico is to advance human rights such occupation is miscalled a conquest. "It is no more than the restoration of moral rights by legal means." The field for such a work is "opened to us by the conduct of Mexico, and such moral and legal means are offered for our use. Shall we occupy it? Shall we now run with manly vigor the race that is set before us? Or shall we yield to the suggestions of a sickly fanaticism, and sink into an enervating slumber. Can we feel no emotion but pity for those whose philanthropy or patriotism or religion has led them to believe that they can prescribe a better course of duty than that of the God who made us all?"[2]

January 12 Senator Rusk, of Texas, called on the President to request him not to commit himself further against the annexation of all of Mexico. Polk told him that his views had been distinctly stated in his message and that his mind had not changed.

As in our own day, foreign pressure in this direction was not lacking. More than a year earlier Bancroft wrote Buchanan from London:

People are beginning to say that it would be a blessing to the world if the United States would assume the tutelage of Mexico.[3]

Rumors, too, were current of a rising annexationist party in Mexico.[4]

The foregoing all show that the agitation for "all of Mexico" was well started and needed only time to become really formidable. It was deprived of that requisite element of time

---

[1] The National Era, August 19, 1847. The article fills three and one-half columns. The plan was presented again February 3, 1848. As these Mexican accessions would probably have preserved their nonslaveholding character, the number of free States would have been immensely reenforced by any such proceeding.

[2] Niles's, Register, LXXIII, 391.

[3] G. T. Curtis's Buchanan, I, 576. In this connection it is interesting to compare the forecast, at a somewhat later date, of Alexander von Humboldt: "Die Vereinigten Staaten werden ganz Mexico an sich reissen und dann selbst zerfallen." Roscher, Kolonien, Kolonialpolitik und Auswanderung, p. 177.

[4] Cf. the citation by Von Holst, III, 342, from Hodgson's Cradle of the Confederacy, 251-252, in regard to the annexation party in Mexico. Hodgson's estimate, however, must be greatly exaggerated.

by the astonishing course of Trist, who despite his recall still lingered with Scott's army and finally negotiated a treaty on the lines of Polk's ultimatum. How this conduct struck the President can best be told in his own words. When he hears, January 4, that Trist has renewed negotiations he says:

> This information is most surprising. Mr. T. has acknowledged the receipt of his letter of recall, and he possesses no diplomatic powers. He is acting, no doubt, upon General Scott's advice. He has become the perfect tool of Scott. He is in this measure defying the authority of his Government. * * * He may, I fear, greatly embarrass the Government.

On the 15th came a long dispatch from Trist, which Polk declares—

> The most extraordinary document I have ever heard from a diplomatic representative. His dispatch is arrogant, impudent, and very insulting to his Government, and was personally offensive to the President. He admits he is acting without authority and in violation of the positive order recalling him. It is manifest to me that he has become the tool of General Scott and his menial instrument, and that the paper was written at Scott's instance and dictation. I have never in my life felt so indignant, and the whole Cabinet expressed themselves as I felt.

Buchanan was directed to prepare a stern rebuke to Trist and Marcy to write Scott to order him to leave the headquarters of the Army.

January 23 Senators Cass and Sevier advised the President to inform the Mexican Government that Trist has been recalled. The next day Buchanan thought such a letter proper if Polk had made up his mind to reject the treaty. This Buchanan thought should be done. Polk said he could not decide till he saw the treaty. On the 25th the question was put before the Cabinet. Walker agreed with Buchanan. In regard to the treaty, Polk said that if "unembarrassed" he "would not now approve such a treaty," but is now in doubt about his duty. Buchanan still favored rejection, while Marcy was in favor of approval if the treaty were on the lines of the ultimatum, and John Y. Mason took sides with Marcy. It was finally decided on the 28th to dispatch the letter to the Mexican Government. The next entry of importance records the arrival of the treaty after nightfall February 19. Polk found it within Trist's original instructions as regards boundary limits, and thought that it should be judged on its merits and not prejudiced by Trist's bad conduct. The next evening, Sunday, the Cabinet discussed the treaty, Buchanan and

Walker advised its rejection. Mason, Marcy, Johnson, and Clifford favored its acceptance. Buchanan announced that he "wanted more territory, and would not be content with less than the lines of Sierra Madre in addition to the provinces secured in this treaty." Polk reminded Buchanan of his entire change of position during the war, and adds in his diary that he believed the true reason of Buchanan's course to be that he was a candidate for the Presidency. If the treaty were well received he would not be injured; if opposed, he could say that he opposed it.

February 21 the President made known his decision to the Cabinet:

> That under all the circumstances of the case I would submit it to the Senate for ratification, with a recommendation to strike out the tenth article. I assigned my reasons for this decision. They were, briefly, that the treaty conformed on the main question of limits and boundary to the instructions given Mr. Trist in April last, and that though if the treaty was now to be made I should demand more, perhaps, to make the Sierra Madre the line, yet it was doubtful whether this could be ever obtained by the consent of Mexico. I looked to the consequences of its rejection. A majority of one branch of Congress is opposed to my Administration; they have falsely charged that the war was brought on and is continued by me with a view to the conquest of Mexico, and if I were now to reject a treaty made upon my own terms, as authorized in April last, with the unanimous approbation of the Cabinet, the probability is that Congress would not grant either men or money to prosecute the war. Should this be the result, the army now in Mexico would be constantly wasting and diminishing in numbers, and I might at last be compelled to withdraw them, and then lose the two provinces of New Mexico and Upper California, which were ceded to us by this treaty. Should the opponents of my Administration succeed in carrying the next Presidential election, the great probability is that the country would lose all the advantages secured by this treaty. I adverted to the immense value of Upper California, and concluded by saying that if I were now to reject my own terms as offered in April last I did not see how it was possible for my Administration to be sustained.

The rumor soon spread in Washington that Buchanan and Walker were exerting their influence to have the treaty rejected. On the 28th Senator Sevier, the chairman of the Committee on Foreign Relations, informs the President that the committee will recommend the rejection of the treaty and advise sending a commission. The other members of the committee were Webster, Benton, Mangum, and Hannegan. Polk declared his opinion unchanged, and expressed his belief that Webster's object was to defeat the treaty. Sevier said Webster wanted no territory beyond the Rio Grande, and Polk comments in his diary:

> Extremes meet. Mr. Webster is for no territory and Mr. Hannegan is for all Mexico. Benton's position can not be calculated.

Polk concludes his entry with:

> If the treaty in its present form is ratified there will be added to the United States an immense empire, the value of which twenty years hence it would be difficult to calculate.

It was surely irony of fate that the eyes of this resolute Augustus, enlarger of empire, were so soon closed in death and that he was not suffered to see in the consequences of his policy the fulfillment at once of the most dismal prognostications of its opponents and of his own confident prophecy.

For several days the treaty hung in the balance. On February 29 Polk records:

> From what I learn, about a dozen Democrats will oppose it, most of them because they wish to acquire more territory than the line of the Rio Grande and the Provinces of New Mexico and Upper California will secure.

On March 2 the outlook appeared more hopeful; on the 3rd Benton and Webster are recorded as the leading opponents. The suspense came to an end March 10, when the treaty was ratified at 10 p. m., 38 to 14, four Senators not voting.

The reception of the treaty and its recommendation to the Senate clearly defined the position of the Administration and tended to discourage the advocates of "all of Mexico." If Trist had returned as ordered and the war had been prolonged, we should probably have acquired more territory, but how much more is, of course, uncertain. Calhoun, in his opposition, realized that every delay in bringing the war to a close would strengthen the expansion party and complicate the situation in ways that would contribute to advance their cause. We can best realize the importance of the element of time in this matter, and so appreciate the significance of Trist's unexpected action in securing a treaty, if we remember how long it took after the battle of Manila Bay for the final policy of acquiring all the Philippines to be developed. Trist's treaty arrived about four months after the news of the capture of Mexico City, and it was at least four months and a half after the battle of Manila Bay before the present Administration decided to demand all of the Philippines. Nor must we forget, in this comparison, that the formation and expression of public opinion through the agency of the press proceeds to-day at a much more rapid pace than fifty years ago.

In conclusion, then, in answer to the question how we escaped the annexation of all of Mexico in 1847-48, the following reasons may be assigned: The growing realization that territorial expansion and the extension of slavery were so inextricably involved with each other that every accession of territory would precipitate a slavery crisis powerfully counteracted the natural inclinations of the people toward expansion which are so clearly revealed to-day. Second, the fact that the elections for the Congress that met in December, 1847, took place over a year earlier, before the great military victories of 1847 had begun to undermine the first revulsion from a war of conquest, gave the control of the House to the Whigs, who, as a party, were committed against the war and consequent annexations. Thirdly, there was the opposition of President Polk, who effectually controlled the policy of the Government; and, finally, the lack of time for the movement to gather sufficient headway to overcome these obstacles.

VI.—THE PROBLEM OF CHINESE IMMIGRATION IN FURTHER ASIA.

By FREDERICK WELLS WILLIAMS,
NEW HAVEN, CONN.

THE PROBLEM OF CHINESE IMMIGRATION IN FURTHER ASIA.

By FREDERICK WELLS WILLIAMS.

The entrance of the United States as landholder and administrator into the regions of the Western Pacific confronts the Government rather unexpectedly with several old problems in new guises. Questions that affect our national policy, like those of the protective tariff and the Monroe doctrine, have already presented themselves for fresh discussion, while other issues of hardly inferior gravity call for immediate arrangement or solution. First among these in the Pacific islands comes the question of labor supply and the admission or restriction in our colonial possessions of those Chinese immigrants whom we have forbidden to come to America. Before our troops in the Philippines became actually an army of occupation the Administration was asked by General Otis whether we should antagonize the Chinese element there by enforcing the embargo against them equally on both sides of the ocean, or treat the yellow race with less rigor in Luzon than in California. The matter is sure to become one of extreme importance if we continue to hold our Eastern conquest, for it has been the experience of all European powers holding possessions near the Chinese Empire that they succeed or fail in exploiting them more or less in proportion to their success or failure in dealing with their Chinese subjects. It should be realized as early as possible that in a tropical region the Chinaman is no longer a rival and competitor, but an assistant to the Caucasian. In his chosen homes in temperate zones the Anglo-Saxon has persistently refused to tolerate the presence of Chinese laborers, and however selfish or illogical his action, there is no gainsaying the decision.[1]

---

[1] Les motifs étaient les mêmes que ceux qui entretiennent l'agitation dans la Colombie anglaise, qui ont suscité les émeutes Kearney à San Francisco, c'est-à-dire la jalousie et la haine que les chinois ne manquent jamais d'inspirer; le cri fut alors le même

The problem as presented to us here must be discussed, therefore, not as an ethical question, but as a politico-economic affair. Being confronted with the task of reducing and ruling a populous territory lying close to Asia, shall we persist in the same policy of Chinese exclusion there as at home, or shall we take counsel of Europeans ruling similar regions and act accordingly?

A consideration of the first magnitude is that of labor supply to exploit the very valuable natural and cultivated products of a tropical region where the white man can not work. The difficulty is an old one, familiar to all European nations with tropical colonies, who have made many experiments in endeavoring to meet it, and to whose experience we naturally look. Though something may be done with the aborigines found in the Tropics, it is often necessary to supplement or replace their work by men imported from other lands. Thus far the world only offers what might be called raw material for the torrid labor market in large quantities from three sources—the Negro, the Hindu, and the Chinese. We have had our share of the first and are not likely to encourage fresh accessions to our Oriental territories from central Africa. The second, though to some extent exported to certain West Indian and African colonies, are very properly protected by legislative enactments of their British rulers at home, and are consequently not available in tempting or remunerative quantities for exploitation abroad. There remain the Chinese, numerous, capable, enduring, superior as a race to either of the others mentioned.[1]

---

qu'aujourd'hui, "Ils enlévent l'argent du pays." Ce cri est si absurde que nous ne nous y sommes pas arrêtés. S'ils gagnent de l'argent, c'est en donnant l'équivalant par leur travail, et cet argent ils ont le droit de l'emporter où ils veulent. Tout absurde que soit ce cri, il n'en est pas moins vrai que partout où les chinois se sont établis, la masse du peuple est arrivée tôt ou tard à les considérer comme des instrus dangereux. Cela peut être injuste, déraisonnable, injustifiable, mais c'est un fait dont il faut tenir compte. Non-seulement les chinois n'inspirent pas de confiance, mais après un certain temps, ils inspirent de la terreur. Et pour celui qui a lu les temoignages recueillis, la raison en est bien simple, elle réside dans leur habileté, leur utilité dans les champs les plus humbles du travail, leur habileté commerciale et leur phénoménale frugalité. Il n'y a rien de tel que le succès, mais aussi il n'y a rien qui soit autant détesté, au moins par ceux qui le peusent conquis à leurs dépens. La finesse des Hollandais elle-même n'égalait pas celle des chinois, et leur prospérité était surpassée. (Commission royale. Rapport sur l'immigration chinoise, Ottawa, 1885, p. cxix.)

[1] No student of Chinese character should omit to read the admirable and comprehensive studies by Rev. Arthur H. Smith, D. D., in his Chinese Characteristics, Shanghai, 1890, republished in New York, 1894, and Village Life in China, New York, 1899, both sociological documents of great value.

The Chinese have had their own problems of exploitation and expansion within the generous confines of an empire more favored by nature for man's support than perhaps any territory of the same extent on the globe. In this region they have, as every one knows, held their own for a very long time with less intermixture from other peoples than has been the case with any other great nation during historical times. An ancient and homogeneous people with room to multiply, have, consequently, developed a policy of preference for their own land, greatly fostered by their governmental and religious polity, which has held the Chinese aloof from the rest of the world during the greater part of their recorded history. To these two causes of national reclusion and solidarity must be added a reluctance to venture on the sea, characteristic of all continental peoples. They have not remained isolated from inherent inability to mingle with other nations, as was at one time supposed; they stayed at home simply because they were fairly comfortable, because their masters wanted them to, and sometimes, perhaps, because they disliked the water; there was very little love or sentiment in the matter, for the Chinaman, generally speaking, lacks the emotion of patriotism. But give him a fighting chance at a fortune, some idea of the manner of going to distant countries and what awaits him on his arrival, and he will not only accept the idea of expatriation, but abandon household gods and ancestral tombs to win the prize.[1] Yet to emigrate is to him always a disagreeable alternative or a last resort. Though he can go abroad and succeed there, he prefers to remain in China; this is his attitude now, as in the past.

While it is unlikely that there was no exodus at all of Chinese to the archipelago in ancient times, no reliable accounts have come to us of such emigration.[2] A few adventurers and traders were all that went abroad. In Ceylon, for instance, "the silk merchants of China, who had collected in their voyages aloes, cloves, nutmegs, and sandalwood, maintained," in the language of Gibbon, "a free and beneficial intercourse

---

[1] See, among many authorities upon their emigrating tendencies, G. F. Seward, Chinese Immigration; W. B. Farwell, The Chinese at Home and Abroad; R. H. Conwell, Why and How; E. Cailleux, La Question Chinoise aux Etats-Unis, etc., 1898.

[2] A body of Chinese, for example, are alleged to have settled in Borneo as early as the Chow dynasty, 1000 B. C.; hardly a reliable tradition, though the island was known then.

with the inhabitants of the Persian Gulf,"[1] and during a part of the fifteenth century that island was reckoned as a tributary vassal of the Ming emperors;[2] but such intercourse as this seems to have been largely political and commercial; it involved no general peopling of the coasts and islands easily within reach of China. A Chinese traveler in Java a century ago writes of his countrymen there:

> Those who ply the oar and spread the sail to go abroad are principally the inhabitants of Fokien and Canton provinces, who have been in the habit of emigrating for the space of four hundred years, from early in the Ming dynasty (circ. 1400) to the present day, while those of our countrymen who have remained and sojourned in these parts after propagating and multiplying amount to no less than a hundred thousand.[3]

If four centuries of "propagating and multiplying" produced a net result of no more than 100,000 Chinese, we must conclude that the immigration to Java, at least, never reached very formidable proportions, and this seems to have been the case generally during the Middle Ages so far as Chinese settlements throughout the archipelago are concerned.

Under normal conditions the people of China never seem to have cared much about occupying the great islands near their coasts. Had there been a disposition to do so certainly opportunities were not wanting to emigrate to Formosa, yet the Chinese did not possess themselves of that island until the present dynasty came to rule over them in the seventeenth century. Magellan's companions make no mention of them in the Philippines in 1521; nor was there any indication of their settlements there when Legaspi effected the conquest of the islands for Spain in 1565, though they had, of course, traded with all the islands of the archipelago for many years before that date. Their evident indifference to Korea, the Liu Kiu Islands, and the tropical wilderness of Indo-China to the south of their great Empire points to the conclusion that the tendency to seek their fortunes abroad is a recent phenomenon among the Chinese.

Like the Israelite, rather than the ancient Phœnician, the Chinaman only goes far afield when compelled by distress at home or tempted by opportunity abroad. He has no desire to rule or conquer but is content to call any one master who

---

[1] Decline and Fall of the Roman Empire, Chap. XL.
[2] C. P. Lucas, Histor. Geogr. of the British Colonies, 1, p. 69.
[3] Ong Tae Hae, A Chinaman Abroad, Chinese Miscellany, Canton, 1849, p. 2.

treats him fairly. This trait is the key to his movements out of China during the past few centuries. Since the Mongol conquest[1] the Empire has been filling up at a more rapid rate than the occasional wars and famines could reduce. As a result of the secular operation of this cause and of the distress arising from the misgovernment of the Manchus, from recent rebellions and such calamities as the flooding of the Yellow River Valley, the past century has compelled a greater exodus from China than has ever before been known. To these expelling forces have lately been added the devices for enticing laborers to emigrate by offering golden inducements, and even by crimping and kidnaping men for the benefit of a few rascals who could make money by transporting coolies to foreign plantations or gold fields.[2]

It might be an interesting and profitable study to trace the palpable connection between periods of storm and distress in modern China and those of increased emigration to foreign parts, but the present occasion only allows a passing reference to this proof of the statement that the Chinese do not leave China except to escape evils they can not endure. Thus they rather suddenly flocked to Formosa and the archipelago during the decline of the Ming dynasty, and the disturbances following the Manchu conquest in the seventeenth century. They have begun a new and even more important exodus within the past fifty years, a period of weakness and dynastic decline marked by three or four foreign invasions and by as many rebellions.[3] On a smaller scale, but in a no less significant fashion, the action of this propelling force is visible in the occasional sudden increases in the population of the British colony of Hongkong, which have almost always been at times of distress in the neighboring provinces on the mainland. Thus the awful carnage of 1850–1852 in Kwangtung gave the infant colony its first great boom when the natives flocked to the island

---
[1] 1280 A. D.

[2] Samples of circulars are given in H. H. Bancroft's New Pacific, p. 593. Here is one posted about Kwangtung province in 1862: "To the countrymen of Ah Lung: Laborers are wanted in the land of California. Good works to be done there, good houses, plenty of food. You get $20 a month and good treatment. Passage money required, $45. I will lend the money on good security, but I can not take your wife or child in pay. Come to Hongkong and I will care for you until the ship sails. The ship is good. Ah Lung." See also Conwell, Why and How.

[3] The most important of these, the Tai-ping revolt, which raged nearly twenty years, is estimated to have cost the Empire more than 25,000,000 lives, and to have devastated the greater portion of the four central provinces of China proper.

for safety and employment. Another important increase in population was received in 1860 after the British capture of Canton and the renewed activity of the insurgents. The Hongkong population tables might be used as a sort of economic barometer to measure the pressure or density of the social mass in its vicinity.

An indication of the Chinaman's dislike to leave his native land unless compelled by circumstances to do so is found in his determination to return home as soon as his money-making object is accomplished. But fate is often stronger than the human will, and time and environment can work changes even in a conservative Chinese, so many indeed stay abroad in the end who never intended to do so. The emigration of this people has ever been marked by this one characteristic which seems to distinguish it from all other movements of population in modern history.[1] The number of emigrants leaving China in a given year, therefore, is no actual measure of the annual exodus, for a great many return. Until quite recently this was the tendency of all emigrating Chinamen, and the ebb and flow of this tide, combined with their losses by death while abroad, kept the aggregate number out of the Empire at any one time down to very moderate figures. Their harsh treatment and the legislation against them in America and Australia have greatly diminished their total in those two continents during the past twenty years, while their influx within that period into Manchuria and all the countries and islands adjacent to Eastern Asia has enormously increased. However, there is nothing exceptional or inexplicable in the phenomena thus observed. The normal working of an economic law is clearly traceable in this exodus of a people to regions, for the most part imperfectly known, whence the reluctant emigrant confidently expects to return home if successful, but where he willingly remains if room and opportunity are found. Were China efficiently governed and its natural resources exploited so as to afford a livelihood for its

---

[1] This trait forms indeed one of the chief counts in the rather inconsistent list of charges brought against the Chinaman as an immigrant to America and Australia. An intelligent Chinese visitor to the Straits Settlements in 1848 says of his countrymen there that "Originally the Chinese came intending to return after three or four years, but only one or two out of ten can do so at that time, and when they do they take very small earnings with them. This (he continues) is due chiefly to their acquiring the opium habit, on which they spend their earnings. The desperate from this vice become the criminal class." (Siah U Chin in Jour. of Indian Archipel., II.)

surplus population to-day it is unlikely that many of her peasants could be induced to go abroad. As it is, being in worse straits socially and economically than she has been for three centuries, her wretched sons are braving every risk and hardship and deserting her shores in the desperate struggle for existence. In other words, the conservative Asiatic yields as inevitably to the action of economic law as the European.[1]

In dealing with the quality and character of the Chinaman as a laborer we must not be misled by the unpopularity that almost invariably attends him wherever he goes. There is the same objection to him in the West and in the East when the white man has to compete and mingle with the yellow,[2] and racial antipathy as universal as this has proved to be within the past half century is reason enough, perhaps, for excluding Chinese labor where the Caucasian inhabits as well as governs the land. But where the laws of nature outweigh the prejudices of men, and white labor can not endure the climate, it is fair to ask if use can not be made of this available supply from Asia. The chief charges brought against Chinese immigrants in the East are (1) their immorality and filth; (2) their insubordination, which usually takes the form of passive resistance, and (3) their clannishness and tendency toward the underground methods of secret societies. Such counts as their alleged vagrancy and thievishness, sometimes heard in the wilder parts of Indo-China, are hardly just when laid at the door of the whole people, for the Chinese are no less apt than Europeans to become vagabonds, pirates, and adventurers when the situation tempts them. In these remote and misgoverned regions, where the offscourings of three continents join in deeds of shame, there is no lack of opportunity for the professional rascal; but there is no clear testimony that the Chinese predominate in this vicious element.[3] Compared

---

[1] Only very general estimates, in some cases mere guesses, are to be had as to the number of Chinese outside of the Empire. Reclus (in his Nouvelle Géographie Universelle) calculated their number at a little less than 3,000,000 all told twenty years ago. Since that time they have probably decreased in South America and increased considerably in Siberia, Indo-China, and throughout the Pacific. Probably the total to-day without the Empire is under 4,000,000—say 1 per cent of the gross population of China—more than one-half of whom live in Burma and Siam.

[2] The dislike of Australians for Chinese is like the dislike of terriers for rats. Sir C. Dilke, Problems of Greater Britain, p. 214.

[3] Mr. W. H. Medhurst calls attention also to the fact that for many years the Chinese in Malacca and thereabouts were largely recruited from the ports of Swatow, Chinchow, and Amoy, long points of escape for the vicious and criminal element of central China. Nineteenth Century, September, 1878.

with the achievements of European adventurers of the sixteenth and seventeenth centuries, their worst escapades in the archipelago to-day seem like children's games.

Taking these complaints against the Chinese immigrant in the order presented:

1. It is impossible not to sympathize with the feeling of disgust aroused in Anglo-Saxon minds by descriptions of the filth and indecency found in Chinese dwellings of the poorer class. It is doubtful, however, if vices are, upon the whole, more deeply rooted in Chinese than in European communities; nor have they proved more difficult of police control when vigorously handled than depravity in other forms among other races. As to their unclean dwellings, the Chinaman has no warmer love for dirt and poverty than the European. He is as totally ignorant of the first principles of sanitary science as were our own ancestors a few generations ago; but it is not impossible to teach him the advantages of clean streets, drainage, ventilation, and the rest. When he has learned the difficult lesson he is quite willing to conform to cleaner and costlier comfort, as is abundantly proved by his residence, in ever-increasing numbers, in the "foreign settlements" of such cities as Shanghai, Hongkong, or Singapore. Because a very numerous and conservative people have not turned from their ancient prejudices and sins at the end of half a century's contact with Western charity and culture, there is no conclusive proof that they may never mend their ways. At least, it is too early yet to despair.

2. As to their insubordination and stubborn resistance to authority, it may be asserted that this trait is due to the democratic instincts of a people long accustomed to ill usage from their officials, both at home and abroad. The Chinaman has survived and prospered in Asia because he has learned to take care of himself. Needing very little paternal attention from his rulers, he tolerates very little interference in personal and domestic affairs.[1] This kind of recalcitrance is, as everyone in authority knows, most difficult to overcome. But fortunately the Chinaman is only persistently rebellious when he is desperate. If met by firmness and a show of reason, he

---

[1] See Dr. A. H. Smith's Chinese Characteristics and Village Life in China for accounts of the Chinese at home; for both sides of the controversy as to their traits in America consult J. A. Whitney, The Chinese and the Chinese Question, and O. Gibson, The Chinese in America.

will succumb. An example of this sort of sedition and its successful treatment is seen in the administration of Sir Hercules Robinson, the first governor of Hongkong, who seems to have properly withstood the exasperating practice of the Chinese of combining in passive obstruction against legislation they did not like.

Unaware what stuff Sir Hercules was made of, the Chinese resorted to this practice three times within four successive years, but gave in on each occasion when they encountered on the part of the governor calm but rigidly uncompromising firmness. The pawnbrokers' ordinance (3, of 1860) evoked a general closing of pawnshops, and the ordinance remained for a long time a dead letter, while the pawnbrokers agitated for certain concessions. They submitted, however, when they found that the governor turned a deaf ear to all their representations. In order to provide a remedy against the habitual plundering to which goods were subjected in transit between ship and shore, an ordinance (15, of 1860) was passed for the registration and regulation of the men employed on cargo boats. As soon as this ordinance came into force (1861) a general strike ensued on the part of cargo-boat people, but by unflinching firmness on the part of the governor and the community they were soon brought to submit to registration. The chair coolies also resorted to a strike (1863) when they were for the first time to be brought under a system of regulating and licensing public vehicles by ordinance 6 of 1863. They also yielded after nearly three months' passive resistance, and the new ordinance proved a great boon to the public.[1]

3. But this kind of resistance to authority is sometimes indistinguishable from their more formidable tendency to combine for all purposes, good or evil. Chinese society everywhere is honeycombed with family and clan leagues, trade guilds, social unions, and secret fraternities. The truth that in union is strength has nowhere in the world such significance as in China. It is applied to the most trivial as well as to the largest matters, and no dealing with a Chinese community will succeed for a moment that does not take into account and work with, rather than against, their organizations. As is the case among other peoples, the combinations are factors of regeneration and social betterment as well as nuclei of conspiracy and crime. The citizens of San Francisco have at length learned to separate the Six Companies, with their regulating influence upon the California Chinese, from the notorious Highbinders, and the distinction is evident everywhere,[2]

---
[1] E. J. Eitel, Europe in China: A History of Hongkong, p. 368.
[2] J. Dyer Ball, Things Chinese, pp. 408–430.

The secret society in China is the natural outcome of arbitrary and inefficient government. Having learned the trick of saving himself by erecting an imperium in imperio, the Chinaman carries it with him to the country of his adoption, where, indeed, it often serves him in good stead. Transplanted to regions where there is no settled rule, the Chinese community provides for and protects itself as effectively as does the Teutonic.[1] But it is true that the secret society also degenerates.

In unsettled localities these combinations do lend themselves to lawlessness, sometimes even to civil war. There are accounts, grotesque as a page of Sinbad's Adventures, of secret conclaves held in mat houses in the jungles of Borneo, Burma, or Malaya, where acts of dakoity are contrived, desperate deeds of revenge plotted, members imprisoned, tortured, and even executed for suspicion of treachery, and fresh recruits cajoled or compelled to join the society.[2] Such institutions have held sway so long in some places as to render the rule of former native chiefs impossible. In the Malay States twenty-five years ago the Chinese banded

[1] Sir Hugh Low gives an account of a typical Chinese community taking care of itself, in a place called Marup, on the Sekarang branch of the Balang Lupar River, among the gold deposits of West Borneo. "About 250 men, forming a cooperative association, lived in a neat village built of planks and palm leaves. There was a common hall in a central position, and each member had one share of stock and was bound to contribute his daily work. There were certain officers of the company, as the engineer, the commissariat officer, the schoolmaster, and others, who were awarded, at the periodical distribution of the profits, extra shares in proportion to their responsibilities. Widows and orphans were provided for, and education was compulsory and free. General meetings of the members took place periodically, but a meeting could at any time be called by a certain number of members, to consider any question of importance. The gold-bearing soil was washed from the rough gravel, collected in heaps under careful inspection until the time arrived for the final separation of the metal, which occurred once in three months, when gold was sold to the Chinese merchants. All the expenses of the community being first defrayed from the produce, any balance which might remain was divided in proportion to their shares among the members of the community. Rations were provided for the single workmen in the central building, while many members were married to Dyak women and lived in separate houses, all being supplied from the public commissariat, vegetables being grown in well-cultivated gardens, the common property of the community.

"On the walls of the council house the rules of the society were posted up. All questions were decided by a majority of votes, and the officers were elected in the same way. I was told by the bookkeeper that each man received from $8 to $10 a month in addition to his subsistence, which was above the average rate of wages prevalent elsewhere at the time. The discipline preserved was extremely strict, no loitering being allowed at the works; the laborers were superintended by overseers, each with a cane in hand. I was informed that this community was affiliated to a great society which had worked on similar lines in the Dutch territory of Sambas for about two hundred years." (British Empire Series, Vol. I. India, etc., p. 480.)

[2] Jour. of the Indian Archipel., Vol. VI, p. 545; Vol. VIII, p. 1; Vol. IX, p. 109; Straits Branch of the Roy. As. Soc., No. 1, 1878, p. 63. G. Schlegel, Thian Ti Hwui. Batavia, 1866.

together under control of capitalists, living in great style in the British settlements, had quite usurped all power on the mainland and necessitated English interference.

<small>The possession of the richest stanniferous land was the prize of victory, and the Malay chiefs, divided among themselves, were quite unable to cope with the Chinese factions. Anarchy, complete as it can be only in Asia, barbarous cruelties . . . were the things that held undisputed possession in the Malay Peninsula when the British Government first began to interest itself in their affairs.[1]</small>

But even under these alarming conditions order has been restored by judicious management. While it is seldom possible and never wise to suppress secret societies among the Chinese, they can, as experience has often shown, be reduced to obedience and even used as instruments for the better government of their members. They must be compelled to live scrupulously within the letter of the law, to submit to a certain amount of surveillance and investigation, while their leaders may be held responsible for their illegal acts. This has been the course pursued in the Straits Settlements and Malay States, and it is everywhere practicable.

We have before us, in entering upon our heritage in the Far East, the example and experience of four European nations in dealing with the important problem of Chinese immigration—the Spanish, the French, the Dutch, and the English. The first and oldest of these has passed at length from the occupation of a few forlorn vestiges of empire which she was no longer fitted to retain, leaving to us, her successors, the sole legacy of her failure. It will be worth while to consider each of these nations in turn.

Legaspi, the founder of Manila, very wisely encouraged the Chinese to settle there in order to promote the trade from the Asiatic mainland which they had hitherto carried on from their junks alone.[2] Scarcely were the Spaniards established, however, when a Chinese filibustering expedition of sixty junks under Lim a-hong, a Cantonese pirate, attacked the settlement (1574) and all but annihilated it. This raid was only one of the many symptoms of disorder in the Government of China which portended the overthrow of the Ming dynasty and the

---

<small>[1] H. Clifford: Lessons from the Malay States, Atlantic Monthly, November, 1899.</small>
<small>[2] J. Crawford, Dictionary of the Indian Islands, p. 349; Consul Stigand in British Parl. Report, F. O. series, No. 1391, 1893; Guillemard, Australasia.</small>

Manchu conquest. It did not at once affect the policy of Legaspi's successors, who tolerated if they did not encourage their coming, until in a score of years their numbers in Luzon amounted to 25,000 or 30,000. In spite of the jealousy of the native islanders and of acts of barbarous oppression on the part of the Spanish, sometimes gallantly reciprocated,[1] the Chinese prospered both by piracy and trade among the Philippines until the first fearful blow fell upon them at the hands of their Christian rulers. In 1603 the Emperor of China is absurdly said to have sent three mandarins "to enquire if Cavite fort was built of gold," as reported. The Spaniards took alarm and fancied that China was preparing an army of invasion to eject them altogether from their islands, and when a little later a Chinese Christian convert of wealth was found building a wall about the Chinese quarter their senses took flight; they undertook with the savage natives, who were like children under control of the priests, a general massacre of Chinese, which in a few awful days destroyed 23,000 of them. The policy of slaughter once begun was more than once renewed. In 1639 some twenty thousand are said to have perished in a six-months' man hunt conducted by Spaniards and Tagals. By the middle of the following century (in 1759), after repeated commands from Madrid, an order was issued at Manila for the total expulsion of every Chinaman that had not been converted to Christianity. For these a special locality was assigned to which they might retire and trade. It was precisely the "hermit-nation" idea of exclusion fostered and entertained by the Chinese and Japanese empires at this period as regards Europeans. In adopting it Spain displayed the barrenness of her polity, as in its execution she revealed the utter inadequacy of her powers. The order of exclusion was suicidal as well as unjust, and apart from the profits of even a waning trade the Spanish officers were threatened with the loss of their best asset in the removal of these subjects of their taxes, fines, and forced contributions. Of course the edict was not enforced, but the net result of these persecutions was the hearty cooperation of the Philippine Chinese with the British invaders when they captured

---

[1] On the Spanish expedition to Malacca in 1593 one hundred and fifty Chinese were forced to row the viceroy's galley; when detached from the rest of the fleet during a calm they arose and slew their tyrant and his escort to a man.

Manila in 1762. Upon the withdrawal of the English the Chinese were visited with another general massacre as a slight token of Spanish esteem; and again they were set upon and killed en masse in a cholera panic in 1819. The final effort to expel at least the whole trading class was undertaken in 1804, exception only being made for plantation laborers. Heavier taxes were then imposed, and remitted upon their consenting to go to the fields. But here the native laborers objected furiously and they were driven back to town. Up to the end of the Spanish occupation the Chinese were taxed $60 per annum for the right to sell goods in the market, while taxation on other occupations ranged from $12 to $100. All their accounts had to be kept in the Spanish language.

In all this melancholy and disgraceful story there appears never a desire on the part of the Spanish to understand or deal fairly with their unpopular subjects. To tax and bully them until they discovered that the colony was threatened with ruin by the withdrawal of these petty traders and patient mechanics, then to weakly receive them again into the community—this was the Spanish method of dealing with one of the most subtle and expert people on the globe. The only success they can be said to have achieved with the Chinese was through captains, whom they allowed them to select from their own number, whose business it was to collect the tribute and arrange all internal dissensions. Thus the Chinese were able to secure a certain degree of liberty at the price of an excessive taxation.[1]

The French have been until recently the nearest neighbors of China proper, though the past five years have brought both the Russian and British empires as close to her populous provinces. Owing to its proximity, therefore, French Indo-China has a military and political as well as an economic problem to solve as regards China. The situation there seems at first sight to be seriously complicated by the legacy of hate left among the Chinese of both sides of the border because of

---

[1] Lawrence Oliphant, writing of Manila in 1858, says: "Manila, like Singapore, owes a great part of its prosperity to the Chinese portion of the population. All Chinese on arriving at Manila are registered and taxed according to their occupations." They were classified as merchants, shopkeepers, artisans, and day laborers. Their number, according to a Spanish authority, in 1842 was only 6,000, but their capitation tax came to $100,000 yearly, while that of all the 3,000,000 natives in the islands only amounted to $800,000. (Lord Elgin's Mission, p. 66.) In 1872 the Chinese there amounted to 50,000; at present they are thought to number 100,000.

their defeat and expulsion from Tongking. Reading into the oriental mind something of their own soreness over the loss of the Rhine provinces, the French conclude that the Chinese have no intention of acknowledging their defeat or abiding by their treaty.[1] The native population of Annamese is separated from Europeans by a moral and intellectual abyss which time and contact seem powerless to bridge. No treatment or education renders them in the least appreciative or sympathetic. But with the Chinese, to whom they have always looked for political and intellectual guidance, they are both friendly and docile. It is easy for the Chinese to tell them that though the European barbarian is a stronger he is not necessarily a better man; that the stranger has succeded only through brute force; that his rule can not long endure. Hence the contempt of the natives for the European, despite his invariable military success and matchless power; hence, also, their imperturbable confidence in the superiority of the defeated Chinese and in their hope of ultimate triumph. Moreover, the Chinese not only come in swarms into the country, but they intermarry with the natives and sedulously train their offspring to maintain the old hatred of the foreign invader. Their well-known ability to combine in secret and other associations is also employed to keep alive a spirit of revolt and to fill the colony with domestic enemies against the time when a new war with China commences.

This reasoning is not without some valid grounds, but on the other side we must remember that as a general rule the Chinaman does not antagonize his own selfish interest. Though his dislike for the European may not disappear, it can be rendered innocuous. Though it may be hopeless to win their affection in Tongking, or convert them to Western customs, religion, or habit of thought, the Chinese can here, as well as elsewhere, be pacified and won by letting him share in local administration, by allowing him a feeling of security and a chance to make money, and above all by permitting him to "save his face" before the natives, which means not interfering with his *amour propre.*

Let us see what the French have accomplished touching this delicate problem in Cochin China and Annam. Thus far

---

[1] The argument is developed in the Report of M. Séville in the Receunie de délibérations du congrès colonial national, 1888-1890, Tome II.

their Government measures have been inspired by political rather than economic motives. Fear of being overwhelmed by their numbers prompted a high taxation upon them, which naturally excited uneasy protests from the Chinese Government, in view of existing treaty stipulations. In order to control, if possible, their immigration and to watch them during their stay, a Service de l'Immigration was established at Saigon immediately after the conquest of Cochin China,[1] and under this or the director of the interior[2] all Chinese and their affairs were brought. An immigrant landing at Saigon not provided with a "certificate of engagement" had to be registered at the immigration bureau and get a card. The immigrant coming overland from Annam or Cambodia was made to buy a pass from the administrator, which was exchanged for a "permis de circulation," good for one month. For breaking these regulations the immigrant was expelled, and if caught returning sent to the penitentiary at Pulo Condor for three years. Exception was made in favor of women and children. The decrees regulating, taxing, fining, punishing (and inevitably irritating) the Chinese follow each other thick and fast during twenty years. In November, 1880,[3] the governor orders every Asiatic not a French citizen, unless a contract laborer or paying a land tax, to provide himself with a workman's book, which should contain his name, prenomen, birthplace, occupation, name or domicile of his parents, if belonging to the colony, his signature, his photograph, a number of order and date of issue, with sundry remarks, if there was room for them. For such a book he paid 2.50 francs, and if lost, a new one cost him 2 francs more. No wonder the French fonctionnaires, though numerous, complained of being overworked in a tropical climate. But these attempts at prevention and control did not in the least affect the influx of Chinese into the colony. In January, 1885, the idea of the little book was applied only to the native Cambodians and Annamese, while immigrating strangers were made to buy a personal card, always to be carried with them, and renewed each January. They were classified for purposes of this new scheme of taxation in three groups: First,

---

[1] Decree of November 24, 1874; also decrees of April 6 and October 13, 1876.
[2] Instructions issued January 10, 1879.
[3] Approved May 6, 1881.

patentees of the first and second class and landed proprietors paying taxes of 60 piasters (Mexican dollars) and over; second, patentees of the second and third classes and landholders paying between 60 and 20 piasters in taxes; third, all others; women, children, and those less than 15 or over 60 years of age excepted. To leave the colony, every Asiatic had to buy a permit for 2 francs.

The present regulations controlling Asiatic immigration into Cochin China date from a decree of February 19, 1890, in accordance with which the incomer has to go to Saigon, get registered at the bureau of immigration, and accept a place in one or another of the groups recognized by Government. He must obtain a traveling certificate and have his permis de séjour renewed every year, and when he departs he must secure a passport. The three groups are those paying 80, 60, and 7 piasters annually. Everyone found associated with a secret society not authorized is heavily punished by fine and imprisonment, and afterwards expelled.

In Tongking the situation was not only complicated by a long conterminous Chinese frontier, but also by a sentiment of disgust for a territory which had cost France so much blood and had proved, apparently, to be of so little value. The legislation respecting this colony has been marked by an illogical feeling of disappointment, which does not reflect credit upon a civilized nation. General Courcy began in 1885 by ordering a general tax to be levied on all Chinese alike. The Chinese Government protested against this invidious distinction against inhabitants of a friendly State. The law as modified in December, 1886, ordered the tax and a personal carte de séjour to be applied to all Asiatics, whether resident or immigrant; also a registration in four categories—those paying 300 francs taxes, those paying over 60 francs, those holding land, licensed laborers, employees, etc., and, finally, common workmen. The cost of the card for each year was fixed at 300, 100, 25, and 10 francs, respectively, according to category. But here, as elsewhere, the European was practically helpless without the assistance of the Chinaman in working the fields and mines and transportation service, as well as in minor business affairs. The Celestial stopped coming. The laws were again tinkered, the categories extended and amended through a long series of changes. To foster the direct trade with China, Chinese traders with certificates from French consuls in the South China treaty ports could travel two months in Annam and Tongking without any payment whatever.[1] Further reductions were also made in the categories during 1893.

Such treatment as the Chinese have thus far received from the French has not tended to remove difficulties or supplant ancient prejudices. Nevertheless the indefatigable Chinaman, who can thrive in tropical jungle or malarial marsh, is indispensable to French success in Indo-China. There may be some apprehension lest they multiply too rapidly in the country, and by absorbing every industry, large or small, leave no room for their French masters. They have already got practically all the trade of Cochin China in their hands.[2] They are not only clever merchants and skillful artisans, but can also work in the fields. They, moreover, know as well as European colonists how to secure goods from Western countries where they are manufactured, to charter and load them on steamers and ship them to India, Réunion, China, and elsewhere. It is said that during the first trying years of occupation, when French merchants had only very irregular and uncertain means of communication between Saigon and Hongkong, the Chinese of Cholon maintained and profited by a courier service direct to Canton. As in many other colonies, the Chinese, who once always returned to China after acquiring a certain competence, are now beginning to get their wives clandestinely out of the Celestial Empire and settle permanently in such places as Cholon and Soctrang, which are pure Chinese cities.[3]

Says one French author:[4]

They have rendered us incontestable service, in helping to establish Saigon and serving as intermediaries between ourselves and the Annamites. To-day it is entirely otherwise. Their selfishness, conservatism, and bigoted attachment to their own customs constitute insuperable obstacles to their fusion with other elements in the population, and not infrequently interfere with our control of the Annamites. Occasionally they become formidable by reason of their famous secret societies, chief among which is the Heaven-Earth League (Tien-Ti Hwui), which gave us trouble during the Tongking war. In northern Tongking there is a constant influx of Chinese, who now populate the mountain districts and coast provinces, and by their intermarriages with native women are gradually transforming this entire region.

---

[1] Decree of May 15, 1890.
[2] Where they chiefly reside in four towns, Soctrang, Sadec, Saigon, and its suburb, Cholon.
[3] E. Cailleux, La question Chinoise aux États-Unis et dans les poss. des puiss. européennes 1896. pp. 86-115. H. Blondel, Le régime du travail et la colonization libre, 1896, p. 138.
[4] A. Rambaud, La France Coloniale.

On the other hand, another Frenchman, Dr. Mougeot, is frank enough to confess that—

> Far from doing us harm, these millions of Chinese, attached to the soil and enjoying in the midst of real security a welfare they never knew at home, will constitute in future the safeguards of our possessions where they will make their fortunes.[1]

In Réunion the Chinese have, with the proverbial ability of their race, monopolized the retail trade and petty shopkeeping of the island, and, in conjunction with their only competitors, the Arabs and Hindus, they have long since pretty much engrosssed the traffic in food stuffs. Here and in the neighboring island of Mauritius, under British rule, both land and commerce seem to be passing into the exclusive conerol of Asiatics. It is with some idea of saving their newest colony, Madagascar, for the Malagassies and for themselves, that the French have imposed a prohibitive tariff ranging from 1,000 francs to 100 francs, according to category, upon all Africans or Asiatics coming to the island.[2] Attempts were made some forty years since to introduce Chinese coolie labor in Guadaloupe and Martinique, but the traffic was revolting and the article of labor proved upon experience to be too costly. Nor was the similar attempt made in Guiana more successful, though here a few Chinese remained long enough to engross all the retail trade and incur the usual unpopularity which seems to be everywhere their lot. In January, 1881, the counseil général there voted a special tax of 1,500 francs, in addition to cost of permit, on every Chinaman who was engaged in any business whatever, while other foreigners paid but 1,000 francs for the same privileges. The bill was, of course, annulled by the home Government, but its passage is significant.[3]

The Dutch, who are to-day the oldest colonial masters remaining in the Indian Archipelago, have made themselves at once disliked and feared by Asiatics to a greater degree, perhaps, than any European nation in the East. They have, it is true, confined their efforts chiefly to the more docile tropical islanders, over whom they rule with an unyielding rigor that rather shocks a European unaccustomed to the ful-

---
[1] Quoted in Essais agricoles et industriels. Publications de la Soc. des Études Indo-Chinoise de Saigon, No. 1, p. 175.
[2] Decree of July 26, 1897. Quinzaine coloniale, 25 septembre, 1897.
[3] H. Blondel, Régime du travail et la colonisation libre, p. 121.

ness of Oriental servility. With the sterner stuff of the Japanese and of the fighting tribes of northern Sumatra they have hitherto been quite unsuccessful. To the educated Chinaman they appear as interlopers in the islands. Ong Tae Hae in 1790 writes:

> The territory of Batavia originally belonged to the Javanese, but the Dutch, having by stratagem and artifice got possession of the revenues, proceeded to give orders and enact laws, until, squatting down all along the seacoast, they have exacted duties, issued passports, guarded ingress and egress, put down robbers, and finally brought the natives under their complete control. The Hollanders have long noses and red hair, and 'tis for this reason that they acquire such influence over the aborigines.[1]

The language is precisely such as Dutch writers have used in describing Chinese colonial activity in these waters.

As is usually the case, however, the Chinese are satisfied to let others rule, provided they can live in peace and earn money. In Borneo, which had remained until early in this century abandoned to native chiefs and the horrors of anarchy, the turbulent conduct of Chinese settlers under their own chiefs threatened soon to annihilate the Malay princes altogether. Under these afflictions they hailed with joy the expedition sent by Holland in 1818 to renew the old rights of the Dutch on these shores. But the mass of the Chinese were hardly less pleased with the change than the Malays. They presently abandoned their old turbulence and remained to the number of 38,000 or 40,000 nominal subjects of the Dutch.[2]

Long before this the attempt had been made, with all the implacable determination of the Dutch, to limit and repress their immigration into Java.[3] All manner of expedients were tried to annoy them, to throttle their trade, to prohibit their landing. It was thought that unless a resolute course was undertaken Java would suffer the same fate as Formosa, from which the Dutch had been driven when the island became

---

[1] The Chinese Miscellany, Canton, 1849, p. 3

[2] Temminck, Coup d'œil général sur les possessions néerlandaises dans l'Inde Archipelagique, and Jour. Ind. Archipel, Vol. II, 1848, p. 444. In 1840 the author calculated that Java gets annually 1,800 or 2,000 out of a total emigration of 8,000 or 9,000 to these islands from China. "If Chinese laws were not severely opposed to the emigration of females," he adds, "Malaysia would soon become a second Chinese Empire." In 1836 some 130,000 Chinese were supposed to live in the states of the western coast of Java alone. The Chinese "captain" of Montrado said that 110,000 were under his orders.

[3] Though in the early period of their colonial activity the Dutch ranged the coasts of Eastern Asia for the purpose of taking Chinese as slaves for their plantations. See Abstract of Instructions, in Calendar of State Papers. East Indies, 1622-1624, p. 100.

subject to China.[1] After years of stupid and thoughtless oppressions the climax was reached in 1740, when Governor Adrien Walkenier, in opposition to his council, tried the good old-fashioned Spanish business of massacre. He set the populace upon the wretched Chinamen, who, taken unawares, defended themselves desperately, but who were butchered and burned in their houses and hounded like beasts of prey by the natives until some 10,000 are supposed to have perished, and the Dutch, frightened at the awful bloodthirst their order had engendered in the excitable Javanese, were compelled to call upon their own troops to reduce them to reason. After this an apologetic letter was sent to the Emperor of China, who snubbed its authors by replying not, caring neither for the Dutch nor for the Chinese who had stolen away from the imperial domain.[2] But none the less, owing to just apprehensions from the surviving Chinese, more forts were built in Java, and the Chinese there were thenceforth made to live in a quarter of the town by themselves. In other islands the native princes were bidden to restrict their immigration and issue certificates of residence, but the princes being in need of their services paid little attention to the injunctions of the European traders. The Dutch authority in Borneo was extremely tenuous at sundry times and places. They were, therefore, content to deal with the Chinese there through their kongris (associations), and accept voluntary gifts from them in lieu of tribute.

The Chinese in Java, though no longer persecuted to-day, are looked upon with very small favor by their rulers. The last decree against their immigration was abrogated in 1837, though the attempt to restrain them is continued by requiring passports and imposing a heavy poll tax and other dues upon them.[3] Their number at present throughout all the Dutch Indies is roughly estimated at 470,000, about half of whom live in Java and Madura. This total does not appear very formidable when arrayed against a population of 35,000,000 in all these regions; but in the affairs of men it is quality rather than quantity that counts.

---

[1] The opinion of Van den Bosch, one of their ablest governors.
[2] Always the attitude of the Chinese Government toward its subjects who had broken the law by leaving China.
[3] Stengel in Jahrbuch der Internat. Vereinigen für Vergleich. Rechswissenschaft, IV, p. 244.

The cardinal principle of control applied by Holland to these subjects in her colonies, that of governing them through intermediaries of their own race, was borrowed from their predecessors, the Javanese sovereigns. This, and the invariable practice of keeping them pretty well segregated in kampongs apart from the natives, is about all the contrivance the Dutch use. It has the merit of simplicity, but it does not relieve the administration from very grave and constant fear of uprisings, which, like their sleepless volcanoes, are liable to break out at any moment.[1] All attempt at absolute uniformity in regimen has been abandoned within the past twenty years. In the three principal centers of Java the Chinese are governed by councils who manage the local affairs and police in their districts; elsewhere authority over them is vested in a "captain" or "lieutenant," usually a headman of some kongri chosen by themselves.[2] It is not regarded as altogether a satisfactory solution of the problem, for the Chinese are known to hate the Dutch and there is always apprehension lest they forget their customary calm, and rebel. But, as all acknowledge by this time, there is no doing without them. Says a French traveler:

These people, essentially intelligent and keen-sighted, who can live upon nothing, can bend to all circumstances, and are marvelously gifted in everything that relates to commerce, are as greedy of gain as of work. The most difficult trades can not disgust them; they understand cleverly how to create needs which they only are in a position to satisfy. * * * They are necessary to the circulation of the wealth of the country, which they certainly understand how to suck up wonderfully; they lay by in store for times of famine—perhaps somewhat forestalling; they unite fraternally in buying wholesale, vying with one another in fraudulent gains on retail sales; they stimulate financial enterprises which would fail without their aid, but like, perhaps a little too well, short loans at exorbitant interest; in short they seem to me to be the Jews of the Dutch Indies.[3]

---

[1] Rather against their will the Dutch find it expedient to admit a number of Chinese to their colonies as artisans, clerks, etc. There exist no stipulations regulating this immigration in their treaty with China. (La main-d'auvre aux colonies, tome I, p. 581, 1896. Biblioth. coloniale Internat.)

[2] E. Cailleux, La question chinoise, p 220. A résumé of regulations affecting the Chinese is given by J. J. Meijer, "La condition politique les chinois aux Indes Néerlandaises," in Toung-pas, tome IV, pp. 1 and 137, 1893.

[3] Comte de Beauvoir, "Voyage Round the World," Eng. trans., Vol. II, p. 75. The Chinese in Java seem to have profited materially by the culture, or forced labor system instituted there by the Dutch, which left them practically free of native competition in their favorite avocations as shopkeepers and middlemen and also afforded them golden opportunities as money lenders and usurers to the wretched natives, impoverished by the oppressive system under which they labored.

Looking now to the British experience in managing Chinese in their colonies in the East, we shall find that they have been more successful than other Europeans precisely in proportion as they have been more liberal. Coming rather later than the Portuguese, Spanish, and Dutch into permanent stations in Further Asia they had the advantage of profiting by their errors. It is more likely, however, that their success is chiefly due to lessons learned in India, whence their earlier administrators were sent to carry on the work of imperial expansion toward the Pacific. As Prof. Morse Stephens has pointed out, the British possessions beyond India constitute four typical groups embodying quite distinct methods of governing Asiatic regions.[1] In each of these and in Burma the problem of the Chinaman looms large, but it is in these colonies of the British Crown alone that it may be said to have nearly found its happy solution. Alone of all Europeans, the English have not recoiled at contemplating a reservoir of hundreds of millions of this persistent and procreating race, ready to swarm into any country and live under any climate. In establishing their strategic posts in Malaya, Borneo, Hongkong, they needed workmen, tradesmen to supply provisions, compradores, and domesties to render living not only possible but even agreeable; if these were not forthcoming their stations were doomed to fail, for these were not localities for European laborers and settlers. The Chinese, as usual, were attracted by a hope of protection and the chance of gain. They flocked into Singapore and Penang early in the century, as they did to Hongkong in its middle decades, and as they are doing in Burma and Borneo at its end. In each colony the success from a commercial and administrative standpoint has been astonishing. Let us look at them one by one.

At its inception the colony of Hongkong was formally and frankly given two different systems of law and administration, one for native Chinese, who were to be governed and judged in accordance with the laws and customs of China, every description of torture excepted, and all persons other than Chinese, who should enjoy the protection of British law.

This natural bifurcation reflected, at the first formation of the settlement, the fundamental incompatibility of the Chinese and European systems of civilization, by creating two separate forms of government and two sepa-

[1] In The American Historical Review for January, 1899, p. 246.

rate codes of law, corresponding with the two separate communities, Chinese and English, which were about to settle at Hongkong and which immediately proceeded to divide the two into separate European and Chinese quarters. But regarding this bifurcation thus provisionally introduced the pleasure of Her Majesty was subsequently made known from time to time, gradually extending by special ordinances and executive regulations the sphere of English forms of government and the application of English law. This was, however, done cautiously and gradually in proportion as the two local communities were by the slow process of the interaction of English and Chinese modes of thought, life, and education brought a little nearer to each other. This process (though hardly perceptible) is still going on at the present day, but executive regulations and legal enactments have all along proved utterly futile whenever they went too far ahead of the successive stages reached by this extremely slow process of race amalgamation, which depends more on the silent influences of English education, English speaking, and English modes of living than on the exercise of the rights and powers of the Crown. The Chinese, though the most docile people in the world when under fair government, proved utterly intractable whenever the executive or the legislature of the colony rushed into any unreconciled conflict with deep-seated national customs of the Chinese people.[1]

It must not be supposed that the task was altogether easy, even though greatly simplified by having her human experiment station located in England's element—the sea. The natives who swarmed over from the shore were not always of the kind wanted; many of them indeed were of the same sort as those who have been bothering the French in Tongking. They brought over their clan feuds, their passion for gambling, and their generally deplorable morals; they had no conception of cleanliness or hygiene; and lastly they introduced their inevitable secret-society system. Yet British patience and system overcame the difficulties involved in managing such a welter of disorderly elements. In the first place they were not too particular. Serene in the consciousness of their ability to control Asiatics they accepted any and all who would come and help build up a settlement on an empty island. Once there, they set the common people apart in a community by themselves, watching them closely, as was necessary, but avoiding needless irritation. The police problem was one of considerable complexity. Chinese constables were inexpensive and easily obtained, but they were liable to be bribed and to become accomplices in crime. Sepoys from

---

[1] E. J. Eitel, Europe in China; the History of Hongkong, 1895, p. 164.

India were more reliable than the natives and were also hardier in this climate than Europeans, but they lacked tact and failed to inspire the same degree of respect as Caucasians. Englishmen, on the other hand, were costly and liable to break down, while their ignorance of the people and the language made them almost useless in patrol and detective service. Though no element alone was effective a combination of all three proved successful for every purpose. A police force was organized in 1860 containing 60 Europeans, mostly officers, 300 Indians, and 110 Chinese, which thirty years later has 100 Europeans, 200 Indians, and 400 Chinese, the latter being secured on a bond of $50 a piece.

Piracy has been for centuries one of the chief activities on the waters along the south China coast. It is still fearfully prevalent in the obscurer bights and channels of the archipelago, but in the early days of both Singapore and Hongkong it had reached the proportions of a profession which engaged all the more enterprising element in the seafaring population and had become a menace to foreign trade. With the cooperation of the Chinese authorities the English set themselves to work to check the monstrous business. But the merciless pursuit of their countrymen and often enough of their near relatives did not arouse the Chinese in Hongkong harbor. On the contrary they respected a power that evidently was determined to make its rule felt on the side of law and order. For the Chinaman whose God is gold knows the excessive risks of its worship under conditions of anarchy. He may not object to the gains to be got by robbery, but he usually prefers to earn a livelihood by work rather than by stealing, not for moral reasons but because it is in the long run more profitable. A stern insistence upon perfect equality of all men before the law was another feature of English rule that not only earned general approval among the natives, but flattered their national pride.

The customs and prejudices of Chinese living under British control are violated as little as possible. Their quarters are always crowded, and their domestic habits often filthy and unwholesome. But unless these unpleasantnesses become a menace to the public health they are ignored. The Chinese, however, who overflow into the better-built portion of Hongkong must conform to European usages. For the rest, education, must be left to accomplish the herculean task of cleaning the Chinaman's habitation by purifying his mind and morals. Schools are opened to the very humblest in the social scale, and their influence and success are encouraging. In 1852, when the colony was 10 years old and had 37,000 inhabitants, there were 134 pupils in five schools; within a shorter space than half a century this has grown to some 6,800 pupils in 109 public schools, and over 2,000 more in private establishments, out of a population reckoned at 250,000. Nor are the English more jealous of the increase of wealth among the Chinese living there than of their increased intelligence. Here is a significant contrast: In 1876 the twenty largest taxpayers in Hongkong included 12 Europeans paying $62,523 and 8 Chinese paying $28,267; in 1881 the same group comprised only 3 Europeans against 17 Chinese, the latter paying about $100,000.[1] At present it is safe to say that the whole first twenty are native Chinamen, including many millionaires. Nevertheless they and the British both know that it is the Englishman that both brings and safeguards all this wealth. A community in eastern Asia needs no fairer assurance of stability than such a conviction.

To understand British methods of dealing with the Chinese it is suggestive to look at some typical experiences in the government of Hongkong. In 1844 the infant colony was naturally alarmed at the influx of the disorderly scum of the population from the mainland. To avoid the imputation of class legislation the governor, Sir John Davis, suddenly and arbitrarily imposed a poll tax on every inhabitant, rich or poor, European or native. Protests from every foreigner and memorials from every firm and organization in the community soon effected a virtual repeal of the ordinance, the abandonment of the poll tax, and the substitution of a registration system applying only to the lower orders of the Chinese. The régime of Sir John Bowring, another former East India Company servant, between 1855 and 1858, was especially notable for attention paid to Chinese rights and interests. Among his acts was one giving natives the privilege of owning British vessels and using the British flag on colonially registered vessels,[2] one of which, by the way, was

---
[1] J. Chailley-Bert, The Colonization of Indo-China, English translation, p. 85.
[2] Ordinances 4, 1855, and 9, 1856.

the famous *Arrow*, the immediate cause of the second war between England and China. Another recognized Chinese wills, made in accord with Chinese law and usage, in local colonial courts.[1] Another established Chinese cemeteries instead of indiscriminate private burial.[2] Another admitted to legal practice qualified Chinese lawyers.[3] Another organized control over Chinese living on the island through their recognized *tipos* or headmen and established a census bureau,[4] while another removed the old monopoly of the market for food stuffs from two or three compradors supposed to enjoy special official patronage.[5]

The so-called cadet system, introduced by another governor, Sir Hercules Robinson, in 1860, for the better government of the Chinese people in the colony, had in view two chief things: First, that the natives should be clearly informed of the nature and purpose of every Government measure affecting their interests, and, second, that the governor should always be as clearly apprised of the desires or objections of every Chinaman. The first of these was fairly secured by having trustworthy translations made of all ordinances touching the Chinese and their affairs, and later expanded by issuing a separate and complete issue of the Hongkong Government Gazette. The next point involved the abandonment of Bowring's application of the Dutch system of control through native leaders[6] and the intrusting of Chinese matters to the registrar-general, who was thereby given the same functions which the colonial secretary performed in relation to the European population. But, to be effective, the governor was careful to intrust the office to men who were both acquainted with the life and language of China and were in sympathy with the people. This difficult end was accomplished by his somewhat famous cadet scheme, which provided the colony with a staff of civil-service young men who were brought to Hongkong to study the language, and promoted, when qualified, to places in the department. From this tried and trained corps the registrar is always chosen, and upon his personal qualifications and ability depends for the most part the peace and happiness of more than 200,000 individuals.

---

[1] Ordinance 4, 1856.   [2] Ordinance 12, 1856.
[3] Ordinance 13, 1856.   [4] Ordinance 8, 1858.
[5] Ordinance 9, 1858.
[6] Ordinance 30 June, 1861. Substantially a return to Captain Elliot's original policy of 1841.

Eitel, the historian of this colony, writes:

> By fifty years' handling of Hongkong's Chinese population Great Britain has shown how readily the Chinese people (apart from Mandarindom) fall in with a firm European régime, and the rapid conversion of a barren rock into one of the wonders and commercial emporiums of the world, has demonstrated what Chinese labor, industry, and commerce can achieve under British rule.

On the other hand, the same author notices on the part of the leading Chinese residents of Hongkong a settled aversion to identifying themselves in any way with the European community:

> The persistent refusal to adopt European costume or English ways of living, the uniform aversion to participation in local politics, coupled with a deep-seated anxiety to keep on good terms with the Chinese mandarins even when these blockaded the port to throttle their trade, the steady increase of the Chinese joint-stock companies from which foreign investors are jealously excluded, the readiness of secret combination to retaliate against unpopular government measures by a general strike—all these symptoms of Chinese clannish exclusiveism, natural enough in people whose just liberties have for centuries been invaded by despotic rulers, clearly indicate that on the Chinese side there is, as yet, no desire to see the chasm that still separates Chinese and European life in this colony bridged over.[1]

The necessity of engaging the Chinese on their side impressed itself upon the founders of Singapore, and here somewhat the same policy was devised as that elaborated in Hongkong.

Says Prof. Morse Stevens:

> The imperial governors, though at first mainly occupied with the question of military defence, were not blind to the necessity of encouraging commerce, and because in the nature of things the continued prosperity of the province of Singapore depended upon the management of the Chinese, a regular Chinese department was established, with a branch at Penang. Certain officers of the Straits Settlements civil service, who showed special ability in mastering the Chinese language and special aptitude for dealing with the Chinese settlers, were detached for this department, and the office of "Protector of the Chinese" was created. It was realized that a special training was necessary for effectually dealing with Chinamen, and the creation of a special Chinese department, trained to keep track of the working of the Chinese community with its secret societies, its peculiar habits, and extraordinary powers of combination, greatly simplified the management of the Chinese problem.[2]

---

[1] E. J. Eitel, Europe in China, pp. v. and 574. See also P. Leroy-Beaulieu, Colonisation chez les peuples modernes; H. Norman, Peoples and Politics in the Far East; and Eitel's Handbook to Hongkong, 1893. The Ordinances of the Legislative Council of Hongkong were published in the colonies in 4 volumes, 4º. in 1890-91.

[2] "Adminstr. hist. of Brit. dependencies in the Further East," Am. Hist. Rev., IV, p. 265.

In these settlements the Chinese came into competition not only with the Malay native but with the Hindu coolie; but the Chinese laborer has proved—both in the sugar plantations, at the mines, and about the towns—to be cheaper than the Indian. They now constitute by far the largest element in the colony [1] and have practically monopolized the retail trade and provision business. It was here that the English, before China was opened, enjoyed their most favorable opportunities of studying the Chinaman individually and in his redoubtable gilds and secret organizations.

From the accounts brought to them in the early days of the formidable nature of these societies, their riotous and unholy conclaves, and their tendency to supplant legitimate government, colonial administrators were at first inclined to suppress them. Such a policy would inevitably have landed the English where the Spanish were at the end of their colonial career in the East. Fortunately, it was early felt, rather than formally demonstrated, that the policy of suppression was impossible. By working in harmony rather than against this profound national instinct of association, by insisting upon the registration of all societies and only moving against the illegitimate, by using them as intermediaries, and by rather ostentatiously engaging the good offices of their head men, a great change for the better has been effected; the poor Chinaman no longer fears to testify against a hwui, nor to call upon courts when they try to oppress or rob him. Probably the chief danger to the peace of the colony lies now in the ancient rivalries between the lower orders of the great tribes of Hokkiens and Cantonese, which, like the strife between Catholic and Orangemen in Ireland, seems to breed a hate that never dies.[2]

On the whole, considering that he is bound to come, that he is determined to live in his own way, that he is indispensible to the material success of these great centers of international commerce, and that he is callous and unimaginative to a degree unknown in other races, the Chinaman has been admirably managed, though it must be frankly confessed he has not been mastered by the Englishman in these coast colonies of the farther East.

---

[1] About 235,000 against 214,000 Malays and 54,000 natives of India.
[2] J. D. Vaughan, Manners and Customs of the Chinese of the Straits Settlements, 1879. Fr. Ratzel, Die Chinesische Auswanderung, pp. 198-219.

In North Borneo, where British sovereignty is exercised through the medium of a chartered company, the protectorate may be said to be passing through some of the phases which marked the early years of Penang and Singapore. Here and in Raja Brooke's dominion of Sarawak, the old hostility between the piratical Chinese and Malays has not been subdued, and often breaks out in bloody contests. The Chinese, of course, accumulate in towns wherever they are established and strengthen the communities by starting and maintaining trade. But they are distrusted here rather more than in other British colonies, and under the influence of this solicitude the English officials have been less successful than elsewhere in managing them.[1] In Burmah, on the contrary, where the cultivation, mining, and building, as well as banking and commerce, have long been entirely in the hands of Chinese and Parsees, the celestial is a welcome guest and assistant to the English administrator. Unhappily, these Chinamen flocking across the border show the same disposition as in Tongking to go about marauding through the loosely settled districts; but they presently marry native girls, treat them much better than do Shan and Burmese husbands, and eventually remain in the country to multiply and implant their characteristic institutions.

The situation in Upper Burmah after the British absorption was in many respects peculiar. The region had long been harried by roving dakoits, the result of King Thebaw's misrule and the shock of British conquest. The Chinese had enjoyed tempting opportunities for crime, and had not altogether neglected them. Their preponderance in Bhamo had years before converted it into a Chinese stronghold and point d'appui for further aggressions; while the nearness of their own borders, across which they could always retire for refuge and assistance, made their pursuit and punishment extremely difficult. These features, combined with the natural obstacles presented by jungle-clad mountains and trackless wildernesses, rendered the task of introducing order very trying. But after some ill-advised severity, the result of inexperience, the chief commissioner adopted a policy of not only conciliating, but of frankly welcoming the Chinese. Instead of show-

---

[1] But Mr. H. H. Bancroft quotes an opinion of the North Borneo Company to the effect that "the Chinese make excellent citizens, always at work." (The New Pacific, p. 597.)

ing fear he encouraged them to come from China and settle. The Irrawaddy Valley is now theirs to occupy and exploit, to cultivate and navigate at will. The certainty of profit is already bringing over a better class of immigrants, who will not tolerate the turbulence of the old set. By engaging the Chinese as their partners in a complicated bit of colonial exploitation the British have, of course, voluntarily surrendered a valuable region to those best able to exploit it; on the other hand, they have here, as in Malaya and other places, secured the warm and even enthusiastic support of a people who will strengthen and enrich the Empire, and will, if only for their own selfish ends, stoutly resist the encroachments of any foreign power desirous of interfering in their prosperity.[1]

There is not much to be said as yet on the attitude which the Russians take in dealing with this problem. Their policy in the Amur and Littoral provinces has heretofore been one of experiment and reserve. Now that they have possessed themselves of Manchuria they have a direct concern in the management of some 25,000,000 Chinese subjects who far surpass the Slavs in industry and pertinacity. In such towns as Vladivostok the Chinese are already in charge of the retail trade and smaller industries of the place, and it is impossible to do without them. It does not appear that either here or in their territories of Central Asia the Russians have succeeded in ingratiating themselves with the Chinese any more than have other Europeans elsewhere. But Russian absolutism and steadfastness of purpose undoubtedly impress and satisfy them; it is something they can deal with and understand.[2]

---

[1] Chailley-Bert, Colonisation of Indo-China, part II; Isabelle Marrieu, "Une colonie anglaise," Rev. des Deux Mondes, 15 September, 1899; Dilke, Problems, p. 461. The English laws applying to labor emigration are brought together in La main d'œuvre aux colonies. (Documents officiels), Tome II, Bruxelles, Institut Colonial International, 1897.

[2] "Vladimir" in his Russia on the Pacific (London, 1899) gives, perhaps, the most favorable glimpse of Russian relations with their Chinese subjects to be found in English. They have had, he says, "the greatest toleration for the customs of the Chinese and for their local self-government, even when it was prejudicial to their legal sovereignty. Russian annexation, therefore, has been favorable to the Chinese people, opening new fields for their trading enterprise. All the Russian towns from Vladivostok to Chita have Chinese quarters, with a numerous population of shopkeepers and workmen; there are far more Chinese living on the Russian banks of the Ussuri and Amur than on their own. Away from the river, in the interior of the Ussuri region, are Chinese villages governed by their own elders and headmen. The relations between the Chinese traders and the aborigines have continued as they were before the treaty of Aigun, the former, artfully supplying the hunters with tobacco, spirits, etc., hold them always in debt, which passes from father to son, constituting a veritable commercial bondage. Besides swindling the natives with their commercial ability, the Chinese in outlying districts even collect tribute as in the time

Mr. Medhurst thus describes the political characteristics of the Chinese:

The Chinaman is by tradition and education a monarchist, regarding autocracy as the only reasonable form of government. He thrives best under its sway so long as his just rights are respected. For the elective franchise he is utterly unfit, nor would he care for the privilege of exercising it if thrust upon him. After generations of association with white races and experience of the advantages of freedom of thought the case might be different, but until his nature is materially modified and the scope of his aims and wants becomes more extended he progresses more safely led than leading. It follows that whatever may be the political changes in the countries to which the Chinese resort, their condition will be happiest for themselves and safest for the country concerned if they are dealt with as a subject people and as a community possessing abnormal characteristics and therefore needing otherwise than ordinary treatment.[1]

In summing up the problem in a few words, it is evident that we have a very different phase of Chinese immigration in the East from that which presents itself in the sparsely populated regions of the temperate zones, where white men can work and dwell. In Indo China and the Archipelago it is palpably impossible to keep them out, and it is as obviously madness to attempt to do so if the rulers of the colonies there desire to check anarchy and make their possessions profitable. Unwelcome and unloved though they may be by all races alike, we can not deny them qualities which make for racial permanence and material success. Their unpopularity may in some degree be attributed to their virtues, which by carrying them triumphantly through the strenuous competition of modern industrial life leave their rivals far behind and incur their lasting enmity. It is this dislike, too, rather than an ineradicable aloofness, that makes it convenient or necessary to segregate them in quarters by themselves when dwelling in foreign countries. If treated with fairness they assist rather than impede the work of administration by setting the machinery of their social organizations to act in its defense. To the charge that their secret societies are a menace to governments under which they live, it may properly be asked whether there is any known instance of their subvert-

---

of their domination. The toleration of the Russians, extended even to such flagrant acts, gives the Chinese far greater advantages than in the pre-Russian period; this is evinced by their growing numbers in regions where before they scarcely appeared." p. 317.

[1] W. H. Medhurst, "The Chinese as colonists," Nineteenth Century, September, 1878.

ing a government that had proved itself fit to rule over them. The fact is that, while the most democratic people in the world in their private and commercial relations, the Chinese are by temperament believers in absolute monarchy and are, for the most part, indifferent to affairs of state and politics, provided they are so conducted as to leave them in peace. They are accused of making a very limited stay in countries to which they emigrate; but the tendency to return to China, once almost universal, is passing with their fuller experience of the advantages to be derived from thorough identification with the peoples and countries of their adoption. Not only is the transitory phase of Chinese immigration, heretofore its distinguishing feature, passing, but the steady increase of a Chinese half-caste population in regions where they have long been settled proves them as capable of intermixture and amalgamation as other races.

With our present knowledge and appreciation of their national characteristics, and relieved somewhat from the almost fanatical hatred which their presence aroused on this continent twenty years ago, it is desirable that Americans should adopt at the outset a settled policy of toleration and control toward the Chinese in their Pacific possessions. From the point of view of the colonial administrator no oriental people are more amenable and useful when rightly managed or more subtly dangerous to the peace and prosperity of the community when thwarted and abused. This is the substance of our inquiry into the history of European relations with them during three hundred years. If entirely unrestricted their numbers and pertinacity presently overwhelm the European system, culture, and control; he is gradually but inevitably effaced and his colony becomes not an affair of a European state but of China, as is the case to-day in Portuguese Macao. If too severely repressed by the foreigner, fearful of his own safety in presence of such overwhelming numerical odds, as in the Philippines under Spain and to some extent in French Tongking, the colony languishes and dies for lack of this most industrious workman and active trader. As the only people who remain effective and ambitious in tropical climes we need their help in our new undertaking, but we also need great caution in handling and guiding them.

VII.—THE DROIT DE BANALITÉ DURING THE FRENCH RÉGIME IN CANADA.

By W. BENNETT MUNRO, Ph. D.,
HARVARD UNIVERSITY.

THE DROIT DE BANALITÉ DURING THE FRENCH RÉGIME IN CANADA.

By W. Bennett Munro.

Among the many oppressive incidents which marked the land-tenure system of the old régime in France, not the least important were the "banal rights" (droits de banalité), or the privileges enjoyed by the seigniors of exclusively controlling certain of the instruments of production within their seigniories and of compelling the censitaires to make use of these mills, ovens, wine presses, slaughterhouses, and so on, to a fixed charge.

Whether in their origin these banal rights were the result of unlawful usurpations on the part of the seigniors—advantages wrested by strength from weakness—or whether they simply grew out of the mutual wants and interests of the parties concerned, has never been satisfactorily determined; their existence as legal rights was recognized, however, in only eleven out of the large number of French coutumes.[1] The other coutumes are either silent upon the whole subject of banalité, or speak of banal rights only as possible "servitudes" arising as the result of mutual agreements made between seignior and dependent.

Notwithstanding this, mention may be found of the droit de banalité in the etablessments and ordonnances as far back as the reign of Louis IX (1226–1270) and by the seventeenth century they had become—to use the words of Championnière[2]—"the most terrible abuse and the most general exaction of the whole seigniorial system."

Like most of the other seigniorial exactions, the banal rights varied very greatly, both in nature and extent, in different parts of France. The French Government, however,

[1] Henrion de Pansey, Dissertations Feodales (Paris, 1789), T. I., p. 175.
[2] De la Proprieté, etc., p. 552.

207

when it undertook to transplant to its North American possessions the system of seigniorial tenure, with all its incidents, endeavored to secure some degree of uniformity by prescribing the Coutume de Paris as the colonial code. And in thus relieving the colony of the legal confusion which necessarily resulted from the existence of so many different coutumes at home, the French authorities acted very prudently. But their choice of a suitable coutume for colonial use was in some respects less sagacious. The greater part of the colonial settlers came from the northern provinces of France,[1] Normandy contributing the largest share. Paris and the surrounding districts contributed little beyond the administrative officials and the members of the religious orders. Furthermore, the immigrants to the colony came, as a rule, from the agricultural class and not from the industrial or commercial, so that upon arrival in Canada they found themselves subject to a code of laws which was not only totally unfamiliar to them, but also out of harmony with the needs of an agricultural colony. This, nevertheless, was the coutume—framed for the use of an urban population—which the French Crown saw fit to introduce, and all the relations of the colonial seignior and censitaire were henceforth regulated according to its provisions.

The Coutume de Paris, as revised in 1580, recognized the enforcement of banal rights by the seigniors, but with two important limitations regarding the rights as applied to mills and ovens. These were:

(1) No seignior can compel his subjects to go to the oven or mill which he pretends banal * * * if he have not a valid title * * * and no title is reputed valid if it has not been executed more than twenty-five years.[2]

(2) A windmill (moulin à vent) can not be banal, nor under this pretext can the neighboring millers be prevented from canvassing for grain (chasser), if there be not a written title or acknowledgment as above.[3]

According to this custom, therefore, the rights of mill and oven banality—which were the only ones ever enforced in Canada—were not prescriptive, but contractual rights. They could be exacted by the seignior only when they had been

---
[1] Sulte, Origin of the French Canadians (Ottawa, 1897), p. 7.
[2] Brodeau, Coutume de Paris, Art. 71.
[3] Ibid., Art. 72.

expressly stipulated for in the title deeds of his subgrants, and in no case could a windmill be deemed a basis for the enforcement of banal rights. As the former of these limitations did not appear in the Coutume de Paris before 1580, but was inserted during the course of the revision in that year, it would seem as if the policy of the French Government was to place more restrictions upon the exercise of the rights of banality by the seigniors.

In Canada, on the other hand, not only were these restrictions disregarded, but, as we shall find, the French Crown and its representatives took active measures to establish and enforce the banal obligations in all parts of the colony. And, paradoxical as it may appear, the chief burden of this enforcement fell not upon the censitaires, but upon the seigniors.

During the period of almost half a century (1627–1663), throughout which the colony was in the hands of the Company of One Hundred Associates, very few of the sixty-odd grants en fief were taken in hand by the grantees. The object of the company was, primarily, to fill its coffers with the profits of the fur trade, and the directors paid very little attention to the matter of colonial settlement or organization. On a few of the seigniories, however, mills were built and used by the somewhat sparse population, under what conditions of payment can not be definitely ascertained. In 1652 we find trace of the first official regulation concerning the management of the seigniorial mills in an ordinance of the governor, M. de Lauzon. This ordinance was, apparently, never enregistered, as no copy of it can be found, but mention is made of it some fifteen years later in an ordinance issued by the intendant and council reiterating its purport and ordering its enforcement. This later ordinance[1] (March 28, 1667) goes on to declare that—

> Considering that it has been represented to us by the attorney-general that several abuses are being committed by the millers of this country with respect to the grinding of grain, and to remedy which it would seem fit to reiterate the ordinance made in 1652 by the late governor of this country, M. de Lauzon, and, reviewing the said ordinance, the council, adjudicating thereon, hath ordained and doth ordain that it shall have its full and entire force, saving the right of adding to it in future should necessity arise.

---

[1] Edits et Ordonnances Concernant le Canada, II, p. 86.

The ordinance then proceeds to provide that " the damages suffered by tenants carrying their grain to be ground " at the seigniorial mills "shall be had from the owners of the said mills, saving to these the right of deducting the same from the wages of their paid millers." These appear to have been the first ordinances relative to the management of banal mills, but others were not long in following. On June 20 of the same year (1667) an ordinance [1] of the intendant and council was issued in response to a petition presented some few days previously on behalf of " most of the proprietors of mills in the colony," wherein it was stated " that the mills of this colony cost double or treble those of France, as well for their construction, maintenance, and repair as for the wages and board of the millers," in consequence of which the petitioners declare that they might with justice ask "that the toll be proportioned to the above expenses and consequently be fixed above the usual toll in France." Notwithstanding this the petitioning seigniors went on to say that they were satisfied with the current rate of toll and ask for the issue of an ordinance fixing this customary rate for general use in the colony.

In accordance with the prayer of this petition, the ordinance of June 20, 1667, ordered the rate of toll to be fixed at one-fourteenth of the grain ground. Furthermore, it empowered the Government officials "to go from time to time from place to place to gauge the measures used in the mills, and to find out generally what is going on," and declared that where seigniors had leased their mills the censitaires should have recourse for damages, "in the event of malversation by the millers," upon the lessee and not upon the proprietor. Finally, in order to guard both against fraud on the part of the miller and the preferring of groundless accusations by the censitaire, the ordinance required that "owners of grain taken to be ground should be held to have their grain weighed, in default of which their complaints should not be heard." This practice of administrative interference in the management of seigniorial mills was not peculiar to the colony; it had been common in France, where it was justified on the grounds of public policy.[2]

---

[1] Edits et ordonnances Concernant le Canada, II, p. 39.

[2] Regarding this Henrion de Pansey observes (Dissertations Feodales. Paris, 1789, p. 215, sec. 19): "But above the authority of the seigniors there is an authority of a higher

In France the amount of toll exacted for the grinding of corn at the banal mills varied in different parts of the Kingdom. In the Coutume de Paris it was fixed at one-fourteenth, and the effect of the ordinance of 1667 was therefore simply to specifically apply this rate to the colony. The remuneration of the seigniorial mill owner, being fixed at a definite percentage of the grist, varied, obviously, with variations in the price of grain, which latter, especially during the closing period of the French régime, were very marked. During the period of thirty years from 1729 to 1759 the price of wheat ranged all the way from 2 francs to 10 francs per minot, or measure of about three French bushels.

But despite the assertions of the seigniors in the petition of 1667 that they would be satisfied with the usual rate of toll, there seem to have been some attempts on the part of certain of their number to exact more than the legal rate. In the lengthy code of "Police regulations," issued by the intendant some years later (1676), a clause was inserted [1] forbidding all millers from "causing more than one-fourteenth to be paid for the toll of grist." Likewise, the millers of each seigniory are forbidden to compete with one another (le chasseur les uns sur les autres), as e. g., by soliciting grist from the inhabitants of seigniories other than their own.

But the number of mills increased very slowly, owing, doubtless, to the poverty of the seigniors, most of whom could ill afford the means necessary to build the mills and to import from France the needed machinery. The stones were quarried in the colony; all else had to be imported. The toll received, except in the case of the more populous seigniories, often scarcely sufficed to pay the wages of a miller and the result was that in many of the seigniories no mills were erected. This state of affairs was soon brought to the notice of the French King, and the latter, in keeping with his usual zeal for the rapid development of the colony and in consonance with his unlimited faith in the efficacy of royal edicts as the general panacea for tardy industrial progress, at once set

---

order to which belongs all that can interest public policy, * * * and which has the right to restrict the liberty of each individual for the good of the greatest number. The mills intended to give the first preparations to the chief article of food must necessarily be subject to the inspection of this supreme authority, which has, then, the right not only to control them but to regulate their number."

[1] Ed. et Ord., II, 66-71, sec. 85.

about a reformation of the colonial milling industry. In 1686 he issued an important arrêt,[1] one of the most important edicts concerning the droit de banalité in the colony. After declaring that he has been informed "that most of the seigniors who are holders of fiefs in New France neglect to erect the banal mills necessary for the subsistence of the inhabitants of the country," and, "in order to remedy an evil so prejudicial to colonial welfare," he proceeded to ordain that "all seigniors who are holders of fiefs within the territory of New France should be bound to erect their banal mills therein within the space of one year after the publication of this decree," in default of their doing which "his majesty permits all individuals, of whatever condition and rank they may be, to erect such mills, granting to them in that respect the right of banality, and prohibits any persons from disturbing them in the right thereof." This edict, the provisions of which were intended to stir up the unprogressive seigniors, was duly registered by the superior council at Quebec,[2] on October 21, 1686, and was ordered to be promulgated at the necessary and accustomed places. Strange to say, this required publication did not take place till some twenty years later. During the period 1686–1707 the seigniors continued to build mills or not, as they found it profitable to do so or not to do so. In the latter case, however, they invariably took care to insert in their contracts of concession the obligation on the part of the grantees to carry their grain to the seigniorial mill "whenever such shall be erected within the seigniory." The long delay in the publication of the arrêt of 1686 is, in all probability, correctly explained by M. Raudot, intendant of Canada, in a dispatch to the French minister, dated November 10, 1707.[3]

He writes:

I should think, My Lord, that it would be necessary * * * that the exclusive right of grinding should be preserved to the seigniors on condition of their building a mill on their seigniories within a year, failing in which their right should be forfeited, and the inhabitants would not be obliged when one was built to have their corn ground there; otherwise, My Lord, they will never be induced to erect mills, from the privation of

---
[1] Ed. et Ord., I, p. 255.
[2] Ibid., p. 256.
[3] Raudot à Pontchartrain, 10 November, 1707, Correspondance Générale (Canadian Archives), Vol. XXVI.

which the inhabitants suffer greatly, being unable, for want of means, to avail themselves of the favor which his majesty has granted them by permitting them to erect mills in case the seigniors do not do so.

The dispatch continues:

This was granted them in the year 1686 by an arrêt which was registered by the superior council of this country, but not having been sent to the subordinate jurisdictions to be promulgated, the inhabitants have not hitherto profited by this favor, and it is only since my arrival here that the decree has been published, the fact of its nonpublication having only come to my knowledge in the course of a lawsuit, recently determined, in which the arrêt was produced, but one of the parties was not able to take advantage of it because it had never been promulgated.

And he goes on to say:

The fault can only be attributed to the Sieur d'Auteuil, whose duty as attorney-general is to transmit such decrees to the subordinate courts, but it was his interest as a seignior, as also that of some of the other councilors who are also seigniors, not to make known this decree.

Raudot proceeded, on the discovery of this nonpublication of the royal arrêt to issue an ordinance ordering its publication without delay.[1] From the foregoing may be seen plainly the desire of Louis XIV to make the droit de banalité obligatory in all parts of the colony, in the interest, however, not of the seignior, but of the habitant, together with the equally strong disinclination of many of the seigniors to conform to the royal will.

By the Coutume de Paris (article 71) no seignior was allowed to exact the droit de banalité from his dependents unless he had stipulated for such right in his deeds of concession. In the colony this limitation was not observed. Wherever a seigniorial mill was erected the censitaires were required to carry their grain thither to be ground whether this condition had been imposed upon them by their title deeds or not, and wherever the seignior met with refusal the aid of the intendant was invoked. For example, some of the censitaires of

---

[1] Ed. et Ord., II, 145-150. The orders of the French Government relative to colonial affairs were communicated to the officials of the colony in two ways: (1) By arrêts or edicts dispatched to the intendant, and registered in the records of the superior council at Quebec, which corresponded to the parliament of Paris in France This council consisted of the governor, intendant, and bishops of the colony ex officio, together with certain other officials (generally drawn from the colonial population) appointed by the King. After registry these arrêts were published by being sent to the royal courts at Montreal, Quebec, and Three Rivers, to be read in open court; (2) By private instructions to the governor and intendant These were not enregistered, nor was any promulgation of their contents made.

Demaure in 1716 refused to avail themselves of the seigniorial mill on the ground that their title deeds contained no provision compelling them to do so. The seignior, François Aubert, brought the matter before the intendant who issued an ordinance[1] ordering the censitaires one and all to bear their grain to the banal mill under penalty of a fine, the ordinance "to be published at the door of the parish church of the seigniory upon the first Sunday or fast day so that it may be diregarded by none."

Again, as has been seen, according to the Coutume de Paris a windmill could not be made banal (article 72). This distinction between mills driven by water power and wind power, as regards seigniorial rights based thereon, was likewise soon removed in the colony by an ordinance of the intendant issued in July, 1675.[2] The immediate cause of the issue of this ordinance was the presentation to the superior council of a petition signed by one Charles Morin, miller of the seigniory of Demaure, praying that he be permitted to grind the grain of the censitaires resident within the neighboring seigniory of Dombourg, inasmuch as the mill of the latter seigniory was workèd by wind power and consequently could not be included within the category of banal mills.

The council, after hearing in defense the lessee of the Dombourg mill, and after taking the opinion of the attorney-general on the matter, decided to "dismiss the demand of the said Morin and to ordain that all mills, whether they be water mills or windmills (soit a eau soit a vent), which the seigniors have built or will hereafter build in their seigniories shall be banal mills, and that their censitaires who shall be bound by their deeds to that effect shall carry their grain to such mills." Furthermore, this ordinance forbade the proprietors of mills to induce censitaires of other seigniories to come to their mills under penalty of fine, together with the confiscation of the grain and the vehicles carrying it. The issue of this ordinance is but one out of the many instances which mark the constant attempt on the part of the central power to adapt the seigniorial system to the changed customs under which it had been established. Every seigniory did not possess an available water power, and to deny the extension of the banal right to windmills would have given most of the seigniors a valid

---

[1] Ed. et Ord., II, 448–449.   [2] Ibid. II, 62.

excuse for neglecting to build their mills whenever they found such a course profitable, and would have thus deprived the censitaires of what was a convenience rather than a burden. There was, however, one disadvantage concerning the windmill—the power was very unreliable. The habitants [1] bringing their grist to the seigniorial windmill often found it necessary to lose many valuable hours waiting for the breeze to blow. A clause in the aforementioned ordinance therefore provided that if the windmill of their own seigniory could not grind their grain within the space of forty-eight hours after it had been brought thither, the habitants should have full liberty to take their grist elsewhere.

It will be seen that by the early years of the eighteenth century the banal right in Canada had differentiated itself in three ways from that existent in France under the custom of Paris.

1. The right could be enforced by the seigniors even although they had not stipulated for it in their contracts of concession.

2. All mills, whether driven by wind power or water power, could be made the basis for the exercise and enforcement of the banality.

3. Any seignior who failed to build a mill within the limits of his seigniory within a given time lost all claim to the right, the latter becoming the property of anyone who was willing to proceed with the erection of the mill.

The arrêt of 1707 was not allowed, like many others of its kind, to become a dead letter. Within a few months after its publication the intendant showed that he was in earnest by pronouncing the forfeiture of the right in the case of the seignior of Mille Isles.

"All the inhabitants of the seigniory of Mille Isles," the decree of forfeiture recites, "have caused the seignior Dupré,[2] proprietor of the said seigniory, to come before us that he may be ordered to build a mill for them, or, if he do not choose to do so, to consent that they should be allowed to build one for themselves, in which case they should be discharged from their banal obligation and allowed to utilize the right for their own benefit."[3] The seignior having admitted

---

[1] The French-Canadian peasant always spurned the terms censitaire or roturier. He invariably spoke of himself as "the habitant."

[2] This is probably a misprint for Dugué or Duguay, who was seignior at this time. (See Titrés des Seigneuries, I, p. 59.)

[3] Judgment of 14 June, 1707, Ed. et Ord., II, 427. In 1720 the arrêt of 1707 was ordered to be enregistered, published, and enforced in Acadia as well as in "Canada," Ed. et Ord., II, 157.

his inability to proceed with the erection of a mill, the judgment proceeded to "permit the said habitants to erect a mill in such part of the seigniory as they shall deem fit, and by so doing to be discharged from the obligation of banality to the seignior forever, being allowed to exact it for their own advantage." Here we have, therefore, under a seigniorial system, the somewhat unusual spectacle of a group of censitaires being permitted to exercise seigniorial rights over themselves.[1] In the same month a somewhat similar judgment was issued against the seignior of Varennes, while others followed from time to time during the course of the next few years. After Raudot's tenure of the intendancy had expired, however, the enforcement of the arrêt of 1707 became more lax, and there can be no doubt that many seigniors neither built their mills nor were deprived of their rights.

Subsequent intendants devoted their attention rather to the reformation of abuses which had sprung up in connection with seigniorial mills already in operation. In 1715 a somewhat lengthy code of regulations[2] was framed, providing among other things "that the owners of banal mills shall be held * * * to have scales and weights, stamped and marked to weigh the wheat which shall be carried there to be ground and the flour which shall be made therefrom." The judges of the royal courts were given power, when this regulation was found not to have been complied with, to have proper scales and weights put in and arranged at the seignior's expense.[3] These judges were, furthermore, instructed to examine the toll measure of each mill and "to have it made exact and stamped, prohibiting all millers from taking toll with any other measure than that which shall have been so stamped." Millers are enjoined to cut the weight of the grain, toll deducted, upon a tally, handing over to the habitants one duplicate half of this, in order that they may verify the weight of their flour when it is handed over to them. They are, finally, forbidden, under penalty "even of corporal chastisement," to wet the grain brought to them in order to have the flour thereof heavier.[4] In addition to this general code of regulations, ordinances were issued from time to time seeking to

---

[1] C. F. Ashley, Economic History, Vol. I, p. 37.
[2] Ed. et Ord., II, 169.
[3] Ibid., Art. 5.
[4] Ibid., Art. 9.

effect improvements in the machinery and management of particular mills, and from the very considerable number of these it would seem that the system of seigniorial flour making was not always wholly satisfactory. For example, in 1714 one of the habitants of the seigniory of Vincelotte, having been brought before the council on a charge of having "sent his grain to strange mills," urged in defense of his action that he had been obliged to take part of his grain elsewhere than to the mill of his own seigniory, because the latter was "no good;" that it "made very bad flour," and that "the miller who worked the mill gave too small return of flour for grain."[1] The council declared the defense of the habitant good, and ordered the seignior to have his mill improved—having done which his right would be enforced. From this decision the seignior made appeal to the king, but the latter confirmed the action of the council, adding that habitants should be allowed to have their grain ground elsewhere whenever the seigniorial mill should be "stopped in any manner and for any reason whatsoever."

In 1728 several inhabitants of the seigniory of Grondines set forth, in a petition to the superior council that "they are compelled to take their grain to the windmill of the seigniory, which is most grievous and prejudicial to them inasmuch as the stones only crack up the wheat, both because the mill has been absolutely ruined by the different persons who have run it heretofore, and because the Sieur Hamelin, who now runs it (Hamelin was himself the seignior of Grondines), not being a miller by trade, simply increases the defects in the flour. [2] As it was flour, and not cracked wheat, which the habitants wanted, they asked that experts should be appointed to examine the mill and to report the state of affairs to the council. The seignior being called on for his defense, declared that his mill was "in excellent order;" that while it was true that he was running—or trying to run—the mill himself, this was not his fault, his miller having been called out to do military service; that he was just about to secure the services of a competent flour maker and, finally, that he invited the appointment of experts who should satisfy themselves of the truth of his statements. The council, taking the seignior at his word, ordered a visit to the mill by a board of experts, with what result is not recorded.

---

[1] Titles and Documents, II, 224.   [2] Ed. et Ord. III, 241.

In the same year the habitants of the seigniory of St. Anne de la Pérade sent a delegation before the authorities at Quebec to complain that the mill of that seigniory was "entirely out of order;" that "the miller was not only a dishonest man, but was known to the seignior as such," and that the mill was not of sufficient capacity to grind out all the flour which was required for the maintenance of the habitants and their families.[1] The inhabitants of the seigniory of Neuville were better provided for, since there were in the seigniory two banal mills—one a windmill, the other a water-power affair. This double facility appears, however, to have availed them little, for in 1733 they made complaint to the council that the former seldom ran, and the latter turned out defective flour. Furthermore, they declared that "when the windmill failed for wind or the water-mill for water the seignior kept them hauling their grain back and forward from one mill to the other as often as three times."[2]

They asked, among other things, that the seignior be ordered to keep a regular miller, who should live near the mill, and that he should provide "stamped weights of iron instead of stones, the weight whereof is not shown." In this last request is an interesting bit of evidence as to the general equipment of the banal mills of the old régime.

Complaints were sometimes made that seigniorial mills had been erected in places which the habitants found it difficult to reach. In one case the intendant ordered a seignior to have his mill built on the riverside, where it could be reached by boat, or else to have a road built up to it.[3] In another case the same official allowed certain habitants exemption from the banal obligation until their seignior should have opened up a passable road.[4] In a country where seigniories extended, as they frequently did, over from 200 to 500 square miles, the difficulty of transporting the grain to the mill was often very serious. As to the choice of a mill site, the seignior was unhampered. If he saw fit to erect it upon land which had been already granted to a habitant, he could obtain a decree from the council reuniting this land to his demesne, the habitant being given the privilege of selecting a new concession of similar extent from any portion of the ungranted lands of

---

[1] Ed. et Ord., II, 497.
[2] Tit. and Docs., II, 155.
[3] Ed. et Ord., II, 210.
[4] Perault's Extracts, p. 71.

the seigniory. In some cases decrees of this kind were granted.[1]

In response to repeated complaints that habitants were being put to much inconvenience by having to wait on windmills to start running during calm weather, an ordinance was issued in 1730 giving all persons liberty to take their grain to a water-power mill, if compelled to leave their grist unground at the seigniorial windmill for more than two days.[2] This provision, which was greatly appreciated by the habitants in general, was issued chiefly through the influence of Giles Hocquart, who with the exception of Jean Talon—the Colbert of New France—was perhaps the most public-spirited as well as the most energetic of the colonial intendants. Hocquart during the course of his régime rigidly obliged seigniors to keep their mills in good repair, going so far as to threaten them with entire deprivation of the banal right in the event of their failure to comply with his demands.[3]

In the course of one of his dispatches, Hocquart advised the French Government that the quality of the flour turned out by the banal mills would be materially improved if the grain were only properly cleaned before being ground, but that there were no fanning mills in the colony. The seigniors, in all probability, deemed it sufficient to build the mills and to run them for the most part at a loss, without providing subsidiary appliances. The French King, however, with his usual zeal for the development of colonial industry, promptly gratified the desire of the intendant by sending out, in 1732, six fanning mills at his own expense. On arrival in the colony, these were distributed, gratis, among six of the most important seignioral mills—those of the seigniories of Sault a la puce, Petit-Pre, Beauport, Point de Levy, St. Nicholas, and St. Famille—and an ordinance[4] was forthwith issued, compelling the owners of those mills "to have all the wheat of whatsoever quality sent to them passed and fanned before its conversion into flour." It was further ordered that the millers should take their toll merely upon the cleaned and fanned grain and not upon the whole, but that in compensation for this the millers should be allowed to exact 6 deniers per minot on the whole grist, in addition to the usual toll of

---

[1] Ed. et Ord., II, 466.
[2] Ibid., 840.
[3] Ibid., II, 519.
[4] Ibid., 852.

one-fourteenth. All "taillings" were to be given back to the habitant.

During the course of the next year five more fanning mills were sent out and distributed among the seignioral mills in the district of Montreal,[1] the King promising to keep up the good work but failing thereafter to do so. The seigniors themselves showed very little industrial enterprise at any time, and this may be accounted for partly by the comparative poverty of the greater portion of their number, and partly, too, by the fact that many of them were retired military and administrative officials with little taste for industrial life. Absenteeism, one of the curses of the seigniorial system in France, was never an evil in Canada, and the writer who declares that "the peasants looked upon their lords in the light of taxpayers wringing money out of labor to spend it in luxury in Quebec and Montreal"[2] has attributed to the colonial seigniorial system a feature which it fortunately never inherited from the motherland. The great majority of the Canadian seigniors shared the rough everyday life of their pioneer dependents—very frequently they numbered among their censitaires men better endowed with worldly goods than themselves—and the number of seigniors whose means permitted luxurious idleness in the towns could be counted upon the fingers of one hand.[3] In France, again, the seignior was almost invariably a member of the noblesse; in the colony this was rarely the case, with the result that there was no legal bar to his engaging in manual work, and the colonial prototype of the haughty seigneur who lounged in the corridors of Versailles might not infrequently be found crushing grain in his little mill on the banks of the St. Maurice.

The seigniorial mills were usually constructed of timber, but in not a few cases they were built of stone, many of the seigniors expressly reserving in the titles of their subgrants the right to take materials for this purpose from the conceded lands without compensation. In a few cases the habitants were obliged to render their *corvées* in preparing the materials and even in erecting the mills, but this practice was never sanctioned by the authorities. The stone mills were usually

---
[1] These were given one each to the mills of Lachine, Isle Jesus, and Isle St. Helene, and two to the mill of the seigniory of Terrebonne.
[2] Watson, Constitutional History of Canada, p. 12.
[3] C. F. Sulte, La Tenure Seigneuriale in Revue Canadienne (August, 1882).

loopholed in order to be available as places of refuge and defense in the event of Indian attacks, and the mill of the seigniory of St. Sulpice at Montreal was one of the chief strongholds of the town. The religious orders were, in fact, able to build much better mills upon their various seigniories than were the individual lay seigniors, and these they almost invariably fortified, for during the greater part of the period of French possession no part of Canada was safe from an Iroquois assault.

Three questions have been much mooted in regard to the extent of the droit de banalité in the colony. The first of these was as to whether all the grain produced by the censitaires was subject to the banal obligation, or only such portion of it as was required for the consumption of the producer and his family. Some of the seigniors took the former view, but the authorities thought differently and ordinances were refused to seigniors who wished thereby to compel habitants to bring all their grain to the seigniorial mills. On the other hand, the intendant never refused, in default of good reason to the contrary, to enforce the obligation in regard to grain used by the habitant and his family.[1] The action of the authorities in this regard has been upheld by the most authoritative writers upon the subject of French-Canadian civil law,[2] and would seem to be borne out by the wording of the long-suppressed arrêt of 1686, which speaks of the neglect of the seigniors to build the banal mills "necessary for the subsistence of the inhabitants," a feature which might be taken to show that in the opinion of the French Crown the primary object of the system of banal mills in the colony was to insure the grinding of grain for home consumption. The question, however, was never of very great importance, for the habitants were generally able to produce but little grain more than was sufficient for their own use. It was by no means an uncommon occurrence to import flour from France for the use of the urban population of the colony.

Then there was the more important question as to whether the banal obligation extended to all grain intended by the habitant for his own use, or the wheat alone. As to the extent of the right in France there is some difference of opinion

---
[1] Cf. Case of the Seignior of Champlain, Ed. et Ord., II, 452.
[2] Cugnet. Traité de la loi des fiefs, p. 36.

among writers. Henrion de Pansey[1] affirms that it extended not only to wheat, but to barley, buckwheat, and all other grains. Denizart, in his decisions,[2] quotes a judgment of the parliament of Bretagne in which a seignior was sustained in his claim that barley should be included within the category of cereals subject to the droit de banalité. Other authorities of equal weight declare that the right usually extended to wheat only.[3] No doubt the extent of the obligation varied in different parts of the country, but on the whole the general weight of opinion seems to be in favor of the view that it was properly applicable to wheat alone.[4] In Canada, on the contrary, the obligation was generally understood to have been applicable to grain of all kinds. The expression made use of in the arrêts and ordinances was invariably "porter moudre leur grains,"[5] and the term "grains" can scarcely be construed to have meant cereals of any one kind. The same expression is used in the titles of lands granted en censive by the Crown in the vicinity of Detroit, Mich.,[6] and it is also the wording usually employed by the various seigniors in their titles of concession. In some few of the latter cases, however, the expression "porter moudre leur bled" occurs, in which case the intention would seem to have been to attach the obligation to wheat alone. These cases were very exceptional, and, in general, the fact that the intendant was apparently only once[7] called upon to decide the question in favor of the extension would go to show that the extension of the right to grain of all kinds was not opposed by the habitant. Finally there was a question as to whether a censitaire purchasing grain outside the limits of the seigniory and having it brought within was or was not bound to have it ground at the seigniorial mill. Henrion de Pansey, on this point, quotes an arrêt de Gonesse, in which it is authoritatively stated that all grain, whether grown within or brought within a seigniory, was subject to the banal right.[8] There is no colonial

---

[1] Dissertationes Feodales I, Vo. Banalité, p. 9.
[2] Nouveau Denizart, p. 648, sec. 5.
[3] Le Febre, III, 168, 173–175; Rousseau de la Combe, II, 67.
[4] Cf. Opinion of Judge Caron (Reports of the Special Seigniorial Abolition Court, 1854), Vol. B, p. 38d.
[5] Cf. Arrêt of 1675, ordinances of 10th June, 1728, and 23d July, 1742, Ed. et Ord. Vol. II.
[6] Titres des Seigneuries, I, pp. 235, 258.
[7] Ed. et Ord, II, 323.
[8] Henrion de Pansey, op. cit., I, pp. 9–10.

arrêt or ordinance bearing directly on the point; but the understanding seems to have been that when grain was both purchased and ground without the seigniory, the flour might be brought home and used without the necessity of any toll being paid to the seignior within whose fief it was brought. But where the grain was purchased outside the seigniory and brought home unground, it ranked on the same footing as grain grown within the seigniory. The general tendency was to look on the right of banality as a personal right. It was not because the grain had been grown within the seigniory that it was subject to the obligation, but rather because the habitant owning it lived within the seigniorial jurisdiction. Thus grain purchased within the limits of a seigniory by a person without was subject to the banal obligation, not in the seigniory within which the grain was bought, but in the seigniory in which he was a censitaire.

The right of banality carried with it the right, not only to prevent the erection of other than seigniorial mills within the seigniory, but even to compel the demolition of such after they had been erected. Instances are on record of the enforcement of these latter rights by ordinances of the intendant, proceedings which were attended with considerable hardship. For example, one of the inhabitants of the seigniory of Lauzon was, in 1698, given permission by the seignior to erect a mill, there being no banal mill in operation. Shortly afterwards the seigniory was sold and the new seignior at once ordered the mill closed, and on the refusal of the owner to comply, an intendant's ordinance was procured to enforce compliance.[1] Similarly the brethren of the hospital (Frères Charron) at Montreal had erected a small windmill to supply their own wants. This mill was, however, within the limits of the seigniory belonging to the Seminary of Sulpice, and the latter applied for permission to have the mill demolished. The intendant ordered this to be done in case the mill should be found to be infringing upon the seigniorial rights of the seminary.[2]

It will be seen, therefore, that on the whole the banal obligation did not in the period of the French régime bear very

---

[1] Ed. et Ord., II, 145.
[2] This arrêt is not printed. Its authenticity is vouched for by Chief Justice Sir L. H. Lafontaine (in his judgment of the special court, 1854, p. 334).

heavily upon the habitant. In the majority of cases the seignior was the loser. With the passing of the colony into the hands of Great Britain, however, this state of affairs was somewhat changed. By the treaty of Paris the seigniors were guaranteed full possession of their ancient privileges, and with the great growth in population which succeeded the change of colonial ownership these rights, not the least important of which was the droit de banalité, became much more valuable. In very many of the seigniories the banal mill was no longer capable of doing all the work required and it became the custom of the seigniors to allow the habitants to take their grist elsewhere upon the payment of a fixed sum.[1] To this necessity of paying two tolls the habitants soon began to strenuously object, but the newly established English courts in the cases which came before them invariably upheld the claims of the seigniors. Prominent among the decisions in this regard was that given in the case of Monk v. Morris,[2] in which the court distinctly declared that the droit de banalité existed in full force under the new régime; that it was enforceable even without the possession of specific title; that it applied to grain of all kinds; that seigniors could compel the demolition of any nonseigniorial mills erected within the limits of their seigniories. The seigniors in these matters had custom on their side, and precedents in the eyes of the English judges were all-powerful. In the eyes of the French intendants of the old régime precedents had counted for almost nothing when the course marked out by them conflicted with what was deemed the general weal. The legal result of the conquest was thus to deprive the habitants of one of their chief sources of protection.

During the whole of the first half of the present century the habitants of French Canada kept clamoring for the abolition of the seigniorial system with its various incidents, of which the droit de banalité now formed one of the most objectionable, and in 1854 their ends were obtained by the passing of the "seigniorial tenures abolition act,"[3] by the terms of which all

---

[1] It is interesting to note that in England, where the droit de banalité existed to some extent for a considerable time, it was frequently the practice of the townsmen within seigniorial jurisdictions to obtain exemption from its exercise by the payment of a sum in commutation. In this, however, they were not always successful, as, e. g., the case of the men of St. Albans (Cunningham, Growth of English Industry and Commerce, Vol. I), who had not obtained exemption as late as 1381.

[2] 3 Lower Canada Reports, pp. 17 et seq.   [3] 18 Vict., 6, III.

lands held en fief, en arrière-fief, en censive, and en roturier were converted into free and common socage holdings, due compensation being awarded to the seigniors, partly in the form of constituted rents upon the land and partly in funds from the public treasury. The questions regarding the extent of rights for which the seigniors claimed compensation was referred to a special court composed of all the judges of the superior courts.[1] In regard to the right of banality this court decided that while, according to the custom of Paris, this obligation was a contractual and not a prescriptive one, the arrêt of 1686 had abrogated this rule and made the droit de banalité a general right incidental to all grants en fief. The court, moreover, decided that the banal right extended to grist mills alone and did not apply to works (usines) of other kinds; that it applied only to such grain as was used by the habitant; and that lands which had been granted within the seigniories en franc aleu[2] were not subject to the obligation. Seigniors who had erected and operated mills were adjudged entitled to compensation, but those who had not done so prior to 1854 were deemed by the court to have forfeited any right to indemnity. The act of 1854 provided that expert valuators should visit all the seigniories and should "estimate the probable decrease (if any) in the net yearly income of the seignior resulting from his loss of his right of banality,"[3] taking into account the foregoing conclusions of the court; the sum so estimated to be apportioned upon the granted lands of the seigniory in proportion to their extent. A large sum was also set aside from the public treasury for the reduction of the sums so apportioned.

Thus ended the droit de banalité in Canada. There was, however, another species of banal right which, though by no means as important in the economic history of New France, calls for a passing notice. This was the droit de fours banalité, or right of oven banality. By the Coutume de Paris[4] the rights of oven and mill banality had been placed upon a similar basis; that is, a seignior could compel his censitaires to carry their dough to the seigniorial oven to be baked only if he had

---

[1] Decisions des Tribunaux, 1854, Vol. A.
[2] Some few freehold grants had been made by seigniors.
[3] 18 Vict. C., 3, Sec. VI, par. 3.
[4] Art. 71.

expressly stipulated for this privilege in his title deeds of concession. As far as I can ascertain there was only one banal oven ever erected in Canada, viz, that of M. Amiot, seignior of Vincelotte, but the obligation was inserted in many of the title deeds. In Raudot's dispatch of November 10, 1707, to which reference has already been made, the writer speaks of the right of oven banality as being one of the abuses of the colonial seigniorial system. He says:

> The seigniors have also introduced in their grants the exclusive right of baking or keeping an oven (fours banal), of which the inhabitants can never avail themselves, because the habitations being at great distances from the seignior's house where this oven must be established (which indeed could not be in a more convenient place for them wherever placed, since the habitations are very distant from one another), they could not possibly at all seasons carry their dough to it; in winter it would be frozen before it got there.

He continues:

> The seigniors, moreover, feel themselves so ill-grounded in claiming this right because of its impossibility that they do not exact it now, but they will at some future time make use of this stipulation to compel the inhabitants either to submit to it or redeem themselves from it by means of a large fine; in this way will the seigniors have acquired a right from which the inhabitants derive no benefit. This, my Lord, is what I call getting a title to vex them afterwards.[1]

Replying to this dispatch, the French minister, M. de Pontchartrain, advised that "with respect to the privilege of baking in the seignioral oven, all that is to be done is to follow and enforce the arrêt of 1686, by which that matter has been settled."[2] The minister was here in error, for the arrêt of 1686 had reference wholly to banal mills, and contained not a word about banal ovens. It had simply ordered that seigniors who claimed the right to erect banal mills should erect them at once or lose the right. The question of ovens had not yet arisen. This advice of the minister did not satisfy the colonial intendant, who, in reply, pointed out that what he wanted was the entire suppression of the right of oven banality, the impossibility of enforcing which, he declared, would become apparent when it was considered that "the inhabitants would have to carry their dough a distance of 2 or 3 leagues in the depth of winter."

---
[1] Raudot á Pontchartrain, 10th November, 1707; Correspondence Génerale, Vol. XXVI.
[2] Pontchartrain á Raudot, 13th June, 1708; Seigniorial Documents (1854), p. 9.

He says:

> It is a right which must be suppressed, because the inhabitants can derive no benefit from it, and the seigniors have established or wish to establish it only to oblige them to redeem themselves from it by condescending to pay in future some heavy charge. It is not so with the banal mills, the latter being always a benefit to the inhabitants who have not the means of erecting mills themselves, whereas the banal oven is a disadvantage, there being not one of them who has not an oven in his own house and as much wood as he wants to heat it.[1]

This correspondence is interesting as showing the valuable services rendered by the colonial intendants in the way of affording protection against unjust seigniorial exactions, a feature which was often sadly lacking in the conduct of the provincial intendants at home. It serves, further, to show that in the colony seigniorial rights were viewed by the authorities as resting upon a much more nearly utilitarian basis than in France.

The forebodings of the zealous intendant were, however, not well founded, for, with the exception of the single case given, the seigniors do not appear to have exacted either the right of oven banality or a money payment in its stead.

In France the seignior enjoyed the right to compel his censitaires to have their grapes pressed in the seigniorial wine press, and this privilege, especially in the southern part of France, was a very remunerative one. But in the colony there were no grapes and consequently no wine presses, seigniorial or otherwise.

It has been the practice of almost all writers on the history of Canada during the French régime to look upon the seigniorial system as one of the chief causes of tardy colonial development, and the action of the French Government in regard to the establishment of seigniorial mills has come in for especial criticism.[2] One writer goes to the other extreme, declaring that the banal right remained "almost a dead letter;"[3] but the fact is, as I have endeavored to show, that the French Government and its colonial representatives sought to develop the system of banal mills in the interests of the poorer habitants and not in the interests of the seigniorial proprietors. From the fact that royal edicts were found

---
[1] Raudot à Pontchartrain, October 18, 1708; Corr. Gén., Vol. XXVII.
[2] Cf. Parkman, Old Régime, p. 300–301.
[3] Goldwin Smith, Canada and the Canadian Question, p. 72.

necessary to force the seigniors to avail themselves of their privilege it is very probable that during the greater part of the French régime there would have been no mills at all had the milling interest been left to private enterprise. Profit was to be found not in agriculture nor the manufacture of the products of agriculture, but in the fur trade, and the French Government must, in all justice, be given the credit of having realized that, so long as that was the case, the habitants must be given all possible facilities for turning their agricultural products to account with the least possible expense to themselves. So long as the population was sparse the system of banal grinding was, to the habitants, convenient and inexpensive. The burden fell upon the seigniors and they, though by no means opulent as a class, were after all best able to bear it.

De Tocqueville has aptly remarked that the physiognomy of a government may be best judged in its colonies:

When I wish to study the spirit and faults of the administration of Louis XIV, I must go to Canada. Its deformity is there seen as through a microscope.

As regards many features of the administration of Canada during the old régime this remark is undoubtedly true, but as regards the respective attitudes of the Government toward the exercise of the *droit de banalité* in Old and in New France, a striking exception to De Tocqueville's generalization makes itself apparent.

VIII.—THE RESTORATION OF THE PROPRIETARY OF MARYLAND AND THE LEGISLATION AGAINST THE ROMAN CATHOLICS DURING THE GOVERNORSHIP OF CAPT. JOHN HART (1714–1720).

By BERNARD C. STEINER, Ph. D.,
LIBRARIAN, ENOCH PRATT FREE LIBRARY, BALTIMORE, MD.

VOL. XVIII, No. 2—THE DECLARATION OF MARYLAND AND THE LEGISLATION AGAINST THE TORIES DURING THE CIVIL WAR; DURING THE CHANCELLORSHIP OF HON. JOHN HARP, 1914–1797.

By BERNARD C. STEINER, PH. D.,

LIBRARIAN, ENOCH PRATT FREE LIBRARY, BALTIMORE, MD.

THE RESTORATION OF THE PROPRIETARY OF MARYLAND AND THE LEGISLATION AGAINST THE ROMAN CATHOLICS DURING THE GOVERNORSHIP OF CAPT. JOHN HART (1714-1720).

By BERNARD C. STEINER.

The Crown of England had governed the province of Maryland for over twenty years when Benedict Leonard Calvert, eldest son and heir of Charles, the third Lord Baltimore, "publicly renounced the Romish errors." Seizing upon the fact of a Protestant revolution in Maryland, which followed hard upon the Protestant revolution in England, King William had deprived the proprietary of his political rights over his palatinate. The change had undoubtedly been for the benefit of the province. It is true the old religious freedom had been succeeded by the establishment of the Church of England; but justice was probably better administered, education for the first time received attention, and the nepotism which was the inevitable consequence of regarding the province as the proprietary's private property had passed away with the change of government. The Roman Catholics chafed at their deprivation from the control of government, and even threatened to remove to the domains of His Most Christian Majesty of France,[1] but the Protestants were the majority and the heads of the great Protestant families formed the council.

The Church of England was established by law, but its adherents were like the squires of England—caring more for it as a national faith than as a rule of life. Scattered on their plantations, there were many planters whose adherence to the Church was merely nominal, and as the livings were in the presentation of the Government, the character of the clergy was often far from immaculate. Good men there were in both laity and clergy of the established church. Many good

---
[1] Scharf, 1, 390.

men were found in the Quaker meetings which Fox, Christison, and the other zealous missionaries had founded. In the Eastern Shore Makemie was introducing Presbyterianism into American soil. The Puritans of Providence had become Quakers or Anglicans, and the "Papists" were far more important from the prominence of their leaders than their number, which was less than one-tenth of the population of the province.[1] The settlements of the 40,000 people in the province were still along the rivers which empty into the Chesapeake Bay. Until the Germans from Pennsylvania drifted along the valleys of the Blue Ridge, after 1730, the back country was unsettled. Annapolis was the only town, and that had only a few hundred inhabitants. St. Marys City had died when the capital had been withdrawn. Almost everyone was engaged in the cultivation of tobacco, and this staple of the province was the common currency, being given in payment at the rate of 1 penny per pound. In England the assembly of the province was represented by Col. Nathaniel Blakiston, who, having been once a governor of Maryland, knew well its circumstances and possessed the full confidence of the provincials.

The proprietary had an agent in Maryland to attend to his private affairs and to watch that the governor and assembly did not encroach upon his lands and revenues. This position had been held by Charles Carroll, a prominent Roman Catholic, since Col. Henry Darnall had laid it down, about 1692. Carroll had acquired a "vast estate in this province by the office he formerly occupied and his practice in the law." We shall frequently come across him as the leader of the Roman Catholics.

Maj. Gen. Edward Lloyd, president of the council, had held the executive power in the province since the death of Governor John Seymour, on July 30, 1709. Head of a family which has remained prominent in Maryland until this day, he was drawing from the treasury two salaries, one as temporary governor and one as councilor. This, we shall see, gave rise to trouble. It was seldom that a locum tenens retained power for four years, as Lloyd did, but probably the last effort of the aged proprietary to regain control of his province caused the delay. In February 17$\frac{12}{13}$ Charles, Lord Balti-

---

[1] Scharf, 1, 370.

more, petitioned[1] that the government might be restored to him. Apparently the Crown was willing at first to commission his nominee, Col. John Corbet, and a commission was made out for him on June 27, 1711. Difficulties arose, however, for on July 21 Sir Edward Northey told the Queen that she has the right to appoint a governor, until satisfied that the proprietor can sufficiently secure the province against the enemy. For this or some other reason Corbet was never sent out. Meantime Benedict Leonard, the heir of the proprietary, "having for some years expressed to several his inclinations to become a member of the Church of England," finally "publicly renounced the Romish errors" and communicated in the Church of England.[2] It is usually supposed that this step was taken through mercenary motives, but we know too little of the circumstances to dogmatize upon the matter. The argument "post hoc, ergo proter hoc" is always dangerous. He had married, in 1698, Charlotte Fitzroy Lee, daughter of the Earl of Lichfield, and had by her four sons and two daughters. Their married life had not been happy, and they had separated some years before this date. The children were sent to "Popish seminaries abroad" by the grandfather and educated there at his expense. To Benedict Leonard the proprietary had given an allowance of £450 per annum until the son's change of faith, when this was withdrawn. Immediately after his becoming a member of the Anglican Church, Calvert sent for his children and placed them at Protestant schools in and about London.

Queen Anne, whose Protestant councilors recognized the value of gaining over the nobility, granted Benedict a pension of £300 per annum during the life of his father for the maintenance of his children, and appointed Capt. John Hart "captain-general and governor in chief of Her Majesty's province of Maryland." Hart's tributes to his patron and friend, that he was a "person of very distinguishing judgment" (June 1, 1715, council) and had a "gentle and sweet disposition" (lower house, April 23, 1716), are the only bits of description extant concerning the character of Benedict Leonard Calvert.

Of Captain Hart himself we know very little, save what the Maryland records show us. He was nephew to John Vesey,

---

[1] Scharf, 1, 377.   [2] Ibid., 379.

the Archbishop of Tuam, whose sister Lettice had married Merrick Hart, of Crobert, County Craven, Ireland. John and Lettice Vesey were children of the venerable Thomas Vesey, and thus Captain Hart came of a family long devoted to the service of the Episcopal Church of Ireland. Archbishop John Vesey was born at Cobrannel, County Derry, Ireland, and was successively Archdeacon of Armagh and Bishop of Limerick before he reached his highest dignity. He died in 1716, shortly after his nephew became governor of Maryland. Captain Hart had served for several years in Spain and Portugal during the wars of the Spanish succession. Beyond these facts his whole life, apart from the six years of his governorship, is almost a blank. How well he bore his honors here we shall see shortly. He was recommended for the governorship by Calvert upon promising to return to him £500 per annum out of the profits of the government. This seems a large amount, but we must remember the governorship of Maryland was an extremely lucrative post.

On January 1, 17¼, Lord Bolingbroke, the secretary of state, directed that a commission be drafted for Hart.[1] This was speedily prepared,[2] as were also a series of instructions to guide him in the conduct of his office.[3] With these in his possession, Hart started from England in the early spring and arrived in Maryland on May 29, 1714. The province had been nearly five years without a permanent governor, and this one might only spend part of the year in Maryland, if he chose to take advantage of the commission given him to reside at New York during the hot season.[4] The first year, at least (and, indeed, we have no evidence that Hart spent any length of time out of Maryland during his administration), the new governor found sufficient to occupy him in his province.

After publishing his commission and the treaty of peace with Spain, Hart at once summoned the provincial assembly, which met at Annapolis on June 22, 1714. It was the third session of this assembly, which had been prorogued in the preceding November. The upper house, or the "council in assembly," consisted of 12 members—wealthy planters, chief

---

[1] March 12, 17¼, the board of trade recommended that Tobias Bowles be made governor.
[2] Drafted January 12 and approved by order in council January 17.
[3] Drafted by board of trade January 29; approved by order in council January 31.
[4] Apparently he never did this.

men of the province. Among them were Edward Lloyd, Thomas Brooke, William Coursey, Richard Tilghman, William Whittington, Thomas Addison, Samuel Young, and Thomas Ennalls. The lower house, representing the 40-shilling freeholders, consisted of 50 members—4 from each of the 12 counties and 2 from the city of Annapolis. Robert Ungle,[1] of Talbot County, was the speaker, and among the prominent members[2] were Henry Peregrine Jowles and Kenelm Cheseldyne, of St. Mary; St. Leger Codd, of Kent; John and Thomas Purnell, of Somerset; John and James Mackall, of Kent; James Smallwood, of Charles; John Fendall, Solomon and Charles Wright, of Queen Anne; Matthew Tilghman Ward and James Lloyd, of Talbot, and Thomas Sprigg, of Prince George. As their clerk[3] they chose Thomas MacNamara, a lawyer, who was a connection of the Carrolls and was to be a great thorn in Hart's side.

The council had no committees, the house had four—on elections and privileges, on laws, aggrievances, accounts. The committees must have carried on their deliberations in the evening. The day was well filled with legislative sessions, for the delegates were always anxious to return to their homes as soon as public business could be dispatched. The quorum[4] was fixed each session, and was 18 or 22 members and the speaker. Two sessions of the lower house were held daily, lasting generally from 8 to 11 a. m. and from 1 to 6 p. m. The council was more leisurely, and met from 9 to 11 a. m. and 2 to 5 p. m.[5]

These meetings were not mere nominal ones. A member who did not appear at the second roll call in the morning lost his allowance, and one absent in the afternoon lost 5 shillings, unless satisfactory cause was shown for the absence.[6]

Questions of privilege come up from time to time, as at the session of 1719, when we find the delegates committing a

---

[1] July 3, 1714 (L. H. J.), he was unanimously chosen treasurer of the Eastern Shore.

[2] October 9, 1714, William Watts was ordered to show cause why he did not attend this session.

[3] L. H. J., June 30, 1714. Bernard White chosen assistant clerk and sworn to keep the secrets of the house.

[4] L. H. J., April 27, 1715; May 28, 1715.

[5] L. H. J., June 24, 1714. October 6, 1714, lower house, 9 a. m. to 4 p. m.; upper house, 10 a. m. to 4 p. m.; May 18, 1715, lower house, 7 to 11 a. m. and 1 to 6 p. m.

[6] L. H. J., June 24, 1714; L. H. J., October 5, 1714. Day's allowance forfeited if delegate "disappears."

man[1] to custody of the sergeant for failure to appear before the election committee, and unseating a member[2] for having been "unduly elected," because the sheriff was "very partial and remiss." The sheriff is fined £5 and ordered to make acknowledgment of his fault and thank the delegates for their lenity, which he accordingly does, while the expressions used by the unseated member in a petition to the governor are pronounced "indecent," and he is ordered to apologize.

A rather mysterious case of privilege is that of Tobias Pollard,[3] a delegate, whose petition to the council is stated by that body basely to affront the governor and the whole legislature, and to tend to create jealousies and distrust between the people and the governor and assembly. If the petitioner, they say, were a tool in the case alleged, what must be thought of representatives who are easily perverted by one single pernicious person to consent to the ruin of their country.

The day after the beginning of every session, both governor and assembly proceeded to St. Anne's Church and listened to a sermon delivered by Rev. Samuel Skippon, of that parish, or Rev. Henry Hall, of St. James Herring Run Parish, lying a few miles to the south of Annapolis.[4]

Each day, after beginning of the session, "was read what was done yesterday." When leave was given to bring in a bill,[5] it was read twice in the house where introduced and then sent to the other house. There the "paper bill" was also twice read, and if neither rejected nor amended was returned to the house whence it came, where it received a third reading and engrossing. The engrossed bill was then sent to the upper house and signed, usually at the close of the session, by the governor in presence of both houses. Money bills, of course, were introduced in the house of delegates. Relations with the Indians were peaceful, and the treaties with them were easily renewed. There were few aborigines in the province, and they were well inclined, though somewhat disturbed that their emperor, Astiquas, had left them and gone

---

[1] George Forbes, L. H. J., May 19, 1719.
[2] Peter Taylor, from Dorchester County, L. H. J., May 19, 1719. He was reelected.
[3] U. H. J., May 19, 1719.
[4] If the sermon was liked, a gratuity followed, vide L. H. J., July 18, 1716. L. H. J., June 1, 1719. Skippon given 2,000 pounds of tobacco for great charge in residing at the seat of government for the service of the public.
[5] Petitions to have bills brought in must be addressed to the "governor and council and to the "house of delegates." (U. H. J., June 24, 1714.)

to the northern Indians. The industrial condition of the province was very bad.¹ During the "consuming war" many industrious planters had suffered, and "the ruin of families in the province has sensibly affected the fortunes of much the greatest number of inhabitants."² Clothing was so difficult to obtain that manufactures had been set up in the province.³ Crops had been poor for several years, and this summer, through lack of rain, the tobacco crop was so burnt up that Hart felt encouragement must be given the planters.⁴ In his opening speech to the legislature Hart expressed the hope that "trade now being free and open, through conclusion of the treaty of peace, there is a fair occasion of restoring the province to its former flourishing condition." He promises to assist all he can therein, but the delegates fear "the lowness of the ebb to which this province is reduced" is such that, even in peace, without royal aid, Maryland will not be able to recover her lost circumstances nor prevent total ruin of the tobacco trade.

Hart advises the reviving of good laws and the making of new ones for their prosperity, and presents some directions of Queen Anne with reference to this last matter. These are eight in number:

(1) That due support and observance of religion be provided, and all debauchery, drunkenness, swearing, and blasphemy may be discountenanced and punished. On these points the house of delegates answers that the laws are sufficient, and if any justice of the peace is not executing them they hope Hart will remove him.

(2) That there be an act restraining inhumane severities by ill masters or overseers toward servants or slaves; that maiming Indians or negroes be punished with a fit penalty, and that the punishment for killing Indians and negroes be made death.

The house replies there is already a law concerning the treatment of slaves, which they will inspect and make more

---
¹ April 29, 1715, L. H. J., lower house, in answer to Hart's address speaks of "present poverty of this province."
² Hart's speech of June 22, 1714.
³ S. P. O., April 16, 1713.
⁴ Hart to board of trade, July 11, 1714. Board of trade later suggested that pitch tar and hemp be produced in Maryland and gave directions therefor. (U. H. J., April 21, 1720.)

stringent if necessary. The latter part of the direction they ignore.

(3) That stocks and public workhouses for the employment of poor indigent people be provided in convenient places, and that idle vagabonds be restrained from burdening the people.

With an air of satisfaction the house states that provision has been made for such persons as are objects of charity, and that vagabonds are so discountenanced by county courts that there are few or none of them in Maryland.

(4) That further supplies necessary for defraying the charges of government be raised; that the public arms be better preserved and kept ready fixed, and that storehouses be settled throughout the province for them. Accounts of disbursements, the Crown acknowledges, should always be laid before the assembly.

The lower house professes that they will always raise sufficient supplies and that, although provision has already been made for the care of the public arms, they will do more if necessary, being thankful for the Queen's interest in the matter.

(5) That for the better administration of justice a minimum property qualification be fixed for jurors.

(6) That creditors of British bankrupts who have estates in Maryland may obtain satisfaction of their claims therefrom.

The house says there are already statutes covering these two points.

(7) That no act be passed lessening or impairing the revenue.

The house rejoins that they would rather enlarge it, if they could, being good subjects.

(8) That no law be passed affecting the property of subjects in Great Britain, unless it be provided that it shall not go into effect until eighteen months after passage in time of war and twelve months in time of peace, to give opportunity to know the royal pleasure therein.

Hart began at once to serve the province, "employing his utmost efforts," and on the second day of the session suggested that the Virginia law with reference to frauds in tobacco might be worthy of adoption in Maryland.

The tobacco industry, which employed 100 ships and 1,600 seamen yearly, was most important,[1] and it was necessary that

---

[1] Scharf 1, 384, upper house approved of law and sent it to lower house (U. H. J., June 27).

"trash" should be separated from the good tobacco and that the annual output of 30,000 hogsheads should preserve its good reputation. In this case, as in many others, the assembly eventually adopted Hart's suggestion, but not at the session when it was made.

As important as any specific recommendation is one of Hart's, at this session, that letters be sent to the agent in England to get the opinion of some of the Queen's counsel and other eminent lawyers as to what statutes are in force in Maryland. The laws are dubious and uncertain, and, though Maryland claims part in common law, it is denied the benefit of some statutes, as plantations are not named therein.[1] The lower house feared that this matter would take up time, and as the season is inconvenient for a session, suggest that the question be postponed until next session.[2]

The committee on laws on June 25 reported that three of the temporary laws would soon expire and should be reenacted at this session: Those regulating the militia, the officers' fees, and for relieving the inhabitants from some aggrievances in the prosecution of suits at law. We note that these temporary acts were important ones. McMahon[3] notes the "general disinclination in Maryland to the enactment of permanent laws." He rightly attributes this to the fact that "no change could be made in such laws but by some new act of legislation requiring the proprietary's assent; and the assemblies were always unwilling to render themselves dependent upon his will for relief from a law which might be found, by experience, to be inconvenient or oppressive." "They preferred temporary laws," continues McMahon, "which would expire by their own limitation and might be reenacted if found salutary." Especially was this the case with revenue bills, as the colonists could thus control the purse strings.

The militia bill[4] produced little debate and continued the previous law, providing for the enrollment of the people in troops and companies under the control of a colonel appointed for each county.

---

[1] U. H. J., June 28, 29, upper house does not see how it can lengthen the session, but does not press matters (July 2).

[2] Ordinarily a vote to postpone until the next session was held equivalent to one to lay on the table or postpone indefinitely.

[3] P. 282.

[4] Act of 1714, ch. 111

The fee bill was a constant cause of friction between the proprietary and his officials on the one hand and the popular representatives on the other. A chronic disease lurked in the body politic which reached an acute stage when either side was obstinate. At each reenactment the house of delegates tried to reduce the emoluments of the officials, and the council, itself largely composed of the proprietary's officers, strove to have the old bill reenacted. The houses were fairly amicable now, but when the lower house sent up this fee bill, changed to suit their views, the upper house[1] protested. The new fee table would discourage men of good learning, integrity, and parts from accepting some of the inferior offices, and would also lessen and debase the state and dignity of the superior officers, who are most useful in the province and ought to be handsomely supported, according to their several characters, not only for the sake of their own merit and capacity, but also for the honor of the Government. Though they insist on the old fee table, the council state they are willing to suppress and punish any officer guilty of bribery, extortion, negligence, or any unfaithful misdemeanors, according to the utmost severity of law.

To this message the house of delegates[2] retorts that, in many particulars, the fees are exorbitant and tend to oppression of the people, and the bill now submitted provided decently for the support of judicial and ministerial officers, considering the multiplicity of their business. They remind the council that in 1709 the latter body had promised to join in a revision of the fee table, whenever a captain-general should come.

The council[3] refuse to recede and say the present fees are in no-way exorbitant, considering the little advantage the several officers have had from tobacco for many years. The lower house[4] yielded on the last day of the session and continued the old law, as they were desirous to keep good correspondence with the council and end the session with the same good temper with which it opened.

In reenacting the third temporary act, there was another controversy,[5] in which the lower house yielded again. From

---
[1] U. H. J., June 30.
[2] L. H. J., July 1.
[3] U. H. J., July 1; upper house also objected that the penalties against sheriffs were too heavy.
[4] L. H. J., July 3, act of 1714, ch. 5.
[5] Act of 1714, ch. 4.

the preamble of the act as passed we learn that, because of losses the provincials sustained from the closing of the continental markets during the late war and the capture of their tobacco cargoes by enemies at sea, the people have become "vastly indebted." Their "miserable and deplorable circumstances" are "much heightened and aggravated" by suits being brought against them in the provincial court at Annapolis, though they live in the remotest parts of the province. The result is truly dreadful. Many of the people "daily desert their habitations and remove themselves to plantations and colonies where they are far less serviceable to her sacred Majesty and her revenue of customs of tobacco." The act was designed to remedy this evil. As originally introduced in the lower house, it provided that claims under £100 or 30,000 pounds of tobacco shall be sued for in the court of the county where the debtor resides. The council[1] pointed out that by this bill, if a debt be of £250 and all but £19 have been paid, there is no remedy, for the provincial court takes cognizance of no sum under £20 and county courts of no debt over £100. The bill was amended,[2] to permit such action to be heard in county courts, and then seemed to be satisfactory. At this juncture, however, the lawyers of the province step in.[3] Charles Carroll, the proprietary's agent, claims that this bill infringes the prerogative by limiting the jurisdiction of the provincial courts, limits the power delegated Hart to erect courts, and opens a great gap for partiality, as it provided for the trial of causes amongst the debtor's relations and friends. The bill visibly attacks trade, for British merchants dealing with the provincials must employ twelve agents to attend the various county courts,[4] whose judgments are generally so erroneous that their jurisdiction should rather be diminished than increased. Then, too—and, I fancy, to Carroll and his brothers this was a most important argument—the bill will lessen the practice of lawyers in the provincial court and thus discourage learning.

---

[1] U. H. J., June 26.
[2] Section 5.
[3] Petition, June 29, hearing by upper house, June 30; similar act previously passed had not met with objection in England.
[4] Hart inquired, U. H. J., June 28, whether justice is well administered in county courts and whether some of them have not delayed business. The council says complaints have come of only one or two, but they agree that for future clerks should yearly send copy of "doggetts" with reason of continuance and adjournment contrary to law.

Philemon Lloyd, secretary of the province, added to these arguments others—such as that, by the constitution of England, the jurisdiction of the county court is very low because men of power often sway it, and that the debts were what caused people to leave the province, not the few 100 pounds of tobacco extra from the costs in the provincial court.

As a result of this hearing, the upper house reduced the maximum of the jurisdiction of the county courts to £20 or 5,000 pounds of tobacco. Hardly had the lower house agreed to this amendment, when their clerk, MacNamara, petitioned the council that a clause about attorneys' fees be added to the bill. The house of delegates sent up the bill engrossed without this clause, which the council recommended. That body stated that the merchants of England may justly complain that for want of due encouragement given attorneys they can not get fit persons to prosecute actions.[1] Finally, a conference committee was appointed and both houses agreed to its report, which was that when the total debt sued for or the balance recovered in the county court be over £10 sterling or 2,000 pounds of tobacco, the attorney should have 200 pounds of tobacco as fee. If a lawyer refuse to take a suit for this fee or ask more, he is to be fined 500 pounds of tobacco and be suspended from practice for a year.[2] This bill was found to be of such utility that it was successively reenacted down to the Revolution. In the discussion over this bill we first meet Carroll and MacNamara. In the light of future events, it seems strange to find the latter an official of one house and championed in his cause by the other. Carroll and Hart were already showing their opposition to each other. Early in the session[3] Carroll suggested retaliation, in the return for some unjust charges said to be laid by Virginia on Maryland tobacco. Hart replied that "if Virginia does wrong, it is no rule for us to walk by."[4] A week later Carroll was summoned before the council to state why a law should not be passed releasing Peter Sewell, who had lain three years in Calvert County jail for a debt of £80 to London merchants, clients of Carroll. We know not what Carroll said, but may judge that it was not very satisfactory, from the fact that, as

---

[1] U. H. J., July 1, 2. Some little friction here. House of delegates desires to avoid messages, which delay the session. Macnamara could not attend hearing against bill because of his duties as clerk.

[2] Not in bills as printed by Bacon.

[3] U. H. J., June 25, July 3.   [4] U. H. J., July 1.

soon as he left the room, it was unanimously resolved and made a standing rule that when a person is called by the council to give them satisfaction, such person shall only answer directly to the questions proposed without offering anything further. The fact was that Carroll led the Roman Catholics, and because of that fact could not be at peace with Hart, the head of the Protestants. The lower house showed its fondness for Hart at this session by passing without demur a bill granting him 3 pence per hogshead of tobacco exported[1] so long as he should continue governor. There was no governor's house, and this was to compensate him for being forced to rent a dwelling. Hart's salary came from one-half of the 2-shilling duty on each hogshead. Further remuneration his instructions forbade him to receive from the province. It will be noted that the fierce struggles of contemporary Massachusetts over the governor's salary are unknown here.

Hart made inquiry with reference to another part of the 2 shillings,[2] the 3 pence appropriated for arms and ammunition. This was a different tax from the 3 pence for public charges, which was appropriated by an especial bill. Lower house also made inquiry as to the expenditure of the ammunition tax and,[3] stating that they believe a considerable sum is due the public thereon, asked that it be spent in building storehouses. They make arrangements at once to have one built of wood on the public grounds at Annapolis.[4] Hart was already planning a much more substantial structure, and induced the delegates to postpone the work. Meanwhile the arms should be hung up in the county court-houses.

Just before the end of each session of the assembly the committee of aggrievances[5] was accustomed to make its report. This year it referred to two inveterate abuses—one, that several places of profit were in the hands of one person, which was bad for public business and a discouragement for qualified persons; and a second, that the places of profit and especially

---

[1] U. H. J., June 24, 25, 30. Hart expresses thanks. Council provided that it be sterling money; for if it were not, only traders would gain, Marylanders paying them in sterling, not ready money. Lower house (J., July 2) did not consider building a governor's house this session because of lack of time.

[2] U. H. J., June 28; U. H. J., October 7. Hart had accounts ready to lay before lower house. Act of 1714, chapter 1.

[3] L. H. J., July 2.

[4] Dimensions 25 by 10, and 10 feet pitch, planed within and without, and shingled. Capt. Thomas Dowra built it.

[5] L. H. J., July 3. On this day the assembly was prorogued.

sheriffs' offices are sold to the highest bidder, and therefore the inhabitants are aggrieved and oppressed, through the commissioning of persons incapable and of too mean capacities and estates. There had been an attempt to remedy this grievance in 1709, but it still remained. Sheriffs were always viewed with suspicion by the popular delegates. Though their term is for three years, by clandestine, secret, understood practices they continue in power many years.[1] They give too slender security for executing their duty, though they are in a manner county treasurers, on whose credit and good demeanor depend the credit and interest of all those who act in public stations.

Religious matters as well as secular demanded Hart's attention. He called together the clergy of Maryland in the month of June and propounded to them queries as to the state of affairs. Twenty clergymen[2] were present and told him that God is duly served throughout this province on Sunday according to the Book of Common Prayer, in every parish where there is an incumbent, and on holidays also in many parishes. The communion is duly administered, the churches are sufficient in number, though some should be put in better order. Most parishes give the clergymen[3] but a bare competency. Glebes are totally lacking in some parishes, while in others they are very poor. Most parishes have been furnished with parochial libraries through the energy of Rev. Thomas Bray, the former commissary; but some have never received a library, which is unfortunate. Every minister is principal vestryman in his parish, and all acknowledge the jurisdiction of the Bishop of London. The remote clergy ask that a councilor be deputed to inspect them. We are told that in the whole province none administer the sacred office without being regularly ordained. In every church there is a table of the prohibited degrees of marriages, and the provincial law against incest is severe. The clergy discountenance all immorality, but complain that the penalty against fornication is too light and that a law is needed against the "damnable sin of polygamy."

---

[1] Anne Arundel County had an especially objectionable sheriff. So had Cecil in 1720.
[2] U. H. J., June 26. Hawks's Eccles. Contribs., II, 137 and ff.
[3] A pleasant light is cast on the clergy by a vote of the assembly on October 8, 1714. Gabriel d'Emiliane, rector of Christ Church in Calvert County, went to England, and the other clergy promised to officiate for him, that his family might receive his salary. He was shipwrecked and died, and the assembly voted his widow his salary.

RESTORATION OF PROPRIETARY OF MARYLAND. 245

The Church of England had been established in Maryland in 1692, as soon as the Crown Government began, and was then supported under the law of 1704, providing for an annual tax of 40 pounds of tobacco for each taxable person. "Many worthy" persons were among the clergy, but Hart was forced to write to the Bishop of London[1] that "there are some whose education and profession are a scandal to their profession," and to express amazement that "such illiterate men came to be in holy orders." From the inefficient character of the Anglican clergy many proselytes were made by the Jesuits. This became so grave a difficulty that Hart meditated using his authority to constrain the Jesuits "from entering the houses of dying persons."[2] It was a difficult matter to get rid of the worthless clergymen. So inconclusive were the proceedings in one[3] instance that Hawks speaks of the establishment "as so profligate in some of its members that even the laity sought to purify it, and yet so weak is its discipline that neither clergy nor laity could purge it of offenders." Both the clergy and the governor asked for a bishop, but in vain.[4] In Maryland, as there was an establishment, the Society for the Propagation of the Gospel had no missionaries, and so there was absolutely no control of the incumbents. A commissary, or representative of the Bishop of London, could only "warn and rebuke," and so his influence was small.[5] Yet it seemed better to revive this office than to do nothing, and so in 1716, in answer to Maryland's request, two commissaries were appointed,[6] Rev. Christopher Wilkinson for the Eastern Shore and Rev. Jacob Henderson for the Western Shore.[7]

During the summer of 1714 Queen Anne died; but before the arrival of the dispatches, sent over in two special vessels, announcing the accession of King George, Hart had a second time called together the assembly.

An important matter is broached by Hart in his opening speech,[1] on October 5. Commands have been received from

---

[1] Hawks, II, p. 139.
[2] Ibid., II, p. 140.
[3] That of William Tibbs, U. H. J., May 4, 1715.
[4] Ibid., II, p. 142.
[5] Grambrall's Ch. Life in Col. Md., p. 79.
[6] Vide Hart's address, U. H. J., April 28, 1716.
[7] Hawks, II, p. 150.

[8] He gives another good piece of advice, that "moderate proceeding in debate will best facilitate business," and "if you dissent, please express yourselves so as to evidence clearness of judgment and not a warmth of resentment." Modern legislators might take this thought to heart to their advantage.

England to have the body of laws revised. Hart says this should be done as inexpensively as possible. The house of delegates respond they will try to perform this and all other duties to God, and that they would "take care to acquit themselves as dutiful and loyal subjects to our sovereign and a grateful people to your excellency and faithful servants to our country." These aims were faithfully pursued by the assemblies while Hart was governor. A conference committee was appointed in the matter of revision,[1] but just as they began their work unofficial news came from Philadelphia that Queen Anne had died. This, of course, put an end to the session, the only act passed being one for laying the public levy.[2] The crop had failed again, and on Hart's suggestion the house of delegates agree to his issuing a proclamation prohibiting the exportation of indian corn from November 10 to March 10. The council rejected the further suggestion of the delegates that no execution issue for a year.[3] The delegates said the tobacco crop was very short, and it would be a hardship to the people to go to jail because of that. The council was desirous of helping the "honest and well-meaning sort of people," but think this[4] repugnant to the laws of England and Maryland. On October 9 Hart prorogued[5] the assembly and then took "a long and expensive journey," possibly to Philadelphia, to assure himself of Anne's death. On October 27 he called his council together. He had no official news as yet, but London papers he had procured gave such definite information that, without delay, at noon on October 28, Prince George of Brunswick Lunerburg was proclaimed King at the statehouse. The militia made a handsome appearance; the governor and council took oaths to the new King; Hart gave a "generous and splendid entertainment," and orders were sent to each county to have the King proclaimed there.[6]

---

[1] L. H. J., October 8.
[2] Hart recommended Blakiston's salary of £100 be included therein, and says the province offered £120, but Blakiston took the smaller sum.
[3] L. H. J., October 8; U. H. J., October 9. There might be suffering if the winter was severe.
[4] U. H. J., June 3, 1715.
[5] For a month, but unless notified the members need not expect a session. Official notice did not arrive until October 29. Council decided then that nothing further as to proclamation was needed. Further official notice on April 13, 1715.
[6] U. H. J., June 13, 1715. Hart celebrated George's birthday also. Coun. Proc.

When the official notice came the council ordered the liturgy to be changed, and November 25 to be observed as a thanksgiving day, wherein all should abstain from bodily labor and repair to the parish churches, where the clergymen shall read service and preach suitable sermons. We must have no Jacobitism here in our province of Maryland.

On January 18, 17$\frac{14}{15}$, summons were issued for a new assembly, and the embargo was taken off the exportation of indian corn, since the winter had been mild and favorable and there was no more danger of a scarcity. There was danger, however, that Hart might not meet the assembly he had summoned. On January 29, 17$\frac{14}{15}$, Lord Stanhope, secretary of state, directed the board of trade to prepare a commission for Brigadier Richard Franks as governor of Maryland. This aroused Benedict Leonard Calvert at once, and on February 2 he petitioned the King to continue Hart, or if he objected to him, to appoint Calvert himself.[1] The King granted this petition at once, and two days later Stanhope directed the board of trade to renew Hart's commission.

On the 20th of the same month Charles Calvert, third Lord Baltimore, died, aged 85 years. The pretext for the suspension of proprietary government in the province having died with the Roman Catholic proprietary, a restoration was now confidently looked for; but before it came Benedict Leonard died, on April 5, 1715. His son Charles,[2] then about 16 years of age, became the fourth proprietary and fifth Lord Baltimore, and his guardian, Francis, Lord Guilford, at once petitioned for a restoration of the government. This was granted "to give encouragement to the educating of the numerous issue of so noble a family in the Protestant religion," and a new commission was issued to Hart, bearing date May 30, 1715. Lord Guilford was a man of Jacobite bearings, and, though he is said to have corresponded rarely with that party after 1714, he was arrested for complicity in the Atterbury plot. He then retired to Paris, joined the Roman Catholic Church in 1728, and died in 1734. Such an influence as his over the young proprietary must have given rise to some apprehensions among the more extreme Hanoverians and Protestants in Maryland.

---

[1] Scharf, 1, p. 379.   [2] Ibid., p. 380.

Meantime, the assembly of 1715 had met on April 26, completed its task, and adjourned on June 2. During this session, lasting little over a month, forty-nine laws were passed, covering the most important concerns of the province. McMahon's encomium on this session, the last ever held in Maryland under the royal government, is well deserved. He writes in 1830[1] that "the assembly of 1715 is as conspicuous in our statute book, even at this day, as the 'blessed Parliament' in that of England. A body of permanent laws was then adopted, which, for their comprehensiveness and arrangement, are almost entitled to the name of 'code.' They formed the substratum of the statute law of the province, even down to the Revolution; and the subsequent legislation of the colony effected no very material alterations in the system of general law then established. Several of the important statutes of that session are in force to-day." Such an achievement as this sheds splendid luster on Hart's administration, and he is entitled to a fair share of the praise.

This was a new assembly, and so, after the council had taken the oaths and the delegates had chosen as their speaker Robert Ungle, of Talbot County, both houses assembled in the council chamber and the governor approved of the speaker. The latter then, in due form, "disabled himself to undergo so weighty a charge." Hart, of course, refused to accept his declination of the office. Sometimes the speaker a second time,[2] "decently and submissively addressing himself to his excellency, offered several reasons disabling himself * * * and made humble suit to be discharged." In this case, too, Hart would "noways admit of" the declination, being well satisfied "of the speaker's skill and knowledge."

The next act in the drama follows English precedent, as do they all. The speaker asks that the delegates may have "freedom of speech, as of right and custom they have used, and all their ancient and just privileges and liberties allowed them, and that in anything he shall deliver in the name of the lower house, if he shall commit any error no fault may be imputed to the lower house, but that he may resort to them again for declaration of their true intent, and that his error may be pardoned 'and that as often as necessity' for the public good shall require it, he may, by the discretion of the

---

[1] History of Maryland, p. 282. [2] E. g., April 23, 1716.

lower house, have access to his excellency." When this was granted the assembly listen to the governor's speech.[1]

On this occasion Hart begins by referring to the new monarch's "lenity and consummate judgment" as of happy omen for his subjects.[2] The Protestant religion is safe because of George's "noble disposition, generous courage, and numerous offspring." So a "continued series of happiness" may be expected. It now behooves the assembly to revise the laws[3] and do it diligently, as long and frequent sessions are a grievous burden to the people. He kindly warns them not to expect too much, since "few things attain perfection at the first setting forth," and this "province is but in its infancy."

He makes two special recommendations that they should enact laws to promote "industry in your trafficks" and "useful learning, but these also are here in their tender age, so they must be nourished with time, care, and patience."

In trade he recommends that they try to reform abuses in the revenue from tobacco, but need not trouble themselves to pass an act encouraging the tobacco trade, as there is an English law thereon. Indeed, though the "inhabitants of the province with commendable industry cultivate tobacco, there are "spacious tracts of this fertile soil, especially on the Eastern Shore, not fitted for tobacco. There good hemp can be grown, and Maryland might "supply Great Britain with cordage forever."[4]

Few send their children to sea, and the result is that there is a want of seamen, which is a "mighty obstacle of trade." Hart advises that if a "certain number of the youth maintained by the several counties be yearly apprenticed as sailors, in a few years there would be a provincial navy."

The education of youth ever lay close to Hart's thought, and he is grieved that "many young men of admirable natural parts grow up without the least improvement of art." It is now "more than time to repair that neglect that is shown

---

[1] Mcnamara clerk again.

[2] He calls him "one of the greatest as well as one of the best of kings that ever yet swayed the British scepter."

[3] U. H. J., April 29, 1715. Hart sent down Anne's instructions to lower house May 7 (L. H. J.) Committee on laws resolve to send a "complete body" home May 9. Hart sends lower house message to hasten; they have done little in fifteen days. Hart's instructions concerning the passage of laws are given in U. H. J., May 15. They were often disregarded in the laws passed at this session.

[4] A hemp law was introduced by delegates, but council rejected it as it put composition for money too high (U. H. J., May 26).

to learning here," and it lies at the assembly's door "to lay a foundation for sufficient schools that your sons may increase in knowledge as well as in wealth and honor." If this be done "you will have blessings of the poor in this life, and posterity will praise you as benefactors." Alas! this blessedness was lost.

The year before[1] the clergy reported that the case of schools is very bad, good schoolmasters are very much wanting, and those professing to teach were very insufficient and rarely had the certificate from the Bishop of London as required by law.[2] At the abortive session preceding this one Hart had complained that it was "deplorable" that there was "no better provision for the education" of the numerous youth, there being but "slender support for one school on the Western Shore and none on the Eastern Shore of this so wide a bay."[3]

At this session the rector and governors and visitors of the free schools came to the assembly with a petition.[4] They complain that the funds for free schools are "so insufficient to answer the pious design of having a free school in each county that they can keep up only one such school—King William's School, in Annapolis—and this with difficulty." They also ask that their quorum[5] be reduced, since they live so far from each other, and that their title be confirmed in a piece of property in Annapolis.[6] The two latter requests are attended to, but their urgency to obtain more funds is ignored.

The libraries, which Rev. Thomas Bray established in several parishes, were for reference; that at the capital, the great Provincial Library of 1,100 volumes, the remnants of which collection are in St. John's College Library to-day, was for circulation. The books were taken out, and, alas, not always brought back, so that when Hart had an inventory made several were missing, and the assembly resolved that the sheriffs publish notices commanding persons having books

---
[1] U. H. J., June 26, 1714.
[2] On May 3, 1715. Hart tells council he will insist on schoolmasters taking oaths and showing certificates of good capacity before he will give them licenses to teach and will obtain lists of schools and school teachers from the county courts.
[3] U. H. J., Oct. 5, 1714.
[4] U. H. J., May 13, 1715.
[5] Act of 1715, ch. 4.
[6] July 6, 1697, Anthony Workman gave £150 sterling for a house on a lot which Governor Nicholson gave to King William's School on condition he might use the house for life and then leave it to the school. The "Kentish Ordinary" was kept there. Workman was dead. His heirs refused to surrender it.

belonging to "the Public Library" to bring them to Rev. Mr. Skippon, who, as rector of St. Ann's parish, Annapolis, was ex-officio librarian.

In the preparation of the laws of this session there was engaged one of the first famous American lawyers, Andrew Hamilton, who achieved most of his fame while practicing his profession at Philadelphia. He was at this time a resident of Kent County, and had thence been elected to this assembly. He was absent from the opening of the session[1] on account of being in attendance as counsel at the supreme court in Pennsylvania. He appeared on May 4, after the sergeant-at-arms had been sent for him, and was at once added to the committee on laws. How much of the excellence of the session's work may be attributable to his efforts we know not. It is interesting to know that his greatest fame probably came to him from an acquaintance he made in Maryland. John Peter Zenger, a young printer, came from New York, at the conclusion of his apprenticeship, to try his fortune in Kent County. In 1720 he petitioned, with apparent success, for leave to print a "body" of the session laws for each county, and he was naturalized by the assembly in the same year.[2] He went back to New York and, when accused of libel some fifteen years later, sent for the lawyer, whom he had doubtless known in Maryland, to act as his counsel. How brilliantly Hamilton filled that position is known by all.

The first act[3] passed was one for the recognition of George I as King. The assembly represented the Protestant party, and so this was easily passed and was loyal in tone.[4] Indeed, in their answer to Hart's opening speech, they thanked him for his most expeditious "proclamation of the King," and for "his extraordinary zeal and diligence for His Majesty's service."[5]

At this time there were intimations of lurking Jacobitism, and "secret insinuations" were uttered that George's seat was in danger.

---

[1] L. H. J., May 2, 4, 1715. Fined 45/, costs for absence. Men who went home without permission were also fined. (L. H. J., July 28, 1716, and May 8, 1718.) The delegates, however, were privileged from arrest for twenty days after adjournment of the assembly. (L. H. J., May 3, 1718.)
[2] Act of 1720, ch. 18.
[3] Act of 1715, ch. 1.
[4] At Hart's suggestion. Introduced in council probably as the more dignified body. L. H. J., May 4, passed both houses day of introduction.
[5] L. H. J., April 29, 1715. June 3, 1715.

The address to Hart, adopted at the close of the session,[1] breathes a loyal spirit and also pays a high tribute to Hart's character. He had been with them nearly a year, and they found him "affable, kind in conversation," "prudent in the management of public affairs," "careful to consult the ease and benefit of the people," and "scrupulous to maintain the prerogative and just rights of the Crown." These were no feigned words. John Hart was one of the best colonial governors.

Besides the recognition act, the one legalizing proceedings taken in Queen Anne's name after her death,[2] and one repealing all laws which had been revised at this session,[3] there were forty-six chapters in the act of 1715. Of the one relating to education we have already spoken. The establishment of religion was not changed, but provision[4] was made when there is no incumbent in a parish the poll tax should be used for repairing, completing, furnishing, or even building a church, and if not needed therefor to be applied to the purchase and stocking of a glebe for the use of the minister. This we see is evidently a result of the meeting of the clergy in 1714, and we shall note other instances where an act recommended to one session is passed at a future one. Evidently the legislators of the province were not to be hurried in their deliberations.

Another act[5] "for the better security of His Majesty * * * and for extinguishing all hopes of the friends" of the "pretended Prince of Wales," provided a form of an oath of abjuration to be taken by all public officers, and especially by vestrymen, in lieu of the former oaths. The Protestant party is beginning to cut off Romanists from the privileges they had enjoyed.

The only other religious matter[6] which engaged the attention of the assembly was a petition of the Quakers to the council stating that the "Yearly meetings" at West River and Tred Haven, which they had held for about forty years for

---

[1] L. H., J. June 3, 1715.
[2] Act of 1715, ch. 8.
[3] Act of 1715, ch. 49. Most of these are revised laws. Act of 1719, ch. 16, specifies what laws were now repealed.
[4] Act of 1715, ch. 24, repeals 1704-12. Taxables were male persons, except Anglican clergymen and paupers and female slaves above 16 years of age. Slaves past labor might be so adjudged by the county court and then ceased to be taxables. Act of 1715, ch. 45, sec. 5.
[5] Act of 1715, ch. 30, repeals 1704-11.
[6] U. H. J., May 10, 1715.

the worship of Almighty God, had been disturbed by the sale of liquor near by. From this "arise drunkenness, fighting, hooping, hollowing, swearing, cursing, wrestling, horse racing, and abundance of wickedness and immoralities." This must be stopped at once, and henceforth let no liquor be sold, save at licensed ordinaries, nor any sports be carried on within 2 miles of either meeting house. Let the sheriffs see that order is preserved. Sheriffs were always disliked and the committee of aggrievances state that sheriffs take advantage of the law which decrees the date when money shall be paid them, but not when they shall pay it out again to the public creditors. In some cases they will not pay it out without reward.[1] This is scandalous, and when the committee of laws examine into it they find not only this but other ill practices need to be guarded against, and so a comprehensive act is passed "for the direction of sheriffs in their offices."[2] Annual appointment by justices of the peace is provided for the constables and the other executive officers of the law, and the duties of their office are defined.[3] It would seem that sheriffs were not the only public officers who had abused their positions. Early in the session[4] Hart calls the attention of the council to "embezzlement" of records, which had taken place in several counties, and recommends that a law be passed against it. The assembly replied with a provision[5] that conviction of "embezzling, impairing, razing, or altering" any record, whereby a freehold should be defeated or injured, should involve the terrible punishment of forfeiture of all property, standing in the pillory for two hours, and loss of both ears.

The election of future assemblies took a considerable part of the attention of this one, and the act now passed[6] was the basis of Maryland's electoral system for nearly a century. It changed little the previous system of one poll for each county, conducted by the sheriff in English fashion, and continued the limitation of suffrage to 40-shilling freeholders,[7] but it

---

[1] L. H. J., May 4, 1715.
[2] Act of 1715, ch. 46, repealing previous laws, 1704–57, 1709–6, 1713–1.
[3] Act of 1715, ch. 15.
[4] U. H. J., May 1, 1715.
[5] Act of 1715, ch. 11.
[6] Act of 1715, ch. 42, reenacted after the restoration of the proprietary act of 1716. (Steiner Citizenship and Suffrage in Maryland, p. 25.)
[7] It provided that only resident freeholders could vote, and not all persons having a visible estate in the county. (L. H., January 12; U. H. J., May 23, 1715.)

added a clause imposing a penalty on a qualified voter who did not exercise his franchise. This compulsory voting law was a suggestion of the upper house.

An attempt was made to limit the number of members to two for each county and one for Annapolis.[1] This was partly through economy, to reduce the charge of the assembly. Each councillor received 110 pounds of tobacco per diem, and each delegate 100 pounds of tobacco and itinerary charges[2] besides. At first the delegates seemed favorably inclined to the lesser number, but the lower house finally rejected the plan, and passed the bill with the old number of delegates retained. It is possible the delegates feared a smaller body might be more pliable to outside interest, and so refused any compromise[3] in the matter. The militia law was re-enacted, and in connection with it we find a proposition from Hart to fine those who refuse to accept commissions and are absent from training. The delegates agree to fine absent officers but say there is no use to fine those refusing to accept commissions, since so few do so.[4]

Evidently military titles were popular at that early day. The danger of war was by no means an imaginary one, and great care was taken that the public arms[5] be not embezzled by their custodians. The colonels of militia, the chief military officers in each county, were ordered to report the condition of the arms[6] since 1709, and Hart now broaches[7] the project of building a permanent stone house at Annapolis, which he was to see realized. After the adjournment he brings the matter before the council, stating that a well-built powder house might be useful for other occasions, particularly as a council chamber, and "to receive the country, as well as strangers, on occasions so requiring it, especially in time of assemblies." He recommended that they build such a house from the proceeds of the 3 pence per hogshead for arms, and pay 10 shillings, or some other fit sum, as ground

---

[1] Hart's instructions urged him to do this.
[2] Apparently an abuse had grown up and law committee said expenses for boats and ferriages ought to come out of itinerary charges. (L. H. J., May 12, 1715; May 18, 21.)
[3] Upper house suggested three members from each county. (J., May 23, 1715.)
[4] L. H. J., May 24.
[5] Three pence of the 2-shilling tax went therefor by act of April 30, 1679.
[6] Col. John Contee had received arms. In 1706 he had died, his widow Mary had since married Philemon Hemsley, and they were rigidly called to account for the arms. (U. H. J., May 10, 11; L. H. J., May 11, 9, 1715.)
[7] U. H. J., May 3, 4, 1715.

rent for the needed land. At the next session the upper house, having approved of Hart's suggestion, recommended to the delegates that a handsome house be built for the public arms, and that a council room be included in the plan, and also an apartment to "receive the country and strangers that may resort to his excellency the governor on any public occasions."[1] The lower house agreed to this plan, and £500 sterling were appropriated therefor. The building was erected forthwith. In 1718 it was reported as completed[2] and well done, so that the assembly agreed to pay Thomas Cooke, the contractor, £100 more than the contract called for.

The laws with reference to the Indians were revised.[3] The committee of aggrievances recommended that careful men be appointed in each county to hear and determine disputes between whites and Indians, and the bill gave power to the governor to appoint such. Other provisions forbade the sale of liquor to Indians, the kidnapping and sale of friendly Indians out of the province, and endeavored to prevent the frequent false rumors about Indian risings. While the assembly was in session, an apparently groundless one caused the dispatch of one of the delegates to the frontiers, to encourage the inhabitants and learn what the truth was.[4]

Laws were amended and reenacted[5] prohibiting the transportation of any person from the province without a pass, lest servants, felons, and debtors might escape from the jurisdiction, and laying a heavy duty on the importation of rum, negroes, and Irish servants. These duties were rather for the purpose of limiting importation than for revenue, and that on Irish servants had a distinctly religious purpose, "the prevention of importing too great a number of Irish Papists."

The slave code was thoroughly revised[6] and regulations were made for the conduct of masters toward those under

---

[1] U. H. J., August 8, 9, 1716.
[2] U. H. J., May 6, 1718.
[3] Act of 1715, ch. 16, L. H. J., May 4, 1715.
[4] U. H. J., May 17, 30, 1715; L. H. J., May 17, 31, 1715. Gifts were made to friendly Indians. These last had reported they had seen "naked Indians." It is possible the latter may have been Tuscaroras.
[5] Act of 1715, ch. 19, 34.
[6] Act of 1715, ch. 46. A petition was presented that a white woman marrying a negro be made slave for life, but the old law was retained, providing that she be bound out for seven years (U. H. J., May 3, 1715). The committee of aggrievances thought that law should be made against negroes gathering without leave of masters. House says law already provides against it (L. H. J., May 16, 17, 1715; U. H. J., May 23, 24, 1715). Heavy penalties were put on those aiding runaway servants.

their control, so that there should not be undue cruelty. For example, only 10 lashes could be given, for any offense, by a master; but, if he carried a peculiarly disobedient or wicked slave to a justice of the peace, that the latter could order a greater penalty, up to 39 lashes. The council proposed that manumission be limited, as in Virginia. Against this the delegates nobly protested. To restrain manumission is to discourage probity of well-deserving negroes or mulattoes, as their masters can not otherwise recompense them.

Other important acts with reference to property were those concerning bounds of lands,[1] an important matter with the rough surveys of the day, concerning conveyance of landed property,[2] and concerning rights of persons to town lands.[3] The whole testamentary law of the province, which was administered by the commissary-general in the prerogative court at Annapolis and by the deputy commissaries in the counties, received a careful amendment and was reenacted.[4]

The tobacco trade, of course, received attention.[5] Early in the session Hart proposed that all tobacco be shipped between October 1 and May 10 in each year, as the longer it hangs the more it loses scent, freshness, substance, weight, and goodness in every respect, and finally only the shape and nothing of the substance of the tobacco remains. Further, the limitation of time of shipment will quicken trade and cheapen freight. The council suggested a conference committee from two houses. This met at Hart's own house, and to it he proposed his plan. He added that the backwardness in preparing the tobacco for shipment was largely due to the delay in getting cask timber properly seasoned and ready to be set up, and this delay of the coopers was largely because of the uncertainty of their pay. Would it not be well to have a law appointing a time yearly to get such cask timber ready and for the coopers to set it up, and granting them the right to take their pay by execution? "The worm bites more" the

---

[1] Act of 1715, ch. 45, U. H. J., May 28, 1715. Proposed in council. Delegates thank them for proposing so useful a law.

[2] Act of 1715, ch. 47. Committee of aggrievances complained that fines and recoveries had been proposed in provincial court to cut off entails. The house said this is a grievance and tends to ruin of many (L. H. J., May 15, 17, 1715).

[3] Act of 1715, ch. 32.

[4] Act of 1715, ch. 39. Clause was inserted preventing the commissary-general from taking fees from estates less value than £30 (L. H. J., May 15, 17, 1715).

[5] U. H. J., May 1, 6, 1715, L. H., May 3, thanked Hart for offering to join in conference and have it at his house.

ships which are forced to stay, and so the sloops, flats, and other craft which carry Maryland's staple would find the proposed law highly beneficial. Under it they would receive a timely cargo, and further, if ships drop in all the year round, the tobacco buyers will purchase no more of it at a time than just from hand to mouth, while if the whole crop went to market at once, the buyers would purchase a whole year's stock at once, and thus the price would always be kept up. Thus argued the governor, and the conference accepted all his plan, save that they decline to fix any date by which the tobacco should be ready. In the pressure of other affairs, however, the matter seems to have been laid aside.

An act was passed[1] for securing merchants' tobacco, to prevent alteration of marks on hogheads and to forbid the packing of "any frost-bitten, trashy, ground leaves, or small, dull scrubs, or any stalks, stems, wood, stones, dirt, or any other manner of trash, or old, decayed tobacco in the inward parts of such hogsheads, when the generality of such tobacco as shall be packed in the outward parts is good, sound, and merchantable." "Small, dull, scrubby tobacco, and ground leaves" might be packed separately and labeled so as not to impose on purchasers. Tobacco being the great source of revenue for government,[2] the act ascertaining the gauge of hogsheads and for laying impositions on tobacco per hogshead, for the support of government, was always an important one, especially as it included a composition in tobacco for the lord proprietary's alienation fines and quit rents. Another important act was one requiring all weights and measures used in the colony to be yearly compared with the standards kept by the justices of each county, that tobacco and other things might be given in full quantity and weight.[3]

While the assembly was sitting came news of the death of the old Lord Proprietary, and a letter from Benedict Leonard, the new lord, announcing to Hart that the King is about to restore him the government. Hart,[4] after taking advice of the council, announces these things to the delegates[5] and requests them to provide an act to take the

---

[1] Act of 1715, ch. 22.
[2] Ibid., 1715, ch. 38.
[3] Ibid., 1715, ch. 10.
[4] U. H. J., May 30, 1715; L. H. J., June 1.
[5] Lower house thanks Hart for news, and expresses joy that proprietary is Protestant.

place of the payment of 12 pence per hogshead of tobacco,[1] which had been given to Charles for his life in return for his receiving tobacco at 2 pence per pound, in lieu of quit rents and alienation fines. The house passed the gauge act we have noticed above, granting a duty of 18 pence per hogshead.[2] The old duty was to be continued for four months more.

An old quarrel was recalled for a moment this session. Sir Thomas Lawrence, who had been secretary of the province twenty years before, had claimed that the ordinaries' fines, or profits from saloon and hotel licenses, as we should say, belonged to the secretary. The popular party and Colonel Blakiston claimed they belonged to the country. Baltimore said he had given them to a relation when he had the government, and would reclaim them were the government again in his hands. Hart thought they belonged to the Crown,[3] and asked the assembly to find out what is their amount. He stated he was willing to have the proceeds used for building a governor's house. The council and lower house agree that they would be willing by law to devote them to this purpose, but the lower house say they are not willing to appropriate additional money therefor for two reasons: They wish, first, to know how much the fines are, and secondly, the circumstances of the province are too low. Hart writes he is content to share their present circumstances, though he thinks it for the honor and interest of the province to have a governor's house.[4]

The house of delegates, as usual, had complaint to make of the revenue officers,[5] who are too many in number, and take extravagant salary from the 3-pence duty for arms while they should be paid from the fines and forfeitures. Hart responds that he will have the number of receivers reduced to one, and will see that salaries are taken from the proper source.[6]

---

[1] Hart told them that Benedict Leonard was not satisfied with the old duty, vide U. H. J., July 29, 1716.

[2] Act of 1715, ch. 19. In 1718, the upper house raised the question as to the disposition of this tax (U. H. J., May 5). Carroll is summoned and says Benedict Leonard knew nothing of the law. Carroll sent the money to England. Carroll was authorized by Benedict's executor to take all his personal estate in the province and took a half year's rent as consideration for sending the money to England (L. H. J., May 7).

[3] U. H. J., May 16, 19, 25, 26, 1715.

[4] The delegates offer to pay Hart's rent. He asks that they appropriate for repairs to his house.

[5] U. H. J., May 15, 1715.

[6] He investigated the matter and reported at a later session.

RESTORATION OF PROPRIETARY OF MARYLAND. 259

Here, as ever, we see both parts of the government working together for the public good.

The procedure of the courts received much attention. Laws were passed establishing[1] court days in the counties, providing[2] that execution be suspended during the summer and autumn months that people might not be imprisoned to the ruin of their crops, regulating[3] the drawing of jurors, directing the manner of suing out attachments,[4] determining the period of limitations for various kinds of actions,[5] providing what shall be good evidence to prove foreign and other debts,[6] and permitting the taking of special bail.[7] Other statutes authorized speedy recovery of small debts before a single justice of the peace,[8] rectified the ill practices of attorneys and fixed a table of fees to the attorney-general and lawyers,[9] arranged for the better administration of justice in the courts,[10] for the more speedy recovery of debts, for preventing officials to plead as attorneys in their courts, and for the collection of amercements.

It was decreed what damages should be allowed upon protested bills of exchange,[11] and several acts for the benefit of poor debtors were passed.[12] One of these was for the relief of the "languishing prisoner," Peter Sewell. Following the rule that no private act be passed without hearing those opposed, the council again had Charles Carroll before it.[13] He opposed the relief of Sewell, saying he mortgaged two negroes several times over and, therefore, is least worthy of commiseration. Hart had been for some time interested in this case and generously repeated a previous offer to give £5 toward making up Sewell's debt, if his creditors have no compassion. Let us hope Sewell, when released, was more care-

---

[1] Act of 1715, ch. 14.
[2] Ibid., ch. 33.
[3] Ibid., ch. 37.
[4] Ibid., ch. 40.
[5] Ibid., ch. 23.
[6] Ibid., ch. 29.
[7] Ibid., ch. 28.
[8] Ibid., ch. 12.
[9] Ibid., ch. 48.

[10] Act of 1715, ch. 41. The justices of Dorchester sold the amercements to the sheriffs for several years at a considerable loss. This is a grievance, say the delegates, as it not only lessens the public credit, but also gives power to the sheriff to burthen the people with several fees (L. H. J., May 4, 1715.) Lower house asks what has been done with amercements in provincial court. Hart says they were given to clerk of council, but small in amount. This explanation was satisfactory.

[11] Act of 1715, ch. 7.

[12] L. H. J., May 15, 16; act of 1715, ch. 17, 20, 21.

[13] U. H. J., May 15. Council May 2, on petition of John Leatherwood, an old and poor inhabitant of Baltimore County, who has been a "good liver," recommend justices of that county court to discharge him from paying public levy.

ful in his future financial dealings. Other private acts[1] were passed, though in general the assembly declined to interfere when there was a remedy in the courts.[2] One of the attempts to secure the passage of a private bill, brought in what looked like an attempt to bribe a member of the council, to whom the applicant wrote that he would reimburse him for any trouble[3] and "would have sent money, but it is a thing a body can not trust everybody with." Two other questions of privilege came up at this session. Hart complained to the council that Mayor Josiah Wilson, delegate for Prince George's, deserved public censure for scurrilously reflecting on him and a second delegate by calling the latter the governor's agent.[4] At another time the governor said one of the council had broken his oath to keep secret its proceedings. In neither case was any answer made.

Revised laws were passed concerning adultery and fornication, cursing, and drunkenness,[5] and for the speedy trial of criminals.[6] The law for ascertaining the height of fences and redressing the great evil arising from the multiplicity of useless horses that run in the woods[7] caused some discussion,[8] but was finally passed. The jealousy of the northern province was shown by an act prohibiting importation of grain, bread, beer, and horses from Pennsylvania.[9]

Such was the legislation of the assembly of 1715, a noble legacy from the royal to the proprietary province.[10] Twice before, in 1692 and 1704, the laws had undergone revision, but neither revision remained long in force. This work of Andrew Hamilton and his colleagues remained the law, with little change, till long after the State of Maryland succeeded the province.

After the adjournment of the assembly[11] Hart called his council together. Grave tidings had come. There was now no question of checking illegal trade with the French, of seeing

---

[1] Act of 1715, ch. 2, 3, 5, 6, 35.
[2] E. g., U. H. J., May 4, 1715.
[3] L. H. J., May 9.
[4] U. H. J., May 20, 30.
[5] Ibid., ch. 27, 34.
[6] Ibid., ch. 26.
[7] Ibid., ch. 31.
[8] U. H. J., May 26, 27; L. H. J., May 27.
[9] Act of 1715, ch. 18.
[10] In this year the merchants of Maryland sent an address to the Crown that Hart's administration had been to the general satisfaction.
[11] A curious petition of two men against the inhabitants of Queenstown, in Queen Anne County, remained unanswered. They complained of oppression because hogs and live stock are raised on the lots in that town, which is so small that the animals trespass on the petitioners' lands. (L. H. J., July 30, 1716.)

that the vessels clearing from Maryland provided themselves with Algerine passes so that they might be safe from the fierce pirates, or of fixing fees in chancery. News had come from Governor Spotswood, in Virginia,[1] that the terrible Tuscarora war had broken out in South Carolina and two hundred families had been massacred at Port Royal.[2] Spotswood sends aid to South Carolina and asks that Maryland do the same and watch her own safety. The council say they can spare no arms; all must be saved for our frontier, whither Hart agrees to go in person. A month later[3] the council met again. The Potomac Indians were said to have gone out. Arms were ordered to be sent to the frontier counties of Prince George, Baltimore, and Cecil. Blakiston[4] was instructed to buy £500 worth of arms and ammunition. A special levy on the province was decided to be made by Hart and any three of the council, if they see need.[5] Lead and powder in the possession of tradesmen should be at once condemned for the public use and lodged with the "colonels."[6] After another month[7] the excitement had calmed down. Spotswood writes again there is no damage from the Virginia Indians. He wishes Maryland, Virginia, and North Carolina would raise 1,500 men and attack the Indian towns. Virginia has already sent 300 men to South Carolina, in return for which South Carolina pays each volunteer and sends a slave to work in his place. May not Maryland make a similar contract? Maryland declines to do so, and the danger dies away. No other Indian trouble disturbs the administration.

Hart was a man of infirm health. He complains of ill health in the fall after his arrival in the province,[8] and is severely ill when Bladen transmits for him the proceedings

---

[1] Vide Coun. Proc., April 13, 1715.
[2] His autograph letter is preserved in the council proceedings. Spotswood had never met Hart.
[3] July 12, 13, 1715.
[4] May 31, 1717, Blakiston reported he had spent £257 10s. 4d. for arms and had saved the rest of the appropriation for future use, as arms were so high at the time of the great rebellion.
[5] The governor had a certain discretionary power over the country stock of arms and ammunition, in case of exigency, e. g., May 31, 1717, he reported having given the necessary amount to several vessels to protect them from pirates.
[6] L. H. J., July 18, 1716. Richard Ledger, of Prince George, is paid for a horse which died in removing arms to oppose the threatened attack from Indians.
[7] August 24, 1715.
[8] Letter of September 14, 1714.

of the assembly and the report of the Indian war. When he recovered he found his position a perplexed one. A letter had come from Lord Guilford announcing that Benedict Leonard was dead and that he was guardian of the young Lord Charles.[1] As such he had nominated Hart "lieutenant and chief governor of the province," and the nomination having royal approval, the commission and instructions would follow at once. They came, but brought no official intimation that the government was restored to the proprietary. The council advise Hart to pay no attention to the new commission until this preliminary be positively known. For four months the doubt continued, and the sessions of the courts of chancery and appeals were postponed until it could be known under whose commission they could sit.[2] Finally the news came, and the council were sent for at Christmas time. The weather was violent and hard and deep snow lay on the ground when the members met on the evening of December 27. The next day at noon, in the public court-house, the accession of the new proprietary was proclaimed and Hart's new commission read.[3] The assembly was dissolved and a new one summoned. Thus the rule of the proprietary was restored over Maryland, though much of the former authority had been shorn away. Theoretically, the second Charles had the same rights as the first; practically, the twenty-five years since the grandfather had ruled had made a vast difference. An unknown youth was at the head of affairs. The people seemed to have cared but little for the change,[4] and, save for the religious quarrels which now arise, the course of events moves on precisely as before. The Protestants knew that the young proprietary was of their faith, but were slightly apprehensive lest he might lean too much toward the adherents of his grandfather's faith. The Romanists were hopeful that they might gain greater influence and be restored to their position in old times, before the proprietary lost the province.

For the time being little difficulty on this score appeared. The new assembly met[5] on April 24, 1716. Matthew Tilgh-

---

[1] Council proceedings August 24.
[2] Council proceedings September 3, 1715.
[3] Council records lost from this on. As early as May 19, 1719, Hart told the council that thirteen months' proceedings of that body while Bladen was clerk were missing.
[4] McMahon, p. 280.
[5] MacNamara chosen clerk lower house and approved by Hart. Records of upper house for this session are lost.

man Ward, of Talbot County, was chosen speaker, and, according to custom, "decently and submissively disabled himself to undergo so mighty a charge," but finally accepted it. Hart's opening speech refers to the new government and to his personal knowledge of the "gentle and sweet disposition" of the young lord. He hopes that the province will be happy under the new régime.

The new government made it necessary to change the style of all laws, and Hart showed his thoughtfulness and kindness of disposition by asking the assembly to "make the change as light as possible to the people, for I am so sensible of the burden of long and frequent assemblies that I am willing to ease them on any part." This was somewhat of a sacrifice from him, as he received a fee as chancellor for affixing the seal to every law. In the end it was found necessary to reenact less than half a dozen acts.

Another point in his speech showed his interest in the people. It was for the interest of the well to do, of whom the assembly was composed, to have quit rents paid in sterling money, according to the terms of the grants, but such payment was a hardship to the common people. A "particular ought always to give way to the general good;" therefore Hart entreats the assembly to remember the poor and pass a composition act, which Lord Baltimore has agreed to accept upon his solicitation. A failure to pass this act would disappoint Baltimore in the due receipt of rents, would injure tenants holding lands under condition of punctual payments, would check the future cultivation of remote and forest parts of the province, and would cause the remoter inhabitants to desert their yet but poor improvements.

This session again was to prove an abortive one. Scarcely had Hart delivered his address when a rumor came that the proprietary had died and that King George is taking all the proprietary governments under royal rule.[1] The assembly ask to be prorogued, as, if this rumor be true, their session would be in vain. Hart grants their request. Before he has found the rumor groundless and called them together again a most vexatious incident occurred.

Early in June Hart went to Cecil County, and in his absence,

---

[1] McMahon, p. 271, speaks at some length of this movement Baltimore petitioned against it and estimated his Maryland revenue at £3,000 per annum.

on June 10, the anniversary of the pretender's birth,[1] "some wicked, disloyal, and traiterous persons" loaded four of the great guns on the court-house hill in Annapolis and fired two of them. This was in honor of the pretender, in contempt of King George, and "to the extreme surprise, dread, and disquiet of all" good people. Hart hurried back and issued a proclamation offering a reward for the guilty persons and pardon for any who would turn state's evidence. William Fitz Redmond, a nephew of Charles Carroll, and Edward Coyle were arrested on suspicion. A special court of oyer and terminer was called. Jacob Fox confessed he fired one of the guns, and sufficient evidence was secured to convict the person who fired the other gun.[2] He was whipped and pilloried. Fitz Redmond and Coyle were convicted of "drinking the pretender's health and speaking contemptibly of the King,"[3] and were heavily fined and imprisoned until the fines were paid. This trial was the beginning of the struggle between the Anglican and the Romanist parties. Thomas MacNamara appeared as attorney for the defense. He was a relation of Carroll and a man of stubborn disposition and of fiery temper.[4] In Philadelphia,[5] where he had lived before coming to Maryland, he had been presented by the grand jury for his insolent behavior in court, especially for appearing there at one time with his sword drawn, and had been disbarred upon this presentment.[6] He was now especially audacious and insulting in his bearing, and is reported to have publicly said: "Let me see who dares try them by this commission."

---

[1] The insurrection in England headed by the pretender had broken out, and the Maryland Jacobites were so elated with hopes of their imaginary success, so open and glaring in their presumption, that Hart felt obliged to check them by a proclamation dated February 14, 1716. (Hart's speech, April 5, 1720.)

[2] Vide U. H. J., July 26, 1716.

[3] Strangely enough complaint was lodged against Hart for permitting this. The complainant, however, was widow Mary Contee, who married Philemon Helmesly.

[4] Barrister at law of Gray's Inn. (U. H. J., May 15, 1719.)

[5] Penn. Col. Rec., 11, 457, June 6, 1709. Remonstrance to assembly by freeholders and inhabitants of Philadelphia, and by them to the governor and council, with request for relief, that MacNamara "vilified and brought" Queen Anne's "royal power into contempt" by saying at the supreme court in Philadelphia, on April 11, 1709, that the Queen had no right to issue the order in council of January 21, 1702, allowing Quakers to affirm, and that the order was against the law. The petitioners ask that MacNamara, for this offence "and others, his insolency's, contempts, and abuses, openly and scandelously committed in the city sessions in the face of the court and country, as by an address or representation of the same, by the grand jury presented, fully is demonstrated, may not have liberty to practise as an attorney at law in any of the courts of this province."

[6] The presentment states that the report is that he was previously disbarred in Maryland. (U. H. J., April 29, 1718; vide May 6.)

From this time the feud between him and the governor was unrelenting. With Carroll there also arose a difficulty which ended only when Hart left the province. Carroll came forth and said he had a commission from the proprietary which gave him such power that he could and would discharge the fines.[1] This was a most distasteful announcement to Hart and he ordered Carroll to record his commission in the secretary's office as "a public trust or employment." Carroll steadfastly refused to take the oath, and Hart told him plainly he should not regard him as a public officer, but would render him all requisite assistance in the execution of any matters with reference to the proprietary's "lands or other private matters."

The facts in the case seem to have been that immediately upon Charles's accession Carroll had gone to England, and making representations of his long and faithful service as private agent of the late proprietary, had secured a commission as "chief agent, escheator, naval officer,[2] and receiver-general of all rents, or arrears of rents, fines, forfeitures, tobaccos, or moneys for land warrants, of all ferries, waifs, strays, and deodands; of duties arising from or growing due upon exportation of tobacco aforesaid, tonnage of ships, and all other moneys, tobaccos, or other effects in any manner or ways now due, or hereafter to grow due, whether by protested bills of exchange or otherwise." He was empowered to appoint inferior officers. It is doubtful whether Guilford fully realized how extensive the powers were, but Hart did at once, and tells the assembly at their meeting on July 17, 1716, that the grant of such powers to another, and "especially to a Papist, is such a lessening of his power and dishonor to his character that he has desired to be recalled unless he can be restored to the full authority he held under the Crown." Powers formerly exercised by Hart's deputies are now put into the hands of Carroll's, who have taken no oath for the fulfillment of law.[3] Hart has always advised the proprietary "never to employ any papists in the public affairs of this province." Yet, probably because Carroll had deceived the

---

[1] Hart's speech of April 5, 1720, said that he remanded the prisoners to custody.

[2] Upper house, August 1, 1716, said royal instructions gave Hart as governor in Maryland the power to appoint naval officers.

[3] 12, 14, ch. 11, for encouragement of shipping. 15, ch. 11, on trade; 7 and 8 William, 111, for preventing frauds. Upper House, July 20, 1716, resolved Carroll could not be naval officer without taking the oaths.

lord proprietary and his guardian, he is made receiver of the duties for defense,[1] public charges, and support of government.[2] He had the impudence to ask Hart to account for 3d. for arms,[3] when Hart flamed out upon him with "I would as soon give you up my heart's blood." Clearly Hart has much to tell this assembly. He asks the council what is their opinion. They all agree that, not having taken the abjuration oath, Carroll can not hold public office, and all save one answer that the proprietary has been imposed upon.[4] They summon Carroll before them and ask him whether he told the authorities in England that he was a Roman Catholic, that he would not take the oaths, that acts of Parliament forbade his holding these offices?[5] How came he to take these offices knowing he could not take the lawful oaths? Who are the surveyors-general and deputy surveyors of the land office?

Carroll answers[6] that he did not tell these things in England, because it was not necessary and because he was not asked to make a profession of faith. He knows an oath should be taken by each public officer and is willing to take one for the punctual performance of duties. For some years he had held without question all the offices that the proprietary could grant, and so did not hesitate to take the additional ones. Further he does not believe that the act of abjuration is of force in the province. His faithful services and the justness of his accounts were the only inducements which led the proprietary to appoint him. As to surveyor-generals, Walter Pye and Henry Sewall, two Roman Catholics, claim that office, but there was difficulty about their qualification.[7] Twelve commissions had been sent over and been put in their hands to be delivered to Protestants, where such formerly held office,[8] but these could not be delivered on account of the council's action. So Carroll declared the land office closed, and thus the people suffered detriment.

---

[1] 3d. each per hogshead.
[2] 12d. per hogshead exported.
[3] Hart in speech of April 5, 1720, said Carroll's commission authorized him to receive all money for the support of government and for purchasing arms and at a time when the pretender was scarce suppressed.
[4] Lloyd, the sole exception, dryly said he could not tell the proprietary's motives.
[5] July 19, 1716, U. H. J.
[6] July 25, 1716, U. H. J.
[7] U. H. J., July 20, 1716, July 25.
[8] Lower house says every county except Queen Anne's, and possibly that, has had a Catholic surveyor, and so Carroll might nominate such again. (L. H. J., July 7, 1716.)

The council said Carroll evades their queries,[1] and Hart told him not to say he has closed the land office, but to have the surveyor's commissions delivered and let the work go on. Hart told the council that before sailing for England Carroll showed him a petition he intended to present to Benedict, asking that Roman Catholics have an equal share of the offices. Hart persuaded him not to present it, saying, "I would oppose it with the utmost vigor," and Carroll promised not to do so; but evidently has broken his word.[2] With this unfaithful dealing Hart taxed him before several of the council.[3] "I acknowledge that I gave that representation," answered Carroll, "but it did not import that the Roman Catholics might be qualified for employments, but that they might be unqualified for them." "A poor and jesuitical evasion," Hart calls this remark. "By what claim of right," asks the governor, "did you offer that representation; for by law Romanists can not hold ministerial offices without qualifying?" "By the instrument granted by Cecilius, Lord Baltimore, which I believe was burnt in the State house," cried Carroll, with great vehemence, "and we will insist on that right, and if the Lord Guilford will not admit of our right, we will appeal to higher powers."

Other matters troubled Hart. The proprietary is using a great seal in England. Thus the governor's perquisites are diminished, while he is held answerable for that over which he has no control, and the people are under great uncertainty, which is still more intolerable. Another difficulty arose in connection with the act for the composition for rents.[4] Henry Darnall, a Romanist, had offered Baltimore £300 annually for his "growing" rents. Carroll says, provided the farmer paid the officers' salaries, he believes Baltimore would have accepted this offer. In fact, there seems to have been made out a lease to Darnall, though the latter, seeing the opposition, said he would not accept it, as he did not wish to "interfere with the interests of his lordship and the country." Hart felt that this lease hurt his honor, as he had sent to Baltimore a pro-

---

[1] Hart said Carroll's commission gave him appointment of rangers contrary to provincial law, which gave it to the governor. Carroll answered he had not thought of the law, and could not help what Baltimore put in his commission.
[2] Vide Hart's address of April 5, 1720; also that of April 22, 1718.
[3] Speech of April 22, 1718.
[4] U. H. J., July 20, 1716; July 23, 24.

posal for the satisfaction of the rents, and assures the delegates that the lease was until now unknown to him. Hart's intention to resign was made known to the delegates on July 20 when he sent them Carroll's commission. He tells them he shall not omit to inform the proprietary of such men, as "either have or may lead him into improper measures so as to give any disgust to the well affected." He attributes his treatment to the advice of some persons who either are not capable or unwilling to give better counsel.

Two days after the session opened[1] the delegates sent Hart an address, which was really an answer to his speech of the preceding April. It is loyal in tone; expresses hope that in the future they shall be happy as in the past, and that the "aspiring interest of those that term us heretics will not be able to prevail against us." It thanks Hart for his words, promises cooperation with him, and praising his "impartiality" and "unbiased administration," states that if the provincials could select a governor he would be their choice.

When Hart announced his purpose to resign, both houses prepared an address[2] condemning "the late audacious, wicked, and rebellious practices of many disaffected persons," which "gave us no small uneasiness," and praising Hart's "zeal" and "exact discharge" of duty. The address expresses regret that the "artifices of every evil-designing person" should influence the proprietary to "lop off so many branches of Hart's power," and especially because the "branches" are given to papists. They promise to address Baltimore against Hart's leaving, "the very thoughts whereof strike such a damp upon our spirits that we are scarce able to express the miseries we may well fear are about to break in upon us by an inundation of popery and slavery."

The address was accordingly drawn up.[3] It is more loyal to Hart than to Baltimore, and, while congratulating the latter upon his restoration to power, pointedly reminds him that this is due to the change of faith. They thank him for the continuance of Hart in office, and complain that his power has been reduced by placing part of it in the hands of a "profest papist" who will not take the oaths, and by granting in

---
[1] U. H. J., July 19, 1716.
[2] U. H. J., July 27, 1716. Signed by all members of the houses.
[3] U. H. J., July 30, 1716. Lower house drew it up.

England blank commissions under the great seal. They ask that Hart's old power be restored and that he be thus induced to remain as governor and continue to foil the plans of "those papists who have very lately soared to that height of impudence as to threaten his person and undervalue his power." The address warns Baltimore not to become obnoxious to King George nor to alienate from himself the people of Maryland, which would be the result of too great favor toward Roman Catholics. There was no danger the council would show them too great favor. A Romanist who "purely offers to take the oaths only for sake of a place" should not be appointed, even though recommended by Baltimore's English agent.[1]

The lower house was not one whit more complaisant. They adopted an address[2] to King George, congratulating him on his success in suppressing the pretender's invasion, referring to the benefits they had enjoyed as a royal province, and asking him to continue his influence for the preservation of the people and the Protestant religion, which has very many adversaries. They voted to repay Hart's expenses in the late disturbance,[3] and they sent for the sheriff of Anne Arundel County. "Why did you release Fitz Redmond and Coyle?" they sternly ask. He showed Carroll's receipt for the fines, and Carroll is sent for. The fines belong to the lord proprietary's prerogative, say the assembly, and not to his private estate, and Carroll, by receiving them without taking the oaths, has acted "contrary to the known laws of this province," and has made "an inroad upon our Constitution."[4]

Words were followed by acts, and the "better security of his Lordship's Government and the Protestant interest"[5] were provided for. The preamble to the act states that it has been found advantageous to Great Britain to exclude all persons from office who will not take oaths, and that here in Maryland the general assembly think themselves indispensably obliged to do their part in securing "to the proprietary and the people their share in these benefits, especially agreeable" to us who

---

[1] U. H. J., July 30.

[2] L. H. J., July 31, 1716. Blakiston to present it.

[3] L. A. J., August 3, 1716. Upper house same day recommended to lower house to pay Richard Evans for his services at that time.

[4] L. H. J., July 27, 1716.

[5] Act of 1716, ch. 5. Act in force throughout provincial history. It was introduced in the lower house. This act was the result of Carroll's acts, not of the acts of the Jacobites, as McMahon says on p. 281.

are under the immediate government of a Protestant[1] lord proprietor. After referring to the late Jacobite excitement in the province, and to the fact that the act of 1704 required all officials to take the oath of abjuration, the statute enacts that all persons now, or in the future, holding office in the province shall take the oaths of allegiance, abhorrency, and abjuration, and subscribe the test against transubstantiation. If persons refuse to take these oaths and still "presume to execute any office," their commission is declared void *ab initio* and they are liable to a fine of £250.[2] The oaths may be required again at any time while the office is held. If they have been taken by any person, and he afterwards be present at any Popish assembly and join in the "service at mass," he shall suffer the same penalty as above.[3] The management of the private affairs of the proprietary is especially exempted from the provisions of this act.[3] On the last point, there was some disagreement, as the lower house[4] at first did not wish even to exempt these, but it finally yielded to the insistence of the council. The delegates wished to have the officers named who were considered to be engaged in Baltimore's private affairs, but this was difficult, and brought up again the old quarrel about ordinary licenses,[5] and, as they did not wish to enter into that matter then, the subject was dropped.

Carroll disturbed the assembly at another point by questioning the validity of the laws passed in 1715. The delegates considered these laws as the entire code of the province and were very unwilling that the time and labor spent in framing them should be wasted. They refused to pass any laws save those which needed to supplement deficiencies, and declined to reenact the body of laws, inasmuch as their authority was undoubted. Carroll reminded the delegates that the King had not considered the acts before the restoration of the proprie-

---

[1] On July 27, Hart submits the council the fifty-seventh article of his instructions directing him to give liberty of conscience to all quiet persons save Papists. He says he has received no instruction contrary to this from the proprietary. The council agree that he ought still to obey the above article.

[2] At suggestion of upper house; one-half to free schools, one-half to informer.

[3] Added by upper house July 28, 1716.

[4] U. H. J., July 31, August 1, 4, 6, 1716.

[5] Hart tried to get the assembly to take action in this matter (U. H. J., August 2, 1716), and to fix ordinary licenses (U. H. J., August 3, 1716), but delegates refused, August 4, 1716 (L. H. J., July 21, 1716.) The upper house insisted that the law as to fines and forfeitures be reenacted so as to transfer the right to them to the proprietary. This was done. (Act of 1716, ch. 38.)

tary, but they answer him that the efficacy of laws dates not from the date of the royal consideration but the time of passage by the assembly.

There was not much legislation at this session. Seven of the twenty-one acts passed were private ones, and several of the others were rendered necessary by the change of rulers. The gauge act and that granting the proprietary 18 pence per hogshead was reenacted.[1] Over the first there was considerable discussion. Guilford had sent over drafts which he wished passed. In these the enactment is stated to have been made by the proprietary and the assembly, as was the custom before 1688. In the reign of Queen Anne, the governor had been mentioned as a separate estate, and the assembly determines to continue such mention.[2]

The revenue laws themselves caused some difficulty. The lower house agreed[3] to lay an additional duty of 6 pence per hogshead in full recompense to the proprietary for his rents and fines for alienation, provided the 3 pence tax for defraying the public charge be repealed, and its place be taken by an increased tax on negroes and Irish servants imported into the province. The upper house agreed to this, but Carroll, as Baltimore's agent, protested against the allowance of a percentage of the tax as fees for the officers collecting it. The upper house refused to raise any further sum as salary for the officers, and Carroll withdrew his objection, saying he did so without precluding Baltimore's right to show that he should not be so burdened.[4] Some days later Carroll wrote to Hart warning him not to sign certain laws,[5] in which phrase he plainly included the revenue ones, and directing him to turn over the residue of the revenue after deducting the governor's salary. This letter is at once transmitted to the assembly, which advises Hart to pay over the 18 pence tax, but not the 15 pence tax raised for support of government unless Carroll

---

[1] To continue five years, till the proprietary was of age. (Act of 1716 ch. 8, and 19, U. H. J., July 20.)

[2] Hart suggested the guardian's (Lord Guilford) name should appear. Lower house (July 21) objected that the proprietary is a body politic and is not mentioned in his natural capacity, therefore he can not be a minor. Hart yielded.

[3] L. H. J., July 29, 1716.

[4] Vide L. H. J., August 3, 1716, where lower house agrees to relieve Baltimore of part of the discount. Hart says he will approve it, if the assembly will repay him in case Baltimore makes him pay therefor.

[5] Council, August 1, 1716, asked Carroll to enumerate them. He said it would be very difficult.

takes the oaths. They pronounce the caution in Carroll's letter unintelligible,[1] a general threat against passing any laws, "designed to disturb Hart in his weak state of health,"[2] and for other secret ends. Carroll has "used a very indecent 'way and freedom' with Hart" in assuming to himself the liberty of directing him in so general a manner. This freedom had never before been "used by a subject to a governor." The council added that Baltimore's agents in Maryland and England "have given signal marks of their disingenuity." Hart then came to the assembly, and the assembly promised to reimburse him for any pecuniary loss he may suffer from signing the bills. He thanks them, signs the bills, complains of the "insults in his sickness" and the barbarous treatment received from Carroll, and prorogues the assembly. The message from Carroll came to Hart at night, at a time he was in such a dangerous condition that he was making his will.[3] The act raising an additional revenue from imported servants was passed,[4] but as we shall see did not receive Baltimore's assent. It was the only act passed at this session which he vetoed, in spite of Carroll's warning to Hart.[5]

Hart had always taken interest in the security of the public papers.[6] Shortly after his arrival he reported to the assembly that he had seen lighted candles in the court-house and secured an order that neither candles nor other fire be carried into offices in the court-house, and that the clerk of the secretary see that the back door be locked every night "before day-

---

[1] U. H. J., August 10, 1716, the last day of the session.

[2] Hart was sick with a violent fever about August 1, and as his instructions said nothing as to his successor in case of his death, he sent to the council to ask what should be done. An act is at once passed (Carroll making no objection) providing for the succession, first, of the president of the council, and then of its members according to seniority. This had been the custom when the matter was mentioned in instructions. (Act of 1716, ch. 21.) Baltimore soon gave similar instructions. (U. H. J., May 29.)

[3] Speech of April 5, 1729.

[4] Upper house suggested the duty be limited to the servants imported from foreign countries. Lower house objected, fearing the act would be eluded, as our more recent Chinese acts have been, and upper house withdrew amendment.

[5] One of Carroll's objections to the laws was that in case of war and a capture of the tobacco fleet, Baltimore, and his five brothers and sisters, would have no support for that year if they gave up their whole revenue for a tobacco duty. (U. H. J., August 7, 1716.) A message from the council to the delegates on August 6 asked that a clause be added that tenants pay tobacco rents in the county where the land is, that such debts have precedence over other debts, and that they may be levied by execution. The lower house objected to this, saying the land was good security. The upper house further said captains of vessels are alarmed and wish a clause permitting them to collect their portion of the tax from shippers of tobacco. As to this last, the lower house says the captains may retain all tobacco until paid.

[6] U. H. J., October 7, 1714.

light be shut in," and opened half an hour after sunrise every morning. Now, through his suggestion, an act is passed[1] for repairing the damages already sustained in the public records and for their future security. A committee was appointed to inspect the records. It reported that some had been lost, and a greater part of those remaining were much worn and damnified from the transportation from St. Mary's city to Annapolis, the want of good and sufficient books, and the negligence of officers. These old records are to be repaired at public expense, and for the future all clerks, who receive the fees of office, must give bond to provide good and sufficient books and deliver the records in good order to their successors. Those who have worked in the ancient records and understand their importance will bless the assembly of 1716 for their act, which continued in force throughout the province's history.[2]

All of the measures Hart advised were not carried. His plan to advance the credit of the province[3] was not transmuted into a law. On the other hand, the projects of the lower house were sometimes blocked. Especially was this the case with reference to the attempt to make Lloyd refund the sums received by him as councillor, while also receiving a salary as acting governor.[4] He claimed he held two different offices and had a right to both salaries. The upper house admitted that it "would have been more generous in him to have forgone" the councillor's salary, but it had been paid, and, while a second instance of this will be guarded against, it is not fitting to unravel the laws as to the past.[5] The delegates grow quite excited, accuse Lloyd of falsehood, and say that when councillors have offices of profit, they are never paid as councillors.[6] The councillor's allowance is only paid to those who have no other way to reimburse themselves for their

---

[1] Act of 1716, ch. 1.

[2] Vide U. H. J., July 21, 23, 1716. A report on the subject showing that progress was being made was given by the committee to lower house on June 7, 1717. 7 words=line, 15 lines=side=¼ tob. pay.

[3] It dealt with payment of debts, vide U. H. J., July 24, 1716.

[4] The matter was postponed from session to session until Lloyd died. Then out of respect to his widow the matter was dropped, but the assembly resolved that no such future grant should be made. (L. H. J., May 30, 1719; U. H. J., May 29, 1719.)

[5] U. H. J., July 30, 1716.

[6] U. H. J., August 3, July 20. He received £52, 13.6 and 29680 pounds of tobacco as councillor while drawing salary as president. August 1, Lloyd had a public hearing before delegates, who resolved he should refund.

expenses in the service of the public. As president and acting governor he was a separate body, distinct from council, and bills were dissented from, because the word president was not in their style of enactment. He had the full negative over laws and received larger remuneration than all the rest of the council. Hart's sickness was one cause why the matter was not pushed further at this time.[1]

The evil practices of sheriffs receive the customary condemnation at this session.[2] It seems that the good people had been "greatly damnified and abused in their estates" by the sheriffs, who seized more goods on writs of fieri facias than were sufficient to satisfy the demands of law. They also kept the goods a long time before they sold them, and finally disposed of them privately, and sometimes for only a tenth part of their value. This is great loss to both debtor and creditor, and ruins their families. For the future, all goods seized must be appraised by four substantial freeholders named by the parties, and the amount due is to be turned over to the creditor at their appraisal.

Another act, permitting inhabitants of the province in their own proper persons to sue out writs when plaintiffs and give judgment when defendants, was passed, though the upper house at first objected[3] that allowing persons to appear in their own behalf as plaintiffs would enable ill-disposed persons to gratify revenge, and cause ignorant ones to mislay their actions, be nonsuited, and have to pay costs. The upper house was more successful in opposing a law allowing plaintiffs to have suits removed to the provincial court when the amount claimed as damages is less than 5,000 pounds of tobacco. In opposition, the council seems to be arguing in behalf of the poorer and debtor classes.[4] The delegates complain of the ignorance of attorneys in the county courts, and say a failure to pass the law will discourage trade and permit persons to evade the act for the recovery of small debts, but the upper house was stubborn and the act failed.

---

[1] Complaints against John Rousby, receiver of taxes, were postponed for the same reason.

[2] Act of 1716, ch. 16. A sheriff who had been appointed to fill a vacancy petitioned for longer time to make collections. The council say a dangerous precedent. Sheriffs will die at inconvenient times for their successors. (U. H. J., August 1, 1716.)

[3] U. H. J., August 6, 1716.

[4] U. H. J., July 25, 26, 1716.

RESTORATION OF PROPRIETARY OF MARYLAND.

Much attention was given at this session to the act[1] amending the law offering a bounty for killing wolves, crows, and squirrels.[2] The upper house thought the amount paid was an intolerable burden, and suggested that an act be passed obligating each taxable to bring in 6 heads yearly or pay 4 pounds tobacco. The lower house, using a true socialistic argument, while admitting the charge is great, claims that the bounty "circulates among the taxable inhabitants." Every person, if he chooses and thinks it worth while, may kill as many as will defray his proportion of the charge. If the expense continues for several years, it may then be changed. Very well, answers the council, at any rate, let us prevent fraud and be sure that the same heads are not used twice to obtain a bounty. Why should not they be brought to county courts and burned by the youngest justice present, after oath taken by the person who brought in the heads that he slew the animals. The lower house agreed that the heads should be burned,[3] but a man can not swear to killing done by his servants, and bringing the heads to court would "discourage many from killing those vermin."

An additional cause of alarm to the Protestants came from the influx of Jacobites transported and sold as indented servants.[4] Shortly after the adjournment of the assembly of 1716, on August 28, Hart and the council issued a proclamation for the sale of 80 rebels transported in the ship *Friendship*, and on October 18 a second shipment of 55 men, mostly Scots, was received on the ship *Good Speed*.

These were all indented for several years.[5] The most prominent men of the province bought their services, and some, unfortunately, soon lost them, as the men ran away.

Hart's desires[6] were that the "gentlemen of the Romish

---

[1] The act of 1712, ch. 11, prohibiting sticking fish, was repealed (act of 1716, ch. 7), as it only affected those living at a distance from the water who may be discovered with fish. (L. H. J., July 25, 1716.)

[2] Act of 1716, ch. 2 (U. H. J., August 1, 1716; August 2, L. H. J., July 28). Last year 45,000 pounds paid St. Mary's; 46,000 pounds Charles; 45,000 pounds Kent; 51,000 pounds Prince George's; 62,000 pounds Calvert; 60,000 pounds Dorchester; 45,000 pounds Talbot; 27,000 pounds Cecil; 140,000 pounds Somerset; 24,000 pounds Queen Anne's; 26,000 pounds Baltimore; 40,000 pounds Anne Arundel. May 31, 1717, lower house again refused to repeal squirrel act.

[3] Lower house amendment excluded Indians from benefit of act. (U. H. J., August 3, 1716.)

[4] Scharf., 1, 385 pp.

[5] Hart's letter of April 28, 1717.

[6] Speech of May 29, 1717.

communion will prudently consider their own interest and will content themselves with the lenity of the government they live under." They have all privileges of citizens, save officeholding, and Protestants in Roman Catholic countries would regard this condition of things as an inestimable blessing." When we place ourselves in the position of the men of that day, we see that this was by no means an unnatural position.

The Protestants were counseled by Hart to show themselves such by their "charitable demeanor toward their neighbors of another persuasion, since it is no longer in their power to do you any injury."[1] "When I was a soldier," says the governor, "I learned this maxim: Whilst the enemy was in arms, to oppose him with a vigorous resolution; but when Providence pleased to bless the juster side with advantage, to treat them with humanity." Bravo! the ruler has the milk of human kindness in him and forgets the insults[2] the Papists have heaped on him, even that distressful time when Carroll wrote him a threatening letter, though he was dangerously ill with a fever and making his will, for he thought himself near death.

When Baltimore and his guardian received the proceedings of the assembly of 1716 they promptly vetoed the servants' importation[3] bill and held the gauge act for further consideration. They had given up the quit rents for "the good and relief of the poor and more numerous part of our people," and are surprised that the act gives Hart his salary directly, rather than to the proprietary for the use of the governor. This, "with our honor, we never can consent to," and the bill must be amended. As amended, it will benefit the "planter by the ease he will find in payment of his rent, and the trader by the advantageous proviso of reshipping free of tax the tobacco upon any loss that shall happen to them at sea in their homeward voyage. The act for the security of the peace is approved with great alacrity, that Protestants and Papists may clearly perceive that "your lord proprietary is

---

[1] Lower house, May 31, promises to accept this advice. (Vide U. H J , April 5, 1720.)

[2] October 9, 1716, Carroll again made demand on Hart to recognize his commission, and warned him against signing act for better security of government. (vide U. H. J., April 5, 1720.)

[3] It did not allow Irish Protestants to come in free, and is dangerous to charter (U. H. J , June 2, 1717).

not, as he has been maliciously suggested by some, a Papist in masquerade, but a true Protestant of the Church of England, in which faith he is resolved to live and die." Thus write Baltimore and his guardian to the assembly, which met on May 29, 1717, and they ask that advice be given them "free and without influence."

A promise is made not to advance any person to any preferment for which he is not qualified by law.[1] This, of course, would take away Carroll's commission. Such was the result of the representations of Hart and the assembly, and it caused Carroll, who insisted that Roman Catholics had the right to hold office, to raise contributions and send emissaries to England to try at the least to secure the removal of Hart.

The address from England was read by Hart to the assembly at its opening. He followed it with an address, stating that he was ignorant of the motives of the house in passing the gauge bill and had found out what the motives were through the revelations of one of their officers in Great Britain.[2] He was not in the upper house when the bill passed there, as it was the time of his sickness, and now he urges the assembly to modify the bill to suit the proprietary.[3] The proprietary, as hereditary governor of Maryland, has by charter a right to the revenue, and he provides generously for Hart. The new gauge bill was drawn up and passed with the change Baltimore requested.[4]

The session was short and harmonious. Hart prorogued it on June 7, after it had lasted a week and a half. Fifteen chapters were added to the statute book, five of which were local or private. The address from Baltimore and Guilford recommended them to lay aside all feuds and animosities, and they seem to have done so. If it had not been for the difficulty with the Romanists nothing would have prevented the province from increasing and flourishing under the family of Baltimore.

The assembly was very loyal to the House of Hanover[5] and grateful to Hart. They speak of his "tenderness of our

---

[1] Lower house acknowledges Baltimore's justice in this (May 31) and thanks Hart. Of course this caused a withdrawal of Hart's resignation (Hart's speech, April 5, 1720). Baltimore's letter was dated October 10, 1716.

[2] He is evidently hurt at this. The delegates apologize (May 31, 1717) vide April 5, 1720.

[3] June 5, 1717. Hart submitted Baltimore's draft of gauge bill to council.

[4] The delegates positively refuse to make any other change. (U. H. J., June 7.)

[5] L. H. J., May 31, 1717, Hart thanks them and hopes for "many halcyon days. (U. H. J., June 1, 1717)

privileges," and tell him the "largest opportunities we have had of demonstrating the esteem we have for your excellency have fallen so far short of amounting to a compliment that we are forced to acknowledge we have failed in doing justice to your merit. * * * Though we are limited in some other respects, we are not so in affection." The assembly's chief cause for which to thank Baltimore is his graciousness in retaining Hart as governor, "of whose loyalty, fidelity, honor, and justice we have had so ample an experience." I know of no colonial governor who received higher praise, and certainly none in Maryland, save Eden, who was ever so well beloved.[1] Thus the assembly sums up his administration for its first three years, "amidst the various shocks he has met with, we may with boldness affirm, he has with a resolute constancy endeavored to promote your lordship's truest interest here by defending the honor of your lordship's government and the rights and privileges of the people under it with impartiality, by whose exhortation and general example we shall never be wanting to show a true Christian principle of charity." The only other thing of which the assembly makes much in its address to Baltimore[2] is its thanks that "he is a Protestant, and that by his recent action he has removed the grounds and motives of jealousies and made room for the truly charitable and Christian spirit of the Church of England to show how indulgent she is to the professors of the Romish religion, although the same time she knows them to be her irreconcilable enemies."[3] The future showed that the grounds and motives of jealousies were as yet far from being removed, but for the present all seems peaceful. This being so, Hart turns his attention to education. He has ever had this in mind, and is Nicholson's worthy successor in zeal for schools. Just at this time, too, the governors of the free schools have a petition prepared. Col. Thomas Smithson, of Talbot County, with ideas kindred to him of the same name, who has so benefited the growth of science, left a bequest of about £200 to the free schools. There was some danger that debts of the estate might diminish or wipe out the legacy, and

---

[1] Address to Baltimore, June 7, 1715.
[2] Address to King very loyal, June 7, 1717.
[3] They urge Baltimore not to listen to Romanists, who are not his true friends. There is obviously still a little doubt as to his position.

the governors[1] wish to be assured against this. They represent public education as in sorry plight. The funds scarce amount to £20 per annum, and were it not for the subscriptions of sundry charitable people the school at Annapolis could not be carried on. It is hopeless to think of opening such a school in each county "for the instructing their youth in good literature and manners." The youths' application and improvement are undoubted, had they the means provided to assist their studies. Hart took up this matter and made especial allusion to the needs of the schools in his opening address. He told the assembly that the province was now in a happy condition and the means were in their hands. Therefore, it was their duty to advance the honor and interest of their country for the particular good of their children, who, were they sensible of the irretrievable loss they would sustain in the want of a liberal education in their youth, would join their tears to his entreaties. The assembly thank him for his zeal for the advancement of learning and apologize for the neglect thereof in Maryland; but attempt to excuse it from the discouragement they have experienced in having moneys raised in the province applied to the maintenance of an institution (William and Mary College) outside of it, "by which never any one inhabitant of this have reaped the least advantage."[2]

This tax they are persuaded arose from the Virginians' misrepresentations, and they ask Hart to help them in trying to have its proceeds transferred to Maryland schools. In the meantime they promise to do all they can, which will not be too burdensome to the public, to support the present school, and ask for suggestions as to how this may be done.

In the address to Baltimore the assembly again refers to educational matters, complain of the "great want of good literature within this province, whereby many good geniuses are of little use that might otherwise be ornaments to the country and serviceable to your lordship's interest." They ask Baltimore to help them to have the proceeds of the tax transferred to Maryland schools, instead of being applied "to a free school in Virginia, which by its remoteness from this province" is "wholly useless to any of its inhabitants."

---

[1] June 7, 1717, U. H. J., a further petition is that in intestate estates when creditors seize them the remainder may be turned over to the free schools.
[2] U. H. J., May 31, 1717.

Two years later,[1] Hart again called to the attention of the assembly that their abilities are not equal to their desires, and suggests that they petition the King for the tobacco duty which goes to William and Mary. The upper house[2] complain bitterly of the failure of Maryland to receive any benefit from that institution. The delegates join in this complaint and add that most of the duty comes from Maryland tobacco.[3] They agree to address the King thereupon, but apparently changed their minds and addressed the proprietary instead.[4] They tell him of their "narrow circumstances," and that "abundance of youth now growing up are unhappily destitute of those common improvements which nature hath made them very capable of, for the rendering them better Christians, better subjects to His Majesty, and better qualified persons for the just discharge of the several trusts to which your lordship * * * may have occasion to appoint them, as well in the offices of State as in the distribution of justice and all other the exigencies of life." They admit with truly aristocratic scorn that the "condition of most of the people here has little claim to a truly generous and liberal education," but feel that there are enough children deserving such education to demand for Maryland a share in the royal bounty. Those who "can pay the charge there choose rather to educate their children in Great Britain, and the middling sort of people, who only stand in need for their children of such pious and charitable foundation, reap no benefit" from the "magnificent college" in Virginia.[5] This petition met with no very favorable response, and, as the people were as yet unwilling to raise anything by an additional tax, nothing was done until the administration of Hart's successor.

The question of ordinary licenses[6] engaged much of the attention of this session of the assembly. Lord Baltimore sent instructions to Hart claiming the right to these and asking that a bill be passed making these fines certain, "so that the consent of the people and not our prerogative" may settle them. The lower house responded that previous assemblies have said ordinary licenses do not belong to the secretary's office. Since Baltimore seemed to claim them by his prerogative "we are unwilling to intermeddle therewith," though they

---

[1] U. H. J., May 14, 1719.
[2] U. H. J., May 15, 1719.
[3] U. H. J., May 19, 1719.
[4] U. H J., June 4, 1719.
[5] Vide U. H. J., April 21, 1720.
[6] Act of 1717, ch. 1.

asked Baltimore to give the proceeds to free schools.[1] The upper house, taking the proprietary's side as usual, said Baltimore has already given these fines to the secretaries,[2] and it would be inconsistent with Baltimore's honor that the assembly should enter upon a matter which he had settled. Further, the secretaries have been active in the happy settlement of the present establishment. Baltimore's command in the matter must be regarded as absolute. The lower house drew up a bill in the matter, to which Hart refused to consent,[3] as it gave the licenses to Baltimore as a compliment and not as a right. A verbal change was made and the act was finally passed. In the address to Baltimore reference is made to the matter and to the previous refusal of assemblies to admit that these licenses could be levied without consent of the people. Therefore, this assembly would think itself "justly liable to the censures of those we represent if we should now give up to your lordship, as a matter of right, what our predecessors have so much contended for and even refused to give up to the Crown." Baltimore thought it wise not to strain the point and accepted the act, though the acknowledgment of his right was not expressed.[4]

Baltimore gained another point at this session. On June 3 the lower house resolved to bring in a gauge bill, as proposed by Baltimore, and this resolve was carried out.[5] A third request of Baltimore, that the recent act for the security of the peace be reenacted so as to disclaim any reference to private affairs, was rejected as needless by the lower house.

The Irish servant bill was reenacted, however, at Baltimore's suggestion, with such amendment as to impose no restriction on the immigration of Protestants. The duty was lowered and the proceeds given to the schools.[6]

Another act made the negro code of the province more stringent. It seems to have been customary for each session of the assembly to take up and act upon the report of the committee of aggrievances made on the last day of the previous session. The report of 1716 complained that negroes

---

[1] L. H. J., June 3, 1717.
[2] Thomas Beake and Charles Lowe.
[3] U. H. J., June 6, 1717.
[4] L. H. J., June 7, 1717. Baltimore asked that it be made permanent. (L. H. J. April 24, 1718.)
[5] Act of 1717, ch. 7.
[6] L. H. J., June 6, 1717; U. H. J., June 1; act of 1717, ch. 10; act of 1717, ch. 13.

were permitted to give evidence in court. This privilege is now only to be exercised in trials of other negroes or Indians. A second grievance was that no penalty was laid on a negro marrying a white person, while the latter is punished. This, too, is now remedied, and it is also provided that slaves may be tried before a single magistrate for misdemeanors for which white men were brought before the county court. To prevent the owner from loss when slaves were condemned to death for crime, it is now enacted that the court should value the slave and the public pay three-fourths of such value to the owner.

The remaining grievance of 1716, that there was not sufficient stringency in the marriage law, was also remedied,[1] and due provision made for marriage according to the forms of the Church of England in the parish where the woman is resident.

A supplementary fee bill, passed this session, fixed the naval officers' fees and provided that officers must henceforth write out their accounts of fees in full.[2]

Baltimore sent word that he wished an act passed punishing the counterfeiting of the great seal. No such law had been passed since the obsolete one of 1649, and this neglect was now remedied.[3] For the future such a criminal must forfeit all his property, receive 39 lashes, stand two hours in the pillory, and be banished forever.[4] The last important act of the session was caused by a complaint from the Indians of Copangus Town, in Somerset County, that the English disturb them by fishing, fowling, hunting, and setting traps for raccoons and the other vermin.[5] A proclamation forbidding this is issued to the sheriffs to be read at the court-house and church doors. Formerly all such differences between Indians and whites had to be brought before the governor and council. This is manifestly inconvenient, and for the future any justice of the peace may hear such causes where the value does not exceed 20 shillings[6] sterling.

In the year 1717 the two commissaries held their first visit-

---

[1] Act of 1717, ch. 15. Act not to refer to marriages of persons of other faiths. The clergy complained of this law, claiming it was passed through dislike to the clergy. Hawks, p. 152.
[2] Act of 1717, ch. 2. The act for ascertaining the bounds of land also receives a supplement.
[3] Act of 1717, ch. 9.
[4] Lower house wished to have both his ears cut off.
[5] U. H. J., June 3, 1717.
[6] Act of 1717, ch. 14.

ations.[1] Wilkinson, the prudent and judicious Eastern Shore man, brought together seven clergymen, delivered a sensible charge, and reported that the meeting was successful. The Eastern Shore clergy addressed the Bishop of London a long letter, thanking him for Mr. Wilkinson's appointment and complaining that a threatened division of parishes would deprive the clergy of support and drive them from the province. Hawks thinks there was more or less of a plan to starve out the clergy, and though this is improbable it must be confessed that many of the clergy did all in their power to make themselves obnoxious to the people of Maryland. In this letter, referred to above, they regret that the jurisdiction of the bishop through the commissaries is impatiently regarded by the gentry, and ask that the governor be instructed to allow no law to pass, relative to ecclesiastical matters, without causing the commissaries or some of the clergy to attend and granting them a hearing. The conclusion of the letter shows how great was the unpopularity of the clergy: "It is a sad truth that we must declare that we have not one friend in the province, except our governor, to make our application to; nor any access to, nor place, nor employ in the government, nor friend in the world that we know of, but your lordship, to stand by us."

Rev. Mr. Henderson, an abler and much more pugnacious man than Mr. Wilkinson, had a far less peaceful time in his visitation.[2] He gathered twelve clergymen and church wardens from thirteen parishes at Annapolis, and propounded to the latter, under oath, a series of queries as to the condition of their parishes. The clergy were then called on to produce their letters of orders and licenses from the Bishop of London. At this point even Dr. Hawks admits that Henderson "indiscreetly asserted his official importance." On the production of his letters by Rev. Henry Hall, of St. James, Herring Run Parish, Mr. Henderson put them in his bag to examine them at his leisure.[3] Mr. Hall, who held such a station among the clergy that he had been the first person proposed for the place Henderson held, immediately resented this and demanded their return. Henderson unwisely refused to do this, and Hall caused a warrant to be issued for their

---

[1] Hawks' Eccles. Contribs., 11, 152.
[2] Hawks, pp. 154 ff.
[3] Gambrall's Church Life in Colonial Maryland, p. 85.

recovery. The matter was at once carried by the commissary before the Bishop of London, whom Henderson thought was insulted in his person. The bishop sustained Hall, but ill-feeling had been engendered which did not soon subside. The governor bore testimony to the bishop of Hall's great worth, and most of the clergy sided with him.

Hart had formerly been a warm friend of Henderson [1] and, as he still continued friendly with Wilkinson, a coldness and suspicion grew up between them. Henderson's course strengthened the already existing predjudice against the exercise of the commissaries' powers. It is not surprising to find that Henderson now thought because Hart will not support him, he is not sincere in his advocacy of Protestantism and of the lord proprietary, but Dr. Hawks, in accepting Henderson's view of Hart's character, attributes an almost impossible Machiavelianism to the governor.

During 1717 another difficulty arises in Hart's path.[2] Mac-Namara, the testy attorney, was continually becoming more insolent. He called the council "the Spanish inquisition." He illegally got out a writ of replevin on a sloop and lading seized by the collector of the Potomac district. When Hart, obeying his instructions to help the collectors, granted a supersedeas, MacNamara in the most insolent manner endeavored to obstruct him, saying he wished he could see the man that dared grant such a writ. Further, he deceitfully took certain attorneys' fees from another naval officer.

Finally in the chancery court, on October 10, 1717, while Hart was presiding as chancellor, MacNamara said to the governor, "You have called me rogue and rascal." Hart denied this, but MacNamara insisted, "You did, to the best of my remembrance." The obstreperous attorney frequently had acted improperly to the court, with threatening words and indecent and irreverent behavior, and frequently, but to no purpose, had he been admonished. Hart will endure no more. "This is contempt, and lessens his lordship's authority and the grandeur of this court by taxing the governor with falsity. As keeper of the great seal, I suspend you from practice, save for pending cases of Crown revenue, till due sub-

---

[1] Hawks, p. 159.

[2] Hart's speech to upper house, April 25, 1718. Indictments were brought against him by the grand jury for some of these things. (U. H. J., May 6, 1718.)

mission is made by you." "I appeal to the King in council," retorts MacNamara. "The appeal is granted, but should be made to the lord proprietary," answers the governor. "Then I appeal to him, and ask that the particular facts or instances of misbehavior alleged against me be set out." On June 22 and July 12 MacNamara had already written to Baltimore and Guilford, complaining he had been impeded in his practice by Hart. In answer they write to Hart not to continue this. There had been all sorts of trouble when Charles Carroll was being examined by Hart on behalf of the commissioners for forfeited estates. MacNamara, "officiously and without call," interrupted and told Carroll not to answer. At other times MacNamara had used "ill language to another practitioner in the face of the court" "and indecent and contumacious tones and gestures" to the court itself. When Hart taxed him with this and rebuked him MacNamara answered "I deny it," thus charging the governor with uttering falsities.[1] At some time or other, in the chancery court, MacNamara publicly told Hart "I had tried to have you removed from your position." As the winter came on matters did not improve. On February 24, 1717–18, in chancery court, in presence of two witnesses, MacNamara said to Hart, "I am sorry that ever I said anything which might offend the governor, but I will not beg the commissioners' pardon." Yet this speech he now denies, and thus again indirectly gives Hart the lie. When Hart suspended him from practice MacNamara said, "You are both judge and party in the case," and circulated the false report that Hart had unmercifully beaten him.

When the assembly met on April 22, 1718, Hart[2] gives the upper house a full account of his difficulties with MacNamara, and refers to them in his address to both houses. He asked them whether MacNamara's insolence should be exempt from punishment, seeing he has given this Government disturbance for almost as many years as he has been in it. MacNamara heard of this and at once went to the clerk of the lower house and demanded a copy of Hart's speech. When the clerk did not comply MacNamara threatened to extort it, and spoke dis-

---
[1] L. H. J., May 7, 1718.
[2] In the fall of 1717 Hart issued proclamation forbidding illicit trade, but writes to England that he knows of no such trade in Maryland.

respectfully of the house. For this he was at once summoned and stated he remembers using no such expressions, and is sorry if he has done so, attributing it to the effect of the wine he had been drinking.[1] He was excused, but the lower house showed its position in the matter clearly on April 28 in their answer to Hart's address. They speak of MacNamara's "plotting, uneasy, and revengeful temper," of his "proud and turbulent behavior," and thoroughly approve of Hart's suspension of him from practice, as necessary to preserve proper decorum. This is strong language, especially when we remember MacNamara was formerly clerk of the house. They thank Hart for his promise to support all magistrates, and promise to do all they can to support him.

Apparently, in two letters,[2] Baltimore and Guilford had expressed approval of Hart's action in the matter, and these letters meet with the warmest commendation on the part of the assembly.[3] The lower house thinks this conduct of the proprietary will discourage such as for the future shall fly in the face of Government, and that MacNamara's troubles came "purely through his own haughty ambitious temper and ill conduct."

Further complaints against the turbulent MacNamara pour in. Bladen,[4] the attorney-general, says he overcharged fees as naval officer of the *Patuxent*.[5] The justices of the provincial court[6] lay complaint that he is a person of "turbulent, refractory, haughty, and abusive temper," who had been already once suspended from practice. The whole course of his life is so turbulent and disorderly that he hath very rarely been clear of some criminal prosecution in the provincial court for many years, though his artful, audacious management of the subtle and tricking part of the law hath often freed him. "We will no longer hold our places," they say, "if so turbulent and insolent a person be allowed to practice.

Baltimore, in a letter to MacNamara, seemingly advised him to submit to Hart, and added, "we are willing the people of our province should reap the benefit of that capacity and

---
[1] L. H. J., April 24, 1718.
[2] Dated November 16, 1717, and February 4, 17½.
[3] U. H. J., April 28, May 10, 1718; L. H. J., April 29, 30.
[4] Captain Pulsifer also charges this (U. H. J., May 7, 1718).
[5] L. H. J., May 2, 1718
[6] William Holland, Samuel Young, Thomas Addison, Richard Tilghman (U. H. J., May 5, 1718).

abilities your enemies allow you have to serve your clients." But he would not bend. The upper house sent for him on May 5, but received no submission from him.[1] Something must be done. The upper house suggests the passage of a bill preventing him from the practice of law. The delegates at once accept the suggestion and the bill is passed. With it are incorporated certain provisions for better supporting the magistrates in the administration of justice.[2]

The clergy call for more attention of the assembly at this session than at any other in Hart's administration. At the same time that the legislature met, the clergy were convened in Annapolis at Hart's summons, that the good government of the church may promote and propagate true religion and virtue.[3] When they were met in the library, Hart addressed them, twenty in number, and called attention to the fact that the commissaries had found difficulty in executing their commissions, through the constitution of the province and the natural situation of the country, filled with great rivers and creeks. He asks them to do what is fitting and to present any grievances to the assembly. The "Jesuits and other popish emissaries are prevailing by their insinuating arts upon the weak and ignorant," and are "vigilant in gaining proselytes and seducing the unwary." He advises the commissaries to "use methods of mildness and gentleness and the clergy to show by their unity and brotherly love they are the disciples of the prince of peace and concord."

The clergy return a grateful answer,[4] regretfully acknowledging that "popery" is increasing. They speak of their "deep sense" of Hart's goodness and favor to them and his zealous inclination for the propagation of our most holy religion "and of their deep feeling of gratitude" to him. Hart replies, saying, more definitely than before,[5] that the clergy should speak plainly concerning the necessity of some legislative sanction to the exercise of the bishop's jurisdiction in Maryland. In this action Dr. Hawks thinks Hart was hypocritical and tried to fortify himself in popular favor by casting odium on the clergy. He adduces no proof of this, however, and there was no possible reason for such a line of

---

[1] U. H. J., May 7, 1718.   [3] Hart's message to lower house, April 29, 1718.
[2] Act of 1718, ch. 16.   [4] Hawks 11, p. 161.
[5] So Hawks says. I have not seen the reply.

conduct. Hawks has undoubtedly attached too much importance to the disappointed vaporings of Henderson. The latter is said to have opposed having the convocation take any action, fearing a failure. Gambrall, however, well says that Henderson was one cause of the failure,[1] for the people did not wish to place ecclesiastical jurisdiction in the hands of a man whose actions had been such as those of Henderson toward Hall. It is noticeable that the clergy insisted that Henderson must withdraw all charges against Hall, and that several of them contributed to the failure of the attempt to establish ecclesiastical jurisdiction by telling the delegates that "the act was tyrannical and would be the means of driving people from the church to the Roman Catholics and the Quakers."

The clergy submitted[2] to the assembly the following requests: (1) That the jurisdiction and authority of the bishop of London be recognized by the assembly; (2) that the province pay the salary of a writer to record the commissary's proceedings; (3) that the sheriffs may serve citations for the clergy; (4) that church wardens who attend the commissary's visitations, with difficulty crossing creeks and rivers, be allowed their traveling expenses from the parochial charges, and (5) that the commissaries and other clergy may be allowed to cross ferries free at all times. Hart sent this paper to the assembly. The upper house seems to have been willing to accept the propositions. The lower house,[3] however, felt that the ecclesiastical jurisdiction might overlap the law courts and be grevious to the people, that consideration of the matter would take time, and that at present it was impracticable to put ecclesiastical laws in force.[4] It was the only attempt to carry the idea of a state church to its logical conclusion, and it fortunately failed at the very outset.

The religious question was a most important one. Hart had hoped[5] to have the rest of his administration peaceful, that he might wholly work for the welfare of the province, but found that "the restless and turbulent spirit of the Papist

---

[1] Church Life in Colonial Maryland, p. 86.
[2] U. H. J., April 30, 1718. The bishop had written to the commissaries, leaving such application to their discretion. Wilkinson read his letter, against Henderson's advice, who said the opponent would claim the bishop was indifferent to the plan. (Hawks II, 163.)
[3] Hawks II, 164, says one-third lower house were dissenters.
[4] L. H. J., May 3, 1718.
[5] Hart's speech, April 22, 1718, to assembly.

party still persecuted and defamed him," because he opposed their claim of an equal share in the administration of government and required them to qualify before they could execute office. MacNamara joined with Carroll in complaining to the proprietary against Hart, and they tried to make people believe there was no law nor justice under Hart's government. So Hart tells the assembly. Carroll,[1] "that profest Papist and first fomenter of the late disturbances, having acquired vast estates by the offices he formerly employed and his practice of law," was "not contented to enjoy this affluence of fortune with more indulgence than he could expect anywhere else," but must "add ambition of rule to his former felicity." It is obvious to all, "save those willfully blind, what steps the Romanists take to introduce themselves into the province." "Indefatigable in their designs," instead of sitting down after their first repulse, "contented and easy under the protection of the government," they calumniate Hart in their disappointed rage. The emissaries sent by them to London were very active against Hart and exclaimed in bitter terms of the persecutions of the Roman Catholics in Maryland and "how cruel manner they were treated in, and even debarred the liberty of a free commerce." They unfairly got the opinions of three eminent lawyers against the act for suspending the persecution of Papist priests, but Hart told Baltimore the truth. An answer from Baltimore[2] sustaining Hart has been received: We "are so far from imagining that any countenance should be given them in that pernicious practice of perverting people to the Romish superstition that we very well approve of the laws made to prevent it." "In the name of God, gentlemen of the assembly," cries out Hart, "inquire into these things and make an impartial representation of the truth."

The addresses of the two houses[3] in answer to this are filled with expressions of devotion to Hart. The council speaks of his "prudent conduct in the late conjunction of affairs, whereby the dark intrigues and secret machinations of popish faction are in a great measure defeated," and states that they feel

---

[1] Carroll had refused to issue patents for land, but when paid one-half the fees of the seals and with the test "our trusty and well-beloved Charles Carroll, esquire, his lordship's chief agent of our land offices." Hart said this was derogatory to the office of keeper of the great seal, and refused to permit it. The lower house supported Hart and said the people entitled may sue Carroll for their patents. (L. H. J., May 5, 1718).

[2] Baltimore's letter of November 16, 1717.   [3] U. H. J., April 26, 1718.

secure against the "further attempts of that restless and ambitious party." They warn them that they will lose their present quiet, "if they continue." Hart's enemies are only the friends of a popish establishment, inflamed by disappointment and centering their malice on Hart. They spread rumors that Baltimore was favorable to them. With rather remarkable boldness, the council express the hope that the proprietary will look upon that body as best qualified to give advice and tell of the true state of the province and will not lean on representations from other quarters. They significantly add: The "restless spirits of a popish enterprising faction" might endanger the proprietary's position if they were allowed a voice.

The lower house [1] praises Hart's "steady and prudent conduct of affairs" and his "unbiased methods" of administration. They feel that the Roman Catholics have no right to further indulgence, and that it might be well to repeal the Maryland laws against Popery, that the sterner English ones might come into force. "Papists under a Protestant government," say the delegates, "if listened to, will not be without complaint, more than fire without warmth or water without moisture." In all Hart's administration the strictest observation can find only justice and "universal satisfaction to all His Majesty's faithful Protestant subjects."

An address of both houses to Hart is adopted and an appropriation of £200 made to recompense him for the expense he has been put to in resisting the attacks of the Romanists.[2] The milder Maryland statutes are repealed [3] and the Roman Catholics come under the harsher English law. Another act,[4] the first of the session, by which the electoral franchise is taken from all Roman Catholics, is hurriedly passed, that a special election for delegates at Annapolis may be held under it. In approving it, Hart says:

I take it to be highly unreasonable the Papists and their adherents, who, whenever it is in their power, show such a notable disaffection to our laws, should be permitted to vote for the election of members of the lower house.

These oppressive laws were in force throughout the whole

---

[1] L. H. J., April 28, 1718.   [2] L. H. J., May 9, 10.   [3] Act of 1718, ch. 4.
[4] Act of 1718, ch. 1; L. H. J., April 29, 30, 1718. It was urged that without this law the Roman Catholics might occasion great disturbance by electing themselves or their adherents as delegates. (L. H. J., April 26, 1718.)

provincial period of Maryland's history. Their intolerance has often been cóndemned.[1] Their passage has been explained by no previous historian. Though we must admit there was much to extenuate the conduct of the assembly in passing these laws, which simply made the condition of Roman Catholics in Maryland similar to that of those in England, we agree with McMahon that "the Catholics were taxed to support a religion and government to which they were emphatically strangers."[2]

Just before adjournment the assembly[3] adopted an address to the proprietary. They thank him for his kindness and express gladness that he is so good a Protestant, though the "assiduous endeavors of a restless faction" tried to prove the contrary. They tell him that the Roman Catholics are members of that party "which kicks against government," and explain why the new measures against them were adopted. "The penalties of the English law are greater than we wish to use, if these gentlemen will demean themselves quietly and peaceably;" and this was true, for the Roman Catholics rarely, if ever, incurred the full rigor of the law, though it remained on the statute book.

At this session comes into notice a third opponent of Hart, Maurice Birchfield, collector of the customs. The committee on grievances complain that he summoned to the chancery court, without demand or notice, in "immethodical manner," many who had small dealings with London merchants and some who had never dealt with them.[4] This he did from the avaricious and litigious temper of MacNamara, his attorney, "desiring to increase the fees." The assembly complained of it in the address to Baltimore.[5]

As usual, we find the report of the last session's grievance committee acted on at this time. There were three points in this report. The first was that executors and administrators were not obliged to deliver the estate to the heirs till accounts are fully stated.[6] This might not be done in seven years. The committee suggested that the heirs should receive a proportionate part of what appears to be due, on the rendering

---

[1] E. g., by Scharf, 1, 370, 383.
[2] History of Maryland, 281.
[3] L. H. J., May 10, 1718.
[4] L. H. J., May 5, 10, 1718.
[5] On Hart's advice. (U. H. J., May 9, 1718.) Baltimore says he'll lay case before the commissioners of the customs. (U. H. J., May 14, 1718.)
[6] L. H. J., June 7, 1717.

of the first account, and (if full age) give security to refund a proportionate part of any claims proven against the estate.[1] This recommendation was favorably received at the next session, and a law passed authorizing heirs and legatees, twelve months after the death of the one from whom they inherit, to demand their shares of the estate from the executors or administrators.[2]

The third grievance[3] was that public business in the several courts was delayed often for six or seven years, thus discouraging suitors and often forcing them to agree their causes to their great disadvantage. The committee suggest the passage of an act obliging county courts to determine cases in six months' time, the provincial court in twelve months, and the court of chancery and the governor and council in eighteen months.[4] The suggestion was accepted, though the periods of time were changed, and an act was passed to "limit the continuance of actions," and to ascertain "the manner of taking the evidence of seafaring men," and to grant "appeals from the chancery court to the governor and council."[5]

The revenue question, of course, came up, this time with reference to the 8 per cent deduction from the 18d. per hogshead. Baltimore, in his letter of November 16, 1717, said that he expects the restoration of this. The lower house[6] answers that the money was raised conditionally for Baltimore's use and not for defraying the public charge, and when he accepted it the assembly wholly resigned their interest therein. But if Baltimore had refused, the money would have been applied to the use of the public. Naval officers then would have had the right by law to deduct their salary of

---

[1] Also that no injunction against orphans remain undetermined over two courts.
[2] Act of 1718, ch. 5.
[3] The only new grievances noted at this session are that, on rehearing a case in chancery, the same judges are present as passed the decree, and that feigned recoveries of lands are practiced. (L. H. J., May 6, 8, 1718.)
[4] L. H. J., April 29, 1718, May 5, 7; act of 1718, ch. 10.
[5] There were nineteen acts passed this session. Eleven of these were strictly private, and another (ch. 3) permitted John Steele to hold office, though he had not been three years in the province. (U. H. J., May 6, 1718.) The bounds of land act was amended and reenacted. (Ch. 18.) It may be added that the assembly was generally careful not to pass a private act unless the parties had notice (L. H. J., May 1, 1718), and that they rarely, if ever, interposed if there was a common-law remedy. (Vide U. H. J., May 3, 1718.) April 2, (L. H. J.), Monason, King of Asotage, and his Indians petition for something (L. H. J., May 1), but apparently without result. One private act, that for the relief of certain languishing prisoners, debtors, raised some discussion as to whether the sheriff or gaolers should have any fees for them. (L. H. J., May 7, 8, 1718.) The treasurer was ordered to procure £20 worth of paper, parchment, and ink powder for public use.
[6] Vide L. H. J., June 8, 1717.

8 per cent against the public. Baltimore took it under the like incumbrance. The dispute, if any, is not between Baltimore and the assembly, but between Baltimore and the officers. This was an adroit shifting of ground.[1] The upper house, however, suggests that it would be well to give the 8 per cent to Baltimore, to make him look favorably upon the assembly proceedings, and this is done by majority vote of the delegates. They give up none of their claim to the right, but grant the money as a favor to Baltimore, for his goodness in admitting good laws.

Hart's health did not improve, and in the winter of 1718–19 he petitioned Baltimore that he might be absent twelve months for his health.[2] Leave was granted by the Crown[3] and by Baltimore, but Hart did not take advantage of it. Probably the troubles with MacNamara caused him to remain. This troublesome man appealed to England, and on his representation of the matter Lord Baltimore vetoed the act disbarring him as an ex post facto one.[4] He told Baltimore that the assembly which made the law[5] did not summon him before it, but acted with such secrecy that he only heard of it by accident, and that his petition to have opportunity of justifying and defending himself was denied. On this partial and false statement Baltimore took the advice of three of the most distinguished lawyers of the day.[6] They all advise him to veto the law, one of their opinions going so far as to say he "never heard that the legislature of any civilized country ever passed an act so arbitrary and unjust as this seems to be." Without trying to get a statement of facts from the legislature, Baltimore vetoes the bill. He does, indeed, suggest that he would approve a general act for better supporting the magistrates.

Upon receiving this news Hart at once calls the assembly together, although at an inconvenient time of the year.[7] In the beginning his speech at the opening of the assembly on May 14, Hart refers to the veto, and tells the legislators that if MacNamara, or any other, be suffered to insult the courts

---

[1] U. H. J., May 10, 1719. [3] On March 19, 1718–19.
[2] Vide L. H. J., April 15, 1720. [4] U. H. J., May 14, 1719
[5] Hart says MacNamara did not appeal to the upper house nor to him before the passage of the act. (U. H. J., May 14, 1719.)
[6] U. H. J., May 15, 1719, John Hungerford, Thomas Pengelly, Edward Northey. Northey said if MacNamara was guilty he should make submission to the courts.
[7] Robert Ungle was chosen speaker by a majority vote, and Michael Jenifer clerk of the delegates. This was a new assembly.

with impunity, as he has so often done, it will destroy the very essence of all authority and power, principally instituted to pull down and punish the haughty and bad and support and cherish the humble and good. He advises the legislature to repass the law so amended as to meet Baltimore's objections.

The second point in his speech refers to the other great quarrel, that with the Roman Catholics. Baltimore and Guilford have written that they are displeased at the indiscreet and malicious proceedings of this party against Hart, who feels bound by public utterance to disabuse all of the notorious untruth that he has persecuted them. All he has done has been to endeavor to prevent "their employing of offices or having any influence, either publicly or privately, on the administration of this government."[1] This has been his indispensable duty as governor, and he challenges any to show when he has gone beyond this and persecuted any for conscience sake. Roman Catholics have never yet been disturbed under the protection of this Protestant government, but must not intermeddle with the ministerial part of the government nor proselyte Protestants. They have nothing better to hope from Lord Baltimore when he comes of age.[2]

Turning to measures of more local character, Hart recommends that the return of juries be better provided for by law, since the lives and fortunes of the people depend on the integrity of juries. In England no commoner is too good to be a juryman; so should it be in Maryland.

Hart urges upon the assembly the importance of good roads. The thing speaks for itself, but there is not a sufficient penalty allowed by law to be inflicted by road overseers on those who disobey them, and only the meanest of the people are appointed overseers. No man should be too good to serve his country. Especially provision should be made for the great road through the heart of the province, which is the usual and shortest passage for travelers to and from the other colonies.[3]

---
[1] He says not all the Roman Catholics have been against him.
[2] The upper house (May 18) says the Romanists have built on the nearness in blood of Baltimore to some gentlemen of Romish communion.
[3] A bridge over the Patuxent at Queen Anne Town and a road over the Kent Marshes are recommended.

Five years earlier, October 5, 1714, Hart threw an interesting side light on means of transportation in Maryland, in suggesting that a provision for certain convenient places

The act offering a bounty on squirrels should be repealed, as the war made on these little animals cost the country in one year £7,000 sterling.[1] The last suggestion in the speech is one concerning the returns of taxables. All who receive protection of the laws should bear an equal proportion of the charge, and it does not seem to Hart that the increase in the number of taxables corresponds with the happy increase of youth and the vast importation of Europeans and negroes. His final sentence is one of the most remarkable to be found in the annals of colonial governments:

As you are, I thank God, a free people, so may you accept or reject what I now deliver to you, as you shall find it for the conveniency or inconveniency of your country.[2]

Eighteen acts were passed at this session. Of these seven were private. The act against MacNamara was passed a second time.[3] In the answer to Hart's speech the upper house say that they think MacNamara purposely made no application to them that he might appeal to England. This address, as all from that body to Hart, is extremely grateful and cordial in tone. The lower house is fully as loyal to Hart, and expresses much more indignation at the opinions of the lawyers, stating that these opinions are worthless, because their authors did not know the facts. MacNamara had not been heard in person before the lower house of assembly because, though they believed he had knowledge of their first vote, he made no application to them until the bill had passed beyond their hands into those of the upper house.[4] Furthermore, the court in which MacNamara pleaded had condemned him. To admit him to a hearing would be to question the veracity of

---

of landing would lower freight charges and give ready dispatch to shipping tobacco in good condition for an early market, which is the life of the province's commerce. Also, sailors would no more have to "rowl" the hogsheads for many miles, which is not "only destructive to navigation, but is a slavish labor unworthy the native liberties of Englishmen." The masters of ships made an unsuccessful petition to the same effect at this session. (L. H. J., May 21, 1719.)

[1] May 25, lower house refused to repeal or amend it.

[2] L. H. J., June 4, 1719, Evan Jones was given leave to print the laws made this session with the governor's speech, answers, and the several addresses, vide July 30, 1715, when he petitioned to write the laws.

[3] Act of 1719, ch. 17. The lower house committee of laws say that the act is not a bill of indictment, and therefore not void for uncertainty, and that the legislature is not tied to common rules of justice. Courts in which MacNamara practiced condemned him, and out of diffidence in their own power asked the legislature to aid them.

[4] He never petitioned the upper house. This, say the delegates' committee of laws, argues "sense of guilt or resolute obstinacy."

that court without cause, and would make the justices parties or defendants in a matter whereof the law made them judges and where the facts are notorious.[1] The very essence of authority and government are nearly concerned here. If there is yielding now, any lawyer may summon the whole country, as suitors, to Great Britain, where they can not with conveniency appear to prove their allegations. The constitution is not worth supporting, if neither court nor country are capable of judging the demeanor of one attorney. MacNamara may be a barrister, but in Maryland he has only appeared as an attorney and should be punished, as any inferior court has power to act toward an attorney misbehaving before it.

The lower house[2] committee on laws go on to say:

If the legislature can not redress the country's grievances and remove nuisances, and they found him both, if this man must be supported in his practices, in spight of courts and country, * * * especially as there is no encouragement by fees or pensions for judges, and the positions are a great burthen, every one qualified will try to avoid them, rather than tamely submit to lies and affronts, or drag themselves into tedious and chargeable contests, then we are not so happy in our constitution as we had hoped for, for what impartiality can there be in judges, where, if they oblige not resenting counsel, they are abused or affronted or become objects of his revenge?

In the address to Baltimore, adopted at this session, the assembly refers to the trouble with MacNamara, and states that to pass the disbarring act was the only way of effectually discouraging this generally troublesome person. The act for better supporting magistrates in the administration of justice is passed separately, so that if Baltimore reject the one the other may be saved. Reference is made to the frequent insults given to magistrates, and authorization is given them to fine officers.[3]

In regard to the troubles with the Romanists, the two houses support Hart most warmly. The upper house says there is no religious persecution in Maryland, "unless wholesome laws to preserve life or property be persecution of felons and murtherers, a principle of so horrid and salvage a nature

---

[1] Hart apparently alludes to MacNamara in his speech of April 5, 1720, when he refers to "one now dead, who with horrid execrations said he did not doubt to see me as fast in prison as ever he was (who had been so for murder and other crimes) and my innocent children set a begging."

[2] L. H. J., June 4, 1719.

[3] Act of 1719, ch. 4.

that every community of reasonable creatures will explode it as destructive of all civil society." The analogy is far-fetched, but there is no doubt of the house's meaning.

The lower house is astonished at the "monstrous structure raised by the partial clamors of Papists." Reference is made to the fact that the laws of Great Britain are more severe against Roman Catholics than those of Maryland. They complain against the justice and lenity of Hart's administration, only because he opposed their attempt to hold the prime offices in this province. The Romanists have endeavored to subvert the government and pervert the more unthinking of our people by alluring them to the superstition of their church. Thus Hart and the assembly have been forced to act defensively.[1] Long may the province continue "under the conduct of so unbiased a ruler."

In pursuance of the recommendation as to juries, an act is passed that each jury may receive 120 pounds of tobacco for each cause and an additional per diem of 15 pounds of tobacco per juror. If any suitor give more, he is to be fined. This is evidently to prevent embracery, and also is a far less important act than the one Hart recommended. The lower house said there was no instance of the sheriffs failing to return the best and most understanding freeholders as jurors.

As to roads, the delegates say the law needs no amendment, but rather enforcement, and that the several counties should make all the roads. Road making should not be a provincial charge. The recommendation as to the return of the taxables was looked on favorably, and a more stringent law was passed which remained in force for many years. Single freemen without settled place of residence had not been returned by employers, as not being members of their families, and so have paid no tax.[2] For the future they must procure a housekeeper to give them in as taxables, or be committed to the sheriff's custody.[3] Other important acts of the session were those for the encouragement of an iron manufacture,[4] and for the administration of intestates' estates, providing that a strict accounting be made of the residue of each estate and that

---

[1] Reference to this matter in address to Baltimore, June 6, 1719, last day of the session.
[2] Act of 1719, ch. 8; U. H. J., May 30, June 1, 2, 1719.
[3] Act of 1719, ch. 12; U. H. J., May 29, 1719.
[4] Act of 1719, ch. 15.

it be not embezzled by the administratosr, who were often creditors of the deceased.[1]

The committee on aggrievances[2] reported early in the session that when servants run away from masters in other colonies they will often lose the servants rather than pay the fees. In such case there is no provision as to the disposition of the servants. To remedy this state of things, an act is passed providing that the sheriff may sell such servants by public vendue and pay the fees out of the produce, only accounting to the owner for the residue.[3]

The last act of this session[4] was one regulating officers' fees, and Hart's action on this occasion was looked back to as a precedent in the later quarrels over fees, even down to that latest and greatest conflict when Governor Eden and the delegates struggled in a fierce contention which only ended when Maryland ceased to be a province and became an independent State. The old fee bill expired at this time and Hart suggested to the assembly that, as he had no instructions about fees and Baltimore had expressed his intention to come in person to the province, the former bill be continued[5] until Baltimore comes of age, on September 20, 1720. The upper house agreed to this, but the delegates said the present fees are so great an oppression to the inhabitants that they rather inclined to be without a law for that purpose till the arrival of the lord proprietary than longer to groan under such hardships.[6] The upper house said in reply that by awaiting Baltimore's arrival in the province they will have an opportunity to argue the reasonableness of things with him, and what will then be done will be lasting. They agree that some offices are grievously burdensome, but consider it better to continue the old act for so short a time rather than involve the country in great difficulties.

The lower house refused to agree to this. The act has expired.[7] Hart directs the man who affixes the great seal to

---

[1] Vide May 25, L. H. J.: If no heirs, residue to public schools. This was all that was done for education at this session. (June 2, L. H. J., act of 1719, ch. 14.)

[2] L. H. J., May 23, 1719. A bill against the villainies of imported servants was introduced, but did not pass. (U. H. J., June 3, 5, 1719.) Importers of convicts were ordered to give bond for their good behavior. (L. H. J., June 3, 1719.)

[3] Act of 1719, ch. 2.   [4] Ibid., ch. 18.   [5] U. H. J., June 1, 1719.

[6] L. H. J., June 1, 1719; U. H. J., June 3, 1719.

[7] Bacon says, May 20, 1718, "If so, the province had already been a year without any fee law."

RESTORATION OF PROPRIETARY OF MARYLAND. 299

documents not to do so without the fee indicated in the old law. This is government by executive authority.

The next day the upper house[1] again addressed the delegates. 'Are not you too positive in resolving to deprive the country of the benefit of the former law, which did somewhat restrain the officers? Some fees are too high, but the bill you would have us pass abridges the perquisites of some officers so as not to afford sufficient support for the stations of the persons who execute them. It is an ungrateful return to Baltimore and Hart for their favors, to lessen extravagantly the revenues of their officers. Why could not we have a joint committee on the matter? Our house is as much a part of the legislature as yours, and has the interest of the country as much at heart. We wish to be just to all.' The lower house at once agrees to a conference, and the report of this committee, made on the following day, is at once adopted by both houses.[2] Hart agrees to pass the bill if limited to three years, or to the first session after Baltimore's arrival. This is done, and the bill thus passed was in force by continuances for some six years. The whole procedure shows the reasonableness of both parties. Hart[3] announced, however, that Philemon Lloyd, deputy secretary of Maryland, formally protests in the council against this bill, saying that by depriving the secretary of so large a part[4] of those perquisites intended by Baltimore to be a handsome support for him, it is an infraction of his rights, and will encourage all litigious spirits in molesting and harassing their innocent neighbors with vexatious suits upon slight and frivolous grounds.

Peace has been made with the Tuscaroras. The delegates thank Hart for this and for his great care in cultivating and preserving good friendship with the bordering Indians. They vote a present of £10 currency to the Tuscaroras. The great men of the Nanticokes, Panquash, and Annatoquin complain that a white man has settled on their lands at Checkacone.

---

[1] U. H. J., June 4, 1719. The lower house, May 28, asked its committee of laws to prepare a bill against the purchase of offices. The bill did not pass, owing to upper house amendments.

[2] U. H. J., Apr. 21, 1720. Baltimore refuses to approve this bill, June 5.

[3] In spite of their good will toward Hart, the assembly refuse to make one Humphries, a particular friend of Guilford and Baltimore, and recommended by them capable of holding office, before he had been three years in the province. They suspended that law once for each governor, they say, and the favor (case of Steele) had already been done for Hart.

[4] He estimated it as one-fourth.

The Choptanks also complain that the English have encroached upon their lands, so they are all driven into Locust Neck.[1] The intruders are ordered to remove, and three men are appointed to decide differences between Indians and whites on the Eastern Shore,[2] but, alas, nothing was done with reference to the complaint of the Nanticokes that the English bring strong drink to their towns and sell it to their great prejudice.

The relations between Hart and this assembly were so friendly that at the conclusion of this session a present of £200 currency is made to him as a partial reimbursement for the great sums of money he has spent for the provincial interest, and because he has been kind and serviceable to Maryland.

All seemed to think this was to be Hart's last assembly, but he was yet to summon another session. After nearly a year more he met with the legislature on April 5, 1720 The session lasted until the 22d, but its contribution to the statute book was a small one. Fourteen acts were passed. Of these ten were strictly private.[3] One continued the ordinary act for a year, a second provided for the public levy, a third continued the gauge act for a year, and the fourth concerned the governor's salary. There seems to have been a restlessness and discontent in the assembly and a trifle less of cordiality toward Hart. In opening the session Hart asks that the gauge act be continued, and refers to it as a considerable achievement of his administration.

As this is his last session, Hart reviews his course toward the Roman Catholics. The "Papists" still seem to keep on foot their pretense to hold all offices, as the Protestants do. He has been a memorable instance of the effects of popish malice, and now doubt not that they await his departure as a more favorable conjecture to put their designs into practice. He traces the course of his struggle against the claims of Carroll, "who by principle is an enemy of the Protestant constitution," and the conflict with MacNamara. If these men have acted so to the governor, what would they do to Protestants if they had the power? The Roman Catholics might have been peace-

---

[1] U. H. J., May 18, 1719.
[2] April 8, 1720, Philip Thomas, of Anne Arundel County, says his servant has run away to the Tuscaroras, who are ordered to give him up.
[3] In explanation of the large number of private acts, on April 21, 1720, the assembly tells Baltimore that the infancy of the country does not permit such extensive administration of courts of justice, but that in some cases the assistance of the legislature may be absolutely necessary to supply defects of law.

fully happy if they had not interfered with government and perverted Protestants, as the Jesuits constantly do. They falsely pretend that Maryland was granted them as an asylum from the rigor of the penal laws of England. They can not have a better right than the charter admits them to, and, in Hart's opinion, there is so far from a provision being made therein that the government should be in their hands in any degree, that there is not even an exception made for the free exercise of their religion. The phrase "God's holy and truly Christian religion," used by Charles I, a Protestant, could only mean the religion that monarch professed. Therefore, Papists only enjoy privileges in Maryland through the connivance of the government. If they win the conflict, it may some day be fatal to the Protestant colonists, especially considering the prodigious settlements which a formidable nation of their own persuasion are extending on our borders. It is easier and safer to prevent than to cure an inveterate distemper.

Let us therefore call some of the principal Papists and examine them before the legislature as to their privileges. If they will not submit their claim to public examination, mankind will be persuaded that it will not bear the light. If they have the right, let justice be done, in the name of God. This course of procedure will prevent imposition on strangers and unguarded minds.

The lower house[1] is loyal to Hart and speaks of his zeal and resolution in defense of the present happy Protestant constitution. They approve of his plan and promise to attend to the gauge act. The upper house[2] joins in approbation of Hart's administration, which is not only approved but also applauded by the Protestants. The Jacobites and Papists are in the opposition, with possibly some few Protestants, gained through misunderstanding. Both houses agree that the Roman Catholics have all the rights which they should enjoy.

Hart at once puts his plan into execution[3] and summons Charles and James Carroll, Henry Darnall (senior and junior), Benjamin Hall, Clement Hill, William Fitz Redmond, Henry Wharton, Charles Diggs, Peter Atwood (a priest), Maj. Nich-

---
[1] L. H. J., April 11, 1720.
[2] U. H. J., April 11, 1720. Hart in his reply acknowledges his success as largely due to the assembly's "just, steady, and well-concerted counsels."
[3] U. H. J., April 12, 1720; vide April 12.

olas Sewall, and Richard Bennett to appear before the assembly. The summonses were sent out and the assembly waited over a week, but no answer came.[1] It was ascertained that the "most eminent of the Papists were in town at the time appointed to hear their pretensions,"[2] but did not think fit to appear. "Therefore," say the upper house, "they tacitly acknowledge that their pretensions are groundless and their exclamations most unreasonable." The lower house agrees that these proceedings were admirable "means to secure and establish to the Protestants their just rights against any future claim of right the Papists may pretend to."

It seems that Baltimore, and Guilford,[3] his guardian, had become more hostile to Hart. On July 4, 1719, he wrote them that on account of ill weather he could not leave at the season formerly appointed, and asked permission to remain a while in Maryland. On December 30 they answer his letter, permitting him to stay until May, 1720, and then positively command him to return. Apparently Hart had told them that no provision is made for him during his absence from the province. In their harsh answer, they call this declaration most ill-advised, and maintain that nothing is due him by the law for the support of government. In a rather labored sentence they tell him he has no ground to suppose that His Majesty's grace and favor to him is evaded by totally removing him, "which we shall do when we think fit."

This letter did not reach Hart[4] until after the April, 1720, session of the assembly, though he told that body that he does not leave the governorship by voluntary choice, but because he prefers integrity to interest. Mr. Rozier, a Papist,[5] had declared that he had done the governor's business, which was the only notice Hart had that he was to be superseded. Hart told the assembly that he hoped the commission of the governor did not "depend on that malicious and insignificant man."[6] "If it does," he cries out, "the Lord have mercy on the governor." Since the last session of the assembly Hart

---
[1] U. H. J., April 20, 1720.
[2] Henry Darnall, sr., Charles Diggs, Clement Hill, Benjamin Hall, William Digges (probably).
[3] L. H. J., October 1, 1720.
[4] In his introductory speech he states he has no recent advice from Baltimore.
[5] U. H. J., April 11, 1720.
[6] U. H. J., April 21, 1720.

had received letters from the proprietary [1] stating that Mac-Namara had made satisfactory submission to him and should be restored to practice. No reparation was made to Hart or to the insulted judges.

Before any proceedings could be taken MacNamara died, and with him died the controversy. It only remained for Hart to transmit Baltimore's letter to the assembly and to state that he was grieved by it and that he feared lest the example may be laid hold of by other practitioners. Some of them are "of his kidney, vehement espousers of the Popish faction," and use the governor "with such indecencies as are inconsistent with the grandeur of an inferior court." One of these other lawyers was undoubtedly the elder Daniel Dulany.[2] He was a "noted favorer of Papists" and comes into notice at this time through a charge of misfeasance he lays against Col. Thomas Addison of the land office. One Mark Brown seems to have also been an accuser in this matter. Addison,[3] an "honest Protestant and lover of the King and country," says Hart, has been taxed with "villainous things" by "little mean fellows," and writes that he has done his duty, but is a "mere pageant of paist board if he must suffer such barbarous affronts." The assembly seems loath to do anything in the matter.

The trouble with Birchfield[4] comes up at this session.[5] On December 13, 1718, the commissioners of customs wrote to Baltimore that Birchfield's course of conduct was correct, but that Hart obstructed His Majesty's service. They ask that he be instructed not to do so, and such instructions were sent. Hart was naturally offended and lays the matter before the assembly. The upper house suggest that the former assembly's address against Birchfield be inspected and that they discover how they came short of explaining things fully. This was done,[6] and the delegates report that they are surprised to find that the commissioners of customs rather countenance than redress abuses, and that Hart is arraigned by Birchfield

---

[1] Dated February 18, 1719 (U. H. J., April 9, 1720).
[2] U. H. J., April 14, 1720; L. H. J., April 9, 1720.
[3] A councillor.
[4] U. H. J., April 9, 1720.
[5] The old statehouse at St. Mary's City was given to William and Mary Parish at this time (April 7, 1720, L. H. J.).
[6] L. H. J., April 15, 1720.

for delaying proceedings, when they know that he "hath been very assiduous and zealous in promoting and expediting the affairs of the Crown."

The upper house[1] thought proper measures should be taken to render the address effectual, since the occasion of it still continued and the aggressors were encouraged, while the impartial conduct of the governor, as the judge in chancery,[2] was reproved. They suggest that Hart be requested to act as the province's agent in the matter.

The lower house[3] tell Hart that the dockets show his promptness, and that "we are so well satisfied with your excellency's integrity and justice, during your administration as chancellor, that the most invidious of your enemies can not in anywise make out the least charge of partiality or corruption." Yet they conceive that MacNamara's management of Birchfield's affairs was largely the cause of the evils in the customs. These are largely removed by MacNamara's death, and the delegates are not inclined to take further steps in the matter, so they decline to make use of Hart as their agent.

This surrender is very unpalatable to the council. They urge the insult to the governor, the danger to let another have opportunity to act as Birchfield did, and the fact that it is easier to prevent aggrievances than to be put to the necessity of seeking redress after suffering them. The commissioners say Birchfield did his duty and Hart was partial. This accusation should be answered. The lower house, however, stood to its position and the matter was dropped.[4]

A bill was brought in by the lower house[5] that Hart might enjoy the 3 pence per hogshead during his absence for a year, or until superseded. Hart thanked them for this,[1] but suggested that the money raised by that duty be paid the treasurer for the public charge, and that in lieu thereof Hart be paid at once a sum approximately equal to what would be raised by this duty in the next six months. The lower house at first thought this prejudicial to the interest of the new governor and wanting in duty to Baltimore, who may soon ap-

---

[1] U. H. J., April 19, 1720.
[2] Hart gave up the seals to Col. William Holland on account of this matter.
[3] L. H. J., April 19, 1720.
[4] L. H. J., April 22, 1720. A conference committee, on the last day of the session, recommended the employment of Hart as agent in the matter.
[5] L. H. J., April 16, 1720.

point another governor. Hart says Baltimore can not supersede him without permission of the Crown, and the latter has granted him leave of absence for twelve months, making no provision but for his absence.[1] He felt that the lower house acted "very cautiously in saving their money, and that he had deserved so much of Maryland that their representatives might have done me a favor, which he is persuaded no private friend would have refused him on less obligations." Further, he will have no support during his absence if not from the 3-pence duty. The lower house say the new governor may ask for this duty, and, having already voted it away, they will lie under his displeasure. Hart writes to the speaker, "I insist upon it that the 3 pence is due to me as governor until my commission is legally superseded, and resolve to take all proper measures to maintain it. His lordship's instructions can not take precedence of a law."[2] The council strenuously aided him, and the lower house, "reassuming" its former vote, grants the governor what he asked.

We notice, in general, throughout this session that the delegates are apt to yield to the influence[3] of Hart, as in former years. There is more friction and a little more stubbornness on the part of the delegates, but they rarely persist in opposition. This is clearly seen in the procedure with reference to an unguarded remark of the delegates that they did not care to enter into the discussion of a certain matter, since the session would be short. For this Hart at once brings them to account. They answer that certain members of the upper house gave them to understand that the end of the session was near.

"This is an insufficient answer," retorts Hart; "your expressions seem to infringe on the undoubted right of the proprietary to summon and adjourn assemblies."

To this the lower house made a submissive reply. They did not pretend to fix the length of the session, but thought it would not be a long one, as there was little public business.

---

[1] U. H. J., April 20, 1720.
[2] U. H. J., April 22, 1720.
[3] On April 22 the upper house recommends the delegates to allow a reasonable recompense to the governor's gardner, who "has been very serviceable and curious in making, leveling, and rolling the shell walk before the public building, for which the country has never been charged anything, though he has been very diligent and laborious therein." In 1715 a flagstaff had been ordered erected, with sufficient braces and a cedar frame, in front of the state house.

They acknowledged fully Baltimore's right.[1] So the incident terminated. Shortly after the close of the session Hart embarked for England and arrived there before August 8, when he answered certain queries of the board of trade in such a way as to show that he had lost none of his affection for the province. He then vanishes from Maryland's records.

In May, 1720, Baltimore and Guilford petitioned the King that Charles Calvert, captain in the First Regiment of Foot Guards and a cousin of the proprietary, be appointed governor of Maryland. They state that they find it necessary to change their governor, but give no reasons. This application is granted, and Calvert shortly leaves for Maryland. The friends of Thomas Brooke, the president of the council, as was reported to Baltimore, had spread rumors that Baltimore had sent a private commission to Brooke while Hart was in Maryland. This and certain undefined hasty proceedings of Brooke caused Calvert's speedy departure from England. On October 12 he met the assembly, read them Baltimore's letter, notifying them of his appointment, and expressing the hope that "old rancor and jealousy will now disappear."[2] Hart returned to London and was nominated by the King, on May 9, 1721, as governor of the Leeward Islands[3] in the West Indies. He arrived at the seat of government at Antigua on December 19, 1721, and found himself ruler of a domain which included the islands of Antigua, St. Christophers, Nevis, Montserrat, and the Virgin Islands.

His career here was fully as stormy as in Maryland. He was at continual variance with the assembly about his salary, and at one time removed his family to St. Christophers. In 1725 various petitions were presented to the British Government against him, and he was replaced by the Earl of Londonderry. Hart sailed for England on January 14, 1727, and of his later life nothing has been discovered.

---

[1] U. H. J., April 22, 1720. I suspect there was a malicious satisfaction felt by the delegates when they refused to draw up an address to the King, as Hart recommended them to do on the last day of the session. They tell Hart they want to go home after so long a detention which has not resulted in "any great service to our country." Many of the members are sick or absent, and they enjoy what we may or reasonably can desire. This they have often told the best of kings, and ask to be excused from repeating it.

[2] In his address to the assembly of 1721, Calvert speaks of "the little heats being at an end."

[3] N. and Q., 8th series, 11, 81; Anderson's Col. Ch., 111, 181, 187; Edwards's West Indies, 11, 453.

A strong, zealous, impetuous man, he was a most devoted member of the Anglican Church and a faithful servant of the English Crown. He was probably overbearing and exacting and had many of the defects of his times and of his Irish blood, but with it all his conscientious devotion to duty, his single purpose to have his province well governed, and his painstaking care of the details of administration make him a man who should not be forgotten. The code of laws which Maryland adopted under his influence remained his best monument and was in force for more than half a century after his departure.

IX.—THE FIRST CRIMINAL CODE OF VIRGINIA.

By WALTER F. PRINCE, Ph. D.,
NEW HAVEN, CONN.

THE FIRST CRIMINAL CODE OF VIRGINIA.

By WALTER F. PRINCE.

Dale's Code is the title commonly employed to denote the first code of laws which was ever written for the colony of Virginia. The period during which it, or any part of it, was at least nominally in force is that extending from the arrival of the first governor under the second charter, Sir Thomas Gates, in May, 1610, to the accession of Sir George Yeardley as governor in April, 1619. There have been so many divergent opinions expressed regarding this code and its application, as well as such a general misapprehension of some of the issues connected with it, that it seems worth while to recanvass the whole subject more thoroughly than has yet been done.

THE LAWS.

The following condensed examples of laws will give a fair idea of their character:[1]

Speaking against the Trinity or Articles of the Christian faith, death.

Blasphemy against God: First offense, severe punishment; second offense, bodkin through tongue; third offense, death.

Deriding God's word, death.

Disrespect to a minister, thrice whipped and pardon asked in public three Sabbath days.

Failure to attend Sunday service: First offense, loss of allowance one week; second offense, same plus whipping; third offense, death.

Murder, adultery, rape, sodomy, perjury in court, death.

Fornication: First offense, whipping; second offense, whipping; third offense, whipping thrice a week for one month, also public apology.

Robbing church or store, death.

---

[1] See Articles, Lawes, and Orders, Historical Tracts collected by Peter Force, Vol. III, No. II. All citations of Dale's Code to be made in this paper will be from this reprint.

Treasonable words against the King, death.

Slander or "unfitting speeches" against the Virginia Company of London, or its council or committees, etc., or against any book which the council publish: First offense, whipping and public contrition; second offense, galleys for three years; third offense, death.

Unauthorized trading with the Indians, death.

Robbing an Indian coming to trade, death.

False account rendered by a keeper of colony supplies of any kind, death.

Mariner selling at higher rates than set by governor and council, death.

Killing any domestic animal or fowl without consent of the general, death.

Failure to keep the regular hours of work for the colony: First offense, to lie neck and heels together all night; second offense, whipping; third offense, galleys for one year.

Running away to the Indians, death.

Robbing garden of flower or vegetable, stealing ears of corn, etc., death.

Refusal to go to the minister to be instructed in religion: First offense, whipping; second offense, whipping twice and public contrition; third offense, whipping every day till public acknowledgment and obedience.

Fraud on part of any baker, cook, or fisherman employed by the colony: First offense, loss of ears; second offense, galleys one year; third offense, galleys three years.

Following these is a long list of laws relating to the duties of soldiers in field and in camp and prescribing penalties for nonperformance of the same.

SEVERITY OF THE LAWS.

Measured by modern standards they were terribly severe. It seems well-nigh incredible that death could ever, in a civilized community, have been threatened him who should pluck a flower from his neighbor's garden or purloin an ear of corn; that the same dreadful doom could have menaced the person who should thrice neglect to attend church, or should kill a hen without permission from the authorities, or sell an article at an illegal price. But many laws of civilized lands in the seventeenth century seem positively barbarous to us now. It is of more importance to inquire whether these Virginia laws were inordinately stern compared with those of England at the same date. A few late writers, indeed, answer in the negative.[1] But the majority think otherwise, and are undoubtedly right. Individual enactments as cruel and almost as grotesque as some of these may have been on the statute books of England, but taken as a whole the laws of Virginia were much bloodier, much more whimsical. Indeed, I venture to say that there was not in western Europe at that day so stern a criminal jurisprudence.

True, William Strachey, secretary of the colony in 1610, seems, by the tenor of the preface that he wrote for the printed laws, to be unconscious that they were liable to censure for unusual harshness. But the question does not hinge on the knowledge of English law which fits or unfits him for making comparisons. Then, too, his remark to the effect that "many of these constitutions and laws divine or marshall may seeme ancient and common" was justified by the fact that many of the laws were drawn from or in the spirit of English laws, but there is a residue which was not so derived and could not by any possibility have impressed one as ancient or common. He names also as one of the reasons for printing the laws that those who had maligned the colony, "as if we lived then lawlesse," might be silenced. We may presume that they were, very effectually.

But the most of Strachey's contemporaries recognized the unusual nature of some of the Virginia statutes. Friends as well as enemies of the management are included in this statement. John Rolfe, an ardent advocate of the colony, foresees an Edenic period of good behavior when "may sleep the rigour of your laws," but thinks that in the meantime they are justified, in fact, are "wholesome lawes."[2]

Ralph Hamor, also at one time secretary of the colony, makes no secret of the "severe and strict imprinted booke of articles," takes note that some are objecting that certain punishments under those articles were "cruel, unusual, and

---

[1] Alexander Brown, for example, in Genesis of United States, II, 528-529. But this writer slips when he asserts that then in England "nearly 300 crimes, varying from murder to keeping company with a gipsy, were punishable with death." This was not the case till the reign of George III.
Also Editor of Notes in Aspinwall Papers, Vol. IX, p. 55.

[2] The new life of Virginia, declaring the former success and present estate of that plantation; being the second part of Nova Brittannia. Published by authoritie of His Majesties councill of Virginia. London, 1613. In Force's Tracts, III, No. VII.

barbarous," and at the same time that he denies that they were so measured by the standards of "France and other countries," admits that "they have been more severe than usuall in England," but defends their severity by the salutary results which they procured.[1] If the impassioned attacks upon the Virginia laws in 1623[2] are to be discounted because made by confessed enemies of the company administration during which they had been passed, then must the defense made by Alderman Johnson, of "that discreet and mild government first nominated,"[3] be likewise discounted, for he himself had been a leading figure in that administration.

Sir Thomas Smythe himself, who, as ruling officer of the Virginia Company, 1607–1619, was especially blamed, found a necessity of adopting an apologetic tone. He did contend, when called upon to reply to a petition of one Captain Bargrave, before the committee of grievances in the House of Commons, that the laws "rightly weighed are justifiable by the laws of England;" but he also affirmed that years ago he had written to Captain Martin in Virginia, and had "signified his dislike in the strickness" of the laws.[4] He would not even say that he thought them justified by circumstances, though he affirmed that the governors of Virginia had so thought. He further excused them by asserting that some of them were published "ad terrorem." Finally, when the colony of Virginia heard news of the attacks upon the New Company, and found that the Old Company, with Smythe at the head, might come into control again, its governor and assembly, embracing many of the old colonists, protested vehemently, not only proclaiming the severity of their past sufferings, but also the bloody and unusual character of the laws under which they had suffered.[5]

---

[1] A True Discourse of the Present Estate of Virginia, Ralph Hamor, 1615. Richmond reprint, 1860.

[2] New Company of Virginia's reply to Alderman Johnson's petition, May 7, 1623. In Abstract of Proceedings of Virginia Company of London, II, 175.

[3] Alderman Johnson's petition, in Abstract of Proceedings of Virginia Company of London, II, 169.

[4] Reply of Sir Thomas Smythe and Alderman Johnson to Captain Bargrave's petition, November, 1621. In Abstract of Proceedings of Virginia Company of London, II, 446.

[5] "The tragical relation. The answere of the generall assembly in Virginia to a declaration of the state of the colonies in the twelve yeers of Sir Thomas Smith's government, exhibited by Alderman Johnson and others." In Abstract of Proceedings of Virginia Company of London, II, 407 et séq.

Also, "A briefe declaration of the Plantation of Virginia duringe the first twelve yeares, when Sir. Thomas Smith was governor of the Companie and down to the present tyme, by the ancient planters now remaining alive in Virginia, 1624." In Colonial Records of Virginia. Richmond, 1874.

WERE THE LAWS CONTRARY TO THE CHARTER?

This question is not entirely settled by our conclusion regarding their severity. A law in Virginia might be more severe than the corresponding law in England, providing that the peculiar circumstances of Virginia made the severity necessary. More than this, the charter warranted the passing of laws in Virginia which had no prototypes in England, provided the circumstances in the colony were really unique and demanded such laws. Article XXIII of the Charter of Virginia of 1609 granted the treasurer and council of the Virginia Company, together with the governors, officers, etc., whom they appointed, according to the nature and limitations of their offices, respectively, to "have full and absolute power and authority to correct, punish, pardon, govern, and rule" the colonists "according to such orders, ordinances, directions, and instructions" as the council shall determine, "and in defect thereof, in case of necessity, according to the good discretions of the said governor and officers, respectively, as well in cases capital and criminal as civil both marine and other; so always as the said statutes, ordinances, and proceedings, as near as conveniently may be, be agreeable to the laws, statutes, governments, and policy of our realm of this England."[1] This certainly leaves all the latitude for lawmaking that we have suggested. But whether a given law was really "as near as conveniently may be" "agreeable to the laws," etc., of England, is a matter concerning which there might well have been, and be, diversity of opinion. For example, one might regard the law forbidding any domestic animal or fowl to be slain on pain of death[2] as contrary to the charter, because so utterly unlike any English law. But others might defend it on the ground that the extreme necessity of keeping up the stock in those early days of danger and scarcity transformed the seemingly trivial act to the proportions of a heinous crime and justified the passing of a law which, though divergent from any

---

[1] The charter may be found in Genesis of United States, by Alexander Brown, I, 206 ff. The instructions issued by the King under the first charter, 1606, are similar touching this point. The "King's council of Virginia" was empowered to give direction to the council of any colony which shall be in "Virginia and America" between the thirty-fourth and forty-fifth parallels for "the good ordering and disposing of all causes," "as near to the common lawes of England and the equity thereof as may be." (See Brown's Genesis, I, 66.)

[2] Articles, Lawes, and Orders, Force's Tracts III, No. II, p. 14, law 21.

English statutes, was nevertheless as near the English laws as conveniently might be.

Again, the law in Virginia which forbade any commodity of the country of what quality soever "to be sent out for private profit"[1] might be susceptible of defense on the ground that it was sufficiently in the spirit of the law of Elizabeth which made the exportation of leather, tallow, and hides felony.[2] But what of a statute which made a seaman who charged a colonist for cheese a penny a pound in excess of the price regularly fixed by the governor liable to death, though it were his first offense?[3] Ingenuity which could extenuate this on account of the peculiar circumstances of Virginia could probably frame an excuse for any murderous statute whatever. It can hardly be claimed that the existence of the colony would be imperiled if a man hired to weed a garden purposely plucked a flower or secreted a turnip, yet death was the penalty proclaimed for such an act.[4] In England, if a man robbed or wasted a garden or orchard he was liable only to damage or a whipping[5] in default. It is a long step from flogging to execution. Even according to the conceptions of the age, three years in the galleys at the very most ought to have been a sufficient penalty. We can not but think, then, that a few such statutes were contrary to the charter because not conformable to the spirit of English law. Yet if a special commission had been appointed to try the code with the object in view to decide if it was in derogation of the charter, it is likely that the result would have been very much influenced by the political prejudices of the members, or perhaps by the wishes of the King. Kings afterwards found a similar indefiniteness in the language of the charter handy when they wished to quash that instrument, since they could procure a decision that it had been violated.

Attacks against the second Charter of Virginia on such grounds had little chance of success, for King James I was friendly to the Smythe administration and apparently in sympathy with the severity of government in Virginia.

But there might be another reason for complaint that the

---

[1] Articles, Lawes, and Orders p. 18, law 36.
[2] I Elizabeth, ch. 10, Statutes of the Realm.
[3] Articles, Lawes, and Orders p. 14, law 20.
[4] Ibid, p. 16, law 31.
[5] 43 Eliz., ch. 7, Statutes of the Realm, Vol. IV, pt. 2, p. 971.

Virginia laws violated the charter. Article XXIV of that instrument authorized the employment of martial law only in time of mutiny and war. Now, if the law, or any part of it, which was in use in Virginia in time of peace as the ordinary law of the land was martial law, then there was a plain and pronounced infraction of chartered limitations. This leads us to consider

THE THREEFOLD DIVISION OF DALE'S CODE.

There has been a tendency on the part of modern writers to speak as though the whole code was one of martial law. Perhaps they have been misled by the contemporaneous charges[1] that the code was translated or extracted from Netherlandish martial law. We shall consider those charges later. Perhaps the impression has been deepened by reading impassioned asseverations that those were "most cruell and tyranneous laws, exceeding the strictest rules of marshall discipline,"[2] and that "though they might serve for marshall government in time of war," yet were they unfit for statutes to govern a people in time of peace.[3] But really only a part of Dale's Code was martial law, and this was not the part by which the colonists, in their capacity as citizens, were to be governed. The title of the code itself announces that it is composed of "Articles, Lawes, and Orders—Divine, Politique, and Martiall." This does not mean that its contents, as a whole, are characterized as at once "divine, politique, and martiall," but that a part of the laws are "divine," a part "politique," and a part "martiall" in their nature. The laws "divine" are those which concern acts which are in their own essence criminal and were so regarded by civilized nations generally. The laws "politique" are those which were only technically criminal; that is, which became so through public exigiencies, often such as were peculiar to the life of a young colony. The laws "martiall" are those which are military in their nature, having application only to soldiers, but to them at all times; not, as is the case with martial law in the ordinary and proper sense of the term, such

---

[1] The charges were first made by the New Company. (See Abstracts of Proceedings of Virginia Company, II, 186–187.)

[2] "A briefe declaration" by the ancient planters of Virginia, 1624. In Colonial Records of Virginia, Richmond, 1874, p. 74.

[3] "Answer to a petition delivered to Her Majesty by Alderman Johnson." Made by New Company of Virginia and Company of Somers Island. In Abstracts of Proceedings of Virginia Company, II, 186–187.

as may be properly invoked in times of war and rebellion only, and then applied to all classes alike. Now, there is no indicated division line between the "divine" and "politique" statutes as printed, yet there seems to be a rough attempt, only partly successful, at classification, the most of the "divine" laws being printed first and the most of the "politique" last. But it is important to note that there is a division plainly marking off and discriminating the "martial" laws from the rest. The distinction is indicated not only in the separate subtitle standing at the head of the "martial laws," but also in various passages in the text. Thus the preamble,[1] referring to the former part of the code, says: "All these prohibited and forefended tresspasses and misdemeanors, with the enjoyned observance of all these thus repeated civill and politique lawes [here a number of them are named]—and others, the rest of the civill and politique lawes and orders—with their due punishments and perils, here declared and published, are no less subject to the marshall law than unto the civil magistrate, and where the alarum, tumult, and practice of arms are not exercised, and where these now following lawes, appertaining only to marshall discipline, are diligently to be observed and shall be severely executed." The sense is as unmistakable as the grammar is defective. The code is made up of laws "divine and politique" on the one hand and martial laws on the other. The former come primarily under jurisdiction of civil magistrates, the latter, of a military tribunal; the former may be made use of by the military judges for the trial and punishment of the crimes of soldiers not especially provided for in the martial section, but the latter has no application to colonists not at the time in military service. Farther on there is given another practical summary of the laws in the first part of the code, "all of which," it is declared, "the Marshall Law, as well as the Civil Magistrate. is to punish."[2] Neither does it appear that any contemporary friend or enemy supposed the whole code was martial law. That notion was reserved for modern writers.[3] Even

---

[1] Articles, Lawes, and Orders, p. 20.
[2] Ibid., p. 32. (See also pp. 33, 42, 47, 55.)
[3] There are many who affirm that the colony was governed by martial law. Consult, for example, H. C. Lodge, in Short History of the English Colonies in America, pp. 7, 8. George Chalmer's Introduction to History of Revolution of American Colonies. 1849, I, 9.

THE FIRST CRIMINAL CODE OF VIRGINIA. 319

the Virginia assembly, in its bitterest denunciation of Dale's government, while it affirmed that his laws exceeded "the strictest rules of Marshall discipline,"[1] never ventured to affirm that they were, as a whole, martial laws.

SOURCE OF THE LAWS.

It is the fashion with writers of our day, almost without exception, to affirm that the Dale Code was derived, compiled, or translated from the military law of the Netherlands.[2] Of course this might well have been, since both Dale and Gates, who were probably the principal authors of the code, had been officers in the service of the Netherlandish Republic for years, and were doubtless familiar with the law which governed the armies there. But what is the evidence they did "derive from," "compile," or "translate" Dutch military laws? The only contemporary witness who affirms it is the spokesman of New Virginia Company, who, May 7, 1623, in reply to Alderman Johnson's petition, affirmed that there was compiled for use in Virginia "a book of most tyrannical laws written in blood, which, although they might serve for marshal government in time of war, being translated, as they were most of them, from the marshal laws of the united provinces, yet was the same far from that mild government commended by the petitioners,"[3] etc. This charge is the original from which all subsequent affirmations of the kind have sprung. It does not appear that anyone has looked up the Netherlands military law code with a view to verify the correctness of the statement. It probably has struck most that it would not have been ventured by the heads of the Virginia Company of 1623 unless they knew it was true. But perhaps the noble lords, not friendly to the former administration, and none too particular to examine the mud they threw at it, relied upon the likelihood that Dale and Gates, so long military officers in the Netherlands, would borrow from the law they were

---

[1] "Brief Declaration of the Plantation of Virginia," in Colonial Records of Virginia, Richmond, 1874.

[2] It is almost superfluous to cite particular writers upon this point, as they so generally give the same testimony. But see Hildreth's History of United States, I, 112; Lodge in Short History of the English Colonies in America, 7; Charles Campbell in History of the Colony and Ancient Dominion of Virginia, p. 104; G. P. Fisher in Colonial Era, p. 40; Burk's History of Virginia, I, 165; Stith in History of Virginia, I, 188.

[3] Abstract of Proceedings of Virginia Company of London, II, 186.

most familiar with when they came to make laws themselves. Now, there were in the Netherlands at the time that Dale and Gates were in service there two separate military codes in operation. They may both be found in the old Groot Placaet-Boeck, published in 1664.[1] One is called "Ordinances and Edicts of War," was issued in 1586, and was intended for the government of the English army serving in the Netherlands[2] under Robert, Earl of Leicester. The other was published in 1590, has for its title Articles or Ordinances of Military Discipline,[3] and was for the government of the native Dutch forces. The writer of this paper took pains to translate nearly the whole of both of these codes in order to ascertain if the Virginia laws were really translated from or even adapted from either of them. Of the two the code of 1586 would be the more likely, as it was that which was established by the English Earl of Leicester and enforced in the English army. Singularly, however, there is more, though little, special resemblance between the Virginia body of laws and the native Dutch code of 1590. Of neither was the Virginia list a translation or compilation. But was it perceptibly influenced by either? Let us answer first for the civil and, afterwards, for the purely military part of the Virginia schedule. It seems unlikely that anyone would build a system of civil government in imitation of a purely military model. Yet there are two laws that, if the eye first fell upon them, would make one think that this was probably done. These are the third and fifth civil statutes of Virginia, which bear a striking resemblance to the first and second of the Dutch list.

DALE'S CODE.	DUTCH CODE OF 1586.
3. "No man shall blaspheme God's holy name upon paine of death, or use unlawful oathes, taking the name of God in vaine, curse or banne upon paine of severe punishment for the first offense, and for the second to have a bodkin thrust through his tongue & if he continue the blas-	1. "No one shall take the name of the Lord in vain or blaspheme the same on pain that he ask pardon and be imprisoned on bread and water for the first offense, for the second have his tongue pierced with a red hot

[1] Groot Placaet-Boeck, Vervattende de Placaten, Ordonnantien ende Edicten, &c., Graven Hage, 1664.
[2] Groot Placaet-Boeck, "Het tweede deel."
[3] Groot Placaet-Boeck, 170 ff.

pheming of God's holy name, for the third time so offending he shall be brought to a marshall Court and there receive censure of death for his offense."

5. "No man shall speak any word or do any act which may tend to the derision or despight of God's holy word, upon pain of death. Nor shall any any unworthily demeane him-selfe unto any Preacher or Minister of the same, but generally hold them in all reverent regard and dutifull intreatie otherwise he the offendor shall openly be whipped three times and ask public forgiveness in the assembly of the congregation three several Sabbath daies."

iron and also be stripped to his shirt and banished out of the United Provinces."

2. "Anyone who says anything in despite or ridicule of the Word of God or of the Minister, shall incur similar penalties for the first and second offense" (as those in law 1.)

The resemblance, I have said, is striking, yet it is very likely illusive. There are at the same time striking differences, and the coincidences are not convincing, taken alone. The language of the colonial is quite different from that of the Dutch laws, except in the first part of the fifth of the Virginia and the second of the Netherlands code, and in the juxtaposition of insult to scripture and minister in both cases. But in the day when exaggerated respect was felt for ministers it was natural that the thought of injury to the Bible should lead to the thought of injury done to the preacher of the Bible. So it may be simply a logical coincidence. The penalties prescribed in the two sets, too, are very different, except that for the second guilt of blasphemy both offenders were to have their tongues thrust through. In one case, however, this was to be done with a bodkin, in the other with a hot iron. And it should be remembered that this was an age when misdeeds of the tongue were often punished by some infliction upon that unruly member.[1] Certainly the icy severity of the Virginian statutes quoted could not have been derived from the Dutch laws, for the latter denounced neither offense with death, as did the former. Further, in Holland the crime of deriding the minister seems to have been regarded coordinate with that of deriding the Holy Scriptures. On the whole, there seems hardly correspondence enough to

---

[1] E. g., tongue of scolds put in cleft stick; tongue of perjurer slit, etc.

be convincing, unless in cumulation with further correspondences between the Virginian and the Dutch laws. But such can not be found. Of course, there are laws directed against similar offenses, and it is to be expected that in both codes the graver crimes were punished with death. But there is no sign of connection. Indeed, an examination of the colonial statutes will show that many of them were evidently called forth by circumstances which did not exist in the Netherlands, but were peculiar to Virginia.[1]

The question still remains, Were the laws of a military nature, contained in the latter part of the Virginia code, derived from either of the two military codes of the Netherlands? This would seem likely. One would proceed to investigate the point with a considerable measure of confidence that this was the case when he remembers how long Dale and Gates were officers in the Low Countries and how freshly they went from that field to the colony in the New World. What more natural, if either or both of them had a part in the making of a system of laws to govern the conduct of soldiers, that they should revert to those with which they had been for years familiar in the United Provinces? And yet, almost strange to say, there is little or no proof from the nature and wording of the military rules and statutes of the colony that they were translated or even derived from the Dutch models. Parallels exist, but just such parallels as exist between some of the Virginia martial laws and certain martial laws of continental Europe. The Dale's seventh martial law, forbidding any quarreling soldier to call upon one of his countrymen to aid him,[2] reminds one of law 39 in the native Dutch code,[3] of similar import, but as vividly reminds one of the seventy-fifth law in an old Swedish code.[4]

Dale's twenty-sixth martial law forbidding interference with a provost-marshal or his officers in the performance of duty[5] is not unlike statutes in both the Netherlandish codes,[6]

---

[1] Especially laws 12, 15, 16, 17, 18, 19, 20, 21, 22, 28, 29, 32, 35, and 36.
[2] Articles, Lawes, and Orders, p. 21.
[3] "Articles and ordinances of military discipline," of 1590. In Groot Placaet-Boeck.
[4] "Divers articles and marshall laws, whereby an army is to be regulated and governed both in camp and garrison. By these lawes the King of Sweden governed his army." In pamphlet entitled Military Law, by Gen. W. T. Sherman, New York, 1880, and taken from Animadversions of Warre, Robert Ward, London, 1639. Book II, Ch. VII, Sec. XVIII.
[5] Articles, Lawes, and Orders, p. 25.
[6] Art. 78 of "Articles and ordinances of military discipline." Art. 30 of "Ordinances of war." Both in Groot Placaet-Boeck, art. 36 of Sweede Deel.

but is also not unlike one in the Swedish code just mentioned. In penalty the Swedish law is more like it,[1] since it as well as Dale's law threatened death, while the native Dutch law prescribed corporal punishment, and the law of the English army denounced the culprit with the penalty that the prisoner in whose behalf it interferes was to suffer. In general, it may be said that with all pains to find parallels between the military laws of Virginia and those of either army in the Netherlands we are able to detect only superficial resemblances, such as exist between it and the Swedish code, which is certainly unrelated. The resemblances arise from similar necessities in active army life.[2] On the other hand, the discrepancies, both substantial and verbal, are manifold. The penalties prescribed in Virginia are often very different from those in Holland, and apt to be more severe. The language and grouping of related offenses in the shape of statutes is very divergent. It should be noted also that stereotyped expressions are used in each code which are not found in the others. "Shall be put to death (or 'hung') without mercy" is a common formula in "Articles and Ordinances." "Shall be put to death with such arms as he carrieth," is a stereotyped form and penalty in Dale's Code.[3] We hear nothing in the Netherlands about passing the pikes. But to "pass the pikes" was a punishment familiar to the military law of Virginia.[4] I do not remember a case where either of the Dutch codes mentioned the galleys, but the Virginia statutes make frequent mention of them as a penalty.[5]

---

[1] "Divers articles and martiall lawes" in Military Law, Gen. W. T. Sherman.

[2] There seems to be a slight connection between "Ordinances of war" and "Articles and ordinances of military discipline" or else both these borrow a little from a common source. Article 22 of "Ordinances of war" says: "No one shall play or pawn away his weapons or arms; moreover, he shall always keep his equipments and weapons clean and serviceable on pain of dismission." Article 73 of "Articles and ordinances" declares that "No one shall play away his weapons or accoutrements or make way with them. Moreover, he shall keep them clean and serviceable on pain of being cashiered from the company without passport." The wording and penalties prescribed are significantly like. Dale's law, numbered 29, is as follows: "No man shall sell, give, imbezzel, or play away his armes, or any part thereof, upon paine of death." There are no special marks of relationship to either of the proceedings. Article 10 in "Ordinances of war" also is probably related to article 12 in "Articles and ordinances of military discipline," but neither find any counterpart in Virginia. And on the whole it is remarkable how dissimilar the two military documents of the low countries are, how slight the evidence of relationship. But the evidence of relationship of either to Dale's law is much slighter.

[3] Articles, Lawes, and Orders, Laws, 3, 7, 8, 9, 21, 23, 34, 37.

[4] Ibid., Laws, 6, 10, 11, 12, 24.

[5] Ibid., Civil Laws, 6, 12, 13, 26, 37, Martial Laws; 2, 3, 13, 18, 19, 20, 28, 36, 41.

There seems to be no other conclusion possible than this, that the charges made by the enemies of Smythe and Dale, in 1623, and meekly repeated by scores of writers since, to the effect that Dale's Code was a translation or compilation of the martial law of the army, whether English or Dutch, of the Netherlands, is quite erroneous. When we come to take up the "divine & politique laws" of Virginia we shall find that some of them were derived from English statutes and some were from the English common law. If the "martial laws" were framed after some model, as is more than likely, that model has not yet been brought forward.

As will hereafter appear, Dale was responsible for the whole of the "martial" laws, as well as some of the laws "divine & politique." His own testimony has been strangely neglected. It ought to clinch the whole matter. In his instructions to the captain of the watch he says:[1]

> Having thus *religion* beside *prescription* and *reason* (which my own breeding hath taught me how to make use of) to be my guide in the new settlement and in this strange and heathenous (contending with all the strength & powers of my mind and body, I confess to make it *like our native*) country * * * And as I have constituted subaltern officers according both to the ancient & modern order of the wars and well approved the government and magistracy, *resembling* [active verb] *and maintaining the laws of England*, so I have taken pains to present so many & such instructions. * * * Let me advise, therefore, every officer now established to hold it a service of duty, faithfully to execute such orders and instructions as I have made it my mindes labour to expresse and draw out for him.

There is no hint of obligation to Dutch models in this, but rather a claim that the author had endeavored to make laws which should resemble the laws of England. He wants to make Virginia like, not Holland, but England. He relies upon three great aids—religion (the Bible), prescription (by which he probably means the existing laws of England, whether civil or martial), and his own reason. This is not the language of a translator or compiler, but of an intelligent and responsible legislator.

Before we leave this section let us consider another possible source of inspiration for a few of the earlier laws of the Dale schedule. William Crashaw, father of the poet, preached a sermon before Lord Delaware and others of the council and

---

[1] Articles, Lawes, and Orders, p. 37.

company of Virginia, just before the noble lord took his departure to be governor of Virginia. Therein he gave the following noteworthy advice:[1]

Suffer no Papists, let them not nestle there; nay, let the name of the Pope or Poperie be never heard in Virginia. Take heed of Atheists, the Divels Champions; and if thou discover any make them exemplarie. And (if I may be so bold as to advise) make Atheism and other Blasphemie Capitall and let that be the first law made in Virginia. Suffer no Brownists, nor factious Separatists, let them keep their canticles elsewhere * * *. Especially suffer no sinful, no leud, no licentious men, nor that live not under the obedience of good lawes, and let your lawes be strict, especially against swearing and other prophaneness. * * * Let the Sabbath be wholly and holily observed, and public praiers daily frequented, idlenesse eschewed and mutinie carefully prevented.

Now, since all these recommendations, except those relating to Papists and obnoxious sects (and probably no representatives of these were in Virginia), are incorporated in the first part of Dale's Code, and in very nearly the same order, the question rises whether here is a case of connection. The question gains in interest when we learn that the long prayer appended to the code to be repeated twice a day in the court of guard was probably the composition of Crashaw.[2]

But Crashaw's sermon was not delivered till March 3, 1610, while Gates, who established the first law of Virginia, surely including the fundamental ones on blasphemy, church attendance, and mutiny, had started for America the year before. He was shipwrecked on the Bermudas and did not actually reach Virginia and proclaim his laws till May, 1610. But in the meantime he could have had no intelligence of Crashaw's sermon, so as to have been influenced by it. When the sermon was delivered Gates was supposed to be lost, and when Crashaw speaks of the first laws to be made in Virginia he means the laws to be made by Delaware. But when Delaware arrived in the colony he found law already established and it is doubtful if he added any, and extremely unlikely that he made any on the subjects mentioned by Crashaw.[3] The only

---

[1] Abstract of Crashaw's sermon in Brown's Genesis of United States, I, 360-375. The citation is from p. 371.

[2] Since it employs verbatim a part of the language of Crashaw's preface to Hamor's Present State of Virginia, published in 1615. Besides, if one examines the prayer itself (Articles, Lawes, and Orders, near bottom of pp. 67, 68), he will find the sentiments in regard to papacy, atheism, etc., curiously similar to those expressed in the sermon.

[3] Despite Neill's conjecture that Delaware established laws in accordance with a suggestion in Crashaw's Sermon. (See English Colonization of America, p. 49.)

possible connection that Crashaw could have had with the laws actually made is on the supposition that he advised with Gates a year previous to the sermon, and is now simply repeating the substance of his views. This would not be unlikely, as ministers were not frequently consulted by lawyers,[1] and Crashaw seems to have been influential in the Virginia Company and was called upon afterwards by the council or, perhaps, by Dale himself to furnish the prayer to be incorporated in the code. But we dare not venture this as a probable hypothesis. It might be that Crashaw had known what sort of laws Gates intended establishing, had approved of the same, and that this passage in his sermon is a reflection of that approval.[2] It might be that it was the strong religious feeling of Dale and Crashaw that led each to put statutes of a religious nature foremost and that whatever else of similarity shows in their ideas is pure coincidence.[3]

WHO WAS DIRECTLY RESPONSIBLE FOR THE LAWS.

It is interesting to compare the opinions of modern writers upon this point. Some say the Virginia Company sent out, authorized, or approved the Dale Code.[4] One says that the colony sanctioned it, but probably he also means the company.[5] One or two lay the onus on the council, seeming to imply that the council acted on its sole authority without reference to the remaining personnel of the Virginia Company.[6] But most authors fix on Sir Thomas Smythe, treasurer and chief

---

[1] This was common in the early history of the New England colonies.

[2] As is the case with a passage in Lord Bacon's essay "Of Plantations." It reads thus: "For government, let it be in the hands of one assisted with some counsel, and let them have commission to exercise martial laws, with some limitation." It has been suggested that this paragraph may have had influence upon the government in Virginia. But the date of the essay is probably later than the establishment of Dale's Code. (See Brown's Genesis of United States, II, 801.) The paragraph is probably based upon reflection concerning the government of Virginia and its reputed success.

[3] The coincidences are not perfect. Gates did not make his law against blasphemy, etc., first in his code, as Crashaw desired it should be. Gates does not mention atheism by name, and speaking against the Trinity or the articles of the Christain religion might amount to a less crime. While the order of Crashaw's recommendations is quite like that of the laws having to do with the subject-matter of those recommendations, yet they do not in the code follow consecutively, but other laws are interspersed, which Crashaw does not mention.

[4] H. C. Lodge in Short History of the English Colonies in America, p. 7. David Ramsay, History of the United States, 1818, I, 48.

[5] John Fiske, in English Colony of America, 49.

[6] W. C. Bryant and Sidney H. Gay, in Popular History of the United States, I, 300, 301.

officer of the Virginia Company, as the culprit. It was "his divine and martial law,"[1] "compiled by Sir Thomas Smythe,"[2] "sent over by Sir Thomas Smythe,"[3] "with directions to apply it,"[4] and all this done by Sir Thomas Smythe "without sanction or authority from the council,"[5] and in fact with "no other sanction than the approval of Sir Thomas Smythe" himself.[1] All this is but an echo of the charges that arose out of the dissensions of the Virginia Company in 1623. The party opposed to him declared that "there was printed here and with great honors dedicated to Sir Thomas Smythe and afterwards sent by him to Virginia without the companie consent, a book of most tyrannicall laws," etc.[6] The truth is, when the code was sent from Virginia to London to be printed in 1612 it was not dedicated to Sir Thomas Smythe at all,[7] but was "with great honors dedicated to" "The Right Honourable, the Lords of the Councell of Virginea," in a sonnet of almost idolatrous praise.[8]

This does not look as though there was any intention to conceal the publication from the Virginia Company. Strachey's preface to the code is addressed to "the Committees, Assistants unto her Majesties Council for the Colonie," and the whole tone of the preface is indicative that the laws are printed for the enlightenment of everyone concerned, the friends of Virginia, including the council and the treasurer himself, its enemies, and every colonist sent out. It is absurd to suppose that any one in the company was ignorant of the printing of the laws. If the company was aggrieved, why did it wait

---

[1] Edward Eggleston, in Beginnings of a Nation, p. 70, note.
[2] Hildreth's History of the United States, I, 112.
[3] Charles Campbell, in History of the Colony and Ancient Dominion of Virginia, 104.
[4] John Daly Burk, in History of Virginia from its First Settlement to 1804, I, 177.
[5] James Graham's History of the United States, I, 60.
[6] Abstract Proceedings of Virginia Company of London, II, 186. Reply of Virginia Company to the petition of Alderman Johnson. The statement quoted is of a piece with another immediately preceding it. "His Majesty's particular instructions for government were clean suppresst and extinguished and the original not now extant.' The reference is to Instructions for the government of the Colonies issued by the King when Virginia was under his personal direction. The document needed not to be "suppresst" after the second charter was granted. It was simply superseded, and all the privileges of government given into the hands of the Virginia Company, with certain limitations. So far from being "not now extant ' the "Instructions ' were at the very moment the charge was made lying in the MS. records of the colony in Jamestown. (See Brown's Genesis of United States, I, 64 ff.).
[7] Articles, Lawes, and Orders, Force's Tracts, III, No. II.
[8] Nova Brittania, published in 1609, was dedicated to Smythe, as was its sequel, New Life of Virginia, published 1612, and Ralph Hamor's Present State of Virginia, of 1615.

eleven years before making any complaint? Sir Thomas Smythe's own testimony was that direction to print the laws was not given by him alone, "but by sundry of his Majesties Councill for Virginia, whereof many are very honorable Lords and Knights and of this honourable House."[1] It is reasonable that this should have been so. He furthermore asserted that the laws "were not framed by Sir Thomas Smythe, as is most untruly alledged, but by those worthy governors in Virginia, as the very title and preface to the book sets down. Which laws and articles Sir Thomas Smythe was so far from framing or making them as in a letter written to Captain Martin, one of the first planters and an especial man at that time in Virginia, that he signified his dislike in the strickness thereof, fearing it would discourage men from going to the plantation."[2] As Smythe says, the preface and title appended by William Strachey, secretary of the colony, to the printed code plainly states that the laws were made by the governors, Gates and Dale. The enemies of Smythe, indeed, in the very philippic which seems to lay on him the onus of the tyrannical laws, affirm, no doubt correctly in this instance, that "as for the government abroad in the plantations it was for the most part left to the governor's absolute pleasure and power only."[3] We have already seen that Sir Thomas Dale expressly acknowledged himself the author and promulgator of the martial part of the code, which is nearly four-fifths of the whole. The direct responsibility for the laws rests upon the governors, Gates and Dale, who constructed them, proclaimed them, and for the most part, as we shall see, probably made them after they reached Virginia; so that when they were sent to England to be printed they were as much a novelty to Smythe as to anyone else. Whether the ultimate responsibility legally could be traced to the Virginia Company—it could not to the treasurer alone—must depend on whether it could legally transfer its legislative functions according to the manner and theory about to be described.

James I looked upon the American colonies as Crown lands, subject to his personal supervision and control. He held

---
[1] Reply of Smythe and Alderman Johnson to Captain Bargrave's petition. (See Brown's First Republic, p. 447.)
[2] Brown's First Republic, p. 446.
[3] Abstract of Proceedings of Virginia Company of London, II, 186.

that Parliament had no authority to interfere,[1] and only called in the advice of his privy council on colonial affairs. The first government of Virginia, lasting from 1605 to 1609, was according to a plan drawn up by the King himself.[2] There was a King's council of Virginia in England, whose members were of royal appointment. There was a colonial council in Virginia whose members were nominated by the King's council, and whose functions and acts were subject to the guidance of the King's council. The colonial council might make ordinances for good government and order, but these must not touch life nor member, and might be annulled at any time by the King or his council for Virginia. Thus the reins of authority were all in the royal hands. The King was in theory himself doing what his subordinates did in respect to Virginia.

But the colony did not prosper. There were other reasons[3] why the King desired to divest himself of responsibility while retaining his share in the prospective profits. On such accounts he acceded to the petition of the Virginia Company for a new charter. Only the first members of the council in England were to be nominated by the King. All vacancies were to be filled by vote of the council itself.[4] The council was to constitute whatever officers it saw fit for Virginia,[5] and to make all laws for government.[6] It was to have, together with the governors, officers, etc., it should appoint, according to the natures and limitations of their offices, respectively, "full and absolute power and authority to correct, punish, pardon, govern, and rule" colonists "according to such orders, ordinances, directions, and instructions" as the council should determine, and "in defect thereof, in case of necessity, according to the good discretion of the said governors and officers, respectively, as well in cases capital and criminal as civil,

---

[1] In 1624, a parliament having been called by the King after an interval of seven years, the Virginia Company petitioned Parliament in the interests of its chartered rights. A committee for the business was already appointed, when James forbade Parliament to meddle, roundly asserting that it was King and privy council alone that had to do with governing colonies. (See Abstract of Proceedings of Virginia Company of London, II, 229, 230.)

[2] "Instructions for the Government of the Colonies." In Brown's Genesis of United States, I, 64 ff.

[3] Brown's First Republic in America, p. 75.

[4] See Art. IX, X of second charter, 1609, in Brown's Genesis of United States, I, 206 ff.

[5] Second charter, Art. XIII.

[6] Ibid., Art. XIV.

both marine and other, so always as the said statutes, ordinances, and proceedings, as near as conveniently may be, be agreeable to the laws, statutes, government, and policy of our realm of this England."[1] This was a giving over of the regal powers of legislation and government into the hands of the company council. With one proviso, the council was empowered to act in place of the sovereign, in so far as making laws for Virginia and enforcing them was concerned. What the council actually did during the term of Smythe's administration was to follow the royal example and pass over its sovereign powers of legislation and administration to the governors of Virginia. This was not done by formal action, so far as appears. Sir Thomas Smythe was an exceedingly busy man, with various affairs on his hands. It was generally difficult to get more than a handful of the council together, so there may have been merely neglect to frame and send laws over.[2] Now, the charter provided that in case of failure to receive instructions the governor and assistants of Virginia should act on their own responsibility, exercising the same functions granted to the council, though the charter probably did not contemplate more than a temporary neglect of the council to furnish such instructions. So if the company had been called to account for delegating its legislative responsibilities in this way, it might and might not have been able to defend its course under this clause of the charter.

To summarize the way by which the direct responsibility for the laws of Virginia got lodged in the hands of the governors, the King originally claimed to exercise the sole right of legislation for Virginia; but in 1609 he invested the Virginia Company with this attribute of sovereignty in respect to the colony, and further provided that if at any time the

---

[1] Second charter, Art. XXIII.
[2] Lord Delaware's commission as lord-governor of Virginia, granted February 28, 1610 by the Virginia Company, gives him power to execute martial law in case of mutiny and rebellion, "and upon all other cases and occasions there happening, to rule, punish, and govern according to such directions, orders, and instructions as by His Majesties said councill, or the greater part thereof here resident in England, shall from tyme to tyme be in that behalf made and given, * * * and in defect of such informations, the said lord-governor and captain-generall shall and may rule and govern by his own discretion or by such lawes for the present government as he with such councill as he shall take unto him, or as the said lord-governor and captain-generall shall think fitt to make and establish." (In Brown's Genesis of United States, I, 379.) This is thoroughly in accordance with the authority granted the council by the terms of the charter. It appears, too as if it were intended presently to legislate for Virginia. No legislation abroad was attempted, however, till after Smythe's administration had expired in 1619.

company's organ, the council, failed to furnish legislation and instructions necessary the colonial governors were to assume the functions of legislation and independent action themselves. The council did neglect, and that for a period of years, and so, from intention or preoccupation, made the governor in so far sovereign over his dominion of Virginia. The only ground on which the council could interfere with whatever laws the governor might choose to make was the same ground which would have given the Crown to interfere with any laws which the council might have devised—that is, on the ground that they were unwarrantably divergent from the laws of England.

DATES AND PARTICULAR AUTHORSHIP OF THE LAWS.

We have already gone so far as to see that the laws were drawn up by the governors of Virginia. Now, the laws composing the "Dale code," so called, were sent to England to be printed in the fall of 1611, a year and a half only after the first of them were established. The title which heads them is as follows:

> Articles, Lawes and Orders Divine, Politique and Martiall for the Colony in Virginea: first established by Sir Thomas Gates Knight, Lieutenant General the 24 of May 1610, exemplified and approved by the Right Honorable Sir Thomas West, Knight, Lord Lawarr Lord Governour and Captaine Generall the 12 of June, 1610. Againe exemplified and enlarged by Sir Thomas Dale Knight Marshall and Deputie Governour, the 22nd of June 1611.[1]

This title was probably written by William Strachey, secretary of the colony, who was about as good a witness of the facts as could have been produced.[2] He again remarks in the preface:

> It hath appeared most necessary unto our Ethnarchie Deputy Governor Sir Thomas Dale, Knight Marshall, not only to exemplifie the old Lawes of the Colony, by Sir Thomas Gates published and put in execution by our Lord Generall Laware during his time one whole yeere of being there, but by virtue of his office to prescribe and draw new, with their due penalties.

Both title and preface testify to the same thing, namely, that while Lord Delaware had a hand in enforcing the laws as

---

[1] Articles, Lawes, and Orders, p. 9.
[2] If not written by Strachey, it doubtless was written by Dale himself, the author of preamble which follows. Of Dale, too, it must be said that no one could have known the facts better than he.

printed in 1612, Sir Thomas Gates and Sir Thomas Dale were the sole authors.[1] Other statutes may have been added after this time. We know that some were proclaimed by Deputy Governor Argall, but none of these were ever authoritatively put in print.

The question what part of the laws should be ascribed to Gates and what to Dale is one which is full of difficulties and has been answered variously,[2] but as far as can be seen none of the answers have been based at all upon internal evidence. But internal evidence, it will appear, is the strongest bearing upon the question. Let it be more clearly explained than has yet been done that the entire code is of the following component parts: A preamble and thirty-seven statutes which are characterized by the quaint epithet divine and politique (11 pages), another preamble, a table of fifty-one marshall lawes (a little over 8 pages), and several sets of instructions addressed by the marshall separately to colonels or local governers (8 pages), captain of the watch (5 pages), captain (4½ pages), lieutenants (2 pages), ensigns (2 pages), sergeants (3 pages), corporals (over 3 pages), and private soldiers (6 pages).

---

[1] Those who favor the notion that Delaware made the first laws and sent them over to Gates may object that all that the title and preface assert as to Gates's connection with the laws is that he "established" them and that he "published and put in execution" the first statutes. But silence gives a testimony nearly as emphatic as affirmative when so well-informed and obsequious a person as Strachey uses expressions not only ignoring any possible connection of Lord Delaware as author, but calculated to convey the unavoidable impression that Gates and Dale were sole authors. Besides, it would be ludicrous to speak of Delaware as having "approved" the laws he himself had written. The language of Dale in the preamble to the civil code, to the effect that he "adhered unto the lawes divine and orders politique and martial of his lordship," do not signify that Lord Delaware was author of the laws. Delaware succeeded Gates as sole and absolute governor and still held that office while Dale was deputy. Having approved and adopted Gates's laws he made them his own.

[2] Alexander Brown's earlier opinion was that Gates (or Delaware) was author of all the general laws of civil and military character and that Dale put forth only the "instructions." (Genesis, I, 461. Cf. Document CXIX.) But this can not be correct, for Dale in the first preamble expressly states (Articles, Lawes, and Orders, p. 9) that to the "lawes divine and orders politique and martial" which he found he had added others. Brown's later opinion (First Republic, 154) is that Gates (or Delaware) was the author of simply the divine and politique laws. But this can not be so, since Dale speaks of the martial laws that he found when he came. (Articles, Lawes, and Orders, p. 9.)

Neill not only says that the code in its earliest form had twenty-one articles (History of Virginia Company in London, 73), which, as stated in the text, may be correct, but he also declares that Dale enlarged the laws and "also introduced the martial code contained in the thirty-two articles of war of the army of the Netherlands." (History of Virginia Company in London, 75.) If this is no better founded than the context, which informs us that Delaware proclaimed a part of the laws and that Dale introduced the martial laws with the cognizance of Sir Thomas Smythe, it is built on sand. We more than suspect that this is the case. Where can any such thirty-two articles of war be found, whether in their original form in the Netherlands or as embodied in Dale's code?

THE FIRST CRIMINAL CODE OF VIRGINIA. 333

Since every one of the sets of military instructions is dated June 22, 1611, which date moreover agrees with the statement, presumably written by Strachey, embodied in the general title, that Dale enlarged the code June 22, 1611; and since, moreover, those instructions purport to emanate from the marshal, which was the title of office of Dale, who did not land till May 10, 1611, it may not be questioned that Dale was the author of this part of the code and that it was proclaimed on the 22d of June of that year. Our inquiry is therefore confined to the first 19 pages, embodying the civil and military code of a general character.

Two fallacious presumptions have usually been allowed to darken the problem. The first is that the laws were all made in England and sent there in two distinct batches. The other is that their original order is exactly the order in which we find them as printed in 1612.

Now as regards the former, it was strange if a man sent to rule and make laws in Virginia should not wait until he was on the spot and had studied the situation before he attempted to suit the peculiar circumstances of the colony. Laws of an ordinary criminal nature, such as those relating to blasphemy, Sabbath breaking, murder, theft, adultery, rape, etc., could as easily be framed before arrival, but not to advantage such as relate to communication with the Indians, sanitary precautions, etc. Since Gates proclaimed his laws May 24, 1610, the very day after his arrival, it would seem that he did indeed almost certainly make them before coming to Virginia or en route thither. Therefore one might with reason argue that the articles of Gates's code were those in the afterwards printed collection which do not show and did not need knowledge of the special circumstances of Virginia for their construction, being those fundamentals which could be derived from the common law of England, with an added pinch of severity, perhaps, to suit a community so far removed from civilization. It is confirmatory of this reasonable hypothesis that none of the fundamental but only the special laws show signs, and will be proved of origin later than Gates's administration—that is, belonging to Dale. Time enough, about forty days, elapsed betwixt the landing of Dale and the date when he is said to have "exemplified and enlarged" the code to give him the opportunity for studying the situation. Observation gave ability to determine which were those enactments which "I have found either the necessities of the present state of the colonies to require or the infancie and weakness of the body thereof as yet able to digest."[1] Neither need we infer from the title that he issued his statutes strictly in a batch, but rather that June 29 saw a kind of codification of proclamations previously issued as there was occasion for them. This would be the natural course; and we know from his own pen that some of his laws were actually put forth before June 22. In a letter[2] written May 25 he remarks that three days previously he had set up on public view several proclamations, "one for the preservation of our cattle amongst ourselves, another for valuation of provisions amongst the mariners." Both of these proclamations may be identified as articles in the code, "copies of which I have sent and leave to your noble consideration," he adds, and thereby confirms the conclusion that he issued the laws on the spot, and not previously in England, and that he issued them from time to time as occasion demanded. The presumption that the order in which we find the statutes is the original order of their promulgation is unwarranted. We shall have no doubt of this when we come to a more detailed examination of internal evidences. If all Strachey had to do was simply to copy an engrossed table of laws he might indeed write of his "pains," but he would hardly mention "gathering of them." But if he was obliged to collect the laws issued by Gates and Dale, and hitherto comprised in various documents, he may well have judged it fitting and been expressly empowered by the deputy governor to attempt some kind of a decent logical classification. This would explain the fact, which we shall make patent, that the statutes issued respectively by Gates and Dale are not, as hitherto supposed, divisible at some particular point in the print of 1612, but occur intermingled, at least to some extent.

Let us now proceed to examine a few of the laws in question, enough of them, and those minutely enough to exhibit the grounds on which we base the conclusions already shadowed forth. The references will be to the "divine and politique" laws in every case except where it is expressly stated that a "martial" law is meant.

---

[1] Brown's Genesis of United States, I, 493. Letter of Dale to council of Virginia Company.
[2] Preamble of first part of Articles, Lawes, and Orders, p. 9.

Law 22, along with a number of excellent sanitary regulations, prohibits that anyone "rench or make clean any kettle, pot, or pan, or such like vessell, within twenty foote of the olde well or new pumpe." This law could not have been made by Gates, for the reason that the new pump did not exist at the time his part of the code was proclaimed. Delaware superseded him June 10, and a month later William Strachey wrote that Jamestown "hath no fresh-water springs serving the Towne but what wee drew from a well six or seven fathoms deepe, fed by a brackish River owzing into it."[1] The next year Dale arrived, and May 25, thirteen days after landing, he wrote to the Virginia Company a letter wherein he mentions that one of the necessities of Jamestown is "a new well, for the amending of the most unwholesome water which the old afforded.[2] According to Brown, on May 20 Dale had a conference with his council and decided to dig the well.[3] Therefore law 22 must be of later date than May 20, 1611, and have Dale as its author.[4] A letter written by Delaware after he came to Virginia throws further light, probably, upon one way in which some of the laws made by Dale sprang naturally from the situation of things in the colony. "So uppon the tenth of June," he says:

I landed at Jamestown, being a verie noysome and unwholesome place, occasioned much bie the mortalitie and idleness of our owne people, so the next daie I set sailors to worke to unlode shippes and the landmen some to cleanse the towne, some to take cole for the forge.[5]

It was this condition and the uncleanly habits veiled in the above paragraph which most likely suggested to Dale the first part of law 22.

Nor shall anyone aforesaid within lesse than a quarter of one mile from the Pallizadoes dare to doe the necessities of nature, since by these unmanly

---

[1] "A true repertory of the wracke and redemption of Sir Thomas Gates," etc. Written July 15, 1610. In Purchas's Pilgrims, IV, 1753.

[2] "Letter of Sir Thomas Dale" to the President and Counsell of the Companie of Adventurers and Planters in Virginia. In Brown's Genesis of United States, I, 492.

[3] Brown's First Republic, 150. I have not happened to trace the statement to its source, but do not doubt its correctness. The date would be May 30, new style.

[4] Capt. George Percy was acting governor during the short interim between the departure of Delaware and the arrival of Dale, March 28 to May 12, but there is no reason to suppose that he ventured any new statutes. Gates's second administration is out of the question in this regard, since it began at almost exactly the same date, the last of August, 1611, that the ships departed bearing to England Strachey's manuscripts of the whole code.

[5] A letter written by Lord Delaware to Salisbury, not dated, but received by the latter September, 1610. (English State Papers, Colonial, James I, Vol. I, No. 22; also Brown s Genesis, I, 415.)

slothful, and loathsome immodesties the whole fort may bee chooked and poisoned with ill aires.

The twenty-first law is that which decrees death to the man who "shall dare to kill or destroy any Bull, Cow, Calfe, Mare, Horse, Colt, Goate, Swine, Cocke, Henne, Chicken, Dogge, Turkie or any tame Cattel or Poultry of what condition soever" without leave from the General. Now, when Delaware reached Virginia he wrote home relating what happened during the winter which preceded Gates's short administration, the winter of 1609–1610, the awful "starving time." He says that "our people, together with the Indians (not to friend) had the last winter destroyed and kil'd all our hoggs, inasmuch as of five or six hundred (as it is supposed) there was not above one sow, that we can heare of, left alive; nor a henn nor chick in the forte (and our horses and mares they had eaten with the first)."[1] It would have been a whimsical proceeding on the part of Gates to have sat down immediately on his arrival[2] and written out a law forbidding the slaughter of horses, mares, hens, chickens, hogs, etc., when there was not a horse, mare, hen, or chicken left in the colony, and only one sow. And, furthermore, when it was so doubtful if an attempt should be made to keep up the colony, that ten days later he decided to abandon it, and on June 10 actually started away. The law was really issued by Dale after several consignments of his stock had reached Virginia.[3] He himself tells us, as before stated, that on May 22 he set up several proclamations, "one for the preservation of our cattle amongst ourselves."[4] This was undoubtedly what afterwards became the twenty-first law, or at least the first draft of it. Had the

---

[1] Governor and council in Virginia to the Virginia Company, July 7, 1610. In Brown's Genesis, I, 408.

[2] He arrived May 23 and established his laws the next day. No ships arrived in Virginia from the winter of 1609–1610 till the coming of Gates.

[3] It would seem that Delaware brought some cattle over, for he testified that the cows passed the winter of 1610–1611 out of doors, and did well. ("A short relation made by Lord De-La-Warre to the lords and others of the councell of Virginia." In Brown's Genesis, I, 481.) In the latter part of 1610 the *Dainty* arrived, with three horses on board. When Dale himself came he brought with him "twelve kine, twenty goates, besides conies, pigeons, and pullen [poultry]." (Howe's Abridgment of Stow's Chronicle, in Brown's Genesis, I, 461.) He knew that a detachment of colonists was soon to follow him with "100 kyne and 200 swine for breed." (Letter of Sir Edwin Sandys, March 21, 1611. In Brown's Genesis, I, 461–462.) Every species named in the law was included in the several consignments except the turkey, which was native in Virginia, and the dog, representatives of which tribe had probably survived the starving time." There was now occasion for the law.

[4] Dale to council of Virginia-Company, May 25, 1611. In Brown's Genesis, I, 493.

remarkably minute law 21 previously existed there would have been no need of a new proclamation. It was the experience of the winter of 1609-1610, when the people fell upon and devoured the live stock, that made this statute in all its terrible severity seem called for. As if to excuse the harshness of the penalty by explaining the extreme importance to the colony of preserving the domestic creatures, the statute is prefaced by a long preamble, in the course of which occurs an adjuration to "forbear to worke into our own wants *againe* by over hasty destroying and devouring the stocks." The significant word *againe* looks back to the starving time and the short-sightedness that accompanied it.

Dale writes that he held council May 21, 1611, and that day "did forbid all manner of tradings with the Indians, least our commodities should grow every day with them more vile and cheap by their plenty."[1] Evidently before that date trading with the Indians was very common indeed. Had any law been issued by Gates on the subject Dale need not have made a new order, but only to have enforced the old. But on May 21 we evidently have the genesis of law 15: "No man of what condition soever shall barter, trucke, or trade with the Indians, except he be thereto appointed by lawful authority, upon pain of death." Not only is the law Dale's, but it was certainly put forth after he had come to the colony and because of the rise of circumstances demanding action.

There are two proofs that law 20, forbidding mariners to sell "provisions of Meale, Oatmeale, Bisket, Butter, Cheese, etc.," at higher than the fixed rates, whether said mariners belong "to any ship or shippe, now within our river or hereafter which shall arrive," was not issued by Gates, but by Dale. In the first place, during the eighteen days of Gates's administration no ships were in the river except the two which he had brought from the Bermudas, and they, after the nine months' stay of 140 shipwrecked emigrants upon the islands, could have contained no provisions of the kind.

The second proof is found in the statement of Dale that among the proclamations he set up May 22, 1611, was one "for the valuation of provisions amongst the Mariners."[2] The proclamation may easily be identified with law 20.

---

[1] Sir Thomas Dale to Virginia Company, May 25, 1611. In Brown's Genesis, I, 493.
[2] Letter of Dale to council of Virginia Company, May 25, 1611. In Brown's Genesis, I, 493.

Law 13 forbids slander, mutiny, disobedience, or neglect contrary to the authority of the lord-governor, lieutenant-general, marshal, council, or any public officer of Virginia.

Law 17 menaces with death any keeper of public stores who deals fraudulently or gives a false account to the lord-governor, lieutenant-general, marshal, or any deputy governor in authority. Law 30 threatens the person who conspires against the person or authority of lord-governor, lieutenant-general, or marshal with the same condign fate. The thirty-seventh law, providing for the case of a soldier who refuses to pay his debts, mentions the marshal, as do also the martial laws numbered 13 and 39. Now, all of these must belong to Dale's share in the authorship of the code, for while there were doubtless provost-marshals previously to enforce purely military discipline,[1] Dale was the first, if not the only, person who ever bore the title of marshal of Virginia.

Laws 13, 17, and 30 summarized above, likewise martial law 50, make mention of the lord governor. That was the title of Delaware, and was his only because he was the only governor of his rank during the term of the second charter. At first it seems perfectly obvious that the laws referred to must therefore date at least as late as the coming of Delaware. But an obscure bit of history must be elucidated before that shall be certain.

The impression derived from many secondary histories[2] is that when Sir Thomas Gates, Admiral Somers, and Captain Newport started for Virginia, it was under the arrangement that whoever reached Virginia first should be governor there. This would be a ridiculous arrangement, but so those who trust the statement of John Smith would have us believe. In consequence quarrels arose between the three and all took passage on the same boat, which would be a still more rediculous thing, since it would leave the question who was to be governor undetermined, after they arrived. Furthermore, we are told that Gates, when he finally did happen into the seat of authority in Virginia, was acting only as deputy governor, while all the while Lord Delaware was the real gov-

---

[1] See Articles, Lawes, and Orders, pp. 22, 24, 25; martial laws, 13, 24, 25, 26.
[2] R. A. Brock, in "Narrative and Critical History of America," III, for example.

THE FIRST CRIMINAL CODE OF VIRGINIA. 339

ernor under appointment for life. Now, this is all wrong. An authoritative document issued by the council of the Virginia colony states what the arrangement really was. According to it Gates, Somers, and Newport, in the order named, were given several commissions, sealed, successively to take place one after another "considering the mortality and uncertainty of human life."[1] Therefore when shipwrecked on the Bermudas, and after arrival at Virginia, Gates administered the government. In what capacity, as deputy for Delaware, already under appointment to be lord governor for life? No, Strachey's words denominating him "our right, famous, *sole* governor then"[2] are justified by the testimony of the council for the Virginia colony, which certainly ought to have known the character of its own acts: "We gave our commission to an able and worthy gentleman, Sir Thomas Gates, whom we did nominate and appoint *sole* and *absolute* governor."[3] The first signer of this statement is Lord Delaware himself, who would not have been likely to subscribe to any derogation of his own title and authority. The document continues:

> Seeing that all the dangers and sicknesses have sprung from *want of affecting our purpose of sending an able governor* [Gates was shipwrecked, and it was not yet known in England but that he was lost], we have concluded and resolved to send forth the Right Honorable the Lord de la Warr by the last of January, and to give him all the liberties and privileges which we have power to derive upon him.

If these powers were yet to be granted him, nine months after Gates left England for Virginia, it is plain that he did not then possess them. His commission, making him absolute

---

[1] "A true and sincere declaration of the purpose and ends of the plantation begun in Virginia." Entered for publication December 14, 1609, under hands of Lord De la Warr, Sir Thos. Smith, etc. Printed, 1610. In Brown's Genesis, I, 345. This very Somers who is represented as quarreling with Gates and Newport on the question of precedence, afterwards unhesitatingly calls Gates "our governor," both as acting in the Bermudas (letter to Salisbury, lord treasurer of England, June 15, 1610. See Brown's Genesis, I, 401) and after arrival in Virginia, although sailing with him in the same vessel. It is true that in another "broadside" the council of Virginia dubs three men, Gates, Somers, and Newport "*Chiefe Governours*" (Brown's Genesis, I, 354-356). But the word is here used in a general sense only, just as when the whole council of the Virginia Company is called the "governours and councillors established for that plantation" (Brown's Genesis, I, 337).

[2] Preface to Articles, Lawes, and Orders, p. 5.

[3] "A true and sincere declaration" signed by Lord De la Warr, Sir Thomas Smith, Sir Walter Cope, etc. Entered for publication December 14, 1609. In Brown's Genesis, I, 345.

governor for life was not given him till February 28, 1609–10.[1] He proceeded to Virginia, where, to quote his own language:

> I caused my commission to be read, upon which Sir Thomas Gates delivered up unto me his commission, both patents and the counsell seale.

Here was the formal transfer of authority from one depositary to another. Confusion has arisen from two facts. One is that the Virginia Company in February 17, 1608–1609, *did* intend to send Lord De la Warr as governor the next month, and so expressed itself.[2] But it changed its mind and sent Gates instead. The other is that while the appointment of Delaware was deferred, yet the programme afterwards carried out was already arranged. Delaware was slated[3] to be lord governor, and the council once proleptically calls him by that title, although not yet his in reality.[4] But the fact remains that he did not receive his appointment till the next year. Therefore it is doubly sure that laws 13, 17, and 30, as likewise martial law 50, were not passed in the time of Gates. The language of the fiftieth martial law clearly shows that it was written by some deputy governor acting in the absence of the lord governor and in his stead and behalf. We are forced to the conviction, then, that it was composed after Delaware had returned home from Virginia in 1611, and that Dale was its author.[5]

Martial law 43, also, was certainly issued by Dale. It says that "all other faults, disorders, and offences that are not mentioned in these Lawes, Articles, and Orders, shall be and are supplied in the instructions which I have set downe and now shall be delivered unto every Captain and other Officer,"

---

[1] Brown's Genesis, 1, 375–384.

Crashaw's sermon, delivered before Delaware and others a week previous to the date of the commission, is indeed entitled, "A sermon preached in London before the Right Honorable the Lord de la Warr, lord governour," etc., but the sermon was not printed till March 19, when Delaware was governor, and the title is significant of nothing except that it was appended after the noble lord received his commission.

[2] Letter from council of Virginia to corporation of Plymouth. February 17, 1609–10. In Brown's Genesis, I, 238ff.

[3] As Brown says: "First Republic," 84.

[4] Broadside published by council of Virginia Company. Date unknown but probably March or April, 1609. Perhaps the reason why Delaware is spoken of as if he were already governor is that it was desired to impress the public with the magic of his noble name, although strictly it was a little tricky to do so.

[5] Martial law 50 enjoins on all officers to execute the statutes of military discipline "as no doubt our Right Honorable Lord Generall doth assure himselfe" that they will do, "wherefore in his Lordship's behalfe I must entreat all Governors, Captains" etc., to govern themselves "according to the intention of his Lordship, declared by these present Ordinances."

etc. These instructions, we have seen, compose the greater part of the entire code, and are severally dated June 22, 1611, showing by that date and by the fact that they are issued by the "marshall" that Sir Thomas Dale, the only marshall of Virginia, was their author. It follows that Dale was the author of martial law 43.

It is perhaps not worth while to mention internal evidences which tend to show, but with less cogency, that certain others of the articles "divine, politique, and martial" were not written by Gates, but by Deputy Governor Dale.

These, then, are four conclusions, in briefest form.

1. The "Articles, lawes, and orders" of Virginia are the work of two men, Sir Thomas Gates and Sir Thomas Dale.

2. No sharp division line can be drawn at any point of the printed code separating the work of Gates from that of Dale.

3. Some of the laws "divine and politique" (pp. 9-19) were by Gates, some by Dale.

4. Some of the laws "martial" (20-28) were by Gates, some by Dale.

5. The laws established by Gates were probably those of a fundamental nature, such as found a place in the civil and military systems of all civilized states.

6. The laws which betray intimate knowledge of the peculiar circumstances of the Virginia colony were probably issued by Dale.

7. Dale's laws were not made in England and brought over in a batch, but issued after he came to Jamestown and as there was occasion for them.

8. It is not probable that the order in which the articles are printed is the order of their original promulgation. Strachey did not simply transcribe, but was obliged to "gather" them, and either did not know their chronological sequences or disregarded it in a rude attempt at classification.

9. The instructions, directed to the various ranks of soldiery, are the work of Dale.

ADMINISTRATION OF THE CODE.

It is needful at this point that we should understand what the "marshall lawes," which occupy so prominent a place in the code, really were, and who were the objects of their application. The term martial law has been used, historically, in two senses.[1] First, it may stand for the rules of military discipline adopted for the government of soldiery during the term occupied by a particular expedition or series of warlike operations,[2] in which case it consists of a set of edicts issued by the king or his representative. Or it may mean what is properly not law at all, but the substitution of arbitrary military authority for the ordinary tribunals of justice in times of mutiny and rebellion.[3] In the first case, those subject to the martial law are soldiers only; in the second case, the whole population may be subjected to "drumhead justice." Really the martial law of Virginia was, in theory at least, of the former kind. Only soldiers were supposed to be subject to it. There was for the ordinary citizen the civil magistrate;[4] for the soldier the marshal and his officers. The citizen would ordinarily be tried by civil courts held by the governor of the colony, assisted by his council,[5] following the lines of jurisprudence marked out in the laws "divine and politique." For the soldier there was the marshal's court, probably meeting at regular intervals and administering discipline according to the special military statutes.[6] It should be observed, however, that by the military code itself soldiers were held to obedience under the "divine and politique lawes" also. "Yee are now further to understand that all these prohibited and forefended trespasses and misdemeanors, with the injoyned observance of all these repeated civill and politique lawes * * * with their due punishments and perils heere declared and published are no less subject to the marshall law then unto the civill magistrate and where the alarum, tumult

---

[1] Commentaries on Martial Law. W. F. Finlason. London, 1867, pp. 91, 92 n.

[2] The attempt to colonize Virginia might well have been considered a warlike expedition. It was an enterprise conducted in a hostile country, in the face of alert and savage enemies. There was as much reason for strict discipline over the soldiers of Virginia as there was in the Netherlands over the English and Dutch armies.

[3] It was this kind of martial law which the charter forbade in times of peace. (Article 24 of second charter.) Whether it was ever exercised in Virginia we have yet to see.

[4] Preamble to the marshall lawes in articles "Lawes" and "Orders," p. 20.

[5] Perhaps minor cases would be attended to by the local governors of towns.
Under the Royal Government, 1605–1609, the president and council constituted the court which was required to punish certain officers with death, while those of a minor character it might punish at discretion. See "Instructions for the government of the colonies," in Brown's Genesis, I, pp. 68–70.

[6] Before the reign of Henry VIII military justice was in the hands for the most part of a high constable and marshal, assisted by officers and civilians versed in military affairs. But after 19 Henry VIII the office of high constable no longer existed, and the marshal (usually the second in command) became the chief judge on military courts. This court met in Henry VIII's reign usually twice a week. (See Military Antiquities, France Grose, F. A. S., London, 1801.)

THE FIRST CRIMINAL CODE OF VIRGINIA. 343

and practise of arms are not exercised and where these now following lawes appertaining only to martiall discipline, are diligently to be observed, and shall be sternly executed."[1] There is considerable obscurity on the subject of military service in early Virginia. Whether there was a class of men who were perpetually soldiers or whether none were liable for military service more than a certain number of weeks a year I have not been able to determine. John Rolfe, in 1617, wrote that all farmers were bound "to watch and ward in the townes where they are resident," and "to do thirty-one dayes service for the colony when they shall be called thereunto."[2] On the other hand soldiers were employed in daily labor, except when their turn for guard duty came around.[3] But though all soldiers were a part of this time laborers, it does not seem that all laborers were soldiers.[4] Certainly soldiers are discriminated from civilians in a number of passages in the marshal's instructions. "Any laborer or souldier,"[5] "any soldier or what manner of man else soever, of what quality or condition he be." These are examples.[6] There were certain classes of citizens who were never liable to military or other public service, such as ministers, bakers,[2] cooks,[7] probably Cape merchants, truckmasters, keepers of public stores,[8] and perhaps some others. But whatever constituted the soldier, and however long he continued a soldier, he was amenable to the martial laws, as well as to the ordinary law of the land.[9] The citizen who was performing military service, though it were only watch and ward, was for the time being a soldier, and so subject to the martial law. But the citizen, not at the time acting in a military capacity, was subject only to the law of the land embodied in the laws "divine and politique." This

---

[1] Preamble to martial division of "Articles, Lawes, and Orders," p. 20.
[2] Relation of the State of Virginia, John Rolfe, 1617. In Virginia. Hist. Reg., I, 107.
[3] Articles, Lawes, and Orders, p. 31, and other places.
[4] This is the cumulative impression gained from many references in the marshal's instructions, but which are difficult to bring together as an exhibit without consuming inordinate space.
[5] Articles, Lawes, and Orders, p. 33.
[6] Ibid., Third martial law, p. 21.
[7] Ibid., Thirty-seventh law, pp. 18, 19.
[8] Ibid., Seventeenth law, p. 13.
[9] But in all cases, if we mistake not, he was answerable at the marshal's court and not before the civil magistrate. In case a soldier refused to pay his debts, though the creditor was a civilian, the latter would bring suit at the court of the marshal. The marshal had a civil officer to prefer such cases. (See Thirty-seventh law, p. 18.)

was the general theory, but it can not be said to have been a thoroughly consistent and well-digested scheme.

Laws 1 and 37 of the civil part of the code are really martial laws out of their true places, having nothing to do with civilians or civil courts.[1] On the other hand, the third martial law presumes to lay hold of a civilian[2] and punish him by a martial court. This may be said to be contrary to the charter. In six cases, also, the civil courts gave over a criminal to the marshal's court. In one case,[3] that of blasphemy, the penalty of death was fixed by statute for the third repetition of the offense, but the sentence was to be pronounced by a martial court. In three cases[4] trading away tools or furniture to mariners, killing domestic stock, and perpetrating unsanitary acts, the statutes prescribe certain penalties, presumably inflicted by civil authorities, but then gave the culprits over to the tender mercies of the marshal's court for such further punishment as it saw fit to direct. In the two remaining cases,[5] failure to take certain other sanitary precautions, and neglect of duty by overseers, the guilty person was to be tried by martial court in the first instance, and that tribunal was free to prescribe the penalties it judged proper. Was the procedure laid down for these six cases in violation of the charter? For the martial law to attack civilians, for the military court to usurp the functions of the civil court in times of peace would be so. Was it so for the civil statutes to require the assistance of the martial courts in certain instances by the express warrant of the law of the land and by express requisition of the civil tribunal? Whether

---

[1] "I do strictly commaund and charge all Captaines and Officers of whatever qualitie or nature soever whether commaunders in the field, or in towne or townes, forts or fortresses, to have a care that the Almightie God bee duly and daily served, and that they call upon their people to heare sermons, as that also they diligently frequent Morning and Evening praier themselves by their own exempler and daily life and dutie herein encouraging others thereunto, and that such who shall often and wilfully absent themselves be duly punished according to the martiall law in that case provided." (Law 1.) "If any souldier indebted, shall refuse to pay his debts unto his creditor, his creditor shall informe his Captaine, if the captaine cannot agree to the same, the creditor shall informe the Marshall's civill and principal officer, who shall preferre for the creditor a bill of complaint at the Marshal's Court, where the Creditor shall have Justice." (Law 37.)

[2] "If any souldier, or what maner of man else soever of what quality or condition soever he be, shall tacitly compact with any seaman" etc. to leave the colony without permission from authority, he shall be put to death. (p. 21.)

[3] Law 3, Articles Lawes, and Orders, p. 3.
[4] Laws 19, 21, and 22. Ibid., pp. 13, 14, 15.
[5] Lawes 25 and 27. Ibid., p. 16.

a trick or an inadvertency, this procedure might successfully evade the letter while it violated the spirit of the charter.

We are now to see, so far as evidence is extant, to what extent and in what spirit the laws of the code were put in force by the various governors of Virginia.

By Gates: The authority of Sir Thomas Gates in Virginia began, of course, with his arrival and the reading of his commission, May 23, 1610. But his gubernatorial authority over the body of colonists which took passage with him began at the time they entered the ships to go to Virginia, June 2, 1609. In the absence of much positive information about the character of his government in Virginia, whether it was severe or otherwise, we are the more indebted to Strachey's account[1] of affairs in the Bermudas, where Gates ruled his shipwrecked company nine months and a half, ere he could get ships ready to complete his journey.

When Governor Gates set the men at work building a ship in which to go to Virginia some of them became mutinous, saying: "How that in Virginia nothing but wretchedness and labour must be expected, with many wants and a churlish intreaty, there being there neither that Fish, Flesh, nor Fowle," which here were plenty, while here hard work, also, was not necessary. So in September, 1609, a conspiracy was formed by six persons to run away to another part of the island and live by themselves. They were found out, and to "fit the punishment to the crime" they were in fact put on a lonely island. There they became very sick of each other's exclusive society and sent petitions and promises of amendment to the governor, "upon which our governor (not easie to admit any accusation, and hard to remit any offence, but at all times sorry in the punishment of him in whom may appear either shame or contrition) was easily content to reacknowledge them again." This was the first mutiny. The second was fomented by one Stephen Hopkins, who gave reasons "both civill and Divine (the Scripture falsely quoted)" why it would be right to refuse to obey the governor, whose authority he said ceased at the time of the shipwreck. This he asserted to two hearers, who reported it to the governor. Hopkins was "generally held worthy to

---

[1] W. Strachey's narrative, 1610. In Memorials of the Discovery and Early Settlement of the Bermudas or Somer's Islands, 1515-1685. Maj.-Gen. J. H. Lefroy, 2 vol., London, 1877. Vol. I, 22-55.

satisfie the punishment of the offence with the sacrifice of his life, such as belonge to Mutinie and Rebellions." But all uniting in intercession for him, the governor readily granted pardon. Encouraged perhaps by this leniency of Gates a third mutiny broke out. Some persons "who conceived that our Governor indeede neither durst nor had authority to put in execution nor passe the act of Justice upon anyone" conspired to seize the stores, abandon the governor, and settle on the island. The affair was betrayed, but the conspirators were not at once arrested, being scattered. One Henry Paine kept stealing articles to use in the rebellion, and one night when it was his turn to watch, and the captain of the guard gave him directions he struck that officer, and when told that the governor should hear of it, roundly declared that the governor had no authority to interfere. This passed all bounds. He was arrested, convicted before the company, and sentenced by the governor to be hanged, "and the ladder being ready, after he had made many confessions, he earnestly desired, being a gentleman, that hee might bee shot to death," which was done. Some of the malcontents now fled to the woods, fearing that they were discovered. Gates sent and offered them pardon if they would return and amend. All did save two, who were left behind when the rest went to Virginia.

What was done by the governor in the three instances just cited was done not in pursuance of any particular statute, but under the chartered authority to hold courts-martial in times of mutiny and punish at the discretion of the judges. Wherefore it is of value, not to show how he actually did carry out the statute law, but rather to show how he would be likely to do so. In the first mutiny he banished instead of putting to death, and pardoned the offenders when they showed contrition. In the second, he pardoned the culprit already condemned to death. In the third, he felt compelled to make an example, the rebellious spirit was getting so rampant, but granted the criminal's request for a more honorable form of execution than had been adjudged. All this speaks a humane man, whom only urgent peril to the state can force to severe measures. There is visible one touch of intolerance, although it is a mark of the times rather than of the man. John Want was "a sectary in points of Religion, and in his own prayers much devout and frequent, but hardly drawne to the publique, insomuch that being suspected by our Minister for a Brownist, he was often compelled to the common Liturgie and form of Prayer." This was probably pursuant to the thirty-third law.

Gates's first administration in Virginia lasted less than three weeks, and was busied with preparations for the abandonment of the colony, which would have taken place had Delaware not opportunely arrived. His second administration lasted from August, 1611, to February, 1614.

The evidence is wholly of a negative character, but it supports the presumption raised by the Bermuda régime that he was personally lenient.

Years later the colonists of Virginia issued passionate statements of the cruel sufferings under the code, but while fiercely denouncing Dale, are silent as to any injury received from Gates.[1] To be sure, the four years which the "extreame slavery and miserye" of the people is charged to have lasted included not only Dale's first and second administration, but also the latter one of Gates, sandwiched between. Nevertheless, Gates comes in for no share of execration. So it is highly probable that he gave over the responsibility for criminal prosecution entirely into the hands of the marshal, who then would become the chief judge. The treasurer of the Virginia colony, characterizing the work of Gates and Dale in Virginia, ascribes to the latter a severity which he does not impute to the former. Where identically the same inference is derivable from testimony of friend and foe, it is probably a just one.

By Delaware: The lord governor was resident in Virginia and active as well as titular ruler there not quite ten months, June 10, 1610, to March 28, 1611. He addressed the colonists upon his arrival in somewhat menacing terms, according to his own report:

I delivered some few words unto the company, laying some blame on them for many vanities and their idlenes, earnestly wishing that I might

---

[1] "A brief declaration of the plantation of Virginia during the first twelve yeares, when Sir Thomas Smith was governor of the companie down to the present tyme, by the ancient planters now remaining alive in Virginia, 1624." In Colonial Record of Virginia, 1874. Also "The tragicall relation" in Neill's History of the Virginia Company of London, 407 ff.

1. Abstract of Proceedings of Virginia Company of London, I, 21.

2. Letter of Lord Delaware and Council of Virginia to Virginia Company, July 7., 1610. In Brown's Genesis, I, 407.

3. Strachey's preface to Articles, Lawes, and Orders, p. 7. But he says that Delaware's residence continued "one whole yeere," when, to be exact, it lasted nine months and eighteen days.

no more find it so, leaste I should be compeld to drawe the sworde of Justice, to cut off such delinquents, which I had much rather drawe in their defence, to protect from enemies.

The colonial secretary affirmed that the laws were "put in execution by Delaware during the whole of his stay in Virginia." Probably not, nevertheless, with a severity such as "thunders in the index." For the colonists, when it became safe and necessary in after years to tell their pitiful story, remembered no more against Delaware than Gates.

By Percy: Percy's administration, after the lord governor was obliged to leave on account of sickness, lasted a month and a half. He was not likely, knowing himself to be simply an ad interim governor till the marshal should come, to undertake any drastic measures involving life and death. There is extant no whisper of complaint about his government.

By Dale: According to the old planters of Virginia,[1] Sir Thomas Dale gave an early proof of his harshness of temper after arriving in Jamestown, May, 1611:

> We must alsoe noat heere that Sir Thomas Dale at his arrivall, finding himself deluded by the aforesaid protestations [by Sir Thomas Smythe, that the colony was flourishing] pulled Captain Newport by the beard and threateninge to hang him for that he affirmed Sir Thomas Smith's relation to be true, demanding of him whether it were meant that the people here in Virginia should feed upon trees.

From quite another quarter an incident has come down to us singularly in accord with this glimpse of the marshal's deposition.[2] Captain Argall brought some French prisoners to Jamestown, captured in an attack upon the settlement at Mount Desert Island. The captains were hopeful of excellent treatment when they learned that they would be given over to the care of Marshal Dale, because he had formerly shown friendliness toward the French, and had received promotion himself by the kindly offices of the French Government. But instead, "he spoke of nothing but of ropes and gallows and of hanging every one of us," and seemed about to carry out his threat, but desisted at the intercession of Argall, who showed him that the prisoners had acted under authority received from the King of France. It may be that his long career in

---

[1] "A brief declaration of the plantation of Virginia, during the first twelve yeares, when Sir Thomas Smith was Governor of the companie and down to this present tyme, by the ancient planters nowe remaining alive in Virginia, 1624." In Colonial Records of Virginia, Richmond, 1874.

[2] Narrative of the French prisoners. See Brown, First Republic, pp. 191, 192.

the military service of the Netherlands, during eight years of which he had been an officer,[1] had not predisposed him to suavity or mildness.

Alexander Whitaker, the "Apostle of Virginia," spoke highly of Dale. But it is not unknown that some ministers of that day were far from disapproving harsh laws and of harsh enforcement. It was Rev. John Cotton who drew up for Massachusetts Bay a code so bloody and cruel that even the stern legislators of that colony would not adopt it.[2] Whitaker says that the marshal was a man "of good conscience in all things."[3] So, very likely, was Torquemada. Nor was the "good conscience" which allowed its owner to become violent and pluck up beards free from the other peculiarities. Dale actually sent to Powhatan offering to make his daughter, the sister of Pocahontas, then 11 years old, "his nearest companion, wife, and bedfellow,"[4] although he then had a wife living in England.

What information comes down to us regarding the enforcement of the law by Dale comes in part from his friends and in part from those who, having suffered under his administration, were foes to his memory. All extant accounts are meager enough, and they overlap only to a certain extent. But so far as they do overlap they reveal no substantial discrepancy. After the second charter had been replaced by the third and Sir Thomas Smythe had resigned from his position as treasurer, dissension arose in the Virginia Company of London. Friends of Sir Thomas Smythe petitioned that the management of the colony under his successor might be investigated. A spirited defense was made, with counter-charges affecting the past régime. The governor and assembly of Virginia heard the distant rattle of the storm that was hailing petitions, counter-petitions, statements, and manifestoes, and fell into a panic of fear lest Virginia should be handed back

---

[1] Aspinwall Papers, Massachusetts Historical Society Collections, fourth series, Vol. IX, pp. 52-59.

[2] An Abstract of the Laws of New England as They are Now Established. London, 1641. In Force's Tracts, III, No. IX. The title is a misnomer. These laws were intended for Massachusetts Bay Colony, not for all New England, and were not then nor thereafter "established."

[3] Quoted in Old Virginia and Her Neighbors, John Fiske, I, 166.

[4] Ralph Hamor's True Discourse of the Present State of Virginia. Hamor was himself the messenger. There is no reason to doubt his story. He was friendly to and an admirer of Dale. Powhatan had just sold his daughter to an Indian for 2 bushels of wampum, and could not take advantage of the offer.

to the tender mercies of Sir Thomas Smythe once more. Consequently, in the spring of 1623 they drew up the "Tragicall Relation," a statement in brief of the sufferings they had endured while Smythe was treasurer. A year later they sent another, already referred to, the "Brief Declaration," which is a little more detailed, yet exasperatingly short. The latter was signed exclusively by men who were in the colony when Dale was there, and so knew what they testified by experience and direct observation. These state that the colonists were forced by starvation to flee to the Indians for relief. Being taken, they were executed by "starving, hanging, burning, breaking on the wheel, and shooting." The crime so terribly punished is elsewhere called "Webb and Price's Design," and took place in the spring of 1612. It was forbidden by the twenty-ninth law, reading thus:

No man or woman (upon paine of death) shall runne away from the Colonie to Powhatan or any savage Weroance else whatever.

The statute does not fix the form of execution, and Dale chose as he pleased and judged would be most effective in warning others not to be guilty of the like offense. The code nowhere hints at any such barbarous practices as burning or breaking on the wheel. The "Brief Declaration" says that one person "was chained to a tree and starved to death." The "Tragicall Relation" had more explicitly rehearsed that his offense was stealing two or three pints of oatmeal, and that he had his tongue pierced with a bodkin ere he was tied up and starved. George Percy's book, probably written after 1824,[1] relates the story and also informs us that the theft was from the store.[2] It was therefore liable to death by the tenth law, but the statute does not say anything about the method of execution. Dale went out of his way to enforce it with savage severity, especially if, as it is asserted and seems nearly certain—else why should a man steal two or three pints of oatmeal?—the perpetrator was drawn to the deed by hunger.

[1] A Trewe Relacyon of the Procedinges and Ocurentes of Moment which have happened in Virginia from the Tyme Sir Thomas Gates was shipwrackte uppon the Bermudas Anno. 1609, untill my departure out of the country, which was in Anno. 1612. George Percy. Only a fragment of this is preserved—4½ pages out of 41. These are to be found in Neill's "Virginia Vetusta," VI, ff. Captain Percy was president of the King's council in Virginia, September, 1609, till the end of the royal government there, June, 1610, and was deputy-governor March 28, 1611 to May 12 of the same year.

[2] Only he says "*some* which robbed the store he cawsed *them* to be bowned faste unto trees and so starved *them* to deathe." A little touch of exaggeration or of carelessness in expression, probably.

The pitiful story of the colonists continues: "Some for stealing to satisfie their hunger were hanged. Others attempting to run away in a barge and a shallop (all the Boates that were then in the Collonye) and therein to adventure their lives for their native countrye, being discovered and prevented, were shot to death, hanged, and 'broken upon the wheel." The leader in the attempt to get to England in open boats was one Abbot, and the offense was punishable by death under the thirty-second statute. Abbot as leader probably suffered the horrible and un-English execution of breaking upon the wheel; the other methods of execution proportioned to the responsibility. These executions occurred in 1612. At some date unknown, when returning from an expedition to the Pamonkey River, a mutiny, caused by the "want and scarcitye," broke out. It was suppressed by Dale, and "the prime actors were duly examined and convicted, whereof sixe, beinge adjudged and condemned, were executed." Since the Pamonkey River was the seat of very troublesome Indians known by the same name, against whom the Virginians are known to have made incursions, it is to be presumed that the expedition was of a military character and broke out among soldiers. They were therefore amenable to the eighth martial law, on the subject of mutiny. If its provisions were exactly carried out, the punishment of each was to be "put to death with such armes as he carrieth." The "ancient planters" testify that to their own knowledge all the barbarities above related happened, "besides continuall whippings, extraordinary punishment, workinge as slaves in irons for a term of yeares (and that for petty offences) weare dayly executed. Under the tiranus Government the Collony continued in extreame slavery and miserye for the space of five yeares, in which time many whose necessities enforced the breach of those laws by the strictness and severitye thereof suffered death and other punishments."

Ralph Hamor, at one time secretary of the colony, a professed friend of and apologist for Sir Thomas Dale, mentions the desertion of Coles, Kitchen, and three others, composing the military guard of Molina, a Spanish prisoner, and induced by him to try and reach the Spanish settlements toward the south. Indians were employed by Dale to track and bring them back, and they were executed.[1] They were guilty of the crime of letting a prisoner of war go, made capital by martial law 35. It is curious that there was no martial law covering all cases of desertion; for the third law specifies only desertion by ship. Probably it was not contemplated that anyone might attempt to desert to the Spaniards, traversing a trackless and dangerous country on foot in the effort.

But the forty-third martial statute reserved the right to try offenses not named in the article, and the instruction of the marshal to the colonel names as one of the disorders liable to be brought up in the martial court, "running unto the enemy, or intending and plotting to runne but prevented." Of course any martial court in the world would award death for such an offense, even in our own day. Hamor,[2] aware that "the manner of their death, may some object, hath bin cruell, unusuall and barbarous," declares that "indeede they have not bin, witnesse France and other Countries," but does not add "witness England," the only country which was germane for comparison. Indeed, in the very next clause he admits that "they have bin more severe than usuall in England," and in the same paragraph that "a cruell, painefull and unusuall death" was quite in the order of things. His defense of such terrible penalties will be noticed later. That defense is somewhat weakened when we learn that he was to become one of the signers of the "Tragicall Relation" of the general assembly in 1623. John Rolfe, the husband of Pocahontas, and another friend of the Dale administration, admits[3] that the laws were enforced by advising the continuance of their enforcement, and, by foreseeing a state of things when "may sleep the rigor of your lawes," further intimates that they were at the time enforced with a fair degree of rigor.

The severity of the law, coupled with the hardship of toil imposed in Virginia, was rumored in London[4] to that extent that thieves preferred to hang than to become colonists with

---
[1] A True Discourse of the Present Estate of Virginia, etc. Ralph Hamor, 1615, Richmond reprint, 1860.
[2] A True Discourse. Richmond reprint, p. 27.
[3] The new life of Virginia. Published by Council of Virginia Company, 1612. In Force's Tracts, Vol. III, No. VII.
[4] According to Gondomar, the Spanish ambassador, a couple of thieves, given the option to be hanged or go to Virginia, chose at once to be hanged, "as they would much rather die on the gallows here than to die slowly of so many deaths as was the case in Virginia." Gondomar to Philip III, October 17, 1611. (See Brown's Genesis, II, 737 ff.)

pardon. Herein they were in hearty accord with the colonists already there, who in 1623 wrote that "rather than to be reduced to live under the like Govennment, we desire his Majestie that Commissioners be sent over to hang us."[1] This may have been hyperbole, but if so it was at least hyperbole suggested by very strong feeling on the subject. Against such testimony, Dale's own statement[2] in 1614, that "here is no one that the people would have govern them but myself," is ineffectual. While Dale was on the spot the people would hardly dare otherwise than feebly cheer, after the manner of the pupils in Dotheboys Hall. Well-grounded fear prevented them also from making complaint at the time the merciless government was proceeding. So we might reasonably conjecture, but are not left to speculation. The old planters themselves testify[3] that Sir Thomas Smythe gave orders to the governor "that all men's letters should be searched at the goinge away of ships, and if anye of them weare found that the true estate of the Collony was declared, they were presented to the Governor and the indighters of them severely punished, by which meanes noe man durst make any true relation to his frendes of his owne or the Collonyes true estate." Since there were laws commanding regular and daily labor, under overseers,[4] this matter comes up for examination. Dale's instructions to the captains[5] mentioned that the men shall be kept at work till 9 or 10 a. m. (he does not say when they shall begin work, but allowing for breakfast, etc., that could not not have been earlier than 5 or 6 a. m.) and, resuming labor at 2 or 3 p. m., be withdrawn at 5 or 6, depending on the time of the year. This would make not over eight hours, perhaps not over six, for a day's labor, which seems moderate enough. One feels inclined to nod assent when Dale himself pronounces it "an easie taske."[6] But the colonists themselves did not afterwards remember that their work was play. They declare that, at least in the building of Henrico, Dale "oppressed his whole companye (three hundred

---

[1] Tragicall Relation. In Neill's History of Virginia Company in London.
[2] Letter of Dale, June 18, 1614. In Purchas's Pilgrimes, IV, 1768.
[3] Briefe Declaration. In Colonial Record of Virginia, Richmond, 1874, p. 79.
[4] Statutes, 26, 27, 28. These severally direct that every tradesman shall ply his trade daily, that overseers shall see the work intrusted them duly performed, and that soldiers and tradesmen shall work from beat to beat of drum, morning and afternoon.
[5] Articles, Lawes, and Orders, page 45.
[6] Ibid., p. 61. Instructions of Marshal to Privates.

in number) with such extraordinarye labors by daye and watchinge by night as may seem incredible to the eares of any who had not the experimentall triall thereof."[1] It is to be suspected that Dale regarded the work at Henrico as an emergency demanding haste, and far exceeded the hours of labor named in his own instructions. How often such emergencies, in his judgment, arose, and how long they continued we have no means of ascertaining. But if any dependence at all is to be placed in human testimony, we can not reject the concurrent voice of a body of eyewitnesses, backed by the approval of the governor and entire general assembly, to whom it was read. That general assembly, council, and governor, had already testified that "yf a man through his sickness had not been able to worke at all, and so perished, many through these extremities being weery of life dug holes in the earth and hidd themselves till they famished."[2] By the twenty-sixth statute if a man refused to work, that part of his food which came from the public stock was withheld one month; for the second offense the time of deprivation was to be three months, and for the third one year. There were times, as is well known, when, with the full share allotted to each from the company provisions, the colonists barely kept from starving; his would have been a remarkable constitution which could survive a year at any time that Dale was in Virginia with such supplies withheld. The marshal must have believed or charged that the persons referred to were shamming sickness and could work if they pleased. But it was a persistent species of malingers which burrowed in the ground and died like rats. If they were really sick, no words would seem excessive which characterized the heartless savagery of the marshal. If they were not sick then their preference of a death by starvation to life under the existing conditions is the most eloquent proof of the horror which those conditions inspired. While we can not be sure that every law in the code saw its fulfillment, nor even that occasion for the invocation of the terrors of everyone arose, yet we may be certain that Dale, at least, felt no hesitation on the score of employing everyone that suited him even beyond the measure

---

[1] "Briefe declaration." In Colonial Records of Virginia, p. 74.
[2] "Tragicall relation." In Neill's History of Virginia Company in London, p. 407.

of its face value. However, in one particular for which he was blamed, in these times he would be considered praiseworthy; that is, for his impartiality in the treatment of the rich and poor, gentry and those of low rank.[1] Hamor's apology for the cruelty of Dale's law and government was that those who suffered were a hard lot "of no use so fit as to make examples to others" and that "the feare of a cruell, painefull, and unusuall death more restrains than death itself."[2]

Modern writers have in many cases taken their cue and declared that though Dale was somewhat severe it was because such severity was absolutely necessary. How easily might any magisterial barbarity be justified on this plea. Why should the officers of the Spanish Inquisition be blamed for torturing their victims? Heresy was crime by the law, and it was found absolutely necessary to torture guilty persons in order to make them renounce it. Or we might easily extend the mantle of charity to cover military atrocities. Weyler was put in Cuba to crush the rebellion, and he found that the reconcentrado policy, so much execrated since, was absolutely necessary if the rebellion was to be crushed. In like manner the friends of Dale put forward the plea of necessity in his behalf. But are we prepared to admit that success in a commercial and political enterprise is sufficient motive for any lengths of inhumanity whatever? The additional apology offered by some late writers, that Dale lived in a severe age, is discredited by the fact that it was in his own age that his harshness was criticised, and with the full knowledge of English customs and penalties.

By Capt. George Yeardley: Captain Yeardley became deputy governor when Sir Thomas Dale finally retired to England, and remained in that office about one year—from the spring of 1616 to that of 1617. No intimation of any harshness in his administration has come down to us. John Smith would give us the impression that he was rather slack in government.

---

[1] "A true discourse," etc. Richmond reprint, 1860, p. 27.
[2] See complaint in "Briefe declaration," as follows: "Divers gentlemen both there [Jamestown] and at Henrico Town, and throughout the wholl colonye (beinge great adventurers and no frendes or alliance to Sir Thomas Smith) [this fling was directed against Smythe's supposed favoritism of Captain Argall, who was his relative] weare feeling members of those generall calamaties, as far forth as the meanest fellow sent over."

He would have seemed so by comparison with his predecessor, at any rate.[1]

By Capt. Samuel Argall: This officer ruled as deputy governor about two years—from May, 1617, to April, 1619. Delaware, the titular lord, sailed governor from England in the meantime to take actual command of the colony, but died en route. It is the general fashion with those who have written of the early history of Virginia to depict Argall's rule as especially severe.[2] He is declared to have been furnished with new and excessive powers to execute martial law, which prerogatives he exercised with inquisitorial cruelties, and to have enacted new laws of absurd and extravagant nature. The original source of these representations is the bitterly hostile statement which Argall's enemies in the Virginia Company made in 1623, impugning the former government of the country by Sir Thomas Smythe. This charges that Argall was sent "armed also with the strength and exercise of martial law, even in time of peace, that no man there might dare even to open his mouth in any complaint against him." It states, further, that he was "furnished with exorbitant power and exemption."[3] But scholars are getting to "sadly mistrust" the ex parte statements of these wrangles of the Virginia Company. It is highly improbable that Argall had any martial powers other than the old ones of keeping discipline among the soldiers, *not* of supplanting the regular courts by military tribunals. There is no evidence that he was extraordinarily severe. No complaint on that score comes from the colony that retained and expressed such vivid memories of the cruelties of Sir Thomas Dale. What glimpses we get of the wide-awake captain tends to show him a man grasping and perhaps dishonest, but not cruel. We find him saving, by his intercession, the lives of French prisoners of war whom Dale would have slaughtered.[4] The edicts issued by him were neither

---

[1] General History of Virginia, New England, and Summer Islands, Capt. John Smith (1619), Richmond, 1819, I, p. 284. See also II, 33, where Smith says Yeardley's successor found in Jamestown "but five or six houses, the Church downe, the Palizadoes broken, the Bridge in pieces, the Well of fresh Water spoiled, the Storehouse they used for the Church * * * the salvages as frequent in their houses as themselves." This is evidence of a weak administration and poor discipline.

[2] See, for example, History of Colony and Ancient Dominion of Virginia, Charles Campbell; History of Virginia, Burk, I, 194; A Short History of English Colonies in America, Lodge (8), etc.

[3] Abstract of Proceedings of Virginia Company of London, II, 196.

[4] Brown's First Republic, 191, 192.

absurd nor extravagant; and relatively to Dale's are moderate. He forbade[1] private trucking with the Indians. I do not know why this was necessary, unless he proposed softening the penalty, which by Dale's code was death. He prohibited pulling down the palisades, erected for defense against the murderous savages. He proclaimed that if anyone taught an Indian to shoot with guns, both learner and teacher must die. Who shall say the offense was not deserving of so severe a punishment in a colony surrounded by Indians full of hatred and cunning and thirsting for white men's blood? With their rude implements of war they had terribly thinned the ranks of the immigrants. What would they do if they got guns and learned to use them?

The edict commanding all to go armed to church and to work was admirably sensible. That compelling every man "to set 2 acres with corn (except tradesmen following their trade)—penalty, forfeit of corn and tobacco and to be a slave a year to ye Colonye," is severe enough, but not excessively so as compared with the statutes of Dale. There was already a law,[2] probably issued by Gates, commanding regular attendance at church on penalty of some undefined "severe punishment for first offense, piercing of the tongue with a bodkin for the second, and death for the third." Argall put forth another on the subject which must have acted as a repeal of the first, substituting lighter penalties, the sharpest of which was service to the colony a year and a day instead of death. Finally, it was enjoined, "no man to shoot but in defense of himself against enemies untill a new supply of ammunition comes." The colony was at this time "slenderly provided of munition." Therefore, though the Indians scoffed, inquiring if the white men's guns were sick, that they could not fire them, yet if Argall had allowed the ammunition to be all used up, the red-skinned foes would soon have done worse than scoff. Finally, we find a proclamation dated June 17, 1617, prescribing certain fixed prices for goods and tobacco, deviation therefrom to be punished by three years' service to the colony. But Dale threatened a very similar offense with death.[2]

---

[1] For statement of the edict, see Brown's First Republic, 278.
[2] Articles, Lawes, and Orders, law 6.

Not only in legislation but in actual penal administration Argall is shown to be more humane than Dale. We find him in June, 1617, reprieving John Hudson, sentenced by the courts to die "for divers crimes."[1] His "hope of amendment" in the man was disappointed, for the latter added other offenses. Yet he was not executed, but banished to the Indians with intimation that if he returned, he would be put to death at once. One George White had run away to the Indians,[2] a crime punishable by death under the old law.[3] Yet in November, 1617, Argall pardoned him. About the same time Anthony Edwards and Henry Potter were pardoned for offenses capital under the Dale code. Such are the glimpses we get of Argall. There is one case, however, which looks like a blot on his administration and may be responsible for the most of the evil reputation that he has had unjustly foisted upon him. That is the case of Captain Brewster, which was, in brief, as follows.[4] Certain servants of Lord Delaware, lately deceased, were set at work in the service of the colony by Deputy Governor Argall. Brewster, on the plea that he had directions from Lord Delaware that he was to govern and set the servants to work, withdrew them from the tasks to which Argall had assigned them, all save one, whom he abused for refusing to go. The deputy governor had Brewster brought before a court, where he was promptly condemned to death. Having rendered the sentence which the letter of the law made obligatory, the members of the court united with some of the clergy in asking that clemency should be shown the offender. Accordingly Argall showed his usual forbearance and commuted the penalty to perpetual banishment, at the same time putting Brewster to oath not to make use of speeches disparaging to the plantation or the governor. But the pardoned man speedily broke his oath on returning to England. He complained to the Virginia Company; and although the authorities in Virginia were supposed to have

---

[1] Letter by Sir Thomas Smythe to Sir Thomas Dale. (See Brown's First Republic, 254.)
[2] Brown's First Republic, 257.
[3] Articles, Lawes, and Orders, law 29.
[4] Abstract of Proceedings of Virginia Company in London, II, 39 ff. It should be remembered that we do not get Argall's side of the case stated here. The editor of the abstract, R. A. Brock, in his account of the Brewster case, printed in Winsor's Narrative and Critical History of the United States, III, 142, by some singular lapse, completely reverses the relations of the two principal actors in the episode, making Argall the culprit, and Brewster the accuser.

plenary jurisdiction, yet the company consented to review the case. The subsequent annulling of the verdict was not put on the ground that Brewster did not deserve banishment or even death, but was put on the purely technical ground that he had been condemned under the martial law, which, by King James' charter, was limited to times of mutiny and rebellion. The English lords who sat on the case showed an utter misapprehension of the nature of the martial law which obtained in Virginia. As we have explained, this was not martial law of the kind meant by the charter, that is, the supersession of civil by military tribunals, summarily and arbitrarily exercising their functions over the whole body of the citizens. It was what would be more properly termed military law, meant for the discipline of soldiers only. It was martial law of the kind that was in force in both the English and native armies of the Netherlands, although, as already shown, the Virginia martial code was not derived from that of the Netherlands. The martial law of the United Provinces was not restrained to times of mutiny and rebellion; neither was that of Virginia. According to the records of the Virginia Company the law under which Brewster was tried was the thirty-second of the martial series, "as appeared by the official record of the court transmitted to London." Argall probably regarded Brewster as an officer violating military discipline in a gross manner. There was a civil law, the thirtieth,[1] by warrant of which the prisoner might have been condemned to death. But be it remembered that Argall did not attempt to have him put to death, but commuted his sentence to banishment. In fact, so far as the evidence goes, Argall's administration was bloodless, and as a comparatively humane man he is undeserving of the obloquy heaped upon him, unless for quite unrelated causes.[2]

Following Argall came Capt. Nathaniel Powell, but his rule

---

[1] It awarded death to whatsoever person "that shall conspire anything against the person of the Lord Governor and Captain Generall, against the Lieutenant-General, or against the Marshall or against any publique service commanded by them for the dignitie and advancement of the good of the Colonie."

[2]. Aspinwall Papers, Massachusetts Historical Society Collections. (Series 4, Vol. IX, p. 28 ff. n.) On the whole the editor supports the view which is given above. He is wrong, however, in saying that Brewster could have been condemned to death under the thirteenth law. This could not have been till the third perpetration of the offense. He is right, however, in saying that under the thirtieth law "the only legal question that could be raised was whether the service was 'for the dignity and advancement of the colony.'"

lasted less than two weeks. He was supplanted by Yeardley, now returned to Virginia with knightly honors. The latter brought a new charter, began a new representative government, and, having banished the old, cruel, and arbitrary code, assisted the general assembly in passing such simple and moderate measures as formed the nucleus of a new jurisprudence.

DID DALE SUCCEED IN BRINGING THE COLONY TO ORDER AND PROSPERITY?

Idleness and disorder characterized the life of the colony under the first charter, 1605–1609. There were several reasons for this. One was the unsettled state of the government. The governing body was a council of thirteen members, one of whom was chosen as president for a term nominally of one year, but since the council was empowered to depose him any time that it saw fit, his term of office was very uncertain, especially as the council seethed with jealousies and petty ambitions. It is no wonder that the government was weak and fitful. Again, homesickness and the new and strange conditions of pioneer life in a strange land, the terrors and panic inspired by stealthy attacks of Indians, and the gnawings of famine when provisions ran low and crops were a failure inclined many to the unwisest course they could take, namely, that of insubordination. But most potent of all causes of disorder was the fact that many of the immigrants during this period, probably the very large majority, had been gathered up from the prisons, brothels, and streets and were simply acting out their accustomed natures when they showed insubordination and idleness.

Gates's first administration was too short and too full of preparations for the intended removal for it to count in the life of the colony. Delaware prefaced his term with a sharp warning, that he would "draw the sword of justice to cut off delinquents"[1] unless they subsided. How much success he had in improving the morals of the settlements we can not exactly measure. At any rate, when Dale came, in August, 1611, he found plenty to do. In spite of the reiterated intentions of the Virginia Company to accept only worthy and

[1] Letter of Delaware and Council to Virginia Company, July 7, 1610. In Brown's Genesis, I, 407.

industrious emigrants,[1] a worse sort continued to be sent, probably because few others could be had, on account of the bad reports that came concerning the colony. The 300 men brought on the very ship with Dale had been found "in riotous, lasie, and infected places," were "full of mutinie and treasonable intendments," and were of "such diseased and crased bodies" that not three score were fit for service.[2] Similar testimony had been given by Strachey earlier[3] and was to be given a year later by one John Chamberlain.[4] The Spanish ambassador, Velasco, wrote to his master August 22, 1611, that the colony of Virginia would be preserved because the authorities of England "sadly want some outlet for all the idle and wicked people such as this Kingdom has."[5] Thus was created the situation which Dale faced and for whose solution he saw no other way than to sharpen the sword of law and wield it remorselessly. The first effect of his peculiar harshness was to aggravate the difficulty. There had never been such a succession of outbreaks and attempts to escape as now followed for a time. But there can be no question that the terrible discipline finally succeeded in bringing the colonists into orderly subjection. The mutinous and discontented could not escape to England, though they tried. If they started to join the Spanish or Indians they were speedily apprehended and brought to doom. What remained to them but to submit? There are many witnesses to the fact of the establishment of good order, and no dissenting voice.

Ralph Hamor was able to write in 1615 that the execution of law was "now much mitigated, for more deserved death in those daies than do now the least punishment."[6] But it is to be suspected that one of the factors leading to this comparatively happy condition was the increasing number of honest and industrious working people whom the company succeeded in persuading to go to Virginia.

The question whether Dale's rule brought prosperity to the

---

[1] Various broadsides issued by the Virginia Company, 1607-09. See Brown's Genesis, I, 352-353, 354-356, 439, 445.

[2] Dale to Salisbury, August 17, 1611. State Papers, Colonial, James I, Vol. I, No. 26.

[3] "A true repertory," William Strachey, written July 15, 1610. In "Purchas's Pilgrimes," London, 1625, IV, 1750.

[4] John Chamberlain to Sir Dudley Carleton, July 9, 1612. In Calendar of State Papers, Colonial, 1574-1660, edited by W. Noel Sainsbury, London, 1860.

[5] Velasco to Philip III, August 22, 1611. In Brown's Genesis, I, 494-495.

[6] A True Discourse. Ralph Hamor, 1615. Richmond reprint, 1860.

colony is quite a different one and is not so easy to answer. A community may be orderly and not prosperous; it may have the quiet primness of a corpse, and for the same reason, that it is destitute of life. Sir Thomas Dale, indeed, with the same optimism or vanity which had impelled him to say that the people wanted no ruler but himself, wrote that he "left the colony in great prosperity and peace."[1] But men are apt to view their own work in roseate colors. Sir Dudley Carleton testified to the States General of the United Provinces, with similar commendation,[2] and in its response the Council of State, apparently basing its opinion on Carleton's representations, referred to the work of the late deputy governor as "very remarkable."[3] Similar phrases might easily be brought forward. On the other hand, the old settlers of Virginia gave no such testimony, and the inference from their statements is rather that the colony saw prosperity at no time before 1619, when the people were permitted to set up a general assembly and help make their own laws. But Alderman Johnson, a friend of Sir Thomas Smythe, asserted that the colony was in worse condition after 1619 than before,[4] and to support him Captain Butler wrote his blundering, if not lying, "unmasking of our colony as it was in the winter of 1622."[5] It may also be observed that when Dale went to Virginia in 1611, he expected to find it in a prosperous condition, for it had been so reported. One is in danger when he pores over such statements, so strangely discordant with each other and the facts, of becoming perturbed, if not to the extent that Dale was when he pulled Captain Newport by the beard for indorsing Sir Thomas Smythe's claim that the colony was prosperous.[6] There were two causes which operated to make the declarations touching Virginia which were published in London questionable. One was the desire of the friends of the colony to have it stand well with the public, that wealthy men might adventure funds and emigrants might offer themselves. The other cause lay in the factional strife which arose

---

[1] Sir Thomas Dale to Secretary Sir Ralph Winwood, June 16, 1616. In Calendar of State Papers, Colonial, 1574–1660, page 17.
[2] Documents Relating to the Colonial History of the State of New York. Collected by J. H. Brodhead and edited by E. D. O'Callaghan. Albany, 1853–1887, I, 16–17.
[3] Ibid., p. 19.
[4] Abstract of Proceedings of Virginia Company of London, II, 169, 170.
[5] Ibid., II, 170 ff.
[6] "A briefe declaration," Colonial Records of Virginia, p. 79.

in the Virginia Company and caused, especially from 1623, reckless charges on both sides. But if there was any class of persons who knew the facts, it ought to have been the people of Virginia, who had experienced twelve years of government during the Smythe treasurership, four of which were passed with Dale as the chief judicial officer, and latterly four years under a different régime, during which they were freemen with all the rights of property and the power to take part in making the laws under which they lived. They spoke by the unanimous voice of the general assembly, in which the governor and his council joined, and their testimony had no uncertain sound. They declared that they were in every way better off since autocratic and arbitrary governors armed with Draconian laws had left them. And it seems reasonable to conclude that they were; that they had hope and energy and motives to ambition and effort, now that their property and time belonged to them as individuals and that they had a voice in the regulation of their own affairs. So, while we can not prove by means of the preponderance of contemporary testimony that it was so, it seems safer to hold that the real prosperity of Virginia dates from 1619, when it became, what it has been not inaptly styled, the "First Republic in America."[1]

---

[1] Alexander Brown's title for his history of the early period of Virginia.

X.—A CRITICAL EXAMINATION OF GORDON'S HISTORY OF THE AMERICAN REVOLUTION.

By ORIN GRANT LIBBY, Ph. D.,
PROFESSOR, UNIVERSITY OF WISCONSIN.

A CRITICAL EXAMINATION OF WILLIAM GORDON'S HISTORY OF THE AMERICAN REVOLUTION.

By ORIN GRANT LIBBY, PH. D.

I.

The most important of the earlier histories of the American Revolution produced in Europe was written by William Gordon, a dissenting clergyman of England.[1]

He had been a pastor in Ipswich, but emigrated to America in 1770, settling at Roxbury, Massachusetts. He remained in this country sixteen years, and during his residence was actively engaged in defending the cause of the colonists. His thanksgiving sermon in 1774 before the Massachusetts provincial congress at Watertown brought upon him the unsparing denunciations of the King's friends in the colony. He early engaged in the work of writing the history of the struggle with England, and he seems to have been favored with unusual opportunities for making himself acquainted with the course of events. Before his return to England, Harvard and Yale conferred upon him the degree of master of arts and the College of New Jersey honored him with a doctorate of divinity.

The history was published in England in 1788, and in the following year the American edition appeared. The English reviews of the work were divided as to its merits. The favorable critics dwelt upon the advantages of the author's being upon the ground where material could be obtained at first hand, and dwelt particularly upon his impartiality. The chief attack upon him was directed against his style,

---

[1] Gordon, The History of the Rise, Progress, and Establishment of the Independence of the United States of America. In 4 volumes. London, 1788. N. Y., 1789; 3 volumes.

which, indeed, not even his friends attempted to defend. The New York newspapers, after the appearance of the American edition, continued for some time to publish long extracts from the history. For the Revolutionary period of our history, since that time Gordon has held high place as an authority, of greater or less value, according to the critical ability of the author using him. Dr. David Ramsay, whose history of the Revolution appeared soon after, spoke in terms of high praise of the work.[1] Bancroft, while criticising Gordon severely, says of him: "His work, notwithstanding all its faults, is invaluable."[2]

Edward Channing also pays high compliment to him:

> The most valuable history of the Revolution from a British pen is Gordon's well-known work. This author was assisted by Gates and Greene, so far as the southern campaigns were concerned. * * * Taken altogether, this work ranks with Ramsay as an authority of the very first importance.[3]

And in the latest exhaustive work on the literature of the Revolution Moses Coit Tyler says of Gordon's History:

> The book, as we have it, though written by a man who strove hard to be accurate, is defaced by many errors both of fact and opinion, and yet with all its faults of whatever kind, and even in competition with the subsequent historical labors of more than a century, this account of the American Revolution holds its ground as one of the best yet produced by anyone upon that vast uprising of human nature. It can hardly be possible for any reader of Gordon's book to resist the impression that he was an honest man and meant to be a truthful and a fair historian. Everywhere, also, in its incidental strokes of information, in a thousand casual hints and glances of meaning, one perceives the immense advantage he derived from his intimate communication with the great civilians and soldiers who conducted the Revolution from its beginning to its end. It is true that his brief residence in the country, which he made his own with so much ardor, rendered it impossible for him to see the real relation of some events, to understand the true character of some persons; but even that disadvantage had its compensation in his freedom from local and hereditary bias, in the unhackneyed freshness of his judgment, in a sort of aloofness of vision which gave something of the just perspective and the impartiality that are conferred by actual distance in space or in time.[4]

In 1758 Robert Dodsley founded that well-known English publication, the Annual Register. Edmund Burke was engaged, at the salary of £100 a year, as editor, and this

---

[1] Belknap Papers, Pt. II., 162.
[2] Bancroft, History of America, IX., 123. Note.
[3] Winsor's Narrative and Critical History, VI, 518.
[4] Tyler, Literary History of the American Revolution, II, 427–428.

position he held for nearly thirty years. In this publication there appeared from year to year a series of articles under the title of History of Europe, describing the leading events in England and America connected with the breach between the mother country and her colonies. The chief part in the production of these articles is ascribed to Burke, though he never acknowledged his share in them.

In the preface to Gordon's History we find the following:

> The Americans remarked that Dodsley's Annual Register contained the best foreign printed summary account of their affairs. * * * That Register and other publications have been of service to the compiler of the present work, who has frequently quoted from them, without varying the language except for method and conciseness.

This apparently innocent statement conceals one of the most complete plagiarisms on record. Instead of quoting from the Annual Register, Gordon copies it wholesale, varying the language so little that it can hardly be said it was done for conciseness. The proof of these charges is easy and conclusive. One needs but to sit down with the Annual Register in one hand and Gordon's History in the other to find parallel readings everywhere, from the beginning to the close of the war.

For some reason, known only to the author or his publishers, Gordon's History is written in the form of letters instead of chapters. The events in America are set forth in thirty-two letters dated from Roxbury, Massachusetts; while the foreign events appear in letters from London, Rotterdam, and Paris, six, ten, and two letters, respectively.

About two-thirds of the material in these foreign letters is copied directly from the Annual Register without substantial change. Barely one-tenth of it can be called original in any sense as intelligent comment on European conditions. The longest single piece of this kind is the description of the naval exploits of Paul Jones, four pages in length. The remainder of the material, while taken from the Register, is changed sufficiently to conceal its origin, though the style is such that it could never have been composed by the reputed author of the history we are examining. The following examples of how Gordon plagiarized his finest passages will serve to bring out more clearly what is meant. All of the material here subjoined is incorporated in the body of the text without the slightest hint of its real source:

Annual Register, 1775, p. 105, c. 2.	*Gordon's American Revolution, I, 495.*
We should deem it inexcusable to quit this part of the subject without laying before our readers the astonishing growth of the colonies within a little more than half a century and the prodigious share they contributed to our greatness—a matter of the first importance to ourselves—which perhaps can not in any degree be paralleled in the history of mankind and which will equally excite the admiration and exercise the scepticism of future ages.	This astonishing growth of the colonies within little more than half a century and the prodigious share they contribute to our greatness makes them a matter of the first importance to ourselves and must excite the admiration of future ages.

Annual Register, 1777, p. 24, c. 2.	*Gordon, II, 436.*
For when, at length, the American cruisers not only scoured the Atlantic Ocean, but spreading their depredations through the European seas, brought alarm and hostility home to our doors; when the destruction which befell the homeward-bound richly laden West India fleets poured equal ruin upon the planters in the islands and the merchants at home; when an account of the failure of some capital house in the city was almost the news of every morning; even in that state of public loss and private distress, an unusual phlegm prevailed, and the same tranquil countenance and careless unconcern was preserved by those who had not yet partaken of the calamity.	When at length the American cruisers not only scoured the Atlantic, but spreading over the European seas, brought alarm and hostility to our doors; when the destruction which befell the homeward-bound richly laden West India fleets poured equal ruin upon the planters in the islands and the merchants at home; even in that state of public loss and private distress an unusual phlegm prevailed, and the same tranquil countenance was preserved by those who had not partaken of the calamity.

Annual Register, 1780, p. 172, c. 1-2.	*Gordon, III, 416.*
Such was the complete and decisive victory gained in behalf of the petitions by the opposition on that extraordinary and memorable day. * * * Without doors, the joy and triumph in most parts of England, as well in most of the counties that did not petition as in those that did, was great and general, and though not displayed in the same manner, would not, perhaps, have been exceeded on occasion of the most decisive victory over a foreign enemy.	Such was the complete and decisive victory gained by the opposition in behalf of the petitions on that extraordinary and memorable day. Without doors, the joy and triumph in most parts of England was great and general, and perhaps would scarcely have been exceeded on occasion of the greatest victory over a foreign enemy.

ACCOUNT OF THE GORDON RIOTS IN LONDON.

Annual Register, 1780, p. 195, c. 1-2.	*Gordon, III, 425.*
Nothing could be more dismal than that night. Those who were on the spot or in the vicinity say that the present darkness, the gleam of the distant fires, the dreadful shouts in different quarters of the rioters, the groans of the dying, and the heavy, regular platoon firing of the soldiers formed altogether a scene so terrific and tremen-	The natural darkness of the night, the gleam of the distant fires, the dreadful shouts of the rioters in different quarters, the frequent firings of the soldiers, and the groans of the dying formed altogether a scene so dreadful that no description can easily reach. London the next day presented in many

dous as no description or even imagination could possibly reach.

The metropolis presented on the following day in many places the image of a city recently stormed and sacked; all business at an end, houses and shops shut up, the Royal Exchange, public buildings, and streets possessed and occupied by the troops; smoking and burning ruins, with a dreadful void and silence in scenes of the greatest hurry, noise, and business.

Annual Register, 1781, p. 139, c. 1.

Thus, after the strongest appearances on every side of an approaching and heavy tempest, the sky was suddenly cleared, and everything went smoothly and prosperously with administration.

Page 141, c. 2.

The proclamation for dissolving the Parliament operated like a thunderclap with respect to suddenness and surprise on those not in the secret.

places the image of a city recently stormed and sacked; all business was at an end, houses and shops were shut up, the Royal Exchange, other public buildings possessed and occupied by the troops; ruins were still burning and smoking, and a dreadful void and silence reigned where scenes of the greatest hurry and noise were habitual.

Gordon IV, 4.

The strong appearances of an approaching storm with which administration was threatened having subsided, and everything going on smoothly and prosperously.

* * *

When the proclamation for the dissolving of it appeared, it wrought like a thunderclap with respect to suddenness and surprise on those who were unacquainted with the design.

ATTACK ON GIBRALTAR.

Annual Register, 1782, p. 104, c. 1-2.

One hundred and seventy pieces of cannon of the heaviest metal and fourscore mortars disgorged their tremendous torrents of fire all at once upon that narrow spot. It seemed as if not only the works, but the rock itself, must have been overwhelmed. This dreadful cannonade and bombardment was continued night and day for a considerable time without intermission. It is said, and may well be supposed, that nothing could be more splendidly magnificent or dreadfully sublime than the view and the report of this tremendous scene to those who observed them from the neighboring hills of Barbary and Spain during the night, especially in the beginning, when, the cannonade of the enemy being returned with still superior power and greater fierceness by General Elliot, the whole rock seemed to vomit out fire, and all distinction of parts was lost in flame and smoke.

Gordon, IV, 73.

One hundred and seventy pieces of cannon of the heaviest metal and eighty mortars disgorged their tremendous torrents of fire all at once upon that narrow spot. This dreadful cannonade and bombardment was continued night and day for a considerable time without intermission. Nothing could be more splendidly magnificent or dreadfully sublime than the view and report of this tremendous scene to those who observed them from the neighboring hills of Barbary and Spain during the night, especially in the beginning, when, the cannonade of the enemy being returned by General Elliot with still superior power and greater fierceness, the whole rock seemed to vomit out fire, and all distinction of parts was lost in flame and smoke.

It is very evident from these examples that Gordon copied with care and impartiality wherever opportunity offered. The selections given cover the entire range of foreign topics even remotely connected with the American Revolution. It will be observed also that each of the four volumes is represented in these parallel quotations.

When we come to the material in the Roxbury letters there is necessarily less taken from the Register, though even here there is evident an astonishing lack of original sources. If anywhere in Gordon's work we should look for original material it is in that part dealing with his adopted State. He was an active participant in the stirring events of the early war, and in more than one instance is known to have personally collected material for his future history. Yet strangely enough some of the most aggravated cases of plagiarism are to be found in these very pages. In the letter dated September 28, 1774, is found an eloquent and remarkably clear statement of the conditions existing in America.

Annual Register, 1775, p. 10, c. 1-2.

The people of America at this time, with respect to political opinions, might, in general, be divided into two great classes. Of these one was for rushing headlong into the greatest extremities; they would put an immediate stop to trade without waiting till other measures were tried or receiving the general sense of the colonies upon a subject of such alarming importance, and, though they were eager for the holding of a congress, they would leave it nothing to do but to prosecute the violences which they had begun. The other, if less numerous, was not less respectable, and though more moderate were perhaps equally firm. These were averse to any violent measures being adopted until all other means were ineffectually tried; they wished further applications to be made to Great Britain and the grievances they complained of, with the rights which they claimed, to be clearly stated and properly presented. This they said could only be done effectually by a general congress, as in any other manner it might be liable to the objection of being only the act of a few men or of a particular colony. We, however, acknowledge a third party which were the friends to the administration in England, or, more properly those who did not totally disapprove of its measures; but their still, small voice was so low that except in a very few particular places it could scarcely be distinguished.

Gordon, I, 578–579.

The people may be divided into two great classes. One is for rushing headlong into the greatest extremities without waiting till other measures are tried or receiving the general sense of the colonies; and, though eager for holding a congress, would leave it nothing to do but to prosecute the violences which they have begun. The other is averse to violent measures till all other means are ineffectually tried. They wish further applications to be made to Britain and the grievances they complain of, with the rights which they claim, to be clearly stated and properly presented. This, they say, can be effectually done only by a general congress. There is a third party, who are friends to the British administration, or, rather, who do not totally disapprove of its measures; but their voice is so low that except in a few particular places it can scarcely be distinguished.

We may, by this time, begin to understand where Gordon acquired his "aloofness of vision" with which he is credited.

It is perhaps the next best thing, when an author does not possess this invaluable quality, for him to know how to acquire a reputation for having it.

In his use of documentary material for this part of his work, our author depends quite often upon the summaries found in the Annual Register, and these he uses so carelessly as to fall into several capital errors.

1. Boston town meetings of May 13 and 18, 1774.

Here Gordon seems to have had the original documents, but follows the Register's mistake in mentioning one meeting only and in compressing the two sets of resolutions into one. This leads him into the further error of giving the wrong date for Gage's landing at Boston.[1]

2. Salem resolution of June 18, 1774, on the Boston port bill, presented to General Gage.

In this case the summary in the Annual Register is used to the almost entire exclusion of the original, but a single phrase being used that shows knowledge of its existence.[2]

3. Proceedings of the Massachusetts provincial congress, October 11, 1774.

Their petition to General Gage and his answer are given from the Annual Register, and a comparison with the original shows certain slight but decisive variations.[3]

4. Action of Suffolk county convention on Gage's fortification of Boston Neck, September 10, 1774.

The resolutions are given in Gordon from the original documents,[4] but in Gage's reply he follows the Annual Register into the serious error of confusing Gage's answer to the Boston Selectmen, September 9, and his later reply to the Suffolk County convention. This is an error which might easily occur in the preparation of the English publication, but our author should have been better informed. As this

---

[1] Gordon, I, 360. Annual Register, 1775, p. 4, c. 2. Boston Evening Post, May 16, 1774, p. 2, c. 2; May 23, 1774, p. 2, c. 3.
[2] Gordon, I, 374. Annual Register, 1775, pp. 8-9. Boston Evening Post, June 20, 1774, p. 2, c. 3.
[3] Gordon, I, 411-412. Annual Register, 1775, pp. 20-21. Essex Gazette, October 11-18, 1774, Vol. VII, 325; Oct. 18-25, 1774, Vol. VII, 326.
[4] I, 389-391. Annual Register, 1775, pp. 18-19.

case illustrates several interesting features of Gordon's methods, the material is subjoined for comparison:

GAGE'S REPLY TO THE BOSTON SELECTMEN, SEPTEMBER 9.

Boston Evening Post, September 12, 1774, p. 3, c. 1.

When you lately applied to me respecting my ordering some cannon to be placed at the entrance of the town * * * I thought you was satisfied the people had nothing to fear from that measure, as no use should be made thereof unless their hostile proceedings should make it necessary. * * * I have thought proper to assure you that I have no intention to prevent the egress and regress of any person to and from the town, * * * neither shall I suffer any under my command to injure the person or property of any of His Majesty's subjects. But as it is my duty, so it shall be my endeavor, to preserve the peace and promote the happiness of every individual.

GAGE'S ANSWER TO THE ADDRESS OF THE SUFFOLK COUNTY CONVENTION OF SEPTEMBER 10, 1774.

Annual Register, 1775, p. 20, c. 1.

To this address General Gage answered that he had no intention to prevent the free egress and regress of any person to and from the town of Boston; that he would suffer none under his command to injure the person or property of any of His Majesty's subjects; but that it was his duty to preserve the peace and to prevent surprise, and that no use would be made of the cannon unless their hostile proceedings should render it necessary.

Gordon, I, 392.

I have no intention to prevent the free egress and regress of any person to and from the town of Boston. I shall suffer none under my command to injure the person or property of any of His Majesty's subjects; but it is my duty to preserve the peace and to prevent surprise: and no use will be made of the cannon unless the hostile proceedings of the people shall render it necessary.

Gage's real address to the Suffolk County convention, which Gordon must have read at the time, as everybody did, differs from his earlier one in so many points that it could not possibly be mistaken for it. A few words quoted from it will illustrate the difference. It begins:

I hoped the assurance I gave the selectmen of Boston on the subject you now address me had been satisfactory to everybody. I can not possibly intercept the intercourse between the town and the country. * * * I would ask what occasion there is for such numbers going armed in and out of the town, and through the country in an hostile manner; or why were the guns removed privately in the night from the battery at Charlestown?[1]

In April 26, 1775, the Massachusetts provincial congress issued an address to the inhabitants of Great Britain. Gordon had been chaplain of this body in 1774 and was, of course, thoroughly familiar with its proceedings, especially at this exciting period in its history. Yet it is sufficient comment

---

[1] Boston Evening Post, September 19, 1774, p. 2, c. 1-2.

on his carefulness as a historian that, in referring to this important address, he copies a summary of it verbatim from the Annual Register. The original document is given below with its variations:

New England Chronicle or Essex Gazette, May 18-25, 1775, Vol. VIII, 356, p. 2.	*Annual Register*, 1775, p. 129, c. 1.	*Gordon, I, 491-2.*
We profess to be his loyal and dutiful subjects. * * * Nevertheless, to the persecution and tyranny of his cruel ministry we will not tamely submit—appealing to heaven for the justice of our cause, we determine to die or be free. We can not think that the honor, wisdom, and valor of Britons will suffer them to be longer inactive spectators. * * *	In the meantime the provincial congress drew up an address. * * * They * * * place much dependence on the honor, wisdom, and valor of Britons, from which they hope their interference in preventing the prosecution of measures which they represent as equally ruinous to the mother country and the colonies; they make great professions of loyalty; but declare that they will not tamely submit to the persecution and tyranny of a cruel ministry, and (appealing to heaven for the justice of their cause) that they are determined to die or be free.	In the address the congress profess to place much dependence on the honor, wisdom, and valor of Britons, from which they hope for their interference in preventing the prosecution of present measures. They make great professions of loyalty, but declare that they will not tamely submit to the persecutions and tyranny of a cruel ministry; and that they are determined to die or be free. They appeal to heaven for the justice of their cause.

Such examples might be multiplied for the history of Massachusetts in the years 1774 and 1775. The Annual Register is depended upon to supply dates, documents, and summaries of conditions in the colony with complete disregard for historical accuracy.

In a somewhat similar fashion are the proceedings of other provincial congresses treated. And even the Continental Congress does not wholly escape, though the paucity of material of this kind in the Annual Register compelled our author to have recourse to the originals. Occasionally, however, he was able to appropriate a passage like the following in regard to the Continental Congress:

Annual Register, 1775, p. 36, c. 2.	*Gordon, I, 409.*
* * * it must be acknowledged that the petition and addresses from the Congress have been executed with uncommon energy, address, and ability; and that considered abstractedly, with respect to vigor of mind, strength of sentiment, and the language, at least of patriotism, they would not have disgraced any assembly that ever existed.	The impartial world will go near to acknowledge that the petitions and addresses from the Congress have been executed with uncommon energy, skill, and ability; and that abstractedly considered, in respect to vigor of mind, strength of sentiment, and patriotic language, they would not disgrace any assembly whatsoever.

In 1780, when Congress was urging the States to make up their respective quotas in order to be ready for any decisive move that might be concerted with the French fleet, letters were sent out by a committee of Congress in support of the measure. The effort put forth at this time is thus described:

Annual Register, 1781, p. 19, c. 2.	*Gordon, III, 575.*
The disgrace of appearing contemptible in the eyes of their great ally and the mischief and ruin which must be the consequence of their being incapable to benefit of his intentions in their favor were strongly urged. And the people were passionately called upon not to suffer the curse of another campaign to rest upon America. The eyes of all Europe were upon them, and their future independence, fortune, and happiness, as they said, depended upon their present exertion.	The disgrace of appearing contemptible in the eyes of their great ally and the mischief which must be the consequence were strongly urged. The people were passionately called upon not to suffer the curse of another campaign to rest upon America. They were told that the eyes of all Europe were upon them, and that their future independence, fortune, and happiness depended upon their present exertion.

Turning now to the military operations of the war, we find the same use of borrowed material varying in amount according to the distance from Boston. The battle of Bunker Hill is quite free from it; the operations about New York City, Long Island, and through New Jersey show considerable evidence of copying. The campaign in Canada and Burgoyne's expedition are full of borrowed phrases, sentences, and even whole paragraphs. And when we reach the operations on the frontier, as in the Wyoming massacre and Clark's expedition, the entire account is taken almost verbatim. The method is quite simple and invariable, since it was the business of our historian to produce as complete a compilation as possible, absence of material must be compensated for by the appropriation of the work of someone better informed, and in this case the greater the deficiency the more complete the theft. Clark's expedition is thus described:

Annual Register, 1779, p. 16, c. 1.	*Gordon, III, 193.*
The situation of this small party in the heart of the Indian country, at the back of some of their most cruel and hostile tribes, in the track of many others, and more or less in the way of all, was converted to peculiar advantage by the extraordinary activity and unwearied spirit of their commander. He directed and timed his attacks with such judgment and executed them with such silence and dispatch that the savages at length found their own mode	* * * the dangerous situation of this small corps in the inner part of the Indian territory, at the back of some of the most cruel and hostile tribes, in the track of many others, and more or less in the way of all, was converted to peculiar advantage by the extraordinary activity and unwearied spirit of the commander. He directed and timed his attacks with such judgment and executed them with such silence and dispatch that the Indians found their own

of war effectually turned upon them. Surprised in their inmost retreats and most sequestered recesses, at those times and seasons when they were scarcely less indisposed for action than unprepared for defense. * * *

mode of war effectually turned upon them. Surprised in their inmost retreats and most sequestered recesses, at those times and seasons when they were scarcely less disposed for action than unprepared for defense. * * *

But while Gordon had the good taste to prefer the lucid statements and beautifully rounded phrases of the Annual Register to his own awkward and limping sentences, yet he does not seem to have been appreciative of figures of speech. The following account of conditions in the Wyoming Valley just preceding the massacre well illustrates this:

Annual Register, 1779, p. 9.

* * * they had no inconsiderable mixture of loyalists among themselves, and the two parties were actuated by sentiments of the most violent animosity. Nor were these animosities confined to particular families or places, or marked by any line of distinction, but creeping within the roofs and to the hearths and boards where they were least expected, served, as it afterwards fatally appeared, equally to poison the sources of domestic security and happiness and to cancel the laws of nature and humanity.

Gordon, III, 185.

But it was their unhappiness to have a considerable mixture of royalists among them, and the two parties were actuated by sentiments of the most violent animosit., which was not confined to particular families or places, but creeping within the roofs and to the hearths and floors where it was least expected, served equally to poison the sources of domestic security and happiness and to cancel the laws of nature and humanity.

Our author betrays his obtuseness by substituting the word "floors" for the original "boards" in Burke's account, thus spoiling the figure and marring the finish of the period.

In his account of Arnold's treason and Andre's death the Annual Register is his source throughout. This ought to be a fair test of an American historian's accuracy—his treatment of a subject so widely discussed in this country and involving so many men of rank on both sides of the contest. A quotation will show the real authorship of Gordon's version of the affair:

Annual Register, 1781, p. 42, c. 2.

This excellent young man, disdaining all subterfuge and evasion, and only studying, by the magnanimity which he should now display, and the intrepidity with which he would encounter the expected sentence, to throw such a luster over his character as might prevent the smallest shade of that imputation which he so much dreaded, voluntarily confessed more than he was asked, and sought not to palliate anything that related to himself, whilst he concealed with the most guarded and scrupulous nicety whatever might involve others, p. 45, c. 2.

Gordon, III, 486, 487.

Andre, disdaining all subterfuge and evasion, and studying only to place his character in so fair a light as might prevent its being shaded by present circumstances, voluntarily confessed more than he was asked and sought not to palliate anything relating to himself, while he concealed with the most guarded and scrupulous nicety whatever might involve others.

Page 488:

Andre was superior to the terrors of death, but that disgraceful mode of dying which the usage of war had annexed to his unhappy situation was to him infinitely dreadful. He encountered his fate with a composure, dignity, and fortitude which equally excited the admiration and melted the hearts of all the spectators. The sympathy which Andre excited in the American army is perhaps unexampled under any similar circumstances.	The major was superior to the terrors of death, but the disgraceful mode of dying which the usage of war had annexed to his unhappy situation was infinitely dreadful to him. Page 489: (He) performed the last offices to himself with a composure that excited the admiration and melted the hearts of all the spectators. Page 490: The sympathy he had excited in the American army was perhaps unexampled under any similar circumstances.

It is of interest to note in this connection that this description of the Andre affair was quoted in one of the London magazines in 1789, as illustrative of Gordon's style.[1]

It may not be surprising after what has been related of the methods of our historian that his only apparent source for the naval operations this side of the Atlantic is the Annual Register. This is more marked for those of the West Indies, and the material is sometimes adapted and abridged, more frequently copied entire without change or acknowledgment. But it does create surprise to find the closing campaign of the war and the surrender at Yorktown described with such evident reference to his English source. He has here, however, one advantage; two authorities had covered the ground already and it was easier to appropriate without detection in this case than in most others. How intricately he wove his narrative from material obtained from the two sources may be seen from the following parallel quotations describing the closing scene at Yorktown:

Annual Register, 1781, pp. 133-134.	Ramsay, II, 326.	Gordon, IV, 194-195.
But things were now drawing to that crisis which could no longer be averted. The works were everywhere sinking under the weight of the enemy's artillery and Lord Cornwallis himself could not but concur in opinion * * * that a continuance of the same fire only for a few hours longer would reduce them to such a condition that it would	By this time the works of the besieged were so broken that they were assailable in many places, and the troops were exhausted by constant watching and unceasing fatigue. The time in which relief from New York was promised had elapsed. Longer resistance could answer no purpose, and might occasion the loss of many valuable lives. Lord Corn-	Matters were now hastening to a crisis, which could not be longer averted. The British works were sinking under the weight of the American and French artillery. The continuance of the allied fire, only for a few more hours, would reduce them to such a condition that it would be rashness to attempt their defence. The time for expecting relief

[1] Literary Magazine, London, 1789, II, 381-383.

GORDON'S HISTORY OF AMERICAN REVOLUTION. 879

then become desperate to attempt their defence. * * * The troops were not only diminished by loss and by sickness, but the strength and spirits of those in the works were exhausted and worn down by constant watching and unremitting fatigue. * * * Lord Cornwallis accordingly wrote a letter to General Washington on the same day, the 17th, proposing a cessation of arms for twenty-four hours, and that commissioners might be appointed on both sides for settling the terms of capitulation. * * * Page 135: It was remarkable that the commissioner appointed by the Americans to settle the terms, and who himself drew up the articles of a capitulation by which a British army became prisoners to his country, was Colonel Laurens, son of that Mr. Laurens, late president of the Congress, who was then, and had been for a considerable time, a close prisoner in the Tower of London.	wallis, therefore, on the 17th, wrote a letter to general Washington, requesting a cessation of arms for twenty-four hours, and that commissioners might be appointed for digesting terms of capitulation. It is remarkable, while lieutenant-colonel Laurens, the officer employed by general Washington on this occasion, was drawing up articles by which a numerous British army became prisoners, that his father was closely confined in the Tower of London.	from New York was elapsed. The strength and spirits of the royal troops were worn down by constant watching and unremitting fatigue. Lord Cornwallis, therefore, sent out a flag at 10 o'clock in the morning of the 17th, with a letter to general Washington, requesting a cessation of arms for twenty-four hours, and that commissioners might be appointed for digesting the terms of capitulation. * * * Commissioners were appointed—the side of the allies, viscount de Noailles, and lieutenant-Colonel Laurens, whose father was in close confinement at the Tower, while the son was drawing up articles by which an English nobleman and a British army became prisoners.

NOTE.—This quotation raises a question regarding the source of some of Ramsey's material. But no one who has read Ramsey would charge him with the gross plagiarism of which Gordon is continually guilty.

Nothing better reveals Gordon's value as an historian than his account of the negotiations of the Howes with Washington. The affair was known very widely through the newspapers and Congress passed resolutions respecting it. In Gordon, however, in spite of his boasted access to Washington's correspondence, we are treated merely with the account at second hand.

Sparks' Life and Writings of Washington, IV, app. 509-511, No. 1, p. 14.	*Annual Register, 1776, p. 168, c. 2.*	*Gordon, II, 301-302.*
The General declined the letter and said that it was true the &c. &c. &c. implied everything, and they also implied anything. Gen. Washington replied that * * * from what had appeared or transpired on this head Lord Howe and	The General replied * * * that it was true et ceteras implied everything, but they also implied anything." Page 169, c. 1: * * * "he received for answer, among other things, that, by what had appeared, their powers were only to	Washington says: * * * it is true the et ceteras imply everything, but it is no less true that they imply anything. Their powers are only to grant pardons. They who have committed no fault want no pardons. The

| General Howe were only to grant pardons; that those who had committed no fault wanted no pardon; that we were only defending what we deemed our indisputable rights. | grant pardons; that those who had committed no fault wanted no pardon, and that they themselves were only defending what they deemed their indisputable right. | Americans are only defending what they think their indisputable rights. |

It may now be clear why the larger part of Gordon's four volumes so conspicuously lacks bibliography. The first volume is an exception, as it contains in the first letter footnotes giving numerous authorities consulted. In the next two letters, however, the number is much less, and from letter IV to the end of the volume but twelve references occur in 300 pages. The remainder of the work is even less well supplied than this. This paucity of references marks the appearance of the material from the Annual Register, which, of course, could not safely be acknowledged. Letter III is in no small part a copy in ideas, arrangement, and phrasing of the Register. This material increases till it swallows up every other, the only exception, of course, being those parts taken from Ramsay.

It was obviously unsafe to be too precise in stating his authority, since it is no easy task to conduct a theft on so large a scale without betraying it to the reader. The single instance in which he refers to the Annual Register is in connection with the fleet of Rochambeau, when he takes pains in a footnote to point out that the list in the "English publications" is in error.[1] A Providence paper is here mentioned as his authority, but he follows it only partially, since material from the Annual Register appears side by side with that from the local newspaper. Apropos of the arrival of the French fleet Gordon mentions an order to the army officers issued by Washington with reference to the wearing black and white cockades. And though this order was published in this local newspaper already referred to, he copies his statement of it from the usual source.

| *Massachusetts Spy*, August 10, 1780, No. 483, p. 3, c. 2. [Extract from General Orders.] | *Annual Register*, 1781, pp. 21-22. | Gordon, III, 380. |
| It is recommended to the officers of the American army to have black and white cockades, a black | In the meantime Washington issued a requisition in public orders to the American officers, soliciting and | The American commander in chief recommended the officers of the Continental Army, in general orders, |

---

[1] Gordon, III, 379. Note.

ground with a white relief, emblematic of the expected union of the two armies.

strongly recommending to them the wearing of black and white cockades (the ground being of the first color and the relief of the second) as a compliment to and a symbol of friendship and affection for their allies.

the wearing of black and white cockades (the ground being of the first color and the relief of the second) as a compliment to and a symbol of friendship and affection for their allies.

Nothing has been said so far respecting the part taken by the Southern States in the war. Before the breaking out of hostilities, and in the first years of the struggle, Gordon's source was quite largely the Annual Register, especially for Virginia and North Carolina. In his preface he mentions the fact that Dr. Ramsay's history of the war in South Carolina was sent him in manuscript, with full liberty to use it as he saw fit. It is so used by him, sometimes as an acknowledged source, more often as a partial one, and a still greater number of times with no acknowledgment whatever. Very little of value indeed does Gordon add to the history of the Southern war. And his manifest unfairness in his use of Ramsay is only exceeded by his dishonest manipulation of the material borrowed from the Annual Register. The following description is thoroughly typical of Ramsay's style at its best, and Gordon uses it as his own:

Ramsay's History of the Revolution in South Carolina, II, 123-125.

In this crisis of danger to the liberties of America the ladies of South Carolina conducted themselves with more than Spartan magnanimity. They gloried in the appellation of rebel ladies. * * * In the height of the British conquests, when poverty and ruin seemed the unavoidable portion of every adherent to the independence of America, the ladies in general discovered more firmness than the men. Many of them, like guardian angels, preserved their husbands from falling in the hour of temptation, when interest and convenience had almost gotten the better of honor and patriotism.

Gordon, IV, 138-139.

Here let me introduce an account of the manner in which most of the whig ladies conducted themselves while they remained in Charleston. They showed an amazing fortitude and the strongest attachment to the cause of their country, and gloried in the appellation of rebel ladies. * * * In the height of the British conquests, when poverty and ruin seemed the unavoidable portion of every adherent to the independence of America, they discovered more firmness than the men. Many of them, like guardian angels, preserved their husbands from falling in the hour of temptation, when interest and convenience had almost gotten the better of honor and patriotism.

Examples similar to this might be multiplied indefinitely. Even where a compiler with only an average amount of industry would abridge or condense, material is copied verbatim. In view of the courtesy by which Ramsay's manuscript was placed at his disposal, this theft on Gordon's part becomes all the more inexcusable. The pursuit by the Americans of Colonel Ferguson is one of the most characteristic descriptions in Ramsay. As it reappears in Gordon, it is given here in parallel version.

Ramsay, II, 181-182.

Each man set out with his blanket, knapsack, and gun in quest of Col. Ferguson, in the same manner he was used to pursue the wild beasts of the forest. At night the earth afforded them a bed and the Heavens a covering; the running stream quenched their thirst, while a few cattle driven in their rear, together with the supplies acquired by their guns, secured them provision.

Gordon, III, 463.

Each man set out with his blanket, knapsack, and gun in quest of major Ferguson, in the same manner he was used to pursue the wild beasts of the forest. At night the earth afforded them a bed and the heavens a covering; the running stream quenched their thirst, while a few cattle driven in their rear, together with the supplies acquired by their guns, secured them provision.

What, then, remains of the two thousand pages in four volumes of Gordon's History of the American Revolution? Of the first part of the first volume, Letters I and II, he may be the author, or at least the compiler. The style is certainly stiff and clumsy enough to be the author's own. But as for the remainder of the work, especially from Letter IX, Volume I, it is conspicuously lacking in that essential unity of thought and style which should pervade a genuine piece of historical writing.[1] In its place we have a sorry patchwork in which selections or adaptations from Burke and Ramsay are raggedly joined to material of quite another kind. Manifestly we can not cut out the portions copied from other writers and in this way make sure that the remainder is genuine. The persistent plagiarism of which he has been guilty vitiates his entire work. There is inevitably a taint of dishonesty about the whole.

---

[1] After this study was completed the attention of the writer was called by Professor Bourne, of Yale, to a citation in Allibone's Dictionary of Authors (art. Gordon) which indicates that Gordon's indebtedness to the Annual Register was early discovered. Allibone quotes from a work which he calls Supp. Vol. Dict. Hist., 1812, the sentence "The best part of it occurs where he made most use of Dodsley's Annual Register." In response to request for a verification of this quotation Mr. Bourne suggests that it was taken from Chalmer's Biog. Dict. (art. Gordon), where the same citation is given and credited to the "Supplemental Volume to the Dictionnaire Historique, 1812, which consists chiefly of American lives probably contributed by an American." This Dictionnaire Historique was the Nouveau Dictionnaire Historique, par L. M. Chandon et Delaudine Lyon, 1804, new ed., Paris, 1810-1812, under the title Dict. Universel, hist. crit. et bibliog., 20 vols. From this source this statement of Gordon's obligations to the Annual Register has been taken up in several of the biographical dictionaries, but so far as I know has never been verified, nor at present can its author be identified. It is, however, the only direct assertion I have ever found indicating anything like an appreciation of Gordon's plagiarism

II.

The question now naturally arises, Was Gordon a conscious plagiarist in our meaning of the term, or was it the fault of the time in which he lived? The question can of course never be satisfactorily answered, but there is some evidence upon it worth consideration. First, as to contemporary opinion regarding Gordon's character, purposes, and writings.

The historian seems not to have made a very favorable impression upon those who knew him in America. John Adams wrote of him in 1775, "I fear his indiscreet prate will do harm in this city. He is an eternal talker and somewhat vain, and not accurate nor judicious."[1] Hamilton in 1779 referred to him contemptuously as "the old Jesuit."[2]

Belknap, writing to Hazard from Boston in 1789 with reference to Gordon's history, says:

I believe it will be no easy matter for G. to find any persons of character and consequence who will stand forth as his vouchers. He was not much beloved nor regarded while he was here, and the stories he has told of one and another in his book have helped to sink him in the general estimation, though now and then I find some who are rather inclined to speak favorably of him.[3]

James Sullivan speaks of him in much the same fashion, and refers also to the low esteem in which he was held in Massachusetts. He adds:

In every part of his history there is a very remarkable want of truth and integrity, but the arrows of his envy and Malevolence are so blunted by the indiscretion of his attacks and the want of decency in his manner that they do no injury.

In his estimation Gordon is a "mercenary scribbler who makes books with no other object than to gain a few pence."[4] This charge of being influenced by mercenary motives is one that appears again and again. It never can be substantiated, but the evidence is very damaging. The letters of John Adams[5] and Jefferson[6] both show traces of it, even before the edition appeared. In 1813 John Adams writes:

It is with grief that I record a fact which I ought to record relative to Gordon's history. His object was profit. He was told that his book

---
[1] Life and Works of John Adams. Boston, 1850, II, 423–424.
[2] Hamilton's Works. Lodge ed., VII, 576.
[3] Belknap Papers. Part II, 161.
[4] Amory, Life of James Sullivan. Boston, 1859, Vol. I, 258. Note.
[5] Works. IX, 550.
[6] Jefferson's Works. Washington, 1853, II, 167.

would not sell if printed according to his manuscript. It was accordingly thrown into a new form of letters between a gentleman in England and one in America. He was told, besides, that the style was so bold that it would damn the work, and that many other things were so favorable to America and others so disgraceful to Britons that neither would be borne. Accordingly the style and spirit was altered and accommodated more to the British taste and feelings. In this labor of love he had the assistance of some of the dissenting clergymen, and among them I can name the Drs. Towers, father and son.[1] Had the original manuscript been printed the work would have appeared very differently.[2]

Thus stated by a contemporary is the whole charge against Gordon's reputation as a man and a historian. Another contemporary of Gordon goes still further and insists that he saw the original manuscript before the author went to England, and that it was changed in one instance of which he was aware.[3] Dr. Luther M. Harris, one of Gordon's friends, claimed that more than 100 pages were struck out of the original manuscript, while others confirm this evidence and add that the author was paid for the alteration.[4] The case against Gordon, as stated by his contemporaries, is certainly strong enough to justify further examination.

Secondly, we may consider the internal evidence of Gordon's history. If the author was paid for changing his manuscript to conform it to the English feeling, the plagiarism from the pages of the Annual Register was conscious and deliberate. For purposes of concealment, transposition of material was resorted to very frequently, as where a three-page description was built up out of eleven fragments taken from material filling fifteen pages of the Annual Register, and rearranged in such an order as to be almost unrecognizable.[5]

The proof of direct change of form in manuscript itself in favor of the English view is not now possible, for Gordon's original manuscript has in all probability perished. But fortunately there is in existence a letter written by him on

---

[1] Dictionary of National Biography, LVIII, 91. Joseph Towers. 1737-1799. Editor of "British Biography;" chief work, Memoirs of Frederick III of Prussia. Joseph L. Towers. 1767-1831. Unitarian preacher, writer, and book collector.

[2] Austin, Life of Elbridge Gerry, Boston, 1828. Appendix, p. 530. Winsor's account of Gordon, Nar. and Crit. History, VIII, 470-471, has been the chief means used in tracing the contemporary opinion of Gordon.

[3] Recollections of a Bostonian: Niles, Principles and Acts of the Revolution. Baltimore, 1822, pp. 482, 483.

[4] Loring in Historical Magazine, VI, 78-82.

[5] Gordon, III, 302-304. Annual Register, 1780, pp. 21-36. Here Gordon's eleven consecutive fragments are to be found in the Annual Register in the order 2, 3, 4, 1, 5, 6, 7, 10, 9, 8, 11.

May 17, 1775, describing the battles of Lexington and Concord.[1] In comparing this early account with that appearing in his later work due allowance must be made for the intervening years and the consequent cooling of the passions of the moment. We should hardly expect, for instance, to find in sober history such a sentence as this: "Eight hundred of the best British Troops in America having thus nobly vanquished a company of nonresisting Yankees while dispersing, and slaughtering a few of them by way of experiment, marched forward in the greatness of their might to Concord." And while we may be able to understand why he omitted in his later account the phrase "inimical torified natives," yet he should have mentioned that they were present in the Lexington-Concord expedition. One of the most curious alterations occurs in connection with the Lexington skirmish. In the first account it is related that as the officers of the regiment rode up toward the Americans one of them shouted, "You damned rebels, lay down your arms;" another, "Stop, you rebels;" and a third, "Disperse, you rebels." But in his history[2] the version of the affair is taken from the Annual Register, as follows: "An officer in the van called out, '*Disperse, you rebels; throw down your arms and disperse.*'"[3]

In his treatment of Major Pitcairn, Gordon shows his change clearly enough. In the letter of 1775 he says: "Major Pitcairn, I suppose, thinking himself justified by Parliamentary authority to consider them as rebels, perceiving that they did not actually lay down their arms, observing that the generality were getting off, while a few continued in their military position, and apprehending there could be no great hurt in killing a few such Yankees, which might probably, according to the notions that had been instilled into him by the tory party, of the Americans being poltroons, end all the contest, gave the command to fire, then fired his own pistol, and so set the whole affair agoing." This hardly reads like the later version: "An instant compliance not taking place, which he might construe into contempt, he rode a little farther, fired his pistol, flourished his sword, and ordered the soldiers to fire;"

---

[1] An Account of the Commencement of Hostilities between Great Britain and America in the Province of Massachusetts Bay Force, American Archives, fourth series, II, 625-631.
[2] Gordon, I, 478.
[3] Annual Register, 1775, p. 126, c. 2.

"undoubtedly," he says, further on, "from the mistaken apprehension he had entertained of American resolution, for he has the character of a good-tempered officer." This last sounds somewhat different from his denunciation of the same officer in 1775, which he concludes by saying, "I have no such great opinion of the Major's character."

With all its mutilation, however, we may be sure that this letter of 1775 was the basis for his later account of the first bloodshed of the Revolution. There are so many agreements of detail, wording, and spirit which no revision could quite destroy. The expedition of 1,100 men, for instance, to Jamaica Plains and Dorchester, resulting in a great destruction to the stone fences; the influence of the Tories in causing Gage to send out the famous expedition; the presence of British officers on the road out of Boston the night before the battle of Lexington; the taking of the grenadiers and light infantry off duty under pretense of learning a new exercise, which made the "Bostonians jealous;" the incident connected with the Lexington meetinghouse, or "meeting" as he calls it, which he proves did not shelter armed Americans; the braining of a wounded British soldier by a young farmer armed with an ax, and his denial of the report the British soldiers were scalped—these details with their exact phraseology reappear as evidence of the essential unity of the two accounts. The most curious feature of the later account occurs in the description of Lord Percy's march to aid the flying British, where Gordon pauses midway to explain at length the origin of the term "Yankee." Stranger still is the alteration of his original story of Lord Percy's playing Yankee Doodle as he marched out of Boston, and being reminded later how he had been made to dance to that tune. This at least has local color; but in his history Gordon tells us that a mocking youth calls out to Lord Percy that he is soon to dance to the tune of Chevy Chase. Now, though we are aware of the uncommon precocity of the Boston boys of 1775, yet it is hard to believe that one of them could so cleverly connect Lord Percy with the hero of Chevy Chase. This smacks decidedly of the atmosphere of some quiet English study, but is out of harmony with everything in Boston at this period of her history.

The net result of the alterations, then, of this original letter of 1775 is to give a view decidedly more favorable to the

British. The incident of the braining of a wounded soldier is retained, while he omits to mention Pitcairn's insolence and brutality, the presence of Tories in the detachment of soldiers sent to Lexington, and the detail of atrocities committed by the British soldiers. Most curious of all is the addition (in parenthesis, to be sure) of the statement that at the battle of Concord Lieutenant Gould would have been killed but for the intervention of a clergyman. Yet in his deposition soon after the battle, Gould gives every important detail of his experience except this one.[1] In his use of Ramsay, also, Gordon shows the same partiality for the British side by attempting to palliate the injustice and cruelty of their soldiers in Charleston by citing cases somewhat similar on the part of the Americans elsewhere,[2] even making use of Washington's losses by dishonest debtors to show how corrupt they had become.[3]

To sum up our conclusions thus far, we may say that Gordon was neither a man of unimpeachable veracity nor a great historian, and that his history must be rejected wholly as a source for the American Revolution. And it is meant to include in this statement not only the three-fourths taken largely from other histories, but also the remaining portion, chiefly contained in the first eight letters of Volume I. We may conclude further that Gordon's letter of 1775 (American Archives), describing the battles of Lexington and Concord, is a fair type of his original history, as he took it to England for publication, and that his later account of these battles shows how the history suffered in contents and spirit by the revision to which it was subjected.

It must be admitted, on the other hand, that while there are abundant evidences of the presence of the original manuscript in Gordon's history, it is by no means easy to verify the hypothesis of his compilation of the work by the aid of friends in England. How many portions of his published history resemble the description of the battles of Lexington and Concord it is impossible to say, and in the absence of similar material for comparison we have little means of knowing. Internal evidence alone can hardly reveal whether it was

---

[1] Hubley, History of the American Revolution. Northumberland, Penn., 1805. I, 242-243.
[2] Gordon, III, 454. Ramsay, II, 169-170.
[3] Ib. III, 260.

Gordon or his clerical friends who mangled this original manuscript and transcribed portions of the Annual Register in the production of the published work. We may be quite sure, however, that Gordon passed judgment upon the whole production and gave to certain portions of it a characteristic animus which is easily recognizable. A good example of this is his treatment of Gates, which betrays his partisanship for this ignoble rival of Washington. This could hardly be the result of a fortuitous selection from Gordon's entire manuscript by an ordinary compiler. The work must have been done under his constant supervision, and nowhere, unless it be in the foreign letters, do we fail to find traces of its presence.

There remains, consequently, the difficult task of disentangling the composite of original and borrowed material and the assignment of each fragment to its proper source. This is by no means the simple problem it at first appears, for after the material of the original has been separated from that of the Annual Register and of Ramsay, we are confronted with the difficulty of distinguishing the particular compiler who copied or abridged the various portions of the plagiarized material. That there were several compilers at work upon the history seems quite apparent; what each contributed to the composite result is exceedingly difficult to determine. These and other similar questions must await a more detailed and careful study of the whole subject at some future time, but even though new evidence may modify, as to minor details, the conclusions so far reached, the main contention is beyond cavil that no part of Gordon's history can any longer be taken as authority on the American Revolution.

XI.—A RECENT SERVICE OF CHURCH HISTORY TO THE CHURCH.

By WILLIAM GIVEN ANDREWS, D. D.,
GUILFORD, CONN.

XI.—A RECENT CHAPTER IN CHURCH HISTORY IN THE CHURCH

BY WILLIAM GIVEN ANDREWS, D. D.

A RECENT SERVICE OF CHURCH HISTORY TO THE CHURCH.

By W. G. ANDREWS.

The period from about 1830 to about 1861, or, approximately, the second third of this century, was one of heated controversy for the church in America. The preceding thirty years had not been free from religious discords; church history would have found it hard to give them recognition if they had been. But for more than thirty, for at least forty or fifty, years there had existed what we may fairly enough call an "era of good feeling," and a review of this will help us to appreciate the change which became manifest not far from the year 1830.

Such good feeling as existed from the close of the Revolutionary war to the end of the eighteenth century was to a large extent an easy-going tolerance, due to the absence of strong religious feeling of any kind. But when the nineteenth century opened religious emotions and religious convictions had been wonderfully intensified. The great evangelical revival of sixty years before had been renewed in a less vehement form, but in a form on the whole more beneficent in spite of strange and even repulsive phenomena in the newer parts of the country. And the evangelical movement, again vigorously in progress and marked by successive revivals for many years to come, began and continued to mold the Christian life of most American Protestants. It has not yet ceased to do this, and we may believe that as respects its underlying principle it never will. But the movement has worn very different aspects in its different stages, and even where it has preserved the revival form that form is very unlike what it once was. It is worth while to try to characterize briefly, even if, perhaps, fancifully, these successive phases, since they illustrate one way in which the living Christianity of modern times adapts itself to new environments and thereby becomes not less but more Christian. The work of Whitefield and Gilbert Tennent and their fiery comrades was as when the rains descended, and the floods came, and the winds blew, and the house on the rock, which could not fall, was half cleansed and half laid waste. The work done a century ago, when ungodliness was for the time so wonderfully beaten back, reminds us (if we adhere to the familiar rendering) of "the swelling of Jordan" which forces the lion to come up from his lair. The task of the "happy warrior," just now fallen asleep upon his shield amidst the grief of millions, the great lay evangelist, from whom priests and elders gladly learned wisdom—in that we see the dew of Hermon which fell upon the hill of Zion.[1]

The primary action of the evangelical movement has been in the sphere of the affections, because its vital principle, never wholly absent from real religion under any form, was the clearer perception of the Fatherhood of God, seen in His giving to His human children what they have often vainly tried to earn. The essence of this perception is implied in the familiar lines of one who is not always recognized as an evangelical poet:

> 'T is heaven alone that is given away;
> 'T is only God may be had for the asking.[2]

And the normal result is a clearer perception of the brotherhood of man and new zeal in the varied tasks of Christian philanthropy. And as they engage together in these tasks Christians should become more conscious of their own still closer brotherhood, closer because it is the relation to each other of men who heartily believe in their divine sonship. They should become more conscious, too, of the supreme importance of what they hold in common as Christians, as contrasted with what they hold severally as members of various denominations. Denominational interests should occupy them less, Christian and catholic interests should occupy them more. And here, in fact, we find the evangelical movement passing into that which has, under strangely diverse aspects, been the dominant force in the Christianity of the present

---

[1] Mr. Moody had been buried the day before.
[2] Lowell, Vision of Sir Launfal.

century, namely, the catholic movement, of which the issue ought to be, though we can not yet know whether it will be, the revelation in some grand and beautiful form of our brotherhood in Christ. That the evangelical movement also produced, through the infirmity of man, what may now, without offense, be called Evangelicalism, one-sided, narrow, and often of a mien most unbrotherly, does not excuse us for failing to see that, as it reappears in vigor at the dawn of the century, it was already transforming itself into the catholic movement, and was the forerunner of what is noblest in the Christianity of our time. And this is something more than a splendid philanthropy; it is also the gradual emancipation of believers from the dogmatism which divides them by offering them a dozen theologies instead of the one faith; the heart is latitudinarian, and it is the heart which believeth.

It is difficult even to enumerate briefly the various ways in which all this was illustrated for thirty years in the American church by that labor of love in which most Christians could unite and by the common proclamation of certain great doctrines as to which most Christians were then agreed. In the widespread revivals at the beginning of our period Methodists and Baptists, often thrown otherwise into sharp competition, worked hand in hand, and Presbyterians, the antagonists of both on matters held by all to be of much importance, worked gladly beside them. The two bodies of Christians first named could not, owing to the nature of their distinctive tenets, permanently maintain a close alliance with Presbyterians or with each other, although the Baptists of Georgia made overtures for some sort of union in 1803.[1] But while both denominations gained largely in numbers and in zeal, the Methodists, by the introduction in 1808 of representative government, and the Baptists, by receiving indirectly from the Congregationalists a powerful impulse toward missionary effort (1814), were brought more nearly into harmony with the spirit of American Christianity.[2] Those early revivals, indeed, cost the Presbyterians a schism in 1810, when Cumberland Presbyterianism began its separate course. The church is never wholly free from strife, and to stimulate activity is to increase

---

[1] Newman, American Church History series, ii, 323-326.
[2] Newman, American Church History series, ii, 388-391; Buckley, ib., v. 328-335; Stevens, History of the Methodist Episcopal Church, iii, 378-379, 403, 411-468-469; iv, 439-442.

the risk of discord.[1] But in the same year a company of Christians, likewise the product of the revivals, announced themselves to the church, and they had their very life in their protest against schism, their longing for unity. These Christians, since known as the Disciples of Christ, were resolutely determined not to become a sect, and resisted the forces which drove them toward that attitude during almost the whole of this period, or until 1828.[2]

In the meantime, in the first year of the century (1801), the Presbyterians and many of the Congregationalists (the two being then one in theology and willing to make sacrifices as to polity which showed the relative weakness of purely denominational instincts) achieved something like organic unity by means of the famous Plan of Union. This had the noble purpose—expressing a high form of philanthropy—of saving new settlements, in which both bodies were represented, from local schisms, and so enabling Christianity to use its full strength against its real foes.[3] The two churches which had originally embodied the Protestantism of Germany, the Lutheran and the Reformed, were more slow than most others to feel the quickening evangelical influences, owing largely, no doubt, to the obstacles interposed by difference of language. They long continued, therefore, to suffer from the spiritual sluggishness which had enfeebled most communions in the latter part of the eighteenth century, and the life of both was at a low ebb. Consequently, when at last the new impulse began to act vigorously upon them, let us say after 1820, not only were they animated on a wide scale with intense evangelical fervor and brought into warm sympathy with the more zealous of their fellow-Christians, but what had marked them among Christians for nearly or quite three centuries almost seemed on the point of disappearing. Owing, as I think, to strong and quite dissimilar personal influences, the obliteration of historic traits went much further in one case than in the other. The Lutherans, or a large part of them, came very near throwing away the one doctrine chiefly characteristic of their great Confession (that about the Lord's Supper)

---

[1] Thompson, American Church History series, vi, 74-75; Foster, ib, xi, 259-285, etc.
[2] Newman, American Church History series, ii, 487-494; Tyler, ib., xii, passim.
[3] Walker, American Church History series, iii, 316-319; Thompson, ib., vi, 72; Gillett, History of the Presbyterian Church, revised edition, i, 436-441, etc.

and making "American Lutheranism" as meaningless a name as "American Panslavism" would have been. But while the stars in their nineteenth century courses have fought against sectarianism, it has not been in order to turn the church universal into a sect by hiding beneath evangelicalism the manifold life of Christianity. In the case of these two churches this stage of their progress extended far beyond 1830, but that their development was retarded only makes more striking its conformity to a general law.[1]

The Protestant Episcopal Church was rather gradually, but profoundly, influenced by the revivals of a century ago. But from causes not discreditable to them American Episcopalians had scarcely felt the "Great Awakening" of 1740, and its less valuable results, in certain opinions and forms of speech current among other Christians, were little apparent among them. Furthermore, the renewed power of the evangelical movement was transmitted to them in part, as I think in large part, through the very men who were foremost in asserting High Church views of polity, notably Bishop Hobart, of New York, and Bishop Ravenscroft, of North Carolina, the latter less widely influential, but if possible more intense alike in his evangelical fervor and in his High Churchmanship. Now, Hobart could not have wrought such a change in his church as he ultimately effected had his belief in a divine and unalterable form of church government not been with him, as with the Puritan Thomas Hooker, of Hartford, "a fundamental point of religion," and had not his personal religion glowed with the same ardor that inspired the revivalists.[2]

As a consequence of the facts mentioned, the presence in the Episcopal Church of the new evangelical life was less readily observed by others, and its normal effect, zealous cooperation with others in tasks of Christian philanthropy, was less manifest than it might have been. It was visible enough, nevertheless. It appeared, of course, in Low Churchmen of the later type developed by the revivals, and in Low Churchmen, at

---

[1] Jacobs, American Church History series, iv, 320-331, 353, 359-372; Dubbs, ib., viii, 330, 336, 339-345; Wolf, Lutherans in America, New York, 1890, introd. (by Dr. Jacobs), x-xi, 279-294; Mercersburg Review, i, 468-477; cf. Baird, Religion in America, New York, 1845, 259.

[2] It is interesting that the year 1830 witnessed the death, somewhat premature, of both Hobart and Ravenscroft, and so is rather significantly marked in this instance as lying between two periods.

first far more numerous, of the eighteenth-century type, like the godly Bishop White, of Pennsylvania, and in such High Churchmen as Bishop Moore, of Virginia, whose views of polity were of less moment to him than the same views were to Hobart and Ravenscroft. The interchange of pulpits was then far from uncommon, and the relations between Episcopalians and their brethren, if much less intimate than those which existed between Presbyterians and Congregationalists, were much more so than they became in the following period. They were, moreover, now in full sympathy with their fellow-Christians as citizens. They had ceased to suffer the old reproach, natural though never very just, incurred by the persistent loyalty of so many of them to the throne which all Americans had long upheld. Bishop Hobart himself, though he loved and honored England, was thoroughly an American, and he exposed himself to severe criticism on the part of some Englishmen for strenuously asserting in his New York pulpit the superiority of American institutions.[1]

Members of all the churches which I have thus far mentioned, and of some others, began to associate themselves early in the century for various forms of Christian work. This had not been absolutely unknown before, but the great union societies which now sprang up constitute one of the striking features of the period before 1830, and more than almost anything else mark it as one of comparative harmony as well as of genuine zeal in the service of God and man. Denominations as such were not united in a Christian league or federation, though denominational legislatures might and often did sanction and regulate cooperation. But individual Christians of most Protestant communions were organically united for the performance of high offices of the church catholic. The task in which it was then possible for all to take part, the circulation of the authorized version of the Scriptures, was, it is said, initiated both in New York and Philadelphia by Baptists, and the president of the oldest local Bible society,

---

[1] Tiffany, American Church History series, vii, 385-387, 410-433, 449-451; Bacon, ib., xiii, 177-179; McConnell, History of the American Episcopal Church, New York, 1890, 142-146, 293-296, 299; Perry, History of American Episcopal Church, Boston, 1885, i, 350-354; ii, 135, 153-166, 174-186, 192-194; Collections of the Protestant Episcopal Historical Society, i, 129-135; White, Memoirs of Protestant Episcopal Church, 2d ed., 193-195, 208, 226-228. See also biographies of Bishops Seabury, White, Griswold, R. C. Moore, Sprague, Annals of the American Pulpit, Vol. V; Hawks, Ecclesiastical Contributions (Virginia, Maryland). Perry's Historical Collections (7 volumes); Whitefield's Journals, first edition, etc.

that established in Philadelphia in 1808, was an Episcopalian, Bishop White, while the national Society, organized in 1816, had little difficulty in enlisting general support. More significant is the case of the oldest of the national societies, the American Board of Commissioners for Foreign Missions, organized in 1810 by Congregationalists. Here full cooperation was not quite so easy, but the board became to a large extent the organ of Presbyterians of British origin, of more than one name, of the Reformed Dutch and German Reformed churches, Presbyterians of continental origin, and of the Lutherans. As much or more might be said with regard to half a dozen other societies which I can not pause to name, but attention should be called to the rather impressive fact that just as this period was closing, in the year 1829, Presbyterians accepted as their own agency the Congregational Education Society.[1]

The theological controversies of that relatively peaceful time, with many aspects that some of us find to regret in them, were nevertheless a training in Christian brotherhood, especially in that liberty of the children of God which fraternity ought to secure. Thus the protest which the Methodists, in their character of Arminians, made against the dominant Calvinism had the result of finally convincing most Christians that the difference between the two systems is relatively unimportant, which was a gain for liberty and fraternity and unity. That this conviction was wrought was shown conclusively, for example, in 1871, when (as Dr. H. M. Dexter admitted in 1880) the Congregational National Council practically and intentionally gave "a good standing to Arminians equally with Calvinists," and in 1883, when the Presbyterian, Dr. Howard Crosby, declared that this theological divergence does not affect piety or the growth of the church.[2] Meanwhile the heroic circuit riders of Methodism were teaching by practice the highest forms of brotherly love. The protest made, and partly against the same system, by the two wings of Liberal Christianity, the Universalists and the Unitarians,

---

[1] Bacon, American Church History series, xiii, 252, 255, 258-259 (also other volumes of the series, to be consulted by index); Schaff-Herzog Encyclopædia (articles on various societies); McClintock and Strong, Cyclopædia (ib); Armitage, History of the Baptists, rev ed., New York, 1893, 514 etc.; Wilson, Memoir of Bishop White, 289-290, note, 293, et seq.

[2] Congregationalism, as seen in Its Literature, 710-711; Handbook of Congregationalism, 78-79; Symposium on "The revision of creeds," North American Review, February, 1888.

was made, it seems to me, under great provocation, and the primary evangelical truth of God's Fatherhood, on which depends the reality of human brotherhood, was, if not more clearly seen, at all events made very much more visible to the average mind by Murray and Channing than by Jonathan Edwards. As respects the Unitarian protest, many of us who are not Unitarians would have joined them in protesting against an orthodoxy which unconsciously offered three gods to be worshiped, and proclaimed a Fatherhood which was divine and yet not eternal. And we, assembled in this home of all blessed human charities, do not need to be reminded how Liberal Christianity has obeyed Christ's law of love; a law not more solemnly uttered in the command to preach the Gospel to every creature than in the words which those who, "in His name" have ministered to the hungry, and the thirsty, and the naked, and the stranger, and the prisoner, still wait to hear, "Ye have done it unto me."[1]

Our survey will not be complete without a glance at the relation of Protestants to the Roman communion during the period before 1830. The First Provincial Council of Baltimore, held in October, 1829, informs us that those relations were then, on the whole, friendly. Hatred and prejudice were vanishing, "holy religion" received honor from her "enemies," priests were venerated by those without. Such cooperation as existed among Protestants was impossible, but besides the occasional lending of churches for Protestant worship, very common in Canada in the last century, but checked by the bishops in the United States, both priests and bishops were invited to preach, and did preach, to Protestant congregations; once, at least, mass was said in a Protestant church; Protestant laymen subscribed readily for the erection of Roman Catholic churches, and Jesuits served as trustees of colleges established by Protestants. And the two classes of Christians were in warm sympathy and hearty cooperation as citizens. It was, indeed, largely the patriotism of Roman Catholics, from the time of the Revolution, which had pro-

---

[1] Drs. Allen and Eddy, American Church History series, x; Stevens, Methodist Episcopal Church, iii, 216-218; Channing, Discourses, etc., Boston, 1830, pp. vii, 215-238, 299-304; Diman on "Religion in America," North American Review, January, 1876; Fisher, Discussions in History and Theology, New York, 1880, 257-258, 270-273; Bushnell, Christ in Theology, Hartford, 1851, 171-187, etc.; Report of Tenth Church Congress (Protestant Episcopal); "Christian doctrine of the Atonement," Address of Rev. (now Bishop) A. C. C. Hall, 44-47.

duced the prevalent good will. Patriotic they continued to be, and they became more and more distinctly American. Their great and justly honored representative, Archbishop Carroll (died 1815), was extremely averse to all unnecessary exercise of external control over the temporal affairs of the church, and would have liked to have our language used in worship. Bishop England, of Charleston (1820-1842), seeking to adapt his administration as much as might be to American usages, gave his diocese a constitution under which representatives of the laity took part in the care of secular interests; and an active and influential portion of the laity desired, and for a while secured, a conformity to American and Protestant usages which went far beyond this. Lay trustees, claiming rights of ownership in the church buildings, claimed the further right of deciding what priests should officiate in them—that is, of choosing their own ministers, like Protestants. The effort to establish this claim (constituting the phenomenon known in the Roman communion as "trusteeism") began soon after the Revolution, was general, persistent, and even violent, and though earnestly opposed by the bishops was hardly checked until after 1830. Had the claim been established, the change, whether an improvement or not, would have been a revolution, substituting at a vital point the authority of the people for that of the Pope.[1]

We see in this case phenomena closely akin to those which we have observed in Protestant bodies; a friendly feeling toward other Christians, a disposition to act with them as far as was practicable (not very far), and a disposition of startling strength to obscure or obliterate some of the most characteristic features of their own system. Now, in the case of Protestants we have found that these phenomena were in a large measure traceable to the revivals of a hundred years ago. Had the revivals anything to do with them in this case? Evidently direct religious effects of a religious movement so strongly Protestant in its forms as the Evangelical were not

---

[1] O'Gorman, American Church History series, ix, 253-254, 255-258, 267-270, 277, 297-299, 305-309, 316-323, 337-339, etc.; J. G. Shea, Life and Times of Archbishop Carroll, New York, 1888, 267, 275-276, 317, 328-329, 418, 426, 434, 438, 505-506, 512; ib., History of the Catholic Church in the United States, 1808-1843, New York, 1890, 114, 182, note 2; 229, note; 237-238, 243, 280, 296, 313, 314, 317, 418, 419 et seq., 435; Report of Proceedings of First Presbyterian General Council, Edinburgh, 1877, 263; Stuart, Church of England in Canada, 1759-1793, 12, 14, 25, 26, 29, 32; Hallam, Annals of St. James's Church, New London, Conn., 95; Church Journal, New York, May 10, 1865.

to be looked for in the Roman communion, at least not so early. And the most striking phenomena, those which exhibit a strongly American feeling, seem plainly traceable to a source not religious. But here there appears to have been a sort of transformation of energy, and in order to see this, and still more in order to get an adequate view of our subject as a whole, it is necessary to observe a very interesting and suggestive parallel between the course of events in the ecclesiastical and in the political spheres.

A fraction of the period before 1830, that covered by the administration of Mr. Monroe, has always been known as the "era of good feeling." But this describes merely the relations existing for a few years between political parties; they had stopped fighting because one of them was past fighting. But the entire period before 1830, extending back to the beginning of our national existence, may be called on the whole an era of good feeling because of the comparatively amicable relations then existing among the political societies called States, which are, far more than political parties, the counterparts of the religious societies called churches or denominations. The great difference between the two groups of societies, in virtue of the fact that the former group was organically united in one larger state, while the latter had not even become a league of sovereignties, need not be much insisted on now, because events were showing, at all events after the revivals, that an even firmer bond of union than attachment to the Constitution of the United States might exist in a common passionate loyalty, acting in many denominations, to one invisible King. State feeling was rather abnormally strong in the early national period—may it never become weak!—and Professor Jameson has given us an illustration of this in the multiplication of State histories at that time.[1]

But that State institution which afterwards became the occasion of raising the feeling to white heat, and nearly destroyed the union of States, was then regarded in very much the same light in the commonwealths which maintained it and those in which it was fast disappearing. It is quite true, and is abundantly proved by the course of Congressional debate and legislation before the compromise of 1820, that as slaveholding

---

[1] Historical Writing in America, pp. 84-86.

became more profitable at the South the desire for immediate emancipation grew weaker. And at the same time the dreadful abuses to which the system is liable multiplied, and began to be sheltered by "barbarous laws" (a Southern characterization), so that States as well as individuals became responsible for them. But as late as 1831 Virginia was thought to be almost ready for emancipation; the new domestic slave trade, by which negroes were transferred in great numbers from Maryland and Virginia to the cotton States, excited the wrath of Southerners like John Randolph, and was fiercely denounced as "remorseless and merciless," the fruit of "insatiable avarice," by a governor of South Carolina; churches and individuals openly protested against various features of the slave codes, and for ten years after the passage of the Missouri compromise there were few men of character, North or South, who defended slavery in the abstract. The organization of the Colonization Society in 1817 meant then, whatever the administration of it meant afterwards, that the wish for the disappearance of slavery had become a purpose, not the purpose of all citizens, but of a multitude of the worthiest citizens irrespective of State lines.

In Virginia, for example, the society was repeatedly and warmly indorsed by the annual convention of the Protestant Episcopal Church between 1819 and 1836. A bishop of Virginia (Dr. Meade, 1829–1862) was a zealous friend of the enterprise, hoped for the ultimate extinction of slavery, and even suffered some reproach, very unreasonably, for his deep interest in the spiritual welfare of the slaves. Since, moreover, the society was organized by Christians, as Christians and philanthropists, it emphasized the fact that the common attitude on the subject was taken in that spirit of love to man which the revivals had so strengthened, and amply warrants the belief that States, or groups of States, were brought so far into sympathy in part by means of the revival.[1]

In the meantime any excess of State feeling, or disposition to insist overmuch on State rights, was checked in a degree by the rising tide of national feeling. This became far more

---

[1] Hildreth, History of the United States, rev. ed., vi, 613–616, 661–676, 682–698, 703–718; Newman, American Church History series, ii, 145; Thompson, ib., vi, 134–136; G. Alexander, ib., xi, 33–34; Thomas, ib., xii, 284; Bacon, ib., xiii, 154, 203–205, 257–258, 268–274; Digest of Councils in Diocese of Virginia, 86, 99, 117–118, 120, 125; Johns, Memoir of Bishop Meade, Baltimore, 1867, pp. 117–125, 473–477.

intense after the war of 1812 in spite of the fact that in New England State feeling was for a while both deepened and embittered by the war. Before very long Americans in general were glorying as never before in their American citizenship and hoping all things for the future of their country. The new American spirit showed itself sometimes in unpleasant, even in offensive, forms—in vanity and vulgar boasting. But men of the highest character and of entire sobriety of mind shared it, as we have seen in the case of Bishop Hobart. And this spirit included not only patriotism, but philanthropy. It began to be believed that America had a mission, a twofold mission, to mankind. She was to offer a refuge to the poor and oppressed of all nations, and she was to teach all nations by her example the lesson of civil and religious liberty. The nation, like the church, was intensely alive, and, like the church, was addressing itself to a work for humanity which had been given it to do. It is hard to resist the conviction that the same powerful religious movement which had produced such results in the church, by which it is certain that the citizens of the nation had in vast numbers been affected, and which was not wholly past and gone, but was from time to time renewing itself with more or less energy, had something to do with the results which appeared in the civic life of the people. Patriotism is certainly a sentiment which religion may strengthen as well as exalt; philanthrophy, even if it may be found apart from religion, belongs to the essence of "pure religion and undefiled;" and the conception of a mission—a great task not assumed, but assigned—is distinctly a religious conception. Church and nation, moreover, seemed called at the same period to grapple with the same problem—that of securing harmonious cooperation on the part of a multitude of individuals, who were also members of various subordinate societies, organized for the attainment of kindred ends, but seeking them in unlike ways. Something was undoubtedly contributed by the religious movements of the period toward the solution of this problem as well as toward the bringing to pass of various kindred conditions in the total life of the American people; a powerful stimulant acting on a living tissue through one of the organs into which that enters may show its energy in all, under modes as different as their various functions. And so, as regards the Roman communion, effects which can not be traced directly to the evangelical movement may easily have flowed from it indirectly through the channels of secular life.

But the time came when it seemed as if the one force which had been applied to so many different forms of Christianity had itself become differentiated. A quickening impulse had visited a large number of religious societies, each of which regarded itself as a distinct church, competent to do all that the church universal can do. Herein, of course, the position of these societies differed from that of the political societies called States (which can not do all that the nation can do), and made it easier for the former to act independently of each other. And each of them had its own methods of doing Christian work, often inherited from an honorable past, associated with proudly cherished memories of godly and heroic fathers, of confessors, perhaps of martyrs; each had a history, however brief; some a history stretching over generations and centuries. And as the members of each entered with new energy on common Christian tasks, it not only grew delightful, but more and more seemed dutiful to do their work in the very way in which it had been done by pious ancestors, their own superiors in zeal and in the spirit of sacrifice. They did not wish to disown their brethren, but they would serve the God of their fathers after the pattern given to their fathers. And so there came on, by a process of evolution, a new stage in the evangelical catholic movement. In nearly or quite every one of the denominations powerfully affected by it there was, sometimes earlier, sometimes later, a vigorous development of its own historic life. Each began to assert itself and to become more thoroughly itself, and to be conscious of a special mission of its own. What had invigorated the American church as a whole was now infusing new vigor into the several lesser churches which composed it, and the result must be not only a parting of ways, but often an angry parting of allies, and rivalry and strife. And sometimes when, within the same church, some denied what others affirmed—that sainted fathers had a stronger claim than living brethren—and so the growth of a more rigid denominationalism was resisted, internal discords arose, and then schisms. And this in large part (by no means altogether), is the history of the next thirty years, or thereabouts, of American Christianity.[1]

It is natural to begin the account of this period with a statement of the way in which the changing action of religious forces affected the relations of Protestants in general to the Roman communion. For while this arrangement, by bringing near together what has to be said of the latter church in the two periods respectively, emphasizes most sharply the contrast between them, it also shows how the Protestant churches as a whole were affected in a manner analogous to that in which they were affected singly. Their common Protestantism, their zeal for the doctrines of the Reformation, above all for what is known as its life principle—which was indeed in its essence the life of the evangelical movement—the doctrine of justification by faith, as Luther taught it; their veneration for the Reformers, were now intensified, and they were ready for a new campaign against Rome.

That communion, having thus far felt the influence of the revivals, if at all, chiefly through their influence on national life, displayed such new energy as came into its own ecclesiastical life, and its disposition to be true to its own historical position, chiefly by resisting the aggressive Americanism of the lay trustees. Trusteeism had been skillfully flanked by Bishop England, in Charleston, as early as 1829; but the first decisive defeat seems to have been inflicted in Philadelphia in 1831, while it was twenty-three years before the final victory was achieved in Buffalo in 1854.[2]

This achievement was of such importance to the church, if it were to continue to be itself, that it places that body fairly in line with others in the matter of internal development. But it was not of a nature to be gravely offensive to Protestants, though it may somewhat have offended their Americanism. And although provocations to the warfare which followed 1830 have been found in the sympathy felt on this side of the Atlantic with the opponents of Catholic emancipation in England accomplished in 1829, and in the alarm

---

[1] The date, 1830, taken as that of the commencement of this troubled time, may be regarded as approximate. That it has not been chosen arbitrarily can be inferred from the language of Professor Thompson, the historian of the Presbyterians: "The years 1830–1850, indeed, were a time of controversies throughout the churches of America." American Church History series, vi, 102.

[2] Shea, Life and Times of Archbishop Carroll, 329, 547, 549; O'Gorman, American Church History series, ix, 352–358, 367, et seq., 400, etc., 449; Bacon, ib., xiii, 310.

excited by Roman Catholic immigration, beginning to attract attention after 1820, and becoming very large after 1840, it does not appear why the first cause should have had great influence in a land of religious liberty, nor why the second should have had so much influence quite so early.[1] It was an awakened Protestantism, feeling its strength anew, and fearing that it had forgotten its ancient mission, which began the war, and began it not because Rome was assuming a new aspect, but because she was believed to be what she always had been, and what Protestantism ought never to have ceased to fight. The second provincial council of Baltimore, meeting in 1833, spoke in very different terms from those employed four years before, and in the tone of the injured party. Complaint was now made of the "increasing virulence" of the attacks upon the church, and of the accusation, which must have been hard to bear, that its members were the enemies of the Republic. And when men like Robert J. Breckinridge, in Baltimore, and Lyman Beecher, in Boston, were fiercely denouncing Rome, it was plain that as far as she was concerned the era of good feeling was over.[2] But it was not to be merely a battle of pulpits and pamphlets. Before the close of January, 1830 (apparently), there was an act of incendiarism at Charlestown, Massachusetts. Near the close of 1831 a Roman Catholic Church was burned in New York. In 1834 occurred that shameful outrage upon helpless women, when the Ursuline Convent at Charlestown was burned, an outrage promptly branded as shameful by the Christianity of Boston, though never, I believe, adequately punished by the civilization of Massachusetts. In 1836 an abominable wrong was done the Roman communion by the circulation, with reputable Protestant indorsement, of what Dr. L. W. Bacon calls the "monstrous stories," the "shameless frauds," of Maria Monk, who sought to bring infamy upon the nuns of Montreal. She was proved a slanderer by Protestant zeal for truth and righteousness, but this did not at once destroy her influence. It is needless to enumerate all the acts of violence committed, East and West; but very significant of the strength

---

[1] Shea, Catholic Church, United States, 1808–1843, 420; O'Gorman, American Church History series, ix, 340–341, cf. 494–496; Bacon, ib., xiii, 312, 315, 318; Jameson, Dictionary of United States History, art. "American Party."

[2] O'Gorman, American Church History series, ix, 342, 343; Shea, Catholic Church, 1808–1843, 435, 449, 451, 466.

of the abhorrence of Rome felt by Protestants of the highest standing is the remark attributed to an eminent Presbyterian, about 1840, that he would rather be an infidel than a Roman Catholic. The antagonism was carried into politics, and so became the occasion of the bloody riots in Philadelphia in 1844, though the lives then lost, according to a Roman Catholic writer, seem all to have been those of Protestants, "killed while burning houses." The great Irish immigration which followed the famine of 1846-47 (giving Americans an opportunity to show by their eagerness to feed the hungry that they had not lost their philanthropy) stimulated hostility, and again, in 1852, engaged a political party in making use of religious antipathy. There were riots and bloodshed in Kentucky; and in Maine, in 1854, an able and cultivated man—Father Bapst, afterwards known and, I am sure, honored in Boston—was tarred and feathered. This was not the latest outrage, and Professor O'Gorman says that bitter feeling "marked the times preceding the war," as if it did not cease to be widely prevalent till then. It would be absurd to suppose, were there no proofs to the contrary, that all the bitterness and all the violence were on one side when on the other side were Irishmen by the million. But which side began the fight is clearly enough indicated by Dr. Bacon when he says, speaking of the prejudice and antipathy made more active by the immigration, that "it was a good time for the impostor, the fanatic, and the demagogue to get in their work." Evidently, however, he does not regard himself as giving in these words a full account of the anti-Roman forces.[1]

And the anti-Roman forces illustrated the sincerity as well as the intensity of their zeal by finding enemies to fight among the children of the Reformation. The Protestant Episcopal Church, having preserved more features of the older Christianity than others, was especially exposed to distrust and dislike. At the death of Bishop Hobart in 1830 the High Church party, which he had led, was about equal in numbers to the Low Church party, and it soon began to gain upon the latter.[2]

---

[1] Shea, Catholic Church, etc., 462, 498-499, 529, 555, 606, 635; Memoir of Rev. William Croswell, D. D., 142-143; O'Gorman, American Church History series, ix, 356-360, 450-454; Bacon, ib., 312-314.

[2] Tiffany, American Church History series, vii, 456-474; Perry, History American Episcopal Church, ii, 194-195; McConnell, ib., 320-323; Stone, Memoir of Bishop Griswold, 370-371, etc.; Johns, Memoir of Bishop Meade, 198-202; Hopkins, Life of Bishop Hopkins, 152, etc.

Both parties had their immediate origin in the evangelical movement, and both were nobly serving the church which both loved. But the more rapid growth at that period of High Churchmanship, which strongly emphasized the distinctive features of this communion, meant that the same process was going forward in it as in others, the development of its historic life, and increasing faith in a mission of its own. In this case the historic life included elements which had come down from the pre-Reformation period, while the mission seemed so divinely sanctioned that for many it was difficult, perhaps impossible, to recognize the legitimacy of any other. To those who had strong faith in a rather different mission, sanctioned at all events by the divine blessing, and who thought that what their reforming ancestors in Scotland and on the Continent had not kept was poisonous superstition, the High Church Episcopalian development was at once irritating and alarming. When, in 1832, a canon was so amended as apparently to exclude ministers not in episcopal orders from the pulpits of the Episcopal Church, the attitude of that church became still more offensive. The amended canon was misunderstood, as was proved when it received a judicial interpretation in 1868, although, for reasons which can not be considered in this paper, a new canon, unmistakably exclusive, was then passed. But in the meantime nearly everybody had misunderstood the action of 1832, including in the end most of the Low Church party, so that its practical effect accorded more and more with its presumed meaning, and exclusiveness appeared to be more and more characteristic of the church.[1]

The Oxford movement, beginning in 1833, and resulting in important secessions to Rome from the Church of England, though not very influential here, caused great alarm both within and without the Episcopal Church. Within, party spirit became very bitter, and each side was very unjust to the other. The essentially evangelical teaching of the High Church clergy was acknowledged with much difficulty by their Low Church brethren, some of whom flatly denied it,

---

[1] Journals of General Convention (Protestant Episcopal Church), 1792, 1808, 1820, 1832, 1856, 1859, 1868; American Church Review, October, 1865, pp. 367–406; newspaper discussion on exchange of pulpits, 1865, in Church Journal, Christian Times, New York Observer, Independent, etc.; reports of the Hubbard case, Churchman, 1868. See also sketch of Episcopalian legislation on "officiating," Church and State, September 30, 1874

though it was generally admitted that there was a class of "Evangelical High Churchmen." In 1852 a bishop went to Rome, and in that year ten prominent ministers of six denominations united in commending a book, written chiefly to prove that High Churchmen and Low Churchmen alike were helping the Pope. In 1860 the New York Independent said of the English Society for the Propagation of the Gospel, with which American High Churchmen were in sympathy, that it "propagates another gospel, which * * * is inimical to the Cross of Christ; * * * the essential spirit of Popery pervades the society." Of course, examples could easily be given of a kinder and juster treatment of opponents on all sides, but what I give may serve my purpose of showing that a deep dislike and distrust of the Protestant Episcopal Church, as represented by the majority of its members, was widely prevalent at the close of our period. I ought probably to add that the dislike, if not the distrust, had vehement expression in the next period, for several years after 1865. But of that and of the subsequent growth of very different feelings I can not speak at length in this paper.[1]

But the enemy watched so jealously was after a while discovered lurking in the very bosom of Presbyterianism. In 1844 the German Reformed Church was beginning to rally from the overpowering effect of the somewhat belated impact of the forces of Evangelicalism and to exhibit the normal influence of the evangelical movement in the renewed energy of its own proper life, as well as in its deepened spirituality and enlarged Christian activity. In 1855 one of its ministers testified that his church had within "the last ten years" become more conscious than ever before "of her denominational character and mission," while it was also true that in few churches was there a more earnest longing for fellowship with the church universal. But in this case development had proceeded under a powerful influence from the so-called Mercersburg movement, and its very able and accomplished leaders, Dr. Nevin and Dr. Schaff. These men had taught a large party in their church to claim an inheritance in a past more venerable than the sixteenth century. Dr. Schaff, on taking in 1844 a chair in the seminary at Mercersburg,

---

[1] Tiffany, as above; Baird, Religion in America, 223; American Church Review, July, 1852, 197-218; July, 1860, 341; etc.

declared that the Reformation was "the legitimate offspring of the Catholic Church," and, speaking as a Protestant, he spoke respectfully of Rome, and not altogether disrespectfully of "Puseyism." What he said, and a good deal more than he said, Dr. Nevin said with equal power and greater vehemence. The result was a long, fierce struggle (not indeed continuous) within the church, nearly ending in a schism, and a bitter quarrel with its ecclesiastical next of kin. The Reformed Dutch Church, almost its twin sister, broke off correspondence with it in 1853, and the Old School Presbyterians did the same thing in 1854, ecclesiastical intercourse being resumed after a while; by the Dutch in 1863.[1]

The revival of denominational life among the Lutherans, whose experience of Evangelicalism had been very like that of the Reformed Church, only more disastrous to traditional beliefs, did not show itself, as far as concerned the majority of American-born Lutherans, until it was well advanced among the Reformed. After 1849, however, the new spirit steadily gained influence. The attachment of Lutherans to the Augsburg Confession, and its distinctive teaching on the Lord's Supper, was growing, and with this stricter confessionalism on the part of one school, internal controversy became more general and acute. But some years earlier, or in 1839, there had arrived in Missouri a body of Saxon Lutherans, imbued with a double portion of the new spirit. They combined a fervid inner life, such as in Germany was fostered by Pietism, and was often of a highly emotional type, with a fiery zeal for the whole body of Lutheran doctrine. Analogous combinations were then to be seen on all sides in America, but it is particularly interesting to find this one, probably surpassing them all in the activity of the separate elements, and the energy and tenacity of their union, flung then into the midst of American Christianity from without. There were conditions in Germany, the spread of rationalism, and the partly successful attempt of the Government in Prussia, to unite organically the Lutherans and the Reformed, which must be recognized in accounting for the peculiar intensity of Lutheran orthodoxy in these immigrants. But their orthodoxy was

---

[1] Dubbs' American Church History series, viii, 345-361, 370-371, 374-379; Schaff's Principle of Protestantism, 49, 181; Mercersburg Review, 1849-1855, passim, and January, 1855, 104, 111-113; Tercentenary Monument, 533-537, 565-566; Appel's Life and Work of John Williamson Nevin, D. D., 115, 157, et seq.

certainly made more intense by the ardor of their piety, and they supply an independent illustration of the tendency of a religious awakening in a body of Christians with a history, at least to carry it through a stage of enthusiastic devotion to historic modes of belief and practice. These Lutherans were so rigid in their Lutheranism that they excluded from both pulpit and altar not only non-Lutherans and Lutherans less orthodox than themselves, but orthodox Lutherans less exclusive than themselves. The union of evangelical fervor with zeal for a system in this case, as in Bishop Hobart's, gave extraordinary power of propagandism, and the few shiploads of Saxon pilgrims have grown into the largest of the Lutheran bodies, the Synodical Conference, while they have helped to raise the general standard of confessional loyalty in this country. Of course they were ready to "contend earnestly," and knowing no open questions in theology, they have had occasion to contend often. But the history of the chief Lutheran controversies, delayed like their whole denominational development, belongs to the next period, and can not be further treated in this paper.[1]

The Methodists and Baptists, having been in a manner compelled to maintain a somewhat sharply defined denominational attitude before 1830, had less occasion for more vehement self-assertion afterwards. But there were various ways in which a quickened vitality might act, and in that very year the Methodists suffered a rather serious schism which looks like an outcome of the energetic Americanism for which we have seemed to find a partly religious origin. The chief issue was lay representation in the general conference, actually granted many years afterwards. In 1844 they suffered a much heavier loss when the Southern conferences withdrew, because it was shown that slaveholders could not become bishops. Here the development of American Christianity on the ethical side, which was carrying Christians toward both a larger philanthrophy and a higher righteousness, is seen to be moving in two distinct channels, and so separating good men who dis-

---

[1] Jacobs' American Church History series, iv, 396-408, etc.; Wolf, Lutherans in America, 346, 364, 406-431, etc.; Köstering, Auswanderung der sächsischen Lutheraner, etc., St. Louis, 1868, passim; Hochstetter, Die Geschichte der Evangelisch-lutheranischen Missouri-Synode, Dresden, 1885, passim. The successive "Transactions" (Verhandlungen) of the Synodical Conference, beginning in 1872, give very full statements as to the doctrinal positions and ecclesiastical relations of the "Missourians."

agreed about the forms under which mercy and justice should be exercised. It is enough to say now that the religious zeal of the Southern Methodists seemed to be undiminished, and that they addressed themselves with peculiar energy and success to the task, religious and philanthropic, of Christianizing the blacks.[1]

In 1832 the Baptists proved that they felt the evangelical impulse in its new form by organizing a Home Missionary Society, which was of immense service in church extension, while incidentally it both extended and intensified sectarian rivalries. In 1836 the support hitherto given by Baptists to the Bible Society was partially withdrawn, and a society was established for the purpose of providing foreign missionaries with translations of the Scriptures "conformed as nearly as possible to the original text." In 1850 the further step was taken (attended by a painful division of the new society) of making provision for a new English version, complying with the same rule, and such as the American Bible Society thought itself unable to furnish. Meanwhile, in 1845, the Southern Baptists had followed the example of the Southern Methodists, and for a very similar reason, the discovery that slaveholders would not be employed as missionaries. This separation was followed by an enormous expansion of missionary work at the South.[2]

Very noteworthy was the course of denominational development after 1830 among the Presbyterians and Congregationalists, so closely united since 1801 in planting churches, indifferently Presbyterian or Congregational, or, strictly speaking, neither, in what was then the West. Conservative Presbyterians were growing impatient of the Plan of Union for both theological and ecclesiastical reasons. They were afraid of the "improvements" in theology which New Eng landers persisted in inventing, and they more and more disliked to see Congregational committeemen sitting in church courts by the side of ruling elders. The conservative attitude as to theology was decisively announced in 1830, when a sermon of Albert Barnes, a Presbyterian, was condemned by the Presbytery of Philadelphia. In 1837 the General

---

[1] Buckley, American Church History series, v, 368, 406-463; Alexander, ib., xi, 15-38.
[2] Newman, American Church History series, ii, 422, 428-432, 446-455; Armitage, History of the Baptists, rev. ed., 520-524.

Assembly, having a conservative, or Old School, majority, abrogated the Plan of Union, naturally withdrawing also from cooperation with Congregationalists in missions and in ministerial education, although, as has been noticed, they had made common cause with them in the latter as recently as 1829. At the same time the assembly cut off four synods as infected with false doctrine, and as being, when tested by Presbyterian standards, disorderly in discipline.

In 1838 a new Presbyterian Church appeared, claiming to be the true one, and maintaining the old alliance with Congregationalism. But Congregationalism was beginning to be more denominational. To borrow the words of its recent historian, Professor Walker, "soon after 1830 the denominational consciousness, largely though not wholly dormant in the early part of the century, began to awake, and Congregationalism all through the Western States began to take a more self-reliant and aggressive attitude." The New School Presbyterians, too, were powerless to resist the differentiating force acting throughout the American churches, and as Professor Thompson says, "on the new-school side there was a decided growth of Presbyterian feeling, which drew them and their Congregationalist allies farther apart." And in fact the Plan of Union had strengthened Christianity (and the Presbyterians) a good deal more than it had strengthened Congregationalism, and in 1852 a great Congregational assembly voted against continuing it. In 1853 a society was formed for propagating pure Congregationalism at the West. And under the pressure of another disintegrating influence belonging to the period the New School Assembly soon after lost the allegiance of its Southern presbyteries. The action of the common philanthropic impulse, growing more and more divergent in the two sections, produced an independent Presbyterian synod at the South in 1858. This body manifested the vigor of its Presbyterianism by at once proposing union with the Old School Assembly, and by securing union, after the war had divided that body too, with the intensely conservative Old School Presbyterians of the South.[1]

It has already appeared that the growth of the denomina-

---

[1] Walker, American Church History series, iii, 370-384, Thompson, ib., vi, 102-128; Johnson, ib , xi, 436-438, Gillett, History of the Presbyterian Church, rev. ed., ii, 446-562; Life of Charles Hodge, 283-320, etc.

tional spirit had lessened the amount of cooperation between denominations so long maintained through the union societies. The Bible Society, in spite of the withdrawal of many Baptists, seems to have suffered least. Others, like the Tract Society and the Sunday School Union, suffered not so much by the discontinuance of all cooperation as by the establishment of denominational institutions under various names to do what an undenominational institution could not do. This was simply an incident of the general movement for promoting denominational growth in all possible ways. But especially significant in this period, as in the preceding one, is the case of the American Board of Commissioners for Foreign Missions, originally established by Congregationalists. In 1831, at the beginning of our period, four denominations were represented in its management, and there were others which contributed to its support. It had then more Presbyterian than Congregational members, and supported more Presbyterian than Congregational missionaries. At the close of our period, or at the beginning of the civil war, each of the four denominations had its own missionary organization, and the American Board had become once more substantially Congregational, although some German Reformed missionaries were under its care until 1873. The Reformed Dutch Church assumed the charge of its own missionaries in 1857, and a writer of that communion said with reference to this: "Since * * * we asserted our denominationalism is the time of our growth." The Lutherans had cooperated with the American Board, but even as early as 1841 a missionary refused to go under any but Lutheran auspices, and thenceforth there were Lutheran missions. The reasons against spreading the divisions of American Christianity over the earth are so abundant that its being freely done by good men is the most striking proof of the power of the revived denominational instinct. And it is not discreditable to any denomination that it includes the great task of the Christian church in its own.[1]

During this turbulent period there were manifestations of the spirit of union, as there had been of the spirit of discord

---

[1] Walker, American Church History series, iii, 325–326; Jacobs, ib., iv, 337; Corwin, ib., viii, 199–201; Dubbs, ib., viii, 395; Encyclopædias, as quoted under first period; Christian Intelligencer, Reformed (Dutch), July 24, 1874; etc.

during the era of good feeling. Such were the establishment of the Young Men's Christian Association, brought hither from England in 1848, and the active participation of Americans in the Evangelical Alliance, though the American branch was not organized until after the war (1867). Memorable appeals in behalf of church unity were made by individuals, as by the Lutheran, Dr. Schmucker, in 1838, and in 1853 by the Episcopalian, Dr. Muhlenberg, also by birth a Lutheran. Vail's Comprehensive Church, first published in 1841, and conveying an invitation to enter the writer's own church (the Protestant Episcopal, in which he became a bishop), was very valuable for its emphasis on the "new idea of comprehensiveness," or the ability of a church to make room for all sorts of Christians.[1]

The parallel development in the national life can not be quite passed by. Soon after 1830 the great philanthropic impulse of the century, constantly making the heart more sensitive to human suffering, and the strengthened sentiment of nationality, seeming to repeat Hamilton's financial achievement in the field of morals, and to make the nation once more assume the debts of the States, so throwing the responsibility for slavery heavily on the conscience of Northern philanthropists, drove many good men in both sections into a new attitude toward the institution. In 1833 the American Antislavery Society was founded, and founded in a deeply religious spirit, to demand immediate abolition. At the South the sense of responsibility, not so much for slavery as for the slaves, was among the best men still more profound, while the prospect of relief, for various reasons, good and bad, was diminishing. And in or near the same year 1833 the Southern Church seemed to become something like a proslavery society, and announced that the Bible not merely sanctions slavery but consecrates it; that God was using it to save the negro race. It is not strange that the announcement was even more welcome to men of Christian spirit than to selfish and worldly men, nor that, just before slavery perished, it was declared by an eloquent preacher to be "a divine trust," which (for the time, not necessarily forever) it was "the duty of

---

[1] See Schmucker's Fraternal Appeal to the American Churches; Muhlenberg's Evangelical Catholic Papers, first series; Bishop A. Potter's Memorial Papers; etc.

the South to preserve and perpetuate," and even to extend. And in such sincerity and humility as may never be seen again the holiest of Southern Christians bowed to "the white man's burden." And they could do it without denying that the majority of Northern Christians were as conscientious as themselves.[1]

Nothing can be clearer than that the most powerful force acting on either side was religious in its origin. And then State feeling rose against nationalism with new ardor, and the political societies, like the ecclesiastical societies, asserted themselves more boldly and fiercely, until, as the communion of churches had been grievously violated, the Union of States was almost dissolved. In each case the result came in the way of development, and the same religious impulses were active, here more, there less, prominently in both cases. Evil came because development necessarily went forward in the midst of human ignorance and passion. But as in the political sphere slavery was destroyed and State sovereignty at least practically renounced, so in the ecclesiastical sphere dogmatism in religion and ethics, the chief occasion of unbrotherly strife, and much less destructible than slavery, was at least terribly discredited, and men's faith in the doctrine that schism is a good thing was somewhat shaken. How these latter results were brought to pass by forces acting during this period of discord we are now to see.

The deepened interest of the various denominations in their several inherited modes of thought and work was itself a summons to their members to know their own past better. And a new zeal for the study of church history, first chiefly of denominational, later somewhat more prominently, of general history, is manifest after 1830. A careful examination of Dr. Jackson's valuable bibliography, in the twelfth volume of the American Church History series, as also of the briefer lists furnished by the writers of the several narratives, with reference to other sources of information, including Dr.

---

[1] Alexander, American Church History series, xi, 33; Johnson, ib., xi, 351, 354 and note, 426, 429, 431–434; Bacon, ib., xiii, 277–278; Perry, History American Episcopal Church, ii, 580 (in monograph, "The Church in the Confederate States," by John Fulton, D. D., LL.D.), Brand, Life of Bishop Whittingham (Maryland, 1840–1879), i, 263–265; ii, 2–6; Green, Memoir of Bishop Otey (Tennessee, 1834–1863), 64; Palmer, Slavery a Divine Trust, passim, and p. 18; Thornwell, The State of the Country, 29 (1860 and 1861).

Dexter's magnificent collection of titles in his "Congregationalism as seen in its literature," has confirmed my previous impressions on this matter. My use of these lists is likely enough to have been unskillful, and I do not pretend to have read or even seen all the books the existence of which I regard as of some significance. Whatever abatement this fact requires in estimating the value of my results will of course be made.

As far as I can judge from titles (where my knowledge of the books themselves is defective), the lists which I have examined indicate that twelve volumes belonging to the department of ecclesiastical history had been published in the United States from the year 1800 to the year 1819, inclusive, and twenty-eight more during the ten years preceding 1830. Interest in the study was therefore already increasing before the close of the first period. And it should have been increasing with the growth of a civilized people in devotion to higher interests in general. But since the special influences which so powerfully stimulated denominational life after 1830 were certainly gathering strength before that time, it is natural that one should find traces of their presence in a special activity of the spirit of research. Of the forty works in all, thus far referred to, I am disposed, with much diffidence, to speak of five, or one-eighth, as important. They are those of the Methodist, Jesse Lee (1810); the Baptist, Semple (1810); the Congregationalist, Trumbull (1818; the second volume of a work almost as much religious as secular); the Moravian, Heckewelder (1820); and the Episcopalian, White (1820, first edition).

Passing to the next decade, the first of the period of intenser denominationalism, I find fifty-four titles from 1830 to 1839, or nearly twice the number assigned to the ten years next earlier, and many more than the total for thirty years preceding. Of this number I am inclined to describe seventeen, or nearly one-third, as important, making more than thrice as many works of this grade as I suppose to have appeared previously in thrice the number of years. If my counting of volumes and my reckoning of values can be trusted, the amount of fruitful historical work done by our countrymen in the ecclesiastical department was very greatly enlarged from about the year

1830. And whether or not this phenomenon is chiefly to be accounted for, as I believe, by the action of the forces described in this paper, such energetic historical labor was at all events fitted to produce certain results, soon to be noticed, which is what now concerns us.

Among the leading names of the decade connected with this form of literature are the following: Allen (1834; second and greatly enlarged edition of Biographical Dictionary), Bacon (1839), Bangs (1839), Callender (1838; reprint), Greenwood (1833; for half a century, according to the lamented Henry Foote, the only authority on the extremely interesting subject of King's Chapel), Hawks (1836, 1839), Hodge (1839), Murdock (1832; translator), Palfrey (1839; first edition of the History of New England, too important ecclesiastically to be omitted here), and White (1836; second and standard edition). More significant, as a proof of new interest in the study, than any single publication is the mission of Dr. F. L. Hawks to England in 1836, under the direction of the Protestant Episcopal General Convention, and the collection by him of material for many volumes of documentary history.

For the remaining twenty years of our period I have found about one hundred titles, and of these perhaps one-third represent important works. As far as these numbers go it would seem that interest in the study of church history was simply holding its own. But it might have done much less than this in the hot atmosphere of controversy, little favorable to the single-minded search for truth which is the historian's business. And if some writers of the time were really constructing historical arguments (a legitimate thing in itself, if it be done with candor), they illustrate equally with the rest the value which was felt to lie in the records of the past. And this sustained interest in history suggests, what is doubtless true, that the interest in controversy was often less absorbing than it seemed or than it would have been had all the participants felt the issues to be vital. Moreover, the contrast is sufficiently striking between the two entire periods of thirty years before and after 1830. We have but forty titles in the first against one hundred and fifty in the second, and but five important works in the first against fifty in the second.

Another fact arrests our attention. The history of the several denominations continues to enlist the labors of students, but instead of one important work of a more general character, issued in the first decade of the second period (Murdock's translation of Mosheim's Institutes of Ecclesiastical History, 1832), we have in the following twenty years nearly a dozen. Among the denominational writers of those years I may name the Congregationalist Punchard (1841), the Lutheran Hazelius (1846), the Unitarian Ellis (1857), the Episcopalian Meade (1857), the Friend (Quaker) Janney (1859), and conspicuously the Roman Catholic John Gilmary Shea, the first results of whose long and useful labors appeared in his Catholic Missions in America, in 1854. There are also the second edition of the Baptist Benedict (1848), a reprint in a periodical of Humphreys' Historical Account of the Society for the Propagation of the Gospel (1851-1853), and the first American edition of Sewell's History of the Quakers (1859). Turning to works of more than denominational interest, if not all of them of general interest, we find Tracy's Great Awakening (1842), Baird's Religion in America (1845; earlier in Europe for European readers), Sprague's Annals of the American Pulpit (1856 and later), the third edition of Allen's Biographical Dictionary (1857), and, in some respects most memorable of all, the first two volumes of Stevens's History of Methodism (1858, 1859), which is in fact a history of the evangelical movement. Almost equally interesting as historical sources to all students are Bradford's History of Plymouth Plantation (1856, from a copy of the original manuscript, itself then in England), the reprints of Winthrop and Cotton Mather (1852, 1853), and Mourt's Relation (1852). Quite disconnected with sectarian divisions here are such works as Merle d'Aubigné's History of the Reformation, of which one issue of a translation printed in New York in 1843 is announced as the eighteenth thousand, and which probably engaged a far larger number of persons in the reading of church history than any work then as yet published. The same year witnessed the appearance in America of Burnett's History of the Reformation, the next (1844) of Ranke's History of the Popes, the next (1845) of Neal's History of the Puritans, and the year 1847 of Torrey's translation of Neander's History of the Christian Religion and Church, of which the first volume passed through nine editions in twelve years. This was a circulation of more significance than that of D'Aubigné's history, because Neander's work was largely designed for students and the guides of opinion, to say nothing of its higher value.

More important for our purpose than anything thus far mentioned was the task performed in America during this period by one who represented both America and Germany, and who, by his learning and insight, his large and reasonable conception of Christianity, his knowledge and his clear presentation of the deeper significance of history, and his power of sympathy, perhaps came into helpful contact with a greater number of the leaders of Christian thought than any man who has lived among us, and whom we of the church history section of the American Historical Association remember so proudly and gratefully—Dr. Philip Schaff. I have mentioned very briefly his part in the Mercersburg movement, and that assertion of a true Christian life in the unreformed church which made him a confessor for catholicity. In 1846 he published an essay on Historical Development, or the doctrine that history in the objective sense, as the "general course of events," is a process of organic growth. Under this general conception church history, specifically, became to Dr. Schaff the unfolding of the life of Christ in His living body, the movement of one unchanging force through change after change, like those which mark the progress of the individual from infancy to maturity, and which various conditions may render more or less abnormal, but which, in virtue of the divine element always present, masters all that is alien to itself and advances toward perfection. The doctrine was applied in Dr. Schaff's History of the Apostolic Church, which appeared in English in 1853, or in the last decade of our period. The author took occasion to state briefly his convictions about the place of the Roman system in the evolution of Christianity. Nevertheless, the book was well received and widely read; it contained so much which was plainly valuable, that what was novel and what was possibly offensive to a zealous Protestantism might be pardoned; at least until it was approved. The novelty might even escape notice. One of the warmest of Dr. Schaff's admirers, as he was one of the ablest and most accomplished, Dr. J. A. Alexander, of Princeton, in writing a very favorable review of the book not only took no notice of the doctrine of development, but, as his distinguished colleague, Dr. Charles Hodge, tells us, "he did not even know it was there."[1] That theory, I may add, was set forth in a somewhat different form in 1853 by one of the strongest of American Calvinists, Dr. W. G. T. Shedd.

Biography is so closely related to history that I would gladly have given, if I could, an account of the progress of biographical literature during this period. One fact easily within my reach I mention as probably indicative of what might be discovered by careful investigation to be true on a larger scale. The first work of this nature relating to a bishop of the Protestant Episcopal Church appeared, I believe, in the year 1831, in the form of a "Memorial of Bishop Hobart," of various authorship. Twelve bishops had died before Hobart, but not one of them seems at that date to have been commemorated in a similar way. But of the eleven who died during the next quarter of a century (including Hobart himself, of whom two elaborate lives were soon written) six had found biographers before the close of 1855.

There is a parallel to be noticed in secular historical literature. Of the seven American historians whose portraits appear in Professor Jameson's Dictionary of United States History six began their work between 1828 and 1859, namely, Irving (1828), Bancroft (1834), Sparks (1834), Prescott (1837), Motley (1851), and Parkman (1859). To these we may here fairly enough add Wheaton, whose History of the Northmen, written in Denmark, was published in London and Philadelphia in 1831; Force, whose invaluable collection of papers was begun in 1833; Botta (as translated by Otis), of whose War of Independence five editions appeared between 1834 and 1838; Hildreth, whose first volume appeared in 1856; Palfrey, whose first appeared in 1859, and Tucker, who wrote a History of the United States at the close of the period. Professor Jameson, in his History of Historical Writing in America (pp. 91-97), finds the explanation of the remarkable development of historical literature which began so near "the revolutionary year 1830,"[2] partly in the awakening of the

---
[1] A. A. Hodge, Life of Charles Hodge, 558.
[2] Revolutions were achieved or begun in France, Belgium, Polland, and Italy, and to Metternich "the Europe of 1830 was a world of ruins." C. M. Andrews, The Historical Development of Modern Europe, i, 205, 257; etc.

national spirit, following the war of 1812, and already noticed in this paper. This naturally showed itself chiefly in those who grew to manhood while that impulse was so active. But since the new historians were largely of New England and even of Massachusetts birth, another cause, aside from more general ones, is found in the exceptional power there of the idea of political development which the study of history illuminates. This is not inconsistent with the belief that some influence was also exerted by the spiritual quickening which has acted so effectively throughout the century in the religious and ethical development of the people of the United States. And our present study seems to indicate both a deep underlying unity of the Christian church in America, and also a certain spiritual and religious unity of the American people. If so, the special tasks which fall to our branch of the Historical Association form an indispensable part of its general task, so far as either has to do with America.

It is needless to dwell on the value of historical study and, in its degree, of simple historical reading, for promoting broader and juster views of men and parties, allaying prejudice, and ultimately producing kinder feelings and friendlier relations, where feelings and relations have been embittered and disturbed. Even a student who studies only in order to find arguments to support his side, if he be not deliberately dishonest, will try to state correctly the facts which are useful to him. A church historian was at work in Great Britain in the early part of the period before us. The result of his labors was described by a famous member of his own party as a "big pamphlet," because it was so bitterly partisan. Another scholar of kindred sympathies ascribed to it two qualities which have been sarcastically commended to writers of history—"wrath and prejudice." Of the sixteen hundred years which this work of nearly five hundred pages professedly deals with, thirteen hundred years are disposed of in fifteen pages. Nevertheless, this historian declares in his preface that "no person ought to attempt to write history who has not both an honest desire to ascertain the truth, and sufficient courage to state it freely and impartially when ascertained." To have attempted to conform to principles so excellent and to have bestowed such effort on the attempt as to be able to believe that it had succeeded, must have been an admirable discipline for such a man. It will not surprise us to find that other writers of the period achieved a success which was perceptible also to their readers.

The student of American church history has unusual opportunities for learning lessons of charity and humility, as well as of impartiality. No other history is so crowded with examples of genuine Christian faith and righteousness seen in Christians of so many different names. All the forms of doctrine and usage found in western Europe have been gathered here, and we can not read the story without seeing that as there have been error and wrong in all, there has been good in all. Nor can we fail to see how much nearly every one has owed to others; how their various lines of progress have crossed and recrossed; how characteristics naturally looked for in one have been found in another most unlike it; how doctrines supposed to be wholly antagonistic have been found here and there in combination, and found, too, in combination with love to God and man. I can take space only for some partial illustrations. Such are the unquestionable presence of Puritanism in the best religious life of early Virginia—that Puritanism, for the most part wholly averse to separatism, not often committed to nonconformity, seldom zealously, if at all, Presbyterian, which had, by the beginning of the seventeenth century, produced a "Puritan England;"[1] the marked courtesy shown to Jesuits by the Boston Puritans, the really fraternal attitude of John Eliot toward one of them, and the very great obligations of members of the same order to Dutch protestant pastors;[2] the combined efforts of Puritans and Anglicans in behalf of Indian missions during a large part of the seventeenth century, above all, the great services to the Puritan Society (or Company) for the Propagation of the Gospel in New England and Parts Adjacent by the Anglicans, especially Robert Boyle, who saved it from ruin at the restor-

---

[1] Johnson, American Church History series, xi, 317-318 Bacon ib., xiii, 43-50; Anderson, Colonial Church of England, 1856, i, 227, 231-241, 265-267, 269-272, ii, 9-10, 16-17, 22, Perry, History American Episcopal Church, 59, etc.; Briggs, American Presbyterianism, 87-90, 109-110; Cooke, Virginia (American Commonwealth series), 88-92, 114-115, 129-132, 159-162, 171-173, 192-194, 200-207; Bancroft, History United States, Cent. ed , i, 109, 159; Hildreth, History United States, rev. ed., i, 133. Green, History of the English People, Am. ed., iii, 8-23, etc.

[2] Shea, Catholic Church in Colonial Days, 229-231, 241-212. Corwin, Manual of Reformed Church, 3d ed., 378-379; ib., American Church History series, viii, 37. Bacon, ib., xiii, 71.

ation and watched over its interests for thirty years, or until the revolution of 1688 had made it easy for dissenters to care for it;[1] and the transmission to one school of American Episcopalians of the Puritan and High Church doctrine of a divine and unalterable form of church government, a doctrine set forth by New England Congregationalists in 1648, and reaffirmed, less distinctly, in Connecticut in 1708, but generally repudiated or disregarded in the Church of England on both sides of the ocean in the eighteenth century, and preserved almost exclusively among the Anglican missionaries of Connecticut, who were distinguished from the majority of their brethren everywhere else by their colonial birth and their Puritan descent.[2]

I have not the ample knowledge of the writers of our period (if I had the time and space) which would enable me to show how large a proportion of them were on the whole impartial and fairly accurate. But I am sure that this was the case with many of the most important of them, even when, as often happened, they had something to prove in a controversial way. For instance, Dr. Charles Hodge's Constitutional History of the Presbyterian Church (1839) is essentially a historical argument in behalf of the Old School party. For this reason it is, or used to be, well to read Dr. Gillett's New School History (the unrevised edition) along with Dr. Hodge's. But the latter, a moderate member of his own party, is eminently candid in spirit, freely recognizes faults on both sides of the great controversy caused by the revival of the eighteenth century (which was the easier for his having points of sympathy with both), and confesses that his studies have

---

[1] Anderson, Colonial Church of England, ii, 10-16, 188-189, 208-209, 495-498 Briggs, American Presbyterianism, 97-99, Appendix V; Walker, American Church History series, iii, 165-166; Bacon, ib., xiii, 66, etc.

[2] Cambridge Platform (1648), Chap. I, 3; Preface to Confession of Faith, issued with Saybrook Platform (1708), Abbey and Overton, English Church in the Eighteenth Century, passim. Abbey, English Church and Bishops, 1700-1800, i, 180, 188, 369, note, 370-371 and note; ii, 80, note, Church, Oxford Movement, 17 note, 90-92; Hawks and Perry, General Convention Journals, i, 427-437, 459-469, 475-477; Perry, Historical Papers, Virginia; ib., Massachusetts; Hawks, Historical Contributions, Virginia, 200. White, Memoirs of Protestant Episcopal Church; Wilson, Memoirs of Bishop White; Dalcho, Historical Account of Protestant Episcopal Church in South Carolina, 432-436, etc ; Meade, Old Churches, Ministers, and Families of Virginia, i, 386; etc , Foote, Annals of King's Chapel, i, 318, 339-341; Beardsley, History of Episcopal Church in Connecticut; ib., Life and Correspondence of Samuel Johnson; ib., Life and Correspondence of Samuel Seabury; Perry, History of American Episcopal Church, i, 626, ii, 194; Sprague, Annals of American Pulpit, Vol. V, Episcopalian, etc. I venture to refer also to a lecture on "The Parentage of American High Churchmanship," published in the Protestant Episcopal Review, January, 1899.

somewhat modified his own opinions and led him to conclusions which differ even more from opinions still current when he wrote than from his own.[1] Dr. Leonard Bacon's Historical Discourses, also published in 1839, is more strictly an historical narrative, with the writer's own Congregational parish in New Haven for its subject. He sustains a relation to the contending parties of the period of the evangelical revival not unlike Dr. Hodge's, and was thereby aided in being fair to both. But fairness to all parties (including the Tories) was aimed at throughout, though the faults of the Puritans were avowedly not made prominent, and a book devoted exclusively to their faults had to be published a few years later.[2]

Dr. Bacon was accused of writing in the interest of the New School Presbyterians, but the manifestation of his natural sympathy with them is merely incidental. His recognition of Dr. Trumbull's bias in favor of the New Lights, toward whom Dr. Bacon's own prepossessions strongly inclined him, along with the recognition of Trumbull's honesty of purpose, is an illustration of his candor. On the whole, these two ecclesiastical historians compare favorably as respects impartiality with two of the most distinguished writers of secular history who have been mentioned, Bancroft and Hildreth, the first somewhat warped by his intense Americanism, the second still more by his vehement sympathy with Federalism.[3]

More obnoxious to censure in this respect are Tracy's Great Awakening (1841) and Baird's Religion in America. But the former shows his wish to be fair just where he disapproves most strongly by his remarks on baptismal regeneration. To his credit, too, is his habitual use of Whitefield's original journals instead of the revised edition which Whitefield issued later, because only so could justice be done to those who opposed him at the beginning of his career on the ground of what he, with a recklessness almost criminal, then printed about them and others.[4] And Dr. Baird's harsh treatment of those Christian bodies which he did not regard as evangelical is more characteristic of the period than of the man. He speaks in a far kindlier tone of those among Episcopalians whose evangelical position he questions. Dr. Stevens's His-

---
[1] Preface to Part II, page 5.
[2] Coit's Puritanism.
[3] See Jameson, Historical Writing etc., 104-108, 112.
[4] Great Awakening, 36, note, 84, note.

tory of Methodism (Vols. I and II, 1858, 1859) seeks to hold the balance fairly between the Arminian and the Calvinistic sides of the evangelical movement, and I used to hear it enthusiastically praised by an accomplished Presbyterian divine and teacher. To be so far impartial was not as difficult at that date as it was to avoid the common error of Evangelicalism, the overvaluation of the forms and accidents of the revival. It is instructive to compare Dr. Stevens's treatment of Wesley's "conversion" (where he honestly gives Wesley's own pregnant distinction between "servants" and "sons") with the fuller account and the far more explicit recognition of a genuine religious life in Wesley for years before the beneficent change of 1738, given by his English biographer, Mr. Tyerman, in 1870.[1] I can mention in addition only the very temperate and reasonable works of Bishop White (second edition, 1836) and Dr. Francis L. Hawks (1836, 1839).

This fact, I think, is tolerably certain, that during a period in which American Christians were diligently fighting each other (though not really forgetting that their worst enemies were the world, the flesh, and the devil) they were also more or less diligently reading church history. And the history which they were reading was much of it of a character to strengthen, indeed, their denominational attachments, but, on the whole, to weaken their sectarian prejudices; to make each communion more conscious of its own historic life, but also more conscious of a mightier life, historic in a far grander sense, which was in each its very lifeblood, and was common to them all. The practical effects of such a consciousness surely ought to have been a growing desire on the part of American Christians to unite again in the common labor of love, as they had done two generations before; to unite, perhaps, not merely as individual Christians, but as Christian societies, each with its special mission, but all with one greater mission, in fulfilling which they must never again hinder, but always and everywhere help each other. It might well be that among these many societies there should be one or another which had obviously fulfilled its special mission, if not any to which no mission had ever been given, and that such should be somehow absorbed. But the tendency of historical study,

---

[1] Stevens, I, 104-5; Tyerman, Life and Times of John Wesley, Am. ed., I, 166-168, 175-180.

whatever might be true as respects other and powerful influences at work in the American church, would certainly be to make permanent various distinct societies, representing various types of Christian life, doing in different, but not discordant, ways the work of the Catholic Church. And so there would be room in the manifested unity of that church for that for which few churches in the secondary sense furnish room enough, and for which a genuine sect has not room at all, the free play of all legitimate activities of Christian thought and feeling, for all proper forms of work and modes of worship. Thus there might come to pass something analogous to what did come to pass in the political life of the people during the years of battle which followed the period that we have been studying, when it was determined, as we trust finally, that the nation must command the supreme allegiance of all the citizens of all the States, while it was proved that the rights of States within their sphere had never before been more freely asserted, and never so frankly conceded by the national authority, executive and judicial.

That something like this has been struggling toward manifestation during the last third of the century I had wished to show by various illustrations. It would be easy, for the desire of Christians to unite was displayed with extraordinary energy while the civil strife was still raging. But it is unnecessary to tell this story, for the general aspects of American Christianity during the past generation are familiar to us. And I think that we all perceive that the desire for uniformity in opinion or in ritual or in administration has nearly vanished, while the longing for unity or for a vigorously cooperative union, though varying in energy with fluctuating conditions, shows inextinguishable vitality. And if what we thus perceive be, as I have wished to show, due in some measure to such studies as this body exists to encourage, and as it has shown its faith in by the publication of the thirteen volumes of the American Church History series, then before that very conspicuous and recent one there was another, less observed but fairly recent, service of Church History to the Church.

We are told that in the extremely hot summer of 1834 the cruciform outline of a great church became visible in the turf of a deserted English hill, where a cathedral had, in fact, been built eight hundred years before.[1] It is not incredible that the more torrid heats of religious controversy should have summoned from a far remoter past a vision of the church as the embodiment of love and sacrifice, a vision of that cross which is as enduring as time. If so, it will only make us all sharers in the vision granted within our generation to one known to most men as a philanthropist, to many Christians as a saint and seer, the dream of whose whole life had been a united church. William Augustus Muhlenberg, dying a poor man in the hospital which he had founded, repeated the words of our Lord: "Love one another as I have loved you," and exclaimed, as a seer in his ecstasy, "'Love one another!' Yes; that's it. That's the church."[2]

---

[1] At Old Sarum. Winkles's Illustrations of the Cathedral Churches of England and Wales, 1, 2, note 3.
[2] Ayres, Life and Work of Dr. Muhlenberg, 497.

XII.—THE ORIGIN OF THE LOCAL INTERDICT.

By ARTHUR CHARLES HOWLAND, Ph D.,
COLUMBIA UNIVERSITY, NEW YORK.

By Arthur C. Howland.

The origin of the local interdict has been the subject of some controversy among writers on canon law, most of whom have considered the question in its legal aspects rather than from the point of view of historical evolution. The most satisfactory discussion is that of Hinschins,[1] who disproves the assertion that the interdict was a censure in common use long before the tenth century and merely extended to districts and provinces at that period. He has failed, however, to take notice of numerous examples of general penalties prior to the year 1000, and has not clearly shown the influences that led to the differentiation of the interdict from general excommunication, giving to the former an independent existence quite distinct from the other censures of the church. It is necessary to observe that there existed from the earliest times an almost irrepressible tendency on the part of church authorities to resort to general censures, a tendency not restricted to any particular period or locality. On the whole, however, this movement was successfully combatted by the more thoughtful ecclesiastics until the imperative demands of the church led to a compromise, best illustrated by the provisions of the council of Limoges, whereby general censures were finally recognized, but with such modifications as guarded the innocent from mortal dangers and brought the penalty into harmony with the religious and legal conceptions of the times.

Interdict is a censure that deprives the faithful of the use of most of the sacraments, of participation in the celebration of divine services, and of burial in consecrated ground. Its most striking characteristic is that whereas other censures affect primarily the guilty, the effects of this are experienced mainly

---

[1] *Kirchenrecht*, V, 19-24.

by the innocent, through whose indignation it is sought to bring pressure to bear upon the real culprits. Interdict is differentiated from excommunication not only by this peculiarity, but also by the fact that it does not entail segregation from other Christians or exclusion from the fold of the church, so that those upon whom it is laid are not menaced with eternal punishment. In the later Middle Ages the penalty was distinguished from suspension, and from cessation of divine services, but in earlier use such a distinction was unknown. Late writers have also classified the interdict as local and personal, either of which may be particular or general, but the personal censures were for the most part employed in disciplining individual members of the priesthood, and do not fall within the scope of this paper; the local interdict, however, coming into common use in the eleventh century, became the most powerful instrument the clergy had at its command for forcing its will upon the secular authorities. Owing its efficiency to the hold of the church upon the thoughts and habits of the people, it contributed more than any other one agency to elevate the spiritual above the temporal power in western Europe.

Unlike excommunication, it could not claim in justification the usage of primitive Christianity. It was developed in the mortal struggle of the church against the anarchy of feudalism; and when the spiritual power had finally won the ascendency, it was retained as the readiest means whereby that position might be maintained against the encroachments of a reviving secular authority. Excommunication, being a censure against individuals, retained much of its efficiency after the downfall of the mediæval papacy; but the interdict was essentially a weapon directed against rulers, and its influence disappeared when the state became supreme. In the fourteenth and fifteenth centuries it was applied with great frequency, but with little result; and though it lingered into the eighteenth century in Spain and even later in the Spanish colonies, the last important example of its use elsewhere is found in Venice in 1605. Thereafter it ceased to be employed, and though the church still maintains its legitimacy, she refrains through motives of policy from laying the censure upon a stiff-necked and recalcitrant generation.

The interdict grew out of a wide use of excommunication,

and owes its peculiar form to the opposition of the great theologians of the church to such an extension of the older penalty. It was, indeed, developed without the sanction of canon law and by subordinate members of the hierarchy, and was not adopted by the papacy until experience had shown its usefulness. Inasmuch as punishments of this kind were foreign to the spirit of the Roman law, its early use was naturally to be looked for in those lands where the barbarian codes had familiarized men's minds with the idea that the community was collectively responsible for the misdeeds of each of its members.

Many instances in the earlier history of the church show how strong was this tendency toward general excommunications and how determined in most cases was the stand of the leading ecclesiastics against it. Thus it is related that in the year 196 Pope Victor excommunicated the church of Asia on account of differences over the observance of Easter. "But," says Eusebius, "this did not please all the bishops, and they besought him to consider the things of peace, of neighborly unity and love." Irenaeus strongly rebuked Victor for cutting off entire churches, and contrasted his action with the charity exhibited by Polycarp and Anicetus, who, though differing on the subject of Easter, continued to partake of the Eucharist together.[1] About the year 375 St. Basil caused a whole village to be excommunicated because a young girl had been carried off by force and held there against the will of her guardians.[2] Marriage by capture seems still to have been a common practice in many communities, but the church set its face strongly against it. In this case the ravisher was probably supported by the village in which he had taken refuge, but the excommunication must, nevertheless, have included many innocent people with the guilty. Some forty years later Bishop Synesius, unable longer to endure the cruelties of Andronicus, governor of Pentapolis, solemnly anathematized him and his associates and all their families. They were excluded from the associations of common life and were to be refused burial at death.[3] Practices such as this, however, were strongly opposed by St. Augustine, as is seen in his rebuke of Bishop

---

[1] Euseb. Hist., V, 24.
[2] St. Basil, Letter 270 (Op. om. S. Basil., Paris, 1730).
[3] Synesius Letters 57, 58, cited in Gibbon, I, 290 (Milman).

Auxilius. A royal officer had violated the rights of sanctuary by seizing an offender who had taken refuge at the altar. Auxilius protested in vain, and finally excommunicated the officer, and with him his entire family. Augustine, being appealed to, condemned this extension of the ban. His tone seems to indicate that such instances were not uncommon, but he declares that censures of this kind are wholly unjustifiable. "How," he says, "can we justify our conduct, either before man or before God, if we inflict spiritual punishments on innocent souls because of another person's crimes?" He would be glad to know on what grounds Auxilius could defend himself for condemning the wife, children, and servants for the sins of the head of the family, or how he could endure the thought of little children dying under the anathema unbaptized.[1] So, too, Pope Leo I deprecated the abuse of the anathema. There was, he said, a legitimate use of the censure, but only such punishments should be inflicted as involved the guilty; the innocent should be spared.[2] A similar sentiment was expressed by the council of Agde in 506.[3]

But it was impossible always to restrain within proper limits the punitive powers exercised by the clergy. However arbitrarily inflicted, ecclesiastical sentences were considered binding, and an innocent man had no recourse from unjust excommunication except an appeal to a higher authority. Even when a priest hesitated to lay the ban directly on his parishioners he might attain the same end by refusing to administer to them any of the rites of religion. This method became so much of an abuse that the thirteenth council of Toledo, in 683, enacted that those members of the clergy should be degraded and held in dishonor who avenged themselves for insults or satisfied personal grudges by stripping the altars and extinguishing the lights of their churches and refusing to celebrate divine services. Such a procedure, which was indeed a virtual interdict, was permissible only when the priest had reason to fear a hostile attack on his church, or when his conscience convicted him of unworthiness to conduct the services.[4] The second council of Nicaea shows that it was not the lower clergy

---

[1] Augustine, Letters 250, in Migne, 33, col. 1066, 1067, cited in Corp. Jur. Can., can. 1, XXIV, q. 3.
[2] Leo I, Letter 10, in Migne, 54, col. 635.
[3] Cited in Corp. Jur. Can., can. 8, XI, q. 2.
[4] Harduin, III, col. 1742.

alone whose greed or personal animosity might result in depriving the faithful of religious consolations. The bishops were accustomed to exact money from their clergy, and when the latter were unwilling to accede to their demands, they sometimes removed them from office or closed their churches, so that the laity were shut out from worship. This evil custom was condemned by the council, which threatened such prelates with removal from office.[1]

But, notwithstanding the abuses to which it was liable, the need of some form of general censure became more and more pressing in the constant struggles of the church within and without. The papal registers throw little light on the subject, but enough is there recorded to make evident the gradual increase in the number of penalties that involved many people in a single sentence. Coming down to the time of John VIII we certainly find general punishments employed without hesitation. His pontificate fell in the troublesome and dangerous period when the Saracens were making themselves masters of the Mediterranean Sea. For fifty years they had been in control of Sicily, and they were now extending their incursions to all points on the mainland. The people of lower Italy, intent on commercial pursuits, did not look upon the infidels with the same horror as did the pope and the more remote Christians. The rulers of Naples, Amalfi, Spoleto, Beneventum, and other cities formed alliances with the Mohammedans and threw open their markets to them. The pope felt the greatest alarm that Christian princes should thus ally themselves with unbelievers, and attempted to put an end to the unnatural friendship. In 875 he threatened Naples with the ban, and the following year commanded the bishop of the city to leave the place unless he could persuade his brother, the duke, to make war on the Saracens. A year later the whole city was excommunicated. The bishop took advantage of the curse to seize the government himself and overthrow his brother, whom he sent blinded to Rome; but no sooner was he in power than he too found it to his interest to continue the forbidden alliance and to disregard the papal anathemas.[2] About the same time Amalfi fell under the displeasure of the church for similar causes. John

---

[1] Harduin, IV, col. 490.
[2] Mansi, XVII, col. 35 sq.—C. f. Langen, *Gesch. der röm. Kirche*, III, 189, 195, 201, 258.

VIII remonstrated in vain, and finally tried the effect of money. He paid the Amalfitans 1,000 *mancusi* down and promised an annual subsidy of 10,000 more, as well as a remission of the papal port taxes, on condition of their breaking their alliance with the Saracens and undertaking the defense of the coast from Tractto to Civita Vecchia. The money was accepted readily enough, but it brought no change of policy, and John finally excommunicated the entire city, together with its rulers.[1]

In the more remote parts of Christendom there seems to have been no question raised as to the right of priests to lay such penalties. Thus it is related that in the latter part of the sixth century, Mouricus, King of Glamorgan in South Wales, murdered a certain noble in violation of an oath taken upon sacred relics. Thereupon Oudoceus, bishop of Llandaff, summoning a council, excommunicated the king and prohibited divine services in all his kingdom. "So casting down the crosses on the ground and at the same time overwhelming the land, the bishop sent the king away without baptism and separated him and his children from Christian communion by a curse, the synod confirming the act in these words: 'May his days be few, his children orphans, his wife a widow.' And the king with his whole country remained for two years or more under the same excommunication. After that the king was no more able to bear an excommunication of such long duration, seeing the destruction of his soul and the damnation of his kingdom, he sought forgiveness from St. Oudoceus of Llandaff."[2] There is reason to believe that in the years 817–823 the kingdom of Mercia also lay under some sort of general censure that very much resembled the interdict. Owing to a quarrel between King Kenulf and Wulfred, Archbishop of Canterbury, the people were said to have been deprived of the spiritual direction of the primate for six years, during which time the sacrament of baptism was not administered in all the kingdom.[3]

The foregoing examples of general excommunication, though they may be considered sporadic, yet show that under certain

---

[1] John VIII, Letter in Migne, 126, col. 889, 901.—Jaffé-Löwenfeld, *Regesta*, No. 3304.
[2] Wilkins, I, 17.—Harduin, III, col. 343.
[3] Haddan and Stubbs, Councils, III, 597. See in Dict. of Christian Biography, art. "Wulfred," by Stubbs.

conditions and with the accepted theory of sacerdotal powers the church from the very nature of her position must have recourse to some such measures to maintain her authority. The birthplace of the interdict as an independent censure, however, was northern France, and the period of its development as a new weapon of defense and aggression was the end of the tenth century, when the disappearance of the old Carolingian dynasty had freed the Gallic Church from its traditional attitude of dependence on the Frankish kings. Here, among a people ignorant of the theories of Roman law and impatient of restraint, a people with Germanic institutions and ideals, the principle was accepted that the community was somehow responsible for the conduct of its rulers, and that punishment might be justly laid upon it to coerce those rulers into listening to the behests of the spiritual powers.

In the Merovingian period, under conditions that were analogous to those of the tenth century, the clergy attempted similar measures, but with comparatively little success. The times were not yet ripe for such coercion. Religion had too little hold upon the natures of these Frankish barbarians, while their rulers, too feeble to keep the church in subjection, retained enough of their Germanic fierceness and license to hold in contempt most forms of ecclesiastical reproof. Still, we can trace here, as elsewhere, the workings of those forces that resulted at a later time in the development of the inderdict. Gregory of Tours relates that when in the year 586 Pretextatus, bishop of Rouen, was secretly murdered, the churches of the city were immediately closed by command of the bishop of Bayeux, in order that the people might not behold the solemnities of divine service until the author of the crime should be discovered through a general investigation. But when certain men, after being put to the torture, revealed that the murder had been perpetrated by Queen Fredegonda, all thought of avenging it had to be given up and public worship was resumed.[1] About the same time the bishop of Poitiers tried to assert his episcopal authority over a body of nuns in a similar manner. Chrodieldis and Basina, daughters of two Merovingian kings, were nuns in a religious house at Poitiers. It seems to have been from no excess of

---

[1] Gregory of Tours, Hist., VIII, 31.

piety that they took the veil. As princesses of the royal blood they looked upon it as an indignity that their abbess should impose the full severity of the discipline upon them. At last they organized a veritable rebellion, broke out of the convent with a number of followers and collected a band of lawless men to support their cause. Then returning, they attacked the abbess, and after killing a number of her supporters took her prisoner. The poor bishop was greatly scandalized at such proceedings, but was helpless before women so ardently bent on asserting their independence of authority. After exhausting other means of persuasion, he finally threatened to prohibit the celebration of the approaching Easter services in Poitiers, and to refuse to receive or baptize any catechumens unless the mother superior were liberated. The threatened interdict, however, was held in scorn by the rebellious nuns, who were only brought to terms upon being excommunicated by a synod of bishops from the domains of King Childebert and King Gunthram.[1] Other instances of the suspension of divine services are mentioned by Gregory, as in the case of the churches of Agde and Aix. A man named Gomacharius had seized a field belonging to the church of Agde, but on falling ill he promised to restore it if he might receive the prayers of the bishop. When he got well he again took possession of the property. The bishop went to his church, and, after spending the night in prayer and weeping, he shattered with his staff the lights that hung suspended there, exclaiming, "Let no light be lighted in this place till God take vengeance on His enemies and restore the property of His house." Whereupon Gomacharius was again taken with the fever, and only recovered on relinquishing forever his claims to the field.[2] At Aix a certain Childeric took possession of land belonging to the church, and Bishop Franco, unable to obtain restitution otherwise, cast himself down before the sepulcher of St. Metrius, exclaiming, "There shall not be a candle lighted here nor a psalm sung, most glorious saint, until thou avenge thy servants on their enemies and cause the property that has been taken violently away from thee to be restored to the holy church." Thus speaking, he scattered thorns upon the tomb, and then going

---

[1] Gregory of Tours, Hist., X, 15 ff.
[2] Id. In Gloria Martyr., c. 78.

out placed other thorns before the closed doors.[1] As usual, the despoiler of the church was seized with a fever a little after, and compelled by fear of death to give back the property to the saint.[2]

The lack of trustworthy authorities for the hundred and fifty years following Gregory's death leaves us in ignorance to what extent the bishops continued to suspend public worship in the defense of their rights; the matter-of-fact tone, however, in which Gregory treats the practice shows that it was so common in his time as to excite no surprise or discussion, though it is certain that the church was too weak to carry out any fixed system of censures in that period. Even excommunication was little regarded by the nobility; and as it was the state rather than the church that first emerged from the anarchy of the time, the interdict remained undeveloped until the prestige of the secular power had in its turn passed away.

After the death of Charles the Great the first instance, apparently, in which a prelate ventured to employ general excommunication was in 869, during the quarrel between Hincmar, bishop of Laon, and Charles the Bald. The former had been raised to the episcopate while still a youth through the favor of his uncle, Hincmar of Rheims, but no sooner did he feel himself secure in his see than he began to assert his independence. Owing to certain high-handed acts against royal vassals in his diocese, the bishop of Laon was called to account by the king, but refused to appear before a secular tribunal. In this he was supported by his uncle, who used his influence to have the affair settled in an ecclesiastical court. Meanwhile the younger Hincmar had appealed the whole matter to Rome, not only in defiance of the king, but of the archbishop also, who in reply called a synod to meet at Verberie in April to discipline him. He was now in an embarrassing situation, for he could hope for no assistance from the other Frankish prelates, and help from Rome would be tardy at the best. So he determined to throw himself on the support of his own diocese, and in order to impress them with the concurrence of their interests with his own he directed that in case he should be imprisoned by the king or forbidden to

---
[1] The custom of scattering thorns at the entrance of an interdicted church is frequently met with in the eleventh and twelfth centuries.
[2] Gregory of Tours. *In Gloria Confess.*, c. 70.

go to Rome his clergy should cease from all sacerdotal functions. They were not to celebrate mass, visit the sick, give absolution or the viaticum, bury the dead, or baptize infants, even though the latter might be in peril of death. Such a sentence, though differing from later interdicts in the refusal of baptism and confession, was not a general excommunication, for the parishioners were not cut off from the church nor were others forbidden to hold intercourse with them. It may therefore be considered a severe form of the interdict. When the younger Hincmar was imprisoned a few weeks later by the king, he sent word to the priests to carry out his commands in full. Not daring to disobey, they secretly appealed to the archbishop of Rheims for advice. The answer of the latter was most emphatic. Never before, he said, had a bishop ventured to treat his clergy in such a manner. They had done well to call upon a higher power, and by virtue of his metropolitan authority he absolved them from their promise of obedience and commanded them to resume their duties in the diocese. This interference of the archbishop gave rise to a bitter controversy with his nephew, but the principle was finally recognized that no bishop had the right to deprive the people committed to his care of the means of salvation. It was not denied that a church might be closed or religious services suspended in a particular community, but priests must not deny baptism to infants, confession to the dying, or burial to the dead. The refusal of these rites formed one of the counts against the bishop of Laon when he was finally deposed and degraded in 871.[1]

With this experience as a warning, no bishop seems to have again attempted a similar exercise of authority for another century. The metropolitan as well as the royal power was still too strong. But the next hundred years saw a great change. Feudalism and the false decretals undermined the two powers, and in the confusion of the Capetian revolution the bishops began again to employ general excommunication. Papal examples of such measures were indeed not wanting, for not only had John VIII excommunicated the cities of southern Italy in the ninth century, but in 942 Pope Stephen had threatened to lay an anathema on France and Burgundy unless the

---

[1] Letter of Hincmar of Rheims in Migne, 125, col. 511–515.—Harduin, V, col. 1231, 1314. See Von Noorden, *Hinkmar*, 241–291.

princes and people received Louis d'Outre-Mer as their king.[1] Under these changed conditions it was once more the diocese of Laon that suffered from the application of general censures. Its bishop, Adalbero, had been accused of unlawful intrigues with Queen Emma, wife of Lothair, and though he was acquitted of the charge her son, Louis V, on coming to the throne in 986, expelled the bishop from his see. The latter, actuated by the same motives as Hincmar, appears to have caused at least the more solemn rites of worship to be suspended in his territory.[2] In a letter to his fellow-bishops he forbade them to perform any episcopal acts within the limits of Loan or to supply his church with the holy chrism during his exile, for he wished his flock to feel the absence of their pastor. No objections were raised to these measures, for Adalbero on being expelled had fled to Hugh Capet, who was in close alliance with the church party.[3] Through this alliance Hugh obtained the crown in the following year, but the death of the archbishop of Rheims and the election in his stead of Arnulf, a Carolingian, divided the ecclesiastical interests in the struggle that followed between the rival dynasties. The first incident of the civil war was the capture of the city of Laon by Charles of Lorraine. Adalbero, who had returned on the death of Louis, was seized and thrown into prison, whence he escaped with some difficulty after several months' confinement. From the safe refuge of the Capetian camp he anathematized the entire diocese that had failed to protect him from attack, forbidding all Christian worship within it, and removing all the priests from the service of the altar. Soon, however, a voice was raised in protest. Arnulf, in spite of oaths and pledges, had deserted the Capetian party and gone over to the side of his kinsman Charles, delivering into his hands the city of Rheims. A greater loss to Hugh, there went with

---

[1] Flodoard, Annales, sub an. 942. C. f. Hist. Rem., IV, 29. In Catalonia, also, at this period we find an example of general excommunication, viz, in 991, when the bishop of Urgel orders all the churches in the two counties of Cerdonna and Berga to be excommunicated because of violence done to church property, excepting only the Countess Ermengard and her children from the workings of the censure. Mansi, XVII, col. 467. Cited by Hinschius, *Kirchenrecht*, V, 20, note 1.

[2] Du Cange, in the Glossarium, s. v. *Interdictum*, quotes from a MS. source a formula of Hildegar, bishop of Beauvais (933–972), for excommunicating a church and its dependent chapels and interdicting all services therein. If this formula is authentic and there has been no mistake made in assigning its date (of which there is some doubt), it shows that Adalbero in forbidding religious services was following a recent example in a neighboring diocese.

[3] Richer, III, 66. Gerbert, Letters 97, 98 (ed. Havet).

him the most conspicuous figure of the time in the church, Gerbert of Aurillac. This man had come to Rheims as a student, but had quickly won his way to the position of confidential clerk and advisor of the archbishop. He now held the same office in relation to Arnulf, and his first act after the latter had deserted to Charles was to write a letter to Adalbero censuring him for the sentence he had laid upon his people. "Because Charles has returned to Laon, his native city," he says, "what decrees of the Roman pontiffs have forbidden children to be baptized? What sacred canons have permitted innocent priests to be removed from their altars? Abraham pled with God, demanding whether in Sodom the just ought to perish with the unjust; but thou, even the pastor of thy flock, dost not hesitate to bring injury upon the guilty and the innocent at the same time."[1]

Such an admonition, it is true, could have no effect, but it shows that from the time of Hincmar no change had occurred in the attitude of the church toward this method of censure. In fact, Gerbert, in reproving Adalbero, employs the very expressions that were used by the elder Hincmar a century before, and no doubt had in his mind those earlier events. It must not be supposed, however, that the practice of suspending services in a single church for a given time was unknown to Gerbert or condemned by him, for when a synod was held at Senlis in 990, in the hope of winning Arnulf back to the king's party, the bishops pretended to believe that their metropolitan had deserted Hugh only through fear of physical violence, and they accordingly ordered the cathedral church of Rheims to be closed. The same sentence was laid on the church of Laon. Gerbert had in the meantime returned to the Capetian party, and in writing of the council's action to an absent bishop he took pains to explain that this decree was passed in the belief that the other churches afforded the faithful sufficient opportunities of worship.[2] But there was no thought in this of depriving the people of religious services; the sentence was only a protest against sacrilege. On the deposition of Arnulf, Gerbert, in acknowledgment of his services and ability, was raised to the see of Rheims, and he used

---
[1] Gerbert, Letter 164.   [2] Id., Letter 176.

the authority of his new office to restrain other bishops from imitating the vindictive measures of Adalbero. One of these, perhaps the bishop of Amiens, he reprimanded for transgressing the rules of the church in refusing baptism and burial in a certain parish, and at the same time preventing the people from enjoying those rights elsewhere. Such a proceeding, he wrote, would bring the bishop under the displeasure of his fellow prelates.[1] Still, Gerbert seems to have had little support in his efforts to maintain the ancient discipline of the church on this point.

In 996 the pope himself threatened to lay an anathema on the whole land of France. Arnulf's deposition and imprisonment had not been strictly legal, but the protests of John XV were disregarded. When Gregory V became pope he did not hesitate to demand Arnulf's release, under threat of a general excommunication. King Hugh was still alive and no attention was paid at first to the threat, but on his death a few months later his successor, Robert, made haste to yield. Abbo, abbot of Fleury, was sent to Rome to lay the king's submission before Gregory, and the danger of an interdict was avoided. Still the threat had greatly alarmed the country, and shown that the higher ecclesiastics had definitely given up the one time principle that the innocent were not to be deprived of religious consolations for the guilt of those who could not be otherwise reached by the arm of the church. Abbo accordingly took the occasion of his embassy to obtain the privilege for his monastery that divine services should never be forbidden there, even though all France should be placed under the papal ban. This is the first privilege of the kind of which we have any mention, and the monk who records it finds it necessary to prove the papal power to grant such concessions by quoting the example of Gregory I, who forbade a certain bishop to suspend the mass or to refuse burial in the monastery of St. George.[2]

Coming at the time it did, the pontiff's threat of a general anathema on France furnished a sufficient precedent to bishops to employ the same censure, and we find that even Gerbert when he became pope was obliged to recognize its legality. He could only urge that rulers should conduct themselves in

---
[1] Gerbert, Letter 203.
[2] Aimoin, Vita Abbonis Floriac., cc. 11, 12, in Bouquet, X, 334, 335.

such a manner that if any bishop attempted to excommunicate their lands unjustly the sentence could be removed by the authority of the pope.[1]

From this time on examples of the interdict under the form of general excommunication become frequent, but the tone of the chroniclers in speaking of them shows that they were looked upon rather as an innovation. Thus Adémar of Chabannes, who wrote about the year 1030, relates that the bishop of Limoges in attempting to preserve order often employed a new measure between the years 990 and 1012. "Then Alduin," he says, "made frequent use of a new kind of enactment on account of the rapine of the soldiery and the harrying of the poor,[2] namely, he directed the churches and monasteries to refrain from divine worship and from the holy sacrifice, and caused the people, like heathen, to cease praising God. This regulation he held to be an excommunication."[3] Bishop Fulbert, of Chartres, used similar methods in his diocese. The vassals of his church in the county of Vendôme refused to render the proper services for the fiefs they held, and in 1007 he summoned them to the performance of their obligations. If they did not appear before him by Easter he threatened not only to place them under the ban of the church but to anathematize the town and the territory of Vendôme so as to prevent burial and all other religious services there.[4]

A few years later the troubles between the bishop and his nobles broke out afresh. One Gaufred began building castles in a position to command the neighboring country. By order of the king they were torn down, but the work was soon resumed and Fulbert attempted to check it by forbidding all solemn services in his church. The bells were not allowed to ring and mass was celebrated only in a subdued voice. When this measure failed he appealed to the king threatening to interdict the divine offices throughout the entire diocese, to close the churches, and himself to migrate to some other land where he could receive royal protection. In answer to this threat King Robert finally put a stop to the castle building.[5] About the same time the bishops of Autun and Lisieux carried out simi-

---

[1] Sylvester, in Migne, 139, col. 274.—Jaffé-Löwenfeld, No. 3906.
[2] Another reading gives the phrase as "on account of the wickedness of the people."
[3] Adémar of Chabannes, Chron., III, 35.
[4] Letter of Fulbert in Bouquet, X, 447.
[5] Id., p. 457, ff.

lar measures in certain portions of their dioceses;[1] while the archbishop of Rouen, when driven from Normandy by Robert the Devil, forced the duke to sue for a reconciliation by laying that duchy under the anathema.[2] So, too, the archbishop of Bourges laid an excommunication on the diocese of Limoges because Jordanus, the newly elected bishop, refusing to give him money for his ordination, had sought consecration at other hands; and the sentence was only removed when Jordanus with one hundred priests and monks had walked barefooted to Bourges to beg reconciliation.[3] To these were added the example of two popes of the period. In 1008 John XVIII threatened to lay an anathema on France if the king did not compel certain bishops to obey his summons and appear before him in Rome;[4] and in 1016 or 1017 the city of Orleans fell under the displeasure of Benedict VIII, because the people had elected as their bishop a man named Theoderic, supposed to be guilty of murder. All services were forbidden in the city, so that when King Robert wished to hold a national council there Fulbert of Chartres advised him not to go to a place cursed with excommunication where it was not permitted to the priests to offer the sacrifices nor to the king to receive the Eucharist. On such a solemn occasion as a council he ought neither to be deprived of hearing the divine offices nor compel them to be unlawfully said. Whether or not this advice was followed the city soon made its peace, for Theoderic was consecrated bishop a little later and a synod was held there in 1018.[5]

During this reign of Robert the Pious anarchy reached its height in the kingdom of France, and in the absence of strong secular authority some form of general censure was absolutely necessary to the church to restrain the evils of the time.

From the end of the tenth century on, constant efforts were made by the clergy, supported by the king, to put down unlawful violence and abolish the right of private warfare. These efforts after a time resulted in the establishment of the Truce of God, but for many years little headway could be made against the turbulence of the nobles. In the first synod held

---

[1] Letter., 25, Id., p. 505; Letter of Fulbert, p. 452.
[2] William of Jumièges., IV, 3.
[3] Ademar of Chabannes, Chron., III, 57.
[4] John XVIII, Letter in Migne, 139, col. 1490.—Jaffé-Löwenfeld, No. 3958.
[5] Fulbert of Chartres, Letters 20-24, in Bouquet, X, 453, ff.

to consider peace ordinances—that of Charroux in 989—the penalty of excommunication was threatened against all those who disregarded the enactments of the council,[1] and this was repeated in most of the subsequent councils. A few years later at the synod of Poitiers, where were assembled the nobles of Aquitaine as well as the clergy, an additional precaution was taken, the nobles being prevailed upon to give hostages as pledges for their observance of the Peace of God.[2] Neither excommunication nor pledges, however, could prevail over the custom of the time, and another method was tried in Burgundy and northern France in 1023. The inhabitants were made to bind themselves by solemn oath to keep the peace and in the future to refrain from all acts of injustice toward each other.[3] These various efforts of the Church at first amounted to little, and affected the nobility only in so far as it added to the crimes of robbery and bloodshed the sin of perjury. But in 1031 a council of Aquitainian bishops met at Limoges where, after settling the question of the apostleship of St. Martial, they proceeded to devise a new measure against the lawless barons. This was nothing less than the formal adoption of the interdict as a means of compelling the lords of the land to refrain from acts of violence. The leading figure in the council was Jordanus, bishop of Limoges, and it was at his urgent request that action was taken in the matter. Nor was it entirely an accident that the first formal legislation of the church in regard to this censure should have occurred at an assembly held in his diocese. Only ten years before Jordanus had been compelled to submit to the archbishop of Bourges by having a general excommunication laid upon his see, and the censure must have been further made familiar to the clergy of the diocese through the measures formerly taken by Bishop Alduin to preserve order.[4] It seems probable that there was in the church a conservative party which, notwithstanding the growing tendency toward excommunication, was opposed to the censure and feared the abuses that might arise from its frequent use.[5] Bearing in mind,

---
[1] Huberti, *Gottesfrieden und Landfrieden*, pp. 34, 35.
[2] Id., 136, 137.
[3] Id., 158-164.
[4] See supra, p. 444.
[5] Otherwise it seems strange, considering the troubles of the time, that the interdict had not been more widely adopted.

therefore, the objections of these men, as well as those of Hincmar and Gerbert, Odolric, abbot of St. Martial, who with his congregation had alone been exempt from the censure of 1021, proposed the following measure to meet the needs of the church and the land:

If the nobles do not keep the peace, lay the whole territory of Limoges under a public excommunication, namely, in this manner, that no one unless a priest or a beggar or a traveler or an infant of two years old or under may be buried in all Limoges nor be carried into another diocese for burial. Let divine service be celebrated secretly in all churches, and let baptism be given those that seek it. About the third hour let the bells be rung in all the churches, and let all, throwing themselves on the ground because of their tribulation, pour forth their prayers for peace. Let confession and the viaticum be administered in the extremity of death. Let the altars in all the churches be stripped as on Good Friday, and let the crucifixes and ornaments be veiled as a sign to all of sorrow and mourning. At mass only, which each priest shall celebrate behind locked doors, may the altars be decorated, and again, after mass, stripped. Let no one marry a wife during the excommunication. Let no one give another a kiss. Let no one in all Limoges, either of the clergy or the laity, whether sojourners in the land or travelers, eat meat or any other food except what is allowed in Lent. Let no one of the clergy or the laity have his hair cut or be shaved until such time as the barons, the leaders of the people, show obedience to the sacred council in all things. And if anyone shall prove to be a violator of this ban, let him not be received except after fitting penance. For the excommunication of the bishops is to be especially observed, lest perchance the wrath of the Lord should fall upon us and upon the people.[1]

Such were the provisions of the famous enactment of Limoges, which has frequently been considered the origin of the interdict, though it is so only in the sense of being the first legislation on the subject[2] and as forming the model for nearly all subsequent penalties of this kind. It was essentially a compromise between the older principles of the canon law and the recent practices of the church. The permission to administer baptism and confession was a concession which brought the censure within the rules prescribed by ecclesiastics such as Pope Leo and Hincmar, and reconciled men's ideas of justice with the requirements of the age. Only rarely is the old severity of a general anathema found after this date, as in the case of Berengar of Narbonne,[3] or Hubert of Bou-

---
[1] Harduin, VI, col. 885.
[2] The canon of the Council of Sens, supposed to have been held in 915, in which the interdict is mentioned as a well-known censure, is undoubtedly a forgery, as are the other canons attributed to the same council. See Gallia Christiana, XII, 28, and Mansi, XXIII, col. 509.
[3] Harduin, VI, col. 1050.

logne.[1] It will be observed that the name "interdict" is not yet employed to distinguish this new form of excommunication. The term did not gain its technical meaning until the middle of the eleventh century[2] in the usage of the Papal chancery, but from 1031 on the interdict was looked upon as a distinct and separate censure embodying certain specific penalties that bore a close resemblance to, and yet were not so severe as, a general excommunication.

---

[1] Jaffé-Löwenfeld, No. 5188.

[2] It is true that the substantive *interdictum* and the verb *interdicere* occur in connection with the censure before this time, as, e. g., in Gerbert, Letter 203, in the formula given by Du Cange and frequently in the letters of Fulbert of Chartres, but in these cases it has the ordinary meaning of "prohibition" or "prohibit" and is not to be taken in the later technical sense. In the same manner, according to Huberti, the term *treuga dei* is used in the sources before it obtained its special signification. See Huberti, op. cit., pp. 171, 219.

XIII.—THE POOR PRIESTS; A STUDY IN THE RISE OF ENGLISH LOLLARDRY.

By HENRY LEWIN CANNON, Ph. D.,
INDIANAPOLIS, INDIANA.

THE POOR PRIESTS; A STUDY IN THE RISE OF ENGLISH LOLLARDRY.[1]

By H. L. CANNON, Ph. D.

Of the Poor Priests, mention of whom is made so frequently in the literature relating to English history of the latter part of the fourteenth century, we possess a surprisingly small amount of exact information. According to the best light we have they appear to have been a loosely associated body of men drawn from the various walks of life who, awakened by Wiclif to a sense of the great need of the English people for religious instruction and somewhat trained by the influences he brought to bear upon them, and supplied moreover by him with matter for their sermons, zealously set out to evangelize all England.

THE DATE OF THE RISE OF THE POOR PRIESTS.

The date of the rise of the Poor Priests of Wiclif is clouded in the obscurity natural to the humble beginnings of such an institution. Perhaps the best way to determine it would be to start with an assured date and work backward.

It is clear that in the year 1382 their preaching was in full swing. Walsingham said that during that time Wiclif strove to spread his opinions both by his own means and by means of his followers; and that not being satisfied with sermons declaimed among the common people, he wrote to the lords and magnates. And again, that he sent out apostates most evilly disposed to the Catholic faith for dogmatizing and preaching.[2] The chronicler of the Continuatio Eulogiarum wrote under the same year that Wiclif's disciples were preaching the doctrine of their master throughout England, weaken-

---

[1] For bibliography, see appendix.   [2] II, 50, 53.

ing the faith of many persons not only among the laity but also among the noble and the learned. The friars that year in consequence had a hard time, being refused alms and bidden to work.[1] Thirdly, in the letter of William Courtenay to Peter Stokys, dated May 28, 1382, the archbishop wrote that through frequent complaint and common report it had come to his hearing that some evil persons were going about in the province of Canterbury without official license, spreading broadcast doctrines which threatened the position of the whole church and the tranquillity of the realm.[2] As the doctrines condemned in this letter were those of Wiclif, it is clear that Wiclif's preachers were the offenders.

Since it was in 1382 that Wiclif left Oxford for the retirement of Lutterworth, if the Poor Priests were notorious at that time they must have received their first impulse from Wiclif while he was at Oxford. This conclusion also agrees with what one would naturally suppose an earnest teacher would do in the way of interesting young men in his plans. Still, it might be hard to point to any particular men and say with certainty that they became Poor Priests from studying under Wiclif at Oxford. According to his confession, reported by a hostile chronicler, John Ball was a pupil of Wiclif for two years, but it might be questioned if Ball would possibly come under the category of Poor Priests.[3] William Thorpe, however, was one, and had studied under Wiclif, Hereford, and others; where, is not stated.[4]

In support of earlier dates we find interesting evidence in the writings of Wiclif and other Lollards.

Wiclif's Sermon for the second Sunday in Lent appears to belong to 1380, or to come but a little later. It contains plain directions to his hearers or readers concerning the delivery of the sermon, such as he often in later times was accustomed to give his Poor Priests.[5]

Again in the Dialogus, believed by the editor, A. W. Pollard, to have been written in 1379, we meet this passage: "Through this (i. e., desire for temporal possessions) the incompetent aspire to the superior ranks of the priesthood and

---
[1] Con. Eul., III, 354, 355.
[2] Fasc. Z., 275.
[3] Id., 273.
[4] Cf. Lechler, I, 413–415; II, kap. 5, ii.
[5] I, Sermones, Intro., xxxiii–xxxiv; Sermon xix, p. 130; II, 330–331.

hinder the preaching of the word of God among the people. Those who strive for this they persecute as being heretics, and this persecution is a manifest proof of their own heresy. Nor do the poor faithful priests[1] suffice to resist unless God, by means of the secular arm or by some other means, shall quickly offer helping hands."[2]

This and other passages in the Dialogus almost lead Mr. Pollard to the conclusion that "Wiclif's Poor Priests must have both begun their work and met with resistance much earlier than is supposed."[3]

In the tract which begins "The first general poynt of pore prestis that prechen in engelond is this," ascribed by the editor, F. D. Matthew, to the year 1377, the writer complains of hindrance from preaching suffered by the clergy, and of lack of safeguards against arbitrary imprisonment by ecclesiastical authorities: (Points by which the land would be strengthened.) "That non of the clergie be lettid to kepe trewely & frely the gospel of ihu crist in good lyuynge & trewe techynge, for no feyned priuelegie or tradicions founden vp of synful wrecchis." "That no prest or religious in oure lond be prisoned with-oten opyn dom & trewe cause, fully knowen to oure kyng or his trewe conseil: for ellis worldly prestis & feyned religious may stoppe trewe men from prechynge of holy writt & magnyfyng of the kyngis regalie, & murthere the kyngis lege men with-outen answere."[4]

Wiclif's tract De Daemonio Meridiano mentions that the faithful in the Lord are prohibited, through imprisonment, privations, and other censures, from declaring the law of Christ openly to the people; and that a false friar preaching manifest heresy will be licensed by the bishop and defended by the secular arm, but that a faithful priest (a common designation for Poor Priests) wishing to preach the gospel gratis will be instantly forbidden to preach in that diocese.[5] R. Buddensieg, the editor, would like to date this tract within a short time after the death of the Black Prince, which he mistakenly ascribes to June 8, 1377, instead of June 8, 1376, but he leaves the date uncertain in deference to "All par-

---

[1] A common designation for Poor Priests. See Lechler, I, 417.
[2] Dialogus, Intro., xx, pp. 10, 11.
[3] Intro., pp. xiv, xv.
[4] Matthew, p. 279.
[5] II, Polemical Works, pp. 424-425.

ticulars hitherto known of the institute of Wiclif's itinerary preachers,"[1] a consideration which has led to the dating by Lechler of the Trialogus and by Loserth of Part I of Sermones.

It should be noted that the dating of these tracts has been done by four different editors, Loserth, Pollard, Matthew, and Buddensieg, and that their constant tendency has been to date these tracts earlier than the accepted belief as to the date of the rise of the Poor Priests would warrant. The tracts referred to apparently belong to the years 1380, 1379, 1377, 1376. Even the two tracts earliest in date speak strongly, as of well-known evils, of hindrances to preaching and of imprisonment for ecclesiastical offenses. One is therefore led to infer that as early as 1376 or 1377 the Poor Priests were rich in experience of opposition, and that consequently the seedtime of their earliest training must lie back of that.

What light do the chroniclers throw upon the possibility of Poor Priests existing in notable numbers in 1376-77?

The Chronicon Angliæ[2] merely hints at Wiclif having helpers in recording the injunction of the archbishop in 1377 to the effect that not only Wiclif should not touch upon forbidden topics, "*sed et omnes qui communicarent eidem.*"

The manuscript in the appendix to the Chronicon Angliæ[3] of the fourteenth century contains a notice under 1377 to the effect that Wiclif gathered to himself many disciples living together in Oxford, clothed with long vestments of russet, all of one cut, going about on foot ventilating his errors among the people and preaching publicly in sermons. After a statement of these errors, the chronicler continues to relate that they asserted and affirmed these so much that lords and magnates of the land and many of the people regarded and honored them as holy prophets. Furthermore, that although the archbishop laid silence upon Wiclif and all others in regard to the forbidden doctrine, and that in no manner either Wiclif or others thereafter or elsewhere [sic] should treat of the matter; yet they did not long keep silence.[4]

Walsingham,[5] apparently working over this or a related

---
[1] Page 414.   [2] Pages 115-117.   [3] MS. 13, D. 1.   [4] Page 391.
[5] Writing before 1388, see Chron. Ang. Intro., xxxii.

text, embellishes the account so far as to say that it was in order to spread his heresy the more cautiously, and under an exquisite coloring to spread it the wider, Wiclif gathered his companions and allies, who stayed at Oxford and elsewhere. Wiclif was forbidden to permit others to teach the matter.[1]

These chronicles, supplementing each other, from the circumstantial nature of their accounts seem hardly guilty of anachronisms; and, moreover, they harmonize with the other testimony given above. If it be contended that the allies of Wiclif referred to were merely the Oxford doctors, like Hereford and Aston, attention might be called to the many disciples, to the garb worn by enough men to become distinctive as the uniform of a sect, to the statement that they stayed both at Oxford and elsewhere, that a deliberate intention is attributed to Wiclif of gathering companions and allies to spread his heresy, that Wiclif was forbidden to permit others to teach.

A curious bit of evidence bearing on the date of the rise of the Poor Priests may be offered for what it is worth. The chronicler, Knighton, treating of the wide spread of Lollardry in 1382, wrote that the principal false Lollards at the first introduction of this horrible sect wore for the greater part garments of russet.[2] But it was under date of 1377 that the chronicler quoted above mentioned the teachers of Wiclif as at that time wearing russet gowns. Slight as this thread may be, to the extent that it holds it binds the rise of the Poor Priests to the period in or just preceding 1376-77.

WICLIF'S VIEW OF THE NEED FOR POOR PRIESTS.

To state the various evils that must have operated to lead Wiclif to originate the Poor Priests would be to review the whole series of complaints which he had to make against the abuses of the times. He set the highest estimate upon the value and importance of preaching. "Evangelization is the supreme work pertaining to the ecclesiastical hierarchy."[3] "Right preching of Goddis Word is the mooste worthy dede that prestis don heere among men."[4] And yet the people for

---
[1] Wals., I, 324-326.
[2] II, 184.
[3] Opus Evangelium (1384), p. 4, ll. 13-15. For a collection of quotations on this point see I, Sermones, Intro. iii, ff.
[4] Matthew, De Officio Pastorali, p. 441

lack of sound preaching were falling into evil ways. "Indeed, (as I have often said) this preaching in which the preachers put aside the Gospel and tell the people what is false, ludicrous, and profane is the greater part of the cause of the perturbation of the church. For if the people should hear regularly the word of God in such preachings, and should somewhat attend to and observe it, the law of Christ would not be sterile as it is now."[1]

How had the Gospel come to be so neglected? "Ant thus ther ben many causis that letten goddis word to renne, * * * o caus is dowing of the chirche & riching ther-of ouer cristis' wille, for bi this prelatis slepen in synne & ben to fatte to preche the puple, * * * & heere breken out thes freris ordris, for al yif thei han no worldly lordchip as han prestis that ben dowid, yit thei spuylen men of moeblis & wasten hem in noumbre & housis, & this excess is more synne than synne of the fend in o persone. & thus they turnen the ende of ther preching for-to gete hem siche godis. & this entent mut nedis make falsed in maner of ther preching, for thei shapen ther sermouns more to gete hem good than to profite to the chirche: & as the firste wile of the fend bigan soone in siluestris tyme, so this secound wile bigan in grounding of thes newe ordris." "the thridde cause that lettith trewe preching is appropring of chirches. for whanne chirches ben approprid, thes curatis tellen not bi this preching, as munkis or chanouns or othere collegies, but bi gedering of godis: & thus they ben maad slowe to preche & stronge to gedere dymes to hem." * * * "the fourthe cause is bringing in of false freris bi many cuntreys: for, as it is seid bifore, thei letten trewe preching to renne & maken curatis bi many weyes to leeue this moost worthy offiss. First they robben hem many weyes & maken hem bisy for to lyue, for they deprauen hem to ther parischens bi floriyshid wordis that they bringen yn; & no drede they shapen ther sermouns bi dyuy siouns & othere iapis that they maken moost plese the puple. & thus they erren in bileue & maken the puple to trowe to hem that sermouns ben nought but in ther foorme & thus thei stoppen symple curatis that thei doren not preche to the puple, & this defaute of preching of crist is more than defaute in hereris."[2]

---
[1] III, Sermones, p. 385, ll. 34-35, l. 38; p. 386, l. 7.
[2] Matthew, De Officio Pastorali, pp. 445-416. Written not later than 1378. See p. 405.

As proofs that friars preach only for gain, Wiclif said: "Friars (i. e., the orders of friars) select as preachers those that can get the most goods from the people. These gloss the sins of the people. They go not where sin is greatest, but where they can gain most. They do not disclose the sins of prelates and great men for fear of losing their favor. They do not preach at times most favorable for edifying the people, but at seasons the most profitable for themselves. When they get rich enough not to need more goods they do not preach. They do not preach to the very poor. They are far more interested in gathering the collection than in confirming the weak faith of the people."[1]

As though this were not enough: "Friars pursue with lies and many fallacious indictments the faithful who in charity expose their defects."[2] As for the prelates: "They scorn the preaching of the gospel as being in the highest degree hateful to them, for its teachings and their lives do not accord. Hence they wish it should be left undeclared to the people."[3]

WICLIF'S AIMS FOR POOR PRIESTS.

Wiclif's Poor Priests were designed to remedy just these evils, so clearly recognized. "Simple Priests should not cease to evangelize on account of excommunications or other censures of Antichrist."[4]

"And if it be asked to what degree we ought to press on to evangelization and the passion of martyrdom, the answer is the same as before, that just as a man should exert all his strength upon cherishing God, thus also he should exert all his strength upon preaching Christ. Nor should he mingle in a consideration of self-love, nor strive to introduce novelty or subtle speech into his sermons, but should consider purely in what manner he can best avail the honor of God and the utility of the people."[5]

This preaching was to consist not of soft flattery, but of hard truth. Evangelical men needed to uncover the sins of the people, and to persist in doing so.[6]

---

[1] II, Sermones, No. VIII, pp. 57-59.
[2] IV, Sermones, No. 63, p. 499.
[3] Dialogus, p. 17, ll. 18-26.
[4] III, Sermones, No. 10, p. 73, ll. 29-32.
[5] II, Sermones, No. 38, p. 279. ll. 1-8.
[6] I, Sermones, No. 42, p. 281, ll. 1-9.

And since the monks and friars were blinding the people to the rule of God, it would be especially the work of an evangelist to destroy those sects.[1]

That Wiclif's Poor Priests were designed to give the people not merely sermons in English, as the friars had done, but were intended to present to the people the gospel itself as clearly as possible, and hence in English, as the other preachers had not done, goes almost without argument.

Wiclif said the clergy feared to give in English the whole gospel, because it would prove themselves to be followers of Antichrist.[2] To him, who as a crowning work presented to Englishmen the Bible in English, it was a commonplace to say: "The wit of goddis lawe shulde be taught in that tunge that is more knowun."[3] "There is no one so simple as not to be able to learn the evangelical words to the extent of the rudiments that will suffice him for salvation."[4]

SELECTION OF POOR PRIESTS.

In the selection of men to perform the work of preaching Wiclif does not appear to have shown any preference.

Of the Oxford doctors that were repressed in 1382 John Aston took up the life of an itinerant Wiclifite preacher, and it would appear likely that others did the same. There appears to be no specific reference to any young Oxford student becoming a Poor Priest unless we take William Thorpe, but such a body of suitable material at hand could hardly have been neglected.

Besides students and doctors there must have been many humble curates scattered about England to whom Wiclif's appeals for gospel reform came in one way or another. It was not a rare thing for curates to leave their benefices for a time in order to study the gospel. "Also yif siche curatis ben stired to gone lerne goddis lawe & teche here parischenys the gospel, comynly thei schullen gete no leue of bischopis but for gold: & whanne thei schullen most profite in here lernynge than schulle thei be clepid hom at the prelatis wille."[5]

---

[1] I, Sermones, No. 27, p. 179, ll. 8-12.
[2] I, Polemical Works, cap. iv., p. 126, ll. 4-15.
[3] De Officio Pastorali, Matthew, cap. 15, p. 429.
[4] Opus Evangelicum, p. 92, ll. 5-8.
[5] Matthew, Why Poor Priests have no Benefice; author and date uncertain, p. 250.

Wiclif himself held the rectorship of the church at Lutterworth while teaching at Oxford.[1] Curates accordingly may well have heard Wiclif teaching. That curates were often not desired to preach the gospel has already been noticed. Consequently, such as did become desirous to preach the gospel were apt to lose their benefices, and these would go to swell the ranks of the Poor Priests. Such a view of the case is supported by the declaration of Wiclif that a simple curate who is deprived of his benefice for preaching is all the better off, for then he can preach the more freely.[2]

Did Wiclif attempt to draw monks and friars into his ranks? The editor of De Apostasia, M. H. Dziewicki, believes that the first two chapters of that treatise were written largely with that design. He writes: "Both these propositions (i. e., A man may, without apostacy, leave any of these private religions, and a man may, without leaving any private religion to which he belongs, incur apostacy) seem intended to bring over to Wiclif's band of 'poor priests' some wavering Franciscans or Dominicans, who, struck and attracted by his austere doctrines, were yet held back for fear of apostacy. This hypothesis is strengthened, first, by the comparative moderation in tone to which Wiclif keeps all through the book; second, by several passages that we shall notice as we go on; and third, by the general tendency and evident à propos of the arguments." Also, "From some passages in De Blasphemia it appears that Wiclif's propaganda amongst the monks was very active at this time (i. e., 1383[3]). He avails himself with much skill of every motive that they could have to be discontented with their superiors."

The passages from De Apostasia referred to are especially two: one in which Wiclif states that some of the more religious and intelligent friars, speaking in reference to the perfidy of the orders, quote the Psalmist: "Let us break their bonds and cast their yoke from us;" and another to the effect that there are many saintly and intelligent clerics among them who do well to flee, despairing on account of the hardened malice of those sects. They do well to flee because otherwise as apostates they are killed or committed to perpetual prison.[4]

---

[1] Fasc. Ziz., pp. 242-243; Bull of Gregory XI. Cf. Matthew, p. 141.
[2] Opus Evang., p. 375, l. 32, p. 376, l. 1.
[3] See vi-vii.
[4] P. 24, ll. 8-12; p. 41, ll. 35-37; p. 42, ll. 1-5.

We have now to consider the question of how far Wiclif drew upon the laity to secure Poor Priests. And here for the sake of clearness it may be well to explain the meaning of certain terms as used in this paper. Whenever the writer wishes to refer to priests regularly ordained according to the rules of the church of that day, he will use the term "regularly ordained;" whenever he refers to men ordained in a fashion that would have been regarded as irregular by the church of that day, he will use the term "irregularly ordained." By "lay preachers" he wishes to signify men who have been neither "regularly ordained" nor "irregularly ordained."

Wiclif set slight value upon episcopal ordination. "Sensible consecration avails little, and thus if the divine ordination be present any priest can confer the ecclesiastical sacraments equally well with the Pope, just as the other apostles ordained bishops equally well with Peter." "Indeed, I suppose, as far as concerns these two ordinations (i. e., sacraments), namely, confirmation and ordination, there is no reason why inferior priests could not give them.[1]

Not only was this doctrine held theoretically by Lollard preachers, but it was actually put into practice. Witness Walsingham under date of 1389: "The Lollards, followers of John Wiclif, at this time seduced very many to their error and acquired so great audacity that their priests, after the custom of pontiffs, created new priests, asserting, as we have frequently told above, that every priest had as great power of binding and loosing and of performing other ecclesiastical functions as the Pope himself gives or can give. They practised this perfidy in the diocese of Salisbury. And they who were thus ordained by the heretics, thinking all things were permitted to them, did not fear to celebrate mass, to treat of divine affairs, and to confer the sacraments. This baseness was disclosed by one who had been ordained by them, but who, pricked by conscience, confessed the error to the Bishop of Salisbury at his manor of Sunnyng."[2]

In John Balle's confession, according to the Fasciculi Zizaniorum, the followers of Wiclif by 1381 were ordaining one another, "*se ordinaverant*."[3]

---
[1] Polemical Works, I, De Quattuor Sectis Novellis, pp. 259–260.
[2] Wals., II, p. 188.
[3] Fasc. Ziz., pp. 273–274.

If the Poor Priests thus believed and practiced ordination among themselves, it follows that it would have been an easy matter for such laymen as joined this group of teachers to become irregularly ordained priests, and thus laymen could have been drawn upon as recruits.

But did Wiclif countenance as preachers laymen who had never become irregularly ordained? Contrary to received opinion as it may be, all the evidence that the writer finds goes to prove well nigh conclusively that Wiclif had no lay preachers, and moreover had no place for them in his scheme for reform. As this point deserves careful consideration, let us first notice what parts Wiclif considered the church properly to be divided into.

In Sermon No. LX, of the First Part, he outlines his ideal church militant: "The church should be divided into these three parts: All members of the church ought to be shepherds or sheep. The shepherds ought to be priests or deacons, teaching the sacred conversation of Christ; and the sheep, which are the people or laymen, are in a twofold function, because they are either defenders or workmen. The defenders are the secular lords, who ought powerfully to defend the church; the workmen are the people, who should minister to the church in the more humble duties. And if this third part performs its office heartily and faithfully then mother church will prosper. * * * But although by reason of haughtiness or avarice of Antichrist ministers are multiplied among the clergy, even beyond the order of the Old Testament, nevertheless priests and deacons would suffice, just as it was at the time of the Apostle."[1]

From this outline one can see that Wiclif had a clear conception of the parts of the church militant, and of the duty of each part. It is to be observed how clearly he lays it down that all members ought to be shepherds or else sheep, that the shepherds are to be priests or deacons, who are to preach; while of the layman, those who are not secular lords are to perform the more humble duties. There certainly appears to be no place in such a system for the lay preacher.

If we follow Wiclif a step farther we shall find him arguing that a certain office can be filled by laymen for the specific

---

[1] P. 401, ll, 2-20.

reason that such offices do not require preaching. Continuing the line of thought he had presented, Wiclif showed how in his opinion there were six superfluous orders among the clergy. Of the archdeacons he said: "In the second rank archdeacons have been introduced, more clearly superfluous (i. e., than the bishops), since if they avail for anything they avail for that infamous twofold duty of burdening, of plundering, poor subject churches, and of calling attention to the ease of the superior bishop." "The faithful therefore should notice that their ministry, and the whole of it, can be prudently filled by a layman, and if the bishop would fully and duly perform his office the ministry of each would be more perfectly executed. For our archdeacons do not preach as did Stephen, nor living without property, as the apostles, do they minister to the poor."[1]

If Wiclif argues that a layman can fill the archdeaconry because it involves no preaching, does he not take for granted that a layman ought not to preach?

On the other hand, where does Wiclif mention or recognize the need for lay preachers? The arguments usually put forth in support of the idea of lay preachers turn out, upon examination, to be without foundation. As these arguments are presented in the greatest array in the writings of Lechler, the writer craves the privilege of taking up seriatim the three arguments whereby Lechler 'believes he can prove that in the lifetime of Wiclif, and with his knowledge and approbation, laymen worked as traveling preachers.' The point of Lechler's arguments is not that Wiclif thought that his irregularly ordained preachers had sufficient authority, but that Wiclif was consciously sending out laymen.

First (Lechler): "The circumstance is plainly not accidental that Wiclif, in the sermons of his later years, when he speaks of his beloved traveling preachers, calls them less and less often 'poor priests,' or 'simple' or 'faithful priests,' but refers to them by the name 'evangelical men,' or 'apostolic men.' That is, he purposely avoids in such places the term priests, because that now was less and less applicable to all traveling preachers." The references given to support this proposition are limited to the Three Festival Sermons, numbered 31, 37, 53, in MS., No. 3928, and presumably now

---

[1] Ibid., p. 402, ll, 11-21.

published under the same numbers in II Sermones. But II Sermones, according to the editor, Loserth,[1] group around 1382, and precede Sermones, III and IV, which remained to be written or revised before Wiclif's death, in December, 1384. If the sermons referred to all come within about a year the proposition is hardly supported. Since these references fail it becomes necessary to make such comparisons of the varying use of these terms as the incomplete indexes of Wiclif's published writings, supplemented with further search, will permit. After the elimination of writings of doubtful date or authenticity, as far as Wiclif is concerned, the following table of the use of these terms appears:

"Priest."	Approximate date.	Approximate date.	More comprehensive term.
Sacerdos fidelis....... De Dæmon. Merid. Pol. W., 424.	1376–7		
Pauperes et pauci........ Fideles sacerdotes......... Sacerdotum simplicum....... Dialogus, 11, 54.	1379		
Pore prestis............ Of Servants & Lords, Matthew, 229.	1381		
Sacerdotes simplices .... I, Sermones, No. 63, p. 289.	1381–2	1381–2	Viri evangelici. I Sermones, No. 62, p. 281.
		1382	Viros apostolicos. Viri evangelici. II, Sermones, No. 31, pp. 227–229.
		1382	Viri evangelici. II, Sermones, No. 38, p. 282.
Simplices sacerdotes .... III, Sermones, No. 6, p. 43.	1382–3		
Sacerdotes simplices .... III, Sermones, No. 10, p. 74.	1382–3		
Sacerdotes fideles .... De Triplico Vinculo Amoris, Pol. W., p. 172.	1383 (close of).		
Nos simplices............ (Filios domini, genus sacerdocium.) IV, Sermones, No. 56, p. 437.	1383–4	1383–4	Nostri prædicantes. IV, Sermones, No. 59, p. 462.
Sacerdotes simplices .... Opus Evang., Pars I, p. 35. (Wiclif died soon after this work.)	1384		
Sacerdotes Christi........... Op. Ev., Pars I, p. 175.	1384		

The just conclusion seems to be that any argument based upon the supposed gradual abandonment of the term "priest" is without foundation. At all times, it should be noted, it would be perfectly natural for a speaker to use the terms "evangelical men," etc., as synonymous with "priests."

---

[1] I Sermones, Intro., xxxi–xxxii,

The second argument is based upon the argument in the Dialogus, which reads: "And as for the fruit it seems certain that an ignorant person, by mediation of God's grace, avails more for building up the church of Christ than many graduates of schools or colleges, because he sows the law of Christ more humbly and more abundantly in works as well as in speech."[1] At first glance this passage would seem to refer to lay preachers. But a closer examination, together with that of the context, shows that Wiclif is here comparing only ignorant men and learned men to the disadvantage of the latter, so far as preaching is concerned. He is censuring scholastic learning. No comparison is instituted between priests and laymen.

That Wiclif is here comparing learned and simple priests is conclusively shown by the next few sentences of his argument. He goes on to explain that the scholastic studies breed heresies, such as that of the nature of the host. The fourth sentence after the one quoted above reads: "And thus it is concerning other heresies newly arising against the faith; for the inspiration of the simple priests, both in knowledge and willing work, will be of more profit to the capacity of the faithful laymen than all the said universities with their studies pertaining or their privileges hypocritically introduced and depressing the laity."[2]

Thirdly, there is the passage in Sermon No. IX, Secunda Pars, quoted to support the theory of lay preachers: "It seems, therefore, that for the existence of such a minister of the church there is required the authority of divine acceptance, and consequently the power and knowledge given of God for the performance of such ministry. When one has these, even though the bishop has not imposed hands upon him according to his traditions, God through himself has established him, and thus it seems (as is expressed in the utterances of Saint Paul and Saint John) that to become such a prelate there is required the effective following after Christ and the due renunciation of all the goods of the world."[3] The context shows that Wiclif was bent upon proving that Pope and prelates had no especial authority as to ordination given

---

[1] Dialogus, p 54, ll, 6–10.   [3] II, Sermones, p. 64, ll. 25–34.
[2] Ibid., ll. 25–30.

them by virtue of the gift of the keys. Accordingly he concludes, in the passage quoted, that one needs not the ordination of bishops; that if the ordination of bishops was not requisite, no ordination from human hands was required does not follow. As noticed some time ago, Wiclif held that "If the divine ordination be present any priest can confer the ecclesiastical sacraments," and that there was no reason why inferior priests could not confer ordination. His whole position was that any priest had as full powers as any prelate. The passage in the Dialogus therefore can not be used to prove that Wiclif believed in lay preachers.

THEIR PREPARATION BY WICLIF.

Wiclif gave considerable attention to the preparation of the Poor Priests, supplying them with great numbers of model sermons, and attempting to train them in their character and behavior as well. These points can be determined from his Latin and his English sermons. In both, but with greater frequency in the latter, are found various directions in regard to the proper use of the sermon.

In the Latin references like these appear: "The preacher can expand the matter of the exhortation according to its applicability to the audience." "The matter of the sermon is to be expanded according as it will benefit the audience." "Since the people are commonly accustomed to receive the Eucharist on this day, the sense is to be adapted pertinently to their instruction."[1] Considerations like these have led the editor of the Latin sermons, Dr. Loserth, to say without qualification that "The Latin sermons belonging to the Lutterworth period) and these form a large proportion of the whole number of sermons) were all composed by Wiclif as model sermons for the use of the 'poor priests,' or the 'wandering' or 'traveling preachers'".[2]

The references to the English sermons are similar,[3] but the

---

[1] I, Sermones, No. 18, p. 128, ll. 3-4; I, No. 19, p. 130, ll. 30-31; I, No. 19, p. 133, ll. 21-22; I. No. 24, p. 164, ll. 1-3; I, No. 24, p. 165, ll. 1-3; I, No. 39, p. 260, ll. 9-12; II, No. 30, p. 226, ll. 30-31.

[2] I, Sermones, Intro., xvi.

[3] Sunday Gospels: I. Arnold, No. 1, p. 3; No. 2, p. 6; No. 3, p. 9; No. 4, p. 12; No. 5, p. 14; No. 21, p. 53. Gospel Sermons: II, Arnold, No. 147, p. 45; No. 50, p. 53; No. 154, p. 60, following No. 178, p. 116; following No. 178, p. 117; No. 204, p. 168; No. 205, p. 169; No. 207, p. 172. Epistle Sermons: II, Arnold, No. 6, p. 240; No. 7, p. 244; No. 9, p. 249; No. 13, p. 259, No. 14, p. 264; No. 16, pp. 271-272; No. 55, p. 376.

additional important feature is that long passages from the New Testament are often quoted in English, thus putting it in the power of any preacher who could read at all to present to the people not merely an exposition of the Gospel, but the Gospel itself in a good translation.

These model sermons would naturally, in an indirect way, instruct the preachers who used them. Wiclif, however, did not stop with that, but also frequently directed his attention to the special edification of priests and preachers. Thus, for instance, sermon No. 31 in Secunda Pars begins: "This Gospel directs apostles and apostolic men in what manner they should conduct themselves in the office of preaching." And No. 31 in Quarta Pars consists of a long disquisition upon the points of good and bad sermons and the character needful for preachers. In the notice of the Wiclifites made by the author of the Continuatio Eulogii under the year 1382 occurs the remark that "The disciples of the aforesaid John studied in the compilation of sermons and gathered the sermons of (their) brothers."

One would much like to know whether Wiclif at times gathered his Poor Priests around him and face to face with them uttered his sermons, or whether his sermons to them and for them were disseminated in written form. Any attempt to answer this question leads only to inconclusive and therefore unsatisfactory results, the reason for which is clear. In the Præfatio to the Latin Sermons, as we have them, Wiclif explained that he had been collecting these sermons with some idea of revision: and at the close of the English Sermons—that is, in the last paragraph of the fifty-fifth of the Epistle Sermons—he apparently so wrote of the Gospel and Epistle Sermons as to indicate that, as we now have them, they had been issued all together.

Consequently, one who should favor the idea that they were issued first in written form may not claim in his favor that they lack the directness which one should expect in them if they were first issued orally, for the revision may have changed the phraseology in this respect. And, too, the cross references from one sermon to another[1] may similarly be explained. On the other hand, he who would favor the idea of their first being issued orally to groups of priests can not

---

[1] I, Sermones, No. 39, p. 260, ll. 9–12, II, Arnold, No. 50, p. 531, No 204, p 168.

deny that such passages as point that way (leaving out of view the forty sermons *dum stetit in scholis*[1] which supposably the Poor Priests could not have heard when first issued) may be merely instances of vivid writing. Or if the passages seem to be particularly addressed to the priests themselves, one can not deny that such sermons, as well as the others, may have been passed from hand to hand.

REASONS FOR THEIR ITINERANCY.

In discussing this question we are fortunate in having peculiarly satisfactory material to draw upon for information. We possess the valuable tract Why Poor Priests have no Benefice,[2] which shows what considerations actually led them to become itinerant; and as further material to draw upon, in the second part of the Sermons (composed 1382+), and in the Dialogus (composed 1379), and in the tract *De Officio Pastorali* (Wiclif, not later than 1378),[3] not to mention other places, we find fully explained the underlying principles that gave those considerations their vitality.

These underlying principles or desirable ends are three in number, namely: to preach in the place and manner most profitable to the people, to live modestly by work or free alms, to avoid simony. In regard to these points Wiclif had strong convictions.

He called it one of the errors of the disciples of Antichrist that they chose places productive to themselves rather than with the view of being the most useful.[4] He likewise used the same phrase "to be most useful" (plus prodesse) in rebuking the system whereby bishops established limitations for preachers and thus "Imply that the region of their jurisdiction is exempt from the dominion of God to be a principality of the devil."[5] Still more clearly did he express himself upon another error of these disciples of Antichrist who believed that they should not preach outside of their own cure. "For it often happens that a preacher is more bound to another people (i. e., than the people in his own jurisdiction); indeed, just as the law of charity and of love requires one to

---

[1] IV, Sermones, Intro., v, etc.
[2] Probably written by a Poor Priest?, Matthew, p. 244.
[3] Matthew, p. 405.
[4] II, Sermones, p. 277, ll. 23-26.
[5] Ibid., p. 278, ll. 1-9.

love everyone, so the law of the gospel requires one to preach to whomsoever he may be able to give the most help (plus prodesse).[1]

He believed that priests should live modestly, limiting their wants to moderate supplies of food and raiment only,[2] the latter to include the protection of dwellings; that they should not hesitate to earn their support by work, provided that it be of a suitable character;[3] that such support as they received from others should be from alms[4] and from alms alone.[5]

Of simony Wiclif said that in the conferring of benefices it should be understood that the goods received were pure alms, not one's own, but belonging to God and the people. And accordingly patrons should look to God, not to the recipients, for their reward.[6]

Coming now to the tract Why Poor Priests have no Benefice, we find that the writer offers at least five reasons why the Poor Priests should not have a benefice, all more or less directly based on the assumption of the duty of preaching in the place and manner to obtain the best results.

If a priest has a benefice he dare not speak out boldly in reproof of sin wherever he may find it. If he reproves sinful prelates and false religions, or exercises the censures of the church against sinful men who, for the revenue they afford, enjoy prelates' protection, he is quickly brought to order.[7] If priests do not bind themselves to a single place, "as a tey dogge," they can not be hindered from speaking out, "for now thei ben free to flee fro o cite to a nother whanne thei ben pursued of anticristis clerkis, as biddith crist in the gospel." Secondly, as an evil incidental to the holding of a benefice, small curates are often in receipt of letters from their ordinaries whereby they are compelled to summon and curse poor men for no reason but the covetousness of Antichrist's clerks.[8] Surely not Gospel preaching nor conducive to the spread of the Gospel. Thirdly, if curates are stirred to get a leave of absence for study of God's Word,

---

[1] II, Sermones, p. 278, ll. 23-29.
[2] Matthew, De Officio Pastorali, pp. 410, 411.
[3] Dialogus, p. 51, l. 12; p. 52, l. 2.
[4] Matthew, De Officio Pastorali, p. 414.
[5] Dialogus, p. 79, l. 31; p. 80, l. 3.
[6] Dialogus, p. 80, l. 3; l. 10.
[7] Matthew, Why Poor Priests have no Benefice, p. 249.
[8] Ibid., p. 250.

thus to bring the Gospel back to their parishoners, they can not get leave of absence but for gold.[1] Fourthly, "also nowe thei may best with-oute chalynge of men goo & dwelle among the peple where thei schullen most profite, & in couenable tyme come & goo aftir stiryng of the holy gost, & not be bounden bi synful mennus iurdiccion fro the betre doynge.[2] Fifthly, the care of a benefice brings in much worldliness and needless business. Priests need more time for prayers and the study of the Scriptures, and ought not be hindered by new songs and more sacraments than Christ and his apostles used. And lords who present clerks to benefices are prone to divert the efforts of the curates entirely from their duties, and employ them for scribes and architects or other worldly offices.[3]

In consideration of their duty to live by alms rather than by tithes the Poor Priests saw that without a benefice this was a simple matter, for thus they were unhampered by any ecclesiastical system of tithes and customary offerings, and the people they taught might give them only what they wished to give freely.[2] Closely connected with this thought was the one that they feared to misspend poor men's goods, gathered by tithes and offerings, in feasting prelates, patrons, and idle vagabonds, and, upon occasion of institution and induction, in feeing bishops' officers, archdeacons, and other officials.[4]

As for simony, "for yif men schulde come to benefices be gift of prelates ther is drede of symonye: for comynly thei taken the firste fruytis or othere pensions, or holden curatis in office in here courtis or chapelis or othere veyn offices,[5] fer fro prestis lif taught & ensaumplid of crist & his apostlis." "And yif lordis schullen presente clerkis to benefices thei wolen haune comynly gold in grett quantite."[3] "for thes dredes & many thousand mo," the writer concludes, "& for to be more lich to cristis lif & his apostlis, & for to profite more to here owene soules & othere mennus, summe pore prestis thenken with goddis helpe to traueile aboute where thei schulden most profiten by euydence that god geueth hem, the while thei han tyme & litel bodily strengthe & youthe."[6]

---

[1] Matthew, Why Poor Priests have no Benefice, p. 250.
[2] Ibid., p. 252.
[3] Ibid., p. 246.
[4] Ibid., pp. 248–249.
[5] Ibid., p. 245.
[6] Matt., p. 253.

Did they look down upon curates? Not at all; "netheles thei dampnen not curatis that don wel here office, so that thei kepen liberte of the gospel, & dwellen here thei schullen most profite, & that thei techen trewly & stabely goodis lawe agenst false prophetis & cursed fendis lymes."[1] One may see that in this tract it is not even implied that all Poor Priests were itinerant. The first sentence declares that "Summe causes meuen summe pore prestis to resceyue not benefices."[2] This is the same phrase as that employed in a closing paragraph just quoted. The thought that some held benefices agrees, too, with Wiclif's teachings, which nowhere, as far as known by the writer, condemn Poor Priests holding benefices provided they do it honorably, and, too, with the last paragraph of this tract, which shows great respect for curates.

The foregoing paragraphs throw a strong light upon the question as to whether the itinerant character of the Poor Priests, considered as an association, was in its nature permanent or temporary. The charms of their life were great. Accountable to no prelate, to no ordinary, to no ecclesiastical system that might thwart their plans of evangelizing, free to live without worldly cares, without routine work, and thus free to study and work where and when they should deem it best, they were certainly in many ways to be envied by the earnest curate, however fortunately he might be located, and the peculiar advantages they enjoyed clearly led them to envy no curate. This itinerant mode of life had at least sufficient inducements to lead to its becoming a characteristic of the typical Poor Priest.

DID THE POOR PRIESTS CONSTITUTE AN ORDER?

Had not Dr. Shirley, in 1858, in the twilight of knowledge preceding the publication of Wiclif literature, declared himself so emphatically on the affirmative side of this question, it never perhaps would have been seriously broached. He stated that "Wiclif was the founder of a new order," compared him to Loyola and Francis of Assisi, and declared that these "'simple priests' were employed under episcopal sanc-

---

[1] Matthew, Why Poor Priests have no Benefice, p. 253.
[2] Ibid., p. 245.

tion, through what was then the immense diocese of Lincoln, and probably in others also."[1]

Now, that for various reasons the Poor Priests would naturally tend to form some sort of an organization, though it might go no further than a thorough good understanding, would not be denied. That they were charged with forming organizations is well known. The Fasciculi contains an account of a confession of John Balle,[2] wherein it is stated "He also said there was a certain company of the sect and doctrine of Wiclif who had formed a confederation (*conspiraverant confœderationem*), and had ordained themselves to go about all England to preach what Wiclif had taught"[3] * * * And in the mandate of the Bishop of Worcester, of August 10, 1387, it is charged that Hereford, Aston, Purvey, Parker, and Swinderby are "*conspirati in collegio illicito* * * * *ritu Lollardorum confœderati.*"[4] These charges of association should not be confounded with the open establishment of an order approved by the church—such as Dr. Shirley believed to have been established. The episcopal sanction which Dr. Shirley claimed for the Poor Priests was deduced by him from very narrow reading of a simple statement made by Wiclif when outlining the treatment to be accorded good priests in general.[5]

Certainly all the Wiclif literature that we now possess indicates that a new order or sect would have been the last thing that Wiclif would have desired, and nowhere does he give any indication of a close organization, an oath, a particular rule, for his Poor Priests. He simply pointed his followers to Christ as their pattern.

It will readily be seen from the examination just made that no cut-and-dried rule can be applied to determine whether this man or that was or was not a Poor Priest, for, as we have reason to believe, the Poor Priests did not form a sharply defined body. John Purvey, the "simple chaplain," who

---

[1] Fasciculi Zizaniorum, Intro., p. xl.
[2] Before his execution, which occurred July 15, 1381; Stubbs, Const. Hist. of Eng., 3d edition, ii, p. 471, note.
[3] Fasc. Ziz., pp. 273-274.
[4] Wilkins, Conc. III, p. 202.
[5] "Videtur meritorium bonas colligere sacerdotes, cum Christus exemplar cujuslibet boni operis ita fecit. Sed eleemosynantes caverent de talibus sacerdotibus præcipue in his tribus. Primo quod sint amovibiles et non hæredati, cum jam non sint immerito confirmati. Sed sub conditione quod vivant digne et juste, habeant de temporali eleemosyna in mensura." Fasc. Ziz., Intro. xli, note 1, MS. Denis, ccclxxviii, fol. 52, v°.

was the intimate friend of Wiclif,[1] and whose version of the English Bible was so successful as to replace the version of Wiclif and Hereford,[2] may be said to have been a Poor Priest. And there was John Aston, the Oxford scholar, who likewise recanted and relapsed again, so active on his feet as to call forth Knighton's simile of being like a dog ready to leap from his couch and bark at the slightest sound.[3] William Swinderby, whose early life was so remarkable, was among the itinerant Lollard preachers; and William Thorpe, who, as a young man, studied under the three men just named, might be termed a Poor Priest. There is no special need of giving their biographies here, however, for their characteristics have been brought out in two recent writings—in G. M. Trevelyan's England in the Age of Wycliffe,[4] and in Prof. Edward P. Cheyney's article, "The recantations of the early Lollards."[5]

DRESS OF THE POOR PRIESTS.

It is noteworthy that in the writings of Wiclif, of the probable date of 1383, are found expressions indicating that he believed that the dress of men was of little importance. Such passages occur when he is attacking the religious orders. "It seems, however, probable to me that neither rite nor bodily habit is essential to any good religion or order, but to every good religious (i. e., a person belonging to a religious order) the rite or bodily habit should be a matter of indifference."[6] "Nor does it seem that variation of habits in color and figure has a probable reason except for prognosticating that these are of an adulterous generation which seeks such signs. * * * At any rate that fiction is to be derided, that black signifies sorrow for sins; white, purity of heart; and russet, assiduous labor in the church militant."[7] If this were Wiclif's position how came it that—as will be seen in a moment—his Poor Priests, and the Lollards generally, adopted a more or less peculiar garb? I should say a key to the explanation lies in another passage of Wiclif's writings, of

---

[1] Knighton, II, pp. 178, 179.
[2] Forshall & Madden, § 59.
[3] Knighton, II, pp. 176–178.
[4] N. Y., Longmans, Green & Co., 1899, 8°, pp. 380, indexed.
[5] American Hist. Rev., Vol. IV, No. 3, pp. 423–438.
[6] De Apostasia, p. 5, l. 38; p. 6, l. 14.
[7] De Fundatione Sectarum, Polemical Works, I, p. 26, ll. 10–12; p. 27, ll. 2–4.

about the same date, where he quotes with approval a passage from Augustine, who condemned certain men who went barefoot "not because they walked thus for the sake of afflicting the body, but because they were of the opinion that they should do thus from Divine command."[1] That shows that while Wiclif thought a peculiar dress of no Scriptural authority, still he believed it might be justified on other grounds.

In the discussion of the date of the rise of Poor Priests, the writer noted the mention made of "many disciples of depravity dwelling together in Oxford, clothed in long vestments of russet of a single cut, going on foot, etc.," an account of which appears in Walsingham expanded to "companions and allies of a single sect dwelling both at Oxford and elsewhere, clothed in vestments of russet reaching to the ankle, in sign of greater perfection, going barefoot, etc."[2] Knighton wrote: "The principal pseudo-Lollards at the first introduction of this horrible sect wore for the most part garments of russet, displaying outwardly as it were simplicity of heart, so that they subtly attracted the minds of the onlookers to themselves and the more securely entered upon the task of teaching and sowing their insane doctrine."[3]

In a poem "Against the Lollards," supposed to have been written soon after the rebellion of 1381, it is taken for granted that the Lollard preachers go barefoot, but it is charged that they do so only when they will be seen: "They take off their shoes at the entrances of the villages when they deceive the people. They go barefoot when they approach the doors of places in which they preach. They make much of their punishments."[4]

The conclusions to be drawn from these passages, that Lollard preachers, including the Poor Priests, went about barefoot and wore clothes that were simple and quiet in tone and apt to be similar, though not necessarily of one cut or color, are supported by the descriptions given by Knighton and Walsingham of John Purvey, William Swinderby, and William Smith. John Purvey was the "simple chaplain, mature in carriage and appearance, * * * like a common man in

---

[1] Freely translated. Sermones, VII, Quarta Pars. Sermones, p. 141, ll. 18-21.
[2] Wals., I, p. 324-326.
[3] Knighton, II, p. 181.
[4] Pol., P. I., p. 233.

clothing and habits."[1] William Swinderby is described as having the appearance and habits of a hermit (*multum et habitum praeferens heremitae.*)[2] William Smith was the fanatic who joined the Lollards (described by Knighton) who, from disappointment in a love affair, renounced the world, wore no linen, ate no fish nor flesh, drank no wine nor beer, and went barefoot for many years.[3]

METHODS.

In the discussion of the Poor Priests given above attention was called to the itinerant tendencies of the Lollard preachers and of the Poor Priests in particular. In Ball's so-called confession, it is recalled, the Lollards were said to have made a conspiracy to go about all England to preach the doctrines of Wiclif.[4] Purvey, it will be remembered, put aside ease of body for the labor of journeying about.[5] Swinderby was always a restless wanderer, and when silenced in one diocese stole off to another.[6] Ball's wanderings were notorious.

Quite in keeping with these facts are the notices in the ecclesiastical documents. Thus in his letter to Stokes, dated May 29, 1382, Archbishop Courtenay complains that the Wiclifites—he really says "*quidam filii damnationis*"[7]—do not hesitate to publicly preach within his diocese, both in churches and on the highways and other profane places. The mandate of the Bishop of Worcester, August 10, 1387, forbidding Lollards to preach within his diocese, after naming several of the chief Lollards, as I have stated elsewhere, speaks of them as preaching publicly in churches and cemeteries, in the streets, and many profane places; also as secretly reaching the ears of the people in halls, chambers, inclosures, and gardens.[8]

As has already been hinted, these preachers were by no means confining their efforts to secret teaching. Wiclif would not have approved such a limitation to their activity, for he said that evangelical men should put aside fear and persist even to death in exposing the sins of the people and in rectifying the church.[9] It may have been some such spirit as this

---

[1] Knighton, II, p. 178.
[2] Wals., II, p. 53.
[3] Knighton, II, p. 190, 191.
[4] Fasc. Z., p. 274.
[5] Kinghton, II, p. 176.
[6] Kinghton, II, p. 198.
[7] Fasc. Z., p. 275.
[8] Wilkins, III, p. 202-203.
[9] I Sermones, p. 281, ll, 1-9.

that actuated Swinderby when he made a pulpit of the millstones at Leicester and declared the bishop could not hinder him from preaching in the King's highway.[1]

In addition to their own determination to spread their teachings the Lollard preachers were supported in their efforts by temporal lords.[2]

Apart from the knights, the people sometimes took a hand in favor of the Lollard preachers, as in the instances of the Londoners impeding the trial of Aston in 1382,[3] and, again, of the London Lollards attacking the friars who sought to silence Patteshulle when denouncing them at St. Christophers in 1387.[4] At Leicester, in 1382, Swinderby was for a time left unmolested, because the bishop of Lincoln feared the crowd, "who heard heard him very willingly and were willing to expose themselves to peril for him before he should be prohibited from preaching or before anything should be done against him in the way of justice."[5]

The force of public opinion was further made use of by the Lollard preachers to win over the weak-kneed who did not dare to belong to a party which the Lollards charged to be composed of people "impious, depraved, malignant, and perverse, worthy of all vituperation, and (living) contrary to the law of God."[6] Knighton asserts: "And thus very many simple ones they perverted and compelled to adhere to their sect. They did so that they might not seem alienated from the law of God and the divine precepts. And many of the weaker ones were seduced, some through fear, others through timidity, that they might not be attacked by them with opprobrious words."

SUCCESS.

One can not estimate the success met with by the Poor Priests apart from the general Lollard movement. Of this a few words might be added relative to the first wave of Lollardry.

---

[1] Knighton, II, p. 192.
[2] For this and related topics see Trevelyan, p. 318, passim.
[3] Wals, II, pp. 65-66.
[4] Ib., II, p. 157.
[5] Ib., II, p. 55.
[6] Knighton, II, p. 185-186.

Walsingham writes that in 1377 the lords and magnates of the land and many of the people favored the Wiclifites.[1] In the poem of 1381, "Against the Lollards," the author says: "A greater pestilence never existed in the church." "This pest now in England, and in no other nation, reigns without remedy." "O land now pestiferous, you were formerly the mother of all sound knowledge, free from the stain of heresy, without share in any error or fallacy. Now you stand forth our standard bearer of schism, discord, error, and madness. You are the faithful patron of every nefarious sect, of every varying doctrine."[2]

In the *Continuatio Eulogii* it is written under 1381 that the Wiclifites were preaching through all England, seducing many laymen as well as nobles and great lords.[3] Under 1382 it is stated that the Wiclifites corrupted the faith and devotion not only of many (common) people and laymen, but also of nobles and scholars, so that in that year the alms of the friars were taken away, the mendicants were ordered to labor, they were not permitted to preach, and were called penny preachers and creepers-in of houses.[4]

Knighton was impressed with the increase of Lollards in 1382: "The body of believers in this sect increased, and germinating, as it were, they were greatly multiplied and filled the whole circle of the Kingdom, and members of this household were made as though they were procreated in one day." "So much did they (i. e., Lollard preachers) prevail in their laborious teachings that they gained a half part or even a majority of the people to their sect." "That sect was held in the greatest honor in those days, and was multiplied to such a degree that you would scarcely meet two men upon the highway of whom one would not be a disciple of Wiclif."[5]

The author of the *Chronicon Angliæ* notes, under the year 1382, that Parliament made a grant to the King on the condition that he would give aid to the church to depress the heretical Wiclifites, "who by their depraved doctrine had deeply infected the whole realm."

These general statements show that the writers of the time

---

[1] Wals., I, p. 325; Appendix Chron. Angl., p. 396.
[2] Pol., P. I., p. 132.
[3] Continuatio Eulogii, III, p. 351.
[4] Ibid., III, pp. 354, 355.
[5] Knighton, II, pp. 183, 185, 191.

regarded Lollardry with great apprehension, and believed it to have had great success among the people. The estimate of one-half the population made by Knighton may be regarded as possibly true for only very limited areas, perhaps those falling under his personal observation. An indirect indication of the number of the Lollard converts which may be regarded as significant is that contained in an item of Lollard preaching of the time reported by Knighton.[1] He says of a certain Lollard whom he had heard preach: "He was also accustomed to assert frequently that scarcely every tenth man will be saved."[2] As Lollards would be apt to think their own numbers saved, it would appear from this that this particular Lollard, if thinking of Englishmen only, estimated that the Lollards formed something less than that fraction of the whole population.

In concluding this paper a summary of results arrived at may be acceptable.

The Poor Priests who entered into the light of history about the year 1376 or 1377 had been established by Wiclif in view of the great ignorance of the people, in order to preach plainly to them and to awake the clergy to their duty. Recruited from all classes, the Poor Priests, if not already ordained, conferred what they considered ordination upon each other, so that none within their ranks were what they would have considered laymen. They were prepared for their work largely by means of Wiclif's sermons, and possibly enjoyed the oral instruction of that great teacher. The most of them, but not necessarily all, led an humble, itinerant life, supported by voluntary alms, because thus they thought to have the most freedom and time for their chosen work. They did not form an order, at least not at the time of the first wave of Lollardry, but undoubtedly enjoyed a thoroughly good understanding among themselves. Good illustrations of the character and life of the Poor Priests are afforded from the accounts of John Purvey and John Aston.

The dress of the Lollard preachers was not considered important, but they appear to have preferred subdued colors, and, possibly out of a feeling of fellow sympathy and cooperation, they adopted a somewhat similar garb.

---

[1] Knighton, 176.   [2] Ibid.

Their methods of evangelizing were to go wherever and to preach whenever their preaching would be most effective. This led them into unaccustomed places, especially when the clergy exerted their influence against them.

The number of converts they made was certainly large, but of course unknown, and it is safe to say that the fears of opponents led to exaggerated estimates, based upon observation extending over only limited areas. The results of the rapid rise of Lollardry seemed to the chroniclers to forbode evil without limit, and they drew harrowing pictures of the confusion that ensued within the realm as a result of its propagation.

BIBLIOGRAPHY.

The Rolls Series contains the following important works:

Fasciculi Zizaniorum Magistri Johannis Wyclif cum Tritico. Ascribed to Thomas Netter of Walden, provincial of the Carmelite order in England and confessor to King Henry V. Edited by the Rev. Walden Waddington Shirley. 8°. 1858.

The editor's introduction is a valuable contribution to Wiclifite literature.

* * * "It seems probable that Patryngton wrote the narrative as far as page 359 of this volume in the course of the years 1392–1394, and subsequently, perhaps, collected the tracts as far as page 411, up to which point they form a nearly regular chronological sequence; that he then abandoned his plan of writing, and some years afterwards gave his papers to Walden. To these, which extend to the year 1400, were added some collected by Walden himself after his return from Pisa, during the years 1414–1428, and the materials thus accumulated were abridged and arranged by another hand after his death." Pages lxxvii–lxxviii.

* * * "Patryngton was * * * an early friend and patron of Walden, and his predecessor as provincial of the Carmelite order; he was also the successor of Cunningham in the same office, circumstances which tally well with the undue prominence given to Cunningham in the narrative and with the papers having passed into Walden's possession." Page lxxvii.

"As the only contemporary account of the rise of the Lollards it well deserves the attention which it has received, but it can scarcely be called a regular chronicle, still less a history of the sect. The documents relating to the lifetime of Wiclif are indeed connected by a narrative which, though broken and inconsecutive, is evidently authentic and of great value, but from the death of Wiclif, or more strictly from the Council of London to the close of the book in 1428, the original papers are given without comment or correction." Page x.

Political Poems and Songs relating to English History, composed during the period from the accession of Edward III to that of Richard III. Edited by Thomas Wright. Vol. I. 8°. civ-462. 1859. Vol. II. 8°. lxxii-357. 1861.

Eulogium (Historiarum sive Temporis) Chronicon ab Orbe condito usque ad Annum Domini 1366: a monacho quodam Malmesbirensi exaratum. Accedunt continuationes duae, quarum una ad annum MCCCXIII, altera ad annum MCCCCXC, perducta est. Edited by Frank Scott Haydon. Three volumes. 8°. 1858–1863.

The third volume contains a continuation (pages 333–421) which extends from 1364 to 1413. Nothing is known of the author (Vol. III, Intro., ii). The account of the Wiclifites under 1382 just precedes a paragraph written before 1404 (Intro., i). The entry telling of the death of Wiclif in 1384 notices his exhumation, which occurred in 1428.

Thomae Walsingham, quondam monachi S. Albani, Historia Anglicana. (Chronica Monasterii S. Albani.) Edited by Henry Thomas Riley. Vol. I, A. D. 1272–1381. 8°. xxvi-484. 1863. Vol. II, A. D. 1381–1422. 8°. xxiv-535. 1864.

For comment, see under Chronicon Angliæ.

Chronicon Angliae, ab anno Domini 1328 usque ad annum 1388, auctore monacho quodam Sancti Albani. Edited by Edward Maunde Thompson. 8°. lxxxiii-449. 1874.

The Chronicon Angliæ is printed from the Harleian Manuscript, No. 2-3634. Walsingham's chronicle has been traced back to the Old Royal MS. 13, E. IX, in the British Museum (Chron. Ang., Intro., xxi). The text of the Harleian and Royal Manuscripts at an early point agree, and run side by side to the year 1369. From that time on the parts in the Chronicon Angliæ which cast reflections upon John of Gaunt are replaced by less offensive expressions in Walsingham. From 1382 the two in the main part company. See Chron. Ang., Intro., xxi–xxiv. According to evidence presented by Thompson (Chron. Ang., Intro. ca., xxxii), Walsingham had written up the rebellion of 1381 before 1388, and so the portions useful for the early history of the Lollards is strictly contemporaneous. Walsingham is regarded as the author of all that is similar in the Chronicon Angliæ and the Historia Anglicana; hence the small type in the edition of the former.

The bitter hatred toward the Lollards felt by Walsingham is shown by his account of Wiclif's death (Wals. II, pp. 119-120).

Chronicon Henrici Knighton, vel Cnitthon monachi Leycestrensis. Edited by Joseph Rawson Lumby. Vol. I. 8°. xx-479. 1889. Vol. II. 8°. ciii-354. 1895.

Knighton begins his account back of the Norman Conquest, and stops in 1395. "The independent, and therefore the valuable, portion of his Chronicle commences only with the last chapter of Book III." (Vol. II, Intro., xcvi.) Book V., beginning with Volume II, page 124, 1377, covers the part useful for the history of the Lollards. As to the author of this book there is some doubt. The editor writes: "With reference to Book V, I incline to the opinion expressed by Dr. Shirley in a note to page 524 of the Fasciculi Zizaniorum, that it is not by the same hand as the rest." (II, xcvii.) Thomas Arnold, however, believes Knighton to have been the author of Book V (Wiclif's English Works, III, pp. 525-527). Even if Knighton be not the author of this portion, it is agreed that the writer "appears, like Knighton, to have known a great deal about Leicester Abbey and the country round about." (II, xcvii.) As Leicester was only 14 miles from Lutterworth and was a center of Lollard activity, this writer is of prime authority. But it is to be remembered that in Book V Knighton groups in one place and under one date, 1382, most of what he has to say about the Lollards. "The Chronicler hates Wicliffe and his followers with a bitter hatred." (II, xcix.)

Wilkins, D.: Concilia Magnæ Britanniæ et Hiberniæ. Tomi IV. Londini, 1737. Folio.

Volume III covers this period. The dating is not altogether trustworthy.

Wiclif's writings are especially helpful in treating of the Poor Priests. All of his numerous writings are not yet published; of those published I have referred to the publications named below. Where the publications include more than one work, the authenticity, nature, and dates of the parts used are touched upon as they are used.

Gothard Lechler: Joannis Wiclif. Trialogus cum supplemento Trialogi. 8°. Oxonii, 1869.

Lechler believes the Trialogus to have been written not earlier than 1381 (p. 3, Prologomena). That his reason is insufficient will appear in the discussion of the Rise of the Poor Priests.

Thomas Arnold: Select English Works of John Wyclif. Edited from original MSS. 3 vols. 8°. Oxford. Clarendon Press.
Vol. I. Sermons on the Gospels for Sundays and Festivals. xxx-112. 1869.
Vol. II. Sermons on the Ferial Gospels and Sunday Epistles. Treatises. xviii-423. 1871.
Vol. III. Miscellaneous Works. xxiii-545, 1871.
F. D. Matthew: The English Works of Wiclif Hitherto Unprinted. 8°. ii-572. 1880. London. Trübner & Co. (E. E. T. S.)
Wiclif's Latin Works. Published for the Wiclif Society, by Trübner & Co., London. 8°.

This list comprises only a part of what the society has published. The dates given are those of actual publication. The date in the series is always that of the year previous.

John Wiclif's Polemical Works in Latin, for the first time edited from the manuscripts, with critical and historical notes by Rudolf Buddensieg. English edition. Vol. I, c-384; Vol. II, vi, 395-840. 1883.
Johannis Wycliffe Dialogus sive Speculum Ecclesie militantis. Now first edited from the Ashburnham MS., xxvii-c. With collations from the Vienna MSS. 1387, 3930 and 4505, by Alfred Pollard, M. A., xxvii-107. 1886. Dated by the editor tentatively in 1379. (Intro., xxi.)
Johannis Wyclif Sermones. Now first edited from the manuscripts, with critical and historical notes, by Dr. Iohann Loserth.
Vol. I. Super Evangelia Dominicalia, xi-417. 1887.
Vol. II. Super Epistolas, ix-533. 1889.
Vol. III. Super Evangelia de Sanctis, xxii-476. 1888.
Vol. IV. Sermones Miscellanei (Quadraginta Sermones de Tempore. Sermones Mixti, xxiv.) 1890.

Part I contains sermons written in 1381-82; Part II, 1382; Part III was written a little before Part IV; of Part IV a great number were composed in 1383-84; the rest were revised then. In Part IV, from the twenty-third sermon, they are probably early ones revised. No. 3 in Part IV goes back to the Schism in 1378. See Part I, Intro., xxx-xxxiv.

Johannis Wyclif Tractatus de Apostasia. Now first edited from the Vienna MSS. 1343 and 3935, by Michael Henry Dziewicki. xxxvi-259. 1889.

This was written about September, 1383. (Intro., vi.)

Johannis Wyclif Opus Evangelicum. Now first edited from the manuscripts, with critical and historical notes by Dr. Iohann Loserth. Vols. I and II bound in one. iv-184. 1895.

Written in 1384. (Intro., v.)

John Fox: Ecclesiasticall historie: contayning the acts and monuments of the church, especially of the persecutions and martyrdoms, from the primitive tyme till the reigne of Henry VIII. London, 1570. folio.

Fox is very zealous in behalf of the Lollards. His work is uncritical, but contains translations of documents and other information not otherwise accessible.

Forshall and Madden (Rev. Josiah Forshall, Sir Frederic Madden, editors): The Holy Bible, containing the Old and New Testaments, with the Apocryphal Books, in the Earliest English Versions, made from the Latin Vulgate, by John Wycliffe and His Followers. 4 vols. 4°. Vol. I, lxiv-683. Oxford University Press. 1850.

The introduction contains valuable information not otherwise obtainable from printed sources. Purvey's Prologue to his Bible is also in this volume.

Lechler, Gotthard: Johann von Wiclif und die Vorgeschichte der Reformation. 2 vols. bound in one. 8°. xxii-743; viii-654. Leipzig, Friedrich Fleischer. 1875.

Lechler's work has justly been the authority for Wiclif and his followers, but Lechler worked under the disadvantage of having to consult Wiclif's writings in manuscript. A reference to the dates of the publications of Wiclif's works will show how much has been done since his work appeared.

XIV.—THE ROMAN CITY OF LANGRES (FRANCE), IN THE EARLY MIDDLE AGES.

By EARLE WILBUR DOW,
UNIVERSITY OF MICHIGAN.

THE ROMAN CITY OF LANGRES (FRANCE), IN THE EARLY MIDDLE AGES, ESPECIALLY THE NINTH CENTURY.

By EARLE W. DOW.

It is well known that no large amount of information has been collected in regard to the towns of the early Middle Ages. Also, since there are but few sources, it has often been said[1] that there is no possibility of our ever having a satisfactory knowledge of the towns at that period. And this no doubt is true; no one will ever be able to write their history in full. But, on the other hand, it is quite probable that the record of them may be carried beyond the point where it is now. It can scarcely be said that the sources are all known, or that all possible use has been made of those that are known. And it seems reasonable to hope that by continuing the study of individual towns we shall be able not only to see more clearly what conditions prevailed in various places here and there, but also shall thus eventually prepare the way for a better knowledge of townspeople in general at that time.

One of the places for which there is a relatively large number of sources now available is the old Roman city of Langres. Indeed, there are probably more documents which contain information of some sort in regard to this city for the period from Roman to feudal times than can be cited for any other French town. It may be of some advantage, therefore, to give such account as seems possible at this time of Langres in the early Middle Ages, but since the greater part of the documents just referred to belong to years between 814 and 887, the study which follows will refer especially to Langres in the ninth century. To be sure, it will not be possible to give specific answers to all the questions that arise concerning a

---

[1] For example, Luchaire, Les communes françaises, p. 11. Also Histoire du Languedoc, nouv. éd., t. I, p. 1131, n. 2.

town of that epoch; for, after all, in the way of providing us with information bearing directly on the subject, the documents do little else than give more or less definite indications, either on the material aspect of the town or on the extent to which government by individuals acting in a private capacity had there gained the upper hand. But these indications will be sufficient to show conclusively what were some of the essential features of the situation in that place at a relatively early period after the fall of the Empire, and so what were at least some of the conditions or influences to which the people of one of the larger and older towns of France had long been accustomed when they began, in the later Middle Ages, their struggle for emancipation.

The most important sources from which data relating to early Langres may be obtained consist of a series of fifteen charters, given by emperors and kings from the time of Louis the Pious to that of King Lothaire. These charters have all been preserved in the original, save possibly one, and they have all been published, some of them several times. The texts used in the present study were made by Monsieur A. Roserot, who has recently edited or reedited these and three other originals of the Carolingian period from the manuscripts in the archives of the Department of La Haute-Marne.[1]

Following is a chronological list[2] of these charters, together with references to other additions or reproductions of them.[3]

(1) 814. September 9. Aix-la-Chapelle. Louis the Pious confirms charters granted by his predecessors to bishops of Langres. Roserot, No. 1. Gallia christiana, IV, Instrumenta, col. 129. Bouquet, VI, p. 461. Migne, CIV, p. 987. Mittheil. des Inst. für Öst. Geschichtsf., VII, p. 437.

(2) 834. August 19. Langres. Confirmation by Louis the Pious of the measures taken by the bishop Alberic in the way of providing the clergy of Langres with suitable buildings and with property of their own.

---

[1] Bulletin de la Société des sciences historiques et naturelles de l'Yonne, t. 47, 1898, pp. 503–539.

[2] In view of the fact that it is no part of the purpose of this study to make known certain sources as such, and also in view of the manner of exposition adopted, I have thought it best not to give full analyses of the charters in question. For the most part it would lead only to unnecessary repetition. It should be said, however, that the analyses of these documents made by Roserot are not always to be depended upon. In some instances they are inadequate. In others they are quite wrong; for example, those for his numbers 15 and 18.

[3] No attempt is made to indicate all other editions. Rather only those which, though not always trustworthy, are perhaps more accessible.

Roserot, No. 2. Gal. christ., IV, Instr., col. 130. Bouquet, VI, p. 595. Migne, CIV, p. 1249.

(3) 846. October 19. "Wadimias." Donation, by Louis the Pious to one Suitgarius, of certain pieces of property which the said Suitgarius has been holding in beneficium. Roserot, No. 3. Sickel, in Forschungen zur deuts. Gesch., IX, p. 409.

(4) 854. September 17. Vernum. Confirmation by Charles the Bald of provisions made in the interest of the chapter at Langres. Roserot, No. 4.

(5) 869.[1] July 22. Ponthion (?). Charles the Bald makes an exchange of possessions with the count Gérard. Roserot, No. 5.

(6) 871. October 7. Langres. Confirmation by Charles the Bald in reference to certain possessions of the chapter at Langres. Roserot, No. 6.

(7) 882. August 8. Vienne. Confirmation by King Carloman of a contract between the bishop of Langres and a priest named Otbertus. Roserot, No. 7. Musée des archives départementales, pp. 22-25. Reproduction, ibid., planche VIII.

(8) 885. May 20. Granges. Donation by Charles the Fat to his vassal Dodo. Roserot, No. 9. Sickel, in Forschungen, IX, p. 415.

(9) 885. August 28. Monastery of Lauresheim. Charles the Fat restores to the bishopric of Langres one of a great number of possessions of which it had been deprived by various seigneurs. Roserot, No. 10, Gal. christ., IV, Instr., col. 133-134. Bouquet, IX, p. 344.

(10) 886. July 30. Metz. Donation by Charles the Fat to one Jacob, his vassal. Roserot, No. 11. Sickel, loc. cit., p. 416.

(11) 886. October 29. Paris. Charles the Fat restores the villa Ulmus to the church of Langres. Roserot, No. 12. Sickel, loc. cit., p. 420.

(12) 887. January 15. Schlettstadt. Donation by Charles the Fat to Otbertus, prévôt of the church of Langres. Roserot, No. 14. Sickel, loc. cit., p. 422.

(13) 887. January 15. Schlettstadt. Charles the Fat grants to the church of Langres the walls and other portions of the city, and confirms measures of Charles the Bald in reference to the money and market privileges at Langres and Dijon. Roserot, No. 15. Bouquet, IX, p. 346.

(14) 889. December 14. Laon. Odo confirms various measures of his predecessors in favor of the church of Langres. Roserot, No. 16. Gal. christ., IV, Instr., col. 135-136. Bouquet, IX, p. 449.

(15) 967. August 30. Dijon. Lothaire grants to the bishops of Langres the "County of Langres" and the dues *in teloneo* collected at the gates of the city. Roserot, No. 18. Mus. des arch. départ., p. 32. Reproduction, ibid., planche XII.

Other sources referring to Langres, scattered and less important, it will be sufficient to indicate in notes.

---

[1] "Data XI Kalendas augusti, indictione III, anno XXX regnante Karolo gloriosissimo rege." Roserot, apparently giving preference to the indiction element, places the act in 870. But if one gives preference to the reigning year of Charles the Bald, assuming that Roserot has transcribed the act correctly, the date should be 869, since the years of Charles's kingship were counted from the 21st of June, 840 (cf. Giry, Manuel de diplomatique, p. 728). It is well known that indiction data are far more likely to be wrong than the count of the years of a reign.

I.

Under the Empire at its height Langres was a city of some importance. No doubt it would be going too far to say, with Monsieur Th. Pistollet de St. Ferjeux, that its size was then almost double what it is to-day.[1] The proofs he offers can not be depended upon for as much as that. But there are other things besides size to be taken into consideration. The industrial and commercial life of the town was promoted by the grand highways that ended or crossed there.[2] And being situated thus, on the roads between other important points in Gaul, it was of necessity constantly visited or traversed by the legions and by magistrates and travelers of all sorts. Also numerous excavations and discoveries have brought to light the remains of public theaters, parts of columns, capitals, fragments of statues, gold medals, mosaic, tombs, and an arch of triumph.[3] Clearly, this ancient city was a place of considerable wealth and a veritable center of Gallo-Roman civilization.

But such prosperity was none too lasting. Naturally enough, the troubles of the later Empire and of the centuries following brought with them serious changes, as well for Langres as for other places. Possibly it was ravaged even before the invasions of the fifth century. Anyway, it seems to have suffered then at the hands either of the Vandals or of the Huns.[4] And evidently it fared ill in the midst of the confusion of Merovingian and early Carolingian times. The charter of 814 would have it that the Saracens occupied and

---

[1] This author says that "les ruines qui ont été découvertes ont prouvé qu'elle s'étendit, au sud, à environ 900 mètres de son enceinte actuelle." And in a note: "Comme la longueur de la ville, depuis l'extrémité sud de la rue des Moulins jusqu'à l'extrémité nord de la rue de Longeporte n'est que d'environ 970 mètres, la ville romaine avait donc une longueur presque double de celle qu'elle a aujourd'hui." Mém. de la soc. hist. et arch. de Langres, t. II, p. 231.

[2] Migneret, Précis de l'histoire de Langres, pp. 33-34.

[3] On this subject see especially an important notice on the Roman antiquities of Langres in the Annuaire du diocèse de Langres, t. I (1838), pp. 253-487. This is followed by some 60 pages of notes referring to communes of the arrondissement of Langres, and there is a supplement containing additional notes. See also some articles in the Mém. de la soc. hist. et arch. de Langres, t. I and II, passim; and Brocard, Catalogue du musée fondé et administré par la société historique et archéologique de Langres.

[4] See Vignier, Décade historique du diocèse de Langres, edition by the Société hist. et arch. de Langres, chs. XII, XIV, and XV, passim. Also it is known that the bishops of Langres had to live in Dijon for some time. Aprunculus, about the year 450, was there (Gregory of Tours., Hist. Franc., Lib. II, ch. 23); and the bishop Gregory, at the beginning of the sixth century, had his residence there (Ibid., Lib. III, ch. 19).

ravaged the city.[1] We may indulge ourselves a strong doubt about this, for in that day "Saracen" was a name applied rather indiscriminately to destroyers of property. But there can be no question that the town suffered severely at somebody's hands; and most likely, too, the devastations referred to in the charter of 814 occurred in the course of the reign of Charles Martel.[2] Moreover, it was not simply faubourgs that were exposed to these devastations; for the charters of the church, which were burned at that time, must have been kept within the fortifications, where alone they could be at all secure. In the last years of the ninth century we hear again of the city's misfortunes, since in 887 the bishop, Geilo, related to Charles the Fat that he had been rebuilding his city.[3] Without doubt the reference here is especially to the fortifications. But it is impossible to say conclusively at exactly what time or by what means they had been destroyed.[4]

Such, in substance, appears to be the extent of our knowledge in regard to the importance and fortunes of Langres in Roman and earliest mediæval times. A meager record, indeed; yet it is at least clear that the material city of the Empire had practically disappeared, and that the city which

---

[1] * * * "venerabilis Betto, Lingonensium urbis episcopus, obtulit nobis auctoritates antecessorum nostrorum regum, in quibus insertum reperimus qualiter olim propter occupationem Saracenorum strumenta cartarum vel etiam immunitates regum quæ ibidem erant, perdita vel dirupta fuissent, et eidem reges sua auctoritate miserandi gratia ad preces predecessorum suorum episcoporum eandem relevassent jacturam, ita videlicet ut per eorum auctoritatem antecessores sui episcopi res et mancipia quæ in eisdem strumentis cartarum incendio exustis continebantur, sive eadem quæ postea a catolicis viris eidem conlata fuerunt ecclesiæ actenus secure et quiete in jure et potestate predictæ tenuissent ecclesiæ."

[2] It is well known that the Saracens continued their operations in France after the famous defeat at Tours. But, for that matter, the mention in the charter of 814 that predecessors of Louis the Pious had taken part in the replacement of titles is in entire harmony with the date of the battle of Tours.

[3] * * * "Geilo * * * innotuit qualiter Lingonis civitatem sibi videlicet a Deo commissam, ob nimiam persecutionem sive infestationem paganorum, et refugium sive salvationem cristianorum et sanctæ Dei ecclesiæ defensionem prope jam reædificatam sine alicujus comitis vel judicis juvamine atque constructam haberet." * * * Charter of 887.

[4] They had probably been exposed at no distant time to ravages of some sort. Certain documents of the period point in this direction, since, by providing for restoring to churches property of which they had been despoiled, they prove what were, or at least what had been, the general situation in the region of Langres. These documents will be cited later. Also, Geilo gave as one of his reasons for the rebuilding of the walls "ob nimiam persecutionem sive infestationem paganorum." Charter of 887. Perhaps he was speaking of contemporary counts, since farther on in the same document one finds that the bishop asked certain concessions, "ob nimias comitum seu judicum inquietudines."

survived must have been one which bore the marks of the troubles through which it had passed.

Its general aspect by the eighth and ninth centuries naturally reflected the experience of the town and the general social conditions of the period. Occupying at that time the same ground as to-day, it was situated on a hill which rises slowly from the south to the height of some fifteen hundred and fifty feet, and then falls off quickly on the west, north, and east.[1] Its wall,[2] inclosing a space somewhat oval in outline, began on the north at the extremity of the hill, and on the south followed a line approximately traced to-day by the streets of the Boullière, Boucherie, and Petit Cloître. A little southeast of the central point within the fortifications were

---

[1] On the topography of Langres see especially Vignier, who wrote in the seventeenth century, and who had special knowledge of such things throughout the diocese of Langres at a period when the remains of the ancient city were much more in evidence than they are to-day. Décade, t. I, ch. V, passim. See, also, various articles on the archæology of Langres in the Mém. de la soc. hist. et arch. de Langres, t. I and II. Migneret, in his Précis, gives a good plan of the town as it was in 1769, drawn from the map published at that time by Nicholas Chalmandrier. It indicates the location of the old walls and gates.

[2] There was a wall at Langres as early as the last years of the third century, since it is known that the Emperor Constance Chlorus, on an expedition against a German army that had crossed the Rhine and advanced to near Langres, was saved by people who "raised him upon the wall with ropes, the gates of the city having been closed." * * * "a Constantio Cæsare in Gallia pugnatum est circa Lingones; die una adversam et secundam fortunam expertus est. Nam quum, repente barbaris ingruentibus, intra civitatem esset coactus, tam præcipiti necessitate, ut, clausis portis, in murum funibus tolleretur; vix quinque horis mediis adventante exercitu sexaginta fere millia Alamannorum cecidit." (Eutropius, Lib. IX, ch. XV.)

Whether the wall here spoken of survived or not, and if so, in what form, can not be definitely proved. Possibly it constituted in later centuries what was meant by the munitio. On the other hand, it may be that it was of considerably greater extent than the mediæval munitio and was the same as the outer wall of the later Middle Ages All that can be said safely is that by the time referred to in the text there was a wall properly so called, and within it a munitio. (See the note following.)

There are those who say with Father Vignier (Décade, t. I, p. 40 and p. 455; also Migneret, Précis, p. 60, note 1) that a new rampart was built after the ravages by the "Saracens" in the middle of the eighth century. And according to this opinion the Place Chambeau (campus bellus) mentioned in the charter of Charles the Fat, of the year 887, as being situated outside the walls, was, on the contrary, inside the city. Father Vignier explains the contradiction between his conclusions and statements in the charter of 887 as follows: "Il y a deux points à remarquer sur ce titre, l'un que les murailles dont il est fait mention font les vieilles qui forment l'enclos du cloître canonial de St. Mammes du côté du midi, lesquelles Geilo fit raccommoder pour servir de fermeture à ce cloître, de défense à l'eglise, de retranchement, de citadelle et de refuge aux habitants de la ville, en cas que les autres qui sont plus loin n'eussent été forcés." (Décade historique, t. I, p. 507.) As a matter of fact, his explanation is nothing but a supposition, and it seems well to stand by the terms of the charter. In this case there is occasion to conclude that whether a new rampart was built after the "Saracen" invasions or not, at all events the wall which included the Place Chambeau, and which survived in part until recent times (see p. 492, n. 3), was not yet in existence at the end of the ninth century; that is to say, at least the south line of that wall near which the Place Chambeau was located was not then in existence.

the cathedral of St. Mammes, formerly dedicated to St. John, and other houses devoted to church purposes. Around these buildings was a special inner wall. The texts call it a munitio.[1] Outside of this fortress, but within the walls properly so called, and to the west of the cathedral, stood the Abbey of St. Peter.[2] About 834, the bishop Alberic, in the interest of his chapter, not only divided the episcopal properties and thus created the canonical properties, but also erected cloisters and other houses for the use of the canons.[3] These buildings were of course located within the fortifications; possibly they were even inside the munitio. Finally, among the churches to be seen later within the outer line of defense, that of the Magdalen, dedicated in the twelfth century to St. Didier, appears to have been there already several centuries.[4] The rest of the space inside the defenses, for aught that the texts tell us of it, must have been occupied by ordinary dwelling houses, or perhaps by other constructions, lay or ecclesiastical, concerning which we have no precise indications.

In regard to what was outside the walls, whether closely adjacent to them or somewhere in the immediate vicinity, spite of sieges, fires, and other ravages, the town extended beyond its defenses, and there was at least one important near-by village. This is surely true for the ninth century; and it seems that if there were suburbs there in the midst of the troubles of that epoch, they were probably in existence also for a long time before. One document says that the churches of St. Amatre[5] and St. Ferreol, or St. Ferjeul, stood "near the faubourg." This would put it south of the town,

---

[1] That it is a question here of a fortress distinct from the walls properly so called, there is no doubt. From the 814 charter of Louis the Pious it is clear that the munitio, enumerated among the things that had belonged to the bishopric at least since the reign of Pippin, father of Charlemagne, protected the church of St. Mammes, and also that it is not at all to be identified with the walls. "Sed ipsam sanctam sedem antecessores nostri reges cum cellulis subjectis vel omnibus rebus juste ad se aspicientibus, munitionem videlicet Lingonicæ civitatis ubi habetur ecclesia in honore sancti Mammetis eximii martyris. * * * Et infra muros jam dictæ Lingonis abbatiam sancti Petri." * * * See, also, the repetition of these expressions in the confirmation of King Odo in 889. Then the donation of the walls in 887, as we shall see, was looked upon by the bishop as a new concession.

[2] "Et infra muros jam dictae Lingonis abbatiam sancti Petri." * * * Charter of 814. See, also, the confirmation by King Odo, December 14, 889.

[3] Charter of 834.

[4] Acta sanctorum, May, vol. V, p. 243. Also Vignier, op. cit., t. II, p. 260, and t. II, p. 271.

[5] It is in an act by the council of Chalons in May, 887, that this expression is to be found. See Vignier, op. cit., t. I, pp. 512–513, who cites it as belonging to the archives of the church of Langres.

on land which was incorporated within the new inclosure made at the time of the English wars. According to other texts, there was a faubourg around the church of St. Geosmes.[1] Indeed one might come to that conclusion without written testimony. St. Geosmes was built in the third century, on the spot where three saint brothers suffered martyrdom, Speusippus, Eleusippus, and Meleusippus.[2] So sacred a place would naturally be surrounded by a little community. In this instance also the location was toward the south, about three kilometers from the center of the city. That was the natural field for expansion, since in other directions, especially toward the north, the hill was too steep; and when new walls were built, what really took place was an extension of the walls to the south.[3]

II.

Turning to the question as to what constitutional and administrative régime existed in the midst of the material conditions just described, we know that in the time of the Romans Langres was at first the capital of a "federated" people.[4] Without doubt, this federated people later became simply the Civitas Lingonum;[5] and as such it had the usual officers of the Roman civitates, or cities.[6] Furthermore, we may infer

---

[1] See, on a council held at Langres "circa kalendas junii, 859," Sirmond, Concilia, t. III, p. 136. Flodoard says that this council was held "in suburbio lingonicae urbis:" Hist. eccl. Remensis, Lib. III, Ch. XVI. That it met in the church of St. Geosmes is attested by the date of a charter in favor of the clergy of Autun by which certain prelates, in council, approve the donation of the village of Sampigny as made to the said clergy by the bishop Jonas: "Actum in territorio Lingonensi in Abbatia Sanctorum Geminorum * * * XIII kalend. maii, XVIII karoli gloriosissimi regis indictione VII * * *" Pérard, Recueil de plusieurs pièces curieuses pour l'historie de Bourgogne, p. 147. On the corrections to be made in this date, see Vignier, Décade, t. I, pp. 486–487. He makes it May 25, and identifies it with the council mentioned by Flodoard, the acts of which are given by Sirmond.

[2] See their lives by Warnharius, who wrote in the seventh century: Acta sanct., January, vol. II, p. 76. See also Vignier, op. cit., Liv. II, ch. II, in t. I, and Liv. III, ch. XXI, in t. II.

[3] For example, the new wall wrongly ascribed by Vignier to the middle of the eighth century: op. cit., t. I, p. 41. At the time when he was writing this wall was in large part still in existence. It followed approximately the line traced to-day by the streets of Terreaux, Grand-Bie, and Petit-Bie. See the plan of the town in Migneret, op. cit.

[4] See Désjardins, Geog. hist. et admr. de la Gaule romaine, t. III, pp. 54, 240, 452. An inscription belonging to the years 198–202 contains the words "Lingones foederati": Mém. de la soc. hist. et arch. de Langres, t. I, pp. 43–44.

[5] That is, it eventually became the same sort of a civitas as were the other civitates; a 'city" without any special status, without any peculiar character in respect to matters of government.

[6] See the incriptions cited by Désjardins, op. cit., p. 452, notes 5 and 6.

that its fortunes were the same as those of the Roman municipalities in general. That is to say, the Civitas Lingonum, once possessed of a highly developed system of aristocratic local self-government, became more and more only a division for the imperial administration. It can not be said that under the later Empire it had any real local autonomy. There, as elsewhere, representatives of the general government must have gradually supplanted the old municipal officers. Local as well as general affairs, instead of being conducted by officers responsible to the people in the municipality, or at least conducted in accordance with laws which might properly be called municipal, must have been almost entirely in the hands of imperial officers. The demands and the law to which the people of the city had to conform from year to year could have been neither of their own making nor under their own control. They were imperial regulations, in force in any particular administrative division in quite the same way as in all others. Also, legally speaking, the words Civitas Lingonum did not indicate simply the town itself, the town in the usual modern sense of the term. For it can not be affirmed, at least of the later period of Gallo-Roman history, that the material, social group known in modern times as a town had any independent public life of its own, or that it was even so much as a unity of some sort for administrative purposes. Constitutional and administrative divisions were not identical with places of habitation. All the arrangements for the management of local affairs appear to have applied to the civitates; that is, to divisions so large that, at the beginning of the fifth century, there were but 112 of them in all Gaul.[1] None of the towns within each civitas, not even the capital, can be said to have had any legal status of its own. Whatever separate community of interests the townspeople may have had in other respects, at least constitutionally and administratively they belonged to a larger unity.

When one seeks to follow Langres into the Middle Ages, he asks instinctively to what extent the governmental organization which prevailed there in the time of the Empire was transmitted to succeeding centuries. As a matter of fact, not the slightest documentary evidence has been found to show

---

[1] See Longnon, Atlas hist. de la France, texte, pp. 13-20.

that any of the Roman institutions for the civitas survived as such at Langres. However, relying upon the conclusions now generally accepted in regard to the Roman municipal régime and its survival, we may be reasonably sure that if any part of that régime at Langres lived on through the invasions, this did not mean at all that the people there surely had some sort of town government in the present sense of the terms. Also, any spirit of local independence that may have existed there during or after the invasions was not, at least in any positive sense, an inheritance from the later Empire.

If town government, properly so called, did not exist under the Romans, at least during the last two centuries of the Empire, the Roman constitutional and administrative régime can scarcely be held to have transmitted any such government to succeeding centuries. In truth, there is no indisputable reason to conclude even that remnants of the old civitas régime became identified with the towns, in the modern sense of the word. Such "city" institutions as were to be found among the new peoples may very well have corresponded to the same large divisions as those to which the old ones had been attached. The diocese extended over any given region for spiritual affairs,[1] and the pagus for temporal. For aught that can be said to the contrary, the defensor, who had once exercised jurisdiction throughout a civitas, continued to do so. The formulæ testify abundantly to the fact that the curia and defensor performed the functions of "juridiction gracieuse;" and they make no provisions in this direction for the count or any of his representatives. But unless the curia and defensor looked after these things for the whole pagus or county, it was evidently in the province of the count or his subordinates to attend to them.

As to the spirit of independence, the Roman régime for at least two centuries of its existence did not stand for real local freedom—did not rest on principles which accorded to the several communities the legal right to a public life entirely and irrevocably their own. On the contrary, the more Roman the administration of Gaul became, the more firmly established

---

[1] As for Langres, we know that under the Burgundians, and after them under the Franks, this ancient Roman city formed, from an ecclesiastical point of view, the diocese of Langres. Under the Empire ecclesiastical and civil divisions followed the same lines, and there is no change to be cited in reference to the diocese of Langres during the following centuries.

grew the principle that the State at large was the source and the instrument of all legal public life, and the more marked appeared the interference of the central government in local affairs. If, during or after the invasions, the spirit of local freedom existed in Roman municipalities, either among the people of the civitas as a whole or among the people of one or more towns therein, it must have developed amidst the circumstances connected with the disappearance of Roman central control—must have arisen through the action of influences quite foreign to things really Roman.

To whatever extent the imperial organization may have survived at Langres, it appears that the governmental organs that were in real effective operation there after the decline of Rome, or at all events under the Carolingians, were those of the county régime. This statement, aside from its being in harmony with the general conclusions already reached in regard to the prevalence of that régime, is supported by a number of facts relating to the particular region in question. In the Carolingian period there were within the bounds of the diocese of Langres some ten different pagi, or counties, among which was the pagus Lingonicus, containing the town of Langres.[1] Several names of counts and viscounts of that region have come down to us, among which at least one belongs to a count of Langres.[2] This is the Milo who, in 887, gave his consent[3] that Charles the Fat should endow Otbertus, prévôt of the church of Langres, with properties situated at Bourg.[4] Villæ and other possessions were usually described in legal documents as situated in such or such a pagus or county.[5] Furthermore, as will be seen later, the authority against which the succeeding régime made progress always appears to have been that of or that represented by the count. There is, indeed, no doubt that the county régime of the Carolingians was established in that district, as elsewhere.

The only question that can possibly arise is, Did the same conditions prevail within as without the walls of the town? Was there a special organization for the town in addition to

---

[1] See Longnon, Atlas hist., texte, pp. 96-97.
[2] Several others have been cited, but, as it seems to me, without precise, sufficient proofs. For all these see Mém. de la soc. hist. et arch. de Langres, t. III, pp. 10-12.
[3] Charter of 887.
[4] Located between 4 and 5 miles from Langres, on the road to Dijon.
[5] See for example the charters edited by Roserot, passim.

that of the county as a whole? It certainly seems entirely rational to suppose that the county régime should not be confined to the little villages and rural districts; that, on the contrary, it should apply also to the city; and that there, just as in the country round about, it should be the real, responsible authority. It is inconceivable that the place which gave its name to the division; which was its industrial, administrative, and religious capital; which was the very center of the interests and activities that the royal agent was commissioned to govern, should not have been under the direct control of that agent. Also, the powers which the different functionaries of the county system in general are known to have possessed were so inclusive and the hypothesis so strong that such duties as may have been performed by officers of the old Roman civitas did not relate simply to property and people located within the town, that one is at a loss to know how there could have been any public administrative divisions other than those characteristic of the pagus as such. And these very rational a priori conclusions are supported by the facts. When we come to study the bishop's relations with the powers that were, we shall find among other things that the county régime was, or had been, the regularly constituted public organization as well within the town as in the country round about it.

But, as time went on, did the count and such other public officials as may have been associated with him find themselves in possession of all authority, or sovereignty, exercised within the county? Did the various organs of the county régime, and such survivals as there may have been of the Roman régime, control all the governmental functions in the division? Or rather, since we know that in general the authority or sovereignty of public officials was in the advancing Middle Ages more and more supplanted by private sovereignty, by the rule of individuals, did public sovereignty disappear among townspeople, especially those in the larger and older towns, just as it did among people in the country and in the smaller communities? And if so, at what time was this change accomplished and in favor of what persons or organizations among the people? In particular, what answer to such questions does the history of Langres provide? As will be seen, the documents give some slight indications for the eighth and considerable really conclusive proof for the ninth century.

First of all, it is noteworthy that many things happened in and about Langres; that conditions existed in that region which strongly favored the rise and development of government by individuals, conditions which contributed eminently toward the formation of the political features of the feudal régime. And quite naturally, for the decline of the old Carolingian organization should be expected to furnish there as elsewhere numberless opportunities to personal ambition.

The sort of things that were happening may perhaps be best observed in the history of ecclesiastical possessions located outside the town. The patrimony of the church of Langres evidently suffered much in the midst of the various troubles of the period, for on several occasions provisions were made in regard to the restoration of property it included. For example, in 814, Louis the Pious confirmed charters granted to bishops of Langres by preceding kings, which charters related that these same predecessors of Louis had repaired the loss of certain documents, titles of some sort, that had been destroyed, or at least had disappeared, in the time of the occupation of the "Saracens;" and, further, that the church of St. Gangulfus, in the county of Port-sur-Saône, with all its belongings, had been unlawfully seized upon by certain princes, and should be restored to the church of Langres.[1] In 885 Charles the Fat restored to the bishopric of Langres the Abbey of Notre Dame and St. John, located at Réomé, in the pagus of Tonnerre, together with the churches and persons legally in its possession. This abbey was but one of a great number of possessions of which the church of Langres had been unlawfully deprived by certain "tyrannical and sacrilegious" princes.[2] In October of the following year Charles restored to this same church its old villa of Ulmus, in the county of Troyes.[3] The act of King Odo, of December 14, 889, confirming provisions made in favor of the church of Langres by his royal and imperial predecessors, states that those predecessors had returned to the church things of which it had been deprived.[4]

But the circumstances that called out such acts were not confined to the country in the neighborhood of Langres. They also appear to have been common inside the town. We

---

[1] Charter of 814.
[2] Charter of 885.
[3] Charter of October 29, 886.
[4] Charter of 889.

have seen already that after the prosperous time of the Empire this place had some hard experiences; that at least a part of the troubles through which it passed affected property within the walls, and that in the late ninth century it bore clear marks of ravages of some sort. In addition, it may be said that the counts and other officers associated with them were accustomed to exercise, in a high-handed manner, such jurisdiction as they possessed in the town; for in 887 the bishop made certain requests of the Emperor, in the course of which he asked that, "because of the excesses of the counts and judges," Charles should give him, among other things, whatever there was in Langres that belonged to the royal fisc and was under the authority of the count.[1]

It is evident, therefore, that both inside and outside the town there was general insecurity; that losses occurred from time to time in consequence of troubles of one kind or another; that the stronger exploited the weaker; that there were many who took possession unlawfully of the property of others; that the royal or county officials either would not or could not carry on their administration so as to assure order and protection. And it is quite clear what one should expect to be the results of these conditions. If the regularly constituted authorities failed to provide the sort of government which private interests demanded, various individuals would undertake to do it for themselves. That is, under such circumstances, governmental functions would naturally drift more and more into the hands of those who owned or managed many resources, moral, material, or both, and who would govern because they were owners or guardians. Also, those who had less resources would gradually become subordinate in various respects to those who had more.

In trying to see whether these results were actually realized at Langres, and if so, when and to what degree, it may be of some service to turn for a moment to the field of episcopal elections. The purpose here is not to discuss the proposition, often advanced in former years, that wherever "the people" took part in the election of bishops there was of

---

[1] "Gello sanctæ Lingonensis ecclesiæ reverendus antistes * * * cum quantis precibus potuit humiliter deprecatus est quatinus ob nimias comitatum seu judicum inquietudines * * * omnia ex fisco nostro infra eandem civitatem ad causam comitis pertinentia." * * *—Charter of 887.

necessity a municipal régime. If evidence of this sort were in any way trustworthy it would be very easy to show that Langres had always had town institutions. As early as 1829 M. Raynouard cited proofs of the action of "the people" there in the matter of episcopal elections in the sixth, ninth, and eleventh centuries.[1] On the contrary, the object is simply to see if in certain facts relating to a particular election there is not at least some indication of what was the real governmental situation at Langres in the ninth century.

For successor of Thibaut I[2] the count Gérard de Roussillon, regent of Provence, proposed Wulfad. The clergy and the people chose Anschar. Charles the Bald took the part of Isaac. Quite naturally, the King's candidate won the place.[3] Most of the folk who took part in this election we know very well: The King, the important personage Gérard, and the clergy. But what is meant by "the people?" The word seems to be defined by some expressions in the confession which was exacted of Anschar after the election of Isaac: "I, Anschar, subdeacon, avow that in usurping the episcopal see against Isaac, to whom it was committed, and in soliciting the support of the clergy, the vassals, and all the familia of his church, I have done that which is contrary to the canon law."[4] That is, by the year 853 things had arrived at the point where the popular or lay elements who took part along with the clergy in the choice of the bishop were designated partly as vassals and partly as the familia of the church. The word "familia" probably refers to non-noble dependents. But even if one gives to it here the sense of ecclesiastical or spiritual family, it is none the less established that by that time the people who occupied at Langres the first place after the clergy and who were considered as having the most influence, whose support was looked upon as of most value in a matter which was really decided by the interplay of political forces, were vassals.

From this it appears reasonably clear that as early as the middle of the ninth century the general political organiza-

---
[1] Histoire du droit municipal, t. II, pp. 84, 95, 105, 110, 112, 114.
[2] About 853.
[3] For all these facts, see Gallia christiana, vol. IV, col. 532-533.
[4] "Ego Anscharius subdiaconus confiteor contra canonica statuta temere me fecisse in Isaac venerabilem pontificem, usurpando sedem ecclesiæ sanctæ sibi commissæ, et sollicitando clericos et vassalos ejus omnemque familiam." * * * See council of Toul "ad Saponarias," 859, canon V, Gallia christ., IV, col. 533.

tion in the region of Langres was one in which feudal principles determined at least the dominant tendencies of the time in reference to the distribution of authority. But one need not stop here. The governmental tendencies and prevailing political principles of that epoch and place can be so set forth as to leave no question whatever concerning what they really were.

In the charter issued by Louis the Pious in the year 814 it is pointed out that the bishopric of Langres possessed at that time certain fortresses—those of Langres, Dijon, and Tonnerre—some churches, some monasteries, together with their dependencies, and numerous other properties. It had held some of these possessions at least as far back as the time of Pippin, predecessor of Charlemange, for Louis confirms what his antecessores had done.[1] Others belonged to it at a period anterior to the disorders commonly referred to as invasions of the "Saracens," since in part it was a matter of replacing titles then lost.[2] It is particularly worthy of note that some of the properties enumerated were situated within the walls of Langres; that is to say, the church of St. Mammes, the Abbey of St. Peter, and the munitio. And the monastery of the Sts. Jumeaux was not far outside the walls.

There is no direct statement in the charter as to who performed the governmental functions in reference to these possessions of the bishopric before 814. It is said there, however, that the bishopric possessed immunities;[3] and it

---
[1] "Sed et ipsam sanctam sedem antecessores nostri reges cum cellulis vel omnibus rebus juste ad se aspicientibus, munitionem videlicet Lingonicæ civitatis ubi habetur ecclesia in honore sancti Mammetis eximii martyris, et castrum Divionense in quo sita est ecclesia in honore sancti Stephani protomartyris, et juxta murum monasterium beati Benigni cum omni eorum integritate. Et in pago Tornetrensi monasterium Melundense, et in eodem pago castrum Tornetrense, Symphoriani in Ladiniaco cum ecclesiis aliisque rebus sibi aspicientibus. Et infra muros jam dictæ Lingonis abbatiam sancti Petri, et juxta eandem civitatem monasterium sanctorum geminorum. Et in comitatum Portense, cum omnibus sibi competentibus, ecclesiam sancti Gangulfi * * * et in pago Atoariorum monasterium Besuense sub plenissima semper defensione et immunitatis tuitione habuissent * * * postulavit * * * Betto * * * ut eorundem regum auctoritates * * * nostra confirmaremus auctoritate. Cujus petitioni libenter adquievimus." * * * Charter of 814.

[2] * * * "Auctoritates antecessorum nostrum regum, in quibus insertum reperimus qualiter olim propter occupationem Saracenorum strumenta cartarum vel etiam immunitates regum, quæ ibidem erant, perdita vel dirupta fuissent, et eidem reges * * * eandem relevassent jacturam, ita videlicet ut per eorum auctoritatem antecessores sui episcopi res et mancipia quæ in eisdem strumentis cartarum incendio exustis continebatur." * * * Charter of 814.

[3] * * * "strumenta cartarum vel etiam immunitates regum * * * monasterium Besuense sub plenissima semper defensione et immunitatis tuitione habissent." Charter of 814.

may well be inferred that these immunities were for the possessions mentioned. Also, the act of 814 was made by way of confirming preceding acts, and the governmental arrangements that it specifically sanctioned had probably been prescribed by the acts confirmed. In any case, for the period after 814, the question is settled in the most explicit manner. It was the bishop who was endowed with political authority on the lands and other possessions of his church. His control there was complete.[1] He was even freed from all obligations therefor to the royal treasury.[2] Evidently, then—quite likely in the eighth, and surely in the early ninth century—it was already the rule at Langres in regard to certain ecclesiastical possessions that he who owned or controlled property also exercised sovereignty over it.

And from time to time this rule became more strongly and more generally established there. First, with reference to the bishopric: In 882 a priest named Otbertus placed some very valuable possessions in the hands of the prévôt of St. Mammes;[3] and we have seen that in 886 the Emperor Charles the Fat restored to the church of Langres the villa of Ulmus and all its belongings, including some thirty "mansa."[4] Can it be that for the people in the domains in question these acts did not entail government by the bishop or by his subordinates? If they did not, they were surely not in harmony with the tendencies then prevailing in that region. Again, when Charles the Fat, in 885, restored to the bishopric the abbey of Notre Dame and St. John, located at Réomé, together with the churches, people, and whatever else legally belonged to it, he prescribed that from that time forth the abbey should be subject to the bishop of Langres.[5] In 887, as will be seen later, the bishop was granted very important possessions and prerogatives within the town itself. And lastly, the charter of King Odo of December 14, 889, in which it is set forth that various predecessors of that king had made or confirmed numerous provisions in regard to donations, restorations, and

---

[1] * * * "Jubemus atque precipimus ut nemo fidelium nostrorum vel quibuslibet ex judiciaria potestate," * * * and other provisions of a formula of immunity. Charter of 814.

[2] "Et quicquid exinde fiscus noster exigere debet ad integrum prædictæ ecclesiæ concedimus." * * * Charter of 814.

[3] Charter of August 8, 882.

[4] Charter of October 29, 886.

[5] Charter of August 28, 885.

immunities to the church of Langres, that referred to property and privileges both inside and outside the city, also conveys proof that for all his possessions in or out of the town the reverend bishop was granted the most complete immunity from the action of other authorities, public or private.

Second, with reference to the chapter: From about 834 it entered into possession of some of the goods and authority formerly all in the hands of the bishop. For in that year Louis the Pious approved the measures taken in this direction by Alberic.[1] This bishop, in trying to better the conditions among his clergy, introduced the chapter organization among them, built cloisters, and set aside numerous pieces of property for their special use.[1] Twenty years afterwards Charles the Bald confirmed the approval, or sanction, given by his father, and also sanctioned new additions made to the chapter's possessions by Bishop Teotbaldus.[2] In 871 Charles acted again in favor of the chapter. This time he confirmed to the clergy the possession of certain properties which Bishop Isaac had acquired especially for them, and to his own previous gift of the villa Aculiacum he added that of Stabulæ.[3] In the case of all these possessions the chapter appears to have been master as well as owner. Louis the Pious specifies quite clearly that those granted by Albericus are to be under the complete control of their new owners.[1] The first act by Charles the Bald is not so definite in its terms, nor so extensive;[2] but it included a confirmation of the measures of Louis the Pious, and its general intent could scarcely have been less than that of the measures it confirmed. As to the second act of Charles the Bald, that of 871, its purport could hardly have been made more clear by incorporating a full formula of immunity. What had been given to the clergy should be henceforth subject to their authority and direction, nor should anyone do aught in reference to the said possessions to disturb or oppose their owners in the control of them; they should be free to use their common property in all respects as they would.[3] Most of the domains mentioned in the enumerations of grants to the chapter were located outside the city. Many of them, to be sure, were not far away, since they were within the county of Langres, and some of them

---

[1] Charter of 834.   [2] Charter of 854.   [3] Charter of 871.

were right near the walls.[1] But one can not say that these formed part of the town. Nevertheless, not all of the chapter's property was in the country. At least the canonical grounds and buildings accorded by Alberic were located inside the fortifications.[2] Here, then, we have upon the scene a second grand seigneur, a virtually independent governor of all the possessions it had, whether these were in the county, faubourgs and city of Langres, or in more distant regions. That is to say, here is a second factor which, by reason of its control of realty, exercised functions that regularly would be public.

Third, with reference to individuals in their private or personal capacity: The charters of which special use is made here furnish several illustrations of the practice of the Carolingians of the ninth century in this direction. In 846 the Emperor Lothaire gave to one of his vassals, by name Suitgarius, certain properties to be held as his own, which before that time he had held by benefice tenure. They consisted of eight "mansos," together with their chapels, dwelling houses and other buildings, cultivated and uncultivated lands, the woods, fields, meadows, pastures, still and running waters, mills, together with proceeds and revenues; and also the mancipia thereon, of both sexes and of all ages, and whatever else went with the said mansos. All these possessions, the persons included, were to pass from under the law and rule of the Emperor and were to be thenceforth under the law and rule of Suitgarius; who, moreover, was to be absolutely free to deal with them as he wished, just as he was in the case of other things he owned, as long as he should be faithful to the Emperor.[3] In 870 Charles the Bald made an exchange of possessions with one of his vassals, the count Gérard; and each was evidently to have full license to do as he chose with both the domains and the persons he thus acquired.[4] In 885 Charles the Fat transferred to one Dodo, his vassal, two mansa and thirty mancipia, with full rights of possession and of authority.[5] The next year he made a similar grant to one

---

[1] * * * "in circuitu murorum ejusdem civitatis colonias duas." Charter of 834.
[2] On the location of these buildings, see Th. Pistollet de St. Ferjeux, Cloître de la cathédrale de Langres, in Mém. de la soc. hist. et arch. de Langres, t. II, p. 3.
[3] Charter of 846.
[4] Charter of 870.
[5] Charter of May 20, 885.

Jacob, likewise a vassal.[1] Finally, it is possible to cite at least one case bearing rather closely upon conditions at Langres. In those indicated so far not only the lands but also the people in question were more or less distant from there. In January of 887 the Emperor gave to a certain Otbert, prévôt of the church of Langres, two pieces of property, one located at Bourg, in the county of Langres, and the other in the county of Ouche. Both of them, including vineyards and mancipia, were placed under the full personal authority of Otbert.[2] To be sure this does not directly concern property inside the town. But the Otbert in question, holding the office of prévôt of the church of Langres, must have been a resident of that city; and the tendencies with which he was identified in this instance may very properly be taken to be those that were followed in all or most such matters by the people among whom he lived.

The foregoing proofs should leave no doubt that the principle of private sovereignty was a part of the regular order of things in and about Langres in the ninth century. We have seen that much before 814 it was sanctioned by the law, by the powers that were; that all authority over landed possessions might belong to him who owned or controlled the same. The provisions in the charters of the Carolingian kings applied to all the property of the church, and therefore the arrangements which they ordered were to be found not alone in certain rural districts. They represented also what had been done concerning at least a large part of the property within the walls of the city. Furthermore, we have every reason to conclude that that which was true in the case of ecclesiastical corporations was also true in the case of individuals. The aim of the great landowners was, in general, to govern as well as to own, and that was what they were actually doing.

III.

Having thus seen what were some of the prevailing conditions in and around Langres long before the end of the ninth century, it will be in order next to observe, as far as possible, just how the actual distribution of authority over or among

---

[1] Charter of July 30, 886. [2] Charter of May 20, 885.

the people living there was affected by these conditions; to see more definitely just what governmental arrangements were brought about at Langres by the operation of influences so far disclosed, and, first, what was the situation with reference to matters relating rather to the whole county or pagus than to the town of Langres as such.

The Count of Langres, like many others whose territories included large or important places, had had, no one knows exactly how long, the control of the money, the annual fairs, and the weekly markets in the capital of his county and in Dijon. According to the old public law of the period, he should have continued to have the control of such things; but new legal principles were being established. The circumstances were such that the exercise of these functions passed naturally into the hands of that person in the locality who had the most moral and material resources, and consequently the most influence. At Langres this was the bishop, administrator of an immense landed estate and possessor, besides, of the arms of the church. Already some years before 887 the bishop had been granted the privilege of coining money at both Langres and Dijon.[1] Also he had received before that time the half of the dues from the annual fairs and all the dues from the weekly markets.[2] The charter of Charles the Fat says that Charles the Bald accorded these last-named privileges, and, as a matter of fact, there is a document emanating from Charles the Bald, published by Pérard,[3] which

---

[1] "Obtulit præterea obtutibus celsitudinis nostræ, auctoritatem præcepti piæ recordationis avunculi nostri Karoli imperatoris qualiter ipse ob deprecationem Isaac, venerabilis episcopi ejusdem Lingonensis ecclesiæ, et in eadem Lingonis civitate et in Divione castro, monetas fieri concessit, ea tamen ratione quo absque alicujus judicis seu comitis inquietudine ad jus sive ordinationem jam sæpe memoratæ ecclesiæ rectorum pertinere perpetuo debeant." Charter of 887.

[2] "Statuit [Charles the Bald] denique, et in eadem auctoritate, ut de mercatis annalibus in supra dictis locis medietas, et de ebdomadalibus summa integritas partibus ejusdem Lingonensis atque Divionensis ecclesiæ cederetur. * * * De mercatis vero et monetis, sicuti diva memoria suprascriptus Karolus imperator avunculus noster sua auctoritate statuit, constatuit et confirmavit, ita et nos ejus redintegrantes et renovantes auctoritatem * * * statuimus, stabilimus atque æternaliter confirmamus." Ibidem.

[3] Recueil, p. 48. According to the document itself, its date is: "duodecimo kal. Septemb. indictione secunda, anno XXXIV regnante Karolo gloriosissimo Rege." Pérard places it in the year 863, which was number 11 in the indiction, and in the month of August, the twenty-fourth year of the reign of Charles the Bald, which should be counted from June 21, 840. Dòm Bouquet, who reproduces the text of Pérard, corrects the indiction number, making it 6, and gives the date as 873. See Rec. des hist. de France, VIII, p. 643. This is in harmony with "the thirty-fourth year of the reign." If importance is to be attached to the terms of the charter of 887, in which Charles the Bald is called emperor, the document ought to be dated between 875 and 877. Father Vignier, Décade, t. I, p. 496, assigns it to the year 876.

bears witness to such a concession in respect to Dijon, but not Langres.[1] Clearly, then, so far as the county functions in general are concerned, that owner or controller of private property at Langres who was most favored by the tendencies toward private sovereignty was the bishop.

But the texts do not restrict themselves to giving indications solely in regard to the bishop's conquest of the prerogatives of the count in the pagus as a whole. They are more specific. They furnish us a series of facts from which it is easy to see that the bishop marched steadily toward the holding of absolute authority over the city of Langres.

When Louis the Pious confirmed the charters which replaced those lost in the midst of the "Saracen" troubles, he also sanctioned what his predecessors had done in the way of conceding to the bishops of Langres the cathedral church at that place and its chapels and all else that was legally in its possession. Among the things thus belonging to the church he mentioned the munitio of the city.[2] If, then, the expression "*antecessores nostri reges*" can be taken literally, the bishop had been master of the citadel of Langres at least since the middle of the eighth century. He continued, too, it appears, to be the absolute controller of that fortress. Also, in the course of the year 887, as can be seen from the charter of Charles the Fat already cited, the bishop's property and power in the town were greatly increased. Geilo related to the Emperor that without the aid of any count or of any other royal officer he had rebuilt his city.[3] Then he addressed to him certain requests, aiming to assure the town against the abuses of the

---

[1] "Simili modo etiam deprecatus est [Isaac, bishop of Langres] de mercatis in sua potestate constitutis, in Lingonensi scilicet et in Divione; de quibus talis antiquitus consuetudo fuit, ut medietas de annalibus et de Ebdomadali in Divione, summa integritas, iam dictæ potestati constitueretur, tale auctoritatis nostræ preceptum sæpe fatas Ecclesias relinqueremus, per quod ipse, ejusque successores, sine aliqua contradictione tenere racionabiliter possent. Cuius laudabilibus petitionibus atque ammonitionibus aurem accommodantes, hoc sublimitatis nostræ præceptum fieri, eique dare jussimus, per quod ipse venerabilis antistes, ejusque successores, et præfatas monatas, et de mercatis quemadmodum supra habetur insertum, quieto ordine, æterna stabilitate obtinere in perpetuum valerent." Pérard, Recueil, p. 48.

[2] "Sed et ipsam sanctam sedem antecessores nostri reges cum cellulis subjectis vel omnibus rebus juste ad se aspicientibus, munitionem videlicet Lingonicæ civitatis." * * * Charter of 814.

[3] "Geilo * * * celsitudini nostræ innotuit qualiter Lingonis civitatem sibi videlicet a Deo commissam, ob nimiam persecutionem sive infestationem paganorum, et refugium sive salvationem cristianorum et sanctæ Dei ecclesiæ defensionem prope jam ræædificatam sine alicujus comitis vel judicis juvamine atque constructam haberet." * * * Charter of 887.

count and to complete the improvements which he had already undertaken.[1] All his desires were satisfied. Charles the Fat granted to Geilo, of course in the interest of his church, the walls of the city, together with a space 15 feet wide extending around the town just inside, and a similar space 60 feet in breadth just outside the walls. Also whatever there was within the fortifications that belonged to the royal fisc and was under the jurisdiction of the count; and likewise whatever there was that belonged to the royal fisc in the Place Chambeau, just without the fortifications.[2] Furthermore, while it is clear that the royal and imperial concessions already cited carried with them immunity from the regular public authorities, it is of interest to note that when King Odo, in 889, confirmed various measures taken by his predecessor in favor of the church of Langres, he provided specifically that the monasteries, abbeys, and possessions of other kinds enumerated in his act of confirmation, and also the rights of the church relating to money, fortresses, and markets, should be under the absolute control of the bishop.[3]

In view of these facts, what may be said to have been the govermental situation at Langres during and after 887 as compared with conditions before that time? We know that before 887 the bishop and the chapter, by virtue of their immunities, controlled at least a large part of the city. And at that epoch, when church officials had once acquired authority they were careful enough not to lose any of it. We know also that before 887 a count and certain other representatives of the old public administration exercised powers inside the city. For it follows from the exposition of the undertakings and requests that Geilo laid before the Emperor, not only that there were such personages and that they were guilty of grave excesses in their administration, but also that the property

---

[1] * * * "et ut ad perfectionem illam perducere posset, modis omnibus satageret; hujus rei causa serenitatem nostram cum quantis precibus potuit humiliter deprecatus est [Geilo] ob nimias comitum seu judicum inquietudines." * * * Ibid.

[2] "Cujus nos laudabilibus petitionibus aurem nostræ celsitudinis accomodantes, hoc auctoritatis nostræ præceptum fieri jussimus, per quod statuentes decernimus et decernendo confirmamus quatinus omnia ex jure fisci nostri ad causam comitis pertinentia infra eandem Lingonis civitatem, et extra, loco qui Campus Bellus dicitur, et ipsam civitatis murum et XV pedes deintus et LX deforis, veluti supra insertum est, et quemadmodum jam sæpefatus Geilo episcopus petiit, ita per hanc nostram imperialem auctoritatem et ipsa Lingonensis ecclesia et ipsae suique successores legitime ordinent, et perpetuo in Dei nomine ordine quieto obtineant." * * * Ibid.

[3] Charter of 889.

which gave them the opportunity of committing such excesses was located within the walls.[1] Again, the right to coin money related without doubt to the entire county; and the bishop had this privilege at Langres in all probability since 876.

Beginning with 887, we can say not only that the bishop controlled the old-time lands and buildings of the church, that he possessed all the fortifications of the city, together with a circular strip of land à l'entour both outside and inside the walls, that he coined money, and that he held the rights over the annual fairs and weekly markets, but also that from that time neither the count nor any of his delegates had any jurisdiction inside the city. On this last point the language of the charter of Charles the Fat is quite clear.[2] And when one passes to the year 967, the year in which King Lothaire endowed the church of Langres with the rights remaining to the royal power in that region, he finds nothing that contradicts this interpretation.

At that time the bishop was given, for his church, all the "county" prerogatives at Langres, including the toloneum exacted at the gates of the city.[3] That is to say, he was given all the privileges and public power still belonging to him who had the title of Count of Langres, not necessarily that he was made the possessor of all the goods belonging to the person or family in whose hands the countship of that region had rested. No mention is made in the act of 967 of any function or privilege necessarily exercised inside the city. Indeed, there was no reason why there should be any such mention. The bishop had been an absolute master there for four score years. Without doubt he had held the keys of the city at least since 887. He was not only the protector, but as well the governor of the town. And he was all this especially by virtue of the possessions in his control. It must have been

---

[1] Charter of 887.

[2] Bishop Geilo "humiliter deprecatus est quatinus ob nimias comitum seu judicum inquietudines * * * et ipsum civitatis murum et quindecim pedes deintus, et LX de foris, sive omnia ex fisco nostro infra eandem civitatem ad causam comitis pertinentia seu etiam et omne illud ex jure fisci nostri quod in Campo Bello juxta sepefatam civitatem consistit." * * * And Charles decreed, "Quatinus omnia ex jure fisci nostri adcausam comitis pertinentia infra eandem Lingonis civitatem, et extra, loco qui Campus Bellus dicitur, et ipsum civitatis murum." * * *

[3] * * * "Res quasdam pertinentes ad supplementum regii honoris * * * concedimus sanctæ praescriptæ ecclesiæ ac sancto Mammeti glorioso martiri, comitatum scilicet Lingonensem atque omne praemium quod exigitur in teloneo de portis civilibus." * * * Charter of August 30, 967.

the relatively vast resources at his disposal that made it possible for him to undertake the repairing of the walls. He ruled on the lands that his church owned; and surely, in view of the circumstances of the time, not the least reason for this was that his church owned these lands. And if he was sovereign over anything more it must still have been mainly because the church he represented was a large owner. Furthermore, the bishop seems thus to have been in perfect harmony with the general conditions of the period. Association between sovereignty and ownership was characteristic to a marked degree even of the old Frankish public law. The king or emperor was accustomed to give to the church things which either he himself or his representatives in a certain sense possessed. To remedy abuses, to better existing situations, or to promote private interests, it was not necessary to follow principles absolutely new. It was more natural, and for the most part the custom, to follow the dominant tendencies of the time, and therefore simply to change proprietors.

Finally, it will be well to notice more definitely against what governmental arrangements at Langres the new régime of private sovereignty was making its way. All concessions of immunity either to individuals or to ecclesiastical corporations appear to have been made at the expense of the count and of the royal government. We know that as a general rule such provisions affected only that authority which the kings or their more or less loyal representatives exercised in the pagi;[1] and there is no reason to make exceptions of those relating to Langres. In fact, the language of at least one concession, that to Otbertus, is quite clear on this point.[2] The Emperor acted with the consent of the counts in whose territory the lands conceded were situated.[3] It is evident from this document that at least in those portions of the county of Langres that were not included within the town the usual public authority was that of the count; and, too, it is no less evident that all the powers which that functionary was accustomed to exercise on any of his domains might be given to some person who would exercise the same powers by reason of his ownership of the domains in question.[4] And when one studies the

---

[1] See, for example, Viollet, t. I, pp. 327-331 and 400-402.
[2] Charter of 887.
[3] * * * "Illis volentibus atque consentientibus." * * * Ibidem.
[4] The real point involved here still holds even if it be true that the counts were already holding such authority as they exercised mainly because of ownership considerations.

immunities accorded to the bishopric and to the chapter,[1] although the terms may not always be precise, he can have no doubt about their meaning. They involved the supplanting of control exercised through the old public administrative organs by control exercised through owners.

It is, however, especially in connection with the events of 887 that it becomes clear what sort of government was declining, as well as what sort was taking its place. Naturally enough, the confirmation of the privilege to coin money, and the grant of rights in reference to the fairs and markets, were made at the expense of the count's prerogatives. But also, just as in the county at large, so in the city, the only public authority prejudiced by the acquisitions of the bishop seems to have been that of the count or of his delegates. The concession of the walls and of authority associated with the royal fisc was made, at least ostensibly, to free the city of the excesses or exactions of the counts and judges;[2] and the bishop rebuilt the city, not without the aid of any local authority surviving from Roman times, but without the aid of any count or judge.[3] It appears, then, that if there still existed at Langres any organs of the old Roman municipal régime, they were of no real, vital importance. The county régime had been in full operation there; but now, by reason of new circumstances, and because they possessed the necessary material and moral resources, ecclesiastical corporations and certain individuals, especially the bishop, were taking its place.

IV.

Briefly resumed, the conclusions reached in the course of this study appear to be as follows:

First. The history of Langres, in so far as it is now known, offers no proof that such or such parts of the Roman municipality survived in that city. And even if certain remnants of it did continue there for a time they were in no way the real governing agencies in the Langres of the ninth century.

---

[1] Charters of 814, 834, 889.
[2] * * * "ob nimias comitum seu judicum inquietudines * * *." Charter of 887.
[3] * * * "civitatem * * * et * * * defensionem prope jam reædificatam sine alicujus comitis vel judicis juvamine atque constructam haberet." * * * Ibidem.

Second. There can be no question that under the Frankish organization the regular legally constituted governmental régime at Langres was that of the county.

Third. By the beginning of the ninth century the county régime at Langres had for a long time been declining before the influences which contributed to the rise and continued progress of private or proprietary sovereignty, and much before the end of the ninth century those influences had fully brought about their logical or natural results. Public government, in so far as the rule of the Merovingians and Carolingians may be so called, had disappeared, and the rule of ecclesiastical corporations and of individuals as such had taken its place.

Fourth. That individual, that representative of private interests and resources whom the conditions and tendencies in and about Langres favored most, was the bishop. In 887 he was the ruler, the virtually absolute master, not likely of the city as such, but *in* the city. The position he had acquired by that date may be looked upon not only as the most striking illustration of the general governmental conditions in that region in and from the ninth century, but also as the most prominent and most defined feature of the governmental régime to which the people of Langres were accustomed, not only at that time but also for some centuries thereafter.

XV.—ROBERT FRUIN, 1823-1899.

A MEMORIAL SKETCH.

By RUTH PUTNAM.

ROBERT FRUIN, 1823-1899—A MEMORIAL SKETCH.

By RUTH PUTNAM.

The name of Robert Fruin, late professor at the University of Leiden, is little known in America even among workers in history. His voice, which should have been welcomed by all interested in the historical topics discussed by him, has been stifled in a language of narrow vogue, current coin in a tiny scrap of a realm. His works, published almost entirely in ephemeral publications, have not been translated, and his message has thus been deadened by its vehicle of expression so that its notes have only been audible to a few.

Now, this narrowness of limit does not apply to the interest in the subject treated by this Dutch scholar in his college lectures and in his monographs on the history of his fatherland. It is unnecessary to recall to you how keen has been American sympathy for the story of Holland and her people.

Here is the testimony of the president of the historical society of this Commonwealth. Last April he said that he deemed the sixteenth century grapple between Spain and Holland, when middle-age feudalism went down and nationalism arose, the most interesting and dramatic episode in modern development, adding: "You can not study or write the history of Massachusetts intelligently without bearing that struggle in mind." This is still more true of the history of New York and of other quarters of the earth beyond our United States. A year ago we heard how, in behalf of the Venezuela Boundary Commission, the trail of the Dutch was carefully scrutinized in South America; in South Africa the past history, present position, and future fortunes of the Dutch Afrikanders is holding the attention of the civilized world to-day.

Between the publications of Motley's Rise of the Dutch Republic, in 1856, and Fiske's Dutch and Quaker Colonies, in

1899, Americans less studious and less scholarly than these Massachusetts authors have busied themselves with Hollanders and their doings at home and abroad. American books receive adequate and discriminating notice in Dutch periodicals, but the repeated complaint of the reviewers in De Gids and the Netherland Spectator is that our trans-Atlantic writers are sound on their own history—one side of the contrasting pictures they present—but often unsound on the real significance of Dutch institutions and generally ignorant of modern Dutch criticism on Holland's past. This rebuke is not unfair. Indiscriminate admiration pleases the Hollanders as little as Irving's History of New York.

Professor Fruin's pen and lectures were devoted to Netherland history. He never left the Netherlands but once, but he was not ignorant of our land. In the three times I had the pleasure of seeing him at Leiden, in 1896, when he was already emeritus, the interest he expressed in the United States was keen and his knowledge discriminating. He knew Boston and New York, and had a fairly clear conception of the differences between North and South, East and West. He was sure that he should like Boston better than any other American city. Many were his questions, and so true were his comments that it seemed to me he must know by instinct, so little apparent opportunity had he had for knowledge.

I may mention here that it was easier to understand his real opinion than that of most Hollanders, who talked to me in a stiff, school English, because he at once proposed that we should each speak his native tongue. Several times he stopped me to query an expression, "Maar, Mejufvrouw, ik geloof dat is Amerikansch." But he never failed to understand my explanation.

Robert Fruin belonged to Holland in part only. His descent was pure Dutch in the maternal line, but his paternal grandfather, Thomas Frewin, was a Warwickshire miller. Unsuccessful in business, he determined to try his fortunes in the new West. In 1774 or 1775 he took his family to Rotterdam, meaning to embark thence for Massachusetts. The rumors of the coming outbreak in America finally determined him to remain in Rotterdam. One son, Robert, became apprentice to an apothecary, married his master's daughter, prospered well in the business, which he inherited, and left a competency to each of his sons, three of whom followed learned professions.

Robert the younger, our Leiden historian, was born November 14, 1823, and educated at the Erasmian Latin School in Rotterdam.

The first book to arouse enthusiasm in the lad was Heeren's Ideen über die Politik, den Verkehr und den Handel der vornehmsten Völker der alten Welt (Ideas about the Politics, the Intercourse and the Commerce of the Chief Peoples of the Ancient World). The romance in commercial relations, the vision seen by the author of links between peoples woven by the trade shuttle carried to and fro by the slow-moving caravans, made a picture fascinating to the boy. "Mere chance threw the volumes"—six dull-looking tomes they are—"into my hands, and I shall never forget the impression of history as a living, moving growth," he says. When Fruin matriculated at Leiden—1842, æt. 19—it was with the intention of devoting himself to ancient history.

It was a barren period at the university. There was no one in history or literature to affect a student of Fruin's inclination. The liberal education he gained came from his peers, chiefly from Opzoomer, three years his senior. Fruin's doctorate thesis was, true to his ancient ideals, on an Egyptian topic, De Manethone librorumque ab eo scriptorum reliquiis (Manetho and his Literary Remains). But that was his last plunge into the remote past.

The following years of 1847 and 1848 were exciting ones. Fruin was in Utrecht, where he worked at Netherland history, while he, his brother, Opzoomer, and a few others watched the European revolutionary crisis with intense interest, amusing their leisure meanwhile with Shakespeare. The impress of those years—Netherland past and present to an accompaniment of Shakespeare's rhythm—was more potent in its effect upon Fruin than the influence of his years at the university. In 1849 he was appointed teacher of Dutch history—divided then for the first time from language—in the Leiden Gymnasium. In 1853 he made his first appearance in print in a controversy with Groen van Prinsterer. This was the beginning of a long public duel upon questions of governmental theory and policy. In private the two were friendly until the publication of Fruin's Political Morality wounded Groen, and the controversy became a quarrel.

Meantime Fruin was working steadily at Dutch historical sources. In 1856 he printed the first result of his investigations—Tien jaren uit den tachtigjarigen oorlog (Ten Years of the Eighty Years' War). This masterly treatise appeared in a most unattractive form as appendix to two successive issues of the Leiden Gymnasium report, a big, ungainly folio. But the merit was recognized. In a long review[1] J. A. Nijhoff, after expressing admiration for the evident research, for the command of the sources, and for the discriminating estimation of their values, says: "Yet with all the impression of authority for every word uttered, there is a marked stamp of freshness over all, which places this little work in a class by itself in comparison with the early histories of the Netherlands."

The monograph was speedily reprinted from the report, making a volume of 400 pages, small octavo. But it is wonderful how much matter is contained therein. The period covered is 1588-1598. Our author draws a brilliant picture of the situation in the Netherlands after the death of William of Orange—Spanish success seemed assured for good and all; then comes a sketch of the Armada expedition, the decline of Spain as a factor in European politics, Leicester's withdrawal from the provinces, the course of the events which succeeded each other until the tide turned gradually, and in 1598 the little republic of the North emerged from chaos and began to show an independent face to the world.

A study of Hugo De Groot (Grotius) and his wife followed this naturally, touching as it does on the first years of the seventeenth century. The next essay deals with an earlier period. This was "The prologue to the eighty years' war," which appeared in 1859 in three successive numbers of De Gids in the form of a review on Motley's Rise of the Dutch Republic, then just translated into Dutch.

Fruin begins:

The perusal of Motley's book led me to a reëxamination of his sources. The investigation has given me a different impression of his facts, their causes and their interconnection, than I gained from his captivating pages. I here take it for granted that everyone knows the American writer's

---

[1] Bijdragen voor vaderlandsche Geschiedenis, N. R. I (1859), p. 95.

work—it would be a scandal if our people neglected to read what a foreigner counted important to write of.

Motley is at his best in description. His style is clever. His sympathy for his subject gives color and glow to his pictures. The color and glow indeed are dominant.

It may be in order here to quote a bit from one of Motley's letters, dated Brussels, 1853, to Holmes. He was then working on his manuscript. He dilates on his keen pleasure in Rubens's work, ending with—

As for color, his effects are as sure as those of the sun rising in a tropical landscape. * * * There are some pictures here, and I often go * * * of a raw, foggy morning merely to warm myself in the blaze of their beauty.

It looks as though Rubens were one source of Motley's highly colored style which impressed many of his early reviewers unfavorably.

To continue Fruin's criticism:

But he (Motley) is less happy in getting to the bottom of hidden motives which affect events—of causes which could not have other results. What the witnesses whom he summons testify he reports far better than they relate. But he does not investigate sharply enough what they say between the lines. The "how" can be read in his narrative; the "why" is not clear. He often loses a sense of perspective. His judgment on Charles V is much too severe, as Bakhuizen has shown. His judgment of certain governmental acts of Philip and Granvelle rests on untenable ground. In general, he has a sense of the love of liberty which animated our people, but he has no conception of the rights of the government which was forming a modern state on the ruins of mediæval privileges, nor of the church as a political factor. There is much that he could learn from Ranke.

Very appreciative, however, is the Dutch scholar of Motley's researches, and very discriminating in the points where he differs from him. The "Prologue" is as masterly as the "Ten years," and shows wonderful initiation into the subject and a very dramatic sense of presentation.

These three articles decided Fruin's reputation as an authority upon national history. In 1860 De Vries, holding the double chair of Dutch history and language in the University of Leiden, asked to have the subjects divided. This was done, and Robert Fruin received the first appointment as Hoogleeraar in Vaderlandsche Geschiedenis, or professor of the history of the Fatherland.

No gift could have been more welcome to him. Joyously he filled out his year's lessons to the schoolboys, and then on

June 1, 1860, he was formally inaugurated into his new office of interpreting Netherland history to the student class.

It is a beautiful speech, his inaugural. It is only printed in the big official records of the Netherland academies—Annales Academiæ Lugduno Bataviæ. I found the series in an unvisited corner of the Astor Library, with their silent pages still uncut. Probably sister sets are equally neglected in Boston and Cambridge. The opening address to the rector, curators, town officers, professors, and students, and other hearers show how many degrees of "honorableness" can exist in a Germanic tongue, while the translation into English gives only monotony to the quality. Fruin then plunges into his subject, "Impartiality in history." An apter title might be "Ideals of an historical writer and teacher of his national history."

Taking Bilderdijyk, an avowed partisan, and Wagenaar, the official state historian of the seventeenth century, as types, he quotes this passage from Wagenaar:

A history which fulfills what may be expected of it represents events just as they occurred, and can properly be compared to a mirror, in which not only the outline but also the color of the objects is shown.

"Now what can be imagined as more impartial than a cold, clear mirror?" continues Fruin. "But shall we take that as an ideal for the imitation of an historian? In the first place, where shall he obtain his mirror in which the past is reflected in its exact form? It is irrational to demand the impossible. The past can not be mirrored, can not be reflected without a medium. A history requires an historian who can not picture the events as they happened, but as they present themselves to his imagination. It can not equal the mirror in truth; it can possess no other merits than those of a portrait which is like. A portrait never can show a person just as he is, but as the artist sees him. Two excellent portraits of one person painted by different masters would differ from each other as two historical narratives of the same period composed by different writers, for the artist's origin and training stamps his work and the production is a combination of personality and of art.

" If then we acknowledge history writing as an art, we can not deny that, like every art, it has its limits, and that we can not demand from the artist what goes beyond the limits.

"To expect an historian to write history other than as he himself sees it, as he himself is impressed by it, is as unrhymed as to make the same demand of the painter.

"Let everyone be artistic enough to express himself. Let a partisan who feels called on to write history write partially. Wagenaar pretends to be impartial when he is not. Bilderdijk's lack is not due to partisan spirit, but to his defective investigation. He simply has no model. He may paint, but it is phantasy.

"But I venture to assert that if every writer be absolutely true to the impressions resulting from his own conscientious and thorough investigations, two descriptions can not tally exactly."

Then follows a long eulogy on Shakespeare and an expression of the speaker's conviction that had this dramatic poet chosen that work, he would have been the most perfect narrative historian the world had ever seen. Having sketched his ideal further of how the history of one's own land should be taught with exactness, with a power of research and an ability to separate truth from falsehood, Fruin adds: "I am handing you a yardstick with which to measure my own shortcomings. Do not think I flatter myself that I can reach my ideal. But life is a continuous struggle and the height of the aim should not prevent striving." To the students he said: "I can do no more than offer the opportunity to learn. Individual study is the only real means of acquiring knowledge. My purpose is to teach you the methods by which you can direct your investigations. * * * I only beg your sympathy, without which my instruction can not be fruitful." ("Sympathy is the keynote of history," he says elsewhere.)

Now Heer Bijvanck—ex Leiden student, librarian of the Royal Library at The Hague, one of the editors of the Gids—says[1] of Fruin: "He was the last of his school of historians." To me in this address of 1860 he seems, as he seemed in the talks of 1896, intensely modern, markedly in touch with one phase of the historical spirit of to-day.

How far did he attain his own ideal? Thirty-four years later, when he retired from the post he had been so proud to fill, he said that he had lacked the eloquence and enthusiasm to give the satisfaction in his lectures given for example by

---
[1] De Gids, 1899, I, et seq.

his predecessor, De Vries. One of his former students says: "Fruin's delivery was not attractive. His voice had a metallic ring. He spoke in too high a key for a man, and often his sentences ended in a falsetto. Nevertheless, if you came for historic knowledge, to learn, to understand historic criticism, it was not long before the speaker won your ear by way of your understanding."

Stellwegen wrote in 1894:

Professor Fruin is a speaker of the greatest simplicity. Clear as a spring in the dunes is his language. His sentences are so perfectly consecutive that they form one logical whole. His lectures read well. He never improvises. Every point is lucid before his mind's eye. He conquers your attention by the vividness of his matter. It is as though he recalls what he had actually seen and been present at and witnessed. Not through the usual ornaments of oratorical style, but through the sequence of narrative and demonstration does he hold his hearers prisoner. He is rather poor than rich in images and dainty turns. Soberness, dignity, justice—those are the characteristics of his words in substance and in form. Historical matter seems part of him, and as soon as the auditor has experienced the charm of this quality, he is convinced of the science of the master. * * * Fruin must not be judged according to the standard of those who followed the course in history for the sake of their certificate, or for the purpose of taking examination in a subject which they never intended to touch again. One must listen to those who chose Fruin's courses inspired by their own love for historical studies. But more than once has it been my experience to see those who chose the lectures for a minor (bijvak.) find that from that moment they became imbued with the subject.

"It is true, Professor Fruin founded no school," says another biographer. "He never tried to make others adopt his line. His one aim was to arouse love for his subject and to give a worthy example of devotion and unselfish performance of the duty in hand. He never urged his own opinions, never made propaganda for certain principles of instruction. His aim was to present the pros and cons, to collect data whereby we might give judgment, and to this watchword he remained true."

Meanwhile Fruin's pen was busy hand in hand with his teaching. No other work appeared in its own two covers like the "Ten Years," but the sum of his monographs, all told, is about 250, according to the quotation in the Amsterdamsche Dagblad of Professor Blok's memorial address at the Royal Academy (Holland) on the 12th of this month (December 12, 1899).

In regard to the worth of these brief studies, I again appeal to Mr. Adams, who considers "the monograph as the foundation and corner stone of the historical edifice of the future."

In full accord with this opinion, I would urge that no one ought to treat Dutch history without a familiarity with this abundant harvest of Professor Fruin's sowing, though naturally the fruit varies in quality.

For some years, too, Fruin was editor of De Gids (1865-1874) and of Nijhoff's series "Historische Bijdragen," or Historical contributions to national history. De Gids, or "The Guide," is and was a rather heavy though dignified monthly. Here is a bit of sanctum gossip repeated by Heer Bijvanck, now on that same editorial board. Sometimes one of the editors wished to refuse an article because it was so deadly dull. Fruin would ask him gently whether harmony were not lovely, and whether he appreciated the character of "our review." Once the four other editors hesitated to accept a certain contribution which they urged was somewhat wanting in taste though fresh in style. "Come, now," said Fruin, "we can safely risk it. We have taste enough and to spare, but no one can deny that we do lack freshness."[1]

It was owing, perhaps, to Fruin's dramatic sense that he usually wrote on a subject brought vividly before him by an anniversary or present event parallel to one in the past. Or again his articles are in the form of a review of new books, but he soon leaves comments upon the author and follows his own thread of thought upon the subject-matter.

There are studies on nearly all divisions of history—military, political, social, financial, economical, ecclesiastical, and religious—as affecting national development; as, for instance:

De Overwinning bij Heiligerlee 1568 (The Victory at Heiligerlee).

De schuld van Willem III en zijn vrienden aan den moord der gebruder de Witt. De Gids, 1867, I, 201 (The blame of William III and his friends in the murder of the de Witts).

Uit het dagboek van een Oud Hollander. De Gids, 1869, 14, 369 (The diary of an old Hollander).

Over de muntverzwakking in de 14de jaarhundert (The depreciation of the currency in the fourteenth century). 1877.

De wederopluiking van het Katholicisme in Noord Nederland. Gids, 1894, p. 240 (The revival of Catholicism in North Netherland in the sixteenth century).

---

[1] De Gids, 1899, II, p. XL, 1.

There are a few studies on the middle ages, like the very interesting article on Philip of Leiden, but in the main the period treated is the sixteenth century, and gradually there came into being a series of papers which pretty well cover the period of the struggle with Spain.

That on the Gorcum martyrs is one of the most interesting. The writer gives a picture of those true and steadfast Catholic victims to De Lumey's Beggars in 1572, before the restraining voice of William of Orange came to urge that revolt against one authority must not mean unbridled license. It is an exquisite bit of historical narrative and a good example of the author's attitude toward his authorities. It is full of discrimination and gives reverent honor where honor was due, even though the martyrs seemed to him mistaken in their zeal.

Fruin often expressed a wish that a Catholic Netherlander would treat the eighty years' war. Asked once why he did not put himself into the position of a Catholic, he answered that it was impossible. Untruth could only result from one trying to see from a strained position.

Later, when the fervent Catholic Nuyens wrote, Fruin reviewed his work very severely in two articles entitled: "Een proeve van averechtsche geschiedschrijving," (A specimen of preposterous history writing.) He attacks the author in detail for his unjust handling of his material, for his his misquotation, and his lack of due estimate of his authorities. In 1896 I asked him what he thought of another Catholic, the Belgian, Kervijn de Lettenhove. He answered that he considered him absolutely honest, only mistaken in points. Nuyens he deemed maliciously wrong, and too clever to be as stupid as his errors would have made him.

Only once do I find him accused of writing without due knowledge. That is in relation to his article in the Gids, "Our rights to Netherland India," wherein he sympathized with the native owners of the soil in Java too markedly to suit colonial statesmen. Again, once I find an acknowledgment that he had pronounced what he thought a last word too hastily. He had a vigorous dispute with Heer Knoop at the Royal Academy in regard to William III's responsibility for fighting the battle of St. Denis and losing hundreds of lives after peace had been signed for four days. The discussion was long and bitter, but it was Fruin himself who finally discovered convincing proof that he had been wrong, that William III had been guilty of absolute falsity in his statements. He made public acknowledgment to Heer General Knoop, and it does not seem to me that his reputation as a scholar or a gentleman suffered at all in the transaction.

Toward the end of his life he drifted into studies on cities, writing much on Rotterdam and Leiden. In 1894 with his seventieth year he had to resign his professional career, according to the law of Holland. I have only been able to find references to his farewell address. There was apparently a note of sadness in it from the opening words: "I have had my time." But there was a note of loving reverence in the reception that followed. Several people who were present told me that it was delightful to see the grateful and surprised astonishment of the new emeritus—who did not feel himself old—at the affection in the greeting given him by his students and townspeople. According to the pretty European university custom, a group of his ex-pupils presented him with a collection of their own original studies on subjects relating to his work and theirs. The names of Blok, the Mullers, the younger De Vries, Beaufort, present minister of foreign affairs, and half a dozen more all bear witness to the impulse he gave them to turn their attention to Vaderlandsche Geschiedenis.

After his retirement from active teaching, Fruin passed the remaining years of his life in the pleasant, roomy house at Leiden, where he had lived his bachelor life with its quiet, uneventful routine of continuous work. In 1895 Queen Emma invited him to instruct Wilhelmina in the past of the land she was to govern. But he declined in favor of his successor, Professor Blok.

In addition to his state pension, the professor emeritus had a comfortable private income. No want ever troubled his scholar's calm, no money pressure ever led him to undue haste in his work. Thus in addition to the fullness of knowledge shown in his monographs, there is also a comfortable sense of leisure and of uniformity as though he had worked it all at a sitting and never been tired at all, as Kipling sings of the artist's dream. Nor did he work for money and certainly not for fame. The two hundred odd articles—I found between sixty and seventy in New York—are scattered in all kinds of publications, almanacs, reports, and society proceedings, as well as in current periodicals. On my third and last visit to him he fished under the masses of papers in the corners of his delightful disorderly scholarly workroom and found a few of his essays taken in pages from the magazines which he presented to me. "The others must be lost," he remarked placidly. His satisfaction had been in the work for its own sake purely.

At a Royal Society meeting in 1895 he had been asked to speak on "Historical method." When he arose, he said he found he had not enough method to give an exposition thereof. It could be put in a word—Research into sources friendly and unfriendly—a vivid picture in the writer's mind of the actors and their relation to the events, and then—the history. Relata refero was not enough, source burrowing was not enough, insight and intuition must be added. He then gave a sketch of the campaign of 1572 as an illustration.

At subsequent meetings of the various societies he always had a word to say; in his study his pen was rarely at rest until January, 1899, when a brief illness silenced his voice and ended his activity.

I deeply regret that this Leiden teacher did not fulfill the ideal sketched by Mr. Adams for the work of a ripe scholar:

At last, throwing all his finished monographs, his preliminary studies and his matured judgments into the crucible, he will analyse, refine, and condense, in the end pouring out the concentrated result—not in thirty volumes, but in two.

I wish we had that masterpiece, compact, self centered, and philosophical, like Shakespeare's man looking before and after. Professor Fruin was the man to produce it for his fatherland, had he only added to his other qualities personal ambition, an excellent thing in an historian, especially to be desired in one so rich in characteristics of integrity, of sympathetic and scholarly insight, and of knowledge of his own national history, as was Robert Fruin.

XVI.—SACRED AND PROFANE HISTORY.

By JAMES HARVEY ROBINSON,
PROFESSOR, COLUMBIA UNIVERSITY, NEW YORK.

SACRED AND PROFANE HISTORY.

By JAMES HARVEY ROBINSON.

Our modern fondness for looking at well nigh everything historically, and the development of several new social sciences, notably economics, sociology, and comparative jurisprudence, have combined to foster so multiform an interest in the past, and have led to so vast and so varied an accumulation of historical knowledge, that the venerable term "history" seems no longer adequate to designate multitudinous and heterogeneous events and conditions, which often appear to have little more than their bygoneness in common. Like an overgrown empire, history threatens to be disrupted into its component parts. If the late Professor Seeley was right, it has already become only "the name of a mere residuum which has been left when one group of facts after another has been taken possession of by some science." This residuum, Professor Seeley believed, must go the way of the rest, the time being "not very distant when a science will take possession of the facts which are still the undisputed property of the historian."

That history will even thus softly and suddenly vanish away, like the baker who met a Boojum, we none of us really fear. But it is clear enough that should such a general dissolution take place, its results would be most unhappy all around. No one can fail, of course, to appreciate the advantages of specialization. It would be as preposterous to impeach it as it would be absurdly gratuitous to defend it. The scientific indispensableness of specialization is everywhere recognized, and many would claim a high educational value for it too. Without the continued productions of monographs like those of Stubbs, Hefele, Rashdall, Lea, Harnack, Voigt, Henry Adams, dealing with some one phase of human organization or interest, or some brief period, progress would cease. Yet this specialization has concomitant disadvantages which need to be emphasized.

Only comparatively recently have constitutional, economic, and legal history, and the development of philosophy, morals, art, and literature become separate fields, subject to intensive cultivation. We have hardly had time as yet to see what effect this subdivision will have upon our educational system or upon the historical treatises which are prepared for the public. But the past furnishes us with a singularly conclusive proof of the disastrous results of putting things asunder which are indissolubly associated by nature. The earliest form of specialization in history, so far as I am aware, was the distinction made between sacred and profane history—a distinction that has been perpetuated by our habit of setting off church history by itself as something concerning only the theologian.

This differentiation was not due, it is true, to that scientific ambition for precision and thoroughness which dictates to-day a careful separation of economic or literary history from what we may vaguely call history at large. While our modern specialization is first and foremost a division of labor, a conscious concession to the exigencies of investigation, the older distinction between sacred and profane history was at first a matter of sentiment, then, later, of prejudice and ill will. That certainly renders its consequences doubly noxious; but if our newer scientific specialization does half as much to distort and obscure our general conceptions of man's past as the older has done, it will do incalculable harm.

We have unwittingly permitted our modern enthusiasm for the principle of the separation of church and state to effect a corresponding divorce in our historical studies. The result has been that we have failed to reckon with a tremendous force whose nature and workings should logically be our first and chief preoccupation in approaching the history of Europe during the past fifteen centuries. I believe that it would not be difficult to prove that no single factor in European history, whether we regard the growth of the state or the development of culture, can in any way be compared in its constant, direct, and obvious influence with the Roman church. Yet our prejudices, or our thoughtlessness, practically exclude the church from consideration in our manuals of general history and in our academic instruction. Something is said, of course, of the mischievous influence of the papacy, of its encroachments on the poor, suffering emperors and kings, of the terrible wickedness and degradation of the ecclesiastical system, which Luther bravely showed up. There is, perhaps, a perfunctory tribute to the monkish scribe busily copying Horace's Satires, or a word about the Truce of God, but the church is known mainly for the pope's arrogance, the wrangling theologians, the inquisition, for its "pigges bones" indulgences, dirty friars, and sly Jesuits. How, it may be asked parenthetically, would the state, that noblest of man's creations, to many the very central theme of historical research, appear if we heard only of royal adulterers, of star chambers, and ship money, of George III's "golden pills," and Tammany's insolence? In short, the church has been represented as a gigantic conspiracy consistently hostile to the normal and beneficent social organization. But in reality it was the most characteristic and natural production of European society as it existed in the Middle Ages. It was brought forth and maintained by the most distinguished men of the period; it included among its officials pretty much the whole educated class. As we revere our Federal Constitution today, so Europe, high and low, clergy and laity alike, revered the constitution of Holy Church for a thousand years.

We all know well enough that no band of conspirators could erect a permanent system opposed to the needs and ideas of the period, but habit and the force of ancient prejudice leads us to relegate a study of the hierarchy to the church historian, while the term history means, as usually received, those matters unconnected with the church, which appears on the scene only as a marplot.

It is true that we no longer speak familiarly of Antichrist, the Scarlet Woman, or the Mystery of Iniquity, as did our ancestors, but centuries of Protestant polemic has transmitted to us a dull, persistent suspicion of the Mediæval Church and all its works, which haunts the minds of otherwise impartial scholars. Another circumstance has, moreover, blinded us still further to the real historic importance of the ecclesiastical organization. We live in an age strikingly secular in its spirit and in a country where the exclusion of the church from all governmental functions and its reduction to a group of voluntary private associations has been carried out with a consistency perhaps unparalleled in the world's history. The mediæval system, which Europe has by no means altogether outgrown, appears to us so monstrous a violation of the principles of civil government that only by a persistent and strenuous cultivation of an artificial historical sympathy can we come to comprehend it, even imperfectly. The position of the church to-day in England and France is full of mystery to us. Court of Arches, church wardens, advowsons, lords spiritual, all are wholly alien to our notions of government and property, and yet they are but the scanty vestiges of a cunningly devised system under which Europe lived for ages—a system which must be understood before there is the least chance of understanding the most serious, perhaps, of all the momentous problems which have faced Europe during the past five centuries.

The Mediæval Church was no exclusively religious organization. It was a state as well, a state rivaling a continental bureaucracy in the importance and variety of its functions and in the precision and efficiency of its mechanism. As Maitland well says: "We could frame no acceptable definition of a state which would not comprehend the church. What has it not that a state should have? It has laws, lawgivers, law courts, lawyers. It uses physical force to compel men to obey its laws. It keeps prisons. In the thirteenth century, though with squeamish phases, it pronounces sentence of death. It is no voluntary society. If people are not born into it, they are baptized into it when they can not help themselves. If they attempt to leave, they are guilty of crimen læsæ majestatis and are likely to be burnt. It is supported by involuntary contributions, by tithe and tax."[1] It is obvious that this ecclesiastical state, the most powerful, extensive, and enduring social organization of which we have any record, bears little resemblance to our Protestant communities. The danger of using the same word for what Innocent III and Mr. Moody understood by church is indeed appalling to a teacher who sees the disparity. If we had occasion to deal with the Council of Jerusalem, as described in Acts, and the Council of Trent, or with the University of Bologna in the

---

[1] Canon Law in the Church of England (1898), pp. 100–101.

thirteenth century and that of South Dakota to-day, we should immediately recognize the necessity of making plain the ambiguity of the terms as the very first step in our explanation. Now, while our students and the general public may well have a shrewd suspicion, after studying one of our current manuals, that the church over which Hildebrand presided must have been very different from the Baptist church around the corner, they have no means of appreciating the real nature of the difference or of estimating its tremendous importance.

The same danger of confusion exists in the case of the civil authority, for we are almost sure to assume a fundamental resemblance between the feudal anarchy and our modern state. When Gregory VII hotly asserted that the civil rule was the invention of evil men, instigated by the devil, it was, after all, no hasty conclusion but the outcome of years of observation. We should doubtless all have agreed, could we have witnessed the conduct of the average ruler of those days, that the Pope's theory of the origin of the state was a fair working hypothesis, all things considered. The dictum of Thomas Aquinas that the secular power is subject to the spiritual, as the body to the soul, was no empty claim. It was not only the most generally accepted opinion, but corresponded pretty well with the actual political and social relations of the Middle Ages.

If, then, both church and state in our modern sense were unknown in Europe until comparatively recently, might it not be worth while to explain so fundamental a matter in our manuals, and endeavor especially to make clear the general organization of the church, its functions, the sources of its power, and the public support which it enjoyed? Indeed, is there the least prospect that the public will understand the history of Europe at all until we mend our ways and give the church its due place? It would hardly be exaggerating its importance if we said that the chief interest of the earlier Middle Ages lies in the development of the Roman Catholic Church; that of the later Middle Ages in its controlling influence at the height of its power; that of the past five centuries in the revolution which overthrew it and replaced it by our modern state and our modern culture.

In spite, however, of my conviction that the neglect of the church is the most conspicuous defect of our instruction in general history, I should be quite misunderstood if it should be inferred that I advocated a more general attention to church history. Not at all; I am not, as I indicated at the start, making a plea for any special field of research, but for a rational reconstruction of our conception of what should be included in a general review of Europe's past. To deal with the Lutheran revolt without understanding how the church was a secular as well as a religious institution is like presenting our civil war as simply the outcome of a different conception in North and South of the nature of the Constitution. To define the French Revolution, as De Tocqueville does, as the destruction of the feudal system is to belittle it. The Civil Constitution of the Clergy betokened as vital a metamorphosis as the decrees of August 4–5 abolishing the feudal dues. So no elementary study of either the Protestant revolt or of the French Revolution can be satisfactory so long as we continue to neglect one of the greatest factors in both movements.

Our attitude toward church history should be on the whole our attitude toward economic or constitutional or literary history. We must divide the vast stock of historical data and conclusions accumulated in all the fields of special research into two separate parts. All that is of a technical nature should be classed "professional," and should usually be so formulated as best to serve the purposes of the expert. The exact contents of St. Francis's first rule, the finances of Glastenbury Abbey at the end of the fifteenth century, or the diplomatic antecedents of the Seven Years' War do not directly concern the public or the students in our schools and colleges. On the other hand, there is much in the thoroughgoing revision which is going on of our notions of man's past which persons with no special knowledge of history will be glad to know and will be the better for knowing.

This distinction between the technical and professional and the popular and general phases of our subject doubtless appears to be very trite and very self-evident. Trite it is not, however, for only modern conditions have rendered it imperative, and so little self-evident is it that some of our most serious perplexities may be ascribed to a failure to recognize it in our instruction and writing. In this country at least history is hardly yet regarded as a technical subject reserved for those who have been prepared by professional training to pursue it. Until recently all our historical works were supposed to meet the needs both of the public at large and of the rare student who might appreciate the purely esoteric. Obviously we can not continue to do this, for, in the first place, the scholar is becoming more exacting and demands a concise, technical statement of the results of research; in the second place, if the public and our college students are to gain the best which history has to give, our whole energy must be directed toward freeing our presentation from every unessential detail which serves only to obscure the great issues and transformation of the past. No detail may be admitted simply because it is true or "interesting" or important to a specialist. Each particular detail chosen must substantiate, enliven, or illustrate the manifold general truths whose number and importance increase daily.

"The history of education," Rashdall well says, "is indeed a somewhat melancholy record of misdirected energy, stupid routine, and narrow one-sidedness. It seems to be only at rare moments in the history of the human mind that an enthusiasm for knowledge and a many-sided interest in the things of the intellect stirs the dull waters of educational commonplace."[1] This depressing reflection is as true of historical instruction as of any other branch of education. But we are now all busy stirring the dull waters of educational commonplace. The development of special historical studies implies a careful reconstructing of our general view of the whole subject; and whether we ultimately accept Ranke's view that the foundation and development of the political order is far the greatest achievement of our race, that it alone gives continuity to the story of the past, or whether we discover in the progress of culture the true import of history, we shall learn to look back with amazement and pity upon a period when general history was taught as if the Church of Rome were a negligible factor.

[1] Universities of the Middle Ages, II, 705.

XVII.—SHOULD RECENT EUROPEAN HISTORY HAVE A PLACE IN THE COLLEGE CURRICULUM?

By CHARLES M. ANDREWS, Ph. D.,
PROFESSOR BRYN MAWR COLLEGE.

SHOULD RECENT EUROPEAN HISTORY HAVE A PLACE IN THE COLLEGE CURRICULUM?

By Charles M. Andrews.

The object of this paper is largely controversial. I do not anticipate any radical changes resulting from its presentation, but by uttering a word of dissent I should like to disturb somewhat, if I may, the complacency with which historical students have placed the events of the last thirty years outside the limits of serious historical study. No propositions in history would seem to be more certainly demonstrable than these: First, that the events of these thirty years are not within the scope of historical treatment; secondly, that in consequence no self-respecting historical writer would concern himself with the problems which these years have to offer; and thirdly, that no teacher who pretends to take a scientific view of historical development would consider himself justified in attempting to deal with the subject. Are these propositions either scientifically or practically sound?

The chief reasons commonly alleged in support of these propositions are as follows: In the first place it is said that the year 1870 marks the close of a clearly defined historical period, one in which a specific set of issues was worked out; that the years since that time are but the first part of an epoch the end of which is not in sight and the characteristic features of which are at present so vague as to defy exact definition; and that this incompleteness renders such a period practically unavailable for historical study and presentation. In the second place, it is said that the material for such study is at present of such a character as to make scientific examination impossible; that much of it is ephemeral, partaking of the nature of newspaper literature, while the real evidence upon which sound conclusions only can be based is still locked up in secret archives, there to remain until the various governments see fit to make it public. In the third place, the objection is raised that these years are too close to give us the proper perspective for even a narrative history and much more for an exposition which aims to explain as well as to record facts, inasmuch as the great problems are scarcely defined and only dimly perceived. And, in the last place, the contention is made that as the majority of those who would exploit this period have lived through the years they are studying, they are bound to be influenced unduly by prejudice and partisan feeling, and, therefore, to be incompetent to present fairly and judicially the evidence at hand.

Each of these objections is weighty, and each has a large foundation of truth upon which to rest. Each is sufficient to render futile any attempt to write of scientific purpose with a view to finality of treatment the history of any one of the European states since 1870, or to determine with precision the problems with which the historian of the future will have to grapple in dealing with the last thirty years of the nineteenth century. We do not know and we can not know what is the final word that posterity will pronounce upon this period of history, and while we can see dimly the nature of the problems with which present society is wrestling we can not determine their proportions, nor can we, with any certainty, forecast their solution. With such an attempt to treat recent history I have nothing to do. The question I would discuss is as to whether recent European history should be made the subject of historical study, particularly in college classes.

In the first place, what is the purpose and end of all historical study and investigation? Is it to train men in powers of criticism and insight; is it to make them more reasonable, cautious, and impartial; is it to awaken the imaginative faculty and render the human mind more competent to interpret truly the thoughts and actions of past generations of men? All these certainly are among the objects to be attained; but are these the only and final objects sought? I think not. The training of men's minds is itself not an end; it is the shaping of a more perfect instrument for the accomplishment of a further work. The more perfect instrument will fashion a more perfect product; the trained mind will produce the more accurate rendering of a past movement or series of movements, but it is the more accurate rendering that is the end, and not the training that has made such rendering possible. Again, is such accurate interpretation of a phase of past history the end and highest purpose of historical study? A student by minute and special investigation, by the employment of accepted canons of criticism, by a truer appreciation of the motives which have actuated men and of the times in which they have lived, may bring forth a monograph upon a particular subject, may rewrite the history of a whole epoch, or may view from a new standpoint the whole of a nation's career. Are each or all of these the end sought, or is each but a means to the accomplishment of something greater still? Do students of to-day recognize no higher aim than the production of the article, the monograph, or the book upon a particular subject? I think that they do. I think that the discovery of truth and the elimination of error, which is the essence and soul of all special historical investigation, is but the preparing of material to be employed in the production of something greater and more comprehensive. The historical world needs the trained and methodical mind; it needs criticism and insight; it needs the exact fact and the honest interpretation, but it needs them for that philosophical synthesis of history, the summing up of all that history is and history means, which, as was said by the first president of this association at its first meeting, is "the highest effort and noblest result toward which these special historical investigations lead."

Now, admitting that historical training and method, historical criticism and minute investigation, are but means to the attainment of this higher end, it is necessary that we determine more exactly what form this historical synthesis should take, and its relation to our subject. Such synthesis is not merely a general history of the world, else the highest end and purpose would be a mere grouping of facts, and our interest in it would be the mere acquiring of information. The object of historical study is not the obtaining of an encyclopedic knowledge of facts. Nor is such synthesis the coordination and correct interpretation of any one set of facts relating to a given subject. The highest end and purpose of history is not to explain the development of political history, nor yet of constitutional, legal, administrative, religious, social, or economic history. Each of these is but a part of a larger whole.

Professor Burgess has concisely and accurately formulated the categories according to which we are to determine the form that the historical synthesis is to take. First, continuity in time; but that is not enough. Secondly, the relation of cause and effect; but that is not enough. Thirdly, the relation of cause and effect, plus the increment of progress. The highest end and purpose of history is, therefore, the synthesis of those facts and phases of history that mark the progressive development of the human spirit. There are histories of nations and states, of institutions and constitutions, but above and over all is History which takes from each those particulars that have made for progress and weaves them into a nobler sequence. We study the Orient, Greece and Rome, the Middle Ages, the Renaissance and Reformation, the seventeenth and eighteenth centuries, the French Revolution and the nineteenth century, in each case for its own sake, but still more in order to determine the part that each has played in producing institutions and ideas destined to shape the civilization of the ages that were to follow. Each period and epoch of history looks back to that which has gone before, and forward to that which comes after; and the character of each is determined not by any one feature, political, religious, or other, but by that one or those several which in that period have done most to expand the human mind and enlarge the human capacity.

But this view of the subject, which is the only logical view, and, therefore, the only scientific one—for history is a science because it is capable of logical treatment—demands that we ask one more question: If we study each epoch for the sake of the light it throws upon that which is to follow, and value the information acquired in proportion to its importance in explaining progress, what is the final goal toward which we are moving? It is inevitably and logically the better understanding of the civilization of the present century, of the present day. There is no possible stopping point short of the present, for all history has been leading up to this, and in the highest sense of our science we study the past that we may better understand the present; not by making historical parallels or in framing arguments drawn from the careers of past nations, but by tracing line by line and sequence by sequence the gradual unfolding of this development of human ideas and human institutions. It is only in this way that we can understand what we have and what we are. Logically the history of the nineteenth century is the culmination of all history; and if one phase of that history was finished in 1870 we must still say, if we would not have our synthesis shamefully incomplete, that we study the period from 1789 to 1870 in order to understand better the character of the unfinished era in which we are now living.

In view of this fact that the last thirty years are the most important years in all history and the logical goal toward which all historical study is directed, are the objections which have been raised sufficient to warrant the widely defended neglect of these years in the college curriculum? I do not think so. Two of these objections are supported by the argument of incompleteness—in one case the incompleteness of the era itself; in the other, the incompleteness of the evidence. But an argument based on the incompleteness of the evidence is dangerous, for it can be raised against half the periods of history. No student of recent events could possibly err so frequently as did Kemble in his history of the institutions of the Anglo-Saxons; nor would he deliberately reject whole groups of evidence as did Niebuhr when he refused to use inscriptions, or Hume when he refused to examine newly discovered papers bearing on the history of the Stuarts. There is plenty of material accessible for a study of the history of Europe since 1870, and it is by no means ephemeral, but official and reliable. Let it be granted, however, that the knowledge to be obtained would be incomplete. Is that a sufficient reason why the students who are graduated from our colleges should be kept in ignorance of the most important era in history? The work to be performed by the college is not professional; it is educational Fifty years ago the cry was that too much time was spent on the history of those "brave men who lived before Agamemnon," and that the student knew more of Marathon and Herodotus, Sphacteria and Thucydides, Cannæ and Polybius than he did of Napier and the Peninsular war, the reform acts, or the unity of Germany. I venture to think that the average reader, whether in college or out of it, finds his darkest ages to be those years since 1870, and even it may be those since 1814, and that, too, in the face of the fact that he is a reader of newspapers and a commentator upon current events. Is it any argument at all that the student should remain in darkness because the light that can be thrown be confessedly fitful and uncertain?

But two stronger arguments remain to be examined. First, that these events are too close to us to be seen in their true proportions; and, secondly, that even if we attempted to interpret them the version would be either perfunctory or biased. To the first objection I would answer, that if the point of view be that of to-day and the glance be backward, then the range is too close and the perspective will be destroyed. But no historical instructor or scholar studies his history backward. I am presenting no brief for "current-events" classes or for courses in the study of modern problems; I am simply urging that the historical continuity which we study in the past be extended to its logical conclusion, and that is down to the present day. History has provided the proper range, and those events which seem confused and amorphous as we look back at them from the present will be found to take on an intelligent and orderly arrangement when approached from the standpoint that history itself has provided—the standpoint of the past. Now, the historical instructor who knows his business teaches general history to 1870 with his glance always forward; why, then, should he change his point of view in considering the history since that time? He may not be a prophet in his diagnosis of the future, for history forbids prophecy, but he will be far better equipped by his knowledge of what problems have been solved in the past to trace the growing importance of those which are becoming the problems of the future. He may see the tendencies dimly, but is it not a gain if he see them at all? Why should the student who leaves college to enter into the world of affairs be left stranded at the years 1870 or 1878 and never be brought to see that which he ought above all things to know, the connection between the Europe of yesterday and the Europe of to-day? The knowledge that he has obtained of the history of the past will fail of its highest value if he be not given this last connecting link.

And now one word about the last objection. We are told

that the treatment of the history of so recent a period must of necessity be one sided and biased. I think that this would be true were the history written by one who has been an active participant in the affairs of the period. But we are also told that such an one ought to do the work; that he who knows diplomacy from the inside, who has sat in legislative chambers, has led troops in battle, or has been a banker, a merchant, or an employer of labor is more competent than the student to write of these things. I believe that there is a fallacy here somewhere, and that unless such persons be trained historians first and men of affairs afterwards they will produce very poor histories. Grote was a banker, Hodgkin, Seebohm, and Lubbock are such still, but we do not trace to that training the excellence of the historical work that each has done. Sybel was for years a member of the Prussian Landtag, but there is no special reason to believe that his historical work owes its high character to the experiences there gained. Gardiner has never held political office, Firth has never been a soldier. That great scholar who has done more for the history of English law than any man living or dead was unable to succeed as a legal practitioner. The best history of the speaker has been written by a woman; and one of the leading authorities upon the battle of Waterloo and the battles of the civil war, whose name stands high abroad as well as at home, never saw a battle or heard a shot fired. That which is true of the past is also true of the present. The writer upon current history need not be and ought not to be a man of affairs. The historical lumber room is full of books; I do not refer to memoirs and recollections, but to historical treatises, which have been written by men who have mistaken their calling. But suppose that that worm, the mere student, the impartial investigator, should give his presentation a twist, would he be doing more than have scores of writers of past times, whose works are standards to the uncritical public—Macaulay, Hume, Froude, even our own Bancroft? Such twist it is the business of the college instructor, if he do his work as he ought, to unwind, that all the strands may be straight.

I have been endeavoring to show thus far that in failing to instruct students in the history of the last thirty years the college has not fulfilled one of its most important functions.

My argument has thus far concerned what is the scientific—that is, logical—demand of the subject, against which no sound objections can be raised. Let me view the subject from the strictly utilitarian standpoint, from the standpoint of the college's educational obligations. The aim of college instruction in history is neither to produce trained historians nor to impart mere information. It is to equip men with habits of thought that we may call scientific, and with an apparatus of knowledge which will have some bearing on the practical sides of life. Every man, whatever be his profession, has an interest in the world in which he is living, and in this country a growing interest in the affairs of the world across the sea. The American is losing his provinciality and is becoming, in the range of his intellectual interests, a cosmopolite. He must know not only the history of the country of which he is a citizen but also the history of those countries whose careers are becoming year by year of greater and greater importance to him. There never was a time, because of the changing material conditions under which we are living, because of rapid communication and transportation, and, above all, because of the changing relations into which this country is entering with the countries of the Old World, when the need to know and the desire to know what the Old World is doing and why it is doing it was greater than it is to-day. Yet in the presence of this fact we are told that though history may be a science and deserving of study and logical treatment up to the year 1870, it is after that date a mere handicraft to be learned, not under the guidance of a competent instructor, but in that worst of practitioner's offices for such a subject, the world of experience. Up to 1870 history may be scientifically treated, after 1870 information regarding it must be got by any haphazard method that happens to be at hand. The student must learn this history from the newspapers, confessedly incomplete and partisan; from editorials written to support a policy, or from magazine articles written to defend a cause. He is to be given no training in the interpretation of recent history, no warning against the dangers of hasty judgments, no word of caution concerning the equal danger of ultra conservatism. The student is taught to feel that he has left his real history behind him with the year 1870, and that what he has learned of history in college has only a remote and not very tangible connection with affairs of to-day. I would not urge that the college instructor use his history as does the Prussian schoolmaster, to arouse a spirit of patriotism and of loyalty to his country. That is well enough, it may be, but it is not the true purpose of history. The college should make it possible for the student to read his newspaper with intelligence, to bring to his reading that attitude of skeptical reserve which will enable him to judge slowly and reasonably; to bring to his reading that knowledge of the events of the last century, of the last decade, of the last year, and it may be of yesterday, which will enable him to determine what issues are vital and what are only incidental, to strike at the heart of a question and not to be misled by multiplicity of details. The newspaper of to-day—and I mean not only the daily, but the weekly, the monthly, and the quarterly—is often a trap for the unwary, and the amount of unintelligent comment upon current events is a characteristic of our present intellectual activity. And in such unintelligent comment there is a great waste of mental ability that ought to be better directed.

Here is the field in which historical instruction in colleges can perform a practical and utilitarian work by virtue of which history will be able to defend its right to be considered a subject of real and immediate value to the unprofessional student. I do not mean by this that an instructor should become the exploiter of every new issue that arises, or should pose as an authority upon technical questions of international or public law. Far from it. I mean that in studying the past he should bring his tale of progress down to the present in such a fashion that the student will have the suitable historical background which the majority of the readers of to-day do not possess. College instruction should show not only the work of the French Revolution and its outworking in the first seven decades of the nineteenth century, but it should show the changing conditions, political, social, and economic, under which we have entered upon the new era. And it should go on to trace in unbroken sequence the chief tendencies of the present so far as an honest and impartial study of the material can disclose them. In such an exposition mistakes will undoubtedly be made, but they will not be comparable with the errors of judgment that are made every day in the newspaper editorial columns, and the hastily written magazine articles that are at the present time to the average man the chief source of information. College instruction should, so far as the practical difficulties that lie in the way can be overcome, act as a corrective to this, and the more completely this can be done the more completely will the college have fulfilled the task which the subject imposes upon it. Historical instruction will also have justified its practical character, creating real values for the student and preparing him for a more intelligent understanding of the events in the issues of which he may be called upon to take part. And furthermore the college in so doing will have prepared the way for that school of diplomacy of which this country stands so greatly in need.

The conclusion that may be drawn from this is as follows: Were European history of the last thirty years made the final stage in a course of modern history, beginning, let us say, with the French Revolution, or, if time allowed, even with the Renaissance and Reformation, the college graduate would face the world better able to understand the great events occurring in it, and at the same time better able to appreciate at their true value the unwieldy commentaries and statements with which he is daily confronted in the press. The French Republic would not fall so often before the man on horseback; the decline and fall of the British Empire, after the fashion of old Rome, would not be so often foretold; Italy would not be so often threatened with utter collapse; Austria-Hungary would not so often break up into fragments; the struggles of the lesser states—Norway, Belgium, Spain, and the Danubian principalities—would take on more orderly and intelligent form; and war, that frequently recurring universal war, would be more commonly discounted on its appearance in newspaper headlines. And, lastly, and perhaps most important of all, were a sounder knowledge possessed of the historical tendencies of the century in America and England as well as in the continental States, there would be, I venture to believe, among those of the next generation who have received their college training in this, fewer jingoes on one side and doctrinaires on the other.

XVIII.—THE COLONIAL PROBLEM.

By HENRY E. BOURNE, B. D.,
PROFESSOR, WESTERN RESERVE UNIVERSITY.

THE COLONIAL PROBLEM.

By Henry E. Bourne.

A year ago the council of this Association appointed a committee to report on the colonial problem. The Economic Association chose a similar committee. These committees divided the field of work so that matters chiefly financial were given to the economists, while administrative affairs and questions of general policy were left to us.

It was concluded that the problems of American colonization, particularly in the Philippines, could be analyzed more successfully if, in a series of detached studies, an explanation were given of the colonial systems, the methods of training officials, etc., of England, Holland, and France, and if accounts were added of their experiments in controlling such possessions as Java, the Malay States, Indo-China, and Madagascar.

An attempt was made to supplement the material already published by forwarding a memorandum of questions, through the State Department, to our diplomatic and commercial agents residing in these dependencies. Not only might fresh impressions be gained in this way, but many things might be learned which, though incidental, really illustrate the process of adjusting a colonial régime to a conquered possession. The State Department, however, sent the questions to the embassies at London, Berlin, The Hague, and Paris, probably believing that satisfactory answers could be procured more readily through the several colonial offices. The replies received up to this time are instructive, and yet are too brief to be more than guides for further investigation.

Of the detached studies planned by the committee only three or four have been undertaken. Two of these—viz, Chinese emigration, and the selection and training of colonial officials—are on the programme this morning.

In discussing some difficulties of American colonization I do not use the word "difficulties" in the sense of objections to the policy of retaining Porto Rico and the Philippines. To a smaller degree, or in a different form, the same difficulties beset the attempt to govern Alaska or the Hawaiian Islands, or any possession distant from our shores and unlikely to be settled by men of American or European descent.

Among the many problems which such a subject suggests I wish to consider chiefly one whose importance is easily lost sight of in these discussions. I refer to the disposition of the authority to make laws.

In the organization of Territories Congress has always sought to promote their early development into self-governing commonwealths, and has therefore allowed the size of the population to determine the time of granting legislative power to a local representative assembly. During the interval, in the Territories carved out of the Northwest Territory, the governor and the judges were to adopt laws from the codes of the older States, subject to the approval of Congress. But in Orleans, according to the act of 1804, legislation was temporarily intrusted to the governor and a council of "thirteen fit and discreet persons of the Territory," chosen by the President. Such a measure marked Orleans as a colony without voice in its own affairs. And this was done intentionally. In the debate on the bill Dr. Eustis, of Boston, declared significantly, "I am one of those who believe that the principles of civil liberty can not be suddenly ingrafted on a people accustomed to a regimen of a directly opposite hue." But the opposition to the bill was so strong that its validity was limited to one year. It set a precedent, however, which may point the way out of some of our present difficulties.

Were Porto Rico not in the Tropics, a thousand miles away, and already peopled by races which have not yet succeeded in managing free institutions, it would bring us no problems not solved long ago; and, in principle, much the same may be said of the Philippine Islands.

Probably in the Hawaiian Islands a modified form of the Territorial system will be workable, and yet the Fifty-fifth Congress, instructed by an elaborate report from its special commission, could not agree upon such modifications in time to establish by law any settled government. Indeed, the old Territorial system is a delicate instrument to intrust to so composite a group of peoples, even if the native Hawaiians are as docile as they are said to be and if political leadership be retained by the comparatively small band of Americans now in control.

In all our new lands race antipathies will probably be aggravated by the influence of the feelings and prejudices which have sprung from our own race conflicts. This danger in a heightened form has already been cunningly used by Aguinaldo and his advisers to convince the Filipinos that they are to be treated like the negro in many of the Southern States. And with the best will in the world we can not look upon dark-skinned peoples, certainly not in Porto Rico, where the negro constitutes a large element of the population, in the same impartial way as would the English or the French, or even the Spaniards. These colonizing nations have no race problem at home, and so they have not merely the intention of fairness toward all—they have the sentiment of it. On the other hand, we feel more as do the Afrikanders. And this attitude is so deeply inbred, the cause of it works with such continuous force in our national life, that the more generous feeling of races toward each other in our new possessions is not likely to affect us. On the contrary, it is likely to be submerged in the volume of our own antipathies. If this is not mere vague foreboding, it will render the problem of Territorial self-government more difficult as union with the United States becomes more intimate.

The situation in Porto Rico is at present less complex than in the Hawaiian Islands, and yet the people, unlike at least the dominant element in Hawaii, have had no training in genuine self-government. It is not surprising, therefore, that the Hawaiian Commission expressly guarded in their report against the supposition that they were incidentally paving the way for a subsequent Porto Rican act. And President McKinley in his message suggested that reconstruction begin in the municipalities, and that the legislative power be at first intrusted to a council, like the council of Orleans. This would place the people of Porto Rico for a time in the position of subjects rather than of citizens, but in the estimation of the President the position would be soon exchanged for one which would carry with it the full privileges of self-government.

Whatever may finally be devised for the Hawaiian Islands and for Porto Rico, it is evident that the Philippines must be treated differently. As the Philippine Commission pointed out in its preliminary report, the most significant fact in this situation "is the multiplicity of tribes inhabiting the archipelago, the diversity of their languages (which are mutually unintelligible), and the multifarious phases of civilization—ranging all the way from the highest to the lowest—exhibited by the natives of the several provinces and islands." It would be no more reasonable for the United States to act as if the inhabitants of these islands possessed national unity than it would be for England to treat the peoples of British India as one nation. If the Territorial régime can be used at all, it must be so adapted to new requirements that it will practically become unrecognizable. The problem is essentially new.

It may not be easy for those who shape public opinion and make wise action by Congress possible to successfully analyze this situation, even if aided by the tests of European experience, for the old way of organizing territory has been found applicable to so many cases that it has become a fixed habit of political thought. Moreover the public mind is not yet quietly settled in the conviction that these islands are permanent parts of American territory. While the majority of the people are unwilling to abandon them at present, it is not clear that this majority would accept without hesitancy, or even positive distaste, such a scheme of administration as the most successful colonial powers of Europe would adopt. This hesitancy is increased by the ceaseless cries of the opponents of annexation that the American people are faithless to their traditions of self-government if the islanders are kept in tutelage. But so long as we are responsible for this territory we should give the inhabitants an effective administration. This should be done while showing every consideration for their natural susceptibilities. But if to good government they prefer liberty after the manner of certain Central American republics, we can only employ the old expedient of appealing "from the Pope badly informed to the Pope better informed."

It can not be assumed that the political education of even the Tagalogs and Visayans will be pushed forward so rapidly that they will soon be fitted for real self-government. It would be strange if what the English, the Dutch, and the French peoples, who also believe sincerely in liberty, have not ventured to attempt we can accomplish in a few years, although, unlike them, we have not been taught by long experience how to deal with Orientals. Nearly twenty years ago the French took a timid step in this direction by the establishment of a colonial council in Cochin China. The minister of the marine, who suggested the measure, said it was his purpose, by successive acts, to prepare for the introduction of French institutions. But great care was taken lest this council become embarrassing to the authorities. The system of elections insured a majority to resident Frenchmen; and the chairman was appointed by the governor-general, who could also suspend the sittings at any time. Political discussion was absolutely excluded. Only four carefully defined things could the council do—adopt decrees regulating private property; deliberate, if the governor-general consented, upon finances and taxation; set forth its opinion upon tariffs, etc., and forward protests to the ministry in France. Obviously a council like this has been hardly more than a school for training in the forms of representative government, and yet it is practically all that has been accomplished in Cochin China toward giving the Annamites a share in legislation. It should be remembered that the communes are under native control, the French having interfered little with municipal institutions.

If we aspire to train the Filipinos for eventual self-government the object can be attained only through a long process of constructive legislation. The new must be skillfully adjusted to the old. To find the proper body in the state to whom a task of this sort should be intrusted is one of the difficulties of American colonization. So long as the Philippines remain under military control the War Department or some commission appointed by the President possesses the power to attempt such work. And the present Philippine commission before its return to this country did begin the establishment of municipal administrations in many towns within the American lines.

But when the war is over and Congress organizes the government of the islands, where is such power to be lodged? Perhaps some will argue that it should be retained by Congress itself. Alaska may, however, furnish a warning. It has been ours for over thirty years, and yet it has neither good local governments nor an effective judicial system. In the newer settlement the inhabitants themselves have been obliged to organize provisional governments and take action without authority of law. Congress has also left the Hawaiian Islands a year longer than appeared necessary without a territorial government, to the serious embarrassment of the local courts, if nothing worse.

But even if the business now thrust upon Congressmen did permit them to give prompt attention to colonial needs they would find impossible the task of legislating for so distant a possession, where all the conditions of life are utterly foreign to American civilization. President Schurman came back with the conviction that "no one but men on the spot can form a judgment as to the machinery for an Asiatic people, or still less of the manner in which that machinery should work."

Every European nation that has dependencies in the Far East has tried to solve this problem on the same principle, though with modifications of detail. The principle has been to leave with the governor and council, and to some extent with officials at home, served by a permanent staff, the duty of meeting by new legislation local needs in such depencies as the Philippine Islands.

In Ceylon and the Straits Settlements England has granted this power to the governor and his council, giving the privy council also the right to issue ordinances. India is naturally treated by itself, but the disposition of the legislative power is particularly suggestive. By successive acts of Parliament it has been granted to the governor-general and his council, composed partly of officials and partly of men unconnected with the service. Within the limits marked out by these tests, according to Lord Selborne, "it is not in any sense an agent or delegate of the Imperial Parliament, but has * * * plenary powers of legislation, as large and of the same nature as those of Parliament itself." And he further explains that it belongs to the courts to decide whether the "prescribed limits have been exceeded." But should critical questions arise the governor-general would doubtless reserve his assent until he had obtained the approval of the secretary of state for India, who, as a member of the cabinet, would act with some sense of his responsibility to Parliament.

The French have managed the matter differently. The governor-general of Indo-China, with theoretically as wide powers as the Viceroy of India, is authorized to issue decrees regulating only the budget, the functions of administrative officers, etc.; legislation, strictly speaking, is reserved to the President of the Republic, acting through a responsible minister. This régime of decrees, as it is called, which controls all colonies except three, the Republic inherited from the Second Empire. In certain cases the President is expected to consult the council of state, but often it is merely upon a report from the minister of the colonies that decrees are issued. Should the chambers at any time enter this field of legislation the President could not subsequently traverse it by decree.

The recent history of Madagascar shows how far such a system may be carried. Since its annexation in 1896, only one important law has been passed by the chambers, and that provided for the application of the tariff of 1892. All other legislation, some of it fundamental in character, has originated in a presidential decree. A judicial and administrative organization has been created, certain sections of the French code have been adopted, changes have been made in the tariff, the system of holding land has been revolutionized, and so on.

Such a solution of the problem is open to obvious objections, which are emphatically stated by M. Leroy-Beaulieu. He calls it "an encroachment of the executive power upon the essential functions of the representatives of the people; its consequence is that colonial questions are settled with the minimum of discussion and information, and then are noiselessly hidden from sight and hearing." But there is much to be said on the other side.

It is difficult to see how the multitude of questions constantly arising in diverse possessions the world over could be wisely and promptly disposed of by a body like the chamber of deputies. Serious evils might go festering on for lack of a remedy, and natives might suffer more in this way than they could from an occasional hasty and ill-considered measure.

Ilbert, Government of India, 206.

In the end the treasury would find it burdensome paying for wars against inconsiderate peoples who could not comprehend the tardy workings of a cumbersome legislative machine.

The prerogatives of the chambers are in no danger, for they can hold the ministers to a full responsibility on these matters, as well as upon the affairs of France itself. The weak spot in the system lies in another quarter. It is exposed to the evils of bureaucracy, to the danger that important matters may be decided by some clerk in the colonial office, rather than by a trained observer on the spot, or even by the minister of the colonies himself.

Evidently the French solution of the problem of legislation for distant dependencies turns, even more than the English, upon the fact of ministerial responsibility. And right here in our case arises a serious difficulty. It would be possible to follow the precedent set in the Orleans act, and grant legislative power to a council somewhat in the way Parliament has given it to the governor-general's council. Further, it would naturally fall to the United States Supreme Court to interpret the act, and to mark the limits within which such a delegated power should work. But what body in the State is to control the decisions of such a Philippine council as the secretary for India controls the governor-general's council? If the President, then, since he is not obliged to act through a responsible cabinet, more power is given to him than by the decree system is conceded to the French Executive. If Congress, there is the old risk of delay or utter neglect.

But this difficulty must be met, and the larger problem of legislation, of which it is an element, must be solved; and, if European experience counts for anything, this will not successfully be solved by a simple extension of the territorial system.

XIX.—A BIBLIOGRAPHY OF THE STUDY AND TEACHING OF HISTORY

Compiled by JAMES INGERSOLL WYER,

LIBRARIAN OF THE UNIVERSITY OF NEBRASKA.

A BIBLIOGRAPHY OF THE STUDY AND TEACHING OF HISTORY.

By James Ingersoll Wyer.

INTRODUCTION.

This bibliography was originally compiled for the Committee of seven on the study of history in schools, and it was expected that it would appear in their report. As time went on both the report and the bibliography grew to such size that it was found impossible to include both of them in the single volume of the extent and cost which the association desired. The bibliography, therefore, is now printed here.

The first section on "The philosophy of history" is, of course, only a selection from the wealth of literature on that subject, and the greater part of the titles included therein represent what perhaps may be called the classics on that subject. The sociologist, the theologian, and the scientist have each their own philosophy of history, and it has been impossible in the scope of this work to attempt to include anything more than the historian's conception of the philosophy of history. If any other titles have been added, it is because they are especially noteworthy. The point of view in the entire work is that of pedagogy and not philosophy, and this in some measure determined what titles to reject or include in this first section.

The second section, "Methodology of history," is explained in the note at its head. In the entire remainder of the bibliography the pedagogical point of view is given first place. The aim has been to include all books and periodical articles in English which are of sufficient note to be of real value to the teacher or student of history. A large number of French and German titles are also included and references made in appropriate places where further information may be had, especially on history teaching in Germany. It is hoped that all foreign titles of importance will be found entered.

It is believed that all abbreviations used will be recognized at once.

Volume and page numbers are separated by a colon; e. g., 6: 170-186 means volume 6, pages 170 to 186.

Price is given for all late books in English, but not for foreign titles.

The following is an outline of the classification by subjects, used in arranging the titles:

Philosophy of history.
Methodology of history.
Educational value of history.
Place in curriculum.
Methods of study and teaching,
    Primary instruction.
    Correlation.
    Use of the sources.
        Collections of sources in American history.
France.
Germany.
Great Britain.
United States.

PHILOSOPHY OF HISTORY.

The most helpful bibliographies of this subject which may be consulted for additional titles are:

Bernheim. Lehrbuch der historischen Methode. p. 522-45.
Flint. Historical philosophy in France.
Adams. Manual of historical literature.
Barth. Die Philosophie der Geschichte als Sociologie.

ADAMS, BROOKS.
    The law of civilization and decay; an essay on history. 393 p. O. N. Y. 1896. Macmillan. $2.50.

BARTH, PAUL.
    Die Philosophie der Geschichte als Sociologie. v. 1. O. Lpz. 1897.
        Examines many systems of sociology and many conceptions of history, finding the true philosophy of history in social development.

BERNHEIM, ERNST.
    Geschichtsforschung und Geschichtsphilosophie. 138 p. D. Göttingen. 1880.

BUCKLE, HENRY THOMAS.
> History of civilization in England. 2 v. O. N. Y. 1875. Appleton. $6.
>> First published in 1857. Not men and institutions, but fixed, unvarying natural laws, govern the course of history.

BUNSEN, CHRISTIAN KARL JOSIAS, FREIHERR VON.
> God in history. 3 v. O. Lond. 1870. Longmans. 42s.
>> See Edinburgh Review 127:496-99. English translation is by Susanna Winkworth. Work first pub. in 1857.

――――.
> Outline of philosophy of universal history. 2 v. O. Lond. 1854. Longmans. 21s.

CARLYLE, THOMAS.
> History. (See his Essays. Houghton ed. 2:228-40; 3:247-56.)
>> First printed in Fraser's Magazine in 1830 and 1833.

COMTE, AUGUSTE.
> The positive philosophy; translated and condensed by Harriet Martineau. 2 v. O. Lond. 1853. Trübner. 16s.
>> Lectures delivered between 1830-42, v. 2 alone concerns history.

DRAPER, JOHN WILLIAM.
> History of the intellectual development of Europe. 2 v. O. Lond. 1876. Bell. 10s.
>> Sees in physiology the philosophy of history. His argument and point of view are much like those of Buckle.

DROYSEN, JOHANN GUSTAV.
> Outlines of the principles of history; trans. by E. B. Andrews. 122 p. D. Bost. 1893. Ginn. $1.10.
>> A good translation of the Grundriss der Historik.

FLINT, ROBERT.
> Philosophy of history in Europe; v. 1, France. 706 p. O. Lond. 1894. Blackwood. 21s.
>> To be initial volume of a comprehensive history of the Philosophy of history.

―――― Philosophy of history in France and Germany. Lond. 1874. Blackwood. 15s.
>> Records all notable attempts at a philosophical study of history. Now almost wholly superseded by preceding title.

FROUDE, JAMES ANTHONY.
> The science of history. (See his Short studies on great subjects. 1868. 1:7-36.)
>> Opposes the theories of Buckle.

HEGEL, GEORG WILHELM FRIEDRICH.
> Die Philosophie der Geschichte. (See his Werke. 1840. Bd. 9.)
>> Best English translation is by J. Sibree. Lond. 1852. An excellent summary is found in Morris, G. S. Hegel's Philosophy of history. Chic. 1887.

LAMPRECHT, KARL.
> Was ist Kulturgeschichte? Beitrag zu einer empirischen Historik. (See Deutsche Zeit. für Geschichtswissenschaft. 1896-97. p. 75-150.)

LAURENT, FRANÇOIS.
>La philosophie de l'histoire. Par. 1870. (Etudes sur l'histoire de l'humanité. v. 18.)
>>A rather over positive review of many of the great writers on philosophy of history.

LOTZE, RUDOLF HERMANN.
>History. (See his Microcosmos. 1894. 2:125-301.)

MONTESQUIEU, CHARLES DE SECONDAT, baron de la Bréde et de.
>Esprit des lois. 2 v. O. Par. 1748.
>>A good English translation is by Thomas Nugent. Attributes great influence to climate and physiography in historical evolution. See Flint. p. 262-80.

MORRIS, GEORGE SYLVESTER.
>Philosophy of the state and history. (See Hall, methods of teaching history. Ed. 2. 1886. p. 149-66.)

PATTEN, SIMON NELSON.
>The development of English thought; a study in the economic interpretation of history. 415 p. O. N. Y. 1899. Macmillan. $3.

ROGERS, JAMES EDWIN THOROLD.
>The economic interpretation of history. 547 p. O. Lond. 1888. Unwin. 16s.
>>Lectures delivered in Worcester college hall, Oxford, 1887-88.

SCHLEGEL, KARL WILHELM FRIEDRICH VON.
>Die Philosophie der Geschichte. 2 v. O. Wien. 1829.
>>The best English translation is by J. B. Robertson. Lond. 1835.

SCHOPENHAUER, ARTHUR.
>History. (See his World as will and idea. Ed. 3. 1896. 3: 220-30.)
>>A theory of the philosophy of history and a denial of a "science" of history.

SHEDD, WILLIAM GREENOUGH THAYER.
>Lectures upon the philosophy of history. D. N. Y. 1873. Draper. 75c.

SIMMEL, GEORG.
>Die Probleme der Geschichtsphilosophie. 109 p. O. Lpz. 1892.
>>Reviewed in Jahresberichte der Geschichtswissenschaft, 1894.

SMITH, GOLDWIN.
>Lectures on the study of history delivered in Oxford, 1859-61. 269 p. N. Y. 1865. Harper.

STRADA, J.
>La loi de l'histoire; constitution scientifique de l'histoire. Paris. 1894.

TOLSTOI, ALEKSYEI KONSTANTINVICH.
>Power and liberty; trans. from the French by Huntington Smith. 132 p. D. N. Y. c1888. Crowell. 75c.
>>Chap. 1, The object of history.
>>Chap. 2, Contradictions of historians.

VICO, GIAMBATTISTA.
>Principi della scienza nuova d'intorno alle commune nature delle nazioni. Napoli. 1725.
>>One of the earliest of the fatalist philosophies of history. Michelet made a partial translation into French in 1827.

VOLTAIRE, FRANÇOIS MARIE AROUET DE.
Philosophie de l'histoire. Par. 1765.
<blockquote>First printed alone, but in 1769 and after it is found as an introduction to his Essai sur les moeurs et l'esprit des nations.
Bernheim says that Voltaire is the first to use the term Philosophy of history. It is notable rather for brilliance than for exactness. A series of brief, loose-woven chapters reveals a vague and imperfect conception of the term Philosophy of history. See Flint, p. 289-304.</blockquote>

METHODOLOGY OF HISTORY.

This section includes titles of articles which are not preeminently and essentially pedagogical. Those are found under Methods of study and teaching. Analytic and synthetic criticism of the materials of history; grouping of results; historical research; the work of the historian rather than the teacher; all that is meant by the German "Historik" is in this section.

An extensive bibliography of Historical method 1450-1850 is given in Bernheim, section 3 of chapter 2 and is not reprinted here.

ACTON, JOHN EMERICK EDWARD DALBERG ACTON, LORD.
A lecture on the study of history delivered at Cambridge, June 11, 1895. 142 p. D. N. Y. 1895. Macmillan. 75c.

ADAMS, HERBERT BAXTER.
Is history past politics? (See Ass'n of colleges and preparatory schools of the Middle States and Maryland. Proceedings. 1894, p. 26-38.)

ARBOIS DE JUBAINVILLE, MARIE HENRI D'.
Deux manierès d'écrire l'histoire; critique de Bossuet, d'Augustin Thierry et de Fustel de Coulanges. Par. 1896.

ARNOLD, THOMAS.
Introductory lectures on modern history . . . with notes by Henry Reed. Ed. 6. O. Lond. 1874. Longmans. 7s. 6d.
<blockquote>First edition was in 1842. The inaugural lecture is especially valuable.</blockquote>

BARNES, MRS. MARY DOWNING (SHELDON).
History, a definition and a forecast. (See Annals Amer. Acad. 1895. 6:128-31.)

BASCOM, JOHN.
The historic sense. 12 p. Chic. 1881.

BIRRELL, AUGUSTINE.
The muse of history. (See his Obiter dicta. 1887. 2:196-223.)

BISSET, ANDREW.
Essays on historical truth. 468 p. O. Lond. 1871. Longmans. 14s.
<blockquote>Important exposition of the methods in which historical investigations should be conducted. The author illustrates by critical reviews of famous men and books.</blockquote>

BODIN, JEAN.
> Methodus ad facilem historiarum cognitionem. Par. 1566.
>> See Flint's Historical philosophy in France, p. 193, and Bernheim's Lehrbuch, p. 152-55, for extended description and comment on this pioneer work, the first French book with any claim to scientific method.

BOURDEAU, LOUIS.
> L'histoire et les historiens. 472 p. O. Paris. 1888.
>> Defines history as "La science des developpements de la raison."

CLEVELAND, ROSE ELIZABETH.
> History. (See her George Eliot's poetry and other studies. 1885, p. 63-83.)

CREIGHTON, MANDELL.
> Picturesqueness in history. (See Cornhill magazine. 1897. 75: 305-20.)
>> Also in Littell's living age. 1897, 213:39-49. A lecture delivered at the Royal Institute.

DOLCI, P.
> Sintesi di scienza storica. Roma (?). 1887.

DROYSEN, JOHANN GUSTAV.
> Grundriss der Historik. Ed. 3. 90 p. O. Lpz. 1882.
>> A philosophical discussion of the nature of history and historical criticism. Translated under title Outline of the principles of history by E. B. Andrews. Ginn. 1893.

DUFF, SIR MOUNTSTUART ELPHINSTONE GRANT.
> Address to the Royal historical society, Feb. 18, 1892. 22 p. O. n. t. p.
>> Also in Royal society transactions. 1892, 6:315-38.

EMERSON, RALPH WALDO.
> History. (See his Essays. Houghton ed. 1892. Ser. 1.)

FLEGLER, ALEXANDER.
> Ueber das Wesen der Historie und die Behandlung derselben; zwei Vorlesungen gehalten bei Eröffnung seiner Vorträge über die Geschichte des Alterthums an der Akademie zu Bern. Bern. 1831.

FREEMAN, EDWARD AUGUSTUS.
> The unity of history; the Rede lecture delivered in the Senate house before the Univ. of Cambridge ... May 24, 1872. 59 p. O. Lond. 1872. Macmillan. 2s.
>> Also forms p. 296-339 of his Comparative politics. 1873.

> ———— The use of historical documents. (See Fortnightly rev. 1871, 16: 321-36.)

FROUDE, JAMES ANTHONY.
> The scientific method applied to history. (See his Short studies on great subjects. 1868. 2:459-87.)

GACHON, P.
> Les methodes historiques et les historiens en France. au 19me siècle. Montpellier. 1891.

GERVINUS, GEORG GOTTFRIED.
>   Grundzüge der Historik. 95 p. O. Lpz. 1837.
>> The first important publication on the subject. Despite its title it is only a monograph summarizing the conditions for artistic historical writing and sketching the various kinds from the æsthetic standpoint.

HARRISON, FREDERIC.
>   Historical method of J. A. Froude. (See Nineteenth cent. 1898, 44: 373-85.)
>> Reviewed in Nation 67: 366.

———.
>   The historical method of Prof. Freeman. (See Ninteenth cent. 1898, 44: 791-806.)

———.
>   Meaning of history . . . 482 p. O. Lond. 1894. Macmillan. $2.25.
>> Chapters 1-4.

JODL, FRIEDERICH.
>   Die kulturgeschichtsschreibung; ihre Entwickelung und ihr Problem. 124 p. O. Halle. 1878.

JOHNSTON, WILLIAM PRESTON.
>   Definition of history. (See Amer. hist. ass'n. Report. 1893, p. 43-53.)

KINGSLEY, CHARLES.
>   Limits of exact science as applied to history. (See his Roman and the Teuton. 1864, pref. p. 9-56.)
>> Inaugural lecture at Univ. of Cambridge. Printed separately. 72 p. D. Lond. 1860.

LACOMBE, P.
>   De l'histoire considérée comme science. 415 p. O. Par. 1894.
>> Reviewed in Revue critique, 1895, v. 1, p. 132, and in Revue historique 59: 408, and the author's point of view declared analogous to that of Frederic Harrison in the Meaning of history.

LAMPRECHT, KARL.
>   Alte und neue Richtungen in der Geschichtswissenschaft. 1. Ueber geschichtlicher Auffassung und geschichtliche Methode. 2. Ranke's Ideenlehre und die Jungrankianer. 79 p. O. Ber. 1897.

LENGLET DU FRESNOY, NICOLAS.
>   Methode pour étudier l'histoire, avec un catalogue des principaux historiens. 4 v. Q. Par. 1713.

———.
>   Supplement. 2 v. 1740.
>> A work of immense industry, the best handbook of history in its day, but of no value now save as history.
>> For description and criticism of the book see Flint, Historical philosophy in France, p. 251.

LILLY, WILLIAM SAMUEL.
>   The new spirit in history. (See Nineteenth cent. 1895, 38: 619-33.)
>> Also in Eclectic mag., 1895, 125: 721-31; Littell's living age, 1895, 207: 737-48, and in his Essays and speeches. 1897, p. 193-223.

LORENZ, OTTOKAR.
> Friedrich Christoph Schlosser und über einige Aufgaben und Principien der Geschichtsschreibung. 91 p. S. Wein. 1878.
>> Also in his Die Geschichtswissenschaft in Hauptrichtungen und Aufgaben. 1886, 1:1-89.

MACAULAY, THOMAS BABINGTON.
> History. (See Edin. rev. 1828, 47: 331-67.)
>> A review of Romance of history by Henry Neele.

MARSELLI, N.
> La scienza della storia. Torino. 1873.

MAURENBRECHER, WILLIAM.
> Geschichte und Politik. 27 p. O. Lpz. 1884.

MODERN critical and historical school, its methods and tendencies (in Dub. Rev. 1898, 123:121-39).

MORISON, JAMES COTTER.
> History. (See Ency. Brit. 1881, 12:19-24.)
>> A suggestive article on the nature and development of historical science.

MORTET, C. AND V.
> La science de l'histoire. (See La grande encyclopédie. 1894. v. 22. 88 p.)
>> Also reprinted separately. One of the best French works on historical method.

PFLUGK-HARTTUNG, JULIUS VON.
> Geschichtsbetrachtungen. 47 p. O. Gotha. 1890.
>> An outline of historical method.

PRIESTLY, JOSEPH.
> Lectures on history and general policy. 2 v. O. Lond. 1793.

RABIER, E.
> Leçons de philosophie. v. 2:316-45. Par. 1892 (?).
>> Judicious treatment of Testimony; Historical criticism; Methodology.

REED, HENRY.
> Study of history. (See his Lectures on English history. 1885. p. 13—).

RHOMBERG, ADOLF.
> Die Erhebung der Geschichte zum Range einer Wissenschaft. 94 p. O. Wien. 1883.

ROGGE, H. C.
> De wetenschap der geschiedenis en hare methode. 42 p. O. Amsterdam. 1890.
>> This sketch of historical method was an inaugural address at the University of Amsterdam.

ROSA, G.
> Storia della storia. Milano. 1884.
>> An excellent general sketch.

ROUND, JOHN H.
> Historical research (in Nineteenth cent. 1898, 44:1004-14).

SCHILLER, JOHANN FRIEDRICH CHRISTOPH.
> Was heisst und zu welchem Ende studiert man Universalgeschichte? 32 p. D. Jena. 1789.

SCHOULER, JAMES.
    Historical grouping. (See Mag. Amer. hist. 1887, 18: 326-29.)
        Paper read at Amer. hist. ass'n meeting, May, 1887. Also in his Historical briefs.

———.
    Historical testimony. (See Amer. hist. ass'n. Report. 1895, p. 435-42.)
        Also in his Historical briefs, 1896.

———.
    The spirit of historical research. (See Amer. hist. ass'n. Papers. 1890, 4: 97-106.)
        Also in Nat. Mag. 1892, 15: 250-57 and in his Historical briefs, 1896.

SEIGNOBOS, CHARLES.
    Les conditions psychologiques de la connaissance en histoire. (See Revue philosophique, 1887, numbers 7 and 8.)
        A careful study of the question, How is any particular historical proposition to be determined?

SMEDT, CHARLES DE.
    Principes de la critique historique. 292 p. D. Paris. 1883.
        Clear rules for criticism of material, use of sources, and formation of narrative. While in no way a systematic treatise and often inadequate and insufficient for the close student, it is still one of the best books on the subject.

STUCKENBERG, JOHN HENRY WILBURN.
    Ranke and his method. (See Andover rev. 1887, 7: 117-37.)

TARDIF, AD.
    Notions elémentaires de critique historique. 30 p. O. Paris. 1883.
        A mere outline.

TAYLOR, ISAAC.
    History of the transmission of ancient books to modern times, together with the process of historical proof . . . 413 p. D. Lond. 1859.

THE study of history. (See Cornhill magazine. 1861, 3: 666-80; 4: 25-41.)
        Discusses the question, Is history a science?

THORNTON, WILLIAM THOMAS.
    History's scientific pretensions. (See his Old fashioned ethics. 1873, p. 84-112.)

WACHSMUTH, WILHELM.
    Entwurf einer Theorie der Geschichte. Halle. 1820.
        The first modern book devoted solely to exposition of the conception and method of historical science.

WORSLEY, HENRY.
    Methods of historical inquiry. (See Dub. rev. 1881, 88: 269-88.)
        Reviews Freeman, Comparative politics; Maine. Ancient law and village communities; Spencer. Study of sociology.

WRIGHT, JOHN HENRY.
    The place of original research in college education. (See Nat. educ. ass'n. Proceedings. 1882, p. 91-115.)

EDUCATIONAL VALUE OF HISTORY.

ANDREWS, CHARLES McLEAN.
    History as an aid to moral culture. (See Nat. educ. ass'n. Proceedings. 1894, p. 397–411.)

———.
    Value of history for moral culture. (See Journal of pedagogy. 1893, 6: 42–43.)

BALDWIN, JOSEPH.
    The study of American history as a training for good citizenship. (See Nat. educ. ass'n. Proceedings. 1895, p. 139–42.)

BARBAULD, ANNA LÆTITIA.
    On the uses of history. (See her Life and works. 1874, 2: 393–99.)

BLACKIE, JOHN STUART.
    What does history teach? 123 p. S. N. Y. 1886. Scribner. 75c.

BLAIR, FRANK G.
    The social function of history. (See Nat. Herbart soc. Yearbook. 1898, 4: 44–56.)

BONA, M.
    Zweck und Behandlung des Unterrichts in der Geschichte. (See Pädagogium. 1887, 9: 246–.)

BRETTSCHNEIDER, HARRY.
    Der Wert des Geschichtsunterrichts für die Jugendbildung. 22 p. Q. Insterburg. 1895.

BRISTOLIENSIS. *Pseud.*
    History as an instrument of education. (Educ. rev. (Lond.) 1900, 2: 162–67.)
        Suggested by The matriculation history of England. C. S. Fearenside.

CAMPE, J. F. C.
    Ueber die ethische Aufgabe des Geschichtsunterrichts. (See Zeit. für das Gym. 1861, 15: 625–38.)

CARRINGTON, HENRY BEEBE.
    History a patriotic force in the schools. (See Nat. educ. ass'n. Proceedings. 1889, p. 333–39.)

CHASE, WAYLAND J.
    Value of history in school training. (See School journal. 1897, 55: 237–38.)
        Address delivered at a convocation of Morgan Park (Ill.) academy.

CROTHERS, SAMUEL M.
    History a teacher of liberal religion. (See New World. 1899, 8: 215–28.)

EDWARDS, WALTER A.
    The chief aim in the study of history. (See Nat. educ. ass'n. Proceedings. 1892, p. 348–53.)

FLEMMING, HANS.
    Geschichtsunterricht und Kulturgeschichte. 47 p. O. Osterwieck. 1897.
        Appeared in Pädagogische Warte for 1896.

FOUILLÉE, ALFRED.
    Historical and political instruction. (See his Education from a national standpoint. 1892, p. 218–25.)
FOULKE, WILLIAM PARKER.
    The right use of history. 44 p. O. Phil. 1856.
        Discourse before the Historical soc. of Penn., Nov. 25, 1850; theme, "The use of history in the elementary education of our people, particularly in the common schools."
FRITZSCHE, R.
    Nach welchen Grundsätzen ist der Geschichtsunterricht zur gestalten, wenn er monarchisch-patriotische Gesinnung wecken und historische Sinn bilden soll? 26 p. O. Bielefeld. 1895. (Sammlung pädagogischer Vorträge, 10.)
HALL, JOHN.
    Uses of history. 27 p. O. N. Y. 1889. N. Y. hist. soc.
        Address before the N. Y. hist. soc., Nov. 21, 1889.
HENZE, E.
    Wie ist der Geschichtsunterricht zu gestalten, wenn er nicht nur Leben wecken, sondern auch zu einer für das Leben bildenden Analyse der Gegenwart führen soll? (See N. Päd. Zg. 1896, nos. 3–6: 17–19, 54–55, 61–63.)
HERBART, JOHANN FRIEDRICH.
    Geschichte. (See his Sämmtliche werke. 1851, 10: 293–301.)
HIGGINSON, THOMAS WENTWORTH.
    Why do children dislike history? (See Hall. Methods of teaching history. Ed. 2. 1886, p. 227–29.)
HILL, FRANK A.
    Aims in teaching civil government. (See Nat. educ. ass'n. Proceedings. 1891, p. 657–65.)
HISTORY, its use and meaning. (See Westminster rev. 1854, 62: 420–48).
    Review of Carlyle's Past and present.
HOWARD, GEORGE ELLIOTT.
    Place of history in modern education. (See Nebr. State hist. soc. Transactions. 1885, 1: 202–17.)
        Also in State Journal, Lincoln, Nebr. Jan. 18, 1885. A thoughtful article which deserves to be better known.
HOWELL, SELAH.
    History in its relations to practical life. (See Education. 1881, 1: 255–59.)
KNEPPRECHT, CHRISTIAN.
    Bedeutung und Aufgabe des Geschichtsunterrichtes. (See Päd. archiv. 1896, 38: 226–33.)
KÖHLER, RICHARD.
    Ueber die Verbindung des Culturgeschichtlichen mit dem Geschichtsunterricht. (See Pädagogium. 1894, 16: 281–303.)
LADENBAUER, W.
    Der historische Unterricht als Grundlage einer religiösen Weltanschauung. 53 p. O. Budweis Gym. 1885.

LECKY, WILLIAM EDWARD HARTPOLE.
    The political value of history. 57 p. O. Lond. 1892. Arnold. 2s. 6d.
        Address before the Birmingham and Midland institute, Oct., 1892.

LIEBER, FRANCIS.
    On history and political economy as necessary branches of superior education in free states. (See his Miscellaneous writings. 1881, 1:179–203.)

LLOYD, J. E.
    History. (See Spencer. Chapters on the aims and practice of teaching. 1897, p. 141–55.)
        A plea for history study in elementary and secondary schools, for its ethical and informative value.

McCULLAGH, W. TORRENS.
    Use and study of history; being the substance of a course of lectures delivered in Dublin in March, 1841. O. Lond., 1842. Chapman. 7s. 6d.

——. Ed. 2. 314 p. O. 1845.

McMASTER, JOHN BACH.
    The social function of United States history. (See Nat. Herbart. soc. Yearbook. 1898, 4:26–30.)
        Also in School journal. 1898, 56:597-98.

MAYDORN, B.
    Der Geschichtsunterricht als Vorbereitung auf das praktische Leben. (See Päd. archiv. 1890, 32:226–40.)

MILLSPAUGH, J. F.
    Ethical value of history in elementary schools. (See Nat. educ. assn. Proceedings. 1896, p. 410–14.)

MOWRY, WILLIAM AUGUSTUS.
    History as a means of teaching patriotism.
    (See School journal. 1897, 50:351–52.)

——
    What special work should be undertaken in the elementary school to prepare the pupils for the duties of citizenship? (See Nat. educ. ass'n. Proceedings. 1893, p. 273–78).

POST, TRUMAN M.
    History as a teacher of social and political science; an address delivered at Springfield, Ill., Feb. 16, 1870. 32 p. O. Springfield, 1870.

PROTHERO, GEORGE WALTER.
    Why should we learn history? (See Nat. rev. 1895, 24:460–74.)
        Also in Eclectic mag. 1895, 124 349–59. Inaugural lecture at Edinburgh univ. Oct. 16, 1894.

ROHMEDER, WILHELM.
    Ohne Vaterlandsgeschichte keine Vaterlandsliebe; eine Studie im Hinblick auf den Geschichtsunterricht in den technischen Unterschulen. 48 p. O. Munchen. 1872.

SEYMOUR, GEORGE E.
> The study of history; its functions. St. Louis. 1889.
> Privately printed.

———.
> Value of historical reading. (See Amer. jour. of educ. Mar.-May, 1896, 29: no. 3-5.)

SIMEONER, A.
> Der Geschichtsunterricht in seiner erziehlichen Bedeutung. 22 p. O. K. K. Staats. Real u. Ober Gym. Ungarisch-Hradisch. 1893.

SLOANE, WILLIAM MILLIGAN.
> How to bring out the ethical value of history. (See School review. 1898, 6: 724-44.)
> An address before the New England association of colleges and preparatory schools.

SPECKMANN, S.
> Humanität und Geschichtsunterricht. (See Pädagogium. 1888, 10: 602– .)

SPENCER, HERBERT.
> Education; intellectual, moral, and physical. 283 p. O. N. Y. 1895. Appleton. $1.25.
> History, p. 64-71.

STODDART, SIR JOHN.
> On the uses of history as a study. (See his Introduction to the study of universal history. 1850, p. 3-103.)

STORRS, RICHARD SALTER.
> Value of historical study. (See Mag. of Amer. hist. 1887, 18: 157-60.)

THOMPSON, ANNA BOYNTON.
> Educational value of history. (See Educ. rev. 1895, 9:359-67.)

ULBRICHT, EDMUND.
> Die Verwertung des Geschichtsunterricht zur politischen Erziehung unseres Volkes. (Program Dresden-Neustadt. 1893.)

WEBER, GEORG.
> Der Geschichtsunterricht auf Schulen ein vorzügliches Mittel zur Bildung des charakters und richtiger Lebensanschauung in der deutschen Jugend. 27 p. O. Heidelberg. 1850.
> From Heidelberger Jahrbücher der Literatur. 1850.

WEIGAND, HEINRICH.
> Der Zweck des Geschichtsunterrichts. (See Pädagogium. 1893, 15: 377-86.)

WHITE, ANDREW DICKSON.
> On studies in general history and the history of civilization. (See Amer. hist. ass'n. Papers. 1886, p. 49-72.

WYLIE, ANDREW.
> The uses of history. (See Indiana hist. soc. Publications. v. 1. 1897, p. 79-117.)
> Discourse delivered before the society Dec. 11, 1831.

ZIEGLER, C.
Der Geschichtsunterricht im Dienste der Erziehung; nach den Grundsätzen der Herbartischen Pädagogik dargestellt. Ed. 2. 44 p. O. Minden. 1894.

PLACE IN CURRICULUM.

APPROVED course of study for high schools and academies in the State of New York. (See School review. 1899, 7:58-60.)
Approved by the Dept. of Public Instruction.

CHAMBERS, HENRY.
Course of study in history for high schools. (See School review. 1899, 7:56-57.)
Adopted by the General conference of Louisiana high school teachers.

COOLIDGE, A.
A plea for study of the history of northern Europe. (See Amer. hist. ass'n. Report. 1895, p. 445-51.)

CROSWELL, T. R.
Courses of study in the elementary schools of the United States. (See Ped. sem. 1897, 4:294-335.)

CURRICULA and programmes of work for higher schools in Prussia, together with explanations and practical directions. (See Gt. Britain—Educ. dept. Special rept's. on educational subjects. 1898, v. 3:253-325.)

ELIOT, CHARLES WILLIAM.
What is a liberal education? (See Century. 1895, 28:203-12.)
One page on the place of history in the curricula of American schools.

ENTRANCE requirements in history. (See School review. 1896, 4:341-80.)

ENTRANCE requirements in history; report of conference. (See School review. 1895, 3:469-85.)

FREEMAN, EDWARD AUGUSTUS.
Office of the historical professor. 61 p. D. Lond. 1884. Macmillan. 2s.
Inaugural lecture at Oxford Oct. 15, 1884. Also in his Methods of historical study. Reviewed by S. R. Gardiner in Acad. 1884, 26:386.

GOODWIN, EDWARD J.
The curriculum of a small high school. (See School review. 1895, 3:268-80.)

GREENE, E. B.
College-entrance requirements with special reference to the problem of the ordinary public high school of the central west. (See Nat. educ. ass'n. Proceedings. 1897, p. 677-79.)

HART, ALBERT BUSHNELL.
Entrance requirements in history. (See Educ. rev. 1895, 10: 417-29.)

HOLCOMBE, WILLIAM P.
Place of history in a college course. (See Ass'n of colleges and preparatory schools of the middle states and Maryland. Proceedings. 1888, p. 52-54.)

JAY, JOHN.
    The demand for education in American history. (See Amer. hist. ass'n. Papers. 1890, p.19-43.)

JOHNSTON, WILLIAM PRESTON.
    History; its place in a liberal education. 15 p. O. n. p. 1872.
        An address to Educational association of Virginia.

KLEMM, L. R.
    A want and how to meet it. (See Education. 1886, 6: 248-56.)

LUEBKER, FRIEDRICH.
    Die Beziehungen der Geschichte zur Pädagogik. (See Allg. monatsschrift. Feb. 1825.)

MACE, WILLIAM HARRISON.
    History in the high schools; how much and in what order? (See Associated acad. prins. of N. Y. State. Proceedings. 1897, p. 164-67.)

MCKELWAY, ST. CLAIR.
    The study of political history in high schools and academies. (See Univ. State of N. Y., 23rd Convocation, 1885. Proceedings, p. 131-38.)
        In regents' report No. 99.

MCLAUGHLIN, ANDREW C.
    The study of history in schools. (See Nation. 1899, 69: 151.)
        Reply to a criticism of the Report of the committee of seven.

MCMURRY, FRANK.
    Concentration. (See Nat. Herbart Soc. Yearbook. 1895, 1: 27-69.)

NATIONAL EDUCATIONAL ASSOCIATION, COMMITTEE OF FIFTEEN.
    Report on history. (See Educ. rev. 1895, 9: 252-57; 282.)

NATIONAL EDUCATIONAL ASSOCIATION—COMMITTEE OF TEN ON SECONDARY SCHOOL STUDIES.
    Report. (See United States Bureau of education. Report of the commissioner, 1892-93. 2: p. 1415-94.)
        Contains a bibliography of the literature evoked by the report. Also published separately by Bureau of educ. as whole No. 205 and by Amer. book co. N. Y. 1894.

NEW ENGLAND ASSOCIATION OF COLLEGES AND PREPARATORY SCHOOLS.
    Report of the conference on entrance requirements in history. (See School review. 1895, 3: 469-85.)
        This report is discussed in the School review for Dec., 1895, 3: 597-631, and in the Educational review for Dec., 1895, 10: 417-29. The report recommends two years of solid work and plenty of written exercises as a minimum and further strongly recommends four years of work, including Greek and Roman history.

PEARSON, CHARLES HENRY.
    History in state schools. (See his Reviews and critical essays. 1896, p. 202-38.)

ROBINSON, EDWARD VAN DYKE.
    An ideal course in history for secondary schools. (See School review. 1898, 6: 672-78.)

SALMON, LUCY MAYNARD.
   Shall historical studies be a necessary part of college-entrance requirements? (See Journal of pedagogy. 1896, 10: 19–22.)

———.
   Unity in college entrance history. (See Educ. rev. 1896, 12: 151–68.)

SCHINDLER, SOLOMON.
   History in public schools. (See Arena. 1889, 1: 41–54.)

SEELEY, LEVI.
   Common-school system of Germany and its lessons to America. 251 p. D. N. Y. 1896. Kellogg.
   The course of study, chap. 14.

STEPHENS, HENRY MORSE.
   Shall historical studies be a necessary part of college-entrance requirements? (See Ass'n of colleges and preparatory schools of the middle states and Maryland. Proceedings. 1896, p. 33–48.)
   Discussion by L. M. Salmon and J. B. McMaster.

THORPE, FRANCIS NEWTON.
   History and political economy in manual training schools. (See Education. 1888, 8: 351–57.)

———.
   In justice to the nation: American history in American schools, colleges, and universities. 22 p. O. 1886.
   Reprinted from Education.

U. S.—BUREAU OF EDUCATION.
   National educational association committee [of ten] on secondary school studies; report with reports of the conferences. 249 p. O. Wash. 1893.
   History, p. 162–203.

WARRINER, HENRY PITT.
   Place of history in the preparatory schools. (See Ass'n of colleges and preparatory schools of the middle states and Maryland. Proceedings. 1894, p. 44–50.)

WARREN, E. C.
   Can American history be put into all courses in the high school? (See School review. 1898, 6: 101–4.)
   Paper read at meeting of Michigan schoolmasters' club.

WHITE, GREENOUGH.
   Plea for expansion in the teaching of American history. (See School and college. 1892, 1: 286–94; 326–36.)

WHITTON, FREDERICK.
   The secondary schools and the colleges. (See Nation. 1899, 69: 108–09.)
   Says that the recommendations of the Report of the committee of seven for four years' history work are impossible.

METHODS OF STUDY AND TEACHING.

Subheads: Primary instruction; Correlation; Use of the sources; France; Germany; Great Britain; United States.

ADAMS, CHARLES KENDALL.
 Manual of historical literature. 665 p. D. N. Y. 1882. Harper. $2.50.

——— ———. Ed. 3. 720 p. O. 1889.
 The 30-page introduction is on The study of history. The body of this work is now sadly out of date, as but little change or addition has been made in it since the first edition in 1882.
 The American library association has in preparation an Annotated bibliography of American history, wh.ch is promised during 1900. It is under competent editorship and will furnish a long-needed supplement to Adams in its field.

———.
 On methods of teaching history. (See Hall. Methods of teaching history. Ed. 2. 1886, p. 203-13.)

———.
 Recent historical work in colleges and universities of Europe and America. (See Amer. hist. ass'n. Papers. 1890, 4: 39-65.)
 Also in Mag. of Amer. hist. 23: 111-31.

ADAMS, HERBERT BAXTER.
 Methods of historical study. (See Johns Hopkins Univ. studies. 1884. Ser. 2, Nos. 1-2, p. 87-94.)

———.
 Special methods of historical study. (See Hall. Methods of teaching history. Ed. 2. 1886, p. 113-47.)

———.
 The study and teaching of history. 18 p. O. Richmond. 1898.
 Phi Beta Kappa address at William and Mary college.

ALLEN, WILLIAM FRANCIS.
 Gradation and topical method of historical study. (See Hall. Methods of teaching history. Ed. 2. 1886, p. 231-321.)

———.
 History topics for the use of high schools and colleges. 121 p. S. Bost. 1890. Heath. 25c.
 Preface explains the topical method.

ALTAMIRA, RAFAEL.
 La enseñanza de la historia. 278 p. O. Madrid. 1891. (Museo pedagógica de instruccion primaria.)

——— ———. Ed. 2. 475 p. D. 1895.
 A very useful and impartial work. First issued in parts. It contains much matter describing secondary and higher historical instruction in Europe and the United States.

AMERICAN HISTORICAL ASSOCIATION, COMMITTEE OF SEVEN.
 Report on the study of history in schools. 267 p. D. N. Y. 1899. Macmillan. 50c.
 Also in Amer. hist. ass'n. Report. 1898, p 427-564.
 Reviewed by G. E. Howard in Educ., Rev., Mar., 1900, 19:257-68, and by N. M. Butler in Amer. Hist. Rev. Jan., 1900, 5: 320-23.

ANDREWS, ELISHA BENJAMIN.
  Brief institutes of general history. 440 p. D. Bost. 1887. Silver, Rogers. $2.
    The division of matter follows the best German text-books. See especially chap. 1 on methods.

——.
  The indispensableness of historical studies for teachers. (See Amer. inst. of instruction. Proceedings. 1889, p. 1-14.)

ATKINSON, WILLIAM PARSONS.
  On history and the study of history; three lectures. 107 p. S. Bost. 1894. Roberts. 50c.

BAAR, JOSEPH.
  Studien über den geschichtlichen Unterricht an den höheren Lehranstalten des Auslandes. Pts. 1-2. 56 p. O. Ostern. 1895-97.
    A Malmedy "programm;" pt. 1, France, Russia, North America; pt. 2, England, Spain, Norway.

BACON, THOMAS R.
  Study of history. (See Overland Monthly. 1896, n. s. 27:427-34.)

BAIN, ALEXANDER.
  Education as a science. 453 p. D. N. Y. 1886. Appleton. $1.50. (Internat. sci. ser.)
    Method in history, p. 281-87.

BALDAMUS, ALFRED.
  Erfüllung moderner Forderungen an den Geschichtsunterricht. (See Neue Jahrb. f. das klass. Alterthum. 1898. v. 2: 307-17.)

BALDWIN, JOSEPH.
  School management and school methods. 395 p. D. N. Y. 1897. Appleton. $1.50. (Internat. educ. ser).
    History, p. 306-11.

BARNES, MRS. MARY DOWNING (SHELDON).
  Methods of teaching general history. (See Nat. educ. ass'n. Proceedings. 1891, p. 673-77.)

——.
  Studies in historical method. 144 p. D. Bost. 1896. Heath. 90c. (Heath's ped. lib.).
    Written especially for the teacher who wishes to specialize his work. Particularly suggestive regarding children's ideas of history.

——.
  Teacher's manual to general history. 172 p. D. Bost. 1894. Heath. 60c.
    Useful for teachers as illustrating the seminary method.

BARNETT, PERCY ARTHUR.
  History and geography. (See his Common sense in education. 1899. p. 245-69.)

BARROWS, WILLIAM.
  Methods of teaching history. (See Mag. Amer. hist. 1888, 19: 245-47.)

BARTH, E.
    Zur Methode des Geschichtsunterrichts. (See Erziehungsschule. 1884, v. 4, nos. 5–7, 10–11.)

BERNHEIM, ERNST.
    Geschichtsunterricht und Geschichtswissenschaft. (Neue Bahnen. 1899, 10:274 ff.)
        A criticism of Lamprecht's historical work and of distinct value to the teacher.

——.
    Lehrbuch der historischen Methode. 530 p. O. Lpz. 1889. Duncker.

——. Ed. 2. 1894.
        Section 3 of chapter 2 contains a bibliography of historical method, 1450–1850. The first real text-book on historical method. Admirable discussion of the nature of historical science, its relations to other subjects, and the principles of historical criticism and interpretation. It has not been translated into English, and is now out of print.

BIEDERMANN, FRIEDRICH KARL.
    Der Geschichtsunterricht in der Schule, seine Mängel und ein Vorschlag zu seiner Reform. 45 p. O. Braunschweig. 1860.

BIGLAND, JOHN.
    Letters on the study and use of ancient and modern history. . . . 610 p. O. Lond. 1806. Longmans.
        Has gone through many editions.

BLACKMAR, FRANK W.
    The study of history and sociology. 69 p. O. Topeka. 1890. Kans. pub. co.

BOONE, JAMES SHERGOLD.
    Essay on the study of modern history. 179 p. O. Lond. 1821. Warren.

BREWER, JOHN SHERREN.
    English studies; or, Essays in English history and literature. 448 p. O. Lond. 1881. Murray. 14s.

BROOKS, EDWARD.
    Normal methods of teaching. 504 p. D. Phil. 1889. Normal pub. co.
        History, p. 485–504.

BRUMBAUGH, M. G.
    Method of the social function of history. (See Nat. Herbart Soc. Yearbook, 1898, 4: 31–43.)

CAMPE, J. F. C.
    Geschichte und Unterricht in der Geschichte. 251 p. O. Lpz. 1859.
        Reviewed in Zeitschrift für das Gym. 1860, 14: 691–700.

CARLYLE, THOMAS.
    On the study of history. (See Old south leaflets. 1883, ser. 1, no. 6.)
        From the Address to the students of Edinburgh university, April 2, 1866.

CLARKE, J. F.
Address on the study of history delivered at the third annual reunion of the Somerville high school association, Feb. 24, 1870. (See Charlestown Chronicle and Somerville Gazette, Feb. 26, 1870, 2, no. 74.)

COLLAR, W. C.
Advice to an inexperienced teacher of history. (See Hall. Methods of teaching history. Ed. 2. 1886, p. 77-88.)

CONDILLAC, ETIENNE BONNOT DE.
De l'étude de l'histoire. (See his Œuvres complètes. 1803, v. 29.)

CORTINA, JOSÉ GOMEZ DE LA.
Cartilla historial, ó método para estudiar la historia. Madrid. 1829.

CZERWENKA, F. J.
Was lehrt Herbart über Geschichtsunterricht? (See Päd. Abhand. Lpz. 1877, Heft 2.)

DABNEY, R. H.
Methods of historical instruction. 6 p. O. Bloomington (Ind.). 1888. (Indiana Univ. Bull., 1, No. 5.)

DEAN, AMOS.
The true method of studying and teaching history; a paper read before the Amer. ass'n for the advancement of education at its annual session, Aug. 5, 1857. 32 p. O. Alb. 1857. Weed.

DIALOGUE on the study of history. (See Common school journal. 1840, 2:366-71.

DIESTERWEG, GEORG FRIEDRICH ADOLPHE WILHELM.
Instruction in history. (See Hall. Methods of teaching history. Ed. 1. 1883. pt. 1.)
 Also published by Heath in 1885.

——.
Wegweiser zur Bildung für Lehrer und die Lehrer werden wollen. Essen. 1834-35.
——— ———. Ed. 5. 3 v. O. 1875-79.
 History, v. 3.

DILCHER, A.
Welche Ausgaben erwachsen dem Geschichtsunterricht in der Volksschule aus dem Wesen des modernen Staates? (See Päd. Bll. f. Lehrerbildung u. Lehrerbildungstansalten. 1896:344-53.)

DITTES, FRIEDRICH.
Schule der Pädagogik. Ed. 4. 1051 p. O. Lpz. 1891.
 Die Weltgeschichte, p. 705-15.

DRESCH, —— VON.
Ueber den methodischen Unterricht in dem allgemeinen Geschichte. (See his Kleine Schriften. 1827, p. 253.)

EMERTON, EPHRAIM.
The practical method in higher historical instruction. (See Hall. Methods of teaching history. Ed. 2. 1886, p. 31-60.)
 Also printed separately.

EMMA Willard's methods of teaching history. (See Amer. journal of educ. 1859, 6: 149–51.)

FITCH, JOSHUA GIRLING.
    Lectures on teaching. 393 p. D. N. Y. 1891. Macmillan. $1.
        History, p. 336-55.

FLING, FRED MORROW.
    Outline of historical method. 124 p. D. Lincoln (Nebr.). 1899. J. H. Miller. 75c.
        Based on Bernheim's Lehrbuch and Langlois and Seignobos. Introduction aux études historiques.

FOSS, RUDOLPH.
    Zum Geschichtsunterricht. (See Päd. archiv. 1898, 40:252–58.)

FOSTER, FRANK HUGH.
    The seminary method of original study in the historical sciences. 129 p. D. N. Y. 1888. Scribner. $1.

FREEMAN, EDWARD AUGUSTUS.
    How the study of history is let and hindered. 32 p. Lond. 1879.
        Address delivered in the Liverpool Institute Nov. 19, 1879.

———.
    The methods of historical study; eight lectures read in the Univ. of Oxford in . . . 1884, with the inaugural lecture on The office of the historical professor. 335 p. O. Lond. 1886. Macmillan. 10s. 6d.

———.
    On the study of history. (See Fortnightly rev. 1881, 35: 319–39.)
        Address at the opening of the Birmingham historical society, Nov. 18, 1880. Also in Eclectic mag. 1881, 96: 577–91.

FRITZSCHE, RICHARD.
    Die Gestaltung der Systemstufe im Geschichtsunterricht. 38 p. O. Langensalza. 1896. (Magazin pädagogisches, 77.)

FROHLICH, JOSEF.
    Zur Reform des geschichtlichen Unterrichts. (See Oesterreich. Schulzg. 1896: 326–28.)
        Plea for one tiny book for use in the primary school which shall contain all the history which the child absolutely must learn.

FROSCHAUER, M.
    Zur Methode des Geschichtsunterrichtes von der Reformation bis Ende des 18en Jahrhundert. (Repertorium der Päd. 1896, 51: 72–78.)

FROUDE, JAMES ANTHONY.
    The study of history. (See Critic. 1885, 6: 176; 187–89.)
        Also in Youths' companion.

GANSEN.
    Geschichte und Unterricht in der Geschichte. 70 p. O. Stuttgart. 1897.

GARDINER, SAMUEL RAWSON.
    Freeman on the teaching of history. (See Academy. 1883, 26: 386.)

GARLICK, A. H.
    A new manual of method. 331 p. D. N. Y. 1896. Longmans. $1.20.
        History, p. 258-76.

GOLDWIN Smith on the study of history. (See Westminster rev. 1861, 76: 293-334.)
        Reviewing Mr. Smith's two lectures at Univ. of Oxford.

GOODRICH, A L.
    History in secondary schools. (See School review. 1899, 7: 29-35.)

GORGE, S.
    Die "Extemporalien" im Geschichtsunterricht. (See Zeit. für das Gym. 1895, 49: 200-3.)

GREENWOOD, JAMES M.
    Teaching of history. (See Education. 1884, 4: 623-32.)

GRIMM, HERMAN.
    Der Geschichtsunterricht in aufsteigender Linie. (Deutsche Rundschau. 1891. 68. 437-56.)

GROTH, ERNST.
    Bemerkungen zum Geschichts-Unterricht. 28 p. O. Lpz. 1894.

GUIZOT, FRANÇOIS PIERRE GUILLAUME.
    Historical studies. (See his Memoires. 1860, 3: 161-74.)

GUNTHER, ADOLF.
    Vorschläge zu ein zeit gemässen Gestaltung des Geschichtsunterrichts. 48 p. O. Gotha. 1891. (Zeit-und Streitfragen pädagogische.)
    ———— ————. Ed. 2. 50 p. O. Wiesbaden. 1897.

GUTH, FRIEDRICH.
    Praktische methodik. Ed. 4. 531 p. O. Stuttgart. 1883.

HALL, GRANVILLE STANLEY. *ed.*
    Methods of teaching history. Bost. 1883. Ginn. $1.30. (Pedagogical library 1.)

————.
    Methods of teaching history. Ed. 2. 385 p. D. Bost. 1886. Ginn. $1.50.
        Entirely recast and rewritten. Diesterweg. Instruction in history is omitted. Every article in this edition appears separately in this bibliography.

HANNAK, EMANUEL.
    Methodik des Unterrichtes in der Geschichte. 90 p. O. Wien. 1891. Lehrbuch der speciellen Methodik. Heft 6.)

HARLEY, LEWIS R.
    Francis Lieber; his life and political philosophy. 214 p. O. N. Y. 1899. Col. Univ. $2.
        Lieber was one of the earliest modern teachers of history in America, and his work had great influence in securing for history a place in the college curriculum.

————.
    Methods of the study of history. (See Education. 1895. 15: 332-40.)

HARRIS, WILLIAM TORREY.
   Syllabus of topics for oral lessons in history. 15 p. St. Louis. 1880. Jones.

HART, ALBERT BUSHNELL.
   How to study history. (See Chautauquan. 1893, 18: 17–21.)
      Reprinted as No. 4 of his Studies in American education, 1895; in Chautauqua studies in American education, and in Wayside course studies, No. 2, 1895.

HARTLEB, PH.
   Die Forderungen der Gegenwart an den Geschichtsunterricht der Volksschule. 31 p. O. Bielefeld. 1899. (Päd. abhd. 4, no. 1.)

HEDGE, FREDERIC H.
   The method of history. (See North Amer. rev. 1870, 111: 311–29.)

HERBST, F. L.
   Zur Frage über den Geschichtsunterricht. 58 p. O. Mainz. 1869.

HINSDALE, BURKE AARON.
   History teaching in schools. (In his Studies in education. 1896. p. 206–22.)
      Read before the Department of Superintendence of the Nat. Educ. Ass'n, Feb., 1895, and is also found in N. E. A. Proceedings for 1895, p. 360–70.
      It is a review of the report of the Conference on history, civil government, and political economy made to the Committee of ten.

———.
   How to study and teach history. 346 p. D. N. Y. 1894. Appleton. $1.50. (Inter. educ. ser.)
      "No effort is made to tell the teacher *just what* he shall teach or *just how* he shall teach it. The aim is rather to state the uses of history, to define in a general way its field, to present and illustrate criteria for the choice of facts, to emphasize the organization of facts with reference to the three principles of association, to indicate sources of information, to describe the qualifications of the teacher, and finally to illustrate causation and the grouping of facts by drawing the outlines of some important chapters in American history."

HISTORY; how she is wrote. (See Saturday rev. 1892, 74: 438–39.)
      Remarks on Mr. Lecky's Birmingham lecture, The political value of history.

HORN, FR.
   Der Geschichtsunterricht vom modernen Gesichtspunkte (See Päd. blätter. 1897, p. 71–74.)

HOWARD, GEORGE ELLIOTT.
   The study of history in schools. (See Educ. rev. 1900, 19: 257–68.)
      Reviews the report of the Committee of seven.

HUGHES, J. L.
   Topical teaching of history. (See Education. 1882, 2: 410–14.)

HÜLLMANN, RITTER KARL D.
   Ueber den Unterricht in der Geschichte. (See Königsberger Archiv für Philosophie. 1811.)

JÄGER, E. F. OSCAR.
   Bemerkungen über den geschichtlichen Unterricht. 47 p. O. Wiesbaden. 1892.

JÄGER, E. F. OSCAR.
Didaktik und Methodik des Geschichtsunterricht. 255 and 110 p. O. München. 1895. Beck. 6-50. (Handbuch der Erziehungs und Unterrichtslehre für höhere Schulen. Bd. 3. Abtlg. 1.)
  Reviewed in Zeit. für die öst. Gym. 1896, 47: 538-43.
  Gives a detailed account of the methods of instruction in the various classes of the German gymnasium.

KAULICH, J.
Wert und Methode der Geschichte. (See Pädagogium. 1893, 15: 430- .)

KEMP, ELLWOOD W.
Outline of method in history. 263 p. O. N. Y. 1896. App. $1.50.

——— ———. Ed. 2. 300 p. D. Terre Haute. 1897. Inland pub. co. $1.50.

KIDDLE, HENRY, and others.
How to teach; a manual of methods for a graded course of instruction. 276 p. D. Cinn. 1877. Van Antwerp. $1.
  History. p. 189-94; 211-16; 238-41.

KLEIN, E.
Aphorismen über Geschichtsunterricht. (See Pädagogium. 1896, 18: 298-307.)
  Reprinted from his Kritische Gänge durch Schule und Welt.

KLEMM, L. R.
Chips from a teacher's workshop. 408 p. D. Bost. 1888. Lee. $1.50.
  History, p. 341-408.

LANDON, JOSEPH.
The principles and practice of teaching and class management. N. Y. 1894. Macmillan.
  History, p. 398-407.

LANG, ANDREW.
History as she ought to be wrote. (See Blackwood's mag. 1899. 166: 266-74.)
  A delightful, graceful plea for style in historical writing. Langlois and Seignobos's Introduction to historical studies is used as the text for a quasi-review.

LANGE, KARL.
Die Sage im Geschichtsunterricht der Volksschule. (See Kehr. Pädagog. blätter. 5: 201-.)

LANGLOIS, CHARLES VICTOR, and SEIGNOBOS, CHARLES.
Introduction aux études historique. 308 p. D. Par. 1898. Hachette. 3 fr. 50c.
  Especially p. 281-92.
  An English translation by G. G. Berry is published by Holt & Co.
  The best brief treatise on the methods of historical investigation.

LAVISSE, ERNEST.
Histoire. (See Buisson. Dictionnaire de pédagogie et d'instruction primaire. 1882. 1: 1264-72.)

LAZARUS, M.
  Erziehung und Geschichte. 51 p. O. Breslau. 1881.
LEVERMORE, CHARLES H.
  Methods and results of instruction in history. (See School and college. 1892. 1:218-28.)
LORENZ, KARL.
  Der moderne Geschichtsunterricht; eine historischpädagogische Studie. 148 p. O. München. 1897.
LORENZ, OTTOKAR.
  Die Geschichtsiwissenschaft in Hauptrichtungen und Aufgaben. 2 v. O. Berlin, 1886-91.

———.
  Der zukünftige Unterricht in der neuesten Geschichte. (See Päd. archiv. 1892, 34:129-45.)
MACDONALD, J. W.
  Teaching history. (See Academy, Syracuse. 1892, 7:36-40.)
MACE, WILLIAM HARRISON.
  Method in history for teachers and students. 311 p. D. Bost. 1897. Ginn. $1.10.
  A plea for the pedagogics of history teaching: illustrated from American history.
  Reviewed in Amer. Hist. Rev., Oct., 1898, and in Educ. Rev., Sept., 1899.
MACKIBBIN, STUART.
  Outline course of study in history. (See Education. 1889, 10:159-67.)
MCMURRY, FRANK M.
  History. (See Nat. educ. ass'n. Proceedings. 1894, p. 160-65.)
MAHAFFY, JOHN PENTLAND.
  On the methods of writing and teaching ancient history. (See his Prolegomena to ancient history. 1871, p. 1-29.)
MANSEL, G. B.
  Two letters on Smith's lectures on history. Lond. 1861-62.
MEAD, EDWIN DOAK.
  On the study of history. (See Amer. inst. of instruction. Proceedings. 1888, p. 1-44.)
    Also issued separately. Bost. 1888.
  Mr. Kingsley on the study of history. (See Westminster rev. 1861, 75:305-36.)
    Review of his inaugural lecture at Cambridge.
MORRIS, GOUVERNEUR.
  Inaugural discourse delivered before the New York hist. soc. Sept. 4, 1816. 24 p. O. N. Y. 1816.
MOWRY, WILLIAM AUGUSTUS.
  Teacher's independent study of history. (See Education. 1888, 9:134-36.)

NEUBAUER, FRIEDRICH.
>Geschichtsunterricht auf höheren Schulen. (See Rein. Encyklopädishes Handbuck der Pädagogik. 1896, 2: 765–801.)
>>Contains a brief bibliography. Also published separately. 39 p. O. Langensalza. 1896.

NEW ENGLAND HISTORY TEACHERS' ASSOCIATION.
>Register and report of the first annual meeting in Bost. Oct. 16, 1897. 51 p. O. Bost. 1897.
>>Reprinted in Educational rev. 1898, 15: 813–30.

NIGHTINGALE, A. F.
>History in the high schools. (See School review. 1899, 7: 11–17.)
>>Read at meeting of American historical ass'n. Dec., 1897.

NOACK, F.
>Alte und neue Ansichten über die Ziele des Geschichtsunterrichts. (See Päd. archiv. 1883, 25: 161–66.)

NORTH CENTRAL ASSOCIATION OF COLLEGES AND PREPARATORY SCHOOLS.
>Proceedings. 1896. (See School rev. 1896. 4: 267–72.)
>>First annual meeting.

ORDINARY teaching of history. (See Christian remembrancer. 1845, 9: 317–37.)

PARK, ABRAHAM.
>Manual of method. . . . 92 p. S. Lond. 1879.
>>History, p. 61–65.

PATRIDGE, LELIA ELLEN.
>"Quincy methods" illustrated. 660 p. D. N. Y. 1886. Kellogg. $1.50.
>>History, p. 641–56.

PEABODY, ELIZABETH PALMER.
>Instruction in history. (See Amer. inst. of instruct. 1850, p. 123–28.)

PEASLEE, JOHN B.
>Methods of teaching history. (See U. S.—Bureau of educ. Report of commissioner, 1883–84, p. 93.)

POMIES, ———.
>Tableaux pour l'enseignement de l'histoire. (See Revue péd. 1883, 11: 49–53.

PORTER, LUTHER HENRY.
>The study of history. (See Education. 1882, 3: 136–47.)

PRACTICAL methods of teaching history. (See Educ. rev. 1898, 15: 313–30.)
>>This is in substance the report to the New England history teachers' association by its Committee on methods of teaching and study.

PRAWITZ, A.
>Ueber (!) Geschichtsunterricht. 13 p. Q. Kgl. Gym. Friedeberg Nm. 1895.

PREPARATORY instruction in history. (See Nation. 1899. 69: 87–88.)
>>Reviews the Report of the Committee of seven and suggests that its recommendations would overcrowd the curriculum and demand more thoroughly trained teachers.

PRINCE, JOHN TILDEN.
   Courses and methods; a handbook for teachers of primary, grammar, and ungraded schools. 344 p. D. Bost. 1890.
   History, p. 162-72.

PTASCHNIK, J.
   Ueber den Unterricht in der Geschichte. (See Zeit. für die öst. Gym. 1862, 13: 866-75.)

———.
   Zur Frage über den geographischen und historischen Unterricht. (See Zeit. für die öst. Gym. 1858, 9: 254-70.

RAUMER, KARL GEORG VON.
   Aphorisms on teaching history. (See Amer. jour. of educ. Barnards. 1860, 8: 101-10.)
   From his History of pedagogy.

REIN, WILHELM, PICKEL, A., and SCHILLER, E.
   Theorie und Praxis des Volksschulunterrichtes nach Herbartischen Grunsätzen. 7 v. O. Dresden. 1884-88.
   Each volume covers one school year, except that the third and fourth years are included in one volume.

RICE, EMILY J.
   History in the common schools. (See Educ. rev. 1896, 12: 169-79.)

RICHTER, ALBRECHT.
   Geschichtsunterricht in 17en Jahrhundert. 27 p. O. Langensalza. 1893. (Magazin pädagogisches. Heft 35.)

ROARK, RURIC NEVEL.
   Method in education. 348 p. D. N. Y. 1899. Amer. book co. $1.
   Chap. 13 (p. 192-214) treats of history.

ROGERS, CHARLES.
   Notes on the study of history. (See Royal hist. soc. Transactions. 1880. 8: 1-11.)

ROSSBACH, F.
   Die Berücksichtigung der Kulturgeschichte im Geschichtsunterricht. 15 p. O. Neuwied. 1897. (Für die Schule aus der Schule 66.)

RUSCH, GUSTAVE.
   Methodik des Unterrichts in der Geschichte. 91 p. O. Wien. 1884. (Handbuch der speciellen Methodik. Thl. 4.)
——— ———. Ed. 3. 87 p. 1895.

ST. JOHN, HENRY, VISCOUNT BOLINGBROKE.
   Letters on the study and use of history. 2 v. O. Lond. 1752.
   Famous and still of value and interest.

SALMON, DAVID.
   The art of teaching. 289 p. D. Lond. 1898. Longmans. $1.25.
   History, p. 212-18.

SAN ROMAN.
   Introducción al estudio de la historia. Guadalajara. 1889.

SCHELLING, F. W. J.
Ueber das Studium der Historie und der Jurisprudenz. (See his Vorlesungen über die Methode des academischen Studium. Ed. 3. 1830. p. 211-37.)
First printed in 1802.

SCHENK, K.
Ueber die Behandlung der von der Kritik verworfenen Erzählungen im Geschichtsunterricht. (See Zeit. für das Gym. 1895. 49: 396-410.)

SCHILLING, Dr.
Ueber die Grundsätze der Auswahl, Anordnung und Behandlung des Lehrstoffes für den Geschichtsunterricht. 43 p. O. Lpz. 1897.

SCHMID, KARL A.
Encyklopädie des gesammten Erziehungs-und-Unterrichtswesens. ... Ed. 2. 10 v. O. Gotha. 1876-87.
Geschichte, v 2: 970-1002.

SCHRADER, W.
Erziehungs und Unterrichtslehre für Gymnasien und Realschulen. Ed. 4. 590 p. Ber. 1882.
Part 3 treats of special branches.

SCHWANN, M.
Über die Methode des Geschichtsstudiums. (See Gesellschaft. 8: 67-83.)

SCIENTIFIC method in study of history. (See Science. 1884. 3: 564-65.)
Review of Hall. Methods of teaching history.

SEARS, BARNAS.
Historical studies in college, their degree of importance and the best way of conducting them. (See Bibliotheca sacra. 1865. 22:251-84.)

SEELEY, JOHN ROBERT.
The teaching of history. (See Journal of educ. Lond. Nov. 1, 1884.)
Reprinted in Hall. Methods of teaching history, Ed. 2, p. 193-202 and in International conference on education, 1884. Proceedings. 3 33-43.
Advocates the scientific and sociological instead of the chronological and purely literary method.

SEIGNOBOS, CHARLES.
Histoire narrative et descriptive des anciens peuples de l'Orient, avec un supplément à l'usage des professeurs. Par. 1891.

———.
Une expérience d'exercices historiques. (See Revue universitaire. 1896, June 15.)

SELIGMAN, EDWIN ROBERT ANDERSON.
The seminarium; its advantages and limitations. (See Univ. of the state of New York. Report of 30th convocation. 1892. p. 59-81.)
In regent's bulletin, No. 9. Followed by a discussion shared by Ephraim Emerton, J. G. Schurman, J. H. Canfield, E. B. Andrews, and others.

SEYMOUR, LUCY M.
> Teaching history. (See Education. 1897, 17:624–31.)

SHEPARDSON, FRANCIS W.
> Points of view in studying history. (See Inland educator. 1895. 1:273–75.)

SMITH, A. L.
> The teaching of modern history. (See Cookson, Christopher, ed. Essays on secondary education. 1898. p. 177–95.)

SMITH, GOLDWIN.
> The study of history. (See Atlantic mo. 1870, 25:44–56.)
>> Lecture delivered at Cornell univ.

SOREL, ALBERT.
> Comment on prépare une leçon d'histoire. (See Rev. péd. 1882, 10:401–8.)

SORLEY, WILLIAM RITCHIE.
> The historical method. (See his Essays in philosophical criticism. 1883.)

SPENCE, C. H.
> The teaching of modern history. (See Cookson, Christopher, ed. Essays on sceondary education. 1898. p. 161–76.)

SPIELMANN, C.
> Der Geschichtsunterricht in ausgeführten Lektionen für die Hand des Lehrers nach den neueren methodische Grundsätzen bearbeitet. 319 p. O. Wiesbaden. 1897.

STAHN, KARL.
> Zur Frage über den Geschichtsunterricht. (See Pädagogische blätter. 1896, p. 418–23.)

STANLEY, ARTHUR PENRHYN.
> Study of modern history. (See his Lectures before the young men's Christian ass'n. . . from Nov. 1853–Feb. 1854. 1854.)

STUBBS, WILLIAM.
> Seventeen lectures on the study of mediæval and modern history and kindred subjects, delivered at Oxford. . . 1867–84. 455 p. D. Oxford. 1887. Clar. press, 8s. 6 d.
>> Especially, no. 1–5.

STUTZER, E.
> Der Lernstoff in Geschichtlichen Unterricht. (See Pädagogisches archiv. 1883, 25: 423–53.)

TECKLENBURG, AUGUST.
> Der Ausbau des Geschichtsunterrichts. (See Bll. für d. Schulprax. Beilage zur preuss. Lehrerzeitung. 1896, no. 7: 51–54.)
>> The selection of material for historical instruction must keep in mind both the ethical and practical ends in view.

THATCHER, OLIVER J.
> Preparation for college in history. (See School review, 1898, 6: 84–88.)

THOMAS Arnold's methods of teaching history. (See Amer. jour. of educ. Barnard. 1857, 4: 575–77.)

THOMPSON, ANNA BOYNTON.
How to study history. (See Educ. rev. 1899, 17: 169–77.)
A philosophical discussion of the nature of history, not a practical plan for its actual study except as true historical study depends on the nature of history.

———.
Suggestions to teachers. (See Channing. Student's history of the United States. 1898. Pref. p. 29–35.)

THWAITES, REUBEN GOLD.
The study of local history in the Wisconsin schools. (See Wis. jour. of educ. 1888, 18: 465–74.)
A plea for more attention to the study of local history.

TIBBEY, THOMAS G.
On the teaching of history. (See Westminster rev. 1899, 151: 516–26.
A plea for more history teaching and better methods.

TREUNTLER, JULIUS.
Zum geschichtlichen Unterricht. 2 v. O. Koln. 1885–86.
Oberrealschule Program.

VAILE, E. O.
Teaching current events in school. (See Nat. educ. ass'n. Proceedings. 1892, p. 142–49.)

VAN WIE, C. B.
Methods in common branches. 197 p. D. Syracuse. 1892. Bardeen. 75c.

VÉRICOUR, L. RAYMOND DE.
The study of history. (See Royal hist. soc. 1872, 1: 9–33.)
Printed separately at different times with varying titles.

WARFIELD, ETHELBERT D.
Teaching of history. (See School rev. 1895, 3: 33–40.)

WEAK side of the historical method. (See Nation. 1887, 24: 217–18.)

WEIGAND, HEINRICH.
Der Geschichts-Unterricht nach den Forderungen der Gegenwart. 61 p. O. Hannover. 1897. (Bibliothek pädagogische, 21.)

———.
Die Heimat im Geschichtsunterricht. (See Rhein-Westf. Schulzeitung. 1896: 322–23.)

———.
Die methode des Geschichtsunterrichts. (See Pädagogium. 1895, 17: 358–80.)

———.
Lehrmittel für Geschichtsunterricht. (See Pädagogium. 1896, 18: 354–72.)

———.
Stoffauswahl und Stoffanordnung für den Geschichtsunterricht in Schulen. (See Pädagogium. 1893, 16: 167–82.)

WHEELER, N. M.
    How to teach history. (See Dial. 1884, 4: 312–13.)
        Review of Hall. Methods of teaching history.

WHY is history read so little? 27 p. O. New Bedford (Mass). 1876.

WICKERSHAM, JAMES PYLE.
    Methods of instruction. 496 p. D. Phil. n. d.
        History, p. 414–50.

WIE studirt Man classische ... Geschichte? 32 p. O. Lpz. 1884.

WILSON, ROLAND KNYVET.
    Should history be taught backward? (See Contemp. rev. 1896, 70: 391–407.)
        Also in Littell's living age, 211: 259–71.

WOLF, JOSEPH.
    Ueber Vortrag und Wiederholung im Geschichtsunterricht. (See Zeit. für die öst. Gym. 1863, 14: 259–73.)

ZEITSCHRIFT FÜR DEN GESCHICHTLICHEN UNTERRICHT.
    v. 1. Apr. 1897–March 1898. 64 p. O. Osterburg. 1898.
        Discontinued.

ZERFFI, GUSTAVUS GEORGE.
    Studies on the science of general history. 3 v. O. Lond. 1887–89. Hirschfeld. 12s. 6d. each.

ZILLER, TUISKON.
    Materialien zur speziellen Pädagogik. Ed. 3. 296 p. O. Dresden. 1886.
        The famous Leipziger Seminarbuch in enlarged form. Contains a valuable chapter on History teaching.

PRIMARY INSTRUCTION.

DETTMER, H., and BAACKE, G.
    Lehr-und Lernbüchlein für den ersten Geschichtsunterricht. 56 p. O.

EGERT, PH.
    Geschichtliche Spuren in unsrer Heimat und ihre Unterrichtliche und erziehliche Bedeutung (Päd. Warte. 1896: 531–42).

GORDY, WILBUR F.
    Essentials of United States history to be taught in elementary schools. (See Nat. educ. ass'n. Proceedings. 1898, p. 70–77.)

HANBIDGE, MARY.
    The teaching of ancient history. (See Work and play in girls' schools. 1898, p. 159–67).
        Primary work.

HOLMAN, H.
    First lessons in history. (See Educational Times (London). 1898, 51: 248–51.)
        Lecture delivered at meeting of preceptors in London, May 11, 1898.

KING, JULIA A.
> History in the elementary school. (See Educ. rev. 1899, 18: 479-500.)

MONROE, WILL SEYMOUR.
> Historic sense of children. (See Journal of educ. Bost. 1897, 45: 406-7.)

MOORE, NINA.
> Local history for primary classes. (See Common school educ. 1888, 2: 259-63; 304-8; 342-45; 398-402.)

N., M.
> A Fröbel method of teaching history. (See Journal of educ. Lond. 1891, 13: 520-21.)

NEWELL, M. A.
> History in elementary education. (See Nat. educ. ass'n. Proceedings. 1892, p. 310-16.)

PEABODY, ELIZABETH PALMER.
> First steps to the study of history. 89 p. D. Bost. 1832.

PEABODY, MRS. MARY H.
> Methods of teaching history to children. (See Nat. educ. ass'n. Proceedings. 1893, p. 284-85.)

PIZARD, ALFRED.
> L'histoire dans l'enseignement primaire. D. Paris. 1891.
> An extract from above was printed in Revue inter. de l'enseign. 1890, 26: 581-35.

RUSCH, GUSTAVE.
> Zur Verbesserung des elementaren Geschichtsunterricht. 136 p. O. Wien. 1893.

SALMON, LUCY MAYNARD.
> History in elementary schools. (See Educ. rev. 1891, 1: 438-52.)

———.
> Study of history below the secondary school. (See Report of the Committee of seven. 1899, p. 158-72.)

SCHMIDT, F.
> Die Verwendung der Heimatkunde im Geschichtsunterricht. 28 p. Q. Bensheim. 1896. (Schulprogram.)

VIERGUTZ, FRANZ.
> Ist im Geschichtsunterricht in der Volksschule ein Handbuch in der Hand der Schuler wünschenswert? (Pomm. Bll. 1896: 225-26.)

WARFIELD, ETHELBERT D.
> Teaching of history in elementary schools. (See Education. 1893, 14: 1-5.)

WILLMANN, OTTO.
> Der elementare Geschichtsunterricht; zugleich Begleitworte für das Lesebuch aus Herodot. 87 p. O. Wien. 1872.
> After Herbart and Ziller.

WILTSE, SARA E.
　　Place of the story in early education, and other essays. 132 p. D. Bost. 1892. Ginn. 60c.

CORRELATION.

ALDEN, EDMUND KIMBALL.
　　Mountains and history. (See Amer. hist. ass'n. Report. 1894, p. 519-29.)

ATKINSON, WILLIAM PARSONS.
　　The study of politics. 63 p. S. Bost. 1888. Roberts. .50c.

BARNES, MRS. MARY DOWNING (SHELDON).
　　Teaching of local history. (See Educ. rev. 1895, 10: 481-88.)

BOUGHTON, WILLIS.
　　Study of local history. (See Education. 1893, 13: 400-8.)

CLARKE, JOSEPH THACHER.
　　Plea for archæological instruction. (See Hall. Methods of teaching history. Ed. 2. 1886, p. 89-103.)

FISCHER, K.
　　Behandlung der Sozialen Frage im Geschichtsunterricht der Prima. (See Zeit. für den gesch. Unterricht. 1897, 1: 226-33.)

FOSS, RUDOLPH.
　　Wie ist der Unterricht in der Geschichte mit dem Geographischen Unterricht zu verbinden? Ed. 2. 48 p. O. Ber. 1874.

HILLARD, GEORGE S.
　　On the connection between geography and history. (See Amer. inst. of instruction. 1845, p. 269-307.)

MCMURRY, CHARLES ALEXANDER.
　　Co-ordination in the field of history and literature. (See Nat. educ. ass'n. Proceedings. 1895, p. 104-9.)

——.
　　Special method for literature and history in the common schools. Ed. 4. 114 p. D. Bloomington, Ill. 1898. Public school pub. co. 35c.

—— ——. Ed. 2. 114 p. D. 1894.

MACY, JESSE.
　　Relations of history to politics. (See Amer. hist. ass'n. Report. 1893, p. 179-88.)

MOSES, BERNARD.
　　The social sciences as aid in teaching history. (See Cal. univ. Bulletin no. 37. 1892.)

NACHTIGALL, KARL.
　　Die Berücksichtigung des Volkswissenschaftlichen Elementes bei dem Geschichtsunterricht in höheren Lehranstalten. 18 p. O. Remscheid. 1883.

NEUBAUER, FRIEDRICH.
Volkswirtschaftliches im Geschichtsunterricht. 63 p. O. Halle. 1894.

NEVINS, WINFIELD SCOTT.
Study of local history. (See New Eng. mag. 1893, 14: 28–30.)

PHILLIPS, J. H.
History and literature in grammar grades. 17 p. D. Bost. 1893. Heath. 15c.
Also in N. E. A. proceedings. 1892, 606–16.

PTASCHNIK, J.
Der geographische und historische Unterricht. (See Zeit. für die öst. Gym. 1860, 11: 474–79.)

PHYSICAL geography and history. (See Hall. Methods of teaching history. Ed. 2. 1886, p. 223–26.)

REDWAY, JACQUES WARDLAW.
Influence of environment on United States history. (See Nat. educ. ass'n. Proceedings. 1898, p. 139–49.)

RICE, EMILY J.
Course of study in history and literature, with suggestions and directions. 67 p. O. Chic. °1891. Flanagan.

SACH, AUGUST.
Die Behandlung der wirthschaftlichen und gesellschaftlichen Fragen im Geschichtsunterricht. 14 p. O. 1896. Hadersleben.

SCHOLZ, ED.
Studie über den historisch-geographischen Unterricht am Gymnasium. (See Zeit. für die öst. Gym. 1870, 21: 454–79.)

TIETZ, ADOLF.
Ueber Verbindung des geschichtlichen mit dem geographischen Unterrichte in der Quinta des Gymnasiums. 39 p. O. Cöthen. 1877.

TITTEL, E.
Die Heimatskunde als Grundlage der Geschichtsunterricht. (See Praktischer Schulmann. 1896, p. 105–27.)

WENDT, G.
Zum geschichtlichen und geographischen Unterricht. 18 p. O. Karlsruhe. 1879.
Gymnasien-program.

WOLF, JOSEPH.
Ueber die Verbindung des geographischen Unterrichtes mit dem Unterricht in der Geschichte. (See Zeit. für die öst. Gym. 1862, 13: 253–63.)

USE OF THE SOURCES.

BARNES, MRS. MARY DOWNING (SHELDON), and BARNES, EARL.
Collections of sources in English for history teaching. (See Educ. rev. 1898, 15: 331–38.)

BECKER, A.
  Quellenbenutzung im Geschichtsunterricht. (See Zeit. für den gesch. unterricht. 1897, 1:158–65.)

BENGEL, JOHANN.
  Quellenbenutzung beim Geschichtsunterrichte. 96 p. O. Wiesbaden. 1898. (Zeit-und-Streitfragen pädagogische. 53.)

CALDWELL, HOWARD WALTER.
  Source-study method of teaching history in high schools. (See Nat. educ. ass'n. Proceedings. 1897, p. 670–76.)

FLING, FRED MORROW. Outline of historical method. 124 p. D. Lincoln, Nebr. 1899. J. H. Miller. 75c.

FLING, FRED MORROW, and CALDWELL, HOWARD WALTER.
  Studies in European and American history. 336 p. O. Lincoln, Nebr. 1898. Miller. $1.
    Explaining and illustrating work by the "source" method in Univ. of Nebr Rev. in Jour. of pedagogy, July, 1898.

HART, ALBERT BUSHNELL.
  The sources and how to find them. Use of sources. (See his American history told by contemporaries. 1898. v. 2, pt. 1, p.1–34.)
    A shorter chapter of similar content prefaces, volume 1.

HART, ALBERT BUSHNELL, and others.
  The use of sources. (In his Source book of American history. 1899, pref. p. 1–46.)

MOELLER, C.
  Traité des études historiques. 673 p. O. Louvain. 1892.
    Contains a critical introduction to modern history and chapters on archives. Important bibliographic catalogs. Historical method.

PAGE, T. W.
  The "source method" of teaching history in schools. (In University chronicle (California), Dec., 1899, 2:421–32.)
    A vigorous arraignment of the "source method" as the author somewhat radically conceives it.

ROBINSON, JAMES HARVEY.
  Ought the sources to be used in teaching history? (See Ass'n of colleges and preparatory schools of the middle states and Maryland. Proceedings. 1894, p. 38–44.)

RUDE, ADOLF.
  Quellen im Geschichtsunterricht . . . 24 p. O. Gotha. 1892. (Päd. Zeit-und-Streitfragen. Heft, 27.)

WOHLRABE, WILHELM, and others
  Einige Präparationen zu profangeschichtlichen Quellenstoffen. 48 p. O. Gotha. 1887.

WOODBURN, JAMES A.
  To what extent may undergraduate students of history be trained in the use of the sources? (See Amer. hist. ass'n. Report. 1897. p. 45–49).

COLLECTIONS OF SOURCES IN AMERICAN HISTORY.

This list includes only such collections as are both good and so inexpensive as to be within reach of all teachers. A much fuller list is found in Channing & Hart's Guide.

HART, A. B. and CHANNING, EDWARD. *eds.*
American history leaflets. American history; colonial and constitutional, 1–30. N. Y. 1892–97. Lovell. 10 cents each.
Published bimonthly.

HART, ALBERT BUSHNELL.
American history told by contemporaries. 4 v. O. N. Y. 1897–1900. Macmillan. $7.
Three volumes have appeared and may be had separately for $2 each.

———.
Source book of American history. . . . 408 p. D. N. Y. 1899. Macmillan. 60c.
From the Columbian discovery to the Spanish war.

JOHNSTON, ALEXANDER. *ed.*
American orations to illustrate American political history. 3 v. D. N. Y. 1884. Putnam. $3.75.

McDONALD, WILLIAM. *ed.*
Select charters and other documents illustrative of the history of the United States. 1606–1775. O. N. Y. 1899. Macmillan. $2.25.

———.
Select documents illustrative of the history of the United States. 1776–1861. 465 p. O. N. Y. 1898. Macmillan. $2.25.

OLD South leaflets. 100 numbers. D. Bost. 1883–99. Pub. and sold by Directors of the Old South work, Old South meeting-house, Boston. 5 cents each; $4 per hundred; the first 100 numbers can be had in 4 volumes at $1.50 each.

POORE, BENJAMIN PERLEY. *ed.*
The federal and state constitutions, colonial charters, and other organic laws of the U. S. 2 v. Q. Wash. 1877.
A reprint is in preparation.

PRESTON, HOWARD W. *ed.*
Documents illustrative of American history. 1606–1863. 320 p. O. N. Y. 1891. Putnam. $1.50.

RICHARDSON, JAMES D. *ed.*
A compilation of the messages and papers of the presidents, 1789–1897. 10 v. O. Wash. 1896–99.
Published by authority of Congress.

FRANCE.

BOURGEOIS, EMILE.
La réforme de l'agrégation d'histoire. (See Revue inter. de l'enseign. 1894, 28: 2–8.)

BRISAC, EDMOND DREYFUS.
Les réformes de l'enseignement secondaire en France. (See Revue inter. de l'enseign. 1881, 1: 1–24.)
Discusses the place of history in the French curricula.

BROUARD, EUGÉNE.
  L'enseignement de l'histoire dans l'école primaire. (See Conferences pédagogiques fait aux instituteurs primaires venus à Paris pour l'Exposition universelle de 1878.)

CAUDEL, M.
  Un enseignement de l'histoire diplomatique à l'école libre des sciences politiques. (See Revue inter. de l'enseign. 1898, 35:541-50.)

CONS, LOUIS.
  L'enseignement de l'histoire de France à l'école primaire. (See Revue péd. 1880, 5:569-75.)

FRÉDÉRICQ, PAUL.
  L'enseignement supérieur de l'histoire à Paris. (See Revue inter. de l'enseign. 1883, 6:742-98.)

———.
  The study of history in Belgium and Holland; trans. by Henrietta Leonard. (See Johns Hopkins Univ. studies. 1890, ser. 8, no. 10, 62 p.)

———.
  The study of history in Germany and France; trans. by Henrietta Leonard. (See Johns Hopkins Univ. studies. 1890, ser. 8, nos. 5-6, 33 p.)

GEOFFROY, A.
  Le concours d'agrégation d'histoire. (See Revue inter. de l'enseign. 1895, 9:329-40; 402-25.)

HASKINS, CHARLES HOMER.
  History in French lycées. (See Report of the Committee of seven. 1899, p. 199-209.)
    Also in Amer. hist. ass'n. Report. 1898, p. 533-38.

———.
  Opportunities for American students of history at Paris. (See Amer. hist. rev. 1898, 3:418-30.)
    Address before the American historical association, Dec. 29, 1897.

HORNER, R.
  L'enseignement de l'histoire et de la géographie dans les colleges. Fribourg, Suisse. 1895.

HUBAULT, GUSTAVE.
  De l'enseignement de l'histoire de France dans les écoles primaires. (See Rev. péd. 1878, 1:382-93.)

JULLIAN, CAMILLE.
  Extraits des historiens français du dix-neuvieme siècle. 684 p. O. Paris. 1898.
    Acc't of the development of historical studies in France during the present century.

LANGLOIS, CHARLES VICTOR.
  L'enseignement des sciences auxiliares de l'histoire du M. A. à la Sorbonne. (See Bibliothèque de l'école des chartes. 1888, 49:609-29.)

LANGLOIS, CHARLES VICTOR.
 Remarques à propos de l'agrégation d'histoire. (See Revue universitaire. 1892, June 15.)

LAVISSE, ERNEST.
 Agrégation d'histoire et de géographie. (See Revue inter. de l'enseign. 1883, 5:371-82.)

———.
 Comment a été réformée l'agrégation d'histoire. (See his A propos de nos écoles. 1895, p. 142-53.)

———.
 De l'enseignement de l'histoire. (See his A propos de nos écoles. 1895, p. 77-107.

———.
 L'enseignement de l'histoire. (See his Instructions concernant les programmes de l'enseignement secondaire classique. n. d.)
  The same matter somewhat abridged is in his A propos de nos écoles, p. 77-107.

———.
 L'enseignement historique en Sorbonne et l'éducation national. (See Revue des deux mondes. 1882, 159: 870-97.)

LEMONNIER, HENRY.
 L'enseignement de l'histoire dans les écoles primaires. (See Recueil des monographies pédagogiques publiées à l'occasion de l'exposition universelle de 1889, 4:221-68, no. 30.)

MENTION, LÉON.
 De l'enseignement de l'histoire dans les écoles normales. (See Rev. péd. 1885, 16:41-46.)

MONIN, H.
 Les progrès de l'enseignement historique. 14 p. Paris, 1891.

SALOMON, HENRY.
 L'enseignement de l'histoire dans les lycées. (See Revue inter. de l'enseign. 1890, 20:471-80.)

SECONDARY history teaching in France. (See Amer. jour. of educ. Barnards. 1872, 23:51.)

SEIGNOBOS, CHARLES.
 L'enseignement de l'histoire dans les Facultés. (See Revue inter. de l'enseign. 1883-84, 6:1076-88; 8:36-60; 97-111.)

TEEGAN, THOMAS HENRY.
 Elementary education in France. 255 p. D. Lond. 1891. Simpkin.
  Detailed programs are given, p. 215-55, showing place of history in the curricula of the French elementary schools.

VAN DAELL, ALPHONSE N.
 Methods of instruction in secondary schools in France. (See Academy, Syracuse. 1889, 4:201-12.)

WERTSCH, FRIEDRICH.
 Ueber den Geschichtsunterricht in Frankreich. Perleberg, 1897.
  A "Programm."

GERMANY.

ACTON, JOHN EMERICK EDWARD DALBERG ACTON, LORD.
    German schools of history. (See English hist. rev. 1886, 1:7–42.)

ASSMANN, W.
    Das Studium der Geschichte insbesondere auf Gymnasien nach den gegenwärtigen Anforderungen. 39 p. Q. Braunschweig. 1847.
        Also in Zeit. f. d. Gymnasialwesen, vol. 1.

BALDAMUS, ALFRED.
    Die Stoffverteilung im Geschichtsunterricht. (See Zeit. für das Gym. 1891, 45:330–36.

BARNARD, HENRY. ed.
    German schools and pedagogy. 2 v. in 1. O. N. Y. 1861.
        Reprinted from American journal of education. Part 2, p. 101-10, contains Aphorisms on teaching history, translated from Raumer's History of pedagogy.

BENGEL, JOHANN.
    Geschichte der Methodik des kulturgeschichtlichen Unterrichts. 74 p. O. Wiesbaden. 1896. (Zeit-und-Streitfragen pädagogische. 49–50.)
        Appeared first in Neue Bahnen.

BIEDERMANN, FRIEDRICH KARL.
    Der Geschichtsunterricht auf Schulen nach kulturgeschichttlichen Methode. 45 p. O. Wiesbaden. 1885.

BLUME, E.
    Geschichtsunterricht auf den Seminarien. (Rein's Studien.)

BOLTON, FREDERICK E.
    The secondary school system of Germany. 398 p. D. N. Y. 1900. Appleton. $1.50. (Inter. educ. ser. v. 47.)
        P. 235-50 give syllabus of work in history and geography in the German schools from the first study of the subjects in the Vorschule through Upper Prima in the Gymnasium.
        Text books, apparatus, and methods of instruction are discussed, with emphasis on the close correlation of the two subjects and the wonderfully unified and thorough work done.

BONGAERTZ, JULIUS.
    Der Geschichtsunterricht in der Volksschule. 278 p. O. Münster. 1892.

BOURNE, EDWARD G.
    Ranke and the beginning of the seminary method in teaching history. (See Educ. rev. 1896, 12:359–67.)

BRETTSCHNEIDER, HARRY.
    Zum Unterricht in der Geschichte vorzugsweise in den oberen Klassen höherer Lehranstalten. 84 p. O. Halle. 1895.

DORPFELD, FRIEDRICH WILHELM.
    Repititorium der Gesellschaftskunde zur Ergänzung des Geschichtsunterrichts. Ed. 3. 48 p. O. Gütersloh. 1890.

EBERHARDT, K. F.
    Ueber Geschichtsunterricht auf den Seminarien. 32 p. O. Wien. 1876. (Rein's pädagogische Studien 4.)

EBERHARDT, K. F.
 Zur Methode und Technik des Geschichtsunterrichts auf den Seminarien. 15 p. O. Eisenach. 1874.

EKERIS, VAN.
 Der Geschichtsunterricht in der Volksschule. Bielefeld. 1891.

ENDRIS, A.
 Der Geschichtsunterricht in der Volksschule. 62 p. O. Lpz. 1887. (Päd. Sammelmappe. 111.)

FELDHAUSEN, G.
 Der Geschichtsunterricht in der Volksschule. 108 p. O. Lpz. 1887. (Hesse's Lehrer-Bibliothek. 8.)

FLING, FRED MORROW.
 The German historical seminary. (See Academy, Syracuse. 1889, 4:129-39; 212-19.)
 Describes the organization and working of Maurenbrecher's seminary at Leipzig in 1888.

FRÉDÉRICQ, PAUL.
 De l'enseignement supérieur de l'histoire en Allemagne. (See Revue de l'instruction publique en Belgique. 1882, 24:18-53; 25:79-92.)

FREE, H.
 Der gänzliche Neugestaltung des Geschichtsunterrichts in der Volksschule. (See Neue Bahnen. 1897, p. 289-305 and 345-72.)

FROBOESE, J.
 Bedenken gegen den neuen preussischen Lehrplan der Geschichte. (See Zeit. für das Gym. 1893, 47:65-76.)

GÄBLER, Dr.
 Zum Geschichtsunterrichte für Mädchen. (See Aus der Schule-für die Schule. 1896, pts 2-3, p. 61-67, 114-21.)

GENZ, HERMANN.
 Die Bedeutung des Geschichtsunterrichts auf den höheren Lehranstalten. (See Zeit. für das Gym. 1888, 42:657-68.)

GOLDMANN, THEODOR.
 Zum Geschichtsunterricht des Gymnasiums. 45 p. O. Darmstadt. 1890. (Program Ludwig-Georges Gym.)

GRAVENHORST, K. TH.
 Ein Wort zur Verständigung über Mass und Ziel des geschichtlichen Unterrichts auf Gymnasien. 15 p. Braunschweig Gym. 1880.

GRÜLLICH, OSKAR ADALB.
 Beitrag zur Methodik des Geschichtsunterrichts an höheren Lehranstalten. 80 p. O. Löbau. 1874.

HAUPT, C.
 Ein Beitrag zu der Frage nach Ziel und Methode des Geschichtsunterrichts an Gymnasien. 38 p. O. Wittenberg. 1883.

HERBST, F. L. W.
 Die neuere und neuste Geschichte auf Gymnasien. 40 p. O. Mainz. 1877.

HERRMANN, E.
   Bemerkungen zum Geschichtsunterricht in den oberen Gymnasialklassen. 46 p. Q. Ber. 1894.

HISTORY in continental schools. (See Industrial educ. ass'n. N. Y. Educ. leaflets no. 5, Jan. 10, 1888.)

HÜBNER, MAX.
   Neuere Bestrebungen auf dem Gebiete des Geschichtsunterrichts. 50 p. O. Breslau. 1891.

———.
   Der Unterricht in der Geschichte mit zahlreichen Lehrproben. 147 p. O. Breslau. 1898.

IMMANUEL, ———.
   Studium der vaterländischen Geschichte; Bemerkungen über den historischen Unterricht auf Gymnasien. (See Archiv für Geschichte und Alterthumskunde Westfalens. 1828, 3:62- .)

DER in preussen geplante Reform des Geschichtsunterrichts. (See Deut. Zeit. f. Geschichtswissenschaft. 6:191-97.)

JACOBI, A. ed.
   Beiträge zur Methodik des Unterrichtes in der Volksschule. Apolda. 1883.

JACOBI, F.
   Grundzüge einer neuen Methode für den vaterländischen Geschichtsunterricht in deutschen Schulen. O. Nürnberg. 1839.

JÄGER, E. F. OSCAR.
   Ueber die Stellung des Unterrichts in der alten Geschichte im Gymnasiallehrplan. (See Humanistische Gymnasium. 1895, 5:5-12.)

JÖRGENSEN, PAUL.
   Der Geschichtsunterricht auf dem Realgymnasium; Beiträge zur Methodik. 23 p. Q. Ber. 1894.

JULLIAN, CAMILLE.
   Notes sur les séminaires historiques et philologiques des universités allemandes. (See Revue inter. de l'enseign. 1884, 8: 289-310; 403-24.)

JUNGE, FRIEDRICH.
   Der Geschichtsunterricht auf Gymnasien und Realgymnasien nach den preussischen Verordnungen von 31 März, 1882. 38 p. S. Ber. 1886.

KEHR, CARL. ed.
   Geschichte der Methodik des deutschen Volksschulunterrichts. 4 v. O. Gotha. 1877-81.
——— ———. Ed. 2. 1887-94.

KEHR, CARL.
   Die Praxis der Volksschule; mit einem Anhange über die besten Lehr-und-Lernmittel auf dem Gebiete des Volksschulunterrichts. Ed. 10. 408 p. O. Gotha. 1885-87.
      Ed. 1 was issued in 1868.

KLEIN, E.
　Ueber Geschichte: Erzählen in Mädchenklassen. (See Schulbote für Hessen. 1896, 48–50.)

KLEMM, L. R.
　European schools. 419 p. D. N. Y. 1889. App. $1.50. (Inter. educ. ser.)
　　A few paragraphs on history in chapters two and three.

KLINGHARDT, JULIUS.
　Die Berücksichtigung der bildenden Kunst beim Unterrichte in der Geschichte und Erdkunde in den mittleren Klassen des Gymnasiums. 16 p. Q. Altenburg. 1896.

KÖCHER, ADOLF.
　Zwei neuere Probleme des Geschichtsunterrichtes auf den höheren Schulen. 23 p. O. Hannover. 1896.
　　The place of history in the curriculum of the grammar school and the treatment of social and economic questions in high school history work.

KORNRUMPF, E.
　Methodische Handbuch für den deutchen Geschichtsunterricht in Volksschulen. Lpz. 1893.

KRIEGER, FERDINAND.
　Der Geschichtsunterricht in Volks-und-Bürgerschulen. 160 p. O. Nürnberg. 1876.

KROUES, F.
　Zum Lehrplane und zur Instruction für den geschichtlichen Unterricht an den Gymnasien in Oesterreich im Jahre 1884. (See Zeit. für die öst. Gym. 1886. 37: sup. 90–98.)

KURTH, GODEFROID.
　De l'enseignement de l'histoire en Allemagne. (See Revue de l'instruction publique en Belgique. 1876, 19: 88–100.)

LEFRANC, ABEL.
　L'enseignement de l'histoire dans les universités de Leipzig et de Berlin. (See Revue inter. de l'enseign. 1888, 15: 239–62.)

LIPP, JOHANN.
　Die Geschichte in der Volksschule. (See Pädagogium. 1888. 10: 653–   .)

LÖBELL, JOHANN WILHELM.
　Grundzüge einer Methodik des geschichtlichen Unterrichts auf Gymnasien. 88 p. O. Lpz. 1847.

LORENZ, OTTOKAR.
　Geschichtsunterricht auf höheren Schulen. (See Nat. Zeitung. 2, May, 1891.)

———.
　Zur Frage über den Geschichtsunterricht am Gymnasium. (See Zeit. für die öst. Gym. 1861, 12: 169–89.)
　　Directed against Campe and Biedermann.

MAHRENHOLTZ, RICHARD.
> Wandlungen der Geschichtsauffassung und des Geschichtsunterrichts besonders in Deutschland. 74 p. O. Hamburg. 1891. (Zeit-und-Streitfragen, 84–85.)

MARTENS, RICHARD.
> Die Neugestaltung des Geschichtsunterrichts auf höheren Lehranstalten. 118 p. O. Lpz. 1892.

MEYER, G. E.
> Der Geschichtsunterricht in der Volksschule. (See Preuss. Schulbl. 1896. Hefte 36–38.)

MIQUÉL, F. W.
> Beiträge eines mit der Herbartischen Pädagogik befreundeten Schulmannes zur Lehre vom biographischen Geschichtsunterricht auf Gymnasien. 61 p. O. Leer. 1847.

MUSTER, F.
> Die Geschichte in der Volksschule; von der Diesterweg Stiftung in Berlin prämiirte Concurrenzschrift. 78 p. O. Köln. 1876.

NEUBAUER, FRIEDRICH.
> Die Kulturgeschichte auf höheren Lehranstalten. (See Zeit. für das Gym. 1897, 51: 257–66.)

NOHASCHEK, H.
> Ueber der Geschichts-Unterricht in einer Volksschule von acht Klassen; ein methodischer Versuch. 40 p. O. Mainz. 1878.

NOHL, CLEMENS.
> Ueber die Nothwendigkeit einer gründlichen Reform des Lehrplans für den Geschichtsunterricht auf Real-und-höheren Bürgerschulen. Neuwied. 1870.

OHL, E.
> Veranschaulichung der Geschichte in der Volksschule. (See Pädagogium. 1890, 12: 308– .)

OMMERBORN, C.
> Der Geschichtsunterricht unter besonderer Berücksichtigung die neueren Erlasse. 64 p. O. Charlottenburg. 1891.

PAULSEN, FRIEDRICH.
> Geschichte der gelehrten Unterrichts auf den deutschen Schulen und Universitaten vom Ausgang des Mittlealters bis zur Gegenwart. 811 p. O. Lpz. 1885.
> Place of history in the German Lehrplan is accurately traced.

PETER, CARL.
> Der Geschichtsunterricht auf Gymnasien. 238 p. O. Halle. 1849.

PIETZSCH, F. W.
> Bericht ü. d. Neugestaltung des Geschichtsunterrichts seit der Berliner Dezemberkonferenz. 18 p. Q. Zwickau Real Gymnasium. 1894.

PRINCE, JOHN TILDEN.
Methods of instruction and organization of the schools of Germany. 237 p. D. Bost. 1892. Lee. $1.15.
History and geography. Chap. 10.

PRUSSIAN elementary school code, translated by A. E. Twentyman. (See Great Britain—House of Commons papers. No. 8447. Special reports on educational subjects. 1896-97. p. 470-80.
Shows the time given to history in the curriculum.

PTASCHNIK, J.
Beitrag zur methodischen Behandlung des geographischen und historischen Unterricht an dem Untergymnasium. (See Zeit. für die öst. Gym. 1853, 4: 455-87; 533-42.)

———.
Die griechische und römische Geschichte im Gymnasium. (See Zeit. für die öst. Gym. 1862, 13: 380-94.)

RAFFAY, ROBERT.
Der Geschichtsunterricht an den österreichischen Mittelschulen. 35 p. Wien. 1889.

RAUSCHEN, GERHARD.
Der Unterricht in der alten Geschichte auf den oberen Klassen des Gymnasiums. Theil. 1. 12 p. Q Andernach. 1890.

RICHTER, ALBRECHT.
Geschichtsunterricht in 17 en Jahrhundert. 27 p. O. Lagensalza. 1893. (Pädagogisches Magazin. Heft 35.)

———.
Die Methodik des Geschichtsunterrichtes der Volksschule in ihrer geschichtlichen Entwickelung. 59 p. O. Gotha. 1889. (Kehr. Geschichte des deutschen Volksschulunterrichtes. 2: 73-132.)

———.
Der Weltgeschichtliche Unterricht in der deutschen Volksschule in seiner methodischen Entwickelung. (See Kehr. Geschichte der Methodik. 1877, 1: 169-211.)

ROSENBURG, HERMANN.
Methodik des Geschichtsunterricht; nach den Grundsätzen der vermittelnden Pädagogik bearbeitet. 120 p. O. Breslau. 1892.
——— ——— Ed. 2. 150 p. 1897.

RUSSELL, JAMES E.
History and geography in the higher schools of Germany. (See School rev. 1897, 5: 257-68; 539-47.)
Reprinted as chapter 15 of his German higher schools. 1899.

SACHSE, FRIEDRICH.
Gesichtspunkte für den Geschichtsunterricht in der Volksschule. (See Praktischer Schulmann. 1875. Heft 1-2.)

SALMON, LUCY MAYNARD.
History in the German gymnasia. (See Educ. rev. 1898, 15: 167-82.)
Also in Report of the Committee of seven. 1899, p. 173-98, and in Amer. hist. ass'n. Report. 1897, p. 75-89

Scheiblhuber, Cl.
Präparationen für den Geschichtsunterricht in der Volksschule. 264 p. O. Straubing. 1897.

Schiller, ———.
Bemerkungen über den Geschichtsunterricht mit besonderer Beziehung auf die bayerischen Schulverordnungen. (See Zeit. für das Gym. 1849, 3:503.)

Schiller, Hermann.
Die neueste Geschichte auf der obersten Stufe des Gymnasialunterrichtes. (See Zeit. für das Gym. 1889, 43:513–36.)

Schmarsow, A.
Die Kunstgeschichte an unseren Hochschulen. 120 p. O. Berlin. 1891.

Seignobos, Charles.
L'enseignement de l'histoire dans les universités allemandes. (See Revue inter. de l'enseign. 1881, 1:563–600.)

Steiner, Karl.
Zur Reform des Geschichtsunterrichts. 16 p. O. Lpz. 1891. (Päd. Sammelmappe. 144.)

Stiehl, F.
Der vaterländische Geschichtsunterricht in unsern Elementarschulen. Koblenz. 1842.

Thiele, R.
Zur Methodik des Geschichtsunterrichts in den unteren und mittleren Klassen höherer Lehranstalten. (See Zeit. für das Gym. 1894, 48:609–16.)

Tieffenbach, Richard.
Wie ist an den humanistischen Gymnasien der geschichtliche Lehrstoff auf die einzelnen Klassen der Oberstufe zu verteilen? (See Zeit. für das Gym. 1891, 45:321–30.)

Uebel, Arthur.
Ueber Geschichtsunterricht in der allgemeinen Fortbildungsschule. (See D. deutsche Fortbildungssch. 1896:106–14.)

Weber, Georg.
Der Geschichtsunterricht in Mittelschulen. Heidelberg. 1864.

White, Andrew Dickson.
European schools of history and politics. (See Johns Hopkins Univ. studies. 1887, ser. 5: no. 12, p. 477–546.)

Würfl, Chr.
Das Lehrpensum der Geographie und Geschichte im 2te Semester der achten Gymnasial classe. (See Zeit. für die öst. Gym. 1890, 41:831–47.)

Zillig, ———.
Der Geschichtsunterricht in der elementaren Erziehungsschulen. (See Jahrbuch des Vereins für wissenschaftlichen Pädagogik. 1882, 14:89–245.)

ZILLIG, PETER.
>   Der Geschichtsunterricht in der Erziehungsschule. (See Rein. Encyklopädisches Handbuch der Pädagogik. 1896, 2:753-65.)

ZIMMERMANN, ———.
>   Die Methode der historischen Unterrichts auf Gymnasien. (See Gymnasialzeitung. 1842, p. 217.)

See bibliographical references accompanying articles on Geschichtsunterricht in the Encyclopedias of Baumeister, Rein, and Schmid for more detailed references on German grade work in history.

Jahresberichte über das höhere Schulwesen and Pädagogischer Jahresbericht are two annuals which list and comment upon the current German literature of this subject.

GREAT BRITAIN.

ADAMS, HERBERT BAXTER.
>   English views on the study of history. (See Index, Dec. 20, 1884.)

ANDREWS, ALICE.
>   Teaching modern history to senior classes. (See Work and play in girls' schools. 1898, p. 124-58.)
>   >   Includes a 20 p. specimen syllabus of English history.

BAKER, ARTHUR.
>   On the teaching of history. (See Journal of educ. Lond. 1891, 13:19-20.)
>   >   Read before the Teachers' Guild.

BARNETT, PERCY ARTHUR. *ed.*
>   Teaching and organization with special reference to secondary schools. 419 p. O. Lond. 1897. Longmans. $2.
>   >   History, p. 161-98. Fresh, clear, and practical.

BROWNING, OSCAR.
>   Teaching of history in schools. 20 p. O. Lond. 1887. Longmans. 1s.
>   >   Also in Royal historical society. Transactions. 1889, p. 69-84.

BURSTALL, S. R.
>   History teaching in schools. (See Journal of educ. Lond. 1895, 17:381-82.)

CHARLES, R. F.
>   History teaching in schools. (See Journal of educ. Lond. 1895, 17:379-81.)

CURRIE, JAMES.
>   Principles and practice of common-school education. 504 p. D. Lond. n. d. Stewart.
>   >   History, p. 473-84.

FOX, GEORGE L.
>   History in English secondary schools. (See Report of the Committee of seven. 1899, p. 210-30.)
>   >   Also in Amer. hist. assn. Report. 1898, p. 539-50.

FRÉDÉRICQ, PAUL.
De l'enseignement supérieur de l'histoire en Écosse et en Angleterre. (See Revue inter. de l'enseign. 1885, 9:500-20; 10:106-28.)

———.
The study of history in England and Scotland; trans. by Henrietta Leonard. (See Johns Hopkins Univ. studies. 1887, ser. 5, no. 10, 54 p.

HARRISON, FREDERIC.
Royal road to history. (See Fortnightly rev. 1893, 60:478-91.)
Reprinted as chapter 4 in his Meaning of history.

HISTORICAL study at Oxford. (See Bentley's Quarterly rev. 1895, 1:282-300.)

HODGKIN, HOWARD.
The study of history in the University of Cambridge, England. (See Alumnus. 1879.)

How English history is not taught in England. (See Rev. of rev. 1897, 16:101.)
Extract from Dr. Miller Maguires' lecture The national study of military history.

SECONDARY history teaching in Scotland. (See Amer. jour. of educ. Barnards. 1871, 22:691-92.)

SMITH, ARTHUR L.
Historical teaching in public schools. (See Academy. 1897, 51: 106-7.)

SOMERVELL, R.
Modern history. (See Barnett. Teaching and organization. 1897, p. 161-79.)

STUBBERT, MARY R. W.
The Cambridge school of history. (See Amer. hist. assn. Report. 1898, p. 383-411.)

STUDY of history at Oxford. (See Nation. 1895, 60:274-5.

WELLS, J.
The teaching of history in schools. Lond. 1892. Methuen.
An Oxford extension lecture.

WITHERS, H. L.
Ancient history. (See Barnett. Teaching and organization. 1897, p. 180-98.)

UNITED STATES.

ADAMS, HERBERT BAXTER.
History in American colleges.
Amherst. (See Education. 1886. 7:177-87.)
Columbia. (See Education. 1886. 7:7-14; 92-100; 177-87.)
Harvard. (See Education. 1886. 6:535-47; 618-33.)
Yale. (See Education. 1887. 7:334-44).

———.
The study of history in American colleges and universities. 299 p. illus. O. Wash. 1887. (Bureau of educ. Circular of information no. 2.)
Revised and very much extended from the articles in Education.

ALLEN, WILLIAM FRANCIS.
 Instruction in American history. (See Wisconsin journal of education. v. 4. Oct., 1874.)

AMERICAN HISTORICAL ASSOCIATION.
 Preliminary report of the Committee of seven on study of history in schools. (See School review. 1897, 5:346-9.)

BALCH, GEORGE T.
 Methods of teaching patriotism in the public schools. 109 p. O. N. Y. 1890. Van Nostrand. $1.50.
 From an address delivered June 28, 1889, before the teachers of the Children's aid society, N. Y. City.

BARNES, MRS. MARY DOWNING (SHELDON).
 General history in the high school. (See Academy, Syracuse. 1889, 4:285-91.)

————.
 Teacher's manual to American history. 155 p. D. Bost. 1893. Heath. 60c.
 "Vital, original, and stimulating." Monroe.

BURGESS, ISAAC B.
 Method of college preparatory teaching of history. (See Academy, Syracuse. 1883, 3:293-305.)

BURGESS, JOHN WILLIAM.
 Methods of historical study and research in Columbia University. (See Hall. Methods of teaching history. Ed. 2. 1886, p. 215-21.)

BUTLER, NICHOLAS MURRAY.
 Reform of secondary education in the United States. (See Atlan. Mo. 1894, 73:372-84.)
 A review of the report of the Committee of ten.

CHANNING, EDWARD, and HART, ALBERT BUSHNELL.
 Guide to the study of American history. 471 p. D. Bost. 1896. Ginn. $2.15.
 The most useful book to the teacher of American history. Treats of method and materials, with full bibliographies and topical references. Thoroughly indexed.

CLOW, F. R.
 Outline of work in professional history in the State normal school, Oshkosh, Wis. 11 p. O. 1897.

DOUGHERTY, NEWTON C.
 The study of history in our public schools. (See Nat. educ. ass'n. Proceedings. 1897, p. 58-67.)

DRAKE, J. H.
 Roman constitutional history in our high schools. (See School review. 1900, 8:146-56.)

FOSTER, WILLIAM EATON.
 Use of a public library in the study of history. (See Hall. Methods of teaching history. Ed. 2. 1886, p. 105-11.)

GORDY, WILBUR F., and TWITCHELL, WILLIS IRA.
 A pathfinder in American history. 261 p. D. Bost. °1893. Lee & Shepard. $1.20.

HALL, C. P.
: History of the civil war; what and how much shall be taught. (See Education. 1887, 7:470-81.)

HART, ALBERT BUSHNELL.
: History in high and preparatory schools. (See Academy, Syracuse. 1887, 2:256-65; 306-15.)
  Reprinted separately. 22 p. O. Syracuse, 1887.

——.
: Methods of teaching American history. (See Hall. Methods of teaching history. Ed. 2. 1886, p. 1-31.)

——.
: Revised suggestions on the study of the history and government of the United States. 164 p. O. Camb. 1895. Harv. univ.
  While designed specially for Harvard students, it is valuable to secondary teachers as showing clearly the nature of the college work to which their students go.

——.
: Studies in American education. 150 p. D. N. Y. 1895. Longmans. $1.25.
  Essays 4 and 5 on History.

HINSDALE, BURKE AARON.
: History teaching in schools. (See Nat. educ. ass'n. Proceedings. 1895, p. 360-70.)
  Abstracted in School Journal. Mar. 9, 1895.

HULING, RAY GREENE.
: History in secondary education. (See Educ. rev. 1894, 7:448-59; 8:43-53.)

JUDSON, HARRY PRATT.
: History in Secondary schools. (See Education. 1885, 6:19-25.)

——.
: Teaching history in secondary schools. (See Univ. state of N. Y.—23rd convocation. 1885. Proceedings. p. 81-96.)
  In regents' report 99 a long discussion follows.

LAURIE, SIMON SOMERVILLE.
: History in the school. (See School review. 1896, 4:649-63.)

MACALISTER, JAMES.
: Syllabus of a course of elementary instruction in U. S. history and civil government. 44 p. Phil. 1887.

MATHES, EDWARD T.
: Teaching American history. (See N. Y. educ. 1898, 1:326-29.)

MOWRY, WILLIAM AUGUSTUS.
: History of our country; how to teach it. (See Common school educ. 1888-89, v. 2-3.)
  Six articles in v. 2; five articles in v. 3.

NEW ENGLAND HISTORY TEACHERS' ASSOCIATION.—COMMITTEE ON TEXT-BOOKS.
: Text-books in American history. (See Educ. rev. D. 1898, 16:480-502.)
  Contains critical and descriptive notes on 19 leading text-books.

NEW YORK (STATE)—UNIVERSITY.
Aims and methods in teaching United States history; a discussion at the 9th annual conference of Associated academic principals. (See Regents' bulletin 30. 1893, p. 538–47.)

ROBINSON, EDWARD VAN DYKE.
An ideal course in history for secondary schools. (See Nat. educ. assn. 1897, p. 679–83.)

———.
Topics for supplementary reading and discussion in United States history. (See School rev. 1897, 5:302–8.)

ROBINSON, JAMES HARVEY.
Teaching European history in college. (See Educ. rev. 1898, 16:28–39.)

ROLLINS, GEORGE W.
American history in preparatory schools. (See Academy, Syracuse. 1886, 1:133–39.)

SALMON, LUCY MAYNARD.
The teaching of history in academies and colleges. (See Academy, Syracuse. 1890, 5:283–92.)
> Also in Women and the higher education, N. Y., 1893, and in the proceedings of convocation of Univ. of the state of New York, 1890, where it is followed by a long discussion.

SCOTT, HENRY E.
Courses of study in history, Roman law and political economy at Harvard univ. (See Hall. Methods of teaching history. Ed. 2. 1886, p. 167–92.)

SEERLEY, HOMER H.
The essentials of United States history to be taught in secondary schools. (See Nat. educ. ass'n. Proceedings. 1898, p. 77–87.)

SLOANE, WILLIAM MILLIGAN.
The department of history in Columbia university. (See Columbia university bulletin, June, 1898, 20:181–94.)

STEPHENS, HENRY MORSE.
History in the secondary schools. (See Nat. educ. ass'n. Proceedings. 1896, p. 623–30.)

THORPE, FRANCIS NEWTON.
History in American schools. (See Education. 1886, 7:234–43; 149–58.)
> Also reprinted with title Study of United States history in schools, colleges, and universities.

———.
Study of current topics as a feature of school, academic, and college education. (See Education. 1890, 11:170–74.)

———.
Teaching American history. (See Education. 1887, 7:686–90.)

TRAINER, JOHN.
> How to teach and study United States history by the Brace system. 335 p. O. Chic. 1895. Flanagan. $1.
>
> The Brace system is a plan of bracket analysis.

U. S.—BUREAU OF EDUCATION.
> The study of history in American colleges and universities, by Herbert B. Adams. 299 p. illus. O. Wash. 1887. (Circular of information no. 2.)

WELSH, CHARLES.
> English history in American school text-books. (See Educ. rev. 1900, 19: 23–35.)
>> Discusses, with illustrative quotations, the unjust and partial picturing of England in our text-books.

WEST, WILLIS M.
> History in the high school. (See Nat. educ. ass'n. Proceedings. 1890, p. 648–55.)

WHITE, ANDREW DICKSON.
> Historical instruction in the course of history and political science at Cornell university. (See Hall. Methods of teaching history. Ed. 2. 1886, p. 71–76.

WINTERBURN, ROSE BARTON.
> History work in high schools. (See Academy, Syracuse. 1891, 6: 510–18.)

WRONG, GEORGE M.
> History in Canadian secondary schools. (See Report of the Committee of seven. 1899, p. 231–38.)

ZELLER, J. W.
> Manual containing suggestions and 500 questions and answers to be used in connection with United States history and civil government study. 45 p. D. Phil. 1896. McConnell. 15c.

ZIMMERN, ALICE.
> Methods of education in the United States. 178 p. D. Lond. 1894. Sonnenschein. $1.
>> History, p. 61–77.

APPENDICES.

APPENDIX A.

The books in English of most value to the teacher of history in secondary schools. Fuller details of each title will be found with its entry in the body of the bibliography.

ADAMS, C. K.
> Manual of historical literature. 1882.
>> See note under this entry in the bibliography.

AMERICAN HISTORICAL ASSOCIATION.
> Report of the Committee of seven on history study in schools. 1899.

BARNES, MRS. MARY D. SHELDON.
    Studies in historical method. 1896.
CHANNING, EDWARD, and HART, ALBERT BUSHNELL.
    Guide to the study of American history. 1896.
FREEMAN, E. A.
    The methods of historical study. 1886.
HALL, G. S. *ed.*
    Methods of teaching history. Ed. 2. 1886.
HINSDALE, B. A.
    How to study and teach history. 1894.
MACE, W. H.
    Method in history. 1897.

APPENDIX B.

Books in German which have not been translated, of most value to the American teacher of history.

BAAR, JOSEPH.
    Studen über den geschichtlichen Unterricht an den höheren Lehranstalten des Auslandes. 1895–97.
BERNHEIM, ERNST.
    Lehrbuch der historischen methode. 1894.
FREE, H.
    Der gänzliche Neugestaltung des Geschichtsunterrichts in der Volksschule. 1897.
JÄGER, E. F. O.
    Didaktik und Methodik des Geschichtsunterricht. 1895.
LORENZ, KARL.
    Der moderne Geschichtsunterricht. 1897.

XX.—TITLES OF BOOKS ON ENGLISH HISTORY PUBLISHED IN 1897 AND 1898.

SELECTED AND ANNOTATED

By W. DAWSON JOHNSTON.

(Reprinted, without the incidental criticism, from annotated titles of books on English history published by the American Library Association. Issued both in pamphlet form and on cards for use in card catalogues.)

TITLES OF BOOKS ON ENGLISH HISTORY PUBLISHED IN 1897 AND 1898.

With notes by W. DAWSON JOHNSTON.

1897.

ABBOTT, EVELYN and CAMPBELL, LEWIS.
Life and letters of Benjamin Jowett. N. Y., Dutton; London, Murray. 1897. 2 v. Portraits, plates, facsim. O. $10.

> Biographia of "the 19th century Dr. Johnson," the Master of Balliol; from some 50 volumes of Jowett's notes of conversations and of his own thoughts and letters, all letters to Jowett having been destroyed; contains much of unique value for the history of English national life and thought since 1836, the church, Oxford, Balliol, and Greek studies, with references to Browning, Eliot, Disraeli, Carlyle, Ruskin, Stanley, Symonds, Toynbee, etc., but with few personalities; with illustrative letters, and list of Jowett's works and portraits. A number of valuable letters on more general topics are reserved for another volume; of general interest and value, being good biographical material.
> Ath. 1897. 1: 437; Nation 64: 418; Sat. R. 83: 385; Ed. R. 185: 405; Quar. 185: 331.

ATKINSON, THOMAS DINHAM.
Cambridge described and illustrated, being a short history of the town and university. London and N. Y. Macmillan. 1897. 37+528 p. illus. plates, maps. O. $7.

> From Cooper, Willis, and Clark, Cambridge Antiquarian Society. *Contents:* Town, 1-241, gilds, topography, architecture, churches, religious houses, fairs, schools; University, 241-502, with bibliographical list, and introduction by J. W. Clark. Another history of the town is by Cooper, of the university, by Mullinger.
> Eng. Hist. R. 13: 389 (J. B. Mullinger); Spec. 79: 900; Nation 66: 117.

BLOMFIELD, REGINALD.
History of Renaissance architecture in England, 1500-1800. London, Bell [N. Y., Macmillan]. 1897. 2 v. Q. $16.

> From the most important sources and authorities, the Soane Museum, Transactions of the Institute of British Architects, etc.; describes the influence of Italy on ornamentation in the southern counties in the time of Henry 8 and Edward 6, and of Germany in the eastern counties in the time of Elizabeth and James, the country house, the Palladianism of Inigo Jones, the block plan, architectural literature, survivals of Gothic, Sir Chris. Wren, French and Dutch influence, the academic Palladians, eclecticism; with information about the stage, the trades, carpentry, masonry, etc., and numerous reproductions of contemporary prints; supplementary to Gotch's views 1560-1630, and Belcher and Macartney, 1640-1800.
> Ath, 1897. 2: 790; Ed. R. 187: 415; Acad. 52: 477.

CUNNINGHAM, WILLIAM.
> Alien immigrants to England. London, Sonnenschein; N. Y., Macmillan. 1897. 23+286 p. D. $1.25.
>
>> A history; contains a brief account of the Norman political invasion, mediæval industrial settlements, Jew, Flamand, Gascon; religious refugees, Dutch, Huguenot; French emigrés 1789; a contribution to the history of economic and social conditions and of foreign relations.
>> Econ. J. 8:214 (H. A. L. Fisher); Econ. R. 8:266 (J. C. Medd); Ath. 1898. 1:273; Nation 66:267.
>> Eng. Hist. R. 13:268 (A. F. Pollard).

EGERTON, HUGH EDWARD.
> Short history of British colonial policy. London, Methuen. 1897. 15+503 p. O. 12s. 6d.
>
>> From the most accessible printed sources and authorities, Bruce, Brown, etc. *Contents:* Beginnings, Trade ascendancy. Systematic colonization and granting of responsible government, Zenith and decline of laissez-aller principles; Greater. Britain; descriptive of events and opinion, with short bibliography) 481-91); a good book for reference, clear, dry, Imperialist. See also introduction to this subject, J. R. Seeley's "Expansion of England," and the constitutional treatise by Alpheus Todd.
>> Econ. R. 8:261 (W. R. Inge); Nation 66:190; Sat. R. 85:558; Ath. 1897. 2:853. Pol. Sci. Q. 8:538 (G. L. Beer); Eng. Hist. R. 13:778 (E. J. Payne).

FLEMING, DAVID HAY.
> Mary Queen of Scots, from her birth to her flight into England. London, Hodder. 1897. 12+543 p. O. 7s. 6d.
>
>> A biographical essay; from the Hamilton Papers, Detectio, Book of Articles, etc.; tabulating for the first time the whole of the evidence of the Register of the Privy Seal regarding her movements in an itinerary, with critical notes, p. 177-491, and a few documents hitherto unpublished, p. 491-515.
>> Ath. 1897. 2:703, 821; Sat. R. 84:754; Spec. 79:932; Acad. 52:521.

GARDINER, SAMUEL RAWSON.
> Cromwell's place in history. London and N. Y., Longmans. 1897. 5+120 p. D. $1.
>
>> A biographical essay, aiming "to estimate his relation to the political and ecclesiastical movements of his time, to show how he was influenced by them and influenced them in turn;" represents Cromwell to have been a warrior rather than statesman, and his work destructive, not constructive, "the greatest because the most typical Englishman of all time."
>> Am. Hist. R. 3:135 (Goldwin Smith); Atlan. 81:842 (J. F. Rhodes); Nation 65:132 (A. V. Dicey); Ath. 1897. 2:873; Hist. Ztsch. 81:330 (A. Stern); Eng. Hist. R. 12:578 (G. P. Gooch).

GARDINER, SAMUEL RAWSON.
> What Gunpowder Plot was. London and N. Y., Longmans. 1897. 8+208 p. illus. plate. D. $1.50.
>
>> A critical essay upon the origin of the Gunpowder Plot in reply to Father Gerard's "What was the gunpowder plot?" (Jesuit); discusses in defense of the traditional story the evidences and the topography of the story, and the policy of the Government toward priests and Catholics. See also the work of David Jardine, 1857.
>> Am. Hist. R. 3:348 (W. D. Johnston); Nation 65:400 (C. W. Colby); Dub. R. 120:299 (B. Cam); Gardiner-Gerard controversy continued in [on the character of

the conspirators] Gerard's "Gunpowder plot and gunpowder plotters," and in articles on Garnet in The Month 63.58,382; 64:41 and [on the character of the evidence] in Gerard's "Thomas Winter's confession," and in the Athenæum, 1897. 2·785,855; 1898. 1:23; 2:352. See also A. Bellesheim in Hist-polit. Blätter 121:8.

GROSS, CHARLES.
Bibliography of British municipal history, including guilds and Parliamentary representation. London and N. Y., Longmans. 1897. 34+461 p. O. $2.50.

A select list of books, pamphlets, magazine articles, and papers of learned societies; bibliographies, catalogues, general public records, general municipal histories, Roman and Anglo-Saxon periods, later mediæval ages, modern times, 19th century, municipal reform, parliamentary history, guilds, county histories, Cinque Ports, Ireland, Scotland, Wales, particular town records and histories, A-Y; with critical notes and an introduction; of special value to the municipal historian, of general value as a supplement to J. P. Anderson, 1881, which is the most complete general bibliography of town history.
Am. Hist. R. 3:528 (G. E. Howard); Nation 66:35; Ath. 1898. 1:629; Acad. 53·148; Pol. Sci. Q. 13:191. Eng. Hist. R. 13:816 (F. W. M).

HAZLITT, WILLIAM CAREW.
Four generations of a literary family: the Hazlitts in England, Ireland, and America, 1725–1896. London and N. Y., Redway. 1897. 2 v. portraits. O. 31s. 6d.

Biography and memoir; from the Diary of Margaret Hazlitt, etc. *Contents:* 1. The American visit, 1783–88. 2. Wm. Hazlitt, artist and writer; Sir. Jas. Mackintosh, Godwin, Jerdan. 3. William Hazlitt, journalist and judge; Carlyle, Turner, Bentham, Hepworth Dixon, Our Club. 4. W. C. Hazlitt, Merchant Tylors' School, the Lamb Letters, London suburban life, Thos. Wright, S. C. Hall, John Forster, the royal family, Gladstone, Browning, Tennyson, Huth, Laing, Sotheby's, the British Museum, etc., anecdotes and characterizations. See also Memoirs of Wm. Hazlitt, 1867.
Acad. 51:198; Sat. R. 83:147.

KING, CHARLES COOPER.
Story of the British army. London, Methuen. 1897. 10+426 p. illus. maps, plans. O. 7s. 6d.

Describes the development of armament, organism, and tactics in different wars, especially in the modern period, 1793–1896 (p. 128–407), in the Peninsula, the Crimea, India, and Africa, with lists of campaigns and battles since 1688, of regiments, badges, mottoes, and nicknames, and illustrations of arms, armor, uniforms, etc.; of interest to the general reader, readable and reliable. See also History of the army, by Sir Sibbald Scott, 3 v., 1868–80.
Ath. 1898. 1:305; Nation 66:465; Eng. Hist. R. 13:762 (J. E. Morris).

LAW, ERNEST.
Short history of Hampton Court. London, Bell [N. Y., Macmillan]. 1897. 11+421 p. illus. portraits. O. $3.

An abridgment of the author's larger work, 3 v., 1885–91, but less topographical, with little about architecture and art; contains much relating to the royal household, court life, and diplomacy, Wolsey, the Conference 1604, the King's confinement 1647, a popular resort; with reproductions of many contemporary prints. See also work by W H. Hutton, 1897.
Ath. 1897. 2:784; Spec. 80:92; M. of Art, 22:234.

McCarthy, Justin.
Story of Gladstone's life. N. Y. and London. Macmillan. 1897c. 12+436 p. Illus. portraits, plates. O. $6.

> A Home ruler's memoir of Gladstone; based upon personal acquaintance. See also biographies by G. B. Smith and G. W. F. Russell. Careful Gladstone bibliography, Notes and queries, Dec. 10, 24, 1892; Jan. 7, 21, 1893.
> Ath. 1898. 1: 182; Sat. R. 85: 178; Spec. 80: 312; Acad. 53: 199.

Mahan, Alfred Thayer.
The life of Nelson the embodiment of the sea power of Great Britain. Boston. Little, Brown. 1897. 2 v. Portraits, plate, map, plans. O. $8.

> From the collection of Hamilton and Nelson letters published by Alfred Morrison, etc.; makes Nelson describe himself as far as possible, tell the story of his own inner life as well as of his external actions. See Macmil. 76: 92 (D. Hannay) "Nelson and his biographers."
> Fortn. 67: 895 (W. O. Morris); Eng. Hist. R. 12: 801 (J. K. Laughton); 19th Cent. 41: 893 (G. S. Clarke); Nation 64: 285 (C. W. Colby); Sat. R. 83: 363 (P. H. Colomb); Ed. R. 186: 84; Atlan. 80: 264; Ath. 1897. 1: 497.

Maitland, Frederic William.
Domesday Book and beyond; three essays in the early history of England. Cambridge [Eng.] University press. 1897. 13+527 p. O. $4.50.

> A discussion of Anglo-Saxon institutions since Kemble; by the authority upon early English law; using Round and Meitzen. *Contents:* 1. Domesday Book a geld book, villeins, sake and soke, manor, borough. 2. England before the Conquest, bookland, folkland, village community. 3. The hide; of value as a criticism, especially of Seebohm, and for its discussion of these theses; no manorial system before the 12th and 13th centuries; the village and agrarian not a political community; origin of the borough military not economic, etc.
> Eng. Hist. R. 12: 768 (James Tait); Am. Hist. R. 3: 130 (C. M. Andrews); Pol. Sc. Q. 12: 715 (C. Gross); Ath. 1897. 1: 274.

Mason, Arthur James.
Ed. Mission of St. Augustine to England, according to the original documents, being a handbook for the 13th centenary. Cambridge [Eng.] University press. 1897. 19+252 p., maps. D. 5s.

> A complete collection of authentic documents relating to Augustine's mission; from the works of Gregory and Bede, with translations and explanatory notes; essay on the sources, the Editor; political outlook of Europe 597, C. W. Oman; Augustine's mission in relation to other agencies in the conversion of England, the Editor; Landing place of, with map, T. M. Hughes; some liturgical points relating to, H. A. Wilson; Anglican. See also Works of G. F. Browne 1897 (Anglican), and Father Brou 1897 (Romanist), and Bassenge 1890.
> Ath. 1897. 2: 313; Sat. R. 83: 640.

Masterman, John Howard Bertram.
Age of Milton. London, Bell [N. Y., Macmillan]. 1897. 21+254 p. D. 3s. 6d.

> A manual of English literature 1632-60; from the most accessible authorities; contains bibliographic notes on Milton, Sir Thos. Browne, Fuller, Hobbes, the dramatic and lyrical poets, theological, historical, and biographical writers, etc., with introduction and articles on Cowley, Hacket, Falkland, and the Cambridge Platonists by J. B. Mullinger.
> Ath. 1897. 2: 64; Acad. 52: 130.

OLIPHANT, MRS. MARGARET OLIPHANT (WILSON).
Annals of a publishing house: William Blackwood and his sons, their magazine and friends. London, Blackwood; N. Y., Scribner. 1897. 2 v. Portraits. O. $10.50.

> Contains much matter illustrative of the history of periodical literature 1815–1861, Blackwood's New Monthly, Quarterly, Spectator, and of the work of Scott, Lockhart, Wilson, Hogg, Maguire, Coleridge, De Quincey, Galt, Croker, Croly, Gleig, Hemans, Thackeray, Lytton, Eliot, Disraeli, Kinglake, etc.
> Longm. 31:117 (H. Maxwell); Fortn. 68:853 (C. Stein); Nation 65:179; Ed. R. 187:40; Ath. 1897. 2:517; Contemp. 72:632; Sat. R. 84:559; Westm. 148:665; Blackw. 162:864.

ORDISH, THOMAS FAIRMAN.
Shakespeare's London. London, Dent; N. Y., Macmillan 1897. 7+257 p. Illus. S.

> A useful study of Shakespeare's London environment; from John Gerrard's Herball, Stowe, Hentzner, etc. *Contents:* The English historical plays, Nature and London, The comedies, Shakespeare's London haunts.
> Spect. 79:859.

POLLARD, ALBERT FREDERICK, *editor*.
Political pamphlets. London, Kegan Paul; N. Y., Holt. 1897. 6+345 p. D. 6s.

> Pamphlets selected for their style and influence: Sexby's Killing no murder, Halifax's Draft of a new model at sea, Halifax's Choice of members of Parliament, Arbuthnot's Political lying, Steele's Crisis, Swift's Present state of affairs, Bolingbroke's State of parties 1714, Swift's Drapier's letters, No. 4, Junius's letter No. 1, Junius's letter to the Duke of Bedford, Junius's letter to the King, Burke's Thoughts on the cause of present discontents, Burke's letters on a regicide peace No. 3; with introduction and notes. See also Collections of Henry Morley, 1890, and George Saintsbury, 1892.
> Acad. 51:623; Spec. 79:464.

ROBERTS, FREDERICK SLEIGH, 1st baron.
Forty-one years in India. London, Bentley; N. Y., Longmans. 1897. 2 v. Portraits, plates, maps. O. $12.

> Reminiscences of the most distinguished soldier of this generation in India. *Contents:* V. 1, 1852–63. V. 2, 1863–93. A most intimate view of the more important military operations, with conclusions upon the political causes and consequences of such momentous events as the Sepoy mutiny and the second Afghan war, with appendices of documents.
> Fortn. 68:750 (J. M. Innes); Sat. R. 83:83 (C. W. Dilke) 84:281; Acad. 51:169 (F. A. Steele); Ed. R. 185:1; Quar. 186:552; Blackw. 161:297; Ath. 1897. 1:39, 75.

TAUNTON, ETHELRED L.
English black monks of St. Benedict. London, Nimmo; N. Y., Longmans. 1897. 2 v. O. $7.50.

> A history of the English Benedictines 597–1897; from original sources, Reyner, etc.; with résumé of the Consuetudinary of St. Augustine's, Canterbury. See also work on English monasticism in general by T. D. Fosbroke.
> Eng. Hist. R. 13:556 (M. Bateson); Dub. R. 122:439; Ath. 1898. 1:461; Am. Cath. Q. 23:442.

TRAILL, HENRY DUFF, *editor*.

Social England, a record of the progress of the people in religion, laws, learning, arts, industry, commerce, science, literature, and manners. London, Cassell; N. Y., Putnams. 1893-97. 6 v. O.

> A popular encyclopedic history; by specialists, of whom at least Maitland. Saintsbury, Prothero, Oman, Bateson, Poole, Powell, Gasquet, Hall, Clowes, Mullinger, Griffiths, and Keltic are authorities. *Contents:* v. 1, to 1372. v. 2, to 1509. v. 3, to 1603. v. 4, to 1714. v. 5, to 1815. v. 6, to 1885.
> V. 1-3. Eng. Hist. R. 9:721; 10:359; Ath. 1894. 2:489; 1895, 2:88;.—v. 4. Eng. Hist. R. 11:378 (S. R. Gardiner).—v. 5. Ath. 1896. 2:153.—v. 6. Ath. 1897. 2:279. Eng. Hist. R. 13:807 (G. W. Prothero).

TURNER, B. B.

Chronicles of the Bank of England. London, Sonnenschein. 1897. 12+296 p., illus. O. 7s. 6d.

> A short history of the Bank of England; by a clerk in the bank; based upon John Francis and the Bankers' magazine; contains a summary of the history of the bank, particularly of the history of forgeries, etc., with little about its organization or position in the monetary world; indicates among other things the relation of the bank to the Revolution of 1688, Whig Party, South Sea Bubble, '45, Loyalty Loan of 1796. See also history by John Francis 2 v. 1862, and bibliography of the subject by Thos. A. Stephens, 1897.
> Ath. 1898, 1:147; Sat. R. 84:758.

WHITE, WILLIAM.

Inner life of the House of Commons; edited by Justin McCarthy. London, Unwin. 1897. 2 v. O. 16s.

> A reporter's sketches of notable debates and debaters in the Commons, 1856-1871; from the Illustrated Times; contains sketches of Brougham, Palmerston, Peel, Lewis, Russell, Cobden, Bright, Lytton, Disraeli, Gladstone, J. S. Mills, Roebuck, Northcote, Miall, Kinglake, Lowe, Stratford, Canning, Salisbury, Lefevre, Hughes, Forster, Dilke, etc.; a supplement to the works of Jennings, Lucy, and others on the later period.
> Stat. R. 83:525 (C. W. Dilke); Westm. 149:708.

WINDLE, BERTRAM COGHILL ALAN.

Life in early Britain, being an account of the early inhabitants of this island and the memorials which they have left behind them. London, Nutt; N. Y., Putnams. 1897. 15+244 p. illus. maps, plans. D. $1.25.

> A good handbook of British archæology. *Contents:* Palæolithic man, Neolithic, Bronze period, Roman, Saxon, tribal and village communities, traces of past races, with list of places where remains are found, and bibliographical list. See also Works of Boyd Dawkins, Seebohm, and others.

1898.

ABBOTT, EDWIN ABBOTT.

St. Thomas of Canterbury, his death and miracles. London, Black; N. Y., Macmillan. 1898. 2 v. O. $7.50.

> A critical discussion of the Becket miracles, and of the early accounts of the murder and miracles; a valuable study of mediæval religious thought, and a good supplement to such works as "The life and miracles of St. William of Norwich by Thomas of Monmouth," edited by A Jessopp, 1896. See also Biography of Becket by John Morris, S. J., 1885, and the Protestant account by J. A. Froude, 1878.
> Church Q. 47:435; Sat. R. 87:115; Ath. 1899. 1:74.

ADDY, SIDNEY OLDALL.
> Evolution of the English house. (Social England series.) London, Sonnenschein; N. Y., Macmillan. 1898. 28+223 p., illus., plate. D. $1.50.
>> A monograph upon the mediæval history of the English house; from such works as Konrad Lange "Haus und Halle" 1885; Anderson "Scotland in early Christian times" 1881; Stokes "Early Christian architecture in Ireland" 1878, and O'Curry "Ancient Irish," 3 v. 1873; describes the underground house, the round house, the rectangular house, manor house, town house, castle, church, with list of authorities. See also Work upon the subject by T. H. Turner and J. H. Parker, "Domestic architecture in England" 1066-1485, 3 v. in 4, 1851-1859.
>> Eng. Hist. R. 14: 588 (Edith Thompson); Nation 68: 336.

ALLEN, WILLIAM OSBORN BIRD and MCCLURE, EDMUND.
> Two hundred years: The history of the Society for promoting Christian knowledge, 1698-1898. London, S. P. C. K. 1898. 6+551 p. Illus. plate. O. 10s. 6d.
>> A manual of historical data; from the records, letter books, reports, and minutes of the society; throws light on the history of the Anglican Church in the 18th century, education, missions, the colonies; with extracts from the correspondence, etc., and a few illustrations.
>> Ath. 1898. 2: 315; Sat. R. 86: 444; Acad. 53: 574; Spec. 81: 51.

ARCH, JOSEPH.
> Story of his life told by himself; edited by the Countess of Warwick. London, Hutchinson. 1898. Second ed. 20+412 p. portrait. O. 12s.
>> Autobiography of a Liberal agitator, 1826-1898; contains much relative to the history of the National agricultural laborers' union, the game laws, emigration, household franchise, land question, and to the social, political, and religious conditions of the laboring class; supplements Arthur Clayden "Revolt of the field," 1874, a sketch of the history of the National agricultural laborers' union, and the Memoir of Arch by F. S. Attenborough.
>> Ath. 1898. 1: 148; Stat. R. 85: 114; Acad. 53: 113; Spec. 80: 273.

ASHBOURNE, EDWARD GIBSON, 1st baron.
> Pitt: Some chapters of his life and times. London and N.Y., Longmans. 1898. 14+395 p., portraits. O. $6.
>> Studies in the life and times of William Pitt, 1759-1806; from new materials among the Bolton papers, the Pitt papers, and the Stanhope collection; contains new light on the events which led up to the Union of 1800 and the failure of Pitt's Irish policy—Rutland, Orde, and the commercial resolution of 1785, the Fitzwilliam vice-royalty of 1795, Lord Clare, Lord chancellor; together with chapters on Pitt's youth, relations with his mother, his one love story, and his relations with his first biographer, Bp. Tomline; supplements T. D. Ingram's "History of the Union" 1887, and Stanhope's standard biography of Pitt, 2d ed. 4 v. 1862.
>> Eng. Hist. R. 14: 574 (R. Dunlop); Am. Hist. R. 4: 527 (Goldwin Smith); Qu. R. 189: 359. Ath. 1898, 2: 531, 919.

AUBREY, JOHN.
> Brief lives, chiefly of contemporaries set down between 1669 and 1696; edited by Andrew Clark. Oxford, Clarendon press. 1898. 2 v. Portrait, plates. O. 25s.
>> Collective biography, writers, politicians, etc., Chaucer to 1696; gives in full all in the four chief MSS. of biographies, the pith of which was extracted by Wood for his Athenae.
>> Eng. Hist. R. 11: 328 (A. Clark), 13: 787 (Douglas Macleane); Nation, 67: 171; Ath. 1898. 2: 150.

BROOKE, STOPFORD AGUSTUS.
   English literature from the beginning to the Norman conquest. London and N. Y., Macmillan. 1898. 9+338 p. D. $1.50.
   A manual, abridged, rewritten, and rearranged from the author's "History of early English literature," which was a history of English poetry to the accession of King Alfred; with a bibliographical note. See also The work by John Earle, 1884, or the critical work by Wülker, "Grundriss zur Geschichte der angelsächsischen Litteratur. Wülker's edition of Grein's Bibliothek der angel-sächsischen Poesie," 3 v. 1883–1897, contains the complete text of all the old English poetry. There is also a study of Aelfric by Caroline L. White, Boston, 1898.
   Ath. 1898. 2:746.

CADELL, SIR ROBERT.
   Sir John Cope and the Rebellion of 1745. Edinburgh, Blackwood. 1898. 12+[2]+282 p., map, plan. O.
   A defense of Sir John Cope, commander of the English forces in Scotland in 1745; by a military authority; from hitherto unused "Proceedings of the Trial of Sir John Cope;" presents an account of the battle of Prestonpans and Cope's responsibility, with criticism of Philip Doddridge's life of Col. James Gardiner 1747, and the Narrative of Murray of Broughton, and list of authorities; of value to the student. See also Alex. C. Ewald's "Life and times of Prince Charles Stuart" 1875, 1883; Walter B. Blaikie's "Itinerary of Prince Charles Edward Stuart," Scot. Hist. Soc. 1897; Robert Chamber's popular Jacobite story 1828, and the contemporary Henderson's Prince Frederick-Whig account.
   Ath. 1899. 1:172.

CAMPERDOWN, ROBERT ADAM PHILIPS HALDANE-DUNCAN, 3d earl of. Admiral Duncan.
   London and N. Y., Longmans. 1898. 11+[2]+416 p. Portraits, plan. O. $5.
   The life of Adam Duncan, 1746–1804; from official letters and orders, Lord Spencer's private letters, etc.; gives an outline of his life and career in the navy, North Sea Squadron, and struggle with France, a detailed account of the battle of Camperdown, 1797, and the history of the Mutiny at Yarmouth and at the Nore from a fresh point of view. See also The naval biographies of Boscawen, St. Vincent, Hawke, Hood, Howe, Rodney, Collingwood, and the "Naval history," 1793–1820 by Wm. James. 6 v. 1860.
   Ath. 1898. 1: 457; Sat. R. 85: 530; Ed. R. 188: 197; Quar. 189: 139.

CARY, ELIZABETH L.
   Tennyson: His homes, his friends, and his work. N. Y., Putnam. 1898. 8+312 p., portraits, plates, facsim. O. $3.75.
   A popular biography of Tennyson; from the most accessible sources; makes reference to the standard works upon the subject, Hallam Tennyson's monumental memoir of his father, 2 v. 1897, Stopford Brooke's "Tennyson: His art and relation to modern life" 1894, George G. Napier's "Homes and haunts of Tennyson" 1892, and George S. Layard's "Tennyson and his pre-Raphaelite illustrators," 1894.
   Nation 67:427.

CLARK, ANDREW.
   Lincoln [college]. (Oxford college histories.) London, Robinson. 1898. 12+220 p. Illus. plates. D. 5s.
   A history of Lincoln; mainly from MS. sources, the college registers, and muniments; describes 14th century intellectual and social life in the university, etc.; shows the constitutional arrangements of a prereformation college. See also the work edited by Andrew Clark, 2d ed., 1892, and the work extending to 1530, by H. C. M. Lyte, 1886.
   Ath. 1898. 2: 289.

LOWES, WILLIAM LAIRD, and others.
   Royal navy. London, Sampson Low. 1897-98. v. 1-2. Illus., portraits. O. $6.50 each.

   A comprehensive naval history of England, to be completed in five volumes; contains 1, the civil history; 2, the military history of the navy; 3, the history of voyages and maritime discovery, with extracts from the sources, fully illustrated; of value to student and reader for reference, but uncritical and undigested. V. 1, to 1603, Voyages and discoveries to 1485, H. W. Wilson; 1485 to 1603, Sir Clements Markham (especially valuable). V. 2, 1603-1714. Military history of the navy 1603-49, L. Carr Laughton; Voyages and discoveries 1603-1714, Sir Clements Markham.
   V. 1, Eng. Hist. R. 13: 342 (F. Y. Powell); Sat. R. 83: 477 (P. H. Colomb); Ath. 1897. 1: 569. V. 2, Stat. R. 85: 397 (P. H. Colomb); Ath. 1898. 1: 683.

CORBETT, JULIAN STAFFORD.
   Drake and the Tudor navy, with a history of the rise of England as a maritime power. London and N. Y., Longmans. 1898. 2 v. Illus., portrait, plates. O. $10.

   A complete biography of Drake, 1540?-1596; uses the sources and latest authorities; presents Drake as an admiral and statesman, as well as an explorer and pirate, with chapters on the Armada, and critical accounts of the sources.
   Eng. Hist. R. 13: 581 (J. K. Laughton); Ath. 1898. 1: 529; Nation, 66: 366; Acad. 53: 415.

EARMER, PERCY, editor.
   Religious pamphlets. London, Kegan Paul; N. Y., Holt. 1898. 380 p. O. $1.75.

   Contents: Wiclif, Septum hereses; Fish, Supplicacyon for beggars; Knox, Monstrous regiment of women; Cartwright, Second admonition to Parliament; Marprelate, Epitome; Nash and Lyly, Pappe with a hatchet; Almond for a parrat. Parsons, Why Catholics refuse to goe to church; Prynne, Looking-glass for lordly prelates; Bastwick, Letany; Baxter, Sheet for the ministry. Fox, Concerning the rule; Halifax, Letter to a dissenter; De Foe, Shortest way; Leslie, Wolf stript; Swift, Abolishing of Ch'y; Law, Second letter to Bp. of Bangor; Syd. Smith; Fifth letter on Catholics; Newman, Seventh Tract for the Times. Tracts selected for style and influence; with introduction and notes.
   Sat. R. 85: 338; Eng. Hist. R. 13: 608; Acad. 53: 546.

FAIRFIELD, CHARLES.
   Some account of George William Wilshere, Baron Bramwell of Hever, and his opinions. London and N. Y., Macmillan. 1898. 4+382 p. portrait. O. $4.

   An account of the public career and opinions of Lord Bramwell, Baron of the Exchequer 1856-1886; contains much of interest and value about the history of law and the court of exchequer, political economy and free trade, political science and socialism, the Liberal party, and the Irish and temperance questions, with few personalities.

FOSTER, VERE.
   The two Duchesses: Georgiana and Elizabeth, Duchesses of Devonshire, 1777-1859. London, Blackie. 1898. 9+497 p. portraits. O. 16s.

   Family correspondence of and relating to Georgiana and Elizabeth, Duchesses of Devonshire, 1777-1859; from recently discovered mss.; contains matter relative to the Earl of Bristol (Bishop of Derry), the Countess of Bristol, Lord and Lady Byron, the Earl of Aberdeen, Sir Augustus Foster, Nelson, and others.
   Ath. 1898. 4: 242; Sat. R. 85: 403; Nation 67: 155; Ed. R. 188: 78.

FOWLER, THOMAS.
    Corpus Christi. (Oxford college histories.) London, Robinson. 1898. 12+[1]+252 p., plates. D. 5s.

    A reproduction, in a shorter form, with corrections, of the author's History of Corpus Christi College, 1515 to the present (Oxford Hist. Soc. 1893); from the collections of Fulman and Wood, and the lives of Edm. Staunton, John Potenger, R. L. Edgeworth, etc. See also Geo. R. M. Ward's "Foundation statutes of Bp. Foxe . . . with life" 1843.
    Ath. 1898. 2:489, Acad. 54:323.

FOXCROFT, H. C.
    Life and letters of Sir George Savile, bart., first marquis of Halifax, with a new edition of his works. London, Longmans. 1898. 2 v. Portraits, genealogical table. O. $12.

    A work upon the life and writings of the Trimmer, Halifax; expanded from an article in the Eng. Hist. R. Oct. 1896; contains a critical account of the sources, the life, letters and works. Character of a Trimmer, Letter to a Dissenter, Maxims of State, etc., together with the works attributed to Halifax.
    Eng. Hist. R. 14:166 (C. H. Firth); Sat. R. 86:508; Ath. 1898. 2:743; Ed. R. 188:386.

GOOCH, GEORGE PEABODY.
    History of English democratic ideas in the 17th century. (Cambridge historical essays, No. 10). Cambridge University press. 1898. 8+363 p. D. 5s.

    From pamphlets, French and German critical works, etc.; discusses the origin of Puritan political ideas in Calvin, the Huguenots, the Ultramontanes; the progress of ideas from Wiclif to Owen, the Levellers, Millenarians, Constitutionalism, Socialism, Communism, Presbyterian, Independent, and Baptist politics; and the writings of Prynne, Lilburne, Harrington, Winstanley, etc.
    Am. Hist. R. 4:148 (F. Strong); Eng. Hist. R. 13:784 (S. R. Gardiner); Ath. 1898. 2:58; Nation 67:14.

GOSSE, EDMUND.
    Short history of modern English literature. London, Heinemann; N. Y., Appleton. 1898. 6+1+416 p. O. $1.50.

    A manual of English literature rather than of the literature of England, Chaucer to the present; describes the works of the most prominent writers, especially poets; expression, form, technique being emphasized rather than biography or sociology; of value for its critical point of view, combating the classical and individualistic schools of literary criticism in favor of a scientific evolutional criticism of motive and circumstance.

GOUGER, ROBERT.
    The founding of South Australia as recorded in the journals of Mr. Robert Gouger, edited by Edwin Hodder. London, Low. 1898. 6+[1]+239 p., portrait, plate. D. 6s.

    A biography of Robert Gouger, 1802-1846, colonizer; from his journals of the years 1830-1838, etc.· contains much relative to the history of the Wakefield system, the National Colonization Society, the South Australian Association, and South Australia to 1838; a supplement to the author's "George F. Angas, father and founder of South Australia" 1891. The author's standard history of South Australia appeared in 1893.
    Ath. 1899. 1:368.

GRAFTON, AUGUSTUS HENRY FITZROY, 3d duke of.
Autobiography and political correspondence; edited by Sir Wm. R. Anson. London, Murray. 1898. 41+417 p. portraits. O. 18s.

> An account of the political career of Grafton, first lord of the treasury and prime minister 1767-1770; presents material of importance for the history of these years; of value to the student for its corrections of misrepresentations of Junius and Walpole; supplemented by "A narrative of the changes in the ministry 1765-1767, told by the Duke of Newcastle," edited by Mary Bateson, Royal Historical Society 1898.
> Eng. Hist. R. 14: 378 (B. Williams); Ed. R. 189: 489; Quar. 189: 219; Ath. 1898. 2: 599; Sat. R. 86: 646.

GRESWELL, WILLIAM PARR.
Growth and administration of the British colonies, 1837-1897. (Victorian era series). London, Blackie. 1898. 253 p. D. 2s. 6d.

> A history of the colonies during the Victorian era; by a specialist in colonial history; describes the factors in colonial development—persons (Wakefield, Roebuck, Buller, Forster), societies, inventions, economic development (slave emancipation and free trade), political relations with France, Germany, etc., and constitutional growth in the American, Australian, and African colonies. See also history of the colonies by H. E. Egerton, 1897. Ath. 1898. 1: 436; Sat. R. 85: 558.
> In 1898 appeared in the excellent "Builders of Greater Britain series" a biography of Wakefield by R. Garnett (Sat, R. 86: 856); in the "Story of Empire series," "The story of the West Indies," by Arnold Kennedy, a small book in a small series (Sat. R. 86: 860).

GRINLING, CHARLES H.
History of the Great Northern Railway, 1845-1895. London, Methuen. 1898. 8+429 p. illus. O. 10s. 6d.

> A complete account of the origin and development of the Great Northern Railway, with much about the other railways of northern England and Scotland; from personal information, the Railway Times, and Herapath's Railway Journal (not using the company records); of great value to the student, impartial and thorough, but dry. See also The general history of English railways by John Pendleton, 2 v. 1894.
> Ath. 1898. 1: 340; Sat. R. 85: 337; Acad. 53: 346; Spec. 81: 310.

HANNAY, DAVID.
Short history of the royal navy. London, Methuen. 1898. [v. I.] O. 7s. 6d.

> A popular history; from the most accessible sources; *Contents:* v. I, to '1688, to be continued to 1815 in a second volume, with valuable bibliographic notes; of general value, well written and in the main trustworthy. (See Contra Ath. 1897. 2: 879.)
> Eng. Hist. R. 13: 342 (F. Y. Powell); Nation 66: 251; Acad. 52: 565; Spec. 80: 880.

HARRIS, MARY DORMER.
Life in an old English town [Coventry]. (Social England series.) London, Sonnenschein; N. Y. Macmillan. 1898. 23+391 p. illus. plates, maps, fac-sim. D. $1.25.

> A short history of Coventry; from official records, Leet Book, etc. *Contents:* The Benedictine monastery, the Chester lordship, municipal government relations between town and commonalty, guilds, prior, earl, and king, Wars of the Roses, Lammas lands, the crafts, the markets, amusements, and religion, with concluding chapter on "How to spend a day in Coventry," and appendices

descriptive of the MS. sources and a list of authorities. See also history of Coventry proper by Benj. Poole, 1870, and History of towns by P. H. Ditchfield. 1897.

Acad. 53: 624; Nation 67: 37.

HUME, MARTIN ANDREW SHARP.
 The great Lord Burghley, a study in Elizabethan statecraft. London, Nisbet; N. Y., Longmans. 1898. 15+511 p. portrait. O. 12s. 6d. $3.50.

 A biographical study of William Cecil 1520-1598, prime minister of Queen Elizabeth; from printed, calendared, and uncalendared sources; presents Cecil as a statesman rather than religious reformer; a study of Elizabethan foreign policy. Most of the Cecil papers are generally accessible in the printed collections of Haynes 1740, Wm. Murdin 1759, and Edw. Nares, 3 v., 1828-31.
 Eng. Hist. R. 14:162 (A. F. Pollard); Ath. 1898. 2:885 (unfav.); Sat. R. 86:854.

HUTTON, WILLIAM HOLDEN.
 St. John's Baptist College. (Oxford college histories.) London, Robinson. 1898. 10+[5]+274 p., plates. D. 5s.

 The first history of St. John's, from its foundation in the Reformation (1555) to the present time; from the Rawlinson MSS., etc.; contains notable chapters on "Social life in the 16th century," "An old Christmas in St. John's," illustrating, in the history of the university, the golden age of the early Stuarts.
 Ath. 1898. 2:344; Acad. 54:168; Literature 2:747.

IRVING, HENRY BRODRIBB.
 Life of Judge Jeffreys. London and N. Y., Longmans, 1898. [9]+380 p. portraits. O. $4.

 A plea for George Jeffreys: "An attempt to reduce the monster to human proportions;" from family papers, etc.; contains much relative to Scroggs, the Popish plot, the courts of law; maintains the good birth and education and essentially Celtic character of Jeffreys, and shows him to be a man of his time; with list of authorities.
 Nation 67: 207; Eng. Hist. R. 13: 816 (C); Ath. 1898. 1: 623; Sat. R. 85: 623.

JONES, R. J. CORNEWALL.
 British merchant service. London, Low. 1898. 17+406 p. plates. O. 14s.

 A history of British navigation from the earliest times to the present day; from the "British Merchant Service Journal," the records of the steamship companies, etc.; contains a sketch of the development of the art of navigation, the rise of the most important merchant lines—Cunard, P. and O., Royal Mail, Orient, etc.—of light-houses, Lloyd's, etc., together with the chief incidents in the history of navigation. See also George Cawston's "Early chartered companies" 1896, Henry Fry's "History of North Atlantic steam navigation" 1896, and A. Frazer-Macdonald's "Our ocean railways" 1893.
 Ath. 1898. 2: 896.

LANG, ANDREW.
 Companions of Pickle. London and N. Y., Longmans. 1898. 9+[2]+308 p. portraits. O. $5.

 A sequel to "Pickle the spy," a character of the rebellion of 1745; from the Cumberland papers, Windsor, the Glengarry MS. Letter Book, the John Macdonell memoirs, etc.; contains biographical studies of some of the Jacobite followers of Prince Charles, the Earl Marischal, George Keith, John Murray of Broughton, Arch. MacDonell of Barisdale, showing the treachery of all but the first, presenting new evidence identifying Glengarry with Pickle the spy, and giving some account of the social condition of the Highlands consequent upon the fall of the clan system. Note also the publication of the "Memorials of John Murray of Broughton, sometime secretary to Prince Charles Edward 1740-1747," Rob't F. Bell, ed. Scot. Hist. Soc. 1898.

Eng. Hist. R. 14: 400; Ath. 1898. 2: 825; Nation 68: 172.

LAUGHTON, JOHN KNOX.

Memoris of the life and correspondence of Henry Reeve. London and N. Y., Longmans. 1898. 2 v. portraits. O. $8.

A biography of Henry Reeve 1813-1895, editor of the Edinburg Review 1855-1895; from a "Chronology of my life," a voluminous correspondence, etc.; contains little about the Review, but much about European and especially French politics, the Eastern question, and the Crimean war; gives early letters to his mother, but few, of later letters to friends, and letters from Guizot, Lord Clarendon, Brougham, etc.

Ath. 1898. 2: 479; Sat. R. 86: 507; Nation 68: 130; Church Q. 47: 406; Yale R. 7: 459 (E. Porritt); Blackw. 164: 682.

LEE, SIDNEY.

Life of William Shakespeare. London, Smith, Elder; N. Y., Macmillan. 1898. 25+476 p. portraits, facsimiles. D. $1.75.

A guide to the life of Shakespeare; an elaboration of the article in the Dictionary of national biography, and the outcome of 18 years study of Elizabethan history and literature; presents a full record of the attested facts of Shakespeare's career and achievements, with new light on the composition of "Love's Labor's Lost" and the "Merchant of Venice," relations with Ben Jonson, financial affairs, and portraits; rejects the sonnets as autobiographical material; with notes on the sources, the Bacon-Shakespeare controversy, the Earl of Southampton, and the Elizabethan sonnet; the imaginative work of Georg Brandes may be compared with this; the documentary materials may be found in Halliwell-Phillips.

Sat. R. 86: 884; Critic, 34: 154 (W. J. Rolfe).

MAITLAND, FREDERIC WILLIAM.

Township and borough. Cambridge, University press; N. Y., Macmillan. 1898. 9+220 p. plate, 2 maps. O. 10s. $2.75.

A monograph upon the history of Cambridge as a village community, being the University of Oxford Ford Lectures for 1897; from old materials and new, using Gierke; emphasizes the rustic basis of the borough, its position as center of the shire, and the differentiation of corporateness from "commonness;" with an appendix of notes relating to the history of the town of Cambridge. See also C. H. Cooper's "Annals of Cambridge."

Eng. Hist. R. 14: 344 (J. Tait); Am. Hist. R. 4: 143 (C. Gross); Pol. Sci. Q. 13: 707 (C. M. Andrews); J. Pol. Econ. 6: 577 (F. A. C.); Ath. 1898, 1: 624; Nation, 66: 506.

MARKHAM, CHRISTOPHER ALEXANDER and COX, J. C., *editors*.

Records of the borough of Northampton. London, Stock. 1898. 2 v. Plates, facsim. plan in pocket. O. 42s.

V. 1. Preface by Mandell Creighton, Introduction on the history of the town, W. R. D. Adkins, Records: Domesday, Pipe rolls, charters, letters patent, acts of Parliament, Liber Custumarum, etc., Chris. A. Markham, with translations, lists, notes, and glossary.

V. 2. History 1550-1835, J. C. Cox. Town muniments, government, jurisdiction, property, commons, trades, charities, churches, plagues, civil war, royal visits, members of Parliament, topography.

Acad. 53: 416; Ath. 1898. 2: 217.

MORRIS, WILLIAM O'CONNOR.
> Ireland 1798–1898. London, Innes. 1898. 21+376 p. O. 10s. 6d.
>> A summary of the history of Ireland in the 19th century; by an Irish landlord and historical scholar; contains in addition to the brief narrative an essay upon the sources and authorities for the history of this period. See also The histories by the Home Rulers, Wm. J. O. Daunt, 2 v. 1886, and J. H. McCarthy 1887, and the political treaties by the Home Ruler R. Barry O'Brien, and the Unionists A. V. Dicey and Sir Gavan Duffy.
>> Eng. Hist. R. 14:176 (G. H. Orpen); Ath. 1898. 2:151 (unfav.).

NICHOLLS, SIR GEORGE.
> History of the English poor law in connection with the state of the country and the condition of the people. Edited by H. G. Willink. London, King; N. Y., Putnam. 1898. New ed. 2 v. Portrait. O. $10.
>> A history 924–1853; with revisions made by the author and list of statutes cited; to be continued to the present time in a third volume, by T. Mackay. v. 1, Life of Sir George Nicholls. Introduction. History 924–1714. v. 2, History 1714–1853. See also Work of Richard Burn 1764 and P. F. Aschrott 1886 (German).
>> Ath. 1898. 1:404; Nation 66:428.

NUGENT, CLAUD.
> Memoir of Robert, Earl Nugent. Chicago, Stone. 1898. [11]+352 p. portraits, plate. O. $3.50.
>> An account of the public career of Earl Nugent, politician, from 1742 to 1784; taken largely from Smollet, Wraxall, Lecky; contains his poems, speeches, and correspondence with Walpole, Pope, Chesterfield.
>> Ath. 1898. 2:669; Literature 3:467 (unfav.).

O'BRIEN, RICHARD BARRY.
> Life of Charles Stewart Parnell 1846–1891. London, Smith, Elder; N. Y., Harpers. 1898. 2 v. portr. fac sim. O. $2.50.
>> A memoir of the great Irish Home Ruler; by a follower; contains much relative to the history of the Land League and the Home Rule movement. See also T. P. O'Connor's "The Parnell Movement" 1890, and J. Henri Cribier's "Parnell et l'Irelande pendant la période aiguë de la crise agraire" 1882.
>> Ath. 1898. 2:667; Nation 68:106, 123; Westm. R. 151:1; Ed. R. 189:543.

OVERTON, JOHN HENRY.
> The Anglican revival. (Victorian era ser.) London, Blackie; Chicago, Stone. 1898. 6+229 p. D. $1.25.
>> Describes the Oxford movement, its effect on the outer world, Hook and Wilberforce, the Hampden and Gorham cases, public worship. See also The author's "English church in the 19th century," 1894, and R. W. Church's "Oxford movement," 1892; also John Tulloch's "Religious thought in Britain during the 19th century," 1895, and the biographies of Newman, Ward, Mozley, Keble, Pusey.
>> Lit. 2:72.

PARKIN, GEORGE ROBERT.
> Edward Thring, head master of Uppingham school; life, diary, and letters.
> London and N. Y., Macmillan. 1898. 2 v. portraits. O. $7.
>> A biography of the eminent English educator, Edward Thring 1821–1887; by a disciple; contains with the diary and letters of Thring, much relative to school and educational conditions and theories about the middle of the century. See also Sketch by John H. Skrine 1889, and Graham Balfour's "Educational systems of Great Britain and Ireland" 1898, may be noted.
>> Educa. R. 17:456; Church. Q. 48:79; Ath. 1898. 2:565; Sat. R. 86:812; Nation, 68:283.

RAMSAY, SIR JAMES HENRY.
Foundations of England B. C. 55–A. D. 1154.
London, Sonnenschein; N. Y., Macmillan. 1898. 2 v. illus. maps. O. $7.50.

> A book of reference for early English history, by a specialist in English mediæval history; presents the more important results of recent work in that subject, particularly upon the side of military history; with list of authorities; like C. H. Pearson's "History of England during the early and middle ages," 2 v. 1867 (to 1307).
> Pol. Sci. Q. 14: 144 (C. Gross); Ath. 1898. 2: 859; Sat. R. 86: 855; Nation, 68: 320.

RAWLINSON, GEORGE.
Memoir of Major-General Sir Henry Creswicke Rawlinson. London, Longmans. 1898. 22 + 358 p. portrait, plate, map. O. $5.

> The authorized biography of Sir. Henry C. Rawlinson 1810–1895, Assyriologist, by his brother, from diaries and letters; contains, with an introduction by Lord Roberts, and a description of his character and of his work as Assyriologist by Sir Henry Rawlinson, an account of Rawlinson's life during the Afghan war 1839–1842, of his cuneiform studies, of his attitude toward Russia, the Afghan frontier question, and of his relations with Sir John Malcolm, Layard, Lord Lytton, etc.
> Ath. 1898. 1: 333; Nation 67: 15; Sat. R. 85: 433.

ROSE, JOHN HOLLAND.
Rise and growth of democracy in Great Britain. (Victorian era ser.) Chicago, Stone. 1898. 8+252 p. D. $1.25.

> An account of the rise of English radicalism, by a specialist in modern history; describes the history of Chartism, the Reform bills, etc., from the point of view of the workman's club rather than of the lobby of St. Stephens. See also Edw. Smith's "English Jacobins," and J. B. Daly's "Radical pioneers of the 18th century" 1886, reprinted as "Dawn of Radicalism" 1892; also "Political defects of the old radicalism," by Wm. Clarke, Pol. Sci. Q. 14: 69, and biographies of Francis Place, Thos. Atwood, and others.
> Acad. 53: 307; Sat. R. 85: 668 (unfav.).

RUSSELL, GEORGE WILLIAM ERSKINE.
Collections and recollections by one who has kept a diary. London, Smith, Elder; N. Y., Harper. 1898. 9+375 p. plate. O. $2.50.

> Reminiscences of the Victorian era; reprinted from the Manchester Guardian, from diary and commonplace books; contains anecdotes about Russell, Shaftesbury, Manning, Houghton, Beaconsfield, Gladstone, the Queen, etc., and about Parliament, the cabinet, and social changes.
> Ath. 1898. 1: 788; Nation 67: 36; Spec. 80: 828; Acad. 53: 656; Sat. R. 86: 279.

SAINTSBURY, GEORGE.
Short history of English literature. London and N. Y., MacMillan. 1898. 20+819 p. D. $1.50.

> A manual of English literature, from the earliest times to the present; presents the chronological facts, with interchapters devoted to generalization; written from the literary rather than the historical or pedagogical point of view. See also The works of Austin Dobson 1897, and Henry Morley 1873.
> Ath. 1898. 2: 746; Sat. R. 86: 738 (unfav.).

SEATON, ROBERT COOPER.
Sir Hudson Lowe and Napoleon. London, Nutt; N. Y., Scribner. 1898. [5]+236 p. portrait. D. $1.40.

> A defense of Sir Hudson Lowe, governor of St. Helena during the imprisonment of Napoleon; from Lowe papers, etc.; contains criticism of Barry O'Meara, "Voice from St. Helena," republished in 1888 as "Napoleon at St. Helena," and of Whig slander and French accusations, with bibliographical list. See also Exhaustive work of Wm. Forsyth, "Captivity of Napoleon."
> Nation 67: 116; Spec. 81: 215.

SELBORNE, ROUNDELL PALMER, 1st earl.
Memorials. Part 2. Personal and political, 1865–1895. London and N. Y., Macmillan. 1898. 2 v. portraits. O. 21s.

> An autobiography of the Earl of Selborne, Lord Chancellor, in continuation of the "Memorials: Family and personal 1766–1865," 2 v. 1896; from family letters and papers; describes his attitude as a high churchman toward church questions, and as an independent conservative toward political questions, with chapters of importance on judicature reform, Parliamentary reform, disestablishment, Irish affairs, the treaty of Washington and Geneva arbitration, the Eastern question in Turkey and in Egypt, the Transvaal.
> Church Q. 48: 54; Ath. 1898. 2: 821; Sat. R. 86: 788; Scot. R. 34: 39 (W. O'Connor Morris).

SIMPSON, MRS. MARY CHARLOTTE MAIR (Senior).
Many memories of many people. London, Arnold. 1898. Third ed. 15+334 p. O. 16s.

> Memoirs 1837–64; partly reprinted from the New Review, the Liberal Unionist, and the 19th Century; from the journals and conversations of her father, Nassau William Senior; contains gossip of interest relative to Whately, De Tocqueville, Guizot, Bright, Stanley, Mrs. Grote, Jenny Lind, and nearly every woman of note of the time, with notes on political and economic questions. See also N. W. Senior's published conversations and journals.
> Ath. 1898. 1: 239; Acad. 53: 282; Spec. 80: 306.

SOLLY, HENRY SHAEN.
Life of Henry Morley. London, Arnold. 1898. 12+410 p. portrait. O. 12s. 6d.

> The life of Henry Morley, 1822–1894, teacher of English literature; from family papers and mostly in his own words; describes his journalistic career as contributor to Household Words, the Examiner, etc., his work as professor of the English language and literature at King's College, and at University College, London, and as editor of various "Libraries" of English literature.
> Ath. 1898. 2: 633; Acad. 55: 326 (portr.).

STERRY, WASEY.
Annals of the King's College of Our Lady of Eton beside Windsor. London, Methuen. 1898. 11+326 p. portraits, plates, facsimiles. D. 7s. 6d.

> A history of Eton, 1440–1898, from printed and MS. sources. See also Work by H. C. Maxwell Lyte, 1889; also Eton bibliography, by L. V. Harcourt, 1898 ed. Biographies of Dr. Hawtrey and Arthur Coleridge.
> Ath. 1899. 1: 48; Sat. R. 86: 744; Nation 67: 448.

TOKES, HENRY PAINE.
Corpus Christi [college]. (Cambridge college histories.) London, Robinson. 1898. [5]+251 p. plates. D. 5s.

> A short history of Corpus Christi from its foundation in the 14th century; from Josselyn, Masters, Lamb, Carter, Willis, and Clark; gives some account of the Benedictine antiquaries, the Library, students' recreations, the masters, and Parker. See also History of Cambridge (to 1625), by J. B. Mullinger. 2 v. 1873-1883; Ath. 1898. 2: 290; Spec. 80: 697.

'TRUTT, JOSEPH.
Sports and pastimes of the people of England . . . from the earliest period; edited by William Hone. London, Chatto. 1898. New edition. 12+530 p., illus., plate. D. 3s. 6d.

> Reprint of the edition of 1826 (original 1801); describes the old English sports of hunting, hawking, horse racing, archery, tournaments, miracle plays, minstrelsy, dancing, baiting, holiday sports, etc. There is a shorter book on holiday sports by P. H. Ditchfield 1891, an elaborate work on children's games by Alice B. Gomme 1894 (Dictionary of British Folklore), besides the special histories of horse racing by Christie Whyte, by J. Rice 1879, J. P. Hore 1886, Rob. Black 1893; of miracle plays by A. W. Pollard 1895, and Sidney W. Clarke 1897; of archery by G. A. Hansard 1841; of pageants by F. W. Fairholt 1844.

'IBART, EDWARD.
Sepoy mutiny as seen by a subaltern from Delhi to Lucknow. London, Smith, Elder; N. Y., Scribner. 1898. 10+308 p., portraits, plates, plan. O. 7s. 6d.

> A soldier's memoir of the Indian mutiny of 1857; reprinted in part from the Cornhill Magazine, from an article by P. V. Luke in the Macmillan Magazine, and from A. R. D. Mackenzie's "Mutiny memoirs," 1891. See also W. Gordon-Alexander's "Recollections of a Highland subaltern" (Ath. 1899. 1:271), and two anglicized "Native narratives of the mutiny," edited by C. T. Metcalfe (Ath. 1898. 2:245); also History of the mutiny, by T. R. Holmes, and the complete chronicle by Sir John Kaye and G. B. Malleson, 6 v., 1864-1880.
> Ath. 1899. 1:271; Spec. 82:273.

VALLAS, GRAHAM.
Life of Francis Place, 1771-1854. London and N. Y., Longmans. 1898. 10+415 p. Portraits. O. $4.

> The biography of the "Father of electoral reform;" from the Place MSS. autobiography and letter books; describes the London corresponding society, Westminster elections, Benthamites, education, economics, libraries, combination laws, parliamentary reform, chartism.
> Am. Hist. R. 3:723 (E. Porritt); Econ. J. 8:209 (L. L. Price); Ath. 1898. 1:368; Nation 66:410.

VILMOT, SYDNEY MAROW EARDLEY-
Life of Vice-Admiral Edmund, Lord Lyons. London, Low. 1898. 14+437 p. portraits, plates, maps. O. 21s.

> A biography of Edmund, Lord Lyons, 1790-1858, Commander in chief of the Mediterranean station 1855-1858; from an immense mass of correspondence hitherto unused; contains chapters upon Lyons's diplomatic career, particularly the Greek mission of 1835, and upon his naval career, especially in the Crimean war 1854-1856, with some account of the change in warships entailed by the introduction of steam. See also The standard history of the Crimea, by Kinglake, who in 1873 failed to get access to Sir Edmund's papers, and the naval history of the period, Sir Aug. Phillimore "Sir Wm. Parker," 3 v. 1876-1880, and John H. Briggs "Naval administrations 1827-1892" 1897.
> Ath. 1898. 2: 857.

YOUNG, ARTHUR.

Autobiography, with selections from his correspondence; edited by M. Betham-Edwards. London, Smith, Elder. 1898. 10+[1]+480 p. illus. portrs. plates, facsim. O. 12s. 6d.

An abridged autobiography of the eminent English agriculturalist and political writer, 1741-1820; from 7 packets of MS. and 12 folio volumes of correspondence; contains correspondence with Dr. Priestley, Dr. Burney, Bentham, etc.; little about his writings, less about his travels; gives history of the Board of Agriculture and Commerce (supplementing the memoir of Sir John Sinclair), and of political thought during the last years of the 18th century. See also Biography of Young as agriculturalist, by John Donaldson, 1854; a Young bibliography, by J. P. Anderson, in Young's Tour in Ireland (A. W. Hutton, editor) 2: 349-374 (1892).

Econ. J. 8: 367 (Henry Higgs); Eng. Hist. R. 13: 797 (Jas. Bonar); Ed. R. 188: 78. Ath. 1898. 1: 176; Sat. R. 85: 498.

XXI.—A BIBLIOGRAPHY OF MISSISSIPPI.

By THOMAS McADORY OWEN, A. M., LL. B.,
BIRMINGHAM, ALABAMA.

ABBREVIATIONS.

P. and pp.—Page and pages.
Ill.—Illustrated.
L. and ll.—Leaf and leaves.
P. l.—Preliminary leaves.
T., t. p., and n. t. p.—Title, title-page, and no title-page.
N. p., n. d.—No place, no date.
1 l.—A leaf printed on one side only and unnumbered.
[1].—An unnumbered page, always verso of a numbered page.
[2].—Two unnumbered pages, i. e., a leaf printed on both sides, neither numbered.
Brackets ([ ]) indicate words supplied in the title.

The following words, placed after a title or note, indicate the library where a copy of the particular work has been seen and examined by the compiler, viz:
Congress.—Library of Congress.
Smithsonian.—Library of Smithsonian Institution.
Surgeon-General.—Library of Surgeon-General.
Bureau of Education.—Library of Bureau of Education.
Johns Hopkins University.—Library of Johns Hopkins University, Baltimore, Maryland.
Peabody.—Peabody Library, Baltimore.
Curry.—Library of Dr. J. L. M. Curry, Washington, District of Columbia.
Hamner.—Library of Dr. George W. Hamner, Washington.
Owen.—Library of Thomas McAdory Owen, the compiler, Birmingham, Alabama.

PREFACE.

This work is a catalogue, arranged alphabetically by authors, of books and articles relating to the State of Mississippi, its history, institutions, and public characters. It is also intended to embrace the general literary product of Mississippi writers and authors. There are doubtless a number of omissions, but the compiler feels that its publication now will be of more practical service than in delaying for greater fullness. It will at least form a convenient basis for further effort by some one having greater facilities.

For the convenience of students, and in order to make it of more practical utility, the work has been cross-indexed under general subject heads.

Its execution has been attended with many difficulties. Acknowledgment is here made to the following for valuable assistance rendered, viz: Hon. Edward Mayes, Jackson, Mississippi; Chancellor R. B. Fulton, University; Hon. John Sharp Williams, Yazoo City; Gov. James T. Harrison, Columbus; Prof. W. L. Weber, Rome, Georgia; Dr. Chiles C. Ferrell, University; Dr. P. H. Eager, Clinton; Prof. Alexander L. Bondurant, University; Gen. E. T. Sykes, Columbus; Prof. Dabney Lipscomb, University; Dunbar Rowland, Esq., Coffeeville; Dr. Joseph B. Stratton, Natchez; Dr. C. H. Otken, McComb City; Rev. L. S. Foster, Jackson; W. L. Hutchinson, Director Mississippi Experiment Station, Starkville; R. C. King, Sr., Mississippi Agricultural and Mechanical College, Starkville; Hon. W. T. Harris, United States Commissioner of Education, Washington, District of Columbia; G. C. Nevill, Esq., Meridian, Mississippi; and the librarian of the Samuel Colgate Baptist Historical Collection, Hamilton, New York. Special thanks are extended Dr. Franklin L. Riley; the able and efficient Secretary of the Mississippi State Historical Society, and professor of history of the State University, for constant helpfulness and suggestions; to Prof. H. S. Halbert, the learned linguist and Indianologist, of Crawford, Mississippi, for many valuable references; to Alfred H. Stone, Esq., for supplying numbers of important titles; and to Theodore L. Cole, Esq., of the Statute Law Book Company, Washington, District of Columbia, for invaluable assistance in perparing the titles on "Laws," "Codes," and "Conventions." I am indebted to my wife for sympathetic interest and encouragement. Mr. A. Howard Clark, Assistant Secretary of the Association, I take pleasure in thanking for courtesies incident to publication.

THOMAS MCADORY OWEN.

BIRMINGHAM, JEFFERSON COUNTY, ALABAMA,
April 12, 1900.

A BIBLIOGRAPHY OF MISSISSIPPI.

By Thomas McAdory Owen, A. M., LL. B.

A.

ABBEY, *Rev.* RICHARD (1805-189-), *D. D.* The Methodist Episcopal Church, South, in Mississippi.
>In Goodspeed's *Memoirs of Mississippi*, vol. ii, pp. 362-368.

—— Sketch of.
>*Ibid.* vol. i, pp. 278-280.
>
>"Dr. Abbey is a hard student; he is the author of the following books and pamphlets, which are mainly of a doctrinal or scientific character: 'Diuturnity,' 'Ecclesiastical Constitution,' 'Letters to Bishop Green on Apostolic Succession,' 'End of Apostolic Succession,' 'Church and Ministry,' 'Ecce Ecclesia,' 'Baptismal Demonstration,' 'Strictures on Church Government,' 'Divine Assessment,' 'City of God,' 'The Priest and the Preacher,' 'The Preacher and the Rector,' etc."—*Ibid.* p. 279. *Also* the following: "Christian Cradlehead, or Religion in the Nursery," "Creed of all Men," and "Call to the Ministry."

ABBOTT, JOHN STEPHENS CABOT (1805-1877), *Author.* The adventures | of the | Chevalier de la Salle | and his companions, | in their explorations of the | prairies, forests, lakes, and rivers of the new world. | And their interviews with the savage tribes, | two hundred years ago. | By | John S. C. Abbott. | New York: | Dodd, Mead & company, | publishers | [1875.]
>12mo. pp. 384.
>
>An interesting preliminary study in the history of French settlement in the old Southwest.
>
>*Copies seen:* Owen.

ABERDEEN. Sketches of.
>In Davis's *Recollections of Mississippi and Mississippians*, pp. 252-285.

ADAIR, JAMES. The | history | of the | American Indians; | particularly | Those Nations adjoining to the Mississippi [*sic*], east and | west Florida, Georgia, South and | North Carolina, and Virginia: | containing | An account of their Origin, Language, Manners, Religious and | Civil Customs, Laws, Form of Government, Punishments, Conduct in | War and Domestic Life, their Habits, Diet, Agriculture, Manu- | factures, Diseases and Method of Cure, and other Particulars, suffi- | cient to render it | a | complete Indian system. | With | Observations on former Historians, the Conduct of our Colony | Governors, Superintendents, Missionaries, &c. | Also | an appendix, | containing | A

Description of the Floridas, and the Mississippi [sic] Lands, with their Produc- | tions—The Benefits of colonizing Georgiana, and civilizing the Indians— | And the way to make all the Colonies more valuable to the Mother Country. | With a new map of the Country referred to in the History. | By James Adair, Esquire, | A Trader with the Indians, and Resident in their Country for Forty Years. | London: | Printed for Edward and Charles Dilly, in the Poultry. | MDCCLXXV [1775.] |
>   4to. 6 p. l., pp. 464. *Map of the American Indian nations.*
>   Reprinted in part as follows:

—— History of the North American Indians, their customs, &c. By James Adair.
>   In King's (E.) *Antiquities of Mexico*, vol. viii, pp. 273–375, London, 1848. Folio.
>   Contains Arguments, i–xxiii, of Adair's work, followed by "Notes and Illustrations to Adair's *History of the North American Indians*," by Lord Kingsborough, pp. 375–400.
>   A German edition was published at Breslau, 1782. 8vo.
>   "Indian trader and author, lived in the 18th century. He resided among the Indians (principally the Chickasaws and Cherokees) from 1735 to 1775, and in the latter year published his 'History of the American Indians.' In this he attempted to trace the descent of the Indians from the Jews, basing his assumption upon supposed resemblances between the customs of the two races . . . . Unsatisfactory as are his vocabularies of Indian dialects, they are the most valuable part of his writings."—Appleton's *Cyclopædia of American Biography*, vol. i, p. 10.

ADAMS COUNTY. Sketch of.
>   In Lowry and McCardle's *Mississippi*, pp. 436–439. Established by proclamation of Gov. Winthrop Sargent, April 2, 1799, and is the oldest county in the State.
>   *See also* Goodspeed's *Memoirs of Mississippi*, vol. i, pp. 173–175.

—— Sketch of. By Judge Joseph D. Shields.
>   Referred to in Lowry and McCardle's *Mississippi*, p. 437.

—— Historic Adams County. *See* Gerard Brandon.

—— Mounds at Natchez.
>   In Ellicott's *Journal*, p. 134. *See*, for incidental mention, Dr. Samuel Morton, *Amer. Journal Science and Art*, 2d ser., vol. ii (1846), p. 6, *note*.
>   There were also mounds at White Apple village, where, according to tradition, the Natchez chief, or "Sun," resided in 1729.

—— Seltzertown mounds.
>   "Described at length in Brackenridge's *Views of Louisiana* (appendix). Brief notice by J. R. Bartlett in the "Progress of Ethnology," pp. 8, 9, published in *Trans. Am. Ethn. Soc.*, vol. 2. Brief description in *Anc. Mon.*, pp. 117, 118. Explored by Joseph Jones and described by him in a communication to the Natchez (Mississippi) *Weekly Democrat and Courier*, June 26, 1884. . . . This is probably the mound alluded to as reported by Prof. Forshey, *Am. Jour. Sci. and Art*, 1st ser., vol. 40 (1841), pp. 376–377."—Thomas' *Prehistoric Works*, p. 123.
>   *See also Twelfth Annual Report Bureau of Ethnology*, 1890–91, pp. 263–267; *plate*.

ADAMS, GEORGE, *Lawyer, U. S. Dist. Judge.* Sketch of.
>   In Claiborne's *Mississippi*, pp. 388–389, *note*.
>   *See also* Goodspeed's *Memoirs of Miss.*, vol. i, pp. 114, 285.

ADAMS, *Prof.* HERBERT BAXTER (1850–), *Ph. D., LL. D.* The study and teaching of history.
>   In *Publications Mississippi State Historical Society*, 1898, vol. i, pp. 73–84.

ADAMS, ROBERT H. (1792–1830), *Lawyer, U. S. Senator from Miss.* Sketch of.
>   In Lynch's *Bench and Bar of Miss.*, pp. 24–27. *See also* Goodspeed's *Memoirs of Mississippi*, vol. i, p. 285.

ADAMS, *Rev.* THOMAS A. S. Enscotidion, or the shadow of death. A poem. Nashville, Tenn. 1876.
> 12mo.

—— Aunt Peggy and other poems. Nashville, Tenn. 1882.
> 12mo.

ADDEY, M. Life and imprisonment of Davis. *See* Jefferson Davis.

ADJUTANT-GENERAL. Biennial report | of the | adjutant-general | of the | State of Mississippi | for the | years 1898–1899, | to the governor. | Printed by authority. | Vance printing Co., | Jacksonville, Fla. | 1900. |
> 8vo. pp. 237.
> Reports were also issued for previous years.

AGRICULTURAL AND MECHANICAL COLLEGE. Report favoring Senate Bill 2699, granting lands to Miss. for College. Feb. 7, 1895. (Sen. Rep. 892, 3d sess. In v. 2.)
> 8vo. p. 1.

—— Origin and location of. *See* J. M. White.

—— The State Grange and A. & M. College. Compiled from the official proceedings by Secretary of State Grange. n. p., n. d.
> 8vo. pp. 7.
> Covers, 1876–1886.

—— Narrative and statistical report of | president and statistical report | of treasurer of the Agricultural | and Mechanical College of Mississippi | to the Secretary of the Interior, and | Secretary of Agriculture, as required | by Act of Congress of August 30th, 1890, | in aid of Colleges of agriculture and | the mechanic arts, Sept. 30th, 1891. | n. p., n. d.
> 8vo. pp. 12.

—— Annual Catalogues, 1880–1899.
> 8vo.
> 1st annual catalogue, 1880–81. pp. —.
> 2d annual catalogue, 1881–82. pp. 47.
> 3d annual catalogue, 1882–83. pp. —.
> 4th annual catalogue, 1883–84. pp. —.
> 5th annual catalogue, 1884–85. pp. 49.
> 6th annual catalogue, 1885–86. pp. —.
> 7th annual catalogue, 1886–87. pp. 47.
> 8th annual catalogue, 1887–88. pp. 40.
> 9th annual catalogue, 1888–89. pp. 45.
> 1st decennial catalogue, 1880–90. pp. 72.
> 11th annual catalogue, 1890–91. pp. 58.
> 12th annual catalogue, 1891–92. pp. 62.
> 13th annual catalogue, 1892–93. pp. 64.
> 14th annual catalogue, 1893–94. pp. 64.
> 15th annual catalogue, 1894–95. pp. 63.
> 16th annual catalogue, 1895–96. pp. 54.
> 17th annual catalogue, 1896–97. pp. 60.
> 18th annual catalogue, 1897–98. pp. 58.
> 19th annual catalogue, 1898–99. pp. 61.

AGRICULTURAL AND MECHANICAL COLLEGE. Biennial reports of the trustees, president and other officers. 1882-1899.
    8vo.
    Biennial Report, 1882 and 1883. pp. —.
    Biennial Report, 1884 and 1885. pp. 84.
    Biennial Report, 1886 and 1887. pp. 108.
    Biennial Report, 1888 and 1889. pp. 79.
    Biennial Report, 1890 and 1891. pp. 91.
    Biennial Report, 1892 and 1893. pp. 79.
    Biennial Report, 1894 and 1895. pp. 73.
    Biennial Report, 1896 and 1897. pp. 64.
    Biennial Report, 1898 and 1899. pp. 65.

—— *See also* J. Z. George, *Dr.* S. A. Knapp, *Gen.* S. D. Lee, Horticultural Society, and Edward Mayes.

AGRICULTURAL EXPERIMENT STATION OF THE AGRICULTURAL AND MECHANICAL COLLEGE OF MISSISSIPPI. Annual Reports. 1888-1899.
    8vo.
    First Annual Report, for 1888, pp. 62.
    Second, for 1889, pp. 44.
    Third, for 1890, pp. 43.
    Fourth, for 1891, pp. 37.
    Fifth, for 1892, pp. 2.
    Sixth, for 1893, pp. 64.
    Seventh, for 1894, pp. 2.
    Eighth, for 1895, pp. 108.
    Ninth, for 1896, pp. 2.
    Tenth, for 1897, pp. 23.
    Eleventh, for 1898, pp. 13.
    Twelfth, for 1899, pp. —.

—— Bulletins, 1888-1899.
    8vo.
    Bulletin No.—
      1. Organization. March 1, 1888, pp. 2.
      2. Cotton Worm. May 20, 1888, pp. 4.
      3. Analysis of Chemical Fertilizers Sold in Mississippi. [*June 20, 1888*], pp. 18.
      4. The Marls of Mississippi. Nov. 7, 1888, pp. 8.
      5. Fertilizers. May 20, 1889, pp. 24.
      6. Charbon. June 25, 1889, p. 1.
      7. Hay Presses. June 20, 1889, pp. 12.
      8. Stock Feeding. pp. —.
      9. Diseases of Sheep and Calves. August 30, 1889, pp. 14.
      10. Dishorning. October 10, 1889, pp. 14.
      11. Charbon. February 15, 1890, pp. 14.
      12. Cotton Leaf Worm. June 25, 1890, pp. 4.
      13. Feeding for Milk and Butter. September 25, 1890, pp. 8.
      14. Injurious Insects. March, 1891, pp. 11.
      15. Feeding and Milk Testing Apparatus. [*June, 1891*], pp. 16.
      16. Glanders. September, 1891, pp. 15.
      17. Injurious Insects to Stored Grain. December, 1891, pp. 19.
      18. Varieties of Corn. January, 1892, pp. 3.
      19. The Southern Tomato Blight. January, 1892, pp. 12.
      20. Grasses and Forage Plants. February, 1892, pp. 17.
      21.   I. Insects Injurious to the Cabbage.
           II. A New Method for Testing Milk.
           III. Feeding for Milk and Butter. June, 1892, pp. 29.

22. Grapes. September, 1892, pp. 16.
  A Chemical Study of the Cotton Plant. December, 1892, pp. 15.
23. Varieties of Cotton. February, 1893, pp. 3.
24. Fertilizers for Cotton. February, 1893, pp. 4.
25. Colic in Horses and Mules. June, 1893, pp. 10.
26. Small Fruits. August, 1893, pp. 15.
27. Insecticides and their Application. November, 1893, pp. 24.
28. The Horn-Fly. January, 1894, pp. 8.
29. Exhaustion and Restoration of Soil Fertility. Fertilizers and their Use. May, 1894, pp. 32.
30. A Kerosene Attachment for Knapsack Pumps. May, 1894, pp. 5.
31. Lameness in Horses and Mules. September, 1894, pp. 15.
32. A New Kerosene Attachment for Knapsack Sprayers. December, 1894, p. 1.
33. Corn. March, 1895, pp. 19.
34. Mississippi Fungi. May, 1895, pp. 45.
35. Hog Raising. September, 1895, pp. 22.
36. Insects Injurious to Corn. November, 1895, pp. 15.
37. Fruits and Vegetables on Gulf Coast. March, 1896, pp. 23.
38. Mississippi Fungi. May, 1896, pp. 20.
39. Feeding for Beef. August, 1896, pp. 12.
40. The Cowpea. December, 1896, pp. 14.
41. The Colorado Potato Beetle in Mississippi. March, 1897, pp. 8.
42. Acclimation Fever, or Texas Fever. November, 1897, pp. 32.
42. Chemical Fertilizers. January 7, 1898, pp. 16.
43. "Natural Plant Food." Claims Made for it and its Value. February, 1898, pp. 14.
44. Winter Pasture. January, 1898, pp. 4.
45. Chemical Fertilizers. February 15, 1898, pp. 20.
46. Cooperative Experiments with Small Fruits. March, 1898, pp. 8.
47. Chemical Fertilizers. March 25, 1898, pp. 23.
48. Chemical Fertilizers. May 1, 1898, pp. 8.
49. Commercial Fertilizers. June 25, 1898, pp. 28.
50. Winter and Summer Pastures. September, 1898, pp. 12.
51. Commercial Fertilizers. June 25, 1899, pp. 12.
52. Commercial Fertilizers. February 15, 1899, pp. 28.
53. Some Insects Injurious to Stock, and Remedies Therefor. March, 1899, pp. 8.
54. Irish Potato Culture. March, 1899, pp. 8.
55. Commercial Fertilizers. March 15, 1899, pp. 24.
56. Grapes. April, 1899, pp. 22.
57. Commercial Fertilizers. April 15, 1899, pp. 8.
58. Soils of Mississippi. May, 1899, pp. 14.
59. Commercial Fertilizers. June, 1899, pp. 30.
60. Value of Cotton to the Farmer. September, 1899, pp. 32.
61. Commercial Fertilizers. January 15, 1900, pp. 16.

AGRICULTURE IN MISSISSIPPI. Sketch of.
  In Wailes's *Report on Agriculture and Geology of Mississippi*, pp. 127–205.
  See Harper's *Report*, 1857; and Hilgard's *Report*, 1860; and also Bulletins of Agricultural Experiment Station, *supra*.

ALABAMA AND CHATTANOOGA RAILROAD. The great | railroad route to the Pacific | and its | Connection, | showing the relation of the | Alabama and Chattanooga Railroad | to the proposed | Southern line to the Pacific. | Boston: | Alfred Mudge & son, printers, . . . | 1870. |
  8vo. pp. 10. *Map.*
  Now the Alabama Great Southern Railroad, a part of the old "Queen and Crescent" system.
  Copies seen: Congress.

ALABAMA AND CHATTANOOGA RAILROAD. Alabama & Chattanooga Railroad | "First Mortgage Indorsed Bonds" | of 1869, | and | 8% State gold bonds of 1870. | First report | of the | council of foreign bondholders acting | under their rules and regulations | with the committee of Alabama | bondholders. | With maps and Appendix. | London: | Councilhouse, No. 10, Moorgate street, | July, 1875. |
>   8vo. pp. 224.
>   *Copies seen:* Owen.

ALABAMA AND MISSISSIPPI RAIL ROAD. Facts | and | figures | illustrative of the value | of the | Alabama and · Mississippi Railroad. | By W. S. B. | Selma: | printed at the Selma Reporter job office. | 1851. |
>   8vo. pp. 27.
>   *Copies seen:* Curry.

ALABAMA AND MISSISSIPPI RIVERS RAIL ROAD. Memorial | of the | Alabama and Mississippi Rivers Rail Road | Company. n. p., n. d. [1861.]
>   8vo. pp. 8.
>   Addressed to Congress of the Confederate States of America, and submits scheme, or plan, by which this body can aid in completing the line. Same road now connecting Selma and Demopolis. Memorial signed by C. G. Griffin, *President*, and W. P. Bocock, Charles Walker, James L. Price, J. M. Lee, P. J. Weaver, J. W. Lapsley, *Directors*.
>   *Copies seen:* Curry.

ALCORN A. & M. COLLEGE. (Colored.) Catalogue | of the | officers and students | of | Alcorn A. & M. College | Westside, Mississippi, | 1898 and 1899 | and | announcement for 1899–1900. | Westside, Miss. | Railroad office, | Lorman, Miss. | 1899. |
>   8vo. pp. 34, 1 l. *Ill.*

ALCORN COUNTY. Sketch of.
>   In Lowry and McCardle's *Mississippi*, p. 439.

ALCORN, JAMES LUSK (1818–1894), *Gov. of Miss.*, *U. S. Senator.* Administration of.
>   In Lowry and McCardle's *Mississippi*, pp. 382–384.

—— Sketch of.
>   In Goodspeed's *Memoirs of Mississippi*, vol. 1, pp. 291–296; *portrait.*
>   *See* Appleton's *Cyclopædia of American Biography*, vol. 1, p. 40, *portrait;* and also Levee Commissioner, *infra.*

—— Messages. *See* State Offices.

ALDEN, T. J. Fox, *Compiler.* Digest of the laws of Mississippi, 1839. *See* Codes of Mississippi.

ALDRICH, TRUMAN H. (1848–), *M. E., M. C. from Ala.* Notes on the Tertiary of Alabama and Mississippi, with descriptions of new species.
>   In *Journal Cincinnati Society of Natural History*, July, 1885, vol. viii, pp. 145–153; *2 plates.*
>   Sections are given of the bluff at Claiborne, Lisbon, White bluff on the east bank of the Tombigbee River, Wood's bluff, and a section half a mile north of St. Stephens.

—— Notes on Tertiary fossils rare or little known.
>   *Ibid.* pp. 153–155.

ALDRICH, TRUMAN H. Notes on the distribution of Tertiary fossils in Alabama and Mississippi.
> *Ibid.* January, 1886, vol. viii, pp. 256-257.
> Mentions the occurrence of *Orbitoides supera* Conrad, *O. Mantelli* Conrad, and a few Nummulites in beds immediately underlying the strata in which the Zeuglodon bones occur at Jackson, on Dry or Town Creek. Mentions also the finding of a *Nautilus* sp. ? at Vicksburg, Miss., in the Oligocene, and also a new species of crab from Alabama.

—— Notes on Tertiary fossils, with descriptions of new species.
> *Ibid.* July, 1887, vol. x, pp. 78-83.

—— Observations upon the Tertiary of Alabama.
> In *American Journal Science*, October, 1885, vol. xxx, pp. 300-308.

—— Preliminary report on the Tertiary fossils of Alabama and Mississippi.
> *See* Geological Survey of Alabama, *Bulletin No. 1.*

—— New or little known Tertiary moll. from Alabama and Texas. Ithaca, N. Y. [1895].
> 8vo. pp. 30.
> *Bulletin No. 2 of American Paleontology*, Cornell University.

—— *and* MYER, OTTO. The Tertiary fauna of Newton and Wautubbee, Miss. *See* Myer, Otto.

ALEXANDER, C. H., *and* BRAME, L. Digest of reports of decisions. *See* L. Brame.

——, —— *Reporters.* Mississippi Reports, vols. 66-72. *See* Supreme Court.

ALEXANDER, *Rev.* W. A. Card playing as a Christian amusement. Richmond, Va. 1892.
> 12mo. pp. 30.

ALFRIEND, FRANK H. Life of Davis. *See* Jefferson Davis.

ALLEN, JAMES. Sketch of.
> In Claiborne's *Mississippi*, p. 182; *note.*
> He intermarried with the Colberts in the Chickasaw Nation.

ALLEN, JOHN M. (1847-), *M. C. from Miss.* Appropriations, expansion, and war. | Speech | of | Hon. John M. Allen, | of Mississippi, | in the | House of Representatives, | Wednesday, March 1, 1899. | Washington | 1899. |
> 8vo. pp. 14.

ALMANAC. The | Alabama | and | Mississippi | Almanac, | for the year of our Lord | 1856, | being bissextile, or leap year, | [-etc., 5 lines]. | Mobile, Ala. | Published and sold by | Strickland & Co. | No. 28 Dauphin street. | Strickland & Co., printers. |
> 12mo. pp. [47].

—— Confederate States | almanac. | For the year of our Lord | 1864. | Being bissextile, or leap year, and the 4th year | of the independence of the Confederate | States of America.—Calculations made at | University of Alabama. | Published for the trade by | Burke, Boykin & Co., | Macon, Ga. | S. H. Goetzel, | Mobile, Ala. |
> 16mo. pp. 20, 4 pp. advertisements.
> Contains several items in reference to the Confederate States government, with lists of battles.
> *Copies seen:* Hamner.

AMES, ADELBERT (1835–), *Gov. of Miss., U. S. Senator from Miss.* The testimony | in | the impeachment of | Adelbert Ames, | as | Governor of Mississippi. | Published by authority. | Jackson, Miss. | Power & Barksdale, State printers. | 1877. |
    8vo. pp. 323.

—— Administration as governor.
    In Lowry and McCardle's *Mississippi*, pp. 379–382, 387–412.

AMITE COUNTY. Sketch of.
    In Lowry and McCardle's *Mississippi*, pp. 439–442.
    See also Goodspeed's *Memoirs of Mississippi*, vol. 1, pp. 183–184.

ANDERSON, FULTON (1820–1874), *Lawyer.* Sketch of.
    In Lynch's *Bench and Bar of Mississippi*, pp. 429–444.
    This sketch contains a copy of Mr. Anderson's address as commissioner to Virginia from Mississippi, delivered February 18, 1861, before the convention of the former State.

ANDERSON, WILLIAM E., *Lawyer.* Sketch of.
    In Lynch's *Bench and Bar of Mississippi*, pp. 258–259.

ANDREWS, CAROLINE. Esther, a Drama by Racine. Translated from the French. Philadelphia, 1876.
    24mo. pp. 63.

ANDREWS, GARNET, *Lawyer.* A digest | of | Mississippi reports, | vols. 45 to 56 inclusive. | Being a supplement to George's Digest. | By Garnet Andrews. | Madison, Wis.: | David Atwood, printer and stereotyper. | 1881. |
    8vo. pp. 760.

ANONYMOUS. (A Mississippian.) Our country—its hopes and fears.
    In De Bow's *Review*, July, 1860, pp. 83–86.

ASHMEAD, W. H. Notes on cotton insects found in Mississippi.
    In *Insect Life*, Washington, D. C., vol. 7, pp. 25–29, 240–247, 320–326.

ANTIQUITIES. *See* Charles C. Jones, J. H. McCulloh, Cyrus Thomas, and W. B. Wilkes. *See also* Prehistoric Works. For mounds, *see* under particular counties.

APPLETON & Co., D., *Publishers.* Appleton's | illustrated | hand-book of American travel. | Part II. | The Southern and Western States, and the | Territories. | [Illustration.] | New York. | D. Appleton & Co., | [etc., 1 line.] | London: Trübner & Co. | [1857.] |
    12mo. pp. 405. *Maps; illustrations.*
    Copies seen: Hamner.

ARNOLD, JAMES M., *Lawyer.* Sketch of James T. Harrison, of Columbus, Miss.
    In *Southern Law Journal*, Tuscaloosa, Ala., September, 1879, vol. 2, pp., 432–436.

—— Some reflections on the school laws and educational | interests of the State. | An address | delivered to | the Alumni Association | of the | University of Mississippi, | at Oxford, Miss., | on the 28th of June, 1881, | by | Judge James M. Arnold, | of Columbus, Miss. | [Ferris & Youngblood, printers, Columbus, Miss.]
    8vo. Cover title only, 1 l., pp. 32.
    Copies seen: Owen.

ARTESIAN WELLS IN MISSISSIPPI. Sketch of.
> In Wailes's *Report on Agriculture and Geology of Mississippi*, pp. 260-268.

ATTALLA COUNTY. Sketch of.
> In Lowry and McCardle's *Mississippi*, pp. 442-444.

AUDITOR OF PUBLIC ACCOUNTS. Biennial report | of the | auditor of public accounts, | to the | Legislature of Mississippi, | for the | years 1898 and 1899. | Printed by authority. | Jacksonville, Fla.: | Vance Printing Co. | 1900. |
> 8vo. pp. 151.
> Contains also "Biennial Report of Wirt Adams, State Revenue Agent."
> Reports were also printed for previous years.

AUTOBIOGRAPHY. *See Mrs.* Fannie Beers, Reuben Davis George H. Devol, Lorenzo Dow, *Maj.* S. S. Forman, H. S. Fulkerson, N. M. Ludlow, Le Clerc Milfort, Matthew Phelps, and Solomon Smith.

B.

BAILY, FRANCIS. Journal | of a | tour in unsettled parts | of North America | in 1796 & 1797. | By the late | Francis Baily, F. R. S., | President of the Royal Astronomical Society. | With a memoir of the author. | London: | Baily brothers, royal exchange buildings. | MDCCCLVI | [1856].
> 8vo. pp. xii, 439.
> The tour extended from Norfolk, Va., to Baltimore, Philadelphia, New York, and then West by way of Washington, Pittsburg, down the Ohio and the Mississippi rivers to New Orleans, and thence by way of Natchez overland ("Departure across the Desert," he says), to Knoxville, Tenn. The latter portion is of much value to an early view of the territory soon (1798) erected into the Mississippi Territory, pp. 346-439.
> *Copies seen:* Congress.

BAKER, *Rev.* DANIEL, *D. D.* Baker's Sermons. By Rev. Daniel Baker, of Holly Springs, Miss.
> 12mo.

BALDWIN, JOSEPH G. (1811-1864), *Lawyer, Judge Calif. Sup. Ct.* The | flush times | of | Alabama and Mississippi. | A series of sketches. | By | Joseph G. Baldwin. | New York: | D. Appleton and company, | 200 Broadway. | London: 16 Little Britain. | MDCCC.LIII. [1853.] |
> 12mo. pp. x, 330. *Illustrations.*
> An edition from the same plates was issued in 1856, which is said on the title-page to be the "Eleventh thousand."
> Originally published in part in the *Southern Literary Messenger.*
> "No other work with which he is acquainted, has been published in the United States designed to illustrate the periods, the characters, and the phases of society, some notion of which is attempted to be given in this volume."—*Preface.*
> "A book replete with the richest anecdote and unsurpassed humor. In conversation he was the most entertaining man I ever knew, and his personal fascination made him the delight of every crowd he entered."—Reuben Davis's *Recollections of Mississippi,* etc.
> *Copies seen:* Owen.

—— The | flush times | of | Alabama and Mississippi. | A series of sketches. | By | Joseph G. Baldwin. | Eleventh thousand. | San Francisco: | Bancroft-Whitney co. | 1889. |
> 12mo. pp. x, 330. *1 illustration.*
> *Copies seen:* Hamner.

BALDWIN, THOMAS, and THOMAS, J., *M. D.* A | new and complete | gazetteer | of the United States; | giving a | full and comprehensive review | [–etc. 9 lines.] | By Thomas Baldwin and J. Thomas, M. D. | [Capital of U. S.] | Philadelphia: | Lippincott, Grambo & co. | 1854. |
>8vo. pp. 1364.
>Contains sketches of counties and towns.
>*Copies seen:* Hamner.

BALL, *Rev.* TIMOTHY H., *and* HALBERT, H. S. The Creek War of 1813 and 1814. *See* H. S. Halbert.

BANKHEAD, JOHN HOLLIS (1842–), *M. C. from Ala.* The Alabama-Mississippi Boundary.
>In *Transactions Alabama Historical Society*, 1897–98, vol. ii, pp. 90–93.
>An account of the manuscript material bearing on this boundary in the General Land Office, Washington, D. C.

BANKING IN MISSISSIPPI. History of. *See* Charles H. Brough. *See also* Union Bank of Mississippi.

BAPTIST (THE MISSIONARY) CHURCH in MISSISSIPPI. Sketch of.
>In Goodspeed's *Memoirs of Mississippi*, vol. ii, pp. 369–374.

—— [Baptist Newspaper Press.]
>"Dr. Crane, writing in 1858, says: 'The *Southwestern Luminary* was conducted by Elder A. Vaughn through the year 1837, and in February, 1838, was merged into the Mobile *Monitor and Southwestern Luminary*, under the care of Elder G. F. Heard. The *Mississippi Baptist* was commenced in January, 1846, by Elder W. H. Taylor, who was associated with Elder W. C. Crane from July, 1847, to July, 1848, in its editorial care. It was then placed under a committee, consisting of W. C. Crane, W. H. Taylor, and L. J. Caldwell. In January, 1849, it was placed under the editorial management of the lamented Elder J. B. Hiteler, and was discontinued in April of that year. A committee, consisting of Elders I. T. Tichenor, G. W. Allen, L. J. Caldwell, and G. H. Martin, edited it for a short time. In January, 1857, it was revived at Grenada, under the editorial care of Elder J. T. Freeman, and removed to Jackson.' . . . The *Mississippi Baptist* was wrecked by the war. . . .
>"A Baptist newspaper was established in Jackson in 1867 called the *Christian Watchman*. It lived only a few months. It was, however, not until 1877 that a successful enterprise of the kind was established. Rev. M. T. Martin began the publication and Rev. J. B. Gambrell became editor of the *Baptist Record*. . . . The general association has an organ called the *Southern Baptist*, which was merged into the *Baptist Record*. It now (1891) has a paper edited by Rev. N. L. Clarke, called the *Mississippi Baptist*."—Goodspeed, vol. ii, pp. 373, 374.

—— Mississippi Baptist State Convention. Minutes. 1836–1899.
>8vo.
>The following is a list of the dates and places of meeting:
>This organization commenced 1822 and lasted only two or three years. In 1836 the present Convention was organized. *See* Ford's *Christian Repository*, vol. viii, p 442. (1858.)
>2d session E. Fork Church, Amite County, 1824.
>Organization. Washington, Miss., 23 and 24 December, 1836.
>1st session, Palestine, Hinds County, 1837.
>2d session, Hepzibah, Meeting House, Lawrence County, 1838.
>3d session, Middleton, Carroll County, 1839.
>4th session, Wahalak, Kemper County, 1840.
>5th session, Brandon, Rankin County, 1841.
>6th session, Tocshish Church, Pontotoc County, 1842.
>7th session, Mound Bluff Church, Madison County, 1843.
>8th session, Palestine Church, Hinds County, 1844.

9th session, Grenada, Yalobusha County, 1845.
10th session, Fellowship Church, Jefferson County, 1846.
11th session, Hernando, De Soto County, 1847.
12th session, Concord Church, Winston County, 1848.
13th session, Raymond, 1849.
14th session, Jackson, 1850.
15th session, Aberdeen, 1851.
16th session, Clinton Church, Hinds County, 1852.
17th session, Columbus Church, Lowndes County, 1853.
18th session.
19th session, Clinton, 1855.
20th session.
21st session.
22d session, Liberty, Amite County, 1858.
23d session.
24th session, Natchez, Adams County, 1860.

This is found in notes in 1866 *Report*. { Crawfordsville 1864
{ Meridian 1865

27th session, Jackson, 1866.
28th session, Holly Springs, Marshall County, 1867.
29th session, Meridian, Lauderdale County, 1868.
30th session, Canton, Madison County, 1869.
31st session, West Point, Lowndes County, 1870.
32d session, Crystal Springs, Copiah County, 1871.
33d session, Meridian, Lauderdale County, 1872.
34th session, Aberdeen, Monroe County, 1873.
35th session, Oxford, 1874.
36th session, Hazelhurst Church, Copiah County, 1875.
37th session, Jackson Church, Hinds County, 1876.
38th session, Starkeville, 1877.
39th session, Summit, 1878.
40th session.
41st session, Okolona, 1880.
42d session, Meridian, 1881.
43d session, Sardis, 1882.
44th session, Crystal Springs, 1883.
45th session, Kosciusko Church, 1884.
46th session, Aberdeen Church, 1885.
47th session, Meridian, 1886.
48th session, Oxford, 1887.
49th session, Jackson, 1888.
50th session, West Point, 1889.
51st session, Columbus, 1890.
52d session, Natchez, 1891.
53d session, Meridian, 1892.
54th session, Summit, 1893.
55th session, Winona, 1894.
56th session, Hazelhurst, 1895.
57th session, Starkeville, 1896.
58th session, Grenada, 1897.
59th session, Brookhaven, 1898.
60th session, Aberdeen, 1899.

The Minutes of 1886 are irregularly numbered as the 32d session, and the session of 1887 is numbered erroneously as the 49th. This erroneous numbering is then regularly followed, making the session of 1899 as the 61st, when it should be the 60th.

Practically a full file of the *Minutes* of the several sessions will be found in the library of Colgate University, Hamilton, N. Y. The compiler is indebted to Virginia A. Willson, of this institution for the above list.

BAPTIST (THE MISSIONARY) CHURCH in MISSISSIPPI. History of Columbus Association. *See Rev.* L. S. Foster.
—— History of Louisville Association. *See Ibid.*
—— Mississippi Baptist Preachers. *See Ibid.*
—— Baptist annals. *See Rev.* Z. T. Leavell.
—— *See also* A. J. Brown, *Capt.* J. T. Buck, *Rev.* Richard Curtis, and *Dr.* R. A. Venable.

BAR ASSOCIATION.—Minutes | of the | Mississippi Bar Association, | at its | third annual meeting, | January 3, 1888. | With | President's address, memorial tributes, | and papers on | tax titles, law reform, and a Code of Civil | procedure, jurisprudence, and law reform, | the Imparlance term. | Jackson, Miss.: | Clarion Ledger steam print. | 1888. |
    8vo, pp. 76.
    There were issues for other meetings, but no copies seen. These volumes contain interesting papers on legal topics.

BARKSDALE, ETHELBERT, *Journalist, M. C., from Miss.* Reconstruction in Mississippi.
    In *Why the Solid South: or, Reconstruction and its Results,* pp. 321–348. Baltimore, 1890. 12 mo.
—— Ancestry of.
    In *Publications Southern History Association,* April, 1897, vol. i, pp. 127–137. Washington, D. C. 8vo.
    Prepared by Thomas M. Owen, Carrollton, Ala., and shows descent from Bryant Lester, of Lunenburg County, Va.

BARKSDALE, WILLIAM (1821–1863), *Brig.-Gen. C. S. A.* Sketch of.
    In Appleton's *Cyclopædia of American Biography,* vol. i, p. 165.
    Brother of Ethelbert Barksdale.

BARKSDALE, WILLIAM ROBERT (1834–1877), *Lawyer, Maj. C. S. A.* Digest of the Criminal Law of Mississippi, 1818–1872.
    In J. Z. George's *Digest Reports of Mississippi* (1872), pp. 787–840.
—— Sketch of.
    In Lynch's *Bench and Bar of Mississippi,* pp. 481–487.

BARNARD, FREDERICK AUGUSTUS PORTER (1809–1889), *LL. D., D. D., L. H. D., Prof. Univ. of Ala., 1838–1854, Pres. Univ. of Miss., 1856–1861, Pres. Columbia College.* Gratitude | due for | national blessings: | a discourse | delivered at Oxford, Mississippi, | on thanksgiving day, November 20, 1856. | By Frederick A. P. Barnard, LL. D. | Rector of the Parish of St. Peter's, Oxford, and President | of the University of Mississippi. | Published by request. | Memphis: | Printed by the Bulletin company, | 15 Madison street. | 1857. |
    8vo. pp. 26.
    Copies seen: Curry.

—— Letter | to | the honorable | the Board of Trustees | of the | University of Mississippi. | By | Frederick A. P. Barnard, LL. D., | President of the University. | Oxford: | University of Mississippi. | 1858. |
    8vo. pp. 112. Errata [1].
    On College education, its demands, requirements, etc.
    Copies seen: Curry.

BARNARD, FREDERICK AUGUSTUS PORTER. Sketch of.
: In Barnard's *American Journal of Education*, v, 753; portrait.

—— Memoirs of; *2 portraits*. See John Fulton.
: See also Waddel's *Memorials of Academic Life*, pp. 282-286.

BARNES, WILLIAM HORATIO. History of the Fortieth Congress. 1867-1869. New York: W. H. Barnes & Co. 1871.
: 8vo. 2 vols.

—— The Forty-second Congress of the United States. 1871-73. Washington, D. C. W. H. Barnes & Co. 1872.
: 8vo.

BARRY, WILLIAM TAYLOR SULLIVAN (1821-1868), *Lawyer, M. C. from Miss., Col. C. S. A.* Sketch of.
: In Lynch's *Bench and Bar of Mississippi*, pp. 295-301; portrait.

BARTON, ROGER (1802-1855), *Lawyer*. Sketch of.
: In Lynch's *Bench and Bar of Mississippi*, pp. 265-272.

BARTRAM, WILLIAM (1739-1823), *Botanist*. Travels | through | North & South Carolina, | Georgia, | East & West Florida, | the Cherokee country, the extensive | territories of the Muscogulges, | or Creek confederacy, and the | country of the Chactaws; | containing | an account of the soil and natural | productions of those regions, toge- | ther with observations on the | manners of the Indians. | Embellished with copper-plates. | By William Bartram. | Philadelphia: | Printed by James & Johnson. | M, DCC, XCI [1791]. |
: 8vo. Title, 1 l.; pp. xxxiv, 522. *Map; 7 plates.*
: Appended as pp. 481-522 is the following title-page for Book iv, viz:
: An | account | of the | persons, manners, customs | and | government | of the | Muscogulges or Creeks, | Cherokees, Chactaws, &c. | aborigines of the continent of | North America. | By William Bartram. | Philadelphia· | Printed by James & Johnson. | M, DCC, XCI [1791].
: *Copies seen:* Congress.

—— Travels | through | North and South Carolina, | Georgia, | East and West Florida, | the Cherokee Country, | the extensive Territories of the Muscogulges | or Creek Confederacy, | and the Country of the Chactaws. | Containing | an Account of the Soil and Natural produc- | tions of those regions; | together with observations on the manners of the Indians. | Embellished with copper-plates. | By William Bartram. | Philadelphia: | Printed by James & Johnson. 1791. | London: | Reprinted for J. Johnson, in St. Paul's Church yard. | 1792.
: 8vo. pp. xxiv, 520, 6 ll. *Map.*

—— Travels | through | North and South Carolina, | Georgia, | East and West Florida, | the Cherokee Country, | the Extensive Territories of the Muscogulges | or Creek Confederacy, | and the Country of the Chactaws; | containing | an Account of the soil and natural produc- | tions of those Regions; | together with | observations on the manners of the Indians. | Embellished with copper-plates. | By William Bartram. | Dublin: | For J. Moore, W. Jones, R. M'Allister, and J. Rice. | 1793. |
: 8vo, pp. xxiv, 520, 6 ll. *Map; 7 plates.*

BARTRAM, WILLIAM. William Bartram's | Reisen | durch | Nord- und Süd-Karolina, | Georgien, Ost- und West-Florida, | das Gebiet | der Tscherokesen, Krihks und Tschaktahs, | nebst umständlichen Nachrichten | von den Einwohnern, dem Boden und den Naturprodukten | dieser wenig bekannten grossen Länder. | Aus dem Englischen. | Mit erläuternden Anmerkungen | von | E. A. W. Zimmermann, Hofrath und Professor in Braunschweig.

<blockquote>
sm. 8vo. pp. xxvi, 1 1, pp. 501 (erroneously numbered 469).

Forms pp. 1–501 of:

Magazin | von | merkwürdigen neuen | Reisebeschreibungen, | aus fremden Sprachen übersetzt | und mit | erläuternden Anmerkungen begleitet. | Mit Kupfern. | Zehnter Band. | Berlin, | 1793. | In der Vossischen Buchhandlung. |

The Carter Brown catalogue titles an edition in Dutch: Haarlaem, Bohn, 1794. 8°. Sabin's Dictionary, No. 3873, titles an edition: Haarlem, 1794–1797; and another (quoting from De Jong): Amsterdam. 1797; 3 parts.

Copies seen: Congress.
</blockquote>

—— Travels | through | North and South Carolina, | Georgia, | east and west Florida, | the Cherokee country, | the extensive territories of the Muscogulges | or Creek confederacy, | and the country of the Chactaws. | Containing | an account of the soil and natural produc- | tions of those regions; | together with | observations on the manners of the Indians. | Embellished with copper-plates. | By William Bartram. | The second edition in London. | Philadelphia: printed by James and Johnson. 1791. | London: | reprinted for J. Johnson, in St. Paul's churchyard. | 1794. |

<blockquote>
8vo. pp. xxiv, 520, 4 ll. *Frontispiece*, a Creek chief; 7 plates.

Copies seen: Congress.
</blockquote>

—— Voyage | dans les parties sud | de l'Amérique | septentrionale; | Savoir: les Carolines septentrionale et méridio- | nale, la Georgie, les Florides orientale et | occidentale, le pays des Cherokées, le vaste | territoire des Muscogulges ou de la confédé- | ration Creek, et le pays des Chactaws; | Contenant des détails sur le sol et les productions natu- | relles des contrées, et des observations sur les | mœurs des Sauvages qui les habitent. | Par Williams [*sic*] Bartram. | Imprimé à Philadelphie, en 1791, et à Londres, | en 1792, et trad. de l'angl. par P. V. Benoist. | Tome premier[-second]. | A Paris, | chez Carteret et Brosson, libraires, rue Pierre- | Sarrasin, Nos. 13 et 7 | Dugour et Durand, rue et maison Serpente. | An VII [1799]. |

<blockquote>
8vo. vol. i, 2 p. l., pp. 457, 1 l. *Map.* Vol. ii, 1 p. l., pp. 436, 1 l.

Copies seen: Congress.

Another edition of this was published in 1801, in which there was no change except in the imprint:

A Paris, | chez Maradan, Libraire, rue Paré Saint-André- | des-Arcs, no. 16. | An IX [1801]. |
</blockquote>

—— Bartram's Travels is partly reprinted in *The Wonderful Magazine and Marvellous Chronicle*, vol. 5, pp. 313–323, 355–366, London, n. d. 8vo.

<blockquote>
The number of the editions, the extensive use made of it by historians, and its constantly increasing market value are evidences of the high character of Bartram's work, all of which is merited. His journeys covered a wide territory, he was eager for knowledge and observant, and his writings preserve incidents, scenes, and pictures of the times and the savage tribes which are of the greatest value.
</blockquote>

BARTRAM, WILLIAM. Observations on the Creek and Cherokee Indians. By William Bartram. With prefatory and supplementary notes. By E. G. Squier.
 In *American Ethnological Society Transactions*, vol. 3, pt. 1, pp. 1-81, New York, 1853. 8vo.
 Bartram, etc., pp. 11-58; Squier's Notes, pp. 59-81.

—— Sketch of John (1699-1777) and William Bartram.
 In *Popular Science Monthly*, 1892. vol. xl, pp. 827-839.
 In the September number is a portrait of William Bartram.

—— Sketch of John and William Bartram.
 In Barnard's *American Journal of Education*, xxviii, 873-874.

B[AUDRY DE] L[OZIÈRES]. Voyage | à la Louisiane, | et sur le Continent | de l'Amérique | Septentrionale, | fait dans les années 1794 à 1798; | Contenant un tableau historique de la Louisiane, | des observations sur son climat, ses riches productions, | le caractère et le nom des Sauvages; des remarques | importantes sur la navigation; des prin- cipes d'adminis- | tration, de législation et de gouvernement propres à cette | Colonie, etc., etc. | Par B x x x D x x x. | Orné d'une belle carte. | [Quotation, 3 lines.] | Paris, | Dentu, imprimeur-libraire, Palais du Tribunal, | galeries de bois, no. 240. | An XI. 1802. |
 8vo. pp. viii, 382. *Map of Louisiana*.
 Résumé of the history of the community, with accounts of the character, manners, and wars of the savages.
 Copies seen: Hamner.

BEERS, *Mrs.* FANNIE A. Memories. | A record of personal experience and | adventure during four | years of war. | By | Mrs. Fannie A. Beers. | Press of J. B. Lippincott Company, | Philadelphia. | 1889. |
 12mo. pp. 336. *Portrait* of author.
 Copies seen: Owen.

BELL, *Mrs.* HELEN D. Glimpses of the past.
 In *Publications of the Mississippi [State] Historical Society*, 1899, vol. ii, pp. 201-206.
 Notes on items of historical interest from a newspaper file, 1836 to 1843.

BENTON COUNTY. Sketch of.
 In Lowry and McCardle's *Mississippi*, pp. 414-445.

BERRYHILL, S. NEWTON (1832-1887), *Journalist, Poet.* Backwoods Poems. By S. Newton Berryhill. [Quotation, 3 lines.] Excelsior printing office, Columbus, Miss., 1878.
 12 mo.

—— Mississippi's "Backwoods Poet." *See* Dabney Lipscomb.

BERTRON, *Mrs.* OTTILLIE. Edith; a novel. 1887.
 12mo.

—— Review of Ingersoll's Attacks on Christianity. 1889.
 8vo.

BESANÇON. Besançon's annual register of the State of Mississippi for 1838. Natchez, 1838.
 16 mo. pp. 232.

BIBLIOGRAPHY. *See* Bureau of Ethnology, Bureau of Education, T. L. Cole, T. W. Field, Miss Mary Morancy, Thomas M. Owen, James Pilling, Ben: Perley Poore, J. L. Power, Joseph Sabin, D. B. Warden, and *Dr.* S. B. Weeks.

BIEDMA, LUYS HERNANDEZ DE. Relation of the conquest of Florida presented by Luys Hernandez de Biedma in the year 1544 to the King of Spain in Council.

In Ternaux-Compan's *Recueil des pièces sur la Floride* (vol. xx of his general collection of *Voyages, relations et mémoires*), pp. 51-106. See *infra*.

This account, which long remained in manuscript in the Archivo General de las Indias at Seville, was first published in the above French edition. A copy of the original Spanish manuscript is in the New York Public Library.

Also in Rye's *Discovery and Conquest of Terra Florida*, pp. 173-200. See Elvas, Gentleman of. Translated for the Hakluyt Society from Ternaux.

Also in French's *Historical Collections of Louisiana*, part ii, pp. 95-109. See French, B. F. Abridged from Ternaux.

Also in Buckingham Smith's *Narratives of the Career of De Soto*, pp. 229-261. See Elvas, Gentleman of. No. 5 of the Bradford Club Series.

Also in Colección | de varios documentos | para la historia de la Florida y tierras adyacentes. | Tomo 1. | En la casa de Trübner y Compañia, | núm. 60, Paternoster Row, | Londres. | [Se han tirado 500 ejemplares | por José Rodriguez, | Madrid, año de 1857.] | pp. 47-64. Folio. 4 p. ll., pp. 208.

"The relation of Biedma adds some curious details to those we already possessed, relating to the fatal expedition of De Soto."—Field's *Indian Bibliography*, p. 390.

BIEN, H. M. Ben-Beor. | A historical story. | In two divisions. | Part I.—Lunar Intaglios. | The Man in the Moon, | a counterpart of Wallace's "Ben Hur." | Part II.—Historical Phantasmagoria. | The Wandering Gentile, | a companion romance to Sue's "Wandering Jew." | By | H. M. Bien, | author [-etc., 1 line.] | Vicksburg, Miss. | Second revised and improved edition. | Baltimore: | Press of the Friedenwald Co. | 1892. |

12 mo. pp. 528, 8.

He is also the author of "Oriental Legends" (1883); "Feast of Lights" (1886); "Samson;" "Purim" (1884); "What is Judaism?" (1888); and "Solar Night" (1887).

BIENVILLE, JEAN BAPTISTE LE MOYNE. Life of. See *Miss* Grace King. See also B. F. French.

BIOGRAPHY. (*Collected.*) See W. H. Barnes, M. B. Brady, H. S. Foote, Rev. L. S. Foster, B. F. French, Goodspeed, Rev. Z. T. Leavell, J. D. Lynch, *Mrs.* Mary Tardy.

—— For individual biographies, see particular names.

BLACK, JOHN (-1854), *Lawyer, U. S. Senator from Miss.* Sketch of.

In Lynch's *Bench and Bar of Mississippi*, pp. 90-92.

BLACK, *Rev.* W. C. A centennial retrospect. 1884.

12mo. pp. 100.

—— Temperance and teetotalism. 1886.

12mo.

—— Christian Womanhood. 1888.

12mo. pp. 300.

—— Philosophy of Methodism. 1879.

8vo.

BLEDSOE, ALBERT TAYLOR (1808-1878), *LL. D., Prof. Univ. of Miss.* Sketch of.

In Waddel's *Memorials of Academic Life*, pp. 279-282.

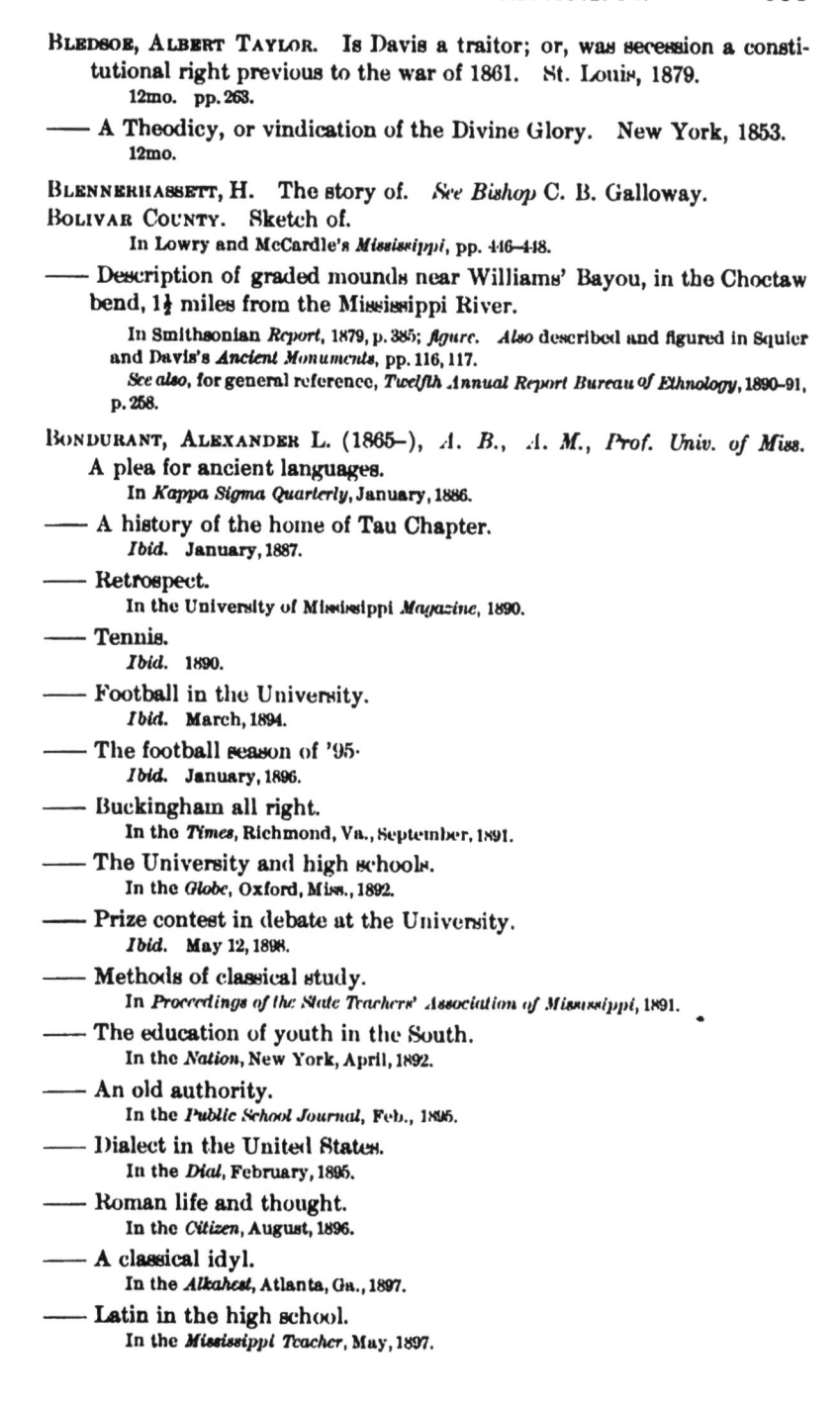

BLEDSOE, ALBERT TAYLOR. Is Davis a traitor; or, was secession a constitutional right previous to the war of 1861. St. Louis, 1879.
12mo. pp. 263.

—— A Theodicy, or vindication of the Divine Glory. New York, 1853.
12mo.

BLENNERHASSETT, H. The story of. *See Bishop* C. B. Galloway.

BOLIVAR COUNTY. Sketch of.
In Lowry and McCardle's *Mississippi*, pp. 416-448.

—— Description of graded mounds near Williams' Bayou, in the Choctaw bend, 1½ miles from the Mississippi River.
In Smithsonian *Report*, 1879, p. 385; *figure*. Also described and figured in Squier and Davis's *Ancient Monuments*, pp. 116, 117.
See also, for general reference, *Twelfth Annual Report Bureau of Ethnology*, 1890-91, p. 258.

BONDURANT, ALEXANDER L. (1865–), *A. B., A. M., Prof. Univ. of Miss.*
A plea for ancient languages.
In *Kappa Sigma Quarterly*, January, 1886.

—— A history of the home of Tau Chapter.
Ibid. January, 1887.

—— Retrospect.
In the University of Mississippi *Magazine*, 1890.

—— Tennis.
Ibid. 1890.

—— Football in the University.
Ibid. March, 1894.

—— The football season of '95.
Ibid. January, 1896.

—— Buckingham all right.
In the *Times*, Richmond, Va., September, 1891.

—— The University and high schools.
In the *Globe*, Oxford, Miss., 1892.

—— Prize contest in debate at the University.
Ibid. May 12, 1898.

—— Methods of classical study.
In *Proceedings of the State Teachers' Association of Mississippi*, 1891.

—— The education of youth in the South.
In the *Nation*, New York, April, 1892.

—— An old authority.
In the *Public School Journal*, Feb., 1895.

—— Dialect in the United States.
In the *Dial*, February, 1895.

—— Roman life and thought.
In the *Citizen*, August, 1896.

—— A classical idyl.
In the *Alkahest*, Atlanta, Ga., 1897.

—— Latin in the high school.
In the *Mississippi Teacher*, May, 1897.

BONDURANT, ALEXANDER L. Five years of football at the University of Mississippi.
: In the *University Record*, December 7, 1898–March 8, 1899.

—— Did Jones County Secede?
: In *Publications Mississippi State Historical Society*, 1898, vol. i, pp. 103–106.
: *See also* Memphis *Commercial-Appeal*, October, 1895.

—— Sherwood Bonner, her life and place in the literature of the South.
: *Ibid.* 1899, vol. ii, pp. 43–68.

—— W. C. Falkner, novelist.
: *Ibid.* 1900, vol. iii. (In press.)

BONNER, SHERWOOD (1848–18), *Author*. Laura Capello, a leaf from a traveler's note book.
: In *The Ploughman*, Boston, circa 1864.

—— A flower of the South.
: In a musical journal, name not ascertained.

—— An exposition on one of the Commandments.
: In *Frank Leslie's Journal*.

—— Miss Willard's two rings.
: In *Lippincott's Magazine*, December, 1875.

—— From '60 to '65.
: *Ibid.* October, 1876.

—— A volcanic interlude.
: *Ibid.* April, 1880.

—— The Valcours.
: *Ibid.* September–December, 1881, pp. 243–258, 345–361, 444–462, 555–570.

—— The revolution in the life of Mr. Ballingall.
: In Harper's *New Monthly Magazine*, October, 1879.

—— Two storms.
: *Ibid.* April, 1881, pp. 728–748.

—— Like unto like. | A novel. | By Sherwood Bonner | New York | Harper and Brothers, publishers | Franklin square | 1878. |
: 12 mo. pp. 169.

—— Dialect tales | By | Sherwood Bonner | Illustrated | New York | Harper and Brothers, Franklin square. | 1883. |
: 12 mo. pp. 187.
: Contains a number of stories first published in magazines. They deal with the negro, the mountaineer, and the Westerner.

—— Suwanee River Tales. Boston. Roberts Brothers, 1884.
: 12 mo. pp. 303.

—— Her life and place in the literature of the South. *See* A. L. Bondurant.
: Mr. Bondurant's paper contains the following summary of her work:
: "Her principal writings may be grouped as follows: Early pieces, '64–'73.—Letters from Boston and Europe, '74–'76.—Short stories published in periodicals between '73 and '83; a number of these were collected after the death of the author and reprinted in a volume entitled 'Suwanee River Tales' (there are many excellent sketches in this little book, but the best are those in which Gran'mammy figures); to this period of her life belong 'Miss Willard's Two Rings,' and 'From '60 to '65.'—'Like unto Like.' a novel; 'The Valcours,' a novelette; 'The Revolution in the Life of Mr. Ballingall;' 'Two Storms;' 'A Volcanic Interlude,' appeared between '78 and '83. She wrote during these years, besides, a number of dialect stories dealing with negro character, the mountaineers of East Tennessee, and the denizens of the Western Prairie."

Bossu, F. (1725–   ) *French traveler.* Nouveaux Voyages aux Indes Occidentales; Contenant une relation des différens Peuples qui habitent les environs du grand Fleuve Saint-Louis, appelé vulgairement le Mississippi; leur Religion; leur gouvernement; leurs mœurs; leurs guerres & leur commerce. Par M. Bossu, Capitaine dans les Troupes de la Marine. A Paris, 1768.

> 12mo. vol. i, pp. xx, 244, and *1 plate;* vol. ii, pp. 264, and *2 plates.*
> There was a Dutch version at Amsterdam in 1769, and the original French was reprinted there in 1769 and 1777.
> Contains much relating to the Southern Indians.
> "The author, an army officer, was first sent up the Tombigbee, and afterward attached to the forces which were posted in Illinois, and was there when Villiers marched on Fort Necessity. He was in the colony twelve years, and bore a good reputation."—Winsor's *Narrative and Critical History of America,* vol. v, p. 67.

—— Travels | through that part of | North America | formerly called | Louisiana. | By Mr. Bossu, Captain in the | French Marines. | Translated from the French, | by John Reinhold Forster, F. A. S. | Illustrated with notes relative chiefly to | natural history. | To which is added by the translator | a systematic catalogue of all the | known plants of English North-America, | or a | Flora Americae Septentrionalis. | Together with | [–etc., 5 lines]. | Vol. I[–II.] | [Quotation, 1 line.] | London: | printed for T. Davies in Russel-street, Covent-Garden. | MDCCLXXI. |

> 8vo. vol. i, pp. viii, 407; vol. ii, pp. 432.
> Only English edition. From the French of the preceding title.
> *Copies seen:* Hamner.

—— Nouveaux | Voyages | dans | l'Amérique Septentrionale, | Contenant | une collection de lettres écrites sur les lieux, par | l'Auteur, à son ami, M. Douin, chevalier, | capitaine dans les troupes du Roi, ci-devant | son camarade dans le nouveau Monde. | Par M. Bossu, | chevalier des l'ordre & militaire de Saint- | Louis, ancien capitaine d'une campagnie de la | Marie. | [Cut.] | A Amsterdam [Paris?], | Chez Changuion à la Bourse. | M.DCC.LXXVII. |

> 8vo. pp. xvi, 392; *4 plates.*
> This volume also contains much information concerning the Indians encountered.
> "Bossu's account of his first two voyages to Louisiana was printed in 1768, after which he made a third voyage, the account of which is given in this volume, which, not having been reprinted or translated into any other language, is a much scarcer work than the former. There are copies with the date of 1778, and with 'nouvelle édition' on the title page, but it is [sic] the same."—*Rich.*
> *Copies seen:* Hamner.

Boundaries. Organization and boundaries of Mississippi.

> In Howard and Hutchinson's *Statutes of Mississippi* (1840), pp. 37–42.

—— Counties and their boundaries.

> *Ibid.* pp. 43–56.

—— An Act defining the limits and divisions of the State of Mississippi.

> In *Revised Code of Mississippi* (1857), pp. 46–69.
> Gives all State and county boundaries.
> The "Introductory Remarks" comprise an admirable discussion of the boundaries of the State, "from treaties and public acts."

BOUNDARIES. An Act in relation to the limits and divisions of the State of Mississippi.
>In *Revised Code of Mississippi* (1880), pp. 48–70.
>Gives all State and county boundaries.

—— Boundaries, State and Counties.
>In *Annotated Code of Mississippi* (1892), pp. 186–206.

—— The line between Mississippi and Tennessee.
>In *Revised Code of Mississippi* (1857), p. 49.
>As early as 1829 doubts arose as to the true dividing line between these States, and whether or not Memphis was in Mississippi. Later, commissioners were appointed by both States, and the line was run, leaving Memphis in Tennessee. This report was adopted by act of the legislature February 8, 1838.

—— Conflicting boundaries in early times.
>In Claiborne's *Mississippi*, pp. 92–101.

—— Southern boundary of Tennessee. Report of select committee . . . instructed to inquire whether any or what steps should be taken . . . for ascertaining . . . the true line between the States of Tennessee and Mississippi. May 6, 1834. (House Rep. 445, 23d Cong., 1st sess.)
>8vo. pp. 18. n. t. p.
>*Copies seen:* Owen.

—— Message | from the | President [John Adams] of the | United States, | transmitting | a Report, and sundry Documents, | from the Secretary of State, | relative to the proceedings of the | Commissioner for running | the boundary line | between the | United States and East and West-Florida. | Published by order of the House of Representatives. | [Philadelphia: Joseph Gales, 1797.] (Ex. Doc., 5th Cong., 1st sess.)
>8vo. pp. 36.
>Reprinted as No. 124, American State Papers: *Foreign Relations*, vol. ii, 20–27; also in *Annals of Congress*, 5th Cong., vol. iii, pp. 3097–3115.

—— Message | from the | President of the United States, | accompanying a report to him | from | the Secretary of State, | and sundry documents | relative to the affairs of the United States | on the | Mississippi; the intercourse with the | Indian Nations, | and the inexecution of the treaty | between the | United States and Spain. | Philadelphia: | printed by W. Ross. | [1798]. (Ex. Doc., 5th Cong., 2d sess.)
>8vo. pp. 91.
>Reprinted as No. 129, American State Papers: *Foreign Relations*, vol. ii, pp. 78–103; also in *Annals of Congress*, 5th Cong., vol. iii, pp. 3175–3238.
>Relates principally to the controversy over the running of the boundary between the United States and Spain, under the treaty of October 27, 1795.

—— The Alabama-Mississippi Boundary. *See* J. H. Bankhead.

—— Boundaries of Mississippi. *See* Henry Gannett.

—— Running Mississippi's South line. *See* P. J. Hamilton.

—— History of the South Carolina Cession and the Northern boundary of Tennessee. *See* W. R. Garrett.

BOURBON COUNTY. Sketch of.
>In Claiborne's *Mississippi*, pp. 96, 155–156, and *notes*.
>This was formed by Georgia, in 1785, in an effort to organize and further settlements in the Western domain. There is no Mississippi county of this name.

BOWLES, WILLIAM AUGUSTUS (1744-1805). Authentic memoirs | of | William Augustus Bowles, | Esquire, | Ambassador | from the United Nations of | Creeks and Cherokees, | to the | Court of London. | London: | Printed for R. Faulder, New Bond-street. | M.DCC.XCI. |
>16mo. pp. vi, 79.
>*Copies seen:* Hamner.

—— Life of George [*sic*] Augustus Bowles, an Englishman, who abandoned civilization to become chief of the Creek Nation.
>In Perrin du Lac's *Voyage dans les deux Louisianes,* chapter III, pp. 456-472. See that title.

—— The life of General W. A. Bowles, a native of America—born of English parents, in Frederick County, Maryland, in the year 1744. From "Public Characters, for 1802." *London.* *New York:* Reprinted by Robert Wilson. 1803.
>8vo. pp. 31.
>*Sabin:* No. 7083.
>Appleton's *Cyclopædia of American Biography* gives the date of birth as 1763.

BOYD, SAMUEL S., *Lawyer.* Sketch of.
>In Lynch's *Bench and Bar of Mississippi,* pp. 142-143.
>See also Claiborne's *Mississippi,* p. 390, note.

BRACKENRIDGE, HENRY MARIE (1786-1871), *Author.* History | of | the late war | between the | United States and Great Britain. | Containing | a minute account of | the various | military and naval operations. | Illustrated with plates. | By H. M. Brackenridge, Esq. | Second edition, | revised and corrected. | Baltimore: | published and sold by Joseph Cushing, | No. 6, N. Howard-street. | J. Robinson, printer. | 1817. |
>12mo. pp. 363.
>It has passed through several editions: Baltimore, two in 1817, and another in 1818; Philadelphia, 1839 and 1846 (pp. 298); besides it has been translated into French and Italian. 6th edition: Philadelphia, 1836. 8vo. pp. 289.
>"One of the earliest, and much the best, of the shorter histories of the war of 1812. Judge Brackenridge was an old acquaintance of General Jackson, and served as his secretary and translator when the General was governor of Florida."—Parton's *Life of Jackson.*
>Contains an account of Creek war.
>*Copies seen:* Hamner.

BRADY, M. B., *and* HANDY, L. C. Brady & Handy's album of the 50th Congress of the United States.
>4to.
>Contains separate portraits, grouped on a single page, of the members of the Mississippi delegation in this Congress. Facing this is a page containing biographical sketches, copied from the *Congressional Directory.*

BRAME, L., *and* ALEXANDER, C. H. A digest | of the | reports of the decisions | of the | Supreme Court of Mississippi | from Volume forty-five to seventy | three inclusive. | By L. Brame and C. H. Alexander. | Nashville, Tennessee: | Marshall & Bruce Co., law publishers, | 1899. |
>8vo. pp. 1456.
>Also bound in 2 volumes, but with same pagination.

—— *and* ALEXANDER, *Reporters.* Mississippi Reports, vols. 66-72. *See* Supreme Court.

HIST 99—VOL I——42

BRANDON COLLEGE. Sketch of.
: In Mayes' *History of Education in Mississippi*, pp. 59-60.
BRANDON, GERARD. Historic Adams County.
: In *Publications Mississippi [State] Historical Society*, 1899, vol. ii, pp. 207-218.
BRANDON, GERARD CHITTAKER (1788-   ), *Lawyer, Gov. of Miss.* Sketch of, with an account of his ancestry and descendants.
: In Goodspeed's *Memoirs of Mississippi*, vol. i, pp. 419-422.

—— Administration as governor.
: In Lowry and McCardle's *Mississippi*, pp. 262-269.

BRANDON, Gen. THOMAS. Sketch of. *See* Wm. T. Lewis.
BRINTON, DANIEL GARRISON (1837-1898), *Author.* The National legend of the Chahta-Muskokee tribes. By D. G. Brinton, M. D.
: In *Historical Magazine, second series*, vol. 7, pp. 118-126, Morrisania, N. Y., 1870. sm. 4º.
: Issued separately as:

—— The | national legend | of the | Chahta-Muskokee tribes. | By | D. G. Brinton, M. D. | Morrisania, N. Y.: | 1870. |
: Large 8vo. pp. 13.
: *See also* Gatschet, A. S.

—— Myths of the New World. A treatise on the symbolism and mythology of the Red Race of America. New York, Leypoldt and Holt, 1868.
: 12mo. pp. 337.

BROOKS UNIVERSAL GAZETTEER. *See* Wm. Darby.
BROOKE, WALKER (1813-1869), *Lawyer, U. S. Sen. from Miss.* Sketch of.
: In Lynch's *Bench and Bar of Mississippi*, pp. 316-319.

BROUGH, CHARLES HILLMAN, *Ph. D.* History of taxation in Mississippi.
: In *Publications Mississippi [State] Historical Society*, 1899, vol. ii, pp. 113-124.

—— History of banking in Mississippi.
: *Ibid*, 1900. vol. iii. (In press.)

BROWN, ALBERT GALLATIN (1813-1880), *Lawyer, Gov. Miss., U. S. Senator, Conf. Senator from Miss.* Sketch of.
: In Lynch's *Bench and Bar of Mississippi*, pp. 277-283.

—— Administration as governor.
: In Lowry and McCardle's *Mississippi*, pp. 304-318.

—— History of the raising of the first American flag in the Capital of Mexico. *See* Mexican War.
: Speech of Senator Brown vindicating claim of Gen. John A. Quitman.

—— Speeches, messages, and writings of. Edited by M. W. Clusky. Philadelphia, 1859.
: 8vo. pp. 614.

BROWN, A. J. History | of | Newton County, | Mississippi, | from 1834 to 1894. | By A. J. Brown, | of Newton County. | Jackson, Miss.: | Clarion-Ledger Company. | 1894. |
: 8vo. pp. xv, 472.
: ILLUSTRATIONS: Judge John Watts, the Court-House, R. H. Henry, Dr. J. B. Bailey, the Baptist Church at Decatur, the Methodist Church at Newton, College at Newton, Hickory Institute, *Elder* N. L. Clarke, A. B. Amis, esq., and A. W. Whatley, esq.
: This is an interesting and valuable local history. It contains graphic accounts of early settlement, customs, Indians, etc., with numerous biographies.

BROWN, SAMUEL R. (1810–1880). The | Western gazetteer; | or | emigrant's directory. | Containing | a geographical description | of the | Western States and Territories, viz, | the States of | Kentucky, Indiana, Louisiana, Ohio, Tennessee | and Mississippi: | and the Territories of | Illinois, Missouri, Alabama, Michigan, and | North-Western. | With an appendix, | containing sketches [-etc., 4 lines.] | By Samuel R. Brown. | Auburn, N.Y. | Printed by H. C. Southwick. | 1817. |

  8vo. pp. 352. Errata slip inset after p. 352.
  Copies seen: Hamner; Congress.

BRUIN, PETER BRIAN, *Territorial Judge of Miss.* Sketch of.
  In Claiborne's *Mississippi*, pp. 152, 161, 172.

BUCK, *Capt.* JOHN T. Historical Sketches of the Baptists of Mississippi.
  In Ford's *Christian Repository.*

BUCKINGHAM, JAMES SILK (1786–1855). The | slave States | of | America. | By | J. S. Buckingham, Esq. | Author of | "America, Historical, Statistic, and Descriptive." | In two volumes. | Vol. I[-II.] | Fisher, Son & Co. | Newgate st. London; rue St. Honoré, Paris. | [1842.]

  8vo. vol. i, 10 prel. leaves, pp. 487; vol. ii, 6 prel. leaves, pp. 588, 4 *plates* in each volume.
  Copies seen: Hamner.

BUCKNER, ROBERT H. (–1846), *Lawyer.* Sketch of.
  In Lynch's *Bench and Bar of Mississippi*, pp. 165-166.

BUFFALO IN MISSISSIPPI. Reference to.
  In Claiborne's *Mississippi*, p. 27, and *note.*

BUREAU OF EDUCATION, THE UNITED STATES. *See* Educational Literature of Mississippi.

BUREAU OF ETHNOLOGY. Catalogue of linguistic Manuscripts. By James C. Pilling.
  In *First Annual Report of the Bureau of Ethnology*, 1879–80, pp. 553–575.
  Mississippi Indian linguistic material noted, *passim.*

BURKITT, FRANK. Our State's finances, and our school system. Okalona, Miss. 1886.
  8vo. pp. 64.

BURKITT, HENRY L. Burkitt's and Reid's church history. 1850.
—— Burkitt's maxims, and guide to youth. 1884.
  No copies seen.

BURR, AARON (1750–1836), *Lawyer, Col. in Rev. War, U. S. Senator, Vice-Pres. U. S.* Capture of.
  In the *American Historical Magazine,* Nashville, Tenn., April 1896, vol. i, pp. 140-153.
  Burr was apprehended in Alabama in 1807. The facts of the capture are here given in a series of original documents, now first published, which, originally belonging to Nicholas Perkins, esq., are now the property of the Tennessee Historical Society.
  They are as follows:
  Feb. 9, 1807, Lemuel Henry to Nicholas Perkins.
  Apr. 6, 1807, The U. S. in account current with Nicholas Perkins for transporting Aaron Burr to Richmond.
  No date. Nicholas Perkins to C. A. Rodney.
  Feb. 19, 1807, Lt. E. P. Gaines to Gen. Wilkinson and Gov. Williams,

Feb. 9, 1807, E. P. Gaines to Nicholas Perkins.
Feb. 23, 1807, Pledge of the guard, or escort, to conduct Burr to the President of the U. S., signed by Nicholas Perkins, John Mertes, Sam'l McCormack, John Jay, Henry H. B. Slade.
No date. Lt. E. P. Gaines to Nicholas Perkins.
Feby. 27, 1807, Passport by Lt. E. P. Gaines to Nicholas Perkins.
March 23, 1807, James Madison, Sec. of State, to Lewis Ford.
March 23, 1807, H. Dearborn to Nicholas Perkins.
No date. G. W. Hay to Nicholas Perkins.
March 29, 1807, *Letter* not signed, not directed.

—— Expedition of.
In Claiborne's *Mississippi*, pp. 278-294.

—— Burr's conspiracy.
In *Transactions Alabama Historical Society*, 1898-99, vol. iii, pp. 167-177.
Consists of six hitherto unpublished letters, bearing upon events in the Southern country in connection with Mr. Burr, from Col. Silas Dinsmore, Judge Harry Toulmin, Gov. W. C. C. Claiborne, and Col. Benj. Hawkins. These are edited by Thomas M. Owen, Secretary of the Alabama Historical Society.

—— *See also* **Daniel Clark** and **A. J. Pickett.**

C.

Cabaniss, Alfred B. (1808-1871), *M. D., Supt. Miss. Lunatic Asylum.* Sketch of.
In Appendix to *House Journal*, 1872, p. 592.
Born in Huntsville, Ala., Dec. 10, 1808, d. in Hinds Co., Miss., Nov. 21, 1871.

Cabeça de Vaca, D'Alvar Nuñez (1507-1559), *Spanish explorer.* Voyages, | relations et mémoires | originaux | pour servir a l'histoire de la decouverte | de l'Amérique, | publes pour la première foie en Français, | par H. Ternaux-Compans. | Relation et naufrages | D'Alvar Nuñez Cabeça de Vaca, | Adelantade et gouverneur du Rio de la Plata, | Valladolid. | 1555. Paris. Arthur Bertrand, libraire-éditeur, | libraire de la Société de Geographie de Paris, | Rue Hautefeuille, No. 23. | M.DCCCXXXVII. |
8vo. 2 prel. leaves, 302.
Vol. vii of the series.
First published at Zamorn, 1542, reprinted at Valladolid, 1555; the latter reprinted by Barcia, *Historiadores primitivos*, 1749; included in Ramusio's *Collection*, 1556; Purchas contains first English version; and in 1871 a new edition by Buckingham Smith appeared, with considerable editorial additions
Copies seen: Hamner.

—— The narrative | of | Alvar Nuñez Cabeça de Vaca. | Translated by Buckingham Smith. | Washington: | 1851. |
Folio. pp. 138. *8 maps, 1 plate.*
From English edition, from the original Spanish edition, Valladolid, 1555.
One hundred copies privately printed by Mr. G. W. Riggs, Washington, D. C., for presentation to societies and personal friends.
The work of Cabeça "is the earliest historic memoir of the Indian races of that portion [Southern] of America, it is also the most minute and full in its narrations of their national traits."—Field's *Indian Bibliography*, p. 55.
Copies seen: Hamner; Congress.

Cage, Henry, *Lawyer, M. C. from Miss.* Sketch of.
In Lynch's *Bench and Bar of Mississippi*, pp. 102-103.

CALHOON, SOL. S., *Lawyer, Pres. Const. Con. 1890.* Negro suffrage. | [Jackson, Miss.: | Commonwealth steam print. | 1890. |]
 8vo. pp. 13.
 First published as a communication to the New Orleans *Times-Democrat*, Feb., 1890.
 Copies seen: Owen.

—— Address at the close of the Constitutional Convention of Miss., 1890.
 In Goodspeed's *Memoirs of Mississippi*, vol. ii, pp. 15-16.

CALHOUN COUNTY. Sketch of.
 In Lowry and McCardle's *Mississippi*, p. 449.

CAMERON, J. D. Mary Singleton, or, The Question answered. 1879. Holly Springs, Miss.
 No copies seen.

CAMPBELL, JOHN L., *and* RUFFNER, W. H. A physical survey | extending from | Atlanta, Ga., across Alabama and Mississippi | to the | Mississippi river, | along the line of the Georgia Pacific Railway, | embracing the | geology, topography, minerals, soils, climate, forests, | and agricultural and manufacturing | resources of the country. | By | John L. Campbell, | Prof. of Chemistry and Geology, | Washington and Lee University, | Lexington, Virginia; | and W. H. Ruffner, | Geologist, | Lexington, Virginia. | New York: | E. F. Weeks, printer and stationer, 52 Cedar street. | 1883. |
 8vo. pp. 147. *3 maps.*
 Copies seen: Owen.

CAMPBELL, *Rev.* JOHN P. The | Southern | business directory | and | general commercial advertiser. | [–etc., 20 lines.] | Charleston: | Steam-power press of Walker & James. | No. 3 Broad street. | 1854. |
 8vo. 2 vols.; 2 parts in vol. i.
 Mississippi, vol. i, part 1, pp. 139-156. Contains brief sketches of the State, the several counties, names of the merchants in each county, statistics, and advertisements.
 Copies seen: Owen.

CANNON, *Mrs.* SUSAN. Turning all to gold. West Point, Miss.
 No copies seen.

CAPPLEMAN, *Mrs.* JOSIE FRAZEE. Importance of the local history of the civil war.
 In *Publications Mississippi State Historical Society*, 1900, vol. iii. (In press.)

—— "Heart Songs," | by | Josie Frazee Cappleman. | [Vignette.] | Richmond, Va.: | B. F. Johnson Publishing Co. | 1899. |
 12mo. pp. 263 [1].

CARPENTER, MARCUS T. Memories of the Past. | Poems. | By | Marcus T. Carpenter. | [Quotation, 2 lines.] | New York: | Baker and Scribner, | 1850. |
 12mo. pp. 168.
 In Jan., 1852, the author, then residing in Jackson, Miss., presented a copy of this book to Hon. Willis G. Clark, of Mobile.

CARROLL COUNTY. Sketch of.
 In Lowry and McCardle's *Mississippi*, pp. 450-453
 This county was the home of the Choctaw chief, Greenwood Leflore.

CARY, JAMES. Halted between two opinions.
 No copies seen.

CASTILIAN SPRINGS. Description of.
: In Lowry and McCardle's *Mississippi*, p. 492.

CATCHINGS, THOMAS C., *Lawyer, M. C. from Miss.* Contested-election case of. *See* cases of Hill *vs.* Catchings, and Jones *vs.* Catchings.

CATHOLIC CHURCH. Sketch | of the | Catholic Church | in the | City of Natchez, Miss., | on the occasion of the consecration of its Cathedral, | September 19, 1886. | n. p. n. d.
: 8vo. pp. 51.
: CONTENTS: Title, 1 leaf; Introduction; I. Early history of Catholicity in Natchez, Miss.; II. Biographical sketch of the Bishops of Natchez; III. Building of St. Mary's Cathedral; IV. Catholic institutions (St. Mary's Asylum, D'Evereux Hall orphan asylum, Cathedral school, and St. Joseph's school); V. Diocesan Synod. Sketches of the following bishops of Natchez are given: Rt. Rev. J. J. Chanche, Rt. Rev. J. O. Van De Velde, Rt. Rev. Wm. Henry Elder, and Rt. Rev. F. Janssens.
: *Copies seen:* Owen.

—— History of the Catholic missions among the Indian tribes of the United States. *See* John D. G. Shea.

—— History of the Catholic Church. *See Ibid.*

—— The Catholic Church in Mississippi.
: In Goodspeed's *Memoirs of Mississippi*, vol. ii, pp. 374-378.

CENTENARY (THE) COLLEGE. Sketch of.
: In Mayes' *History of Education in Mississippi*, pp. 106-117.

CENTRAL FEMALE INSTITUTE. *See* Hillman College.

CHALMERS, JAMES R., *vs.* MORGAN, J. B. Contested-election case | of | James R. Chalmers vs. J. B. Morgan, | from the | Second Congressional district of Mississippi. | Washington: | Government printing office. | 1889. |
: 8vo. pp. 1164.
: *Copies seen:* Owen.

—— Report with resolution that Chalmers is entitled to seat. June 20, 1890. (House Rep. 2503, 51st Cong., 1st sess.)
: 8vo. pp. 101. No title page.
: *Copies seen:* Owen.

CHALMERS, JOSEPH WILLIAMS (1807-1853), *Lawyer, Miss. Chancellor, U. S. Senator from Miss.* Sketch of.
: In Lynch's *Bench and Bar of Mississippi*, pp. 177-181.
: He was styled the "Apostle of Democracy," in North Mississippi.

CHAMBERLAIN-HUNT ACADEMY. Sketch of.
: In Mayes' *History of Education in Mississippi*, pp. 71-72.

CHAMBERS, HENRY E., *Ph. D.* Time and place relations in history with some Mississippi and Louisiana applications.
: In *Publications Mississippi State Historical Society*, 1898, vol. i, pp. 67-72.

CHANCHE, JOHN JOSEPH (1795-1853), *First Bishop of Natchez.* Sketch of.
: In *Sketch of the Catholic Church in Natchez*, pp. 21-25.

CHAPMAN, A. W., *M. D.* Flora of the Southern United States. New York: Ivison, Phinny & Co., 1860.
: 8vo.
: Contains "abridged description of the flowering plants and ferns of Tennessee, North and South Carolina, Georgia, Alabama, *Mississippi*, and Florida, arranged according to the natural system." The part on Ferns was prepared by Daniel C. Eaton.

CHAPMAN, H. P. *and* BATTAILE, J. F. Picturesque Vicksburg. | A description of the resources and prospects of that city | and the famous Yazoo Delta, | its agricultural and commercial interests, | to which is attached a series of sketches of | representative industries. | Profusely illustrated. | By H. P. Chapman and J. F. Battaile. | Vicksburg, Miss.: | Vicksburg printing and publishing co. | 1895. |
    8vo. Ill. cover title, 1 leaf. pp. 167 [1].
    Copies seen: Congress.

CHAPPELL, ABSALOM HARRIS (1807–1878), *Lawyer.* Miscellanies | of | Georgia, | historical, | biographical, descriptive, &c. | By Absalom H. Chappell. | Part I [–III] | [Contents for each part.] | Printed by Thos. Gilbert, printer and binder, | Columbus, Ga., 1874. |
    8vo. Part l., 2 prel. leaves, pp. 73, 1 l.; part ii, pp. 137; part iii, pp. 24.

CONTENTS:

Part I:
    Chapter i, The Oconee war.
    Chapter ii, The Oconee war continued.
    Chapter iii, Alexander McGillivray.
    Chapter iv, Gen. Elijah Clark.
    Chapter v, Col. Benjamin Hawkins.
Part II:
    Chapter i, Middle Georgia.
    Chapter ii, Middle Georgia (continued) and the negro.
    Chapter iii, Middle Georgia (continued) and the land lottery system.
    Chapter iv, The pine mountain.
    Chapter v, King's gap and King's trails.
    Chapter vi, The pine barren speculation in 1794–95.
    Chapter vii, The Yazoo fraud.
Part III:
    Chapter i, Gen. James Jackson—Gen. Anthony Wayne.
    Copies seen: Owen.

CHEROKEE INDIANS. A narrative of their official relations with the Colonial and Federal Governments. *See* Charles C. Royce.

—— *See also* John Haywood.

CHICKASAW BLUFF. Account of.
    In Claiborne's *Mississippi*, p. 181, *note.*

CHICKASAW COUNTY. Sketch of.
    In Lowry and McCardle's *Mississippi*, pp. 453–456.

CHICKASAW INDIANS. Tattoo of.
    In *Tenth Annual Report of the Bureau of Ethnology*, 1888–89, p. 394.

—— De Soto's camps in the Chickasaw country in 1840–41. *See* T. H. Lewis.

—— Reminiscences of. *See Rev.* Frank Patton.

CHILD, JOSHUA, *Lawyer.* Sketch of.
    In Lynch's *Bench and Bar of Mississippi.*, pp. 99–100.

CHOCTAW COUNTY. Sketch of.
    In Lowry and McCardle's *Mississippi*, pp. 456–457.

CHOCTAW INDIANS. Conversations on the Choctaw Mission. *See* Sarah Tuttle.

—— Mortuary customs.
    In *First Annual Report of the Bureau of Ethnology*, 1879–80, pp. 120, 155, 169, 186.
    See also H. S. Halbert, *infra.*

CHOCTAW INDIANS. Use of discoidal stones by.
> Ibid. 1891-92, p. 99.

—— Ancient notices of.
> Ibid. 1888-89, p. 347.

—— Mode of divination of.
> Ibid. pp. 494-495.

—— Description of communal burial of.
> Ibid. 1890-91, p. 677.

—— [Evidence in behalf of the claimants in Case No. 12742, The Choctaw Nation of Indians *v.* The United States, in the U. S. Court of Claims. Washington, 1881.]
> 8vo. 2 volumes, continuously paged. pp. 1707. No title page.
> A mine of information in relation to Choctaw affairs.
> Prof. H. S. Halbert has a set of this valuable publication.

—— National legend of the Chahta-Muskokee tribes. *See* D. G. Brinton.

—— *See also* A. J. Brown, J. F. H. Claiborne, Emmaus, H. S. Halbert, Rev. F. E. Marine, Pushmataha, and E. C. Tracy.

CHRISTIAN, JOHN T., *A. M., D. D.* Immersion, | the act of Christian baptism | By | John T. Christian, A. M., D. D. | corresponding secretary of the Convention Board of Mississippi Baptists. | Louisville, Ky. | Baptist Bank Concern | 1891. |
> 8vo. pp. 256.
> He is also the author of a paper on "Close Communion," 1893.

—— The Missionary Baptist Church in Mississippi.
> In Goodspeed's *Memoirs of Mississippi*, vol. ii, pp. 369-374.

CHRISTIAN (THE) CHURCH IN MISSISSIPPI. Sketch of.
> In Goodspeed's *Memoirs of Mississippi*, vol. ii, pp. 368-369.

—— "The Unitist."
> "In 1875 S. R. Jones edited a paper known as the *Unitist*, in the interest of the church [the Christian]. It continued for a year or more and suspended. An attempt or two has since been made to publish a church paper, but owing to the weak condition of the churches, and perhaps more properly to bad, inefficient management in the projectors, none of these attempts have amounted to much."—Goodspeed, vol. ii, p. 369.

CIVIL GOVERNMENT. *See Miss* Mary V. Duval.

CIVIL LISTS. Judges of the Supreme Court, Circuit Judges, Chancellors, and Attorneys-General of Mississippi, since the organization of the State Government.
> In James D. Lynch's *Bench and Bar of Mississippi*, pp. 533-538.

—— United States Senators and Members of the National House of Representatives.
> In Lowry and McCardle's *History of Mississippi* (1891), pp. 624-633.

—— The Judiciary of Mississippi.
> Ibid. pp. 634-636.

—— Governors of Mississippi.
> In Lowry and McCardle's *History of Mississippi for schools* (1892), p. 262.

CIVIL LISTS. Roster of State Officers. Compiled by J. L. Power, Secretary of State.
> In *Biennial Report of the Secretary of State* to the Legislature of Mississippi, 1896 and 1897 (1897), pp. 88-103.
> Includes Governors, Lieutenant-Governors, Secretaries of State, Auditors of Public Accounts, State Treasurers, Attorneys-General, Clerks of Court of Errors and Appeals and Supreme Court, Superintendents of Public Instruction, R. R. Commission, State Librarians, Swamp Land Commissioner, State Revenue Agent, Supreme Court Judges, Supreme Court of Chancery, U. S. Senators, Representatives in Congress, and Members of the Confederate Congress from Mississippi.

—— Federal Courts, Judges, Attorneys and Marshals in Mississippi, 1798-1898. Compiled by Thomas M. Owen.
> In *Publications of the Mississippi [State] Historical Society*, 1899, vol. II, pp. 147-155.

—— Representatives in the Senate and House of Representatives of Mississippi, arranged by Counties.
> In Lowry and McCardle's *History of Mississippi* (1891).
> See under each County.

CIVIL WAR. The gray jackets: | and | how they lived, fought and died, | for Dixie. | With incidents & sketches of life in the Confederacy. | Comprising narratives of personal adventures, army life, naval | adventure, home life, | partisan daring, life in the camp, | field and hospital: together with the songs, ballads, | anecdotes and humorous incidents of the War for Southern Independence. | Issued [-etc. 2 lines.] | By a Confederate. | Jones Brothers & Co., | Richmond, Va.: [and 5 other places, 2 lines.] | [1867.]
> 8vo. pp. 574. *Maps; illustrations*.
> Many references to Mississippians and incidents.
> *Copies seen:* Hamner.

—— Mississippi in the great War between the States.
> In Lowry and McCardle's *Mississippi*, pp. 637-639.
> See also Waddel's *Memorials of Academic Life*, pp. 366-410, for valuable references; and Davis's *Recollections of Mississippi and Mississippians*, pp. 387-439.

—— Importance of the local history of. *See* Mrs. Josie F. Cappleman.

—— My cave life in Vicksburg. With letters of trial and travel. By a lady. New York, 1864.
> 12mo. pp. 196.

—— The | War of the Rebellion: | a compilation of the | official records | of the | Union and Confederate Armies. | [-etc., Board of Publication] | Washington: | Government Printing Office. | 1880 [-1900.] |
> 8vo.
> A serial publication of the United States Government.
> Many local references in reports, orders, etc.

—— Harvey's Scouts. *See* J. F. H. Claiborne.

—— Confederate military history. By Col. Charles E. Hooker, and Allan J. Hooker.
> In Goodspeed's *Memoirs of Mississippi*, vol. 1, pp. 115-172.
> Contains rosters of the General Officers, and of the several regiments and their commanding officers, from Mississippi.

—— Ordinance of Secession.
> *Ibid.* pp. 115-116.

CIVIL WAR. *See also* Almanac, Confederate Veterans, *Rev.* R. H. Crozier, Jefferson Davis, *Col.* Freemantle, *Mrs.* Fannie A. Beers, John Esten Cooke, Judge M. F. Force, Francis V. Greene, Joseph Hodgson, Thomas Jordan, *Gen.* S. D. Lee, A. T. Mahan, D. D. Porter, John C. Portis, A. C. Roach, J. T. Scharf, J. T. Trowbridge, and J. A. W,eth.

CLAIBORNE COUNTY. Sketch of.
    In Lowry and McCardle's *Mississippi*, pp. 457-460.
    See also Goodspeed's *Memoirs of Mississippi*, vol. i, pp. 178-180.

—— Remains of an ancient wall.
    Mentioned in Smithsonian *Report*, 1879, p. 444.

CLAIBORNE, *Gen.* FERDINAND LEIGH (1773-1815). Sketch of.
    In Claiborne's *Mississippi*, pp. 333-340.

CLAIBORNE, JOHN FRANCIS HAMTRANCK (1809-1884), *LL. D., M. C. from Miss., Journalist, Author.* Life and times | of | Gen. Sam. Dale, | the | Mississippi partisan. | By | J. F. H. Claiborne. | Illustrated by John M'Lenan. | New York: | Harper & Brothers, publishers, | Franklin square. | 1860. |
    12mo. pp. 233. *13 illustrations* in text.
    "Condensed from authentic MSS. never yet published. The personal adventures of Gen. Dale were taken down from his own lips by Franklin Smith, esq., the late Henry A. Garrett, esq , and myself, at different periods."
    "Those gentlemen—both accomplished scholars—turned over their notes to me some years ago, and I incorporated a memoir of Dale with a 'History of the Southwest,' on which I had been long engaged. When ready for the press the MSS. were lost by the sinking of a steamer on the Mississippi. Until within a few weeks past I have never had leisure to reproduce the life of Dale."—*Preface.*
    Copies seen: Owen.

—— Life and correspondence | of | John A. Quitman, | Major-General, U. S. A., and Governor of the State of | Mississippi. | By | J. F. H. Claiborne. | In two volumes. | Vol. I [-II.] | New York: | Harper & Brothers, publishers. | Franklin square. | 1860. |
    8vo. vol. i, pp. 400; vol. ii, pp. 392. *Portrait.*

—— Mississippi, | as a | Province, Territory, and State, | with | biographical notices of eminent citizens, | by J. F. H. Claiborne. | Volume I. | [Monogram of publishers.] | Jackson, Miss.: | Power & Barksdale, publishers and printers. | 1880. |
    8vo. pp. xxiii, 545 [1].
    While in an advanced state of preparation vol. ii was destroyed by fire.
    PORTRAITS: Gov. W. C. C. Claiborne, Gov. Don Manuel Gayoso de Lemos, Gov. Don Estevan Minor, Gov. David Holmes, Wm. M. Gwin, Jacob Thompson, and Greenwood Le Fleur.
    "In writing this work I have not been prompted by a desire for fame or profit, but to preserve the time-worn papers and documents confided to me by those who have long since passed away. I should have executed this trust earlier, but have been prevented by the vicissitudes of war and the demands of everyday life. I have written these volumes in declining health, in pain and suffering, and hope that this may plead for many imperfections."
    "Diodorus Seculus, one of the Fathers of History, introduced in his work minute details of remarkable events, and individual adventures and incidents, which some critics consider inconsistent with the dignity of the historic muse. I adopt his view, and have aimed to collect facts, to illustrate even the most obscure periods. Most of these facts are derived from the MS. of the most prominent actors in the scenes described."—*Introduction.*
    Copies seen: Owen.

CLAIBORNE, JOHN FRANCIS HAMTRANCK. Historical account | of | Hancock County | and the | Sea Board of Mississippi. | An address | delivered by Hon. J. F. H. Claiborne, | of Bay St. Louis. | At the request of the citizens, and in compliance with a resolution | of Congress, and the recommendation of the President of the | United States, and the Governor of the State of | Mississippi. | July 4th, 1876. | Hopkins' printing office, | 26 Camp street, corner Common, New Orleans, La. |
>   8vo. Cover title only, 1 leaf. pp. 16.
>   Of considerable local value.

—— The Pine District of Mississippi.
>   In the *Weekly Clarion*, Jackson, Miss., Dec. 27, 1876.
>   A letter descriptive of the timber, agricultural, and other advantages, dated "Bay St. Louis, Miss., May 6th, 1876."

—— [Sketch of Harvey's Scouts.]
>   8vo.
>   First published, partly in the *Clarion*, Jackson, and partly in *East Mississippi Times*, Starkeville.
>   No copy seen. Reference from Goodspeed, vol. ii, p. 492.

—— [Exposé of the frauds practiced on the Choctaw Indians in the disposition of their claims under the 14th article of the Treaty of Dancing Rabbit Creek.]
>   8 vo.
>   Referred to in Lynch's *Bench and Bar of Mississippi*, p. 522.

—— Interesting Centennial Reminiscences.
>   In the *Natchez Democrat*, 1876; Centennial Number.

—— Sketch of.
>   In Lynch's *Bench and Bar of Mississippi*, pp. 516–529.
>   See also Goodspeed's *Memoirs of Mississippi*, vol i, pp. 544–546.

—— Some inaccuracies in Claiborne's History in regard to Tecumseh. *See* H. S. Halbert.

CLAIBORNE, NATHANIEL HERBERT (1777–1859), *M. C. from Va.* Notes | on the | war in the South; | with | biographical sketches | of the lives of | Montgomery, Jackson, | Sevier, | the late Gov. Claiborne, | and others. | By Nathaniel Herbert Claiborne, | of Franklin County, Va. | A member of the Executive of Virginia during the late war. | Richmond: | published by William Ramsay. | 1819. |
>   16mo. pp. 112.
>   "The following Notes were written while the war was going on. They are now published without alteration. . . . The stile (sic) of this book will not stand the knife of criticism; but the feelings under the influence of which it was produced, are above the reach even of malice."—*Preface*.
>   "A little volume much sought after by collectors because it is scarce; but it is of scarcely any value."—Parton's *Life of Jackson*.
>   *Copies seen:* Congress.

CLAIBORNE, WILLIAM CHARLES COLE (1775–1817), *Gov. of Miss. Territory.* Sketch of.
>   In Claiborne's *Mississippi*, pp. 250–257; *portrait*.

—— Administration of.
>   *Ibid.* pp. 220–244.

CLAIBORNE, WILLIAM CHARLES COLE. Biographical sketch of. *See* N. H. Claiborne.
>A *Life* is said to have been prepared by Mrs —— Darcy, of Mississippi, but in what form, or when published, has not been ascertained.

CLARK, *Gen.* CHARLES (1811-1877), *Gov. of Miss.* Administration as governor.
>In Lowry and McCardle's *Mississippi*, pp 350-363.

—— Sketch of.
>In Goodspeed's *Memoirs of Mississippi*, vol 1, pp. 549-552.

CLARK, DANIEL (1766-1813). Proofs | of the | corruption | of | Gen. James Wilkinson, | and of his | connexion with Aaron Burr, | with | a full refutation of his slanderous allegations in | relation to the character of the prin- | cipal witness against him. | By Daniel Clark, | of the City of New Orleans. | [Quotation, 5 lines.] | Wm. Hall, Jun. & Geo. W. Pierie, printers, No. 51, Mar- | ket-street, Philadelphia. | 1809. |
>8vo. Title, 1 l. pp. 199
>*Copies seen:* Hamner.

—— Sketch of.
>In Claiborne's *Mississippi*, pp. 247-248.

CLARKE COUNTY. Sketch of.
>In Lowry and McCardle's *Mississippi*, pp. 460-462

CLARKE, JOSHUA G. (-1828). *Lawyer, First Chancellor of* **Miss.** Sketch of.
>In Lynch's *Bench and Bar of Mississippi*, pp. 89-90.

CLAY COUNTY. Sketch of.
>In Lowry and McCardle's *Mississippi*, pp. 463-464.

CLAY, *Hon.* HENRY. Account of visit to Jackson, Miss., 1844.
>In Lowry and McCardle's *Mississippi*, pp. 317-318

—— Address on life, character, and public services of. *See* A. K. McClung.

CLAYTON, ALEXANDER M. (1801-1889). *Lawyer, Judge Sup. Ct. Miss.* Centennial address | on the | history of Marshall County | delivered by | A. M. Clayton, | at | Holly Springs, Mississippi, | August 12th, 1876. | Washington, D. C. | R. O. Polkinhorn, printer. | 1880. |
>8vo. pp. 32.
>A valuable historical sketch, with some biographical data.

—— Limitation of estates.
>In J. Z George's *Digest Reports of Mississippi* (1872), pp. 497-505.
>This is more than a digest of the decisions; it is a critical commentary of the entire body of the law up to this time, as it existed in Mississippi.

—— Jurisprudence of Mississippi.
>In Claiborne's *Mississippi*, Chapter XXXII, pp. 466-482
>Goodspeed's *Memoirs of Mississippi*, vol. 1, p. 101, says Judge Clayton contributed this chapter.
>"Judge Clayton was a man of profound legal learning, particularly fond of constitutional law and the limitations of estates. He was patient and laborious in research, impartial and of incorruptible integrity. His opinions are most highly respected by the bar, and it has been well said of him that not one of the illustrious men who have adorned the State's judicial annals ever contributed more to the establishment of her admirable system of jurisprudence."—Edward Mayes, esq., in Goodspeed's *Memoirs of Mississippi*, vol 1, p. 127.

—— Sketch of.
>In Lynch's *Bench and Bar of Mississippi*, pp 500-507, portrait.
>*See also* Waddel's *Memorials of Academic Life*, pp 289-290.

CLAYTON, GEORGE R. (1808–1867), *Lawyer.* Sketch of.
: In Lynch's *Bench and Bar of Mississippi,* pp. 301-307.

CLIMATOLOGY. *See* Meteorology.

CLOWNEY, SAM. Sketch of. *See* Wm. T. Lewis.

CLUSKY, M. W., *Editor.* Speeches, messages, and writings of Albert G. Brown. Philadelphia, 1859.
: 8vo. pp. 614.

COAHOMA COUNTY. Sketch of.
: In Lowry and McCardle's *Mississippi,* pp. 464-466.

—— Mounds in.
: In *Twelfth Annual Report Bureau of Ethnology,* 1890-91, pp. 253-258; 2 plates and 2 figures.
: Contains descriptions of the "Carson Group," the "Dickerson Mounds," and the "Clarksdale Works."

COBB, JOSEPH B. Mississippi scenes. Philadelphia, 1850.
: 12 mo. pp. 250.
: He is also the author of "The Maid of Melos," 1848; "The Creole, or, The Siege of New Orleans," 1850; "A Review of Macaulay's History of England," 1851; and "Leisure Labors," 1852.

COCKE, STEPHEN, *Lawyer.* Sketch of.
: In Lynch's *Bench and Bar of Mississippi,* pp. 167-174.

COCKE, WILLIAM (1748–1828), *U. S. Senator from Tenn., Brig. Gen. of Tenn., Chickasaw Indian Agent.* Sketch of.
: In Claiborne's *Mississippi,* p. 383, note.

CODES OF MISSISSIPPI.
: This title embraces only the revisions and general compilations of the State laws, together with such unofficial papers as have been found bearing on them. Special compilations are entered under their respective authors.

LAWS, 1799.

—— Laws | of the | Mississippi Territory; | published at a session of the Legislature began in the | town of Natchez, in the County of Adams, and | Territory aforesaid, upon the 22d day of January, | Anno Domini 1799, and in the 23d year of | the independence of the United States | of America: and continued by | adjournments to the 25th day | of May, in the | same year | — | By authority. | — | Natchez: | printed by A. Marschalk, | and sold at the store of Messrs. Hunts, & Co.: | 1799. |
: 8vo. Title, 1 leaf, pp. ii, 209.

CONTENTS·

Title, 1 leaf, verso blank;
Table of contents, pp. i-ii;
[Laws of the] Mississippi Territory, pp. [2]-209.
From pp. 3 to 63, inclusive, the verso is numbered *odd.* Page 64 is dropped, thus making p 65, verso p. 66, follow p. 63, etc.

TOULMIN'S STATUTES, 1807.

—— *First title:* The | statutes | of the | Mississippi Territory, | revised and digested | by the | authority | of the | General Assembly. | By the Honorable | Harry Toulmin, | one of the United States Judges for | the Mississippi Territory. | Published by authority. | Natchez: | printed by | Samuel Terrell, | printer to the Mississippi Territory. | 1807. |

CODES OF MISSISSIPPI. *Second title:* A | digest | of the | statutes | of the— Mississippi Terrtiory, | containing all the | laws | now in force: | the constitution of the United States, | with the several amendments thereto: | the Ordinance | for the Government of the Territory of the United States | Northwest of the river Ohio: | and such | acts of Congress | as relate to the Mississippi Territory, | to land titles within the same, to crimes and misdemeanors, | and the intercourse with the Indian nations, together | with the articles of agreement and cession | between the United States and | the State of Georgia. | 1807. |

8vo. Titles, 2 leaves, pp. xiii, 616.

CONTENTS:

Titles, 2 leaves; index, pp. i–xiii; errata, p. xiii; statutes, pp. 1–426; list of private acts, p. 427; acts of Congress, pp. 429–607; contents, pp. 609–616.

The Territorial general assembly at the session of 1805–6, by resolution, engaged Harry Toulmin, then the newly appointed judge of Washington District (now in Alabama), to compile a digest of the laws, etc., a work which he undertook and completed by the next session. By act of Feb. 10, 1807, it was adopted. Two hundred copies were ordered printed and distributed as the acts of the general assembly. He was allowed the sum of $1,200 "in full compensation" for his labors.

"This work he performed with fidelity and skill. This first digest, or code, of Mississippi laws is not only clear and comprehensive, but it also shows a thorough acquaintance of the author with the common law, and an accurate conception of the needs of the territory by way of statutory modifications."—Edward Mayes, esq., in Goodspeed's *Memoirs of Mississippi*, vol. i, p. 107.

TURNER'S STATUTES, 1816.

—— Statutes | of the | Mississippi Territory; | the | constitution of the United States, with the | several amendments thereto; | the ordinance | for the government of the territory of the | United States, North-West of the | river Ohio; | the | articles of agreement and cession, between the | United States and the State of Georgia; | and | such acts of Congress | as relate to the | Mississippi Territory. | Digested by authority of the General Assembly. | Natchez: | printed by Peter Isler, printer to the Territory. | 1816. |

8vo. pp. 495. [28.]
Edition, 1,200 copies.—*Statutes*, etc., pp. 249–251.

The digest proper comprises all laws from 1798 through the session of the Territorial assembly of 1815. The appendix contains all laws of the 2nd sess. of the 9th general assembly, Nov. 4 to Dec. 13, 1816. This was the last session of the Territorial legislature.

Copies seen: Owen.

REVISED CODE, 1823.

—— The revised code | of the | laws of Mississippi, | in which | are comprised all such acts | of the | General Assembly, | of a public nature as were in force | at the end of the year 1823; | with a | general index. | Published according to an act of the general assembly, entitled An act, declaring | what laws of a public nature shall be incorporated in the revised code, and | providing for the publication thereof, passed June 30, 1822, and an act supple- | mental thereto, passed January 21, 1823. | Natchez, | printed by Francis Baker. | 1824. |

8vo. pp. iv, 1–743.

CONTENTS:

Title and preface. pp. iv.
Revised code of Mississippi. pp. 1–488.
Constitution of the U. S. pp. 489–502.
Acts of Congress (pertaining to Miss.). pp. 502–539.
Constitution of Miss. pp. 539–558. Names of delegates appended.
Summary of private and local acts. pp. 558–650.
Index. pp. 651–743.

The material in pp. 502–539 and 558–650 is of considerable historical interest, and contains many facts not condensed elsewhere.

"In 1821 an act was passed to 'revise and consolidate the statutes of the State, with amendments and additional bills, and to report them to the legislature for their concurrence and approval.' And George Poindexter, then governor of the State, was requested to undertake it, and was authorized to call on the attorney-general and the supreme judges for advice and cooperation. It was further enacted, that all acts of a general and public nature, not contained in the revision, should be considered repealed, but not to the extent of impairing existing rights, or preventing prosecutions for previous offences. Private or local acts were to continue in force.

"This code was modeled somewhat after the revised code of Virginia of 1819, by that great lawyer, Benjamin Watkins Leigh, and was executed with marked ability. It was adopted by the legislature, then sitting at Columbia, in 1822; not, however, without opposition, particularly that portion relating to the police of slaves and their assembling for worship, which was obnoxious to the religious classes, and defeated Mr. Poindexter in the canvass for Congress at the ensuing election."—Claiborne's *Mississippi*, p. 469.

LAWS, 1838.

)DES OF MISSISSIPPI. Laws | of the | State of Mississippi; | embracing all acts of a public nature from January session, 1824, to | January session, 1838, inclusive. | Published by authority. | Jackson: | printed for the State of Mississippi. | 1838. | [John D. Toy, printer, Baltimore.]

8vo. pp. xviii, 17–932.

CONTENTS:

Title, 1 l., verso blank.
Contents (table of). pp. iii–xviii.
Laws. pp. 17–902.
Index. pp. 903–932.

This compilation was never adopted.

"Mr. P. was a native of Maine, had a collegiate education, and taught school for a while in Westchester County, New York. He was industrious and methodical, with abundant learning, but his code was not a success. It was by no means satisfactory to the profession. It was too ambitious of originality, and was too much flavored with the civil law. * * * The leaning in the new code to the Roman law made it unpalatable to the disciples of Coke."—Claiborne's *Mississippi*, p. 473.

DIGEST, 1839.

A | digest | of the | laws of Mississippi, | comprising all the | laws of a general nature, | including the | acts of the session of 1839. | By T. J. Fox Alden and J. A. Van Hoesen. | New York: | Alexander S. Gould, printer, 144 Nassau street. | 1839. |

8vo. pp. 1009.

Contains const. of U. S.; articles of agreement and cession; const. of Miss., 1832; acts of Congress, etc.; and laws.

STATUTES, 1840.

CODES OF MISSISSIPPI. The | statutes | of the | State of Mississippi | of a public and general nature, | with | the Constitutions | of the | United States and of this State: | and an | appendix | containing acts of Congress affecting land titles, | naturalization, &c., | and | a manual | for clerks, sheriffs, and justices of the peace. | Compiled by | V. E. Howard and A. Hutchinson. | By authority. | New Orleans: | E. Johns & Co., Stationers' hall. | 1840. |

8 vo. pp. xii, 1-885.

CONTENTS:

Title, preface, analytical index. pp. xii.
Constitution of the U. S. pp. 1-14.
Constitution of Miss. pp. 15-36.
Statutes. pp. 37-740.
Appendix: Nos. I-III. pp. 741-828.
Index. pp. 828-885.

Appendix I is of value to historical students from the very full reprint of all laws relating to public lands in Mississippi.

CODE, 1848.

——— Code of Mississippi: | being an | analytical compilation | of the | public and general statutes | of the | Territory and State, | with | tabular references to the local and private acts, | from 1798 to 1848: | with the | National and State Constitutions, cessions of the country | by the Choctaw and Chickasaw Indians, and Acts of | Congress for the survey and sale of the lands, | and granting donations thereof to the | State. | By A. Hutchinson. | Jackson, Miss.: | published for the compiler, | by Price and Fall, State printers. | 1848. |

8 vo. pp. 1111.

This work was prepared as an independent venture by the compiler, and grew out of his dissatisfaction with his work on the Howard and Hutchinson *Statutes*, of 1840. To it he gave five years of unremitting labor. The legislature in 1848, after its examination by a commission, adopted it, and two thousand copies were purchased for the State.

It is an invaluable compendium for reference to all statute laws prior to 1848.

REVISED CODE, 1857.

——— The | revised code | of the | statute laws | of the | State of Mississippi. | Published by authority of the Legislature. | Jackson, Mississippi: | E. Barksdale, State printer. | 1857. |

8 vo. pp. iv, 943.

CONTENTS.

Title, etc. pp. iv.
Declaration of Independence. pp. 1-4.
Constitution of the United States and amendments. pp. 5-14.
The ordinance for the government of the territory of the United States northwest of the river Ohio. pp. 15-20.
An act to enable the people of the Western part of the Mississippi Territory to form a constitution and State government. March 1, 1817. pp. 21-22.
"Constitution of the State of Mississippi. Adopted October 26, 1832." pp. 23-30. Includes the five amendments adopted between said date and the promulgation of the code.

Laws of Mississippi. pp. 41-643.
Appendix. I. Acts of Congress relating to the public lands. pp. 645-701. Includes all that pertain to Mississippi.
II. Treaties with Indians. pp. 702-722.
III. Acts of Congress now in force on the subject of naturalization. pp. 723-726
IV. Authentication of records. pp. 727-728.
Index. pp. 729-943.

Under act of March 1, 1854, the judges of High Court of Errors and Appeals appointed William L. Sharkey, Samuel S. Boyd, and Henry T. Ellet as three commissioners "to revise, digest, and codify the laws" of the State; and Mr. Boyd having resigned, Wm. L. Harris was appointed in his place.

The commissioners made their report to the legislature January, 1856, and after a part was considered and passed, the consideration of the residue was postponed until December, 1856. At this time a special session convened and continued its deliberations upwards of sixty days. This code is the result of the work of the special session.

REVISED CODE, 1871.

CODES OF MISSISSIPPI. The | revised code | of the | Statute laws | of the | State of Mississippi. | As adopted at January session, A. D. 1871, and published by | authority of the Legislature. | [Vignette.] | Jackson, Mississippi: | Alcorn & Fisher, State printers. | 1871. |

8 vo. pp. 788.

CONTENTS.

Title and preface. pp. 4.
Revised code. pp. 5-638.
Declaration of Independence. pp. 641-643.
Articles of Confederation. pp. 643-647.
Constitution of the United States. pp. 648-655.
Constitution of Mississippi. pp. 656-668.
Ordinance, July 13, 1787. pp. 668-671.
Ordinances of convention of 1865. pp. 672-674.
Ordinances of convention of 1868. pp. 674-675.
Admission of Mississippi. Act of Congress, February 23, 1870. pp. 675-676.
Index. pp. 677-788.

Prepared by J. A. P. Campbell, Amos R. Johnston, and Amos Lovering, as commissioners, appointed by the governor under act of June 9, 1870. The arrangement for the press, the preparation of the index, and the supervision of the printing was done by Amos R. Johnston.

—— Chapter IX. | of | Revised Code of Mississippi, | 1871, | in relation to | Chancery Courts, | consolidated | with its amendments, | with an index and notes. | Jackson, Miss.: | Clarion Steam printing establishment. | 1876. |

8 vo. pp. 119.
Compiled by C. V. Gwin and W. S. Epperson.

REVISED CODE, 1880.

—— The | revised code | of the | Statute laws | of the | State of Mississippi, | prepared by | J. A. P. Campbell, | and | reported to and amended, and adopted by the Legislature at its | biennial session, in 1880. | With references to decisions of the High Court of Errors | and Appeals, and of the Supreme Court, | applicable to the statutes. | Published by authority of the Legislature. | Jackson, Miss.: | J. L. Power, State printer. | 1880. |

8 vo. pp. 941.

CONTENTS.

Title and introduction. pp. 4.
Constitution of the United States. pp. 4-18.
Constitution of the State of Mississippi. Adopted May 15, 1868, and ratified by the people Dec. 1, 1869. pp. 19-40. Includes the four amendments in force to this period.
An act to adopt a revised Code of statutes, March 5, 1880. pp. 41-43.
Revised Code. pp. 44-814.
Appendix: Revised Statutes of the United States, 1878, as to election of Senators in Congress, naturalization, and authentication of records. pp. 815-819.
Index. pp. 821-941.
Prepared under act of Feb. 27, 1878, reported to the succeeding legislature, and adopted by act of March 5, 1880. For last-named act *see supra*.

ANNOTATED CODE, 1892.

CODES OF MISSISSIPPI. The annotated code | of the | general statute laws | of | the State of Mississippi, | prepared by | R. H. Thompson, George G. Dillard, | and R. B. Campbell, | and | reported to and amended and adopted by the Legislature at its regular | session in 1892. | Published by authority of the Legislature. | Nashville, Tenn.: | Marshall & Bruce, law publishers. | 1892. |

8vo. pp. iv, 1253.

CONTENTS.

Title and prefatory. pp. iv.
Declaration of Independence. pp. 1-4.
Constitution of the United States. pp. 5-41.
The constitution of the State of Mississippi, adopted Nov. 1, 1890. pp. 43-111.
An act to adopt the annotated code, approved April 2, 1892. pp. 112-116.
Annotated code of public statute laws. pp. 117-984.
Appendix: Naturalization and authentication of records. pp. 985-988.
Index. pp. 989-1253.
Prepared by three commissioners appointed by the governor, under section 278 of the constitution of 1890, reported to the succeeding legislature and adopted by act of April 2, 1892. For last-named act *see supra*.

COLBERT, LEVI, *Chickasaw Chief.* Sketch of.
In Lowry and McCardle's *Mississippi.* pp. 493-4.

COLE, THEODORE LEE (1852-). Bibliography of the statute law of the Southern States.—Part I. Alabama.
In *Publications of the Southern History Association*, January, 1897, vol. i. pp. 61-75. 8vo.
This is an accurate and well executed piece of bibliographic work, with an account of the early Mississippi compilations.
100 copies reprinted from same type, with pagination unchanged.

—— Statute laws of Mississippi.
In *Report Secretary of State of Mississippi*, 1896-1897. pp. 107-109.
Check list: Includes laws, 1799-1896.
The compiler of this Bibliography is greatly indebted to Mr. Cole, who resides at Washington, D. C., for valuable aid in preparing the titles: "Codes of Mississippi," "Conventions and Constitutions," and "Laws." Mr. Cole is the greatest living authority on all matters pertaining to American statute law.

COLLINS, JACOB C., *Teacher.* Collins' | Poems, | Copyright—Mrs. L. E. Collins—1883. | Memphis: | Rogers & Co., printers and book publishers, | [-etc., 1 line.] | 1883. |

8vo. pp. 296.

COLUMBUS. The | charter and ordinances | of the | city of Columbus, | in | Lowndes County, Mississippi. | With an appendix. | Published by the order and authority of the Board of | Mayor and Aldermen of the city. | Columbus, Miss. | Printed at the Excelsior book and job office, 89 Main street. | 1874. |
    8vo. pp. 139.

—— The | charter and ordinances | of the | City .of Columbus, Lowndes County, Mississippi. | Charter approved March 8, 1884. | Published by the order and authority of the Mayor and | City Council of the City of Columbus. | Columbus, Mississippi. | Index Book and Job Printing Establishment. | 1884. |
    8vo. pp. 200.
    Copies seen: Owen.

—— Public men and early settlers.
    In Lowry and McCardle's *Mississippi*, pp. 524-526.

—— Sketch of.
    In Davis's *Recollections of Mississippi and Mississippians*, pp. 97-102.

—— History of Columbus Baptist Association. *See Rev.* L. S. Foster.

COLUMBUS BAPTIST ASSOCIATION. History of. *See Rev.* L. S. Foster.

—— Minutes. 1838-1899.
    8vo.
    Organized Nov., 1838, at Mount Zion Church, Lowndes County, Miss.
    Minutes have been published for each session. In the preparation of the *History*, Mr. Foster had access to a full file, excepting the years 1838, 1839, and 1840.

COLUMBUS, UNIVERSITY OF. Catalogues. 1867-1891.
    8vo.

—— *See also Rev.* S. A. Goodwin, and Rev. W. S. Harrison.

COMPTON, WILLIAM M., *M. D.* The | influence of alcohol. | By Wm. M. Compton, M. D., | Superintendent Mississippi State Lunatic Asylum. | n. p. n. d.
    8vo. Cover title only, 1 leaf. pp. 30.
    From *Annual Report* Mississippi State Board of Health, Dec. 1, 1877.

CONFEDERATE VETERANS OF MISSISSIPPI. Sketch of.
    In Goodspeed's *Memoirs of Mississippi*, vol. ii, p. 52.

——Proceedings | of the | second annual grand camp | Confederate Veterans | of | Mississippi, | at | Natchez, October 7-8, 1891. | Jackson, Miss.: | The Clarion printing establishment | 1892 |
    8vo. pp. 45.

——Proceedings | of the | third annual session | of the | Grand Camp Confederate Veterans, | hereafter to be known as | The Mississippi Division | of the | United Confederate Veterans, | at Jackson, July 12, 1892. | See revised constitution, page 14. | Jackson, Miss.: | The Clarion printing establishment. | 1892. |
    8vo. pp. 17. Double columns.
    Contains oration of Hon. J. A. P. Campbell.

——Fourth | annual session | of the | Mississippi | Division | United | Confederate Veterans, | at | Jackson, | December 12-13, 1893. | Clarion-Ledger print, Jackson, Miss. |
    8vo. pp. 24.

CONTRACTS, BOARD OF. Biennial report of the Board of Public Contracts.
> 8vo. pp. 11. No title page.
> Dated Jan. 10, 1898, and covers preceding biennial period.
> Made under Sec. 2316 of the Annotated Code of Miss., 1892.

CONRAD, TIMOTHY ABBOTT (1803-1877), *Naturalist.* Observations on the Eocene formation, and descriptions of 105 new fossils of that period from the vicinity of Vicksburg, Miss., with an Appendix.
> In *Journal Academy Natural Science*, Philadelphia, 1848, vol. iii, pp. 111-134. 1 plates.
> The author separates the Eocene into the upper or newer Eocene found at Vicksburg, and includes the white limestone at St. Stephens and Claiborne, Ala. The lower Eocene consists of the fossiliferous soils of Claiborne and St. Stephens, Ala., etc.

—— Description of new species of Cretaceous and Eocene fossils of Mississippi and Alabama.
> *Ibid.* 1860, vol. iv, p. 275.

CONVENTIONS AND CONSTITUTIONS OF MISSISSIPPI.

CONVENTION OF 1817.

—— Letter | from | his excellency David Holmes, | Governor of the State of Mississippi, | transmitting | a copy of the constitution and form of government | of | the said State. | Washington: | printed by E. De Krafft, | 1817. | (House Doc. No. 2, 15 Cong. 1st sess. In vol. 1.)
> 8vo. pp. 23.
> Contents: Title, 1 leaf; Letter, dated Nov. 6, 1817, p. 3, verse blank; Const., pp. 4-23.

—— Standing orders and resolutions for conducting business in the Convention.
> In *Journal of the Convention*, etc., (Reprint, 1831), pp. 19-24.
> "Ordered, That one hundred copies of said rules and orders be printed for the use of the Convention."—*Ibid.*, p. 24.
> No separates seen.

—— [Proposition as to House of Representatives, its membership, etc.]
> In *Journal of the Convention*, etc., (Reprint, 1831), pp. 30-31
> "Mr. [Wm. J.] Minton offered the following proposition, as a section in the Constitution, which was read."
> "*Ordered*, That sixty copies of said proposition be printed for the use of the Convention."
> Mr. Thomas Barnes offered a resolution on the same subject, and sixty copies were ordered printed. pp. 31-32.
> Neither of the foregoing could have exceeded a single sheet.

—— Journal | of the | Convention | of the | Western part | of the | Mississippi Territory. | Began and held at the town of Washington, | on the seventh day of July, 1817. | Port-Gibson: | reprinted by Benj. F. Stockton: | 1831. |
> 12mo. pp. 108.
> Reprinted for the use of the Convention of 1832.
> CONTENTS: Title, 1 leaf, Journal, July 7-Aug. 15, 1817, pp. 3-108.
> This convention was held under act of Congress, March 1, 1817.
> An edition of 800 copies of the original edition ordered printed (p 101), but none have been found.

CONVENTIONS AND CONSTITUTIONS OF MISSISSIPPI. Constitution | and | form of government | of the | State of Mississippi. | Port-Gibson: | printed by Benj. F. Stockton. | 1831. |
    12mo. pp. 36.
    Reprinted for the use of the Convention of 1832.
    CONTENTS: Title, 1 leaf; Constitution, pp. 3-35; Ordinance, p. 35-6.

——Memorial | of | the Mississippi Convention, | praying | an extension | of | the limits of the State. | December 17, 1817. | Read [-etc., 2 lines.] | Printed by order of the House of Representatives. | Washington: | Printed by E. De Krafft. | 1817. |
    8vo. p. 8.
    An effort to bring about an extension of the eastern boundary, as set forth in Act of Congress, to the Tombigby river and Mobile Bay.

——Petition from the citizens of the counties of Clarke, Monroe, Washington, Mobile, and Baldwin, in the Alabama Territory, dated: Fort Stoddert, Nov. 12, 1817. (H. Doc. 23, 15th Cong. 1st sess.)
    8vo. pp. 12. No title page.
    Letter from Judge H. Toulmin, as well as the petition protesting against the Memorial of the Mississippi Constitutional Convention to extend the eastern limits of that State. Several hundred names signed to the petition.
    Copies seen: Owen.

——Sketch, with list of delegates.
    In Lowry and McCardle's *Mississippi*, pp. 236-241.
    See also Lynch's *Bench and Bar of Mississippi*, pp. 79-80; and Claiborne's *Mississippi*, pp. 352-360.

——Chapters in State history. By J. L. Power. The constitutional convention of 1817.
    8vo. pp. [4].
    Reprinted from the *Gazette*, Magnolia, Miss., Sept. 1, 1897.
    Contains list of delegates.

CONVENTION OF 1832.

——Journal | of the | convention | of the | State of Mississippi, | held in the | town of Jackson. | Published by authority. | Jackson: | printed by Peter Isler. | 1832. |
    8vo. pp. 304. Not indexed.
    Contents: Title, 1 leaf; Journal (Sept. 10-Oct. 20, 1832), pp. 3-304; errata, p. 304.

——The | constitution | of the | State of Mississippi. | As revised in convention, on the twenty-sixth day of October, | A. D. 1832. ' Jackson: | printed by Peter Isler. | 1832. |
    8vo. pp. 27.
    Contents: Title, 1 leaf: Constitution, pp. 3-27.
    Edition, 5,000 copies. - *Journal*, p. 301.

——Constitution of the State of Mississippi. Adopted, October 26, 1832.
    In *Revised Code of Mississippi* (1857), pp. 23-39.
    Includes the five amendments.
    Not included in the *Code* of 1880.

——Sketch, with list of delegates.
    In Lowry and McCardle's *Mississippi*, pp. 270-273.
    See also Lynch's *Bench and Bar of Mississippi*, pp. 187-189.

—— Chapters in State history. By J. L. Power. The constitutional convention of 1832. n. p. n. d.
    8vo. pp. [4].
    Contains list of delegates.

CONVENTION OF 1851.

CONVENTIONS AND CONSTITUTIONS OF MISSISSIPPI. *Caption, p. 3:* Journal of the convention of the State of Mississippi. Convened at the capitol, in the city of Jackson, on Monday, the 10th day of November, in the year of our Lord one thousand eight hundred and fifty-one, and of the independence of the United States of America the seventy-sixth, in pursuance of "An Act" of the Legislature of said State, entitled "An Act to provide for a convention of the people of the State of Mississippi," approved November 30th, 1850.

8vo. pp. 79. Title page lost of the copy seen.

Contents: Title, 1 leaf; Journal, Nov. 10–17, 1851, pp. 3–46; preamble and resolulutions as adopted, pp. 47–48; Act to provide for Convention, pp. 49–50; Const. of U. S., pp. 51–64 [2]; and Farewell Address of Washington, pp. 67–79.

Edition, 5,000 copies, pp. 17–18.

CONVENTION OF 1861.

—— Journal of the State convention and ordinances and resolutions adopted in January, 1861, with an Appendix. Published by order of the convention. Jackson, Miss., E. Barksdale, State printer. 1861.

8vo. pp. 256 + 1 leaf at p. 50, and also 1 folded table at p. 221.

Contents: Title, 1 leaf; Journal, Jan. 7–26, pp. 3–90; Const. (1832) and am'dts to 1861, pp. 91–117; Ordinances, pp. 119–147; Authentication, p. 148. *Appendix:* Reports of Com'rs to States, Rept. of Auditor and of Adj. Gen., pp. 119–246; indexes, pp. 247–256.

Edition, 2,000 copies, p. 146.

—— Proceedings of the Mississippi State Convention, held January 7th to 26th, A. D. 1861. Including the ordinances, as finally adopted, important speeches, and a list of members, showing the post office, profession, nativity, politics, age, religious preference, and social relations of each. By J. L. Power, Convention reporter. Jackson, Miss.: Power & Cadwallader, book and job printers. 1861.

8vo. pp. 128, 1 leaf folded.

—— Journal | of the | State Convention, | and | ordinances and resolutions | adopted in March, 1861. | Published by order of the Convention. | Jackson: | E. Barksdale, State printer. | 1861. |

8vo. pp. 104.

Contents: Title, 1 leaf, verso blank; Journal March 25–30, 1861, pp. 3–48; Constitution of Miss., pp. 49–75; Ordinances, pp. 77–95; Index, pp. 97–104.

The "Journal" contains a communication from Howell Cobb, Pres. Conv. Conf. States America, followed by the "Constitution of the Confederate States" *in extenso*, pp. 5–20, of which 200 copies were ordered separately printed for use of the Convention, p. 21.

Edition, 2,000 copies, p. 85.

Copies seen: Owen.

—— An address | setting forth the declaration of the immedi- | ate causes which induce and justify the | secession of Mississippi | from the | Federal Union | and the | Ordinance of Secession. | Jackson: | Mississippian Book and Job Printing Office. | 1861. |

8vo. pp. 8.

The names of the signers of the Ordinance are given.

Copies seen: Owen.

CONVENTIONS AND CONSTITUTIONS OF MISSISSIPPI. Sketch, with list of delegates.
    In Lowry and McCardle's *Mississippi*, pp. 341-349.
    See also Lynch's *Bench and Bar of Mississippi*, pp. 493-499.

—— Text of Ordinance of Secession.
    Ibid. pp. 342-343.

CONVENTION OF 1865.

—— Journal | of the | proceedings and debates | in the | Constitutional Convention | of the | State of Mississippi, | August, 1865. | By order of the Convention. | Jackson, Miss.: | E. M. Yerger, State printer. | 1865. |
    8vo. pp. 296, 1 l. No pp. 80-81; p. 50 for p. 84.
    Edition, 2,500 copies, p. 45.
    In session Monday, Aug. 14, to Thursday, Aug. 24, 1865, inclusive, excepting Sunday, Aug. 20. Contains the debates in full, stenographically reported by order of the Convention.
    Copies seen: Owen.

—— Constitution of the State of Mississippi, as amended, with the ordinances and resolutions adopted by the constitutional convention, August, 1865. By order of the convention. Jackson, Miss.: E. M. Yerger, State printer. 1865.
    8vo. pp. 56.
    Edition, 2,500 copies. - *Journal*, p. 45.

—— Sketch of.
    In Lowry and McCardle's *Mississippi*, pp. 354-356.

CONVENTION OF 1868.

—— Journal of the proceedings in the constitutional convention of the State of Mississippi, 1868. Printed by order of the convention. Jackson, Mississippi: E. Stafford, printer. 1871.
    8vo. pp. 776.
    Contents: Title, 1 leaf; Journal, Jan. 7-May 18, 1868, pp. 3-720; Const., pp. 720-744; Appendix, etc., pp. 745-753; Index to Journal, pp. 755-770; and Index to Const., pp. 771-776.

—— Constitution and ordinances of the State of Mississippi, adopted in convention assembled in pursuance of the Reconstruction Acts of Congress, and held, by order of General E. O. C. Ord, in the city of Jackson in 1868. Jackson, Miss.: Mississippi State Journal Office. 1868.
    8vo. pp. 46.

—— Sketch of.
    In Lowry and McCardle's *Mississippi*, pp. 372-379.
    See also Lynch's *Bench and Bar of Mississippi*, pp. 494-496.

CONVENTION OF 1890.

—— Journal of the proceedings of the constitutional convention of the State of Mississippi. Begun at the city of Jackson on August 12, 1890, and concluded November 1, 1890. Printed by authority. Jackson, Miss.: E. L. Martin, printer to the convention. 1890.
    8vo. pp. 757 [1]
    Contents: Title, 1 leaf; Journal, pp. 3-703; Members, pp. 704-708; Index to Journal, pp. 709-730; Index to Const., pp. 731-757; Errata, p. [1].

CONVENTIONS AND CONSTITUTIONS OF MISSISSIPPI. [Propositions, Reports, etc.]
>Sheets.
>Nos. 1-332.

—— Constitution | of the | State of Mississippi, | adopted November 1, 1890. | Printed by authority. | Jackson, Miss.: | R. H. Henry & Co., Convention printers. | 1890. |
>8vo. Cover title. 1 leaf. pp. 64.

—— Constitution | of the | State of Mississippi, | adopted November 1, 1890. | Printed by authority. | Jackson, Miss.: | E. L. Martin, Convention printer. | 1891. |
>8vo. Cover title only, 1 leaf. pp. 81.
>*Copies seen:* Owen.

—— Annotated edition. | Constitution of the State of Mississippi | Adopted November 1, 1890 | As prepared by | R. H. Thompson, Geo. G. Dillard and R. B. Campbell | commissioners to revise the Statutes | with full index. | Jackson, Miss. | Clarion-Ledger printing establishment. | 1891. |
>8vo. pp. 104.

COOKE, JOHN ESTEN (1830-1886). Wearing of the gray; | being | personal portraits, scenes and adventures | of the | war. | By John Esten Cooke, | formerly of General Stuart's staff, and author [–etc., 2 lines.] | [Quotation, 7 lines.] | New York: | E. B. Treat & Co., [–etc., 3 lines.] | 1867. |
>8vo. pp. 601.
>*Copies seen:* Hamner.

COOPWOOD, *Capt.* THOMAS (1793-18—). Sketch of.
>In Livingston's *Biographical Magazine,* June, 1853, vol. iii, No. 2, pp. 631-644; portrait.

COPELAND, JAMES. Life and bloody career of. *See* Dr. J. R. S. Pitts.

COPIAH COUNTY. Sketch of.
>In Lowry and McCardle's *Mississippi,* pp. 466-470.
>*See also* Fulkerson's *Random Recollections of Early Days in Mississippi,* pp. 28-33.

COPPÉE, H. ST. L., C. F. Standard levee sections. Transactions of American Society of Civil Engineers. New York. 1898.
>8 vo. pp. 45.
>He is also the author of the following papers: "The Yellow River and the P. O." 1896; "Bank revetment on the Mississippi River," 1896; "Improvement of the Mississippi River by dredging," 1898; and a "Discussion of Ockerson's Paper on 'Dredges and Dredging of the Mississippi River,'" 1898.

COTTON IN MISSISSIPPI. Its origin and varieties, and its enemies and diseases.
>In Walles' *Report on Agriculture and Geology of Mississippi,* pp. 138-180, *illustrations.*
>*See also* Claiborne's *Mississippi,* pp. 110-144.

—— Memoir on the cotton-plant. *See* Isaac Croom.

—— Cotton insects. *See* W. H. Ashmead. *See also* R. W. Jones.

—— Production and price of, for one hundred years. *See* James L. Watkins.

—— Statistics. *See* Wm. T. Winn.

—— Climatology of. *See* P. H. Mell.
>*See also* Bulletins of the Agricultural Experiment Station.

COTTON GIN PORT. Sketch of.
> In Claiborne's *Mississippi*, p. 59, and *note*.

COUNTERFEITERS. Execution of Hugh Tally and others.
> In Lowry and McCardle's *Mississippi*, pp. 464-5.
> *See also* p. 492, for other references.

COUNTIES. Boundaries of.
> In Poindexter's *Code of Mississippi*, 1823, pp. 474-480.
> *Statutes of Mississippi*, 1840, pp. 43-56.
> Hutchinson's *Code of Mississippi*, 1848, pp. 70-96.
> *Revised Code of Mississippi*, 1857, pp. 50-69.
> *Revised Code of Mississippi*, 1871, pp. 11-30.
> *Revised Code of Mississippi*, 1880, pp. 49-70.
> *Annotated Code of Mississippi*, 1892, pp. 187-206.

—— *See also* the names of the several counties for particular detail; and E. G. Wall.

COURTS. Brief exposition of the organization of the judiciary of the State.
> In W. C. Smedes' *Digest, 1818 to 1847* (1847), pp. ix-xxii. *Preface.*
> Valuable sketch.

—— Names of the Judges of the Supreme Court of Mississippi, 1817-1833.
> *Ibid.* pp. xxiii.

—— Judges of the High Court of Errors and Appeals of Mississippi, 1833-1847.
> *Ibid.* pp. xxiv-xxv.

—— Chancellors and Vice Chancellors.
> *Ibid.* p. xxvi.

—— Attorney-Generals, since 1833.
> *Ibid.* p. xxvi.

—— The judiciary of Mississippi.
> In Lowry and McCardle's *Mississippi*, pp. 634-636.

—— Federal courts, judges, attorneys, and marshals in Mississippi, 1798-1898. *See* Thomas M. Owen.

COVINGTON COUNTY. Sketch of.
> In Lowry and McCardle's *Mississippi*, pp. 471-472.
> *See also* Goodspeed's *Memoirs of Mississippi*, vol. 1, pp. 196-197.

COVINGTON, *Gen.* LEONARD (1768-1813), *Soldier.* Sketch of.
> In Claiborne's *Mississippi*, p. 259, *note.*

CRAVEN, *Dr.* J. J. Prison life of Davis. *See* Jefferson Davis.

CREEK INDIANS. The national legend of the Chahta-Muskokee tribes. *See* D. G. Brinton.

—— A migration legend of the Creek Indians. *See* A. S. Gatschet.

—— A Sketch of the Creek Country. *See* Benj. Hawkins.

—— Reminiscences of. *See* Thomas S. Woodward.

—— *See also* J. D. Dreisback, H. S. Halbert, A. B. Meek, Le Clerc Milfort, James Pilling.

CREEK WAR. Account of.
> In Claiborne's *Mississippi*, pp. 315-346.
> *See also* Goodspeed's *Memoirs of Mississippi*, vol. 1, pp. 134-139, 271-275.
> Pages 271-275 of the latter comprise rosters of Mississippi commands.

—— Reminiscences of the Jefferson Troop. *See* John A. Watkins.

CREEK WAR. The Creek War of 1813 and 1814. *See* H. S. Halbert and T. H. Ball.

—— Notes on the War in the South. *See* N. H. Claiborne.

—— *See also* J. D. Dreisback, J. H. Eaton, Gen. Thomas Flournoy, George S. Gaines, Maj. A. L. Latour, B. J. Lossing, Henry Trumbull, and Gen. James Wilkinson.

CROOM, ISAAC. A memoir, on the subject of the cotton-plant, its history, influence on commerce, politics, and the welfare of the human race, and its probable destiny as the great product of the Southern United States.
> In *Transactions Alabama Historical Society*, 1851, pp. 30-54.

CROZIER, *Rev.* R. H., *D. D.* The bloody junto, – Or the escape of John Wilkes Boothe, 1869.
> 12mo.
> He is also the author of "The Confederate Spy," 1867; "Fiery Trials," 1882; "Araphel; or the Falling Stars of 1833," 1884; "The Cane of Hegobar," 1885; and "Deep Waters," 1887.

CUMBERLAND PRESBYTERIAN CHURCH IN MISSISSIPPI. Sketch of.
> In Goodspeed's *Memoirs of Mississippi*, vol. II, pp. 358-362.

CUMING, F. Sketches of a Tour | to the Western Country, | through | the States of Ohio and Kentucky; | a voyage | down the Ohio and Mississippi rivers, | and a trip | through Mississippi Territory, and | part of West Florida. | Commenced at Philadelphia in the winter of 1807, and concluded in 1809. | By F. Cuming. | With notes and appendix, | containing | some interesting Facts, together with | a notice of an expedition through | Louisiana. | Pittsburg, | printed & published [–etc. 3 lines] | 1810. |
> 12mo. pp. 504.
> The observations and references are of great interest, and are important as showing a picture of the government of the Territory and of the people.
> *Copies seen:* Congress.

CURRENCY. Circulating medium of Mississippi Territory.
> In Claiborne's *Mississippi*, pp. 300-302.

CURRY, *Dr.* JABEZ LAMAR MONROE (1825-), *LL. D., D. D., Educator.* [Educational address before the Legislature of Mississippi, 1894.]
> 8vo.

CURTIS, *Rev.* RICHARD (1755-1811). Sketch of.
> In Foster's *Mississippi Baptist Preachers*, pp. 176-182.
> He was "the first Baptist preacher who ever lived in Mississippi."

D.

DALE, *Gen.* SAM. Life and times of. *See* J. F. H. Claiborne. *See also* H. S. Halbert, and A. B. Meek.

DANCING RABBIT CREEK TREATY. Text of.
> In United States *Statutes at Large*, vol. vii, pp. 333-341.
> It was printed shortly after ratification, as House Executive Doc. No. 123, accompanying a *Message*, March 2, 1831, by President Andrew Jackson. 8vo. pp. 20.
> Copies are also found in—
> *Treaties between the U. S. and Indian Tribes, 1778 to 1857* (1837);
> Hutchinson's *Code of Mississippi* (1848), pp. 121-128;
> Mississippi *Revised Code* (1857), pp. 702-722; and
> Sprott and Smith's *Special Laws of Sumter County, Ala.* (1890).

A BIBLIOGRAPHY OF MISSISSIPPI. 683

Dancing Rabbit Creek Treaty. Sketches of. *See* A. W. Dillard and H. S. Halbert.

Daniel, John W., *U. S. Senator from Va.* Oration on life of Davis. *See* Jefferson Davis.

Darby, William (1775–1855). A | geographical description | of the | State of Louisiana, | the Southern part of the | State of Mississippi, | and | territory of Alabama; | presenting | a view of the soil [–etc., 5 lines.] | Together with | a Map, | from actual survey and observation, projected [–etc., 2 lines] of | the State of Louisiana, | and | adjacent countries. | Second edition, enlarged and improved. | By William Darby. | [Quotation, 6 lines.] | New York: | published by James Olmstead, | sold also by B. Levy & co. booksellers, New-Orleans. | J. Seymour, printer. | 1817. |

> 8vo. pp. 356. *2 maps. Chart of Mobile, Perdido, and Pensacola Bays*
> Large map described in title issued separately.
> Contains extracts from Robert's *Florida*.
> *Copies seen:* Owen.

—— The | Emigrants Guide | to | the Western and Southwestern States | and territories: | comprising | a geographical and statistical description of the States of | Louisiana, Mississippi, Tennessee, Kentucky, and Ohio; | the territories of Alabama [–etc., 8 lines.] | Accompanied by a map of the United States, including | Louisiana, projected and engraved expressly | for this work. | By William Darby, | member of the New-York Historical Society [–etc., 2 lines.] | New-York: | Published by Kirk & Mercein, | no 22 wall-street. | And for sale by Wells & Lilly— | [–etc., 6 lines.] | William A. Mercein, printer, 98, gold-street. | 1818. |

> 8vo. 3 p. l. pp. 311, xiii. *Map.*
> *Copies seen:* Hamner.

—— Darby's edition | of | Brook's | Universal gazetteer; | or, a new | geographical dictionary: | [–etc., 16 lines.] | The third American edition, with ample additions and | improvements. | By William Darby, | [–etc., 3 lines.] | Philadelphia: | published by [–etc., 3 lines.] | 1823. |

> 8vo. pp. 1119; Appendix, 133. *Map of U. S.*
> Contains sketches of counties and towns.
> *Copies seen:* Hamner.

—— View | of the | United States, | historical, geographical, and | statistical; | exhibiting, in a convenient form, | the natural and artificial features | of the | several States, | and embracing those leading branches of | history and statistics best adapted to develop the | present condition of the | North American Union. | Illustrated with maps, etc. | By William Darby. | Philadelphia: | published by H. S. Tanner. | 1828. |

> 18mo. pp. 654. *Map* of Ga. and Ala., 5 x 7 in., bet. pp. 84–85.
> *Copies seen:* Congress.

Darden, John P. The secret of success. By John P. Darden, of Jefferson County, Miss., 1850.

> No copies seen.

DAVENPORT, BISHOP. A | new | gazetteer, | or | geographical dictionary, | of | North America and the West Indies, | [–etc., 14 lines.] | By Bishop Davenport. | Baltimore: | published by George McDowell. | 1835. |
> 8vo. pp. 471. *Maps; illustrations.*
> Contains sketches of counties and towns.
> *Copies seen:* Hamner.

DAVIS, GEORGE. A | concise sketch | of the | debates and proceedings | of the | House of Representatives | of the Mississippi Territory, | convened at the town of Wash- | ington, on the fifteenth of Sep- | tember, in the year one thousand | eight hundred and eight. | By Mr. George Davis. | Natchez: | printed By John W. Winn & Co: | No. 29 main street. | 1808. |
> 18mo. pp. 66.
> In Vol. 108, *Political Pamphlets*, Library of Congress.
> *Copies seen:* Congress.

DAVIS, JEFFERSON (1808–1889), *M. C. from Miss., Col. in Mexican War, U. S. Sen. from Miss., U. S. Sec. of War, President Confederate States of America, Author.*
> The following incomplete list of titles is given as only a meager basis for future work by some student who may undertake an exhaustive bibliography of this distinguished Mississippian.
> In the *Magazine of Western History*, vol. xiii, page 263, there is a list of the papers of Mr. Davis in possession of the Louisiana Historical Association.

—— Remarks | of | Messrs. Clemens, Butler, and Jefferson Davis, | on | the Vermont resolutions relating to slavery. | Delivered | in Senate of the United States, January 10, 1850. | Washington: | printed at the Congressional Globe office. | 1850. |
> 8vo. pp. 15.

—— *Caption:* Speech | of | Mr. Davis, of Mississippi, | on the subject of | slavery in the territories. | Delivered in the Senate of the United States, February 13 and 14, 1850. | [Towers, print.]
> 8 vo. pp. 32. No title page.
> *Copies seen:* Owen.

—— *Caption:* Speech | of the | Hon. Jefferson Davis, | of Mississippi, | on the | measures of compromise. | Delivered in the Senate of the United States, June 28, 1850. |
> 8vo. pp. 16. No title page.

—— *Caption:* Speech | of | Hon. Jefferson Davis, | of Mississippi, | on his resolutions relative to | the rights of property in the Territories, etc. | Delivered in the Senate of the United States, May 7, 1860. | [Printed by Lemuel Towers.]
> 8vo. pp. 16. No title page.
> *Copies seen:* Owen.

—— Inaugural address | of | President Davis | delivered at the Capitol, | Monday, February 18, 1861, at 1 o'clock, p. m. | Montgomery, Ala.: | Shorter & Reid, printers, Advertiser office. | 1861. |
> 8vo. pp 8.
> Reprinted in *Southern Historical Society Papers*, Jan , 1876, vol. 1, No. 1, pp. 19–23.
> *Copies seen:* Curry.

A BIBLIOGRAPHY OF MISSISSIPPI. 685

Davis, Jefferson. The Administration and the Confederate States, 1861.
 8vo. pp. 7.
 Letters from John A. Campbell to Hon. W. H. Seward, and also a letter from him to Mr. Davis, President Confederate States of America.
 Title from Johns Hopkins University *Catalogue*.

—— Message. December 7, 1863. Richmond, Va., 1863.
 8vo. pp. 29.

—— A | short history | of the | Confederate States | of America | By | Jefferson Davis | [Quotation, 2 lines.] | New York | Belford Company, publishers | [–etc., 1 line] | 1890 | [–etc., 1 line.] |
 8vo. pp. xii, 505.

—— The | rise and fall | of the | Confederate Government. | By | Jefferson Davis. | Volume I [–II] | New York: | D. Appleton and Company, | 1, 3, and 5 Bond street. | 1881. |
 8vo. vol. i, pp. xxiii, 707; vol. ii, pp. xix, 808.

—— Resolutions submitted by Mr. Sumner and by Mr. Johnson, calling on the President of the United States for information as to "the rebel Jefferson Davis." Jan. 31, 1865. (Sen. Mis. Doc. 18, 38th Cong., 2nd sess. In vol. 1.)
 8vo. p. 1. No title page.
 This was reintroduced in the 39th Cong., 1st sess.
 Copies seen: Owen.

—— Treason of Jefferson Davis and others. Dec. 20, 1865. (House Mis. Doc. 6, 39th Cong., 1st sess. In vol. 1.)
 8vo. p. 1. No title page.
 Resolutions submitted by Hon. W. Lawrence.
 Copies seen: Owen.

—— Message of the President [Andrew Johnson] of the United States, communicating, in compliance with a resolution of the Senate of December 21, 1865, information upon what charges and for what reasons Jefferson Davis is still held in confinement, and why he has not been put upon his trial. Jan. 10, 1866. (Sen. Ex. Doc. 7, 39th Cong., 1st sess. In vol. 1.)
 8vo. pp. 4. No title page.
 Contents: Message, Jan. 5, 1866; Communication from Edwin M. Stanton, Sec. of War, Jan. 4, 1866; Resolution of Dec. 21, 1865; and an Opinion from James Speed, Attorney-General, Jan. 4, 1866.
 Copies seen: Owen.

—— Resolution, submitted by Mr. Howard, recommending to the President that "Jefferson Davis and Clement C. Clay be, without unnecessary delay, tried by a military commission." Jan. 16, 1866. (Sen. Mis. Doc. 39, 39th Cong., 1st sess. In vol. 1.)
 8vo. p. 1. No title page.
 Copies seen: Owen.

—— Message from the President of the United States, in answer to a resolution of the H. of R. of the 10th ultimo relative to the imprisonment of Jefferson Davis and others. Feb. 9, 1866. (House Ex. Doc. 46, 39th Cong., 1st sess. In vol. 7.)
 8vo. pp. 2. No title page.
 Contents: Message, Feb. 9, 1866; Communication from Edwin M. Stanton, Sec. of War, Feb. 7, 1866; and an Opinion from James Speed, Attorney-General, Jan. 31, 1866.
 Copies seen: Owen.

DAVIS, JEFFERSON. Resolutions of the Legislature of Nevada in favor of a speedy trial of Jefferson Davis. Feb. 28, 1866. (Sen. Mis. Doc. 69, 39th Cong., 1st sess. In vol. 1.)
    8vo. pp. 2. No title page.
    Same also printed as *House Mis. Doc. 140*, 39th Cong., 1st sess. In vol. 3. p. 1.
    Copies seen: Owen.

—— Letter of the Secretary of War [Edwin M. Stanton], communicating, in compliance with a resolution of the Senate of the 24th ultimo, the evidence upon which the awards for the apprehension of Jefferson Davis were made. April 30, 1866. (Sen. Ex. Doc. 64, 39th Cong. 1st sess. In vol. 2.)
    8vo. pp. 39. No title page.
    Contents: Letter from Sec. of War, April 30, 1866; Letter from E. D. Townsend, Adj. Gen., April 28, 1866; Report of Gen. J. H. Wilson, May 19, 1865; Report of Col. Minty, May 18, 1865; Report of Lt. Col. Harnden, 1st Wis. Cavalry, May 13, 1865; List of officers and men of the 1st Wis. Cavalry, reported as engaged in the pursuit; Report of Capt. Hathaway, 4th Mich. Cavalry, May 15, 1865; List of officers and men of the 4th Mich. Cavalry that left camp on the night of May 7, 1865, on the expedition which resulted in the capture; Lt. Col. Pritchard's report, May 25, 1865; Bvt. Brig. Gen. Minty's letter of July 6, 1865, forwarding report of Lt. Col. Pritchard, July 2, 1865, with two inclosures; Supplemental report of Lt. Col. Pritchard, Aug. 28, 1865, with inclosures; Supplemental report of Lt. Col. Harnden, Dec. 11, 1865, with inclosures; Copy of proclamation by the President of May 2, 1865, offering a reward for the apprehension of Jefferson Davis and others.
    Copies seen: Owen.

—— Assassination of Lincoln. Report of the Committee on the Judiciary, to whom were referred the resolutions of the H. of R. of April 9 and April 30, 1866, instructing the committee to inquire into the nature of the evidence implicating Jefferson Davis and others in the assassination of President Lincoln, etc. July —, 1866. (House Rep. 104, 39th Cong., 1st sess. In vol. 1.)
    8vo. pp. 41. No title page.
    Majority Report, by Mr. Boutwell; and the Minority Report, by Mr. A. J. Rogers. Valuable as presenting the contemporary legal contentions of the respective sides.
    Copies seen: Owen.

—— Letter of the Secretary of War communicating, in compliance with a resolution of the Senate of the 26th inst., the report of Major-General J. H. Wilson on the capture of Jefferson Davis. Jan. 31, 1867. (Sen. Ex. Doc. 13, 39th Cong. 2d sess. In vol. 2.)
    8vo. pp. 8. No title page.
    Copies seen: Owen.

—— Capture of Jefferson Davis. Evidence submitted to the Committee of Claims by the claimants for the reward for the capture of Jefferson Davis. March 2, 1867. (House Mis. Doc. 82, 39th Cong. 2d sess. In vol. 1.)
    8vo. pp. 27. No title page.
    Copies seen: Owen.

—— Concurrent resolution, by Mr. Wilson, recommending the speedy and public trial of Mr. Davis, "or that he be released from confinement on bail, or on his own recognizance." March 22, 1867. (Sen. Mis. Doc. 23, 40th Cong. 1st sess. In. vol. 1.)
    8vo. p. 1. No title page.
    Copies seen: Owen.

DAVIS, JEFFERSON. Capture of Jefferson Davis. Letter from the Secretary of War [Edwin M. Stanton], transmitting all information on file in that Department relative to the capture of Jefferson Davis. Jan. 24, 1868. (House Ex. Doc. 115, 40th Cong. 2d sess. In vol. 11.)
> 8vo. pp. 4. No title page.
> Contains list of officers and men of the 4th Mich. Cavalry present at capture, May 10, 1865.
> *Copies seen:* Owen.

—— Report, by W. B. Washburn, from the Committee of Claims on the payment of the rewards offered by the President of the U. S. in May, 1865, for the capture of Jefferson Davis. June 17, 1868. (House Rept. 60, 40th Cong. 2d sess. In vol. 2.)
> 8vo. pp. 14. No title page.
> *Copies seen:* Owen.

—— Letter from the Secretary of War [Wm. W. Belknap], in answer to a resolution of the House of Dec. 15, in relation to the payment of the reward authorized by law for the capture of Jefferson Davis. Jan. 13, 1870. (House Ex. Doc. 35, 41st Cong. 2d sess. In vol. 5.)
> 8vo. p. 1. No title page.
> *Copies seen:* Owen.

—— Bounty for the capture of Jefferson Davis. Letter from the Secretary of the Treasury [Geo. S. Boutwell], in answer to a resolution of the House of the 15th Dec., relative to the payment of the bounty for the capture of Jefferson Davis. Jan. 13, 1870. (House Ex. Doc. 34, 41st Cong. 2d sess. In vol. 5.)
> 8vo. pp. 7. No title page.
> *Copies seen:* Owen.

——The First Wisconsin Cavalry at the Capture of Jefferson Davis. By Henry Harnden.
> In *Collections State Historical Society of Wisconsin*, vol. xiv, pp. 516–532.
> For other papers and articles on the capture of Mr. Davis, see Official Reports by Colonels Harnden and LaGrange, *Wis. Adj. Gen.'s Report*, 1865, pp. 594–597; correspondence and reports of all Union officers concerned, in *Official Records, War of Rebellion*, series I, vols. xlvii, xlix; Mr. and Mrs. Davis's accounts are in her *Memoir*, etc., vol. ii, chap. lxiv; articles by Gen. J. H. Wilson, commander of the Union Cavalry, and William P. Stedman, of the Fourth Michigan Cavalry, in the Century Magazine, vol. xvii, pp. 586–596; and an article by Col. Burton N. Harrison, C. S. A., one of Pres. Davis's party, in *Ibid.*, vol. v, pp. 130–145.

——Stoneman's last campaign and the pursuit of Jefferson Davis.
> In *Sketches of War History, 1861–1865* (*Papers read before the Ohio Com., Loyal Legion U. S., 1883–1886*) vol. iii. Cincinnati. 1888. 8vo.

——Prison life | of | Jefferson Davis. | Embracing details and incidents in his captivity, parti- | culars concerning his health and habits, to- | gether with many conversations on | topics of great public interest. | By | Bvt. Lieut.-Col. John J. Craven, M.D., | late surgeon, U. S. Vols., and physician of the prisoner during his confinement | in Fortress Monroe, from May 25, 1865, up to December 25, 1865. | [Quotation, 5 lines.] | New York: | Carleton, publisher, 413 Broadway. | London; S. Lawson & Co. | MDCCCLXVI. |
> 12mo. pp. 377.

DAVIS, JEFFERSON. Is Davis a traitor; | or | was Secession a constitutional right | previous to | the War of 1861? | By | Albert Taylor Bledsoe, A. M., LL. D., | late professor of Mathematics in the University of Va. | Baltimore: | printed for the author, by Innes & Company, | 1866. |
    12mo. pp. vi, 263 [1.]

—— Life and imprisonment of, including the life and military career of Stonewall Jackson, by M. Addey. New York, 1866.
    12mo. pp. 440. *3 portraits.*

—— *and* JACKSON, STONEWALL. The life and public services of each, with the military career and death of the latter. Philadelphia, 1866.
    12mo. pp. 300. *Ill.*

—— The life | of | Jefferson Davis. | By Frank H. Alfriend, | late editor of The Southern Literary Messenger. | Cincinnati and Chicago: | Caxton publishing house. | [–etc., 5 lines.] | 1868. |
    8vo. pp. 645. *Portrait* of Mr. Davis.

—— Life of. By Edward A. Pollard. Philadelphia, 1869.
    8vo. pp. 536. *Portrait.*

—— Jefferson Davis v. J. H. D. Bowmar, executor, et al.
    In 55th Mississippi Supreme Court *Reports*, pp. 671–814. (1879.)
    In the opinion by Judge Chalmers, there is much concerning the character and the domestic life of Mr. Davis.

—— Jeff. Davis and the Mexican | War Veterans. | Debate | in the | United States Senate, | Saturday, March 1, 1879. | Washington. | 1879.]
    8vo. pp. 48.

—— Funeral oration | pronounced in the opera house | in | Augusta, Georgia, | December 11th, 1889, | upon the occasion of the memorial services | in honor of | President Jefferson Davis | by | Col. Charles C. Jones, jr., LL. D. | President of the Confederate Survivors' Association | Augusta, Ga. | Chronicle printing establishment. | 1889. |
    8vo. pp. 18. *Portrait.*
    Copies seen: Owen.

—— Address of Hon. Thos. H. Watts, | on the | life and character of ex-President Jefferson Davis, | delivered at the Montgomery theatre, Dec. 19, 1889. | n. p. n. d.
    8vo. Title, 1 leaf, pp. 19.
    Copies seen: Owen.

—— Oration | by | Hon. John W. Daniel | on the | life, services, and character | of | Jefferson Davis, | delivered under the auspices of the | General Assembly of Virginia | at | Mozart Academy of Music, January 25, 1890. | Richmond: | J. H. O'Bannon, superintendent of public printing. | 1890. |
    8vo. pp. 46.
    Copies seen: Owen.

—— In Memoriam. | Jefferson Davis. | A tribute of respect offered by the | citizens of Charleston, S. C. | [Quotation, 4 lines.] | Charleston, S. C. | Walker, Evans & Cogswell Co., publishers, | [–etc., 1 line] | 1890.]
    8vo. pp. 79.
    Copies seen: Owen.

DAVIS, JEFFERSON. Life and reminiscences. By distinguished men of his times. Introductory by Hon. John W. Daniel. Baltimore, 1890.
    8vo. pp. 490. *Portraits.*

—— Sketch of.
    In John Savage's *Our Living Representative Men,* Phila., 1860.
    An abstract of this sketch is in De Bow's *Review,* July, 1860, pp. 96-97.

—— Sketch of.
    In Lowry and McCardle's *Mississippi,* pp. 640-648.
    See also Davis's *Recollections of Mississippi and Mississippians,* p. 310.

—— A memoir by his wife. *See* Varina Jefferson Davis.
    In the *Courier-Journal,* Louisville, Ky., Aug. 3, 1891, a federal official, Jerome Titlow, who was present, gave his recollections of the facts concerning the manacling of Mr. Davis after his arrest.

DAVIS, JOSEPH EMORY (1784-1870), *Lawyer.* Sketch of.
    In Lynch's *Bench and Bar of Mississippi,* pp. 73-78; portrait.
    See also Claiborne's *Mississippi,* p. 355.
    He was an elder brother of Hon. Jefferson Davis.

DAVIS, REUBEN (1813-1890), *Lawyer, Judge Sup. Ct. Miss., M. C. from Miss., Col. C. S. A.* Recollections | of Mississippi | and Mississippians | By Reuben Davis | [Design] | Boston and New York | Houghton, Mifflin and Company | * * | 1889. |
    8vo. pp. vi, 446.
    Largely autobiographical. Vividly written, and full of incident.
    Copies seen: Owen.

DAVIS, VARINA JEFFERSON. Jefferson Davis | ex-President of the Confederate States | of America | A memoir | by | his wife | In two volumes | Vol. I. [-II] | New York | Belford Company, publishers | 18-22 East 18th street | [1890.]
    8vo. Vol. I, pp. xvii, 699; vol. ii., pp. xxxii, 939. *Portraits; illustrations.*
    Copies seen: Owen.

DAVIS, VARINA ANNE JEFFERSON ("Miss Winnie") (1864-1898). The Veiled Doctor. | A Novel. | By | Varina Anne Jefferson Davis. | New York: | Harper & Brothers, publishers, | 1895 |
    8vo. pp. ii, 222.

—— A romance of | summer seas. | A novel. | By | Varina Anne | Jefferson-Davis, Au- | thor of "The Veiled Doctor" | New York: | Harper & Brothers, publishers, | 1898. |
    8vo. pp. iv, 278.

—— Sketch of. *See* C. C. Ferrell.
    Prof. Ferrell's paper is a carefully compiled account of her life, in which he was assisted by her mother. It embraces a critical summary of her literary work.

DEAF AND DUMB. Seventeenth biennial report | of the | Board of trustees and superintendent | of the | Mississippi Institution | for the Education of | the Deaf and Dumb | for the | two years ending September 30, 1899. | Vance printing co., | State printers for Mississippi, | Jacksonville, Fla. | 1899. |
    8vo. pp. 29. *Portraits.*
    Reports were also printed for previous years.

DE SOTO COUNTY. Sketch of.
> In Lowry and McCardle's *Mississippi*, pp. 473-476.

DE SOTO, HERNANDO. *See* Biedma, Elvas, B. F. French, H. S. Halbert, Charles C. Jones, Grace King, T. H. Lewis, A. B. Meek, Rodrigo Ranjel, Barnard Shipp, Ternaux-Compans, and Garcilasso de la Vega.

DEUPREE, J. G., *A. M., LL. D., Prof. Univ. of Miss.* Sketch of Dr. W. S. Webb.
> In Foster's *Mississippi Baptist Preachers*, pp. 701-713; *portrait.*
> A list of Dr. Deupree's writings cannot be presented owing to lack of detail, but he has been a prolific writer on educational, psychological, economic, and social problems. His work is most frequently found in the *Mississippi Teacher*, *Southwestern Journal of Education*, the *Sword and Shield*, the *Proceedings* of the Miss. State Teachers' Association, and the State press.

DEVOL, GEORGE H. Forty years | a gambler | on the | Mississippi | by | George H. Devol. | A cabin boy in 1839; could steal cards and cheat the boys | at eleven; stock a deck at fourteen; bested soldiers on | the Rio Grande during the Mexican War; won hundreds | of thousands from paymasters, cotton buyers, default- | ers, and thieves; fought more rough-and-tumble fights | than any man in America, and was the most daring gam- | bler in the world. | Illustrated. | First edition. | Devol & Haines. | Cincinnati: | 1887. |
> 8vo. pp. 300. *Portrait* of author; *ill.*

DICKSON, DAVID (–1836), *M. C. from Miss.* Sketch of.
> In Claiborne's *Mississippi*, p. 357-358, *and note.*

DICKSON, HARRY. The Black Wolf's Breed. A story of France in the old world and the new, happening in the reign of Louis XIV. The Bowen-Merrill Company, Indianapolis, Ind. 1899.
> 12mo. pp. 288.
> Mr. Dickson is a lawyer of Vicksburg, Miss. For an appreciative review, and a short biographical sketch, *see* the *Alkahest*, Atlanta, Ga., May, 1900.

DIGESTS OF DECISIONS.
> Andrews, G. Reports, vols. 45-56.
> Brame and Alexander. Reports, vols. 45-73.
> George, J. Z. Reports, vols. 1-45.
> Heidelberg, D. W. Reports, vols. 45-64.
> Smedes, W. C. Reports, vols. 1-.
> Harris, J. Bowmar. Railway Decisions Reports, vols. 1-71.

DIGESTS OF LAWS. *See* Codes of Mississippi.

DILLARD, ANTHONY WINSTON (1827-1900), *Lawyer.* The treaty of Dancing Rabbit Creek between the United States and the Choctaw Indians in 1830.
> In *Transactions Alabama Historical Society*, 1898-99, vol. iii, pp. 99-106.

DISEASES. *See Dr.* Wm· M. Compton, *Dr.* Daniel Drake, Insane Asylum, *Dr.* J. M. Toner, *Dr.* B. A. Vaughn.

DONALDSON, THOMAS. The public domain. Its history, with statistics. Washington: Government printing office. 1884.
> 8 vo. pp. 1343.
> A valuable publication, which should be consulted by every student of the history of public lands.

DORSEY, *Mrs.* SARAH A. Agnes Graham. Philadelphia. 1869.
>12 mo.
>
>She is also the author of "Recollections of H. W. Allen, ex-Governor of La.," 1866; "Lucia Dare," 1867; "Atalie," 1871; and "Panola," 1877.
>
>Mrs. Dorsey bequeathed her estate at Beauvoir, Miss., to Jefferson Davis.

DOW, LORENZO (1777–1834), *Methodist Clergyman.* History | of | cosmopolite: | or the writings of | Rev. Lorenzo Dow: | containing | his experience and travels, | in | Europe and America, | up to near his fiftieth year. | Also, his | polemic writings. | To which is added, | the "Journey of Life," by Peggy Dow. | Revised and corrected with notes. | Sixth edition—averaging 4;000 each. | Cincinnati: | H. M. Rulison, . . | Philadelphia. | Duane Rulison, . . | . . | 1856. |
>8vo. pp. 720.
>
>Contains accounts of two trips made to Natchez and the Tombigbee settlements in 1803 and 1804, and also an account of a journey through the Alabama portion of the Miss. Territory, about 1810–1813, by Peggy Dow.
>
>The Mississippi trips are summarized by P. J. Hamilton in *Transactions Alabama Historical Society*, 1897–98, vol. ii, pp. 51–53.
>
>*Copies seen:* Owen.

—— The life | travels, labors, and writings | of | Lorenzo Dow; | including his | singular and erratic wanderings in Europe and America. | [–etc. 12 lines.] | Complete in one volume. | Philadelphia, Pa.: | The Keystone publishing company, [–etc., 2 lines.] | n. d.
>12mo. Title, 1 leaf. pp. 508. *Portrait* of Dow.
>Apparently a late reprint.
>*Copies seen:* Hamner.

DOWD, WILLIAM FRANCIS (1820–1878), *Lawyer, Col. C. S. A.* Sketch of.
>In Lynch's *Bench and Bar of Mississippi*, pp. 396–427.

DRAKE, *Rev.* B. M., *D. D.* The life of Elijah Steele.
>No copies seen.

DRAKE, BENJAMIN (1794–1841), *Author.* Life | of | Tecumseh | and of his brother | the Prophet; | with a | historical sketch | of the | Shawanoe Indians. | By Benjamin Drake, | Author [–etc., 2 lines.] | Cincinnati: | Published by H. S. & J. Applegate & Co., | No. 43 Main street, | 1852. |
>12mo. pp. 235.
>Same apparently as edition of 1850.
>
>"Important, because but for the machinations of Tecumseh, Jackson would never have become a famous general. It was Tecumseh who gave Jackson his opportunity."—Parton's *Life of Jackson.*
>
>*Copies seen:* Hamner.

DRAKE, DANIEL (1785–1852), *M. D.* A | systematic treatise, | historical, etiological, and practical, | on the | principal diseases | of the | interior valley of North America, | as they appear in the | Caucasian, African, Indian, and Esquimaux varieties of | its population. | By Daniel Drake, M. D. | Cincinnati: 1850. |
>8vo. pp. 878.
>
>Based on personal observation. Valuable for its topographical notes and discussion of influence of topography on the diseases of the State.
>
>*Copies seen:* Hamner.

DRAKE, SAMUEL GARDNER (1798-1875). The | aboriginal races | of | North America; | comprising | biographical sketches of eminent individuals, | and | an historical account of the different tribes. | From | the first discovery of the Continent | to | the present period | with a dissertation on their | origin, antiquities, manners and customs, | illustrative narratives and anecdotes, | and a | copious | analytical index | By Samuel G. Drake. | Fifteenth edition, | revised, with additions, | by Prof. H. L. Williams. | [Quotation, 6 lines.] | New York. | Hurst & Company, Publishers. | 122 Nassau Street. | [1880]. |
>8vo. pp. 788.
>The best edition of this work.
>Contains extended accounts of the Southern tribes, biographical sketches, etc.
>*Copies seen:* Owen.

DRAMA, THE. *See* N. M. Ludlow and Solomon F. Smith.

DRAPER, LYMAN C. *See Maj.* S. S. Forman.

DREISBACK, *Maj.* JAMES D. (-1896). Weatherford—"the Red Eagle."
>In *Alabama Historical Reporter*, Tuscaloosa, Ala., Feb., Mar., and April, 1884.
>This is a valuable sketch, prepared by a man long resident in South Alabama, and whose wife was related to Weatherford. It contains the fullest genealogical account of the Weatherfords, family connections, and descendants, that has been prepared.

—— The tragic death of Gen. Wm. McIntosh, a leading chief of the Muscogee or Creek Indians.
>*Ibid.* July, 1885.

—— A man of blood—one-handed "Savannah Jack."
>*Ibid.* July, 1885.

[DUANE WILLIAMS] (1760-1835), *Journalist.* The | Mississippi question | fairly stated, | and | the views and arguments | of those who clamour for war, | examined. | In seven letters. | Originally written for publication in the | Aurora, at Philadelphia. | By Camillus, [*anon.*] | Philadelphia: | Printed by William Duane, No. 106, Market street. | 1803. |
>8vo. pp. 48.
>In Vol. 89, *Duane Pamphlets*, Library of Congress.

DUMOND, ANNIE NELLES. The hard times | The cause and the remedy. | By Annie Nelles Dumond, | [author, etc., 6 lines.] | Jackson, Miss. | Messenger Publishing Company. | 1896. |
>12 mo. pp. 318. *Portrait of author.*
>She is also the author of "The Life of a Book Agent," "Scraps, or Sabbath School Influence," "Ravenia, or The Outcast Redeemed," "Happy at Last, or a Sequel to The Life of a Book Agent," "National Reform, or Liquor and its Consequences," and "Church and Sunday School Influence."

DUNBAR, SIR WILLIAM (1749-1810). Sketch of. By Dr. F. L. Riley.
>In *Publications of the Mississippi Historical Society*, 1899, vol. ii, pp. 85-111.
>*See also* Claiborne's *Mississippi*, pp. 200-201.
>"Dr. Riley collates all of the authorities and minor sources, with references to Mr. Dunbar's writings. His work evinces wide research, and portrays in an able way the work and attainments of a gentleman of rare scientific spirit, but of whom little had heretofore been written.
>Mr. Dunbar was born in Scotland, but located in America, on the lower Mississippi, near Baton Rouge. In a few years he removed to the neighborhood of Natchez, nine miles south, where he lived and died. Dr. Riley thus summarizes his work:

"1. He helped to locate and to survey part of the present boundary line between Mississippi and Louisiana.

2. He first directed the attention of the world to the manufacture of cotton-seed oil.

3. He invented the screw press for packing cotton and helped to perfect the process of packing it in square bales.

4. He made the first accurate meteorological observations in the valley of the Mississippi.

5. He made a critical scientific study of the Mississippi River and its Delta.

6. He made important contributions to geographical knowledge by determining the latitude and the longitude of many places.

7. He was the first to give a scientific account of the Hot Springs and an analysis of its water.'

See also Wailes' *Report on Agriculture and Geology of Miss.*, pp. 364-367.

DU PRATZ, LE PAGE (1695-1775), *Author.* Histoire de la Louisiane, Contenant la Decouverte de ce Vaste Pays, sa Description geographique, un Voyage dans les Terres; l'Histoire Naturelle; les Moeurs, Coutumes & Religion des Naturels avec leurs Origines; deux Voyages dans le Nord du Nouveau Mexique, dont un jusqu a la Mer de Sud; ornee de deux Cartes & de 40 Planches en Taille-douce. Par Mr. Le Page du Pratz. A Paris, 1758.

12 mo. Vol. i, half title, title, pp. xvi, 359; vol. ii, half title, title, pp. 441; vol. iii, half title, title, pp. 454.

Title from Field.

"The presence of Le Page du Pratz in the colony for sixteen years (1718 to 1734) gives to his *Histoire de la Louisiane* a value which his manifest egotism and whimsical theories can not entirely obscure. It was an authority in the boundary discussions."—Winsor's *Narrative and Critical History*, vol. v, p. 65.

"The work teems with facts and particulars relating to the Natchez and other tribes of Louisiana. * * * It is from his relation that most of the details of the life of the Natchez and other Mississippi tribes have been derived. It is difficult to procure his work complete in all the plates and maps, which should number forty-two."—Field's *Indian Bibliography*, p. 234.

—— The history of Louisiana, or the Western parts of Virginia and Carolina; containing a description of the countries that lye on both sides of the river Miss[iss]ippi: with an account of the settlements, inhabitants, soil, climate, and products. Translated from the French, (lately published), by M. Le Page Du Pratz; with some notes and observations relating to our colonies. London, printed for T. Becket, 1763.

12mo. Vol. i, 1 leaf; pp. vii, 368; 2 maps; vol. ii, prel. pp. vi, 272.

Title from Field.

"The English translator, with an assurance which is perfectly satire proof, not only abridges the work, but reconstructs and distorts it, and then calls upon us to admire his dexterity in subverting the labor and plan of the author.—Field's *Indian Bibliography.*

—— The | history of Louisiana, | or of | the western parts | of | Virginia and Carolina: | containing a description of the | countries that lie on both sides of the river Mississippi: | with an account of the | settlements, inhabitants, soil, | climate, and products. | Translated from the French | of M. Le Page Du Pratz; | with some notes and observations relating to our colonies. | A new edition. | London, | printed for T. Becket, corner of the Adelphi, in the Strand. | MDCCLXXIV. |

8vo. 4 prel. leaves. pp. xxxvi, 387. 2 maps.

Copies seen: Hamner.

DUVAL, *Miss* MARY V. (1850-), The students' history | of | Mississippi | arranged | for use in the public schools of Mississippi | by | Mary V. Duval, A. M. | [Quotation, 3 lines.] | Louisville, Ky. | Courier-Journal Job-printing Co. | 1887 |
    12mo. pp. 280. Profusely *illustrated*.

—— History of Mississippi | compiled and arranged for the use of the public schools | of Mississippi | By | Mary V. Duval, A. M. | author of Students' History of Mississippi. | With an appendix containing the Constitution of Mississippi | adopted November 1, 1890. | Louisville, Ky. | Courier-Journal Job Printing Co. | 1892. |
    12mo. pp. 323.
    ILLUSTRATIONS: State House, Jackson; Seal of the State; Lyceum of the Univ. of Miss.; Bienville; Gov. David Holmes; Sargent S. Prentiss; Observatory of Univ. of Miss.; Earl Van Dorn; Judge Wm. L. Sharkey; Jefferson Davis; Gen. E. C. Walthall; Stephen D. Lee; James R. Chalmers; L. Q. C. Lamar; A. & M. College, Starkeville; I. I. and College, Columbus; Judge H. T. Ellet; Whitworth Female College, Brookhaven.

—— A treatise on civil government | arranged for the use of the public schools | of Mississippi | by | Mary V. Duval, A. M. | author of Students' History of Mississippi | and History of Mississippi. | Louisville, Ky. | Courier-Journal Job Printing Co. | 1892. |
    12mo. pp. 200.
    The History of Mississippi, and the Civil Government, also appear together: 12mo. pp. x, [2], 387; *illustrations*.

—— The Queen | of the South | a drama | by | Mary V. Duval, | Sardis, Miss. | Dedicated to the United Daughters of | the Confederacy. | Copyrighted 1899 | by | Mary V. Duval. | The Citizen print, | Pulaski, Tenn. | 1899. |
    12mo. pp. 23. *Portrait* of author on cover.

—— The making of a State.
    In *Publications Mississippi State Historical Society*, 1900, vol. iii. (In press.)

DWIGHT, TIMOTHY (1752-1817), *Pres. Yale College.* Travels in New England and New York. London, 1823.
    8 vo. 4 vols. *Portrait and maps.*
    In vol. i will be found facts relating to a party of emigrants to what later became Mississippi Territory.

E.

EAGER, *Rev.* ELEAZER C. (1813-189-). Sketch of.
    In Foster's *Mississippi Baptist Preachers*, pp. 212-228; *portrait*.

EAGER, P. H., *Prof. Miss. College.* [Mississippi literature.]
    In preparation.
    This work will present a full survey of the literature of the State, etc.

EATON, JOHN HENRY, *and* REID, JOHN. The life | of | Andrew Jackson, | Major General | [of the Seventh Division of the Army of] the United States: | comprising | a history of the War in the South, | from the commencement of the | Creek campaign, | to the termination of hostilities before | New Orleans. | Commenced | by John Reid, | brevet Major, United States' Army. | Completed | by John Henry Eaton. |

Philadelphia: | published by M. Carey and son. | For the benefit of the children of John Reid. | Lydia R. Bailey, printer. | 1817. |

<blockquote>
8vo. pp. 425. *Portrait* of Jackson, *5 maps*, one of which is of the Battle of Talladega.

A second edition was issued: Cincinnati, 1827. 12mo, pp. 454. A third was issued, omitting the name of Reid altogether.

Revised and corrected by the author. Philadelphia, 1828. 12mo. pp. 335.
</blockquote>

EATON, JOHN HENRY (1790-1856), *U. S. Senator from Tenn.* The life | of | Andrew Jackson, | Major-General in the service of the United States: | comprising | a history | of the | War in the South, | from the | commencement of the Creek campaign, | to the | termination of hostilities before | New Orleans. | By John Henry Eaton, Senator of the United States. | Philadelphia: | published by Samuel F. Bradford. | Joseph Harding, printer. | 1824. |

<blockquote>
8vo. pp. 468. *Portrait* of Jackson.

Of this edition Parton, in his *Life of Jackson*, says:

"Published originally about 1818. The basis of all the popular lives of Jackson; valuable for its full details of the Creek War. Not designedly false, but necessarily so, because written on the principle of omitting to mention every act and trait of its subject not calculated to win general approval. The author was a neighbor and friend of General Jackson, afterwards a member of his Cabinet."

The statement as to the original publication in 1818 has reference to the first edition, 1817, by Eaton and Reid. *See* preceding title.
</blockquote>

ECHOLS, OBADIAH. Autobiography. 1869.
<blockquote>No copies seen.</blockquote>

EDUCATION. Elizabeth Female Academy. *See Bishop* C. B. Galloway.

—— Early History of Jefferson College. *See* J. K. Morrison.

—— Schools during Territorial period. *See* W. H. Magruder.

—— History of Education in Mississippi. *See* Edward Mayes.

—— Educational progress in the State.
<blockquote>In Lowry and McCardle's *Mississippi*, pp. 417-421.</blockquote>

—— Common schools.
<blockquote>*Ibid.* pp. 421-430.

See also Mayes' *History of Education in Mississippi*, pp. 278-290.</blockquote>

—— Chickasaw school fund.
<blockquote>*Ibid.* pp. 430-432.</blockquote>

—— *See also* J. M. Arnold, Deaf and Dumb, J. G. Deupree, Dr. C. C. Ferrell, H. S. Halbert, Rev. W. S. Harrison, Dr. R. W. Jones, Dr. S. A. Knapp, Dabney Lipscomb, W. H. Magruder, Edward Mayes, Dr. F. L. Riley, G. S. Roudebush, Dr. John N. Waddel, W. L. Weber, *Rev.* T. D. Witherspoon.

—— *See also* the next succeeding title.

EDUCATIONAL LITERATURE OF MISSISSIPPI IN U. S. BUREAU OF EDUCATION.
<blockquote>
The following list of documents and papers, bearing upon Mississippi schools and educational history, has been supplied by the U. S. Bureau of Education, Washington, D. C., through the courtesy of the Commissioner, Dr. W. T. Harris. In order to preserve the list in its entirety, as showing all the literature of the subject in one place, the usual bibliographical rules have not been observed. It is believed that it will be of more practical value in this form.

<blockquote>
Barnard, H. Education and public schools in Mississippi. Barnard's *Am. Jour. Educ.*, vol. 18, 1869.

—— Constitutional provisions respecting education in Mississippi in 1867-68. *Ibid.*, vol. 24, 1873 : 718.
</blockquote>
</blockquote>

Barnard, H. Development of schools from 1803-1872. *Ibid.*, vol 24, 1873
Common schools in Mississippi. *N. E. Jour. Educ.*, vol. 11:264.
Education in Mississippi. *Am. Ann. Ed.*, 1837·427,570.
The educational test in the Mississippi Constitutional Convention. *Christian Statesman*, Sept. 25, 1890.
Elizabeth Female Academy. *Am. Jour. Educ.*, vol. 3, 1828.
Edwards, B. B. Education and literary institutions. 1832. Barnard's *Am. Jour. Educ.*, vol. 27, 1877.
Forshey, C. G. State of education in Mississippi. *Trans. Coll. Prof. Teach.*, vols. 6-7:101-102.
Mason, J. C. Letter pertaining to educational matters. *Am. Jour. Educ.*, St. Louis, vol. 7. June 5.
Morris, R. Mississippi schools. *Ohio Sch. Jour.*, vol. 2, pp. 163-165, 179-181.
Speech of Chas. W. Clarke on the subject of education, June 30, 1870. Jackson. 1870.
University of Mississippi. *De Bow's Review*, vol. 27, 1859.

CITY SCHOOLS.

Ackerman. An. cat. 4th An. session. 1892.
Bolton. Annual Report. 1893.
Brandon. High School. 1891-92.
Canton. Rules and regulations. 1891-92.
Cascilla. 4th Annual Report. 1893-94.
Columbia. Board of Trustees. Catalogue of High School. 1892-93, 1893-94, 1894-95.
Gloster. Board of Trustees. Male and Female School. 1893-94, 1894-95.
Greenville. Board of Education. Annual Report. 1898.
Harperville. 21st Annual Catalogue and announcement. 1896-97.
Jackson. Graded schools. Course of study; rules and regulations. 1887-88.
Macon. Board of Education. Catalogue and report Graded and High schools. 1893-94.
Magnolia. Board of Trustees. 9th Annual Catalogue. 1896-97.
Meridian. Board of Education. Annual Reports. 1885-86, 1886-87. Curriculum, rules, etc. 1896.
Ocean City. Board of Trustees. 2d Annual announcement 1898-99.
Oxford. Graded schools. "Excelsior." 1898.
Polo. Board of Education. Rules and regulations and a course of study 1892.
Poplarville. Trustees:
    2d Annual catalogue. 1893-94.
    3d Annual catalogue. 1894-95.
    4th Annual catalogue. 1895-96.
    5th Annual catalogue. 1897-98.
Port Gibson. Graded Public School No 2 1895.
Terry. Board of Trustees. Rules for Graded schools.
Tupelo. Board of Trustees. Annual Report and Catalogue. 1895-96.
Vandalia. Board of Education. Rules and regulations and course of study 1894-95.
Vicksburg. Board of Education. Rules and regulations. 1893-94.
Wesson. Board of Trustees. Annual Catalogue. 1897-98.
Winona. Principal of Schools. Annual Report. 1898-99.

INDUSTRIAL EDUCATION.

Mississippi industrial institute and college for the education of white girls of Mississippi. Third biennial report of the president and other officers. Columbus, 1889.

JOURNALS.

Mississippi Educational Journal. H R. Pease. Vol. 1. 1871–72.
Mississippi Journal of Education, vols. 1-2, 1894-95.
Mississippi Teacher, vol. 1, 1887-88.
Mississippi Teacher, vol. 2, 1875-76.
Rust Enterprise, Aug., 1892; June, 1893-94; Dec., 1894; Feb.-Mar., 1895.
Semi-Monthly, The. Vol. 3 1877.
Union Literary Magazine, vol 5, 1893.

LAWS.

Compilation of constitutional provisions and legislative acts pertaining to common schools. 1872-76. Jackson.
Free public schools in Mississippi Chap. xvi of the revised code. 1880. Jackson
Laws for the establishment and government of common schools. 1870. Jackson.
Laws in relation to free public schools in the State, with constitutional provisions for the same 1886. Jackson.
School laws. 1873, 1878, 1890, 1894, 1896.

SUPERINTENDENT'S REPORTS.

Reports, 1871–1897. 8vo.

EELKING, MAX VON. Die | Deutschen Hülfstruppen | im | Nordamerikanischen Befreiungskriege, | 1776 bis 1783. | Von | Max Von Eelking, | herzogl. Sachsen-Meiningischer Hauptmann und correspondirendes Mitglied | der historical Society zu New-York. | 1 Theil | [–11. Theil] | Hanover, 1863. | Helwing'sche Hofbuchhandlung. | (Theaterplatz 3, Ende der Sophienstrasse.)
    8vo. vol i, pp. xii. 397; vol, ii. pp. 271. Appendix, pp. 245-271.
    Copies seen: Hamner.

—— The | German allied troops | in the | North American War of Independence, | 1776–1783. | Translated and abridged from the German of | Max Von Eelking, | Captain Saxon-Meiningen Army; member of the Historical Society of New York. | By | J. G. Rosengarten. | Albany, N. Y.: | Joel Munsell's Sons, publishers, | 1893. |
    8vo. pp 360. Portrait of *Lt. Gen.* Knyphausen.
    Liberal translation, but somewhat condensed.
    Copies seen: Hamner

EGGLESTON, GEORGE CARY (1839–), *Author* Red Eagle | and the | wars with the Creek Indians | of Alabama. | By | George Cary Eggleston. | New York: | Dodd, Mead & company, | publishers. | [1878.]
    12 mo. pp. 346. *5 illustrations.*
    "Famous American Indians" Series.
    "A work of this kind necessarily makes no pretension to originality in its materials."—*Preface.*
    Copies seen: Owen.

ELDER, WILLIAM HENRY (1819–), *Third Bishop of Natchez.* Sketch of.
    In *Sketch of the Catholic Church in Natchez,* pp 28–33.

—— Address to the Gov. of Miss., James S. Alcorn, "in behalf of the liberty of education."
    In appendix to Journal of the Senate of Miss., pp. 1200–1209.
    Dated: "Jackson, Miss., March 25, 1871."

ELECTIONS. Registration and elections. For the information of registrars and commissioners. n. p. n. d. [c. 1892.]
>8vo. pp. 17. No title page. Double columns.
>Forms chapter 172 of *Annotated Code* of Statute Laws of Mississippi, 1892.
>*Copies seen:* Owen.

ELIZABETH FEMALE ACADEMY. Sketch of. *See Bishop* C. B. Galloway. *See also* Educational Literature of Mississippi, *supra*.

—— History of.
>In Mayes' History of Education in Mississippi, pp. 38-46.

ELLETT, HENRY T., *Lawyer, M. C. from Miss.* Sharkey and Harris, Compilers. Revised Code of Miss., 1857. *See* Codes of Mississippi.

ELLIS, POWHATAN (1794-1844), *Lawyer, U. S. Senator from Miss., Federal Judge in Miss.* Sketch of.
>In Lynch's *Bench and Bar of Mississippi*, pp. 87-88.
>*Also* Claiborne's *Mississippi*, pp. 358, *note*, and 470.

ELVAS, GENTLEMAN OF. Relaçam verdadei | ra dos trabalhos *que* | ho gouernado | dõ Fernãdo d' | souto e cer | tos fidal | gos portugueses passarom | no d'scobrimẽto da | prouincia da Fro | lida. Agora | nouamẽte feita por hũ | fidalgo Deluas. | Foy vista por ho señor inquisidor. | [Colophon:] *Foy impressa esta relaçam do | descoubrimento da Frolida | em casa de andree de Bur | gos impressor & cauallei | ro da casa do se- | nhor Cardeal | iffante. | acabouse aos des dias de Febrei- | ro do anno de mil & quinhentos | & cincoenta & sete annos. | Na nobre & sempre leal cidade de Euora.* | [1557.]
>8vo. clxxx leaves.
>"A volume of the greatest rarity. The only known copy [1873] in America is in Mr. Lenox's library. Rich priced it, in 1830, at thirty guineas, and says 'Frodida,' which is an error, repeated by Ternaux, No. 76, and Brunet. It is reprinted in facsimile in vol. i of *'Collecção de opusculos reimpressos relativos á historia das navigações. . . . Lisbon. 1844.'* 4to. pp. 8, xii, 139."—Sabin's *Dictionary*, No. 24895.
>The Elvas narrative is the first and best of the several accounts of Soto's expedition.
>"It ranks second only to the relation of Cabeça de Vaca, in the information it affords us, regarding the aborigines of the southern States, on their first introduction to Europeans."—Field's *Indian Bibliography*, p. 340.

—— Virginia | richly valued. | Being the description of the maine land of | Florida, her next neighbor: | Out of the foure yeers continuall trauell discouerie, | for above one thousand miles East and West, of | Don Ferdinando de Soto, and sixe hundred | able men in his companie. | Wherein are truly obserued the riches and fertilitie of those parts, | abounding with things necessarie, pleasant, and profitable | for the life of man: with the natures and dispo- | sitions of the inhabitants. | Written by a Portugall gentleman of Eluas, emploied in | all the action, and translated out of Portugese | by Richard Haklvyt. | *At London | Printed by Felix Kyngston for Matthew Lownes*, and are to be sold at the signe of the Bishops | head in Pauls Churchyard. | 1609. |
>Small 4to. pp. [8] 180.
>A rare volume. Reprinted in Force's *Tracts*, vol. iv, no. 1; in the supplement to Hakluyt's *Voyages;* and omitting Hakluyt's preface, in French's *Historical Collections of Louisiana*, vol. ii. *See* below for full titles.
>Sabin: No. 24896.
>A second edition appeared under the following title:

ELVAS, GENTLEMAN OF. The | Worthye and Famovs His- | tory of the Travailes, Discouery, & Conquest, of that Great | Continent of Terra Florida, being lively | Paraleld, with that of our now Inha- | bited Virginia. | As also | The Commodities of the said Country, | with diuers Excellent and rich Mynes, of Golde, | Siluer, and other Mettals, &c. which cannot but | giue vs a great and exceeding hope of our | Virginia, being so neare | of one Continent. | Accomplished and effected, by that worthy | Generall and Captaine, Don Ferdinando | de Soto, and six hundreth (sic) Spaniards, his followers. | *London* | *Printed for Mathew Lownes,* | . . . . 1611. |
    4to.
    Sabin: No. 24897.

—— Histoire de la Conqueste de la Floride, parles Espagnols. sous Ferdinand de Soto. Ecrite en Portugais par un Gentil-homme de la ville d'Elvas. [Tradvite] par M. D. C. [Citri de la Guette.] *Paris:* Denys Thierry. 1685.
    12mo. 13 prel. leaves. pp. 300.

—— Another edition: Paris: Edme Couterot. 1699.
    12mo. 13 prel. leaves. pp. 300.
    Sabin says there is no difference in these editions except as to the imprint.
    Sabin: No. 24864.
    "The following is an English translation of this French version. It is 'erroneous as to numbers, distances, and names of places, and very inferior to that by Hakluyt,' published in 1609, as 'Virginia richly valued,' and in 1611 as 'Discovery and Conquest of Terra Florida,' "—(Sabin), viz:

—— A relation of the Invasion and Conquest of Florida by the Spaniards, Under the Command of Fernando de Soto. Written in Portuguese, by a Gentleman of the Town of Elvas. Now Englished. To which is Subjoyned Two Journeys of the present Emperour of China into Tartary in the Years 1682 and 1683. With some Discoveries made by the Spaniards in the Island of California, in the Year 1683. *London:* John Lawrence. 1686.
    16mo. 8 prel. leaves. pp. 273.
    "Kennett's Bibl. Am. Prim. gives this title, with some variations, dated 1687. *See also* Purchas, iii, 807; 1532, 1603."—Sabin: No. 24865.

—— Virginia | richly valued, | by the description of the Maine Land of | Florida, | her next neighbor: | out of the foure yeeres continuall trauell | and discouerie, for aboue one thousand | miles east and west, | of | Don Ferdinando de Soto, | and sixe hundred able men in his companie. | Wherein are truly obserued | the riches and fertilitie of those parts, | bounding with things necessarie, pleasant | and profitable for the life of man: | With the natures and disposi- | tions, of the inhabitants: | Written by a Portugall Gentleman of Eluas, emploied in | all the action, and translated out of the Portugese | by Richard Hakluyt. | At London: | printed by Felix Kyngston for Matthew Lownes, and are | to be sold at the signe of the Bishops head | in Paul's Churchyard. | 1609. |
    In *The Voyages | of | the English nation | to America. | Collected by | Richard Hakluyt, preacher, | and | edited by | Edmund Goldsmid (sic), F. R. H. S | Vol. II. | Edinburgh. | E & G. Goldsmid,* pp. 537-616. 8vo.
    Copies seen. Hamner.

ELVAS, GENTLEMAN OF. Narrative of the expedition of Hernando de Soto into Florida, by a Gentleman of Elvas, translated from the Portuguese by Richard Hackluyt, in 1609.

In French's *Historical Collections of Louisiana*, part ii, pp. 111-220. See French, B. F.

—— The | discovery and conquest | of | Terra Florida, | by | Don Ferdinando de Soto, | and six hundred Spaniards | his followers. | Written by a Gentleman of Elvas, employed in all the action, and | translated out of Portuguese, | by Richard Hakluyt. | Reprinted from the edition of 1611. | Edited, | with notes and an introduction, | and a translation of a narrative of the expedition | by Luis Hernandez de Biedma, factor to the same, | by | William B. Rye, | of the British Museum. | London: | printed for the Hakluyt Society. | MDCCCLI. |

8vo. 2 prel. leaves, pp. lxvii, 1 l., 200 v. *Map* of Soto's route.

—— Virginia | richly valued, | by the description of the main land of | Florida, her next neighbor: | [-etc., 17 lines.] |

In Force's *Tracts and other papers*, vol. iv no. 1, pp. 132.
Title page as in the Hakluyt *translation*, 1609.
Copies seen: Congress.

—— *General title:* Narratives | of the career of | Hernando De Soto | in the | conquest of Florida | as told by a Knight of Elvas | and in a relation by | Luys Hernandez de Biedma | factor of the expedition. | Translated by | Buckingham Smith | [Monogram.] | New York | MDCCCLXVI |

4to. pp. xxviii, 324. *Portrait* of Soto, *map and plates*
Special title: True relation | of the | vicissitudes that attended | the | Governor Don Hernando De Soto | and some | nobles of Portugal in the discovery | of the | Province of Florida, | now just given by a | Fidalgo of Elvas. | Viewed by the Lord Inquisitor. |
pp. 1-228
Special title: Relation | of the | Conquest of Florida, | presented by | Luys Hernandez De Biedma | in the year 1544 | to the | King of Spain in Council | Translated from the original document |
pp. 229-261.
Edition, 125 copies.
No. 5 of the *Bradford Club Series*.
Contains Life of De Soto, pp. ix-xxvi; the two narratives, pp. 1-228 and 229-261; and an Appendix of *Translations*, pp. 263-312, of sundry documents obtained from the *Archivo de Indias* at Sevilla and other places relating to Soto, his family, and his expedition.

"The author of the Relaçam is unknown. At the time of making the original publication, as appears from the printer's notice, he was yet living No doubt he was one of the eight Portuguese gentlemen, spoken of in the text who went from Elvas to join Soto at Sevilla, three of whom lost their lives in Florida. In the order they are mentioned, it is perhaps worth the remark as possibly indicating the writer, that two named Fernandez are placed last, first Benito who was drowned near Achese, then Alvaro, a survivor.

"The narrative, as an early record of the country and condition of the inhabitants, merits attention and study. The facts are stated with clearness and evident care. It is likewise an outward picture of affairs as they stood in the camp, or appeared from the marquee of the Adelantado. Some hints of their inner working, up to the time of the death of Soto, may be learned from the *Historia General y Natural do las Indias*. Documents of the age, now published, attest the exactness of many statements, and time simply has unveiled the truthfulness of others. . . .

"That this account, fraught with instructive incident, has come to us untouched from the hand that wrote it is a matter for gratulation, since in two chronicles we have to lament over ruins that mark as many narratives to have existed, possessing a scope and interest not inferior to the present one. The production of Rodrigo Rangel, the private secretary of the Adelantado, afforded the material for the chapters, now incomplete, of Oviedo; and an account, composed by a captain who remained in America—for which pictures in colours of the battle scenes with the Indians of Florida were at one time in the cabinet of Philip II— was the source whence Herrera drew supplies; while the dry and brief itinerary of Biedma has escaped to us undisturbed in the same official repository—the Council of the Indias. The *Florida* of the Ynca, on the same subject, belongs less to history than to romance."—*Proem* to Smith's *translation*.

Copies seen: Congress.

EMMAUS. Methodist Choctaw Mission.
In Lowry and McCardle's *Mississippi*, p. 461.

ENABLING ACT. An act to enable the people of the western part of the Mississippi Territory to form a constitution and State government, and for the admission of such State into the Union, on an equal footing with the original States. March 1, 1817.
In U. S. *Statutes at Large*, vol. iii, pp. 348–349.
Copies are also in the codes of Miss., 1823, 1840 and 1857; and in Lowry and McCardle's *Mississippi*, pp. 235–236.

——— *See also* Organic acts for the Territories of the United States. Washington, 1900. (Sen. Doc. 148, 56th Cong., 1st sess.)
8vo.

EPISCOPAL (THE PROTESTANT) CHURCH IN MISSISSIPPI. Sketch of.
In Goodspeed's *Memoirs of Mississippi*, vol. ii, pp. 348–354.

——— Bishop Otey as Provisional Bishop of Mississippi. *See Rev.* A. H. Noll.

——— Diocesan Journals. 18– –1899.
8vo.

ESTES, MATTHEW. A defence | of | negro slavery, | as it exists in the | United States. | By Matthew Estes, | of Columbus, Mississippi. | Montgomery: | press of the "Alabama Journal." | 1846. |
24mo. Title, 1 leaf; verso, copyright, pp. vii–x. [11]–260.
"A work which, in a small compass, contains much that should be familiar to every slave holder."—In appendix containing a list of works on slavery.
Copies seen: Curry.

EVARTS, *Rev.* JEREMIAH. Memoir of the life of. *See* E. C. Tracy.

F.

FALKNER, W. C. Rapid ramblings | in Europe. | By | W. C. Falkner. | Philadelphia. | J. B. Lippincott & Co. | 1884. |
12mo. pp. 556.
Mr. Falkner is also the author of the "White Rose of Memphis," 1880; "Life of the Murderer, McCannon," 1857; "The Lost Diamond," 1867; "The Little Brick Church," 1882; and "Henry and Ellen," 1853.

——— Sketch of. *See* A. L. Bondurant.

FAUNA OF MISSISSIPPI. Description of.
In Wailes' *Report on Agriculture and Geology of Mississippi*, pp. 309–340.

FEATHERSTON, WINFIELD SCOTT (1820–1891), *Lawyer, Brig. Gen., C. S. A., M. C. from Miss.* Speech | of | Hon. W. S. Featherston, | of Mississippi, | on | rivers and harbors. | Delivered in the House of Representatives, February 15, 1851. | Washington: | printed by Jno. T. Towers. | 1851. |
8vo. pp. 15.

—— Sketch of.
In Goodspeed's *Memoirs of Mississippi*, vol. i, pp. 721–726; portrait.

FEATHERSTONHAUGH, GEORGE WILLIAM (1780–1866), *Geologist, Traveler.* Excursions through the slave States from Washington on the Potomac to the frontier of Mexico, with sketches on popular manners and geological notices. New York. 1844.
8vo. pp. 168.

FEDERAL COURTS IN MISSISSIPPI. *See* Thomas M. Owen.

FEMALE COLLEGES IN MISSISSIPPI. Sketch of.
In Mayes' *History of Education in Mississippi*, pp. 93–105.

FERRELL, CHILES CLIFTON (1865–), *M. A., Ph. D. (Leipzig), Prof., Univ. of Miss.* Novel reading.
In the *Vanderbilt Observer*, Nashville, 1884.

—— The genius of G. W. Cable.
Ibid. 1886.

—— The New South again.
Ibid. 1887.

—— The Gladstone-Ingersoll controversy.
In the *Kentucky New Era*, Hopkinsville, Ky., 1888.

—— In Craddock's Mountains.
Ibid. 1888.

—— Letter from Germany.
In the *Hopkinsville Kentuckian*, 1889.

—— Teutonic antiquities | in the | Anglosaxon Genesis. | A dissertation | presented to the philosophical faculty | of the | University of Leipzig | for the acquisition of the degree of | Doctor of Philosophy | by | C. C. Ferrell, M. A. | Halle, | Ehrhardt Karras, printer | 1893. |
8vo. pp. 52.

—— The strange Child-Neighbors. Translated from the German of Goethe.
In the *University of Mississippi Magazine*, 1893.

—— Old Germanic life in the *Wanderer* and the *Seafarer*.
In *Modern Language Notes*, Baltimore, Md., 1894.

—— Review of the "Veiled Doctor," by Varina Anne Jefferson Davis, 1895.
In the *University of Mississippi Magazine*, 1896.

—— Sappho | Trauerspiel in fünf Aufzügen | von | Franz Grillparzer | Edited with introduction and notes | by | Chiles Clifton Ferrell, Ph. D. (Leipzig) | Professor in the University of Mississippi | Boston, U. S. A. | Ginn & Company, publishers | The Athenæum press | 1899 |
12mo. pp. 176.
College text-book.

—— 'The Daughter of the Confederacy,' her life, character, and writings.
In *Publications Mississippi [State] Historical Society*, 1899, vol. ii, pp. 69–84.

FICTION. *See Mrs.* Ottilie Bertron, H. M. Bien, Sherwood Bonner, Joseph B. Cobb, *Miss* Winnie Davis, Harry Dickson, *Mrs.* Sarah A. Dorsey, *Miss* A. N. Dumond, *Miss* Mary V. Duval, W. C. Falkner, *Rev.* L. S. Foster, John T. Griffith, C. W. Hatson, Ann Hayward, A. B. Longstreet, *Miss* Ellen Martin, E. F. Moody, J. S. Peacocke, Lulah Ragsdale, *Rev.* W. D. Red, Irwin Russell, M. Ozella Shields, and Mary Welsh.

FIELD, THOMAS WARREN (1820–1881). An essay | towards an | Indian bibliography. | Being a | catalogue of books, | relating to the | history, antiquities, languages, customs, religion, | wars, literature, and origin of the | American Indians, | in the library of | Thomas W. Field. | With bibliographical and historical notes, and | synopses of the contents of some of | the works least known. | New York: | Scribner, Armstrong & Co. | 1873. |

 8vo. pp. iv, 430.
 Contains numerous Mississippi titles *passim.* A valuable work; not the least important part being the notes.
 Copies seen: Hamner; Congress.

FISHER, EPHRAIM S. (1845–1876), *Lawyer.* Sketch of.
 In Lynch's *Bench and Bar of Mississippi*, pp. 356–359.

FISHER, RICHARD SWAINSON, *M. D.* A | new and complete | statistical gazetteer | of the | United States of America, | Founded on [–etc., 4 lines.] | By | Richard Swainson Fisher, M. D., | Author [–etc., 3 lines.] New York: | published by J. H. Colton, | No. 86 cedar street. | 1853. |
 8vo. pp. 960.
 Contains sketches of counties and towns.
 Copies seen: Hamner.

FLINT, TIMOTHY. The | history and geography | of the | Mississippi Valley. | To which is appended | a condensed physical geography | of the | Atlantic United States, | and the whole | American continent. | Second edition. | By Timothy Flint, | [–etc., 2 lines.] | [Quotation, 1 line.] | In two volumes [in one]. | Vol. I [–II.] | Cincinnati: | E. H. Flint and L. R. Lincoln. | 1832. |
 8vo. Vol. i, pp. 464; vol. ii, pp. 276.
 Title page of vol. ii is slightly different from above.
 The general observations on the aborigines, population, etc., are interesting and valuable. Much of vol. ii is purely statistical.
 Copies seen: Hamner.

FLORA OF MISSISSIPPI. Description of.
 In Wailes' *Report on Agriculture and Geology of Miss.*, pp. 341–356.
—— *See also* Dr. A. W. Chapman.

FLOURNOY, *Maj. Gen.* THOMAS. Sketch of.
 In Claiborne's *Mississippi*, pp. 318–319, and *note.*
 He was in command of the 7th Military Division during the Creek war.

FOOTE, HENRY STUART (1800–1880), *Lawyer, U. S. Senator from and Governor of Mississippi, Author.* The | bench and bar | of the | South and Southwest. | By Henry S. Foote. | St. Louis: | Soule, Thomas & Wentworth. | 1876. |

 8vo. pp. viii, 264.
 By far the best prepared and most entertaining of all so-called histories of the Bench and Bar.
 Contains sketches of several Mississippians.
 Copies seen: Owen.

FOOTE, HENRY STUART. *Caption:* The war with Mexico. | Speech | of | Hon. Henry S. Foote, of Mississippi, | in the Senate of the United States, January 19 and 20, 1848, | on the bill reported from the Committee on Military Affairs to raise, for a limited time, | an additional military force. | n. p. n. d.
> 8vo. pp. 16. No title page. Double columns.

—— Administration as governor.
> In Lowry and McCardle's *Mississippi*, pp. 322–339.

—— Sketch of.
> In *Representative Men of the South*, pp. 326–328. See also Lynch's *Bench and Bar of Miss.*, pp. 286–288. See also Davis's *Recollections of Mississippi and Mississippians*, p. 310.

FORCE, *Judge* M. F. Campaigns of the Civil War. From Fort Henry to Corinth. New York, 1883.
> 12mo. pp. 204.

FORMAN, *Rev.* A. P., *D. D.* Prophecy. By Rev. A. P. Forman, D. D., of Canton, Miss. 1875.
> No copies seen.

FORMAN, *Maj.* SAMUEL S. Narrative | of a | Journey | down the Ohio and Mississippi | in 1789–90. | By | Maj. Samuel S. Forman | With a memoir and illustrative notes | by | Lyman C. Draper | Cincinnati | Robert Clarke & Co. | 1888. |
> 12mo. pp. 67.
> Gen. David Forman, of New Jersey, in 1789 entered into a negotiation with the Spanish minister, Don Dirgo de Gardoque, for his brother, Ezekiel Forman, of Philadelphia, to emigrate with his family and about sixty colored people—men, women, and children—and settle in the Natchez country, then under Spanish authority. Maj. Samuel S. Forman accompanied this emigrating party, and in this narrative gives a minute account of their trip, the places they passed through and at which they stopped, prominent people they met, with many curious particulars.

FORREST, N. B., *Lieut. Gen., C. S. A.* Campaigns of. *See* Thomas Jordan and J. P. Pryor. *See also* John A. Wyeth.

FORT ADAMS. Sketch of.
> In Claiborne's *Mississippi*, p. 21, and *note*.

FORT PANMURE. *See* Natchez.

FORT ROSALIE. *See* Natchez.

FOSTER FAMILY. Genealogy of.
> In Goodspeed's *Memoirs of Mississippi*, vol. i, pp. 758–761.

FOSTER, *Rev.* L. S. History | of the | Columbus Baptist Association | from 1840 to 1880, | by L. S. Foster. | [Quotation, 9 lines.] | [Design.] | Starkville, Miss.: | "Novelty" Job Printing Office. | 1881. |
> 12mo. pp. 132. *Portrait of Author.*
> Contains a full denominational history—organization, religious training, religious activity, religious life, etc.
> Also short biographical sketches of laymen of the past and present, and the ministry of the past and present.
> *Copies seen:* Owen.

—— History | of the | Louisville Baptist Association | from 1840 to 1882. | By L. S. Foster. | [Quotation, 3 lines.] | Jackson, Miss.: | Baptist Record book and job print. | 1886. |
> 8vo. pp. 57 [1].
> Prepared after the same general plan as the *History* of the Columbus Association.
> *Copies seen:* Owen.

FOSTER, *Rev.* L. S. Mississippi | Baptist preachers. | By | L. S. Foster, | pastor of Senatobia Baptist Church, | Senatobia, Mississippi. | St. Louis, Mo.: | National Baptist Publishing Company, | 1895. |
> 12mo. pp. 750. *Profusely illustrated.*
> Contains a short sketch of the introduction of the Baptist Church in the State. There are about four hundred and fifty biographies.
> *Copies seen:* Owen.

—— From | error's chains; | or the | story of the religious struggles | of an | accomplished young lady: | By | L. S. Foster, | Jackson, Mississippi. | [Quotation, 4 lines.] | Jackson, Miss. | Baptist Orphanage press. | 1899. |
> 12mo. pp. c. 400.

—— Sketch of.
> In Foster's *Mississippi Baptist Preachers,* pp. 271-274.

FRANKLIN ACADEMY. Sketch of.
> In Mayes' *History of Education in Mississippi,* pp. 72-79.

FRANKLIN COUNTY. Sketch of.
> In Lowry and McCardle's *Mississippi,* pp. 476-477.
> *See also* Goodspeed's *Memoirs of Mississippi,* vol. i, pp. 184-186.

FRANKLIN, FREEMAN E. Eulogies on death of.
> In Appendix to *Journal* of the Senate of Mississippi, pp. 388-401. *See* State Offices

FRANTZ, *Mrs.* VIRGINIA, J. Ina Greenwood, and other poems. 1877.
> No copies seen.

FREEMAN, *Gen.* JOHN D., *Lawyer.* Sketch of.
> In Claiborne's *Mississippi,* pp. 388-389, *notes.*

FREEMAN, THOMAS (d. 1821), *Surveyor-General Mississippi.* Sketch of.
> In Claiborne's *Mississippi,* p. 207, *note.*

FREEMANTLE, *Col.* Three Months | in | the Southern States: | April, June, 1863. | By | Lieut. Col. Freemantle, | Coldstream Guards. | Mobile. S. H. Goetzel. | 1864. |
> 8vo. pp. 158.
> Wall-paper covers.
> The author was an Englishman who made a trip through the Confederacy, and recorded his observations in diary form.

FRENCH, BENJAMIN FRANKLIN (1799–1877), *Author.*
> Not all of the documents and papers in these seven volumes relate, by any means, to all of Mississippi. The full contents of each part are given from the important character of the collection and for the sake of a complete presentation. The special papers relating to the field covered by this bibliography can be readily distinguished.
> "Mr. French was a pioneer in a class of work the value of which has come to be fully appreciated. His *Collections* close a gap on the shelves of many libraries which it would be difficult otherwise to fill. The work was necessarily an education to him, and in some instances new material which came to his hands revealed errors in previous annotations. The value of the work would have been increased if abridgments and omissions had been noted. . . . The labors of Mr. French, as a whole, have been of great service to students of American history."— Winsor's *Narrative and Critical History of America,* vol. v.

FRENCH, BENJAMIN FRANKLIN. Historical collections | of | Louisiana, | embracing | many rare and valuable documents | relating to the | natural, civil and political | history of that State. | Compiled with | historical and biographical notes, | and an | introduction, | by | B. F. French, | honorary member [-etc., 2 lines]. | Part I. | Historical documents from 1678 to 1691. | New York: | Wiley and Putnam. | 1846. |

    8vo. Part i., pp. ix. 1 l. 222.

    Contents: Discourse before the Historical Society of Louisiana, by Henry A. Bullard, president, pp. 1-23; Memoir of Robert Cavalier de la Salle on necessity of fitting out expedition to take possession of Louisiana, pp. 25-34. Letters patent to La Salle, pp. 35-36. Memoir of La Salle reporting to Monseigneur de Seigrelay the discoveries made by him, pp. 37-44. Account (Procès verbal) of the taking possession of Louisiana by La Salle, pp. 45-50; Will of La Salle, p. 51. Memoir sent in 1693 on discovery of the Mississippi, and the neighboring nations, by La Salle from 1678 to the time of his death, and by Sieur de Tonty to the year 1691, pp. 52-78; Chevalier de Tonty's petition to the King, pp. 79-81. Chevalier de Tonty's account of the route from the Illinois by the River Mississippi to the Gulf of Mexico, pp. 82-83; Joutel's historical journal of La Salle's last voyage to discover the river Mississippi, pp. 85-193; Account of discovery of river Mississippi and adjacent country, by Father Louis Hennepin, pp. 195-214; Account of La Salle's undertaking to discover the river Mississippi by way of the Gulf of Mexico, by Father Louis Hennepin, pp. 214-222.

    Copies seen: Hamner; Congress; Owen.

—— Historical collections | of | Louisiana, | embracing translations of | many rare and valuable documents | relating to the | natural, civil and political | history of that State. | Compiled with | historical and biographical notes, | and an | introduction, | by | B. F. French, | member [-etc., 4 lines]. | Part II. | Philadelphia: | Daniels and Smith. | [-etc., 2 lines.] | 1850. |

    8vo. pp. vi, 1 l. 301. *Facsimile* of Delisle's "Carte de la Louisiane et du cours du Mississipi.

    A second edition of this part was also published in 1850.

    Contents: Account of Louisiana Historical Society, by James Dunwoody-Brownson De Bow, pp. 1-16; Discourse on life, character, and writings of Francois Xavier Martin, by Henry A. Bullard, pp. 17-40; Analytical index of the whole of the public documents relative to Louisiana in the archives of the department "De la Marine et des Colonies" et "Bibliotheque du Roi ' at Paris, by Edmund J. Forstall, pp. 41-87, Translation of an original letter of Hernando de Soto on the conquest of Florida [dated July 9, 1539, "port of Saint Esprit, in the province of Florida"], pp. 89-93; Translation of a recently discovered manuscript journal of the expedition of Hernando de Soto into Florida, by Luis Hernandez de Biedma, pp. 95-109; Narrative of the expedition of Hernando de Soto into Florida, by a Gentleman of Elvas, translated from the Portuguese by Richard Hackluyt, in 1609, pp. 111-220; Description of the English province of Carolana, by the Spaniards called Florida, and by the French Louisiane. As also of the great and famous river Meschacebe, or Mississippi, the five vast navigable lakes of fresh water, and the parts adjacent. With an account of the commodities of the growth and production of the said province, by Daniel Coxe (omitting the preface and appendix), pp. 221-276; Translation of Marquett and Joliet's account of a voyage to discover the Mississippi River, in 1673, pp. 279-297; Table of distances, elevation, and latitude of the Mississippi and Missouri rivers, pp. 298-301.

    Copies seen: Hamner; Congress; Owen.

FRENCH, BENJAMIN FRANKLIN. Historical collections | of | Louisiana, | embracing translations of | many rare and valuable documents | relating to the | natural, civil and political | history of that State. | Compiled with | historical and biographical notes, | and an | introduction, | by | B. F. French, | member [–etc., 5 lines.] | Part III. | New-York: | D. Appleton & Company, | [–etc., 1 line.] | 1851. |

    8vo. Title, 1 leaf. pp. 252 *Facsimiles* of autographs of La Harpe, 1721; Frontenac, 1673; Law, 1717; LePage, 1719; DeVergennes; Perier, 1731; and O'Reilly.

    Contents Memoir of H. A. Bullard president of the Louisiana Historical Society, pp. 5-8; Translation of Bernard de la Harpe's Historical Journal of the Establishment of the French in Louisiana, pp. 9-118. The editor has given full notes to the journal on the following: Marquette; Joliet; Iberville; Bienville; Saint Denys, Le Sueur; Tonty; Crozat; Law; Marigny; translation of letters patent granted M. Crozat; translation of letters patent granted to the Western Company; an account of the Indian tribes of Louisiana, translation of Bienville's correspondence with Don Martin d'Allarconne and Father Marcillo; account of the grants or concessions of land in Louisiana; treaty of the Company of the Indies with the Ursuline nuns; description of the military fortifications and posts in Louisiana; translation of the Black Code of Louisiana; rules and regulations for the government of the colony of Louisiana; memoir on the importance of colonizing Louisiana; Translation of the Historical Journal of Father Pierre Francois Xavier de Charlevoix, pp. 119-196. There are, besides biographical notes, the following extended historical notes: Account of the manners and customs of the Arkansas, Choctaws, Chicachas, Cherokee, and Creek Indians; account of the antiquity, manners, and customs of the Natchez Indians; account of the massacre of the French by the Natchez Indians; account of the first inhabitants of New Orleans; account of the Belize and mouths of the Mississippi; Letter on the settlement of the first colony of Huguenots in New France (Florida), 1562, pp 197-202, Account of Jean Ribaut's last expedition, and fate of the French colony in New France, 1565, pp. 203-222; Historical Journal of M. de Sauvole, 1699-1701, pp. 223-240, Memoir of M. de Richebourg on the first Natchez war, pp. 241-252.

    Copies seen: Hamner, Congress; Owen.

—— Historical collections | of | Louisiana, | embracing translations of | many rare and valuable documents | relating to the | natural, civil, and political | history of that State. | Compiled with | historical and biographical notes, | and an | introduction, | by | B. F. French, | member [–etc., 5 lines.] | Part IV. | Redfield, | Clinton hall, New York. | 1852. |

    8vo. pp. lxxx. 267 [1]. *Facsimile* of the autograph map of the Mississippi or Conception River, drawn by Father Marquette at the time of his voyage. Also *facsimile* of letter of Alloucz.

    This part has also been issued in a separate edition, with the following title page, but otherwise identical with the foregoing, viz:

—— Discovery and exploration | of the | Mississippi Valley: | with | the original narratives of Marquette, | Allouez, Membré, Hennepin, and | Anastase Douay. | By | John Gilmary Shea. | With a facsimile of the newly-discovered map of Marquette. | [Design.] | Redfield, | Clinton hall, New York. | 1852. |

    8vo. pp. lxxx. 267 [1].

    This part is the work of John Gilmary Shea. The annotations, which are numerous, are of the highest character and value.

    Contains the following original material: Relation of the voyages, discoveries, and death of Father James Marquette, pp. 1-66 (Pp. 231-257 contain same in French); Narrative of a voyage made to the Illinois, by Father Claude Allouez, pp. 67-77; Narrative of the first attempt by M. Cavelier de la Salle to explore the

Mississippi, by Father Le Clercq, pp. 83-97; Narrative of the voyage to the upper Mississippi, by Father Louis Hennepin, from his "Description de La Louisiane," printed at Paris, 1683, pp. 107-145; Narrative of the adventures of La Salle's party, from Feb. 1680, to June 1681, by Father Zenobius Membré, pp. 147-163; Narrative of La Salle's voyage down the Mississippi, by Father Membré, pp. 165-184; Account of La Salle's attempt to reach the Mississippi by sea, and of the establishment of a French colony in St. Louis Bay, by Father Christian Le Clercq, pp. 185-196; Narrative of La Salle's attempt to ascend the Mississippi in 1687, by Father Anastasius Douay, pp. 197-229; Unfinished letter of Father Marquette to Father Claude Dablon, containing journal of his last visit to the Illinois, pp. 258-264; La Salle's patent of nobility, pp. 265-266; La Salle's second commission, pp. 267+.

Contains the following extended notes: History of the discovery of the Mississippi valley, pp. vii-xxxix; Life of Father James Marquette, of the Society of Jesus, first explorer of the Mississippi, pp. xli-lxxviii; Notice of Sieur Joliet, pp. lxxix-lxxx; Notice of Father Claudius Dablon, p. 2; Notice of Father Claude Allouez, pp. 67-70; Bibliographical notice of the "Establissement de la Foi," of Father Christian Le Clercq, Recollect, pp. 78-82; Notice of La Salle, pp. 83-84; Bibliographical notice of the works of Father Louis Hennepin, pp. 99-106; Notice of Father Zenobius Membré, pp. 147-148.

Copies seen: Hamner; Congress; Owen.

FRENCH, BENJAMIN FRANKLIN. Historical memoirs | of | Louisiana, | from the first settlement of the colony to the | departure of Governor O'Reilly in 1770, | with | historical and biographical notes, | forming the fifth of the series of historical collections of Louisiana | by | B. F. French, | member | [-etc., 5 lines.] | New-York: | Lamport, Blakeman & Law, | No. 8 Park-place | 1853. |

8vo. pp. vii, 291. *Steel portrait* of Bienville, engraved from a copy belonging to J. D. B. DeBow, of an original painting in the family of Baron Grant, of Longueil in Canada.

Contents: History of Louisiana, translated from the Historical memoirs of M. Dumont, pp. 1-125; Memoir of the Present State of Louisiana, by Chevalier de Champigny, translated from the French, pp. 127-233.

Appendix: Preliminary convention between the kings of France and Spain, for the cession of Louisiana to the latter, Nov. 3, 1762, pp. 235-236; Definite act of cession by the King of France to the King of Spain, Nov. 23, 1762, pp. 236-239; Seventh article of the definite treaty of peace between kings of France, Spain and England, signed at Paris, Feb. 10, 1763, pp. 239-240; Note respecting the transfer of Louisiana from the French minister to the Spanish ambassador, April 21, 1764, pp. 240; Commission of Don Louis de Unzaga y Amezaga, as military and political governor of the city, New Orleans and province Louisiana, Aug. 17, 1772, pp. 240-243; Commission of Don Bernardo de Galvez, as same, May 8, 1779, pp. 243-245; Dispatch respecting granting lands from Marquis de Grimaldi to Don Louis Unzaga, Aug. 24, 1770, pp. 245-246; Loyal order respecting the government of the province to Don Pedro Garcia, Mayoral, Jan. 28, 1771, pp. 246-247; Report to the King of Spain by the Council and Chamber of the Indies, Feb. 27, 1772, on Lieutenant-General Don Alexander O'Reilly's statements, Feb. 27, 1772, pp. 248-253; Ordinances and instructions of Don Alexander O'Reilly [Full body of laws and regulations], pp. 254-291.

Copies seen: Hamner; Congress; Owen.

—— Historical collections | of | Louisiana and Florida, | including | translations of original manuscripts relating to their | discovery and settlement, | with numerous | historical and biographical notes. | By B. F. French, | Member [-etc., 2 lines.] | New series. | New York: | J. Sabin & Sons, 84 Nassau street. | 1869. |

8vo. 3 prel. leaves. pp. 362.

Contents: Rémonville's Memoir to Count de Pontchartrain, on the importance of establishing a colony in Louisiana, pp. 1-16; Le Moyne d'Iberville's Narrative of his Voyage to La., 1698, pp. 17-81: Penicaut's Annals of La., 1698-1722, pp. 83-162. Réne Laudonnière's History of First Attempt of the French to colonize Florida. pp. 165-175. Réne Laudonnière's History of Jean Ribault's First Voyage to Florida pp 177-362.

Copies seen: Hamner. Congress: Owen.

FRENCH, BENJAMIN FRANKLIN. Historical collections | of | Louisiana and Florida, | including | translations of original manuscripts relating to their | discovery and settletlement, | with numerous | historical and biographical notes. | By B. F. French, Member [–etc., 2 lines.] | Second series. | Historical memoirs and narratives, 1527-1702. | New York: | Albert Mason, publisher. | 1875. |

8vo. pp. xvii 300.
Contains the following original material:

Louisiana.

Memoir of La Salle, addressed to Monsigneur de Seignelay, translated from the French, with notes, pp. 1-15. Official account of La Salle's exploration of the Mississippi (Colbert) River to its mouth, 1682, translated from the French, with note, pp. 17-27: Narrative of the expeditions made by order of Louis XIV, King of France, to colonize Louisiana, under command of Le Moyne d'Iberville, 1698, with an account of explorations of the Mississippi River, physical features of the country, and manners and customs of the Indian tribes he visited, translated from the French, and now first printed, pp. 29-121; Extract [in note] of a letter to Father Jean de Lamberville by Father Jacques Gravier, who descended the Mississippi River to meet M. d'Iberville on his arrival to take possession of Louisiana, pp. 79-93; Memoir (Procès verbal) of the taking possession of the country of the Upper Mississippi in the name of the King of France, 1689, p. 122; Historical memoir sent by Louis XIV, King of France, to M. de Denonville, Governor-General of New France, 1668, translated from the French, with notes, pp. 123-142.

Florida.

Letter [in note] from Christopher Columbus to Luis de Santangel on his first discoveries 1493, pp. 145-152; Proclamation of Pamfilo de Narvaez, Governor-General, to the inhabitants (Indians) of Florida, pp. 153-158; Extract [in note] from the memoir of De las Casas on the barbarous treatment of the Indians of Florida by the Spaniards, pp. 156-158: Narrative of the first voyage of Jean de Ribault, made in the reign of Charles IX, King of France, under the orders of Gaspard de Coligny, to make discoveries and found a colony of French Protestants (Huguenots) in Florida, 1562, pp. 159-190; Memoir, by Francisco Lopez de Mendoza Grojales, of the Spanish expedition by order of Philip II, in 1565, under command of Don Pedro Menendez de Aviles, to take possession of and colonize the eastern coast of Florida, and to expel the French Protestants (Huguenots) established there in 1564, translated from the French, pp. 191-234: Narrative [in note] by Don Salis de las Meras brother-in-law of Menendez, of the massacre of the shipwrecked French colonists, officers and men of the expedition sent out under the command of Captain Ribault in 1565 to reinforce the colony, translated from Barcia, "Ensayo chronologico para la Historia General de la Florida" (Madrid, 1723), pp. 216-222; Letter [in note] from Pope Pius V to Don Pedro Menendez de Aviles on the expulsion of the French colonists, in 1565, from Florida, on his return to Spain, pp. 222-223. Memoir of Hernando d'Escalante Fontanedo, on the country and ancient Indian tribes of Florida, translated from Ternaux Compan's French translation from the original memoir in Spanish, pp. 235-265; Extract [in note] from the narratives of Guido de las Bazares and Don Angel de la Villafane, describing the bays and ports of the east and west coasts of Florida, translated from the French translation of the original memoirs, 1559, pp. 236-242, La reprinse de la Floride, par Cappitaine Gourgues, pp. 265-289. Memoria de Joan de la Vandera en que se hace relacion de los lugares y tiera de la Florida por donde el capitan Juan Pardo entró á descubrir camino paro Nueva Espana por los Anos de 1566-1567, pp. 289-292; Carta en que se da noticia de un viaje hecho a la bahia de Espiritu Santo, Tejas; y de la poblacion que tenian ahi los Franceses, 1689, pp. 293-295.

Contains the following *extended* notes: Biographical sketch of Pierre le Moyne d'Iberville, pp. 31-33; Biographical sketch of Sieur Louis Joliet, pp. 139-141; Introduction to the colonial history of Florida, pp. 145-152; Biographical sketch of Gaspard de Coligny, pp. 159-161; Roman Catholic missions and missionaries in Florida, pp. 229-230; Historical summary and geographical account of the early voyages and explorations of the Gulf of Mexico and the Atlantic coast of Florida, by the French and Spaniards, pp. 242-249; Historical account of works on the Indian languages of Florida and Texas, p. 296.

Copies seen: Hamner; Congress; Owen.

FRUITS. *See* Bulletins of the Agricultural Experiment Station.

FULKERSON, H. S.   Random recollections | of | early days in Mississippi, | by | H. S. Fulkerson. | Price 50 cents in paper cover; $1.00 in cloth. | [Quotation, 3 lines.] | Vicksburg, Miss.: | Vicksburg printing and publishing company. | 1885. |

8vo. pp. 158.
Entertaining and vivid sketches.
Copies seen: Owen.

—— The negro; | as he was; as he is; as he will be. | By H. S. Fulkerson, | author of | early days in Mississippi. | Vicksburg, Miss. | 1887. | Price 50 cents—postage paid. | Vicksburg, Miss.: | Commercial Herald, printers. | 1887. |

8vo. pp. 119.
Copies seen: Owen.

FULTON, JOHN.   Memoirs | of | Frederick A. P. Barnard | D. D., LL. D., L. H. D., D. C. L. | tenth president of Columbia College in the city of New York | By | John Fulton | [Design.] | New York | Published for the Columbia University press by | Macmillan and Co. | New York and London | 1896 | All rights reserved. |

8vo. pp. xii, 485. *2 portraits:* one in 1848 while he was in the University of Alabama, and one in 1888 while president of Columbia College, New York.
Contains full account of his life, and connection with the University of Alabama, 1838-1854; also of his life and services at the University of Mississippi, 1854-1861.
Copies seen: Congress.

FULTON, ROBERT BURWELL (1849-), *A. M., LL. D., Professor of Physics and Astronomy, University of Mississippi, since 1875; Chancellor, University of Mississippi, since 1892.*   The article on Mississippi. (State.)

In Encyclopedia Britannica, 9th edition.

—— A Prehistoric Lapidary.

Printed in the *Proceedings* of the American Association for the Advancement of Science, 1889.

—— Memorial to the Congress of the United States from the Board of Trustees of the University of Mississippi (asking for the grant of an additional township of land to the State for the University of Mississippi.)

—— Memorial from the National Association of State Universities in support of the bill (S. 1246) to make an equitable adjustment of the grants of land to the several States of the Union for seminaries of learning or universities.

8vo.
Printed as Senate Document No. 206, 54th Congress, 1st session, 1896.

FULTON, ROBERT BURWELL. Memorial from the Trustees of the University of Mississippi to the Legislature of the State. Jackson, The News Publishing Co., 1899.
8vo.

—— Cooperation between High Schools and Colleges.
Read before the New Orleans meeting of the Southern Educational Association in 1898, and published in the *Proceedings*.

—— Growth of confidence between High Schools and Colleges.
Read before the Los Angeles meeting of the National Educational Association in 1899, and published in the *Proceedings*.

—— A Textile University.
Read before the Memphis meeting of the Southern Educational Association in 1899, and published in the *Proceedings*.

—— Sundry reports to the Board of Trustees of the University of Mississippi since 1892.

—— Pre-historic Jasper ornaments in Mississippi.
In *Publications Mississippi State Historical Society*, 1898, vol. i, pp. 91-95.

—— Origin and location of the University of Mississippi.
Ibid. 1900, vol. iii. (In press.)

FUNGI. *See* Bulletins of the Agricultural Experiment Station.

G.

GAINES, GEORGE STROTHER (1784-1873). Reminiscences of early times in the Mississippi Territory.
In the *Daily Register*, Mobile, Ala. [new series, vol. v], June 19, 27, July 3, 10, and 17, 1872.
Reprinted in part in *Alabama Historical Reporter*, Tuskaloosa, Ala., May, 1884, vol. ii.
Prepared at the suggestion of Hon. Percy Walker, of Mobile, and by him presented to the "Franklin Society," of Mobile. Interesting and valuable, covering the years 1805-1815. The author was a part of all he describes.
Copies seen: Owen.

GALLATIN, ALBERT (1761-1849). A synopsis of the Indian tribes within the United States East of the Rocky Mountains, and in the British and Russian possessions in North America.
In *American Antiquarian Society Transactions* (Archæologia Americana), vol. 2. pp. 1-422. Cambridge, 1836. 8vo.
Copies seen: Hamner.

GALLOWAY, Rev. CHARLES BETTS (1846-) LL. D., D.D., Bishop M. E. Church S. The Methodist Episcopal Church South in Mississippi.
In Goodspeed's *Memoirs of Mississippi*, vol. ii, pp. 362-368.

—— Elizabeth Female Academy—the Mother of Female Colleges.
In *Publications Mississippi [State] Historical Society*, 1899, vol. ii, pp. 169-178.

—— The Story of Blennerhassett.
Ibid. 1900, vol. iii. (In press.)

—— Sketch of.
In Goodspeed's *Memoirs of Mississippi*, vol. i., pp. 773-775; *portrait*.

GAMBRELL, JAMES B. (1841–   ), *D.D.* Sketch of.
　In Foster's *Mississippi Baptist Preachers*, pp. 235-294, *portrait*.

GANNETT, HENRY. Boundaries | of | the United States | and of the | several States and Territories, | with a | historical sketch of the territorial changes, | by | Henry Gannett | chief topographer. | [Vignette.] | Washington. | Government Printing Office. | 1885. |
　8vo. pp. 135.
　Bulletin No. 13, U. S. Geological Survey.
　Mississippi, pp. 103-104.
　Copies seen: Owen.

—— A | dictionary of altitudes | in | the United States. | Second edition. | Compiled by | Henry Gannett | chief topographer. | [Vignette.] | Washington. | Government Printing Office. | 1891. |
　8vo. p. 393.
　Bulletin No. 76, U. S. Geological Survey.
　Contains altitudes of various sections of Mississippi.
　Copies seen: Owen.

GARNER, *Prof.* JAMES W. The Revolution of 1875.
　In *Publications Mississippi State Historical Society*, 1900, vol. iii. (In press.)

GARRETT, W. R., *A. M.* Tennessee Historical Society Papers. | History | of the | South Carolina Cession | and the | Northern boundary of Tennessee. | By W. R. Garrett, A. M. | Nashville, Tenn. : | Southern Methodist publishing house. | 1884. |
　8 vo. pp. 32. *1 map.*
　Bibliography, p. 32.
　"South Carolina Cession," read before the Society, Nov. 8, 1881; and "Northern Boundary of Tennessee," March, 1884.
　First paper treats of Northern boundary of Alabama and Mississippi.
　Copies seen: Owen.

GATHRIGHT, THOMAS S. The responsibilities and obligations of a student's life, in connection with the present political situation. An address delivered before the Philomathean and Herenenian Societies of Mississippi College, June 27, 1871.
　8vo. pp. 20.

GATSCHET, ALBERT SAMUEL (1832–), *Ethnologist.* Brinton's library of | Aboriginal American literature. | Number IV. | A | migration legend | of the | Creek Indians, | with a linguistic, historic and ethnographic | introduction, | by | Albert S. Gatschet, | of the U. S. Bureau of Ethnology, Washington, D. C. | Volume I. | [Greek quotation, 3 lines.] | Philadelphia: | D. G. Brinton. | 1884. |
　8vo. pp. 251.

　Vol. ii was issued with titles as follows:
—— *General title:* A | migration legend | of the | Creek Indians, | texts and glossaries in Creek and Hitchiti, with | a linguistic, historic, and ethnographic | introduction and commentary, | by | Albert S. Gatschet, | of the U. S. Bureau of Ethnology, Washington, D. C. | Volume II. | St. Louis, Mo.: | printed for the author. | 1888. |

GATSCHET, ALBERT SAMUEL. *Special title:* Tchikilli's Kasi'hta legend | in the | Creek and Hitchiti languages, | with a | critical commentary and full glossaries to both texts, | by | Albert S. Gatschet, | of the U. S. Bureau of Ethnology, Washington, D. C. | [Greek quotation, 3 lines.] | Copyrighted. 1888. All rights reserved. | St. Louis, Mo. | Printed by R. P. Studley & Co. | 1888. |

    8vo. pp. 207. Accompanied by two maps: 1. Town map of the old Creek Country; and 2. The linguistic families of the Gulf States, both of which are, however, to be referred to vol. 1.

    Copies seen: Owen.

GAYOSO DE LEMOS, *Gov.* DON MANUEL. Administration of.

    In Claiborne's *Mississippi*, pp. 135-201. *Portrait* facing p. 134.

GAZETTEERS. *See* T. and T. J. Baldwin, S. R. Brown, Wm. Darby, Bishop Davenport, R. S. Fisher, Timothy Flint, John Hayward, John Melish, *Rev.* J. Morse, Robert Sears, J. E. Worcester.

GENEALOGY.

Barksdale family.	*See* E. Barksdale.
Dabney family.	Susan D. Smedes.
Foster family.	that title.
Grayson family.	Spence M. Grayson.
Humphreys family.	that title.
Kelly family.	Thomas M. Owen.
Ker family.	David Ker.
Lacey family.	Thomas M. Owen.
Lewis family.	W. T. Lewis.
McWillie family.	Wm. McWillie.
Robert family.	that title.
Routh family.	that title.
Waddel family.	Jno. N. Waddel.
Weatherford family.	J. D. Dreisback.
Webb family.	Robt. D. Webb.
Welsh family.	Mary Welsh.

GENERAL ASSEMBLY. Concise sketch of debates and proceedings of House of Representatives, Mississippi Territory, fifteenth September, 1808. *See* George Davis.

—— Discussion of the legality of the extra session of January, 1835, with the Report of the Committee of the Senate, John Henderson, *chairman*, and the protest of Stephen Cocke.

    In Lynch's *Bench and Bar of Mississippi*, pp. 167-174.

—— House of Representatives. Journals, 1818-1898.

    8vo.

—— Senate. Journals, 1818-1898.

    8vo.

    Journals for some of the sessions of the Territorial House of Representatives and Legislative Council, 1801-1816, were published. No complete collection is known to exist, and a list has not been attempted.

GEOGRAPHY AND GEOGRAPHICAL DESCRIPTION. *See* T. and T. J. Baldwin, S. B. Brown, Wm. Darby, Bishop Davenport, R. S. Fisher, Timothy Flint, John Hayward, John Melish, *Rev.* J. Morse, Wm. Roberts, Bernard Romans, Walter B. Scaife, Robert Sears, C. F. Volney, and J. E. Worcester.

GEOLOGICAL MAPS. *See* Maps.

GEOLOGICAL SURVEY. Report on the agriculture and geology of Mississippi. 1854. *See* B. L. C. Wailes.

—— Preliminary report on the geology and agriculture of Mississippi. 1857. *See* L. Harper.

—— Report on the geology and agriculture of Mississippi. 1860. *See* E. W. Hilgard.

—— Sketch of.
In Mayes' *History of Education in Mississippi*, pp. 213-226.

—— *See also* T. M. Aldrich, Jno. L. Campbell, T. A. Conrad, G. W. Featherstonhaugh, D. W. Langdon, Otto Myer, and E. A. Smith.

GEOLOGIST, THE STATE. *See* L. Harper, E. W. Hilgard, E. A. Smith, and B. L. C. Wailes. *See also* Geological Survey.

GEORGE, JAMES ZACHARIAH (1826-1898), *Sawyer, U. S. Sen. from Miss.* A digest | of the | reports of the decisions of the Supreme Court | and of the | High Court of Errors and Appeals, | of the | State of Mississippi, | from the organization of the State, to the present time. | By James Z. George, esq., late reporter of the High Court of Errors and Appeals. | Philadelphia: | T. & J. W. Johnson & Co., | [- etc., 2 lines.] | 1872. |
8vo. pp. [4]. 966.
Dedicated to Francis Marion Aldridge, esq., "'a profound lawyer,' 'who fell at the battle of Shiloh.'"
The title, "Limitation of Estates," was prepared by Judge A. M. Clayton, and the title, "Criminal Law," was prepared by W. R. Barksdale, esq.
Contains Table of Cases.

—— Relations between the Senate and | Executive Departments. | Speech | of | Hon. J. Z. George, | of Mississippi, | in the | Senate of the United States, | March 23, 1886. | Washington. | 1886. |
8vo. pp. 33.
Copies seen: Owen.

—— Letters | of | Hon. J. Z. George | on the | legal obligations and indebtedness of the State | to the | Agricultural and Mechanical College, | Alcorn University and Industrial Female Institute. | The origin and object | of the | Agricultural Land Scrip Fund. | Jackson, Miss.: | Clarion Steam printing establishment. | 1887. |
8vo. pp. 20.
Copies seen: Owen.

—— The Federal election bill. | Speech | of | Hon. J. Z. George, | of Mississippi, | in the | Senate of the United States, | December 10, 1890. | Washington. | 1890. |
8vo. pp. 50.

—— *Reporter.* Mississippi Reports, vols. 30-39. *See* Supreme Court.

—— Memorial addresses | on the | life and character | of | James Z. George | (late a Senator from Mississippi), | delivered in the | Senate and House of Representatives, | Fifty-fifth Congress, | second session. | Washington: | Government printing office. | 1898. |
8vo. pp. 137. *Portrait.*

—— Character sketch of. *See* Dunbar Rowland.

GEORGIA LAND CLAIMS. *Half title:* An address and remonstrance of the Legislature of the State of Georgia. [1801] (Ex. Doc., 6 Cong., 2d sess.)
8vo. pp. 18.
Relates to the controversy over Georgia's claim to the domain included in Miss. Territory.

—— Message from the President of the United States, accompanying certain articles of agreement and cession, which have been entered into and signed by the Commissioners of the United States, and the Commissioners of the State of Georgia. [Th. Jefferson.] April 26, 1802. (Ex. Doc., 6th Cong., 1st sess).
8vo. pp. 11.
No. 69, American State Papers: *Public Lands*, Vol. I, p. 125.
Contains message; letter of transmittal by the Commissioners; and the articles, etc.

GEORGIA MISSISSIPPI COMPANY. Grant | to the | Georgia Mississippi Company, | the | Constitution | thereof, | and | extracts relative to the situation, soil, | climate, and navigation of the western | territory of the State of Georgia; | and particularly of that part | thereof in which the compa- | ny's lands are situated. | Published by order of the directo[rs.] | Augusta: | printed by John Erdman Smith. | MDCCXCV. | And reprinted with an appendix, by desire | of the purchasers in Connecticut. | n. p. [1796.]
12mo. pp. 39.
Contents: Title, 1 leaf; Grant, pp. 3-6; Constitution of the company, pp. 7-16; Extracts from Thos. Hutchins' narrative of 1784, pp. 17-24; Appendix, by Jos. Purcell, pp. 25-29; Correspondence and papers as to the Spanish claim to territory purchased by the company, pp. 31-39.

GEORGIA PACIFIC RAILWAY. Charter rights | of | The Georgia Pacific | Railway Company. | Compiled by | Bernard Peyton, | of the | Richmond & Danville Extension Co. | 1882. | Dodson & Scott, printers, Atlanta, Ga. |
8vo. pp. 106.

—— Consolidation | of the | Georgia Pacific Railroad Company | (of Georgia), | The Georgia Pacific Railroad Company | (of Alabama), | The | Elyton & Aberdeen Railroad Company, | The | Columbus, Fayette and Decatur | Railroad Company, | and the | Greenville, Columbus and Birmingham | Railroad Company, | into | The Georgia Pacific Railway Company. | Compiled by | Bernard Peyton. | 1882. |
8vo. pp. 52, 1 l.

GEORGIA WESTERN COUNTRY. Acts of the State [Georgia], Dec. 1794, and Jan. 1795, for the sale of vacant and unappropriated lands, etc. n. d. [Augusta.]
4to. pp. 10.
Brinley, Part II, No. 3930.

—— Land laws of Georgia. Augusta, 1794.
4to. pp. 80.
Brinley, Part II, No. 3930.
This copy has "15 pages of manuscript additions, severally certified by the Secretary of State."

GEORGIA WESTERN COUNTRY. Report of U. S. Senate committee on the South Western Territory. 1798.
> 8vo. pp. —.
> Brinley, Part II, No. 3930.

—— ANDERSON, J. C., and HOBBY, WM. J.: The contract for the purchase of the Western Territory, made in 1795, considered. Augusta, 1799.
> 4to. pp. 98.
> Brinley, Part II, No. 3930.

—— Report | of | the commissioners [James Madison, Albert Gallatin, and Levi Lincoln] | appointed in pursuance | of | an act | for the | amicable settlement [of limits] | with the | State of Georgia | and | authorizing the esta[blishment] | of a Government | in the | Mississippi Territory. | Deposited in the executive office by [—] | senators in Congress. | Republished by order of the legislature [of]Georgia. | Savannah, | printed by Lyon & Morse. | 1803. |
> 8vo. pp. 25, 95.
> Contents: Title, 1 leaf; Report, pp. 3-25; Documents accompanying report, pp. 1-95.

—— Act of Feb., 1796, declaring null and void the act of January, 1795, appropriating the unlocated Territory. n. p. n. d.
> 4to. pp. 6.
> Brinley, Part II, No. 3930.

—— Description of the Georgia Western Territory; with a *map*. Boston, 1797.
> 8vo. pp. 24.
> Brinley, Part II, No. 3930.

—— The | case | of the | Georgia sales on the Mississippi | considered. | With a reference | to law authorities and public acts, | and an | appendix, | containing certain extracts, records, and official papers. | Phila.: | printed for Benjamin Davies, No. 68, | High-street. | 1797. |
> 8vo. pp. 109.
> Contents: Title, 1 leaf; Advertisement, 1 p.; Case considered. pp. 1-58; Appendix, Nos. 1-17, pp. 59-109.
> No. 17 is an opinion by Alexander Hamilton that the grant is valid (provided Georgia had a good title before the first act) notwithstanding the act of repeal.

—— Georgia speculation unveiled. Hartford, 1797-98.
> 8vo. pp. 39. Part second, pp. 41-144.
> By Abraham Bishop.
> Brinley, Part II, No. 3930.

—— State of the facts, showing the right of certain companies to lands purchased from the State [Georgia.] n. p. 1795.
> 8vo.
> Brinley, Part II, No. 3930.

—— A | report | of | the Atty. Genl. | [of the U. S. | Charles Lee] | to | to (sic) Congress; | containing, | a collection of charters, | treaties, | and | other documents, | relative to and explanatory of | the title to the land situate in the southwestern parts | of the United States; and claimed by certain companies | under a law of the State of Ga., passed | January 7, 1795. | Printed by order of the Senate of the United States. | Phila.: | printed by John Fenno, | printer to the Senate of the United States, | 1796. |
> 8vo. pp. 171.
> Contents: Title, 1 leaf; Letter of transmittal, p. 3; Reports to Congress, pp. 4-12; Letter from George Chalmers, pp. 13-26; Document, pp. 27-171.

GEORGIA WESTERN COUNTRY. General discussion and explanation.
In Claiborne's *Mississippi*, pp. 92-104.

GHOLSON, SAMUEL JAMESON (1808–1883), *Lawyer, Federal Dist. Judge, M. C. from Miss.* Sketch of.
In Lynch's *Bench and Bar of Mississippi*, pp. 497-500.
Also Goodspeed's *Memoirs of Mississippi*, vol. i, p. 787.

GLADNEY, Rev. RICHARD. The Devil in America. A satire. By Rev. Richard Gladney. Aberdeen, Miss. 1858.
No copy seen.

GLENN, DAVID CHALMERS (1824-186-), *Lawyer.* Sketch of.
In Lynch's *Bench and Bar of Mississippi*, pp. 307-315.

GOODSPEED. Biographical and | historical | memoirs | of | Mississippi. | Embracing an | authentic and comprehensive account of the chief events in | the history of the State, and a record of the | lives of many of the most worthy and | illustrious families and individuals | [Vignette] | In two volumes [vols. I-II.] | Illustrated | Chicago | The Goodspeed publishing company | 1891 |
4to. vol. i, pp. 1270: vol. ii, pp. 1124.
These volumes contain the following chapters:

Volume I.

Chapter i. Topography, natural history and paleontology;
ii. The Indians, their cessions, fortresses and wars;
iii. Exploration and settlement;
iv. Organization and governmental form;
v. The legal and judicial history;
vi. The early wars;
vii. Confederate military history;
viii. Counties of the old Natchez district;
ix. Counties of the first Choctaw cession and the coast addition;
x. Counties of the second Choctaw cession or new purchase of 1820;
xi. Counties of the third (final) Choctaw cession;
xii. Counties of the Chickasaw cession;
xiii-xxv. Biography and family history.

Volume II.

Chapter i. Post-bellum organization;
ii. Later legal and judicial history;
iii. Institutions and societies;
iv. Water transportation, levees;
v. Railway transportation;
vi. Growth and development;
vii. Political history;
viii. Cities, towns and villages;
ix. The press of Mississippi with a cursory glance at the literature of the State;
x. Physicians and their associations;
xi. Educational history;
xii. Religious history of Mississippi;
xiii-xxiv. Biography and family history.

These volumes are a mine of facts embracing every topic of the State's history. Important titles are entered herein under their authors or subjects.

GOODWIN, *Rev.* S. A. Commencement sermon | delivered before the students | of the | University of Columbus, | Sunday, June 26, 1876, | by | S. A. Goodwin, | (pastor of the Baptist Church, Columbus, Miss.) | Subject: | The Excellency of the Knowledge of Christ. | [Vignette.] | Published by the president, | T. C. Belsher, A. M. | [–etc., 2 lines.] | Columbus, Miss.: | printed at the Excelsior Book and Job Office. | 1876. |
>8vo. Cover title only, 1 leaf, pp. 8.
>*Copies seen:* Owen.

GOVERNORS OF MISSISSIPPI. Administrations of.
>In Lowry and McCardle's *Mississippi*, pp. 259–416.

—— Portraits of.
>In Lowry and McCardle's *Mississippi for Schools, passim.*
>*See also* under names of the individual governors herein.

GRAPES. *See* Bulletins of the Agricultural Experiment Station.

GRAVES, RICHARD S., *State treasurer.* Account of the defalcation of.
>In Lowry and McCardle's *Mississippi*, pp. 299–308.

GRAYSON, SPENCE MONROE (1803–1839). *Lawyer.* Sketch of.
>Lynch's *Bench and Bar of Mississippi*, p. 132.
>For sketch of the Grayson family, *see* Claiborne's *Mississippi*, pp. 259, note.

GRAYSON, W. S. The ruler and the ruled. The right of human rule—the authority of civil governments.
>In De Bow's *Review*, Aug., 1860, pp. 168–175.

GREENE COUNTY. Sketch of.
>In Lowry and McCardle's *Mississippi*, pp. 478–479.
>*See also* Goodspeed's *Memoirs of Mississippi*, vol. i, pp. 189–190.

GREENE, FRANCIS V. Campaigns of the Civil War. The Mississippi. New York, 1883.
>12mo. pp. 276.

GREEN, *Col.* THOMAS MARSTON, *Miss. Territorial Delegate.* Sketch of.
>In Claiborne's *Mississippi*, p. 228, and *note.*
>*See also* Dr. Alexander Brown's *Cabells and their Kin.* (1897.)

GREENVILLE. Sketch of.
>In Goodspeed's *Memoirs of Mississippi*, vol. ii, pp. 168–171.

GRENADA. Some facts relating to early history of. *See* Capt. L. Lake.

GRENADA COLLEGIATE INSTITUTE. Sketch of.
>In Mayes' *History of Education in Mississippi*, pp. 97–99.

GRENADA COUNTY. Sketch of.
>In Lowry and McCardle's *Mississippi*, pp. 479–80.

GRIFFITH, JOHN T. The fawn's leap. A novel.
>No copies seen.

GRIFFITH, WILLIAM B. (–1829), *Lawyer.* Sketch of.
>In Lynch's *Bench and Bar of Mississippi*, pp. 112–113.

—— Oration delivered on the Fourth of July, 1819, at Natchez, Miss.
>*Ibid.* pp. 113–126.

GUION, *Capt.* ISAAC. Sketch of.
>In Claiborne's *Mississippi*, p. 186.
>He was one of the public men in the early days of Mississippi, coming to the Territory in the Army.

GUION, JOHN ISAAC (1802-1858), *Lawyer, Gov. of Miss.* Sketch of.
    In Lynch's *Bench and Bar of Mississippi*, pp. 245-247.

—— Administration as governor.
    In Lowry and McCardle's *Mississippi*, p. 321.

GULLY, *Prof.* F. A. The elementary principles of agriculture.
    No copies seen.

GWIN, WILLIAM MCKENDREE (1805-1885), *M. C. from Miss., U. S. Sen. from Cal.* Sketch of.
    In Claiborne's *Mississippi*, pp. 427-446; *portrait*.
    See also Appleton's *Cyclopædia of American Biography*, vol. iii, pp. 19-20; *portrait*.

H.

HAINES, T. M. The resurrection of the dead and restitution of all things. By T. M. Haines, a locomotive engineer. 1892.
    8vo. pp. 19.

HALBERT, HENRY SALE (1837-), *Teacher, Indian linguist.* Muscogee battle pits.
    In *American Antiquarian*, Oct., 1881, vol. iv.

—— Muscogee pits and ambushes.
    Ibid. July 1883, vol. v.
    Supplementary to the preceding.

—— The legend of Chicameca's head.
    Ibid. May 1886, vol. viii.

—— A fragment of Shawnee history.
    Ibid. Jan. 1887, vol. ix.
    Traditions of an ancient war of the Choctaws and Shawnees.

—— The Choctaw Achahpi (Chungkee) Game.
    Ibid. Sept. 1888, vol. x.

—— The last of the Apalachees.
    Ibid. May 1891, vol. xiii.

—— Pyramid and old road in Mississippi.
    Ibid. Nov. 1891, vol. xiii.
    Description of the Nanih Waiya and vicinity, so famed in the traditions and folklore of the Choctaws.

—— Okla Hannali, or the Six Towns District of the Choctaws.
    Ibid. May 1893, vol. xv.

—— A Choctaw migration legend.
    Ibid. July 1894, vol. xvi.

—— The Choctaw Robin Goodfellow.
    Ibid. May 1895, vol. xvii.

—— A relic of De Soto's expedition found in Alabama.
    Ibid. Sept. and Oct., vol. xix, pp. 257-259.
    Reprinted in the *West Alabamian*, Carrollton, Ala., Jan. 12, 1898.

—— Courtship and marriage among the Choctaws of Mississippi.
    In *American Naturalist*, March 1882.

—— The vengeance of Olohtie.
    In *Alabama Historical Reporter*, Tuscaloosa, Ala., July, 1884.

HALBERT, HENRY SALE. The visit of Pushmataha to Fort Glass.
Ibid. Jan. 1885.

—— Relics from the Creek Holy Ground in Alabama.
In the *Archæologist*, June 1895, vol. iii.

—— The treaty of Dancing Rabbit Creek.
In *Mississippi School Report*, 1894-95, 1895-96.
He has a fuller and more exhaustive account of this treaty in preparation.

—— The small Indian tribes of Mississippi.
In Lake Como *Educational Journal*, 1897.

—— and BALL, TIMOTHY H. The | Creek War | of | 1813 and 1814. | By | H. S. Halbert and T. H. Ball. | Chicago, Illinois: | Donohue & Henneberry. | Montgomery, Alabama: | White, Woodruff & Fowler. | 1895. |
8vo. pp. 331 [3]. *8 maps; illustrations.*
Portraits of the authors, Isham Kimball, and Jeremiah Austill.
Contents: Chapter I, Choctaw-Muscogee tribes. II, Causes of the Creek War; III, Tecumseh among the Chickasaws and Choctaws; IV, Tecumseh among the Creeks; V, The war cloud gathering; VI, The stockades; VII, Inter-tribal councils of the Creeks and Choctaws, VIII, The battle of Burnt Corn; IX, Fort Mims; X, The Kimball-James massacre; XI, Attack on Fort Sinquefield; XII, The night courier; XIII, Incidents of the war in the Fork; XIV, Choctaws and Chickasaws join the American Army; XV, The Bashi skirmish; XVI, Beard and Tandy Walker; XVII, The canoe fight; XVIII, Battle of the Holy Ground; XIX, The war in the Indian country; XX, Closing events, 1814; Conclusion.
Appendix: 1, The great Mississippi panic; 2, Names from court records; 3, Highhead Jim or Jim Boy; 4, Death of Pushmataha; 5, Christianity and the Creeks; 6, Mrs. A. E. W. Robertson's letters; 7, Old St. Stephens; 8, Indian names; 9, Indian border warfares; 10, Population of the Five Indian Nations; 11, A card of thanks; 12, Historical paper.
"This work does not propose to give in full that part of the conflict waged in the Indian country which broke the power of the fierce Muscogees, but rather that part which has not been as yet so fully given, connected with the white settlers in what is now South Alabama. This portion of our American history, as connected with Indian border warfare, the authors of this work believe will be given more accurately and fully than has ever been done before. They propose to do justice to the Indians and justice to the whites."—*Introduction.*
The work shows much painstaking effort. The citation and discussion, however, of too many *secondary* authorities is carried to excess. The authors are at their best when giving facts at first hand and patiently working out local detail and description.
Copies seen: Owen.

—— Creek War Incidents.
In *Transactions Alabama Historical Society*, 1897-98, vol. ii, pp. 95-119.
The following are the subjects of the several incidents, viz:
1. Capt. Sam Dale.
2. The First blood shed in Clarke County, [Ala.]
3. The Canoe Fight.
4. The Holy Ground.
5. Abandoning the forts.
6. James Cornells.
7. The fate of Seekaboo, the Shawnee Prophet.
8. Creek War Adventure.
9. Creek reconnoissance of Fort Madison.
10. Indian depredations.
11. Pushmataha.

The last named comprises an elaborate biography of this famous Choctaw chief, and corrects numerous errors in current accounts.

In the sketch of Pushmataha will be found an extended description of "Nanih Waiya," the sacred mound of the Choctaws, and a correction of the incident noted by Pickett's *Alabama*, vol. i, p. 124, in reference to this chief and Col. George S. Gaines. Mr. Halbert shows that Nittakechi was the chief who figured in the incident.

HALBERT, HENRY SALE. Choctaw Indian names in Alabama and Mississippi.
: Ibid. 1898-99, vol. iii, pp. 64-77.
: In the list there are twenty-nine Alabama and fifty-nine Mississippi words which comprise the names, of Choctaw derivation, of towns, rivers, and creeks in these States.

—— Some inaccuracies in Claiborne's History [of Mississippi] in regard to Tecumseh.
: In *Publications of the Mississippi State Historical Society*, 1898, vol. i, pp. 101-108.

—— Nanih Waiya, the Sacred Mound of the Choctaws.
: Ibid. 1899, vol. ii, pp. 223-234.

—— Funeral customs of the Choctaws.
: Ibid. 1900, vol. iii. (In press.)

—— An interpretation of Danville's Map of East Mississippi in 1732.
: Ibid.
: Originally published in part in the Mobile *Register*, July 8, 1899.

—— The Indians in Mississippi and their schools.
: In *Report* of Superintendent of Education of Mississippi, 1893-95, pp. 534-541.

—— Choctaw schools in Mississippi.
: Ibid. 1895-97, pp. 23-27.

—— The Indian named counties in Mississippi.
: Ibid. 1895-97, pp. 27-30.
: Derivation suggested, with translation.

—— The Mississippi Choctaws.
: Ibid. 1897-99, pp. 35-38.

HALL, BASIL (1788-1844), *Author*. Travels | in | North America | in the | years 1827 and 1828. | By Captain Basil Hall, | Royal Navy. | In two volumes. | Vol. I. [-II.] | Philadelphia: | Carey, Lea & Carey, | Chestnut street, | 1829. |
: 12 mo. Vol. i, pp. vi, 5-322; vol. ii, pp. iv, 8-339.
: *Copies seen:* Hamner.

HALL, JAMES (1744-1826), *A. M., Presbyterian Clergyman*. A | brief history | of the | Mississippi Territory, | to which is prefixed, | a | summary view of the country | between the settlements on | Cumberland River, | and the Territory. | By James Hall, A. M. | Salisbury: | printed by Francis Coupee. | 1801. | Copyright secured according to law. |
: 24mo. Title, 1 leaf. pp. 70.
: Contents: Summary view of the country from the settlements on Cumberland River to the Mississippi Territory. pp. 1-7; Boundaries of the territory. pp. 7-8; The time of its settlement. pp. 8-9; The massacre of the French. pp. 9-15; Repopulation and revolutions. pp. 15-16; The late and present form of government. pp. 16-19; Propriety of the soil. pp. 19-23; Face of the county. pp. 24-28; Soil and produce. pp. 28-31; Climate. pp. 31-34; Manners, customs, and character. pp. 34-41; Population. pp. 41-42; Trade and commerce. pp. 42-46; Curiosities. pp. 46-60; Hurricanes. pp. 60-66; Appendix. pp. 67-69; Contents and errata. p. 70.

"In May 1800 a commission was transmitted to me by the General Assembly of the Presbyterian Church, convened in Philadelphia, directing me on a mission to the Mississippi Territory. The Synod of the Carolinas commissioned two other missionaries to accompany me on the tour.

"We arrived at Nashville about the middle of the following November, where we intended to take boating for the territory; but the extreme lowness of Cumberland River rendered our passage that way impracticable. We therefore proceeded on horseback by the way of the Chickasaw Nation.

"We arrived at the territory on the first week of December and left it on the third week of April.

"As I have been solicited by sundry persons to publish an account of my travels through that part of the Union, and having my own geographical curiosity highly gratified by traveling through such a vast tract of country, the history of which is little known; presuming that a brief view of the interjacent space between the settlements of Cumberland and the territory, together with a sketch of the history of that territory would afford some gratification to my fellow-citizens, the following pages are with deference submitted to the candor of the public, by their humble servant, the author. Iredell County, N. C., Aug. 25, 1801."—*Preface.*

The first history of the territory. A well-written and interesting work.
Copies seen: Congress.

HAMBERLIN, L. R. Lyrics. By L. R. Hamberlin. 1881.
No copies seen.

HAMILTON, PETER JOSEPH (1859-), *A. M., Lawyer.* Colonial Mobile | an historical study, largely from | original sources, of the Alabama- | Tombigbee Basin from the dis- | covery of Mobile Bay in 1519 | until the demolition of | Fort Charlotte | in 1821. | By | Peter J. Hamilton, A. M. | late fellow of Princeton; author of [-etc., 1 line.] | Illustrated. | [Vignette.] | Boston and New York | Houghton, Mifflin and Company | the Riverside press, Cambridge, | 1897. |
8vo. pp. xii, 1 l, 446. *Maps; illustrations.*
This valuable work contains many references to the history and region now embraced in Mississippi.
Copies seen: Owen.

—— Running Mississippi's south line.
In *Publications Mississippi* [State] *Historical Society,* 1899, vol. ii, pp. 157-168

—— French exploration from Mobile.
In *Transactions Alabama Historical Society,* 1898-99, vol. iii, pp. 80-98.

HAMM, J. S., *Dist. Judge.* Charge | delivered by | Hon. J. S. Hamm, | Judge of the 7th Jud. Dist., Miss., | to the grand jury of Kemper County, | at Sept. Term, 1877, of the Circuit Court. | Published by request of many members of the Bar and other persons. | Meridian, Miss.: | Shannon & Powell, book & job printers. | 1877. |
8vo. Title, 1 leaf, pp. 19.

—— Charge | delivered by | Hon. J. S. Hamm, | Judge of the 7th Jud. Dist., Miss., | to the grand jury of Lauderdale County, | at February term, 1879, of the Circuit Court. | Meridian, Miss.: | Shannon & Powell, book and job printers. | 1879. |
8vo. pp. 28.

HAMMET, WILLIAM H., *M. C. from Miss.* Sketch of.
In Claiborne's *Mississippi,* p. 451, *note.*

HAMPTON, JOHN P., *Lawyer, First Chief Justice of Miss.* Sketch of.
In Lynch's *Bench and Bar of Mississippi,* pp. 81-83.

HANCOCK COUNTY. Sketch of.
> In Lowry and McCardle's *Mississippi*, pp. 480-482.
> See also Goodspeed's *Memoirs of Mississippi*, vol. 1, pp. 191-192.

—— Historical account of. *See* J. F. H. Claiborne.

HANDY, ALEXANDER H. (1809-   ), *Lawyer*. Sketch of.
> In Lynch's *Bench and Bar of Mississippi*, pp. 508-510.

—— Secession considered as a right in the States composing the late American Union of States, and as to the grounds of justification of the Southern States in exercising the right. 1862.
> 8vo.
>
> Title from Lynch, p. 509, who says: "The work is a profound and instructive constitutional argument, which every lawyer should read who seeks a thorough knowledge of the history, character, and interpretation of the Constitution of the United States."

HARDING, LYMAN (-1820), *Lawyer*. Sketch of.
> In Lynch's *Bench and Bar of Mississippi*, pp. 26-27.
> See also Claiborne's *Mississippi*, pp. 359-360.

HARDY, WILLIAM H. The evil tendencies of the age: Moral and religious education the only corrective. An address delivered before the Philomathean and Hermenian Societies of Mississippi College, June 24, 1873.
> 8vo. pp. 15.

HARMON, *Rev.* M. F. The Christian Church in Mississippi.
> In Goodspeed's *Memoirs of Mississippi*, vol. ii, pp. 868-869.

HARPER, L., *LL. D., State Geologist*. Preliminary report | on the | geology and agriculture | of the | State of Mississippi, | by | L. Harper, LL. D., | correspondent of the Imperial Museum for Nat. Science of France, etc. | State Geologist of Mississippi. | By order of the Legislature of Mississippi. | E. Barksdale, State printer, | Jackson. | 1857. |
> 8vo. pp. 350. Errata, 1 leaf. *Geological map; 52 Diagrams;* and 7 *tables*. *Geological maps* of Pontotoc, Tippah, and Tishomingo counties.
> Edition, 5,000 copies.
> See Mayes' *History of Education in Mississippi*, pp. 216-219.

HARPER, *Capt.* W. L. Centennial address, 1876.
> Referred to and quoted in Claiborne's *Mississippi*, p. 227.
> He was of Jefferson County.

HARRIS, BUCKNER C., *Lawyer*. Sketch of.
> In Lynch's *Bench and Bar of Mississippi*, pp. 139-140.

HARRIS, J. BOWMAR, *Lawyer*. A digest | of | Mississippi Railway decisions | from vol. 1 to and including vol. 71 | Mississippi Reports. | Compiled by | J. Bowmar Harris, | attorney at law, | Jackson, Miss. | Press of Clarke & Courts, Galveston. | 1894. |
> 12mo. pp. 191.
> He is also the compiler of the "Ordinances" of Jackson, Miss., 1890; 8vo. pp. 218.

HARRIS, WILEY P. (1818-1891), *Lawyer, M. C. from Miss.* Memorials | of the | life and character | of | Wiley P. Harris, | of | Mississippi. | Jackson, Miss.: | Clarion printing establishment. | 1892. |
> 8vo. pp. 40.
> Contains Remarks at the funeral, by Rev. John Hunter; Proceedings of the Supreme Court of Mississippi, including addresses of Messrs. T. M. Miller, S. S. Calhoon, Frank Johnston, T. J. Wharton, and of Chief Justice Campbell; Tribute, by Bishop C. B. Galloway; and sundry Editorial Tributes.
> *Copies seen:* Owen.

HARRIS, WILEY P. Sketch of.
> In Henry W. Scott's *Distinguished American Lawyers*.
> Also Goodspeed's *Memoirs of Mississippi*, vol. 1, pp. 879-880.

—— Address on the condition of Mississippi under carpet-bag and alien government, delivered in Jackson, Aug. 23, 1875.
> In Lowry and McCardle's *Mississippi*, pp. 392-400.

HARRIS, WILLIAM LITTLETON (1807-1868), *Lawyer*. Sketch of.
> In Lynch's *Bench and Bar of Mississippi*, pp. 342-355.
> This sketch contains a copy of Mr. Harris' address as commissioner to Ga. from Miss., delivered Dec. 15, 1860, before the legislature of the former State.

—— Sharkey and Ellett. *Compilers*. Revised Code of Miss., 1857. *See* Codes of Mississippi.

HARRISON COUNTY. Sketch of.
> In Lowry and McCardle's *Mississippi*, pp. 482-483.

HARRISON, JAMES THOMAS (1811-1879), *Lawyer, Member Conf. Congress*. Sketch of.
> In Lynch's *Bench and Bar of Mississippi*, pp. 377-388; *portrait*.
> *See also* Baldwin's *Flush Times*, etc., for paper entitled "Jim T."; and James M. Arnold.

HARRISON, *Rev*. W. S. Life culture, | a sermon | preached June 20th, 1875, to the faculty and | students of the University of Columbus, in the | M. E. Church, South, Columbus, Miss. | By Rev. W. S. Harrison, pastor. | [Cut of M. E. church.] | Columbus, Miss.: | printed at the the Excelsior Book and Job Office. | 1875. |
> 8vo. pp. 8.
> He is also the author of "Creation; Life; Life-culture, three sermons," 1875; and "Sam Williams, a tale of the Old South," (1892; 12mo. pp. 303.)

HASKINS, *Rev*. W. Atlantis, 1881.
> No copies seen.

HATSON, CHARLES W. The beginnings of civilization. New York, John B. Alden. 1887.
> 12mo.
> He is also the author of "Out of a besieged city," 1887; "The story of Beryl," 1888; and "French literature," 1889.

HAWKINS, BENJAMIN (1754-1816), *Col. in the Revolution, U. S. Sen. from N. C., Indian Agent*. Collections | of the | Georgia Historical Society, Volume III. | Part 1. | [Motto, 1 line.] | Savannah: | printed for the Society. | MDCCCXLVIII. | [New York: William Van Norden printer.]
> 8vo. pp. 88.
> Contents: Introduction; Biographical sketch of Benjamin Hawkins; The Creek confederacy, by W. B. Hodgson; A sketch of the Creek country, in 1798 and 1799. by B. Hawkins.
> Appendix: Indian treaties, 1773-1796.
> No other part of this volume of collections was issued.
> "The author of this treatise [Sketch of the Creek country] was for more than thirty years employed by the Government of the United States in its intercourse with the Indians. He was styled by the Creeks, Choctaws, Chickasaws, and Cherokees the Beloved Man of the Four Nations. He wrote eight volumes of material relating to the history of the various Indian tribes with whom he treated These volumes of MSS. are filled with details of treaties, his correspondence on

behalf of the tribes with the General and State governments, vocabularies of Indian languages, and records of the manners and customs, religious rites, and civil polity of these wonderful aboriginal nations. This treatise is filled with sketches of all these particulars as existing in the Creek nation."—Field's *Indian Bibliography*, p. 162.

HAWKINS, BENJAMIN. [Journal of a tour through the Creek country, November 19th, 1796, to May 21st, 1797.]
> Folio. pp. 250.
> Manuscript.
> The original of which this is a copy is in the *Georgia Historical Society* library. It contains the author's observations upon the country and its inhabitants at that time. Numbers of others of the Hawkins manuscripts also are in this Society's collection. This copy was made for and is owned by Dr. George W. Hamner, of Washington, D. C.

—— Sketch of. *See* Absalom Chappell.

HAYDEN, *Rev.* HORACE EDWIN. A biographical sketch of Hon. Oliver Pollock, United States Commercial Agent at New Orleans and Havana, 1776–1783.
> In *Harrisburg (Pa.) Daily Telegraph*, Nov. 13, 1880.
> *See also* Egles' *Notes and Queries*, Series II, pp. 147–151.
> Mr. Pollock spent his last years in Miss., and died in the State.

HAYWARD, ANN. Emma Stanley. A novel. By Ann Hayward, of Kemper County, Miss. 1842.
> No copy seen.

HAYWARD, JOHN (1781–1862), *Author*. A | gazetteer | of the | United States of America; | comprising | [–etc., 13 lines.] | By John Hayward, | [–etc., 2 lines.] | Hartford, Ct.: | Case, Tiffany, and company. | 1853. |
> 8vo. pp. 861. *Illustrations*.
> *Copies seen:* Hamner.

HAYWOOD, JOHN (1762–1826), *Atty. Gen. of N. C., Judge of Sup. Ct. of N. C., lawyer in Tenn.* The | natural and aboriginal | history | of | Tennessee, | up to the | first settlements therein | by the | white people | in the | year 1768. | By John Haywood | of the County of Davidson, in the State of Tennessee. | Nashville, | printed by George Wilson, | 1823. |
> 8vo. pp. viii, 390, 1 l. [2.]
> "In this book, now exceedingly rare and highly prized, the author has brought together a very large number of curious facts relating to the origin and character of the natives of his State prior to the settlement by the whites. He does not favor the hypothesis of great antiquity in the Indian nations of America, and believes in their common origin with the Caucasian race. He describes with great minuteness and care the relics of the race which once inhabited the territory, its utensils, skeletons, crania, and fortifications, most of which he appears to have personally inspected."—Field's *Indian Bibliography*, p. 162.

—— The | civil and political | history | of the | State of Tennessee | from its | earliest settlement | up to | the year 1796 | including the | boundaries of the State | by John Haywood. | Printed for the author | by Heiskel and Brown | Knoxville, Tenn. | 1823. |
> 8vo. 2 p l. pp. 504.
> "This work, only less rare than the *Aboriginal History of Tennessee* by the same author, contains a large portion of the material relating to the border warfare with the Indians, narrated in the last-mentioned work. The speculative and

antiquarian portions and descriptions of mounds are omitted in this volume, but the story of Indian conflicts and massacres is narrated with greater detail and minuteness, filling much the larger portion of the work. The story of the formation of the State of Franklin, and the civil war which ensued, is a chapter of American history but little known, and scarcely exceeded in interest by any other."—Field's *Indian Bibliography.* p. 163.

HAYWOOD, JOHN. The | Civil and Political History | of the State of Tennessee | from its | earliest settlement up to the year 1796, | including the | boundaries of the State. | By John Haywood. | Exact reprint of the edition of 1823, published by | W. W. Haywood, great-grandson of the author; | with a biographical sketch of Judge John Haywood. | By Col. A. S. Colyar. | Printed for W. H. Haywood. | Publishing House of the Methodist Episcopal Church, South. | Barbee & Smith, agents, Nashville, Tenn. | 1891. |
    8vo. pp. 518.

HEALTH, STATE BOARD OF. Report of Commission to study yellow fever and sanitary conditions in Cuba. n. p. [1898.]
    8vo. pp. 24.
    Made to the Mississippi State Board of Health.

HEBRON, ELLEN E. Songs from the South. By Ellen E. Hebron. Baltimore, Eugene R. Smith. 1875.
    16mo. pp. 245.

—— Faith, or earthly paradise; and other poems. Chicago. 1890.
    12mo. pp. 28.

HEIDELBERG, DANIEL W., *Lawyer.* A digest | of | Mississippi Reports, | from Vol. 45 to 64 inclusive, | being a digest of all the Mississippi reports not embraced in George's Digest. | By Daniel W. Heidelberg. | Albany, N. Y.: | Weed, Parsons and Co., printers. | 1888. |
    8vo. pp. [4], 743.

HENDERSON, JOHN (1795-1857), *Lawyer, U. S. Senator from Miss.* Sketch of.
    In Lynch's *Bench and Bar of Mississippi,* pp. 145-146.
    He is also the author of "A reply to Tom Paine." (Natchez, 1820.)

HENDERSON, Miss J. P. Annie Balfour. Richmond, Va. Pres. Com. of Publication. 1870.
    12mo.

HENDERSON, JOHN W. A competitive essay on The Sabbath. New Orleans, 1877.
    12mo.

HENDERSON, *Mrs.* LIZZIE GEORGE, *Pres. U. D. C.* Private letters of Mrs. Humphreys, written immediately before and after the ejection of her husband from the Executive Mansion.
    In *Publications Mississippi State Historical Society,* 1900, vol. iii. (In press.)

HERSEY, *Rev.* JOHN. Sketch of. *See Rev.* F. E. Marine.

HILGARD, EUGENE WOLDEMAR (1833-), *Ph. D., Chemist, State Geologist.* Report on the condition of the geological and agricultural survey of Mississippi. 1858.
    8vo. pp. 22.

HILGARD, EUGENE WOLDEMAR. Report | on the | geology and agriculture | of the | State of Mississippi: | by | Eug. W. Hilgard, Ph. D., | State Geologist. | Printed by order of the Legislature. | E. Barksdale, State printer. | Jackson, Mississippi, | 1860. |
    8vo. pp. xxiv, 391. *Geological map; 2 plates;* and several *figures*, unnumbered.
    This report is justly regarded as a production of great value.
    Edition, 5,000 copies.
    Copies seen: Owen.

—— Sketch of.
    In Appleton's *Cyclopædia of American Biography*, vol. iii, p. 202.
    Mr. Hilgard edited vols. v and vi on "Cotton Production," of the "U. S. Census Reports for 1880," to which he contributed the monographs on Mississippi, Louisiana, and California.
    See also Mayes' *History of Education in Mississippi*, pp. 219–226.

HILL, JAMES, *vs.* CATCHINGS, T. C. Contested-election case | of | James Hill vs. T. C. Catchings, | from the | third Congressional district of Mississippi. | Washington: | Government printing office. | 1889. |
    8vo. pp. .
    Copies seen: Owen.

—— Majority and minority reports of the Committee on Elections. Feb. 25, 1891. (House Rep. 4005, 51st Cong., 2d sess.)
    8vo. pp. 9. No title-page.
    Copies seen: Owen,

—— Contested-election case | of | James Hill | vs. | T. C. Catchings, | from the | Third Congressional District of Mississippi. | Brief for contestee. | Dabney, McCabe & Anderson, | attorneys for contestee. | Washington, D. C.: | Geo. R. Gray, printer and publisher. | 1889. |
    8vo. Cover title only, 1 leaf. pp. 264.
    Copies seen: Owen.

HILL, ROBERT ANDREWS, *Lawyer, U. S. Dist. Judge.* Sketch of.
    In Claiborne's *Mississippi*, p. 472, *note.*

HILLMAN COLLEGE. Catalogues. 1856–1890, 1891–1898.
    8vo. *Ills.* in each.
    See Mayes' *History of Education in Mississippi*, pp. 99–100.
    Located at Clinton, Hinds County, Miss. Originally, and until 1891, the "Central Female Institute." In latter year, changed to present name.

HILLYARD, M. B. The | new South | A description of the Southern States, noting each State separately, | and giving their distinctive features and most | salient characteristics. | By M. B. Hillyard. | Published by | the Manufacturers' Record Co. | Baltimore, Md. | 1887. |
    8vo. pp. 413. *Illustrations.*
    Copies seen: Hamner.

—— Letters descriptive of the climate, soil, and resources of Central Mississippi. McComb City, 1876.
    8vo. pp. 203.

HINDS COUNTY. Sketch of.
    In Lowry and McCardle's *Mississippi*, pp. 483–490.
    Jackson, the State capital, is located in this county.

HISTORICAL SOCIETY. Publication | of the | Mississippi State | Historical Society. | For 1898. | Contents: | [–etc., 23 lines.] | Oxford, Miss. | Published by the Society. | June, 1898. | Price, $2.00. |
    8vo. Cover title only, 1 leaf, pp. 106. Index, pp. [4.]

CONTENTS:

1. Mississippi's "Backwoods Poet," by Dabney Lipscomb, A. M.
2. Mississippi as a field for the student of literature, by W. L. Weber.
3. Suffrage in Mississippi, by R. H. Thompson, LL. D.
4. Spanish policy in Mississippi after the Treaty of San Lorenzo, by F. L. Riley. Ph. D.
5. Time and place relations in history with some Mississippi and Louisiana, applications, by Prof. H. E. Chambers.
6. The study and teaching of history, by Herbert B. Adams, Ph. D., LL. D.
7. Some facts in the early history of Mississippi, by R. W. Jones, A. M., LL. D.
8. Pre-historic jasper ornaments in Mississippi, by R. B. Fulton, A. M., LL. D.
9. Suggestions to local historians, by Franklin L. Riley, Ph. D.
10. Some inaccuracies in Claiborne's History in regard to Tecumseh, by H. S. Halbert.
11. Did Jones County secede? By A. L. Bondurant.

Copies seen: Owen.

HISTORICAL SOCIETY. The | Mississippi Historical Society | I. General Information. | II. Personal Endorsements. | III. Publications. | IV. List of members. | [By Dr. F. L. Riley.] | Printed at the | Up-to-date Job Printing Office | Oxford, Miss. | [1899.]

8vo. pp. 16.
Administrative circular.

—— Publications | of | the Mississippi | [State] Historical Society. | Edited by | Franklin L. Riley, | Secretary. | Vol. II. | Oxford, Mississippi: | published by the Society. | 1899 |

8vo. pp. 234 [15.]

CONTENTS:

Title; Officers of the Society for 1899; and Contents.
The historical element in recent Southern literature, by Prof. C. Alphonso Smith.
Irwin Russell—First fruits of the Southern romantic movement, by Prof. W. L. Weber.
William Ward, a Mississippi poet entitled to distinction, by Prof. Dabney Lipscomb.
Sherwood Bonner, her life and place in the literature of the South, by Prof. Alexander L. Bondurant.
"The Daughter of the Confederacy," her life, character, and writings, by Prof. Chiles Clifton Ferrell.
Sir William Dunbar, the pioneer scientist of Mississippi, by Prof. Franklin L. Riley.
History of taxation in Mississippi, by Prof. Charles H. Brough.
Territorial growth of Mississippi, by Prof. J. M. White.
The early slave laws of Mississippi, by A. H. Stone, esq.
Federal courts, judges, attorneys, and marshals in Mississippi, 1798-1898, by Thomas M. Owen, esq.
Running Mississippi's South line, by Peter J. Hamilton, esq.
Elizabeth Female Academy—the mother of female colleges, by Bishop Chas. B. Galloway.
Early history of Jefferson College, by J. K. Morrison.
The rise and fall of Negro rule in Mississippi, by Dunbar Rowland.
Glimpses of the past, by Mrs. Helen D. Bell.
Historic Adams County, by Gerard Brandon, esq.
The historical opportunity of Mississippi, by Prof. R. W. Jones.
Nanih Waiya, the sacred mound of the Choctaws, by H. S. Halbert, esq.
Index.

Copies seen: Owen.

HISTORICAL SOCIETY. Sketch of.
In Goodspeed's *Memoirs of Mississippi*, vol. ii, pp. 52-53.

HISTORY. Works relating to Mississippi. *See* J. G. Baldwin, Besançon, J. F. H. Claiborne, Reuben Davis, Le Page Du Pratz, *Miss* Mary V. Duval, *Rev.* L. S. Foster, B. F. French, H. S. Fulkerson, H. S. Halbert, James Hall, P. J. Hamilton, John Haywood, M. B. Hillyard, Historical Society, Joseph Hodgson, Charles C. Jones, *Rev.* John G. Jones, Edward King, *Miss* Grace King, Louisiana, Lowry and McCardle, Hugh McCall, A. T. Mahan, *Miss* Louise Manly, A. B. Meek, Andrew Miller, J. W. Monette, Charles Nordhoff, Thomas M. Owen, *Rev.* Frank Patton, A. J. Pickett, A. W. Putnam, J. G. M. Ramsay, Wm. Roberts, Bernard Romans, Chas. C. Royce, Susan D. Smedes, Amos Stoddard, C. B. Walker, E. G. Wall, *Rev.* Geo. White.

HODGSON, JOSEPH (1838-), *Col. C. S. A., Journalist.* The Cradle | of the | Confederacy; | or, the Times of | Troup, Quitman and Yancey. | A Sketch of Southwestern Political History | from the Formation of the Federal | Government to A. D. 1861. | By Joseph Hodgson, | of Mobile. | [Quotation, 1 line.] | Mobile: | Printed at the Register Publishing Office. | 1876. |
8vo. xv, 528.
Maintains "that the Southwestern States were driven by Northern enemies rather than by Southern leaders into the act of secession."—*Preface.*
Copies seen: Owen.

HOGUE, ADDISON. The irregular verbs of Attic prose. By Addison Hogue, Prof. of Greek in the University of Mississippi. Boston. 1889.
12mo.

HOLLY SPRINGS. Sketch of.
In Davis's *Recollections of Mississippi and Mississippians*, pp. 86-96.

—— Female Institute. -
In Mayes's *History of Education in Mississippi*, pp. 46-51.

HOLMAN, D. A. Development. A great primary law of nature. An address delivered before the Hermenian and Philomothean Societies of Mississippi College, June 25, 1877.
8vo.

HOLMES COUNTY. Sketch of.
In Lowry and McCardle's *Mississippi*, pp. 490-493.

HOLMES, DAVID (1769-1832), *M. C. from Va., Territorial and State Gov. of, and U. S. Sen. from Miss.* Sketch of.
In Claiborne's *Mississippi*, pp. 302-303; *portrait.*

—— Administration as governor.
Ibid. pp. 304-360.
Also Lowry and McCardle's *Mississippi*, pp. 213-245, 259.

HOLT, JOHN S. The life of Abraham Page. Philadelphia. 1868.
He is also the author of "What I know about Ben Eacles," 1869; and "The Quines," 1870.

HOLT, JOSEPH (1807-1895), *Lawyer, P. M. Gen., Sec. of War.* Sketch of.
In Lynch's *Bench and Bar of Mississippi*, pp. 247-250.

HOOKER, ALLAN J. Confederate military history of Mississippi.
In Goodspeed's *Memoirs of Mississippi*, vol. i, pp. 145-172.
In collaboration with his father, Hon. Charles E. Hooker.

HOOKER, CHARLES E., *Col. C. S. A., M. C. from Miss.* Confederate military history of Mississippi.
: In Goodspeed's *Memoirs of Mississippi*, vol. i, pp. 145-172.

—— Sketch of.
: *Ibid.* pp. 951.

—— Contested election case of. *See* Kernaghan *vs.* Hooker.

HOOKER, CHARLES E., Jr. Political history of Mississippi.
: In Goodspeed's *Memoirs of Mississippi*, vol. ii, pp. 127-146.

HORTICULTURAL SOCIETY. Transactions | of the | Mississippi Horticultural Society, | at the | regular semi-annual meeting, | held | Wednesday, June 18, 1884, | at the | Agricultural and Mechanical College, | Starkville, Miss. | By J. B. Yellowly, | Secretary pro tem. | Jackson, Miss.: | Clarion steam printing establishment. | 1885. |
: 8vo. pp. 32.
: *See also* Bulletins of the Agricultural Experiment Station.

HOUSTON. Recollections of.
: In Davis's *Recollections of Mississippi and Mississippians*, pp. 174-185.

HOWARD, H. R. The History | of | Virgil A. Stewart, | and his | Adventure | in Capturing and Exposing the Great "Western Land | Pirate" and his Gang, in Connection | with the Evidence; | also of the | Trials, Confessions, and Execution | of | a Number of Murrell's Associates in the State of | Mississippi during the Summer of 1835, and the | Execution of Five Professional Gamblers | by the Citizens of Vicksburg, | on the 6th July, 1835. | [Quotation, 3 lines]. | Compiled by H. R. Howard. | New York: Harper & Brothers, Cliff-St. | 1836. |
: 12mo. pp. 273.
: Compiled under the direction and assistance of Mr. Stewart, and is full and circumstantial in detail.
: *Copies seen:* Congress.

HOWARD, VOLNEY F., *Lawyer, M. C. from Texas.* Sketch of.
: In Lynch's *Bench and Bar of Mississippi*, pp. 250-251.

—— *Reporter.* Mississippi Reports, vols. 2-8. *See* Supreme Court.
: "His reports are distinguished for regularity and systematic arrangement, and his captions and syllabuses are lucid, comprehensive, and exact.—Lynch, p. 250.

HOWRY, JAMES MOORMAN (1804-1884), *Lawyer.*
: In Lynch's *Bench and Bar of Mississippi*, pp. 511-515.
: *See also* Waddel's *Memorials of Academic Life*, pp. 290-291.

HUME, ALFRED (1866-), *C. E., D. Sc., Prof. Univ. Miss.* Some physical constants, | (Length of second's pendulum, force of magnetism, latitude, and longitude.) | by Alfred Hume, C. E. | Fellow in Civil Engineering, Vanderbilt University | A thesis presented to the Faculty of Vanderbilt Univ. | for the degree, Doctor of Science | June, 1890. | Cumberland Presbyterian Publishing House, | Nashville, Tennessee. |
: 8vo.
: Mr. Hume has articles in the Vanderbilt University weekly, monthly, and annual. He also has papers in the *Proceedings* of the Engineering Ass'n of the South, 1895; *Miss. School Journal*, 1897; *Proceedings* of the Southern Ass'n of Colleges and Schools, 1899; the *School Review*, Chicago, Feb., 1900; and the *American Mathematical Monthly.*

A BIBLIOGRAPHY OF MISSISSIPPI. 731

HUMPHREYS, BENJAMIN GRUBB (1808–1882), *Brig. Gen. C. S. A.*, *Gov. of Miss.* Administration as governor.
    In Lowry and McCardle's *Mississippi*, pp. 360–371.

—— Genealogy of the Humphreys family.
    In Goodspeed's *Memoirs of Mississippi*, vol. I, pp. 979–988.

HUNT, ABIJAH. Duel with George Poindexter.
    In Lowry and McCardle's *Mississippi*, p. 503.
    See also Claiborne's *Mississippi*, p. 371–372.

HUNTINGTON, *Miss* IRWIN. The | Wife of the Sun. | A legend of the Natchez. | [Quotation, 3 lines.] | By Irwin Huntington, | ("Frances Irwin,") | Mobile, Ala.: | the Gossip printing co. | 1892. |
    8vo. pp. 52. *Illustrations.*

HUTCHINS, *Col.* ANTHONY. Sketches of.
    In Claiborne's *Mississippi*, pp. 118–123, 135, 170–175, 203.

HUTCHINSON, ANDERSON (–1853), *Lawyer.* Sketch of.
    In Lynch's *Bench and Bar of Mississippi*, pp. 252–253.

—— *Compiler.* Code of Miss., 1798–1848. *See* Codes of Mississippi.

—— Manual | of | judicial, ministerial, and civil | forms, | revised, Americanized, and divested | of useless verbiage: | comprising [etc., 9 lines.] | By A. H. Hutchinson, | compiler of the Code of Mississippi, | Jackson, Miss.: | published for the author, by Barksdale & Jones: | 1852. |
    8vo. pp. 325.

HUTCHINSON, *Rev.* J. R. Reminiscences. Sketches and addresses. 1852.
    8vo.

I.

INDIANS. Document 512. | Correspondence | on the subject of the | Emigration of Indians, | between | the 30th November, 1831, and 27th December, 1833, | with abstracts of expenditures by disbursing agents, | in the | Removal and Subsistence of Indians, &c., &c. | Furnished | in answer to a Resolution of the Senate of 27th December, 1833, | by the Commissary-General of Subsistence [George Gibson]. | Vol. I [–V]. | Washington: | Printed by Duff Green, | 1834. (Sen. Doc. 512, 23 Cong., 1st sess. Vols. 7–11.)
    8 vo. Vol. I, pp. vii, 3–1179; vol II, 1 l., pp. 972; vol. III, 1 l., pp. 846; vol. iv, 1 l. pp. 771; vol. v, 1 l., pp. 503.
    Copies seen: Owen.

—— The Natchez, Chickasaw, Choctaw, and other Indian tribes.
    In Lowry and McCardle's *Mississippi*, pp. 246–268.

—— Antiquities of the Southern Indians. *See* Charles C. Jones.

—— The Mississippi Indians.
    In Claiborne's *Mississippi*, pp. 483–526.
    This sketch collates many interesting facts, but it contains also many errors.

—— The Indians, their cessions, fortresses, and wars.
    In Goodspeed's *Memoirs of Mississippi*, vol. I, pp. 27–53.

—— Dancing Rabbit Creek treaty. *See* that title.

—— History of the American Indians. *See* James Adair.

—— Aboriginal races of North America. *See* S. G. Drake.

INDIANS. Life of Tecumseh. *See* Benj. Drake.
—— Essay toward an Indian bibliography. *See* T. W. Field.
—— A synopsis of Indian tribes. *See* Albert Gallatin.
—— *See also* Wm. Bartram, Baudry de Lozieres, Biedma, F. Bossu, Wm. A. Bowles, D. G. Brinton, A. J. Brown, Bureau of Ethnology, Cabeça de Vaca, A. W. Dillard, J. D. Dreisback, Le Page Du Pratz, Elvas, B. F. French, A. S. Gatschet, H. S. Halbert, Benj. Hawkins, John Haywood, Indian Treaties, Helen M. F. Jackson. Louisiana, Hugh McCall, J. H. McCulloh, Thomas L. McKenny, and *also* McKenny and Hall, A. B. Meek, Le Clerc Milfort, J. W. Monette, *Rev.* J. Morse, Panton, Leslie & Co., Pascagoula Indians, Perrin du Lac, A. J. Pickett, John Pope, Pushmataha, A. W. Putnam, J. G. M. Ramsay, Bernard Romans, J. D. G. Shea, Barnard Shipp, Ternaux-Compans, Sarah Tuttle, Henry Trumbull, and Garcilasso de la Vega, *Rev.* George White, and Thomas S. Woodward.

INDIAN TREATIES. Indian treaties, | and | laws and regulations | relating to Indian affairs: | to which is added | an appendix, | containing the proceedings of the old Congress, and other | important state papers, in relation to Indian affairs. | Compiled and published under orders of the Department of War of | the 9th February and 6th October, 1825. | Washington City: | Way & Gideon, printers. | 1826. |
   8vo. pp. xx, 661. Pp. 531-661 consists of a supplement, with the following half-title: "Supplement containing additional treaties, documents, &c., relating to Indian Affairs, to the end of the twenty-first Congress. Official."
   Copies seen: Owen.

—— Treaties | between the | United States of America | and the several | Indian tribes, | from 1778 to 1837: | with | a copious table of contents | Compiled and printed by the direction, and under the supervision, | of the | Commissioner of Indian Affairs. | Washington, D. C. | published by Langtree and O'Sullivan. | 1837. |
   8vo. pp. lxxxiii, 699.
   Copies seen: Owen.
   Issued also with title as follows:

—— Treaties | between the | United States of America, | and the several | Indian tribes, | from 1778 to 1837: | with | a copious table of contents. | New edition, | carefully compared with the originals in the Department of State. | Compiled and printed by the direction, and under the supervision, | of the | Commissioner of Indian Affairs. | Washington, D. C. | Published by Langtree and O'Sullivan. | 1837. |
   8vo. pp. lxxxiii, 699.
   See also Goodspeed's *Memoirs of Mississippi*, vol. l, pp. 27-53.
   Copies seen: Owen.

—— Treaties with Indians.
   In *Revised Code of Mississippi* (1857), pp. 702-722.
   Extracts from all treaties with Mississippi Indians.

—— Dancing Rabbit Creek Treaty. *See* that title.
—— *See also* HUGH M'CALL.

INDUSTRIAL INSTITUTE AND COLLEGE. Circular No. 1.
   8vo. pp. 8.

INDUSTRIAL INSTITUTE AND COLLEGE. Plan of organization.
>   8vo. pp. 11.

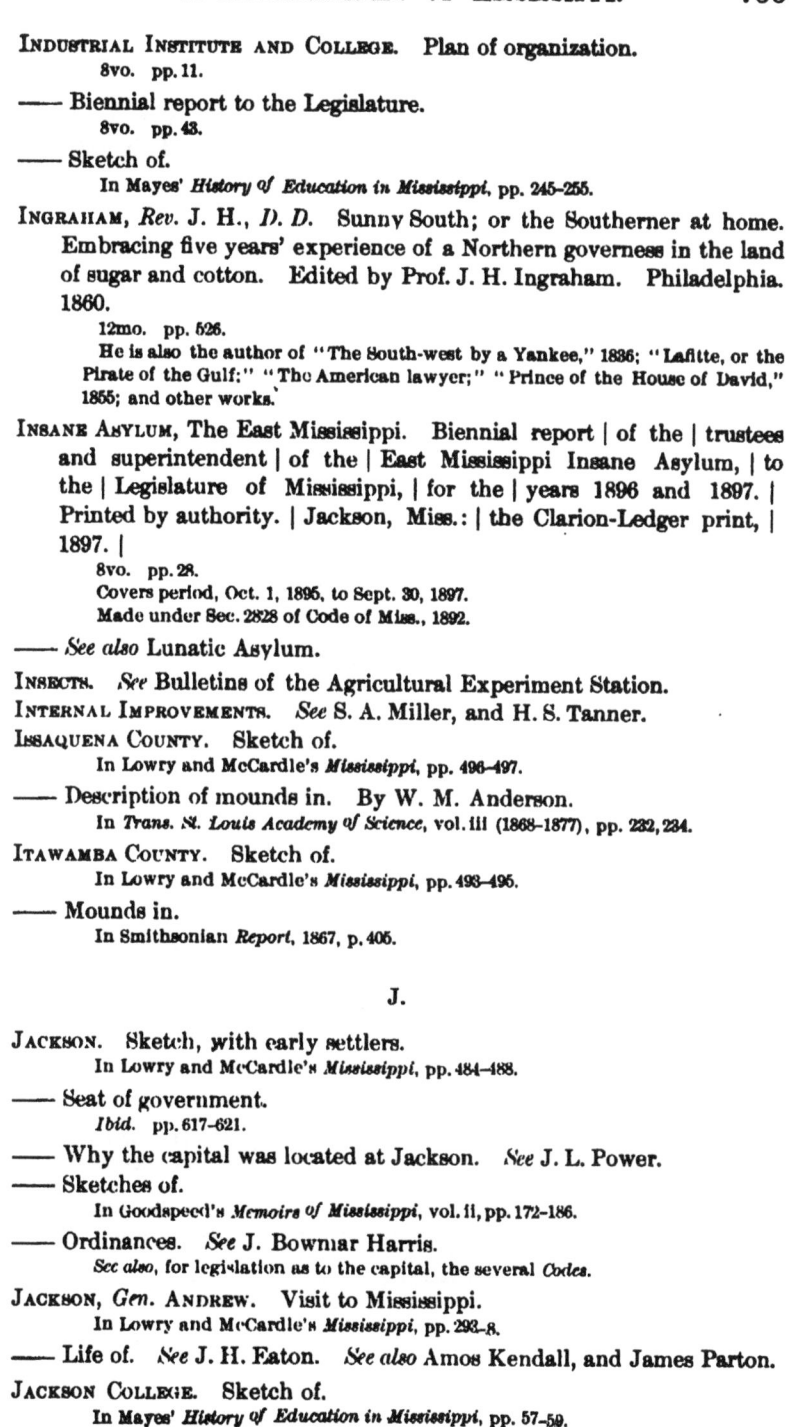

—— Biennial report to the Legislature.
>   8vo. pp. 43.

—— Sketch of.
>   In Mayes' *History of Education in Mississippi*, pp. 245-255.

INGRAHAM, *Rev.* J. H., *D. D.* Sunny South; or the Southerner at home. Embracing five years' experience of a Northern governess in the land of sugar and cotton. Edited by Prof. J. H. Ingraham. Philadelphia. 1860.
>   12mo. pp. 526.
>   He is also the author of "The South-west by a Yankee," 1836; "Lafitte, or the Pirate of the Gulf;" "The American lawyer;" "Prince of the House of David," 1855; and other works.

INSANE ASYLUM, The East Mississippi. Biennial report | of the | trustees and superintendent | of the | East Mississippi Insane Asylum, | to the | Legislature of Mississippi, | for the | years 1896 and 1897. | Printed by authority. | Jackson, Miss.: | the Clarion-Ledger print, | 1897. |
>   8vo. pp. 28.
>   Covers period, Oct. 1, 1895, to Sept. 30, 1897.
>   Made under Sec. 2828 of Code of Miss., 1892.

—— *See also* Lunatic Asylum.

INSECTS. *See* Bulletins of the Agricultural Experiment Station.

INTERNAL IMPROVEMENTS. *See* S. A. Miller, and H. S. Tanner.

ISSAQUENA COUNTY. Sketch of.
>   In Lowry and McCardle's *Mississippi*, pp. 496-497.

—— Description of mounds in. By W. M. Anderson.
>   In *Trans. St. Louis Academy of Science*, vol. iii (1868-1877), pp. 232, 234.

ITAWAMBA COUNTY. Sketch of.
>   In Lowry and McCardle's *Mississippi*, pp. 493-495.

—— Mounds in.
>   In Smithsonian *Report*, 1867, p. 405.

J.

JACKSON. Sketch, with early settlers.
>   In Lowry and McCardle's *Mississippi*, pp. 484-488.

—— Seat of government.
>   *Ibid.* pp. 617-621.

—— Why the capital was located at Jackson. *See* J. L. Power.

—— Sketches of.
>   In Goodspeed's *Memoirs of Mississippi*, vol. ii, pp. 172-186.

—— Ordinances. *See* J. Bowmar Harris.
>   *See also,* for legislation as to the capital, the several *Codes.*

JACKSON, *Gen.* ANDREW. Visit to Mississippi.
>   In Lowry and McCardle's *Mississippi*, pp. 293-8.

—— Life of. *See* J. H. Eaton. *See also* Amos Kendall, and James Parton.

JACKSON COLLEGE. Sketch of.
>   In Mayes' *History of Education in Mississippi*, pp. 57-59.

JACKSON COUNTY. Sketch of.
>   In Lowry and McCardle's *Mississippi*, pp. 497-499.
>   *See also* Goodspeed's *Memoirs of Mississippi*, vol. i, pp. 192-198.

JACKSON, HELEN MARIA FISKE (1831-1885), *Author*. A century of dishonor | A sketch | of the United States Government's dealings | with some of the Indian tribes | By H. H. [anon.] | Author [-etc., 1 line] | [Quotation, 7 lines.] | New York | Harper & Brothers, Franklin square | 1881 |
>   12mo. pp. x, 457.
>   Chapter viii, pp. 257-297, treats of the Cherokees.
>   A sketch, with *portrait*, is in Appleton's *Cyclopedia of American Biography*, vol. iii, p. 386.

JANSSENS, FRANCIS (1843-   ), *Fourth Roman Catholic bishop of Natchez.* Sketch of.
>   In *Sketch of the Catholic Church in Natchez*, pp. 33-34.

JASPER COUNTY. Sketch of.
>   In Lowry and McCardle's *Mississippi*, pp. 499-502.

JEFFERSON COLLEGE. Sketch of. *See* J. K. Morrison.
>   *See also* Mayes' *History of Education in Mississippi*, pp. 25-37.
>   "It is noteworthy that not only was this the first institution of learning established by authority of the State, but also that its charter was the first act of incorporation for any purpose in Mississippi."—*Ibid.*, p. 25.

JEFFERSON COUNTY. Sketch of.
>   In Lowry and McCardle's *Mississippi*, pp. 502-507.
>   *See also* Goodspeed's *Memoirs of Mississippi*, vol. i. pp. 175-178.

—— Reminiscences of the "Jefferson Troop." *See* John A. Watkins.

—— Recollections of. *See Ibid.*

—— History of. *See* P. K. Montgomery.

JEFFERSON TROOP. Reminiscences of. *See* John A. Watkins.

JOHNSTON, AMOS R. (-1879), *Lawyer.* Sketch of.
>   In Lynch's *Bench and Bar of Mississippi*, pp. 371-377.

JOHNSON, JOHN LIPSCOMB (1835-   ), *D. D., LL. D.* Sketch of.
>   In Foster's *Mississippi Baptist Preachers*, pp. 396-407; *portrait.*

JOHNSON, Col. RICHARD M. Account of visit to Jackson, Miss.
>   In Lowry and McCardle's *Mississippi*, pp. 303-4.

JOHNSTONE, GEORGE (———), *Gov. of West Fla.* An | appeal | to the | public | in behalf of | George Johnstone, esq.; | Governor of West Florida. | In answer to the North Briton Extraordinary, | and in consequence of other matters not taken notice | of in that extraordinary publication. | London: | printed for C. Moran, under the Piazza, Convent-garden. | MDCCLXIII.   (Price one shilling.) |
>   12mo. pp. 44.
>   In the *Gentleman's Magazine*, Oct. 1763, vol. xxxiii, p. 475 and p. 516, and also in the *Monthly Review*, vol. xxix, p. 392, this pamphlet is referred to, but the author's name is not given.
>   It is a friend's defense of Gov. Johnstone. On Sept. 17, 1763, there appeared in the *North Briton* a paper "strongly reflecting on the appointment of Scotchmen to the Government of Fla." Gov. J. only recently appointed, and not yet having left the country, became incensed at this article, and addressed a note about it to the editor. Believing he had evidence that a Mr. Brooke wrote it, he went to the lodgings of Mr. B. and after questioning him without satisfaction, he assaulted him. Thereupon a warrant was issued for him. This pamphlet is written concerning these events.
>   It has practically nothing in it of local reference.

Jones County. Sketch of.
    In Lowry and McCardle's *Mississippi,* pp. 507-508.

—— Did Jones County secede? *See* A. L. Bondurant.

Jones, Charles Colcock, Jr. (1831-1893), *LL. D.* Antiquities | of the | Southern Indians, | particularly of the | Georgia tribes. | By Charles C. Jones, Jr. | New York: | D. Appleton and Company, | 549 & 551 Broadway. | 1873. |
    8vo. pp. xvi, 532. *30 plates; 3 woodcuts.*
    'A striking similarity exists among the customs, utensils, implements, and ornaments of all the Southern Indians, consequently, in elucidating the archæology of a region often occupied in turn by various tribes, it seemed appropriate to mention and contrast the antiquities of Virginia, the Carolinas, Florida, Alabama, Louisiana, Mississippi, and Tennessee."—*Preface.*
    Copies seen. Congress; Hamner.

—— Hernando De Soto. | The adventures encountered and the route pursued by the Adelantado | during his march through the territory embraced within | the present geographical limits of the | State of Georgia. | By | Charles C. Jones, Jr. | (Read before the Georgia Historical Society.) | Printed for the author. | J. H. Estill, | Morning News steam printing house. | Savannah, Ga., 1880. |
    8vo. pp. 42. 1 l. *Portrait* of Soto.
    Copies seen: Owen.

—— The | history of Georgia. | by | Charles C. Jones, Jr., LL. D. | Volume I. | Aboriginal and colonial epochs. [–Volume II. Revolutionary epoch.] | [Design.] | Boston: | Houghton, Mifflin and Company. | New York: 11 East Seventeenth street. | The Riverside press, Cambridge | 1883. |
    8vo. Vol I., pp. xiv, 1 l., 556, vol. II, pp. xiv, 1 l., 540. *Illustrations.*
    Valuable for its treatment of the Indians, border life, boundaries, etc.
    Copies seen: Hamner; Congress.

—— Funeral oration pronounced in honor of Davis. *See* Jefferson Davis.

Jones, Cornelius J., *vs.* Catchings, T. C. Contested-election case | of | Cornelius J. Jones v. T. C. Catchings | from the | third Congressional district of Mississippi. | Washington: | Government printing office. | 1897. |
    8vo. pp. 252.
    Copies seen: Owen.

—— Contested election case | of | Cornelius J. Jones vs. Thos. C. Catchings, | from the | third congressional district of | the State of Mississippi. | Washington: | Government printing office. | 1899. |
    8vo. pp. 87.
    Copies seen: Owen.

Jones, *Rev.* John G., *Methodist Clergyman.* A complete | history of Methodism | as connected with | the Mississippi Conference | of the | Methodist Episcopal Church, South. | Written at the unanimous request of | the Conference. | By Rev. John G. Jones, | one of its members. | Volume I. | From 1799 to 1817. | Nashville, Tenn.: | Southern Methodist Publishing House. | Printed for the author. | 1887. |
    12mo. pp. 461.
    Volume II never published.

An invaluable contribution, not only to the Church history of Mississippi, and of that part of Mississippi Territory now Alabama, but to the history of pioneer life and times in these States.

He is also the author of "The Bishop's Council," 1867; "Appeal against dancing," 1867; and "Protestantism in Mississippi and the South-West," 1866.

Copies seen: Owen.

JONES, LACEY. Summer Land. By Lacey Jones, of Columbus, Miss.
No copy seen.

JONES, RICHARD WATSON, *M. A., LL. D., Prof. Univ. of Miss.* Sketch of the life of Gen. Robert Edward Lee.
In the *Rural Messenger*, Petersburg, Va., 1870.

—— Report on the relative disciplinary value of linguistic and scientific studies.
In the *Virginia Educational Journal*, 1872.

—— How to teach a bible class.
In M.E. Church South, *Sunday School Magazine*, 1872.

—— Progress of education in the South.
In the *Holston Methodist*, Knoxville, Tenn., 1874.

—— Establishment of schools related to the State University.
In *Proceedings of the Mississippi State Teachers' Association*, 1876.

—— Personality of the teacher.
Ibid. 1878.

—— Address before the State Teachers' Association on Unification of State Educational Work.
Ibid. 1890.

—— Facts in the life of the rattlesnake (*Crotalus horridus*) of the Mississippi Delta.
In *Science*, New York, 1891.

—— How chemistry is best taught. Papers before the International Congress of Chemists, at Chicago, Ill.
Ibid. 1893.

—— The cotton army worm. Washington, D. C., 1879.
8vo.
Report to C. V. Riley, chief of U. S. Entomological Commission.

—— The boll worm. Washington, D. C., 1879.
8vo.
Report to C. V. Riley, chief of U. S. Entomological Commission.

—— Some facts in the early history of Mississippi.
In *Publication Mississippi State Historical Society*, 1898, vol. i, pp. 85-89.

—— The historical opportunity of Mississippi.
Ibid. 1899, vol. ii, pp. 219-222.
Also reprinted.

JORDAN, THOMAS, *and* PRYOR, J. P. The campaigns | of | Lieut.-Gen. N. B. Forrest, | and of | Forrest's Cavalry, | with portraits, maps, and illustrations. | [Quotation, 1 line.] | By | General Thomas Jordan and J. P. Pryor. | [Monogram.] | Blelock & Company, | New-Orleans, La., Memphis, Tenn., and New-York. | 1868. |
8vo. pp. 704.
Contains a full and probably the best account of Forrest's campaigns.
Copies seen: Hamner; Morgan.

JUDAISM. *See* H. M. Bien.

JUDICIARY OF MISSISSIPPI. *See* Courts.

JURISPRUDENCE OF MISSISSIPPI. Account of.
In Claiborne's *Mississippi*, pp. 467-482.

—— The legal and judicial history.
In Goodspeed's *Memoirs of Mississippi*, vol. i, pp. 100-131; vol. ii, pp. 23-36.

K.

KELLS, *Mrs.* H. B. Sketch of the Woman's Christian Temperance Union.
In Goodspeed's *Memoirs of Mississippi*, vol. ii, pp. 379-383.

KEMPER COUNTY. Sketch of.
In Lowry and McCardle's *Mississippi*, pp. 509-510.

—— The Chisholm massacre. *See* J. M. Wells.

—— Kemper County vindicated. *See* J. D. Lynch.

—— Charge to grand jury of. *See* J. S. Hamm.

KEMPER, *Col.* REUBEN. Sketch of.
In Claiborne's *Mississippi*, pp. 260-262; 308-311.
He was one of the bold and daring spirits in Mississippi in its early settlement.

KENDALL, AMOS (1789-1869), *Postmaster-General.* Life of Andrew Jackson, private, military, and civil, with illustrations. New York. 1844.
8vo.
To have been completed in fifteen, but seven numbers only appeared, bringing the life down to nearly the end of the Creek war.

KENNEDY, WILLIAM. Sketch of. *See* Wm. T. Lewis.

KERNAGHAN, HENRY, *vs.* HOOKER, CHARLES E. Contested-election case | of | Henry Kernaghan vs. Charles E. Hooker, | from the | seventh Congressional district of Mississippi. | Washington: | Government printing office. | 1889. |
8vo. pp 547.

—— Report with resolution that Hooker retain seat. Feb. 25, 1891. (House Rep. 3991, 51st Cong., 2d sess.)
8vo. pp. 15. No title-page.
Copies seen: Owen.

KER, DAVID. *Territorial Judge of Miss.* Sketch of.
In Claiborne's *Mississippi*, pp. 141; 231, *note.*
See also Goodspeed's *Memoirs of Mississippi*, vol. ii, p. 521, for genealogy.

KING, EDWARD (1848-   ), *Author.* The | great South: | a record of journeys | in . . . Mississippi [etc., 4 lines.] | By Edward King. | Profusely illustrated from original sketches | by J. Wells Champney. | American publishing company, | Hartford, Conn. | 1875. |
4to. Title, 1 leaf, pp. 802, iv. *Illustrations.*
Copies seen: Hamner.

KING, *Miss* GRACE, *Authoress.* Makers of America. | Jean Baptist Le Moyne | Sieur de Bienville | By | Grace King | [— etc., 1 line.] | New York | Dodd, Mead and Company | 1893. |
12mo. pp. 330. *Portrait.*

KING, *Miss* GRACE. De Soto and his men in | the Land of Florida | By | Grace King | [— etc., 3 lines.] | With illustrations by George Gibbs | New York | The Macmillan Company | London: Macmillan & Co., Ltd. | 1898 | All rights reserved |
    12mo. pp. xv, 326.

KNAPP, *Dr.* S. A. "Let us enlarge the domain of | industrial knowledge." | An address | delivered by | Dr. S. A. Knapp, | of | Lake Charles, La. | at the | Mississippi | Agricultural and Mechanical College | commencement day, June 20th, | 1894. | Starkville, Miss.: | E. L. Reid, printer. |
    8vo. pp. 24.

KNIGHTS OF PYTHIAS. The constitution | of the | Grand and Subordinate Lodges, | Knights of Pythias, | of the | Grand Domain of Mississippi. | Adopted at Aberdeen, Miss., | May, 1895. | Meridian, Mississippi: | John M. Murphey, printer and stationer, | 1895. |
    8vo. pp. 96.

L.

LACEY, *Gen.* EDWARD. Life of. *See* S. A. Moore. *See also* Thomas M. Owen.

LAFAYETTE COUNTY. Sketch of.
    In Lowry and McCardle's *Mississippi*, pp. 510–512.

—— Mounds in Northwest part of T. 7 S., R. 4 W.
    In Squier and Davis' *Ancient Monuments*, pp. 110–111. *Map No. 2, pl. 33.*

—— Mounds on left bank of Clear Creek, near Mount Sylvan.
    Ibid. pp. 111–112. *Map No. 3, pl. 33.*

LAKE, *Capt.* L. Some facts relating to the early history of Grenada.
    In *Publications Mississippi State Historical Society*, 1900, vol. iii. (In press.)

LAKE, WILLIAM A. (1808–1861), *Lawyer, M. C. from Miss.* Sketch of.
    In Lynch's *Bench and Bar of Mississippi*, pp. 450–452.

LANDS. Acts of Congress relating to the public lands.
    In *Revised Code of Mississippi*, 1857, pp. 645–701.
    All Federal legislation affecting Mississippi to date.

—— Land titles.
    In B. L. C. Wailes' *Report on Agriculture and Geology of Mississippi*, pp. 117–125.
    See also Claiborne's *Mississippi*, pp. 233–237; 295–299.

—— Report | of the | Committee, | to whom were referred, on the 24th of December, and on | the 1st and 13th of Jan'y last, | the | several petitions, | of Thomas Burling and others; of John Cal | lier and others; & of Cato West & others. | [Philadelphia. 1800.] (Ex. Doc., 6th Cong., 1 Sess.)
    12mo. pp. 17.
    Reprinted as No. 52, Am. St. Papers: *Public Lands*, vol. i, pp. 99–102.
    Careful review of claims to lands in Miss. Territory; an examination of charters, treaties, and other documents relating to titles and jurisdiction; and an enumeration of the several classes of land claims in the Territory.

LANDS. Letter | from the | Secretary of the Treasury [A. Gallatin], | transmitting | information relative to the Claim of the Board | of Commissioners West of Pearl river, | in the | Mississippi Territory, | to | additional compensation for their services. | Washington City: | Printed by R. C. Weightman. | 1811. | (Ex. Docs., 11 Cong., 3 Sess.)
> 8vo. pp. 4.
> Additional compensation recommended for actual attendance by members of Board.

—— Homesteads and exemptions in Mississippi. Public and railroad lands for sale. n. p. [1896.]
> 8vo. pp. 8. No title page.
> Circular from the Secretary of State's Office.
> *Copies seen:* Owen.

—— *See also* Georgia Western Lands, Thomas Donaldson, and Edward Mayes.

LANGDON, DANIEL WEBSTER, Jr. (1864–), *A. M.* Observations on the Tertiary of Mississippi and Alabama, with descriptions of new species.
> In *American Journal Science*, 3d series, New Haven, Conn., March, 1886, vol. xxxi, pp. 202-209.

—— Observations on the Tertiary of Mississippi and Alabama, with descriptions of new species.
> In *Nature*, London and New York, 1886, vol. xxxiv, p. 46.
> Noticed in *American Journal Science*, March, 1886.

LANMAN, CHARLES (1819–1895). Adventures | in the | Wilds of the United States | and | British American Provinces. | By | Charles Lanman, | [–etc., 1 line.] | Illustrated by the author and Oscar Bessau. | [Quotation, 1 line.] | With an appendix by Lieut. Campbell Hardy. | In two volumes. | Vol. I [–II.] | Philadelphia: | John W. Moore, [–etc., 1 line.] | 1856. |
> 8vo. Illustrated.
> *Copies seen:* Congress.

LA SALLE. Adventures of. *See* J. S. C. Abbott. *See also* B. F. French.

LATOUR, *Major* A. LACARRIERE. Historical memoir | of | the war | in | West Florida and Louisiana | in 1814–15. | With an Atlas. | By Major A. Lacarriere Latour, | principal engineer in the late Seventh Military District, United States Army. | Written originally in French, and translated for the author, | by H. P. Nugent, esq. | [Quotation, 5 lines.] | Philadelphia: | published by John Conrad and Co. | J. Maxwell, printer. | 1816. |
> 8vo. pp xx, 264, cxc. *Portrait* of Gen. Andrew Jackson; *9 plates.*
> Perhaps the leading work on the subject.
> Full account of operations in Mobile Bay, with 3 maps, showing forts, etc. Contains nearly all the documents relating to the campaign.
> *Copies seen:* Hamner.

LATTIMORE, *Dr.* WILLIAM (d. 1843), *Miss. Territorial Delegate.* Sketch of.
> In Claiborne's *Mississippi*, p. 262-263, and *notes.*

LAUDERDALE COUNTY. Sketch of.
> In Lowry and McCardle's *Mississippi*, pp. 517–518.

—— Charge to grand jury of. *See* J. S. Hamm.

LAW, JOHN (1671-1729), *Scotch Financier.* Biography of. *See* Adolphe Thiers.

LAWRENCE COUNTY. Sketch of.
  In Lowry and McCardle's *Mississippi*, pp. 512-516.
  See also Goodspeed's *Memoirs of Mississippi*, vol. I, pp. 193, 194.

LAWS.
  This title embraces only session laws. *See also* Codes of Mississippi, Conventions and Constitutions of Mississippi, Courts and Supreme Court, and T. L. Cole.
  Owing to the rarity of early session laws, it has been found impossible to give titles in full for the period 1799-1816. The check list for the period gives all the data in the hands of the compiler. He is much indebted to Theodore L. Cole, esq., Washington, D. C., for invaluable aid in this connection.

MISSISSIPPI—TERRITORY.

First grade.

Laws (Enacted by the Governor and Judges) Jan.-May, 1799. 4to T., 1 l., pp. 209. (*See* Codes of Miss. for full title.)
Laws (Enacted by the Governor and Judges) Sept.-Oct., 1799. 4to. N. t. p. pp. 16.
Laws (Enacted by the Governor and Judges). Oct. 4to. N. t. p. pp. 47.

Second grade.

1st General Assembly, 1st sess. Never convened.
1st General Assembly, extra sess., July, 1801. No laws cited in Digests of 1807 and 1816.
1st General Assembly, 2d sess., Oct.-Dec. 1801-Feb., 1802. pp. 267.
1st General Assembly, 2d extra sess., May, 1802. Acts cited in Digests of 1807 and 1816, but not by pp.
2d General Assembly, 1st sess., Dec., 1802-March, 1803. 8vo. pp. 59+.
2d General Assembly, extra sess., May, 1803. Digest of 1816 cites acts, but not by pp.
2d General Assembly, 2d sess., Oct.-Nov., 1803. Fol. T. 1 l., pp. 28, 1 l.
3d General Assembly, 1st sess., Dec., 1804-March, 1805. 8vo. pp. 136.
3d General Assembly, extra sess., July, 1805. 8vo. pp. 38, 1 l.
3d General Assembly, 2d sess., Dec., 1805-March, 1806. Digests of 1807 and 1816 cite acts, but not by pp.
4th General Assembly, 1st sess., Dec., 1806-Feb., 1807. Acts printed in *Digest*, 1807, only.—*See Ibid.*, p. 25.
4th General Assembly, 2d sess., Dec., 1807-March, 1808. 12mo. pp 44.
5th General Assembly, 1st sess., Feb., 1809. 8vo. T., 1 l., pp 19.
6th General Assembly, 1st sess., Nov., 1809. 8vo. T 1 l. pp. 23-156 [12]. This and the preceding sess. form one volume, pp. 1-19 + [3] + 156 [12].
6th General Assembly, 2d sess., Nov., 1810. 8vo. pp. 39 [10].
7th General Assembly, 1st sess., Nov., 1811. 8vo. pp. 117 [1] [2], 1 l.
7th General Assembly, 2d sess., Nov., 1812. 8vo pp. 147 [2], iiii.
8th General Assembly, 1st sess., Nov., 1813. 8vo. pp. 68, iv.
8th General Assembly, 2d sess., Nov., 1814. 8vo. pp. 77 vii.
9th General Assembly, 1st sess., Nov., 1815. 8vo. pp. 108, viii.
9th General Assembly, 2d sess., Nov., 1816. 8vo. pp. 100, viii.

STATE OF MISSISSIPPI.

—— Acts | passed at the first session | of the | first General Assembly | of the | State of Mississippi. | [Cut.] | Andrew Marschalk—State printer. | 1818.]
  8vo. pp. 214, 219-224 [24].
  Convened at the town Washington.

LAWS. Acts | passed at the first session | of the | second General Assembly | of the | State of Mississippi. | Natchez: | printed by Marschalk and Evens—State printers. | 1819. |
    8vo. pp. 138 [14].
    Convened at Natchez.
    No copies of the acts from 1819 to 1824 have been seen.

—— Laws | of the | State of Mississippi: | passed at | the Seventh Session [Dec. 1823] | of the | General Assembly, | held in the | town of Jackson. | Published by authority. | Jackson: | printed by Isler and Cutcher, | 1824. |
    8vo. pp. 110, 7 ll.

—— Laws | of the | State of Mississippi, | passed at | the eighth session [Jan. 1825] | of the | General Assembly, | held in the | town of Jackson. | Published by authority. | Jackson: | Silas Brown, State printer. | 1825. |
    8vo. pp. 148, 8 ll.

—— Laws | of the | State of Mississippi, | passed at | the ninth session [Jan. 1826] | of the | General Assembly, | held in the town of Jackson. | Published by authority. | Jackson: | Peter Isler, State printer. | 1826. |
    8vo. pp. 135, vii, 5 ll.

—— Laws | of the | State of Mississippi, | passed at | the tenth session [Jan. 1827] | of the | General Assembly, | held in the | town of Jackson. | Published by authority. | Jackson: | Peter Isler, State printer. | 1827. |
    8vo. pp. viii, 155, 5 ll.

—— Laws | of the | State of Mississippi, | passed at | the eleventh session [Jan. 1828] | of the | General Assembly, | held in the | town of Jackson. | Published by authority. | Jackson: | Peter Isler, State printer. | 1828. |
    8vo. pp. 147, viii, 5 ll.

—— Laws | of the | State of Mississippi, | passed at | the twelfth session [Jan. 1829] | of the | General Assembly, | held in the | town of Jackson. | Published by authority. | Jackson: | Peter Isler, State printer. | 1829. |
    8vo. pp. 123, vi, 5 ll.

—— Laws | of the | State of Mississippi, | passed at | the thirteenth session [Jan. 1830] | of the | General Assembly, | held in the | town of Jackson. | Published by authority. | Jackson: | Peter Isler, State printer. | 1830. |
    8vo. pp. 206, viii, 7 ll.

—— Laws | of the | State of Mississippi, | passed at | the fourteenth session [Nov. 1830] | of the | General Assembly, | held in the | town of Jackson. | Published by authority. | Jackson: | Peter Isler, State printer. | 1830. |
    8vo. pp. 146, vii.

Laws. Laws | of the | State of Mississippi, | passed at | the fifteenth session [Nov. 1841] | of the | General Assembly, | held in the | town of Jackson. | Published by authority. | Jackson: | Peter Isler, State printer. | 1831. |
    8vo. pp. xviii, 172.

—— Laws | of the | State of Mississippi, | passed at | the sixteenth session [Jan. 1833] | of the | General Assembly, | held in the | town of Jackson. | Published by authority. | Jackson: | Peter Isler, State printer. | 1833. |
    8vo. pp. xxv, 252.

—— Laws | of the | State of Mississippi, | passed at the | seventeenth session [Nov.,1833] | of the | General Assembly, | held in the | town of Jackson. | Published by authority. | Jackson: | George R. Fall, State printer. | 1834. |
    8vo. Title, 1 l., pp. 200.

—— Laws | of the | State of Mississippi; | passed at a regular biennial session | of the | Legislature, | held at | Jackson, in January & February, A. D. 1836. | Jackson, Mi., | G. R. & J. S. Fall, State printers. | 1836. |
    8vo. pp. 440.

—— Laws | of the | State of Mississippi, | passed at an adjourned session | of the | Legislature, | held in the | town of Jackson, in January, 1837. | Jackson: | printed by G. R. & J. S. Fall. | 1837. |
    8vo. pp. 67.

—— Laws | of the | State of Mississippi, | passed at a called session | of the | Legislature, | held at | Jackson, in April, 1837. | Jackson: | G. R. & J. S. Fall. | 1837. |
    8vo. pp. 392.

—— Laws | of the | State of Mississippi; | passed at a regular biennial session | of the | Legislature, | held at | Jackson, in January & February, A. D. 1838. | Jackson, Mi., | B. D. Howard, State printer. | 1838. |
    8vo. pp. 368.

—— Laws | of the | State of Mississippi: | passed at an adjourned session | of the Legislature, | held in the | city of Jackson, | from January 7, to February 16, A. D. 1839. | Jackson: | B. D. Howard, State printer. | 1839. |
    8vo. pp. 491.

—— Laws | of the | State of Mississippi, | passed at a regular session | of the Legislature, | held in the | city of Jackson, | in the months of January and February, A. D. 1840. | Printed by authority. | Jackson: | C. M. Price, State printer. | 1840. |
    8vo. pp. xii, 1 l. 13–366.

—— Laws | of the | State of Mississippi, | passed at an adjourned session | of the | Legislature, | held in the | city of Jackson, | in the months of January and February, A. D. 1841. | Printed by authority. | Jackson: | C. M. Price, State printer. | 1841. |
    8vo. pp. 302.
    Contains Const. of Miss., 1832.

LAWS. Laws | of the | State of Mississippi, | passed at a regular biennial session | of the | Legislature, | held in the | city of Jackson, | in the months of January and February, A. D. 1842. | Jackson: | C. M. Price, State printer. | 1842. |
　8vo. pp. 285.

—— Laws | of the | State of Mississippi, | passed | at a called session | of the | Legislature, | held in the | city of Jackson, | in July, A. D. 1843. | Jackson: | C. M. Price & G. R. Fall, State printers. | 1843. |
　8vo. pp. 135.

—— Laws | of the | State of Mississippi, | passed at a regular biennial session | of the | Legislature, | held in the | city of Jackson, | in January and February, A. D. 1844. | Jackson: | C. M. Price & S. Rohrer, State printers. | 1844. |
　8vo. pp. xxi, 395.
　Contains Const. of Miss., 1832.

—— Laws | of the | State of Mississippi, | passed at a regular biennial session | of the | Legislature, | held in the | city of Jackson, | in January, February, and March, A. D. 1846. | Jackson: | C. M. Price & G. R. Fall, State printers. | 1846. |
　8vo. pp. 613.
　Contains Const. of Miss., 1832.

—— Laws | of the | State of Mississippi, | passed at a regular session of the | Mississippi Legislature, | held in the city of Jackson | January, February, and March. 1848. | Jackson: | Price & Fall, State printers. | 1848. |
　8vo. pp. 584.
　Contains Const. of Miss., 1832.

—— Laws | of the | State of Mississippi, | passed at a regular session | of the | Mississippi Legislature, | held in the city of Jackson | January, February, and March, 1850. | Jackson: | Fall & Marshall, State printers. | 1850. |
　8vo. pp. 544.
　Contains Const. of Miss., 1832.

—— Laws | of the | State of Mississippi, | passed at a called session | of the | Mississippi Legislature, | held in the city of Jackson | Jackson, November, 1850. | Jackson: | Fall & Marshall, State printers. | 1850. |
　8vo. pp. 48.
　Contains Const. of Miss., 1832.

—— Laws | of the | State of Mississippi, | passed at a regular session | of the | Mississippi Legislature, | held in the city of Jackson, | January, February, and March, 1852. | Jackson: | Palmer & Pickett, State printers. | 1852. |
　8vo. pp. xxviii, 537.
　Contains Const. of Miss., 1832.

—— Laws | of the | State of Mississippi, | passed at a called session | of the | Mississippi Legislature, | held in the city of Jackson | October, 1852. | Jackson: | Palmer & Pickett, State printers. | 1852. |
　8vo. pp. xvi, 219.
　Contains Const. of Miss., 1832.

LAWS. Laws | of the | State of Mississippi, | passed at a regular session | of the | Mississippi Legislature, | held in the city of Jackson from | 2nd of January to 2nd of March, 1854. | Jackson: | Barksdale & Jones, State printers. | 1854. |
    8vo. pp. 613.
    Contains Const. of Miss., 1832.

—— Laws | of the | State of Mississippi | passed at a regular session | of the | Mississippi Legislature | held in the city of Jackson, | January, February, and March, 1856. | Jackson: | E. Barksdale, State printer. | 1856. |
    8vo. pp. xvi, 455.
    Contains Const. of Miss., 1832.

—— Laws | of the | State of Mississippi, | passed at an adjourned session | of the | Mississippi Legislature, | held in the city of Jackson, | December, January, and February, 1856–'7. | Jackson: | E. Barksdale, State printer. | 1857. |
    8vo. pp. 125.
    Contains Const. of Miss., 1832.

—— Laws | of the | State of Mississippi, | passed at a regular session | of the | Mississippi Legislature, held in the | city of Jackson, November, 1857. | Jackson: | E. Barksdale, State printer. | 1858. |
    8vo. pp. 197.
    Contains Const. of Miss., 1832.

—— Laws | of the | State of Mississippi, | passed at a called session | of the Mississippi Legislature, | held in the | city of Jackson, November, 1858. | Jackson: | E. Barksdale, State printer. | 1859. |
    8vo. pp. 256.
    Contains Const. of Miss., 1832.

—— Laws | of the | State of Mississippi, | passed at a regular session | of the | Mississippi Legislature, | held in the | city of Jackson, November, 1859. | Jackson: | E. Barksdale, State printer. | 1860. |
    8vo. pp. 608.
    Contains Const. of Miss., 1832.

—— Laws | of the | State of Mississippi, | passed at a called session | of the | Mississippi Legislature, | held in the | city of Jackson, November, 1860. | Jackson: | E. Barksdale, State printer. | 1860. |
    8vo. pp. 45, 1 leaf.
    Contains Const. of Miss., 1832.

—— Laws | of the | State of Mississippi, | passed at a called session | of the Mississippi Legislature, | held in the | city of Jackson, January, 1861. | Constitution revised. | Jackson: | E. Barksdale, State printer. |
    8vo. pp. 56.
    Contains Const. of Miss., 1861.

—— Laws | of the | State of Mississippi, | passed at a called session | of the | Mississippi Legislature, | held in the | city of Jackson, July 1861. | Jackson, Miss. | E. Barksdale, State printer. | 1861. |
    8vo. pp. 86.
    Contains Const. of Miss., 1861.

LAWS. **Laws** | of the | State of Mississippi, | passed at a regular session | of the | Mississippi Legislature, | held in the | city of Jackson, November & December | 1861, and January, 1862. | Jackson, Miss. | Cooper & Kimball, State printers. | 1862. |
 8vo. pp. 333.
 Contains Const. of Miss., 1861.

—— **Laws** | of the | State of Mississippi, | passed at a called and regular session | of the | Mississippi Legislature, | held in | Jackson and Columbus, | Dec. 1862, and Nov. 1863. | Selma, Ala. | Cooper & Kimball, State printers. | 1864. |
 8vo. pp. 256.
 Contains Const. of Miss. 1861, and also the Constitution of the Confederate States.

—— **Laws** | of the | State of Mississippi, | passed at a called session | of the | Mississippi Legislature, | held in | Macon, | March and April, 1864. | Meridian, Miss. | J. J. Shannon & Co., State printers. | 1864. |
 8vo. pp. 106.
 Contains Const. of 1832, with amendments.

—— **Laws** | of the | State of Mississippi, | passed at a called session | of the | Mississippi Legislature, | held in | Macon, | August, 1864. | Meridian, Miss. | J. J. Shannon & Co., State printers. | 1864. |
 8vo. pp. 64.

—— **Laws** | of the | State of Mississippi, | passed at a called session | of the | Mississippi Legislature, | held in | Columbus, | February and March, 1865. | Meridian, Miss. | J. J. Shannon & Co., State printers. | 1865. |
 8vo. pp. 71.

—— **Laws** | of the | State of Mississippi, | passed at a regular session | of the | Mississippi Legislature, | held in the | city of Jackson, October, November and December, 1865. | Jackson: | J. J. Shannon & Co., State printers. | 1866. |
 8vo. pp. 509.
 Contains Const. of Miss., 1865.

—— **Laws** | of the | State of Mississippi, | passed at a called session | of the | Mississippi Legislature, | held in the | city of Jackson, | October, 1866, and January and February, 1867. | Jackson, Miss.: | J. J. Shannon & Co., State printers. | 1867. |
 8vo. pp. xliv, 800.

—— **Laws** | of the | State of Mississippi, | passed at a regular session | of the | Mississippi Legislature, | held in | the city of Jackson, commencing January 11th, 1870, | and ending July 21st, 1870. | Jackson, Miss.: | Kimball, Raymond & Co., State printers. | 1870. |
 8vo. pp. lxiii, 720.
 Contains Const. of Miss., 1868.

—— **Laws** | of the | State of Mississippi, | passed at a regular session | of the | Mississippi Legislature, | held | in the city of Jackson, | commencing January 1st, 1871, and ending | May 13th, 1871. | Jackson, Miss.: Alcorn & Fisher, public printers. | 1871. |
 8vo. pp. xl, 948.
 Contains Const. of Miss., 1868.

LAWS. Laws | of the | State of Mississippi, | passed at a regular session | of the | Mississippi Legislature, | held | in the city of Jackson, commencing January 2, 1872, and ending | April 5, 1872. | Printed by authority of law. | Jackson, Miss.: | Kimball, Raymond & Co., State printers. | 1872. |
    8vo. pp. xxvi, 515.
    Contains Const. of Miss., 1868.

—— Laws | of the | State of Mississippi, | passed at a regular session | of the | Mississippi Legislature, | held in the | city of Jackson, commencing January 21, 1873, and ending April 19, 1873. | Printed by authority of law. | Jackson, Miss.: | Kimball, Raymond & Co., State printers. | 1873. |
    8vo. pp. xxxii, 708.
    Contains Const. of Miss., 1868.

—— Laws | of the | State of Mississippi, | passed at a | called session, | of the | Mississippi Legislature, | convened in the | city of Jackson, October 20th, 1873. | Printed by authority. | Jackson, Miss.: | Kimball, Raymond & Co., State printers. | 1874. |
    8vo. pp. 50.

—— Laws | of the | State of Mississippi, | passed at the | regular session | of the | Mississippi Legislature, | convened in the | city of Jackson, January 20, 1874. | Printed by authority. | Jackson, Miss.: | Pilot publishing company, State printers. | 1874. |
    8vo. pp. xxiii, 324.
    Contains Const. of Miss., 1868.

—— Laws | of the | State of Mississippi, | passed at the | regular session | of the | Mississippi Legislature, | convened in the | city of Jackson, January 20, 1874. | Printed by authority. | Jackson, Miss.: | Pilot publishing company, State printers. | 1874. |
    8vo. pp. xxiii, 224.

—— Laws | of the | State of Mississippi, | passed at a | regular session | of the | Mississippi Legislature, | convened in the | city of Jackson, January 5, 1875. | Published by authority. | Jackson, Miss.: | Pilot publishing company, State printers. | 1875. |
    8vo. pp. xxiii, 284.

—— Laws | of the | State of Mississippi, | passed at a called session | of the | Mississippi Legislature, | convened | in the city of Jackson, July 27, 1875. | Published by authority. | Jackson, Miss.: | Pilot publishing company, State printers. | 1875. |
    8vo. pp. 39.

—— Laws | of the | State of Mississippi, | passed at a regular session | of the | Mississippi Legislature, | held in the | city of Jackson, | commencing January 4th, 1876, and ending April 15th, 1876. | Printed by authority of law. | Jackson, Mississippi: | Power & Barksdale, State printers. | 1876. |
    8vo. pp. xxiv, 362.

LAWS. **Laws** | of the | State of Mississippi, | passed at a regular session | of the | Mississippi Legislature, | held in the | city of Jackson, | commencing January 2d, 1877, and ending February 1st, 1877. | Printed by authority. | Jackson, Miss.: | Power & Barksdale, State printers. | 1877. |
8vo. pp. xvi, 362.

—— Laws | of the | State of Mississippi, | passed at a regular session | of the | Mississippi Legislature, | held in the | City of Jackson, | commencing Jan. 8th, 1878, and ending March 5th, 1878. | Printed by authority. | Jackson, Miss.: | Power & Barksdale, State printers. | 1878. |
8vo. pp. xxix, 1 l., 761.

—— Laws | of the | State of Mississippi, | passed at a regular session | of the | Mississippi Legislature, | held in the | city of Jackson, | commencing January 6th, 1880, and ending March 6th, 1880. | Printed by authority. | Jackson, Miss.: | J. L. Power, State printer. | 1880. |
8vo. pp. xxxi, 739.

—— Laws | of the | State of Mississippi, | passed at a | regular session of the Legislature, | held in the | city of Jackson, | commencing Jan. 3d, 1882, and ending March 9, 1882. | Printed by authority. | Jackson, Miss.: | J. L. Power State printer. | 1882. |
8vo. pp. iv, 1105.

—— Laws | of the | State of Mississippi, | passed at a | regular session of the Legislature, | held in the | city of Jackson, | commencing January 8, 1884, and ending March 15, 1884. | Printed by authority. | Jacr[k]son, Miss. | J. L. Power, State printer. | 1884. |
8vo. pp. [4], 1052.

—— Laws | of the | State of Mississippi, | passed at a regular session | of the | Mississippi Legislature, | held in the | city of Jackson, | commencing January 5, 1886, and ending March 18, 1886. | Printed by authority. | Jackson, Miss.: | R. H. Henry, State printer, | 1886. |
8vo. pp. xxx, 1 l., 883.

—— Laws | of the | State of Mississippi, | passed at a regular session | of the | Mississippi Legislature, | held in the | city of Jackson, | commencing Jan'y 3, 1888, and ending March 8, 1888. | Printed by authority. | Jackson, Miss.: | R. H. Henry, State printer. | 1888. |
8vo. pp. 706.

—— Laws | of the | State of Mississippi, | passed at a regular session | of the | Mississippi Legislature, | held in the | city of Jackson, | commencing January 7, 1890, and ending February 24, 1890. | Printed by authority. | Jackson, Miss.: | R. H. Henry, State printer. | 1890. |
8vo. pp. 808.

—— Laws | of the | State of Mississippi, | passed at a regular session | of the | Mississippi Legislature, | held in the | city of Jackson, | commencing January .5, 1892, and ending April 2, 1892. | Printed by authority. | Jackson, Miss.: | R. H. Henry, printer. | 1892. |
8vo. pp. 492.

LAWS. Laws | of the | State of Mississippi, | passed at a special session | of the | Mississippi Legislature, | held in the | city of Jackson, | commencing January 2, 1894, and ending February 10, 1894. | Printed by authority. | Jackson, Miss.: | the Clarion-Ledger publishing Company. | 1894. |
> 8vo. pp. 163.
> Contains the general and special messages of the session; and also the Report of the Committee on "State Flag" and "Coat of Arms."

—— Laws | of the | State of Mississippi, | passed at a regular session | of the | Mississippi Legislature, | held in the | city of Jackson, | commencing January 7, 1896, and ending March 24, 1896. | Printed by authority. | Jackson, Miss.: | Clarion-Ledger, State printers. | 1896. |
> 8vo. pp. 254.

—— Laws | of the | State of Mississippi, | passed at an | extraordinary session of the Legislature, | held in the | city of Jackson, | commencing April 27th, 1897, and ending May 27th, 1897. | Printed by authority. | Jackson, Miss.: | Clarion-Ledger print. ! 1897. |
> 8vo. pp. 52.

—— Laws | of the | State of Mississippi, | passed at a special session | of the | Mississippi Legislature, | held in the | city of Jackson, | commencing Jan. 4, 1898, and ending Feb. 11, 1898. | Printed by authority. | Jackson, Miss.: | Clarion-Ledger Co., State printers. | 1898. |
> 8vo. pp. 157.

LEAKE COUNTY. Sketch of.
> In Lowry and McCardle's *Mississippi*. pp. 519-520.

LEAKE, WALTER (1760-1825), *Lawyer, Gov., and U. S. Senator from Miss.* Sketch of.
> In Lynch's *Bench and Bar of Mississippi*, pp. 135-137.
> *See also* Claiborne's *Mississippi*, p. 356.

—— Administration as governor.
> In Lowry and McCardle's *Mississippi*, pp. 260-262.

LEATHERMAN, P. R. Elements of morality. By P. R. Leatherman, of Woodville, Miss. 1860.
> No copies seen.

LEAVELL, *Rev.* ZACHARY TAYLOR (1847-), *D. D.* In the saffron plague.
> In the *Western Recorder*, Louisville, Ky., 1898.
> Account of yellow fever at Jackson, Miss., 1898.

—— Mississippi Baptists; their past. A speech delivered before the Baptist Young People's Union of Mississippi, at West Point, in March, 1898.
> In the *Baptist Layman*, 1898.

—— Sixteen years among Mississippi Baptists.
> In the *Baptist Record*, 1894.

—— Twenty years with Mississippi Baptists. A speech delivered before the Mississippi Baptist Historical Society in 1897.
> Manuscript; filed in the archives of the Society.

—— Baptist annals | or | twenty-two years | with | Mississippi Baptists | 1877-1899 | By | Z. T. Leavell, D. D. | With introduction | by | H. F. Sproles, D. D. | Philadelphia | American Baptist Publication Society | [—etc., 1 line.] |
> 8vo. pp. 128. *Portraits of author, and others.*

LEAVELL, *Rev.* ZACHARY TAYLOR. Sketch of.
> In Foster's *Mississippi Baptist Preachers*, pp. 431–432.
> Also in Goodspeed's *Memoirs of Mississippi*, vol. 1, pp. 1110–1111.

LEE COUNTY. Sketch of.
> In Lowry and McCardle's *Mississippi*, pp. 520–521.

—— Mounds in.
> In Smithsonian *Report*, 1867, pp. 404–405.

LEFLORE COUNTY. Sketch of.
> In Lowry and McCardle's *Mississippi*, pp. 522–523.

LEE, STEPHEN DILL (1833–), *Maj. Gen., C. S. A.* The South since the war.
> In *Confederate Military History* (Atlanta, Ga.), vol. 12. 8vo.

—— Inaugural address.
> In *Publications Mississippi State Historical Society*, 1900, vol. iii. (In press.)
> Opening address as president of the society at the annual meeting, Jackson, February 1, 1900.

—— The | Agricultural and | Mechanical College | of Mississippi. | Its origin, object, management, | and results, | discussed in a series of papers, | by Gen. S. D. Lee, president. | Jackson, Miss.: | Clarion-Ledger publishing house. | 1889. |
> 8vo. pp. 18.
> General Lee has been a voluminous writer on military and educational topics.

—— Sketch of.
> In Mayes' *History of Education in Mississippi*, pp. 243–244.

LEFLORE, GREENWOOD. Incident in the life of.
> In Lowry and McCardle's *Mississippi*, p. 451.
> See also Claiborne's *Mississippi*, pp. 116, *note;* and 515, *portrait.*
> See also Trans. Ala. Hist. Society, 1898–99. vol. iii, pp. 101–102.

LEVEE COMMISSIONER. Brief | of the | counsel for defendant in error | in the case of | Aaron Shelby vs. James L. Alcorn, | levee commissioner of Coahoma County, | in the High Court of Errors and Appeals | of the State of Mississippi. | Fulton Anderson and J. W. C. Watson | for the defendant in error. | Jackson: | Mississippian Job office. | 1858. |
> 8 vo. pp. 31.
> See also Transportation, *infra.*

—— Report of the Committee of the House of Representatives to investigate Levee Matters.
> In Appendix to *Journal* of the Senate of Miss., pp. 479–499. See State offices.
> See H. St. L. Coppeé.

LEWIS FAMILY. Sketch of.
> In Claiborne's *Mississippi*, pp. 108–109, *note.*

LEWIS, T. M. De Soto's Camps in the Chickasaw Country in 1540–41.
> In the *National Magazine*, Nov., 1891.
> Also separately printed. 8 vo. pp. 5.

LEWIS, WILLIAM TERRELL (1811–1893). Genealogy | of the | Lewis Family | in America, | from the middle of the seventeenth century | down to the present time. | By | Wm. Terrell Lewis, | of Perryville, Winston County, Miss. | Price $2.00. | Louisville, Ky.: | Published by the Courier-Journal job printing co., | 1893. |
> 8 vo. pp. 2 ll, 454.
> An elaborate and exhaustive work on the Lewis's and related families.
> *Copies seen:* Owen.

LEWIS, WILLIAM TERRELL. Centennial history of Winston County, Mississippi.
In the Winston County *Signal*, Louisville, Miss., 1876-77.

—— Wm. Kennedy, Esq.—General Thomas Brandon—Miss Ann Kennedy, a heroine of the Revolution—Sam Clowney, and others.
In the *Sentinel*, Pickens C. H., S. C., May 7, 1885.

LIBRARY, The State. Biennial report | of the | State Librarian | and | keeper of the Capitol, | to the | Legislature of Mississippi, | for the | years 1890 and 1891. | Printed by authority. | Jackson, Miss.: | Pow & McNeily, State printers. | 1892. |
8 vo. pp. 27.
Copies seen: Owen.

—— Catalogue of. *See* Mrs. Mary Morancy.

LINCOLN COUNTY. Sketch of.
In Lowry and McCardle's *Mississippi*, p. 523.

LINGUISTICS. *See* Bureau of Ethnology, A. S. Gatschet, and James Pilling.

LIPSCOMB, *Prof.* DABNEY, *A. M.* College Y. M. C. A. work: its needs and methods.
In *Proceedings Mississippi Y. M. C. A. Convention*, Apr. 25-28, 1889.

—— School government as a means of moral training.
In *Proceedings Mississippi State Teachers' Association*, Dec. 28-31, 1890.

—— Education a prime factor in Mississippi history.
Ibid. July 5-6, 1894.

—— Objects, methods, and results of Sunday school work.
In the *Christian Advocate*, New Orleans, Mar. 3, 1891.

—— A library in every school. Why not?
In the *Mississippi Teacher*, Nov., 1897.

—— Mississippi teachers at the National Educational Association.
Ibid. Sept., 1889.

—— How to spend the vacation.
Ibid. June, 1889.

—— The Keswick Convention of 1899.
In the *Christian Advocate*, Nashville. Sept. 28, 1899.

—— At service in old St. Giles's, Edinburgh.
Ibid. Nov. 2, 1889.

—— Paris and the next International Exposition.
In the *University of Mississippi Magazine*, Oct., 1899.

—— English in the high school.
In the *Mississippi Journal of Education*, Jan., 1900.

—— A tribute to the memory of Judge William M. Rogers.
In *East Mississippi Times*, Starkville. Oct. 2, 1890.

—— Pledges on examinations.
In the *Reflector*, A. & M College, Miss., Jan., 1891.

—— Negro wit and humor in Irwin Russell's Poems.
In the *Record*, University, Miss., March, 1899.

LIPSCOMB, *Prof.* DABNEY, *A. M.* Mississippi's "Backwoods Poet."
In *Publications Mississippi State Historical Society*, 1898, vol. i, pp. 1-15.
Critical sketch of S. Newton Berryhill and his work.

—— William Ward, a Mississippi poet entitled to distinction.
Ibid. 1899, vol. ii, pp. 23-42.

—— James D. Lynch of Mississippi, Poet Laureate of the World's Columbian Exposition.
Ibid. 1900, vol. iii. (In press.)

LOGAN, *Rev.* NOWELL. History of the Protestant Episcopal Church in Mississippi.
In Goodspeed's *Memoirs of Mississippi*, vol. ii, pp. 348-354.

—— Sketch of Mr. Logan.
Ibid. vol. i, pp. 1141-1144.

LONGSTREET, *Rev.* AUGUSTUS BALDWIN, LLD., D. D. (1790-1870). Sketch of.
In Waddel's *Memorials of Academic Life*, pp. 274-277.
See Mayes' *Lamar: Life, Times, and Speeches*, pp. 37-42; *portrait*.
The wife of Hon. L. Q. C. Lamar was Virginia Lafayette, daughter of Mr. Longstreet.
See also Goodspeed's *Memoirs of Mississippi*, vol. i, pp. 1144-5.

—— Georgia scenes, | characters, incidents, etc. | in the | first half century of the Republic. | By | a native Georgian. | [Quitman, Ga.] | 1894. |
12 mo. pp. 238. *Illustrations.*
Previous editions: Augusta, 1835, 12 mo. pp. 235. Second edition, New York: Harper & Brothers, 1840, 12 mo. pp. 214, plates; *same*, 1843, 1848, 1850, 1858, 1869. Macon, Ga.; Burke, Boykin & Co. 1864, 8 vo. pp. 239. Copies of these have not been seen.
Contains a series of pictures of life and manners, graphically presented, and applicable to the South generally. A book widely read and popular.
Copies seen: Congress.

LOSSING, BENSON JOHN (1813-1891), *Author.* Scenes in the War of 1812: IX. War with Creek Indians.
In *Harper's New Monthly Magazine*, April 1864, vol. xxviii, pp. 598-616.
Contains the following portraits and plans: Weatherford in Jackson's Tent; Plan of Fort Mims (after Pickett); General Andrew Jackson; General John Coffee, and plan of Battle of Talladega.

—— The | pictorial field book | of the | War of 1812; | or, | illustrations, by pen and pencil, of the history, biog- | raphy, scenery, relics, and traditions of the | last war for American independence. | By Benson J. Lossing. | With several hundred engravings on wood, by Lossing and Barritt, | chiefly from original sketches by the author. | New York: | Harper & Brothers, publishers. | Franklin Square. | [1896.]
8vo. 2 p. l. pp. 1084. *882 illustrations.*
The first edition was published in 1868, and a second, 1869, the title pages, pagination, etc., of each being the same as this edition. First issued in twelve parts.
Contains account of the War against the Creek Indians, pp. 738-782; and Operations in the Gulf region, pp. 1016 et seq., with numerous *illustrations, maps, and plans*. Portraits of Gens. Jackson, Coffee, and Claiborne. His account appears to be based principally on Pickett's *Alabama* and Claiborne's *Life of Sam Dale.*
Copies seen: Congress.

LOUISIANA. Topographical and statistical | account of the | Province of Louisiana, | containing, | a description of its soil, climate, trade, and produce, | its divisions, rivers, lakes, cities, towns, &c. | Laws, customs, habits and manners—civil, com- | mercial, political, and ecclesiastical es- | tablishments—numbers and pursuits, of | its inhabitants, together with new and | interesting particulars, relative | to the | Indian tribes: | to which is annexed, a | copious preface; and, | the recent conventions, between the | United States, | and the | French Republic. | Compiled by different individuals, possessed of the | best information, and from the documents com- | municated to Congress, by the President. | From the Franklin press: | Baltimore, | printed for John Rice, | Samuel Butler, and Warner & Hanna. | By Martin & Pratt. | 1803. |
>   24mo. 3 p. l. pp. 13–80. 1 l. folded.
>   Contains *passim* references to Mobile and the contiguous region.
>   In Vol. 51, *Thorndike pamphlets* and Library of Congress.
>   *Copies seen:* Congress.

LOUISVILLE BAPTIST ASSOCIATION. History of. *See Rev.* L. S. Foster.

—— Minutes. 1838–1899.
>   8vo.
>   Minutes have been published for each session, but no complete file is known. Mr. Foster, after the most diligent search, was unable to locate copies for 1838, 1839, 1840, 1847, and 1865.

LOVE, WILLIAM FRANKLIN (1852–1898), *M. C. from Miss.* Memorial addresses | on the | life and character | of | William F. Love | (late a Representative from Mississippi), | delivered in the | House of Representatives and Senate, | Fifty-fifth Congress, | third session. | Washington. | Government printing office. | 1899. |
>   8vo. pp. 54. *Portrait.*

LOWELL, JOHN (1769–1840), *Author.* The | impartial inquirer. | Being | a candid examination | of the | conduct of the president of the United States, | in execution of the | powers vested in him, | by | the Act of Congress of May 1, 1810: | to which is added, | some reflections | upon the | invasion of the Spanish Territory | of West-Florida. | By a citizen of Mass. | (Boston). | Russell & Cutler, printers. | 1811. |
>   8vo. pp. 96.
>   Originally published in the *Columbian Centinel*, Boston.
>   In Vol. 48, *Wolcott Pamphlets*, Library of Congress.
>   *Copies seen:* Congress.

LOWNDES COUNTY. Sketch of.
>   In Lowry and McCardle's *Mississippi*, pp. 523–528.

LOWREY, MARK PERRIN (1828–), *D. D.* Sketch of.
>   In Foster's *Mississippi Baptist Preachers*, pp. 458–464; *portrait.*

LOWRY, ROBERT (b. 1830), *and* MCCARDLE, WILLIAM H. A history | of | Mississippi, | from the | discovery of the Great River | by Hernando De Soto, | including the | earliest settlement made by the French, | under Iberville, | to | the death of Jefferson Davis. | By Robert Lowry and William H. McCardle. | Jackson, Miss.: | R. H. Henry & Co. | 1891. |
>   8vo. pp. viii, 5–648.
>   The value of this publication consists in the several sketches of the counties of the State, chapters xxiii–xxxv.
>   *Copies seen:* Owen.

LOWRY, ROBERT (b. 1830), *and* MCCARDLE, WILLIAM H. State history series. | A | history of Mississippi | for use in schools | by | Robert Lowry | and | William H. McCardle | New York and New Orleans | University Publishing Company | 1892. |
> 12mo. pp. 262, lviii. Profusely *illustrated*.
> The pp., lviii, contain the constitution of Nov. 1, 1890.
> *Copies seen:* Owen.

—— Administration of Mr. Lowry as governor.
> In Lowry and McCardle's *Mississippi*, pp. 415–416.

LUDLOW, NOAH MILLER (1795–1886), *Actor*. Dramatic life | as I found it: | a record of personal experience; with an account of the rise | and progress of the drama in the West and South, with | anecdotes and biographical sketches of the prin- | cipal actors and actresses who have at times appeared upon the stage in | the Mississippi valley. | By | N. M. Ludlow | actor and manager for thirty-eight years. | [Quotation, 3 lines.] | | St. Louis: | G. I. Jones & Co. | 1880. |
> 8vo. pp. xix, 733.
> At some time or other during its early years the author played in all of the principal towns of the South and West.
> *Copies seen:* Hamner.

LUNATIC ASYLUM. Annual report of the superintendent [Wm. M. Compton, M. D.] of the Mississippi State Lunatic Asylum, for the year 1870.
> In Appendix to *Journal* of the Senate of Mississippi, 1871, pp. 66–107.
> This report is a "Synoptical History of the Mississippi State Lunatic Asylum," from its inception to Dec. 1870.

—— *See also* Insane Asylum.

LYELL, CHARLES (1797–1875), *Bart., English Geologist*. A second visit | to | the United States | of | North America. | By Sir Charles Lyell, F. R. S., | President of the Geological Society of London, author of "The Principles | of Geology" and "Travels in North America." | In two volumes. | Vol. I. [–II.] | New York: | Harper and Brothers, publishers. | London: John Murray. | 1849. |
> 12mo. Vol. i, pp. 273; vol. ii, pp. 287. *Illustrations*.
> *Copies seen:* Hamner.

LYNCH, CHARLES, (d. 1853), *Gov. of Miss.* Administration as governor.
> In Lowry and McCardle's *Mississippi*, p. 278.

LYNCH, JAMES DANIEL (1836–), *Lawyer*. The bench and bar | of | Mississippi. | By | James D. Lynch. | New York: | E. J. Hale & Son, publishers * * | 1881. |
> 8vo. pp. 539. Inset, "Correction," between pages 536 and 537. *12 steel portraits*.
> Contains *passim* some account of the jurisprudence of the State: and in the appendix lists of the judges of the supreme court, circuit judges, chancellors, and attorneys-general of Mississippi from the organization of the State government.
> Contains the following biographical sketches:
>
> Adams, Robert H.
> Anderson, Fulton.
> Anderson, William E.
> Barksdale, William R.
> Barry, William S. (*portrait*).
> Barton, Roger.
> Black, John.
> Boyd, Samuel S.
>
> Brooke, Walker.
> Brown, Albert G.
> Buckner, Robert H.
> Cage, Harry.
> Chalmers, Joseph W.
> Child, Joshua.
> Claiborne, J. F. H.
> Clayton, Alexander M. (*portrait*).

Clayton, George R.
Clarke, Joshua G.
Cocke, Stephen.
Davis, Joseph E. (*portrait*).
Dowd, William F.
Ellis, Powhatan.
Fisher, Ephraim S.
Foote, Henry S.
Gholson, Samuel J.
Glenn, David C.
Grayson, Spence M.
Griffith, Wm. B.
Guion, John I.
Hampton, John P.
Handy, Alexander H.
Harding, Lyman.
Harris, William L.
Harris, Buckner C.
Harrison, James T. (*portrait*).
Henderson, John.
Holt, Joseph.
Howard, Volney E.
Howry, James M.
Hutchinson, Anderson.
Johnston, Amos R.
Lake, William A.
Leake, Walter.
Magee, Eugene.
Marsh, Samuel P.
Martin, John H.
Mayes, Daniel.
McMurran, John T.
McNutt, Alexander G.
Mitchell, James C.

Montgomery, Alexander.
Nicholson, Isaac R.
Peyton, Ephraim G.
Phelan, James (*portrait*).
Poindexter, George.
Pray, P. Rutilius R.
Prentiss, Sergeant S. (*portrait*).
Potter, George L.
Quitman, John A.
Rankin, Christopher.
Reed, Thomas B.
Sale, John B. (*portrait*).
Scott, Charles (*portrait*).
Sharkey, Wm. L. (*portrait*).
Smiley, James M. (*portrait*).
Smith, Cotesworth P.
Stockton, Richard.
Tarpley, Collin S.
Taylor, John.
Thacher, Joseph S. B.
Tompkins, Patrick W.
Toulmin, Harry.
Trotter, James F.
Turner, Edward.
Vannerson, Wm.
Walker, Robert J.
Walter, Harvey W. (*portrait*).
Webber, Richard H.
Wilkinson, Edward C.
Winchester, George.
Wright, Daniel W.
Yerger, George S.
Yerger, Jacob S. (*portrait*).
Yerger, Wm.

Copies seen: Owen.

LYNCH, JAMES DANIEL. The | bench and bar | of | Texas. | By | James D. Lynch, | [Author's work, 2 lines.] | [Quotation, 3 lines.] | Published by the author. | St. Louis: | Nixon-Jones Printing Co. | 1885. |
8vo. pp. 610. *8 steel portraits.*

—— Robert E. Lee, or Heroes of the South. A poem. By J. D. Lynch, West Point, Miss. 1876.
8vo. pp. 31.

—— Redpath, or The Kuklux Tribunal. Dedicated to Thomas F. Bayard. Columbus, Miss. 1877.
8vo. pp. 59.

—— Kemper County vindicated. New York, E. J. Hale & Son. 1878.
12mo. pp. 420.

—— Industrial history of Texas. St. Louis. 1888.
8vo.

—— Columbia saluting the Nations. Adopted as the salutation ode at the opening of the World's Fair, Chicago. 1893.
12mo.

He is also the author of many other poems.

LYNCH, JAMES DANIEL. Poet laureate of the World's Columbian Exposition. *See* Dabney Lipscomb.

—— Sketch of.
>In Goodspeed's *Memoirs of Mississippi*, vol. i, p. 1164.

M.

M'CALL, HUGH (1767-1824). The | history of Georgia, | containing | brief sketches | of the | most remarkable events, | up to the present day. | By Capt. Hugh M'Call. | In two volumes. Vol. I [-II.] | [Quotation, 3 lines.] | Savannah: | printed and published by Seymour & Williams [Vol. ii., by William T. Williams.] | 1811 [-1816]. |
>8vo. Vol. i, pp. viii, 376; vol. ii, pp. vii, 424.
>The narrative is not brought down later than 1783. The author does not confine himself to mere local detail, but gives accounts of the numerous encounters and transactions of the whites with the Indians. Much data as to the natives and of their leaders is preserved in this way. The work is based on early manuscripts and incidents gathered from the pioneers.
>In Appendix, vol. i, are the following documents:
>The charter for the settlement of Georgia. pp. 329-356.
>Oglethorpe's first treaty with the Indians, Oct. 18, 1733. pp. 357-362.
>Oglethorpe's second treaty with the Indians, dated at the Coweta town, Aug. 21, 1739. pp. 363-367.
>Acknowledgment by sundry chiefs and others of Malatche Opiya Mico as "our rightful and natural prince," pp. 367-368.
>*Copies seen:* Congress.

McCARDLE, WILLIAM H., *and* LOWRY, ROBERT. History of Mississippi. *See* Robert Lowry.

McCLUNG, *Col.* ALEXANDER KEITH (1812-1855), *Lawyer.* Address on the life, character, and public services of Henry Clay, delivered before the Legislature of Mississippi, Jan., 1853.
>In Lowry and McCardle's *Mississippi*, pp. 324-337.

McCULLOH, JAMES HAINES, Jr. (1793-   ), *M. D., Author.* Researches, | philosophical and antiquarian, | concerning the | aboriginal history of America. | By J. H. McCulloh, Jr., M. D. | Baltimore: Published by Fielding Lucas, Jr. | 1829. |
>8vo. pp. x, 13-535. *Maps* showing route of Soto expedition.
>Pp. 150-168 relates to "the Natchez and other Indians of Florida;" and appendix iii, pp. 523-529, to the "Expedition of Soto to Florida."
>*Copies seen:* Hamner.

McINTOSH, *Gen.* WILLIAM. Tragic death of. *See* J. D. Dreisback.

M'KENNEY, THOMAS LORRAINE (1785-1859), *Author.* Memoirs, | official and personal; | with | Sketches of travels | among the | Northern and Southern Indians; | embracing | a war excursion, | and descriptions of | scenes along the western borders. | By | Thomas L. M'Kenney, late chief of the bureau of Indian Affairs | [-etc., 2 lines]. | Two volumes in one. | Vol. I. [-II.] | New York: Paine and Burgess, 60 John-st. | 1846. |
>8vo. Vol. i, pp. viii, 17-340; vol. ii, pp. vi, 136. *Illustrated.* Contains also *plate: Death of Pushmataha.*
>*Copies seen:* Hamner.

McKENNEY, THOMAS LORRAINE, *and* HALL, JAMES. History | of the | Indian Tribes | of | North America, | with | biographical sketches and anecdotes | of the | principal chiefs. | Embellished with one hundred and twenty portraits. | From the | Indian gallery | in the | Department of War, at Washington. | By Thomas L. McKenney, | late of the Indian Department, Washington, and James Hall, esq., | of Cincinnati. | In three volumes, | volume I. [-III.] | Philadelphia: | published by D. Rice & A. N. Hart, | No. 27 | Minor street | 1854. |

    4to. Vol. i, title, 1 leaf, pp. 333; vol. ii, pp. xvii, 9-290; vol. iii, pp. iv, 17-392.

    The following biographical sketches of Indians belonging to Southern tribes are given, viz:

    Volume I: Yoholo Micco, a Creek chief (*portrait*), pp. 69-70; Neamathla, a Seminole chief (*portrait*), pp. 77-85; Menawa, a Creek warrior (*portrait*), pp. 103-115; Pushmataha, a Choctaw war chief (*portrait*), pp. 185-193; Selocta, a Creek chief (*portrait*), pp. 207-212; Paddy Carr, a Creek interpreter (*portrait*), pp. 245-247; Tahchee, a Cherokee chief (*portrait*), pp. 251-260; Micanopy, a Seminole chief (*portrait*), pp. 271-279; Opothle Yoholo, speaker of the Creek councils (*portrait*), pp. 281-294; Timpoochee Barnard, a Uchee warrior (*portrait*), pp. 297-302; McIntosh, a Creek chief (*portrait*), pp. 307-314.

    Volume II: Tustennuggee Emathla, a Creek chief (*portrait*), pp. 71-74; Major Ridge, a Cherokee chief (*portrait*), pp. 77-101; John Ridge, a Cherokee (*portrait*), pp. 103-106; Asseola, a Seminole leader (*portrait*), pp. 141-166.

    Volume III: This volume contains general view of Indian tribes

    Copies seen: Hamner.

McMURRAN, JOHN T., *Lawyer.* Sketch of.
    In Lynch's *Bench and Bar of Mississippi*, pp. 140-142.

McNUTT, ALEXANDER GALLATIN (1802-1848), *Lawyer, Gov. of Miss.* Sketch of.
    In Lynch's *Bench and Bar of Mississippi*, pp. 133-135.
    See also Goodspeed's *Memoirs of Mississippi*, vol. i, p. 1236.

—— Administration as governor.
    In Lowry and McCardle's *Mississippi*, pp. 279-298.
    See also Fulkerson's *Recollections of Early Days in Mississippi*, pp. 14-15

McRAE, JOHN JOHNSON (1815-1868), *Gov. of Miss., Lawyer, U. S. Senator and M. C. from Miss.* Speech | of | Hon. J. J. McRae, of Mississippi, | on | the compromise question. | Delivered | in the Senate of the United States, January 29, and February 2, 1852. | Washington: | printed at the Congressional Globe office. | 1852. |
    8vo. pp. 24. Double columns.

—— The | Governor's [John J. McRae] Message. | November, 2d, 1857. | Jackson: | E. Barksdale, State printer. | 1857. |
    8vo. pp. 15.

—— Administration as governor.
    In Lowry and McCardle's *Mississippi*, pp. 339-340.

McWILLIE, WILLIAM (1795-1869), *Gov. of Miss.* Administration as governor.
    In Lowry and McCardle's *Mississippi*, p. 340.

—— Genealogy of the McWillie family.
    In Goodspeed's *Memoirs of Mississippi*, vol. i, pp. 1243-1247.

MADISON COLLEGE. Sketch of.
    In Mayes' *History of Education in Mississippi*, pp. 60-63.

MADISON COUNTY. [Alabama.] Letter | from | the Secretary of the Treasury [Albert Gallatin,] | transmitting | a report, | prepared | in obedience to a resolution of the first instant, | requesting information | touching any settlement contrary to law, | on the | public lands, in the County of Madison, | in the | Mississippi Territory. | December 18th, 1809. | Referred to the committee appointed to inquire into the expediency of allowing a | representative to Madison County, in the Mississippi Territory. | Washington City: | printed by Roger Chew Weightman. | 1809. |
 4to. pp. 36.
 This report relates to troubles growing out of the claims to lands under Georgia titles, these being asserted against the United States soon after the surveys consequent on the Cherokee and Chickasaw cessions. It contains many documents descriptive of local conditions and settlement; and is the beginning for the history of the county. It contains two full lists of the settlers. The first is a register of applications and permissions to settle, issued by Thomas Freeman, surveyor, which shows dates of applications and location of residence of settlers. The other is a census of the county, taken in January, 1809, which gives full details as to the number in families and ages, with number of slaves.
 Copies seen: Owen.

MADISON COUNTY. Sketch of.
 In Lowry and McCardle's *Mississippi*, pp. 528–531.

MAGEE, EUGENE, *Lawyer.* Sketch of.
 In Lynch's *Bench and Bar of Mississippi*, p. 137.

MAGRUDER, *Prof.* W. H. Mississippi schools during the Territorial period.
 In *Publications Mississippi State Historical Society*, 1900, vol. iii. (In press.)

MAHAN, A. T. The Navy in the Civil War.—III. | The gulf | and | inland waters. | By | A. T. Mahan, | commander U. S. Navy | New York, | Charles Scribner's Sons. | 1883. |
 12mo. pp. viii., 1 l., 267 *8 maps.*
 Battle of Mobile Bay, 1864, pp. 218–249; *map.*
 Copies seen: Congress.

—— Great commanders | * * * * | Admiral Farragut. | By | Captain A. T. Mahan, U. S. Navy. | President | [–etc. 3 lines.] | [Publishers, trade design.] | New York | D. Appleton and Company | 1892. |
 12mo. 3 prel. leaves. pp. 333. *Portrait* of Farragut; *5 maps.*
 Mobile Bay fight, 1864, pp. 237–293; *map.*
 This map of the fight is more detailed than that of the same action in the preceding title.
 Copies seen: Congress.

MALONE, WALTER. Claribel and other poems. 1882.
 12mo.

—— The outcast and other poems. 1885.
 12mo.

MANLY, *Miss* LOUISE. Southern Literature | from 1579–1895. | A comprehensive review, with copious extracts | and criticisms | for the use of schools and the general reader | containing an appendix with a full list of Southern | authors | By | Louise Manly | Illustrated | Richmond, Va. | B. F. Johnson Publishing Company | 1895 |
 12mo. pp. 514.
 "The primary object of this book is to furnish our children with material for becoming acquainted with the development of American life and history as found in Southern writers and their works."—*Preface.*
 Copies seen: Congress.

MAPS OF MISSISSIPPI.
>No attempt is made to present any approximation to a complete list of maps of the State, or of its several counties and towns.

MISSISSIPPI: STATE.

—— Bowen, E. A map of the country comprised in the State of Mississippi as known in the year 1764, by Eman Bowen, geographer.
>In B. L. C. Wailes' *Report on the Agriculture and Geology of Mississippi*, 1854.

—— British West Florida.
>In Lowry and McCardle's *Mississippi for Schools*, p. 45.

—— De Soto's route.
>In Lowry and McCardle's *Mississippi for Schools*, p. 11.

—— Diagram of the surveying district south of Tennessee.
>In U. S. Senate *Doc.* 17, as No. 7, 25th Cong., 3d sess., vol. 1.
>Shows the bounds of the several Indian cessions.

—— Goodspeed. Map of the Mississippi Country in 1764.
>In Goodspeed's *Memoirs of Mississippi*, vol. i, facing p. 58.
>Same as Bowen's *Map, supra*.

—— —— Battle of Shiloh, April 6, 1862.
>*Ibid.* p. 107.

—— —— Battle of Iuka, Sept. 19, 1862.
>*Ibid.* p. 139.

—— —— Battle of Chickasaw Bluffs, Dec. 29, 1862.
>*Ibid.* p. 139.

—— —— Battle of Port Hudson, June, 1863.
>*Ibid.* p. 202.

—— —— Battle of Big Black River Bridge, May 17, 1863.
>*Ibid.* p. 202.

—— —— Battle of Champion's Hill, May 16, 1863.
>*Ibid.* p. 682.

—— —— Indian cession map of Mississippi.
>In Goodspeed's *Memoirs of Mississippi*, vol. ii, p. 26.

—— —— Siege of Vicksburg, May 25 to July 4, 1863.
>*Ibid.* p. 250.

—— —— Battle of Tupelo, July 14, 1864.
>*Ibid.* p. 458.

—— —— Battle of Jackson.
>*Ibid.* p. 458.

—— —— Battle of Raymond, May 12, 1863.
>*Ibid.* p. 714.

—— —— Battle of Brice's Cross Roads.
>*Ibid.* p. 714.

—— —— Battle of Helena, July 4, 1863.
>*Ibid.* p. 714.

—— —— Battle of Corinth.
>*Ibid.* p. 842.

MAPS OF MISSISSIPPI. Hardee, T. S. Hardee's geographical, historical and statistical | official map | of | Mississippi | embracing portions of | Alabama, Arkansas, Louisiana and Tennessee, | from recent surveys and investigations | and | officially compiled under authority from the State Legislature | By | T. S. Hardee State engineer | A. D. 1872. | Hugh Lewis, lithographer and publisher, New Orleans, La. |
> Scale: One-twelfth of an inch to a mile.

—— Harper, L. The prairies above Tibby Creek.
> In Harper's *Preliminary Report on the Geology and Agriculture of Mississippi*, 1857.

—— Harper, L. Mississippi bottom in the State of Mississippi.
> In Harper's *Preliminary Report on the Geology and Agriculture of Mississippi*, 1857, p. 259.

—— Harper, L. Geological chart of Mississippi.
> In Harper's *Preliminary Report on the Geology and Agriculture of Mississippi*, 1857.
> Scale: 20 miles to an inch.

—— Hilgard, E. W. Geological map of Mississippi.
> In Hilgard's *Report on the Geology and Agriculture of Mississippi*, 1860.
> Scale: 20 miles to an inch.

—— La Tourrette, John. An accurate map | or delineation of | Mississippi | with a large portion of | Louisiana & Alabama: | showing the communication by land and water | between the cities of New Orleans and Mobile, | carefully reduced | from the original surveys of the United States, | being laid off into Congressional townships, and divided into mile squares or sections, on the plan adopted by | the General Government for surveying public lands; so that persons may point to the tract on which they live. | Compiled & published by John La Tourrette, Mobile, Alabama, A. D. 1839. | Engraved | by | S. Stiles, Sherman & Smith, | New York. | Walter S. Cosine | printer. |
> Scale: 6 miles to an inch. Size: 6 x 5 feet.
> Contains the following on the margin:
> Town maps: Columbus, Grand Gulf, Jackson, Natchez, Norfolk, Port Gibson, Vicksburg, Waverly, Woodville, Yazoo City.
> For historical purposes this is the most valuable map extant.

—— Lieber, O. M. Geological map of Mississippi.
> In "A sketch of the geology of the State of Mississippi" in *The Mining Magazine*, New York, July, 1852, vol. iii, p. 42.
> Black etching and geological indications.

—— Meridian, Miss. | 1891. | Population 15,000. | Drawn and published by C. J. Pauli, 726 Central ave., Milwaukee, Wis. |
> Bird's-eye-view map. *Circa*, 18 x 36 inches.

—— Mississippi Territory in 1792.
> In Lowry and McCardle's *Mississippi for Schools*, p. 68.

—— Mississippi in 1817, showing counties and Indian tribes.
> In Lowry and McCardle's *Mississippi for Schools*, p. 94.

—— Mitchell, S. A., *Publisher*. Map of Louisiana, Mississippi, and Alabama. Philadelphia. 1845.
> Scale: *Circa* 30 miles to an inch.
> Shows steamboat and stage routes through these States.

—— Post-route map of Mississippi. Published by the Post-Office Department.
> Several editions.
> Shows post-offices, with intermediate distances on the mail routes.

MAPS OF MISSISSIPPI. Regional map, showing peculiarities of surface and soil.
>In Lowry and McCardle's *Mississippi for Schools*, p. 258.

COUNTIES.

—— County map of Mississippi in 1892.
>In Lowry and McCardle's *Mississippi for Schools; Frontispiece.*

Pontotoc.

—— Harper, L. Special map of Pontotoc County.
>In Harper's *Preliminary Report on the Geology and Agriculture of Mississippi*, 1857.

Tippah.

—— —— Special map of Tippah County.
>In Harper's *Preliminary Report on the Geology and Agriculture of Mississippi*, 1857.

Tishomingo.

—— —— Special map of Tishomingo County.
>In Harper's *Preliminary Report on the Geology and Agriculture of Mississippi*, 1857.

TOWNS.

—— For Columbus, Grand Gulf, Jackson, Natchez, Norfolk, Port Gibson, Vicksburg, Waverly, Woodville, and Yazoo City, *See* La Tourrette's *Map of Miss., supra.*

MARINE, *Rev.* FLETCHER E. Sketch | of | Rev. John Hersey, | minister of the gospel, | of the | M. E. Church. | By Rev. F. E. Marine. | [Quotation, 5 lines.] | Baltimore, Md. | Hoffman & Co., printers | No. 296, W. Baltimore street. | 1879. |
>12mo. pp. vi [i]. [3]-228. *Port. of Rev. Mr. Hersey.*
>Rev. Mr. Hersey was Choctaw Indian factor at Cahaba, 1819-1822, and a short account of his work in that capacity is given.
>*Copies seen:* Hamner.

MARION COUNTY. Sketch of.
>In Lowry and McCardle's *Mississippi*, pp. 531-533.
>*See also* Goodspeed's *Memoirs of Mississippi*, vol. 1, pp. 190-191.

—— Ancient mounds in.
>Mentioned in Smithsonian *Report*, 1879, p. 444.

MARSCHALK, ANDREW, *First printer in Mississippi.* Sketch of.
>In Claiborne's *Mississippi*, pp. 194, 376, 530.

MARSH, SAMUEL P., *Lawyer.* Sketch of.
>In Lynch's *Bench and Bar of Mississippi*, p. 144.

MARSHALL COUNTY. Sketch of.
>In Lowry and McCardle's *Mississippi*, pp. 533-537.

—— Centennial address on the history of. *See* A. M. Clayton.

MARSHALL, C. K., *A. M.* A key, with general observations, explanations, and questions. Designed to accompany the Astronomical Atlas. Philadelphia. 1847.
>12mo. pp. 184.

MARSHALL, THOMAS A., *and* Smedes, Wm. C. *Reporters.* Mississippi Reports, vols. 9–22. *See* Supreme Court.

MARSHALL, T. DABNEY. Everything, nothing, and other things. Poems by T. Dabney Marshall. 1886.
12mo.

MARTIN, JOHN M. (1790–1841), *Lawyer.* Sketch of.
In Lynch's *Bench and Bar of Mississippi*, pp. 288–289.

MARTIN, *Miss* ELLEN. The feet of clay. A novel. By Miss Ellen Martin, of Vicksburg, Miss. 1881. New York.
12mo.

MARTIN, *Rev.* G. H. Responsibilities of educated men. An address delivered before the Philomathean and Hermenian Societies of Mississippi College, July 25, 1859.
8vo. pp. 28.

MASON, TOM. Sketch of.
In Claiborne's *Mississippi*, pp. 225–226.
He was at the head of a notorious robber band which infested Mississippi in Territorial times. Associated with him were Big Harp, Little Harp, and others. *See also* Lowry and McCardle's *Mississippi*, pp. 504–505.

MASONS, ANCIENT FREE AND ACCEPTED. Proceedings | of the | Grand Lodge of Mississippi, | Ancient Free and Accepted Masons, | from its organization July 27, 5818, to include the | communication held in the year 5852, | compiled from the "Extracts from the Proceedings." | By a committee of the Grand Lodge. | Jackson, Miss.: | Clarion steam printing establishment. | 1882. |
8vo. pp. xviii, 5–728.

—— Proceedings | of the | Grand Lodge of Mississippi, | of | Free and Accepted Masons, | at its | eighty-first annual communication, | Vicksburg, February 8–9, 1899. | [Design.] | Jackson, Miss.: | Harmon Publishing Co. | 1899. |
8vo. pp. 219, [19], 107. *Port. of J. M. Stone.*
Copies of the *Proceedings*, etc., for each annual communication have appeared.

—— Proceedings | of the | Grand Royal Arch Chapter | of the | State of Mississippi, | at its | forty-ninth annual convocation, | held at | Biloxi, February 10–11, 1897. | [Design.] | Jackson, Miss.: | Clarion-Ledger Co., printers. | 1897. |
8vo. pp. 117.
Copies of the *Proceedings*, etc., are regularly issued after each annual convocation.

—— Proceedings | of the | Grand Council | of | Royal and Select Masters, | in the | State of Mississippi, | 1856–1866. | Including those of the | Grand Council, organized in 1855. | Reprinted from the originals. | Vicksburg: | Vicksburg Printing and Publishing Co. | 1897. |
8vo. Title, 1 leaf, pp. 183, xvi.
As indicated, the above is a reprint from pamphlet *Proceedings*, etc., issued at the time. These are regularly issued each year.

—— Thirty-eighth annual conclave | of the | Grand Commandery | Knights Templar, | of the | State of Mississippi, | held at | Water Valley, February 8–10, | 1898. | [Design.] | Jackson, Miss.: | Clarion-Ledger print. | 1898. |
8vo. pp. 145, [5].
The proceedings of each annual conclave are regularly issued.

MATHEWS, JOSEPH, *Gov. of Miss.* Administration as governor.
In Lowry and McCardle's *Mississippi,* p. 319.

—— Sketch of.
In Goodspeed's *Memoirs of Mississippi,* vol. II, p. 414.

MAYES, DANIEL, *Lawyer.* Sketch of.
In Lynch's *Bench and Bar of Mississippi,* pp. 254-257.

MAYES, EDWARD (1846-), *Lawyer, LL. D., ex-Chancellor Univ. of Miss.* The voices of the past as heard through life | An | anniversary address | delivered before the Hermæan Society | of the | University of Mississippi, | Feb. 22nd, 1868. |
8vo. pp. 24.

—— Possible future of the South.
In the *XIX Century,* Charleston, S. C., Jan. and Feb., 1870.

—— Equatorial Africa.
Ibid. 1870.
Review of Du Chailler's work of above title.

—— The future of the negro.
Ibid. 1870.

—— Christianity versus anarchy: Address of the Hon. Edward Mayes, LL. D., delivered before Grenada Collegiate Institute, Grenada, Miss., June 16, 1887.
8vo. pp. 16.

—— The State University: its endowment.
In the *Weekly Clarion,* Jackson, Miss., Oct. 26, 1887, and Jan. 4, 1888.
Subsequently published as a pamphlet.
The first was a reply to an article of Senator J. Z. George, in which he assailed the right of the University endowment; and the second was a reply to his rejoinder.

—— The progress of education in Mississippi. Essay delivered by Chancellor Mayes before E. M. T. Association at Tupelo, July 11, 1889.
In the *Mississippi Teacher,* Sept., 1889.

—— The legal and judicial history of Mississippi.
In Goodspeed's *Memoirs of Mississippi,* vol. I, pp. 100-131; vol. II, pp. 23-36.

—— Educational history of Mississippi.
Ibid. vol. II, pp. 300-348.

—— The Christian resources of the New World. Address before the Ecumenical Conference of the Methodist Episcopal Church, at Washington, Oct., 1891.
In the *Minutes* of the Conference, 1891.

—— A glance at the fountains of our land titles. Read before the Miss. State Bar Association, Jan. 3, 1887.
In the *Minutes* of the Miss. State Bar Association, 1887, pp. 5-14.

—— The administration of estates in Mississippi. Read before the Miss. State Bar Association, Jan. 6, 1891.
Ibid. 1891, pp. 52-121.

—— Origin of the State's Colleges.
In the *Clarion-Ledger,* Jackson, April 8, 1897.
Delivered at the dedication of Webster Hall, of Millsaps College, March 31, 1897.

MAYES, EDWARD. Lucius Q. C. Lamar: | his life, times, and speeches. | 1825–1893. | By Edward Mayes, LL. D., | Ex-Chancellor of the University of Mississippi. | [Quotations, 2 lines.] | Nashville, Tenn.: | Publishing House of the Methodist Episcopal Church, South. | Barbee & Smith, Agents. | 1896. |

> Large 8vo. pp. 820.
>
> ILLUSTRATIONS: Justice L. Q. C. Lamar; Mirabeau B. Lamar; Judge L. Q. C. Lamar of Ga.; Rev. Augustus B. Longstreet; Group of Mississippi Senators and Congressmen at the time of secession; Gen. Edward C. Walthall; Group of liberal Republican leaders, 1870-75; Charles Sumner; Senator L. Q. C. Lamar; Group of Democratic Senators; Group of Republican Senators; Group of Mr. Lamar's children; Group of President Cleveland and Cabinet; Funeral of the Bloody Shirt; Group of the Supreme Court of 1891; and Campus Views at Emory College.
>
> 2 editions, 1,000 copies each.
>
> The facts and events of Mr. Lamar's long and brilliant public life have been presented with great prolixity and detail, with an examination of all contemporaneous public matters with which he was connected.
>
> Mr. Lamar's speeches and writings are here reprinted *in extenso*.
>
> The following extracts from press estimates indicate the flattering reception accorded the work:
>
> "Aside from its inestimable historical value, it presents a most fascinating portrait of its many sided subject."—*Charleston News and Courier.*
>
> "In this finely illustrated volume the able ex-Chancellor of the University of Mississippi has given to the public a most admirable and valuable biography of the distinguished Georgian."—*Richmond (Va.) Times.*
>
> "A book which is of general interest because of the light which it sheds upon the reconstruction of the South, and the gradual restoration of Southern men to public positions. * * * The story is well told."—*San Francisco Chronicle.*
>
> "A fitting picture of the great statesman and jurist, one [and] all who know him will recognize. * * * A most valuable contribution to the history of the times. A vast amount of hard and careful work has been done in its preparation."—*Nashville American.*
>
> "Replete with interesting matter pertaining to a most momentous period in our national history, presented in a very attractive manner."—*Columbia (S. C.) Register.*
>
> "One of the most valuable contributions to American history."—*Memphis Commercial-Appeal.*
>
> "One of the most valuable additions to biographical and historical literature. * * * Complete and exceedingly well written. * * * This book will fill a long-felt want."—*Florida Times-Union.*
>
> "A literary production of rare merit. * * * The book will remove unreasonable prejudice, and will inspire, not only mutual respect, but a more cordial feeling among those who participated in the great struggle between the sections."—*Washington (D. C.) Silver Knight.*
>
> "A lifelike presentation of the great statesman's personality, prepared with great care. Related in a finished literary style, and the whole gives a perfect portrait of the man as he really was."—*Houston (Tex.) Post.*
>
> "It will take its place among American classics."—*Washington Post.*
>
> "This element of fairness runs all through the book. * * * As a picture of the reconstruction period this book stands amongst the first."—*Milwaukee Journal.*
>
> "Written with such honesty and fairness as to make it as interesting to the people of the North as to those of the South."—*Inter Ocean.*
>
> "Written in the true historical spirit. With almost judicial impartiality."—*Newark News.*
>
> "With great care and with discriminating judgment."—*Brooklyn Eagle.*
>
> "One of the lives which let the reader deeper into the secret of the civil war than almost any history. A straightforward, frank, and unpassionate narrative."—*N. Y. Independent.*

"A delightful biography—such discrimination and charm as to render it an invaluable contribution."—*Portland (Me.) Argus*.

"A valuable contribution to the history of the stirring times in which his subject was a principal actor. The work is evidently the result of vast and painstaking labor, and is written in a lucid and agreeable style."—*New Orleans Picayune*.

"An excellent biographical work, which tells of an interesting career."—*Boston Globe*.

"An exhaustive and comprehensive biography of the South's great statesman and patriot."—*Detroit Free Press*.

"Interesting to Southern and Northern men alike. '—*Review of Reviews*.

"One of the most important to the South of all the historical contributions that have been made to her annals of the period just before, during, and after the civil war."—*Baltimore Sun*.

MAYES, EDWARD. United States Bureau of Education. | Circular of Information No. 2, 1899. | Contributions to American Educational History. | Edited by Herbert B. Adams. | No. 24. | History of Education | in | Mississippi. | By | Edward Mayers, LL. D., | [-etc., 2 lines.] | Washington: | Government printing office. | 1899. |

8vo. pp. 290. *Illustrations*.

MAYES, R. B. The Tenobaptist; a discourse, wherein an honest Baptist, by a course of argument to which no honest Baptist can object, is convinced that infant Christians are proper subjects of Christian baptism. 1857.

12mo. pp. 172.

MAYHEW. Missionary station.

In Lowry and McCardle's *Mississippi*, p. 549.

MEAD, *Gen.* COWLES, *M. C. from Ga., Sec. Miss. Ty.* Sketch of.

In Claiborne's *Mississippi*, pp. 275–277.

MECKLIN, *Rev.* R. W. The twin parables, or the mysteries of the Kingdom of God. Richmond, Va. 1892.

12mo.

MEDICAL ASSOCIATION. Physicians and their associations.

In Goodspeed's *Memoirs of Mississippi*, vol. ii, pp. 252-299.

Contains a history of the association, biographies of physicians, accounts of the several schools of medicine in the State, an account of the State Board of Health, and notes on yellow fever and other epidemics.

—— Transactions | of the | Mississippi | State Medical Association, | at the | twenty-second annual session, | held at | Jackson, April 17, 18, 19, 1889, | with the | roll of members and reports on medical topics. | Published by the Association. | Jackson, Miss.: | Clarion-Ledger printing establishment. | 1889. |

8vo. pp. 185[3].

25th annual session, at Natchez, April 20–22, 1892, pp. 169[1].

26th annual session, at Jackson, April 19–21, 1893, pp. 155.

—— The Journal of the Mississippi State Medical Association.

8vo.

Vol. ii, Nos. 1–12, April, 1898–March, 1899.

Vol. iii, Nos. 1–12, April, 1899–March, 1900.

Organ of Miss. State Med. Ass'n, and the successor of the *Medical Record of Mississippi*.

Edited by Dr. H. M. Folkes, Biloxi, Miss., and published by the Herald Printing Co., Biloxi, Miss.

MEDICAL RECORD OF MISSISSIPPI.   Herald Printing Co., Biloxi, Miss., 1897–1898.
> 8vo.
> Vol. I, Nos. 1–12, April, 1897–March, 1898, pp. 433.
> The number for March, 1898, contains the *Proceedings* of the 30th Annual Meeting of the Medical Society, April 21, 1897.
> The *Proceedings* of the 29th sess. of the Ass'n was the last published separately.
> H. H. Haralson, M. D., Biloxi, Miss., editor and proprietor.
> Succeeded by "The Journal of the Miss. St. Med. Ass'n."

MEEK, ALEXANDER BEAUFORT (1814–1865), *LL. D., Author and Lawyer.* The Southwest: | Its history, character, and prospects. | A discourse | for the eighth anniversary of | the Erosophic Society | of the | University of Alabama. | December 7, 1839. | By Alexander B. Meek. | Tuscaloosa: | C. B. Baldwind, P'r. . . 1840. |
> 8vo. pp. 40.
> Reprinted in his *Romantic Passages in Southwestern History*, pp. 11–69.

—— Romantic passages | in | Southwestern history; | including | orations, sketches, and essays. | By A. B. Meek, | [–etc., 1 line.] | Mobile: | S. H. Goetzel & Co., 33 Dauphin street. | New York:—117 Fulton street. | 1857. |
> 12 mo. pp. 330.
> Contents: Title, Preface, Contents, etc., pp. x; The Southwest: an oration before the Erosophic Society of the University of Alabama, Dec. 7, 1839, pp. 11–69; Claims and characteristics of Alabama history: an oration before the Historical Society of Alabama, at its anniversary at Tuscaloosa, July 9, 1855, pp. 70–106; Americanism in literature: an oration before the Phi Kappa and Demosthenian Societies of the University of Georgia, at Athens, Aug. 8, 1844, pp. 107–143; Jack-Cadeism and the fine arts: an oration before the literary societies of La Grange College, Alabama, June 16, 1841, pp. 145–190; National welcome to the soldiers returning from Mexico: an oration delivered by appointment, at Mobile, Alabama, July 4, 1848, pp. 191–210; The pilgrimage of De Soto, pp. 213–234; The massacre at Fort Mims, with a historical sketch of the first white settlements in Alabama, the Battle of Burnt Corn, and the other events that led to the Creek War of 1813-14, pp. 235–258; Sketch of Weatherford, or the Red Eagle, the great Chief of the Creeks in the War against General Jackson, with incidental accounts of many of the leading chiefs and warriors of the Muscogee Indians, pp. 250-293; The Canoe Fight, with a sketch of the first American settlements in the interior of Alabama, and of many romantic and sanguinary incidents in the Creek War; also biographies of Gen. Sam. Dale, Jere Austill, and James Smith, the heroes of that fight, pp. 295–322; The Fawn of Pascagoula; or, the "Chumpa" girl of Mobile, pp. 323–330.
> "About half this volume has been published before, in isolated portions, in pamphlets or periodicals. The author has been gratified that his researches in Southwestern History have been recognized as valuable by Bancroft, Theodore Irving, Simms, and Pickett, in their more capacious and dignified performances. This has induced him to revive his articles as they were originally produced with the addition of other and more copious sketches, elucidating our early history. These were written for incidental purposes while preparing a more elaborate work yet to be published, but they may serve in their present form to gratify the general reader better than in a more staid and regular connection."— *Preface.*
> *Copies seen:* Owen.

MELISH, JOHN (1771-1822). A geographical description | of the | United States, | with the | contiguous countries, | including | Mexico and the West Indies; | intended as an accompaniment to | Melish's | map of these countries. | By' John Melish. | A new edition, greatly improved. | Philadelphia: | published by the author. | 1822. |
> 8vo. pp. 491. [15.] *Map of U. S.*
> *Copies seen:* Hamner.

MELL, PATRICK HUES (1850-), *Ph. D.* Report | on the | climatology of the cotton plant. | By | P. H. Mell, Ph. D. | Professor [-etc., 2 lines.] | Published by authority of the Secretary of Agriculture. | Washington, D. C.: | Weather Bureau. | 1893. |
> 8vo. pp. 68, 1 l. 7 charts paged with text.
> *Copies seen:* Owen.

MERIDIAN. Meridian | and | East Mississippi. | By Gray & Murphey. | [John M. Murphey, printer, Meridian, 1894.]
> 8vo. pp. 77. *Illustrated.*
> Prepared to induce immigration.
> Contains short historical sketch, pp. 5-8.
> *Copies seen:* Owen.

—— Sketches of.
> In Goodspeed's *Memoirs of Mississippi*, vol. ii, pp. 153-158.

—— Meridian, Miss., | metropolis | of the Southwest. | A descriptive, historical | and | statistical review. | Industry, development, and enterprise. | P. J. Maloney, publisher, | 1888. |
> 8vo. pp. 99. *Map; and illustrations.*

—— Resolution of the legislature, and the testimony of the committee in reference to the riot at Meridian, 1871.
> In appendix to Senate *Journal*, 1871, pp. 1128-1181.

—— The charter | and | code of ordinances | of | the city of Meridian. | Compiled by | C. W. Gallagher, | and printed by order of the Board of Mayor and Aldermen. | 1872. | Meridian, Miss.: | Printed at the Meridian Gazette Job Office. |
> 8vo. pp. 119.

—— The original charter | together with the | amendments thereto, | and the | revised code | of | ordinances | of the city of | Meridian, Miss. | Meridian, Miss.: | Democrat Book & Job print, | 1889. |
> 8vo. pp. 215, 29, 1 l.
> Lists of the municipal officers, 1860 to 1889, are given.

—— Maloney's | Meridian | city directory | 1890. | Alphabetically arranged and classified. | Price, $1.50. | P. J. Maloney, publisher. |
> 8vo. pp. [150.]

—— Volume 1. | Chittenden's | 1899 | [Design.] | Meridian | City Directory. | Price, $3.00. | Containing | [-etc., 9 lines.] |
> 8vo. pp. 212.
> *See also* Maps, and State officers.

METEOROLOGY OF MISSISSIPPI. Sketch of, with statistics.
> In Walles' *Report on Agriculture and Geology of Mississippi*, pp. 297-308.

—— *See also* Goodspeed's *Memoirs of Mississippi*, vol. i, pp. 12-13. And P. H. Mell.

METHODIST (THE) EPISCOPAL CHURCH SOUTH IN MISSISSIPPI. A complete history of Methodism as connected with the Mississippi Conference. 1799 to 1817. *See Rev.* John G. Jones.

—— Sketch of.
    In Goodspeed's *Memoirs of Mississippi*, vol. ii, pp. 362-368.

—— *See also* Rev. Richard Abbey, *Rev.* W. C. Black, *Bishop* C. B. Galloway, Dr. Anson West, and Emmaus.

MEXICAN WAR. The | history of the raising | of | the first American flag | on | the Capitol of Mexico. | Proceedings in the United States Senate. | Washington: | printed by C. Wendell. | 1856. |
    8vo. pp. 34.
    Contains reprint of Senate Rept. Com., No. 32, 34th Cong., 1st sess., in the Senate March 6, 1856.
    A controversy arose over who first raised the flag, etc. Senator Brown, of Mississippi, in the Senate, Dec. 31, 1855, vindicated the claim of Gen. John A. Quitman.
    Copies seen: Curry.

—— Mississippi troops in.
    In Lowry and McCardle's *Mississippi*, pp. 305-317.
    See also Goodspeed's *Memoirs of Mississippi*, vol. i, pp. 139-145. The latter contains rosters.

—— Mississippi in the Mexican War.
    In Davis's *Recollections of Mississippi and Mississippians*, pp. 211-'51.

—— Jeff. Davis and the Mexican War Veterans. *See* Jefferson Davis. *See also* H. S. Foote.

MIDDLETON, *Rev.* HOLLY, of Panola County, Miss. Truth unmasked and error exposed.
    12mo.
    He is also the author of "Polemic theology."

MILFORT, LE CLERC (1750-1817). *Half title:* Mémoire | ou | coup-d'oeil rapide | sur mes différens voyages et mon | séjour dans la nation Crĕck. |

Title: Mémoire | ou | coup-d'oeil rapide | sur mes différens voyages et mon séjour | dans la nation Crĕck. | Par le G^{al}. Milfort, | Tastanégy ou grand Chef de guerre de la | nation Crĕck, et Général de brigade au service | de la République Française. | A Paris, | de l'imprimerie de Gignet et Michaud, | Reu des Bons-Enfans, N°. 6. | An xi. | (1802.)
    8vo. 2 prel. leaves, pp. 331 [1].
    [Memoir, or rapid view of my different voyages and of my residence in the Creek Nation. By General Milfort, Tastanegy, or great war chief of the Creek Nation, and brigadier-general of the French Republic, Paris, 1802.]
    After his arrival among the Indians, through the influence of McGillivray, he was rapidly advanced in position, and married the latter's Indian sister. He left the nation at the breaking out of the revolution in France. The memoir has only a general value.
    "These memoirs are interesting, but they could not have been written by Le Clerc, who was quite illiterate, and had almost forgotten his native language in the course of his travels."—Appleton's *Cyclopædia of American Biography*, vol. iii, pp. 651.
    Copies seen: Hamner,

MILITIA AND PATROL LAWS.

"*Resolved*, by the legislative council and house of representatives of the Mississippi Territory, in general assembly convened, That five hundred copies (sic) of the act, passed at the present session of the general assembly, entitled 'An act, concerning the militia of the Mississippi Territory,' and five hundred copies of the 'Rules and article of war,' together with five hundred copies of the laws 'Respecting patrols,' be printed under the direction of the governor, for the use of the militia officers: to be printed by the public printer on the same terms as the laws are printed.

"*Resolved*, That seventy-five dollars be, and hereby are appropriated, under the directions of the governor, for the purchase of   copies of Duane's Infantry Handbook, to be by him distributed among the militia officers of the Territory, and his order on the auditor of public accounts, for that sum, for the aforesaid purpose, shall authorize a warrant on the treasury of this Territory for that amount."—*Acts of the Mississippi Territory, 1812*, p. 136.

The militia act referred to is not printed in the laws of the session. The patrol act, or at least one act on that subject, appears under the following title: "An act to amend an act entitled 'An act, establishing patrols, and for other purposes.'" pp. 42–46.

No separates have been seen.

MILLER, ANDREW. New | States and Territories, | or the | Ohio, Indiana, Illinois, Michigan, | North-Western, | Missouri, Lou- | isiana, Mississippi and | Alabama, | in their real characters, | in | 1818; | Showing, in a new and short way, the sit- | uation, size, number of inhabitants, | whites and Indians—the number of | counties, villages, printing offices, | banks, factories, furnaces, forges, mills, | &c. of each; and the *name, situation, ex-* | *tent*, and number of inhabitants of each | county, with its county-town, & num- | ber of houses, stores, banks, &c. in each, | by a map table. Also, a description of | the rivers, roads, settlements, quali- | ties and prices of lands; the timber, | water, climate, diseases, prices of pro- | duce, stock and goods—and the ad- | vantages and disadvantages of each, and | of their particular parts; and of the new | parts of York State, Pennsylvania, Vir- | ginia and Kentucky; with a few words | concerning the impositions and difficul- | ties experienced in moving, settling, &c. | By Andrew Miller. | Printed for the benefit of emigrants, | and others, intending to visit | the Western country. | 1819. |

24mo. pp. 96.

"Mississippi and Alabama," pp. 85–88.

A curious and scarce little book. The promises of the title are sustained, however, in a very limited way, and all of its statements are exceedingly meager.

Copies seen: Congress.

MILLINGTON, JOHN, M. D., *Prof. Univ. of Miss.* Sketch of.

In Waddel's *Memorials of Academic Life*, pp. 277–279.

He was principal professor of geology.

See Wailes' *Report on Agriculture and Geology of Mississippi*, p. 363–364.

MILLSAPS (THE) COLLEGE. Sketch of.

In Mayes' *History of Education in Mississippi*, pp. 256–258.

MINERAL SPRINGS. *See* Albert C. Peale. *See also* Castillian Springs.

MINOR, *Gov.* DON ESTAVAN. Sketch of.

In Goodspeed's *Memoirs of Mississippi*, vol. II, pp. 446.

See also Claiborne's *Mississippi* for sundry references, account of administration.

Portrait faces, p. 170.

MISSIONS. History of the Catholic missions among the Indian tribes of the United States. *See* J. D. G. Shea. *See also* Emmaus and Mahew.

A BIBLIOGRAPHY OF MISSISSIPPI.

MISSISSIPPI. Sketch of.
> In *Encyclopædia Britannica* (9th ed.), vol. xvi, pp. 521–524; map.

—— Origin of name.
> In Claiborne's *Mississippi*, p. 31, and *note*.

MISSISSIPPI COLLEGE. Catalogues of the Mississippi College, Hinds County, Mississippi. 1852–1860, 1869–1898.
> 8 vo. 39 numbers. *Ills.* in each.

—— Laws, enacted Dec., 1852.
> 8 vo.

—— History of.
> In Mayes' *History of Education in Mississippi*, pp. 80–92.
> *See also* A. V. Rowe.

—— Society addresses. *See* T. S. Gathright, W. H. Hardy, D. A. Holman, and G. H. Martin.

MISSISSIPPI SOUND. Mobile entrance and Eastern part of Miss. Sound; chart 189 of Coast and Geodetic Survey. Sept. 1894.
> Scale: st. m. = .79 in. Size: 32 x 40 in.

—— Report of survey of 1884 for channel between Mobile Bay and Miss. Sound. Dec. 21, 1894. (House Ex. Doc. 134, 3d sess. In v. 28.)
> 8 vo. pp. 9.

MITCHELL, *Rev.* B. G. The Cumberland Presbyterian Church in Miss.
> In Goodspeed's *Memoirs of Mississippi*, vol. ii, pp. 358–362.

MITCHELL, JAMES C: (-1843), *Lawyer, M. C. from Tenn.* Sketch of.
> In Lynch's *Bench and Bar of Mississippi*, pp. 320–323.

MITCHELL [SAMUEL AUGUSTUS] (1792–1868), *Geographer*. Mitchell's compendium | of the | internal improvements | of the | United States; | comprising | general notices of all the most important | canals and railroads, | throughout | the several States and Territories | of the Union: | together with | a brief notice of works of internal improvement in Canada and Nova Scotia. | Philadelphia: | published by Mitchell & Hinman, | No. 6 North-fifth street. | 1838. |
> 16mo. pp. 84.
> *Copies seen:* Hamner.

MOBILE AND OHIO RAILROAD. Proceedings | of the | public meeting and Board of Directors | of the | Mobile and Ohio Rail Road. | Together with the opinion of | Lewis Troost, Esq. | Civil Engineer. | Printed by order of the Board. | Mobile: | printed at the office of the Herald & Tribune, | 1847. |
> 8vo. pp. 24.
> Originally published in part in De Bow's *Review*, April, 1846.

—— Sketch of.
> In Hunt's *Merchants' Magazine and Commercial Review*, Dec., 1848.
> Reprinted without title page. 8vo. pp. 15. *Map.*

—— Report of committee on private land claims recommending grant of right of way over public lands, the use of timber for construction, and grant of alternate sections of public land on which the road may be located, to the Mobile and Ohio Railroad Company. May 17, 1848. (House Rep. 615, 30th Cong. 1st sess. In vol. 3.)
> 8vo. pp. 11. No title page.
> *Copies seen:* Owen.

MOBILE AND OHIO RAILROAD. Proceedings | of the | second annual meeting | of the | stockholders | of the | Mobile and Ohio Rail Road Company, | held in Mobile, February 5, 1850: | with an appendix. | [Design] | Mobile: | printed by Thompson & Harris. | 1850. |
    8vo. pp. 46. *Map.*
    Contains act of legislature of Alabama, Jan. 5, 1850, amending charter.
    Copies seen: Owen.

—— Proceedings | of the | twenty-second annual meeting | of the | stockholders | of the | Mobile and Ohio Railroad Co. | held in | Mobile, May 17, 1870. | Mobile: Thompson & Powers, printers, [–etc., 1 line.] | 1870. |
    8vo. pp. 24. 2 l.
    Copies seen: Owen.

—— [Address to the Mobile delegation, dated Dec. 9, 1853, by Sidney Smith, *president*, giving information relative to the condition and resources of the Mobile and Ohio Railroad. n. p. n. d.]
    8vo. pp. 7. No title page.
    Copies seen: Curry.

—— Annual report | of the | Mobile and Ohio R. R. Co. | for the year ended | the 31st day of August, 1876. | Mobile: | Thompson & Powers, printers, [–etc., 1 line.] | 1876. |
    8vo. pp. 36. 2 l.

—— Mobile & Ohio Railway | industries. | 1883. | Shields & Co., printers, Mobile, Ala. |
    8 vo. Cover title only, 1 leaf. pp. 32. *Illustrated.*
    An advertising pamphlet.
    Copies seen: Owen.

—— Facts and figures | describing the climate, soil, rainfall, products and | general character of the | Mobile & Ohio Railroad lands, | situated in the States of | Alabama and Mississippi. | 750,000 acres of | choice timber, farming, fruit, vineyard | and grazing lands, | for sale in tracts to suit purchasers. | Published by the | Alabama Land and Development Company | Mobile, Alabama. | 1890. |
    8 vo. pp. 14. 1 l.
    Copies seen: Owen.

—— Statistics of.
    In De Bow's *Review,* May, 1860. pp. 591, 665.

MONETTE, JOHN WESLEY (1803–1851), *M. D., Author.* History | of the | discovery and settlement | of | the Valley of the Mississippi, | by | the three great European Powers, | Spain, France, and Great Britain, | and | the subsequent occupation, settlement, and extension of | civil government by | the United States, | until the year 1846. | By | John W. Monette, M. D. | [Quotation 1 line.] | In two volumes. | Vol. I [–II] | Harper & Brothers, publishers, | 82 Cliff street, New York. | 1848. |
    8vo. Vol. I, pp. xiii, 567; Vol. II, pp. xv, 595. *3 maps and illustrations.*
    "For its completion and perfection, so far as the nature and extent of the plan will admit, and its faithful adherence to truth and accuracy, the author has spared neither labor nor expense, and he throws himself upon the generous approbation of the American people for the first systematic arrangement of this portion of the history of the United States."—*Preface.*

This work brings into convenient compass a full and thorough treatment of the history of the territory covered by the subject, and gives in order the history of the holdings, settlement, and government of the several European Powers with reference to the present States forming a part of the region. The Mississippi and Alabama Territories are treated both in their general and in their local relations.

He is also the author of "The origin and history of yellow fever epidemics in the South West."

Copies seen: Owen.

Money, Hernando De Soto (1839–), *Lawyer, M. C. and U. S. Sen. from Miss.* Shall we have a navy? | Speech | of | Hon. H. D. Money, | of Mississippi. | In the | House of Representatives, | February 15, 1895. | Washington. | 1895. |
8vo. pp. 16.

——— The Cuban question: | Our responsibility and duty. | [Quotation, 5 lines.] | Speech | of | Hon. H. D. Money, | of Mississippi, | in the | Senate of the United States, | Monday, March 28, 1898. | Washington. | 1898. |
8vo. pp. 16.

——— Speech | of | Hon. Hernando D. Money, | of Mississippi, | on | the resolution relating to the | treaty with Spain, | in the | Senate of the United States, | Friday, February 3, 1899. | Washington. | 1899. |
8vo. pp. 20

——— Right of suffrage in North Carolina. | Speech | of | Hon. H. D. Money, | of Mississippi, | in the | Senate of the United States, | Thursday, January 25, 1900. | Washington. | 1900. |
8vo. pp. 36.

MONROE COUNTY. Sketch of.
In Lowry and McCardle's *Mississippi,* pp. 538–542.

MONTGOMERY, ALEXANDER, *Lawyer.* Sketch of.
In Lynch's *Bench and Bar of Mississippi,* pp. 107–108.
See also Claiborne's *Mississippi,* p. 390, *note.*

MONTGOMERY COUNTY. Sketch of.
In Lowry and McCardle's *Mississippi,* pp. 542–543.

MONTGOMERY, P. K. History of Jefferson County.
Referred to in Mayes' *History of Education in Mississippi,* p. 24, *note.*

MONUMENTS. Confederate Monument at Liberty, Amite County.
In Lowry and McCardle's *Mississippi,* pp. 440–441.
Received April 31, 1871. First Confederate monument erected in the State.

——— Monument to Adam Rum, a Revolutionary soldier, at Fayette, Miss.
In Goodspeed's *Memoirs of Mississippi,* vol. i, p. 176.

——— Monument to the Confederate dead of Mississippi, at Jackson.
Ibid. vol. ii, pp. 18, 181; cut of as *frontispiece.*

MOODY, EDWIN F. Bob Rutherford and his wife | An historical romance | By Edwin F. Moody, | Meridian, Miss. | [Vignette.] | Printed for the author, | by John P. Morton & Company, Louisville, Ky. | 1888. |
12 mo. pp. 212.
He is also the author of "Helen Vernon," 1890.

MOONEY, JAMES. The end of the Natchez | by | James Mooney | From the American Anthropologist (n. s.) Vol. 1, July, 1899 | New York | G. P. Putnam's sons | 1899. |
    8vo. pp. 510-521. Cover title only.
    The best monographic treatment of the subject.
    Copies seen: Owen.

MOORE, JOHN QUITMAN. The attitude of the South.
    In De Bow's *Review*, July, 1860, pp. 25-31.

—— Southern statesmanship.
    Ibid. Oct., 1860, pp. 401-409.

—— Quo tendimus?
    Ibid. pp. 441-448.

—— William Gilmore Simms.
    Ibid. Dec., 1860, pp. 702-712.

—— Feudalism in America.
    Ibid. June, 1860, pp. 615-624.

—— American letters.
    Ibid. June, 1860, pp. 657-667.

MOORE, M. A., Sr., *M. D.* The life | of | Gen. Edward Lacey, | with a list of | battles and skirmishes in South Carolina, | during the Revolutionary War. | By | M. A. Moore, Sr., M. D., | of Spartanburg District, S. C. | Spartanburg, S. C.: | Douglass, Evins & Co., Express office. | 1859. |
    8vo. pp. 32.
    Ancestor of the numerous Lacey and Sandefur families of Mississippi and Alabama.
    Copies seen: Owen.

MOORE, MARTIN V. The rhyme of the | Southern rivers. | With notes historical, traditional, | geographical, etymological, etc. | For the use of teachers, schools, | and general readers. | By Martin V. Moore, | [-etc., 3 lines.] | Publishing house M. E. Church, South, | Barbee & Smith, agents, Nashville, Tenn. | [1897.] |
    12 mo. pp. 107.
    Mississippi, pp. 67-71.

MORANCY, *Mrs.* MARY. Catalogue | of the | Mississippi State Library, | 1877. | Mrs. Mary Morancy, librarian. | Jackson, Miss.: | Power & Barksdale, State printers. | 1877. |
    8vo. Title, 1 leaf, pp. 194.
    Arranged in the following sections: I. Elementary and miscellaneous law books; II. Reports and digests; III. Statute law; IV. Miscellaneous; V. Medical books; and Appendix: Mississippi Documents.
    Copies seen: Owen.

MORGAN, J. B. Contested election case of. *See* Chalmers vs. Morgan.

MORRIS, JOSHUA S., *Lawyer, Atty. Gen. Miss., Reporter.* Mississippi Reports, vols. 43-48. *See* Supreme Court.

MORRIS, JOSHUA S. Mississippi State Cases: | being criminal cases decided | in | the High Court of Errors and Appeals, | and in the | Supreme Court, | of | the State of Mississippi; | from the June term 1818 to the first Monday in January 1872, inclusive. | With | explanatory notes of English and American decisions and | authorities; and a manual of forms for making | up records, entries, criminal | proceedings, etc. | By J. S. Morris, | attorney general of Mississippi: | In two volumes. | Volumes I [-II] | Jackson, Miss., | published by the compiler. | 1872. |

    8vo. Vol. i, pp. xi, 1035; vol. ii, pp. 1037-1965.
    Compiled under the provisions of an Act, passed July 17, 1870, "to authorize a compilation of the criminal laws."
    Vol. i contains a biographical sketch of Chief Justice William Lewis Sharkey, with *portrait*.
    Vol. ii contains "Precedents for Pleadings in Criminal Cases," and "Entries" for making up "Records" in criminal proceedings. It also contains a sketch of S. S. Prentiss, with *portrait*.

MORRISON, J. K. Early History of Jefferson College.
    In *Publications Mississippi [State] Historical Society*. 1899, vol. ii, pp. 179-188.

MORSE, *Rev.* JEDIDIAH (1761-1826), *D. D.* The American Gazetteer [detailed statement of extent of topics treated], with a particular description of the Georgia Western Territory. Printed according to Act of Congress. Boston. 1797.
    8vo. pp. not numbered. 7 *maps*, including two of the *Georgia Western Country*. First edition.
    Copies seen: Hamner.

—— The | American Gazetteer, | exhibiting [-etc. 19 lines.] | with a particular description of | the Georgia Western Territory. | The whole comprising [-etc. 4 lines.] | By Jedidiah Morse, D. D. | Author of [-etc. 2 lines.] | The second edition, corrected, | illustrated with seven new and improved maps. | To which are added | [-etc. 2 lines.] | Published according to act of Congress. | Printed in Boston, New England. | London: | Reprinted [-etc. 2 lines.] | 1798. |
    8vo. pp. viii, 633. 7 *maps*.
    Copies seen: Hamner.

—— The | American Geography; | or, a | view of the present situation | of the | United States of America: | containing | [-etc. 4 lines.] | a particular description of | Kentucky, the Western territory, the territory South of Ohio, | and Vermont: | Of their extent [-etc. 8 lines.] | By Jedidiah Morse, A. M. | A new edition, | revised, corrected, and greatly enlarged, by the author, | and illustrated with twenty-five maps. | London: printed for John Stockdale, Piccadilly. | 1794. |
    4to. pp. —. Title, 1 leaf, viii, 714. *25 maps*.
    Second edition.
    Contains many references to settlements and life in the old Southwest, with observations on the Indians; also sketches of the Spanish Floridas. There are *maps* of the *Southern States* (including Georgia and the Spanish provinces of East and West Florida), separate maps of Georgia, East and West Florida, and the Tennessee government, 1794.
    Copies seen: Hamner.

MORSE, *Rev.* JEDIDIAH (1761-1826), *D. D.* The | American | Universal Geography, | or, a | view of the present state | of all the | empires, kingdoms, states, and republics | in the known world, | and of the | United States of America in particular. | In two parts. | [-etc. 33 lines.] | By Jedidiah Morse, D. D. | minister of the congregation in Charlestown. | Published according to Act of Congress. | Third edition, corrected and considerably enlarged. | [-etc. 2 lines.] | Part I. | Printed at Boston, | by Isaiah Thomas and Ebenezer T. Andrews. | [-etc. 4 lines.] | June, 1796. |

    8vo. pp. 808. *28 maps and charts.*
    Georgia, pp. 693-718; Spanish dominions of East and West Florida, pp. 718-720; Map of Ga. and the two Floridas.
    Copies seen: Owen.

—— A | Report | to the | Secretary of War | of the United States, | on Indian Affairs, | comprising a Narrative of a Tour | performed | in the summer of 1820, [etc. 4 lines.] | Illustrated by a Map of the United States; ornamented by a | correct Portrait of a Pawnee Indian. | By the Rev. Jedidiah Morse, D. D. | Late Minister of the First Congregational Church in Charlestown, near Boston, now resident | in New Haven. | New Haven: | Published by [-etc. 6 lines.] | Printed by S. Converse. | 1822. |

    8vo. pp. 96. 400. 1 l. errata.
    Contains *passim* accounts of the Indian tribes: Creeks, Cherokees, Chickasaws and Choctaws.

MORTON, OLIVER P. Speech | of | Hon. O. P. Morton, | delivered in the | United States Senate, | January 19, 1876, | on the | Mississippi election. | The spirit of the White-line Democracy | vividly portrayed. | Washington. | 1876. |

    8vo. pp. 16.

MUCKENFUSS, *Dr.* A. M. History of scientific industries in Mississippi.
    In *Publications Mississippi State Historical Society*, 1900, vol iii. (In press.)

MURRELL, JOHN A. *See* H. R. Howard, and A. Q. Walton.

MUSCOGEE INDIANS. *See* Creek Indians.

MYER, OTTO, *Ph. D.* Notes on tertiary shells.
    In *Proceedings Academy Natural Sciences*, Philadelphia, 1884, p. 104.
    Describes *Tibiella marshi*, n. gen. et n. spe., *Bulla biumbilicata*, and *Cadulus depressus*, with figures, all Claiborne.

—— The classification and paleontology of the United States Tertiary deposits.
    In *Science*, New York, Aug. 21, 1885, pp. 143-144.

—— The genealogy and the age of the species in the Southern old Tertiary. Part 1 [-3].
    In *American Journal Science*, New Haven, Conn., 3d series, 1885.
    Part 1: Tabulated list showing the successional relations of the Vicksburg, Jackson, and Claiborne species. Vol. xxix, p. 457.
    Part 2: The age of the Vicksburg and Jackson beds. Vol. xxx, p. 60. *Profile* of bluff at Claiborne, Ala.
    Part 3: Reply to criticisms. Dec., 1885, vol. xxx, p. 421.
    E. W. Hilgard criticises this reply in *Science*, New York, Jan., 1886, vol. vii, p. 11.

MYER, OTTO. Contributions to the Eocene paleontology of Alabama and Mississippi.
>In Geological Survey: *Bulletin No. 1, 1886*, pp. 61–85; *3 plates.*

—— The genealogy and the age of the species in the Southern old Tertiary. Part III, reply to criticisms.
>In *Nature*, London and New York, 1886, vol. xxxiv, p. 285.
>Abstract of in *American Journal Science*, Dec., 1888.

—— Observations on the Tertiary and Grand Gulf strata of Mississippi.
>In *American Journal of Science*, 3d series, New Haven, Conn., July, 1886, vol. xxxii, pp. 20–25.
>Mentions the occurrence of several fossils, and concludes: (1) That he does not know any place where Grand Gulf strata can be seen in actual superposition over the Marine Tertiary. (2) There are two places where strata which can not be distinguished from unquestioned Grand Gulf can be seen actually overlain by Marine Tertiary. In one of these cases, moreover, there is actual evidence that these strata were dry land, or nearly dry land, before the Marine Tertiary was deposited upon them. (3) The Grand Gulf formation, at least for its main part, is not a marine formation; it contains fresh-water shells. (4) A thick and extended marine green sand formation with a numerous fauna is found in eastern Mississippi. It is parallel to the strata immediately below the Claiborne profile. Its fauna is Claibornian, but approaches the Jacksonian.

—— Observations on the Tertiary and Grand Gulf strata of Mississippi.
>In *Nature*, London and New York, 1886, vol. xxxiv, p. 330.
>Noticed in *American Journal Science*, July, 1886.

—— Notes on the variations of certain Tertiary fossils in overlying beds.
>In *American Naturalist*, Philadelphia, Pa., July, 1886, vol. xx, pp. 637, 638.
>Describes variations in *Cytherea sobrina* Conrad, and *Ficus mississippiensis* Conrad from the profile near Vicksburg, Miss.

—— Observations on the Tertiary and Grand Gulf strata of Mississippi.
>In *American Naturalist*, Philadelphia, Pa., Nov., 1886, vol. xx, p. 969.
>Abstract of.

—— Invertebrates from the Eocene of Mississippi and Alabama.
>In *Proceedings Academy Natural Sciences*, Philadelphia, 1887, pp. 51–56.

—— Beitrag zur Kenntniss der Fauna des Altertertiärs von Mississippi und Alabama.
>In Bericht über den Senkenbergische naturforschende Gesellschaft in Frankfort am Main, 1887, pp. 1–22, pls. I, II.

—— On miocene invertebrates from Virginia.
>In *Proceedings American Philosophic Society*, Philadelphia, 1888, p. 135.

—— Upper tertiary invertebrates from the west side of Chesapeake Bay.
>In *Proceedings Academy Natural Sciences*, Philadelphia, 1888, pt. II, pp. 170–171.

—— Bibliographical notes on the two books of Conrad on Tertiary Shells.
>In *American Naturalist*, Philadelphia, 1888, vol. xxii, pp. 726–727.

—— Some remarks on the present state of our knowledge of the North American Eastern tertiary.
>In the *American Geologist*, Minneapolis, Minn., 1888, vol. ii, pp. 88–94.

—— and Aldrich, T. H. The tertiary fauna of Newton and Wautubbee, Miss.
>In *Journal Cincinnati Society Natural History*, Cincinnati, O., July, 1886, vol. ix, pp. 40–50; plates II.
>These fossils are all of Eocene age.

MYER, OTTO. Geological Survey | of | Alabama. | Eugene A. Smith, Ph. D., State geologist. | Bulletin No. 1. | I. | Preliminary report on the tertiary fossils of Alabama and | Mississippi. | By Truman H. Aldrich, M. E. | II. | Contributions to the eocene paleontology of Alabama and | Mississippi, | by Otto Meyer, Ph. D. | Printed for the Geological Survey. | 1886. |

    8vo. pp. 85. *Plates,* 6, iii. 1 leaf of explanations, extra and unnumbered, faces each plate.

    Title, etc. pp. 1-64.

    Contents: Summary of the lithological and stratigraphical features and subdivisions of the tertiary of Alabama, pp. 7-14. Aldrich's report, pp. 15-60. *6 plates.* Meyer's report, pp. 61-85; *iii plates.* Prepared at the expense of Mr. Aldrich and Dr. Meyer.

    Copies seen: Owen.

MYERS, MINNIE WALTER. Romance and realism of the Southern Gulf coast. Cincinnati, Robert Clarke Co.
    12mo.

N.

NANIH WAIYA MOUND. Sketch of.
    See H. S. Halbert, *supra.*

NATCHEZ. The Queen City of the South. | Natchez, Mississippi, | on top, not "under the hill" | [-etc., 4 lines.] | Adams County | and the neighboring territory, | [-etc., 3 lines.] | Natchez: | Daily Democrat, steam print. |

    8vo. pp. 28. Numerous *illustrations* of prominent local characters, and business and dwelling houses.

    Copies seen: Owen.

—— Sketch of Natchez.
    In the *Mid-Continent,* Chicago, vol. vi, no. 1; *illustrations.*

—— Natchez in the olden times.
    In Claiborne's *Mississippi,* pp. 527-533.
    Recollections of Mr. George Willey.
    Mr. Claiborne's *History* contains a vast mass of interesting facts concerning Natchez, which for years was the center of settlement, business, and society, with accounts of Fort Panmure, Fort Rosalie, etc.

—— Sketches of.
    In Goodspeed's *Memoirs of Mississippi,* vol. ii, pp. 159-167.

—— *See also* Francis Bailey; *Bishops* J. J. Chanche, Wm. H. Elder, Francis Janssens; J. D. Shields, and *Rev.* J. B. Stratton.

NATCHEZ INDIANS. Sketches of.
    In Claiborne's *Mississippi,* pp. 22-56.

—— The end of the Natchez. *See* James Mooney.

—— The wife of the sun. *See* Miss Irwin Huntington.

NATURAL HISTORY OF MISSISSIPPI.
    In Goodspeed's *Memoirs of Mississippi,* vol. i, pp. 11-27.

NAVY (THE) IN THE CIVIL WAR. *See* A. T. Mahan, D. D. Porter, and J. T. Scharf.

NEGROES. *See* Slavery and the Negro

NEW ENGLAND MISSISSIPPI LAND COMPANY. New England Mississippi Land Company; articles of association, etc. 1798.
>8vo. pp.
>Brinley, Part II, No. 3930.

—— Memorial of the A. [sic] E. Mississippi Land Company to Congress; with a vindication of their title. Washington, 1804.
>8vo. pp. 109.
>Brinley, Part II, No. 3930.

NEWSPAPER PRESS. The Press of Mississippi.
>In Goodspeed's *Memoirs of Mississippi*, vol. ii, pp. 242-251.

—— The Press of Mississippi—Historical Sketch by I. M. Patridge.
>In De Bow's *Review*, Oct., 1860, pp. 500-509.

—— [Early Printing in Mississippi.] By Wm. Nelson.
>In *Archives of the State of New Jersey*, vol. xix, pp. xvii-xxiv.

—— Proceedings of the Mississippi Press Association, from its organization, May, 1866, to May, 1884. Jackson, Miss., 1885.
>8vo.
>Much valuable detail in reference to the several issues, names of editors, etc., will be found in the various editions of George P. Rowell & Co.'s *American Newspaper Directory*, and N. W. Ayer & Son's *American Newspaper Annual*.

NESHOBA COUNTY. Sketch of.
>In Lowry and McCardle's *Mississippi*, pp. 543-544.

NEWTON COUNTY. Sketch of.
>In Lowry and McCardle's *Mississippi*, pp. 547-548.

—— History of, 1834 to 1894. See A. J. Brown.

NICHOLSON, ISAAC R., *Lawyer*. Sketch of
>In Lynch's *Bench and Bar of Mississippi*, pp. 103-107.

NOLL, *Rev.* ARTHUR HOWARD. Bishop Otey as Provisional Bishop of Mississippi.
>In *Publications Mississippi State Historical Society*, 1900, vol. iii. (In press.)
>Mr. Noll had access to the diaries of Bishop Otey.
>He is also the author of "A short history of Mexico" (1890; 12mo., pp. 294).

NORDHOFF, CHARLES. The cotton States | in the | Spring and Summer of 1875. | By Charles Nordhoff, | author of | [–etc., 4 lines.] | New York: | D. Appleton & Company, | 549 and 551 Broadway. | 1876. |
>8vo. pp. 112.
>*Copies seen:* Hamner.

NORTH, RALPH. A | treatise | on the | laws and practice | of the | probate courts of Mississippi: | comprising | a compilation of the statutes of the State on the | subject of the probate courts, last wills and testaments, estates | of decedents, infants and persons non compos mentis, dower, and partition of lands; | the whole methodically arranged, and illustrated with notes | on the common law, and American jurisprudence. | To which is added an | appendix | of forms and precedents: | being a full and complete manual of practice, | adapted to the use of lawyers, judges and clerks of courts, sheriffs, | executors, administrators and guardians: by | Ralph North. | Philadelphia: | Thomas, Cowperthwait & Co. | 1845. |
>8vo. pp. 531.

NOXUBEE COUNTY. Sketch of.
: In Lowry and McCardle's *Mississippi*, pp. 544-547.

NOXUBEE COUNTY AGRICULTURAL SOCIETY. Third | annual fair | of the | Noxubee County Agricultural Society | at Macon, Miss., | October 20, 21 and 22, 1886. | Only stock owned in the county can compete. | Memphis. | S. C. Toof & Co., [–etc., 1 line.] | 1886. |
: 8vo. pp. 40.
: *Copies seen:* Owen.

NUTT, *Dr.* RUSH. Sketch of.
: In Claiborne's *Mississippi*, p. 141, *note*.

O.

OAKLAND COLLEGE. Sketch of.
: In Mayes' *History of Education in Mississippi*, pp. 63-70.

OFFICIALS OF MISSISSIPPI. *See* Civil Lists, *supra*.

OKALONA. Recollections of.
: In Davis's *Recollections of Mississippi and Mississippians*, pp. 174-185.

OKTIBBEHA COUNTY. Sketch of.
: In Lowry and McCardle's *Mississippi*, pp. 548-551.

OLIVER, JAMES MCCARTY. The | battle of Franklin, | The little girl at Spanish Fort, | and | other poems. | By James McCarty Oliver. | [Monogram.] | Philadelphia: | J. B. Lippincott & Co. | 1870. |
: 12mo. pp. 118.
: The preface bears this place and date: "Lake, Miss., Sept. 23, 1869."

ORR, WILLIAM GATES, *Lawyer*. Surrender of Weatherford.
: In *Transactions Alabama Historical Society*, 1897-98, vol. II, pp. 57-59.
: A letter to H. S. Halbert, communicating his recollections of this occurrence as detailed to him by his grandfather, William Gates.
: A footnote on page 57 contains a brief genealogical *Excursus* on the Orr family.

OTEY, *Bishop* JAMES HERVEY (1800-1863). Sketch of. *See Rev.* A. H. Noll.

OTKEN, CHARLES HENRY (1839-), *A. M., LL. D.* The | ills of the South | or | related causes hostile to the | general prosperity of the | Southern people | By | Charles H. Otken, LL.D. | G. P. Putnam's sons | [–etc., 3 lines.] | 1894. |
: 8vo. pp. xii, 277.
: "Beginning with the state of things in 1865, he shows fully the bad influence of the credit system in vogue, the advantage given to merchants of the lien law, the overproduction of cotton, the underproduction of food crops and live stock, the degeneration rather than progress of the negroes, and their inefficiency as farm laborers. Dr. Otken believes that the two races can not subsist permanently side by side; hence the one remedy is colonization."—*Literary World*, Boston.
: "A volume by Dr. Charles H. Otken on the 'Ills of the South' has created quite a sensation among our Northern friends. It is conservatively written, and its statements are well supported by the facts and figures he gives. Dr. Otken finds all the progress of the negroes limited to the mulattoes, quadroons, and octoroons. His book, however, has created a decided impression in the North, has been well received, and has succeeded in correcting a great many erroneous impressions that prevailed there. It is too much in earnest and all its statements are too well supported by facts for anyone to deny them or challenge the conclusions Dr. Otken reaches."—*Times-Democrat*, New Orleans.
: *Copies seen:* Owen.

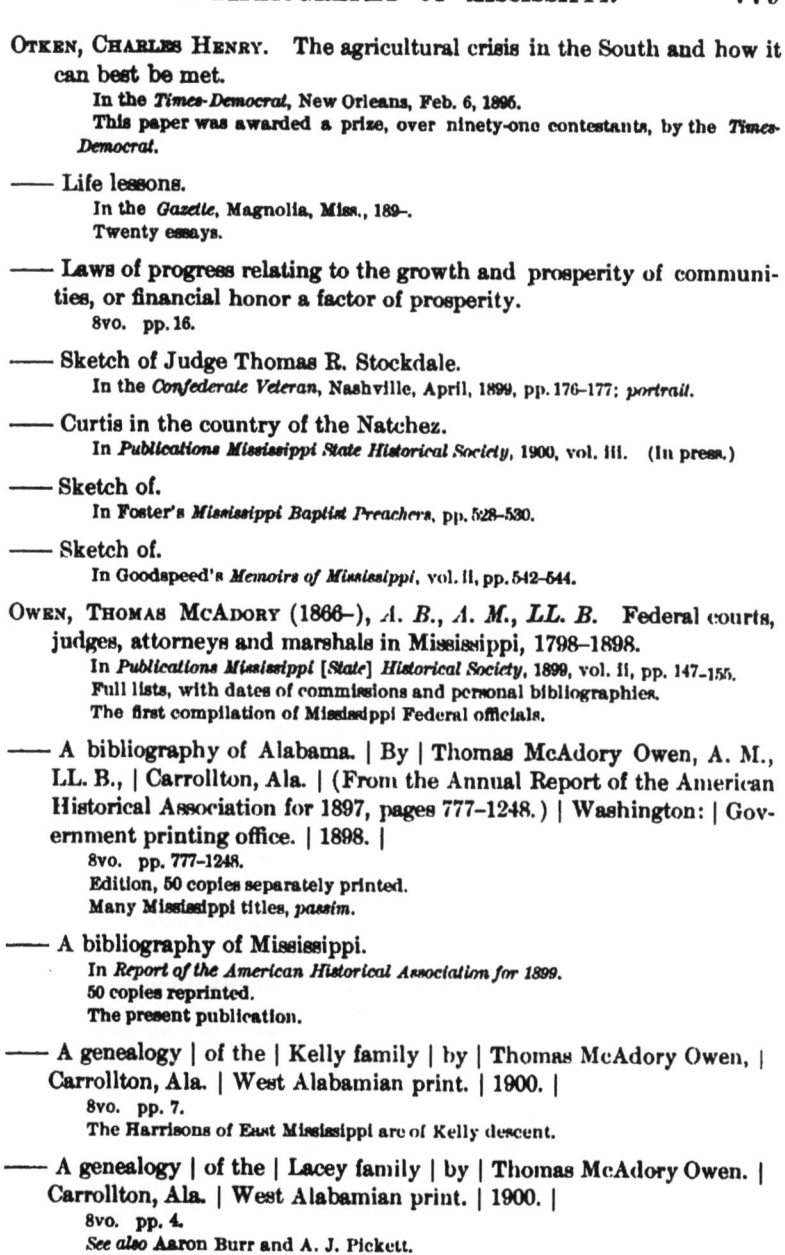

OTKEN, CHARLES HENRY. The agricultural crisis in the South and how it can best be met.
> In the *Times-Democrat*, New Orleans, Feb. 6, 1895.
> This paper was awarded a prize, over ninety-one contestants, by the *Times-Democrat*.

—— Life lessons.
> In the *Gazette*, Magnolia, Miss., 189–.
> Twenty essays.

—— Laws of progress relating to the growth and prosperity of communities, or financial honor a factor of prosperity.
> 8vo. pp. 16.

—— Sketch of Judge Thomas R. Stockdale.
> In the *Confederate Veteran*, Nashville, April, 1899, pp. 176–177; *portrait*.

—— Curtis in the country of the Natchez.
> In *Publications Mississippi State Historical Society*, 1900, vol. iii. (In press.)

—— Sketch of.
> In Foster's *Mississippi Baptist Preachers*, pp. 528–530.

—— Sketch of.
> In Goodspeed's *Memoirs of Mississippi*, vol. II, pp. 542–544.

OWEN, THOMAS MCADORY (1866–), *A. B., A. M., LL. B.* Federal courts, judges, attorneys and marshals in Mississippi, 1798–1898.
> In *Publications Mississippi [State] Historical Society*, 1899, vol. II, pp. 147–155.
> Full lists, with dates of commissions and personal bibliographies.
> The first compilation of Mississippi Federal officials.

—— A bibliography of Alabama. | By | Thomas McAdory Owen, A. M., LL. B., | Carrollton, Ala. | (From the Annual Report of the American Historical Association for 1897, pages 777–1248.) | Washington: | Government printing office. | 1898. |
> 8vo. pp. 777–1248.
> Edition, 50 copies separately printed.
> Many Mississippi titles, *passim*.

—— A bibliography of Mississippi.
> In *Report of the American Historical Association for 1899*.
> 50 copies reprinted.
> The present publication.

—— A genealogy | of the | Kelly family | by | Thomas McAdory Owen, | Carrollton, Ala. | West Alabamian print. | 1900. |
> 8vo. pp. 7.
> The Harrisons of East Mississippi are of Kelly descent.

—— A genealogy | of the | Lacey family | by | Thomas McAdory Owen. | Carrollton, Ala. | West Alabamian print. | 1900. |
> 8vo. pp. 4.
> *See also* Aaron Burr and A. J. Pickett.

OXFORD. Sketch of.
> In Lowry and McCardle's *Mississippi*, p. 511.

OXFORD FEMALE ACADEMY. Sketch of.
> In Mayes' *History of Education in Mississippi*, pp. 93–95.

P.

PALEONTOLOGY OF MISSISSIPPI. Sketch of.
   In Wailes' *Report on Agriculture and Geology of Mississippi*, pp. 269-289; *illustrations*.
   See Goodspeed's *Memoirs of Mississippi*, vol. i, pp. 11-27.
   See also T. H. Aldrich, T. A. Conrad, L. Harper, E. W. Hilgard, and Otto Myer.

PANOLA COUNTY. Sketch of.
   In Lowry and McCardle's *Mississippi*, pp. 552-554.

—— Earthwork three miles east of Panola.
   In Squier and Davis' *Ancient Monuments*, p. 113.

PANTON, LESLIE & Co., *Merchants and traders*. Sketch of.
   In Claiborne's *Mississippi*, pp. 116, *note*, and 132-133, *note*.
   This was a great firm of merchants and traders, having establishments at Pensacola, Mobile, and other places. It commanded the Indian trade and exercised a vast influence.

PARTON, JAMES (1822-1891), *Author*. Life | of | Andrew Jackson. | In three volumes. | By James Parton.—author [-etc., 1 line.] | [Quotation 1 line]. | Vol. I [-III]. | New York: | Mason Brothers, | 5 & 7 Mercer street | 1861, |
   8vo. Vol. i, pp. xxx. 1 l. [29]-636; vol. ii, pp. 672; vol. iii, pp. 734. *4 portraits* of Jackson.
   The most exhaustive and, while it can be corrected in some points, perhaps the best life of Jackson. He played an important part in the early annals of the whole of the Mississippi Territory. Vol. i, pp. 399-636, and all of vol. ii, relate to his military exploits in Alabama, Louisiana, and Florida.
   "The most extensive narrative * * *. It is very readable and not over-partial, but, like most of Parton's biographies, not wholly in good taste."—Winsor's *Narrative and Critical History of America*.
   Copies seen: Owen.

PASCAGOULA INDIANS. Mysterious music on Pascagoula River.
   In Lowry and McCardle's *Mississippi*, p. 498.

PATRIDGE, I. M. The press of Mississippi—historical sketch.
   In De Bow's *Review*, Oct., 1860, pp. 500-509.

PATTON, *Rev.* FRANK. Reminiscences of the Chickasaw Indians.
   In the *Electra*, 1884-1885, pp. 293-295, 329-331, 389-392, 533-536, 616-619, and 670-671.
   Although marred by a discursive method of narration, there are many valuable facts preserved in these sketches.
   Copies seen: Owen.

—— Centennial discourse, 1876.
   Referred to in Claiborne's *Mississippi*, pp. 8, 61.
   Delivered at Tupelo, Miss.
   "Dr. Patton resided in Lee County, has made the Chickasaw traditions a study, and is a recognized authority in all such matters."—Claiborne, p. 61.

PATTON, *Gen.* JAMES. Sketch of.
   In Claiborne's *Mississippi*, p. 356.

PEACOCKE, J. S., *M. D.* The Creole orphans. A novel. New Orleans, 1855.
   12mo.

PEALE, ALBERT C., *M. D.* United States Geological Survey | J. W. Powell, Director | Lists and analyses | of the | mineral springs | of the | United States | (A preliminary study) | by | Albert C. Peale, M. D. | [vignette.] | Washington | Government printing office | 1886 |
> 8vo. pp. 235.
> *Bulletin No. 32* of the Survey.
> *Copies seen:* Owen.

PEARL RIVER COUNTY. Sketch of.
> In Lowry and McCardle's *Mississippi*, p. 554.

PENITENTIARY. Reports of the inspectors, superintendent, physician and chaplain, for fiscal year ending Oct. 31, 1857. Jackson: 1857.
> 8vo. pp. 43.
> *Copies seen:* Owen.

—— Biennial report | of the | superintendent, physician, and chaplain | of the | Mississippi Penitentiary, | to the | Legislature of Mississippi, | for the years 1880–81. | Printed by authority. | Jackson, Miss.: | J. L. Power, State printer. | 1882. |
> 8vo. pp. 166.

PERCY, WILLIAM A., *Col., C. S. A.* Sketch of.
> In Lowry and McCardle's *Mississippi*, pp. 599–600.

PERRIN DU LAC, FRANÇOIS MARIE (1766–1824). Voyage | dans | les deux Louisianes, | et | chez les Nations Sauvages du Missouri, | par les Etats-Unis, l'Ohio et les Provinces | qui le bordent, | en 1801, 1802, et 1803; | Avec un aperçu des moeurs, des usages, du caractère | et des contumes religieuses et civiles des peuples de | ces diverses contrées. | Par M. Perrin du Lac. | [Monogram.] | A Paris, | chez Capelle et Renaud, libraires—commissionaires, | rue J.-J. Rousseau. | Et à Lyons, chez Bruysset ainé et Buynaud. | An xiii. | [1805.] |
> 8vo. 2 prel. leaves [6], pp x–479. *1 map; 1 plate.*
>
> "Chapters xxix to xl, pp. 257 to 364, the author has entirely devoted to the narration of his observations on the Indians then inhabiting the territory he visited. Chapter III. pp. 456 to 472, is entitled 'Life of George [William?] Augustus Bowles, an Englishman, who abandoned civilization to become chief of the Creek Nation.' The life of this worthy was printed in a small duodecimo volume in England, whither he had gone to negotiate some treaty for his tribe.
>
> "The volume contains the narration of the personal experience of a traveler whose curiosity was not sated with what he saw, but who sought from books the particulars he did not himself observe, and thus fills out the form of which he himself observed but the mere outlines. Although there is little produced that is new, the author gives it to us in a pleasing and readable style, and thus, without adding much to our stock of information, makes that we already possessed more available."—Field's *Indian Bibliography*, p. 308.
> *Copies seen:* Hamner.

—— Travels through the Louisianas, and among the Savage Nations of the Missouri; also, in the United States, along the Ohio, and the adjacent provinces, in 1801, 1802, and 1803, with a sketch of the manners, customs, character, and the civil and religious ceremonies of the people of those countries. By M. Perrin Du Lac. Translated from the French. London. Printed for Richard Philips, 1807.
> 8vo. pp. 106. Index, pp. 2.
> A translation, greatly abridged.

PERRY COUNTY. Sketch of.
> In Lowry and McCardle's *Mississippi*, pp. 554-556.
> See also Goodspeed's *Memoirs of Mississippi*, vol. i, pp. 197-198.

PETTUS, JOHN JONES (1813-1867), *Gov. of Miss.* Administration as governor.
> In Lowry and McCardle's *Mississippi*, pp. 341-349.

—— Genealogy of the Pettus family.
> In Goodspeed's *Memoirs of Mississippi*, vol. ii, pp. 589-590.

PEYTON, EPHRAIM GEOFFREY (1802-1876), *Lawyer, Chief Justice Sup. Ct. Miss.* Sketch of.
> In Lynch's *Bench and Bar of Mississippi*, pp. 359-365.

PHELAN, JAMES (1820-1873), *Lawyer, Conf. States Sen. from Miss.* Sketch of.
> In Lynch's *Bench and Bar of Mississippi*, pp. 455-480, *portrait*.
> This sketch contains his speech on the judiciary bill, while he was a member of the Confederate States Senate.

PHELPS, the robber. Capture of.
> In Lowry and McCardle's *Mississippi*, p. 492.

PHELPS, *Capt.* MATTHEW. Memoirs and adventures of Captain Matthew Phelps—formerly of Harwington in Connecticut, now resident in Vermont—particularly in two voyages from Connecticut to the River Mississippi from Dec., 1773, to Oct., 1780. Bennington, Vt., 1802.
> 12mo. pp. 286.
> Exceedingly rare.

PICKETT, ALBERT JAMES (1810-1858), *Planter, Author.* Arrest of Aaron Burr in Alabama, in 1807. By Albert J. Pickett, of Montgomery. n. p. n. d.
> 8vo. pp. 11. No title-page. Double columns.
> Reprinted as *Flag and Advertiser* (Montgomery, Ala.)—*Extra;* prefaced by an *editorial* published, originally with the *sketch*, in that paper.
> Reviewed in *Southern Quarterly Review*, Charleston, S. C., July, 1850, vol. i, n. s., pp. 524-526.
> *Copies seen:* Curry.

—— History | of | Alabama, | and incidentally of | Georgia and Mississippi, | from the earliest period. | By Albert James Pickett, | of Montgomery. | In two volumes, | Vol. I [-II.] | Second edition. | Charleston: | Walker and James, | 1851. |
> 12mo. Vol. i, pp. xix, 377; vol. ii, pp. viii, 445.

> ILLUSTRATIONS:
> All separate from and not paged with text except as noted.
> *Volume I.*—Indians employed in planting corn. Drawn from life by Jacob le Moyne in 1564.
> Chiefs, with their ornaments and war implements, upon their march against the enemy. *Ibid.*
> A chief addressing his warriors, who are armed, painted, and plumed, and ready to march against the enemy. *Ibid.*
> Indians engaged in scalping and cutting up the slain enemy. *Ibid.*
> Indians preparing meats to be deposited in their winter hunt houses. *Ibid.*
> Indians bearing in a chair a young girl who has been selected as one of the future wives of the king. *Ibid.*
> Cut of copperplate (in text).
> Cut of brass plate (in text).

Indian drawing (in text).

Ancient Indian fortifications and mounds in Early County, Georgia, from a sketch by the visitor, Dr. C. A. Woodruff.

Volume II.—Ancient Indian fortifications at Little River Falls, Cherokee County, Alabama, from a sketch by the author, who visited that place in October, 1850.

Map of the war in South Alabama in 1813 and 1814.

Drawing of Fort Mims, found among General Claiborne's manuscript papers.

Plan of the Battle of Talladega.

Battle of Cholocco Litabixee: or, The Horse-Shoe.

CONTENTS:

Volume I.—Chapter I. Expedition of De Soto through Florida, Georgia, Alabama, and Mississippi, A. D. 1539, 1540, and 1541. pp. 1-53.

Chapter II. Part I: Aborigines of Alabama and the surrounding States, A. D. 1540, 1564. pp. 54-73. Part II: The Modern Indians of Alabama, Georgia, and Mississippi—beginning with the Creeks or Muscogees. pp. 74-127. Part III: The Mobilians, Chatots, Thomez, and Tensas. pp. 128-133. Part IV: The Choctaws and Chickasaws. pp. 134-153. Part V: The Cherokees. pp. 154-163.

Chapter III. Ancient mounds and fortifications in Alabama. pp. 164-179.

Chapter IV. The French in Alabama and Mississippi. pp. 180-206.

Chapter V. Alabama and Mississippi granted by the King of France to the rich Parisian merchant, Crozat. pp. 207-239.

Chapter VI. Alabama and Mississippi surrendered by Crozat to the King of France, who grants them to the French India or Mississippi Company. pp. 240-273.

Chapter VII. Terrible massacre of the French at Natchez. pp. 274-303.

Chapter VIII. The colonization of Georgia by the English. pp. 304-316.

Chapter IX. French Jesuit priests or missionaries of Alabama and Mississippi. pp. 317-327.

Chapter X. The French battles upon the Tombigby. pp. 328-353.

Chapter XI. Bienville leaves the Colony—his character. pp. 354-359.

Chapter XII. Horrible death of Beaudrot and the Swiss soldiers. pp. 360-365.

Chapter XIII. Bossu's visit to the French forts upon the Alabama and Tombigby rivers. pp. 366-377.

Volume II.—Chapter XIV. The occupation of Alabama and Mississippi by the English. pp. 1-15.

Chapter XV. Hardships of the early emigrants. pp. 16-23.

Chapter XVI. Journey of Bartram through Alabama. pp. 24-29.

Chapter XVII. An account of the McGillivray family—The Revolutionary War. pp. 30-42.

Chapter XVII[I]. [Ex]treme perils and sufferings of the Natchez refugees. pp. 43-57.

Chapter XIX. The Spaniards in Alabama and Mississippi. pp. 58-73.

Chapter XX. Bloody scenes in Alabama and Georgia. pp. 74-82.

Chapter XXI. The deep intrigues of McGillivray. pp. 83-111.

Chapter XXII. The first Yazoo sale—Bowles, the freebooter. pp. 112-122.

Chapter XXIII. Singular inhabitants of Alabama. pp. 123-135.

Chapter XXIV. Death of McGillivray—Bloody scenes. pp. 136-150.

Chapter XXV. The French minister, Genet—His designs upon the Southwest. pp. 151-157.

Chapter XXVI. The second Yazoo sale. pp. 158-177.

Chapter XXVII. The Americans in Alabama and Mississippi. pp. 178-197.

Chapter XXVIII. Governor Troup, or the McIntosh family—Incidents in the Mississippi Territory. pp. 198-212.

Chapter XXIX. The arrest of Aaron Burr, in Alabama. pp. 213-231.

Chapter XXX. St. Stephens—Huntsville—Indian commerce—Kemper expeditions. pp. 232-239.

Chapter XXXI. Tecumseh—Civil war among the Creeks. pp. 240-254.

Chapter XXXII. Battle of Burnt Corn—Arrival of General Claiborne's army. pp. 255-263.
Chapter XXXIII. Terrible massacre at Fort Mims. pp. 264-284.
Chapter XXXIV. Daring of Heaton—Bloody scenes—Gaines and the Choctaws. pp. 285-292.
Chapter XXXV. Battles of Tallasehatche, Talladega, and Auttose. pp. 293-303.
Chapter XXXVI. Remarkable canoe fight—Battle of the Holy Ground—March to Cahaba Old Towns. pp. 304-328.
Chapter XXXVII. Battles of Emuckfau, Enitachopco, and Calabee. pp. 329-340.
Chapter XXXVIII. Battle of the Horse-Shoe—Weatherford surrenders himself at Fort Jackson. pp. 341-354.
Chapter XXXIX. Treaty of Fort Jackson—Attack upon Mobile Point—March upon Pensacola. pp. 355-370.
Chapter XL. The British take Mobile Point—Peace declared—The Alabama Territory. pp. 371-385.
Chapter XLI. Modern French colony in Alabama, or the Vine and Olive Company. pp. 386-399.
Chapter XLII. Last Territorial legislature—State Convention. pp. 400-433.
Chapter XLIII. The first Legislature of the State of Alabama—Governor Bibb. pp. 434-445.

PICKETT, ALBERT JAMES. History | of | Alabama—and incidentally of | Georgia and Mississippi, | from the earliest period. | By | Albert James Pickett. | Republished by | Robert C. Randolph, | of Sheffield, Ala. | 1896. |

8vo. pp. 669. *Portrait of author. Illustrations* same as in first and subsequent editions.

A verbatim reprint. The only additions are the portrait of Mr. Pickett and the placing of the name of Mr. Randolph on the title-page. There are 47 chapters for the 43 of the early edition, the increase being due to the change of Chapter II, with its parts i-v, of the early edition to Chapters II-VI of the present one. The old pagination has not been preserved, neither has an index been added. The illustrations are facsimiles of the ones of the early edition. The typographical work is good.

Copies seen: Owen.

—— *and* THOMAS M. OWEN. History | of | Alabama | and incidentally of | Georgia and Mississippi, | from the earliest period. | By | Albert James Pickett. | Annals of Alabama, | 1819-1900 | By | Thomas McAdory Owen. | Birmingham: | The Webb book company, | publishers, | 1900. |

8vo. pp. 773. *Ills.*

Excepting the revised title page, the entire first part of this work, pp. 1-669, is the same as the preceding title, being a part of that edition. The addition, pp. 671-773, which contains, however, no data as to Mississippi, was prepared to bring the work to date. The whole is thoroughly indexed, neither the original edition nor the first edition of the reprint having this great essential to a well-made book.

PIKE COUNTY. Sketch of.
In Lowry and McCardle's *Mississippi*, pp. 556-559.
See also Goodspeed's *Memoirs of Mississippi*, vol. i, pp. 195-196.

PILLING, JAMES CONSTANTINE (1846-1893), *Philologist.* Smithsonian Institution | Bureau of Ethnology: J. W. Powell, director. | Bibliography | of the | Muskhogean languages | by | James Constantine Pilling. | [Vignette.] | Washington | Government printing office | 1889. |

8vo. pp. v, 114.
Contains titles of all works, printed or in manuscript, relating to the subject. A valuable critical compilation.

Copies seen: Owen.

PITCHLYNN, PETER P. (1806–1881), *Choctaw Chief.* Sketch of.
    In Appleton's *Cyclopædia of American Biography*, vol. v, pp. 31–32.

PITTMAN, *Rev.* HENRY (1817–1892), *Baptist Clergyman.* Sketch of.
    In Foster's *Mississippi Baptist Preachers*, pp. 543–550; *portrait.*

PITTS, *Dr.* J. R. S. Life and bloody career | of the executed criminal, | James Copeland, | the great | Southern land pirate | leader of a devastating clan | ranging over a great portion of the nation, | particularly the Gulf States, spreading terror and insecu- | rity everywhere. | Mystic alphabet of the clan, | for their secret correspondence, | giving a list of all the members throughout the Union, | with an appendix of | profound research, | bringing to light more of crime, corruption and dissimu- | lation, unveiling the many ways in which talent, | wealth and influence have given assistance. | By Dr. J. R. S. Pitts. | Jackson, Miss.: | Pilot Publishing Company, printers and binders. | 1874. |
    8vo. Ill cover title. pp. 220. *4 illustrations.*
    Second edition.
    Copies seen: Owen.

PLANTERS', MANUFACTURERS', and MECHANICS' ASSOCIATION. Premium list | and | general regulations | for the | second annual fair | of the | Planters', Manufacturers', | and | Mechanics' Association, | to be held at the fair grounds in | Columbus, Mississippi, | beginning Tuesday, September 30th, 1873, | and continuing four days. | Columbus, Mississippi: | printed at the Excelsior Book and Job Office. | 1873. |
    8vo. pp. 48.
    Copies seen: Owen.

PLUMMER, FRANKLIN E. (–1852), *Lawyer, M. C. from Miss.* Sketch of.
    In Claiborne's *Mississippi*, pp. 423–427.

POETRY AND POETICAL WORKS. *See* H. M. Bien, S. Newton Berryhill, Sherwood Bonner, Mrs. J. F. Cappleman, M. T. Carpenter, J. C. Collins, Miss Mary V. Duval, Mrs. V. J. Frantz, L. R. Hamberlin, Ellen E. Hebron, Miss Irwin Huntington, J. D. Lynch, Walter Malone, T. D. Marshall, Col. M. V. Moore, J. M. Oliver, J. F. Simmons, and Wm. Ward.

POINDEXTER, GEORGE (1779–1855), *Lawyer, Governor, U. S. Senator, and M. C. from Miss.* Sketch of.
    In Claiborne's *Mississippi*, pp. 347–414.
    See also Lynch's *Bench and Bar of Mississippi*, pp. 27–73.
    Goodspeed's *Memoirs of Mississippi*, vol. i, pp. 115–116.
    Appleton's *Cyclopædia of American Biography*, vol. v, p. 48.
    Mr. Claiborne's sketch is an elaborate monograph, in which is presented much of Mississippi history and politics during the first half of the present century. He used in its preparation the papers and manuscripts of Mr. Poindexter, which the latter appears to have preserved with great care. Several letters and documents are presented in full. These papers now form a part of the "Claiborne Manuscripts," in the University library, Oxford, Miss.
    Copious extracts from sundry of Mr. Poindexter's speeches are given in Mr. Lynch's sketch.
    A "Biographical Sketch" of Mr. Poindexter was published at Washington, 1835.
    See also T. J. Wharton, *infra.*

POINDEXTER, GEORGE. Administration as Governor.
In Lowry and McCardle's *Mississippi*, pp. 259-260.
—— *Compiler*. Revised Code, 1823. *See* Codes of Mississippi.
—— Portrait.
In Lowry and McCardle's *History of Mississippi for Schools*, p. 101.
POLLARD, EDWARD A. Life of Jefferson Davis. *See* Jefferson Davis.
POLLOCK, OLIVER (1737-1823), *Merchant, Patriot*. A Biographical Sketch of. *See* Rev. H. E. Hayden.
PONTOTOC. Sketch of.
In Davis's *Recollections of Mississippi and Mississippians*, pp. 86-96.
PONTOTOC COUNTY. Sketch of.
In Lowry and McCardle's *Mississippi*, pp. 559-561.
—— Quadrangular mound, between Butchiecunifila and Oconitahatchie creeks.
Mentioned by Samuel Agnew in Smithsonian *Report*, 1867, p. 404.
—— Map of.
In Harper's *Preliminary Report on the Geology and Agriculture of Mississippi*, 1857.
POORE, BEN: PERLEY (1820-1887), *Journalist*. A | descriptive catalogue | of | the Government publications | of | the United States, | September 5, 1774-March 4, 1881. | Compiled by order of Congress | by Ben: Perley Poore, | clerk of printing records. | Washington: | Government printing office. | 1885. |
4to. pp. iv, 1392.
Contains *passim* titles of all such publications as relate to Mississippi, the Indians, etc.
Copies seen: Owen.

POPE, JOHN. A | tour | through the | southern and western territories | of the | United States | of | North America; | the | Spanish dominions | on the river Mississippi, | and the | Floridas; | the countries of the | Creek nations; | and many | uninhabited parts. | By John Pope. | Multorum, paucorum, plurium, omnium, interest. | Richmond: printed by John Dixon. | For the author and his three children, Alexander D. | Pope, Lucinda C. Pope, and Anne Pope. | M,DCC,XCII.
8vo. pp. 104.
"It is the genuine Offspring of positive Observation, taken sometimes on Horseback, sometimes on a Stump, but always in Haste, amidst the Hurly Burly of uninformed and generally Indian Companions."—*Note to the public*.
The original is very rare, commanding a high price. It has been: "Reprinted—with Index, for Charles L. Woodward, New York, 1888." Title, pagination, etc., the same as the original. Index, after p. 104, pp. i-iv.

PORT GIBSON. Yellow fever at, 1853.
In Fulkerson's *Recollections of Early Days of Mississippi*, pp. 118-127.
PORT GIBSON FEMALE COLLEGE. Sketch of.
In Mayes' *History of Education in Mississippi*, pp. 96-97.
PORTER, DAVID DIXON (1813-1891), *Admiral U. S. N.* The naval history | of the | Civil War | by | Admiral David D. Porter, U. S. Navy | Illustrated from original sketches made by Rear-Admiral Walke and others | New York | The Sherman publishing company | 1886 |
4to. Title, 1 leaf, pp. 843. Errata slip. *Numerous portraits, maps, and plans.*
Battle of Mobile Bay, pp. 565-600, *10 illustrations;* Joint operations in Mobile Bay by Rear-Admiral Thatcher and General Canby, pp. 780-791.

PORTER, *Rev.* R. G.   Gilderoy's stories; a book for boys.   1881.
12mo.
He is also the author of "Odd Hours," 1891.

PORTIS, JOHN C.   Resaca's bloody field. | Interesting reminiscences of a Confederate soldier. | [1896.] n. p.
8vo. pp. 4.
Copies seen: Owen.

POSEY, CARNOT (1818–1863), *Brig. Gen., C. S. A.*   Sketch of.
In Appleton's *Cyclopædia of American Biography*, vol. v, p. 83.

POTTER, GEORGE LEMUEL (1812–   ), *Lawyer.*   Sketch of.
In Lynch's *Bench and Bar of Mississippi*, pp. 445–450.

POWELL, F. S., A. M.   Five years in South Mississippi.   Cincinnati, 1889.
12mo.

POWER, *Col.* J. L.   The black and tan convention.
In *Publications Mississippi State Historical Society*, 1900, vol. III. (In press.)

—— The epidemic of 1878 in Mississippi, being a report of the yellow-fever relief work.   Clarion Office, Jackson, Miss., 1879.
8vo. pp. 221.

—— Roster of State officers from 1798 to 1898.   Compiled from official and unofficial sources.
In *Biennial Report of the Secretary of State for 1896 and 1897*, pp. 88–103.
Includes all classes of State officials.

—— List of Mississippi Reports.
Ibid. pp. 104–106.

—— Why the capital was located at Jackson.
In the *Gazette*, Magnolia, Miss., 1897.
Reprinted in the *Mobile Register*, Mar. 21, 1897.

—— *Reporter.*   Proceedings Mississippi State convention, 1861. *See* Conventions and Constitutions of Mississippi.

—— The constitutional convention of 1817.   n. p. n. d.
8vo. pp. [4].
Reprinted from the *Gazette*, Magnolia, Sept. 1, 1897.

—— The constitutional convention of 1832.   n. p. n. d.
8vo. pp. [4].
Reprinted. *Ibid.*

—— Institutions and societies of Mississippi.
In Goodspeed's *Memoirs of Mississippi*, vol. ii, pp. 37–60.

—— Sketch of.
Ibid. pp. 610–612.

—— *and* WEBB, GEORGE F.   Mississippi manual | of legal & business forms: | containing | forms for justices of the peace, county officers, attorneys, | and professional and business men generally, | in the | State of Mississippi, | to which is added the new constitution, Federal Constitu- | tion, reconstruction acts, | acts of Legislature, chancery rules, | [–etc., 4 lines] | By George F. Webb and J. L. Power. | Third edition [vignette] revised & enlarged. | Jackson, Mississippi: | Clarion steam book and job establishment. | 1870. |
8 vo. pp. xv, 199, 60, 68.

POWER, *Col.* J. L., *and* BRIDEWELL, L. O. The | Mississippi form book | and | court, railroad and postoffice guide. | A manual | for | justices of the peace, | attorneys, and | business men generally. | Adapted to annotated code, 1892. | By L. O. Bridewell and J. L. Power. | Jackson, Miss.: | the Clarion-Ledger printing establishment. | 1893. |
    8vo. pp. 312.

POWERS, RIDGLEY CEYLON, *Gov. of Miss.* Administration as governor.
    In Lowry and McCardle's *Mississippi*, pp. 385-386.

PRAY, PUBLIUS RUTILIUS RUFUS (1795-1840), *Lawyer, Pres. Con. Conv. 1832.* Sketch of.
    In Lynch's *Bench and Bar of Mississippi*, p. 204.
    See also Appleton's *Cyclopædia of American Biography*, vol. v, p. 104.

—— *Compiler.* Revised Statutes, 1836. *See* Codes of Mississippi.

PREHISTORIC REMAINS. Nanih Waiya Mound. *See* H. S. Halbert.

—— Prehistoric jasper ornaments in Mississippi. *See* R. B. Fulton.

—— Researches, philosophical and antiquarian, concerning the aboriginal history of America. *See* J. H. McCulloh.

—— Catalogue of prehistoric works East of the Rocky Mountains. *See* Cyrus Thomas.

—— Articles of stone art from.
    In *Thirteenth Annual Report Bureau of Ethnology*, 1891-92, pp. 74-174, *passim*.

—— Mounds in.
    Ibid. 1890-91, pp. 253-278; *ill.*

PRENTISS COUNTY. Sketch of.
    In Lowry and McCardle's *Mississippi*, pp. 561-562.

—— Mound near Baldwyn.
    Mentioned by Samuel Agnew in Smithsonian *Report*, 1867, p. 405.

PRENTISS, SARGENT SMITH (1808-1850), *Lawyer, Orator, M. C. from Miss.* Sketch of.
    In Lynch's *Bench and Bar of Mississippi*, pp. 216-247; *portrait*.
    See also Fulkerson's *Recollections of Early Days in Mississippi*, pp. 100-109.
    Appleton's *Cyclopædia of American Biography*, vol. v, pp. 107-8; *portrait;* and Joshua S. Morris's *Mississippi State Cases*, vol. ii; *portrait*.

—— A | memoir | of | S. S. Prentiss. | Edited by his brother. | Vol. I [-II] | New York: | Charles Scribner, 124 Grand St. | 1855. |
    8vo. Vol. I, pp. 362. vol. II, pp. 578.

—— Life and Times of. *See* Joseph D. Shields.

PRESBYTERIAN CHURCH IN MISSISSIPPI. Extracts | from the | records of the Synod | of | Mississippi and South Alabama, | from 1829 to 1835. | Re-printed by order of Synod, at its meeting, 1878. | Jackson, Miss.: | Clarion steam publishing establishment. | 1880. |
    8vo. pp. 42.
    The first session bears date "Mayhew, Choctaw Nation Nov. 11, 1829." Ministers were present from the Presbytery of Mississippi, the Presbytery of South Alabama, and of the Presbytery of Tombeckbee.
    The original not seen.
    First meeting, at Mayhew, Choctaw Nation, Nov. 11, 1829.
    Second meeting, at Hopewell, Covington County, Oct. 28, 1830.
    Third meeting, at Concord, Greene County. Ala., Oct. 27, 1831.
    Fourth meeting, at Clinton, Oct. 25, 1832.
    Fifth meeting, at Greensborough, Ala., Oct. 30, 1833.
    Sixth meeting, at Port Gibson, Oct. 29, 1834.

PRESBYTERIAN CHURCH IN MISSISSIPPI. Extracts | from the records | of the | Synod of Mississippi, | from 1835 to 1837. | Published by order of Synod. | S. H. B. Black, printer, | Natchez, Mi. | 1838. |
> 8vo. Title, 1 leaf, pp. 54, 1 l.
> First meeting, at Natchez, Oct. 28, 1835.
> Second meeting, at Union Church, Jefferson County, Oct. 26, 1836.
> Third meeting, at Clinton, Oct. 25, 1837.

—— Extracts | from | the records | of the | Synod of Mississippi, | from the year 1838 to the year 1847, inclusive. | Published by order of the Synod. | New Orleans: | printed by D. Davies & Son, | 60 Magazine street. | 1849. |
> 8vo. pp. 96+.
> Fourth meeting, at Vicksburg, Oct. 24, 1838.
> Fifth meeting, at Pine Ridge, Oct. 23, 1839.
> Sixth meeting, at Jackson, Oct. 28, 1840.
> Seventh meeting, Baton Rouge, La., Oct. 27, 1841.
> Eighth meeting, Oakland College, Oct. 26, 1842.
> Ninth meeting, Yazoo City, Oct. 25, 1843.
> Tenth meeting, Oakland College, Oct. 23, 1844.
> Eleventh meeting, Columbus, Oct. 22, 1845.
> Twelfth meeting, Holly Springs, Oct. 28, 1846.
> Thirteenth meeting, Oakland College, Oct. 27, 1847.

—— Minutes | of the | Synod of Mississippi, | from | 1847 to 1854, | inclusive. | Published by order of the Synod. | Jackson, Miss.: | printed at the office of the True Witness. | 1855. |
> 8vo. pp. 111, vi.
> Thirteenth meeting, at Oakland College, Oct. 27, 1847.
> "1848. Meeting for this year failed."
> Fourteenth meeting, at Natchez, Dec. 12, 1849.
> Fifteenth meeting, at Vicksburg, Nov. 27, 1850.
> Sixteenth meeting, at New Orleans, La., Jan. 14, 1852.
> Seventeenth meeting, at Jackson, Dec. 14, 1853.
> Eighteenth meeting, at Canton, Nov. 22, 1854.
> No meeting numbered 19th, etc.

—— Minutes. n. p. n. d.
> 8vo No title page.
> Twentieth meeting, at Kosciusko, Miss., Nov. 28, 1855, pp. 11.
> Twenty-first meeting, at Natchez, Jan. 7, 1857, pp. 16.
> Twenty-second meeting, at New Orleans, La., Jan. 6, 1858, pp. 28.
> Twenty-third meeting, at Vicksburg, Nov. 24, 1858, pp. 24.
> Twenty-third (sic) meeting, at Columbus, Dec. 7, 1859, pp. 17.
> Twenty-fourth meeting, at Shreveport, La., Jan. 17, 1861, pp. 44.

—— Minutes | of the | meeting of the | Synod of Mississippi, | held at | Vicksburg, Miss., | November 4th, 1868. | Jackson, Mississippi: | Clarion steam book and job printing establishment. | 1869. |
> 8vo. pp. 31.

—— Minutes | of the | Synod of Mississippi, | from | 1861 to 1867. | Printed by order of Synod, at its meeting, 1878. | Jackson, Miss.: | Clarion steam publishing establishment. | 1880. |
> 8vo. pp. 92.
> Twenty-fifth meeting, at Oakland College, Oct. 28, 1861.
> Twenty-sixth meeting, at Port Gibson, Nov. 12, 1862.
> Twenty-seventh meeting, at Enterprise, Oct. 28, 1863.
> Twenty-eighth meeting, at Brandon, Oct. 12, 1864.
> Twenty-ninth meeting, at Kosciusko, Oct. 25, 1865.
> Thirtieth meeting, at Canton, Oct. 17, 1866.
> Thirty-first meeting, at Meridian, Oct. 9, 1867.

PRESBYTERIAN CHURCH IN MISSISSIPPI. Minutes. 1869-1899. Jackson, Miss. 1870-1899.

8vo.

Annual meeting, at Prytania Street Church, New Orleans, La., Dec. 8, 1869, pp. 27.
Annual meeting, at Jackson, Nov. 2, 1870, pp. 28.
Annual meeting, at Vicksburg, Dec. 6, 1871, pp. 28.
Annual meeting, at Aberdeen, Nov. 6, 1872, pp. 24.
Annual meeting, at Hazlehurst, Oct. 29, 1873.
Annual meeting, at Canton, Nov. 18, 1874, pp. 40. This and preceding sessions bound together.
Annual meeting, at New Orleans, La., Nov. 10, 1875, pp. 20.
Annual meeting, at Natchez, Nov. 16, 1876, pp. 19.
Annual meeting, at Baton Rouge, La., Nov. 21, 1877, pp. 32.
Annual meeting, at Monroe, La., Nov. 27, 1878, pp. 20.
Annual meeting, at Brandon, Miss., Dec. 3, 1879, pp. 30.
Annual meeting, at Meridian, Nov. 10, 1880, pp. 30.
Annual meeting, at Vicksburg, Nov, 16, 1881, pp. 47.
Annual meeting, at Kosciusko, Nov. 22, 1882, pp. 42.
Annual meeting, at Natchez, Nov. 7, 1883, pp. 36.
Annual meeting, at Crystal Springs, Oct. 29, 1884, pp. 30.
Annual meeting, at Shreveport, La., Nov. 18, 1885, pp. 24.
Annual meeting, at New Orleans, La., Nov. 10, 1886, pp. 41.
57th session, at Meridian, Nov. 23, 1887, pp. 38.
58th session, at Yazoo City, Nov. 14, 1888, pp. 163-192. (Pagination not understood.)
59th session, at Jackson, Nov. 6, 1889, pp. 31.
60th session, at Columbus, Nov. 19, 1890, pp. 225-261. (Pagination evidently intended to be continuous.)
61st session, at Brookhaven, Nov. 11, 1891, pp. 263-307.
62d session, at Baton Rouge, La., Nov. 2, 1892, pp. 309-341.
63d session, at New Orleans, La., Nov. 22, 1893, pp. 343-398.
64th session, at Aberdeen, Nov. 7, 1894, pp. 395-448.
65th session, at Crystal Springs, Miss., Oct. 30, 1895, pp. 449-482.
66th session, at Winona, Nov. 18, 1896, pp. 483-520.
67th session, at Monroe, La., Nov. 15, 1897, pp. 521-558.
68th session, at Vicksburg, Nov. 22, 1898, pp. 559-597.
69th session, at Crowley, La., Nov. 21, 1899, pp. 599-643.

—— Sketch of.

In Goodspeed's *Memoirs of Mississippi*, vol. ii, pp. 354-358.

—— *See also* James Hall and Rev. J. B. Stratton.

PRESS OF MISSISSIPPI. *See* Newspaper press.

PUSHMATAHA (1764-1824), *Choctaw Indian Chief*. Biographical sketch. By H. S. Halbert.

In *Transactions Alabama Historical Society*, 1897-98, vol. ii, pp. 107-119.

This is the best sketch of the chief extant, and corrects numerous errors in current accounts.

The following is a summary of the principal remaining bibliographical references: McKenney and Hall's *Indian Tribes* (1854), vol. i, pp. 185-193; Drake's *Aboriginal Races of North America* (15th ed.), pp. 402-3; Claiborne's *Mississippi*, pp. 514-515, Claiborne's *Life of Dale* (1860); Lowry and McCardle's *History of Mississippi* (1891); Brewer's *Alabama*, p. 16, *note;* Parton's *Life of Andrew Jackson* (1861, 3 vols.); Reuben Davis' *Recollections of Mississippi and Mississippians* (1889); Peter J. Hamilton's *Colonial Mobile* (1897); Ball's *Clarke County, Alabama* (1882); Halbert and Ball's *Creek War* (1895); Riley's *History of Conecuh County, Alabama* (1881); Meek's *Romantic Passages in Southwestern History* (1857); George S. Gaines' "Reminiscences of Early Times in the Mississippi Territory," in the Mobile *Register*, June and July, 1872; Pickett's *History of Alabama* (1851, 2 vols.); Appleton's *Cyclopædia of American Biography*, vol. v, p. 138; Goodspeed's *Memoirs of Mississippi* (2 vols.); and a *Life of*, in manuscript, by Gideon Lincecum. *See also* a paper by Hurlosco Austill in the Mobile *Register*, Aug. 21, 1897.

Copies of the inscription on his tomb in the Congressional Cemetery, Washington, D. C., are to be found in *Trans. Ala. Hist. Society*, 1897-98, vol. ii, p. 118; and Drake's *Aboriginal Races*, p. 408.

Likenesses of him are in McKenney and Hall's *History*, etc., (1854); and in Lowry and McCardle's *History of Mississippi, for Schools* (1892), p. 125.

PUTNAM, A. W.   History | of | Middle Tennessee; | or | life and times | of | Gen. James Robertson. | [cut of State house of Tenn.] | By | A. W. Putnam, esq., | president of the Tennessee Historical Society. | Nashville, Tenn.: | printed for the author. | 1859. |

8vo. pp. 668. *10 illustrations; 3 maps.*

While dealing primarily with Tennessee, this book contains, besides, a wealth of incident and illustration of life in the pioneer days of the old Southwest, with accounts of the pioneers.

Copies seen: Congress.

Q.

QUITMAN COUNTY. Sketch of.
In Lowry and McCardle's *Mississippi*, p. 563.

QUITMAN, JOHN ANTHONY (1799-1858), *LL. D.*, *Lawyer, Gov., M. C. from Miss.* Sketch of.
In Lynch's *Bench and Bar of Mississippi*, pp. 151-164.
See also Davis's *Recollections of Mississippi and Mississippians*, p. 310.
Appleton's *Cyclopædia of American Biography*, vol. v, p. 156.

—— Administration as governor.
Lowry and McCardle's *Mississippi*, pp. 320-322.

—— Life and correspondence of. *See* J. F. H. Claiborne.
See also Joseph Hodgson, Mexican War, and Dunbar Rowland.

R.

RAGSDALE, LULAH. A shadow's shadow. New York, Lippincott & Co. 1892.
12mo.

RAMSAY, JAMES GATTYS MCGREGOR (1796-1884), *A. M., M. D.* The | annals | of | Tennessee | to the | end of the eighteenth century: | comprising its settlement, | as | the Watauga Association, | from 1769 to 1777; | a part of North-Carolina, from 1777 to 1784; | the State of Franklin, | from 1784 to 1788; | a part of North-Carolina, | from 1788 to 1790; | the Territory of the U. States South of the Ohio, | from 1790 to 1796; | the State of Tennessee, | from 1796 to 1800. | By | J. G. M. Ramsay, A. M., M. D., | corresponding secretary [–etc., 3 lines.] | Philadelphia: | J. B. Lippincott & Co. | 1860. |

8vo. pp. xvi, 744. *Map.*

RANJEL, RODRIGO. [Official Report of Soto's expedition, based on his Diary kept on the march.]
In Amador de los Rios's edition of Oviedo's *History*, etc., 1851.
See Winsor's *Narrative and Critical History of America*, vol. ii, pp. 291, 346.

RANKIN CHRISTOPHER (-1826), *Lawyer, M. C. from Miss.* Sketch of.
    In Lynch's *Bench and Bar of Mississippi*, pp. 22-23.
    See also Claiborne's *Mississippi*, p. 354.

RANKIN COUNTY. Sketch of.
    In Lowry and McCardle's *Mississippi*, pp. 563-567.

—— Ancient ruin known as the "Platform."
    Mentioned in Smithsonian *Report*, 1879, p. 444.

RAUM, GREEN BERRY (1829-). The | existing conflict | between | republican government | and Southern oligarchy | by | Green B. Raum | Washington, D. C. | 1884. |
    12mo. pp. 479. *Illustrations.*
    Contains sketches of political affairs in Mississippi during the seventies; refers to Kuklux Klans.
    Copies seen: Hamner.

RECONSTRUCTION. Evidence taken by the committee on reconstruction [showing condition of affairs in Mississippi]. Jan. 6, 1869. (House Mis. Doc. 53, 40th Cong., 3d sess.)
    8vo. pp. 299, 1 l.

—— *See also* E. Barksdale, Conventions of Miss., 1868, Prof. J. W. Garner, Wiley P. Harris, Oliver P. Morton, and G. B. Raum.

RED, *Rev.* W. D. The Devil's parlor; or the ball room unmasked. 1900.
    8vo.

REED, THOMAS B. (-1829), *Lawyer, U. S. Senator from Miss.* Sketch of.
    In Lynch's *Bench and Bar of Mississippi*, pp. 23-24.
    See also Claiborne's *Mississippi*, p. 358, *note*.
    Appleton's *Cyclopædia of American Biography*, vol. vi, p. 211.

RELIGION. Introduction of Protestant Christianity.
    In Lowry and McCardle's *Mississippi*, pp. 432-435.

—— Religious history of Mississippi.
    In Goodspeed's *Memoirs of Mississippi*, vol. ii, pp. 348-383.
    Embraces authorized sketches of all denomininations.

—— *See also* Baptists, Christian Church, Cumberland Presbyterians, Episcopal Church, Methodist, and Presbyterian.

REPORTS OF STATE OFFICIALS. *See* State Offices.

REPUDIATION IN MISSISSIPPI. Sketch of.
    In Fulkerson's *Recollections of Early Days in Mississippi*, pp. 85-94.

REVENUE AGENT, STATE. Biennial report. *See* Auditor of Public Accounts.

REVENUE DISTRICT. Letter from the Secretary of the Treasury, accompanying a Statement of Goods, Wares and Merchandizes, exported from the Mississippi District, during the year 1801, in addition to the general statement of Exports, received by the House, on the 11th of February last. [By Albert Gallatin] April 5, 1802. (Ex. Doc., 7th Cong., 1st sess.)
    8vo. pp. 6.

REYNOLDS, REUBEN O. (-1887), *Lawyer.* In memoriam. | Proceedings | of the | Aberdeen Bar Association, | commemorative of the life and character | of | Reuben O. Reynolds. | Including tributes from members of the bar at Jack- | son, Meridian, Oxford, Kosciusko, Okolona, | Saltillo and Tupelo. | Jackson, Miss.: | Clarion-Ledger printing establishment. | 1888. |
    8vo. pp. 30.
    Copies seen: Owen.

REYNOLDS, REUBEN O. Sketch of.
>In Goodspeed's *Memoirs of Mississippi*, vol. ii, pp. 34, 661-662.

—— Reporter. Mississippi Reports, vols. 40-42. *See* Supreme Court.

RICHARDSON, LEE, Jr. *and* GODMAN, THOMAS D. In and about Vicksburg. An illustrated guide book to the city of Vicksburg, Mississippi. Its history: its appearance: its business houses. To which is added a description of the resources and progress of the State of Mississippi, as an inviting field for immigration and capital. The Gibraltar Publishing Co., Vicksburg, Miss. 1890.
>12mo. pp. 271. *Map* of Vicksburg; profusely *illustrated*.
>*Copies seen:* Congress.

RILEY, FRANKLIN LAFAYETTE (1868–), *A. B., A. M., Ph. D.* (J. H. U.), *Prof. Univ. of Miss.* American Chivalry.
>In *Mississippi College Magazine*, March, 1889.
>An Oration.

—— Salutatory.
>*Ibid.* March, 1889.
>Written upon assuming the work of editor in chief of the *Magazine*.

—— All Deeds that glitter are not Golden.
>*Ibid.* April, 1889.
>An essay.

—— Notes from the Moral Battlefield.
>*Ibid.* May, 1889.

—— Does Mississippi College need a Y. M. C. A.?
>*Ibid.*

—— May.
>*Ibid.*
>An essay.

—— Random Pages from my Scrapbook.
>*Ibid.* July, 1889.

—— The Gravity of Small Things.
>*Ibid.*
>An essay

—— Farewell.
>*Ibid.*

—— Is Education the Best Solution of the Negro Problem?
>In *The New Mississippian*, Jackson, Miss., July, 1889.

—— County Institutes.
>In *Proceedings* Mississippi State Teachers' Association, 1892.
>A paper read before the Mississippi State Teachers' Association.

—— Study of Church History in the Johns Hopkins University.
>In *The Baptist Record*, April, 1894.

—— The Talmud.
>*Ibid.* Dec., 1894, and Jan., 1895.

—— Some educational tendencies of the present day.
>In *Lawrence County Press* (Miss.), May 31, 1894.
>An address delivered before the Hebron High School.

—— Outline of institute work on United States history.
>In *Mississippi Journal of Education*, June, 1895.

RILEY, FRANKLIN LAFAYETTE. Colonial origins | of | New England senates. | [n. p., n. d.]
    8vo. pp. 76.
    In Johns Hopkins *University Studies in Historical and Political Science.* Fourteenth series. No. iii.
    A dissertation for the degree of Ph. D.

—— Address.
    In *The Baptist Layman,* June 10, 1897.
    Delivered before the graduating class of Hillman College, June 1, 1897.

—— Study of history in Southern colleges, | by Franklin L. Riley, Ph. D., | professor of history and rhetoric in the University of Mississippi. |
    8vo. pp. 10. Double columns.
    Reprinted from the *Mississippi Teacher,* Aug., 1897, vol. 1, no. 5
    Read before the Mississippi State Teachers' Association, July 16, 1897.

—— Outline of work for the University Historical Society.
    In Memphis *Commercial Appeal,* Apr. 11, 1898.
    In *Oxford Globe* (Miss.), Apr., 1898.
    An accompanying report contains an account of the organization of the University of Mississippi Historical Society.

—— Some centennial suggestions.
    In New Orleans *Picayune,* Apr. 14, 1898.
    Written upon the one hundredth anniversary of the creation of the Territory of Mississippi.

—— State Historical Societies, | their financial support and sphere | of activity. | By Franklin L. Riley, Ph. D., professor of history in the | University of Mississippi and Secretary and Treas- | urer of the Mississippi Historical Society. | n. p., n. d.
    8vo. pp. 8. Double columns.
    Read at the First Annual Midwinter Meeting of the Mississippi State Historical Society, Jan. 8, 1898.
    Copies seen: Owen.

—— Spanish policy in Mississippi after the treaty of San Lorenzo.
    In *Publications Mississippi State Historical Society,* 1898 pp. 50–66.
    Also in *Report* American Historical Association for 1897, pp. 175–192.

—— Suggestions to local historians.
    Ibid. pp. 96–100.
    500 copies reprinted.
    Contains substance of the "Centennial Suggestions," above.

—— Sir William Dunbar, | the pioneer scientist of Mississippi. | By | Franklin L. Riley, Ph. D., (Johns Hopkins.) | Professor of history, University of Mississippi | [Oxford, Miss., 1899].
    8vo. pp. 85–111.
    Edition, 300 copies.
    Reprinted from the *Publications of the Mississippi Historical Society,* 1899, vol. ii; pagination unchanged.
    This monograph indicates extended research, and portrays in an admirable way the life work of a gentleman of rare scientific attainments, but of whom little had heretofore been written.

—— Memorial.
    In the New Orleans *Picayune,* Jan. 26, 1900.
    Addressed to the Legislature of Mississippi by the Executive Committee of the State Historical Society, asking for the appointment of a History Commission and the granting of an appropriation to the Society.

A BIBLIOGRAPHY OF MISSISSIPPI. 795

RILEY, FRANKLIN LAFAYETTE. School history | of | Mississippi | for public and private schools. | [Richmond, Va., B. F. Johnson & Co., 1900.]
 8vo. *Circa*, pp. 395.

—— *Editor.* Publications of the Mississippi State Historical Society. *See* Historical Society.

RIVERS AND HARBORS. *See* W. S. Featherston.

ROACH, A. C. The | prisoner of war, | and | how treated. | Containing a history of Colonel Streight's expedition to the | rear of Bragg's army, in the spring of 1863, and a correct | account of the treatment and condition of the Union | prisoners of war in the rebel prisons of the South, | in 1863-4. Being the actual experience of a Union | officer during twenty-two months' imprison- | ment in rebeldom. With personal adven- | tures, biographical sketches, and his- | tory of Andersonville prison pen. | By Lieutenant A. C. Roach, A. A. D. C. | Published by | the Railroad City publishing house, | A. D. Streight, proprietor, | North-East corner Washington and Meridian Streets, Indianapolis, Ind. | 1865. |
 12mo. pp. 244.
 Contains short account of Streight's raids, and has the approval of that commander.
 Copies seen: Hamner.

ROBERT FAMILY. Genealogy of.
 In Goodspeed's *Memoirs of Mississippi*, vol. ii, pp. 685-687.
 This family represents, in part, a branch of the descendants of Landgrave Thomas Smith, of S. C.

ROBERTS, ROBERT W., *M. C. from Miss.* Sketch of.
 In Claiborne's *Mississippi*, p. 451, *note.*

ROBERTS, WILLIAM. An account of the | first discovery, | and | natural history | of | Florida. | With a | particular detail of the several expeditions and | descents made on that coast. | Collected from the best authority | by William Roberts. | Illustrated by a general map, and some particular plans, together | with a geographical description of that country. | By T. Jefferys, geographer to his majesty. | London: | Printed for T. Jefferys, at Charing-Cross. | MDCCLXIII. |
 4to. pp. viii. 1 l. 102. *6 maps or plans; 1 plate.*
 Pp. 95-102 contain a letter on Florida, dated June 22, 1763, by Thomas Robinson; with a plan of the Bay and Island of Mobile.
 Copies seen: Hamner.

ROBERTSON, *Rev.* NORVELL. Church members' hand book of Theology. Memphis, 1874.
 12mo.

RODNEY. Sketch of.
 In Lowry and McCardle's *Mississippi*, pp. 504-505.

—— Yellow fever at, 1843.
 In Fulkerson's *Recollections of Early Days in Mississippi*, pp. 37-42.

ROGERS, *Judge* WILLIAM M. Tribute to. *See* Dabney Lipscomb.

ROMANS, BERNARD (1720–1784), *Engineer*. A concise | natural history | of | East and West Florida; | containing an account of the natural produce of all the Southern part of British America, in the three | kingdoms of nature, particularly the animal and | vegetable. | Likewise, | the artificial produce now raised, or possible to be raised, | and manufactured there, with some commercial and po- | litical observations in that part of the world; and a cho- | rographical account of the same. | To which is added, by way of appendix, | plain and easy directions to navigators over the bank of | Bahama, the coast of the two Floridas, the North of | Cuba, and the dangerous Gulph Passage. Noting also, | the hitherto unknown watering places in that part of | America, intended principally for the use of such ves- | sels as may be so unfortunate as to be distressed by | weather in that difficult part of the world. | By Captain Bernard Romans. | Illustrated with twelve copper plates, | and two whole sheet maps. | Vol. I. | New-York: | printed for the author, M, DCC, LXXV. |

8vo. pp. 4, viii, 342. [2.] lxxxix. [3.] *1 folded sheet; 10 engravings, including the frontispiece, the dedication to John Ellis, and 3 full-page maps.*

The copperplates were designed and engraved by the author, and are: (1) *Frontispiece*, vol. I; (2) Dedication "To *John Ellis Esqr.*," the naturalist, "Agent for the Province of West Florida;" (3) "*Arena equiatica Sylvestris*" (Wild Oats), facing p. 31; (4) "*Characteristick Chicksaw Head*," p. 59; (5) *Characteristick Choctaw Busts*, p. 62; (6) Treatment of the dead, by the Choctaws, p. 89; (7) *Characteristick head of a Creek War Chief*, p. 92. Maps in the appendix; (8) *Entrance of Tampa Bay*, p. lxxviii; (9) *Pensacola Bay*, p. lxxxi; and (10) *Mobile Bar*, p. lxxxv.

Vol. II was never published.

"This extremely rare work is so seldom found in any other than a fragmentary condition that we are unable to refer to the full collation of any complete copy. No copy has ever been found with either of the whole sheet maps, and all are more or less deficient in the number of plates referred to in the title page. From the arrangement and tenor of the title, as well as from the sense of the "advertisement," at the end of the volume, we are clearly of the opinion that it was the author's design to distribute the "twelve copper plates, And Two whole Sheet Maps" throughout the two volumes into which he intended to divide the work."—Menzies' *Catalogue*.

A. S. Gatschet, H. S. Halbert, and the Alabama Historical Society have tracings of the large *Map*, which shows the Tombigby River basin, and the "Country" of the Choctaws in Mississippi, 1772.

"Bernard Romans was an enlightened physician and observer, who spent several years in Florida. . . . The whole book, indeed, is a valuable and interesting account of the manners of the Florida savages, and the face and products of their country."—Volney's *View of the United States*.

Extracts appear in Volney's work.

Title and collation from Menzies' *Catalogue* [1875], No. 1722. *See also* Brinley's *Catalogue* [1881], pt. 3, No. 4365.

The Menzies' copy sold for $175, and the Brinley for $265.

—— A | concise | natural history | of | East and West-Florida. | Containing, | an account of the natural produce of | all the Southern part of British America, in the | three kingdoms of nature, particularly the animal | and vegetable. | Likewise, | the artificial products now raised, or possible to be raised, and | manufactured there, with some commercial and political observa- | tions in that part of the world; and a cho-

ROMANS, BERNARD—Continued.

rographical account | of the same. | By Captain | Bernard Romans. | ... | New York, sold by R. Aitken, 1776. |

8vo. pp. [2], 4, 342. *Engraved dedication; 6 other copperplate engravings; and folded table.*

The sheets of the original edition, with a new title page and reprinted introduction (2 pp.). The Frontispiece, Lists of Subscribers, Appendix, Errata, and final "Advertisement" are omitted; but there is *one copperplate engraving* that is *not found in the earlier issue*, though mentioned in the text (p. 102). It represents two "Indian hieroglyphick paintings," executed by Choctaws and Creeks.

Title, collation, and note from Brinley's *Catalogue*, pt. 3, No. 4366.

This copy sold for $70.

ROUDEBUSH, G. S., *D. D.* A plea | for | a higher education | for the | women of Mississippi, | by | G. S. Roudebush, D. D., | professor of English language and litera- | ture in the Mississippi Agricultural | and Mechanical College. | 1881. | Jackson, Miss.: | Clarion Steam Publishing House. | 1881. |

8vo. pp. 23.

Copies seen: Owen.

ROUTH FAMILY. Genealogy of.

In Goodspeed's *Memoirs of Mississippi*, vol. II, pp. 522-523.

ROWE, A. V. History of Mississippi College. Jackson, 1881.

8vo. pp. 32.

ROWLAND, DUNBAR (1867-), *Lawyer, B. S., LL. B.* What of the South? Address before the Alumni Association of the A. & M. College of Mississippi, June, 1888.

In the *Times-Democrat*, New Orleans, 1888; and the *Starkeville Times*, 1888.

—— The poet as a factor in civilization. A paper read before the Bohemian Club of Memphis, Tenn.

In the Memphis, Tenn., *Ledger*, April, 1891; and the *University Magazine*, Oxford, Miss., 1891.

—— An evening with the poets. Address before the students of Union Female College, Oxford, Miss.

In the *College Mirror*, April, 1898.

—— The new constitution of Mississippi.

In the Memphis *Commercial-Appeal*, March, 1897.

—— Success. Address before Grenada Female College, March, 1899.

In Grenada *Sentinel*, March, 1899.

—— A series of papers on politics in Mississippi.

In Memphis *Commercial-Appeal*, January-July, 1895.

—— Character sketch of Gen. J. Z. George.

Ibid. Feb., 1897.

"A masterly sketch of a great man, by one of the rising young men of North Mississippi."—*Water Valley Herald.*

—— Character sketch of John A. Quitman.

Ibid. Oct., 1896.

—— System of taxation in Mississippi.

Ibid. April, 1898.

—— Character sketch of Robert J. Walker.

In the Atlanta *Constitution*, Nov., 1896.

ROWLAND, DUNBAR. Series of letters on "The Money Question."
>In the *Times-Democrat*, New Orleans, April-June, 1896.

—— The race question.
>In the Louisville *Courier-Journal*, April, 1896.

—— Farmers' Institutes.
>In the *Picayune*, New Orleans, March, 1896.

—— Industrial and agricultural growth of Mississippi.
>8vo. pp. 50.

—— The rise and fall of negro rule in Mississippi.
>In *Publications Mississippi [State] Historical Society*, 1899, vol. ii, pp. 189-200.

—— Plantation life in Mississippi before the war.
>*Ibid.* 1900, vol. iii. (In press.)

ROYCE, CHARLES C. The Cherokee Nation of Indians: | a Narrative of their official relations with the | Colonial and Federal Governments. |
>In *Fifth Annual Report of the Bureau of Ethnology*, 1883-'84, pp. 121-378, 2 maps. Washington. 1887. 4to.
>"It is believed the care and skill devoted by Mr. Royce to make the statement both accurate and comprehensive, fortifying it also by the citation of the best authorities, will render it valuable to statesmen, historians, and lawyers."— Director Powell's *Introduction to the General Report*.

—— Cessions of land by Indian tribes in the United States.
>*Ibid.* 1879-80, pp. 249-253.

RUNNELS, *Col.* HARMAN. Sketch of.
>In Claiborne's *Mississippi*, p. 356.

RUNNELS, HIRAM G., *Gov. of Miss.* Administration as governor.
>In Lowry and McCardle's *Mississippi*, pp. 276-278.
>Son of Col. Harman Runnels.

RUSSELL, IRWIN (1853-1879), *Poet.* Poems | by | Irwin Russell | [Vignette.] | New York | The Century Co. | n. d. | [*Verso:* Copyright, 1888, by the Century Co.   The DeVinne Press.]
>12mo. pp. 109.

—— [Uncollected Poems.]
>The Romaunt of Sir Kuss: *Scribner's Monthly*, March, 1880, p. 799.
>Summer Idyllers: *Puck*, vol. vi, p. 745.
>Coroner Jordan: *Ibid.*, vol. vi, p. 797.
>A symbol—Birds and all Nature: *Ibid.*, Dec., 1898, p. 208.

—— [Uncollected Prose.]
>The Hysteriad: *Scribner's Monthly*, Sept., 1878.
>The Fools of Killogue: *Ibid.*, Oct., 1879.
>Of the Uncertainty and Vanity of the Sciences: *Popular Science Monthly*, July, 1876.
>Sam's Four Bits: *St. Nicholas*, Aug., 1876.
>On the Ice: *Ibid.*, March, 1877.
>Sam's Birthday; *Ibid.*, May, 1878.
>Fulton's Seamen: New Orleans *Times*, Aug. 24, 1879. An inconsequential introduction to a poem of 21 six-line stanzas, entitled, "A Pun Her Travels."

—— Sketch of.   By C. C. Marble.
>In the *Critic*, Oct. 27, and Nov. 3, 1888.
>Contains extracts from Russell's letters.

—— Negro wit and humor in Irwin Russell's poems. *See* Dabney Lipscomb.

——Irwin Russell—first fruits of the Southern Romantic movement. *See* W. L. Weber.

S.

SABIN, JOSEPH (1821–1881), *Bibliophile.* A | dictionary | of | books relating to America, | from its discovery to the present time. | By Joseph Sabin. | Volume I [–XIX.] | [Quotation, 3 lines.] | New York: | Joseph Sabin, 84 Nassau street. | 1868[–1891.] |
>8vo. 19 volumes.
>Includes titles from "A" through "Simms." No more published.
>Contains numerous Mississippi titles *passim.*
>*Copies seen:* Library of Congress.

—— Catalogue | of the | books manuscripts and engravings | belonging to | William Menzies | of | New York. | Prepared by Joseph Sabin | [Monogram.] | New York | 1875 |
>8vo. pp. xviii. 1 l. 471. [2.]
>Contains a number of Mississippi titles *passim.*
>*Copies seen:* Congress.

SABINE EXPEDITION. Account of.
>In Claiborne's *Mississippi,* pp. 264–274.
>*See also* Goodspeed's *Memoirs of Mississippi,* vol. i, pp. 131–134.

SALE, JOHN BURRUSS (1818–   ), *Lawyer, Col. C. S. A.* Sketch of.
>In Lynch's *Bench and Bar of Mississippi,* pp. 391–396; portrait.

SARGENT, WINTHROP (1753–1820), *First Gov. of Miss. Territory.* Papers | in relation to the | official conduct | of | Governor Sargent. | Published by particular desire of his friends. | [Design]. | Printed at Boston, | by Thomas & Andrews. | Aug. 1, 1801. |
>8vo. pp. 64.
>*Copies seen:* Owen.

—— Papers in relation to the official conduct of Winthrop Sargent. Jan. 2, 1801. (Ex. Doc., 6th Cong., 2d sess.)
>8vo. pp. 29. No title page.
>Letter of Governor S., charge to the grand jury, with presentment, etc.

—— Report of the committee appointed to enquire into the official conduct of Winthrop Sargent, Governor of the Mississippi Territory. Feb. 19, 1801. (Ex. Doc., 6th Cong., 2d sess.)
>8vo. pp. 10.
>*Reprinted* as No. 143, American State Papers: *Miscellaneous,* vol. i, p. 233; also in *Annals of Congress,* 6th Cong., p. 1376.

—— Administration of.
>In Claiborne's *Mississippi,* pp. 202–219.

SAVANNAH JACK. A man of blood. *See* J. D. Dreisback.

SCAIFE, WALTER B., Ph. D. (Vienna.) America | its geographical history | 1492–1892. | Six lectures delivered to graduate students of | the Johns Hopkins University | with a | supplement | entitled | Was the Rio del Espiritu Santo of the Span- | ish geographers the Mississippi? | By Walter B. Scaife, Ph. D.   (Vienna) | Baltimore | the Johns Hopkins press | 1892 |
>8vo. 6 p. l. pp. 176.
>Opposes view of John Gilmary Shea and others that it was the Mississippi, and holds that it was either the Mobile or the Apalachicola.
>*Copies seen:* Iamner.

SCHARF, JOHN THOMAS (1843-1898) *A. M., LL. D.* History | of the | Confederate States Navy | from its organization | to the surrender of its last vessel. | Its stupendous struggle with the great navy of the | United States; the engagements fought in the rivers | and harbors of the South, and upon the high seas; | blockade-running, first use of iron-clads and torpedoes, and privateer history. | By | J. Thomas Scharf, A. M., LL. D. | an officer of the late Confederate States Navy. | Author of [-etc., 5 lines.] | Profusely illustrated. | Second edition. | Albany, N. Y.: | Joseph McDonough, | 1894. |
    8vo. pp. 824. *Illustrations.*
    Copies seen: Hamner.

SCHOOLS. *See* Education; Educational Literature, etc.

SCOTT, ABRAM M. (d. 1833), *Gov. of Miss.* Administration as governor.
    In Lowry and McCardle's *Mississippi*, pp. 269-276.

SCOTT, CHARLES (1811-1861), *Lawyer.* Sketch of.
    In Lynch's *Bench and Bar of Mississippi*, 175-177. *portrait.*
    See also Goodspeed's *Memoirs of Mississippi*, vol. ii, pp. 725-726.
    Mr. Scott was a Mason of national reputation. He was the author of two works which obtained general commendation from the craft. These were "The Keystone of the Masonic Arch," and "The Analogy of Ancient Craft Masonry to Natural and Revealed Religion."

SCOTT COUNTY. Sketch of.
    In Lowry and McCardle's *Mississippi*, pp. 567-569.

SEARS, ROBERT. A | new and popular | pictorial description | of the | United States: | containing | an account of the topography, settlement, history, revolution- | ary and other interesting events, statistics, progress in | agriculture, manufactures, and population, &c., | of each State in the Union. | Illustrated with engravings | of the principal cities, places, buildings, scenery, curiosities, seals of the States, | &c., &c. | Edited by Robert Sears. | Fourth edition. | New York: | Published by Robert Sears, 128 Nassau street. And sold by F. S. Saxton, Boston, | [-etc., 7 lines] | MDCCCXLIX. [1849.] |
    8vo. pp. 608.
    Copies seen: Hamner.

SEAT OF GOVERNMENT. *See* Jackson.

SECRETARY OF STATE. Biennial report | of the | Secretary of State, | to the | Legislature of Mississippi, | for the | years 1896 and 1897. | Printed by authority. | Jackson, Miss.: | the Clarion-Ledger print. | 1897. |
    8vo. pp. 117.
    Besides much valuable current data, contains the following of general interest: Votes for Governor, 1817-1895; Roster of State officers from 1798 to 1898, including Governor, Lieutenant-Governor, Secretary of State, Auditor of Public Accounts, State Treasurer, Attorney-General, Clerk High Court of Errors and Appeals and Supreme Court, Superintendent of Public Instruction, Railroad Commissioners, State Librarian, Swamp Land Commissioner, State Revenue Agent, Supreme Court Judges, Chancellors, U. S. Senators, and Representatives in Congress, List of Mississippi Reports, and the Statute Laws of Mississippi.
    Reports also issued for other years.
    Copies seen: Owen.

SELMA AND MERIDIAN RAILWAY. Plan of organization | of the | Selma & Meridian Railway | Company, and its agreement with the mortgage bondholders, creditors and | stockholders of the Selma and Meridian Railroad Co. | New York: | Sackett & Mackay, stationers and printers, | cor. Pine and Williams streets. | 1868. |
    8vo. pp. 11.
    Copies seen: Owen.

SESSIONS, JOSEPH, *Lawyer.* Sketch of.
    In Claiborne's *Mississippi,* p. 355.

SHARKEY COUNTY. Sketch of.
    In Lowry and McCardle's *Mississippi,* pp. 573-574.

—— Mounds on Deer Creek.
    Mentioned in Smithsonian *Report,* 1879, p. 442.

SHARKEY, WILLIAM LEWIS (1797-1873), *Lawyer, Chief Justice, Governor, U. S. Senator from Miss.* Sketch of.
    In Lynch's *Bench and Bar of Mississippi,* pp. 189-198; *portrait.*

—— Administration as provisional governor.
    In Lowry and McCardle's *Mississippi,* pp. 353-359, 622-623.

—— Harris and Ellet. *Compilers.* Revised Code of Mississippi, 1857 *See* Codes of Mississippi.

SHARON COLLEGE AND ACADEMY. Sketch of.
    In Mayes' *History of Education in Mississippi,* pp. 51-56.

SHEA, JOHN DAWSON GILMARY (1824-1892), *Author.* History | of the Catholic Missions | among the | Indian tribes of the United States, | 1529-1854. | By John Gilmary Shea, | Author [-etc., 3 lines.] | [Design.] | New York: | P. J. Kenedy, | Excelsior Catholic publishing house, | 5 Barclay street. | [1854.] |
    12mo. pp. 514. *Illustrations.*
    Contains accounts of missions among the Appalachian and Creek Indians. pp. 499-506 contains lists of missionaries, and bibliography.
    Copies seen: Hamner.

—— History | of the | Catholic Missions | among the | Indian tribes of the United States. | 1529-1854. | By John Gilmary Shea. | Author [&c., 3 lines.] | [Design.] | New York: | Edward Dunigan & Brother, | 151 Fulton street, near Broadway. | 1855. |
    12mo. pp. 514.
    Copies seen: Congress.
    There are copies with the date, 1857, but none seen.

—— Geschichte | der | katolischen Missionen | unter den | Indianer-Stämmen der Vereinigten Staaten. | 1529-1860. | von | John Gilmary Shea, | Verfasser [&c. two lines]. | Aus dem Englischen übersetzt | von | J. Roth. | Sr. Heiligkeit Papst Pius IX gewidmet. | Mit 6 Stahlstichen. | Würtzburg. | Verlag von C. Etlinger. | [1858.] |
    12mo. pp. 668.
    No copy seen. Title from Pilling's *Bibliography of the Muskhogean Languages.* Washington, 1889. 8vo.

SHEA, JOHN DAWSON GILMARY. History | of the | Catholic missions | among the | Indian tribes of the United States, | 1529–1854. | By John Gilmary Shea, | author of [&c., three lines]. | [Design.] | New York: | T. W. Strong, | Late Edward Dunigan & Brother, | Catholic publishing house, | 599 Broadway. [1870.]
    12mo. pp. 514.
    Copies seen: Congress.

—— A history | of the | Catholic Church | within the | limits of the United States, | from the first attempted colonization to the | present time. | With portraits, views, maps, and fac-similes. | By | John Gilmary Shea. | [Design.] | New York: John G. Shea. | 1886[–1888, 1890, 1892.] |
    8vo. 4 vols.
    Vol. i, Colonial days, 1521–1763.
    Vol. ii, Life of Archbishop Carroll, and history, 1763–1815.
    Vol. iii, History, 1815–1843.
    Vol. iv, History, 1843–1866.
    Contains *passim* full history of this church in Mississippi.
    Copies seen: Congress.

SHELTON, S. M. The lottery: a discussion. Vicksburg, Miss. 1888.
    No copies seen.

SHIELDS, JOSEPH D. The | life and times | of | Sargent Smith Prentiss. | By | Joseph D. Shields. | Philadelphia: | J. B. Lippincott & Co. | 1883. |
    8vo. pp. 442.

—— [Historical Sketches of Natchez.]
    Referred to in Claiborne's *Mississippi*, p. 47, *note*.

SHIELDS, M. OZELLA. Izma; or, Sunshine and shadow. A novel. J. S. Ogilvie, Chicago. 1889.
    12mo.
    She is also the author of "Sundered Hearts," "Vernon's Mistake," and "A Sinless Crime."

SHIELDS, *Col.* WILLIAM BAYARD, *Lawyer, U. S. District Judge.* Sketch of.
    In Claiborne's *Mississippi*, p. 260, and *note*.

SHIPP, BARNARD (1813–), *Author.* The history | of | Hernando de Soto and Florida; | or, | record of the events of fifty-six years, | from | 1512 to 1568. | By | Barnard Shipp. | Philadelphia: | Collins, printer, 705 Jayne street. | 1881. |
    8vo. pp. xii, 689. 3 vols in 1. *1 plate; 2 maps.*
    "Everything related in the following pages has been taken from the accounts of those who were participators in the events they describe.
    "There is probably no Spanish hero of America whose fame is more widespread throughout the United States than that of Hernando de Soto, and yet, at the same time, of whom so little is known. The expedition of De Soto into 'Florida' was, in fact, the beginning of the history of this country, whose vast domain is now the unrivaled region lying between the oceans, the Mexican gulf, and the Great Lakes. It is to make more particularly known the first great expedition that revealed to the world the interior of our country, to trace the route by which De Soto traveled, and to tell the names and indicate the location of the Indian towns and tribes of 'Florida,' first mentioned in history, that has led me to compile and publish this book."—*Preface.*

CONTENTS:

Volume I.—Chapters I-X, pp. 1-213; Account of early expeditions and voyages to the New World, including Francisco Hernandez de Cordova to Yucatan, 1517; Juan de Grijalva to Mexico, 1518; Cortes to Mexico, 1519; Pamfilo de Narvaez to Mexico. 1520; Francisco de Garay to Panuco, 1519-23; Juan Ponce de Leon, discovery of Florida, 1509-1521; voyage of Juan Verazzian along the Atlantic coast of North America, 1524; Pamfilo de Narvaez to Florida, and the wanderings of Alvaro Nunez Cabeza de Vaca, 1527-1536; Francisco Vasquez Coronado to Cibola and Tiguez, 1539-1543; De Soto in Nicaragua, 1523-1526; Cortes in Honduras, 1524-1526; and De Soto in Peru, 1532-1536.

Volume II.—pp. 215-487; History of the Conquest of Florida; or, a narrative of what occurred in the exploration of this country by Hernando de Soto. By the Inca Garcillasso de la Vega. Translated from the French version of Pierre Richelet [Lisle edition, 1711], from the original Spanish.

Volume III.—Chapters I-VI, pp. 490-589; Events from termination of Expedition of Soto to settlement of French in Florida, 1543-1562; First voyage of Jean Ribault to Florida, 1562; Voyage of Rene Laudonnierre to Florida, 1564; Voyage of Pedro Menendez de Aviles to Florida, 1565; Expedition of Dominique de Gourgue to Florida, 1567; The country and ancient Indian Tribes of Florida, by Hernando d'Escalante Fontanedo, 1551-1568. Appendix. [Notes, etc.] pp. 591-689.

The maps, which are in fac simile, are: (1) General view of the whole peninsula of Florida, with the seacoast of Georgia and South Carolina, by Jacob le Moyne de Morgues, 1564; and (2) Map of North America, by Dr. Mitchelle, corrected in 1776 by Brigadier Hawkins.

Mr. Shipp was born near Natchez, April 30, 1813. His father, William Shipp, a native of Virginia, was a merchant of Natchez for thirty years.

Copies seen: Congress; Hamner; Owen.

SIMMONS, *Judge J. F.* The welded link, | and other poems. | By | Judge J. F. Simmons. | Philadelphia. | J. B. Lippincott & Co. | 1881. |
12 mo. pp. 264.
He is also the author of "Rural Lyrics and other poems," 1884.

SIMPSON COUNTY. Sketch of.
In Lowry and McCardle's *Mississippi*, pp. 569-573.

SIMPSON, JOSIAH, *Territorial Judge of Miss.* Sketch of.
In Claiborne's *Mississippi*, p. 353.

Slavery and the Negro. Early slave laws of Mississippi. *See* A. H. Stone.
—— Rise and fall of negro rule in Mississippi. *See* Dunbar Rowland.
—— Negro suffrage. *See* S. S. Calhoon.
—— Suffrage in Mississippi. *See* R. H. Thompson.
—— Defence of negro slavery. *See* Matthew Estes.
—— Plantation life in Mississippi before the war. *See* Dunbar Rowland.
—— Treatment of slaves.
In Fulkerson's *Random Recollections of Early Days of Mississippi*, pp. 128-140.
See also Claiborne's *Mississippi*, pp. 144-149.

—— Negro population.
In Goodspeed's *Memoirs of Mississippi*, vol. ii, pp. 95-101.

—— Education of the colored race.
In Mayes' *History of Education in Mississippi*, pp. 259-277.

—— The negro; as he was; as he is; as he will be. *See* H. S. Fulkerson.
—— History of negro suffrage in the South. *See* S. B. Weeks.
—— *See also* J. S. Buckingham, Dr. F. L. Riley, Dunbar Rowland, and J. A. Sloan.

SLOAN, J. A., *M. A.* Is slavery a sin in itself? Answered according to the scriptures. Hatton, Galloway & Co., Memphis, Tenn. 1857.
    12mo. pp. 294.

SMEDES, SUSAN DABNEY. Memorials | of a | Southern planter. | By | Susan Dabney Smedes. | [Quotation, 5 lines.] | Baltimore: | Cushings & Bailey. | 1887. |
    12mo. pp. 341. *Port.* of Thomas S. Dabney.
    The introduction, pp. 7-16, contains a genealogy of the Dabney and related families; and also of the Smiths of "Shooters Hill," Gloucester County, Va.

SMEDES, WILLIAM C. A | digest | of the | cases decided and reported | in the | High Court of Errors and Appeals | and the | Superior Court of Chancery | of the | State of Mississippi. | From 1818 to 1847. | By | W. C. Smedes, | one of the reporters to the State. | [Quotation, 5 lines.] | Boston: | Charles C. Little and James Brown. | 1847. |
    8vo. pp. xxxvi, 441.

—— *and* MARSHALL. *Reporters.* Mississippi Reports, vols. 9–22. *See* Supreme Court.

SMILEY, JAMES MALCOLM (1812–1879), *Lawyer.* Sketch of.
    In *Lynch's Bench and Bar of Mississippi*, pp. 181–185; portrait.

SMITH COUNTY. Sketch of.
    In Lowry and McCardle's *Mississippi*, pp. 574–578.

SMITH, C. ALPHONSO, *A. M., Ph. D.* The historical element in recent Southern literature.
    In *Publications Mississippi [State] Historical Society*, 1899, vol. II, pp. 7–14.

—— Southern oratory before the war.
    Ibid. 1900, vol. iii. (In press.)

SMITH, COTESWORTH PINCKNEY (–1863), *Lawyer, Chief Justice Miss.*
    In Lynch's *Bench and Bar of Mississippi*, pp. 198–202.

SMITH, EUGENE ALLEN, *Ph. D.* Geology of the Mississippi bottom.
    In *Proceedings of the American Association for the Advancement of Science*, 1871, pp. 252–261.
    Report of an exploration made by him as Assistant Geologist of Mississippi.

SMITH, SOLOMON FRANKLIN (1801–1869), *Actor.* The | theatrical journey-work | and | anecdotical recollections | of | Sol. Smith, | comedian, attorney at law, etc., etc. | Comprising a sketch of the second seven years | of his professional life; together with | sketches of adventure in after years. | With a portrait of the author. | [Quotation, 2 lines.] | Philadelphia: | T. B. Peterson, No. 102 Chestnut street. |
    12mo. pp. 254.
    Copies seen: Hamner.

—— Theatrical management | in the West and South | for thirty years. | Interspersed with | anecdotical sketches: | autobiographically given | by Sol. Smith, | retired actor. | With fifteen illustrations and a portrait of | the author. | [Quotation, 1 line.] | New York: | Harper & Brothers, publishers, | Franklin Square. | 1868. |
    8vo. pp. 275 [1].
    Copies seen: Hamner.

SMITH, WILLIAM RUSSELL (1815-1896), *Lawyer, M. C. from Ala., Author.*
The | jurisdiction | of | justices of the peace, | in | civil and criminal cases; | and the office and duties of | judges of probate: | with explanations and forms for the use of executors, | administrators and guardians, | and the | commissioners of roads and revenue. | To which is added the | duties of every subordinate civil officer in commission | in the | State of Alabama, | all arranged under the laws as now in force. | By William R. Smith, | with an | appendix, | containing numerous forms for conveyancers, | and the school law. | Montgomery, | White, Pfister & co. | 1859. |
    8vo. pp. 558.
    First edition not seen.
    Third edition, 1860. 8vo. pp. 5-255. Index, 297-304.
    An edition similar in all respects to this was issued, 1860. It may be termed the *Mississippi edition,* the apparent gap, pp. 257-295, in the third edition being filled in this one as *Appendix—Laws of Mississippi.* The title-pages are different. 8vo. pp. 5-255; Miss., etc., pp. 257-295; Index, 297-304.
    Copies seen: Owen.

SOCIAL PROBLEMS. *See* Miss A. N. Dumond and C. H. Otken.

SPANISH EXPLORATION. *See* Biedma, Elvas, Vega. *See also* D. G. Brinton, J. F. H. Claiborne, B. F. French, P. J. Hamilton, A. B. Meek, A. J. Pickett, Barnard Shipp, and Ternaux-Compans.

SPARKS, *Col.* RICHARD. Sketch of.
    In Claiborne's *Mississippi,* p. 221, *note.*

SPARKS, W. H. The memories | of | fifty years: | containing | brief biographical notices of distinguished | Americans, and anecdotes of | remarkable men; | interspersed with scenes and incidents occurring | during a long life of observation chiefly | spent in the Southwest. | By W. H. Sparks. | Third edition. | [Monogram.] | Philadelphia: | Claxton, Remsen & Haffelfinger, | Macon, Ga.: J. W. Burke & Co. | 1872.
    8vo. pp. 489.
    Many references to Mississippi.

SPEIGHT, JESSE (1795-1847), *U. S. Sen. from Miss.* Sketch of.
    In Wheeler's *History of North Carolina,* vol. ii, p. 168.

SPENCER, JOHN F. Spencer's English grammar. Revised edition. 1866.
    12mo.

SPRAGUE, JOHN TITCOMB (1810-1878), *Col. U. S. A.* The | origin, progress, and conclusion | of the | Florida War; | to which is appended | a record of officers, non-commissioned officers, musicians, and | privates of the U. S. Army, Navy, and Marine Corps, | who were killed in battle or died of disease. | As also the names of | officers who were distinguished by brevets, and | the names of others recommended. | Together with the | orders for collecting the remains of the dead in Florida, and the | ceremony of interment at St. Augustine, East Florida, | of the 14th day of August, 1842. | By | John T. Sprague, | Brevet Captain, Eighth Regiment, U. S. Infantry. | New York: | D. Appleton & Company, 200 Broadway. | Philadelphia: | Geo. S. Appleton, 148 Chestnut street. | MDCCCXLVIII. |
    8vo. pp. 557. *Map; illustrations.*
    Copies seen: Hamner.

STARLING, WILLIAM, *C. E.* The improvement of the mouths of the Mississippi River. By William Starling, member Am. Soc. C. E.; member Inst. C. E.; member of the Southwest Pass Board. New York: 1900.
> 8vo.
> He is also the author of "Improvement of the Mississippi River," 1889; "On flood heights in the Mississippi River," 1889; "The Mississippi River, its phenomena and physical treatment," 1890; "Keeping the Mississippi within her banks," 1891; "The Mississippi problem up to date," 1892; "Some notes on the Holland dikes," 1892; "Floods of the Mississippi River," 1894; "The discharge of the Mississippi River," 1895; "The transportation of solid matter by rivers," 1896; and "Floods of the Mississippi River," 1897.

STATE OFFICES. Appendix | to the | Journal | of | the Senate, | for the session of 1871. | Printed by authority. | Jackson, Miss.: | Kimball, Raymond & Co., State printers. | 1871. |
> 8vo. pp. 1292.
> *Also* as an Appendix to House Journal, 1871.
>
> CONTENTS.
>
> Annual Message of Governor James L. Alcorn, 1871.
> Report Mississippi State Lunatic Asylum, 1870.
> Report of the Committee on Public Buildings.
> Report of the Trustees and Treasurer of the Blind Institute.
> Report of the Secretary of State.
> Report of the Auditor of Public Accounts.
> Report of the Superintendent of the State Penitentiary.
> Eulogies on the death of Speaker Freeman E. Franklin and other members (No other members named except Mr. Franklin.)
> Special Messages of Governor James L. Alcorn to the Legislature of Mississippi.
> Treasurer's Report.
> Report of Committee of the House of Representatives to Investigate Levee Matters.
> Lands held by State for Taxes.
> Report of Committee on the Riot at Meridian.
> Special Messages of Governor James L. Alcorn to the Legislature of Mississippi.
> Report of Superintendent Public Education.

—— Appendix, 1872.
> 8vo. pp. 919. No title-page.
>
> CONTENTS.
>
> Governor's Annual Message.
> Annual Report Secretary of State.
> Annual Report Attorney-General.
> Annual Report Board of Trustees, Mississippi State Hospital, at Vicksburg.
> Annual Report Institution for Deaf and Dumb.
> Annual Report Quartermaster-General.
> Annual Report State Treasurer.
> Annual Report Superintendent Public Education. Contains reports of a large number of educational institutions.
> Annual Report State Board of Education.
> Annual Report Mississippi State Lunatic Asylum.
> Annual Report Superintendent Blind Institute.
> "Report of the Chancellor of Oxford University."
> Report Joint Standing Committee on Public Buildings.
> Annual Report of the Auditor of Public Accounts.

—— Appendix | to House Journal, | regular session, 1874. |
> 8vo. pp. 1054.

CONTENTS:

Annual Report Board of Trustees State Lunatic Asylum.
Annual Report Board of Trustees Deaf and Dumb Institute, 1873.
Annual Report Board of Trustees Blind Institute.
Annual Report Board of Inspectors State Penitentiary.
Annual Report Auditor, 1873.
Annual Report of the Commissioner of Immigration.
Report of the Levee Commission.
Annual Report State Treasurer, 1873.
Annual Report Secretary of State, 1873.
Annual Report Adjutant-General.
Annual Report Superintendent Public Instruction.

STATE OFFICES. Biennial reports | of the | departments | and | benevolent institutions, | of the | State of Mississippi, | for the | years 1896–97. | [Seal.] | Jackson, Miss.: | Clarion-Ledger Co., printers. | 1898. |

    8vo. Each report separately paged.
    Contains the following: Message of Gov. A. J. McLaurin; and the biennial reports of the Auditor of Public Accounts, State Treasurer, Attorney-General, Secretary of State, State Librarian, State Land Commissioner, Adjutant-General, Superintendent of Public Instruction, Penitentiary Board of Control, Railroad Commission, State Lunatic Asylum, East Mississippi Lunatic Asylum, Institute for Deaf and Dumb, Institute for the Blind, State Board of Health, and Board of Contracts.
    There were also bound, similar to the above, sets for the years 1890–91, 1892–93, and 1894–95.

STEELE, ELIJAH. Life of. *See Rev.* B. M. Drake.

STEELE, JOHN (1755–1816), *Sec. Miss. Territory.* Sketch of.
    In Claiborne's *Mississippi*, p. 355.

STEWART, VIRGIL A. History of. *See* H. R. Howard and A. Q. Walton.

STOCKDALE, *Judge* THOMAS R. Sketch of. *See* C. H. Otken.

STOCKTON, RICHARD, *Lawyer.* Sketch of.
    In Lynch's *Bench and Bar of Mississippi*, pp. 92–99.

STODDARD, AMOS (1762–1813), *Soldier.* Sketches, | historical and descriptive, | of | Louisiana. | By Major Amos Stoddard, | Member of the U. S. M. P. S. and of the New York Historical Society. | [Quotation, 4 lines.] | Philadelphia: | published by Mathew Carey. | A. Small, printer. | 1812. |
    8vo. pp. viii, 488.

STONE, ALFRED M. The early slave laws of Mississippi.
    In *Publications Mississippi [State] Historical Society*, 1898, vol. ii, pp. 133–145.
    Also reprinted with the following title:
    The early slave laws | of | Mississippi. | Being some brief observations thereon, in | a paper read before the Mississippi | Historical Society, at a meeting | held in the city of Natchez, | April 20th–21st, 1899. | By | Alfred H. Stone, Esq., | Greenville, Miss. |
    Mr. Stone is one of the most cultivated literary men of Mississippi. He has contributed greatly toward the preparation of this work.

STONE, JOHN MARSHALL (1830–1900), *Gov. of Miss.* Administration as governor.
    In Lowry and McCardle's *Mississippi*, pp. 413–414.

—— Sketch of.
    In Goodspeed's *Memoirs of Mississippi*, vol. ii, pp. 850–853.

STONE, JOHN MARSHALL. The pocket veto | of the | Barry railroad bill. | A review of the | arguments of the friends of the measure, | and the | strictures of the press, | particularly of the | elaborated legal argument of the "Clarion." | By J. M. Stone, Governor of Mississippi. | Jackson, Miss.: | "The Cornet" book printing establishment. | 1879. |
8vo. pp. 29.

STONE, Rev. LEWIS MAXWELL, D. D. Sketch of.
In Foster's *Mississippi Baptist Preachers*, pp. 642-616; portrait.
He is a great-grandson of Thomas Stone, of Maryland, one of the signers of the Declaration of Independence.
See also Goodspeed's *Memoirs of Mississippi*, vol. ii, pp. 853-854.

STORMS. Tornado of 1840.
In Lowry and McCardle s *Mississippi*, p. 437.

STRATTON, Rev. JOSEPH BUCK (1815-), D. D. Semi-Centennial discourse | delivered by | Rev. J. B. Stratton, D. D. | pastor, | December 31, 1893, | in the | Presbyterian church, Natchez, Miss. | With biographical sketch, | sketch of church, | and | letter from Rev. Dr. B. M. Palmer. | [Printed at office of Natchez Democrat, | February, 1894.]
8vo. pp. 50. *Portrait* of Dr. Stratton, and *cut* of the church at Natchez.
During the past fifty or more years Dr. Stratton has been a liberal contributor to the religious press North and South, his work including sermons, reports, addresses, etc., only a partial list of which is, however, preserved.
He contributed a series of papers to the *Southwestern Presbyterian*, entitled "Summer Letters from the Seasides." He made a trip to Europe in 1859, and his notes of that trip were published as a series of papers entitled "Sabbaths Abroad."
He delivered anniversary discourses, which were published in pamphlet form, Natchez, 1859 and 1884.

—— Truth in the household. A sermon preached by appointment before the General Assembly of the Pres. Ch. in the U. S. of A. at Lexington, Ky., May 28, 1857, in behalf of the Assembly's Board of Publication. Philadelphia, Presbyterian Board of Publication.
8vo.

—— Confessing Christ. A manual for inquirers in religion. Philadelphia, 1880.
8vo. pp. 168.
Now published by Publication Committee of the Pres. Church, Richmond, Va.

—— Following Christ. A manual for church members. Presbyterian Board of Publication, Phila., Pa. 1884.
8vo. pp. 235.

—— Prayers for the use of families. Richmond, Va. Presbyterian Com. of Publication. 1888.
12mo. pp. 185.

—— Hymns to the Holy Spirit. Richmond, Va. Presbyterian Com. of Publication. 1893.
12mo. pp. 93.

—— Extracts from an elder's diary. Richmond, Va. Presbyterian Com. of Publication. 1898.
8vo. pp. 171.

—— The Presbyterian Church in Mississippi.
In Goodspeed's *Memoirs of Mississippi*, vol. ii, pp. 354-358.

A BIBLIOGRAPHY OF MISSISSIPPI. 809

STUART, JAMES (1776–1849), *Traveller.* Three years | in | North America. | By | James Stuart, esq. | [Quotation 2 lines.] | From the second London edition. | In two volumes. | Vol. I [–II] | New-York: | Printed and published by J. & J. Harper, | No. 82 Cliff-street, | and sold by the booksellers generally throughout the | United States. | 1833. |
 12mo. Vol. i, pp. 334; vol. ii, pp. 337.
 Copies seen: Hamner.

SUNFLOWER COUNTY. Sketch of.
 In Lowry and McCardle's *Mississippi*, pp. 579–580.

—— Mounds in.
 In *Twelfth Annual Report Bureau of Ethnology*, 1890–91, pp. 258–259; *1 figure.*

SUPREME COURT OF MISSISSIPPI. Reports. 1818–1895.
 8vo. 73 volumes.
 The following is a complete list up to and including 1895, showing the book number, the period covered, the special volume number, and the reporter.

R. J. WALKER, REPORTER.

Book No. 1.—June term, 1818, to December term, 1832...................... vol. 1

VOLNEY E. HOWARD, REPORTER.

Book No. 2.—January terms, 1834, 1835, 1836, and 1837........................ vol. 1
Book No. 3.—January term, 1837, January term, 1838 .... vol. 2
Book No. 4.—December term, 1838, January term, 1839 .... vol. 3
Book No. 5.—December term, 1839, January term, 1840 .... vol. 4
Book No. 6.—December term, 1840, January term, 1841 .... vol. 5
Book No. 7.—December term, 1841, January term, 1842 .... vol. 6
Book No. 8.—January term, 1843 .... vol. 7

SMEDES AND MARSHALL, REPORTERS.

Book No. 9.—July term, 1843, January term, 1844........................... vol. 1
Book No. 10.—July term, 1843, January term, 1844........................... vol. 2
Book No. 11.—January and November terms, 1844 .... vol. 3
Book No. 12.—January term, 1845 .... vol. 4
Book No. 13.—January terms, 1845 and 1846................................. vol. 5
Book No. 14.—January term, 1846 .... vol. 6
Book No. 15.—January and November terms, 1846 .... vol. 7
Book No. 16.—January term, 1847 .... vol. 8
Book No. 17.—January terms, 1847 and 1848................................. vol. 9
Book No. 18.—January term, 1848 .... vol. 10
Book No. 19.—November term, 1848 .... vol. 11
Book No. 20.—January term, 1849 .... vol. 12
Book No. 21.—January and November terms, 1849, and January term, 1850. vol. 13
Book No. 22.—November term, 1850 .... vol. 14

JOHN F. CUSHMAN, REPORTER.

Book No. 23.—January term, 1851, November term, 1851, January term, 1852. vol. 1
Book No. 24.—January and October terms, 1852............................ vol. 2
Book No. 25.—October term, 1852, and April term, 1853...................... vol. 3
Book No. 26.—December special term, 1853, and part of April term, 1854.... vol. 4
Book No. 27.—April and October terms, 1854 .... vol. 5
Book No. 28.—October term, 1854, and April term, 1855..................... vol. 6
Book No. 29.—April term, 1855, and general index to 7 vols................. vol. 7

JAMES Z. GEORGE, REPORTER.

Book No. 30.—December special term, 1855, and part April term, 1856....... vol. 1
Book No. 31.—April term, 1856, and part October term, 1856.................. vol. 2
Book No. 32.—Part October term, 1856 .... vol. 3
Book No. 33.—April term, 1856, and part October term, 1857 .... vol. 4
Book No. 34.—Part October term, 1857, and part April term, 1858 .... vol. 5
Book No. 35.—Part April term, 1858, and part October term, 1858........... vol. 6
Book No. 36.—Part October term, 1858, and part April term, 1859............ vol. 7
Book No. 37.—Part April term, 1859, and part October term, 1859............ vol. 8
Book No. 38.—Part October term, 1859, and part April term, 1860............ vol. 9
Book No. 39.—February and October terms, 1860, April and October terms, 1861, and April term, 1863 .... vol. 10

R. O. REYNOLDS, REPORTER.

Book No. 40.—October term, 1864, January term, 1866, April and October terms, 1866 .... vol. 1
Book No. 41.—October term, 1866, June term, 1867, April and July terms, 1868 .... vol. 2
Book No. 42.—October term, 1868, and October term, 1869................... vol. 3

J. S. MORRIS, REPORTER.

Book No. 43.—May term, 1870, October term, 1870, May and October terms, 1871 .... vol. 1
Book No. 44.—October term, 1870 .... vol. 2
Book No. 45.—April and October terms, 1871................................. vol. 3
Book No. 46.—April and October terms, 1872................................. vol. 4
Book No. 47.—April and October terms, 1872................................. vol. 5
Book No. 48.—April term, 1873 .... vol. 6

HARRIS AND SIMRALL, REPORTERS.

Book No. 49.—October term, 1873, and April term, 1874...................... vol. 1
Book No. 50.—April and October terms, 1874................................. vol. 2
Book No. 51.—October term, 1875... vol. 3
Book No. 52.—April term, 1876 .... vol. 4

BROWN AND HEMMINGWAY, REPORTERS.

Book No. 53.—October term, 1876... vol. 1
Book No. 54.—October term, 1876, April and October terms, 1877 .... vol. 2
Book No. 55.—October term, 1877, and April term, 1878...................... vol. 3
Book No. 56.—April term, 1878, January term, 1879, and April term, 1879 .... vol. 4
Book No. 57.—April and October terms, 1879, and April term, 1880.......... vol. 5
Book No. 58.—October term, 1880, and April term, 1881...................... vol. 6
Book No. 59.—October term, 1881, and April term, 1882...................... vol. 7
Book No. 60.—October term, 1882, and April term, 1883...................... vol. 8
Book No. 61.—October term, 1883, and April term, 1884...................... vol. 9
Book No. 62.—October term, 1883 and 1884, and April term, 1885 .... vol. 10
Book No. 63.—October term, 1885, and April term, 1886...................... vol. 11
Book No. 64.—October term, 1886, and April term, 1887...................... vol. 12
Book No. 65.—October term, 1887, April and October terms, 1888 .... vol. 13

BRAME AND ALEXANDER, REPORTERS.

Book No. 66.—October term, 1888, and April term, 1889...................... vol. 1
Book No. 67.—October term, 1889, and April term, 1890...................... vol. 2
Book No. 68.—October term, 1890, and April term, 1891...................... vol. 3
Book No. 69.—October term, 1891, and April term, 1892...................... vol. 4
Book No. 70.—October term, 1892, and March term, 1893..................... vol. 5
Book No. 71.—October term, 1893, and March term, 1894..................... vol. 6
Book No. 72.—October term, 1894, and March term, 1895..................... vol. 7

A BIBLIOGRAPHY OF MISSISSIPPI.

T. A. M'WILLIE, REPORTER.

Book No. 73.—October term, 1895, and March term, 1896 .... vol. 1

SUPREME COURT OF MISSISSIPPI. Mississippi State Cases, 1818-1872. *See* Joshua S. Morris.

—— Chancery Reports. *See Gen.* John D. Freeman.

—— *See also* Civil Lists, Courts.

SWANEY, JOHN L. Reminiscences of.
    In the *Gallatin (Tenn.) Examiner*.
    Referred to in Claiborne's *Mississippi*, p. 182, *note*, and p. 226.
    He was the old Nashville and Natchez mail rider.

SWAYZE, *Rev.* SAMUEL. Sketch of.
    In Claiborne's *Mississippi*, p. 107.
    The first Protestant minister in Mississippi.

T.

TALLAHATCHIE COUNTY. Sketch of.
    In Lowry and McCardle's *Mississippi*, pp. 580-582.

TALLY, HUGH. Execution of.
    In Lowry and McCardle's *Mississippi*, pp. 464-465.

TANNER, HENRY S. (1786-1858), *Geographer*. A | description | of the | canals and rail roads | of the | United States, | comprising | notices of all the works | of | internal improvement | throughout | the several States. By H. S. Tanner. | New York: | T. R. Tanner & J. Disturnell, | 124 Broadway. | 1840.
    8vo. pp. 272.
    Contains an account of the canals and railroads of Mississippi in 1840.
    Copies seen: Hamner.

TANNER, ROBERT. Sketch of.
    In Claiborne's *Mississippi*, *note* p. 242, .
    He was an early and influential settler.

TARDY, *Mrs.* MARY. Southland writers. | Biographical and critical sketches | of the | living female writers of the South. | With extracts from their writings. | By Ida Raymond. | In two volumes | Vol. I[-II] | [Monogram] | Philadelphia: | [Publishers, 2 lines]. | 1870. |
    8vo. 2 vols.
    Contains sketches of indifferent value of several accredited to Mississippi.

TARPLEY, COLLIN S. (1802-1860), *Lawyer*. Sketch of.
    In Lynch's *Bench and Bar of Mississippi*, pp. 366-369.

TATE COUNTY. Sketch of.
    In Lowry and McCardle's *Mississippi*, pp. 582-583.

TAX TITLES IN MISSISSIPPI. *See* R. H. Thompson.

TAXATION IN MISSISSIPPI. History of. *See* C. H. Brough and R. H. Thompson.

—— Lands held by the State of Mississippi for taxes, April 4, 1871.
    8vo. p. 616. No title-page.
    Same, with repagination, as an Appendix to Senate *Journal*, 1871.

TAYLOR, JOHN (—1823), *Lawyer, First C. J. of Miss.* Sketch of.
    In Lynch's *Bench and Bar of Mississippi*, pp. 88-89.
    See also Claiborne's *Mississippi*, pp. 353-354.

TECUMSEH, *Shawnee Indian Chief.* Account of his trip to the Southern Indians to incite them to arms against the Americans.
> In Claiborne's *Mississippi*, pp. 315-318.

—— Life of. *See* Benj. Drake.

—— *See also* H. S. Halbert.

TEASDALE, THOMAS COX (1808-1891), D. D. Sketch of.
> In Foster's *Mississippi Baptist Preachers*, pp. 655-660; portrait.

—— Reminiscences and incidents of a long life. By Rev. Thomas C. Teasdale, D. D. With a brief introduction, by Rev. C. E. W. Dobbs, D. D., of Columbus, Miss. St. Louis, 1887.
> 12mo. pp. xiii, 385.

TERNAUX-COMPANS, H. (1807-1864), *French historian.* Voyages, | relations et mémoires | originaux | pour servir à l'histoire de la découverte | de l'Amérique, | publiés pour la première fois en Français, | par H. Ternaux-Compans. | Recueil de pièces | sur | La Floride. | Médit. | Paris. | Arthus Betrand, libraire-éditeur, | Libraire de la Société de Géographie de Paris, | Rue Hautefeuille, No. 23. | MDCCCXLI. |
> 8vo. pp. [8] 368.
> Vol. xx of the general collection of Ternaux's *Voyages*, etc.
> Contents: Proclamation to be made to inhabitants of the regions and provinces that lie between the River of Palms (Panuco) and the Cape of Florida, pp. 1-7; Fontanedo's Memoire on Florida, its coasts, and its inhabitants, pp. 9-42; Letter from Soto to municipal council of Santiago, Cuba, pp. 43-50; Biedma's relation of De Soto's Florida expedition, pp. 51-106; Father Bateta's account of Melendez's expedition in Florida, pp. 107-142; Account of Guido de las Bazares's voyage to East coast of Florida in 1559, pp. 143-156; Velasco's letter to the King of Spain on the affairs of Florida, pp. 157-164; Chaplain Mendoza's account of voyage of the Melendez expedition to Florida, 1565, pp. 165-232; Copy of a letter on Florida, with plan, etc., of Fort Caroline. In 1565, pp. 233-246; History of Capt. John Ribault's last voyage to Florida, 1565, pp. 217-248; another account of same, pp. 249-300; De Gourgue's reprisal, pp. 301-366.
> *Copies seen:* Hamner.

THACHER, JOSEPH S. B., *Lawyer.* Sketch of.
> In Lynch's *Bench and Bar of Mississippi*, pp. 211-213.

THOMPSON, HUGH MILLER (1830-), D. D., *P. E. Bishop of Miss.* Sketch of.
> In Appleton's *Cyclopædia of American Biography*, vol. vi, p. 91.
> Consecrated assistant bishop of Mississippi Feb. 24, 1883; and on the death of Bishop Green, of Mississippi, he succeeded to his office.
> He is the author of *Unity and its Restoration* (New York, 1860); *Sin and its Penalty* (1862); *First Principles* (1863); *Absolution* (1864); *Copy* (1871); *Is Romanism the Best Religion for the Republic?* (1873); *The Kingdom of God* (1873); *The World and the Logos* (1885); *The World and the Kingdom* (1888), and *The World and This Man* (1890).

THOMPSON, JACOB (1810-1885), *Lawyer, M. C. from Miss.* Sketch of.
> In Claiborne's *Mississippi*, pp. 447-466; portrait.
> *See also* Waddel's *Memorials of Academic Life*, p. 290.

THOMPSON, R. H., LL. D. *Compiler.* Annotated code of general laws of Mississippi, 1892. *See* Codes of Mississippi.

—— *Compiler.* Annotated edition Constitution of Mississippi, 1891. *See* Conventions and Constitutions of Mississippi.

—— Tax titles in Mississippi.
> In *Proceedings* of the Mississippi Bar Association, 1889.
> Read before this body at its meeting, 1889.

THOMPSON, R. H. Suffrage in Mississippi. | R. H. Thompson. | Reprinted from the publication of the Mississippi Histori- | cal Society for June, 1898. |
>8vo.
>In the *Publications*, etc., pp. 25-49.

—— Millsaps College. Lessons to be drawn from its history and the life of its founder. An address before the Lamar Society of the College, April, 1896.
>In the Jackson *Evening News*, April, 1896.

THORNTON, THOMAS C. (1794-1860), *Methodist Clergyman.* Sketch of.
>In Appleton's *Cyclopædia of American Biography*, vol. vi, p. 104.
>He was the author of *Inquiry into the History of Slavery in the United States* (Washington, 1841), in which work he replied to the anti-slavery arguments of Wm. E. Channing; and also of *Theological Colloquies*.

TIPPAH COUNTY. Sketch of.
>In Lowry and McCardle's *Mississippi*, pp. 583-585.

—— Mound on Camp creek, in southeastern part of county.
>Mentioned by Samuel Agnew, in Smithsonian *Report*, 1867, p. 404.

—— Map of.
>In Harper's *Preliminary Report on the Geology and Agriculture of Mississippi*, 1857.

TISHOMINGO COUNTY. Sketch of.
>In Lowry and McCardle's *Mississippi*, pp. 585-588.

—— Map of.
>In Harper's *Preliminary Report on the Geology and Agriculture of Mississippi*, 1857.

TOBACCO IN MISSISSIPPI. Cultivation of.
>In Wailes' *Report on Agriculture and Geology of Mississippi*, pp. 132-138.

TOMPKINS, PATRICK W., *Lawyer, M. C. from Mississippi.* Sketch of.
>In Lynch's *Bench and Bar of Mississippi*, pp. 283-285.

TOPOGRAPHY OF MISSISSIPPI.
>In Goodspeed's *Memoirs of Mississippi*, vol. i, pp. 11-27.

TRANSPORTATION IN MISSISSIPPI. History of.
>In Goodspeed's *Memoirs of Mississippi*, vol. ii, pp. 60-89.
>Includes chapters on water and railway transportation, and an account of the Levee system.

TROTTER, JAMES FISHER (1802-1866), *Lawyer, Judge in Miss., U. S. Senator from Miss., Prof. of Law Univ. of Miss.* Sketch of.
>In Lynch's *Bench and Bar of Mississippi*, pp. 205-211.
>This sketch contains an address by him in 1866, as circuit judge, to the grand jury of De Soto County.

TUCKER, TILGHMAN M. (d. 1859), *Gov. of Miss., M. C. from Miss.* Administration as governor.
>In Lowry and McCardle's *Mississippi*, pp. 299-304.

TUNICA COUNTY. Sketch of.
>In Lowry and McCardle's *Mississippi*, pp. 588-589.

TURNER, EDWARD (1778-1860), *Lawyer, Chief Justice of Miss.* Sketch of.
>In Lynch's *Bench and Bar of Mississippi*, pp. 84-87.
>*See also* Claiborne's *Mississippi*, pp. 354-355; Goodspeed's *Memoirs of Mississippi*, vol. ii, pp. 928-929.

—— *Compiler.* Statutes of the Mississippi Territory, 1816. *See* Codes of Mississippi.

[TUTTLE, SARAH.] Conversations | on the | Choctaw mission. | By the author of | conversations on the Bombay mission. | Revised by the committee of publication. | Second edition. | Boston: | Massachusetts Sabbath School Society. | [-etc., 1 line.] | 1834. |
18mo. pp. 222.
Relates to the work of the "American Board of Missions," through its missionaries and their assistants, at the mission stations of Elliot and Mayhew in the Choctaw Nation in the State of Mississippi.

TERRITORIAL DELEGATES IN CONGRESS. Sketches of.
In Lowry and McCardle's *Mississippi*, pp. 242-245.

THIERS, ADOLPHE. The Mississippi Bubble: a Memoir of John Law. By Adolphe Thiers. Translated and edited by Frank S. Fiske. New York: W. A. Townsend & Co. 1859.
12mo. pp. 338.
Copies seen: Peabody.

THOMAS, CYRUS (1825-   ). Smithsonian institution | Bureau of ethnology: J. W. Powell, director. | Catalogue of prehistoric works | east of the Rocky mountains | by | Cyrus Thomas | [vignette] | Washington | Government printing office | 1891. |
8vo. pp. 246.
Mississippi, pp. 122-6.
Copies seen: Owen.

TONER, JOSEPH MERIDETH (1825-1896), *M. D., Author.* Contributions to the study of yellow fever. | A paper read before | the American Public Health Association, | New York, November 12, 1873, | on the | Natural history and distribution | of | yellow fever | in | the United States, | with | chart showing all the localities, and the eleva- | tion of each place above sea-level, | where it has appeared, | from | A. D. 1668 to A. D. 1874. | Reprinted from annual report Supervising Surgeon U. S. | Marine-Hospital Service, 1873. |
8vo. pp. 36. *Chart.*
Copies seen: Owen.

TRACY, EBENEZER CARTER (1796-1862), *Author.* Memoir | of the Life | of | Jeremiah Evarts, Esq. | Late corresponding secretary of the American Board of | Commissioners for Foreign Missions. | By E. C. Tracy. | Boston: | Published by Crocker and Brewster, | 47 Washington-street. | 1845.
8vo. pp. 448. *Portrait of author.*
Contains much data relating to the missionary establishments of the American Board of Commissioners for Foreign Missions, among the "Southern Indians" before their removal by the General Government beyond the Mississippi River.
Copies seen: Hamner.

TRACY, S. M. Mississippi | as it is. | A handbook | of | facts for immigrants. | Prepared by S. M. Tracy, | director of State Experiment Station, | Agricultural College, Miss. | 1895. | Jackson, Miss.: | Messenger Publishing Company, printers. | 1895. |
8vo. pp. 138. *Map; illustrations.*

TRAVEL. *See* Appleton & Co., Francis Bailey, William Bartram, Baudry de Lozieres, Biedma, F. Bossu, J. S. Buckingham, Cabeça de Vaca, F. Cuming, Lorenzo Dow, Le Page Du Pratz, Timothy Dwight, Elvas, W. C. Falkner, G. W. Featherstonhaugh, *Maj.* S. S. Forman, B. F. French (*Collections, passim*), Basil Hall, Charles Lanman, Charles Lyell, *Rev.* J. Morse, Perrin du Lac, Matthew Phelps, John Pope, Barnard Shipp, James Stuart, and Ternaux-Compans.

TRIALS. Trial of Aaron Burr in Mississippi.
: In Claiborne's *Mississippi*, pp. 278-294.

TROWBRIDGE, JOHN TOWNSEND (1827-   ), *Author.* The | South: | a tour of its battlefields and ruined cities, | a journey through the desolated States, | and talks with the people. | [-etc. 11 lines.] | From personal observations and experience during months of Southern travel. | By J. T. Trowbridge, | Author [-etc. 1 line.] Illustrated. | Sold by agents only. | Hartford, Conn.: | Published by L. Stebbins. | 1866. |
: 8 vo. pp. 590.
: *Copies seen:* Hamner.

TRUMBULL, HENRY. History of the discovery of America. . . . To which is annexed the particulars of . . . the Creek and Seminole wars. Boston, 1831.
: 8vo. pp. 256.
: "A most miscellaneous collection, which happens to contain some early accounts of events preceding the Creek war; among others, one of the first narratives of the massacre at Fort Mims, written near the scene."—Parton's *Life of Jackson.*

—— History of Indian Wars. New edition. Revised and re-arranged. Boston. 1841.
: 8vo.
: Creek wars, chapter 19.

TUPELO. Recollections of.
: In Davis's *Recollections of Mississippi and Mississippians.* pp. 174-185.

U.

UNION BANK OF MISSISSIPPI. Report | of the | select committee | on the | Union Bank bonds, | to the | Mississippi Legislature. | Presented February, 1842. | Printed by order of the House. | Jackson: | Price & Fall, State printers. | 1842. |
: 8vo. pp. 44.
: Contains report and testimony.
: *Copies seen:* Owen.

—— High Court of Errors and Appeals | of the | State of Mississippi. | The State of Mississippi, | vs. | Hezron A. Johnson. | Involving the liability | of the | State of Mississippi | for the | payment of the bonds | issued for and on account of the | Mississippi Union Bank. | Opinion of the Judges | and | final decision of the cause. | Jackson: | Thomas Palmer, printer. | 1853. |
: 8vo. pp. 55.
: Holds the State liable for the payment of the bonds.
: *See* Campbell vs. The Union Bank, *6 Howard's Miss. Reports,* and State of Mississippi vs. Johnson, *25 Miss. Reports. See also,* for account of bank legislation, controversy, etc., Claiborne's *Mississippi,* 479-480.

UNION BANK OF MISSISSIPPI. *See also* Lynch's *Bench and Bar of Mississippi*, p. 328.

—— *See also* Lowry and McCardle's *Mississippi*, pp. 281-293.

UNION COUNTY. Sketch of.
> In Lowry and McCardle's *Mississippi*, pp. 590-1.

—— Mounds in.
> Reported by Samuel Agnew, in Smithsonian *Report*, 1867, p. 404.
> *See also Twelfth Annual Report Bureau of Ethnology*, 1890-91, pp. 267-278; *9 figures*.

UNIVERSITY OF MISSISSIPPI. Sketch of.
> In De Bow's *Review*, 1859.
> *See Ibid.* Sept., 1860, p. 398, for notice of the Catalogue of 1860.

—— Report, by T. C. McRae, amending and favoring H. R. 5778, to supply deficiency in grant of public lands for University. Feb. 15, 1894. (House Rep. 436, 2d sess. In v. 1.)
> 8vo. pp. 5.

—— History of.
> In Mayes' *History of Education in Mississippi*, pp. 118-212.

—— Origin and location of. *See* R. B. Fulton.

—— Mississippi | University | Magazine. | [Quotation, editors, etc., 6 lines.] | Vol. III. November, 1877. No. 1 | [Vignette] | Published by the | two Literary Societies of the University of Mississippi | Marshall & Bruce, stationers, Nashville, Tenn. |
> 8vo. pp. 33.

—— *Cover title:* Historical and current | catalogue | of the | University of | Mississippi. | Fiftieth year | forty-seventh session | 1849-99. | 1898-9 |

—— *Title page:* Historical and current catalogue | of the | officers and students | of the | University of Mississippi, | forty-seventh session | 1898-'99. | Clarion-Ledger book print. | Jackson, Miss. | 1899. |
> 8vo. pp. xiii, 328.
> The "Preface and Historical Sketch" comprise pp. iii-xiii. Contains, also, lists of trustees, members of the faculty, and alumni.

—— The "Ole Miss" of the University of Mississippi. Published by the Fraternities. Vol. I. 1897.
> Pp. 161.
> Vol. II, 1898. pp. 206.

—— *See also* J. M. Arnold, F. A. P. Barnard, John Fulton, R. B. Fulton, Dr. John N. Waddell, and T. D. Witherspoon.

V.

VAN DE VELDE, JAMES OLIVER (1795-1855), *Second Bishop of Natchez.* Sketch of.
> In *Sketch of the Catholic Church in Natchez*, pp. 25-28.

VAN HOESEN, J. A. *Compiler.* Digest of the laws of Mississippi, 1839. *See* Codes of Mississippi.

VANNERSON, WILLIAM (-1874), *Lawyer.* Sketch of.
> In Lynch's *Bench and Bar of Mississippi*, pp. 126-131.

VAUGHN, B. A., *M.D.* Public health. | An address | delivered before | the Mississippi State Medical Association, | by the president, | B. A. Vaughn, M.D., | of Columbus, Miss., | at the eleventh annual session, held in Jackson, April 3d, 1878. n. d. [*Colophon:* Excelsior book and job printing establishment, Columbus, Miss.]
 8vo. Cover title only, 1 leaf, pp. 10.

—— Restoration | of the | practice of medicine | to the | medical profession. | How can it be done? By B. A. Vaughn, M.D., | Columbus, Miss. | Jackson, Miss.: | State Ledger printing establishment. | 1892. |
 8vo. pp. 12.

VEGA, GARCILASSO DE LA (1537-1617), *Peruvian historian.* La Florida | del Inca. | Historia | del Adelantado, | Hernando de Soto, | Gobernador, y Capitan General | del Reino de la Florida. | Y de otros hervicos cabelleros, | Españoles, e Indios. | Escrita | por el Inca Garcilasso | de la Vega, | Capitan de su Magestad, natural | de la Gran Ciudad de Cozco, | Cabeça de los Reinos, y provincias del Perú. | Dirigda | A la Reina | neustra señora. | Van enmendadas en esta impression, | muchas erratas de la Primera: Y añadida Copiosa Tabla | de las Copas Notables. | Y el ensado cronologico, | que contrene, las sucedidas, | hasta en el Año de 1722. | Con privilegio: en Madrid. En la Oficina Real, y à Costa de Nicolas Rodriguez Franco, Impresor | de Libros. | Año CIƆ IƆCCXXIII. | Se hallarán en su Casa. |
 Folio. 16 p. l. 268. [12.]
 Copies seen: Hamner; Congress.

—— Histoire | de la conquête | de la | Floride: | ou | relation de ce qui s'est passé dans | la découverte de ce païs | par Ferdinand de Soto; | composée en Espagnol | par L'Inca Garcillasso de la Vega | & traduite en François | por Sr. Pierre Richelet. | Nouvelle edition | corrigée & augmentée | de très belles cartes, de figures en taille douce & | d'un indice. | Tome premier [-second.] | A la Haye, | Chez Jean Meaulme. | MDCCXXXV. |
 12mo. vol. I, prel. leaves 26 pp. 290; vol. II, 291-582. *8 plates; 1 map.*
 Copies seen: Hamner.

—— History of the Conquest of Florida; or a narrative of what occurred in the exploration of this country by Hernando de Soto. By the Inca Garcillasso de la Vega. Translated from the French version of Pierre Richelet, from the original Spanish.
 In Shipp's *History of Hernando de Soto and Florida,* vol. II, pp. 215-487. See Shipp, Barnard.
 This is the only English version.

VENABLE, ROBERT ABRAM, (1849-) *A. M., D. D.* The | Baptist layman's | hand-book. | By | R. A. Venable, A. M. D. D., | President Miss. College, for eleven years pastor of First Baptist Church, | Memphis, Tenn. | Louisville, Ky.: | Baptist Book Concern. | 1894. |
 8vo. pp. 262.

—— Sketch of.
 In Foster's *Mississippi Baptist Preachers,* pp. 689-692.

VICK, *Rev.* NEWITT. Sketch of.
 In Claiborne's *Mississippi,* pp. 534-535.

VICKSBURG. Public men and early settlers.
In Lowry and McCardle's *Mississippi*, pp. 593-596.

—— Picturesque Vicksburg. *See* H. P. Chapman.

—— In and about Vicksburg. *See* Lee Richardson, jr.

—— Official | reports of battles, | embracing | the defense of Vicksburg, | by Major-General Earl Van Dorn, | and the | attack upon Baton Rouge, | by Major-General Breckenridge, | together with | the reports of the battles of Corinth and Hatchie Bridge; the | expedition to Hartsville, Tennessee; the affair at Pocotaligo | and Yemassee; the action near Coffeeville, Mississippi; the | action and casualties of the brigade of Colonel Simonton, at | Fort Donelson. | Richmond, Va.: | Smith, Bailey & Co., printers. | 1863. |
8vo. pp. 170.

—— Hanging the gamblers, and the flatboat war at.
In Fulkerson's *Recollections of Early Days in Mississippi*, pp. 96-99.

—— Pioneers of Vicksburg and Warren County.
In Claiborne's *Mississippi*, pp. 534-536.

—— Sketches of.
In Goodspeed's *Memoirs of Mississippi*, vol. II, pp. 147-153.

—— *See also* T. A. Conrad and Otto Myer.

VIDAL, DON JOSÉ. Sketch of.
In Claiborne's *Mississippi*, p. 195 and *note*.

VIRGINIA YAZOO COMPANY. Memorial of the Virginia Yazoo Company to Congress, 1803.
Brinley, Part II, No. 3930.

VOLNEY, CONSTANTIN FRANÇOIS (1757-1820). A view | of | the soil and climate | of the | United States of America: | with supplementary remarks | upon Florida; on the French colonies of the Mississippi | and Ohio, and in Canada; and on the aboriginal tribes | of America. | By C. F. Volney, | member of the Conservative Senate, &c. &c..| Translated, with occasional remarks, | by C. B. Brown. | With maps and plates. | Philadelphia, | Published by [–etc., 3 lines.] | Printed by T. & G. Palmer, 116 High street. | 1804. |
8vo. pp. xxviii, 446. *2 maps; plates.*
Pp. 17 *et seq.* refer briefly to the Mississippi Territory; pp. 269-316 treat of Florida and quote at length from Bernard Romans' *History of Florida* [1776].

W.

WADDEL, JOHN NEWTON (1812-188-) *D. D., LL. D.* Memorials of academic life: | being an | historical sketch | of | the Waddel family, | identified through three generations with the history | of the higher education in the South and Southwest. | By | John N. Waddel, D. D., LL. D., | ex-chancellor of the University of Mississippi, and of the | Southwestern Presbyterian University. | Richmond, Va.: | Presbyterian committee of publication. | 1891. |
12mo. pp. 583. *Portrait of author.*
Contains biographies of Rev. Moses Waddel, (1770-1840) D. D., and Prof. Wm, Henry Waddel; and also an autobiography of the author.
Much Mississippi educational history.
Copies seen: Owen.

WADDEL, JOHN NEWTON. Moral heroism: | an oration delivered before | the Ciceronian and Phi-Delta Societies | of | Mercer University, | Penfield, Georgia. | On Commencement Day, July 28, 1852. | By | John N. Waddel, D. D. | Prof. Ancient Literature, University of Mississippi. | Penfield, Ga. | printed at the Banner office. | 1852. |
8vo. pp. 26.
Copies seen: Stansel.

WAILES, BENJAMIN L. C. Report | on the | agriculture and geology | of | Mississippi. | Embracing a sketch of the | social and natural history of the State. | By | B. L. C. Wailes, | geologist of Mississippi; | [–etc., 3 lines.] | Published by order of the Legislature. | E. Barksdale, State printer. | 1854. |
8vo. pp. xx, 17–371. *Bowen's Map, 1764*, covering a part of the present States of Alabama and Mississippi.

ILLUSTRATIONS:

Plate I, figure 1. Seals of the British Province of West Florida. Figures 2 and 3, old French copper coins.
Plate II. Facsimiles of signatures and seals of the Spanish governors of Louisiana.
Plate III. The cotton plant. 1st view.
Plate IV. The cotton plant. 2d view.
Plate V. Caterpillar, chrysalis, and moth on cotton.
Plate VI. Rot in cotton bolls.
Plate VII, figure 1. Primitive roller gin; figure 2, roller gin with treadle and balance wheel; figure 3, Whitney's gin of 1807; figure 4, section of cylinder with flattened wire teeth; figure 5, section of same with pointed wire teeth.
Plate VIII. Cotton plantation in the West Indies in 1764.
Plate IX. Geological strata.
Plate X, figures 1 and 2. Illustrations of stratification.
Plate XI, figure 1. Artesian well at Columbus; figure 2, principles of artesian wells.
Plate XII. Sections on Brandon Railroad.
Plate XIII. Boring artesian wells.
Plates XIV-XVII. Fossil shells from the Eocene marl beds at Jackson.

CONTENTS:

Title, Preface, Contents, Illustrations. pp. xi.
Introduction. pp. xiii-xx.
I. Historical outline: Expedition and discovery by De Soto; as a colony of France; as a British province; as a province of Spain, pp. 17-116.
II. Land titles. pp. 117-125.
III. Agriculture. pp. 127-205.
IV. Geology. pp. 207-296.
V. Meteorology. pp. 297-308.
VI. Fauna. pp. 309-340.
VII. Flora. pp. 341-356.
Appendix. pp. 357-371.

The historical outline presents a continuous narrative from 1699 to 1798, based on the usual authorities, and some hitherto unused manuscripts. The subjects of land titles and agriculture, both of great importance in the history of Mississippi, are treated with a fullness and detail not elsewhere found. The historical illustrations are of great value.
Edition, 2,000 copies.

"The son-in-law of General [Leonard] Covington, the late B. L. C. Wailes, at the time of his death State Geologist of Mississippi, was a man of rare ability and attainments. In literature and science he was the foremost man in the State, and would have achieved the greatest eminence had his life been spared."—Claiborne's *Mississippi*, p. 259, *note*.

As shown by the U. S. Blue Book of 1830, Mr. Walles was born in Georgia, and was on September 30, 1829, register of the land office at Washington, Miss.

Copies seen: Owen.

WALKER, C. B. The Mississippi Valley and prehistoric events: giving an account of the original formation and early condition of the great valley; of its vegetable and animal life; of its first inhabitants, the mound builders; its mineral treasures and agricultural developments. All from authentic sources. By C. B. Walker. R. T. Root, publisher. Burlington, Iowa. 1879.

8vo. pp. 539.

"The object of this book is to supply the means of acquiring a clear idea of the Origin, Extent, Resources and Development of the Miss. Valley. No work before the public embraces this information."—*Preface*.

The work does not rise to the dignity claimed. No citations of authorities.

Copies seen: Congress.

WALKER, ROBERT JOHN (1801–1869), *Lawyer, Sec. of the U. S. Treas., U. S. Senator from Miss., Territorial Gov. of Kansas*. *Caption:* Public dinner, | given in honor | of the | Chickasaw and Choctaw Treaties, | at Mr. Parker's hotel, | in the city of Natchez, | on the 10th day of October, 1830. | n. p. n. d.

8vo. pp. 16. No title page.

Contains a patriotic address by Robert J. Walker, Esq., depicting results to follow opening the lands, etc.

—— Speech | of | Rob't J. Walker, Esq. | Delivered at the union meeting, held in the city of Natchez, | on the first Monday of January, 1833. | Published by request. | Natchez: | printed by N. Wooster, office of the Mississippi Journal. | 1833. |

8vo. pp. 16.

Mississippi Journal—extra.

—— Speech | of | Hon. Robert J. Walker, | of Mississippi, | on the bill to provide further remedial justice | in the | courts of the United States: | delivered | in the Senate of the United States, | June 21, 1842. | Washington: | printed at the Globe office. | 1842. |

8vo. pp. 19. Double columns.

—— *Reporter*. Mississippi Reports, 1818–32, vol. 1. *See* Supreme Court.

—— Character sketch of. *See* Dunbar Rowland.

—— Sketch of.

In Claiborne's *Mississippi*, pp. 415–423.

Also Lynch's *Bench and Bar of Mississippi*, pp. 109–112.

Appleton's *Cyclopædia of American Biography*, vol. vi, p. 329; portrait.

In 1863 he joined James R. Gilmore in the conduct of the "Continental Monthly," which the latter had established the year preceding to advocate emancipation as a political necessity, and for it he wrote some of his ablest political articles.

WALL, E. G., *Compiler*. The State of Mississippi. | Resources, condition and wants. | Compiled and arranged by order of | the State Board of Immigration and Agriculture. | By E. G. Wall, Commissioner. | 1879. | Jackson, Miss.: | Clarion Steam Printing Establishment. | 1879. |

8vo. pp. 200

WALL, E. G. Hand-book | of the | State of Mississippi. | By E. G. Wall, Commissioner. | Published by order of the Board of Immigration and Agriculture. | [Seal,] | Jackson, Miss.: | the Clarion Steam Printing Establishment. | 1885. |
>   8vo. pp. 100. Map.
>   Historical sketch. pp. 3–6.
>   Much statistical information. Separate sketches of the several counties.

WALTER, HARVEY WASHINGTON (1819–1879), *Lawyer.* Sketch of.
>   In Lynch's *Bench and Bar of Mississippi,* pp. 487–492; *portrait.*

WALTHALL, EDWARD CARY (1831–1898), *Brig. Gen. C. S. A., U. S. Senator from Miss.* The federal election bill. | Speech | of | Hon. E. C. Walthall, | of Mississippi, | in the | Senate of the United States, | Friday, December 12, 1890. | Washington. | 1890. |
>   8vo. pp. 27.

—— Memorial addresses | on the | life and character | of | Edward C. Walthall | (late a Senator from Mississippi), | delivered in the | Senate and House of Representatives, | Fifty-fifth Congress, | second and third sessions. | Washington: | Government Printing office. | 1899. |
>   8vo. pp. 154. *Portrait.*

WALTON, AUGUSTUS Q. A | history | of the | detection, conviction, life and designs | of | John A. Murel [sic], | the Great Western Land Pirate. | Together with his system of villainy, and plan of exciting a | Negro Rebellion. | And a catalogue of the names of four hundred and forty-five of his | mystic clan, fellows and followers, and their | efforts for the destruction of | Mr. Virgil A. Stewart, | the young man who detected him. | To which is added a biographical sketch of | Mr. Virgil A. Stewart. | By Augustus Q. Walton, Esq. | Re-published by George White. | Printed at the Journal Office, Athens, Tennessee, 1835. |
>   8vo. pp. 75.
>   Prepared from papers and documents of Mr. Stewart, who committed them to the author for that purpose, the latter being on what was then thought to be his dying bed.
>   *Copies seen:* Congress.

WAR OF 1812. *See* H. M. Brackenridge, N. H. Claiborne, J. D. Dreisback, Wm. Duane, J. H. Eaton, *Maj.* A. L. Latour, B. J. Lossing, John Lowell, John T. Sprague, and James Wilkinson.

WARD, WILLIAM (1823–1887). Sketch of. *See* Dabney Lipscomb.
>   Mr. Lipscomb has a volume of Mr. Ward's poems about ready for the press.

WARDEN, DAVID BAILLIE (1778–1845). A statistical, political, and historical | account | of | the United States | of | North America; | from the period of their first colonization | to the present day. | By D. B. Warden, | late consul for the United States at Paris, | &c., &c. | Volume I [–III]. | Edinburgh: | printed for [–etc., 3 lines]. | 1819. |
>   8vo. *Maps.*
>   Vol. iii, chapter 27, contains an account of Mississippi for the period. Contains meager bibliography.
>   *Copies seen:* Owen.

WARREN COUNTY. Sketch of.
>   In Lowry and McCardle's *Mississippi*, pp. 591–597.
>   See also Goodspeed's *Memoirs of Mississippi*, vol. i, pp. 186–187.

—— Pioneers of Vicksburg and Warren County.
>   In Claiborne's *Mississippi*, pp. 534–536.

—— Mounds on Mississippi and Yazoo Rivers.
>   Mentioned in Smithsonian *Report*, 1879, p. 442.

WASHINGTON. Sketch of.
>   In Goodspeed's *Memoirs of Mississippi*, vol. ii, pp. 167–168.

WASHINGTON COUNTY. Sketch of.
>   In Lowry and McCardle's *Mississippi*, pp. 597–601.

—— Description of mounds in. By James R. Gage.
>   In *Trans. St. Louis Academy Science*, vol. iii (1868–1877), pp. 227–232.
>   See also Twelfth Annual Report Bureau of Ethnology, 1890–91, pp. 259–260; 1 figure.
>   This contains a description of the "Avondale Mounds."
>   See also Smithsonian *Report*, 1879, pp. 383, 384.

WATKINS, JAMES LAWRENCE (1850–). Production and price of cotton | for | one hundred years. | By | James L. Watkins, | special agent. | . [Seal of the Dept.] | Washington: | Government Printing Office. | 1895. |
>   8vo. pp. 20.
>   Miscellaneous series, *Bulletin*, No. 9, U. S. Dept. of Agriculture, Division of Statistics.
>   *Copies seen:* Owen.

WATKINS, JOHN A. (1808–1898). Reminiscences of the Jefferson Troop.
>   In the *Chronicle*, Fayette, Miss.
>   Col. Watkins is in error in saying the Troop was at the battle of the Holy Ground.
>   Two rosters are given.

—— Recollections of Jefferson County.
>   Referred to in Goodspeed's *Memoirs of Mississippi*, vol. i, p. 176.

—— The great Mississippi panic, 1813.
>   In Halbert and Ball's *Creek War*, pp. 296–300.
>   The unabridged original of this paper is now in possession of Mr. Halbert, Crawford, Miss.

WATTS, THOMAS H. Address on life of Davis. *See* Jefferson Davis.

WAYNE COUNTY. Sketch of.
>   In Lowry and McCardle's *Mississippi*, pp. 601–604.
>   See also Goodspeed's *Memoirs of Mississippi*, vol. i, pp. 187–189.

WEATHERFORD, WILLIAM, *Indian Warrior*. Sketch of. *See* J. D. Dreisback.

—— Red Eagle and the wars with the Creek Indians of Alabama. *See* George C. Eggleston.

—— *See also* H. S. Halbert, A. B. Meek, Wm. G. Orr.

WEBB, ROBERT DICKENS (1824–1894), *M. D.* The Webb Family | by | Robert Dickens Webb, M. D. | Yazoo City, Miss. | January, 1894 | [–etc., 4 lines.] | [*Colophon:*—Moss Engraving Co., N. Y.]
>   8vo. pp. 68, 1 l. Numerous *portraits*.
>   *Copies seen:* Owen.

WEBB, *Rev.* W. S. (1825–), *D. D., LL. D.* Sketch of.
    In Foster's *Mississippi Baptist Preachers*, pp. 701-713, *portrait.*

WEBBER, RICHARD H., *Lawyer.* Sketch of.
    In Lynch's *Bench and Bar of Mississippi*, pp. 146-147.

WEBER, WILLIAM LANDER (1866–), *A. B., A. M., Teacher.* Word-Lists | for | the study of | English Etymology. | Compiled by | William Lander Weber | Professor of English, Millsaps College | Jackson, Mississippi | [R. W. Bailey printing co., Jackson, Miss., 1898.]
    8vo. pp. 31.

—— Mississippi as a field for the student of literature.
    In *Publications Mississippi State Historical Society*, 1898, vol. i, pp. 16-24.
    This is a really valuable study, emphasizing the importance and extent of the local field, with comments on the use and value of bibliography.

—— Irwin Russell—First-fruits of the Southern romantic movement.
    Ibid. 1899, vol. ii, pp. 15-22.

WEBSTER COUNTY. Sketch of.
    In Lowry and McCardle's *Mississippi*, pp. 604-605.

WEEKS, STEPHEN BEAUREGARD (1865–), *Ph. D.* [Learned and educational societies in Mississippi.]
    In *Report* [*U. S.*] *Bureau of Education*, 1893-94, pp. 1493-1661, Washington, 1896. 8vo.

—— The history | of | Negro suffrage | in the South | by Stephen B. Weeks | Reprinted from Political Science Quarterly, Vol. IX, No. 4. | Boston | Ginn & Company, | 1894. |
    8vo. pp. 671-703.
    Reference to Mississippi, *passim.*

WELLS, JAMES M. The Chisholm massacre. A picture of "Home Rule" in Mississippi. Chicago, 1877.
    12mo. pp. 291. *Ill.*

—— The Chisholm massacre: a picture of "Home Rule" in Mississippi, by J. M. Wells. Washington, 1878.
    8vo. pp. 331. *Portrait.*

WELSH, *Miss* MARY. Reminiscences of old Saint Stephens [Ala.], of more than sixty-five years ago.
    In *Transactions Alabama Historical Society*, 1898-99, vol. iii, pp. 208-226.
    In a foot-note are to be found a few genealogical references to the Welsh and Gordy families. Miss Welsh resides at Shuqualak, Miss. She is the author of "The Model Family," 1858; "Aunt Abbie," 1859; and the "Baptist Denomination," 1860.

WEST, ANSON, *D. D., Methodist Clergyman.* A history | of Methodism in Alabama. | By the Rev. Anson West, D. D. | Printed for the author. | Publishing house Methodist Episcopal Church, South. | Barbee & Smith, agents, Nashville, Tenn. | 1893. |
    8vo. pp. 755.
    Portraits: Frontispiece, Robert Kennon Hargrove, *D. D.*, Daniel Jones Hargrove, Mrs. D. J. (*Brantley*) Hargrove, *Rev.* Thomas Stringfield, *Judge* William B. Wood, *Chancellor* J. R. John, *Hon.* William H. Thornton.
    "The plan of this book is to begin with the beginning and write the history as it begins, develops, enlarges, and goes on, and give the history everywhere in the order of time, both in the opening and the progress. In the plan thus pursued the history is given from 1808 to 1818. During that time there were only two appointments in the State. Then the history is given from 1818 to 1832. At the

close of that time the Alabama Conference was organized. Then in the order of the design the history is given from 1832 to 1845. Then it was that the jurisdiction of the Methodist Episcopal Church South commenced. Finally, in the on-going of the plan the history from 1845 to 1865 is given. Then the emancipation of slaves was consummated and a new order of things inaugurated. There this history closes."—*Preface.*

Perhaps one of the most important features of this work is the introduction of numerous biographical and family sketches, both of ministers and laymen. The accounts of the first settlements and pictures of early life in the early years of Statehood are unusually full.

Many references to Mississippi Territory.

Copies seen: Owen.

WEST, *Col.* CATO. Sketch of.

In Claiborne's *Mississippi*, pp. 212, 228, and *notes*.

WEST FLORIDA. Petition | of the | inhabitants of West Florida; | signed | by George Patterson, | and four hundred and ten others. | November 20th, 1811. | Ordered to lie on the table. | Washington City: | Printed by R. C. Weightman. | 1811. |

8vo. pp. 7.

Prays to be incorporated with the Mississippi Territory, and opposes the prospect of continuing as a separate territory, or of being attached to the territory of New Orleans.

Copies seen: Johns Hopkins Univ.

—— An account of the "revolution" in what are now the West Florida parishes of Louisiana.

In Claiborne's *Mississippi*, pp. 304-314.

WHARTON, T. J. (1817-), *Lawyer.* What I know of public men and measures in Mississippi in the last sixty-two years.

In *Publications Mississippi State Historical Society*, 1900, vol. iii. (In press.)

—— George Poindexter, founder of the jurisprudence of Mississippi.

In *Commercial-Appeal*, Memphis, Dec. 22, 1895.

Mr. Wharton has been a frequent contributor to the press, and has also published a number of briefs, arguments, etc.

WHITE, *Rev.* GEORGE, *M. A.* Historical collections | of | Georgia: | containing the most interesting | facts, traditions, biographical sketches, anecdotes, etc. | relating to its history and antiquities, from its first | settlement to the present time. | Compiled from original records and official documents. | Illustrated by nearly | one hundred engravings | of | public buildings, relics of antiquity, historic localities, natural scenery, | portraits of distinguished men, etc., etc. | [Georgia seal] | By the | Rev. George White, M. A. | Author of the "Statistics of Georgia." | New-York: | Pudney & Russell, publishers, | No. 79 John-street. | 1854. |

8vo. pp. xiv, 688.

This work is of great value, from its accuracy and extent of material. Contains numbers of biographies of celebrated Indians of the Southern tribes; also much concerning the Western Territory of Georgia.

Copies seen: Hamner.

WHITE, J. M., *M. S.* Territorial growth of Mississippi.

In *Publications Mississippi [State] Historical Society*, 1899, vol. ii, pp. 125-132.

—— Original location of the A. and M. College of Mississippi.

Ibid. 1900, vol. iii. (In press.)

WHITFIELD, JAMES, *Gov. of Miss.* Administration as governor.
: In Lowry and McCardle's *Mississippi*, p. 321.

WHITWORTH FEMALE COLLEGE. Sketch of.
: In Mayes' *History of Education in Mississippi*, pp. 101-103.

WILKES, W. B. [Mississippi archæoloy and antiquities.]
: In Aberdeen *Examiner*.
: Referred to in Claiborne's *Mississippi*, p. 7, *note*.

WILKINS, JAMES C., *Merchant.* Sketch of.
: In Claiborne's *Mississippi*, p. 353.

WILKINSON COUNTY. Sketch of.
: In Lowry and McCardle's *Mississippi*, pp. 605-607.
: *See also* Goodspeed's *Memoirs of Mississippi*, vol. i, pp. 180-183.

WILKINSON, EDWARD C., *Lawyer.* Sketch of.
: In Lynch's *Bench and Bar of Mississippi*, pp. 138-139.
: *See also* Waddel's *Memorials of Academic Life*, pp. 287-288.

WILKINSON, JAMES (1757-1825), *Maj. Gen'l, U. S. A.* Memoirs | of | my own times. | By | General James Wilkinson. | [Quotations, 10 lines] | In three volumes. | Vol. I. [-III.] | Philadelphia: | Printed by Abraham Small. | 1816. |
: 8vo. Vol. i, pp. xv, 855 [52]; vol. ii, title, 1 l., pp. 578 [246]; vol. iii, title, 1 l., pp. 496 [64].
: "These documents will be valuable to the historian, as they contain important details of occurrences in Louisiana [and the Southwest] from 1789 to 1809, and of events of the war with England of 1812-15."—*North American Review*, vol. vi, p. 78.
: *Copies seen:* Hamner.

—— Diagrams and plans, | illustration | of the | principal battles and military affairs, | treated of in | memoirs of my own times. | By James Wilkinson, | late a Major General in the service of the United States. | Philadelphia: | Printed by Abraham Small. | 1816. |
: 4to. *20 maps or plans.*
: Forms vol. iv of the preceding title.
: *Copies seen:* Hamner.

—— Sketch of.
: In Claiborne's *Mississippi*, pp. 245-250.

—— Proofs of the corruption of. *See* Daniel Clark.

WILLEY, GEORGE. Natchez in the olden times.
: In Claiborne's *Mississippi*, pp. 526-533.

WILLIAMS, JOHN SHARP (1854-), *M. C. from Miss.* Against Philippine Annexation. Speech of, in House of Representatives, Dec. 20, 1898.
: 4to. pp. 8. No title page.
: Reprinted from *Congressional Record*, 55th Cong., 3d sess.

—— The Philippine Question—Answer to a Challenge. Two short talks in House of Representatives, Jan. 17 and 31, 1900.
: 8vo. pp. 8. No title page.

—— Philippine Annexation. Speech of, in House of Representatives, Feb. 6, 1900.
: 4to. pp. 8. No title page.
: Reprinted from *Congressional Record.*

WILLIAMS, ROBERT (1768–1837), *Lawyer, M. C. from N. C., Gov. Miss. Territory.* Administration of.
    In Claiborne's *Mississippi*, pp. 258–302.

WILLIAMS, THOMAS HILL (1795–1839), *U. S. Sen. from Miss.* Sketch of.
    In Claiborne's *Mississippi*, p. 258, *note.*

WINCHESTER FORT. Description of.
    In Lowry and McCardle's *Mississippi*, pp. 602–603.
    Erected in Wayne County during the Creek war, for protection against the Indians.

WINCHESTER, GEORGE (–1851), *Lawyer.*
    In Lynch's *Bench and Bar of Mississippi*, pp. 100–102.

WINN, WILLIAM T., *U. S. treasury expert.* Sketch of Mississippi.
    In *Report on Internal Commerce of the U. S. Part II. The Southern States*, pp. 468–505. Washington: Government Printing Office. 1886. (Ex. Doc. 7, Pt. 2, 49th Cong., 2d sess.) 8vo.
    Valuable for its commercial, agricultural, and industrial statistics.

WINSTON COUNTY. Sketch of.
    In Lowry and McCardle's *Mississippi*, pp. 608–609.

—— Centennial history of. *See* William T. Lewis.

WITHERSPOON, *Rev.* T. D. The appeal | of the | South to its educated men. | An address | before the Alumni Association of the University of Mississippi, delivered | in the hall of the university, | on Wednesday, June 26, 1867. | By | Rev. T. D. Witherspoon, | of Memphis, Tennessee. | Of the class of 1856. | Memphis: | published by the association. | 1867. |
    8vo. pp 20.
    Copies seen: Owen.

WOMAN'S CHRISTIAN TEMPERANCE UNION. Sketch of.
    In Goodspeed's *Memoirs of Mississippi*, vol. ii, pp. 379–383.
    See also Rev. W. C. Black.

WOODWARD, THOMAS SIMPSON (1797–1861), *Maj. Georgia Volrs., Lt. Col. Cmt. Indn. Volrs., Brig. Gen. of Militia.* Woodward's reminiscences | of the | Creek, or Muscogee Indians, | contained in letters to friends in | Georgia and Alabama. | By Thomas S. Woodward, of Louisiana, | (formerly of Alabama.) | With an appendix, | containing interesting matter relating to the general subject. | Montgomery, Ala.: | Barrett & Wimbish, book and general job printers. | 1859. |
    8vo. pp. 168.
    The greater number of these letters were originally published in the *Montgomery Mail.*
    A very valuable book, now quite rare.
    "Few men have had better opportunities for studying the Indian character and investigating their customs than General Woodward. Very early in life . . . he was brought into contact with the Red Man; and, stirred by the Indian blood in his own veins, he studied his character and traditions lovingly and earnestly. . . . The unpretending pages which follow contain a very great deal of matter of high historical value to the people of Alabama and Georgia."—*Introduction.*
    "A small volume of reminiscences about the Indians, which attempts to confute many of the statements made by Pickett, Meek, Coxe, and others, which have been in part adopted in this volume. He was an interesting man, tall and erect, and brusk [sic] in manner."—Brewer's *History of Alabama.*
    Copies seen: Curry.

WORCESTER, JOSEPH EMERSON (1784–1865), *A. M.* A | gazetteer | of the | United States | abstracted from | the universal gazetteer | of the author; with enlargement of the principal articles. | By J. E. Worcester, A. M. | Andover: | printed for the author by Flagg and Gould: | 1818. |
>8vo. Not paged.
>*Copies seen:* Hamner.

WRIGHT, DANIEL W., *Lawyer.* Sketch of.
>In Lynch's *Bench and Bar of Mississippi* p. 203.

WYETH, JOHN ALLAN, *M. D.* Life of General | Nathan Bedford Forrest | By | John Allan Wyeth, M. D. | With illustrations by | T. de Thulstrup, Rogers, Klepper | Redwood, Hitchcock, & Carleton | [Design.] | New York and London | Harper & Brothers publishers | 1899 |
>8vo. pp. xxii, 656. *Portraits; ills.*
>His early life was spent in Mississippi.

Y.

YALOBUSHA COUNTY. Sketch of.
>In Lowry and McCardle's *Mississippi*, pp. 609–611.

YAZOO COUNTY. Sketch of.
>In Lowry and McCardle's *Mississippi*, pp. 611–616.

—— Mound on Yazoo River, 20 miles below Satartia.
>Briefly described by J. W. C. Smith, in Smithsonian *Report*, 1874, p. 370.

—— The Champlin mounds.
>In *Twelfth Annual Report Bureau of Ethnology*, 1890–91, pp. 260–263; *3 figures*.

YAZOO FRAUDS. Account of.
>In Claiborne's *Mississippi*, pp. 156–159.

—— Letter from the Secretary of State, accompanied with an abstract of all the evidences of title of lands claimed under any act or pretended act of the State of Georgia; passed or pretended to be passed in the years 1789 and 1795; recorded in the office of the said Department of State, in pursuance of a resolution of the House, on the fifth instant. [By James Madison] Feb. 14, 1805. Washington City: Printed by William Duane & Son. 1805. (Ex. Doc., 8th Cong., 2d sess.)
>4to. pp. 38.
>*Copies seen:* Owen.

—— Sundry papers, in relation to claims, commonly called the Yazoo Claims. Dec. 18, 1809. City of Washington: A. and C. Way, Printers. 1809. (Ex. Docs., 11th Cong., 2d sess.)
>12mo. pp. 195.
>A collection of various papers, hitherto separately published. Never reprinted in this complete form.
>*Copies seen:* Owen.

—— *See also* Absalom H. Chappell.

YELLOW FEVER. Contributions to the study of. *See* Dr. Joseph M. Toner.

—— Treatise on principal diseases of the interior valley of North America. *See* Dr. Daniel Drake.

—— In Mississippi.
In Fulkerson's *Recollections of Early Days in Miss.*, pp. 34–42, 118–127.

YERGER, GEORGE S. (1808–1860), *Lawyer.* Sketch of.
In Lynch's *Bench and Bar of Mississippi*, pp. 261–265.

YERGER, JACOB SHALL (1810–1867), *Lawyer.* Sketch of.
In Lynch's *Bench and Bar of Mississippi*, pp. 272–277; *portrait.*

YERGER, WILLIAM (1816–1872), *Lawyer.* Sketch of.
In Lynch's *Bench and Bar of Mississippi*, pp. 326–341.

XXII.—BIBLIOGRAPHY OF PUBLICATIONS OF THE AMERICAN HISTORICAL ASSOCIATION, 1885 TO 1900.

BIBLIOGRAPHY OF THE PUBLICATIONS OF THE AMERICAN HISTORICAL ASSOCIATION, 1885 TO 1900.

I.—PAPERS OF THE AMERICAN HISTORICAL ASSOCIATION.

Papers of the American Historical Association. Vol. I. New York and London, 1885.
8vo. pp. v, 502.

CONTENTS.

No. 1. Secretary's Report of the Organization and Proceedings, Saratoga, September 9, 10, 1884, pp. 5–44. Prefaced by a reprint of an article by H. B. Adams on "A New Historical Movement," from *The Nation*, September 18, 1884.

No. 2. On Studies in General History and the History of Civilization, by Andrew D. White, President of the Association, pp. 1-28 [45-72].

No. 3. History and Management of Land Grants for Education in the Northwest Territory, by George W. Knight, pp. 1-175 [73-247].

No. 4. The Louisiana Purchase in its influence upon the American System, by the Right Reverend C. F. Robertson, D. D., Bishop of Missouri, pp. 1-42 [249-290].

No. 5. History of the Appointing Power of the President, by Lucy M. Salmon, pp. 1-129 [291-419].

No. 6. Report of the Proceedings of the American Historical Association, Second Annual Meeting, Saratoga, September 8-10, 1885, by Herbert B. Adams, Secretary of the Association, pp. 173 [421-493]; index, pp. 75-82 [495-502].

Papers of the American Historical Association. Vol. II. New York and London, 1887.
8vo. pp. iv, 565.

CONTENTS.

No. 1. Report of the Proceedings of the American Historical Association at Washington, D. C., April 27-29, 1886, Third Annual Meeting, by Herbert B. Adams, Secretary of the Association, pp. 1-104. Includes abstracts of the following papers: Columbus, by Gen. James Grant Wilson; Graphic Methods of Illustrating History, by Dr. Albert Bushnell Hart; The Neglect and Destruction of Historical Materials in this Country, by Prof. Moses Coit Tyler; New Views of Early Virginia History, 1606-1619, by Alexander Brown, Esq.; The part taken by Virginia under the Leadership of Patrick Henry in Establishing Religious Liberty as a Foundation of American Government, by Hon. William Wirt Henry; The Causes of the Revolution, by Dr. Edward Channing; The Development of Municipal Government in Massachusetts, by T. Jefferson Coolidge; The March of the Spaniards across Illinois, by Edward G. Mason; The Northwest Territory, its Ordinance and its Government, by Dr. Israel W. Andrews; Did the Louisiana Purchase include Oregon? by William A. Mowry; The Settlement of the Lower St Lawrence, by Eben Greenough Scott; The Origin of the Highest Functions of the American Judiciary, by Prof. Austin Scott; Jefferson's Use of the Executive Patronage, by J. M. Merriam; The Early Protective Movement and the Tariff of 1828, by Dr. F W. Taussig; The Attack on Washington City in 1814, by Maj.

Gen. George W. Cullum; Confederate and Federal Strategy in the Pope Campaign before Washington in 1862, by Col. William Allan; The State-Rights Theory: Its Evolution and Involution in American Politics, by James C. Welling; The Reconstruction of History, by Dr. George E. Ellis; William Usselinx, by J. F. Jameson; Franklin in France, by Dr. Edward Everett Hale; Historical Studies in Canada, by George Stewart, Jr.

No. 2. A History of the Doctrine of Comets, by Andrew D. White, President of the Association, pp. 1-43 [105-147].

No. 3. William Usselinx, Founder of the Dutch and Spanish West Indian Companies, by J. Franklin Jameson, Ph. D., pp. 1-234 [149-382].

No. 4. Church and State in the United States, or the American Idea of Religious Liberty and its Practical Effects, by Philip Schaff, D. D., LL. D., pp. 1-161 [383-543]; Index [546-565].

Papers of the American Historical Association. Vol. III. New York and London, 1889.

8vo. pp. iv, 536.

CONTENTS.

No. 1. Report of the Proceedings at Boston and Cambridge, May 21-24, 1887, Fourth Annual Meeting, by Herbert B. Adams, Secretary of the Association; Manuscript Sources of American History—The conspicuous Collections extant, by Justin Winsor, pp. 9-27; Diplomatic Prelude to the Seven Years' War, by Herbert Elmer Mills, pp. 29-40; A Short Account of the Life and Times of Silas Deane, by Charles Isham, pp. 40-47; Historical Grouping, by James Schouler, pp. 48-52; The Constitutional Relations of the American Colonies to the English Government at the Commencement of the Revolution, by Mellen Chamberlain, pp. 52-74; On the Peace Negotiations of 1782-83 as Illustrated by the Secret Correspondence of France and England, by John Jay, pp. 79-100; Biographical Sketch of Leopold von Ranke, with an account of Ranke and the Historical Commission of the Bavarian Academy of Science, and Bibliographical Notes on Leopold von Ranke, by Herbert B. Adams, pp. 101-133; A Reminiscence of Ranke, by Frederic A. Bancroft, pp. 121-124; The Parliamentary Experiment in Germany, by Kuno Francke, pp. 133-146; A Study in Swiss History, by John Martin Vincent, pp. 146-164; The Spaniard in Mexico, by W. W. H. Davis, pp. 164-176; Abstract of paper by Prof. Moses Coit Tyler: The Historical Name of Our Country, pp. 176-178; The Biography of a River and Harbor Bill, by Dr. Albert Bushnell Hart, pp. 180-197; Extract from a paper by Col. Carroll D. Wright on The Study of Statistics in American Colleges, pp. 197-202; Abstract of a paper by Prof. Arthur M. Wheeler on The Government of London, pp. 203-205; Religious Liberty in Virginia, and Patrick Henry, by Charles J. Stillé, pp. 205-211; Abstract of a paper by Philip Schaff on The American Chapter in Church History, pp. 211-213; Notes on Historical Studies in Canada, by George Stewart, Jr., pp. 213-215; A letter written in 1500 from Hispaniola by a Franciscan Missionary, pp. 215-219; Necrology: Calvin Holmes Carter and James Carson Brevoort, pp. 223-227; List of members of the American Historical Association, pp. 229-238.

No. 2. Report of the Proceedings, Washington, D. C., December 26-28, 1888, Fifth Annual Meeting, by Herbert B. Adams, Secretary of the Association, pp. 1-30 [245-274]; The Early Northwest, Inaugural Address by William F. Poole, LL. D., President of the Association, pp. 31-56 [275-300]; Remarks by Hon. George B. Loring on Dr. Poole's Address, pp. 56-64 [300-308]; The Influence of Governor Cass in the Development of the Northwest, by Prof. A. C. McLaughlin, pp. 65-83 [309-327]; The Place of the Northwest in General History, by William F. Allen, pp. 85-104 [329-348]; Internal Improvements in Ohio, 1825-1850, by Charles N. Morris, pp. 105-136 [349-380]; The Old Federal Court of Appeal, by Prof. J. Franklin Jameson, pp. 137-148 [381-392], Canadian Archives, by Douglas Brymner, pp. 149-163 [393-407]; The States-Rights Conflict over the Public Lands, by James C. Welling, LL. D., pp. 165-188 [409-432]; The Martyrdom of San Pedro Arbués, by Henry Charles Lea, pp. 189-209 [433-453]; A Reply to Dr. Stillé upon Religious Liberty in Virginia, by Hon. William Wirt Henry, pp. 211-220 [455-464]; American

Trade Regulations before 1789, by Willard Clark Fisher, pp. 221-249 [465-493]; Museum-History and History of Museums, by George Brown Goode, LL. D., pp. 251-275 [495-519]; Appointment of Committees, etc. Index, pp. 276-292 [520-536].

Papers of the American Historical Association. Vol. IV. New York and London, 1890.

8vo. pp. viii, 537.

CONTENTS.

Part 1, January, 1890. Report of the Proceedings of the American Historical Association at the Sixth Annual Meeting, Washington, D. C., December 28-31, 1889, by Herbert B. Adams, Secretary of the Association, pp. 1-21; List of members, pp. 23-34; Report of the Treasurer, Clarence W. Bowen, p. 35; Recent Historical Work in the Colleges and Universities of Europe and America; Inaugural Address of President Charles Kendall Adams, LL. D., pp. 37-65; A Catechism of the Revolutionary Reaction, by Andrew D. White, pp. 67-92.

Part 2, April, 1890. The Origin of the National Scientific and Educational Institutions of the United States, by G. Brown Goode, Ph. D., LL. D., pp. 3-112 [93-202].

Part 3, July, 1890. The Mutual Obligation of the Ethnologist and the Historian, by Otis T. Mason, pp. 3-13 [203-213]; Historical Survivals in Morocco, by Talcott Williams, pp. 13-34 [213-234]; The Literature of Witchcraft, by Prof. George L. Burr, pp. 35-66 [235-266]; The Development of International Law as to Newly Discovered Territory, by Walter B. Scaife, Ph. D., pp. 67-93 [267-293]; The Spirit of Historical Research, by James Schouler, pp. 95-106 [295-306]; A Defense of Congressional Government, by Dr. Freeman Snow, pp. 107-128 [307-328].

Part 4, October, 1890. Materials for the History of the Government of the Southern Confederacy, by John Osborne Sumner, pp. 3-19 [329-345]; The Constitutional Aspect of Kentucky's Struggle for Autonomy, 1784-1792, by Ethelbert D. Warfield, pp. 21-39 [347-365]; The Pelham Papers—Loss of Oswego, by William Henry Smith, pp. 41-53 [367-379]; Notes on the Outlook for Historical Studies in the South, by Prof. William P. Trent, pp. 55-65 [381-391]; Economic and Social History of New England, 1620-1789, by William B. Weeden, pp. 67-78 [393-404]; The Early History of the Ballot in Connecticut, by Prof. Simeon E. Baldwin, pp. 79-96 [407-422]; Bibliography of the American Historical Association, by Paul Leicester Ford, pp. 97-103 [423-429]; Brief Notes on the Present Condition of Historical Studies in Canada, by George Stewart, Jr., D. C. L., LL. D., pp. 105-109 [431-435]; The Trial and Execution of John Brown, by Gen. Marcus J. Wright, pp. 111-126 [437-452]; A Few Facts from the Records of William and Mary College, by President Lyon G. Tyler, pp. 117-141 [453-467]; The Impeachment and Trial of President Johnson, by Dr. William A. Dunning, pp. 143-177 [469-503]; Committees, Historical Societies, etc., 179-211 [505-537].

Papers of the American Historical Association. Vol. V. New York and London, 1891.

8vo. pp. iv, 503.

CONTENTS.

Parts 1-2, January and April, 1891. Report of the Proceedings of the American Historical Association, at the Seventh Annual Meeting, Washington, D. C., December 29-31, 1891, by Herbert B. Adams, Secretary of the Association, pp. 1-16; The Demand for Education in American History: Inaugural Address of Hon. John Jay, LL. D., President of the Association, pp. 19-43; The Theory of the Village Community, by Dr. Charles M. Andrews, pp. 47-60; Remarks on Dr. Andrews's Paper, by William B. Weeden, pp. 60-61; Karl Follen and the German Liberal Movement (1815 to 1819), by Prof. Kuno Francke, pp. 65-81; Bismarck as the Typical German, by William G. Taylor, pp. 85-109; State Activities and Politics, by William F. Willoughby, A. B., pp. 113-127; Mirabeau's Speech of May 20, 1790, by Dr. Fred. Morrow Fling, pp. 131-139; The Organization of Historical Material, by W. H. Mace, M. A., pp. 143-161; The Origin of American Institutions, as Illustrated in the History of the Written Ballot, by Douglas Campbell, pp. 165-185; Remarks on Mr. Campbell's

Paper, by Dr. Williston Walker, pp. 185-186; Remarks on Mr. Campbell's Paper, by Prof. J. F. Jameson, p. 186.

Part 3, July, 1891. The Fate of Dietrich Flade, by Prof. George L. Burr, pp. 3–57 [189-243]; The Philosophic Aspects of History, by Wm. T. Harris, LL. D., pp. 61-68 [247-254]; Brief Notes on the Present Condition of Historical Studies in Canada, by George Stewart, D. C. L., LL. D., D. Litt., F. R. G. S., F. R. S. C., pp. 71–74 [257-260]; Is History a Science? by Prof. R. H. Dabney, Ph. D., pp. 77–86 [263-272]; Canada and the United States: An Historical Retrospect, by John George Bourinot, C. M. G., LL. D., D. C. L., pp. 89–147 (275-333].

Part 4, October 1891. Slavery in New York: The Status of the Slave under the English Colonial Government, by Edwin Vernon Morgan, A. M., pp. 3–16 [337-350]; Amendments to the Constitution of the United States, by Dr. Herman V. Ames, pp. 19–29 [353-363]; Congressional Demands upon the Executive for Information, by Edward Campbell Mason, pp. 33–41 [367-375] A Plea for Reform in the Study of English Municipal History, by Dr. Charles Gross, pp. 45–58 [379-392]; The Yazoo Land Companies, by Dr. Charles H. Haskins, pp. 61–103 [395-437]; The Lost Colony of Roanoke: Its Fate and Survival, by Prof. Stephen B. Weeks, Ph. D., pp. 107–146 [441-480]; Index, pp. 147-169 [481-503].

II.—ANNUAL REPORTS OF THE AMERICAN HISTORICAL ASSOCIATION.

Annual Report of the American Historical Association for the year 1889. Washington: Government Printing Office, 1890.

8vo. pp. viii, 427.

Transmitted by the Secretary of the Association to the Secretary of the Smithsonian Institution and submitted to Congress in accordance with the Act of Incorporation of the Association. Printed as Senate Miscellaneous Document No. 170 of the Fifty-first Congress (first session).

CONTENTS.

Report of Proceedings at Sixth Annual Meeting, Washington, D C., December 28–31, 1889, by Herbert B. Adams, pp. 1–18; Recent Historical Work in the Colleges and Universities of Europe and America, by Charles Kendall Adams, pp. 19–42; The Spirit of Historical Research, by James Schouler, pp. 43–51; The Origin of the National Scientific and Educational Institutions of the United States, by G. Brown Goode, pp. 53–161; A Partial Bibliography of the Published Works of Members of the American Historical Association, by Paul Leicester Ford, pp. 163–386; Index, pp. 387-427.

Annual Report of the American Historical Association for the year 1890. Washington: Government Printing Office, 1891.

8vo. pp. x, 310.

Transmitted by the Secretary of the Association to the Secretary of the Smithsonian Institution and submitted to Congress in accordance with the Act of Incorporation of the Association. Printed as Senate Miscellaneous Document No. 83 of the Fifty-first Congress (second session).

CONTENTS.

Report of Proceedings of the Seventh Annual Meeting of the American Historical Association, held in Washington, D. C., December 29-31, 1890, by Herbert B. Adams, pp. 3–12; The Demand for Education in American History, Inaugural Address by Hon. John Jay, LL. D., pp. 15–36; The following references are abstracts of papers read by the persons named: Canada and the United States from Historical Points of View, by J. G. Bourinot, C. M. G., LL. D., pp. 39–40; New England Settlements in Acadia, by Benjamin Rand, Ph. D., pp. 41–42; The Legislative Work of the First Parliament of Upper Canada, by William Houston, M. A., pp. 43–44; The fate of Dietrich Flade, by Prof. George L. Burr, p. 47; Theory of Village Community, by Dr. Charles M. Andrews, pp. 49–50; A Plea for Reform in the Study of English Municipal History, by Dr. Charles Gross, pp. 51–52; Mirabeau's speech of May 20, 1790, by Dr. Frederick M. Fling, pp. 53–54; The Formation of the French Constitution, by Prof. Adolphe Cohn, pp. 55–56; Karl Follen and the Liberal Movement in Germany, by Prof. Kuno Francke, pp. 57–58; Bismark the Typical German, by William G. Taylor, p. 59; How the Written Ballot came into the United States, by Douglas Campbell, pp. 63–65; A Virginia Bill of Attainder—The Case of Josiah Philips, by Prof. William P. Trent, pp. 67–68; Amendments to the Constitution of the United States, by Herman V. Ames, pp. 66–70; Congressional Demands upon the Executive for Information, by Edward Campbell Mason, pp. 71–72; Responsible Government in Canada, by J. G. Bourinot, C. M. G., LL. D., pp. 73–74; Bills of Rights in State Constitutions, by General R. D. Mussey, pp. 75–77; Development of the Budget in the United States, by E. D. Adams, p. 81; The Yazoo Land Companies, by Dr. Charles H. Haskins, p. 83; State Activities and Politics, by Wm. F. Willoughby, pp. 85–86, Slavery in New York—The Status of the Slave under the English Colonial Government, by Edwin Vernon Morgan, A. B., pp. 87–88; Slavery in the District of Columbia—The Policy of Congress and the Struggle for Abolition, by Mary Tremain, A. M., pp. 89–91; Remarks on Miss Tremain's Paper, by William Birney, pp. 91–93; Raleigh's Settlements on Roanoke Island—An Historical Survival, by Dr. Stephen B. Weeks, pp. 97–98; The Political Ideas of the Puritans, by Dr. Herbert L. Osgood, pp. 99–100; State Historical Societies, by Gen. C. W. Darling, pp. 101–102: Organization of Historical Material, by W. H. Mace, A. M., pp. 103–107; Is History a Science? by Prof. A. H. Dabney, Ph. D., p. 109; Webster's Seventh of March Speech, by James Schouler, pp. 111–112; The Border Land between the Historian and the Archæologist, by Prof. Otis T. Mason, p. 113; Bibliography of the Writings of the Members of the American Historical Association for the year 1890, by Paul Leicester Ford, pp. 117–160; Bibliography of the Historical Societies of the United States, by Appleton Prentiss Clark Griffin, pp. 161–267; Index, pp. 269–310.

Annual Report of the American Historical Association for the year 1891. Washington: Government Printing Office, 1892.

8vo. pp. ix, 499.

Transmitted by the Secretary of the Association to the Secretary of the Smithsonian Institution and submitted to Congress in accordance with the Act of Incorporation of the Association. Printed as Senate Miscellaneous Document No. 173 of the Fifty-second Congress (1st session).

CONTENTS.

Report of Proceedings of the Eighth Annual Meeting of the American Historical Association, held in Washington, D. C., December 29–31, 1891, by Herbert B. Adams, pp. 3–11; Inaugural Address of Hon. William Wirt Henry, LL. D., President of the Association, on The Causes which Produced the Virginia of the Revolutionary Period, pp. 15–29; The Expenditures of Foreign Governments in Behalf of History, by Prof. J. Franklin Jameson, pp. 33–61; The United States and International Arbitration, by Prof. John Bassett Moore, pp. 65–85; Some Recent Discoveries Concerning Columbus, by President Charles Kendall Adams, pp. 89–99; The History and Determination of the Lines of Demarcation Established by Pope Alexander VI, between the Spanish and Portuguese Fields of Discovery and Colonization, by Prof. Edward G. Bourne, pp. 103–130; Slavery in the Territories, by President James C. Welling, pp. 133–160; The Enforcement of the Slave Trade Laws, by W. E. B. Du Bois, pp. 163–174; State Sovereignty in Wisconsin, by Albert H. Sanford, pp. 177–195; The Earliest Texas, by Mrs. Lee C. Harby, pp. 199–205; Governor William Leete and the Absorption of New Haven Colony by Connecticut, by Dr. Bernard C. Steiner, pp. 209–222; The Visitorial Statutes of Andover Seminary, by Prof. Simeon E. Baldwin, LL. D., pp. 226–241; Some Neglected Characteristics of the New England Puritans, by Prof. Barrett Wendell, pp. 245–253; Henry Clay as Speaker of the United States House of Representatives, by Mary Parker Follett, pp. 257–265; Lord Lovelace and the Second Canadian Campaign, 1708–1710, by Gen. James Grant Wilson, pp. 269–297; Commerce and Industry of Florence during the Renaissance, by Walter B. Scaife, Ph. D., pp. 301–308; Parliamentary Government in Canada—A Constitutional and Historical Study, by J. G. Bourinot, C. M. G., LL. D., D. C. L., pp. 311–407; Bibliography of Published Writings of Members of the American Historical Association for 1891, by A. Howard Clark, pp. 411–463; Index, pp. 465–499.

Annual Report of the American Historical Association for the year 1892.
Washington: Government Printing Office, 1893.
>8vo. pp. vii, 698.
>
>Transmitted by the Secretary of the Association to the Secretary of the Smithsonian Institution and submitted to Congress in accordance with the Act of Incorporation of the Association. Printed as Senate Miscellaneous Document No. 57, Fifty-second Congress (2nd session).
>
>CONTENTS.
>
>Summary of the work of the American Historical Association during the year 1892, by Herbert B. Adams, Secretary, pp. 1-16; Copy of Tracts relating to America (17th and 18th centuries) found in the Bodleian Library, at Oxford, by Prof. James E. Thorold Rogers, and by him obtained for the American Historical Association, pp. 17-70; Some Account of George Washington's Library and Manuscript Records and their Dispersion from Mount Vernon with an Excerpt from his Diary in 1774 during the First Session of the Continental Congress, with Notes by J. M. Toner, M. D., pp. 71-169; Lotteries in American History, by A. R. Spofford, Librarian of Congress, pp. 171-195; United States Provisional Court for the State of Louisiana, 1862-1865, by Judge Charles A. Peabody, pp. 197-210; Bibliography of Published Writings of Members of the American Historical Association for the year 1892, by A. Howard Clark, Assistant Secretary, pp. 211-302; Bibliography of Historical Societies of the United States and British America, by Appleton Prentiss Clark Griffin (Continued from Annual Report for 1890), pp. 305-619; Index, pp. 621-698.

Annual Report of the American Historical Association for the year 1893.
Washington: Government Printing Office, 1894.
>8vo. pp. x, 605.
>
>Transmitted by the Secretary of the Association to the Secretary of the Smithsonian Institution and submitted to Congress in accordance with the Act of Incorporation of the Association. Printed as Senate Miscellaneous Document No. 104, Fifty-third Congress (2d session).
>
>CONTENTS.
>
>Report of Proceedings of Ninth Annual Meeting in Chicago, July 11-13, 1893, by Herbert B. Adams, secretary, pp. 1-9; Report of the treasurer, pp. 10-11; List of committees, p. 12; Inaugural address of President James B. Angell on the Inadequate Recognition of Diplomatists by Historians, pp. 13-24; The Value of National Archives, by Mrs. Ellen Hardin Walworth, pp. 25-32; American Historical Nomenclature, by Ainsworth R. Spofford, pp. 33-42; The Definition of History, by William Preston Johnston, pp. 43-53; Historical Industries, by James Schouler, pp. 55-66; The Historical Method of Writing the History of Christian Doctrine, by Charles J. Little, pp. 67-75; The Requirements of the Historical Doctorate in America, by Ephraim Emerton, pp. 77-90; The First Fugitive Slave Case of Record in Ohio, by William Henry Smith, pp. 91-100; The Present Status of Pre-Columbian Discovery of America by Norsemen, by James Phinney Baxter, pp. 101-110; Prince Henry, the Navigator, by Edward Gaylord Bourne, pp. 111-121; The Economic Condition of Spain in the Sixteenth Century, by Bernard Moses, pp. 123-133; The Union of Utrecht, by Lucy M. Salmon, pp. 135-148; English Popular Uprisings in the Middle Ages, by George Kriehn, pp. 149-161; Jefferson and the Social Compact Theory, by George P. Fisher, pp. 163-177; The Relation of History to Politics, by Jesse Macy, pp. 179-188; Early Lead Mining in Illinois and Wisconsin, by Reuben Gold Thwaites, pp. 189-195; The Significance of the Frontier in American History, by Frederick J. Turner, pp. 197-227; Roger Sherman in the Federal Convention, by Lewis Henry Boutell, pp. 229-247; The Historical Significance of the Missouri Compromise, by James A. Woodburn, pp. 249-297; The First Legislative Assembly in America, by William Wirt Henry, pp. 299-316; Naturalization in the English Colonies of America, by Miss Cora Start, pp. 317-328; The Establishment of the First Southern Boundary of the United States, by B. A. Hinsdale, pp. 329-366; The Historic Policy of the United States as to Annexation, by Simeon E. Baldwin,

pp. 367-390; The Origin of the Standing Committee System in American Legislative Bodies, by J. Franklin Jameson, pp. 391-399; Gen. Joseph Martin and the War of the Revolution in the West, by Stephen B. Weeks, pp. 401-477; The Annals of an Historic Town, by F. W. Blackmar, pp. 479-499; Contributions toward a Bibliography of American History, 1888-1892, by John Martin Vincent, pp. 501-572; Index, pp. 573-605.

Annual Report of the American Historical Association for the year 1894. Washington: Government Printing Office, 1895.

8vo. pp. xii, 602.

Transmitted by the Secretary of the Association to the secretary of the Smithsonian Institution, and submitted to Congress in accordance with the Act of Incorporation of the Association. Printed as House Miscellaneous Document No. 91, Fifty-third Congress (3d session).

CONTENTS.

Report of Proceedings of Tenth Annual Meeting in Washington, D. C., December 26-28, 1894, by Herbert B. Adams, Secretary, pp. 1-16; The Tendency of History, by Henry Adams, President of the Association, pp. 17-24; Rise of Imperial Federalism (abstract), by Prof. George B. Adams, pp. 25-28; The Historical Work of Prof. Herbert Tuttle, by Prof. Herbert B. Adams, pp. 29-38; Turning Points in the Civil War, by Dr. Rossiter Johnson, pp. 39-54; Tributes to Hamilton Fish, Hon. John Jay, Hon. Robert C. Winthrop, and others, by Gen. James Grant Wilson, pp. 55-62. The Tejas; their Habits, Government, and Superstitions, by Mrs. Lee C. Harby, pp. 63-82; Why Coronado went to New Mexico in 1540, by George Parker Winship, pp. 83-92; The Casa de Contratacion of Seville, by Prof. Bernard Moses, pp. 93-124; Some European Modifications of the Jury System, by Dr. Walter B. Scaife, pp. 125-140; The Regulators of North Carolina (1765-1771), by Prof. John S. Bassett, pp. 141-212; A Chapter in the Life of Charles Robinson, the First Governor of Kansas, by Prof. Frank W. Blackmar, pp. 213-226; The Continental Congress: A neglected Portion of American Revolutionary History, by Dr. Herbert Friedenwald, pp. 227-236; The Labor Movement in English Politics, by Edward Porritt, pp. 237-246; The Organization of the First Committee of Public Safety, by Prof. Henry E. Bourne, pp. 247-272; The Quebec Act and the American Revolution, by Victor Coffin, pp. 273-280; The Historical Archives of the State Department, by Andrew Hussey Allen, pp. 281-298; Appeals from Colonial Courts to the King in Council, with special reference to Rhode Island, by Harrold D. Hazeltine, pp. 299-350; Rhode Island and the Impost of 1781, by Frank Greene Bates, pp. 351-360. The Constitutional Controversy in Rhode Island in 1841, by Arthur May Mowry, pp. 361-370; Party Struggles over the Pennsylvania Constitution, by Samuel B. Harding, pp. 371-402; Evolution of Township Government in Ohio, by James Alva Wilgus, pp. 403-412; The Western Posts and the British Debts, by Prof. A. C. McLaughlin, pp. 413-444; Existing Autographs of Christopher Columbus, by William Eleroy Curtis, pp. 445-518; Mountains and History, by Prof. Edmund K. Alden, pp. 519-530; Causes and Consequences of the Party Revolution of 1800, by Prof. Anson D. Morse, pp. 531-540; The Tennis Court Oath, by Prof. James H. Robinson, pp. 541-548; What the United States Government has done for History, by A. Howard Clark, pp. 549-562; Bibliography of the Colonial History of South Carolina, by Edson L. Whitney, pp. 563-586; Index, 587-602.

Annual Report of the American Historical Association for the year 1895. Washington: Government Printing Office, 1896.

8vo. pp. x, 1247.

Transmitted by the Secretary of the Association to the Secretary of the Smithsonian Institution and submitted to Congress in accordance with the Act of Incorporation of the Association. Printed as House Document No. 291, Fifty-fourth Congress (1st session).

CONTENTS.

Report of Proceedings of Eleventh Annual Meeting in Washington, D. C., December 26-27, 1895, by Herbert B. Adams, Secretary, pp. 1-11; Report of the

Treasurer; List of Committees; Necrology, pp. 13-18; Inaugural Address, by Hon. George F. Hoar, President of the Association, on Popular Discontent with Representative Government, pp. 19-43; The Surroundings and Site of Raleigh's Colony, by Talcott Williams, pp. 45-61; Governor Edward Winslow: His Part and Place in Plymouth Colony, by Rev. William C. Winslow, D. D., pp. 63-77; Arent Van Curler and His Journal of 1634-35, by Gen. James Grant Wilson, D. C. L., pp. 79-101; Political Activity of Massachusetts Towns during the Revolution, by Harry A. Cushing, pp. 103-113; The Land System of Provincial Pennsylvania, by William R. Shepherd, pp. 115-125; The Electoral College for the Senate of Maryland and the Nineteen Van Buren Electors, by Dr. B. C. Steiner, pp. 127-167; Libraries and Literature of North Carolina, by Dr. S. B. Weeks, pp. 169-267; Suffrage in the State of North Carolina (1776-1861), by Prof. J. S. Bassett, pp. 269-285; Locating the Capital, by Gaillard Hunt, pp. 287-295; "Free Burghs" in the United States, by James H. Blodgett, pp. 297-317; The Employment of the Indians in the War of 1812, by Ernest Cruikshank, pp. 319-335; Commodore John Barry, by Martin I. J. Griffin, pp. 337-365; Agreement of 1817: Reduction of Naval Forces upon the American Lakes, by J. M. Callahan, pp. 367-392; "The Underground Railroad," for Liberation of Fugitive Slaves, by Prof. W. H. Siebert, pp. 393-402; Some Bold Diplomacy in the United States in 1861, by Gen. Marcus J. Wright, pp. 403-410; The Battle of Gettysburg, by Harold P. Goodnow, pp. 411-432; Historical Testimony, by Dr. James Schouler, pp. 433-442; A Plea for the Study of History of Northern Europe, by Prof. A. C. Coolidge, pp. 443-451; The French Revolution as seen by the Americans of the Eighteenth Century, by Prof. C. D. Hazen, pp. 453-466; Napoleon's Concordat with Pope Pius VII, 1801, by Prof. Charles L. Wells, pp. 467-485; The German Imperial Court, by O. G. Villard, pp. 487-497; Dismemberment of the Turkish Empire: An Historical Sketch, by Prof. E. K. Alden, pp. 499-511; Colonies of North America and the Genesis of the Commonwealths of the United States, by Dr. J. M. Toner, pp. 513-614; Classification of Colonial Governments, by Prof. H. L. Osgood, pp. 615-627; Slavery in the Province of South Carolina (1670-1770), by Edward McCrady, pp. 629-673; Bibliography of Historical Societies, by A. P. C. Griffin, pp. 675-1158; Index to Griffin's Bibliography, by A. Howard Clark, pp. 1159-1236; General Index, pp. 1237-1247.

Annual Report of the American Historical Association for the year 1896. Washington: Government Printing Office, 1897.

8vo. 2 vols., pp. 1313, 442.

Transmitted by the Secretary of the Association to the Secretary of the Smithsonian Institution and submitted to Congress in accordance with the Act of Incorporation of the Association. Printed as House Document No. 353, Fifty-fourth Congress (2nd session).

CONTENTS.

Vol. I. Report of Proceedings of Twelfth Annual Meeting in New York, December 29-31, 1896, by Herbert B. Adams, Secretary, pp. 11-25; Report of the Treasurer; List of Committees; Necrology, pp. 27-34; Inaugural Address by Dr. Richard S. Storrs, President of the Association, on Contributions made to our National Development by Plain Men, pp. 35-63; Leopold von Ranke, by E. G. Bourne, pp. 65-81; The Journal and Papers of the Continental Congress, by Herbert Friedenwald, pp. 83-135; The Antirent Episode in the State of New York, by David Murray, pp. 137-173; A Know-Nothing Legislature, by G. H. Haynes, pp. 175-187; Peale's Original Whole-length Portrait of Washington; A plea for Exactness in Historical Writings, by Charles Henry Hart, pp. 189-200; Political Science and History, by J. W. Burgess, pp. 201-219; The Use of History made by the Framers of the Constitution, by E. G. Bourne, pp. 221-230; Schemes for Episcopal Control in the Colonies, by Arthur Lyon Cross, pp. 231-241; The Teaching of History, by Herbert B. Adams, pp. 243-263; The Teaching of European History in the College, by James Harvey Robinson, pp. 265-278; The West as a Field for Historical Study, by Frederick J. Turner, pp. 279-319; A Plea for the Study of Votes in Congress, by Orin Grant Libby, pp. 321-334; The Northern Lake Frontier

BIBLIOGRAPHY OF PUBLICATIONS, 1885 TO 1900. 839

during the Civil War, by J. M. Callahan, pp. 335-359; Langdon Cheves and the United States Bank, by Louisa P. Haskell, pp. 361-371; The Influence of the American Revolution on England's Government of her Colonies, by George B. Adams, pp. 373-390; The Government of Federal Territories in Europe, by Edmund C. Burnett, pp. 391-454; The Value of Maps in Boundary Disputes, by P. Lee Phillips, pp. 455-462; Report of the Historical Manuscripts Commission of the American Historical Association, pp. 463-1107; Public Documents of Early Congresses, by Gen. A. W. Greely, pp. 1109-1248; List of books relating to America in the Register of the London Company of Stationers from 1562 to 1678, by P. Lee Phillips, pp. 1249-1261; An Essay toward a Bibliography of Leopold von Ranke, by William Price, pp. 1263-1274.

Vol. II. Proposed Amendments to the Constitution of the United States during the First Century of its History, by Herman V. Ames. (Chap. I. A General Survey of the Attempts to Secure Amendments; Chap. II. Amendments Affecting the Form of Government—Legislative; Chap. III. Amendments Affecting the Form of Government—Executive; Chap. IV. Amendments Affecting the Form of the Judiciary Department; Chap. V. Amendments Affecting the Powers of the Government; Chap. VI. Procedure as to Constitutional Amendments.)

Annual Report of the American Historical Association for the year 1897. Washington: Government Printing Office, 1898.
8vo. pp. ix, 1272.

CONTENTS.

Report of Proceedings of Thirteenth Annual Meeting at Cleveland, Ohio, December 28-30, 1897, by Herbert B. Adams, Secretary, pp. 1-11; Report of the Treasurer, List of Committees and Officers, pp. 13-17; President's Address, A New Federal Convention, by James Schouler, pp. 19-34; John Cabot and the Study of Sources, by George Parker Winship, pp. 35-41; To What Extent May Undergraduate Students be Trained in the Use of the Sources, by James A. Woodburn, pp. 43-49; The Functions of State and Local Historical Societies with Respect to Research and Publication, by J. F. Jameson, pp. 51-59; State-Supported Historical Societies and their Functions, by Reuben Gold Thwaites, pp. 61-71; History in the German Gymnasia, by Lucy M. Salmon, pp. 73-89; Discussion of the Relation of the Teaching of Economic History to the Teaching of Political Economy, by Gardner, Knight, and Seager, pp. 91-98; Introduction to Southern Economic History—The Land System—by James Curtis Ballagh, pp. 99-129; Mirabeau and Calonne in 1785, by Fred Morrow Fling, pp. 131-147; Some of the Consequences of the Louisiana Purchase, by Samuel M. Davis, pp. 149-160; National Politics and the Admission of Iowa into the Union, by James A. James, pp. 161-173; Spanish Policy in Mississippi after the Treaty of San Lorenzo, by Franklin L. Riley, pp. 175-192; Cuba and Anglo-American Relations, by J. M. Callahan, pp. 193-215; The Diplomacy of the United States in regard to Cuba, by John H. Latané, pp. 217-277; The Protestant Revolution in Maryland, by Bernard C. Steiner, pp. 279-353; European Blue Laws, by J. M. Vincent, pp. 355-372; The Founding of the German Reformed Church in America by the Dutch, by James I. Good, pp. 373-384; First Suggestions of a National Observatory, by James C. Courtenay and William A. Courtenay, pp. 385-396; Second Annual Report of the Historical Manuscripts Commission, pp. 397-679; Guiana and Venezuela Cartography, by P. Lee Phillips, pp. 681-776; Bibliography of Alabama, by Thomas M. Owen, pp. 777-1248; Index, 1249-1272.

Annual Report of the American Historical Association for the year 1898. Washington: Government Printing Office, 1899.
8vo. pp. ix, 745.

CONTENTS.

Report of Proceedings of Fourteenth Annual Meeting in New Haven, Conn., December 28-30, 1898, by Herbert B. Adams, pp. 1-8; Report of the Treasurer, List of Committees and Officers, pp. 9-12; Inaugural Address of Prof. G. P. Fisher, on the Function of the Historian as a Judge of Historic Persons, pp. 13-33; The

Historical Manuscripts in the Library of Congress, by Herbert Friedenwald, pp. 35-45; American Colonial History (1690-1750), by C. M. Andrews, pp. 47-60; Study of American Colonial History, by H. L. Osgood, pp. 61-76; A Forgotten Danger to the New England Colonies, by Frank Strong, pp. 77-95; An Examination of Peters's "Blue Laws," by W. F. Prince, pp. 97-138; The Connecticut Gore Land Company, by Albert C. Bates, pp. 139-162; The Society of Separatists in Zoar, Ohio, by George B. Landis, pp. 163-220; Southern Economic History—Tariff and Public Lands—by J. C. Ballagh, pp. 221-263; Diplomatic Relations of the Confederate States with England (1861-1865), by J. M. Callahan, pp. 265-283; American Diplomacy, by Edwin A. Grosvenor, pp. 285-300; Lessons from the Recent History of European Dependencies, by Henry E. Bourne, pp. 301-312; The Constitutional Questions Incident to the Acquisition and Government by the United States of Island Territories, by Simeon E. Baldwin, pp. 313-343; Germans in America, by Ernest Bruncken, pp. 345-353; The Real Origin of the Swiss Republic, by William D. McCracken, pp. 355-362; Erasmus, the Prince of the Humanists, by George Norcross, pp. 363-380; The Cambridge School of History, by Mary R. W. Stubbert, pp. 381-411; Municipal Government in the Twelfth Century, by J. M. Vincent, pp. 413-425; The Study of History in Schools, Report of the Committee of Seven to the American Historical Association, pp. 427-564; Third Annual Report of the Historical Manuscripts Commission, pp. 565-708; Bibliography of Annual Reports of the American Historical Association, pp. 709-714; Index, 715-745.

Annual Report of the American Historical Association for the year 1899. Washington: Government Printing Office, 1900.

8vo. 2 vols., pp. 817, 1218.

Transmitted by the Assistant Secretary of the Association to the Secretary of the Smithsonian Institution and submitted to Congress in accordance with the Act of Incorporation of the Association.

CONTENTS.

Vol. I. Report of Proceeding of Fifteenth Annual Meeting at Boston and Cambridge, December 27-29, 1899, by A. Howard Clark, Assistant Secretary, pp. 1-42; Inaugural Address of President James Ford Rhodes, on History, pp. 43-63; Removal of Officials by the Presidents of the United States, by Carl Russell Fish, pp. 65-85; Legal Qualifications for Office in America, 1619-1899, by Frank Hayden Miller, pp. 87-153; The Proposed Absorption of Mexico in 1847-48, by Edward G. Bourne, pp. 155-169; The Problem of Chinese Immigration in Farther Asia, by Frederick Wells Williams, pp. 171-204; The Droit de Banalité during the French Régime in Canada, by W. Bennett Munro, pp. 205-228; The Restoration of the Proprietary of Maryland and the Legislation against the Roman Catholics during the Governorship of Capt. John Hart (1714-1720), by Bernard C. Steiner, pp. 229-307; The First Criminal Code of Virginia, by Walter F. Prince, pp. 309-363; A Critical Examination of Gordon's History of the American Revolution, by Orin Grant Libby, pp. 365-388; A Recent Service of Church History to the Church, by William Given Andrews, pp. 389-427; The Origin of the Local Interdict, by Arthur Charles Howland, pp. 429-448; The Poor Priests: A Study in the Rise of English Lollardry, by Henry Lewin Cannon, pp. 449-482; The Roman City of Langres (France), in the Early Middle Ages, by Earle Wilbur Dow, pp. 483-511; Robert Fruin, 1823-1899, by Ruth Putnam, pp. 513-526; Sacred and Profane History, by James Harvey Robinson, pp. 527-535; Should Recent European History have a place in the College Curriculum? by Charles M. Andrews, pp. 537-548; The Colonial Problem, by Henry E. Bourne, pp. 549-558; A Bibliography of the Study and Teaching of History, by James Ingersoll Wyer, pp. 559-612; Titles of Books in English History published in 1897 and 1898, selected and annotated by W. Dawson Johnston, pp. 613-632; A Bibliography of Mississippi, by Thomas McAdory Owen, pp. 633-828; Bibliography of Publications of the American Historical Association, 1885 to 1900, pp. 829-844; Index, pp. 845-871.

Vol. II. Fourth Annual Report of Historical Manuscripts Commission—Correspondence of John C. Calhoun, edited by J. Franklin Jameson; Contents, Preface, pp. 11-19; Chronology of John C. Calhoun, pp. 21-24; Calendar of letters heretofore printed, pp. 25-46; List of letters now printed, pp. 47-64; Account of Calhoun's early life, by Col. W. Pinkney Starke, pp. 65-89; Part I, Letters of Calhoun, pp. 91-787; Part II, Letters to Calhoun, pp. 789-1212. Index, 1213-1218.

Bibliography of American Historical Societies (the United States and the Dominion of Canada). By Appleton Prentiss Clark Griffin. (From the Annual Report of the American Historical Association for 1895.) Washington: Government Printing Office, 1896.

8vo. pp. 559.

Historical Manuscripts Commission of the American Historical Association, First Annual Report, December 30, 1896. By J. Franklin Jameson, Talcott Williams, Frederick J. Turner, and William P. Trent. (From the Annual Report of the American Historical Association for 1896.) Washington: Government Printing Office, 1897.

8vo. pp. 644.

CONTENTS.

Contains list of printed guides to, and descriptions of, archives and other repositories of historical manuscripts; Letters of Phineas Bond to the Foreign Office of Great Britain, 1787, 1788, 1789; Intercepted letters to the Duke de Mirepoix, 1756; Letters of Stephen Higginson, 1783-1804; Diary of Edward Hooker, 1805-1808; Clark-Genet correspondence.

Historical Manuscripts Commission of the American Historical Association, Second Annual Report, December 30, 1897. By J. Franklin Jameson, Talcott Williams, William P. Trent, Frederick J. Turner, and James Bain, jr. (From the Annual Report of the American Historical Association for 1897.) Washington: Government Printing Office, 1898.

8vo. pp. 282.

CONTENTS.

Contains Colonial Assemblies and their Legislative Journals; Letters of Phineas Bond, 1790 to 1794; The Mangourit Correspondence in respect to Genet's Projected Attack upon The Florida, 1793-94.

Historical Manuscripts Commission of the American Historical Association, Third Annual Report, December 30, 1898. By J. Franklin Jameson, William P. Trent, Frederick J. Turner, and James Bain, jr. (From Annual Report of American Historical Association for 1898.) Washington: Government Printing Office, 1899. 8vo. pp. 143.

Contains Items Respecting Historical Manuscripts; Calendar of the Letters of John C. Calhoun heretofore printed; Guide to the Items Relating to American History in the Reports of the English Historical Manuscripts Commission and their Appendixes.

Historical Manuscripts Commission of the American Historical Association, Fourth Annual Report, December 27, 1899. By J. Franklin Jameson, William P. Trent, Frederick J. Turner, James Bain, jr., and Herbert Friedenwald. (From the Annual Report of the American Historical Association for 1899.) Washington: Government Printing Office, 1900.

8vo. pp. 1218.

CONTENTS.

Correspondence of John C. Calhoun, edited by J. Franklin Jameson: Containing, Preface, pp. 1-24; Calendar of letters heretofore printed, pp. 25-46; List of letters now printed, pp. 47-64; Account of Calhoun's early life, by Col. W. Pinkney Starke, pp. 65-89; Part I, Letters of John C. Calhoun, pp. 91-787; Part II, Letters to John C. Calhoun, pp. 789-1212; Index, 1213-1218.

III.—THE CHURCH HISTORY SECTION OF THE AMERICAN HISTORICAL ASSOCIATION.

The American Society of Church History, organized March 23, 1888, was on December 31, 1896, constituted the Church History Section of the American Historical Association. The publications of the Society from 1889 to 1897, comprising eight volumes of "Papers," edited by Rev. Samuel Macauley Jackson, M. A., secretary, have been transferred to the American Historical Association.

Papers of the American Society of Church History. Vol. I. Report and papers of the first annual meeting, held in the city of Washington, December 28, 1888. New York and London, 1889.
    8vo. pp. xxx (2), 271. (Out of print.)

CONTENTS.

Organization of the Society; Constitution; First annual meeting; Letters from the honorary members; The progress of religious freedom, as shown in the history of toleration acts, by Philip Schaff; Indulgences in Spain, by Henry Charles Lea; A crisis in the Middle Ages, by James Clement Moffat; Melanchthon's "Synergism," by Frank Hugh Foster; Some notes on syncretism in the Christian theology of the second and third centuries, by Hugh McDonald Scott; The influence of the golden legend on pre-Reformation culture history, by Ernest Cushing Richardson; Notes on the New Testament canon of Eusebius, by Arthur Cushman McGiffert; A note on the need of a complete missionary history in English, by Samuel Macauley Jackson; List of members; Index.

Papers of the American Society of Church History. Vol. II. New York, 1890.
    8vo. pp. xx (2), 104.

CONTENTS.

Constitution; Second annual meeting; Some remarks on the Alogi, by G. P. Fisher; The Camisard uprising of the French Protestants, by H. M. Baird; Parochial libraries of the colonial period, by J. F. Hurst; Dante's theology, by Philip Schaff; The corruption of Christianity through paganism during the first two centuries, by Abraham H. Lewis; Some relics of early Presbyterianism in Maryland, by J. W. McIlvain; List of members.

Papers of the American Society of Church History. Vol. III. Report and papers of third annual meeting, December 30, 31, 1890. Edited by Samuel Macauley Jackson. New York, 1891.
    8vo. pp. xiii, 251.

CONTENTS.

The Renaissance, the revival of learning and art in the fourteenth and fifteenth centuries, by Philip Schaff; The historical geography of the Christian Church, by Henry W. Hulbert; The Anabaptists of the sixteenth century, by H. S. Burrage; The vicissitudes of the doctrine of the Lord's Supper in the English Church, by J. W. Richard; Villegaignon, founder and destroyer of the first Huguenot settlement in the New World, by T. E. V. Smith; Report on a proposed series of denominational histories, to be published under the auspices of the American Society of Church History, by Albert Henry Newman; The place of church history in the college course of study, by Henry M. MacCracken; List of members of the Society.

Papers of the American Society of Church History. Vol. IV. Report and papers of the fourth annual meeting, December 29 and 30, 1891. Edited by Samuel Macauley Jackson. New York, 1892.
8vo. pp. lviii, 235.

CONTENTS.

Works of interest to the student of church history which appeared in 1891; The religious motives of Christopher Columbus, by William Kendall Gillett; The "heads of agreement" and the union of Congregationalists and Presbyterians based on them in London, 1691, by Williston Walker, Christian unity, or the Kingdom of Heaven, by Thomas Davidson; The bulls distributing America, by John Jordan; The confessional history of the Evangelical Lutheran Church in the United States, by John Nicum; Christian thought in architecture, by Barr Ferree; The friendship of Calvin and Melanchthon, by Philip Schaff; Recent researches concerning mediæval sects, by Albert Henry Newman; List of members of the Society.

Papers of the American Society of Church History. Vol. V. Report and papers of the fifth annual meeting, held in the city of Washington, December 27 and 28, 1892. Edited by Samuel Macauley Jackson, M. A. New York, 1893.
8vo. pp. lxii, 143.

CONTENTS.

Bibliography of works of interest to the student of church history which have appeared in 1892, compiled by the Secretary; St. Thomas of Canterbury, by Philip Schaff; The Absolution Formula of the Templars, by Henry Charles Lea; The services of the Mathers in New England religious development, by Williston Parker; Holland and religious freedom, by Rev. Talbot Wilson Chambers; The Italian Renaissance of to-day, by Rev. George Robert White Scott; List of members; Index.

Papers of the American Society of Church History. Vol. VI. Reports and papers of the sixth annual meeting, December 27 and 28, 1893. Edited by Rev. Samuel Macauley Jackson, M. A. New York, 1894.
8vo. pp. xxx, 224.

CONTENTS.

The Schaff memorial meeting, December 27, 1893; Dr. Schaff as a Bible student and reviser, by T. W. Chambers; Dr. Schaff as uniting Teutonic and Anglo-Saxon scholarship, by J. F. Hurst; Dr. Schaff and the Lutheran Church, by H. E. Jacobs; Dr. Schaff and the Episcopal Church, by C. C. Tiffany; Dr. Schaff and the Roman Catholic Church, by T. J. Shahan; Dr. Schaff as a literary worker, by E. C. Richardson; Tribute from Joseph Henry Allen; Life and work of Bishop Francis Asbury, by Asbury Lowry; Benjamin Schmolck, by J. E. Rankin; Life and work of St. Thomas Aquinas, by Thomas O'Gorman; The Gospel of Peter, by A. C. McGiffert; Faust and the Clementine recognitions, by E. C. Richardson; The contest for religious liberty in Massachusetts, by H. S. Burrage, D. D.; The doctrine of apostolic succession in the Church of England, by H. C. Vedder; Prayers for the dead, by G. F. Williams; List of members; Index.

Papers of the American Society of Church History. Vol. VII. Reports and papers of the seventh annual meeting, held in the City of Washington, D. C., December 27 and 28, 1894. Edited by Rev. Samuel Macauley Jackson, M. A., secretary, New York, 1895.
8vo. pp. ccxlviii, 65.

CONTENTS.

Works of interest to the student of church history published in 1893, a bibliography compiled by the secretary; Dr. Schaff as an historian, by G. P. Fisher; Some elements in the making of the United States, by C. H. Small; Judge Samuel Sewall (1652-1730), A typical Massachusetts Puritan, by J. L. Ewell; List of members.

Papers of the American Society of Church History. Vol. VIII. Reports and papers of the eighth and ninth annual meetings, held in the city of New York, December 26 and 27, 1895, and December 29 and 30, 1896. Edited by Rev. Samuel Macauley Jackson, M. A., secretary. New York and London, 1897.

8vo. pp. xxxi, 323.

CONTENTS.

Constitution of the Society; Eighth Annual Meeting; Ninth Annual Meeting; a brief sketch of the United Synod of the Presbyterian Church in the United States of America, by Rev. Thomas Cary Johnson; The teachings of Antonio Rosmini and the censures passed upon them by ecclesiastical authority, by Rev. Henry Clay Sheldon; The ecclesiastical situation in New England prior to the Revolution, by Rev. Joseph Henry Allen; Amsterdam correspondence, by Rev. Edwin Tanjore Corwin; John Eliot, the Puritan missionary to the Indians, by Rev. Ezra Hoyt Byington; The Labadist colony in Maryland, by Rev. Bartlett Burleigh James; Wesley as a churchman, by Rev. John Alfred Faulkner; The attitude of the western church toward the study of the Latin classics in the early Middle Ages, by Dana Carelton Munro; The development of the appellate jurisdiction of the Roman See, by Rev. Joseph Cullen Ayer; Hincmar, an introduction to the study of the Revolution in the organization of the church in the ninth century, by Guy Carelton Lee; The attitude of the Society of Friends toward slavery in the seventeenth and eighteenth centuries, particularly in relation to its own members, by Allen Clapp Thomas; List of members, honorary and active; Index.

INDEX.

A.

Abbe, Mrs. Robert, 18, 36.
Abbey, Richard, 637.
Abbot on religious test for officeholders, 107.
Abbott, Edwin Abbott, 620.
Abbott, Evelyn, 615.
Abbott, Ira A., 39.
Abbott, John Stephens Cabot, 637.
Abolition, struggle for, 835.
Absolution formula of Templars, 843.
Acadia, New England settlements in, 834.
Acton, Lord, 565, 599.
Adair, James, 637.
Adalbero, Bishop, intrigues of, 441.
Adams, Brooks, 562.
Adams, Charles Francis, VII, 24, 26, 31, 32.
  on military history, 14.
Adams, Charles Kendall, VII, IX, 31, 577, 611, 833, 834, 835.
Adams, George, 638.
Adams, George Burton, VIII, X, 31, 837, 839.
Adams, Henry, VIII, IX, 31.
Adams, Herbert B., IV, V, VII, IX, 4, 24, 28, 31, 32, 42, 565, 577, 606, 607, 638, 832, 833, 834, 835, 836, 837, 838, 839.
Adams, John, 70, 109, 131, 383.
Adams, John Quincy, 73.
Adams, Robert H., 638.
Adams, Thomas A. S., 639.
Addison, Thomas, 235.
Addey, M., 639.
Addy, Sidney Oldall, 621.
Adémar of Chabannes, quoted, 444.
Agassiz, Alexander, 39.
Agassiz, Mrs. Louis, 37, 39.
Age qualifications for office, 126, 130–132.
Agreement of 1817, 838.
Alabama, bibliography of, 839.
  history of, 782.
  residence qualification in, 123.
Alcorn, James Lusk, 642.
Alcorn, James S., 697.
Alden, Edmund K., 593, 837, 838.
Alden, Lewis, 39.
Alden, T. J. Fox, 642.
Aldrich, Truman H., 642, 643.
Alderman, E. A., 33.
Alexander, C. H., 643, 657.
Alexander, J. A., 419.
Alexander, W. A., 643.
Alfred the Great, thousandth anniversary of death of, 27, 32.
Alfriend, Frank H., 643, 688.
Algonquin Club, hospitality of, 26.
Alien immigrants to England, 616.
Allan, William, 832.
Allen, Andrew Hussey, 837.
Allen, James, 643.
Allen, John M., 643.
Allen, Joseph A., 39.
Allen, Joseph Henry, 844.
Allen, Justin, 39.
Allen, William Francis, IX, 577, 608, 832.
Allen, William H., 39.
Allen, William Osborn Bird, 621.
Alogi, remarks on, 842.
Altamira, Rafael, 577.
Amendments to Constitution, 834, 835, 839.
America, history of name, 832.
American diplomacy, 840.
American history, books on sources of, 596.
American Revolution, a heroine of, 750.
  battles of, 15.
  causes of, 831.
  German troops in, 697.
  Gordon's history of, 367–388.
  in the West, 837.
  peace negotiations, 832.
  Quebec act, 837.
  Southern campaign, 381.
American tracts in Bodleian Library, 836.
Ames, Governor Adelbert, 644.
Ames, Herman V., 834, 835, 839.
Amsterdam correspondence, 844.
Anderson, F. M., 33.
Anderson, Fulton, 644.
Anderson, William E., 644.
Andover Seminary, visitorial statutes of, 835.
Andre's execution, Gordon on, 377.
Andrews, Alice, 606.
Andrews, Caroline, 644.
Andrews, Charles M., 18, 29, 32, 34, 37.

845

INDEX.

Andrews, Charles M., 570, 833, 834, 840.
　on Justin Winsor prize, 25.
　on study of recent European history, 539–548.
Andrews, Elisha Benjamin, 578.
Andrews, Garnet, 844.
Andrews, Israel W., 831.
Andrews, W. G., 10, 35, 840.
　on a recent service of church history to the church, 391–427.
Angell, James Burrill, VIII, IX, 31, 836.
Anglo-Saxon institutions, 618.
Annatoquin Indians, 299.
Annexation, historic policy as to, 836.
Anson, William R., 625.
Anthropology, early British, 620.
Antirent episode in New York, 838.
Appeals from Colonial courts, 837.
Appellate jurisdiction of Roman See, 844.
Appleton, Francis H., 39.
Appointing power of President, 831.
Apostolic succession in English Church, 843.
Aquinas, St. Thomas, 843.
Arbitration, international, United States and, 835.
Arbois de Jubainville, Marie Henri d', 565.
Arbués, San Pedro, martyrdom of, 832.
Arch, Joseph, 621.
Archæological instruction, plea for, 593.
Archæologist and historian, 835.
Architecture, Christian thought in, 843.
　early English, 621.
　English renaissance, 615.
Archives, Canadian, 832.
　national, value of, 836.
　State Department, 837.
Argall, Samuel, 356.
Arkansas, religious test in, 121.
Arnold, James M., 644.
Arnold, Thomas, 481, 565, 590.
Arnold's treason, Gordon on, 377.
Arnulf, imprisonment of, 443.
Asbury, Bishop Francis, 843.
Ashbourne, Edward Gibson, 621.
Ashley, W. J., 16, 30.
Ashmead, W. H., 644.
Assmann, W., 599.
Atkinson, Thomas Dinham, 615.
Atkinson, William Parsons, 578, 593.
Attainder, Virginia Bill of, 835.
Atwood, Peter, 301.
Aubrey, John, 621.
Augustine, on excommunication, 434.
Augustine's mission to England, 618.
Auxilius, Bishop, 434.
Ayer, Joseph Cullen, 844.

B.

Baacke, G., 591.
Baar, Joseph, 578, 612.
Bacon, L. W., 405.
Bacon, Thomas B., 578.
Baily, Francis, 645.
Bain, Alexander, 578.
Bain, James, jr., 31, 33, 841, 842.
Baker, Arthur, 606.
Baker, Daniel, 645.
Balch, George T., 608.
Baldamus, Alfred, 578, 599.
Baldwin, Joseph, 570, 578.
Baldwin, Joseph G., 645.
Baldwin, Simeon E., 833, 835, 836, 840.
Baldwin, J. Thomas, 646.
Baldwin, Thomas, 646.
Baltimore, Lord, veto by, 276.
Ball, John, pupil of Wicliff, 452, 460.
Ball, Timothy H., 646, 720.
Ballagh, James Curtis, 839, 840.
Balle, John, 460.
Ballot, written, history of, 833, 835.
Banalité, droit de, 207, 228, 840.
Bancroft, Frederic A., 32, 832.
Bancroft, George, IV, IX, 158.
Bank of England, history of, 620.
Bankhead, John Hollis, 646.
Baptists, evangelical impulse among, 411
　in Georgia, 393.
　in Mississippi, 646, 648.
Barbauld, Anna Letitia, 570.
Bargraves, Captain, 314.
Barksdale, Ethelbert, 648.
Barksdale, William, 648.
Barksdale, William Robert, 648.
Barksdale family, 713.
Barnard, Frederick Augustus Porter, 648, 649, 710.
Barnard, H., 606.
Barnard, Henry, 599.
Barnard, William F., 39.
Barnes, Albert, 411.
Barnes, Mrs. Mary Downing, 565, 578, 598, 594, 608, 612.
Barnes, William Horatio, 649.
Barnett, Percy Arthur, 578, 606.
Barrows, William, 578.
Barry, Commodore John, 838.
Barry, William Taylor Sullivan, 649.
Barth, F., 579.
Barth, Paul, 562.
Barton, Roger, 649.
Bartram, William, 649–651.
Bascom, John, 565.
Basina, nun, rebellion organized by, 438.
Bassett, John S., 33, 837, 838.
Batavia, Chinese in, 191.
Batcheller, Robert, 40.

Bates, Albert C., 840.
Bates, Frank Green, 837.
Battaile, J. F., 663.
Baxter, James Phinney, 836.
Beatty, Franklin T., 40.
Becker, A., 595.
Becket miracles, 620.
Beer, William, 25, 33.
Beers, Mrs. Fannie A., 651, 666.
Bell, Mrs. Helen D., 651.
Benedictine Monks, history of, 619.
Bengel, Johann, 595, 599.
Bennett, Richard, 302.
Berengar of Narbonne, 447.
Bernhiem, Ernst, 562, 579, 612.
Bertron, Mrs. Ottillie, 651.
Berryhill, S. Newton, 651.
Besançon, 651.
Bibliography, Alabama, 839.
   American history, 25, 837.
   books on study of history, 840.
   British municipal history, 617.
   church history, 416, 843.
   early books on America, 839.
   English history, 25, 613-632.
   Louisiana, 25.
   members of American Historical Association, 834, 835, 836.
   Mississippi, 25, 633-828.
   publications of American Historical Association, 831-844.
   publications of historical societies, 835, 836, 838, 841.
   South Carolina colonial, 837.
   witchcraft literature, 833.
Biddle, Nicholas, 144.
Biedermann, Friedrich Karl, 599.
Biedma, Luys Hernandez de, 652.
Bien, H. M., 652.
Bienville, Jean Baptiste Le Moyne, life of, 562.
Bigelow, Melville M., 32.
Bigland, John, 579.
Bijvanck, Heer, 521.
Bill of Attainder, in Virginia, 835.
Bills of Rights in State constitutions, 835.
Bingham, Governor, 150.
Birchfield, Maurice, 291, 308.
Birney, William, 835.
Birrell, Augustine, 565.
Bishop of London, 288.
Bismarck as a typical German, 833, 835.
Bisset, Andrew, 565.
Black, John, 652.
Black, W. C., 652.
Blackie, John Stuart, 570.
Blackman, Frank W., 579, 837.
Blackwood, William, 619.
Bladensburg, battle of, 15.

Blair, Frank G., 570.
Blake, George B., 40.
Blakiston, Colonel, 258.
Blasphemy, penalty for, 311.
Bledsoe, Albert Taylor, 652, 653, 688.
Blennerhassett, H., 653.
Blinn, George R., 40.
Blodgett, James H., 838.
Bloomfield, Reginald, 615.
Blue laws, European, 839.
   Virginia, 311.
   Peters's, 840.
Blume, E., 599.
Bodier, Jean, 566.
Bodleian Library, American tracts in, 836.
Bolingbroke, Lord, 234.
Bolton, C. K., 40.
Bolton, Frederick E., 599.
Bona, M., 570.
Bond, Phineas, letters of, 841.
Bondurant, Alexander L., 635, 653, 654.
Bongaertz, Julius, 599.
Boone, James Shergold, 579.
Borneo, North, Chinese in, 201.
Bossu, F., 655.
Boston meeting, proceedings of, 3.
Boston, town meetings of, in 1774, 373.
Boughton, Willis, 598.
Boundary, first southern, of United States, 836.
Bourdeau, Louis, 566.
Bourgeois, Emile, 596.
Bourne, Edward G., 21, 31, 32, 37, 599, 835, 836, 838, 840.
   on proposed absorption of Mexico, 157-169.
Bourne, Henry E., 5, 6, 29, 32, 35, 42, 837, 840.
   on the colonial problem, 551-558.
Bourinot, John George, x, 834, 835.
Boutell, Lewis Henry, 836.
Bowen, Clarence, W., IV, VII, IX, 24, 25, 29, 30, 31, 833.
Bowles, William Augustus, 657.
Bowman, J. H. D., 688.
Bowring, John, 197.
Boyd, Samuel S., 657.
Boyle, Robert, 422.
Brackenridge, Henry Marie, 657.
Bradford, Gamaliel, 40.
Brady, M. B., 657.
Bramo, L., 643, 657.
Brandon, Gerard, 658.
Brandon, Gerard Chittaker, 658.
Brandon, Thomas, 658, 750.
Bray, Thomas, 250.
Breckinridge, Robert J., 405.
Brettschneider, Harry, 570, 599.
Brevoort, James Carson, 832.

848 INDEX.

Brewer, John Sheren, 579.
Bribery, disqualification for, 141.
   laws against, 141.
Bridwell, L. O., 788.
Briedermann, Friedrich Karl, 579.
Briggs, Frank Harrison, 40.
Brinton, Daniel Garrison, 658.
Brisac, Edmond Dreyfus, 596.
Bristoliensis, 570.
Britain, early inhabitants of, 620.
British army, history of, 617.
British methods of treating Chinese, 197.
Brooke, Stopford Augustus, 622.
Brooke, Thomas, 235, 306.
Brooke, Walker, 658.
Brooks, Edward, 579.
Brouard, Eugène, 597.
Brough, Charles Hillman, 658.
Brown, A. J., 658.
Brown, Albert Gallatin, 658.
Brown, Alexander, 313, 831.
Brown, John, trial and execution of, 833.
Brown, Samuel R., 659.
Browning, Oscar, 606.
Bruin, Peter Brian, 659.
Brumbaugh, M. G., 579.
Bruncken, Ernest, 840.
Brymner, Douglas, 832.
Buchanan, President, officials removed by, 81.
Buchanan, Secretary, on absorption of Mexico, 160.
Buck, Capt. John T., 659.
Buckingham, James Silk, 659.
Buckle, Henry Thomas, 563.
Buckner, Robert H., 659.
Budget, history of, 835.
Bugbee, L. G., 32.
Bulls, Papal, distributing America, 843.
Bunker Hill, battle of, 15, 376.
Bunsen, Christian Karl Josias, 563.
Bureau of Education, U. S., 659.
Burghley, Lord, 626.
Burke, Edmund, 368.
Burke, Thomas, 119.
Burkitt, Frank, 659.
Burkitt, Henry L., 659.
Burnett, Edmund C., 839.
Burr, Aaron, 659, 660.
   arrest of, 783.
   trial of, 815.
Burr, George L., 833, 834.
Burrage, Henry S., 35, 848.
   on banishment of Roger Williams, 10.
Burgess, Isaac B., 608.
Burgess, John William, x, 542, 608, 838.
Burstall, S. R., 606.
Butler, Nicholas Murray, 608.
Byington, Ezra H., 12, 35, 844.

C.

Cabaniss, Alfred B., 660.
Cabeça de Vaga, D'Alvar Nunez, 660.
Cabot, John, and study of sources, 839.
Cadell, Robert, 622.
Cage, Henry, 660.
Caldwell, Howard Walter, 32, 33, 595.
Caldwell on religion in office, 107.
Calhoun, John C., against absorption of Mexico, 163.
   early life of, 841.
   letters of, 25, 840, 841.
Calhoun, Sol. S., 661.
Calhoun County, sketch of, 661.
California, residence qualifications in, 128.
Callahan, James M., 38, 838, 839, 840.
Calvert, Charles, appointed governor of Maryland, 306.
   death of, 247.
Calvin and Melanchthon, friendship of, 843.
Cambridge, historical scenes in, 23.
Cambridge School of History, 840.
Cambridge University, history, 615.
Cameron, J. D., 661.
Camisard uprising, 842.
Campbell, Douglas, 833, 835.
Campbell, John L., 661.
Campbell, John P., 661.
Campbell, Lewis, 615.
Campe, J. F. C., 570, 579.
Camperdown, Earl of, 622.
Canada, historical studies in, 832, 833, 834.
   parliamentary government in, 835.
   responsible government in, 835.
   the droit de banalité in, 207-228.
   United States and, 834.
   Upper, first parliament of, 834.
Canadian archives, 832.
Canadian campaign of 1708-1710, 835.
Çanadian schools, history in, 611.
Cannon, Henry Lewin, 38, 840.
   on English Lollardry, 451-482.
Cannon, Susan, 661.
Canton, British capture of, 178.
Capen, Elmer H., 39.
Capital, locating the, 838.
Cappleman, Mrs. Josie Frazee, 661.
Carlyle, Thomas, on study of history, 563, 579.
Carpenter, Marcus T., 661.
Carpetbag government, 724.
Carrington, Henry Beebe, 570.
Carroll, Archbishop, 399.
Carroll, Charles, 232, 264, 301.
Carroll, James, 301.
Carter, Calvin Holmes, 832.
Carter, Franklin, 39.

INDEX. 849

Cary, Elizabeth L., 622.
Cary, James, 661.
Casa de Contratacion of Seville, 837.
Cass, Governor, influence of, 832.
Cass, Lewis, on annexation of Mexico, 163, 164.
Catchings, Thomas C., 662, 727, 735.
Catholic Church in America, history of, 802.
Catholic interdict, origin of, 431.
Catholic missions among Indians, 768, 801.
Catholics as officeholders, 116.
  legislation against, 231-307.
  patriotism of, 308.
  (See also Roman Catholics.)
Caudel, M., 597.
Cecil, William, 626.
Chalmers, James R., 662.
Chalmers, Joseph Williams, 662.
Chamberlin, John, 361.
Chamberlain, Mellen, 832.
Chambers, Henry, 574.
Chambers, Henry E., 662.
Chambers, Talbot Wilson, 843.
Channing, Edward, 388, 506, 608, 612, 831.
Chapman, A. W., 662.
Chapman, H. P., 663.
Chappell, Absalom Harris, 663.
Charles, R. F., 606.
Charles the Bald, 502, 503.
Charles the Fat, 503.
Charters of city of Langres, 486.
Chase, Philip A., 40.
Chase, Wayland J., 570.
Chanche, John Joseph, 662.
Cheseldyne, Kenelm, 235.
Cheves, Langdon, 839.
Cheney, E. P., 32.
Chick, Charles G., 40.
Chickasaw Indians, 731.
Child, Joshua, 663.
Chinese at Hongkong, treatment of, 199.
  Highbinders, 181.
  immigration in Farther Asia, 173-204.
  immorality and filth, 179.
  in Far East, 840.
  insubordination, 180.
  laborers in Pacific islands, 174.
  love of native country, 177, 178.
  political characteristics of, 203.
  restrictions in America, 178.
  secret societies, 182.
  society, characteristics of, 181.
Chisholm massacre, 823.
Choctaw Indians, 690, 731.
  mission, 814.
Choptank Indians, 300.
Christian, John T., 664.

Christian alliance with Mohammedans, 435.
  doctrine, method of writing history of, 836.
  knowledge, society for promoting, 621.
  philanthropy, 392.
Christianity, corruption of, through paganism, 842.
  primitive, the interdict in, 432.
Chrodieldis, nun, 437.
Church and nation, relation of, 402.
  and State in United States, 832.
  Catholic, in Mississippi, 662.
  early English, 621.
  history, American chapter in, 832.
    Andrews on, 10.
    from 1800 to 1830, 416.
    service of, Andrews on, 391-427.
  mediaeval, 532.
  power of, during ninth century, 508.
  punishment for neglect of, 312.
Church of England in America, 231.
Citizenship qualifications for office, 91, 111, 121.
Civilization, and decay, law of, 562.
  history of, 831.
  in England, 563.
Civil rule, evil of, 513.
Civil war, map of battles of, 758.
  northern lake frontier during, 838.
  Southern prisons, 795.
  strategy in Pope's campaign, 832.
  turning points, 837.
Civitates, government of, 493.
Claflin, William, 40.
Claiborne, Gen. Ferdinand Leigh, 666.
Claiborne, John Francis Hamtranck, 666, 667.
Claiborne, Nathaniel Herbert, 667.
Claiborne, William Charles Cole, 667, 668.
Clark, Andrew, 621, 622.
Clark, A. Howard, v, vii, ix, 3, 4, 24, 25, 28, 29, 31, 32, 635, 835, 836, 837, 838.
Clark, Charles, 668.
Clark, Daniel, 668.
Clark, George Rogers, 376.
Clarke, Charles W., 696.
Clarke, J. F., 580.
Clarke, Joseph Thacher, 593.
Clarke, Joshua G., 668.
Clark-Genet correspondence, 841.
Clay, Henry, 668.
Clay, Henry, as Speaker of House, 835.
Clayton, Alexander M., 668.
Clayton, George R., 669.
Clergy, civil constitution of, 534.
Clergymen excluded from public office, 106, 135.
Cleveland, Rose Elizabeth, on history, 566.

HIST 99, VOL I———54

850 INDEX.

Clifford, Attorney-General, 160.
Clow, F. R., 608.
Clowes, William Laird, 623.
Clowney, Sam, sketch of, 669.
Clusky, M. W., 669.
Cobb, Joseph B., 669.
Cochin-China, Chinese in, 186.
Cocke, Stephen, sketch of, 669.
Cocke, William, 669.
Codd, St. Leger, 235.
Coes, Mary, 42.
Coffin, Victor, 837.
Cohn, Adolphe, 835.
Colbert, Levi, sketch of, 674.
Colby, C. W., 33.
Cole, Theodore Lee, 635, 674.
Collar, W. C., 580.
College, Alcorn A. and M., 642.
　agricultural and mechanical, report of, 639, 640.
　Brandon, sketch of, 658.
　education, place of research in, 569.
Collins, Jacob C., 674.
Colonial assemblies, journals of, 841.
　constitutions on office qualifications, 105.
　courts, appeals from, 837.
　governments, classification of, 838.
　history, American, Andrews on, 840.
　　of South Carolina, 837.
　officials, Lowell on selection of, 6.
　period, office qualifications during, 90.
　policy of England, 616.
　　of France, 19, 557.
　problem, by H. E. Bourne, 551-558, 840.
Colonies, American, constitutional relations to England, 832.
　Crown lands, 328.
　genesis of, 838.
　British, growth and administration of, 625.
　committee on, 32.
Colonization Society, 401.
Color and sex qualifications for office, 104.
Columbus, Christopher, autographs of, 837.
　religious motives of 843.
　remains of, 535.
Comets, history of doctrine of, 832.
Committee of seven, report of, 608, 840.
Committees of the association, list of, 28, 31.
Compton, William M., 675.
Comte, Auguste, 563.
Concord, battle of, 385.
Concord Antiquarian Society, 27.
Condillac, Etienne Bonnot de, 580.
Confederacy, Southern, history of, 833.
Confederate States, almanac, 643.
　diplomatic relations of, 840.

Confederate States navy, history of, 800.
Congregationalists in 1814, 393.
Congressional government, defense of, 833.
Connecticut, blue laws in, 840.
　early history of ballot in, 833.
　New Haven colony absorbed in, 835.
　convention on religion in office, 108.
Connecticut Gore Land Company, 840.
Cons, Louis, 597.
Conrad, Timothy Abbott, 676.
Constitution, applied to foreigners, 20.
　applied to Territories, 22.
　island territories and, 840.
　use of history by framers of, 838.
Constitutional amendments, 834, 839.
　controversy in Rhode Island, 837.
　conventions, debates of, 106.
　relation of American colonies to England, 832.
Constitutions, carpet-bag, 122.
Continental Congress, Friedenwald on, 837.
　journal and papers of, 838.
Cooke, John Esten, 666, 680.
Coolidge, A., 574.
Coolidge, Archibald Cary, 42, 838.
Coolidge, T. Jefferson, 831.
Coopwood, Capt. Thomas, 680.
Cope, John, 622.
Copeland, A. M., 40.
Copeland, James, 680, 785.
Coppeé, H. St. L, 680.
Corbet, John, 233.
Corbett, Julian Stafford, 623.
Corey, Deloraine P., 40.
Coronado in New Mexico, 837.
Corporation officers excluded from public office, 144.
Corpus Christi College, 624.
Cortina, José Gomez de la, 580.
Corwin, Edwin Tanjore, 844.
Cotton plant, climatology of, 766.
Counterfeiting law in Maryland, 282.
Count of Langres, authority of, 505.
County régime of Langres, 511.
Coursey, William, 235.
Courtenay, William, 452.
Courtenay, William A., 839.
Coutume de Paris, 213.
Coventry, history of, 625.
Covington, Gen. Leonard, 681.
Cox, J. C., 627.
Coxe, Tench, quoted, 109.
Coyle, Edward, 264.
Crafts, James M., 39.
Crashaw's sermon mentioned, 325.
Craven, Dr. J. J, 681.
Creek Indians, legend of, 712.
Creek war of 1813 and 1814, 720.

INDEX. 851

Creighton, Mandell, 566.
Criminal code of Virginia in 1610, 311-363.
Cromwell's place in history, 616.
Croom, Isaac, 682.
Cross, Arthur Lyon, 838.
Crosby, Howard, 397.
Croswell, T. R., 574.
Crothers, Samuel, 24.
Crothers, Samuel M., 570.
Crozier, J. H., 666, 682.
Cruikshank, Ernest, 838.
Cuba and Anglo-American relations, 830.
  diplomacy of United States regarding, 837.
  McMaster on government of, 20.
Cuban question, Senator Money on, 771.
Cullum, George W., 832.
Cuming, F., 682.
Cunningham, William, 616.
Currie, James, 606.
Curry, Jabez Lamar Monroe, 682.
Curtis, Richard, sketch of, 682.
Curtis, William Eleroy, 837.
Cushing, Harry, 838.
Cushing, J. P., 38.
Czerwenka, F. J., 580.

D.

Dabney, R. H., 580, 834, 835.
Dabney family, 713.
Dale, Gen. Sam, 682.
Dale, Thomas, 328, 332.
Dale's code of Virginia laws, 317.
Daniel, John W., 683, 688, 689.
Dante's theology, 842.
Darby, William, 683.
Darden, John P., 683.
Darling, C. W., 835.
Darnall, Henry, 301.
Daughter of the Confederacy, the, 702.
Daughters of the Confederacy, 604.
Davenport, Bishop, 684.
Davidson, Thomas, 843.
Davis, Andrew McFarland, 42.
Davis, George, 684.
Davis, Jefferson, 666, 684, 689, 786.
Davis, Joseph Emory, sketch of, 689.
Davis, Reuben, 689.
Davis, Samuel M., 839.
Davis, Varina Anne Jefferson, 689.
Davis, Varina Jefferson, 689.
Davis, W. W. H., 832.
Day, Clive, 7, 36.
Deane, Amos, 580.
Deane, Charles, ix.
Deane, Silas, life and times of, 832.
Dearmer, Percy, 623.
Death penalty in Virginia, 311.
Definition of history, 836.

Delaware, Lord, 331, 332, 336, 347.
Delaware, property qualifications in, 113.
Democracy and peace, Macvane on, 22.
Denny, Henry G., 40.
De Soto, Hernando, 690, 700, 736, 738, 802.
Dettmer, H., 591.
Deupree, J. G., 690.
Devol, George H., 690.
Dexter, Franklin Bowditch, ix.
Dexter, Henry M., 10, 397.
Dickson, David, 690.
Diesterweg, Georg Friedrich Adolphe Wilhelm, 580.
Diggs, Charles, 301.
Dilcher, A., 580.
Dillard, Anthony Winston, 690.
Diplomacy, American, 840.
  during civil war, 838.
  United States, regarding Cuba, 839.
Diplomatic relations of Confederate States, 840.
Diplomatists, inadequate recognition of, 836.
Dittes, Friedrich, 580.
Doctorate, historical, requirements of, 836.
Documents of early Congresses, 839.
Dodsley, Robert, 368.
Dolci, P., 566.
Domesday Book, history of, 618.
Donaldson, Thomas, 690.
Dorpfeld, Friedrich Wilhelm, 599.
Dorsey, Sarah A., 691.
Dougherty, Newton C., 608.
Dow, Earle Wilbur, 38, 840.
  on Roman city of Langres, 485-511.
Dow, Lorenzo, 691.
Dowd, William Francis, 691.
Drake, Benjamin, 691.
Drake, B. M., 691.
Drake, Daniel, 690, 691.
Drake, J. H., 608.
Drake, Samuel Gardiner, 692.
Drake and the Tudor navy, 623.
Drama in the South, 753.
Draper, John William, 563.
Draper, Lyman C., 704.
Dresch, —— von, 580.
Droit de Banalité in Canada, 217-228.
Droysen, Johann Gustav, 563, 566.
Duane, Williams, 692.
Du Bois, W. E. B., 835.
Dudley, N. A. M., 40.
Dueling, defense of, 140.
  disqualification for, 138.
Duff, Sir Mountstuart Elphinstone Grant, 49, 566.
Duke de Mirepoix, letters of, 841.
Dumond, Annie Nelles, 692.
Duncan, Adam, 622.

Dunbar, William, 692, 704.
Dunning, William A., VIII, x, 24, 31, 42, 833.
Du Pratz, Le Page, 693.
Durrett, R. T., 33.
Dutch code of 1586, 320.
  history, 516.
  Reformed Church founded by the, 839.
  treatment of Chinese, 191.
Duval, Mary V., 664, 694.
Dwight, Timothy, 694.

E.

Eager, Eleazer C., 694.
Eager, P. H., 635, 694.
Eaton, John Henry, 694, 695.
Eberhardt, K. F., 599, 600.
Ecclesiastical history, 1800 to 1830, 416.
Echols, Obadiah, 695.
Economic history, New England, 833.
  Ashley on, 16.
Eddy, Richard, 40.
Education, Herbert Spencer on, 573.
Education, history as an instrument of, 570.
Educational Association, National, 575.
  institutions, American, origin of, 833, 834.
  qualifications for office, 132.
Edwards, Anthony, 358.
Edwards, B. B., 696.
Edwards, Walter A., 570.
Eelting, Max von, 697.
Egert, Ph., 591.
Egerton, Hugh Edward, 616.
Eggleston, Edward, VII, IX, 24, 31.
Eggleston, George Cary, 697.
Ekeris, Van, 600.
Elder, William Henry, 697.
Election of association officers, 24.
Electoral college for Maryland senate, 838.
Eliot, Charles D., 40.
Eliot, Charles W., 39, 574.
  address of welcome by, 23.
Eliot, John, 844.
Ellett, Henry T., 608.
Ellis, George E., 832.
Ellis, Powhatan, 608.
Ellsworth on property qualifications for office, 108.
Elvas, gentleman of, 697.
Emerson, Ralph Waldo, on history, 566.
Emerton, Ephraim, IX, 580, 836.
Emery, Samuel Hopkins, 40.
Emma, Queen, intrigues of, 441.
Endicott, William, 39.
Endris, A., 600.
England, Church of, established in Maryland, 245.
  history of civilization in, 563.

English authors, works of, 619.
  history, books on, 613-632, 840.
  Historical Manuscripts Commission of, 841.
  literature, history of, 622.
  manual of, 618, 624.
  thought, development of, 564.
Ennalls, Thomas, 235.
Episcopal Church in America, 395.
  control in colonies, 838.
Erasmus, the prince of humanists, 840.
Estes, Matthew, 701.
Esty, C. C., 40.
Ethnologist and historian, 833.
Europe, history of intellectual development of, 563.
European blue laws, 839.
  dependencies, lessons from, 840.
  history in colleges, 838.
  recent, study of, 539-548, 840.
Eusebius, New Testament canon of, 842.
  quoted, 433.
Evangelical movement, 393.
Evans, Governor, quoted, 132.
Evarts, Jeremiah, 701, 814.
Ewell, J. L., 843.
Excommunication, practice of, 432.
Executive, Congressional demands on, for information, 834, 835.
Expansion, British, 616.
  President Polk on, 158.
  United States policy of, 836.
Expenditures of foreign governments for history, 835.

F.

Fairfield, Charles, 623.
Falkner, W. C., 701.
Farrand, Max, 32, 42.
Faulkner, John Alfred, 844.
Featherston, Winfield Scott, 702.
Featherstonhaugh, George William, 702.
Federal Convention adopts resolution on President's term of office, 109.
  new, 839.
  on property qualifications for office, 108.
Federal court of appeal, 832.
  election bill, 821.
  territories in Europe, government of, 839.
Feldhausen, G., 600.
Fendall, John, 235.
Ferrell, Chiles Clifton, 635, 702.
Fessenden, Anson D., 40.
Fessenden, Edward S., 40.
Field, Thomas Warren, 703.
Fillmore, President, officials removed by, 79.
Finance committee, 32.

Fischer, K., 593.
Fish, Carl Russell, 38, 42, 840.
  on removal of officials by Presidents, 67-85.
Fish, Hamilton, 837.
Fisher, Ephraim S., 703.
Fisher, George Park, VIII. IX, x, 12, 31, 839, 842, 843.
Fisher, Richard Swainson, 703.
Fisher, Willard Clark, 833.
Fiske, John, 13, 326.
Fitch, Joseph Girling, 581.
Fitzroy, Augustus Henry, 625.
Flade, Dietrich, fate of, 834.
Flegler, Alexander, 566.
Fleming, David Hay, 616.
Flemming, Hans, 570.
Fling, Fred Morrow, 32, 33, 581, 595, 600, 833, 835, 859.
Flint, Robert, 563.
Flint, Timothy, 703.
Florence, early commercial industry of, 835.
Florida, clergymen excluded from office, 135.
  first discovery of, 795.
  history of east and west, 796.
  proposed attack on, in 1798, 841.
  Spanish conquest of, 699, 805, 817.
  war of 1812 in, 738.
  war, history of, 805.
Flournoy, Thomas, 703.
Follen, Karl, 835.
Follett, Mary Parker, 835.
Foote, Henry Stuart, 703, 704.
Force, M. F., 666, 704.
Ford, Paul Leicester, 833, 834, 835.
Foreign relations, papers on, 20.
Forman, A. P., 704.
Forman, Samuel S., 704.
Formosa, Chinese in, 177.
Forrest, N. B., 704, 736.
Forrest's Cavalry, campaigns of, 736.
Forshall, Josiah, 482.
Forshey, C. G., 696.
Foss, Rudolph, 581, 593.
Fossils, Tertiary, notes on, 642, 643.
Foster, Frank Hugh, 581, 842.
Foster, L. S., 635, 704, 705.
Foster, Vere, 623.
Foster, William Eaton, 31, 608.
Foster family, genealogy of, 704, 713.
Fouillée, Alfred, 571.
Foulke, William Parker, 571.
Fox, George L., 608.
Fox, Jacob, 264.
Fox, John, 482.
Foxcroft, H. P., 624.
Fowler, Thomas, 624.
Franchise during colonial period, 91.

Francke, Kuno, 832, 833, 835.
Franck, Bishop, 438.
Franklin, Freeman, E. 705.
Franklin in France, 832.
Franklin on property qualifications for officers, 108.
Frantz, Virginia, 705.
Fredegonda, Queen, 437.
Frédéricq, Paul, 597, 600, 607.
Free, H., 600, 612.
Free Burghs in United States, 838.
Freehold qualification for office, 97.
Freeman, Edward Augustus, 566, 574, 581, 612.
Freeman, John D., 705.
Freeman, Thomas, 705.
Freeman, colonial, definition of, 92, 93.
Freemantle, Colonel, 666, 705.
Freemasons of Mississippi, 761.
French, Benjamin Franklin, 705, 706, 707.
French colonial policy, 19, 557.
  colonies, Chinese in, 190.
  Constitution, formation of, 835.
  Indo-China, Chinese in, 185.
  régime in Canada, banal rights during 207-228.
  Revolution, Hazen on, 838.
Frewin, Thomas, 516.
Friedenwald, Herbert, 31, 837, 838, 840, 841.
Friends, Society of, and slavery, 844.
Fritzsche, Richard, 571, 581.
Froboese, J., 600.
Frohlich, Josef, 581.
Frontier, importance of, in American history, 836.
Froschauer, M., 581.
Froude, James Anthony, 563, 566, 581.
Fruin, Robert, memorial sketch of, 18, 515-526, 840.
Fugitive slave case, first in Ohio, 836.
Fugitive slaves, liberation of, 838.
Fulkerson, H. S., 710.
Fuller, Melville Weston, VIII. x, 31.
Fulton, John, 710.
Fulton, Robert Burwell, 635, 710, 711.

G.

Gäbler, Dr., 600.
Gachon, P., on historians of France, 566.
Gage's address to Suffolk convention, 374.
Gaines, George Strother, 711.
Gallatin, Albert, 711, 716.
Gallaudet, Edward Miner, x.
Galloway, Charles Betts, 711.
Gambler, most noted Mississippi, 690.
Gambrell, James B. 712.
Gannett, Henry, 712.
Gansen, 581.
Gardiner, Samuel Rawson, 24, 27, 50, 581, 616.

Garfield, President, quoted, 47.
Garlick, A. H., 582.
Garner, James W., 712.
Garrett, W. R., 712
Gates, Thomas, 311, 332, 339, 345.
Gathright, Thomas S., 712.
Gatschet, Albert S., 712, 713.
Gayoso de Lemos, Don Manuel, 713.
Genz, Hermann, 600.
Geography of Christian Church, 842.
George, Julius A., 40.
George, James Zachariah, 714.
George, S., 582.
Georgia, historical collections of, 824.
  history of, 735.
  land claims of, 715.
  property qualifications in, 112.
  religious tests in, 816.
Georgia Mississippi Company, 715.
Georgia Pacific Railway, 715.
Georgia Western Country, 715, 716, 717.
Georgiana and Elizabeth, 623.
Gérard de Roussillon, 499.
Gerbert reproves Adalbero, 442.
German allied troops in American Revolution, 697.
  gymnasia, history in, 839.
  Imperial Court, 838.
  Reformed Church, 839.
Germans in American colonies, 232, 840.
Germany, common school system of, 576.
  history study in, 599.
Gerry, quoted, 110.
Gervinus, Georg Gottfried, 567.
Gettysburg, battle of, 838.
Gholson, Samuel Jameson, 717.
Gibbon on Tacitus, 52.
Gillett, William Kendall, 843.
Gladney, Richard, 717.
Gladstone, life of, 618.
Gladstone-Ingersoll controversy, 702.
Glenn, David Chalmers, 717.
God in history, 563.
Godman, Thomas D., 793.
Goldmann, Theodor, 600.
Gooch, George Peabody, 624.
Good, James I., 839.
Goode, George Brown, x, 833, 834.
Goodell, Henry H., 39.
Goodnow, Harold P., 838.
Goodrich, A. L., 582.
Goodwin, Edward J., 574.
Goodwin, Elliot H., 42.
Goodwin, S. A., 718.
Gordon, William, biography of, 367.
Gordon's History of American Revolution, Libby on, 367–388, 840.
Gordy, Wilbur F., 591, 608.
Gosse, Edmund, 624.
Gouger, Robert, 624.

Government, civil, aims in teaching, 571.
Government work in history, 837.
Governors disqualified as Senators, 149.
Graham, Agnes, 691.
Gravenhorst, K. Th., 600.
Graves, Richard S., 718.
Grayson, Spencer Monroe, 718.
Grayson, W. S., 718.
Grayson family, 713.
Green, Samuel A., 40.
Green, Thomas Marston, 718.
Greene, E. B., 574.
Greene, Francis V., 666, 718.
Greenwood, James M., 582.
Greswell, William Parr, 625.
Griffin, Appleton Prentiss Clark, 31, 835, 836, 838, 841.
Griffin, Martin I. J., 838.
Griffith, John T., 718.
Griffith, William B., 718.
Grimm, Herman, 582.
Grinling, Charles H., 625.
Groffroy, A., 597.
Gross, Charles, 617, 834.
Grosvenor, Edwin A., 840.
Grote on Thucydides, 51.
Groth, Ernst, 582.
Grüllich, Oskar Adalb., 600.
Guild, Curtis, 40.
Guilds, books on, 617.
Guion, Isaac, 718.
Guion, John Isaac, 719.
Guizot, François Pierre Guillaume, 582.
Gully, F. A., 719.
Gunpowder plot, Gardiner on, 616.
Gunther, Adolf, 582.
Guth, Friedrich, 582.
Gwin, William McKendree, 719.

H.

Haines, T. M., 719.
Halbert, Prof. H. S., 635, 646, 719.
Hale, Edward Everett, 5, 832.
Hall, Basil, 721.
Hall, Benjamin, 301.
Hall, C. P., 609.
Hall, G. Stanley, 39, 582, 612.
Hall, James, 721, 755.
Hall, John, 571.
Hall, Henry, 236, 283.
Hamberlin, L. R., 722.
Hamilton, Andrew, 260.
Hamilton, Peter Joseph, 722.
Hamilton on qualifications of Senators, 111.
  on reelection of Presidents, 110.
Hamm, J. S., 722.
Hammet, William H., 722.
Hamor, Ralph, 313, 351, 361.

INDEX. 855

Hampton Court, history of, 617
Hampton, John P., 722.
Hanbridge, Mary, 591.
Handy, Alexander H., 723.
Handy, L. C., 657.
Hannak, Emanuel, 582.
Hannay, David, 625.
Harby, Mrs. Lee C., 835, 837.
Harding, Lyman, 723.
Harding, Samuel B., 837.
Hardy, William H., 723.
Harley, Lewis R., 582.
Harmon, M. F., 723.
Harnden, Henry, 687.
Harper, L., 723, 759.
Harper, W. L., 723.
Harris, Benjamin W., 40.
Harris, Buckner C., 723.
Harris, George, 39.
Harris, J. Bowman, 723.
Harris, Mary Dormer, 625.
Harris, Wiley P., 723, 724.
Harris, William Littleton, 724.
Harris, William Torrey, 583, 635, 834.
Harrison, Frederic, 567, 607.
Harrison, James T., 635, 724.
Harrison, W. S., 724.
Harrison and Tyler, officials removed by, 76.
Hart, Albert Bushnell, VIII, X, 25, 26, 29, 31, 32, 42, 49, 574, 583, 595, 596, 608, 609, 612, 831, 832.
Hart, Charles Henry, 838.
Hart, Gov. John, of Maryland, 231, 840.
Hart, Merrick, 234.
Hartleb, Ph., 583.
Harvard University, meeting at, 23, 26.
Harwood, Herbert J., 40.
Haskell, Louisa P., 42, 839.
Haskins, Charles H., 24, 32, 37, 42, 597, 834, 835.
Haskins, W., 724.
Hatson, Charles W., 724.
Haupt, C., 600.
Hawaiian Islands, territorial system in, 552, 553.
Hawkins, Benjamin, 724.
Hayden, Horace Edwin, 725.
Hayes, Rutherford Burchard, x.
Haynes, G. H., 838.
Hayward, Ann, 725.
Hayward, John, 725.
Haywood, John, 725.
Hazard, Caroline, 39.
Hazeltine, Harrold D., 837.
Hazen, C. D., 838.
Hazlitt family, 617.
Hazlitt, William Carew, 617.
Hebron, Ellen E., 726.
Hedge, Frederic H., 583.

Hegel, Georg Wilhelm Friedrich, 583.
Heidelberg, Daniel W. 726.
Henderson, E. F., 37.
Henderson, Miss J. P., 726.
Henderson, Rev. Jacob, 245, 283.
Henderson, John, 726.
Henderson, John W., 726.
Henderson, Lizzie George, 726.
Hendrickson, C. D., 40.
Henneman, J. B., 33.
Henry, Patrick, 831.
Henry, William Wirt, VII, IX, 31, 831, 835, 836.
Henze, E., 571.
Herbart, Johann Friedrich, 571.
Herbst, F. L., 583.
Herbst, F. L. W., 600.
Herodotus and Thucydides compared, 49.
Herrmann, E., 601.
Hersey, John, 726.
Higginson, Stephen, 841.
Higginson, Thomas Wentworth, 27, 571.
Highbinders in California, 181.
Hilgard, Eugene Woldemar, 726, 727, 759.
Hill, Clement, 301.
Hill, Don Gleason, 40.
Hill, Frank A., 571.
Hill, James, 727.
Hill, Robert Andrews, 727.
Hillard, George S., 598.
Hillyard, M. B., 727.
Hincmar, imprisonment of, 440.
Hinschins on local interdict, 431.
Hinsdale, Burke Aaron, 583, 609, 612, 836.
Hispaniola, early letter from, 832.
Historian as judge of historic persons, 839.
Historic sense, the, 565.
Historical doctorate, requirements of, 836.
  grouping, 569, 832.
  industries, Schouler on, 836.
  inquiry, methods of, 569.
  manuscripts commission, members of, 31.
  report by, 25, 840, 841.
  manuscripts in Library of Congress, 840.
    printed guides to, 841.
    special committee on, 27, 29.
  material, organization of, 835.
  nomenclature, American, 836.
  research, 568, 569.
  societies, bibliography of, 838, 841.
    in Massachusetts, 39.
    State, 835.
    sphere of, 794, 839.
  studies in Canada, 832, 833, 834.
    in the South, 833.
  study, purpose of, 540.
    value of, 573.

Historical survivals in Morocco, 833.
   testimony, 569, 838.
   training and method, 541.
   truth, essays on, 565.
   work in colleges, 833, 834.
History, a science, 834, 835.
   an aid to moral culture, 570.
   as means of teaching patriotism, 570, 572.
   as teacher of religion, 570.
   bibliography of study of, 561-612.
   books on sources of, 596.
   chief aim in study of, 570.
   considered as science, 467.
   definition and forecast, 565, 836.
   demand for education in, 834.
   economic interpretation of, 564.
   English, books on, 613-632.
   entrance requirements in, 574.
   ethical value of, 572, 573.
   expenditures of foreign governments for, 835.
   God in, 563.
   handbook of, 567.
   historians and, by Bourdeau, 566.
   in American colleges, 607.
   in German gymnasia, 839.
   in high schools, 574.
   in modern education, 571.
   its use and meaning, 571.
   lecture by Acton, 565.
   lectures on, by Priestly, 568.
   lectures on modern, 565.
   limits of science applied to, 567.
   local, study of, 563.
   methodology of, 565.
   methods of illustrating, 831.
   methods of study and teaching, 577-612.
   mountains and, 563, 837.
   muse of, 565.
   new spirit in, 567.
   outlines of the principles of, 563.
   patriotic force in school, 570.
   philosophic aspects of, 834.
   philosophy of, 562.
      by Laurent, 564.
      by Voltaire, 565.
      in Europe, 563.
      in France and Germany, 563.
      in social development, 562.
   political value of, 572.
   primary instruction in, 591-593.
   picturesqueness in, 566.
   related to practical life, 571.
   right use of, 571.
   relation of politics to, 836.
   Rhodes on, 840.
   sacred and profane, 529-535.
   science of, 563, 569.
   scientific method applied to, 566.
   social function of, 570.

History, sources of, 595.
   study of, 568, 569, 573, 638, 833.
   teaching of, 838.
   treatise on, 45.
   unity of, 566.
   universal, outline of philosophy of, 563.
   uses of, 570, 571, 572, 573.
   value of, for moral culture, 570.
      in school training, 570.
   ways of writing, 565.
   why children dislike, 571.
   why should it be learned, 572.
Hoar, George Frisbie, VIII, IX, 31, 838.
Hobart, Bishop, 395, 406.
Hodder, Edwin, 624.
Hodge, Charles, 420.
Hodgkin, Howard, 607.
Hodgson, Joseph, 666, 729.
Hogue, Addison, 729.
Holcombe, William P., 574.
Holland and religious freedom, 843.
Hollanders, history of, 516.
Holman, D. A., 729.
Holman, H., 591.
Holmes, David, 729.
Holt, John S., 729.
Holt, Joseph, 729.
Hongkong, Chinese and British government of, 194.
Hooker, Allan J., 729.
Hooker, Charles E., 730, 737.
Hooker, Charles E., jr., 730.
Hooker, Edward, diary of, 841.
Hooker, Thomas, 395.
Hopkins, Stephen, 345.
Horn, Fr., 583.
Horner, R., 597.
Horton, W. Edgar, 40.
House of Commons, reporters' sketches of, 620.
Houston, William, 834.
Howard, George Elliott, 571, 583.
Howard, H. R., 730.
Howard, Volney E., 730.
Howe, Joseph Sidney, 40.
Howell, Selah, 571.
Howland, Arthur Charles, 38, 840.
   on origin of local interdict, 431-448.
Howry, James Moorman, 729.
Hubault, Gustave, 597.
Hübner, Max, 601.
Hudson, John, 358.
Hugh Capet, allied with church, 441.
Hughes, J. L., 583.
Huguenot settlement, first American, 842.
Hulbert, Henry W., 842.
Huling, Ray Greene, 609.
Hüllman, Ritter Karl D., 583.
Hume, Alfred, 730.

INDEX. 857

Hume, Martin Andrew Sharp, 626.
Humphreys, Benjamin Grubb, 731.
Humphreys family, 713.
Hunt, Abijah, 731.
Hunt, Gaillard, 838.
Huntington, Miss Irwin, 731.
Hurst, J. F., 842, 843.
Hutchins, Anthony, 731.
Hutchins, F. Lincoln, 40.
Hutchinson, J. R., 731.
Hutchinson, Thomas, 12.
Hutchinson, W. L., 635.
Hutton, William Holden, 626.

I.

Iles, George, 31.
Iles's bibliography of American history, 25.
Illinois, early lead mining in, 836.
 march of Spaniards across, 831.
Imperal Federalism, rise of, 837.
India, Chinese in, 201.
 military operations in, 619.
Indiana, corporation officers disqualified in, 144.
Indian trading, death penalty for, 312.
Indian treaties, 732.
Indians, American, history of, 637.
 Cherokee, 663.
 Chickasaw, tattoo of, 663.
 Choctaw, 663, 664.
 Creek, 681.
 in war of 1812, 838.
 Maryland, 299.
 Mississippi, 731.
 Southern, antiquities of, 735.
Indian wars, history of, 815.
Indulgences in Spain, 842.
Industrial education in Mississippi, 696.
Ingraham, J. H., 733.
Instruction, historical and political, 571.
Interdict, local, origin of, 840.
International arbitration, United States and, 835.
Iowa, admission of, 839.
Iredell on religion in office, 107.
Ireland, Alleyne, 7, 35.
Irish immigration after 1846, 406.
Irving, Henry Brodribb, 626,
Isham, Charles, 832.
Italian renaissance of to-day, 843.

J.

Jacobi, A., 601.
Jacobs, H. E., 843.
Jackson, Andrew, 16, 73, 604, 695, 733, 780.
Jackson, Helen Maria Fiske, 734.
Jackson, Samuel Macauley, VII, 29, 32, 842, 843.

Jäger, E. F. Oscar, 583, 584, 601, 612
James, Bartlett Burleigh, 844.
James, James A., 839.
Jameson, J. F., 24, 25, 27, 400, 420, 832, 834, 835, 839, 840, 841.
Janssens, Francis, 734.
Java, Chinese in, 176, 191.
Jay, John, IX, 575, 832, 833, 834, 837.
Jebb, Professor, quoted, 50.
Jefferson and social compact theory, 836.
Jefferson, President, officials removed by, 70.
Jefferson's use of Executive patronage, 831.
Jefferson Troop, 822.
Jeffreys, Judge, 626.
Jesuit priests of Alabama, 783.
Jesuits and Boston Puritans, 422.
Jews as officeholders, 119.
Jodl, Friederich, 567.
Johnson, Alderman, 362.
Johnson, Amos R., 734.
Johnson, President Andrew, impeachment of, 833.
 officials removed by, 83.
Johnson, Edward F., 40.
Johnson, John Lipscomb, 734.
Johnson, Richard M., 734.
Johnson, Rossiter, 837.
Johnson, Thomas Cary, 844.
Johnston, Alexander, 596.
Johnston, Governor, on religion in office, 108.
Johnston, W. Davison, 25, 840.
 bibliography by, 613-632.
Johnston, William Preston, 567, 575, 836.
Johnstone, George, 734.
Jowett, Benjamin, life and letters of, 615.
Jones, Charles Colcock, 688, 735.
Jones, Cornelius J., 735.
Jones, John G., 735.
Jones, Lacey, 736.
Jones, R. J. Cornewall, 626.
Jones, Richard Watson, 736.
Jordan, John, 843.
Jordan, Thomas, 666, 736.
Jörgensen, Paul, 601.
Jowles, Henry Peregrine, 235.
Judicial officers, qualification for, 147.
Judiciary, American, origin of functions of, 831.
Judson, Harry Pratt, 22, 31, 33, 37, 609.
Jullian, Camille, 597, 601.
Junge, Friedrich, 601.
Jury system, European modifications of, 837.
Justices of the peace, jurisdiction of, 805.
Justin Winsor prize, 25, 27, 29.
 circular offering, 33.

K.

Kaulich, J., 584.
Kehr, Carl, 601.
Kells, H. B., 737.
Kelly family, 713, 779.
Kemp, Ellwood W., 584.
Kemper, Reuben, 737.
Kendall, Amos, 737.
Kendall, Elizabeth, 42.
Kennedy, Anne, 750.
Kennedy, William, 737.
Kentucky, educational qualification in, 133.
Kentucky's struggle for autonomy, 833.
Kenulf, King, 436.
Ker, David, 737.
Ker family, 713.
Kernaghan, Henry, 737.
Keyes, John S., 40.
Kiddle, Henry, 584.
King, Charles Cooper, 617.
Klein, E., 602.
King, Edward, 737.
King, Grace, 737, 738.
King, Julia A., 592.
King, R. C., 635.
King, Rufus, on property qualifications for office, 109.
King, Warren D., 40.
Kingsley, Charles, 567.
Kingsley, Mr., on study of history 585.
Klein, E., 584.
Klemm, L. R., 575, 584, 602.
Klinghardt, Julius, 601.
Knapp, S. A., 738.
Knepprecht, Christian, 571.
Knight, George W., 831.
Know-Nothing legislature, 838.
Köcher, Adolf, 602.
Köhler, Richard, 571.
Kornrumpf, E., 602.
Krieger, Ferdinand, 602.
Kriehn, George, 836.
Krones, F., 602.
Kurth, Godefroid, 602.
Kwangtung, massacre at, 177.

L.

Labidist colony in Maryland, 844.
Labor movement in English politics, 837.
Lacey, Edward, 738, 772.
Lacey family, 713.
Lacombe, P., 567.
Ladenbauer, W., 571.
Lake, L., 738.
Lake, William A., 738.
Lakes, naval forces on the, 818.
Lamar, Lucius Q. C., 763.
Lamprecht, Karl, 563, 567.

Land claims, Georgia, 715.
  grants, history of, 831.
  system of provincial Pennsylvania, 838.
  system of South, 839.
Land-tenant system in French Canada, 207.
Landis, George B., 840.
Landon, Joseph, 584.
Lands, public, and States rights, 832.
Lane, Ira Remsen, 32.
Lane, W. C., 31.
Lang, Andrew, 584, 626.
Langdon, jr., Daniel Webster, 738.
Lange, Karl, 584.
Langley, S. P., III, v.
Langlois, Charles Victor, 584, 597, 598.
Langres, Roman city of, 485-511, 840.
Lanman, Charles, 738.
Lapsley, Gaillard T, 42.
Larned, J. N., 24, 31.
La Salle's adventures, 738.
  explorations, 707.
Latané, John H., 839.
Latin classics, study of, in Middle Ages, 844.
Latour, A. Lacarriere, 739.
La Tourrette, John, 759.
Lattimore, William, 738.
Laughton, John Knox, 627.
Laurent, François, on philosophy of history, 564.
Laurie, Simon Somerville, 609.
Lavisse, Ernest, 584, 598.
Law, Ernest, 617.
Law, John, 740.
Lawrence, Sir Thomas, 258.
Laws, Blue, of Virginia, 311.
  colonial, severity of, 312.
  criminal, early Virginian, 311.
  Mississippi, 740.
  Virginia, administration of, 341.
Lazarus, M., 585.
Lea, Henry Charles, 832, 842, 843.
Lead mining in Illinois and Wisconsin, 836.
Leake, Walter, 748.
Leatherman, P. R., 748.
Leavell, Zachary Taylor, 748.
Lechler, Gotthard, 482.
Lecky, William Edward Hartpole, 572.
Lee, Charles, 716.
Lee, Charlotte Fitzroy, 233.
Lee, Guy Carleton, 844.
Lee, Robert E., 754.
Lee, S. D., 666.
Lee, Sidney, 627.
Lee, Stephen Dill, 749.
Leete, Governor William, 835.
Leflore, Greenwood, 749.
Lefranc, Abel, 602.

INDEX. 859

Legal qualifications for office, 87-153, 840.
Legaspi, founder of Manila, 183.
Legislative assembly, first American, 836.
Lehy, John F., 39.
Lemonnier, Henry, 596.
Lenglet du Fresnoy, Nicolas, 567.
Leonard, Benedict, 233, 262.
Le Rossignol, J. E., 33.
Levermore, Charles H., 585.
Lewis, Abraham H., 842.
Lewis, T. M., 749.
Lewis, William Terrell, 749.
Lewis family, 713, 749.
Lexington, battle of, 385.
Lexington Historical Society, 27.
Libby, Orin Grant, 838, 840.
 on Gordon's history of American Revolution, 367, 388.
Liberal movement in Germany, 836.
Libraries and literature of North Carolina, 838.
Libraries, parochial, 842.
Library of Congress, manuscripts in, 840.
Licenses in Maryland, 260.
Lieber, Francis, 572.
Lieber, O. M., 759.
Lilly, William Samuel, 567.
Lincoln College, history of, 622.
Lincoln, President, officials removed by, 82.
Lincoln, Solomon, 39.
Lipp, Johann, 602.
Lipscomb, Dabney, 635, 750.
Literature, English, history of, 622.
Little, Charles J., 836.
Little, William, 40.
Livermore, Thomas L., 40.
Lloyd, Edward, of Maryland, 232, 235.
Lloyd, James, 235.
Lloyd, J. E., 572.
Lloyd, Philemon, 242.
Löbell, Johann Wilhelm, 602.
Local interdict, origin of, 431-448.
Lodge, H. C., 326.
Logan, Nowell, 751.
Lollard preachers, 460.
Lollardry, English, Cannon on, 451-482, 840.
London, government of, 832.
London, Shakespeare's, 619.
Longfellow, Alice M., 37.
Longfellow, Miss Alice, courtesies by, 26
Longstreet, Augustus Baldwin, 751.
Lord, Arthur, 7, 35, 40.
Lorenz, Karl, 585, 612.
Lorenz, Ottokar, 568, 585, 602.
Loring, George B., 832.
Lossing, Benson John, 751.
Lotteries in American history, 836.

Lotze, Rudolf Hermann, 564.
Loud, John J., 41.
Louis, d'Outre-Mer, 441.
Louis the Pious, 502, 506.
Louisiana, bibliography of, 25.
 educational qualification in, 123.
 history of, 696.
 provisional court of, 836.
 purchase, influence of, 831.
  Oregon and, 831.
  some consequences of, 839.
 residence qualification in, 126.
Love, William Franklin, 752.
Lovelace, Lord, 835.
Low, Sir Hugh, on Chinese, 182.
Lowell, A. Lawrence, 26, 32, 35, 42.
 on selection of colonial officials, 6.
Lowell, John, 752.
Lower St. Lawrence, settlement of, 831.
Lowrey, Mark Perrin, 752.
Lowry, Asbury, 843.
Lowry, Robert, 752.
Ludlow, Noah Miller, 692, 753.
Luebker, Friedrich, 575.
Lutheran Church in America, 843.
Lutherans, American, 394.
Luzon, Chinese in, 184.
Lyell, Charles, 753.
Lynch, Charles, 753.
Lynch, James D., 751, 753.

M.

MacAlister, James, 609.
Macaulay, Thomas Babington, 568.
McCall, Hugh, 755.
McCardle, William H., 752, 755.
McCarthy, Justin, 618, 620.
McCarvey, T. C., 33.
McClurg, Alexander Keith, 755.
McClure, Edmund, 621.
McCracken, Henry M., 842.
McCracken, William D., 840.
McCrady, Edward, 838.
McCullagh, W. Torrens, 572.
MacDonald, J. W., 585.
MacDonald, William, 28, 32, 576.
Mace, W. H., 612, 833, 835.
Mace, William Harrison, 575, 585.
McGiffert, A. C., 843.
McGillivray family, 783.
McIlvain, J. W., 842.
McIntosh, William, 692, 755.
Mackall, James, 235.
Mackall, John, 235.
McKelway, St. Clair, 575.
M'Kenney, Thomas Lorraine, 755.
McKenzie, Alexander, 41.
Mackibbin, Stuart, 585.
McKinley, President, 553.

INDEX.

McLaughlin, A. C., VIII, x, 28, 31, 575, 832, 837.
McMaster, John Bach. x, 32, 37, 572.
  on government of foreigners, 30.
McMurran, John T., 756.
McMurray, Charles Alexander, 593.
McMurry, Frank, 575.
McMurry, Frank M., 585.
MacNamara, Thomas, 235, 264, 284, 285.
McNutt, Alexander Gallatin, 755.
McPherson, J. H. T., 33.
McRae, John Johnson, 755.
MacVane, S. M., 22, 37.
McWillie, William, 755.
McWillie family, 713, 755.
Macy, Jesse, 593, 836.
Macy, William F., 41.
Madden, Frederic, 482.
Madison, James, 716.
Madison, President, officials removed by, 71.
Madison on foreigners holding office, 111.
Magee, Eugene, 757.
Magruder, W. H., 757.
Mahaffy, John Pentland, 585.
Mahan, Alfred Thayer, 618, 666, 757.
Mahrenholtz, Richard, 603.
Maine, residence qualification in, 123.
Maitland, Frederic William, 618, 627.
Malone, Walter, 757.
Manchus, misgovernment of the, 177.
Mangourit correspondence, 841.
Manila captured by British in 1762, 185.
  Chinese in, 183.
Manly, Louise, 757.
Mansel, G. B., 585.
Mansfield, Charles F., 41.
Manuscripts, in Library of Congress, 840.
  on history of Southern Confederacy, 833.
  printed guides to, 841.
  Washington's, 836.
Maps, battlefields of civil war, 758.
  Mississippi, 758–760.
  value of, in boundary disputes, 839.
Markham, Christopher Alexander, 627.
Markham, Sir Clements, 623.
Marquette, Father James, voyages of, 707.
Marine, Fletcher E., 760.
Marselli, N., 568.
Marsh, Samuel P., 760.
Marshall, C. K., 760.
Marshall, T. Dabney, 761.
Marshall, Thomas A., 761.
Marshalk, Andrew, 760.
Martens, Richard, 603.
Martial laws of Virginia, 317, 342.
Martin, Ellen, 761.
Martin, G. H., 761.
Martin, John M., 761.
Martin, Joseph, 837.

Marvel, John C., 41.
Maryland, clergymen excluded from office in, 136.
  council meetings in, 235.
  early free schools in, 250.
  early manufactures in, 237.
  electoral college for Senate of, 838.
  Protestant revolution in, 839.
  restoration of proprietary in, 231–307.
  seal of, 282.
  tobacco trade in, 256.
Mary, Queen of Scots, 616.
Mason, Arthur James, 618.
Mason, Edward Campbell, 834.
Mason, Edward Gay, IX, 831.
Mason, J. C., 696.
Mason, John Y., 160.
Mason, Otis T., 833, 835.
Mason, Tom, 761.
Massachusetts, convention on religion in office, 108.
  during Revolution, 838.
  historians of, 12.
  historical societies in, 40.
  municipal government in, 831.
  property qualifications in, 113.
  provincial Congress in 1775, 374.
  residence qualifications in, 129.
Masterman, John Howard Bertram, 618.
Mathers, the, services of, in New England, 843.
Mathes, Edward T., 609.
Mathews, Joseph, 762.
Matthew, F. D., 453.
Maurenbrecher, William, 568.
May, John J., 41.
Maydorn, B., 572.
Mayes, Daniel, 762.
Mayes, Edward, 635, 762.
Mayes, R. B., 764.
Mead, Cowles, 764.
Mead, Edwin D., 41, 585.
Mead, Elizabeth S., 39.
Mecklin, R. W., 764.
Medhurst, Mr., quoted, 203.
Mediæval Church, 532.
  industrial settlements, 616.
  religious thought, study of, 620.
  sects, 843.
Meek, Alexander Beaufort, 765.
Melanchthon's Synergism, 842.
Melish, John, 766.
Mell, Patrick Hues, 766.
Mendenhall, T. C., 39.
Mention, Léon, 598.
Merriam, J. M., 831.
Methodism in Mississippi, 637, 735.
Methodists, evangelical impulse among, 410.
Mercersburg movement, 408.

INDEX. 861

Mexico, Bourne on proposed absorption of, 21, 157-169, 840.
  the Spaniard in, 832.
Mexican war, history of, 767.
Meyer, G. E., 603.
Middle Ages, Langres during, 485.
  popular uprisings in, 836.
  the interdict in, 432.
Middleton, Holly, 767.
Milfort, Le Clerc, 767.
Military history, Adams on, 14.
  of England, 617.
Mill and oven banality in Canada, 208.
Miller, Andrew, 768.
Miller, Frank Hayden, 38, 840.
Miller, Frank Hayden, on legal qualifications for office, 87-153.
Millington, John, 768.
Mills, Herbert Elmer, 832.
Millspaugh, J. F., 572.
Minor, Don Estavan, 768.
Miquél, F. W., 603.
Mirabeau and Calonne in 1785, 839.
Mirabeau's speech of May 20, 1790, 833, 834.
Miracles of Becket, 620.
Missionary history, need of, 842.
Mississippi, bibliography of, 25, 633-828.
  codes of, 669-674.
  history of banking in, 646.
  laws of, 740-748.
  property qualifications in, 112.
Mississippi question, 602.
Mississippi river, gambling on the, 690.
Missouri compromise, historical significance of, 836.
Mitchell, B. G., 769.
Mitchell, Samuel Augustus, 769.
Moeller, C., 595.
Moffat, James Clement, 842.
Mohammedans, alliance of Christians and, 435.
Monette, John Wesley, 770.
Money, Hernando De Soto, 771.
Monin, H., 598.
Monk, Maria, 405.
Monks of St. Benedict, 619.
Monroe, President, officials removed by, 72.
Monroe, Will Seymour, 562.
Montesquieu, Charles de Secondat, baron de, 564.
Montgomery, P. K., 771.
Moody, Edwin F., 771.
Mooney, James, 772.
Moore, Bishop, 396.
Moore, John Bassett, 22, 27, 37, 835.
Moore, F. W., 31.
Moore, John Quitman, 772.
Moore, M. A., 772.
Moore, Martin V., 772.

Moore, Nina, 592.
Moral qualifications for officeholders, 103.
Morancy, Mary, 772.
Morey, Frederick A., 41.
Morgan, Edwin Vernon, on Samoa, 23.
Morgan, Edwin Vernon, 37, 42, 834, 835.
Morgan, J. B., 772.
Morison, James Cotter, 568.
Morocco, historical survivals in, 833.
Morris, Charles N., 832.
Morris, George Sylvester, 564.
Morris, Gouverneur, 111, 585.
Morris, Joshua S., 772.
Morris, R., 606.
Morris, William O'Connor, 628.
Morrison, J. K., 773.
Morse, Anson D., 17, 24, 32, 36, 837.
Morse, Horace H., 42.
Morse, Jedediah, 773.
Morton, Governor, 149.
Morton, Oliver P., 774.
Moses, Bernard, 593, 836, 837.
Motley, Fruin's criticism of, 519.
Mougeot, Dr., on Chinese, 190.
Mounds at Seltzertown, 638.
Mountains and history, 837.
Mount Vernon, manuscripts at, 836.
Mouricus, excommunication of, 436.
Mowry, Arthur May, 837.
Mowry, William Augustus, 572, 585, 609, 831.
Muckenfuss, A. M., 774.
Muhlenberg, William Augustus, 427.
Mullan, W. G. Read, 39
Municipal government in Massachusetts, 831.
  ninth century, 493.
  twelfth century, 840.
Municipal history, books on, 617.
  study of, 834.
Munro, Dana Carleton, 844.
Munro, W. Bennett, 840.
  on the droit de banalité in Canada, 207-228.
Murel, John A., 821.
Murray, David, 838.
Murrell, John A., 774.
Museum history, Goode on, 833.
Mussey, R. D., 835.
Muster, F., 603.
Myer, Otto, 774.
Myers, Minnie Walter, 776.

N.

Nachtigall, Karl, 593.
Nanticoke Indians, 299, 300.
Napoleon's concordat with Pope Pius VII, 838.
Natchez, history of, 776.
  mounds at, 638.

Natchez Indians, 731, 776.
National archives, value of, 836.
National Observatory, 839.
Naturalization during colonial period, 94, 836.
Naval forces on the lakes, 838.
Naval history of England, 623.
Navy, Confederate States, 800.
   Royal, history of, 625.
Negro, as he was and as he is, 710.
Negro code in Maryland, 281.
   suffrage in the South, 803, 823.
Negroes in Mississippi, 803.
Nelson, life of, 618.
Neubauer, Friedrich, 586, 594, 603.
Nevill, G. C., 635.
Nevins, Winfield Scott, 594.
Newell, M. A., 592.
New England association of colleges, etc., 575.
New England-Mississippi Land Company, 777.
New Haven colony, absorption of, 835.
Newman, Albert Henry, 842, 843.
New Orleans, battle of, 16.
Newport, Captain, 362.
New York, anti-rent episode in, 838.
   residence qualifications in, 127.
   slavery in, 834, 835.
Nicæan council, 434.
Nicholls, Sir George, 628.
Nichols, Edward P., 41.
Nicholson, Isaac R., 777.
Nicum, John, 843.
Nightingale, A. F., 586.
Noack, F., 586.
Nohaschek, H., 603.
Nohl, Clemens, 603.
Noll, Arthur Howard, 777.
Nomenclature, American historical, 836.
Norcross, A. D., 41.
Norcross, George, 840.
Nordhoff, Charles, 777.
Norman political invasion, 616.
Norse discovery of America, 836.
North, Ralph, 777.
North Carolina, libraries and literature of, 838.
   Regulators of, 837.
   religious test in, 116, 121.
   suffrage in, 771, 838.
Northern lake frontier during civil war, 838.
Northey, Edward, 233.
Northwest, development of, 832.
   place of, in history, 832.
   the early, 832.
Northwest territory, ordinance of, 831.
   history of educational land grants in, 831.

Norton, Charles Eliot, 41.
Nugent, Claud, 628.
Nutt, Rush, 778.

O.

Oakes, William H., 41.
O'Bannon, J. H., 688.
O'Brien, Richard Barry, 628.
Office, legal qualifications for, 87-153.
Officials, removal of, by Presidents, 67.
O'Gorman, Thomas, 843.
Ohio, age qualification in, 131.
   first fugitive slave case in, 836.
   internal improvements in, 832.
   separatists in Zoar, 840.
   township government in, 837.
Ohl, E., 603.
Oliphant, Lawrence, 185.
Oliphant, Mrs. Margaret, 619.
Oliver, James McCarty, 778.
Ommerborn, C., 603.
Ordinance of 1787, 831.
Ordish, Thomas Fairman, 619.
Oregon, Louisiana purchase and, 831.
Origin of local interdict, 431, 448.
Orr, William Gates, 778.
Osgood, Herbert L., 32, 835, 838, 840.
Oswego, loss of, 833.
Otey, James Hervey, 778.
Otken, Charles Henry, 635, 778.
Oudoceus, Bishop of Llandaff, 436.
Overton, John Henry, 628.
Owen, Thomas McAdory, 25, 633, 637, 784, 839.
   bibliography of Mississippi by,
Oxford, historical study at, 607.
Oxford movement in 1833, 407.

P.

Page, T. W., 595.
Paine, Henry, 346.
Panquash Indians, 299.
Papists in American colonies, 232.
Papists, Virginia laws against, 325.
Pard, Abraham, 586.
Parker, Williston, 843.
Parkin, George Robert, 628.
Parkman, Francis, 15.
Parliamentary experiment in German 832.
   government in Canada, 835.
Parsons, W. Frank, 41.
Parton, James, 780.
Party revolution of 1800, 837.
Pascagoula Indians, 780.
Patridge, J. M., 780.
Patridge, Lelia Ellen, 586.
Patten, Simon Nelson, 564.
Patton, Frank, 780.

INDEX. 863

Patton, James, 780.
Paulsen, Friedrich, 603.
Payson, Rev. Mr., on religion in office, 108.
Peabody, Charles A., 836.
Peabody, Elizabeth Palmer, 586, 592.
Peabody, Mrs. Mary H., 592.
Peace negotiations of 1782-83, 832.
Peacocke, J. S., 780.
Peale, Albert C., 781.
Peale's whole-length portrait of Washington, 838.
Pearson, Charles Henry, 575.
Peaslee, John B., 586.
Pelham papers, 833.
Pennsylvania, bribery laws in, 143.
   constitution, party struggles over, 837.
   convention on holding office, 110.
   provincial land system of, 838.
   religious test in, 120.
Percy, William A., 781.
Pericles's oration, 63.
Periodical literature, history of, 619.
Perkins, James Breck, 19, 37.
Perrin, J. W., 33.
Perrin du Lac, François Marie, 781.
Peter, Carl, 603.
Peters's blue laws, 840.
Pettus, John Jones, 782.
Peyton, Ephraim Geoffrey, 782.
Pflugk-Harttung, Julius Von, 568.
Phelan, James, 782.
Phelps, Matthew, 782.
Philippines, Chinese in, 173, 184.
   government for, 554.
   McMaster on government of, 20.
   question of, 825.
   retention of, 157.
Philips, Josiah, 835.
Phillips, J. H., 594.
Phillips, P. Lee, 839.
Philosophic aspects of history, 834.
Philosophy, of history, lectures on, 564.
Philosophy positive, 563.
Pickel, A., 587.
Pickett, Albert James, 782.
Pierce, President, officials removed by, 80.
Pietzsch, F. W., 603.
Pilling, James C., 659, 784.
Pinckney, Charles, 108, 109.
Piracy on Chinese coast, 196.
Pirate, James Copeland, 785.
Pitcairn, Major, 385.
Pitchlynn, Peter P., 785.
Pitt, William, life and times of, 621.
Pittman, Henry, 785.
Pitts, J. R. S., 785.
Pizard, Alfred, 592.
Platner, John Winthrop, 18, 36.
Plimpton, J. Edward, 41.
Pliny quoted, 52.

Plummer, Franklin E., 785.
Plurality of offices, 103, 145.
Puseyism, 409.
Pocahontas, 352.
Poindexter, George, 731, 735, 824.
Political pamphlets, English, 619.
   science and history, 838.
Politics, study of, 593.
Polk, President, officials removed by, 77.
   on absorption of Mexico, 158, 167, 168.
Pollard, Albert Frederick, 619.
Pollard, A. W., 452.
Pollard, Edward A., 688, 786.
Pollard, Tobias, 206.
Pollock, Oliver, 725, 786.
Poole, William F., IV, IX, 882.
Poore, Ben: Perley, 596, 786.
Poor Priests of Wicliff, H. L. Cannon on, 451-482.
   dress of, 472.
   history of, 840.
   methods of, 474.
   origin and aim of, 455, 457.
Pope, John, 786.
Popular discontent with representative government, 838.
Popular uprisings in middle ages, 836.
Porritt, Edward, 837.
Porter, Edward Griffin, 41, 42.
Porter, David Dixon, 666, 786.
Porter, Luther Henry, 586.
Porter, R. G., 787.
Portis, John C., 666, 787.
Porto Rico, government of, 552, 553.
   McMaster on government of, 20.
Portuguese on Spanish fields of discovery, 835.
Posey, Carnot, 787.
Post, Truman M., 572.
Potter, George Lemuel, 787.
Powell, F. S., 787.
Powell, Nathaniel, 369.
Power, J. L., 787, 788.
Power and liberty, Tolstoi on, 564.
Powers, Ridgley Ceylon, 788.
Prawitz, A., 586.
Pray, Publius Rutilius Rufus, 788.
Pre-Columbian discovery of America, 836.
Prentiss, Sargent Smith, 788.
Presbyterian Church, in Mississippi, 788.
   United Synod of, 844.
Presbyterianism, early, in Maryland, 842.
   in American colonies, 232.
   in 1838, 412.
Presidency, property qualifications for, 109.
President, appointing power of, 831.
   Congressional demands on, for information, 834.
   removal of officials by, 67-85.

864 INDEX.

Preston, Howard W., 596.
Pretextatus, Bishop, murder of, 437.
Price, William, 839.
Priestly, Joseph, 268.
Prince, John Tilden, 587, 604.
Prince, Thomas, 12.
Prince, Walter F., 28, 840.
   on first criminal code of Virginia, 311-363.
Prince Henry, the Navigator, 836.
Prize essay, circular regarding, 33.
Programme committee, 31.
Programme of Boston meeting, 35.
Property qualifications in holding offices, 95, 106, 112.
Proprietary in Maryland, restoration of, 231-307, 840.
Protective movement of 1828, 831.
Protestant revolution in Maryland, 839.
Protestants and the Roman communion, 398.
   as office holders, 117.
Prothero, George Walter, 572.
Prussia, plan of work for higher schools in, 574.
Ptaschnik, J., 587, 594, 604.
Public Archives Commission, 24, 28, 32.
Public domain, Donaldson on, 690.
Public lands and States' rights, 832.
   and tariff, 840.
   laws relating to, 738, 739.
Public safety, first committee of, 837.
Puritans, characteristics of, 835.
   political ideas of, 835.
   typical Massachusetts, 843.
Purnell, John, 235.
Purnell, Thomas, 235.
Purvey, John, 471.
Pushmataha, Choctaw Indian, 790.
Putnam, Alfred P., 41.
Putnam, A. W., 791.
Putnam, Herbert, 31.
Putnam, Ruth, 18, 36, 840.
   sketch of Robert Fruin by, 515-526.
Pye, Walter, 266.

Q.

Quakers as officeholders, 90.
   in American colonies, 222.
Quebec, Adams on capture of, 15.
Quebec Act and American Revolution, 837.
Quincy, Josiah, 35.
Quitman, John A., 164, 791, 797.

R.

Rabier, E., on lessons of philosophy, 568.
Radcliffe College, hospitality of, 26.
Raffay, Robert, 604.

Ragsdale, Lulah, 791.
Railroad, Alabama and Chattanooga, 641, 642.
   Mobile and Ohio, 769.
Railway, Georgia Pacific, 715.
   Great Northern, history of, 625.
Raleigh's settlement at Roanoke, 835, 838.
Ramsay, James Gattys McGregor, 791.
Ramsay, James Henry, 629.
Rand, Benjamin, 834.
Rand, Edward A., 41.
Randolph, John, 131, 401.
Ranjel, Rodrigo, 791.
Ranke, Leopold von, 509, 832, 838, 839.
Rankin, Christopher, 792.
Rankin, J. E., 843.
Rantoul, Robert S., 41.
Raum, Green Berry, 792.
Raumer, Karl Georg von, 587.
Rauschen, Gerhard, 604.
Ravenscroft, Bishop, 395.
Rawlinson, George, 629.
Rawlinson, Henry Creswicke, 629.
Raymond, Ida, 811.
Rebellion of 1745, 622.
Recent European history, study of, 539-548.
Reconstruction in Mississippi, 792.
Red, W. D., 792.
Redmond, William Fitz, 264, 301.
Redway, Jacques Wardlaw, 594.
Reed, Henry, on study of history, 568.
Reed, Thomas B., 792.
Reed, Thomas H., 42.
Reeligibility clauses in States, 151.
Regulators of North Carolina, 837.
Reid, John, 694.
Rein, Wilhelm, 587.
Religious freedom, Holland and, 843.
   progress of, 842.
   liberty in Massachusetts, 843.
      in Virginia, 832.
   observances in Maryland, 237.
   pamphlets, early English, 623.
   tests for officeholders, 99, 106, 115.
Removal of officials by Presidents, 67, 840.
Residence qualification for officeholders, 98, 106, 111, 121.
Revolutionary reaction, White on, 833.
Reynolds, Reuben O., 792, 793.
Rhode Island, appeals from colony courts of, 837.
   constitutional controversy in, 837.
   impost of 1781 in, 837.
Rhodes, James Ford, VIII, IX, 4, 14, 26, 29, 31, 32, 36, 840.
   opening remarks by, 4.
   on history, 45.
Rhomberg, Adolf, 568.
Rice, Emily J., 587, 594.

Richard, J. W., 842.
Richardson, Ernest C., 33, 842, 843, 844.
Richardson, James D., 596.
Richardson, J. K., 41.
Richardson, Lee, Jr., 793.
Richter, Albrecht, 587, 604.
Riley, Dr. Franklin L., 33, 635, 692, 793, 839.
River and harbor bill, biography of, 832.
Roach, A. C., 666, 795.
Roanoke, Raleigh's settlement at, 834, 835, 838.
Robbery, death penalty for, 312.
Robert family, 713, 795.
Roberts, Frederick Sleigh, 619.
Roberts, Robert W., 795.
Roberts, William, 795.
Robertson, C. F., 831.
Robertson, James, 791.
Robertson, Norvell, 795.
Robert the Pious, 445.
Robinson, Charles, 837.
Robinson, Edward Van Dyke, 575, 610.
Robinson, Henry, 181.
Robinson, Hercules, 198.
Robinson, James H., 16, 31, 36, 505, 610, 837, 838, 840.
Robinson, James H., on sacred and profane history, 529-535.
Rogers, Charles, 587.
Rogers, James E. Thorold, 564, 836.
Rogers, William M., 795.
Rohmeder, Wilhelm, 572.
Rolfe, John, 313, 352.
Rollins, George W., 610.
Roman Catholics, immigration in 1820, 405.
in Middle Ages, 533.
Maryland, legislation against, 231-307, 840.
opposition to, 405.
patriotism of, 398.
Roman city of Langres during ninth century, 485-511.
Romanist and Anglican parties in Maryland, 264.
Romanists disqualified for office, 267.
Romans, Bernard, 796.
Ropes, John C., 5, 15, 55.
Rosa, G., 568.
Rose, John Holland, 629.
Rosenburg, Hermann, 604.
Rosmini, Antonio, 844.
Rossbach, F., 587.
Roudebush, G. S., 797.
Round, John H., 568.
Routh family, 713, 797.
Rowe, A. V., 797.
Rowland, Dunbar, 635, 796.
Royal Historical Society, address to, 566.
Royal navy, history of, 623.

Royce, Charles C., 796.
Rude, Adolf, 595.
Ruffner, W. H., 661.
Rum, Adam, 771.
Runnels, Harman, 798.
Rusch, Gustave, 587, 592.
Rusk, Senator, 165.
Russell, Irwin, 796.
Russell, George William Erskine, 629.
Russell, James E., 604.
Russell, William E., 114.
Russian treatment of Chinese, 202.
Rutherford, Bob, 771.
Roark, Ruric Nevel, 587.

S.

Sabin, Joseph, 799.
Sabine expedition, 799.
Sach, August, 594.
Sachse, Friedrich, 604.
Sacred and profane history, Robinson on 16, 529-535, 840.
St. Augustine in England, 618.
St. Basil, cited, 433.
St. John, Henry, Viscount Bollingbroke, 587.
St. Martial, apostleship of, 446.
St. Thomas of Canterbury, 843.
Saintsbury, George, 629.
Sale, John Burruss, 799.
Salisbury, Stephen, 41.
Salmon, David, 587.
Salmon, Lucy Maynard, 576, 592, 604, 610, 831, 836, 839.
Salomon, Henry, 598.
Samoa, Baron Speck von Sternburg on, 21.
Sanford, Albert H., 835.
San Roman, 587.
Saracens, invasions of, 500.
Sargent, Winthrop, 799.
Savannah Jack, 799.
Savile, George 624.
Scaife, Walter B., 799, 833, 835, 837.
Schaff, Philip, 408, 419, 832, 842, 843.
Schaff memorial meeting, 843.
Scharf, John Thomas, 800.
Schark, J. T., 666.
Scheiblhuber, Cl., 605.
Schelling, F. W. J., 588.
Schenk, K., 588.
Schiller, E., 587.
Schiller, Hermann, 605.
Schiller, Johann Friedrich Christoph, 568.
Schilling, Dr., 588.
Schindler, Solomon, 576.
Schlegel, Karl Wilhelm Friedrich von, 564.

INDEX.

Schmarsow, A., 605.
Schmid, Karl A., 588.
Schmidt, F., 592.
Schmolck, Benjamin, 843.
Scholz, Ed., 594.
School, modern critical and historical, 568.
Schopenhauer, Arthur, 564.
Schouler, James, VIII, IX, 31, 32, 569, 832, 833, 834, 835, 836, 838, 839.
Schrader, W., 588.
Schwann, M., 588.
Schwill, Ferdinand, 19, 32, 37.
Scientific institutions in United States, origin of, 833, 834.
Scott, Abram M., 800.
Scott, Austin, 831.
Scott, Charles, 800.
Scott, Eben Greenough, 831.
Scott, George Robert White, 843.
Scott, Henry E., 610.
Scott, Hugh McDonald, 842.
Sears, Barnas, 588.
Sears, Robert, 800.
Seaton, Robert Cooper, 630.
Secession, right of, 723.
Seeley, John Robert, 568.
Seeley, Levi, 576.
Seelye, L. Clark, 39.
Seerley, Homer H., 610.
Seigniorial mills in Canada, 220.
Seignobos, Charles, 569, 584, 588, 598, 605.
Selborne, Lord, quoted, 556.
Selborne, Roundell Palmer, 630.
Selegman, Edwin Robert Andersen, 588.
Senators, United States, governors disqualified as, 149.
Separatists in Zoar, 840.
Sessions, Joseph, 801.
Seven Years War, diplomatic prelude to, 832.
Sewall, Henry, 266.
Sewall, Nicholas, 302.
Sewall, Samuel, 843.
Sewell, Peter, release of, 259.
Seymour, George E., 573.
Seymour, John, 232.
Seymour, Lucy W., 589.
Shahan, T. J., 844.
Shakespeare as a historian, 46.
Shakespeare's London, 619.
Shambaugh, B. F., 33.
Sharkey, William Lewis, 801.
Shea, John Dawson Gilmary, 801.
Shedd, William Greenough Thayer, 420, 564.
Sheldon, George, 41.
Sheldon, Henry Clay, 844.
Shelton, S. M., 802.
Shepardson, Francis W., 589.
Shepherd, William R., 838.

Sherman, Roger, in Federal Convention, 836.
Shields, Joseph D., 802.
Shields, M. Ozella, 802.
Shields, William Bayard, 802.
Shiff, Barnard, 802.
Shiloh, battle of, 758.
Shute, Rev. Mr., on religion in office, 1
Siebert, W. H., 838.
Simeoner, A., 573.
Simmel, Georg, 564.
Simmons, J. F., 803.
Simms, William Gilmore, 772.
Simpson, Josiah, 803.
Simpson, Mary Charlotte Mair, 630.
Skippon, Samuel, 236.
Slafter, Edmund F., 41.
Slave laws of Mississippi, 807.
Slave-trade laws, enforcement of, 835.
Slavery and the church, 401.
Slavery and the negro in Mississippi,
    in District of Columbia, 835.
    in New York, 834, 835.
    in South Carolina, 1670-1770.
    in the Territories, 835.
    Society of Friends and, 844.
Slaves, fugitive, liberation of, 838.
    in Ohio, 836
    treatment of, in Maryland, 237.
Sloan, J. A., 804.
Sloane, William M., 32, 573, 610.
Small, C. H., 843.
Smallwood, James, 235.
Smedes, Susan Dabney, 804.
Smedes, William C., 804.
Smedt, Charles de, 569.
Smiley, James Malcolm, 804.
Smith, Arthur L., 589, 607.
Smith, C. Alphonso, 804.
Smith, Charles L., 33.
Smith, Cotesworth Pinckney, 804.
Smith, Eugene Allen, 804.
Smith, Gustavus, 41, 564, 582, 589.
Smith, Huntington, translation by, 564.
Smith, Solomon Franklin, 692, 804.
Smith, T. E. V., 842.
Smith, Theo. Clarke, 32.
Smith, William Henry, 833, 836.
Smith, William Russell, 805.
Smithson, Thomas, 278.
Smyth, Egbert C., 9, 35.
Smythe, Thomas, 314, 326, 327, 328, 349, 353.
Snow, Freeman, 833.
Snow, M. S., 33.
Social compact theory, Jefferson and, 836
Social England, history of, 620.
Social history of New England, 833.
Society for promoting Christian knowledge, 621.

INDEX. 867

Society of Separatists in Zoar, 840.
Solly, Henry Shaen, 630.
Somers, Admiral, 338.
Somervell, R., 607.
Sorel, Albert, 589.
Sorley, William Ritchie, 589.
Sources, books on use of, 594.
  collections of, 596, 832.
  study of, 839.
South, historical studies in the, 833.
  Trowbridge on the, 815.
South Australia, founding of, 624.
South Carolina, books on colonial history of, 837.
  property qualifications in, 112.
  religious test in, 121.
  slavery in, 1670-1770, 838.
Southern Confederacy, history of, 833.
  female writers, 811.
  land system, 839.
  literature, 757.
  rivers, the rhyme of, 772.
Southwest, the, history of, 765.
Sowdon, A. J. C., 41.
Spain, economic condition of, in sixteenth century, 836.
Spaniard in Mexico, 832.
Spaniards, march of, across Illinois, 831.
Spanish and Portuguese fields of discovery, 835.
  conquest of Florida, 700.
  explorations, 805.
  policy in Mississippi, 839.
Sparks, Richard, 805.
Sparks, W. H., 805.
Speckmann, S., 573.
Speight, Jesse, 805.
Spence, C. H., 589.
Spencer, Herbert, 573.
Spencer, John F., 805.
Spencer, Lord, letters of, 622.
Spencer on religion in office, 107.
Spikemann, C., 589.
Spofford, A. R., 836.
Spotswood, Governor, 261.
Spirit of historical research, 833, 834.
Sprague, John Titcomb, 805.
Sprigg, Thomas, 235.
Stahn, Karl, 589.
Standing committee system, origin of, 837.
Stanley, Arthur Penrhyn, 589.
Starling, William, 806.
Start, Cora, 836.
State activities and politics, 835.
State and history, philosophy of, 564.
State Department archives, 837.
States' rights and public lands, 832.
State-rights theory, history of, 832.
State sovereignty in Wisconsin, 835.
Statistics, college study of, 832.

Steele, Elijah, 807.
Steele, John, 807.
Steiner, Bernard C., 38, 605, 835, 838, 839, 840.
  on restoration of proprietary in Maryland, 231-307.
Stellwegen on Robert Fruin. 522.
Stephens, H. Morse, x, 7, 24, 27, 32, 35, 199, 610.
Sterry, Wacey, 630.
Stevens, Solon W., 41.
Stevenson, E. L., 33.
Stewart, George, jr., 832, 833, 834.
Stewart, Virgil, 807.
Stiehl, F., 605.
Stockdale, Thomas R., 807.
Stockton, Commodore, 164.
Stockton, Richard, 807.
Stoddard, Amos, 807.
Stoddart, Sir John, 573.
Stokes, Henry Paine, 631.
Stokys, Peter, 452.
Stone, Alfred H., 635.
Stone, Alfred M., 807.
Stone, C. C., 41.
Stone, John Marshall, 807.
Stone, Lewis Maxwell, 808.
Storrs, Richard Salter, VIII, IX, 31, 573, 838.
Strachey, William, 313, 331.
Strada, J., on the law of history, 564.
Stratton, Joseph Buck, 635, 808.
Streight, Colonel, expedition of, 795.
Strong, Frank, 840.
Strutt, Joseph, 631.
Stuart, James, 809.
Stubbert, Mary R. W., 607, 840.
Stubbs, William, 24, 27, 589.
Stuckenberg, John Henry Wilburn, 569.
Study of history, demands for, 833, 834.
  in colleges, 834.
  in England, 606.
  in France, 596.
  in Germany, 599.
  in schools, 840.
  of Northern Europe, 838.
Stutzer, E., 589.
Suffrage in Mississippi, 803, 813.
  in North Carolina, 771, 838.
  negro, 823.
  question, 89.
Sullivan, James, quoted, 383.
Sumner, George Frederick, 41.
Sumner, John O., 42.
Sunny South, or the Southerner at home, 733.
Suter, John W., 41.
Swaney, John L., 811.
Swayze, Samuel, 811.
Swift, Charles F., 41.
Swiss history, a study in, 832.
Swiss Republic, origin of, 840.

868 INDEX.

Sykes, Gen. E. T., 635.
Synesius, Bishop, 433.

T.

Tacitus and Thucydides compared, 58.
Tacitus as an historian, Rhodes on, 52.
Tai-ping revolt, 177.
Tally, Hugh, execution of, 811.
Tanner, Henry S., 811.
Tanner, Robert, 811.
Tardif, Ad., 569.
Tardy, Mary, 811.
Tariff and public lands, 840.
Tariff of 1828, 831.
Tarpley, Collin S., 811.
Taunton, Edward L., 619.
Taussig, F. W., 831.
Taylor, Isaac, 569.
Taylor, John, 811.
Taylor, William G., 833, 835.
Taylor, Zachary, officials removed by, 78.
Teaching of history, improvement in, 48.
Teasdale, Thomas Cox, 812.
Technology Club, hospitality of, 26.
Tecklenburg, August, 589.
Tecumseh, life of, 691, 732, 812.
Teegan, Thomas Henry, 598.
Tejas, the, 837.
Templars, absolution formula of, 843.
Tennent, Gilbert, 392.
Tennessee, history of, 726, 797.
Tennis court oath, 837.
Tennyson, biography of, 622.
Ternaux-Compans, H., 812.
Territories, Federal, in Europe, 839.
 island, constitution and, 840.
 organization of, 552.
 the Constitution and, 22.
Texas, the earliest, 835.
Thacher, Joseph H., 812.
Thatcher, Oliver J., 589.
Thiele, R., 605.
Thiers, Adolphe, 814.
Thomas, Allen Clapp, 844.
Thomas, Cyrus, 814.
Thompson, Anna Boynton, 573, 590.
Thompson, Hugh Miller, 812.
Thompson, Jacob, 812.
Thompson, R. H., 812, 813.
Thornton, Thomas C., 813.
Thornton, William Thomas, 560.
Thorpe, Francis Newton, 576, 610.
Thorpe, William, 458.
Thring, Edward, life of, 623.
Thucydides and Herodotus compared, 49.
Thucydides and Tacitus compared, 58.
Thwaites, Reuben G., 24, 28, 31, 33, 590, 836, 839.
Tibbey, Thomas G., 590.

Tiffenbach, Richard, 605.
Tietz, Adolf, 594.
Tiffany, C. C., 843.
Tilghman, Richard, 235.
Tillinghast, C. B., 39.
Tittel, E., 594.
Tobacco industry in Maryland, 238.
 taxes paid in, 275.
 tax on, in Maryland, 245.
Tolstoi, Aleksyei Konstantinvich, 564.
Tompkins, Patrick, 813.
Toner, Joseph Meredith, 690, 814, 836, 838.
Tongking, Chinese in, 188.
Toppan, Robert N., 31, 32.
Township government in Ohio, evolution of, 837.
Tracy, Ebenezer Carter, 814.
Tracy, S. M., 814.
Trade regulations before 1789, 833.
Traill, Henry Duff, 620.
Trainer, John, 611.
Treason, death penalty for, 312.
Treasurer's report, 30.
Treaties, Indian, 732.
Treaty, Dancing Rabbitt Creek, 683.
 San Lorenzo, 839.
Tremain, Mary, 835.
Trent, William P., 27, 32, 833, 835, 841.
Treuntler, Julius, 590.
Trimble, Henry L., 33.
Trist, Mr., 159, 160, 166.
Trotter, James Fisher, 813.
Trowbridge, John Townsend, 666, 815.
Trumbull, Henry, 815.
Tucker, Tilghman M., 813.
Turkish Empire, dismemberment of, 838.
Turner, B. B., 620.
Turner, Edward, 813.
Turner, Frederick Jackson, x, 24, 27, 31, 32, 836, 838, 841.
Tuscaroras Indians in Maryland, 299.
Tuttle, Herbert, historical work of, 837.
Tuttle, Sarah, 814.
Twitchell, Willis Ira, 608.
Tyler, Lyon G., 33, 833.
Tyler, Moses Coit, VIII, IX, 9, 18, 24, 31, 32, 831, 832.
 on Gordon's History of American Revolution, 368.

U.

Uebel, Arthur, 605.
Ulbricht, Edmund, 573.
Ungle, Robert, 235, 248.
United States Bank, 839.
Ursuline Convent, burning of, 405.
Usselinx, William, 832.
Utrecht, Union of, 836.

INDEX.

V.

Vaile, E. O., 590.
Van Buren, President, officials removed by, 75.
Van Buren electors in Maryland, 838.
Van Curler, Arent, 888.
Van Daell, Alphonse N., 596.
Van de Velde, James Oliver, 816.
Van Hoesen, J. A., 816.
Vannerson, William, 816.
Van Wie, C. B., 590.
Vaughn, B. A., 817.
Vedder, H. C., 843.
Vega, Garcilasso de la, 817.
Venable, Robert Abraham, 817.
Venezuela cartography, 839.
Véricour, L. Raymond de, 590.
Vermont, plurality of officers in, 148.
    religious tests in, 116.
Vesey, Lettice, 234.
Vesey, John, 233.
Vesey, Thomas, 234.
Vilvart, Edward, 631.
Vick, Newitt, 817.
Vico, Giambattista, 564.
Vidal, Don José, 818.
Viergutz, Franz, 592.
Village community, theory of, 833, 834.
Villard, O. G., 838
Villegaignon, 842.
Vincent, John Martin, 18, 32, 36, 832, 837, 839, 840.
Virginia, age qualifications in, 131.
    bill of attainder, 835.
    condition of, in 1605–1609, 360.
    during Revolutionary period, 835.
    early history of, 831.
    first criminal code of, 840.
    first legislative assembly in, 836.
    martial laws of, 317.
    plan for holding office, 110.
    religious liberty in, 832.
    source of laws of, 319.
    under Patrick Henry, 831.
Virginia Company, laws under, 314.
Virginia Yazoo Company, 818.
Visitorial statutes of Andover Seminary, 835.
Volney, Constantin François, 818.
Voltaire, François Marie Arouet de, 565.
Von Ranke, Leopold, Adams on, 832.
Von Sternburg, Baron Speck, 21, 37.
Votes of Executive Council, 27.
Votes of the Association, 28.
Votes in Congress, study of, 838.

W.

Wachsmuth, Wilhelm, 569.
Waddel, John Newton, 818, 819.
Waddel family, 713, 818.
Wailes, Benjamin L. C., 819.
Wait, William Cushing, 41.
Walker, C. B., 820.
Walker, M. H., 41.
Walker, Robert J., 159, 162, 797, 820.
Walker, Williston, 834, 843.
Wall, E. G., 820, 821.
Wallas, Graham, 631.
Walter, Harvey Washington, 821.
Walthall, Edward Cary, 821.
Walton, Augustus O., 821.
Walworth, Ellen Hardin, 836.
Want, John, 346.
War of 1812 in Florida, 738.
    Indians in, 838.
Ward, Charles E., 41.
Ward, Matthew Tilghman, 235, 263.
Warden, David Baillie, 821.
Warfield, Ethelbert D., 590, 592, 833.
Warren, E. C., 576.
Warren, Joseph Parker, 41, 42.
Warren, William F., 39.
Warren, Winslow, 41.
Warriner, Henry Pitt, 576.
Washburn, W. B., 687.
Washington, George, library and manuscripts of, 836.
    Peale's whole-length portrait of, 838.
    officials removed by, 69.
Washington City, attack on, in 1814, 831.
    locating the capital at, 838.
Waters, T. Frank, 41.
Watkins, John A., 822.
Watkins, James Lawrence, 822.
Watts, Thomas H., 688, 822.
Weatherford, William, 822.
Weatherford family, 713.
Weatherly, U. G., 33.
Webb, George F., 787.
Webb, Robert Dickens, 822.
Webb, W. S., 823.
Webb family, 713, 822.
Webber, Richard H., 823.
Webber, W. L., 635.
Weber, George, 605.
Weber, William Lander, 823.
Webster, Daniel, on religious tests, 119.
Webster's seventh of March speech, 835.
Weeden, William Babcock, ix, 833.
Weeks, Stephen B., 823, 834, 835, 837, 838.
Weigand, Heiwrich, 573, 590.
Wellesley College, hospitality of, 26.
Welling, James C., 832, 835.
Wells, Charles L., 838.
Wells, J., 607.
Wells, James M., 823.
Welsh, Charles, 611.
Welsh, Mary, 823.
Welsh family, 713.

INDEX.

Wendell, Barrett, 835.
Wendt, G., 594.
Wertsch, Friedrich, 596.
Wesley as a churchman, 844.
West, Anson, 823.
West, Cato, 824.
West, Willis M., 611.
West Florida, petition from, 824.
Western pests and British debts, 837.
West, the, as field for historical study, 836.
Wharton, Henry, 301.
Wharton, T. J., 824.
Wheeler, Arthur Martin, x, 832.
Wheeler, N. M., 591.
Wheelwright, Edward, 41.
Whipple, A. B., 41.
Whitaker, Alexander, 349.
White, Bishop, 396.
White, Andrew D., IV, VII, IX, 31, 573, 605, 611, 831, 832, 833.
White, George, 824.
White, Greenough, 576.
White, J. M., 824.
White, John Williams, 41.
White, Peter, VIII, X, 24, 31, 33.
White, William, 620.
Whitfield, James, 825.
Whitney, Edson L., 837.
Whittington, William, 235.
Whitton, Frederick, 576.
Wickersham, James Pyle, 591.
Wicliff, Poor Priests of, 451-482.
Wilgus, James Alva, 837.
Wilhelmina, Queen, 525.
Wilkes, W. B., 825.
Wilkins, James C., 825.
Wilkinson, Christopher, 245.
Wilkinson, Edward C., 825.
Wilkinson, James, 825.
Willard, Emma, method of teaching history, 581.
Willey, George, 825.
William and Mary College, records of, 833.
Williams, F. Wells, 6, 32, 35, 840.
Williams, Frederick Wells, on Chinese immigration in Farther Asia, 173-204.
Williams, G. F., 843.
Williams, H. L., 692.
Williams, John Sharp, 635, 825.
Williams, Robert, 826.
Williams, Roger, Burrage on banishment of, 10.
Williams, Talcott, 833, 838, 841.
Williams, Thomas Hill, 826.
Willis, Henry A., 41.
Willoughby, William F., 835.
Willmann, Otto, 592.
Wilmot, Sidney Marow Eardley, 631.
Wilshere, George William, 623.
Wilson, H. W., 623.

Wilson, James Grant, 831, 835, 837, 838.
Wilson, Joseph, 260.
Wilson, Roland Kuyvet, 591.
Wilson in Pennsylvania convention, 110.
Wilson on excluding Popish priests from office, 107.
Wilson on foreigners in office, 111.
Wiltse, Sara E., 598.
Winchester, George, 826.
Windle, Bertram Coghill Alan, 620.
Winn, William T., 826.
Winship, George Parker, 837, 839.
Winslow, Edward, 838.
Winslow, William C., 838.
Winsor, Justin, IV, IX, 832.
Winterburn, Rose Barton, 611.
Winthrop, Robert C., 837.
Winwood, Ralph, 362.
Wisconsin, early lead mining in, 836.
Witchcraft, literature of, 833.
Withers, H. L., 607.
Witherspoon, T. D., 826.
Wohlrabe, Wilhelm, 595.
Wolcott, Roger, 36.
  address by, 12.
Wolcott, Oliver, in Connecticut convention, 108.
Wolf, Joseph, 591, 594.
Wolfe's capture of Quebec, 15.
Wolkers, George G., 42.
Woodberry, George E., 42.
Woodburn, James A., 33, 595, 836, 839.
Woodward, Thomas Simpson, 826.
Worcester; Joseph Emerson, 827.
Worsley, Henry, 569.
Wright, Carroll D., 42, 832.
Wright, Charles, 235.
Wright, Daniel W., 827.
Wright, John Henry, 569.
Wright, Marcus J., 833, 838.
Wright, Solomon, 235.
Wrong, George M., 32, 33, 611.
Wulfred, Archbishop of Canterbury, 436.
Würfl, Chr., 605.
Wyclif, John, English works of, 481.
Wyer, James Ingersoll, bibliography by, 561.
Wyeth, John Allan, 666, 827.
Wylie, Andrew, 573.
Wyoming massacre, 376, 377.

Y.

Yager, Arthur, 33.
Yarmouth mutiny, 622.
Yazoo Company of Virginia, 818.
  frauds, 827.
  land companies, 834, 835.
  sale, the first, 783.
Yeardley, George, 311, 355.

Yellow fever, Toner on, 814, 828.
Yerger, George S., 828.
Yerger, Jacob Shall, 828.
Yerger, William, 828.
Yorktown surrender, Gordon on, 378.
Young, Arthur, 632.
Young, F. G., 33.
Young, Samuel, 235.
Young Men's Christian Association, establishment of, 414.

Z.

Zeller, J. W., 611.
Zenger, John Peter, 256, 257.
Zerffi, Gustavus George, 591.
Ziegler, C., 574.
Ziller, Tuiskon, 591.
Zillig, Peter, 606.
Zimmern, Alice, 611.

INDEX

Yellow fever, Paper on, 206, 228.
Yegger, George S., 362.
Yerger, Jacob Shall, 362.
Yerger, William, 362.
Yorktown surrender, Services on, 156.
Young, Arthur, 352.
Young, P. B., 74.
Young, Samuel, 352.
Young Men's Christian Association, organization of, 154.

Z.

Zeller, J. W., 371.
Zenner, John Peter, 350, 387.
Zerah, Caesarea Georgea, 361.
Ziegler, C., 377.
Ziller, Tuiskon, 29.
Zilz, Peter, 362.
Zimmern, Max, 311.